Preface to the Eleventh Edition

The CAT 2022 and 2023 did not surprise us this time and showed a lot of consistency, especially in the VARC section.

The number of questions remained the same as CAT 2021.

However, we saw a little change in the verbal ability part of the CAT 2022 which introduced a new question type called as the Deleted Statement and the removal of Irrelevant Statement questions. CAT 2023 brought back the Irrelevant Statement questions and retained the new Deleted Statement questions but it lessened the number of Para jumble questions.

The CAT examination is changing from time to time. We, as authors and trainers, try our best to keep abreast of the latest pattern of the exam and provide content to you which is up to date and relevant for the exam.

Some changes in the CAT exam that have been seen over the years are as follows:

- The number of questions as well as the number of sections has again changed.
- Now there are three sections in the exam as opposed to the earlier two and four sections.
- The number of questions in each of the three sections is variable, adding up to a total of 66 questions in CAT 2021.
- A totally new question type of questions without options was introduced in CAT 2015, where one has to type in the answer [TITA]. This has now remained the same from CAT 2016 to CAT 2023.
- CAT has introduced 3-4 different question types over the years in the verbal section like: Summary of the Paragraph, Phrasal Verbs, Irrelevant Sentence, Deleted Statement and Paragraph Completion or the Last Sentence of the Paragraph.
- The size of the comprehension passages has also reduced to a maximum of one-page passage as opposed to longer passages in the earlier CAT exam.
- The number of questions in the comprehension section is now limited to 16-18 questions with a break up of 3-6 questions per passage.
- The verbal section fluctuates between 8 to 10 questions.
- The VARC Section had a total of 34 questions in CAT 2015, 2016, 2017, 2018 and 2019.
- CAT 2019, like CAT 2018, had 24 questions on Reading Comprehension and 10 questions on Verbal Ability.
- CAT 2021, 2022 and 2023 had just 24 questions totally comprising of 16 questions in Reading Comprehension and 8 questions in Verbal Ability.

Keeping in mind the new trends, we have introduced the following changes and chapters in this 11th edition of the book:

(1) Fully solved original CAT 2021, CAT 2022 and CAT 2023 papers [of all slots] with detailed solutions to give you the latest perspective of the exam.

(2) A brand new section called 'The CAT Experience', containing CAT-level mock tests with detailed solutions.

(3) A new chapter titled 'Missing Sentence of the Paragraph' in Part 2 (Verbal Ability) of the book.

The other highlights of the book are as follows:

(1) Totally new and solved Reading Comprehension sections LOD 1 and 2 with detailed solutions added. All the questions are as per the latest pattern of CAT examinations.

(2) Inclusion of the new TITA question type without options in the Para Jumbles and Odd Man Out/Irrelevant Statement chapters.

(3) **The CAT Experience:** This is a totally new section of the book which has CAT level questions according to the latest CAT pattern. These questions are with detailed solutions and give you a feeling of solving the actual CAT paper. An important section for the students to solve and analyse as this will make their preparation perfect for the exam.

(4) **Deleted Statement Questions:** this is a totally new question type which has appeared in the CAT 2022 and 2023. This chapter has been added in the book with adequate practice questions and detailed solutions to help the students in their preparation.

(5) Inclusion of tips and tricks for solving grammar-related Sentence Correction questions.

(6) Inclusion of three important chapters (topics) from which questions have started coming in the CAT exam regularly in the last 2-3 years. This includes Summary of the Paragraph, Deleted Statement and Irrelevant Statement.

(7) Inclusion of all the latest CAT papers with detailed solutions.

(8) Addition of fully solved tests in Reading Comprehension with solutions according to the latest CAT pattern.

(9) Addition of the Chapter on Phrasal Verbs with a comprehensive list of Phrasal Verbs which will be a good resource for the student for revision and learning for non-CAT exams.

(10) Removal of questions from the book which have lost their relevance now, due to the changing pattern of the CAT.

(11) All the newly added question types have fully solved questions with detailed solutions and theory which would be helpful for reference.

The book is totally in sync with the exam and aims to provide a one-stop solution for CAT and other MBA exam aspirants.

As a student preparing for these highly competitive examinations, we would like to remind you that a thorough preparation of the English Section is imperative for success in CAT.

Through this book, we aim to provide the reader an invaluable resource for improving the language section score drastically. Contained in this book is the very best advisory for every question type as also for developing your skills in comprehending and understanding the English language. Your job is to ensure that you follow the process diligently.

To quote an often repeated saying,

"Champions do not become champions when they win the event, but in the hours, weeks, months and years they spend preparing for it. The victorious performance itself is merely the demonstration of their championship character."

So, prepare well and gear up to face your challenges.

Good Luck!

Arun Sharma
Meenakshi Upadhyay

COUNTER THE COUNTERFEIT & BUILD A STRONG FOUNDATION FOR SUCCESS

Books are our best friends, is the adage we have grown up with. However, the pirates of piracy are continuously forging 'our best friends'. Our books and their supplementary online resources are copyrighted, and we don't lend any right-to-copy. Piracy is synonymous to stealing books.

Knowledge comes real, let's not encourage its counterfeit. Therefore, we appeal all our readers to discourage pirated books and **choose authentic ones**.

HOW TO IDENTIFY THE PIRATED BOOKS?

1 Transparency Code on the Book

Congratulations! The book you have purchased is protected by Transparency. Transparency by Amazon is a unit-level product serialization service that verifies a unit's authenticity and enables you to view rich information about the product you purchased.

Scan with the Transparency app XXXXXXXX

Please look for the Transparency logo and code on the book back cover (Transparency barcode is a square code that can be found next to the "T" symbol). You can scan the barcode with the Transparency app to verify the book's authenticity. Simply download the Transparency app from the App Store or Google Play. Scan the barcode with the app. The app will display a green checkmark when the book has been verified as authentic.

2 Cover and Spine

- Look and feel (new or used book)
- Blurred images on the cover
- Hologram pasted on front
- Defective spine (wrinkles) or air pocket at its bottom
- Unclear ISBN/bar codes
- Missing/non-operational access codes for supplemental online or e-learning materials

3 Text/Printing/Binding

- Uneven inking of pages
- Poor quality or blurred photographs/images/charts
- Substandard paper quality and opacity
- Misaligned pages
- Missing pages
- Inferior binding quality

You can further watch this video on How to identify a pirated book

For more information about identifying piracy, visit **https://www.mheducation.co.in/piracy**

To report a pirated book, send 'Hi' on WhatsApp code given on the back cover or write to us at **support.india@mheducation.com**.

Reported pirated books are examined to combat their piracy.

Let's fight the Pirates of Piracy and resolve to go for original!

About the Authors

Arun Sharma is a post graduate from the prestigious Indian Institute of Management (IIM), Bangalore. He has been training corporate houses and CAT aspirants since 1996 and has personally trained over a thousand students who have made it into the IIMs and other top B Schools. He also holds the unique distinction of clearing CAT successfully 22 times in a row, with a score of 99.99 percentile in CAT 2008.

Meenakshi Upadhyay is an alumnus of IIM Bangalore and has been deeply involved in training students for CAT, CSAT, other management and aptitude entrance examinations for more than 25 years. A British Council certified trainer for Communications and Business English, she is also a Corporate Trainer in the fields of personality, language, etiquette and communication training.

11e

HOW TO PREPARE FOR

VERBAL ABILITY & READING COMPREHENSION

FOR

CAT

Common Admission Test
& Other Management
Examinations

Arun Sharma
Meenakshi Upadhyay

Mc Graw Hill
McGraw Hill Education (India) Private Limited

Published by McGraw Hill Education (India) Private Limited
Registered Office: Anjana Complex No: 5/90 A, Butt Road, St. Thomas Mount, Chennai – 600016

How to Prepare for Verbal Ability and Reading Comprehension for CAT, 11e

First reprint 2024

Print Edition
ISBN-13: 978-93-5532-715-4
ISBN-10: 93-5532-715-3

E-Book Edition:
ISBN-13: 978-93-5532-872-4
ISBN-10: 93-5532-872-9

02 03 04 05 06 RAJ 28 27 26 25 24

Typeset at Transcend Content Solution, 163F Jaigirghat Road, Panchanantala, Kolkata 700 063 and printed and bound in India at Rajkamal Electric Press, Plot No. 2, Phase-IV, Kundli, Haryana

Cover Design: Neeraj Dayal
Cover Image Source: Shutterstock

Visit us at: www.mheducation.co.in; Phone (Toll free in India): **1800 103 5875**
Write to us at: support.india@mheducation.com

CIN: U80302TN2010PTC111532

To

our son

Shaurya

Preface to the First Edition

The English section, comprising Verbal Ability and Reading Comprehension, is one of the most crucial components of the Common Admission Test (CAT). Questions worth 50 marks have been appearing from this section regularly for the past five years. As teachers in this field for the past 11 years, we have found it extremely difficult to recommend one single book that would comprehensively cover the entire English portion of the CAT. This constant dilemma, coupled with the overwhelming response that we received for *How to Prepare for* ***Quantitative Aptitude*** *for CAT and How to Prepare for* ***Data Interpretation*** *for CAT,* prompted us to think of preparing a book on *How to Prepare for* ***Verbal Ability and Reading Comprehension*** *for CAT.* Besides CAT, this book would effectively meet the requirements of exams like XAT, IIFT, IRMA, CET, MAT, UPMCAT, and Bank PO examinations, where the English section is essentially a very vital component.

However, conceptualising and compiling a book which would provide a one-stop solution for English was not an easy task. And the inputs that we got from our sources regarding the expectations from such a book were no less demanding. They talked about a book which should help students:-

(a) *improve* their reading,
(b) give substantial inputs on how to read and *retain* it,
(c) teach accurate ways of *interpreting* the written material (*refer to Part I on* ***Reading Skill Development***),
(d) have exhaustive *practice of Reading Passages,*
(e) have exhaustive *practice for Reading Comprehension questions,*
(f) have *CAT questions,*
(g) provide the *correct approach to solve CAT questions* in the limited timeframe (*see section on* ***Illustrated CAT Passages***),
(h) have *solved examples* of previous year CAT Reading Comprehension questions,
(i) have *difficulty-based exercises* (one of the unique features of our previous books–*see the* ***Level of Difficulty (LOD)*** *exercises given at various sections*),
(j) provide students with a *rich vocabulary*–graded, if possible and suggest ways of enriching it,
(k) have sections on root words, origin of words, foreign words, prefixes, and suffixes,
(l) cover all *vocabulary-based question types* (like Antonyms, Synonyms, Odd-mans outs, and Analogies),
(m) cover question types and solving techniques for Fill in the Blanks/Cloze Tests; single and double blanks,
(n) provide a comprehensive solution to the all important question types of Paragraph Jumbles and Critical Reasoning (areas which we have covered in an extensive manner),
(o) have a section on Sentence Correction since it puzzles everyone and
(p) cover the all important Verbal Reasoning portion (where the inputs are too enormous to write in a single line).

Efforts have been made to accommodate the all these points. Basically, the book has been prepared in such a fashion that it would help students having varying requirements.

STRUCTURE

The book has been divided into four parts.

(1) Reading Comprehension
(2) Verbal Ability
(3) Verbal Reasoning
(4) Mock Test Papers

Let us now briefly look at the suggested approach for each part of the book.

PART I: READING COMPREHENSION

While going through the first part on Reading Comprehension your focus should be on:

(a) Improving your reading skills (ability to read, grasp and retain information)
(b) Improving your ability to predict questions that might be framed on a passage even as you read the passage (In fact, there is an entire chapter devoted to CAT passages which illustrate what you should perceive at each stage within the reading of a passage)
(c) Understanding the various types of questions that are framed under Reading Comprehension and how to solve these question types
(d) Gaining extensive practice through the Level of Difficulty (LOD) 1, LOD 2 and CAT Exercises provided

PART II: VERBAL ABILITY

The second part of the book concentrates on three levels of the language viz., word level, sentence level and paragraph level.

The word level, apart from giving you a glimpse and practice of the various vocabulary-based question types asked in competitive exams, also contains an exclusive section to help you develop your vocabulary. This section has Word Lists based on three levels of difficulty–the words segregated on the basis of the frequency of appearance of the word in the CAT examination. To make full use of this feature in this book, you are required to work under a proper routine and go through the Word Lists in increasing order of difficulty.

Besides we have also given a comprehensive and rare collection of roots, prefixes and suffixes as well as foreign origin words, which is rather a unique feature of this book.

You will also get adequate question exposure and practice questions under the following question types: Fill in the blanks, Grammatical error-based questions, Paragraph Jumbles, etc.

PART III: VERBAL REASONING

This section exposes you to the various questions types in verbal reasoning viz., Critical Reasoning, Adequate practice sets for each of theses question types have been provided for improving your skills.

PART IV: TEST PAPERS

This part has Test Papers of CAT questions.

Efforts have been made to make the book as student-friendly as possible. Any suggestion for improvement will be highly acknowledged and appreciated.

Arun Sharma
Meenakshi Upadhyay

Acknowledgements

I would like to begin by being grateful for the guidance and inspiration given by my late grandparents Dr. S. N. Upadhyay and Smt. Indira R. Upadhyay. The values and beliefs that they instilled in me have been a source of constant inspiration in my life.

I am thankful to my late father, Mr. G. S. Upadhyay, whose stories and knowledge inculcation have had a very special significance for me, and my mother, Sandhya, who, with her unflinching support through thick and thin, has helped me reach where I am today. I also owe thanks to my sister, Jaysashree, who introduced me to the wonderful world of books and unfolded the voracious reader in me, and my brother, Sachindra, who has always been there whenever I needed him. Special mention and thanks are also due to my brother-in-law Dr. Rajarshi and sister-in-law, Aparna.

I am also thankful to my parents-in-law, Mr. M. K. Sharma and Mrs. Renu Sharma, my brother-in-law, Ravi, whose vocabulary has always inspired me and my sister-in-law Aditi who has always been a big help.

My nephews, Harsh, Rishi, Arjit, Shrey and Rakshit, and my son, Shaurya, have always been happy to extend their help to me!

My husband, Arun, has been a pillar of strength in whatever I have done. This book would have been impossible without him.

Meenakshi Upadhyay

We would like to thank our students and readers across India who remain our primary motivation to discover better and more efficient ways of thinking. Special thanks to Sanjeeta, Ritika and Kavita, who were ready to pitch in wherever required. Our team members at Mindworkzz are a constant source of support and encouragement and we would like to especially mention Arun Chaturvedi for standing with us through thick and thin.

The wonderful people at McGraw Hill Education, with their amazing insights and professional guidance, are responsible in bringing out this book. They are a constant source of learning for us. We extend our special thanks to the team—Mr. Tanweer Ahmad, Mr. Tanmoy Roychowdhury, Mr. Nikhil Wadhera, Mrs. Aarooshi Garg-Khattar, Mr. Atul Gupta and Mrs. Anjali Nair.

Arun Sharma

Key Issues in Preparation

For many CAT aspirants, especially those who do not have an English-medium education background, this section represents the biggest hurdle in the CAT and indeed so, in most other management entrance exams.

At the same time, even for students who have the best education and are seemingly good at English, the experience of the past few years' CAT papers shows us that being good at speaking and conversing in English might not guarantee you a top percentile score.

THE ROLE OF READING IN DEVELOPING YOUR LANGUAGE SKILLS

The most commonly heard advice for career aspirants when it comes to preparing for all important sections is "read more and more". So, it is your right to ask, "If I read more and more, would I get a solution to my problem in the language section in a time frame of say, four months?"

The answer to this question is largely in the negative. The reason is that for you to develop your scores in Verbal Ability (VA) and Reading Comprehension (RC) by just reading more and more, you require maybe a two-to-three years cycle of preparation. Four months would be more like merely scratching the surface.

We are not saying for a moment that reading is not important for preparing yourself for this section. Reading more and more remains one of the primary activities that you would still need to do, but rather than doing it blindly, it would be better for you if you did it with a clear purpose.

First, let us try to set the objectives of reading more and more.

1. Sentence Comprehension is the Core Skill in English

One of the key problems aspirants face when they take the CAT is that the language is too complex and the options for the answer to the question asked are too close to each other for comfort.

Your comfort with the language you read in the examination is going to depend on three broad factors. These give rise to the possibilities of the kind of language you are going to face:

(1) Short Sentences (10–15 words long) versus Long Sentences (25+ words long)

(2) Easy Vocabulary versus Tough Vocabulary

(3) Familiar Topic versus Unfamiliar Topic

So obviously, short sentences, easy vocabulary and familiar topics would be the easiest to handle while you would have to grapple with long sentences, tough vocabulary and unfamiliar topics.

Needless to say, when aspirants face such language they lose control over the solving of questions based on such paragraphs and passages.

So obviously, one of your primary objectives must be to improve your skill in handling the most complex language scenarios that the above three dimensions can throw up.

What we are referring to would be clear from the following example:

Consider this paragraph from a reading comprehension section of the CAT 2008 question paper:

"Finally, while we still have some other past societies to consider before we switch our attention to the modern world, we must already be struck by some parallels between the Maya and the past societies. As on Mangareva, the Maya environmental and population problems led to increasing warfare and civil strife. Similarly, on Easter Island and at Chaco Canyon, the Maya peak population numbers were followed swiftly by political and social collapse. Paralleling the eventual extension of agriculture from Easter Island's coastal lowlands to its uplands, and from the Mimbres floodplain to the hills, Copan's inhabitants also expanded from the floodplain to the more fragile hill slopes, leaving them with a larger population to feed when the agricultural boom in the hills went bust. Like Easter Island chiefs erecting ever larger statues, eventually crowned by Pukao, and like Anasazi elite treating themselves to necklaces of 2000 turquoise beads, Maya kings sought to outdo each other with more and more impressive temples, covered with thicker and thicker plaster - reminiscent in turn of the extravagant conspicuous consumption by modern American CEOs. The passivity of Eater chiefs and Maya Kings in the face of the real big threats to their societies completes our list of disquieting parallels."

The above paragraph contains 202 words and has six sentences, giving an average sentence length of 33.66 words! And this is more of a rule than exception. An aspirant whose comfort level consists of 10-word sentences would be badly out of his depth in such a paragraph.

So, the first point we would like to make here is:

You should focus on improving your ability to comprehend longer sentences with complex vocabulary on unfamiliar topics.

Do all your reading activity with this goal in mind and you would suddenly realise that a three-year cycle of development would crash into four months.

Remember, improved comprehension of sentences could well be the game-changer you are looking for in your language preparations!

2. CAT Questions are More about Logic Than about Language

Consider a Sample Question and its Options

The question was based on a passage in Reading Comprehension (which obviously cannot be reproduced here due to space constraints) but we want you to focus just on reading the options well. Very often one sees that aspirants make an error in an answer simply because they have not understood what the question is asking and what the options are saying.

So, read the options carefully and try to slot them into clear-cut compartments.

The question was:

What is the thematic highlight of the passage?

(1) In the absence of strong biological linkages, reciprocal roles provide the mechanism for coordinating human behaviour.

(2) In the absence of reciprocal roles, biological linkages provide the mechanism for coordinating human behaviour.

(3) Human behaviour is independent of biological linkages and reciprocal roles.

(4) Human behaviour depends on biological linkages and reciprocal roles.

(5) Reciprocal roles determine normative human behaviour in society.

If you were to observe the options carefully you would realise that all the options are talking about the interrelationship between three concepts viz:

A. Biological Linkages

B. Reciprocal Roles

C. Human Behaviour

With this understanding if you were to look at the options they can be rewritten as:

(1) In the absence of strong A, B provides the mechanism to coordinate C

(2) In the absence of B, A provides the mechanism to coordinate C

(3) C is independent of A and B

(4) C depends on A and B

(5) B determines C

Once you have this kind of clarity in your mind about what each of these options is saying all you need to do is to understand the purpose of what the author is saying in the passage. Now if you were to read the following random extracts from the passage, what do you conclude is the author saying?

Statements from the First Paragraph

Human Biology does nothing to structure human society.

Giving birth is certainly not sufficient to be a mother but, as adoption and fostering show, it is not even necessary!

Statements from the Second Paragraph

The fine detail of what is expected of a mother or a father or a dutiful son differs from culture to culture, but everywhere behaviour is coordinated by the reciprocal nature of roles. Husbands and wives, parents and children, employers and employees, waiters and customers, teachers and pupils, warlords and followers–each makes sense only in its relation to the other.

Statements from the Fourth Paragraph

The American sociologist Erving Goffman built an influential body of social analysis on elaborations of the metaphor of social life as drama. Perhaps his most telling point was that it is only through acting out a part that we express character.

Correct Option

It is clear that the author is indeed talking about a relationship between B (reciprocal roles) and C (human behaviour). So, clearly 2 and 3 are rejected. Option 4 can be rejected based on the fact that the author is saying the opposite of the dependence of C on A. In fact, he is saying that C does not depend on A. So, we are in between Options 1 and 5.

In order to choose the correct option from these, you need to read the options clearly and take a call.

Option 1 is talking about the "absence of strong biological linkages" in a society. Hence, all you need to do to eliminate this option is to ask yourself the question–"Can biological linkages ever be absent in a society?" Your mind would tell you clearly that this cannot happen. Hence, we are only left with Option 1 which indeed is the key argument that the author is taking.

Key Arguments

Obviously, the point of discussing this question with you is to make a certain argument about your preparation process for the language section. And the key arguments one is trying to make are:

(1) Solving a language question is an exact science, i.e., just as solving a Quantitative Aptitude or Data Interpretation question. This section too always has one clear answer. The only issue is whether you have developed your mind enough to see it!

(2) Even if you have good command over English you should not take this section lightly and do your preparations to develop your reliability to score well always. Remember they test more of your logical thinking ability rather than your level of English. So, knowing English is no guarantee to scoring well in this section. Focus on clearing the cobwebs from your mind, induce clarity in your thought and you should be well on your way!

3. Concluding Note

It has always been our effort to help and guide you with the best possible study material and practice questions so that you get a simulated experience of the whole process before you take the actual exam. As the saying goes, "The will to win is not nearly as important as the will to prepare to win. Everyone wants to win, but not everyone wants to prepare to win. Preparing to win is where the determination that you will win, is made. Once the game or test or project is underway, it is too late to prepare to win. The actual game, test or project is just the end of a long process of getting ready, in which the outcome was really determined. So, if you want to win, you must want to prepare to win. Once you prepare to win, winning is almost anti climatic."

ALL THE BEST!!

Arun Sharma

Meenakshi Upadhyay

Frequency Analysis Table of Question types in VA and RC in CAT 2014 to 2023

Topic	No. of Qs 2014	No. of Qs 2015	No. of Qs 2017-2019	Comments for No. of Qs 2017-2019	No. of Qs 2020-2021	No. of Qs 2022	No. of Qs 2023
1. Reading Comprehension	16	18-20	24	4-6 Passages with 3-6 Questions (Total 24 Qs)	16	16	
2. Paragraph Jumbles	4	3-5 without options	4 (TITA) without options		4 TITA	4	2
3. Paragraph Completion/						4	2
Last sentence of the paragraph	3	3-4					
4. Phrasal Verbs							
+ Sentence Correction	4						
5. Irrelevant Sentence	4	3-4 (TITA)	3 (TITA) without options		2 TITA		2
6. Critical Reasoning	3	1-2					
7. Summary of the paragraph (New question type)		3-4	3		2	2	2
Total		34	34		24	24	24

Contents

Part 2: Verbal Ability

Part 3: Verbal Reasoning

Part 4: The CAT Experience

Part 5: The CAT Experience

PART 1 Building Skills for Reading Comprehension

All the chapters in this part will help you to hone your reading comprehension (RC) skills in the following ways:

- Helping you to create your daily reading scheme underlining the importance of RC in CAT papers.
- Making you (i) understand vocabulary in context, main ideas and implied main ideas, and transition and idea organisation patterns; (ii) identify supporting details, facts, inferences, and judgements; (iii) recognise author's purpose and tone; and (iv) evaluate strength of argument.
- Helping you understand (i) what is RC; (ii) how to read RC passages; and (iii) how to think and react while reading a CAT reading comprehension passage.
- Helping you practice RC exercises at different difficulty levels.

Key Components of this part:

- **Seven-Dimension approach to better reading skills**
- **An introduction to the various types of RC questions**
- **Thorough explanation and analysis of RC**
- **Bit-by-bit explanation of CAT passage from CAT papers of 2003, 2006, 2017, 2018 and 2019**
- **LOD Exercises**

Go through the introduction and the Seven Dimension Approach to better reading skills

↓

Comprehend the theory of RC

↓

Go closely through the illustrated CAT passages noting the key gaps between *what you understand out of and how you react to a CAT passage versus what should be the ideal reaction and comprehension while solving a CAT passage*

↓

Solve the two Levels of Difficulty and the CAT passages and while doing so make sure that you closely analyse each question and also focus on recognising the mental thought errors you are making while solving each level of difficulty. Solve Level of Difficulty I with detailed analysis (Chapter 5)

- Solve Level of Difficulty II with detailed analysis (Chapter 6)
- Solve CAT passages with detailed analysis (Chapter 7)

In This Part

Section 1: **Reading Comprehension** *Section 2:* **LOD Exercises**

SECTION 1: Reading Comprehension

In this section, we will be concentrating on helping you build your reading comprehension (RC) skills. We start this chapter with a basic introduction **(Chapter 1)** of RC and by giving you a basic framework for developing your reading skills.

Chapter 2 increases the focus on the development of reading skills by dividing reading skills into seven clear-cut dimensions. The reader is expected to first understand each of these skill dimensions and then to focus his self development efforts on each of these reading skill dimensions.

Chapter 3 focusses on the theory and question types of RC giving the reader a clear glimpse into the various question types to expect in RC.

Chapter 4 gives the reader a rare insight into the mind and the mental processes of CAT cracker by taking the reader through the actual thinking that goes towards the solving of real CAT passages.

CHAPTER 1

Introduction

Reading Comprehension (RC) forms one of the most critical parts of the CAT question paper.

To Bell the CAT

Every year, over the past 20 years of the CAT, RC has constituted anything between 15-30 per cent of the total number of questions in the exam.

Thus, for instance, while CAT 2003 (re-exam) had 25 marks out of 150 from the RC section, CAT 2004 had 25 marks out of 150 (16.66 per cent) and CAT 2005 had 20 marks out of 150 (13.33 per cent). Since CAT went online, 10 questions out of the total 60 from the whole paper are from RC carrying 16.66 per cent weightage in the exam. Hence, developing the appropriate level of skills for tackling the reading comprehension section is something that a student preparing for CAT simply cannot afford to ignore during the preparation phase for the CAT exam. Needless to say, the correlation between good Reading Ability and good Reading Comprehension Ability is very high. Hence, in order to develop your ability to solve reading comprehension questions, your first focus should be to take your reading ability up from its current level (whatever that might be.)

READ MORE AND MORE

This advice is what you will come across from every trainer across the country. However, what is not so readily available for students is what skills should one focus on developing while reading, as well as under what framework of self development should one take up the task of reading more and more. Consequently, in our decade long experience of training students, we have seen that students normally end up trying to blindly read more and more without a framework, a direction or a focus. As a result, the returns from reading that students achieve are not proportional to the effort that they put into their reading.

Picking Contextual Clues

We have always believed that blindly reading, without working in a framework, will result in sub-optimal results. Hence, a major thrust of our initial emphasis in this section will be to give you a framework for developing your reading habits. Before we go into that aspect, let us look at another issue which we believe is of utmost importance for you to understand.

THE PROCESS OF WRITING AND ITS RELEVANCE TO THE PROCESS OF READING

Language can be defined as a set of sounds which has been developed in order to convey ideas from one mind to another. Prior to the invention of the first languages, humans used to convey ideas either through sign language or through pictorial representations (as borne out in the paintings in caves through which messages were conveyed). The invention of language represented a paradigm shift in man's ability to communicate his thoughts and ideas to other fellow humans. Initially, all communication used to be oral and passed on orally from generation to generation. Speaking and listening were the two opposite ends of this chain of communication.

As the complexity of human life increased, the introduction of the written word was necessitated. In this chain of communication, reading is basically the reverse process of writing. A piece of writing is incomplete unless it is read by a reader. In this context, understanding the act of writing can take you a long way towards becoming a good reader.

The Cream of the Piece

Since any and every reading that you do involves comprehending and connecting to the author of the passage, in order to become a good reader you need to understand the process through which a good writer goes while writing any piece–(be it as short as a paragraph long to a passage of 1000 words to a full length book).

Let us suppose that you are asked to write a 500 word essay on 'The Relevance of Management Education in India'. Would you straightaway put your pen to paper and start putting down whatever comes to your mind or would you first formulate the outline of the idea structure that you might want to convey through the piece? If you are not an amateur writer, chances are that you would do the latter.

As a matter of fact, all good writers will follow this approach, i.e., they would formulate a kind of a skeleton (map or outline) of the idea they want to convey through their essay, before they put their pen to paper for the first time. This skeleton/map often includes the main idea, the supporting ideas, supporting evidences as well as the conclusion.

Most writers see the skeleton in the form of a picture of the idea structure. (A picture that consists of flowcharts, symbols, etc.) It is only after this that the pen is put to paper and the idea structure conveyed through a sequence of words, sentences and paragraphs.

As a reader, your task essentially, is to decode this sequence of words, sentences and paragraphs and come up with your own picture or interpretation of the idea conveyed by the author. The closer this picture is to the original one in the mind of the author, the better is the comprehension of the passage. In other words, you can even define the objective of reading as 'to photocopy the idea structure of the author into your mind'. Remember a crucial point:

The Cream of the Piece

The closer your skeleton/map is to what the author must have formulated, the more comprehensive will be your understanding of the passage you are reading.

It is in the light of the above that you should embark on what follows below. The following approach, if applied consistently to your daily dose of reading, will help you develop your level of reading from your current levels.

HOW READING SKILLS ARE IMPORTANT FOR ASPECTS OTHER THAN THE READING COMPREHENSION QUESTIONS OF THE CAT ENGLISH SECTION

The relevance of preparing well for the RC section does not simply end there. In fact, a closer look at the questions and question types asked under the head of Verbal Ability in the CAT, XLRI and other management entrance papers of the past few years, clearly points at the overwhelming requirement of good reading habits for this section. Let us take a closer look at the question types in Verbal Ability asked in the CAT over the past few years to illustrate the importance of good reading habits for solving the same.

☞ **Verbal Ability Question Type 1: *Paragraph Jumbles (Frequency of use: Consistently used every year over the last 12 years)***

This has been one of the most favorite question types of examiners over the last 12 years. In this question type, a set of sentences which constitute a paragraph, are jumbled. The student is supposed to find out the correct order of sentences so as to form a coherent paragraph. For instance, try solving this question, which appeared as a two mark question in CAT 2005.

✔ ***The sentences given in the question, when properly sequenced, form a coherent paragraph. Each sentence is labeled with a letter. Choose the most logical order of sentences from among the given choices to construct a coherent paragraph.***

(a) Similarly, turning to caste, even though being lower caste is undoubtedly a separate cause of disparity, its impact is all the more greater when the lower-caste families also happen to be poor.

(b) Belonging to a privileged class can help a woman to overcome many barriers that obstruct women from less thriving classes.

(c) It is an interactive presence of these two kinds of deprivation–being low class and being female–that massively impoverishes women from the less privileged classes.

(d) A congruence of class deprivation and gender discrimination can blight the lives of poor women very severely.

(e) Gender is certainly a contributor to societal inequality, but it does not act independently of class.

1. EABDC
2. EBDCA
3. DAEBC
4. BECDA.

The correct answer here is EBDCA. The skills required to solve a question of this type (which is discussed in detail in Part Two of this book) include:

(a) Identification of opening sentence,
(b) Identification of the topic sentence,
(c) Getting and understanding the main idea in the question,
(d) Identifying transitions of ideas,
(e) Ordering of ideas,
(f) Slotting in the details in their right places,
(g) Understanding Vocabulary in context.

All the above are reading skills which we will learn about in the later part of this chapter.

☞ Verbal Ability Question Type 2: *Inappropriate usage of word*

Here, we would look into the usage of a single word in four different contacts. These type of questions were first introduced in CAT 2003.

In each question, the word at the top is used in four different ways. Choose the option in which the usage of the word is incorrect or inappropriate.

Hand

1. I have my hand full, I cannot do it today.
2. The minister visited the jail to see the breach at first hand.
3. The situation is getting out of hand.
4. When the roof of my house was blown away, he was willing to lend me hand.

Reason

1. Your stand is beyond all reason.
2. Has she given you any reason for her resignation?
3. There is little reason in your pompous advice.
4. How do you deal with a friend who doesn't listen to a reason?

Other words that have been asked are: help, paper, business, service, for, near, etc.

There is no way you can study grammatical rules to help you improve your ability to solve these kinds of questions–nor does it have anything to do with vocabulary since the words given are extremely easy in nature.

The Cream of the Piece

As you must have understood, your ability to solve these questions depends directly on the extensiveness of your reading habits and how often and in what form of usage you have seen the word earlier.

☞ Verbal Ability Question Type 3: *Paragraph Completion*

In this question type, introduced for the first time in CAT 2005, the question contains a paragraph where the last statement has been removed. The student is expected to decide the appropriate option which best completes the paragraph.

Consider the following question that was a two mark question in the CAT 2005 paper:

The following question has a paragraph from which the last sentence has been deleted. From the given options, choose the one that completes the paragraph in the most appropriate way.

Federer's fifth grand slam win prompted a reporter to ask whether he was the best ever. Federer is certainly not lacking in confidence, but he wasn't about to proclaim himself the best ever. "The best player of this generation, yes," he said, "but nowhere close to ever. Just look at the records that some guys have. I'm a minnow."

1. His win against Agassi, a genius from the previous generation, contradicts that.
2. Sampras, the king of an earlier generation, was as humble.
3. He is more than a minnow to his contemporaries.
4. The difference between 'the best of this generation' and 'best ever' is a matter of perception.

The correct answer here is 3.

CAT aspirants in 2005 faced a lot of difficulty in solving this question type. Needless to say, solving this question needs an ability to catch:

(a) the author's topic,
(b) the main idea he/she is trying to convey and
(c) understand the transitions he/she is using in the paragraph.

Needless to say, it is not possible to eliminate the doubts that crop up in one's mind while solving such questions... only a good reader with a lot of reading exposure would be able to clearly see an answer to such a question. If you want to be able to see the answer to such questions, minus any ambiguities, development of good reading skills is the only way out.

(And considering that there were a clear 8 marks in 4 questions, it gave a clear advantage to the 'good reader'.)

☞ Verbal Ability Question Type 4: *Identifying grammatically correct/incorrect sentence(s):*

Consider the following question asked in CAT 2005.

This question consists of four sentences on a topic. Some sentences are grammatically incorrect or inappropriate. Select the option that indicates the grammatically correct and appropriate sentence(s).

A. People have good reason to care about the welfare of animals.

B. Ever since Enlightenment, their treatment has been as a measure of mankind's humanity.

C. It is not a coincidence that William Wilberforce and Sir Thomas Foxwell Buxton, two leaders of the movement to abolish the slave trade, helped found the Royal Society for the Prevention of cruelty to animals in 1820s.

D. An increasing number of people go further: mankind has a duty not to cause pain to animals that have the capacity to suffer.

1. A&D 2. B
3. A&C 4. C&D

The correct answer here is 1.

As you must have realized, solving these questions is not about cramming up complex grammatical rules. Even if you are given a comprehensive book on grammar to consult while solving these questions, you are unlikely to come out with the relevant rule which applies to the particular sentence under consideration. Then, on what skills would you depend to solve these kinds of questions? To draw a parallel, let us ask you a question in turn. How would you solve a similar question if it were asked in your mother tongue? Would you rush to the nearest available grammar book? Unlikely! In fact, your ability to solve such a question would depend solely on the frequency of the number of times that you have seen the particular nuance of the language being used. If you have not been exposed to the same, it is unlikely that you will be able to apply any sort of logic to solving this question type.

☞ Verbal Ability Question Type 5: *Summarising a paragraph.*

Consider the following question which appeared in CAT 2003.

Four alternative summaries are given below. Choose the option that best captures the essence of the text.

Some decisions will be fairly obvious–"no-brainers." Your bank account is low, but you have a two week vacation coming up and you want to get away to some place warm to relax with your family. Will you accept your in-laws' offer to free use of their Florida beachfront condo? Sure. You like your employer and feel ready to move forward in your career. Will you step in for your boss for three weeks while she attends a professional development course? Of course.

A. Some decisions are obvious under certain circumstances. You may, for example, readily accept a relative's offer to free holiday accommodation or step in for your boss when she is away.

B. Some decisions are no-brainers, You need not think when making them. Examples are condo offers from in-laws and job offers from bosses when your bank account is low or boss is away.

C. Easy decisions are called " no-brainers" because they do not require any cerebral activity. Examples such as accepting free holiday accommodation abound in our lives.

D. Accepting an offer from in-laws when you are short on funds and want a holiday is a no-brainer. Another no-brainer is taking the boss's job when she is away.

1. A 2. B
3. C 4. D

The correct answer here is 1.

As for the previous questions, solving this question depends on your ability to understand the author's topic sentence, get a grip of the main idea, identify where the details are and what is the message conveyed through them–all skills of reading rather than anything else.

> **The Cream of the Piece**
>
> A closer look at other question types on Verbal Ability will further bear out this fact that–**strong reading exposure, habits and skills are a must in order to solve questions of Verbal Ability.**

It is due to this fact that Part I of this book on English is devoted to helping the student develop the skills set required to be a good reader. You are required to clearly understand the framework required for developing good reading habits, which is explained in the following part of the chapter. After that, you need to follow through consistently by applying the same framework in your daily reading scheme.

YOUR DAILY READING SCHEME

How Much Time Should I Spend on Reading Daily?

If you want to have any hope of developing your reading skills, the authors recommend a minimum of two hours per day of reading, over a year's time. (Needless to say, if you are trying to achieve this in a shorter time span, the minimum recommended reading will go up proportionately.)

WHAT KINDS OF STUFF SHOULD I READ?

Well, a true and frank answer to that question would be more like everything and anything under the sun. But where and at what level you start off your reading (under the framework we will be mentioning below) would depend on how much of a reader you have been during your school and college life. Remember, whatever your current reading skills are, there is always a level of writing which will challenge you. The basic concept that you need to adhere to for your reading exercises is that you should read things that constantly challenge and invigorate your mind. However, be careful to ensure that the challenge that the reading material puts forth to you should be small and not too big. If the material you choose to read is too challenging, the end result might be that you lose comprehension and subsequently, your interest in reading–an end result we are definitely not targeting!

So, when deciding the sources from which you are going to do your daily dose of reading, first of all define what level of writing represents a challenge for you. Then, you should identify the source/s (newspapers, magazines and books) that will give you that level of writing.

Thus, for instance, for some students, the editorials in a national daily represent a challenge, while for some others, the same level of challenge might be experienced in advanced philosophical (read: heavy) text.

In our experience, based on their reading exposure levels, students might be classified under four categories:

1. The Poor Reader This category of students has had no exposure to reading in English. Most students whom we have encountered under this category come from vernacular medium schooling backgrounds (although that is not an absolute rule since even convent school educated students might belong to this category if their reading exposure has been poor).

Consider the following excerpt, which will prove challenging for students belonging to this category:

"I was deeply embarrassed last week before a distinguished audience of sophisticated investors abroad-they virtually called me a liar. A year ago, I had reassured them that our stellar reformers–Manmohan Singh, Chidambaram and Montek–would not only ensure that our economic reforms would continue but they might even accelerate. A year later, the reforms are stuck and they were angry. I could not pretend that the reformers had become victims of coalition politics, for insiders tell me that the problem is with the Congress Party itself, which has lost the will of reform.

Luckily, I was bailed out by the Indian economy, which continues to grow robustly, and has been doing so for two decades, contemptuously ignoring our governments. The only way to explain this contradiction is that politics and economics are increasingly getting divorced in India, and we may have become like Italy, where they used to say, the economy grows at night when the government is asleep. Stephen Roach, the chief economist of Morgan Stanley, who exercises considerable influence on investor minds explains: 'India is on the cusp of something big. After my third trip there in 18 months, I am as enthusiastic about India as I was about China in the late 1990s. What excites me is the potential for an increasingly powerful internal consumption dynamic–the missing link in most development models."

The Cream of the Piece

If you think you belong to *the poor reader* category, your initial reading should start off with editorials of good quality national level newspapers (like *The Hindu, The Hindustan Times, The Deccan Herald, The Times of India, The Pioneer, The Indian Express,* etc.), analysis based articles in these newspapers and analytical articles in national level current issues magazines (like *India Today, Frontline, Week,* etc.). You can also graduate to books written in simple English (both fictional and non fictional).

2. The Average Reader In this category, students do not have a basic problem in reading and understanding English (since most of them are educated in English Medium schools). However, what we have seen is that in spite of the advantage of having studied in English medium schools, this category of students have not developed their reading skills, simply because they have not worked towards developing their reading habits. This group of students faces problems the moment they are confronted with a slightly complex or an unfamiliar topic. Thus, they might have no problem reading about the latest exploits of the Indian cricket team, but give them a topic about the latest advances in medical technology or for that matter, Freud's interpretation of a dream and they lose contact with the subject matter of the passage.

Consider the following extract which might prove challenging to a reader of this category:

"What reader could resist so delicious a topic: a book that sets out to explain how cuisine came to be deeply ingrained in France's cultural and intellectual make-up? Unfortunately, little of this hard-to-digest work concerns the actual history of French cuisine and how it came to 'triumph'. Much of it seemed at embedding the subject in a sociological framework to prove that food is worthy of academic study. Accordingly, it piles on jargon, including sentences such as: 'The cluster of activities that surround cooking and eating stakes out culinarity as a privileged entry into the social order.'

This is a pity, because beneath the layers of intellectual stodge, the author, a professor of sociology at Columbia University, offers some tantalizing morsels. Almost in passing, she mentions such iconic moments as the suicide of 17th century chef Vatel, when the fish arrived late for a banquet he was preparing for Louis XIV. She also cites the banquets of the Sun king at Versailles as a defining moment in French cuisine, but sadly does not describe them. Nor does she consider the influence of his minister Cardinal Rachelieu. Yet it was in this nation-building era of the Sun King that the first specifically French cookbooks were written."

The Cream of the Piece

If you think you belong to *the average reader* category, your reading scheme should start off with reading editorials from newspapers mentioned above, as also from Economic newspapers and should also include higher level magazines which use good quality English in their writing (like *Time, Fortune* and *Economist*).

3. The Good Reader This category of reader has developed himself through consistently being in touch with reading. His/her reading exposure includes reading novels (fictional mainly), coffee table books on self development and newspapers on a daily basis. He/she will not face problems in reading and connecting to the author's message in either of the above two extracts.

However, for this level of reader, something which goes beyond his/her comfort level of reading poses a problem. Consider this extract which might pose problems for this category of reader:

Philosophers have discussed the mode of existence which belongs to works of art, debating whether they are material things or mental constructs or whether perhaps they are more correctly to be described as 'types' of which the mental objects which come to awareness of this or that observer in moments of appreciation are the 'tokens'. To sturdy common sense it seems at first sight obvious that some works of art are material things: pictures and sculptures are transported from place to place in lorries; they are hung on walls or set up on pedestals; they are weighed and measured, their physical properties can be tested and verified. Yet when we consider such arts as poetry, music, and dance the case is different. Wordworth's Prelude and Verdi's Requiem are unique entities which we agree to be works of art: but there is no one material thing anywhere, and no one happening, which can be identified with either of them. Moreover, as has already been seen, even in the case of painting and sculpture we ascribe to the art work properties which are incompatible with its being merely a material thing. There are important senses in which the picture which we talk about and enjoy as a work of art is not identical with the material piece of pigmented canvas which is crated and carried about in a lorry.

The Cream of the Piece

If you belong to *the good reader* category, your objective should be to raise fair level through consistently reading material that challenges your comprehension. Magazines like Time & Economist & articles/books on Philosophy, advanced Scientific texts etc. should from your daily reading scheme.

4. The Excellent Reader This category of reader has gone beyond the levels required to connect to any of the above three extracts. He/she has typically read a lot on diverse topics and at varying levels of language usage. If you think you belong to this category, you can skim through the reading lessons and frameworks in the next part of this chapter (since we believe you might already be aware of all the points we are making). All you need to do is to continue your good work and further expand your level of exposure and increase the coverage of topics with which you are familiar.

Consider this extract, that might prove challenging to you if you belong to this level:

Man is seen as a component of this order of things, and his psychic-mental life as reproduction of the life of the cosmos, in both its material and its mode of organization. This view was advanced in the sixth century B.C. by the thinkers of the Miletian school (Thales, Anaximander, Anaximenes) and by Heraclitus of Ephesus. They were all products of the commercial-industrial and cultural centres of Asia Minor–the Greek colonial city-states, in which new social and economic relationship were being formed, with maximum destructive effect upon the old order of tribal society.*

*These thinkers of classical times did not all take the same form of matter to be the primary material of the world: Thales held that this was water ; Anaximander, that it was vague, boundless essence (apeiron**); Anaximenes, that it was air; and Heraclitus, that it was fire. The "nature philosophers" of classical times, explaining the natural world as proceeding from a single, all-penetrating primary principle, supposed that the particular form of life and behaviour which language (still reflecting the level of mythological thinking) designated as "the soul", must likewise be a manifestation of this principle.*

The Cream of the Piece

Whichever level you belong to, a common objective for you as an MBA/CAT aspirant will be to increase and develop the scope of subjects with which you can claim familiarity.

To Bell the CAT

A closer analysis of the CAT question papers of the past decade reveals very clearly, that familiarity with certain topics is a must for all aspirants. Not just the passages but even the shorter Verbal Ability questions are normally extracted from one of the following topics/subjects:

(1) Economics
(2) Management
(3) History
(4) National and International Polity
(5) Sociology
(6) Humanities
(7) Philosophy
(8) Psychology
(9) Art, Music and culture
(10) Science and Technology (incl. Medicine and Information Technology.)
(11) Miscellaneous

A WORD OF CAUTION: THINGS THAT DO NOT WORK

Why Speed Reading Does Not Work, and in Fact is not Needed

There are a lot of books and trainers around who talk about speed reading, promising inexperienced readers a never before and almost magical jump in their reading abilities. However, in our experience of training thousands of students, we have seen the futility of speed reading techniques. The fact that the 'magic' wears off the moment you try to read anything outside the provided exercises has been a constant in our years of experience of having trained students. In fact, the moment a 'speed reading trained student' is confronted with something remotely heavy, the speed reading techniques stop working.

The basic reason why these reading techniques do not work under the examination reading conditions is that these techniques are designed for sparse and easy reading materials. (Speed reading is typically defined for ordinary, non technical matter). On the contrary, the passages and extracts used in the CAT, XLRI and other top management entrance exams are dense in terms of their content. They contain too much information and any attempt at skimming and scanning (which are recommended speed reading techniques) results in a loss of comprehension. Sometimes, missing on a crucial sentence might just end up making you lose your connection with the author totally.

Furthermore, at what speed (in words per minute) do you think you need to read in order to do well in the RC section? Take a guess... 400, 500, 700, or even more??? Incidentally, these are the kinds of reading speeds that speed reading books promise you that they will help you achieve.

Now consider this fact. A typical CAT passage is anywhere between 800 to 1200 words. The questions further form approximately 300 to 500 words. This means that in order to read a passage and solve the questions, all you need to do is read and completely understand anywhere between 1100 to 1700 words. CAT 2005 had 3 passages constituting 20 marks in all, and students had approximately 20 to 22 minutes to solve the same. A total of 3073 words – translates to a ridiculous reading speed requirement of 139.68 words per minute if you want to solve all the three passages. If you add the fact that most successful CAT aspirants solved only two out of the three passages, the statistic becomes even more ridiculous–especially in the light of the tall claims of 600 to 800 words per minute that these speed reading trainers and books claim that they can help a student achieve. Looking at it from another angle–if someone was able to achieve these reading speeds he/she should have been able to complete the 20 marks in the RC section in CAT 2005 in about five minutes flat!! Doesn't happen, does it?

To Bell the CAT

A look at CAT 2003 gives a similar picture:

5702 words in five passages (including their questions) were required to be read for 25 questions (reading speed of 228.08 wpm if you were, to solve all five passages). CAT qualifiers attempted at most, 3 passages out of the five, in about 25 minutes. This required a reading speed of approximately 134 wpm.

Where does the need for speed reading arise? It simply does not.

CHAPTER 2 The Seven Dimension Approach to Better Reading Skills

INTRODUCTION

The reading skills that you need to develop to improve your reading ability can be categorised into seven dimensions, which are divided into Basic and Advanced reading skills:

Basic Dimensions	Dimension 1:	Understanding Vocabulary in Context
	Dimension 2:	Identifying and Understanding Ideas
	Dimension 2 (A):	Identifying and Understanding Main Ideas
	Dimension 2 (B):	Identifying Implied Main Ideas
	Dimension 3:	Identifying Supporting Details
	Dimension 4:	Identifying Relationships between Ideas
	Dimension 4 (A):	Understanding the Use of Transitions
	Dimension 4 (B):	Idea Organisation patterns.
Advanced Dimensions	Dimension 5:	Identifying Facts, Opinions and Inferences
	Dimension 5 (A):	Facts and Opinions
	Dimension 5 (B):	Inferences
	Dimension 6:	Identifying Purpose and Tone
	Dimension 7:	Recognising Arguments and their Common Structures

Fig. 2.1 Seven Dimensions of Reading Skills

BASIC DIMENSIONS OF READING SKILLS

DIMENSION ONE: DEVELOPING THE ABILITY OF UNDERSTANDING VOCABULARY IN CONTEXT

As mentioned above, any piece of writing is a sequence of words, sentences and paragraphs. The *word* is the most basic building block of any piece of writing.

During the process of reading, we often come across situations where we are unaware of the meaning of particular words. The presence of unfamiliar words in a piece of writing might lead to one of two types of situations:

(a) The meaning of the word totally breaks the comprehension of the sentence, leading to uncertainty in the interpretation of the passage.

Consider the following example:

(i) *And the courtier said "May I **genuflect**?"*

(ii) *Since, Ecuador's presidents are limited to one term, Mr. Gutierrez might also back his former boss. If so, things really could get loco.*

In each of the above sentences, the italicised words make the reader lose comprehension with what the author is trying to get across. Unless you happen to know the exact meaning of the word, you will be at a loss to understand the author's message. The best you can do is to create alternatives in your mind with respect to what the particular word could mean.

(b) The meaning of the word can be understood (or pieced together) based on the context in which it is used.

If you were asked to define the words *testimony, charismatic or clannism,* you might face some discomfort. However, if you saw these words in sentences, the chances are that you would come up with fairly accurate meanings of the same words.

Consider the following examples. See whether you can define the words in italics in the following three sentences:

Judge John Hass imposed a publication ban on the testimony of Philip Sartre, former head of Amans and Mather, an advertising agency, as he is to stand trial on fraud charges.

✔ ***Here, the word* testimony *means statement.***

The charismatic leader's homecoming will further complicate Ecuador's already turbulent political scene.

✔ ***Here,* charismatic *means magnetic.***

The revival of village clannism is among the party's main worries about it's grip on rural stability. In Beihe, more than half of the villagers share the surname Zhang. Among the rest, Yan is the biggest clan.

✔ ***Here,* clannism *means the tendency to stick to one's tribe or family.***

In each of the above sentences, the context (the previous and the following words and ideas) provides us with clues for defining the unfamiliar word.

In most situations, the meaning of the word can be derived from the context of the passage. However, this is an ability that gets better with use.

Picking Contextual Clues Generally, contextual clues are seen in the form of:

(a) Illustrations & Examples
(b) Cause & Effect relationships
(c) Synonyms (Parallelisms or similarities)
(d) Antonyms (Opposites or contrasts)
(e) General sense of the paragraph or passage.

Let us now look at examples of each type one by one:

(A) Illustrations or examples One of the ways of making a point which is commonly used by authors is through the use of illustrations or examples to reiterate the point. In such cases, if the unfamiliar word has an illustration or an example to support what it means, it provides us with a contextual clue for solving the question.

Let us look at the following examples:

(1) The ***impoverished*** state of the castle told a sorry tale of holding on to past glories–the walls were barren, the paint had peeled off and the glory of the past had clearly worn off.

In the above sentence, ***impoverished*** means:

(a) poor (b) rich
(c) inadequate

(2) His ***obsequious*** nature made him a favorite of all– he only had complimentary words to say about everybody.

In the above sentence, ***obsequious*** means:

(a) Deceiving (b) Critical
(c) flattering

✔ ***In the first sentence above, the examples provided to illustrate, impoverished, clearly point to 'poor' as its meaning. In the second, the illustration provides only one meaning, i.e., flattering, to the word in the context of the sentence.***

(B) Cause & effect Cause and effect relationships are again very commonly used in most writing structures. If we come across an unfamiliar word in either the cause or the effect of a cause-effect structure, the context is likely to tell us what the intended meaning of the word is. This principle is amply illustrated in the example below:

Asked to explain the rosier outlook, manufacturers cite one factor above all–the sharp decline in interest rates in the past five years, which besides beautifying company balance sheets is encouraging consumers to borrow, to buy cars, for example and build houses.

In the above sentence, ***rosier*** means:

(a) Optimistic (b) Pessimistic
(c) Indifferent

✔ ***In the sentence, rosier obviously means optimistic, considering the illustrations in the later part of the sentence. The cause-effect relationship is extremely clear here. Dropping of interest rates has led to improved company balance sheets, as well as to greater demand in the form of consumers buying cars and building houses. The effect of all this has been to create an optimistic outlook on the part of the manufacturers.***

(C) Synonyms (parallelisms or similarities) Often, context clues occur in the form of synonyms– wherein one or more words mean the same as the unfamiliar word. The presence of the synonym gives a context clue that is useful to understand the meaning of the unfamiliar word.

Consider the following examples where the italicised word has its synonym in the form of the emboldened word/s.

(1) ***The exhilaration*** experienced by the parents when their child starts to walk is common to all cultures. The child's first steps give a feeling of **intense happiness** to the parents.
(2) Coming face to face with his first love, left Sameer in a ***poignant*** mood. He was **touched** by the irony of the situation.
(3) The ***felony*** committed by the robber was sure to make him pay. After all, serious **crime** seldom goes unpunished.
(4) Although he had sworn not to ***divulge*** her secret, he **revealed** it to his best friend, Rajeev.
(5) The *emancipatory* or **liberatory** significance of situating ordinary life and the world of duality and dualism in terms of a philosophy of non duality, lies in the fact that ultimately most of the categorical errors, those deep fundamental errors constitutive of our misunderstanding of being, which are at

the same time constitutive of the superficial, oppressive and mystifying levels of social beings which dominate and screen our life world, is the fact that they turn on misidentifications.

(6) Let us look at how a block operates, how potentially free, unbound energy becomes *fixated* or **stuck** or alternatively-in the case of a weakness of attention/ one-pointedness/mindfulness-becomes *dissipated* or **dispersed**.

(D) Antonyms (Opposites or contrasts) Just like same meaning words, there are situations where opposite meaning words give the contextual clues. Antonyms normally are signaled by a contrast statement/phrase, like however, on the other hand, but, yet, as against, although, etc.

Consider the following examples. In these examples, the italicised words are antonyms (have opposite meanings):

(1) Although my grand father was always ***profuse*** in his criticism, his praise was always **scarce**.

(2) A ***sedentary*** lifestyle is the root cause of all diseases, hence, regular exercise to stay **active** is a must to prevent disease.

(3) The ***homogeneity*** of the mixture was broken by the presence of a **variety** of stuff in it.

(E) General sense of the paragraph or passage In many cases, the contextual clues can be seen on the basis of the general sense of the paragraph (or sometimes, even the entire passage.)

Consider the following paragraph as an example.

Oddly, things are looking up for American International Group (AIG). Yes, the embattled global insurer has admitted overstating past earning and has postponed filing its financial statement with the Securities and Exchange Commission(SEC), provoking questions about how much the company is really worth; yes, there was an embarrassing kerfuffle between lawyers over the possible removal of critical documents in Bermuda; yes, regulators are looking through an ever-expanding list of suspect deals; and yes, Maurice "Hank" Greenberg, the brilliant executive who built AIG, has been forced to sever his formal ties with the firm. But a company as aggressive as this has faced litigation before. Even as the headlines seem ever more dire, AIG and Mr. Greenberg already looked poised for a modest comeback.

In the context of the above paragraph:

embattled means:

(a) Healthy (b) Profitable

(c) Stressed or beleaguered

The answer is obviously, stressed, and this can be deduced from the overall meaning of the passage.

Kerfuffle means:

(a) dialogue (b) talks (c) **commotion**

The answer is obviously, c.

In your normal everyday reading exercises, try to identify sentences and paragraphs where contextual clues fitting in one of the patterns above, help you to understand the meaning of a word with which you were unfamiliar.

Dimension Two (A): Ability to Identify and Understand Main Ideas

The ability to identify main ideas is perhaps the most important factor for good reading skills.

The main idea is the answer to the question: What is the main point that the author is trying to make in the paragraph?

For instance, read the following paragraph:

Most people do not worry much about physics or politics when for example, they look at the colours of a rainbow. Nor do they pause much when they use a remote control for their T.V. set, talk on the mobile phone, listen to the radio, cook food in their microwave oven, open their car door from a distance, or surf the internet without wires. Yet, these are all phenomena of electromagnetic radiation. How humans harness electromagnetic waves– and specifically those in the radio frequency part of the spectrum–has become so important that old and new ways of thinking are now lining up for a tense confrontation that will affect numerous businesses and billions of consumers.

The old mindset, supported by over a century of technological experience and 70 years of regulatory habit, views spectrum–the range of frequencies, or wave lengths, at which electromagnetic waves vibrate–as a scarce resource that must be allocated by government or bought and sold like property. The new school, pointing to cutting edge technologies, says that spectrum is by nature, abundant and that allocating, buying or selling parts of it will one day seem as illogical as, say, apportioning or selling sound waves to people who would like to have a conversation.

What is the main point that the author is trying to make in this paragraph? In order to discover the main idea, you should first determine the topic being discussed. In the above paragraph, for example, the topic is 'harnessing of electromagnetic radiation'. The main idea is that 'old and new ways of thinking are confronting each other with respect to the way we are harnessing electromagnetic waves.'

The main idea is something like an umbrella idea– the author's primary point about the topic. All the other material in the paragraph falls under the main idea (and is called the supporting detail, which consists of examples, illustrations, causes and reasons, evidence in the form of factual information, etc.).

(A) The Concept of the Idea Sentence In a paragraph, authors often present the main idea to the readers, in the form of a single sentence, called the **'Idea Sentence'.**

For example, in the given extract both the topic and the point about the topic are expressed in the last sentence of the first paragraph. Thus, the outline of the above paragraph can be shown as:

Topic: Harnessing of Electromagnetic radiation.

Main idea (as expressed in the idea sentence): There is a conflict of opinion about the harnessing of electromagnetic radiation between the old and the new way of thinking.

Supporting details:

(1) The old way of thinking is that the spectrum of radiation is a scarce resource and its scarcity must be respected by making people buy and sell it like property.

(2) The new way of thinking is that the spectrum is abundant by nature and buying and selling it will seem illogical one day.

The Cream of the Piece

You should always remember that the topic is the subject of a selection. It is normally expressed in a few words. Since Reading Comprehension passages do not have the topic mentioned, your first objective while reading a passage should be to identify the topic of the passage. In such a case, the question–'Who or what is the passage about?', is a useful question to ask oneself, as the answer to this question is the topic of the selection.

Once you have found the topic of the selection, the next step is to find the main idea which the author is trying to convey. For this purpose, you should ask yourself the question: 'What is the main point of the author about the topic?'

Note that it is not necessary that authors present the entire main idea of the paragraph in one sentence.

Sometimes, the main idea might be distributed across two to three sentences in the paragraph.

Consider the following selections. The topic and the idea sentence/s in each of these passages have been described below it.

They have a dismal track record when it comes to predicting economic growth, exchange rates or the direction of the stock market. So, you might have expected economists to despair at the thought of forecasting sports result. Not at all. Efforts to work out the numbers of medals which countries are likely to get in the Athens Olympics, which start on August 13th, are well under way.

The topic is forecasting sports results and the last sentence is the idea sentence.

"You want rubies! We can do business!" the anonymous caller promised a lucrative deal over the phone: stump up dollars in advance and he would produce a glittering hoard in Johannesburg. But your correspondence refused; so the caller instead produced some colorful abuse, sneered at British sexual prowess, and hung up.

It is rare for any attempted African scam to be executed so inelegantly. Advance-fee frauds often lure victims to part with tens of thousands of dollars on the promise of huge, but somehow plausible, later gains. Nigerians, especially, are renowned for elaborate and persuasive tales: "my uncle the president, died leaving me a million to smuggle to your country; let me use your bank account to hide the cash and you will get a slice; oh, and pay me a few thousand dollars in advance for handling fees".

The topic and the main idea are visible in the second sentence of the second paragraph. The topic is 'advance fee frauds in Africa' and the main idea is–what is done in these frauds.

"Our everyday life is much stranger than we imagine, and rests on fragile foundation." This is the intriguing first sentence of a very unusual new book about Economics, and much else besides: "The company of Strangers", by Paul Seabright, a professor of Economics at the University of Toulouse. Why is everyday life so strange? Because, explains Mr Seabright, it is so much at odds with what would have seemed, as recently as 10000 years ago, our evolutionary destiny. It was only then that "one of the most aggressive and elusive bandit species in the entire animal kingdom" decided to settle down. In no more than the blink of an eye, in evolutionary time, these suspicious and untrusting creatures, these "shy, murderous apes", developed co-operative networks of staggering scope and complexity-networks that rely on trust among strangers. When you come to think about it, it was an extraordinarily improbable outcome.

The topic is the 'unlikely evolution of the human species' and the idea conveyed is that the human species has moved 'from being an aggressive and elusive bandit species to a species which has developed cooperative networks of staggering scope and complexity, something that seemed highly unlikely in the context of what was our evolutionary destiny'.

"In the first weekend of every August, the town of Twinsburg, Ohio, holds a parade. Decorated floats, cars and lorries roll slowly past neat, white houses and clipped lawns, while thousands of onlookers clap and wave flags in sunshine. The scene is a perfect little slice of America. There is though, something rather strange about the participants: they all seem to come in pairs. Identical twins of all colours, shapes, ages, and sizes are assembling for the world's largest annual gathering of their kind.

The Twinsburg meeting is of interest to more people than just the twins themselves. Every year, the festival attracts dozens of scientists who came to prod, swab, sample and question the participants. For identical twins are natural clones: the odd mutation aside, they share 100 per cent of their genes. That means studying them can cast light on the relative importance of genetics and environments in shaping particular human characteristics."

The topic is 'identical twins' and the main idea as expressed in the second last and last sentences of the second paragraph is that 'studying identical twins can help us understand better, the relative importance of genetics and environment in shaping particular human characteristics.'

"The twin rule of pathology states that any heritable disease will be more concordant (i.e. more likely to be jointly present or absent) in identical twins than non-identical twins–and in turn, will be more concordant in non-identical twins than in non-siblings. Early work, for example, showed that the statistical correlation of skin mole counts between identical twins was 0.4, while non-identical twins had a correlation of only 0.2 (A score of 1.0 implies perfect correlation, while a score of zero implies no correlation). This result suggests that moles are heritable, but it also implies that there is an environment component to the development of moles, otherwise, the correlation in identical twins would be close to 1.0.

The topic is 'the twin rule of pathology' and the main idea about it is 'the relative concordance of heritable diseases between identical twins, non identical twins and non siblings. The idea sentence here is the first sentence of the selection. (In this case, the topic is also in the same sentence.)

The Cream of the Piece

(1) The idea sentence is usually supported by all the information in the remaining part of the paragraph. Hence, a useful way to check if you have got the idea sentence and hence, the main idea correctly is by asking yourself the question–"Is the sentence you have identified as the idea sentence supported by all the other material in the paragraph?"

(2) Be careful not to select a topic that is too broad or too narrow.

(3) The idea sentence can occur at either the start or the middle or the end of the paragraph. Paragraphs could be written in any of the following structures.

(A) Idea Sentence at the start of the paragraph (within the first two sentences). This is the most commonly used structure in writing. In such cases, the paragraph can follow any of the following structures:

(i) **Idea Sentence**–Supporting Detail/comment – Supporting Detail/comment–Supporting Detail/comment –Supporting Detail/comment

(ii) Introductory detail/comment/question–**Idea Sentence**–Supporting Detail/comment–Supporting Detail/comment–Supporting Detail/comment.

(B) Idea Sentence in the middle of a paragraph (Beyond the first two sentences). In such cases, the paragraph would typically follow the following structure:

(i) Introductory detail/comment–Introductory detail/comment/question—Idea Sentence–Supporting Detail/comment–Supporting Detail/comment –Supporting Detail/comment

(C) Idea Sentence at the end of the paragraph will follow the following structure:

(i) Introductory detail/comment–Supporting Detail/comment–Supporting Detail/comment–Supporting Detail/comment–**Idea Sentence**

(D) Idea Sentence at the beginning and the end of the paragraph

Some authors like to make a point at the beginning of the paragraph and reiterate it at the end of the paragraph. In such cases, the following structure will be used:

Idea Sentence–Supporting Detail/comment–Supporting Detail/comment–Supporting Detail/comment/question–**Idea Sentence**

Whatever we have been discussing above has been in the context of single paragraphs, how does it apply to a reading comprehension passage? This is a very obvious query that comes to mind. Well, the answer is that in a long passage consisting of 4-5 paragraphs, each paragraph will have its own main idea (or its own theme). This is due to the fact that the main idea of the entire passage is broken down into its component parts. What you need to realize is that just as the alphabet is the building block of a word and the word is the building block of the sentence, so also the paragraph is the building block of the passage. Just as we need to read all the alphabets used in the formation of a word in order to make sense of the word, and just as we need to read all the words in a sentence in order to make sense of a sentence, similarly, we need to read and grasp each paragraph of a passage to get the true meaning of the entire passage.

Comprehending individual paragraphs without linking them, often leaves us with an incomplete idea structure. Seen from the author's point of view, the writing process as described earlier, is: he/she formulates the main idea in his mind and then breaks it down into its component parts. Each component part is then normally put into separate paragraphs and the supporting details are filled in to complete the passage.

Dimension Two (B): Identifying Implied Main Ideas

Many a times, the main idea may not be expressed inside one sentence. In such cases, authors typically imply or suggest a main idea without actually stating it clearly in one sentence. In such cases, the reader needs to be able to figure out the main idea by stringing together multiple statements giving the idea. Even in such cases, the main idea will be got by the answer to the question:

What is the main point that the author is trying to make in the paragraph? The only difference will be that the answer to the question will not be found in one or more idea sentences.

In fact, it will not be stated anywhere in the paragraph. In such cases, the main idea gets identified by the fact that most of the supporting details will be pointing towards the implied main idea. The student is encouraged to locate and experience such situations in his/her normal reading exercises.

For Your Better Understanding

In the following paragraphs, identify the topic and the idea.

(1) Even by the standards of ASEAN, it was a dismal performance. The leaders of the other nine members of the Association of South-East Asian Nations used their summit in Bali this week to ladle praise on Myanmar for its "positive" and "pragmatic" recent policies. These, it appeared, meant the transfer of Myanmar's most famous citizen, the Nobel laureate Aung San Suu Kyi, from prison to house arrest, and the publication of a "road map" for democracy. Since a return to democracy has been promised by Myanmar's current junta ever since it took power in 1988, and since Miss Suu Kyi won an election in 1990 that has never been recognised, the Myanmar map looks as forlorn as the Middle Eastern one.

The disgraceful treatment meted out to Miss Suu Kyi is only the most obvious outrage committed by South-East Asia's most repressive and incompetent government. The generals do not just imprison thousands of political prisoners: they have turned their country into a place where life expectancy has collapsed to around 55, and growth has vanished. The World Health Organisation ranks the efficacy of Myanmar's health system at 190 out of 191 nations.

Topic: __________

____

Main Idea: __________

____

____

(2) In Pakistan–they are katchi abadis, in Cuba–focos isalubres, in India–bustees and in Brazil–favelas. Whatever the local name of slums, there are a lot of them and they are growing fast. A new report, "The Habitat," by the United Nations agency responsible for "human settlements", says that in 2001, just under a billion people were living in slums–about a third of the world's city dwellers. In the last decade, urban populations in less developed regions increased by a third. On present trends, says the UN report, 2 billion people could be living in slums by 2030.

In Africa, many parts of the middle East, Latin America and Asia, migrants are leaving farm land which is unable to support them, and arriving in cities which are unprepared to deal with them. This has been a long term trend, and is unlikely to abate no matter how awful the slums become. In 1800, only 2 per cent of the world's population was urbanized; by 2008, more than half of the world will be. Because such migration is so predictable, and long established, it might seem surprising that many governments are ill-equipped for it. But there is little new in that either: the now–rich countries fared just as badly when their cities first began to grow rapidly.

Topic: __________

____

Main Idea: __________

____

____

(3) The main factor in the California recall election is the economically underestimated effect of charisma, or rather Governor Grey Devis's utter lack of it. No one can calculate the cost of having uninspiring leaders but we would do well to consider past American presidents.

America struggled in the Depression, but eventually rebounded under brilliant Franklin Roosevelt, in spite of the war. We boomed under the spell of dashing young John Kennedy and declined under smart-but-creepy Richard Nixon and dull Gerald Ford. We muddled along under earnest Jimmy Carter and boomed, after a rough start, under ebullient Ronald Reagan. We fell into recession under the often-unintelligible George Bush senior and then boomed under charming Bill Clinton, before declining once again under plain-spoken George Bush junior. Mr. Davis's problem is that he is perceived not only as ineffectual but insipid; a bad combination for any leader.

Topic: __________

____

Main Idea: ____________

____

____

(4) Pre-Election budgets are not what they used to be. Once upon a time, governments could be relied on to ply the electorate with extravagant giveaways in the run-up to polling day. But today's voters are an edgeable-lot, so a more subtle approach is required. Gordon Brown's second pre-election budget, like his first, avoided traditional tax bribes to the electorate as a whole. Instead, Britain's chancellor opted for a selection of sweeteners, carefully directed at vital electoral target groups such as pensioners, poorer families and aspiring home-buyers.

But the similarity between the two budgets ends there. In 2001, the public finances were exceeding healthy. Including measures announced in his pre-budget report, Mr. Brown was able to give away £8 billion ($12billion) in the fiscal year ahead while still forecasting a comfortable surplus. In this budget, Mr. Brown was in a much weaker position. Even the wee sweeties he handed out were far too much, bearing in mind how bad the figures now look.

Topic: ____________

____

Main Idea: ____________

____

____

(5) The World Bank is the world's biggest development agency–a sprawling bureaucracy that is extremely difficult to run well. Its leader needs to know about development, be able to articulate a workable vision and be a good manager. Mr. Wolfowitz scores passably on two counts. He is not an economist or a banker, but has first-hand experience of developing countries. He has public-sector management experience–not least as number two at the Pentagon, although the bungling in Iraq raises questions about just how good his management skills are.

The biggest concern is that Mr. Wolfowitz is an idealist some would say a Utopian, whose career has been guided by zeal to bring democracy to the world–regardless of what the world might make of that ambition. Thus far,–Mr. Wolfowitz has focused on the relationship between democracy and security, but his belief in the power of democracy will surely colour his views of economic development as well.

Topic: ____________

____

Main Idea: ____________

____

____

(6) If one considers how Nigeria has handled its oil revenues over the past 30 years, its quest for debt relief seems laughable. Its oil wells have yielded hundreds of billions of dollars, which its politicians have largely stolen or squandered. Nigeria is scarcely less poor than before its oil boom began. And, since successive governments borrowed against future oil receipts and wasted that money too, the country is saddled with some $34 billion in foreign debt. Such a record suggests that extra cash freed up by debt relief would be frittered away.

But look at the past year and a half, and a different picture emerges. A new economic team, led by the finance minister, a former World Bank Director called Ngozi Okonjo-Iweala, has made strenuous efforts to impose discipline. Recent high oil prices have generated an unexpected revenue surplus, which previous Nigerian governments would have spent. This one has saved it, on the wise assumption that prices will eventually fall. The federal government has also cajoled Nigeria's 36 states to save their share of the windfall. This is unprecedented. State governments are powerful, jealous of their prerogatives and often the kind of folk who, ahem, are glad that a governorship confers immunity from prosecution.

Topic: ____________

____

Main Idea: ____________

____

____

(7) Will China and Russia be the new Axis of Oil? Supply and demand trends, plus this week's surprise from the OPEC cartel, suggest that these emerging giants may yet up-end energy market.

With oil prices above $30 a barrel, OPEC was not expected to cut output quotas at its meeting in Algeria this week, merely to clamp down on quota busting, which adds some 1.5m barrels per day (bpd) to official quotas of 24.5m bpd. But, on February 10th, it agreed to cut quotas by 1m bpd from April.

Why? "The second quarter is a bad quarter," explained one oil minister. He was talking of the risk of price collapse as the northern-hemisphere winter (when demand peaks) gives way to warmer spring (when oil use declines). Yet, OPEC may be playing with fire. Edward Morse of HETCO, an energy trader, points out that inventories are currently unusually low. Even if OPEC cuts output by half of what it threatens, he says, there may still be sharp price spikes: "There's no cushion left."

Topic: ____________

____

Main Idea: ____________

____

____

(8) There are now, according to Ben Bradshaw, a farming minister, about 1.5m deer roaming Britain–more than at any time since the last Ice Age. One reason is milder weather. Another is that farmers increasingly sow grain and rape seed in autumn rather than spring, because crops grow more vigorously in spring and so produce better yields. That provides fodder for deer in winter. At last, it seems, an agricultural technique which improves farmers' profits and boosts wildlife.

Not quite. Autumn planting may help see deer through hard times. But it is also blamed for a decline in numbers of certain bird species.

Graham Appleton, of the British Trust for Ornithology, says that autumn and winter planting means less grain lying around fields in winter. Naturalists think that may explain why corn bunting numbers are down by 41 per cent since 1994, grey partridge by 18 per cent and yellowhammer by 13 per cent. Autumn-seeded crops also grow all too quickly for field nesters such as skylarks (down 14 per cent).

Topic: ____________

____

Main Idea: ____________

____

____

(9) The poison pill is one of the most egregious creatures of American corporate law. It exists to stop shareholders enjoying their full ownership right by threatening, if triggered, to dilute the value of those shares in certain circumstances by a firm's board. They first caught on in the 1980s, when boards used them to deter hostile takeover bids–hostile atleast, to the board, though not necessarily to shareholders.

How strange, then, to find a poison pill being used (seemingly) in a good cause, against somebody who has (apparently) given many shareholders a lousy deal. This is the latest twist in the remarkable affair involving Hollinger International, a newspaper group, and its long time controlling owner, Conrad Black. This week, Hollinger International board launched a campaign, including the creation of a poison pill, to stop Lord Black selling control of the firm to wealthy Barclay brothers.

Topic: ____________

____

Main Idea: ____________

____

____

(10) A new computer virus, the fastest spreading ever, was this week making the rounds among unprotected computers running on Microsoft Windows. Such incidents of online vandalism by what are often presumed to be geeky teenage hackers are, sadly, routine. But this virus, called MyDoom by some and Novarg by others, seems to be of a different nature–conpriratorial and political. That is because its main feature, besides humiliating Microsoft, is to turn infected machines into weapons against a controversial company called SCO.

SCO, a tiny software firm in Utah, and Microsoft, the world's largest software firm, have only one thing in common. Both are passionately hated by "open-source" software programmers, who typically believe that computer code should be freely shared instead of sold as property. Microsoft is hated chiefly because it represents the opposite model, proprietary software, and because its operating system, Windows, is the main rival to Linux, the best-known open-source software today.

Topic: ____________

____

Main Idea: ____________

____

____

Solutions

(1) *Topic:* Myanmar's failure in ASEAN

Main Idea Sentence: Even by.... recent policies (First two sentences)

(2) *Topic:* Spiraling Slums

Main Idea: Whatever the local name of slums, there are a lot of them and they are growing fast.

(3) *Topic:* Economic effects of Inappropriate Leadership

Main Idea: No one can calculate the cost of having uninspiring leaders but we would do well to consider past American presidents.

(4) *Topic:* Gordon Brown's Pre-Election Budget

Main Idea: Gordon Brown's second pre-election budget, like his first, avoided traditional tax bribes to the electorate as a whole.

(5) *Topic:* Mr. Wolfowitz's Selection as World Bank chief

Main Idea: Its leader needs to know about development, be able to articulate a workable vision and be a good manager.

(6) *Topic:* Nigeria's changing face

Main Idea: A new economic team, led by the finance minister, a former World Bank Director called Ngozi Okonjo-Iweala, has made strenuous efforts to impose discipline.

(7) *Topic:* A surprise cut in oil supplies.

Main Idea: Price collapse as the northern-hemisphere winter (when demand peaks) gives way to warmer spring (when oil use declines).

(8) *Topic:* Deer Oh! Dear

Main Idea: Farmers increasingly sow grain and rape seed in autumn rather than spring, because crops grow more vigorously in spring and so produce better yields. That provides fodder for deer in winter.

(9) *Topic:* A new use for the poison pill

Main Idea: It exists to stop shareholders enjoying their full ownership right by threatening, if triggered, to dilute the value of those shares in certain circumstances, by a firm's board.

(10) *Topic:* Computer security

Main Idea: This virus, called My Doom, seems to be of a different nature–conspritorial and political. That is because its main feature, besides humiliating Microsoft, is to turn infected machines into weapons against a controversial company called SCO.

Now we will graduate from **Understanding Paragraphs** to **Understanding Passages**

DIMENSION TWO (C): IDENTIFYING CENTRAL POINTS

A passage is a series of paragraphs connected to each other through a logical idea flow. Each paragraph has its own main idea. However, when the ideas of each of the paragraphs are connected to each other, one idea stands out as it is surrounded and supported by all the ideas of the passage. Besides, it will also be supported by the details throughout the passage. Such an idea, then, is called the central idea or the central point of the passage.

The Cream of the Piece

Some useful questions that need to be answered in order to determine the central point of the passage are:

"What is the idea that the author is consistently referring to throughout the passage?"

"With what point are all the ideas in the passage connected to?"

"What central idea is supported by all the supporting details in the entire passage?"

The answer to one or more of these questions will help you to identify the central point of the passage.

Being able to identify the central point is a critical skill in the development of RC skills. The student should concentrate on honing this skill through his/her reading exercises. We have demonstrated this skill as applied to actual CAT passages in the detailed solved CAT passages at the end of this chapter.

DIMENSION THREE: ABILITY TO PREDICT AND IDENTIFY SUPPORTING DETAILS

Supporting details are generally in the form of illustrations, reasons, factual evidences, examples, etc. that explain a main idea.

Since supporting details are always supportive of the main idea, developing the skill to predict, an oncoming supporting detail, or to identify the supporting detail when you see one is closely related to the ability to identify main ideas–something we saw in detail in the previous Dimension.

Let us look closely at some of the ways of putting in supporting details.

1. Supporting details as examples: Read the following extract, where the supporting details appear as examples.

Some decisions will be fairly obvious–"no-brainers." Your bank account is low, but you have a two week vacation coming up and you want to get away to some place warm to relax with your family. Will you accept your in-laws' offer to free use of their Florida beachfront condo? Sure. You like your employer and feel ready to move forward in your career. Will you step in for your boss for three weeks while she attends a professional development course? Of course!

Here, The topic and main idea come out of the first sentence of the paragraph. The supporting details are in the form of examples which make the main idea clearer. There are two supporting details:

Supporting Detail 1: Your bank account is low, but you have a two week vacation coming up and you want to get away to some place warm to relax with your family.

Will you accept your in-laws' offer to free use of their Florida beachfront condo? Sure.

Supporting Detail 2: You like your employer and feel ready to move forward in your career. Will you step in for your boss for three weeks while she attends a professional development course? Of course!

2. Supporting Details as a Reason or a Series of Reasons: Read the following extract, where the supporting details appear as reasons.

Is your credit card your biggest source of worries? Unsolicited calls, indecipherable language, hidden charges, rude customer (un)care executives... Well, the Reserve Bank of India has just put an end to all these unfair practices. Arm yourself with details of the RBI notification and make sure you throw the rules at the bank if you are troubled again.

To begin with, banks have been asked to keep the language simple. Most important terms and conditions should be highlighted and advertised, and sent separately to customers. RBI has also instructed card issuers to dispatch bills on time and the customer should be given at least one fortnight for making payments before the interest is charged. Banks should quote annualised percentage rates on cards and the rate along with the annual fee should be shown with equal prominence. The RBI has also directed banks to provide explanation to the customer within 60 days if he questions any bill. Besides, the credit card companies would be responsible for all acts of omission or commission of their agents, so they should be extremely careful about the quality of service while out-sourcing various credit card operations. Further, the banks should ensure confidentiality of the customer's records and privacy.

Here, the topic is credit card companies, while the main idea is the RBI's putting an end to the unfair practices of credit card companies. (These are seen in the first two sentences.)

There are four supporting details in the second paragraph.

Supporting Detail 1: To begin with, banks have been asked to keep the language simple.

Supporting Detail 2: The RBI has also directed banks to provide explanation to the customer within 60 days if he questions any bill.

Supporting Detail 3: Besides, the credit card companies would be responsible for all acts of omission or commission of their agents.

Supporting Detail 4: Further, the banks should ensure confidentiality of the customer's records and privacy.

Consider another example which includes both reasons and examples as supporting details:

Foreign jaunts on business, after the first few times, can get rather boring. Jet lag, early morning meetings, bad weather, local language, and even bland food can turn these trips into a chore rather quickly. Software professionals soon realise that there are just so many parks or castles you can visit when you are in the US or Europe. You can get used to countries rather quickly. If you have been visiting Korea a few times, chances are that you are no longer thrilled about going to Taiwan even if it has a completely different history.

There is a way around it. You could try collecting old maps, for instance. Pradip Shah, a seasoned finance professional, still looks forward to his trips to Manhattan, even if they are just for a couple of days. And that's after years of going to the US. His visits to Amsterdam include a mandatory visit to the same shop on the Dam Street for as long as he can remember. And in Sydney and London, it is the same story. Shah's rendezvous has everything to do with maps. He collects them and puts them up in his office in South Mumbai.

In the first paragraph above, the supporting details are first given in the second sentence of the paragraph, in the form of reasons. The sentence 'Jet lag, early morning meetings, bad weather, local language, and even bland food can turn these trips into a chore rather quickly,' gives a set of reasons for the main idea–'why foreign business jaunts can get rather boring.'

These are followed by two examples as further supporting details–

There are just so many parks or castles you can visit when you are in the US or Europe.

If you have been visiting Korea a few times; chances are that you are no longer thrilled about going to Taiwan, even if it has a completely different history.

In the second paragraph, the author gives us one way of avoiding the boredom–collecting maps. Pradip Shah's example and the three examples he uses to explain what he does are supporting details in the form of examples.

Supporting Detail: His visits to Amsterdam include a mandatory visit to the same shop on the Dam Street for as long as he can remember.

Division of Supporting Details into Major and Minor Supporting Details: In the last paragraph of the above passage, we came across an instance of major and minor details. Let us first understand the distinction between the two. We will then look at how the two are present above.

The Cream of the Piece

In any piece of writing, the major details are used to explain and develop the main idea. Minor details, on the other hand, help to explain and clarify the major details.

For instance, in the last paragraph of the above passage, the example of Pradip Shah has been taken to explain the strategy of collecting old maps as one of the ways of getting over boredom. Pradip Shah represents the major detail, while the specific examples of Manhattan, Amsterdam, Sydney and London have been used in order to explain and clarify the major detail.

Strategies for Identifying Supporting Details Apart from the fact that you need to practice these skills more and more, there are some specific strategies that will help you predict upcoming supporting details.

Strategy one: anticipating Lists When the author uses what can be called a 'list word', as a reader you can predict an oncoming list (of reasons, causes, effects, examples, factors, merits/demerits, etc).

Being prepared for the same will help you better map the author's idea structure. Some words that announce an oncoming list are:

(1) A few
(2) Some
(3) A series of
(4) Several
(5) A number of
(6) First of all
(7) Sometimes, the author might use a specific number to prepare you for an oncoming list. Thus, he might use something like–Three specific reasons, Two examples, etc.
(8) Another common structure used by authors involves the relative grading of the components of a list. Thus, the author might talk about **Principal and subsidiary reasons** or **effects**

Strategy two: identifying Additions: Additions introduce major details. Words that announce additions include:

(1)	On top of	(2)	Moreover
(3)	Also	(4)	In addition to
(5)	Next	(6)	After this
(7)	Lastly	(8)	Firstly
(9)	Secondly, etc.		

The Cream of the Piece

Mind Mapping–Understanding the structure of the passage to get a better grip of the same: As already explained earlier, your objective while reading is to create your own skeleton/map of the passage and the closer it is to the skeleton/map of the author, the better will be your understanding. Supporting details are a crucial factor while trying to create these mental structures. Improving your skill in identifying and then predicting supporting details will go a long way towards helping you gain a closer insight to what the author is trying to convey.

Before moving on to the next dimension, the student is advised to work on his ability to identify supporting details in the structures mentioned above.

Dimension Four (A): Understanding the use of Transition and Idea Organisation Patterns

Most writers have a tendency to use structures/words/phrases that show relationships between ideas. The use of these structures/words/phrases in writing, guides the reader in a similar way as a road sign helps a tourist understand directions.

These relationship structures and words/phrases can be classified under the following categories:

(A) Transitions
(B) Idea Organisation

Let us now look closely at each of these relationships:

(A) Transitions Transitions are words or phrases that show the relationship between ideas. They are like milestones on a road that guides travelers. Consider the following statements:

Your skills at the English language can be substantially improved. You need to improve your vocabulary.

Your skills at the English language can be substantially improved. First of all, you need to improve your vocabulary.

You might have found the second item easier to understand. The only difference between the two items is the presence of the words 'first of all'. They give you an indication that the writer is planning on explaining several ways of improving your English language. Hence, you can anticipate an upcoming list of ways in the next few sentences. Based on this anticipation, you can prepare a mental framework of the structure of the idea presented by the author.

Transition words or phrases, can be classified in the form of:

(a) Addition words These words signify an addition to the thought. An addition transition can be identified with the use of any of the following types of words.

also	further	secondly
next	in addition	furthermore
firstly	lastly	finally
moreover	another	one
additionally		

The following examples will clarify addition transitions for you:

(i) An important dental warning sign is bleeding of gums. Another is a tooth that shows sensitivity to hot or cold.

(ii) In the early seventies, there were three youngsters who broke into the world of professional tennis simultaneously. The first was Jimmy Connors, the next Bjorn Borg and the third Vijay Amritraj. Together, they were known as the ABC of tennis.

(iii) The diesel passenger car is a peculiarity seen exclusively in the Indian transportation scenario. Another is the steam engine driven train. You would not find these anywhere in the world.

(b) Chronology Words These words signify a chronological relationship between the ideas presented under the structure. The following words signify chronology.

before	first	last
eventually	soon	next
after	then	previously
finally	until	now
while	since	following
preceding	second	immediately
during	often	later
as soon as	frequently	when
during	subsequently	one after the other

The following examples will clarify the concept of chronology words.

(i) The performance of the company has been extremely encouraging during the last quarter.

(ii) During the winter months, the whole of the Indian Railway system is paralysed due to the fog that prevails across the breadth of North India.

(iii) Tiredness sets into an office worker by the time he has his lunch. It worsens by the time he gets home.

(B) Idea Organisation Patterns Very often, authors use standard structures to connect between different ideas. The ideas might be **supportive to** or **illustrative of** the central idea.

The Cream of the Piece

Idea organisation might occur in one of the following formats:

(1) The list of items format
(2) The chronological format
 (a) The Idea-Example/Illustration format
 (b) The Idea-Restatement/Reiteration format
(2) The Comparison format
 (a) The Contrast format
 (b) The Parallelism/Similarity format
(5) (a) The Cause and Effects format (Single cause and multiple effects)
 (b) The Causes and Effect format (Multiple causes and single effects)

Before we take a closer look at each of these, it is imperative for you to understand that these idea organisation patterns may be applied in a format where the entire structure appears in a short span of two to three lines at one extreme. On the other hand the structure might be used in such a format that it is applied to an entire paragraph. In fact, at times, an idea structure might span the length of an entire passage.

The following examples to illustrate each type are mostly two to three sentences long and at the maximum, up to a paragraph long. However, we would like to advise the readers that they should try to locate these idea organisation patterns in varying lengths of paragraphs and passages whenever they are reading anything.

Let us now take a closer look at these idea organisations one by one:

While the theoretical contents of this book have been created after a lot of painstaking research, language being a field of endless possibilities, there will always be more idea organisation structures which might come across while you read. Hence, we would like to encourage the readers of this book to not only try to identify one of the above listed idea organisation structures during their reading, but to also try to discover more methods of idea organisation whenever they read.

Idea Organisation Pattern 1 **The list of items format:** The following extract will clarify to you how this format is used to present ideas.

There are four broad categories of new technologies that could make this idea reality. The first is called "spread spectrum", or "wideband". As both names imply, this is a way of spreading an electromagnetic signal across wide bands of frequencies at low power, instead of booming a high power wave through a narrow band. Wi-Fi is one good example of wideband technology–the large range of frequencies and the low power allow it to co-exist with cordless phones and other devises. Hopes are highest, however, for a new technology called "ultra-wideband", which will communicate by whispering its signals so softly across the frequency band of other, higher power transmitters, such as broadcasters, that these will not even notice the presence of another signal.

Another approach is to use "smart" antennae. These are systems of multiple antennae that can "aim" a signal in a particular direction (instead of radiating it out indiscriminately) or pick out a particular signal from background noise by calculating the wave's angle of arrival (for example, from a satellite instead of a source on the ground).

A third technology is "mesh networking". In a mesh, each receiver of a signal also re-transmits it. Every meshed laptop computer, for instance, in effect becomes a node or router on its network. This has three advantages. One is that, as with spread spectrum, signals can be sent at very low power, since they only have to travel to the next user's node, which will be hundreds of meters, instead of kilometers, away. Another is that each newcomer to the network not only uses, but also adds, capacity. A third is that the network will be robust, since traffic can be rerouted easily if nodes fail, the approach already taken by the internet.

As you can clearly see above, a list of items points to a series of reasons, examples or other details that might support an idea. The items have no particular chronological ordering, hence, they are referred to in the order the author most prefers.

Words signifying additions or numericals are often used in order to denote the position of the idea/example in the list.

We would encourage you to familiarise yourself with this style of writing of the author since it is one of the most common ways of writing used currently. Look for more instances where an author uses a list of items as the principle structure in a paragraph or even in a passage.

***Idea Organisation Pattern 2:* The chronological format:**

As the name itself suggests, in such idea organisation structures, the crucial element defining the interrelationships between the ideas/examples is the factor of time. Under this structure of idea organisation, authors normally present things in the order in which they occur. For example, a passage might talk about the events leading up to the Economic Liberalisation in India.

The Cream of the Piece

Most passages on historical occurrences use chronological idea structuring. For that matter, even in the case of the description of events, the same structuring of ideas is used.

Obviously, the chronology words listed under Transitions will be an integral part of Chronology based Idea Structuring. Besides, other signs of the use of this pattern of idea organisation are words such as stages, series, process, steps, sequence, etc. Passages involving a series of events and passages involving a series of steps are the most common under this pattern.

Consider the following example that illustrates the same:

No President wants to hear that the economy has stopped producing new jobs three months before election-day. But for George Bush, the news that only 32,000 new jobs were created in July is doubly troubling. This paltry number makes it almost certain that he will be the first president since Herbert Hoover to face the electorate with an economy that has fewer jobs than when he took office (as John Kerry's campaign delights on pointing out). What makes this all the more embarrassing, however, is that the White House has lately gone out of its way to claim responsibility for the short-term performance of the jobs market.

After enduring months of a "jobless" recovery, George Bush's team was quick to claim credit earlier this year when the pace of jobs growth finally accelerated. John Snow, the Treasury Secretary, argued that the creation of over 300,000 new jobs in March "clearly demonstrated" that Mr. Bush's tax cuts were working. These tax cuts, he suggested, were "driving job creation". The administration did not simply claim that the huge fiscal expansion of the past three years had helped cushion America's recession (which would have been correct). It went much further. Tax cuts, intoned every Bush official, were the elixir behind the jobs recovery.

Now that the payroll figures have weakened, the Bush team is squirming. White House aides offer a slew of reasons why the statistics which just a few month ago " clearly demonstrated" the wisdom of Mr. Bush's economic policies should now be discounted. The president himself pretends the bad news simply does not exist. "We have a strong economy and it's getting stronger," he claimed only hours after the jobless figures were released on August 6th.

The truth is that America's economy has cooled during recent months. Consumer spending slowed during the second quarter, particularly in June......

The chronological format of organisation is an extremely widely used structural format. It is very common in most writing that you will come across. We would advise you to look for more instances where an author uses a chronological format as the principle structure in a paragraph or even in a passage.

Idea Organisation Pattern 3

(a) Idea-Example/Illustration

(b) Idea-Restatement/Reiteration

Most authors will give you multiple chances to understand the idea that they are presenting to you. This is because, in order to communicate successfully, an author must help his readers understand the words and ideas that he is expressing. Many a times, authors realize that writing a key idea in one sentence might not be able to successfully communicate the same–as a reader might miss the idea. To overcome this problem, most authors prefer to clarify their key ideas through examples/illustrations or through restatement/reiteration to make the reader connect better to the idea.

This is typically done through two structures of writing:

(a) The Idea-Example/Illustration format

(b) The Idea-Restatement/Reiteration format

(a) The Example/Illustration format One of the most common styles of idea presentation is the example/illustration format.

> **The Cream of the Piece**
>
> Under this structure, an author first introduces a new idea and then, follows it up with an explanation of the same. The explanation is in the form of an example/illustration.

The following example serves the purpose of clarifying the idea in the mind of the reader.

The following paragraphs use the example based structure of writing:

(i) The truth is that America's economy has cooled during recent months. *Consumer spending slowed down during the second quarter, particularly in June. Employers are once again leery of hiring new workers. Production indicators are showing a down-ward trend.*

The italicised part of the paragraph above has the author using three examples to explain the point that the American economy has cooled during recent months.

(ii) Progress is being made, albeit slowly. *Democracy has brought increased (and better directed) social spending. Economic growth has returned after several years of stagnation. New political forces and the alternation of power are making politics more representative.*

The italicised part of the paragraph above has the author using three examples to explain the point how progress is being made.

(iii) Setting up a business abroad has always been risky, and not just financially. *To create a colony of 90,000 white settlers that, in the late 17th century, earned enormous profits from growing tobacco in Virginia, required the immigration of around 116,000 people. The chaps who sailed for India a century later had to endure even worse. "The variety of means by which a man could be carried off was quite bewildering," observes a recent book on the East India Company." Malaria, typhoid or enteric fever, cholera, dysentery and small pox were the most common diseases, and the bites of scorpions and mad dogs were frequently lethal."*

The italicised part of the paragraph above has the author using two examples to explain the point that setting up a business abroad has always been risky.

The following paragraphs use the illustration based structure of writing (Note that there is a very thin line between example and illustration):

(i) A resident of Najaf, who loathes the militants, was scornful of the Iraqi forces' capabilities. *"The national guard of the Iraqi army fires into the air," he said. "The Mahdi army shoots to kill."* The ill trained fighters of the Mahdi army are in fact, rotten shots. But no one doubts their eagerness to shed blood, whether their own or other people's.

In the paragraph above, the italicised statement of the resident of Najaf is an illustration of his scorn for the capabilities of the Iraqi forces.

(ii) *To his supporters, both inside and outside Venezuela, Hugo Chavez is a cross between Che Guevera and Mother Teresa.* He is, as they see it, the standard bearer of a superior alternative to a Latin America impoverished by 'neo-liberal' economics and elitist, merely formal, democracy.

In the paragraph above, the italicised sentence has illustrated the idea the author is trying to present. The idea is in the next sentence, i.e., a superior alternative to 'impoverishment' (illustrated in his comparison with Che Guevera) and 'merely formal democracy' (illustrated in his comparison to Mother Teresa).

The following words show example/illustration usage:

for example	for instance	to illustrate
as an example	including	
like	such as	to be specific
specifically	for one, etc.	

(b) The Restatement/Reiteration format This format of idea presentation is again commonly used by authors.

> **The Cream of the Piece**
>
> Under the **Restatement format**, the author first presents an idea and then rephrases the same idea in other words. Most often, the restatement is in simpler words than the original statement and hence easier to understand.

Consider the following extract from an article:

A very tentative conclusion is that while America is practicing for another September 11th, the threat of Islamic militancy is becoming less spectacular, more general and more unpredictable. *In short, it may be becoming more like the sort of insurgencies that Britain has fought during many decades.*

The italicised part of the paragraph above has the author restating the point, making it clearer to the reader.

> **The Cream of the Piece**
>
> Under the **Reiteration format**, the author restates the original idea, with greater emphasis or force. This style serves to push through the point more emphatically into the reader's mind.

Consider the following extracts:

(i) The Indian policy of having a closed economy proved to be an impediment to the growth of the economy. *So severe was the negative impact of these policies, that by the late 1980s the Indian economy started to look increasingly fractured and handicapped.*

The italicised part of the paragraph above has the author reiterating the point not only making it clearer to the reader, but also increasing the force used in stating the same.

(ii) Roger Federer is considered to be a great tennis player. *In fact, he is considered to be one of the greatest of all time.*

The Cream of the Piece

Note that the restatement/reiteration, like all idea organisation structures, might come immediately after the original idea is presented or might come later in the passage.

Idea Organisation Pattern 4 Often, in order to explain a point completely, one needs to make a comparison between two or more ideas. The comparison might be in the form of a similarity or a contrast.

A similarity uses the structure–'A is like B'. In such a case, the similarity between A and B is brought about.

A contrast uses the structure–'A is different from B'. In such a case, the differences between A and B are highlighted.

The Cream of the Piece

a comparison format might show how two or more things are similar or how they are different or both. In this structure of idea organisation, the author compares/contrasts two or more ideas/points/examples.

As is clear from the above description, the Comparison format can be divided into two sub types:

(a) The Contrast format

(b) The Parallelism/Similarity format

(a) The Contrast format In figurative terms, contrasts can be visualised as Y junctions–where a fork in a road leads towards two different directions. Looking at it, one notices the difference between the two forks.

Consider the following statements:

The organisation pays the executive handsomely. He doesn't work very hard.

The organisation pays the executive handsomely even though he doesn't work very hard.

It is clear that the second style of writing is much superior than the first, since it is easier to read.

The following words can be used to show contrast.

but	instead	on the one hand
on the other hand	still	even though
yet	in contrast	as opposed to
against this	in another way	however
in spite of	differs from	although
on the contrary	despite	inspite of
unlike	nonetheless	nevertheless
conversely	rather than	while
difference	opposite	

The following examples use this structure of Idea organisation:

(i) For any American President hoping to claim victory in the war on terror, such an analysis brings both good news and bad. *Massive, potentially election-wrecking attacks look less likely, though not impossible. On the other hand, it would no longer be possible to claim-as Mr. Bush would doubtless like to claim-that by knocking out Mr. Bin Laden, the war has been taken to its final round.*

(ii) *Has brave America got Mr. Bin Laden cornered? Or is America bravely stepping up to face head on a renewed threat from Mr. Bin Laden?* Both, is the answer.

In each of the paragraphs above, the italicised statements make a contrast between two ideas.

(iii) *A common myth about electromagnetic waves is that they bounce off one another if they meet. They do not. Instead, they travel onwards through other waves forever (even though they eventually attenuate to the point where they become undetectable.)*

The paragraph above uses a flip-flop-flip structure of argumentation, i.e., an idea is presented, it is then contrasted and then, the contrast itself is contrasted.

(b) The Parallelism/Similarity format Similar to the contrast format, the parallelism format is the discussion of the likeness of two or more ideas.

In figurative terms, it can be seen as two parallel roads, which are similar to each other. Looking at them, one notices the similarities between the two.

Consider the following statements:

The use of computers for printing bills has made a tremendous negative impact on the printing industry, since orders for printing cash memos have disappeared. The introduction of FM radio has greatly affected the music industry, as the sales of cassettes has dropped drastically.

Now consider the same sentences, written differently:

The use of computers for printing bills has made a tremendous negative impact on the printing industry, since orders for printing cash memos have disappeared. Similarly, the introduction of FM radio has greatly affected the music industry, as the sales of cassettes have dropped drastically.

As you can see, the clarity of the second style of writing is much higher than that of the first.

The following words are used to create similarities/ parallelisms:

as	just as	similar
similarly	likewise	just like
same	alike	in the same way
in a similar manner	equally	in like fashion
in a similar fashion	resembling	

***Idea Organisation Pattern 5:* The Cause and Effect format:** Cause and Effect is another extremely common idea structure. As the name suggests, the cause is the reason for the effect (which is an outcome of the reason). The typical cause and effect relationship is–the cause leads to the effect.

Below are listed some words which commonly signal a cause and effect format:

- therefore, hence, so, thus, as a result, results in, because of, thus, causes, effect, is the effect of,
- reason as a consequence of explanation consequently leads to if...then
- accordingly due to since owing to

The cause and effect format is used in a variety of forms as under:

(a) Single Cause–Single Effect Consider the following extract:

Since the failure of the Americans' to crush the Sunni insurgents in Fallujah(CAUSE), the central government has largely given up trying to run many of the Sunni areas of the country (EFFECT).

(b) Single Cause–Multiple Effects Consider the following extract:

*In the early part of the 21st century, the introduction of low cost airlines to the Indian skies (SINGLE CAUSE) caused paradigm shifts (MULTIPLE EFFECTS) in the way people traveled in India. There was a shift of air conditioned train travellers from trains to aeroplanes. Middle class and even lower middle class families experienced air travel for the first time. The distance measured between cities in terms of the time of travel suddenly started sounding much more manageable** Mumbai–Delhi was suddenly two hours instead of sixteen. Businesses started to use the opportunity to expand like never before.*

In some cases, the effects will have their own hierarchy where one effect might be the principal effect and there might be other supporting effects.

(c) Multiple Causes–Single Effect Consider the following paragraph, which can be classified under this format:

If Mr. Chavez wins this, as his supporters now predict, it will be for a mixture of three reasons.

The first is that high oil prices have brought Venezuela a windfall that Mr. Chavez is busily spending on social programs (known as "mission"). These programs have a political purpose and message: the government has mobilised all the resources of the state to secure a vote against recall.

Second, there are other doubts as to how free and fair the vote will be. The referendum is a device inserted into the constitution by Mr. Chavez himself. But he spent almost two years manoeuvring to avoid what his supporters portrayed as an underhand attempt by an American-financed opposition to unseat a democratically elected president. The electoral authority has a pro-Chavez majority. It has placed restrictions on observers. If the outcome is close, fraud is a real fear.

Third, Mr. Chavez is genuinely liked by many Venezuelans. Not all the poor are with him. But he has inspired a sense of political inclusion among many neglected by the previous, increasingly corrupt two-party pact. By contrast, his fractious opposition is unattractive. Most are democrats, but some are not: they staged a failed coup against Mr. Chavez in April 2002.

Another example of this format is given below:

But Londoners aren't ending up on the streets, or at least, not for long.

Why not? There are several reasons. Compared to America, the benefits system is relatively generous and fairly stable, which may be more important: abrupt reforms in the late 1980s sent many young men on to the streets. And the alternatives to living alfresco are better than in New York, and better than they used to be. London's direct-access hostels have converted dormitories into single rooms, which means fewer beds (about 3,000 today, compared with almost 10,000 in the early 1980s) but more enticing ones.

(d) Multiple Causes–Multiple Effects Consider the following extract:

In the later part of the 20th century, the increasing prominence of private sector jobs coupled with the disillusionment with government jobs (MULTIPLE CAUSES), precipitated a series of changes in the psyche of the Indian career aspirant (MULTIPLE EFFECTS). For starters, their conception of what they wanted in a job changed. Job security gave way to job profile as the principle word that defined the way they made their choices. Private sector jobs started to become more lucrative and more appealing to career aspirants in general. The focus of the way they spent their time in their universities also underwent a major change as a result of this.

> **The Cream of the Piece**
>
> Although sometimes an author will use only one idea organisation pattern in a passage, very often authors use multiple idea organisation patterns within the same passage. Hence, you need to be open to identifying and interpreting multiple idea organisations when you see them inside a passage.
>
> It is not necessary for authors to use addition or chronological words prior to using an idea organisation pattern. In some passages, you will come across the use of idea organization patterns without the use of any words which will signal an oncoming pattern.

Dimension Five: Facts, Opinions and Inferences

Let us first understand what facts and opinions are. We often come across situations where a person gets emotional about an issue and starts to speak and give his/her opinions on the basis of emotions, wherein he/she is expected to speak objectively. Especially in formal situations, people want to hear facts rather than emotional opinions.

Consider the following statements:

Opinion	Fact
Jawaharlal Nehru is to date the best Prime Minister India has produced.	Jawaharlal Nehru is the first Prime Minister India has produced.
The Indian Economic Tiger is all set to capture the world.	The Indian economy has grown by over 7 per cent for the last three years.
State Bank of India is India's best bank.	State Bank of India is India's largest bank.
Around the turn of the century, Sachin Tendulkar was the greatest batsman in the world.	During his playing career, Sachin Tendulkar went on to make the highest number of test centuries by any batsman in the world.
IIM Calcutta is a very good institute. (Author's note: Even though this is largely accepted as a fact, this is still an opinion, since what is very good is a subjective issue and hence, cannot be defined or verified.)	IIM Calcutta was the first IIM.
The government has met all its promises in the first hundred days of its office.	The government has been in office for hundred days.
There is little symbolism in Greek art.	Greek art dates back to the BC era.
Internal conflicts are always psychologically interesting.	An internal conflict can be defined as a conflict within a person's mind about his objectives.
The detective story by Erle Stanley Gardner can be described as a glorification of intellectualized conflict.	Erle Stanley Gardner, is a leading detective story writer.
Derrida's work is complex in the extreme.	Derrida's work is based on the theory of deconstruction.

What is the principal difference that you notice between the two columns above?

Each of the entries under the **Fact** column is something which can be easily verified and proven to be true/false, i.e., the statement can be put through the truth test. This is the essential nature of a fact.

> **The Cream of the Piece**
>
> *A fact is information that can be proved through objective evidence.*

This evidence may be in the form of physical proof or spoken and written testimony of witnesses.

A statement of fact might be found to be untrue on verification. However, that does not change it's classification as a factual statement, since the only thing we are concerned about is that a fact can be physically verified.

> **The Cream of the Piece**
>
> An opinion on the other hand, can be seen as someone's point of view about an issue. There is no way to physically verify the truth of the statement.

Hence, there can always be an opposite point of view that can be justified. An opinion is basically a belief, judgment or conclusion that might be based on observable facts, but cannot be objectively proved true. The opinion may be agreed with or disagreed with as it is open to question. Thus, if someone tells you that the food at Taj Lucknow is great, it might be his/her individual opinion. You might dine at the same hotel and come to a very different conclusion. Normally, it is widely accepted that more the number of opinions within a piece of writing, the greater is the bias present in the article.

It can be seen from the table above that in simple writing not involving advanced ideas and language structures, it is extremely easy to identify the difference between a fact and an opinion, but when the ideas presented start to become complex, the differentiation starts to become more and more difficult.

To Bell the CAT

The skill to differentiate between fact and opinion is a key skill possessed by expert readers and it is tested extensively in the CAT examination.

Hence, mastering this key skill is extremely crucial for the student. The only way to do so is to continuously practice and apply the differentiation between fact and opinion while reading any piece of writing.

The Cream of the Piece

A handy way to identify opinions is that normally, opinions contain a set of 'value' words–words which show judgment. These words are subjective in nature because they interpret reality from the writer/speaker's point of view.

Given below is a list of some value words:

Best, The best, worst, bad, good, wonderful, disgusting, interesting, dull, better, amazing, beautiful, fanciful, excellent, etc.

Whenever you come across any statement using value words similar to the list above, you should realize that an opinion is being expressed. Besides, words such as should, would, ought to, must, etc. signal an upcoming opinion.

The Cream of the Piece

In most writing that you will come across, purely factual information is not easy to come by. When most writers and speakers communicate, they rapidly alternate between stating facts and opinions about an issue being discussed. Hence, what is communicated has a sprinkling of bias (which is almost unavoidable.)

However, a lot of writers do try to remain as objective as possible. News items based on event reporting, scientific reports, descriptions of events/experiments, etc. are examples of writing that is mostly factual and hence, unbiased. On the other hand, other types of materials such as editorials, political speeches, advertisements, analysis of events, etc. are examples of writing which contain opinions and hence, are biased by nature.

As a reader, both facts and opinions are crucial for you. All good readers have the ability to differentiate between fact and opinion. Knowing the difference is important in evaluating what is read, because most of what we come across as readers is a mixture of fact and opinion.

It is important to note that, even though opinions cannot be verified to be true, their relevance to everyday life is immense. Some of our most basic foundations and ways of living are built upon opinions. Discarding them is likely to lead to utter chaos in our minds and our lives–since some of those opinions are central to our way of life. Consider trying to live without the following opinions. Each of the list below is an opinion since it cannot be verified and proven to be true.

One should respect one's parents.

Democracy is the best form of governance.

Human life is valuable. (Some of the world's worst tyrants have gone against this opinion, leading to disastrous outcomes for humanity.)

The Cream of the Piece

The relationship between fact and opinion is similar to a pillar supporting a building structure. Writers state facts in order to give support to their opinions. In the absence of facts to support one's opinions, they are unlikely to stand the test of any logical interrogation.

For example: B.S. Chandrasekhar is the best batsman produced by India.

(Surely, you must be kidding!! You just need to look at the records of some of the batsmen India has produced and compare them to B.S. Chandrasekhar's batting records. The facts simply do not support this opinion.)

Directly opposite to an opinion which is negated by facts, is the opinion which is supported by it. This kind of an opinion can be called an informed opinion. The more the facts that support an opinion, the more the people that are likely to agree with it. And the more people agree with an opinion, the more it starts to be accepted as a generic opinion which is not to be questioned–it gets closer to be accepted as a pseudo fact.

For Your Better Understanding

In each of the following sentences, identify whether the author is stating a fact or is making an opinion or using a mixture of both.

(1) If you are a rural parent, you would see little point in most of the news reported in the media on matters of education, including some of the controversies and debates concerning ideology in textbooks.

(2) The urban world, in which middle class children routinely move on from one level to the next, and eventually seek admission to a college, dominates current reporting and writing about education.

(3) Pass percentages are not calculated separately for rural and urban schools, and research which might provide such differentiated awareness has not been done.

(4) The NCERT, that I saw four months ago, looked rather difficult to recognize in terms of its original memorandum.

(5) In mid-November, when the plan to review the National Curriculum Framework was announced, I met the press and found it stuck to its oppositional mood.

(6) Sceptics and critics will undoubtedly continue to see politics in everything.

(7) In matters which constitute the frontier of educational services, the specific requirements of rural education are quite poorly appreciated.

(8) Productivity growth is probably the single most important indicator of an economy's health: it drives real income, inflation, interest rates, profits and share prices.

(9) Since 1996, America's productivity in terms of output per man hour has grown by 3 per cent every year, which is double the pace of the first half of the 1990s.

(10) America's growth in labour productivity is likely to slow, even though it should remain faster than in the decade before 1996.

Solutions

(1) Opinion. This cannot be proved to be true.

(2) Fact + Opinion (The last part *'dominates current reporting and writing about education'* is an opinion.)

(3) Fact, since whatever the author states here can be put through the truth test.

(4) Opinion.

(5) Fact + Opinion. The author's mid-November meeting with the press can be verified, but the press being stuck to its oppositional mood is something that cannot be verified to be true or false.

(6) Truth of the statement cannot be verified. Hence, clearly an opinion.

(7) Opinion.

(8) Opinion supported by facts.

(9) Fact.

(10) Opinion.

Dimension Five (B): Inferences

'Reading between the lines' is a phrase that best summarises what is meant by an inference. An inference is an idea that you pick up in your reading, even though it is not directly stated in what you are reading. In essence, an inference is akin to an implied idea, and is extremely crucial for a full understanding of the author's ideas.

Making inferences is a common mental activity that happens everyday in our lives. It is not just confined to our reading, but even to our experiences in all other activities. Consider the following situations:

- Suppose, you are going to the railway station and find that the road leading into the railway station is jam packed, with many more cars than normal. You might infer that the trains are likely to be much more crowded than normal.
- You meet a woman with a 3 month old child in her arms. You would most likely conclude that she is married and the child is her baby.
- You see a cavalcade of cars going on the road, and infer that someone important is inside the same.
- You see a person driving an expensive car and conclude that he is rich.
- Based on the behavior of a person you meet, you make inferences about his upbringing, his education and exposure in life.

Thought Gems from an Expert

In each of the above situations, you are drawing inferences–conclusions about things that you cannot see or experience directly in front of you. Yet, you are in a position to make conclusions about things that you have not seen, on the basis of past experiences and their outcomes. These conclusions happen reactively and instinctively after the first experience. In everyday life, we make so many inferences, that it is impossible to live the way we live life without making inferences. In fact, the ability to make inferences is one of the parameters on which intelligence is judged.

Similarly, the making of inferences while reading is extremely natural. We have been doing it ever since we learnt our first words. What you need to realize is that the quality of a reader's abilities are defined by the quality of the inferences he/she is able to make. The deeper the inferences that you can make by reading what is written, the superior you are as a reader. In fact, I would go as far as saying that this skill, coupled with the skill to differentiate between fact and fiction, are the most important skills for RC. These are skills that differentiate between a capable/good reader and an expert/excellent reader.

The Cream of the Piece

Why Reading Between the lines/ Making Inferences is critical for Reading Comprehension

(1) It takes you closer to the idea structure of the author:

(2) It gives you an indication of the direction the author is likely to take.

(3) It gives you a better hold on questions based on inferences, implied meanings and questions that go beyond the passage.

As already mentioned elsewhere, when the author puts pen to paper, he/she has already formulated his/her opinions on the topic, his/her idea structure, his/her style of presentation and even the supporting details. With every sentence the author writes, he starts to unravel his thinking.

Before you start reading the passage, you are blank about what the author is going to say. As you start reading the first sentence of the first paragraph, the mind of the author starts to get revealed. Since the author has written each sentence with his own thoughts in the background, he often reveals more than what he says in the sentence. The choice of words, phrases and the structure of the sentence used often gives us an insight into what the author is thinking. Some of these thoughts might be subsequently stated, while some of them might never be directly stated. Understanding what is not said, serves to fill in the gap that is left by virtue of the unstated ideas.

Hence, it serves to give a clearer understanding of the author's thoughts.

Reading being the art of decoding the author's view point about an issue, reading more than what the author has said invariably helps the reader connect better to the ideas of the author.

The ability to make inferences from reading can be further classified into three skill steps:

(a) Skill Level One: Making inferences from single sentences.

(b) Skill Level Two: Making inferences from groups of sentences/from paragraphs.

(c) Skill Level Three: Making inferences from groups of paragraphs/from passages.

Let us now look at Skill Level One in detail:

Consider the following statements/extracts and the inferences we might draw from these:

(1) Statement: Productivity growth is probably the single most important indicator of an economy's health: it drives real income, inflation, interest rates, profits and share prices.

Inference: There are several indicators of an economy's health–out of which productivity growth is one of the most important.

(2) Does Turkey qualify as a European country in order to qualify itself for EU membership?

Inference:

(a) Turkey is not an EU member presently;

(b) In order to become a part of the EU, a country needs to meet the parameters set for being a European country;

(c) EU membership is still open for discussion.

(3) Those countries opposed to extending Europe's borders up to Syria and Iran feel that such a Europe would have little consistency.

Inference:

(a) Some countries are in favor of extending Europe's borders up to Syria and Iran;

(b) There is currently no clear demarcation of the geographical boundaries of Europe;

(c) Countries that will be included in Europe by extending its borders up to Syria and Iran will be culturally, sociologically and economically different to the conventionally defined European countries.

Skill Levels Two and Three mentioned above with respect to drawing inferences are more complex for two principal reasons.

Drawing inferences out of groups of sentences (Level Two as defined above) or from groups of paragraphs (Level Three as defined above) involves being able to

(a) Draw a string of inferences related logically to one another; or

(b) Draw a common inference hinting at something that can be commonly inferred throughout one paragraph or across the entire passage.

Since inferences do not announce their arrival and simply creep in behind what is explicitly stated doing either of this is a complex skill.

Consider the following paragraph:

Astrologers habitually prone to goof-ups now have an excuse for why their predictions have been going haywire: the emergence of newer and newer planets that have caused their calculations to go awry. For the international team of astronomers who recently discovered eight new planets, the new arrivals are, however, a cause for excitement. Indeed, even as the rest of the world continues to be consumed by a morbid passion for shiny new war machines, deadly chemicals and sinister war tactics, astronomers have been doggedly searching the heavens for more heavenly bodies in the belief that the search will take us closer to a more exalted goal that of knowing the truth about us and the universe. "Reality is much bigger than it seems... the part we call the universe is the merest tip of the iceberg," one scientist remarked. How true. In the beginning skeptics wouldn't accept that the earth actually moves, let alone that it revolves around the sun, because of an unshaken belief that the earth was the centre of the universe. We've come a long way. Today, scientists have spotted nearly 80 extra-solar planets using sophisticated instruments.

Inferences:

Astrologers make their predictions based on their calculations of known planetary positions.

Newer Planets are always discovered.

The author is against war and spending on war.

The author has a positive disposition towards scientific discoveries in general.

The instruments used by astronomers today are much more sophisticated than what was used in the past.

Astrologers' have little scientific basis for their predictions.

As you can experience in the paragraph above, and indeed in full length passages, being able to draw a series of correct inferences creates a kind of a *'net of understanding'*, which runs parallel to and below the explicit understanding of the passage. The denser this *'net of understanding'*, the better is your comprehension of the passage and the author's intention.

As you continue to read a passage, the creation of this parallel net of understanding helps you connect better to the author's idea structure as well as to the probable future direction the author is likely to take in the remainder of the passage.

ADVANCED DIMENSIONS OF READING SKILLS

DIMENSION SIX: IDENTIFYING PURPOSE AND TONE

As we already saw through dimension five, behind everything ever written, there is always a living person, who has his own collection of facts and his own opinions about the issue being talked about.

The author also has his own **purpose** for writing the passage, and typically conveys the ideas he wants to convey by using a particular **tone**–something that gives us an insight into his/her attitude and feeling.

Purpose. We first look at **Purpose**: Identifying the authors' purpose of writing helps us in several ways:

(a) It improves our connection with the author

(b) It helps to improve the anticipation about the direction the author is likely to take.

There are three common purposes for writing any piece:

1. Informative/Descriptive Writing This type of writing is one whose objective is to inform/teach the reader about a subject, an event, a process or an issue.

The Cream of the Piece

Informative Descriptive Writing is the most common purpose of writing. It can be in two forms:

(a) Narratives (informing in a narrative fashion, the outlines of an event/happening) or

(b) Informative Articles: (Articles informing about the various dimensions of an issue.)

Writers writing with the purpose of informing/ teaching normally stick to facts and verifiable information. In such writing, the facts are presented as part of the main idea structure, while the supporting details are in the form of examples, illustrations, parallelisms and contrasts. Opinions are mostly conspicuous by their absence in such writing.

To Bell the CAT

An analysis of the various passages of the CAT paper of the past few years will clearly show you that the CAT (and indeed all other Management entrance exams) are filled with passages that can be classified as informative writing.

The passages on Derrida's work (Passage II of the CAT 2005 paper solved in the chapter on solved CAT passages) and on Game theory (Passage I of the CAT 2005 paper solved in the chapter on solved CAT passages) in the CAT 2005 paper are examples of informative writing. Similarly, the CAT 2003 paper had four of the five passages that could be classified as primarily descriptive passages: As given in the chapter on solved CAT passages they appear as: Passage 1 (Topic: Panchayati Raj Institutions), Passage 2 (Greek Architecture), Passage 4 (Education in the twelfth century) and Passage 5 (Development of Aviation).

Hence, as an aspirant, your focus should be on improving your ability to convert factual informative writing into symbols and pictures inside your mind.

2. To Persuade This is another common purpose of writing.

Such writing is opinion driven and has the primary purpose of convincing the reader about the author's point of view.

However, there is a fair sprinkling of facts on which writers draw upon to support their point of view and convince the reader about the same. Hence, such writing contains a mixture of facts (which act as supporting details) and opinions (which give the main ideas of the passage). The bias towards one opinion is clearly reflected in such writing–since all the facts presented as supporting details are normally in favor of the author's opinion. Words such as *should, must, ought to, need to,* etc. are clear giveaways of persuasive writing since they are clear indicators of the author's opinion.

To Bell the CAT

Like Informative writing, persuasive writing is also commonly used in CAT and Management entrance passages.

In the context of the CAT 2005 paper the passage starting with the words 'Crinolene and croquet are out' (Passage III of the CAT 2005 paper, solved in the next chapter on solved CAT passages) and the passage on Straddlers starting with the words 'When I was in class in Columbia' (passage 4 of the CAT 2003 paper in the next chapter on solved CAT passages) can be classified under this type of writing.

3. To Amuse/entertain Another common purpose of writing is to lighten up the reader by amusing/entertaining him/her. Such writing might be in the form of fictional or non-fictional writing.

In either case, there is normally satire or adventure involved.

Most leisure reading comes in this category of writing and every newspaper worth it's name has satirical articles with the sole aim of entertaining the reader.

The Cream of the Piece

However, for some reason, Management entrance exams have kept off such writing for the extracts they use to form their questions.

As a student of English, we would encourage you to find writing of each of the three types mentioned above in your day to day reading.

Tone We now move to the **Tone** of the author:

The tone of an article indicates the author's predisposition towards the subject. By identifying the tone of the author, we can judge his/her attitude/emotional standing towards the subject.

This helps us improve our predictions for questions which go beyond the boundaries of the passage.

The author of any piece of writing gives a fair view of the tone of the passage through the words and the details used in expressing his ideas. Hence, the tone is decoded through the words and the details that the author uses in his writing.

Especially concentrate on the kinds of adjectives and adverbs the author uses while trying to identify the tone of the passage.

The tone of the author can be identified by making a mental list of the adjectives and adverbs he/she uses. Words such as:

- Little, lovely, plain, exquisite, beautiful,
- incongruent, depressing, disgusting, bright,
- optimistic, factually, neutral, doubtful, surely,
- serious, grim, joyous, playful, sympathetic,
- nice, intransigent, flexible, tragic, happy, sad,
- delightful, delicious, inane, etc.

Depending on the basis of the adjectives/ adverbs used, as well as by the force with which they are used, we can get hints about the author's emotional orientation towards the topic. Some examples of tone, with their cue words are given as follows:

Tone	Types of Words Signifying the Tone
Critical	Words with a negative meaning such as incongruent, depressing, disgusting, doubtful, grim, etc.
Humorous	Words and situations with irony, punch lines and double meanings.
Disappointed	Words with a negative connotation– used in a lesser degree than in a critical or a depressing tone

Other examples of tones are factual, analytical, critical, disparaging, tolerant, neutral, hopeful, matter of fact, admiring, nostalgic, regretful, amused, arrogant, etc. As an aspirant for competitive exams, you should try to develop a sense of identifying the author's tone while reading a passage.

Dimension Seven: Recognising and Evaluating Arguments and their Common Structures

There is an undeniable relationship between writing and thinking. During the process of writing, the writer opens up his mind's thought processes for the readers. Being on the reader's side of a written piece, one of the most important tasks before us is to be able to separate the principal arguments that the author is making, from the supporting reasons and other details that are mentioned in the passage.

This is especially important for articles that are written to persuade. In such articles, being able to decipher the author's argument has to be the principal purpose of the reading. It is therefore, essential to be able to recognize and evaluate arguments.

The Cream of the Piece

An Important point to note: Even though the full and final argument of the author will normally only be clear at the end of the article, most authors write in such a style so as to leave enough clues for the reader to understand the drift of the argument prior to actually stating it. It is obvious that the earlier you are able to catch the argument, the better it will be for you. This is because of two principal reasons. They are:

(1) **The predictive value of understanding the author's argument early in the passage:** If you are able catch the author's argument early, you will be able to predict the future course that the author is likely to take. This results in better understanding of why the author is using particular examples and/or phrases in the passage–during your first reading itself. Hence, you will be able to easily answer commonly asked questions that are based on the use of particular examples and/or statements in the passage. (In this context, it is important for you to realize at this point that one of the question types that creates major problems for students–where the question asks why the author has used the particular example/statement–cannot be answered until and unless you have read the example/statement with the author's argument in your mind. Going back to the particular example/statement after reading the question does not help, since it ends up wasting time. Besides, the reader can never get a full perspective of the idea structure by reading a small part of the passage, thus, you will never be able to answer such a question with certainty, by going back to the passage.)

(2) **Faster reading speeds:** Being able to predict what the author's principle argument is, early on in your reading is important since it helps you in reading the remainder of the passage much faster than normal. This is because your reading's objective will change from being driven by the need to explore the idea, to the need to confirm your predictions. You will only need to slow down a bit when the passage's idea structure takes a turn that you might not have expected. At such a stage, as the reader, you just need to expand your prediction of the author's argument to include the new argumentative direction and then continue to read at a faster rate.

[Reading can be compared to driving. Just as during driving, you vary your speed depending on the traffic situation, similarly, during reading, you can vary your speed depending on how much *'idea catching'* you have to do. Just as when there is no traffic on the roads, you might vary your speed of driving by as much as five times, so also during reading, the speed of reading can be easily multiplied by 5 when you are clued to the idea of the author. In our experience, you can and should vary your reading speed between 50 words per minute to up to 500 words per minute in the same passage–sometimes this variance might occur between two consecutive sentences also. Just as the art of driving is about knowing the optimal speed at which to drive, the art of reading is to understand when to slow down and when to speed up while reading. Predicting arguments helps you in improving this skill.]

What is an Argument? Arguments are social phenomena. In our daily life, we are surrounded by numerous arguments–in fact, they are so common that we might feel their absence more than their presence. At the core of every communication going beyond mere factual information exchange is an argument. Every advertisement, every editorial, every conversation, every analytical exchange of ideas contains an argument

The Cream of the Piece

The core of an argument is a claim with reasons. In successful arguments, these reasons are linked to values, beliefs and assumptions held by the audience.

This is important since the purpose of an argument is to persuade. While persuading someone, we are concerned with influencing the way people think or act. In order to do so, we have to make an appeal to the reason of the reader/listener. It is a necessity that there are two conflicting points of view, each of which has its own reasons supporting it. While writing an argumentative passage, the author imagines the reader as an absent listener and hence, tries to address his/her mental frameworks. Hence, while reading, thinking of the author as a live person writing for some real purpose is important to catch the argument. When you start reading the passage, as soon as you recognize the objective of the writer as one of persuasion, you should start looking for the principle argument he/she is making. Ask yourself the question–'What point is the author trying to convey to me as a reader?' 'The details and the reasons used in the passage are supporting which principle argument?' The quicker that you identify the answer to these questions, the quicker you will have the main argument of the author.

Arguments are extensively referred to in passages written for description purpose. For example, consider this statement from the passage on Greek architecture in the CAT 2003 paper: 'Greek art is intellectual art, the art of men who were clear and lucid thinkers, and it is therefore, plain art.' The sentence is an entire argument in itself. The author is making a claim and justifying the same in the same sentence. The likelihood is that the author will either build upon or further support this argument throughout the remainder of the paragraph in which this sentence appears as a starting sentence. As a gentle reminder, I would like to remind you that we had identified this article as primarily description based. This goes to prove the point that arguments are at the heart of every communication. Hence, they are at the heart of every paragraph and every passage of any kind.

Evaluating arguments: Why is it important to be able to evaluate arguments?

Evaluating arguments for their strength and forcefulness is an important aspect of our lives.

The ability to critically determine how much of an argument one should accept and on what points to attack someone else's arguments is a crucial skill needed for success in every sphere of life today. In fact, it is doubly important in the field of management.

To Bell the CAT

In the context of aptitude based exams like CAT, XLRI, other management entrance exams as well as for Bank PO exams, the ability to evaluate arguments is important from three points of view:

(a) In the context of Reading Comprehension, since all passages are filled with arguments, besides being able to identify the argument structure used by the author, we also need to be able to recognize the strength and relevance of the supports used in the arguments.

(b) Critical Reasoning Questions, another important aspect of the CAT exam (explained in details in the Part 3 of this book) is mostly about evaluating arguments, their support, the adequacy and the relevance of the supports.

(c) A specific type of question evaluating the strength and weakness of arguments is asked in Banking and other exams. Such questions are outside the scope of this book, but are also to be solved using the principles explained here.

How do we evaluate arguments?

The evaluation of the strength or weakness of an argument is done by critically looking at the supports the author has used for his argument. In this regard there are two critical questions that you have to ask yourself with regards the argument's supports in order to evaluate how strongly supported the argument is:

(1) Is the support used by the author relevant to the claim he is trying to support? This is seen by evaluating the question against the argument that the supporting point is trying to answer.

Let us take an example to illustrate this point:

Suppose an argument goes like this:

Argument: Mr. Francis should not be made the principal of the school.

Support: His mother was an uneducated woman.

The support here is irrelevant since it does not answer any questions that are likely to be raised against the argument. If it is being argued that Mr. Francis should not be made the principal of the school, opponents of the arguments are likely to attack the argument by talking about his abilities and qualifications that make him suited for the post. Giving a support by talking about his mother's illiteracy does not answer any possible opposition to the claim of the argument.

On the other hand, an example of a relevant claim could be:

Argument: You should buy the car of Brand X.

Support: Brand X cars are amongst the most respected cars in the world and are known for their safety.

(2) Is the support used by the author adequate to cover all possible attacks against the claim?

The adequacy of the support of an argument is a slightly different story. In order to check the adequacy of the support of an argument, one needs to anticipate all the issues on which the claim of the argument can be attacked. Supports should then be created for the argument, which would cover all possible dimensions of attacks on the claim.

If an argument is supported in this way, where all possible counter arguments are effectively dealt with, the argument is adequately supported.

Needless to say, an argument that is relevantly and adequately supported, is a strong argument.

Some Standard Structures of Arguments

Type A: Truth or factual arguments: Truth arguments involve differing points of view about how reality is (or was or will be). They are different than facts because while facts can be confirmed or rejected by physical verification, a truth argument involves an interpretation of facts. The interpretation of facts, like all arguments, should be supported by strong reasons.

Consider the argument stated above:

'Greek art is intellectual art, the art of men who were clear and lucid thinkers, and it is therefore, plain art.'

This is a factual argument, since it is based on an interpretation of certain facts.

It is important to note that there is a very thin line separating a plain fact and a truth argument based on an interpretation of facts. Authors utilise truth arguments as a basis of a larger framework.

There are three types of truth arguments:

- Definitional Arguments
- Causal Arguments
- Similarity Arguments

Definitional Argument: X is/is not a Y such arguments are normally built on the basis of criteria matching. This means that when X is found to be similar to or different from Y, the criteria match is used as the most important support to show the truth of the argument. For this purpose, the criterion on the basis of which Y is defined, is first listed out and then it is shown that X is an instance of Y by matching the criteria and its presence/absence in X. Needless to say, definitional arguments are a very important means of argumentation.

Causal Argument: X is/was/will cause Y OR X will not/ does not/did not Cause Y again, a commonly used and very important argument structure. It can also be termed as the cause and effect structure.

Similarity Argument: X is/is not like Y similarity argument or a resemblance argument. In this argument structure, two different situations/things/eras/events that have no relation to one another, are compared on the basis of an analogy between them. A perfect case of this argument structure is the CAT 2005 passage on Edwardian summer– the passage which starts with 'Crinolene and croquet are out...' (Passage III of the CAT 2005 paper solved in the next chapter on Solved CAT passages)

Type B: Values or Judgmental arguments: Values or Judgmental arguments, as the name suggests, have a value based judgment at their heart. There are two principal types of such arguments:

- Evaluation Argument
- Proposal Argument

Evaluation Argument: X is/isn't a good Y or X is a Bad Y

Proposal Argument: One should/should not do Y

We encourage the readers to try to start identifying each of these types of arguments in their daily reading scheme.

CHAPTER 3 Theory of Reading Comprehension

SOLVING READING COMPREHENSION (RC) IS AN EXACT SCIENCE

Perhaps the first thing that you should know, as you set out to go about improving your RC skills, is that RC is an exact science. What we mean to say is that there is exactness and a precision to RC and the way its questions are answered. We would go as far as saying that the degree of precision in RC is close to that found in Mathematics.

The reason for the exactness is not hard to find. Consider what an examiner trying to create RC questions based on a passage will be trying to achieve through his questions. His objective is to test your understanding of the ideas contained in the passage. At the same time, he has to create questions that should stand the test of logic and reason. Especially, if the passage happens to be for a paper of CAT or XLRI or similar level exams. The examiner definitely realizes that his questions are going to become a subject of intense analysis by lakhs of students and dozens of training institutes and their trainers across the country. Hence, any scope for doubt or ambiguity about the correct answer in a question is something that a question setter cannot afford to leave. Hence, even though his primary objective will be to confuse an imperfectly trained mind, the examiner will definitely focus on keeping the correct answer unambiguous. The logic supporting the correct answer hence, is always so strong, that it can be defended against the scrutiny of the entire community of students and analysts.

From the CAT/MBA/aptitude test aspirants' point of view, this translates into the fact that solving reading comprehension is an exact skill–as exact as mathematics is. All you need to do is to be able to think straight and remove self-created confusion in your mind.

The Cream of the Piece

Confused thought being the reason for selecting the incorrect options, your ability to think straight will invariably help you develop your ability for spotting the correct answer.

In this context, working on the seven dimension approach to develop reading skills (explained in detail in the previous chapter of this book) becomes extremely crucial for you as a student. The more you practice and develop those skills inside your mind, the higher will be your ability to get a correct picture of the authors' idea. The more qualitatively superior your picture of the authors' idea, the better your ability to prephrase the answer to the question asked. (As will be explained subsequently, prephrasing your answer is an extremely crucial skill for solving RC well.)

TACKLING READING COMPREHENSION ON THE BASIS OF EVALUATION OF SUPPORTS

There is another useful process of solving RC questions– Consider each option of the RC question as a building supported by the foundation–the option being the building and the logic that supports the option being its foundation. As a student trying to solve the question, your objective is to spot the foundation which is the strongest. An analysis of typical questions set in RC yields that normally two out of the four options fall by the wayside pretty easily since they have weak or 'false' logical supports.

Getting to the correct answer then depends upon your ability to evaluate the strength of the logic that supports each of the options.

ALL PASSAGES HAVE A TOPIC, A PURPOSE AND A PLAN

As already seen in the previous section on reading skills, every written piece that you will come across is written with a purpose. The author decides what his message about the topic is, at the very outset–before he writes his first words. Closely related to the topic of the passage is the scope of the passage–which can be looked at as the boundary of the passage. Concentrate on not just what the topic of the passage is but also on the scope of the passage.

By scope, we mean the specific components of the topic that the author wants to talk about.

This is also crucial since a lot of times incorrect options are created by going outside the scope of the passage.

Next, again before putting down his first words, the author creates a plan of how he /she is going to achieve his/her purpose. On the basis of this plan, the author creates a series of paragraph divisions.

In the context of an exam like CAT and other aptitude tests, passages contain about, 800–1200 words and have about five-six paragraphs in them. As a reader, you need to recognize that contained within each paragraph, will be an idea with its relevant supporting details.

Your first task is to discover the topic of the passage–something, which is usually revealed by the time you finish the first paragraph. As a reader your objective should be to decode each paragraph, as it comes in front of you. The decoding of each additional idea will help you in decoding out the author's structure, bit by bit. While reading, remember to consciously review at the end of each paragraph, how the same added to your understanding of the idea structure.

By the time you finish reading your mind should be clear about

- The purpose of the passage
- And the plan of organisation of the passage.

You need to remember that as a reader, you need to manage each passage strategically. Most often, the purpose of the paragraph will be clear by the time you are through reading one-third of the passage.

Getting to this point should be the primary purpose of your reading. If by the end of your reading, you have not identified the purpose, the plan and the idea contained in each paragraph of the passage, it is unlikely that you will be able to answer questions based on the passage accurately. You are likely to get confused by options that are meant to confuse students who do not have a clear picture of the idea.

The Cream of the Piece

There are typically three ways in which confusing but incorrect options are created:

1. Creating Options that are inconsistent with the passage's point of view.
2. Creating Options that go outside the scope of the passage.
3. Creating eyewash options–options that contain words/ phrases/sentences used in the passage, but in a way that is not related to the specific question being asked.
4. Creating an option by using a superfluous or irrelevant detail.

OTHER THINGS YOU NEED TO PICK UP WHILE READING THE PASSAGE

The Tonality and Other 'Software' Related to the Author's Viewpoint in the Passage

Apart from the idea structure (plan) and the purpose of the writing, there are several other things that should be picked up during you reading of the passage.

These include–keeping an outlook of the author's choice of words, his/her use of adverbs and adjectives, the strength and quality of his/her argumentation, the tonality of the author, the degree of the force with which he is communicating the idea, the writing style of the author, the use of analogies and comparisons/contrasts by the author, etc.

These aspects can be described as the software in the passage since most of it is intangible–something not very easily describable.

Grasping the intangibles is crucial since there are a lot of questions that are asked on these–and there is no way you can go back to a part of the passage and find an answer to such questions without reading the whole passage again.

Specific Details and Their Use in the Passage

Specific details are always used to support the author's view point about the topic. They are never used frivolously, since they have an inherent connection with the plan of the passage. As a reader, during your reading, you should skim over the details of the passage. The idea is to only catch what specific detail is mentioned and where it is mentioned.

You really do not need to go into the details of the specific details by themselves. What you need to do on the other hand, is to look for the logic of why a particular detail has been used in the passage and with which specific idea is the detail connected and how the detail is connected with this idea. The answer to the 'How' might be: to support/strengthen the idea's credibility or to attack/weaken it.

Getting this perspective will help you, since the questions asking about the specific details in the passage, are invariably phrased so as to see whether you have connected 'correctly' with the 'correct' idea.

Getting a view of the author's purpose in mentioning a specific detail will help you prephrase answers to questions the passage puts forth. Another point is that while reading the passage you should be able to distinguish between facts and interpretations that the author makes on the basis of the facts. Interpretations of facts signal idea transitions and the unfolding of fresh ideas from the author's viewpoint. Hence, you need to slow down while reading the same.

In terms of where the idea of a paragraph is placed within the paragraph, most authors stick to one way of writing throughout the passage. When you start reading a passage, try to identify the authors' specific choice of where he is placing his ideas in the paragraph. The most convenient readings are ones in which the author states the idea within a paragraph in either the first or the last sentence of the paragraph. These are also the most commonly used. However, many a time, the author will write his idea in the middle of the paragraph. The point is, whichever style the author uses, he is most likely to be consistent through all the paragraphs of the passage. If you happen to identify a consistent pattern in the first two paragraphs, you can zip through the passage because you will know exactly where to slow down while reading the remainder of the passage.

The following flowchart could be used as a reference point for improving RC skills:

Identify topic, scope, purpose and plan of the passage as you read

↓

Watch for the idea structure evolution through the different paragraphs of the passage. Watch for significant shifts from one paragraph to the next. Read mainly to get the gist of each paragraph. Remember every paragraph contains an idea which is different from the other ideas contained in the passage.

↓

Get a rough sense of the purpose of the details and facts used in the passage and how they relate to the idea of the paragraph they are in

↓

Do not worry about specific content. Read through the details at a speed approximately five times the speed at which you read the ideas. If required, come back to a detail if there is a specific question about it.

Fig. 3.1

TYPES OF QUESTIONS ASKED FROM READING COMPREHENSION PASSAGE

GLOBAL QUESTIONS (MAIN IDEA, OVERALL ORGANIZATION/STRUCTURE OF THE PASSAGE)

The answers to global questions are to be found throughout the length of the passage. These include questions about:

- The Main Idea about the Passage;
- Logical Structure of the Passage; and
- Questions that ask about the style and Tonality of the Passage.

(a) The Main Idea of the passage Here, you might be asked to recognize a correct restatement or a paraphrase of the main idea of a passage. Besides, main idea questions also include questions about the author's purpose and objectives in writing the passage, as also to guess a title for the passage–one which summarizes briefly, the main idea developed in the passage.

The following is an example of this question:

The central theme of the passage can be best summarized as:

a. Our grassroots development at the panchayat level is now driven by the "foreign aid" syndrome.
b. Panchayati raj is firmly entrenched at the lower level of our federal system of governance.
c. A truly federal polity has not developed since PRIs have not been allowed the necessary political space.
d. The Union government and State-level parties are engaged in a struggle for the protection of their respective rights.

(b) Logical Structure of the Passage These questions ask you to analyze and evaluate the construction, organization and the logical structure of the passage.

For instance, they may ask about the construction of the passage–whether it defines, whether it compares and contrasts, whether it presents and supports a new idea or whether it refutes and opposes an ides. Questions might be framed on the assumptions that the author makes in presenting his ideas, or to evaluate how the author's ideas can be strengthened or weakened from amongst a given set of options.

These questions measure your ability not only to comprehend a passage, but also to evaluate it critically. Your answering of such questions depends only on your ability to clearly understand the plan of the passage and your common sense.

You might be given options like:

- A historical point of view is stated, its contours are examined and a later supporting study is described in detail.

- Two opposing points of views about one topic are placed against each other and each is critically examined.
- An assumption is stated, relevant facts are examined, leading to the rejection/acceptance of the assumption.
- A traditional view point is outlined, its supporting structure is analysed and refuted in the light of new evidence.
- A less understood theory is reexplained using fresh contemporary examples.

(c) Questions that ask about the style and tonality of a passage These questions are based on the language used in the passage. The most common question under this type is the one where you might be asked to describe the author's tone in the passage with options like–'critical', 'supportive' 'enthusiastic', 'pragmatic', 'analytical', 'narrative', etc.

In order to answer such questions, you need to look for the language that is common to the entire passage. Remember the famous English saying–"One swallow does not a summer make." Similarly, one or even a few words of criticism do not make the tone of the passage critical.

Only a tone that is consistently present in each and every paragraph of the passage can be defined as the tone of the passage. You might also be asked to infer the author's attitude towards an idea, a fact, or a situation from the words that he or she uses to describe it.

At times, these questions may also ask about the kind of source that the passage was probably drawn from, for what kind of audience was the passage written and so forth. Tonal questions are answered by discerning the use of words as well as the reason for the use of words in a passage. In order to deduce the answer to such questions you need to go beyond the literal meanings of the words used in the passage.

The Cream of the Piece

- Do not guess while solving global questions. Guesses do not work since you cannot answer these questions unless you have created a photocopy of the author's idea structure into your own mind.
- Answering global questions correctly gives us confidence since it allows us to verify our overall view of the author's purpose and plan.
- If you have read the passage using the reading skills mentioned above and throughout the last section, global questions are easy and sure marks.
- Confirmation of your opinions through solving global questions, makes the solving of specific questions easier.

Inferential Questions

There are broadly two types of inferential questions:

(a) Questions that ask for inferences based on information presented in a passage Often, ideas are implied in a passage without actually stating the idea explicitly. These types of questions ask about ideas or meanings that can be deduced from the information that is explicitly stated. Hence, they measure your ability to 'read between the lines.'

Answers for such questions are strongly suggested, but they are not specifically stated in the passage. The challenge is to figure out from which part of the passage does the inference arise and then read the nearby sentences in order to find the implied idea/s.

For a clear understanding of inferences, go through the section on Reading Skills given in the previous part of this book. An example of this question type is given below.

It can be inferred from the passage that nitro-glycerine is of value in treating heart-attacks because it

1. lowers the blood pressure.
2. stimulates healing of an infarct.
3. causes cardiac acceleration.
4. dilates blood vessels.

Some common question structures of inferential types:

- The author implies which of the following?
- Which of the following can be inferred about the passage?
- The following *'Quote from passage'* suggests that?
- With which of the following statements would the author most likely agree/disagree?
- Which of the following is most consistent with 'something' in the passage?

(b) Questions that ask how information given in a passage can be applied to a context outside the passage These are one of the most difficult question types in RC. Solving such questions require the advanced skill of discerning relationships between situations or ideas presented in the passage and other parallel situations outside the boundaries of the passage. You need a crystal clear understanding of the passage to understand and solve these kinds of questions. In order to answer such questions, you need to more than just recall what you have read. You need to recognize the essential attributes of the ideas and situations presented in the passage when they appear in an entirely new context.

The following is an example of such a question from the CAT 2005 paper. Perhaps a testimony of the fact about the difficulty of such questions is the fact that there was a tremendous dispute about the answer to this question amongst most national level coaching institutes of repute. Obviuosly, some of them got this answer very wrong.

Which, according to the author, would qualify as interesting psychology?

1. A statistician's dilemma over choosing the best method to solve an optimisation problem.
2. A chess player's predicament over adopting a defensive strategy against an aggrcssive opponent.
3. A mountaineer's choice of the best path to Mt. Everest from the base camp.
4. A finance manager's quandary over the best way of raising money from the market.

Logical or Cause and Effect Questions

These questions are relatively easier to solve since they are very direct and most of the time, are explicitly stated in the passage. The only skill required in such questions is your ability to distinguish between the cause and the effect. Remember the cause always comes before the effect.

A clear idea of the idea structure and the plan used in the passage is normally enough to answer such questions.

According to the passage, internal conflicts *are psychologically more interesting than* external conflicts *because*

1. internal conflicts, rather than external conflicts, form an important component of serious literature as distinguished from less serious genres.
2. only juveniles or very few "adults" actually experience external conflict, while internal conflict is more widely prevalent in society.
3. in situations of internal conflict, individuals experience a dilemma in resolving their own preferences for different outcomes.
4. there are no threats to the reader (or viewer) in case of external conflicts.

In the above question, (CAT 2005 again), the effect is that internal conflicts are more interesting than external conflicts. The reason for the same is sought as the answer. Besides cause and effect, logical questions might also ask about what additional details might strengthen or weaken an argument in the passage, questions about supporting and opposing idea, the purpose of a particular paragraph, etc.

Specific Details Questions

These are one of the most common types of questions. In such questions, a specific part/phrase/sentence from the paragraph is taken and a question is created with respect to the reason for citing the detail and/or what the detail represents. Since these details are specifically stated in the passage, answering such questions is easy if you have understood the passage well. The options created for these questions are either picked up directly from the sentences surrounding the specific detail being asked about or are rephrases of these sentences.

The Cream of the Piece

- According to the author, one result of the attacks was:
- The author states which of these about the impact of global warming?
- The passage gives information for answering which of the following questions?
- What is the author trying to say by 'Specific phrase from the passage'?

AN IMPORTANT STRATEGY: PREPHRASING THE ANSWER

Prephrasing, i.e., trying to answer the question on the basis of your understanding of the passage without looking at the options given, is one of the most effective ways of solving RC. In order to prephrase an answer to a question, read the question carefully and explore your understanding of the passage to answer the same. Then phrase the answer to the question.

Once you have what you think is an accurate answer to the question, all you need to do is compare the answer you have phrased with the options and find the option that matches your answer most closely.

Needless to say, the better your understanding of the passage, the more accurate you will be while prephrasing the answer.

Why Prephrasing Helps?

(a) It saves time since you are only confirming your predictions from amongst the answer choices. Hence, you do not need to look at the options too closely.

(b) It decreases risk since if you find an answer close to what you are looking for, you are extremely unlikely to go wrong.

(c) Getting an answer close to your prephrased answer helps you build confidence about your understanding of the passage.

The Cream of the Piece

It would be wise to keep the following additional points at the back of your mind in order to help you solve RC better:

Careful reading of the question is extremely important. You should make certain that you are clear about what is being asked. One of the common errors occurs by choosing an incorrect option that is stated in the passage, but does not answer the question asked. Avoiding this error is crucial since such an error is essentially a silly error. [Author's note: CAT punishes silly errors extremely stringently. An indication of the same can be got by calculating that if you made a silly error in just 4 two mark questions in the CAT 2005 paper, you would end up with –2.66 marks instead of +8 marks. A net effect of 10.66 marks. An analysis of the past results reveals that 10.66 marks can count for as much as 30 percentile in the CAT. Four silly errors will effectively see you trading a ticket to IIM, Ahmedabad with a ticket to a C grade B-school. A difference of life and death in the context of the CAT and other aptitude exams!]

Read each of the options carefully. Refrain from assuming that you have selected the best answer without first reading and eliminating the other options.

While answering questions, do not rely on information or general knowledge that comes from outside the passage. Focus exclusively on the information contained within the passage in order to select the correct option.

In terms of the contrasting merits of Speed vs. Understanding, remember that one hundred times out of a hundred, understanding and not speed is the critical factor in reading comprehension.

CHAPTER 4 Illustrative CAT Passages (Solved)

The following eleven passages are a reproduction of the Reading Comprehension (RC) section of the **CAT** paper. The first three passages are from **CAT 2006** paper & the later eight passages are from **CAT 2003** paper. The choice of papers from these two years is due to the following reasons:

- Upto 2005, CAT paper had four-option questions. CAT 2003 paper would give you a feel of these questions.
- CAT 2006 passages have five-option questions which is the current trend. CAT 2006 paper would give you the practice needed to solve CAT RC questions according to the latest pattern.

CAT 2006 has been given preference over the later CAT papers because of the fact that Reading Comprehension in CAT 2006 is supposed to be the toughest in the history of CAT. Detailed solutions have been provided for each of the eleven passages (including the ideal process of reading the passages, as also the reason for the elimination of each of the incorrect options.) First try to solve these and then look at the detailed thought processes involved for each passage.

However, since such a detailed analysis (the best way to read a passage) is rarely available anywhere, we would like the reader to first solve each passage on his own, by reading it in his normal reading style. Once you have read and solved the passage completely, reread the passage–which is reproduced for your benefit, with detailed comments by the authors–understanding each of the points completely. Then try adopting this approach in your own reading style–by practicing it in everything you read (be it a newspaper article, a journal, a magazine, a fictional or non fictional book). As an additional exercise, you might also want to see what errors of comprehension occurred in case you had wrong answers.

CAT 2006

PASSAGE I

Directions for the questions (1-5): The passage given below is followed by a set of five questions. Choose the most appropriate answer to each question.

Fifteen years after communism was officially pronounced dead, its spectre seems once again to be haunting Europe. Last month, the Council of Europe's parliamentary assembly voted to condemn the "crimes of totalitarian communist regimes," linking them with Nazism and complaining that communist parties are still "legal and active in some countries." Now Goran Lindblad, the conservative Swedish MP behind the resolution, wants to go further. Demands that European Ministers launch a continent-wide anti-communist campaign–including school textbook revisions, official memorial days, and museums–only narrowly missed the necessary two-thirds majority. Mr. Lindblad pledged to bring the wider plans back to the Council of Europe in the coming months:

He has chosen a good year for his ideological offensive: this is the 50th anniversary of Nikita Khrushchev's denunciation of Josef Stalin and the subsequent Hungarian uprising, which will doubtless be the cue for further excoriation of the communist record. Paradoxically, given that there is no communist government left in Europe outside Moldova, the attacks have if anything, become more extreme as time has gone on. A clue as to why that might be can be found in the rambling report by Mr. Lindblad that led to the Council of Europe declaration. Blaming class struggle and public ownership, he explained "different elements of communist ideology such as equality or social justice still seduce many" and "a sort of nostalgia for communism is still alive." Perhaps the real problem for Mr. Lindblad and his right-wing allies in Eastern Europe is that communism is not dead enough – and they will only be content when they have driven a stake through its heart.

The fashionable attempt to equate communism and Nazism is in reality a moral and historical nonsense. Despite the cruelties of the Stalin terror, there was no Soviet Treblinka or Sorbibor, no extermination camps built to murder millions. Nor did the Soviet Union launch the most devastating war in history at a cost of more than 50 million lives–in fact it played the decisive role in the defeat of the German war machine. Mr. Lindblad and the Council of Europe adopt as fact the wildest estimates of those "killed by communist regimes" (mostly in famines) from the fiercely contested Black Book of Communism, which also underplays the number of deaths attributable to Hitler. But, in any case, none of this explains why anyone might be nostalgic in former communist states, now enjoying the delights of capitalist restoration.

The dominant account gives no sense of how communist regimes renewed themselves after 1956 or why western leaders feared they might overtake the capitalist world well into the 1960s. For all its brutalities and failures, communism in the Soviet Union, Eastern Europe, and elsewhere delivered rapid industrialization, mass education, job security, and huge advances in social and gender equality. Its existence helped to drive up welfare standards in the west, and provided a powerful counterweight to western global domination.

It would be easier to take the Council of Europe's condemnation of communist state crimes seriously if it had also seen fit to denounce the far bloodier record of European colonialism–which only finally came to an end in the 1970s. This was a system of racist despotism, which dominated the globe in Stalin's time. And while there is precious little connection between the ideas of fascism and communism, there is an intimate link between colonialism and Nazism. The terms *lebensraum* and *konzentrationslager* were both first used by the German colonial regime in South-West Africa (now Namibia), which committed genocide against the Herero and Nama peoples and bequeathed its ideas and personnel directly to the Nazi parry.

Around 10 million Congolese died as a result of Belgian forced labor and mass murder in the early twentieth century; tens of millions perished in avoidable or enforced famines in British-ruled India; up to a million Algerians died in their war for independence, while controversy now rages in France about a new law requiring teachers to put a positive spin on colonial history. Comparable atrocities were carried out by all European colonialists, but not a word of condemnation from the Council of Europe. Presumably, European lives count for more.

No major twentieth century political tradition is without blood on its hands, but battles over history are more about the future than the past. Part of the current enthusiasm in official Western circles for dancing on the grave of communism is no doubt about relations with today's Russia and China. But it also reflects a determination to prove there is no alternative to the new global capitalist order - and that any attempt to find one is bound to lead to suffering. With the new imperialism now being resisted in the Muslim world and Latin America, growing international demands for social justice and ever greater doubts about whether the environmental crisis can be solved within the existing economic system, the pressure for alternatives will increase.

Q1. Among all the apprehensions that Mr. Goran Lindblad expresses against communism, which one gets admitted, although indirectly, by the author?

(a) There is nostalgia for communist ideology even if communism has been abandoned by most European nations.

(b) Notions of social justice inherent in communist ideology appeal to critics of existing systems.

(c) Communist regimes were totalitarian and marked by brutalities and large scale violence.

(d) The existing economic order is wrongly viewed as imperialistic by proponents of communism

(e) Communist ideology is faulted because communist regimes resulted in economic failures.

Q2. What, according to the author, is the real reason for a renewed attack against communism?

(a) Disguising the unintended consequences of the current economic order such as social injustice and environmental crisis.

(b) Idealising the existing ideology of global capitalism.

(c) Making communism a generic representative of all historical atrocities, especially those perpetrated by the European imperialists.

(d) Communism still survives, in bits and pieces, in the minds and hearts of people.

(e) Renewal of some communist regimes has led to the apprehension that communist nations might overtake the capitalists.

Q3. The author cites examples of atrocities perpetrated by European colonial regimes in order to:

(a) compare the atrocities committed by colonial regimes with those of communist regimes.

(b) prove that the atrocities committed by colonial regimes were more than those of communist regimes.

(c) prove that, ideologically, communism was much better than colonialism and Nazism.

(d) neutralise the arguments of Mr. Lindblad and to point out that the atrocities committed by colonial regimes were more than those of communist regimes.

(e) neutralise the arguments of Mr. Lindblad and to argue that one needs to go beyond and look at the motives of these regimes.

Q4. Why, according to the author, is Nazism closer to colonialism than it is to communism?

(a) Both colonialism and Nazism were examples of tyranny of one race over another.

(b) The genocides committed by the colonial and the Nazi regimes were of similar magnitude.

(c) Several ideas of the Nazi regime were directly imported from colonial regimes.

(d) Both colonialism and Nazism are based on the principles of imperialism.

(e) While communism was never limited to Europe, both the Nazis and the colonialists originated in Europe.

Q5. Which of the following cannot be inferred as a compelling reason for the silence of the Council of Europe on colonial atrocities?

(a) The Council of Europe being dominated by erstwhile colonialists.

(b) Generating support for condemning communist ideology.

(c) Unwillingness to antagonize allies by raking up an embarrassing past.

(d) Greater value seemingly placed on European lives.

(e) Portraying both communism and Nazism as ideologies to be condemned.

Detailed Explanation

Have you read and solved this passage? Now go through it again with our comments. "Check your answers with those given below along with their explanatory notes or author's advice on how they should be read. The passage in italics is the reproduction of relevant section from the original passage, and this will be followed by an explanation or author's interpretation of the same."

Directions for the questions (1-5): The passage given below is followed by a set of five questions. Choose the most appropriate answer to each question.

Fifteen years after communism was officially pronounced dead, its spectre seems once again to be haunting Europe.

(Introduction of an idea—communism is raising its head again??)

Last month, the Council of Europe's parliamentary assembly voted to condemn the "crimes of totalitarian communist regimes" linking them with Nazism

(New idea—link of totalitarian communist regimes with Nazism)

and complaining that communist parties are still "legal and active in some countries." Now Goran Lindblad, the conservative Swedish MP behind the resolution, wants to go further.

(Introduction of the person behind the resolution—Goran Lindblad)

Demands that European Ministers launch a continent-wide anti-communist campaign - including school textbook revisions, official memorial days, and museums - only narrowly missed the necessary two-thirds majority. Mr. Lindblad pledged to bring the wider plans back to the Council of Europe in the coming months.

(The author is mentioning specific details here—so all you need to gather here is that Lindblad is trying to intensify the anti communism campaign through a variety of means) (New papragraph coming up—start to focus on what ideas are going to be thrown at you)

He has chosen a good year for his ideological offensive: this is the 50th anniversary of Nikita Khrushchev's denunciation of Josef Stalin and the subsequent Hungarian uprising, which will doubtless be the cue for further excoriation of the communist record. Paradoxically, given that there is no communist government left in Europe outside Moldova, the attacks have if anything, become more extreme as time has gone on.

(new idea introduced here—that the attacks on communism have got intensified as time goes on in spite of the fact there are almost no communist governments in Europe)

A clue as to why that might be can be found in the rambling report by Mr. Lindblad that led to the Council of Europe declaration.

(idea coming up—tentacles on!!)

Blaming class struggle and public ownership, he explained "different elements of communist ideology such as equality or social justice still seduce many" and "a sort of nostalgia for communism is still alive."

(Obviously the author is hinting at the fact that Lindblad is not content that communism as a form of government is not thriving—he even has a problem with the fact that the ideals of communism like class struggle and public ownership of resources still sound seductive to the minds of many—the next sentence confirms this predictive thought.)

Perhaps the real problem for Mr. Lindblad and his right-wing allies in Eastern Europe is: that communism is not dead enough – and they will only be content when they have driven a stake through its heart.

(New paragraph—new idea coming up)

The fashionable attempt to equate communism and Nazism is in reality a moral and historical nonsense.

(The author starts off with a strong statement about what he feels on the issue of the equation of Nazism and communism. Obviously he has to go on and support his argument—that Nazism and Communism cannot be compared!! Look out for what he says to support his argument as you read the next few lines.)

Despite the cruelties of the Stalin terror,

(even if you do not know that Stalin's regime represented communism, you would have known by now.)

there was no Soviet Treblinka or Sorbibor, no extermination camps built to murder millions. Nor did the Soviet Union launch the most devastating war in history at a cost of more than 50 million lives - in fact it played the decisive role in the defeat of the German war machine. Mr. Lindblad and the Council of Europe adopt as fact the wildest estimates of those "killed by communist regimes" (mostly in famines) from the fiercely contested Black Book of Communism, which also underplays the number of deaths attributable to Hitler. But, in any case, none of this explains why anyone might be nostalgic in former communist states, now enjoying the delights of capitalist restoration.

(Again the author leaves us here with food for thought—if communism was so bad and capitalism so good—why would anybody in a previously communist state be nostalgic about communism—especially after he has supposedly got a taste of capitalism through capitalist restoration!! Strong opinion expressed by the author and he is clearly pointing out that communism is not nearly as bad as Mr. Lindblad is trying to suggest.)

The dominant account gives no sense of how communist regimes renewed themselves after 1956 or why Western leaders feared they might overtake the capitalist world well into the 1960s.

(The author is again raising a serious point here—if communism was so bad for everyone—how did it renew itself after 1956—50 years ago when the Khrushchev Stalin standoff referred to earlier in the passage must have occurred.)

For all its brutalities and failures, communism in the Soviet Union, Eastern Europe, and elsewhere delivered rapid industrialization, mass education, job security, and huge advances in social and gender equality.

(and how did it develop all these wonderful things!!)

Its existence helped to drive up welfare standards in the west, and provided a powerful counterweight to western global domination.

(another brownie point for communism!!)

(New paragraph—the author is likely to take a new turn!!)

It would be easier to take the Council of Europe's condemnation of communist state crimes seriously if it had also seen fit to denounce the far bloodier record of European colonialism

(hmmm! Colonialism—new concept added—and most likely interchangeably used by the author as a precursor to capitalism!!)

- which only finally came to an end in the 1970s. This was a system of racist despotism, which dominated the globe in Stalin's time. And while there is precious little connection between the ideas of fascism and communism, there is an intimate link between colonialism and Nazism.

(Hoo! Now the author comes out of defending communism and starts off with a full frontal attack on colonialism and its offspring capitalism).

The terms lebensraum and konzentrationslager were both first used by the German colonial regime in South-West Africa (now Namibia), which committed genocide against the Herero and Nama peoples and bequeathed its ideas and personnel directly to the Nazi party.

Around 10 million Congolese died as a result of Belgian forced labor and mass murder in the early twentieth century; tens of millions perished in avoidable or enforced famines in British-ruled India; up to a million Algerians died in their war for independence, while controversy now rages in France about a new law requiring teachers to put a positive spin on colonial history. Comparable atrocities were carried out by all European colonialists, but not a word of condemnation from the Council of Europe. Presumably, European lives count for more.

(Huge criticism of colonialism here!! Last paragraph coming up—the author is likely to move us into a conclusion—Increase your focus at this point.)

No major twentieth century political tradition is without blood on its hands, but battles over history are more about the future than the past. Part of the current enthusiasm in official Western circles for dancing on the grave of communism is no doubt about relations with today's Russia and China. But it also reflects a determination to prove there is no alternative to the new global capitalist order - and that any attempt to find one is bound to lead to suffering. With the new imperialism now being resisted in the Muslim world and Latin America, growing international demands for social justice and ever greater doubts about whether the environmental crisis can be solved within the existing economic system, the pressure for alternatives will increase.

1. Among all the apprehensions that Mr. Goran Lindblad expresses against communism, which one gets admitted, although indirectly, by the author?

(Read the question properly—we have to identify which of Lindblad's apprehension has the author admitted indirectly!!)

(a) There is nostalgia for communist ideology even if communism has been abandoned by most European nations.

(This is not an apprehension of Lindblad against communism—so cannot be the answer!!)

(b) Notions of social justice inherent in communist ideology appeal to critics of existing systems.

(This is again not an apprehension of Lindblad against communism.)

(c) Communist regimes were totalitarian and marked by brutalities and large scale violence.

(First line of the last paragraph—'No major twentieth century political tradition is without blood on its hands', means that the author is agreeing that even communism has blood on its hands.)

(d) The existing economic order is wrongly viewed as imperialistic by proponents of communism.

(Irrelevant point—option has been created by picking up words from the last paragraph and has no relevance to the question asked.)

(e) Communist ideology is faulted because communist regimes resulted in economic failures.

(Again an irrelevant point)

2. What, according to the author, is the real reason for a renewed attack against communism?

(Read the question clearly and understand exactly what they are asking you to do—the question is pretty clear—we are looking for the 'real reason' for a renewed attack against communism—which means that we are essentially looking for the motives of the people who have attacked communism.)

(a) Disguising the unintended consequences of the current economic order such as social injustice and environmental crisis.

(Check the truth of the statement: "Disguising the unintended consequences of the current economic order is the real reason for a renewed attack against communism—Maybe a reason but not the real reason. Hence cannot be the answer.)

(b) Idealising the existing ideology of global capitalism.

(Obviously this looks right. The people attacking communism are actually trying to idealise the ideology of global capitalism. Clearly stated in "But it also reflects a determination to prove there is no alternative to the new global capitalist order - and that any attempt to find one is bound to lead to suffering" in the last paragraph. Hence, this option is correct.)

(c) Making communism a generic representative of all historical atrocities, especially those perpetrated by the European imperialists.

(This is clearly not a reason for the attack—although this might be partially the outcome of the attack. These are the kinds of options students get confused with—due to their misreading the question and what it is asking.)

(d) Communism still survives, in bits and pieces, in the minds and hearts of people.

(Again a fact – but cannot be attributed to be the reason behind the attack.)

(e) Renewal of some communist regimes has led to the apprehension that communist nations might overtake the capitalists.

(This is something that has again been said in the passage—but for it to be the answer to the present question it has to have a cause-effect relationship with the renewed attack on communism. For this to hold true the sentence you need to construct in your mind and check for its truth goes as: "The real reason for the renewed attacks on communism is due to the apprehension that communist nations might overtake the capitalists. Obviously this is not true!")

3. The author cites examples of atrocities perpetrated by European colonial regimes in order to

(Look for what exactly the author is trying to prove by citing the examples of the atrocities of the European colonial regime—means look for the main tilt of the argument the author is making in the last couple of paragraphs where this point is mentioned.)

(a) compare the atrocities committed by colonial regimes with those of communist regimes.

(This is not his point although he might be doing it.)

(b) prove that the atrocities committed by colonial regimes were more than those of communist regimes.

(Similar to the first option—only goes one step further—and is not what the author is trying to prove.)

(c) prove that, ideologically, communism was much better than colonialism and Nazism.

(He does not go on to say that—the author is obviously more balanced than that—he says in the first line of the last paragraph that all regimes had blood on their hands—so he is obviously not trying to defend communism on that count.)

(d) neutralise the arguments of Mr. Lindblad and to point out that the atrocities committed by colonial regimes were more than those of communist regimes.

(e) neutralise the arguments of Mr. Lindblad and to argue that one needs to go beyond and look at the motives of these regimes.

(Obviously the author is trying to neutralise Mr. Lindblad's arguments—however you need to discern the difference between the two options—Again here the fourth option fails because the author is clearly not trying to prove that the atrocities committed by the colonial regime were greater than those of the communist regimes. Hence, option 5 is correct.)

4. Why, according to the author, is Nazism closer to colonialism than it is to communism?
   (a) Both colonialism and Nazism were examples of tyranny of one race over another.

(By the terms lebensraum and konzentrationslager the author is trying to allude to racial tyranny – which was one of the cornerstones of Nazism and originated as an idea from the German colonial regime. Hence, this option is correct.)

   (b) The genocides committed by the colonial and the Nazi regimes were of similar magnitude:

(Magnitutes are not being compared—ideologies are!!)

   (c) Several ideas of the Nazi regime were directly imported from colonial regimes.
   (d) Both colonialism and Nazism are based on the principles of imperialism.

(They are not—imperialism was the precursor of capitalism – not of colonialism and neither of Nazism.)

   (e) While communism was never limited to Europe, both the Nazis and the colonialists originated in Europe.

(Again not an important point)

5. Which of the following cannot be inferred as a compelling reason for the silence of the Council of Europe on colonial atrocities?

"Please note—we are looking for what cannot be inferred!!"

   (a) The Council of Europe being dominated by erstwhile colonialists.

(The council of Europe is silent because of being dominated by erstwhile colonialists—true, this can be inferred, hence this cannot be the answer.)

   (b) Generating support for condemning communist ideology.

(Check this option too by making a statement as illustrated in the previous option. True—can be inferred. Hence, cannot be the answer.)

   (c) Unwillingness to antagonize allies by raking up an embarrassing past.

(True—can be inferred. Hence, cannot be the answer.)

   (d) Greater value seemingly placed on European lives.

(This is said in the passage verbatim—but is not a reason why the council of Europe is silent. Hence, cannot be inferred. This is the correct option.)

The normal incorrect thought process from a confused mind would say that this has been explicitly mentioned – hence will not qualify as something that cannot be inferred. Notice that the CAT has a propensity to create such dummies for students—where they pick up a word or a phrase from the passage and use it to create a wrong option. Confused minds think that this has been said in the passage and fall for the trap. Hence, make sure that you are very clear about what the question is asking you and also make sure that you answer the question asked and not something else. Very often reading the question/options carefully will help you avoid errors!!)

   (e) Portraying both communism and Nazism as ideologies to be condemned.

(True, they are trying to do this! Hence, cannot be the answer.)

Passage II

Directions for the questions (6-10): The passage given below is followed by a set of five questions. Choose the most appropriate answer to each question.

My aim is to present a conception of justice which generalizes and carries to a higher level of abstraction the familiar theory of the social contract. In order to do this we are not to think of the original contract as one to enter a particular society or to set up a particular form of government. Rather, the idea is that the principles of justice for the basic structure of society are the object of the original agreement. They are the principles that free and rational persons concerned to further their own interests would accept in an initial position of equality. These principles are to regulate all further agreements; they specify the kinds of social cooperation that can be entered into and the forms of government that can be established. This way of regarding the principles of justice, I shall call justice as fairness. Thus, we are to imagine that those who engage in social cooperation choose together, in one joint act, the principles which are to assign basic rights and duties and to determine the division of social benefits. Just as each person must decide by rational reflection what constitutes his good, that is, the system of ends which it is rational for him to pursue, so a group of persons must decide once and for all what is to count among them as just and unjust. The choice which rational men would make in this hypothetical situation of equal liberty determines the principles of justice.

In 'justice as fairness', the original position is not an actual historical state of affairs. It is understood as a purely hypothetical situation characterized so as to lead to a certain conception of justice. Among the essential features of this situation is that no one knows his place in society, his class position or social status, nor does anyone know his fortune in the distribution of natural assets and abilities, his intelligence, strength, and the like. I shall even assume that the parties do not know their conceptions of the good or their special psychological propensities. The principles of justice are chosen behind a veil of ignorance. This ensures that no one is advantaged or disadvantaged in the choice of principles by the outcome of natural chance or the contingency of social circumstances. Since all are similarly situated and no one is able to design principles to favor his particular condition, the principles of justice are the result of a fair agreement or bargain.

Justice as fairness begins with one of the most general of all choices which persons might make together, namely, with the choice of the first principles of a conception of justice which is to regulate all subsequent criticism and reform of institutions. Then, having chosen a conception of justice, we can suppose that they are to choose a constitution and a legislature to enact laws, and so on, all in accordance with the principles of justice initially agreed upon. Our social situation is just if it is such that by this sequence of hypothetical agreements we would have contracted into the general system of rules which defines it. Moreover, assuming that the original position does determine a set of principles, it will then be true that whenever social institutions satisfy these principles, those engaged in them can say to one another that they are cooperating on terms to which they would agree if they were free and equal persons whose relations with respect to one another were fair. They could all view their arrangements as meeting the stipulations which they would acknowledge in an initial situation that embodies widely accepted and reasonable constraints on the choice of principles. The general recognition of this fact would provide the basis for a public acceptance of the corresponding principles of justice. No society can, of course, be a scheme of cooperation which men enter voluntarily in a literal sense; each person finds himself placed at birth in some particular position in some particular society, and the nature of this position materially affects his life prospects. Yet a society satisfying the principles of justice as fairness comes as close as a society can to being a voluntary scheme, for it meets the principles which free and equal persons would assent to under circumstances that are fair.

Q6. A just society, as conceptualized in the passage, can be best described as:

(a) A Utopia in which everyone is equal and no one enjoys any privilege based on their existing positions and powers.

(b) A hypothetical society in which people agree upon principles of justice which are fair.

(c) A society in which principles of justice are not based on the existing positions and powers of the individuals.

(d) A society in which principles of justice are fair to all.

(e) A hypothetical society in which principles of justice are not based on the existing positions and powers of the individuals.

Q7. The original agreement or original position in the passage has been used by the author as:

(a) A hypothetical situation conceived to derive principles of justice which are not influenced by position, status and condition of individuals in the society.

(b) A hypothetical situation in which every individual is equal and no individual enjoys any privilege based on the existing positions and powers.

(c) A hypothetical situation to ensure fairness of agreements among individuals in society.

(d) An imagined situation in which principles of justice would have to be fair.

(e) An imagined situation in which fairness is the objective of the principles of justice to ensure that no individual enjoys any privilege based on the existing positions and powers.

Q8. Which of the following best illustrates the situation that is equivalent to choosing 'the principles of justice' behind a 'veil of ignorance'?

(a) The principles of justice are chosen by businessmen, who are marooned on an uninhabited island after a shipwreck, but have some possibility of returning.

(b) The principles of justice are chosen by a group of school children whose capabilities are yet to develop.

(c) The principles of justice are chosen by businessmen, who are marooned on an uninhabited island after a shipwreck and have no possibility of returning.

(d) The principles of justice are chosen assuming that such principles will govern the lives of the rule makers only in their next birth if the rule makers agree that they will be born again.

(e) The principles of justice are chosen by potential immigrants who are unaware of the resources necessary to succeed in a foreign country.

Q9. Why, according to the passage, do principles of justice need to be based on an original agreement?

(a) Social institutions and laws can be considered fair only if they conform to principles of justice.

(b) Social institutions and laws can be fair only if they are consistent with the principles of justice as initially agreed upon.

(c) Social institutions and laws need to be fair in order to be just.

(d) Social institutions and laws evolve fairly only if they are consistent with the principles of justice as initially agreed upon.

(e) Social institutions and laws conform to the principles of justice as initially agreed upon.

Q10. Which of the following situations best represents the idea of justice as fairness, as argued in the passage?

(a) All individuals are paid equally for the work they do.

(b) Everyone is assigned some work for his or her livelihood.

(c) All acts of theft are penalized equally.

(d) All children are provided free education in similar schools.

(e) All individuals are provided a fixed sum of money to take care of their health.

Detailed Explanation

Have you read and solved this passage? Now go through it again with our comments. "Check your answers with those given below along with their explanatory notes or author's advice on how they should be read. The passage in *italics* is the reproduction of relevant section from the original passage, and this will be followed by an explanation or author's interpretation of the same."

Directions for the questions (6-10): The passage given below is followed by a set of five questions. Choose the most appropriate answer to each question.

*My **aim** is to present a conception of justice which generalizes and carries to a higher level of abstraction the familiar theory of the social contract.*

(The author is trying to generalize the abstract theory of the social contract—at this stage even if you do not know what the social contract theory is, you would still need to carry the idea ahead—and trust that the author is going to explain the theory.)

In order to do this we are not to think of the original contract as one to enter a particular society or to set up a particular form of government.

(He is going ahead with the explanation of what he means by the social contract—in this sentence he has named it as the original contract. Look out for what he is trying to hint at in the next few sentences—concentration time)

Rather, the idea is that the principles of justice for the basic structure of society are the object of the original agreement.

(Catch a new concept here called the 'original agreement'. Look out for the definition of this!!)

They are the principles that free and rational persons concerned to further their own interests would accept in an initial position of equality.

(There you go—the original agreement is defined!! Catch it at this point. From here you can move faster.)

These principles are to regulate all further agreements; they specify the kinds of social cooperation that can be entered into and the forms of government that can be established. This way of regarding the principles of justice, I shall call justice as fairness. Thus, we are to imagine that those who engage in social cooperation choose together, in one joint act, the principles which are to assign basic rights and duties and to determine the division of social benefits. Just as each person must decide by rational reflection what constitutes his good, that is, the system of ends which it is rational for him to pursue, so a group of persons must decide once and for all what is to count among them as just and unjust. The choice which rational men would make in this hypothetical situation of equal liberty determines the principles of justice.

In 'justice as fairness', the original position is not an actual historical state of affairs. It is understood as a purely hypothetical situation characterized so as to lead to a certain conception of justice.

(Further explanation of 'justice as fairness', a concept the author had introduced in the first paragraph. Light reading but grasp the essence of what the author is saying.)

Among the essential features of this situation is that no one knows his place in society, his class position or social status, nor does anyone know his fortune in the distribution of natural assets and abilities, his intelligence, strength, and the like. I shall even assume that the parties do not know their conceptions of the good or their special psychological propensities. The principles of justice are chosen behind a veil of ignorance.

(crucial idea)

This ensures that no one is advantaged or disadvantaged in the choice of principles by the outcome of natural chance or the contingency of social circumstances. Since all are similarly situated and no one is able to design principles to favor his particular condition, the principles of justice are the result of a fair agreement or bargain.

Justice as fairness begins with one of the most general of all choices which persons might make together, namely, with the choice of the first principles of a conception of justice which is to regulate all subsequent criticism and reform of institutions. Then, having chosen a conception of justice, we can suppose that they are to choose a constitution and a legislature to enact laws, and so on, all in accordance with the principles of justice initially agreed upon. Our social situation is just if it is such that by this sequence of hypothetical agreements we would have contracted into the general system of rules which defines it. Moreover, assuming that the original position does determine a set of principles, it will then be true that whenever social institutions satisfy these principles, those engaged in them can say to one another that they are cooperating on terms to which they would agree if they were free and equal persons whose relations with respect to one another were fair. They could all view their arrangements as meeting the stipulations which they would acknowledge in an initial situation that embodies widely accepted and reasonable constraints on the choice of principles. The general recognition of this fact would provide the basis for a public acceptance of the corresponding principles of justice. No society can, of course, be a scheme of cooperation which men enter voluntarily in a literal sense; each person finds himself placed at birth in some particular position in some particular society, and the nature of this position materially affects his life prospects. Yet a society satisfying the principles of justice as fairness comes as close as a society can to being a voluntary scheme, for it meets the principles which free and equal persons would assent to under circumstances that are fair.

(This paragraph was much lighter reading than the previous one. Let us now move onto the questions asked and see what is asked.)

6. A just society, as conceptualized in the passage, can be best described as:
   (a) A Utopia in which everyone is equal and no one enjoys any privilege based on their existing positions and powers.

(The situation does not describe equality for everyone.)

   (b) A hypothetical society in which people agree upon principles of justice which are fair.

(We are definitely not talking about a hypothetical society!!This cannot be the correct answer.)

   (c) A society in which principles of justice are not based on the existing positions and powers of the individuals.
   (d) A society in which principles of justice are fair to all.
   (e) A hypothetical society in which principles of justice are not based on the existing positions and powers of the individuals. *(We are definitely not talking about a hypothetical society!!This cannot be the correct answer.)*

Between (c) and (d) options, (c) fits better as it gives a closer analysis of the main idea of the passage—that we are talking about a society where the initial agreement is not based on existing powers and positions of individuals. Option (d) is also correct but the question asks us to choose the option which best describes a just society. Between options (c) and (d) option (c) is obviously better.

7. The original agreement or original position in the passage has been used by the author as:
   (a) A hypothetical situation conceived to derive principles of justice which are not influenced by position, status and condition of individuals in the society.
   (b) A hypothetical situation in which every individual is equal and no individual enjoys any privilege based on the existing positions and powers.

(Nowhere is it mentioned that in the original position every individual is equal as we are talking about a hypothetical situation of equal liberty and not of equality).

   (c) A hypothetical situation to ensure fairness of agreements among individuals in society.

(Ensure?? Does not fit)

   (d) An imagined situation in which principles of justice would have to be fair.

(Irrelevant—this is not how the original position has been used by the author!)

   (e) An imagined situation in which fairness is the objective of the principles of justice to ensure that no individual enjoys any privilege based on the existing positions and powers.

(Again this is not the objective—we are not trying to create a society where everyone is equal.)

Option (a) is the correct answer as the author uses the original position as a hypothetical situation which is used to derive the principles of justice which are not influenced by position, status and condition of individuals in the society.

8. Which of the following best illustrates the situation that is equivalent to choosing 'the principles of justice' behind a 'veil of ignorance'?
   (a) The principles of justice are chosen by businessmen, who are marooned on an uninhabited island after a shipwreck, but have some possibility of returning.

(Not the correct answer as businessmen would know what they are good at and more skilled at—so they would have their own preferences).

(b) The principles of justice are chosen by a group of school children whose capabilities are yet to develop.

(Tempting answer!! Again the school children would already have their preferences—so no veil of ignorance.)

(c) The principles of justice are chosen by businessmen, who are marooned on an uninhabited island after a shipwreck and have no possibility of returning.

(Possibility of returning makes no difference to the fact that the businessmen would know their special skills and psychological propensities—hence this situation is not akin to one where things are done behind a veil of ignorance.)

(d) The principles of justice are chosen assuming that such principles will govern the lives of the rule makers only in their next birth if the rule makers agree that they will be born again.

(e) The principles of justice are chosen by potential immigrants who are unaware of the resources necessary to succeed in a foreign country.

(Again these people would know their skills and psychological prospensities)

Option (d) is the best answer because in that case we know for sure that an individual is not going to know his position, skills and psychological inclinations in his next birth—so he would have to be fair to everyone while choosing the principle of justice.

9. Why, according to the passage, do principles of justice need to be based on an original agreement?

(a) Social institutions and laws can be considered fair only if they conform to principles of justice.

(Conformity is not talked about here—the principles of justice are likely to be too abstract to demand exact conformity with them from social institutions and laws.)

(b) Social institutions and laws can be fair only if they are consistent with the principles of justice as initially agreed upon.

(c) Social institutions and laws need to be fair in order to be just.

(Does not answer the question asked.)

(d) Social institutions and laws evolve fairly only if they are consistent with the principles of justice as initially agreed upon.

(e) Social institutions and laws conform to the principles of justice as initially agreed upon.

(Again conformity is going a tad too far here.)

Between options (b) and (d) the only difference is of the words 'can be fair' in option (b) and 'evolve fairly' option (d). Obviously the whole passage is not about fair evolution of social institutions and laws—rather they are about these being fair. Hence, option (b) is correct.

My observation is that these kind of options appear close to test takers. The only feasible reason one can pinpoint in such cases is that aspirants do not learn how to read the crucial differences between two sentences which look very similar but are drastically different in their meanings – like this case. A single word or a word relationship can drastically change the meaning of the option—something that the CAT does regularly and something that you should learn to take care of.)

10. Which of the following situations best represents the idea of justice as fairness, as argued in the passage?

(a) All individuals are paid equally for the work they do.

(Equal pay is not close to justice of fairness.)

(b) Everyone is assigned some work for his or her livelihood.

(Again not something that is necessarily required as a conception of justice—although someone with a socialist mindset might like this option!!)

(c) All acts of theft are penalized equally.

(d) All children are provided free education in similar schools.

(Very clearly the best option here—as in a just society one would want to reduce all differentiation between children at the school level and give all children an equal chance to mould themselves and their lives.)

(e) All individuals are provided a fixed sum of money to take care of their health.

PASSAGE III

Directions for the questions (11-15): The passage given below is followed by a set of five questions. Choose the most appropriate answer to each question.

Our propensity to look out for regularities, and to impose laws upon nature, leads to the psychological phenomenon of dogmatic thinking or, more generally, dogmatic behaviour: we expect regularities everywhere and attempt to find them even where there are none; events which do not yield to these attempts we are inclined to treat as a kind of 'background noise'; and we stick to our expectations even when they are inadequate and we ought to accept defeat: This dogmatism is to some extent necessary. It is demanded by a situation which can only be dealt with by forcing our conjectures upon the world. Moreover, this dogmatism allows us to approach a good theory in stages, by way of approximations: if we accept defeat too easily, we may prevent ourselves from finding that we were very nearly right.

It is clear that this dogmatic attitude; which makes us stick to our first impressions, is indicative of a strong belief; while a critical attitude, which is ready to modify its tenets, which admits doubt and demands tests, is indicative of a weaker belief. Now according to Hume's theory, and to the popular theory, the strength of a belief should be a product of repetition; thus it should always grow with experience, and always be greater in less primitive persons. But dogmatic thinking, an uncontrolled wish to impose regularities, a manifest pleasure in rites and in repetition as such, is characteristic of primitives and children; and increasing experience and maturity sometimes create an attitude of caution and criticism rather than of dogmatism.

My logical criticism of Hume's psychological theory, and the considerations connected with it, may seem a little removed from the field of the philosophy of science. But the distinction between dogmatic and critical thinking, or the dogmatic and the critical attitude, brings us right back to our central problem. For the dogmatic attitude is clearly related to the tendency to verify our laws and schemata by seeking to apply them–and to confirm them, even to the point of neglecting refutations, whereas the critical attitude is one of readiness to change them - to test them; to refute them; to falsify them, if possible. This suggests that we may identify the critical attitude with the scientific attitude, and the dogmatic attitude with the one which we have described as pseudo-scientific. It further suggests that genetically speaking the pseudo-scientific attitude is more primitive than, and prior to, the scientific attitude: that it is a pre-scientific attitude. And this primitivity or priority also has its logical aspect. For the critical attitude is not so much opposed to the dogmatic attitude as super-imposed upon it: criticism must be directed against existing and influential beliefs in need of critical revision - in other words, dogmatic beliefs. A critical attitude needs for its raw material, as it were, theories or beliefs which are held more or less dogmatically.

Thus, science must begin with myths, and with the criticism of myths; neither with the collection of observations, nor with the invention of experiments, but with the critical discussion of myths, and of magical techniques and practices. The scientific tradition is distinguished from the pre-scientific tradition in having two layers. Like the latter, it passes on its theories; but it also passes on a critical attitude towards them. The theories are passed on, not as dogmas, but rather with the challenge to discuss them and improve upon them.

The critical attitude, the tradition of free discussion of theories with the aim of discovering their weak spots so that they may be improved upon, is the attitude of reasonableness, of rationality. From the point of view here developed, all laws, all theories, remain essentially tentative, or conjectural, or hypothetical, even when we feel unable to doubt them any longer. Before a theory has been refuted we can never know in what way it may have to be modified.

Q11. In the context of science, according to the passage, the interaction of dogmatic *beliefs* and critical attitude can be best described as:

(a) A duel between two warriors in which one has to die.

(b) The effect of a chisel on a marble stone while making a sculpture.

(c) The feedstock (natural gas) in fertilizer industry being transformed into fertilizers.

(d) A predator killing its prey.

(e) The effect of fertilizers on a sapling.

Q12. According to the passage, the role of a dogmatic attitude and of dogmatic behaviour in the development of science is:

(a) critical and important, as, without it, initial hypotheses or conjectures can never be made.

(b) positive, as conjectures arising out of our dogmatic attitude become science.

(c) negative, as it leads to pseudo-science.

(d) neutral, as the development of science is essentially because of our critical attitude.

(e) inferior to critical attitude, as a critical attitude leads to the attitude of reasonableness and rationality.

Q13. Dogmatic behaviour, in this passage, has been associated with primitives and children. Which of the following best describes the reason why the author compares primitives with children?

(a) Primitives are people who are not educated, and hence can be compared with children, who have not yet been through school.

(b) Primitives are people who, though not modern, are as innocent as children.

(c) Primitives are people without a critical attitude, just as children are.

(d) Primitives are people in the early stages of human evolution; similarly, children are in the early stages of their lives.

(e) Primitives are people who are not civilized enough, just as children are not.

Q14. Which of the following statements best supports the argument in the passage that a critical attitude leads to a weaker belief than a dogmatic attitude does?

(a) A critical attitude implies endless questioning, and, therefore, it cannot lead to strong beliefs.

(b) A critical attitude, by definition, is centered on an analysis of anomalies and "noise".

(c) A critical attitude leads to questioning everything, and in the process generates "noise" without any conviction.

(d) A critical attitude is antithetical to conviction, which is required for strong beliefs.

(e) A critical attitude leads to questioning and to tentative hypotheses.

Q15. According to the passage, which of the following statements best describes the difference between science and pseudo-science?

(a) Scientific theories or hypothesis are tentatively true whereas pseudo-sciences are always true.

(b) Scientific laws and theories are permanent and immutable whereas pseudo-sciences are contingent on the prevalent mode of thinking in a society.

(c) Science always allows the possibility of rejecting a theory or hypothesis, whereas pseudo-sciences seek to validate their ideas or theories.

(d) Science focuses on anomalies and exceptions so that fundamental truths can be uncovered, whereas pseudo-sciences focus mainly on general truths.

(e) Science progresses by collection of observations or by experimentation, whereas pseudo-sciences do not worry about observations and experiments.

Detailed Explanation

Have you read and solved this passage. Now go through it again with our comments. "Check your answers with those given below along with their explanatory notes or author's advice on how they should be read. The passage in italics is the reproduction of relevant section from the original passage, and this will be followed by an explanation or author's interpretation of the same."

Directions for the questions (11-15): The passage given below is followed by a set of five questions. Choose the most appropriate answer to each question.

Our propensity to look out for regularities, and to impose laws upon nature, leads to the psychological phenomenon of dogmatic thinking or, more generally, dogmatic behavior:

(The author is directly starting off with an idea heavy sentence—catch this and in case you do not understand what dogmatic means then understand the meaning of that from the next part of the sentence—the author is almost obligated to define that more clearly as general writing styles always use idea-elaboration or idea- explanation structures of writing.)

we expect regularities everywhere and attempt to find them even where there are none;

(Here he has defined dogmatic for you!! You can try to move ahead faster from here);

events which do not yield to these attempts we are inclined to treat as a kind of 'background noise'; and we stick to our expectations even when they are inadequate and we ought to accept defeat: This dogmatism is to some extent necessary. It is demanded by a situation which can only be dealt with by forcing our conjectures upon the world. Moreover, this dogmatism allows us to approach a good theory in stages, by way of approximations: if we accept defeat too easily, we may prevent ourselves from finding that we were very nearly right.

(New Paragraph—look for a shift of the idea. Slowdown!!)

It is clear that this dogmatic attitude; which makes us stick to our first impressions, is indicative of a strong belief; while a critical attitude, which is ready to modify its tenets, which admits doubt and demands tests, is indicative of a weaker belief.

(Key idea introduced—the difference between strong and weaker beliefs)

Now according to Hume's theory, and to the popular theory, the strength of a belief should be a product of repetition; thus it should always grow with experience, and always be greater in less primitive persons. But dogmatic thinking, an uncontrolled wish to impose regularities, a manifest pleasure in rites and in repetition as such, is characteristic of primitives and children; and increasing experience and maturity sometimes create an attitude of caution and criticism rather than of dogmatism.

(A dichotomy is pointed out here—the author is saying that stronger beliefs should come to less primitive and more mature people as strength of belief is a function of repetition. However, in truth, dogmatism and rigid beliefs are more characteristic of children and primitives and maturity and experience make people more cautious about being dogmatic in their beliefs.)

My logical criticism of Hume's psychological theory,

(whew...a totally different direction...look out...caution advocated!!)

and the considerations connected with it, may seem a little removed from the field of the philosophy of science. But the distinction between dogmatic and critical thinking,

(recognize that dogmatism and critical attitude are being used as opposites by the author here. If you do so then the next part of the paragraph is likely to be easier for you.)

or the dogmatic and the critical attitude, brings us right back to our central problem. For the dogmatic attitude is clearly related to the tendency to verify our laws and schemata by seeking to apply them–and to confirm them, even to the point of neglecting refutations, whereas the critical attitude is one of readiness to change them - to test them; to refute them; to falsify them, if possible.

(This is almost predictable if you have caught the idea that the author is using—distinction between dogmatic attitude and critical attitude.)

This suggests that we may identify the critical attitude with the scientific attitude, and the dogmatic attitude with the one which we have described as pseudo-scientific. It further suggests that genetically speaking the pseudo-scientific attitude is more primitive than, and prior to, the scientific attitude: that it is a pre-scientific attitude. And this primitivity or priority also has its logical aspect. For the critical attitude is not so much opposed to the dogmatic attitude as super-imposed upon it: criticism must be directed against existing and influential beliefs in need of critical revision - in other words, dogmatic beliefs. A critical attitude needs for its raw material, as it were, theories or beliefs which are held more or less dogmatically.:

Thus, science must begin with myths, and with the criticism of myths; neither with the collection of observations, nor with the invention of experiments, but with the critical discussion of myths, and of magical techniques and practices. The scientific tradition is distinguished from the pre-scientific tradition in having two layers. Like the latter, it passes on its theories; but it also passes on a critical attitude towards them. The theories are passed on, not as dogmas, but rather with the challenge to discuss them and improve upon them.

The critical attitude, the tradition of free discussion of theories with the aim of discovering their weak spots so that they may be improved upon, is the attitude of reasonableness, of rationality. From the point of view here developed, all laws, all theories, remain essentially tentative, or conjectural, or hypothetical, even when we feel unable to doubt them any longer. Before a theory has been refuted we can never know in what way it may have to be modified.

11. In the context of science, according to the passage, the interaction of dogmatic *beliefs* and critical attitude can be best described as:
    (a) A duel between two warriors in which one has to die.

(Both survive—so one does not need to die.)

    (b) The effect of a chisel on a marble stone while making a sculpture.

(The passage talks about co-existence and continuous to and fro iterations between the dogmatic beliefs and critical attitude. Critcal attitude acts like a chisel on a marble stone—this is something that can be inferred. Hence, this is the correct answer.)

    (c) The feedstock (natural gas) in fertilizer industry being transformed into fertilizers.

(Although dogmatic beliefs have been talked about as the raw material for a critical attitude—this is not the central relationship between the two. Hence, in this question this answer will not fit as the question asks for the best description of the relationship—so between option (b) and (c) we would always take (b).

    (d) A predator killing its prey.

(Too drastic. Both coexist infinitely.)

    (e) The effect of fertilizers on a sapling.

(Irrelevant and would be marked only by a person who has not understood the passage at all.)

12. According to the passage, the role of a dogmatic attitude and of dogmatic behaviour in the development of science is
    (a) critical and important, as, without it, initial hypotheses or conjectures can never be made.

(This is the very gist of the third last paragraph. Hence, we can choose this option to be correct.)

    (b) positive, as conjectures arising out of our dogmatic attitude become science.
    (c) negative, as it leads to pseudo-science.
    (d) neutral, as the development of science is essentially because of our critical attitude.
    (e) inferior to critical attitude, as a critical attitude leads to the attitude of reasonableness and rationality.

13. Dogmatic behaviour, in this passage, has been associated with primitives and children. Which of the following best describes the reason why the author compares primitives with children?
    (a) Primitives are people who are not educated, and hence can be compared with children, who have not yet been through school.
    (b) Primitives are people who, though not modern, are as innocent as children.

(Tempting option for someone who thinks emotionally)

    (c) Primitives are people without a critical attitude, just as children are.

(Too drastic)

    (d) Primitives are people in the early stages of human evolution; similarly, children are in the early stages of their lives.
    (e) Primitives are people who are not civilized enough, just as children are not.

(Takes an irrelevant track altogether.)

Between (a) and (d), we would select option (d) because by primitives we do not refer to lack of education – rather we refer to people who have not gone through the stages of human evolution. In case the author wanted to allude to non-educated people instead of primitives he would have said so directly and not used this word.

14. Which of the following statements best supports the argument in the passage that a critical attitude leads to a weaker belief than a dogmatic attitude does?

We are looking for support to the above-mentioned argument. Be clear about what the question is asking—an invaluable principle for CAT.

(a) A critical attitude implies endless questioning, and, therefore, it cannot lead to strong beliefs.

(b) A critical attitude, by definition, is centered on an analysis of anomalies and "noise".

(Not true—a critical attitude is centered around questioning older beliefs on the basis of anomalies and noise)

(c) A critical attitude leads to questioning everything, and in the process generates "noise" without any conviction.

(Nowhere is it mentioned that critical attitude generates noise!?!)

(d) A critical attitude is antithetical to conviction, which is required for strong beliefs.

(Antithetical – too strong a word)

(e) A critical attitude leads to questioning and to tentative hypotheses.

Again here we are between option 1 and 5. A close analysis of the two options would help us reject the first option as it is too drastic- makes a statement like critical attitude cannot(??) lead to strong beliefs!! Hence, option 5 is correct.

15. According to the passage, which of the following statements best describes the difference between science and pseudo-science?

(a) Scientific theories or hypothesis are tentatively true whereas pseudo-sciences are always true.

(Clearly wrong)

(b) Scientific laws and theories are permanent and immutable whereas pseudo-sciences are contingent on the prevalent mode of thinking in a society.

(Clearly wrong—no way are scientific theories permanent and immutable.)

(c) Science always allows the possibility of rejecting a theory or hypothesis, whereas pseudo-sciences seek to validate their ideas or theories.

(This is the key point being made. All through the author is trying to tell us that science has a critical attitude and would always allow the possibility of rejecting a theory, whereas pseudo science would always try to prove its theory even by negating contrary information. Hence, this is the correct option.)

(d) Science focuses on anomalies and exceptions so that fundamental truths can be uncovered, whereas pseudo-sciences focus mainly on general truths.

(Clearly wrong)

(e) Science progresses by collection of observations or by experimentation, whereas pseudo-sciences do not worry about observations and experiments. (You would mark this option only due to preconceived notions about what science is.)

Fact of the Matter

1. CAT 2006 is supposed to be the toughest VA/RC paper ever.
2. 6 questions out of 25 were enough to give you around 85-90 percentile.
3. At 8 questions correct you would end up with 95+ percentile in this section.
4. There you go! In a paper of 2006 that was the toughest CAT language paper ever, you had the possibility of clear thinking based undisputable answers to 20 out of the 25 question–at the very least. And all that one needed to do was 6 questions in 50 minutes for a 90 percentile score!!

Scores at various marks:

The following table would give you an analysis of the percentile obtained at various score levels:

Table 4.1 Percentile table for 2006 passages

Percentile	Percentage Marks	Number of questions to be solved correctly
99.9	60	15
99.5	40	10
99	30	7-8
95	26	6-7
90	24	6
80	18	4-5
70	16	4
60	12	3
50	8	2
40	4	1
30	0	0
20		

CAT 2003

Passage I

Directions for the questions (1-25): Each of the five passages given below is followed by five questions. Choose the best answer to each question. Go through the following passages and answer the questions that follow:

At first sight, it looks as though panchayati raj, the lower layer of federalism in our polity, is as firmly entrenched in our system as is the older and higher layer comprising the Union Govemment and the States. Like the democratic institutions at the higher level, those at the panchayat level, the panchayati raj institutions (PRIs), are written into and protected by the Constitution. All the essential features, which distinguish a unitary system from a federal one, are as much enshrined at the lower as at the upper level of our federal system. But look closely and you will discover a fatal flaw. The letter of the Constitution as well as the spirit of the present polity have exposed the intra-State level of our federal system to a dilemma of which the inter-State and Union-State layers are free. The flaw has many causes. But all of them are rooted in a historical anomaly, that while the dynamics of federalism and democracy have given added strength to the rights given to the States in the Constitution, they have worked against the rights of panchayats.

At both levels of our federal system there is the same tussle between those who have certain rights and those who try to encroach upon them if they believe they can. Thus, the Union Government was able to encroach upon certain rights given to the States by the Constitution. It got away with that because the single dominant party system, which characterised Centre-State relations for close upon two decades, gave the party in power at the Union level many extra-constitutional political levers. Firstly, the Supreme Court had not yet begun to extend the limits of its power. But all that has changed in recent times. The spurt given to a multi-party democracy by the overthrow of the Emergency in 1977 became a long-term trend later on because of the ways in which a vigorously democratic multi-party system works in a political society which is as assertively pluralistic as Indian society is. It gives political clout to all the various segments which constitute that society. Secondly, because of the linguistic reorganisation of States in the 1950s, many of the most assertive segments have found their most assertive expression as States. Thirdly, with single-party dominance becoming a thing of the past at the Union level, governments can be formed at that level only by multi-party coalitions in which State-level parties are major players. This has made it impossible for the Union Government to do much about anything unless it also carries a sufficient number of State-level parties with it. Indian federalism is now more real than it used to be, but an unfortunate side-effect is that India's panchayati raj system, inaugurated with such fanfare in the early 1980s, has become less real.

By the time the PRIs came on the scene, most of the political space in our federal system had been occupied by the Centre in the first 30 years of Independence, and most of what was still left after that was occupied by the States in the next 20. PRIs might have hoped to wrest some space from their immediate neighbour, the States, just as the States had wrested some from the Centre. But having at last managed to checkmate the Centre's encroachments on their rights, the States were not about to allow the PRIs to do some encroaching of their own.

By the 1980s and early 1990s, the only national party left, the Congress, had gone deeper into a siege mentality. Finding itself surrounded by State-level parties, it had built walls against them instead of winning them over. Next, the States retaliated by blocking Congress proposals for panchayati raj in Parliament, suspecting that the Centre would try to use panchayats to bypass State governments. The suspicion fed on the fact that the powers proposed by the Congress for panchayats were very similar to many of the more lucrative powers of State Governments. State-level leaders also feared, perhaps, that if panchayat-level leaders captured some of the larger PRIs, such as district-level panchayats, they would exert pressure on State-level leaders through intra-State multi-party federalism.

It soon became obvious to Congress leaders that there was no way the panchayati raj amendments they wanted to write into the Constitution would pass muster unless State-level parties were given their pound of flesh. The amendments were allowed only after it was agreed that the powers of panchayats could be listed in the Constitution. Illustratively, they would be defined and endowed on PRIs by the State Legislature acting at its discretion.

This left the door wide open for the States to exert the power of the new political fact that while the Union and State Governments could afford to ignore panchayats as long as the MLAs were happy, the Union Government had to be sensitive to the demands of State-level parties. This has given State-level actors strong beachheads on the shores of both inter-State and intra-State federalism. By using various administrative devices and non-elected parallel structures, State Governments have subordinated their PRIs to the State administration and given the upper hand to State Government officials against the elected heads of PRIs. Panchayats have become local agencies for implementing schemes drawn up in distant State capitals. And their own volition has been further circumscribed by a plethora of "Centrally-sponsored schemes". These are drawn up by even more distant Central authorities, but at the same time tie up local staff and resources on pain of the schemes being switched off in the absence of matching local contribution. The "foreign aid" syndrome can be clearly seen at work behind this kind of "grass roots development".

Q1. Which of the following best captures the current state of Indian federalism as described in the passage?
- (a) The Supreme Court has not begun to extend the limits of its power.
- (b) The multi-party system has replaced the single party system.
- (c) The Union, state and panchayati raj levels have become real.
- (d) There is real distribution of power between the Union and State level parties.

Q2. The central theme of the passage can be best summarized as:
- (a) Our grassroots development at the panchayat level is now driven by the "foreign aid" syndrome.
- (b) Panchayati raj is firmly entrenched at the lower level of our federal system of governance.
- (c) A truly federal polity has not developed since PRIs have not been allowed the necessary political space.
- (d) The Union government and State-level parties are engaged in a struggle for the protection of their respective rights.

Q3. The sentence in the last paragraph, "And their own volition has been further circumscribed. ..", refers to:
- (a) The weakening of the local institutions' ability to plan according to their needs.
- (b) The increasing demands made on elected local leaders to match central grants with local contributions.
- (c) The empowering of the panchayat system as implementers of schemes from State capitals.
- (d) The process by which the prescribed Central schemes are reformulated by local elected leaders.

Q4. What is the "dilemma" at the intra-State level mentioned in the first paragraph of the passage?
- (a) Should the state governments wrest more space from the Union, before considering the panchayati system?
- (b) Should rights similar to those that the States managed to get be extended to panchayats as well?
- (c) Should the single party system which has withered away be brought back at the level of the States?
- (d) Should the States get "their pound of flesh" before allowing the Union government to pass any more laws?

Q5. Which of the following most closely describes the 'fatal flaw' that the passage refers to?
- (a) The ways in which the democratic multi-party system works in an assertively pluralistic society like India's are flawed.
- (b) The mechanisms that our federal system use at the Union government level to deal with States are imperfect.
- (c) The instruments that have ensured federalism at one level, have been used to achieve the opposite at another.
- (d) The Indian Constitution and the spirit of the Indian polity are fatally flawed.

Detailed Explanation

Have you read the above passage and solved its questions?

Then check your answers with those given below (along with their explanatory notes or author's advice on how it should be read).

The passage in *italics* is the reproduction of relevant section from the original passage, and this will be followed by an explanation/author's interpretation of the same.

At first sight, it looks as though panchayati raj, the lower layer of federalism in our polity, is as firmly entrenched in our system as is the older and higher layer comprising the Union Govemment and the States.

(The above sentence is the idea sentence since it gives a very fair idea of the passage. As a reader, you can very fairly predict the next path the author will take. The author is obviously trying to compare the provisions for Panchayati Raj with the provisions for the Union Government and the States. Because of the usage of 'At first sight', as a reader, you should expect that the author will move into first talking about similarities to explain as to why the two look similar at first sight. The author will then have to obviously move towards why the two are different.

Sidelight: In fact, this can be held true for all phrases using the phrase 'at first sight'. Consider the following examples:

Example 1: At first sight, we thought we had seen a tiger. It's eyes had shone a bright red in the glare of the spotlight. But when we got closer it turned out to be just a deer.

Example 2: At first sight, the CAT paper appeared to be a simple one. It had only 90 questions spread evenly over three sections. But when the aspirants started to solve the questions, the doubts created in their mind in solving even seemingly simple questions made them review their initial estimation.

As can be seen above, all language is based on extremely structured logic. As a student of the English language, you need to get more and more familiar with the existing standard word structures of the language. The more often you will see them, the more you experience them, the more will you develop your ability to predict the future course of passages, i.e., what course the author is likely to follow in the coming sentences.

The ability to predict the next few sentences in the passage is a key skill that is common amongst all good readers. If you have developed this skill, you will read only to confirm your prediction and to spot any pattern shifts from what you expect. Once you gain such an outlook/perspective, while reading you will feel a new kind of power in your ability to understand passages better—your reading speed will automatically increase without any associated loss of comprehension.)

Now let's read further on:

Like the democratic institutions at the higher level, those at the panchayat level, the panchayati raj institutions (PRIs), are written into and protected by the Constitution. All the essential features which distinguish a unitary system from a federal one, are as much enshrined at the lower as at the upper level of our federal system.

The above are reasons why at first sight, the two look similar, as expected.

Let's read further. But look closely and you will discover a fatal flaw.

There is a change of track as expected. Now expect the reasons for the change of track.

The letter of the Constitution as well as the spirit of the present polity have exposed the intra-State level (new word used for panchayati raj) of our federal system to a dilemma of which the inter-State and Union-State layers are free. The flaw has many causes.

Another defining sentence telling you what to expect further—something about the causes of the flaw.

But all of them (the causes) are rooted in a historical anomaly, that while the dynamics of federalism and democracy have given added strength to the rights given to the States in the Constitution, they have worked against the rights of panchayats.

This is a key idea sentence in the passage. Losing comprehension here could be dangerous. Reread if required.

At both levels of our federal system there is the same tussle between those who have certain rights and those who try to encroach upon them if they believe they can.

This is a key idea sentence.

Thus, the Union Government was able to encroach upon certain rights given to the States by the Constitution. It got away with that because the single dominant party system, which characterised Centre-State relations for close upon two decades, gave the party in power at the Union level many extra-constitutional political levers. Firstly, the Supreme Court had not yet begun to extend the limits of its power. But all that has changed in recent times. The spurt given to a multi-party democracy by the overthrow of the Emergency in 1977 became a long-term trend later on because of the ways in which a vigorously democratic multi-party system works in a political society which is as assertively pluralistic as Indian society is. It gives political clout to all the various segments which constitute that society. Secondly, because of the linguistic reorganisation of States in the 1950s, many of the most assertive segments have found their most assertive expression as States. Thirdly, with single-party dominance becoming a thing of the past at the Union level, governments can be formed at that level only by multi-party coalitions in which State-level parties are major players. This has made it impossible for the Union Government to do much about anything unless it also carries a sufficient number of State-level parties with it. Indian federalism is now more real than it used to be, but an unfortunate side-effect is that India's panchayati raj system, inaugurated with such fanfare in the early 1980s, has become less real.

This entire paragraph is focused on explaining through various reasons, the last sentence of the previous paragraph. It explains how the dynamics of federalism and democracy have given strength to the rights given to the States in the Constitution. A good reader would be able to predict most of what was written in this paragraph on the basis of the idea sentence in the last line of the previous paragraph. If you too had understood that sentence, you must not have faced a problem with this entire paragraph and read it extremely fast. At this stage, a good reader will realize that the author still has not told us why the States getting their rights affected the Panchayati Raj Institutions negatively. Why this happened would be expected from the author.

By the time the PRIs came on the scene, most of the political space in our federal system had been occupied by the Centre in the first 30 years of Independence, and most of what was still left after that was occupied by the States in the next 20. PRIs might have hoped to wrest some space from their immediate neighbour, the States, just as the States had wrested some from the Centre. But having at last managed to checkmate the Centre's encroachments on their rights, the States were not about to allow the PRIs to do some encroaching of their own. (Author's Note:Answers the question outlined above.)

By the 1980s and early 1990s, the only national party left, the Congress, had gone deeper into a siege mentality. Finding itself surrounded by State-level parties, it had built walls against them instead of winning them over. Next, the States retaliated by blocking Congress proposals for panchayati raj in Parliament, suspecting that the Centre would try to use panchayats to bypass State Governments. The suspicion fed on the fact that the powers proposed by the Congress for panchayats were very similar to many of the more lucrative powers of State Governments. State-level leaders also feared, perhaps, that if panchayat-level leaders captured some of the larger PRIs, such as district-level panchayats, they would exert pressure on State-level leaders through intra-State multi-party federalism.

Here, the author continues to answer the same question, only explains it in more detail.

It soon became obvious to Congress leaders that there was no way the panchayati raj amendments they wanted to write into the Constitution would pass muster unless State-level parties were given their pound of flesh. The amendments were allowed only after it was agreed that the powers of panchayats could be listed in the Constitution. Illustratively, they would be defined and endowed on PRIs by the State Legislature acting at its discretion.

The minor details are continued here.

This left the door wide open for the States to exert the power of the new political fact that while the Union and State governments could afford to ignore panchayats as long as the MLAs were happy, the Union Government had to be sensitive to the demands of State-level parties. This has given State-level actors strong beachheads on the shores of both inter-State and intra-State federalism. By using various administrative devices and non-elected parallel structures, State Governments have subordinated their PRIs to the State administration and given the upper hand to State government officials against the elected heads of PRIs. Panchayats have become local agencies for implementing schemes drawn up in distant State capitals. And their own volition has been further circumscribed by a plethora of "Centrally-sponsored schemes". These are drawn up by even more distant Central authorities, but at the same time tie up local staff and resources on pain of the schemes being switched off in the absence of matching local contribution. The "foreign aid" syndrome can be clearly seen at work behind this kind of "grass roots development".

Now let us solve the questions.

1. Which of the following best captures the current state of Indian federalism as described in the passage?

   (a) The Supreme Court has not begun to extend the limits of its power.

Clearly incorrect option because the passage explicitly states that the Supreme Court has in fact, begun to exert its power. The sentence 'But all that has changed in recent times' in the second paragraph clearly illustrates this fact.

   (b) The multi-party system has replaced the single party system.

This option seems correct but is not true since multi party system has overshadowed the single dominant party system. There is nothing called the single party system.

   (c) The Union, State and panchayati raj levels have become real.

Illogical answer since the whole passage concentrates on why the PRIs never got real power. Further, what does the option mean by saying 'have become real'? These words are irrelevant in the context of the passage.

   (d) There is real distribution of power between the Union and State level parties.

This option is correct since the passage clearly talks about the balancing of powers between parties at the Centre and those at the State levels.

2. The central theme of the passage can be best summarized as:

   (a) Our grassroots development at the panchayat level is now driven by the "foreign aid" syndrome.

This option uses an eyewash, since it uses words directly from the passage. However, describing this as the central theme will be incorrect because it just has a passing mention at the end of the passage—and the rest of the passage is not driving towards this.

   (b) Panchayati raj is firmly entrenched at the lower level of our federal system of governance.

The whole passage is negating this option.

   (c) A truly federal polity has not developed since PRIs have not been allowed the necessary political space.

This is the correct answer since this is what the whole passage concentrates on. Note that there is no explicit usage of words from the passge in this option—yet it turns out to be correct.

   (d) The Union government and State-level parties are engaged in a struggle for the protection of their respective rights.

Yes definitely, but this is just a supporting detail of the entire logic of the passage.

3. The sentence in the last paragraph, "And their own volition has been further circumscribed. ..", refers to:

   (a) The weakening of the local institutions' ability to plan according to their needs.

This is the **correct** option since it is essentially a restatement of the sentence above, which talks about the restriction of the self wish of the Panchayats.

(b) The increasing demands made on elected local leaders to match central grants with local contributions.

This is the next point of the author. Hence, cannot be the correct answer.

(c) The empowering of the panchayat system as implementers of schemes from State capitals.

The sentence means 'Their own wish has been further restricted'. It definitely does not refer to the empowering of the Panchayat system.

(d) The process by which the prescribed Central schemes are reformulated by local elected leaders.

This option is out of context.

4. What is the "dilemma" at the intra-State level mentioned in the first paragraph of the passage?

(a) Should the state governments wrest more space from the Union, before considering the panchayati system?

This dilemma has not been discussed. Further, it is a Union–State dilemma

(b) Should rights similar to those that the States managed to get be extended to panchayats as well?

This is the **obvious answer**—since we are talking about a dilemma at the intra state level.

(c) Should the single party system which has withered away be brought back at the level of the States?

Out of context

(d) Should the States get "their pound of flesh" before allowing the Union government to pass any more laws?

Again, a Union–State dilemma, even if it exists.

5. Which of the following most closely describes the 'fatal flaw' that the passage refers to?

(a) The ways in which the democratic multi-party system works in an assertively pluralistic society like India's are flawed.

There is nothing wrong in the democratic multi party system. Hence, this cannot be the fatal flaw.

(b) The mechanisms that our federal system uses at the Union government level to deal with States are imperfect.

The fatal flaw does not refer to the mechanisms that the Union uses to deal with the State.

(c) The instruments that have ensured federalism at one level, have been used to achieve the opposite at another.

This is the **correct** answer, since the fatal flaw is the central idea of the entire passage—and this option correctly describes what the passage describes.

(d) The Indian Constitution and the spirit of the Indian polity are fatally flawed.

This option is too drastic to be considered.

PASSAGE II

The endless struggle between the flesh and the spirit found an end in Greek art. The Greek artists were unaware of it. They were spiritual materialists, never denying the importance of the body and ever seeing in the body a spiritual significance. Mysticism on the whole was alien to the Greeks, thinkers as they were. Thought and mysticism never go well together and there is little symbolism in Greek art. Athena was not a symbol of wisdom but an embodiment of it and her statues were beautiful grave women, whose seriousness might mark them as wise, but who were marked in no other way. The Apollo Belvedere is not a symbol of the sun, nor the Versailles Artemis of the moon. There could be nothing less akin to the ways of symbolism than their beautiful, normal humanity. Nor did decoration really interest the Greeks. In all their art they were preoccupied with what they wanted to express, not with ways of expressing it, and lovely expression, merely as lovely expression, did not appeal to them at all.

Greek art is intellectual art, the art of men who were clear and lucid thinkers, and it is therefore plain art. Artists than whom the world has never seen greater, men endowed with the spirit's best gift, found their natural method of expression in the simplicity and clarity which are the endowment of the unclouded reason, "Nothing in excess," the Greek axiom of art, is the dictum of men who would brush aside all obscuring, entangling superfluity, and see clearly, plainly, unadorned, what they wished to express. Structure belongs in an especial degree to the province of the mind in art, and architectonics were pre-eminently a mark of the Greek. The power that made a unified whole of the trilogy of a Greek tragedy, that envisioned the sure, precise, decisive scheme of the Greek statue, found its most conspicuous expression in Greek architecture. The Greek temple is the creation, par excellence, of mind and spirit in equilibrium.

A Hindoo temple is a conglomeration of adornment. The lines of the building are completely hidden by the decorations. Sculptured figures and ornaments crowd its surface, stand out from it in thick masses, break it up into a bewildering series of irregular tiers. It is not a unity but a collection, rich, confused. It looks like something not planned but built this way and that as the ornament required. The conviction underlying it can be perceived: each bit of the exquisitely wrought detail had a mystical meaning and the temple's exterior was important only as a means *for* the artist to inscribe thereon the symbols of the truth. It is decoration, not architecture.

Again, the gigantic temples of Egypt, those massive immensities of granite which look as if only the power that moves in the earthquake were mighty enough to bring them into existence, are something other than the creation of geometry balanced by beauty. The science and the spirit are there, but what is there most of all is force, unhuman force, calm but tremendous, overwhelming. It reduces to nothingness all that belongs to man. He is annihilated. The Egyptian architects were possessed by the consciousness of the awful, irresistible domination of the ways of nature; they had no thought to give to the insignificant atom that was man.

Greek architecture of the great age is the expression of men who were, first of all, intellectual artists, kept firmly within the visible world by their mind, but, only second to that, lovers of the human world. The Greek temple is the perfect expression of the pure intellect illumined by the spirit. No other great buildings anywhere approach its simplicity. In the Parthenon straight columns rise to plain capitals; a pediment is sculptured in bold relief; there is nothing more. And yet–here is the Greek miracle–this absolute simplicity of structure is alone in majesty of beauty among all the temples and cathedrals and palaces of the world. Majestic but human, truly Greek. No superhuman force as in Egypt; no strange supernatural shapes as in India; the Parthenon is the home of humanity at ease, calm, ordered, sure of itself and the world. The Greeks flung a challenge to nature in the fullness of their joyous strength. They set their temples on the summit of a hill overlooking the wide sea, outlined against the circle of the sky. They would build what was more beautiful than hill and sea and sky and greater than all these. It matters not at all if the temple is large or small; one never thinks of the size. It matters not how much it is in ruins. A few white columns dominate the lofty height at Sunion as securely as the great mass of the Parthenon dominates all the sweep of sea and land around Athens. To the Greek architect man was the master of the world. His mind could understand its laws; his spirit could discover its beauty.

Q6. Which of the following is NOT a characteristic of Greek architecture, according to the passage?

(a) A lack of excess.

(b) Simplicity of form.

(c) Expression of intellect.

(d) Mystic spirituality.

Q7. From the passage, which of the following combinations can be inferred to be correct?

(a) Hindoo temple–power of nature.

(b) Parthenon–simplicity.

(c) Egyptian temple–mysticism.

(d) Greek temple–symbolism.

Q8. According to the passage, what conception of man can be inferred from Egyptian architecture?

(a) Man is the centre of creation.

(b) Egyptian temples save man from unhuman forces

(c) Temples celebrate man's victory over nature.

(d) Man is inconsequential before the tremendous force of nature.

Q9. According to the passage, which of the following best explains why there is little symbolism in Greek art?

(a) The Greeks focused on thought rather than mysticism.

(b) The struggle between the flesh and the spirit found an end in Greek art.

(c) Greek artists were spiritual materialists.

(d) Greek statues were embodiments rather than symbols of qualities.

Q10. "The Greeks flung a challenge to nature in the fullness of their joyous strength." Which of the following best captures the 'challenge' that is being referred to?

(a) To build a monument matching the background colours of the sky and the sea.

(b) To build a monument bigger than nature's creations.

(c) To build monuments that were more appealing to the mind and spirit than nature's creations.

(d) To build a small but architecturally perfect monument.

Have you read the above passage and solved it's questions?

Then, check your answers with those given below (along with their explanatory notes or author's advice on how it should be read). The passage in *italics* is a reproduction of relevant section from the original passage, and this will be followed by an explanation or author's interpretation of the same.

The endless struggle between the flesh and the spirit found an end in Greek art.

Idea Sentence... Gives us an inkling of the topic of the passage—the expression of the struggle between the flesh and the spirit in Greek art.)

The Greek artists were unaware of it. They were spiritual materialists

Key word to understand—a spiritualist is one who has a strong spiritually awakened mind, a materialist is one who tilts more on the side of the body, hence, a material spiritualist has to be one who gives importance to both the aspects together...what the author next says could have been predicted.

Never denying the importance of the body and ever seeing in the body a spiritual significance.

You need not have read the italicised part as you could very easily have guessed this, if you got what the author meant by spiritual materialists.

Mysticism on the whole was alien to the Greeks, thinkers as they were. Thought and mysticism never go well together and there is little symbolism in Greek art.

Key idea sentences. You need to slow down to understand this, else there is a danger of losing comprehension. The author introduces us to a duality between mysticists and thinkers. You need to understand what the author means by mysticism here in order to move further. Otherwise, you will move on with half baked comprehension. The following are the alternate meanings of the word—

1. the experience of mystical union or direct communion with the ultimate reality reported by mystics.
2. the belief that direct knowledge of God, spiritual truth, or ultimate reality can be attained through subjective experience (as intuition or insight).
3. (a) vague speculation: a belief without sound basis;
   (b) a theory postulating the possibility of direct and intuitive acquisition of ineffable knowledge or power.

The sense in which mysticism is used here, is most likely that of vague speculation, since a thinker would not be expected to indulge in vague speculation. Even if you had not known the exact meaning of the word, you could have guessed it in the context of its usage as the opposite of thought. Further, how would you interpret the use of the word 'Symbolism'? Since mysticism was alien to the Greeks, there is little symbolism in Greek art.... Obviously, symbolism here has something to do with mysticism. Further, it must also have something to do with its root word 'symbol'. Hence, symbolism as used here, must mean the use of symbols to create vagueness in art.)

Athena was not a symbol of wisdom but an embodiment of it and her statues were beautiful grave women, whose seriousness might mark them as wise, but who were marked in no other way. The Apollo Belvedere is not a symbol of the sun, nor the Versailles Artemis of the moon. There could be nothing less akin to the ways of symbolism than their beautiful, normal humanity.

The author is using examples to illustrate his point–the lack of symbolism in Greek art. You can go through this quickly, and not worry about 100 per cent comprehension here since these are minor details.

Nor did decoration really interest the Greeks.

A new point about what Greek artists were not interested in, apart from mysticism and symbolism. You need to add this to the idea structure formed in your mind till now.

In all their art they were preoccupied with what they wanted to express, not with ways of expressing it, and lovely expression, merely as lovely expression, did not appeal to them at all.

Reiteration of the same points. Nothing new is said here—hence, go for a quick read. Now, since there is a change of paragraph, upgrade your concentration for catching new points.)

Greek art is intellectual art, the art of men who were clear and lucid thinkers, and it is therefore plain art. Artists than whom the world has never seen greater, men endowed with the spirit's best gift, found their natural method of expression in the simplicity and clarity which are the endowment of the unclouded reason, "Nothing in excess," the Greek axiom of art, is the dictum of men who would brush aside all obscuring, entangling superfluity, and see clearly, plainly, unadorned, what they wished to express. Structure belongs in an especial degree to the province of the mind in art, and architectonics....

Key word signalling a shift in the focus of the paragraph and perhaps, the entire passage—from art to architecture. However, in case you do not catch this word fully, the next sentence of the paragraph should make this shift clear.

... were pre-eminently a mark of the Greek. The power that made a unified whole of the trilogy of a Greek tragedy, that envisioned the sure, precise, decisive scheme of the Greek statue, found its most conspicuous expression in Greek architecture. The Greek temple is the creation, par excellence, of mind and spirit in equilibrium.

What is said in the itailcised sentences at the start of this paragraph fits rather easily in our mind—nothing new is said as it is just carrying on from where it left off in the previous paragraphs.

A Hindoo temple is a conglomeration of adornment. The lines of the building are completely hidden by the decorations. Sculptured figures and ornaments crowd its surface, stand out from it in thick masses, break it up into a bewildering series of irregular tiers. It is not a unity but a collection, rich, confused.

It looks like something not planned but built this way and that as the ornament required. The conviction underlying it can be perceived: each bit of the exquisitely wrought detail had a mystical meaning and the temple's exterior was important only as a means for the artist to inscribe thereon the symbols of the truth. It is decoration, not architecture.

The author ended the last paragraph by introducing a comment on the Greek temple in this paragraph, he is describing a Hindoo temple. You can safely expect the author to elaborate on the Greek/other temples in the next paragraphs.

Again, the gigantic temples of Egypt, those massive immensities of granite which look as if only the power that moves in the earthquake were mighty enough to bring them into existence, are something other than the creation of geometry balanced by beauty. The science and the spirit are there, but what is there most of all is force, inhuman force, calm but tremendous, overwhelming. It reduces to nothingness all that belongs to man. *He is annihilated, the Egyptian architects were possessed by the consciousness of the awful, irresistible domination of the ways of nature; they had no thought to give to the insignificant atom that was man.*

In the context of the paragraph, these are minor details. The concentration is on describing the temples of Egypt. There is no significant shift in the direction of the passage. Hence, you can afford to skim this passage at a fast rate—even to the point of losing some comprehension. The emboldened sentence is the topic sentence.

Greek architecture of the great age is the expression of men who were, *first of all*, intellectual artists, *kept firmly within the visible world by their mind, but, only second to that, lovers of the human world. The Greek temple is the perfect expression of the pure intellect illumined by the spirit.* No other great buildings *anywhere* approach its simplicity.

The author is explaining the intellectualism and simplicity of the Greek architecture.

In the Parthenon straight columns rise to plain capitals; a pediment is sculptured in bold relief; there is nothing more. And yet–here is the Greek miracle–this absolute simplicity of structure is alone in majesty of beauty among all the temples and cathedrals and palaces of the world. Majestic but human, truly Greek. No superhuman force as in Egypt; no strange supernatural shapes as in India; the Parthenon is the home of humanity at ease, calm, ordered, sure of itself and the world.

The italicised sentences just follow the script of what has been said before—It is just that the repetition is using new words.

The Greeks flung a challenge to nature in the fullness of their joyous strength.

A new sub idea is introduced...

They set their temples on the summit of a hill overlooking the wide sea, outlined against the circle of the sky. They would build what was more beautiful than hill and sea and sky and greater than all these. It matters not at all if the temple is large or small; one never thinks of the size. It matters not how much it is in ruins. A few white columns dominate the lofty height at Sunion as securely as the great mass of the Parthenon dominates all the sweep of sea and land around Athens.

....and illustrated through examples.

To the Greek architect man was the master of the world. His mind could understand its laws; his spirit could discover its beauty.

This is the author's concluding note about Greek architects, where he says how they put man over nature.

6. Which of the following is **Not** a characteristic of Greek architecture, according to the passage?
   (a) A lack of excess. (Author's Note: Definitely a characteristic of Greek architecture as explained in the passage.)
   (b) Simplicity of form. (Author's Note: Another definite characteristic.)
   (c) Expression of intellect. (Author's Note: Another definite characteristic)
   (d) Mystic spirituality. (Author's Note: This is the obvious answer. It is specifically mentioned in the passage that the Greeks were intellectuals and did not believe in mysticism. Do not confuse with the term 'spiritual materialists')
7. From the passage, which of the following combinations can be inferred to be correct?
   (a) Hindoo temple–power of nature.

The Hindoo temple was not connected to the power of nature, this is a characteristic of the Egyptian temple.

(b) Parthenon - simplicity

Simplicity is definitely a characteristic of Greek architecture, since the Greeks believed in a 'lack of excess'. Hence (b) is correct

(c) Egyptian temple–mysticism.

No mention about mysticism is made with respect to the Egyptian temples. As a matter of fact, mysticism was more connected to the Hindoo temple.

(d) Greek temple–symbolism.

The Greeks did not believe in symbolism. Hence, this cannot be the answer.

The options for the above questions are confusing. This is an implicit question. You have to understand the components of the passage correctly.

8. According to the passage, what conception of man can be inferred from Egyptian architecture?
   (a) Man is the centre of creation.

The Egyptians believed the opposite of this, hence this cannot be correct.

(b) Egyptian temples save man from unhuman forces.

Nowhere is this mentioned. Hence, you can safely reject this option.

(c) Temples celebrate man's victory over nature.

Quite the contrary.

(d) Man is inconsequential before the tremendous force of nature.

This is the obvious answer. This comes out clearly from the interpretation of the paragraph on Egyptian temples.

9. According to the passage, which of the following best explains why there is little symbolism in Greek art?

(a) The Greeks focused on thought rather than mysticism.

This is the immediate reason for the lack of symbolism in Greek art.

(b) The struggle between the flesh and the spirit found an end in Greek art.

Although this is explicitly stated, this is not the reason for the lack of symbolism in Greek art.

(c) Greek artists were spiritual materialists.

Again, though this is also explicitly stated, this is not the reason for the lack of symbolism in Greek art.

(d) Greek statues were embodiments rather than symbols of qualities.

This point is mentioned about one particular statue and cannot be generalised.

Options confuse you by using words from the passage. However, the answer to this question is in the line: **'Thought and mysticism never go well together and there is little symbolism in Greek art.' Hence, the first option is correct.**

10. "The Greeks flung a challenge to nature in the fullness of their joyous strength." Which of the following best captures the 'challenge' that is being referred to?

(a) To build a monument matching the background colours of the sky and the sea.

This option is irrelevant.

(b) To build a monument bigger than nature's creations.

Size of the monument did not matter.

(c) To build monuments that were more appealing to the mind and spirit than nature's creations.

Not stated expilicitly, but this is what is implied.

(d) To build a small but architecturally perfect monument.

This choice is irrelevant.

PASSAGE III

While I was in class at Columbia, struggling with the *esoterica du jour*, my father was on a bricklayer's scaffold not far up the street, working on a campus building. Once we met up on the subway going home–he was with his tools, I with my books. My father wasn't interested in Thucydides, and I wasn't up on arches. My dad has built lots of places; in New York City he can't get into: colleges, condos, office towers. He made his living on the outside. Once the walls were up, a place took on a different feel for him, as though he wasn't welcome anymore. Related by blood, we're separated by class, my father and I. Being the white-collar child of a blue-collar parent means being the hinge on the door between two ways of life. With one foot in the working-class, the other in the middle class, people like me are Straddlers, at home in neither world, living a limbo life.

What drove me to leave what I knew? Born blue-collar, I still never felt completely at home among the tough guys and anti-intellectual crowd of my neighbourhood in deepest Brooklyn. I never did completely fit in among the preppies and suburban royalty of Columbia, either. It's like that for Straddlers. It was not so smooth jumping from Italian old-world style to US professional in a single generation. Others who were the first in their families to go to college, will tell you the same thing: the academy can render you unrecognisable to the very people who launched you into the world. The ideas and values absorbed in college challenge the mom-and-pop orthodoxy that passed for truth for 18 years. Limbo folk may eschew polyester blends for sea-isle cotton, prefer Brie to Kraft slices. They marry outside the neighbourhood and raise their kids differently. They might not be in church on Sunday.

When they pick careers (not *jobs*), it's often a kind of work their parents never heard of or can't understand. But for the white-collar kids of blue-collar parents, the office is not necessarily a sanctuary. In Corporate America, where the rules are based on notions foreign to working-class people, a Straddler can get lost. Social class counts at the office, even though nobody likes to admit it. Ultimately, corporate norms are based on middle-class values, business types say. From an early age, middle-class people learn how to get along, using diplomacy, nuance, and politics to grab what they need. It is as though they are following a set of rules laid out in a manual that blue-collar families never have the chance to read.

People born into the middle class to parents with college degrees have lived lives filled with what French sociologist PierreBourdieu calls 'cultural capital'. Growing up in an educated environment, they learn about Picasso and Mozart, stock portfolios and *creme brulee.* In a home with cultural capital, there are networks: someone always has an aunt or golfing buddy with the inside track for an internship or some entry-level job. Dinner-table talk could involve what happened that day to mom and dad at the law firm, the doctor's office, or the executive suite. Middle-class kids can grow up with a sense of entitlement that will carry them through their lives. This 'belongingness' is not just related to having material means, it also has to do with learning and possessing confidence in your place in the world. Such early access and direct exposure to culture in the home is the more organic, 'legitimate' means of appropriating cultural capital, Bourdieu tells us. Those of us possessing 'ill-gotten Culture' can learn it, but never as well. Something is always a little off about us, like an engine with imprecise timing. There's a greater match between middle-class lives and the institutions in which the middle class works and operates–universities or corporations. Children of the middle and upper classes have been speaking the language of the bosses and supervisors forever.

Blue-collar kids are taught by their parents and communities to work hard to achieve, and that merit is rewarded. But no blue-collar parent knows whether such things are true in the middle-class world. Many professionals born to the working-class report feeling out of place and outmanoeuvred in the office. Soon enough, Straddlers learn that straight talk won't always cut. Resolving conflicts head-on and speaking your mind doesn't always work, no matter how educated the Straddler is.

In the working-class, people perform jobs in which they are closely supervised and are required to follow orders and instructions. That, in turn, affects how they socialise their children. Children of the working-class are brought up in a home in which conformity, obedience and intolerance for back talk are the norm–the same characteristics that make a good factory worker.

Q11. According to the passage, which of the following statements about 'cultural capital' is NOT true?

(a) It socializes children early into the norms of middle class institutions.

(b) It helps them learn the language of universities and corporations.

(c) It creates a sense of enlightenment in middle-class children.

(d) It develops bright kids into Straddlers.

Q12. According to the passage, the patterns of socialization of working-class children make them most suited for jobs that require:

(a) diplomacy.

(b) compliance with orders.

(c) enterprise and initiative.

(d) high risk taking.

Q13. When Straddlers enter white collar jobs, they get lost because:

(a) they are thrown into an alien value system.

(b) their families have not read the rules in corporate manuals.

(c) they have no one to guide them through the corporate maze.

(d) they miss the 'mom and pop orthodoxy'.

Q14. What does the author's statement, "My father wasn't interested in Thucydides, and I wasn't up on arches", illustrate?

(a) Organic cultural capital.

(b) Professional arrogance and social distance.

(c) Evolving social transformation.

(d) Breakdown of family relationships.

Q15. Which of the following statements about Straddlers does the passage NOT support explicitly?

(a) Their food preferences may not match those of their parents.

(b) They may not keep up some central religious practices of their parents.

(c) They are at home neither in the middle class nor in the working-class.

(d) Their political ideologies may differ from those of their parents.

Have you read the above passage and solved its questions?

Then check your answers with those given below (along with their explanatory notes or author's advice on how it should be read). The passage in *italics* is a reproduction of relevant section from the original passage, and this will be followed by an explanatory note or interpretation on the same.

While I was in class at Columbia, struggling with the esoterica du jour, my father was on a bricklayer's scaffold not far up the street, working on a campus building.

This sentence gives us an idea of what the author is going to talk about— the contrast between a son studying in a college and his father who is a building worker.

Once we met up on the subway going home–he was with his tools, I with my books. My father wasn't interested in Thucydides, and I wasn't up on arches. My dad has built lots of places; in New York City he can't get into: colleges, condos, office towers. He made his living on the outside. Once the walls were up, a place took on a different feel for him, as though he wasn't welcome anymore.

Quick reading as these are minor details in the context of the passage.

Related by blood, we're separated by class, my father and I. Being the white-collar child of a blue-collar parent means being the hinge on the door between two ways of life. With one foot in the working-class, the other in the middle class, people like me are Straddlers, at home in neither world, living a limbo life

These are Idea sentences.

What drove me to leave what I knew?

Shift of emphasis. Expect an answer to this question in the remaining part of the paragraph.

Born blue-collar, I still never felt completely at home among the tough guys and anti-intellectual crowd of my neighbourhood in deepest Brooklyn. I never did completely fit in among the preppies and suburban royalty of Columbia, either. It's like that for Straddlers.

The author has earlier described himself as a straddler. He is putting forward an opinion that straddlers like him never fit in completely in either the blue collar surroundings that they were born into, or the academic world, which he has described as suburban royalty.

It was not so smooth jumping from Italian old-world style to US professional in a single generation. Others who were the first in their families to go to college, will tell you the same thing: the academy can render you umecognisable to the very people who launched you into the world.

Read Parents.

The ideas and values absorbed in college challenge the mom-and-pop orthodoxy that passed for truth for 18 years. Limbo folk may eschew polyester blends for sea-isle cotton, prefer Brie to Kraft slices. They marry outside the neighbourhood and raise their kids differently. They might not be in church on Sunday.

Minor details, hence skim while reading.

When they pick careers (not jobs), it's often a kind of work their parents never heard of or can't understand. But for the white-collar kids of blue-collar parents, the office is not necessarily a sanctuary.

A new shift of direction, as the author moves into talking about the experience of people like him in modern offices.

In Corporate America, where the rules are based on notions foreign to working-class people, a Straddler can get lost. Social class counts at the office, even though nobody likes to admit it.

This is an Idea sentence.

Ultimately, corporate norms are based on middle-class values, business types say. From an early age, middle-class people learn how to get along, using diplomacy, nuance, and politics to grab what they need. It is as though they are following a set of rules laid out in a manual that blue-collar families never have the chance to read.

Minor details. Skim.

People born into the middle class to parents with college degrees have lived lives filled with what French sociologist Pierre Bourdieu calls 'cultural capital'. Growing up in an educated environment, they learn about Picasso and Mozart, stock portfolios and creme brulee. In a home with cultural capital, there are networks: someone always has an aunt or golfing buddy with the inside track for an internship or some entry-level job. Dinner-table talk could involve what happened that day to mom and dad at the law firm, the doctor's office, or the executive suite. Middle-class kids can grow up with a sense of entitlement that will carry them through their lives. This 'belongingness' is not just related to having material means, it also has to do with learning and possessing confidence in your place in the world. Such early access and direct exposure to culture in the home is the more organic, 'legitimate' means of appropriating cultural capital, Bourdieu tells us. Those of us possessing 'ill-gotten Culture' can learn it, but never as well. Something is always a little off about us, like an engine with imprecise timing. There's a greater match between middle-class lives and the institutions in which the middle class works and operates–universities or corporations. Children of the middle and upper classes have been speaking the language of the bosses and supervisors forever.

The author continues to contrast the middle class upbringing with the lower class upbringing. He is just continuing from the last idea introduced in the previous paragraph, i.e., 'Social class counts at the office.'

Blue-collar kids are taught by their parents and communities to work hard to achieve, and that merit is rewarded. But no blue-collar parent knows whether such things are true in the middle-class world. Many professionals born to the working-class report feeling out of place and outmanoeuvred in the office. Soon enough, Straddlers learn that straight talk won't always cut. Resolving conflicts head-on and speaking your mind doesn't always work, no matter how educated the Straddler is.

In the working-class, people perform jobs in which they are closely supervised and are required to follow orders and instructions. That, in turn, affects how they socialise their children. Children of the working-class are brought up in a home in which conformity, obedience and intolerance for back talk are the norm–the same characteristics that make a good factory worker.

11. According to the passage, which of the following statements about 'cultural capital' is **Not** true?
    (a) It socialises children early into the norms of middle class institutions.

Cultural capital does this. Hence, this cannot be the answer.

(b) It helps them learn the language of universities and corporations.

Explicitly mentioned about the effects of cultural capital. Hence, this cannot be the answer.

(c) It creates a sense of enlightenment in middle-class children.

This can be inferred from the third last paragraph.

(d) It develops bright kids into Straddlers.

This is the appropriate answer, since this clearly is not an effect of cultural capital.

12. According to the passage, the patterns of socialization of working-class children make them most suited for jobs that require
    (a) diplomacy.
    (b) compliance with orders.

This is the obvious choice. It is clear from the last sentence of the passage.

(c) enterprise and initiative.
(d) high risk taking.

13. When Straddlers enter white collar jobs, they get lost because:
    (a) they are thrown into an alien value system.

This is the main idea the author is trying to convey in the last three paragraphs.

(b) their families have not read the rules in corporate manuals.

Irrelevant. An eye wash which can be easily caught.

(c) they have no one to guide them through the corporate maze.

This is not necessarily true.

(d) they miss the 'mom and pop orthodoxy'.

This can confuse you, but option (a) is superior.

14. What does the author's statement, "My father wasn't interested in Thucydides, and I wasn't up on arches", illustrate?
    (a) Organic cultural capital.

This statement is not at all connected to organic cultural capital.

(b) Professional arrogance and social distance.

There is no arrogance involved here.

(c) Evolving social transformation.

The statement is used to illustrate the social transformation brought about by education within one generation in a family. Hence, this is the correct option.

(d) Breakdown of family relationships.

There is no breakdown of family relationships involved.

15. Which of the following statements about Straddlers does the passage **Not** support explicitly?
    (a) Their food preferences may not match those of their parents.

Explicitly mentioned in the words 'prefer Brie to Kraft slices'.

(b) They may not keep up some central religious practices of their parents.

Can be inferred from the last sentence of the second paragraph 'They might not be in church on Sunday.'

(c) They are at home neither in the middle class nor in the working-class.

Clearly mentioned in the second and third sentences of the second paragraph 'Born blue-collar, I still never felt completely at home among the tough guys and anti-intellectual crowd of my neighbourhood in deepest Brooklyn. I never did completely fit in among the preppies and suburban royalty of Columbia, either. It's like that for Straddlers'

(d) Their political ideologies may differ from those of their parents.

There is no explicit mention about differing political ideologies anywhere in the passage. Hence, this is the correct option.

PASSAGE IV

Pure love of learning, of course, was a less compelling motive for those who became educated for careers other than teaching. Students of law in particular had a reputation for being materialistic careerists in an age when law was becoming known as "the lucrative science" and its successful practice the best means for rapid advancement in the government of both church and state. Medicine too had its profit-making attractions. Those who did not go on to law or medicine could, if they had been well trained in the arts, gain positions at royal courts or rise in the clergy. Eloquent testimony to the profit motive behind much of twelfth-century education was the lament of a student of Abelard around 1150 that "Christians educate their sons. ..for gain, in order that the one brother, if he be a clerk, may help his father and mother and his other brothers, saying that a clerk will have no heir and whatever he has will be ours and the other brothers." With the opening of positions in law, government, and the church, education became a means for advancement not only in income but also in status. Most who were educated were wealthy, but in the twelfth century, more often than before, many were not and were able to rise through the ranks by means of their education. The most familiar examples are Thomas Becket, who rose from a humble background to become chancellor of England and then archbishop of Canterbury, and John of Salisbury, who was born a "plebeian" but because of his reputation for learning died as bishop of Chartres.

The instances of Becket and John of Salisbury bring us to the most difficult question concerning twelfth-century education: To what degree was it still a clerical preserve? Despite the fact that throughout the twelfth century the clergy had a monopoly of instruction, one of the outstanding medievalists of our day, R. W. Southern, refers with good reason to the institutions staffed by the clergy as "secular schools". How can we make sense out of the paradox that twelfth-century schools were clerical and yet "secular"?

Let us look at the clerical side first. Not only were all twelfth-century teachers except professionals and craftsmen in church orders, but in northern Europe students in schools had clerical status and looked like priests. Not that all really were priests, but by virtue of being students all were awarded the legal privileges accorded to the clergy. Furthermore, the large majority of twelfth-century students, outside of the possible exception of Italy, if not already priests became so after their studies were finished. For these reasons, the term "cleric" was often used to denote a man who was literate and the term "layman" one who was illiterate. The English word for cleric, clerk, continued for a long time to be a synonym for student or for a man who could write, while the French word *clerc* even today has the connotation of intellectual.

Despite all this, twelfth-century education was taking on many secular qualities in its environment, goals, and curriculum. Student life obviously became more secular when it moved out from the monasteries into the bustling towns. Most students wandered from town to town in search not only of good masters but also of worldly excitement, and as the twelfth century progressed they found the best of each in Paris. More important than environment was the fact that most students, even though they entered the clergy, had secular goals. Theology was recognized as the "queen of the sciences," but very few went on to it. Instead they used their study of the liberal arts as a preparation for law, medicine, government service, or advancement in the ecclesiastical hierarchy.

This being so, the curriculum of the liberal arts became more sophisticated and more divorced from religion. Teaching was still almost exclusively in Latin, and the first book most often read was the Psalter, but further education was no longer similar to that of a choir school. In particular, the discipline of rhetoric was transformed from a linguistic study into instruction in how to compose letters and documents; there was a new stress on logic; and in all the liberal arts and philosophy texts, more advanced than those known in the early Middle Ages were introduced.

Along with the rise of logic came the translation of Greek and Arabic philosophical and scientific works. Most important was the translation of almost all the writings of Aristotle, as well as his sophisticated Arabic commentators, which helped to bring about an intellectual revolution based on Greek rationalism. On a more prosaic level, contact with Arabs resulted in the introduction in the twelfth century of the Arabic numeral system and the concept of zero. Though most westerners first resisted this and made crude jokes about the zero as an ambitious number "that counts for nothing and yet wants to be counted," the system steadily made its inroads first in Italy and then throughout Europe, thereby vastly simplifying the arts of computation and record keeping.

Q16. According to the passage, which of the following is the most noteworthy trend in education in twelfth-century Europe?

(a) Secularization of education.

(b) Flowering of theology as the queen of the sciences.

(c) Wealthy people increasingly turning to education.

(d) Rise of the clergy's influence on the curriculum.

Q17. What does the sentence "Christians educate their sons... will be ours and the other brothers" imply?

(a) The Christian family was a close-knit unit in the twelfth century.

(b) Christians educated their sons not so much for the love of learning as for material gain.

(c) Christians believed very strongly in educating their sons in the Church.

(d) The relationship between Christian parents and their sons was exploitative in the twelfth century.

Q18. According to the passage, twelfth century schools were clerical and yet secular because:

(a) many teachers were craftsmen and professionals who did not form part of the church.

(b) while the students had the legal privileges accorded to the clergy and looked like priests, not all were really priests.

(c) the term 'cleric' denoted a literate individual rather than a strict association with the church.

(d) though the clergy had a monopoly in education, the environment, objectives and curriculum in the schools were becoming secular.

Q19. According to the author, in the twelfth century, individuals were motivated to get higher education because it:

(a) was a means for material advancement and higher status.

(b) gave people wealth with an opportunity to learn.

(c) offered a coveted place for those with a love of learning.

(d) directly added to the income levels of people.

Q20. According to the passage, what led to the secularization of the curriculum of the liberal arts in the twelfth century?

(a) It was divorced from religion and its influences.

(b) Students used it mainly as a base for studying law and medicine.

(c) Teaching could no longer be conducted exclusively in Latin.

(d) Arabic was introduced into the curriculum.

Have you read the above passage and solved it's questions?

Then, check your answers with those given below (along with their explanatory notes or author's advice on how they should be read). The passage in *italics* is a reproduction of relevant section from the original passage, and this will be followed by an explanatory note or interpretation on the same.

Pure love of learning, of course, was a less compelling motive for those who became educated for careers other than teaching.

Idea Sentence. You need to grasp this well and if you do so, the next few sentences become easy minor details, reading.

Students of law in particular had a reputation for being materialistic careerists in an age when law was becoming known as "the lucrative science" and its successful practice the best means for rapid advancement in the government of both church and state. Medicine too had its profit-making attractions. Those who did not go on to law or medicine could, if they had been well trained in the arts, gain positions at royal courts or rise in the clergy. Eloquent testimony to the profit motive behind much of twelfth-century education was the lament of a student of Abelard around 1150 that "Christians educate their sons... for gain, in order that the one brother, if he be a clerk, may help his father and mother and his other brothers, saying that a clerk will have no heir and whatever he has will be ours and the other brothers." With the opening of positions in law, government, and the church, education became a means for advancement not only in income but also in status.

Minor idea.

Most who were educated were wealthy, but in the twelfth century, more often than before, many were not and were able to rise through the ranks by means of their education. The most familiar examples are Thomas Becket, who rose from a humble background to become chancellor of England and then archbishop of Canterbury, and John of Salisbury, who was born a "plebeian" but because of his reputation for learning died as bishop of Chartres.

The italicised part of the above paragraph can be skimmed at a rapid pace if you have understood the first idea sentence, where the author is just talking about the fact that getting educated had a motive other than the pure love of learning.

The instances of Becket and John of Salisbury bring us to the most difficult question concerning twelfth-century education: To what degree was it still a clerical preserve?

Here, we can witness a shift of emphasis.

Despite the fact that throughout the twelfth century the clergy had a monopoly of instruction, one of the outstanding medievalists of our day, R. W. Southern, refers with good reason to the institutions staffed by the clergy as "secular schools." How can we make sense out of the paradox that twelfth-century schools were clerical and yet "secular"?

The shift of emphasis continues by ending the paragraph with another question, the answer to which we need to find in the next paragraph.

Please take note that from this paragraph, you get to understand that by the words 'clerk' in the first paragraph and 'clerical' in this paragraph, the author is referring to the Christian clergy and not the clerk we understand in our normal day to day life. Further, since the paragraph ends with a question, you can expect an answer to the question in the next paragraphs.

Let us look at the clerical side first.

A list word is used signifying an upcoming list. This sentence has introduced a first dimension to the answer to the question. You can expect at least a second dimension or perhaps more.

Not only were all twelfth-century teachers except professionals and craftsmen in church orders, but in northern Europe students in schools had clerical status and looked like priests. Not that all really were priests, but by virtue of being students all were awarded the legal privileges accorded to the clergy. Furthermore, the large majority of twelfth-century students, outside of the possible exception of Italy, if not already priests became so after their studies were finished. For these reasons, the term "cleric" was often used to denote a man who was literate and the term "layman" one who was illiterate. The English word for cleric, clerk, continued for a long time to be a synonym for student or for a man who could write, while the French word clerc even today has the connotation of intellectual.

Details which can be read fast.

Despite all this

Signals a contrast point coming up

Twelfth-century education was taking on many secular qualities in its environment, goals, and curriculum. Student life obviously became more secular when it moved out from the monasteries into the bustling towns. Most students wandered from town to town in search not only of good masters but also of worldly excitement, and as the twelfth century progressed they found the best of each in Paris. More important than environment was the fact that most students, even though they entered the clergy, had secular goals. Theology was recognized as the "queen of the sciences," but very few went on to it. Instead they used their study of the liberal arts as a preparation for law, medicine, government service, or advancement in the ecclesiastical hierarchy.

Details, what you need to do is understand the point and skim while reading.

This being so,

Another use of transition, suggesting an upcoming effect of the previous paragraph, something that can be predicted.

the curriculum of the liberal arts became more sophisticated and more divorced from religion. Teaching was still almost exclusively in Latin, and the first book most often read was the Psalter, but further education was no longer similar to that of a choir school. In particular, the discipline of rhetoric was transformed from a linguistic study into instruction in how to compose letters and documents; there was a new stress on logic; and in all the liberal arts and philosophy, texts more advanced than those known in the early Middle Ages were introduced.

Identify the shift of the author to the sub topic of 'how liberal arts went away from religion' in this paragraph.

Along with the rise of logic came the translation of Greek and Arabic philosophical and scientific works. Most important was the translation of almost all the writings of Aristotle, as well as his sophisticated Arabic commentators, which helped to bring about an intellectual revolution based on Greek rationalism. On a more prosaic level, contact with Arabs resulted in the introduction in the twelfth century of the Arabic numeral system and the concept of zero. Though most westerners first resisted this and made crude jokes about the zero as an ambitious number "that counts for nothing and yet wants to be counted" the system steadily made its inroads first in Italy and then throughout Europe, thereby vastly simplifying the arts of computation and record keeping.

16. According to the passage, which of the following is the most noteworthy trend in education in twelfth-century Europe?
    (a) Secularisation of education

This is obviously the correct answer. The entire passage is based on this issue.

(b) Flowering of theology as the queen of the sciences.

Irrelevant detail

(c) Wealthy people increasingly turning to education.

Irrelevant detail.

(d) Rise of the clergy's influence on the curriculum.

This cannot be the answer, as it is talking of the opposite.

17. What does the sentence "Christians educate their sons. ..will be ours and the other brothers" imply?
    (a) The Christian family was a close-knit unit in the twelfth century.
    (b) Christians educated their sons not so much for the love of learning as for material gain.

This point is explicitly made prior to the statement. Hence, this has to be correct.

(c) Christians believed very strongly in educating their sons in the Church.

Irrelevant option.

(d) The relationship between Christian parents and their sons was exploitative in the twelfth century.

Irrelevant option

18. According to the passage, twelfth century schools were clerical and yet secular because:
    (a) many teachers were craftsmen and professionals who did not form part of the church.

Irrelevant point.

(b) while the students had the legal privileges accorded to the clergy and looked like priests, not all were really priests.

Although this is stated, it is not the cause of the clerical, yet secular nature.

(c) the term 'cleric' denoted a literate individual rather than a strict association with the church.

Might confuse some students, but is not accurate enough to be the answer.

(d) though the clergy had a monopoly in education, the environment, objectives and curriculum in the schools were becoming secular.

This option is the most accurate and consistent with the idea expressed in the third and fourth passages.

19. According to the author, in the twelfth century, individuals were motivated to get higher education because it:
    (a) was a means for material advancement and higher status.

This is the correct answer since this idea is expressed explicitly in the sentence: "With the opening of positions in law, government, and the church, education became a means for advancement not only in income but also in status."

(b) gave people wealth with an opportunity to learn.

This option is inconsistent with the sense of the passage as expressed in the first paragraph.

(c) offered a coveted place for those with a love of learning.

Incorrect, since it contradicts the idea expressed in the first paragraph.

(d) directly added to the income levels of people.

Income was one of the factors. Status was also a factor. Also, this option is structured too drastically to be the correct answer.

20. According to the passage, what led to the secularization of the curriculum of the liberal arts in the twelfth century?

(a) It was divorced from religion and its influences.

This is just a restatement of 'secularization of the curriculum.' Hence, this cannot be the cause of the same.

(b) Students used it mainly as a base for studying law and medicine.

The second last paragraph talks about the secularization of education. However, it starts with the transitory— "This Being so..." which indicates that we are reading a cause and its effect. Hence, as a student, you should look for the cause in the in the prelude to the second last paragraph. The idea of this option is expressed in the last sentence of the third last paragraph. Hence, this option is correct.)

(c) Teaching could no longer be conducted exclusively in Latin.

The second last paragraph discusses the opposite of this option.

(d) Arabic was introduced into the curriculum.

Irrelevant point.

Passage V

The invention of the gas turbine by Frank Whittle in England and Hans von Ohain in Germany in 1939 signalled the beginning of jet transport. Although the French engineer Lorin had visualized the concept of jet propulsion more than 25 years earlier, it took improved materials and the genius of Whittle and von Ohain to recognise the advantages that a gas turbine offered over a piston engine, including speeds in excess of 350 miles per hour. The progress from the first flights of liquid propellant rocket and jet-propelled aircraft in 1939 to the first faster-than-sound (supersonic) manned airplane (the Bell X-I) in 1947 happened in less than a decade. This then led very rapidly to a series of supersonic fighters and bombers, the first of which became operational in the 1950s. World War II technology foundations and emerging Cold War imperatives then led us into space with the launch of Sputnik in 1957 and the placing of the first man on the moon only 12 years later–a mere 24 years after the end of World War II.

Now, a hypersonic flight can take you anywhere in the planet in less than four hours. British Royal Air Force and Royal Navy, and the air forces of several other countries are going to use a single-engine cousin to the F/A-22 called the F-35 Joint Strike Fighter. These planes exhibit stealthy angles and coatings that make it difficult for radar to detect them, among aviation's most cutting-edge advances in design. The V-22, known as tilt-rotor, part helicopter, part airplane, takes off vertically, then tilts its engine forward for winged flight. It provides speed, three times the payload, five times the range of the helicopters it's meant to replace. The new fighter, F/A-22 Raptor, with more than a million parts, shows a perfect amalgamation of stealth, speed, avionics and agility.

It seems conventional forms, like the Predator and Global Hawk are passe, the stealthier unmanned aerial vehicles (UAVs) are in. They are shaped like kites, bats and boomerang, all but invisible to the enemy radar and able to remain over hostile territory without any fear of getting grilled if shot down. Will the UAVs take away pilots' jobs permanently? Can a computer-operated machine take a smarter and faster decision in a war-like situation? The new free-flight concept will probably supplement the existing air traffic control system by computers on each plane to map the altitude, route, weather and other planes; and a decade from now, there will be no use of radar any more.

How much bigger can the airplanes get? In the 1950s they got speed, in the 1980s they became stealthy. Now, they are getting smarter thanks to computer automation. The change is quite huge: from the four-seater to the A380 airplane. It seems we are now trading speed for size as we build a new superjumbo jet, the 555 seater A380, which will fly at almost the same speed of the Boeing 707, introduced half a century ago, but with an improved capacity, range, greater fuel economy. A few years down the line will come the truly larger model, to be known as 747X. In the beginning of 2005, the A380, the world's first fully double-decked superjumbo passenger jet, weighing 1.2 million pounds, may carry a load of about 840 passengers.

Barring the early phase, civil aviation has always lagged behind the military technologies (of jet engines, lightweight composite materials, etc.). There are two fundamental factors behind the decline in commercial aeronautics in comparison to military aeronautics. There is no collective vision of our future such as the one that drove us in the past. There is also a need for a more aggressive pool of airplane design talents to maintain an industry that continues to find a multibillion dollar-a-year market for its product.

Can the history of aviation technology tell us something about the future of aeronautics? Have we reached a final state in our evolution to a mature technology in aeronautics? Are the challenges of coming out with the 'better, cheaper, faster' designs somehow inferior to those that are suited for 'faster, higher, further'? Safety should improve greatly as a result of the forthcoming improvements in airframes, engines, and avionics. Sixty years from now, aircraft will recover on their own if the pilot loses control. Satellites are the key not only to GPS (global positioning system) navigation but also to in-flight communications, uplinked weather, and even in-flight e-mail. Although there is some debate about what type of engines will power future airplanes–lightweight turbines, turbocharged diesels, or both–there is little debate about how these power plants will be controlled. Pilots of the future can look forward to more and better on-board safety equipment.

Q21. According to the first paragraph of the passage, which of the following statements is NOT false?
(a) Prank Whittle and Hans von Ohain were the first to conceive of jet propulsion.
(b) Supersonic fighter planes were first used in the Second World War.
(c) No man had traveled faster than sound until the 1950s.
(d) The exploitation of jet propulsion for supersonic aviation has been remarkably fast.

Q22. What is the fourth paragraph of the passage about?
(a) Stealth, speed, avionics, and agility of new aircraft.
(b) The way aircraft size has been growing.
(c) Use of computer automation in aircraft.
(d) Super-jumbo jets that can take more than 500 passengers.

Q23. What is the most noteworthy difference between V-22 and a standard airplane? The V-22:
(a) can take off vertically.
(b) has winged flight.
(c) has excellent payload.
(d) has a very high range.

Q24. Why might radars not be used a decade from now?
(a) Stealth technology will advance so much that it would because pointless to use radar to detect aircraft.
(b) UAVs can remain over hostile territory without any danger of being detected.
(c) Computers on board may enable aircraft to manage safe navigation on their own.
(d) It is not feasible to increase the range of radars.

Q25. According to the author, commercial aeronautics, in contrast to military aeronautics, has declined because, among other things,
(a) speed and technology barriers are more easily overcome in military aeronautics.
(b) the collective vision of the past continues to drive civil and commercial aeronautics.
(c) though the industry has a huge market, it has not attracted the right kind of aircraft designers.
(d) there is a shortage of materials, like light weight composites, used in commercial aeronautics.

Have you read the above passage and solved its questions?

Then, check your answers with those given below (along with their explanatory notes or author's advice on how they should be read). The passage in *italics* is a reproduction of relevant section from the original passage, and this will be followed by an explanatory note or interpretation on the same.

The invention of the gas turbine by Frank Whittle in England and Hans von Ohain in Germany in 1939, signalled the beginning of jet transport. Although the French engineer Lorin had visualized the concept of jet propulsion more than 25 years earlier, it took improved materials and the genius of Whittle and von Ohain to recognize the advantages that a gas turbine offered over a piston engine, including speeds in excess of 350 miles per hour. The progress from the first flights of liquid propellant rocket and jet-propelled aircraft in 1939 to the first faster-than-sound (supersonic) manned airplane (the Bell X-I) in 1947 happened in less than a decade. This then led very rapidly to a series of supersonic fighters and bombers, the first of which became operational in the 1950s. World War II technology foundations and emerging Cold War imperatives then led us into space with the launch of Sputnik in 1957 and the placing of the first man on the moon only 12 years later– a mere 24 years after the end of World War II.

This defines the topic as 'air transport'. Note that the above paragraph is structured on the basis of time-based technological advances in flight technology. There might be some confusion in your mind in case you do not understand the technologies mentioned. But such confusion is totally avoidable since there is no need to understand these in order to comprehend the paragraph. All you need to do is to catch the chronology defined. Then, you will broadly understand that the author is talking about advances in technology from the 1910s to the 1950s.

Now, a hypersonic flight can take you anywhere in the planet in less than four hours.

The author is continuing in the direction of further improvements in aeronautics. You should expect that the author will continue in this direction by giving us more examples of the trend.

British Royal Air Force and Royal Navy, and the air forces of several other countries are going to use a single-engine cousin to the F/A-22 called the F-35 Joint Strike Fighter. These planes exhibit stealthy angles and coatings that make it difficult for radar to detect them, among aviation's most cutting-edge advances in design. The V-22, known as tilt-rotor, part helicopter, part airplane, takes off vertically, then tilts its engine forward for winged flight. It provides speed, three times the payload, five times the range of the helicopters it's meant to replace. The new fighter, F/A-22 Raptor, with more than a million parts, shows a perfect amalgamation of stealth, speed, avionics and agility.

As expected, two specific examples of the trend.

It seems conventional forms, like the Predator and Global Hawk are passe, the stealthier unmanned aerial vehicles (UAVs) are in.

A new direction in the development of aeronautics is introduced here. Details about UAVs are bound to follow.

They are shaped like kites, bats and boomerang, all but invisible to the enemy radar and able to remain over hostile territory without any fear of getting grilled if shot down. Will the UAV s take away pilots' jobs permanently? Can a computer-operated machine take a smarter and faster decision in a war-like situation? The new free-flight concept will probably supplement the existing air traffic control system by computers on each plane to map the altitude, route, weather and other planes; and a decade from now, there will be no use of radar any more. (Author's Note: As expected.)

How much bigger can the airplanes get?

Notice the shift in the direction and expect details to follow.

In the 1950s they got speed, in the 1980s they became stealthy. Now, they are getting smarter thanks to computer automation. The change is quite huge: from the four-seater to the A380 airplane. It seems we are now trading speed for size as we build a new superjumbo jet, the 555 seater A380, which will fly at almost the same speed of the Boeing 707, introduced half a century ago, but with an improved capacity, range, greater fuel economy. A few years down the line will come the truly larger model, to be known as 747X. In the beginning of 2005, the A380, the world's first fully double-decked superjumbo passenger jet, weighing 1.2 million pounds, may carry a load of about 840 passengers.

Barring the early phase, civil aviation has always lagged behind the military technologies (of jet engines, lightweight composite materials, etc.)

New dimension of the idea.

There are **two fundamental factors**

List words—look for the two factors.

behind the decline in commercial aeronautics in comparison to military aeronautics. There is no collective vision of our future such as the one that drove us in the past. There is also a need for a more aggressive pool of airplane design talents to maintain an industry that continues to find a multibillion dollar-a-year market for its product.

Can the history of aviation technology tell us something about the future of aeronautics? Have we reached a final state in our evolution to a mature technology in aeronautics? Are the challenges of coming out with the 'better, cheaper, faster' designs somehow inferior to those that are suited for 'faster, higher, further'? Safety should improve greatly as a result of the forthcoming improvements in airframes, engines, and avionics. Sixty years from now, aircraft will recover on their own if the pilot loses control. Satellites are the key not only to GPS (global positioning system) navigation but also to in-flight communications, uplinked weather, and even in-flight e-mail. Although there is some debate about what type of engines will power future airplanes-lightweight turbines, turbocharged diesels, or both— there is little debate about how these power plants will be controlled. Pilots of the future can look forward to more and better on-board safety equipment.

21. According to the first paragraph of the passage, which of the following statements is **Not** false?
    (a) Prank Whittle and Hans von Ohain were the first to conceive of jet propulsion.

    False statement, they just used the concept formulated by Lorin.

    (b) Supersonic fighter planes were first used in the Second World War.

    False, they were used first in the 1950s.

    (c) No man had traveled faster than sound until the 1950s.

    It happened in 1947.

    (d) The exploitation of jet propulsion for supersonic aviation has been remarkably fast.

    This is true, hence, not false. Therefore, this is the correct answer.

22. What is the fourth paragraph of the passage about?
    (a) Stealth, speed, avionics, and agility of new aircraft.
    (b) The way aircraft size has been growing.

    It is obviously the correct option, since the paragraph tries to answer the question 'How much bigger can airplanes get?'

    (c) Use of computer automation in aircraft.
    (d) Super-jumbo jets that can take more than 500 passengers.

23. What is the most noteworthy difference between V-22 and a standard airplane? The V-22
    (a) can take off vertically.

    This is the correct option. Although each of the other options is mentioned specifically in the context of the V-22, the question is specific about the difference between the V-22 and a standard airplane.

(b) has winged flight.
(c) has excellent payload.
(d) has a very high range.

The options (b), (c) and (d) do not mention the feature that is different from what a standard airplane would have.

24. Why might radars not be used a decade from now?

A cause and effect question. The question is asking you to identify the cause for the effect mentioned.

(a) Stealth technology will advance so much that it would become pointless to use radar to detect aircraft.
(b) UAV s can remain over hostile territory without any danger of being detected.
(c) Computers on board may enable aircraft to manage safe navigation on their own.

The third paragraph clearly mentions this cause for the non use of radars a decade from now.

(d) It is not feasible to increase the range of radars.

25. According to the author, commercial aeronautics, in contrast to military aeronautics, has declined because among other things,
(a) speed and technology barriers are more easily overcome in military aeronautics.
(b) the collective vision of the past continues to drive civil and commercial aeronautics.
(c) though the industry has a huge market, it has not attracted the right kind of aircraft designers.

This is obviously the correct answer, and this must have been be clear to you if you had interpreted the final sentence of the passage correctly.

(d) there is a shortage of materials, like light weight composites, used in commercial aeronautics.

Irrelevant option.

Passage VI*

A game of strategy, as currently conceived in game theory, is a situation in which two or more "players" make choices among available alternatives (moves). The totality of choices determines the outcomes of the game, and it is assumed that the rank order of preferences for the outcomes is different for different players. Thus the "interests" of the players are generally in conflict. Whether these interests are diametrically opposed or only partially opposed depends on the type of game.

Psychologically, most interesting situations arise when the interests of the players are partly coincident and partly opposed, because then one can postulate not only a conflict among the players but also inner conflicts within the players. Each is torn between a tendency to cooperate, so as to promote the common interests, and a tendency to compete, so as to enhance his own individual interests.

Internal conflicts are always psychologically interesting. What we vaguely call "interesting" psychology is in very great measure the psychology of inner conflict. Inner conflict is also held to be an important component of serious literature as distinguished from less serious genres. The classical tragedy, as well as the serious novel, reveals the inner conflict of central figures. The superficial adventure story, on the other hand, depicts only external conflict; that is, the threats to the person with whom the reader (or viewer) identifies them in these stories exclusively from external obstacles and from the adversaries who create them. On the most primitive level this sort of external conflict is psychologically empty. In the fisticuffs between the protagonists of good and evil, no psychological problems are involved or, at any rate, none are depicted in juvenile representations of conflict.

The detective story, the 'adult' analogue of a juvenile adventure tale, has at times been described as a glorification of intellectualized conflict. However, a great deal of the interest in the plots of these stories is sustained by withholding the unraveling of a solution to a problem. The effect of solving the problem is in itself not a conflict if the adversary (the unknown criminal) remains passive, like Nature, whose secrets the scientist supposedly unravels by deduction. If the adversary actively puts obstacles in the detective's path toward the solution, there is genuine conflict. But the conflict is psychologically interesting only to the extent that it contains irrational components such as tactical error on the criminal's part or the detective's insight into some psychological quirk of the criminal or something of this sort. Conflict conducted in a perfectly rational manner is psychologically no more interesting than a standard Western. For example, Tic-tac-toe, played perfectly by both players, is completely devoid of psychological interest. Chess may be psychologically interesting but only to the extent that it is played not quite rationally. Played completely rationally, chess would not be different from Tic-tac-toe.

In short, a pure conflict of interest (what is called a zero-sum game) although it offers a wealth of interesting conceptual problems, is not interesting psychologically, except to the extent that its conduct departs from rational norms.

Q1. According to the passage, which of the following options about the application of game theory to a conflict-of-interest situation is true?

*This question appeared in CAT 2005 paper.

(a) Assuming that the rank order of preferences for options is different for different players.
(b) Accepting that the interests of different players are often in conflict.
(c) Not assuming that the interests are in complete disagreement.
(d) All of the above.

Q2. The problem solving process of a scientist is different from that of a detective because:
(a) scientists study inanimate objects, while detectives deal with living criminals or law offenders.
(b) scientists study known objects, while detectives have to deal with unknown criminals or law offenders.
(c) scientists study phenomena that are not actively altered, while detectives deal with phenomena that have been deliberately influenced to mislead.
(d) scientists study psychologically interesting phenomena, while detectives deal with "adult analogues of juvenile adventure tales."

Q3. According to the passage, *internal conflicts* are psychologically more interesting than external conflicts because:
(a) internal conflicts, rather than external conflicts, form an important component of serious literature as distinguished from less serious genres.
(b) only juveniles or very few "adults" actually experience external conflict, while internal conflict is more widely prevalent in society.
(c) in situations of internal conflict, individuals experience a dilemma in resolving their own preferences for different outcomes.
(d) there are no threats to the reader (or viewer) in case of external conflicts.

Q4. Which, according to the author, would qualify as interesting psychology?
(a) A statistician's dilemma over choosing the best method to solve an optimisation problem.
(b) A chess player's predicament over adopting a defensive strategy against an aggrcssive opponent.
(c) A mountaineer's choice of the best path to Mt. Everest from the base camp.
(c) A finance manager's quandary over the best way of raising money from the market.

Have you read the above passage and solved its questions?

Then, check your answers with those given below (along with their explanatory notes or author's advice on how they should be read). The passage in *italics* is a reproduction of relevant section from the original passage, and this will be followed by an explanatory note or interpretation on the same.

A game of strategy, as currently conceived in game theory, is a situation in which two or more "players" make choices among available alternatives (moves).

Introduces the topic and straightaway starts with an idea.

The totality of choices determines the outcomes of the game, and it is assumed that the rank order of preferences for the outcomes is different for different players. Thus the "interests" of the players are generally in conflict.

Continues to go deeper into the idea.

Whether these interests are diametrically opposed or only partially opposed depends on the type of game. Psychologically, most interesting situations arise when the interests of the players are partly coincident and partly opposed, because then one can postulate not only a conflict among the players but also inner conflicts within the players.

The idea transits into a new direction, through the introduction of the 'psychologically interesting situation.'

Each is torn between a tendency to cooperate, so as to promote the common interests, and a tendency to compete, so as to enhance his own individual interests.

Internal conflicts are always psychologically interesting. What we vaguely call "interesting" psychology is in very great measure the psychology of inner conflict. Inner conflict is also held to be an important component of serious literature as distinguished from less serious genres. The classical tragedy, as well as the serious novel, reveals the inner conflict of central figures. The superficial adventure story, on the other hand, depicts only external conflict; that is, the threats to the person with whom the reader (or viewer) identifies stem in these stories exclusively from external obstacles and from the adversaries who create them. On the most primitive level this sort of external conflict is psychologically empty. In the fisticuffs between the protagonists of good and evil, no psychological problems are involved or, at any rate, none are depicted in juvenile representations of conflict.

A whole paragraph of details where no new idea is introduced. Should be quickly read.

The detective story, the 'adult' analogue of a juvenile adventure tale, has at times been described as a glorification of intellectualized conflict. However, a great deal of the interest in the plots of these stories is sustained by withholding the unraveling of a solution to a problem. The effect of solving the problem is in itself not a conflict if the adversary (the unknown criminal) remains passive, like Nature, whose secrets the scientist supposedly unravels by deduction. If the adversary actively puts obstacles in the detective's path toward the solution, there is genuine conflict. But the conflict is psychologically interesting only to the extent that it contains irrational components such as tactical error on the criminal's part or the detective's insight into some psychological quirk of the criminal or something of this sort. Conflict conducted in a perfectly rational manner is psychologically no more interesting than a standard Western. For example, Tic-tac-toe, played perfectly by both players, is completely devoid of psychological interest. Chess may be psychologically interesting but only to the extent that it is played not quite rationally. Played completely rationally, chess would not be different from Tic-tac-toe.

Again, a full paragraph of details illustrating what the author refers to or does not refer to while talking about psychologically interesting situations.

In short, a pure conflict of interest (what is called a zero-sum game) although it offers a wealth of interesting conceptual problems, is not interesting psychologically, except to the extent that its conduct departs from rational norms.

Restatement of an idea already mentioned earlier in the passage. Hence, quick reading.

1. According to the passage, which of the following options about the application of game theory to a conflict-of-interest situation is true?

This question tests your understanding of the ideas mentioned in the passage.

(a) Assuming that the rank order of preferences for options is different for different players.
(b) Accepting that the interests of different players are often in conflict.
(c) Not assuming that the interests are in complete disagreement.
(d) All of the above.

All the above options are true about the application of game theory to a conflict of interest situation.

2. The problem solving process of a scientist is different from that of a detective because:

This question is about a specific detail mentioned by the author in the second to last paragraph. In order to be able to solve such questions, one needs to understand the exact flow of ideas through the passage—leading upto and following the specific point where this particular detail is given. In fact, this is true for solving all details based questions.

(a) scientists study inanimate objects, while detectives deal with living criminals or law offenders.
(b) scientists study known objects, while detectives have to deal with unknown criminals or law offenders.
(c) scientists study phenomena that are not actively altered, while detectives deal with phenomena that have been deliberately influenced to mislead.

This is what the author mentions while comparing scientists and detectives.

(d) scientists study psychologically interesting phenomena, while detectives deal with "adult analogues of juvenile adventure tales."

3. According to the passage, *internal conflicts* are psychologically more interesting than external conflicts because

This question is asking about the cause behind why internal conflict situations are more interesting than situations where the conflicts are external.

(a) internal conflicts, rather than external conflicts, form an important component of serious literature as distinguished from less serious genres.

The detail being referred to is too narrow to connect as the reason asked for.

(b) only juveniles or very few "adults" actually experience external conflict, while internal conflict is more widely prevalent in society.

Irrelevant idea.

(c) in situations of internal conflict, individuals experience a dilemma in resolving their own preferences for different outcomes.

This is the main idea the author is trying to convey throughout the passage. There should be no ambiguity in choosing this option as the correct one.

(d) there are no threats to the reader (or viewer) in case of external conflicts.

Irrelevant idea

4. Which, according to the author, would qualify as interesting psychology?

(a) A statistician's dilemma over choosing the best method to solve an optimisation problem.

This is the only option that has an inherently built inner conflict. A statistician trying to solve an optimisation problem has an internal conflict, since he has to first decide for himself as to what objectives he should set for the optimisation problem.

(b) A chess player's predicament over adopting a defensive strategy against an aggressive opponent.
(c) A mountaineer's choice of the best path to Mt. Everest from the base camp.
(d) A finance manager's quandary over the best way of raising money from the market.

PASSAGE VII

While complex in the extreme, Derrida's work has proven to be a particularly influential approach to the analysis of the ways in which language structures our understanding of ourselves and the world we inhabit, an approach he termed *deconstruction.* In its simplest formulation, deconstruction can be taken to refer to a methodological strategy which seeks to uncover layers of hidden meaning, in a text that have been denied or suppressed. The term 'text', in this respect, does not refer simply, to a written form of communication, however. Rather, texts are something we all produce and reproduce constantly in our everyday social relations, be they spoken, written or embedded in the construction of material artifacts. At the heart of Derrida's deconstructive approach is his critique of what he perceives to be the totalitarian impulse of the Enlightenment pursuit to bring all that exists in the world under the domain of a representative language, a pursuit he refers to as *logocentrism.* Logocentrism is the search for a rational language that is able to know and represent the world and all its aspects perfectly and accurately. Its totalitarian dimension for Derrida at least, lies primarily in its tendency to marginalize or dismiss all that does not neatly comply with its particular linguistic representations, a tendency that, throughout history, has all too frequently been manifested in the form of authoritarian institutions. Thus logocentrism has, in its search for the truth of absolute representation, subsumed difference and oppressed that which it designates as its alien 'other'. For Derrida, western civilisation has been built upon such a systematic assault on alien cultures and ways of life, typically in the name of reason and progress.

In response to logocentrism, deconstruction posits the idea that the mechanism by which this process of marginalization and the ordering of truth occurs is through establishing systems of binary opposition. Oppositional linguistic dualisms, such as rational/irrational, culture/nature and good/bad are not, however, construed as equal partners as they are in, say, the semiological structuralism of Saussure. Rather, they exist, for Derrida, in a series of hierarchical relationships with the first term normally occupying a superior position. Derrida defines the relationship between such oppositional terms using the neologism *difference.* This refers to the realization that in any statement, oppositional terms differ from each other (for instance, the difference between rationality and irrationality is constructed through oppositional usage), and at the same time, a hierarchical relationship is maintained by the deference of one term to the other (in the positing of rationality over irrationality, for instance). It is this latter point which is perhaps the key to understanding Derrida's approach to deconstruction.

For the fact that at any given time one term must defer to its oppositional 'other', means that the two terms are constantly in a state of interdependence. The presence of one is dependent upon the absence or 'absent-presence' of the 'other', such as in the case of good and evil, whereby to understand the nature of one, we must constantly relate it to the absent term in order to grasp its meaning. That is, to do good, we must understand that our act is not evil, for without that comparison the term becomes meaningless. Put simply, deconstruction represents an attempt to demonstrate the absent-presence of this oppositional 'other', to show that what we say or write is in itself not expressive simply of what is present, but also of what is absent. Thus, deconstruction seeks to reveal the interdependence of apparently dichotomous terms and their meanings relative to their textual context; that is, within the linguistic power relations which structure dichotomous terms hierarchically. In Derrida's own words, a deconstructive reading "must always aim at a certain relationship, unperceived by the writer, between what he commands and what he does not command of the patterns of a language that he uses... [It] attempts to make the not-seen accessible to sight."

Meaning, then, is never fixed or stable, whatever the intention of the author of a text. For Derrida, language is a system of relations that are dynamic, in that all meanings we ascribe to the world are dependent not only on what we believe to be present but also on what is absent. Thus, any act of interpretation must refer not only to what the author of a text intends, but also to what is absent from his or her intention. This insight leads, once again, to Derrida's further rejection of the idea of the definitive authority of the intentional agent or subject. The subject is decentred; it is conceived as the outcome of relations of *difference.* As author of its own biography, the subject thus becomes the ideological fiction of modernity and its logocentric philosophy, one that depends upon the formation of hierarchical dualisms, which repress and deny the presence of the absent 'other'. No meaning can, therefore, ever be definitive, but is merely an outcome of a particular interpretation.

Q5. According to the passage, Derrida believes that the system of binary opposition:
(a) represents a prioritization or hierarchy.
(b) reconciles contradictions and dualities.
(c) weakens the process of marginalization and ordering of truth.
(d) deconstructs reality.

Q6. According to the passage, Derrida believes that:
(a) Reality can be construed only through the use of rational analysis.
(b) Language limits our construction of reality.

(c) A universal language will facilitate a common understanding of reality.

(d) We need to uncover the hidden meaning in a system of relations expressed by language.

Q7. Derrida rejects the idea of '*definitive authority of the subject*' because:

(a) interpretation of the text may not make the unseen visible.

(b) the meaning of the text is based on binary opposites.

(c) the implicit power relationship is often ignored.

(d) any act of interpretation must refer to what the author intends.

Q8. To Derrida, logocentrism does not imply:

(a) a totalitarian impulse.

(b) a domain of representative language.

(c) interdependence of the meanings of dichotomous terms.

(d) a strategy that seeks to suppress hidden meanings in a text.

Have you read the above passage and solved its questions?

Then, check your answers with those given below (along with their explanatory notes or author's advice on how they should be read). The passage in *italics* is a reproduction of relevant section from the original passage, and this will be followed by an explanatory note or interpretation on the same.

While complex in the extreme, Derrida's work has proven to be a particularly influential approach to the analysis of the ways in which language structures our understanding of ourselves and the world we inhabit, an approach he termed deconstruction.

A very idea heavy sentence. The author is introducing the topic and starting off with an idea straightaway. Make sure that you do not go further unless you understand this sentence—otherwise you might end up finding yourself in choppy waters. Ask yourself the question: Who or What is the author talking about—the answer 'Derrida's work' gives you the topic of the passage. Then ask yourself the question: What is the author's idea about the topic? The answer that 'his work has thrown light on the ways in which language structures our understanding of ourselves—called 'deconstruction'—gives you the idea conveyed.

In its simplest formulation, deconstruction can be taken to refer to a methodological strategy which seeks to uncover layers of hidden meaning, in a text that have been denied or suppressed.

Deconstruction is further defined, throwing more light on the idea the author is trying to convey.

The term 'text', in this respect, does not refer simply, to a written form of communication, however. Rather, texts are something we all produce and reproduce constantly in our everyday social relations, be they spoken, written or embedded in the construction of material artifacts.

This sentence is about details and should be read much faster than the first two sentences.

At the heart of Derrida's deconstructive approach is his critique of what he perceives to be: the totalitarian impulse of the Enlightenment pursuit to bring all that exists in the world under the domain of a representative language, a pursuit he refers to as logocentrism. Logocentrism is the search for a rational language that is able to know and represent the world and all its aspects perfectly and accurately.

Another idea is defined – that of logocentrism. You need to slow down to take in what the author is trying to say in this sentence and connect it to the previous ideas in the paragraph.

Its totalitarian dimension for Derrida at least, lies primarily in its tendency to marginalize or dismiss all that does not neatly comply with its particular linguistic representations, a tendency that, throughout history, has all too frequently been manifested in the form of authoritarian institutions. Thus logocentrism has, in its search for the truth of absolute representation, subsumed difference and oppressed that which it designates as its alien 'other'. For Derrida, western civilization has been built upon such a systematic assault on alien cultures and ways of life, typically in the name of reason and progress.

Details and opinions being mentioned here. No significant new idea emerges in the above sentences. You should be able to read this extremely rapidly.

In response to logocentrism, deconstruction posits the idea that the mechanism by which this process of marginalization and the ordering of truth occurs is through establishing systems of binary opposition.

The author is connecting the two ideas of deconstruction and logocentrism mentioned in the previous paragraph by showing the principal difference between the two approaches. You need to grasp this here or if not here, in the next two to three sentences, which are likely to be details explaining the idea expressed in the first sentence of this paragraph.

Oppositional linguistic dualisms, such as rational/irrational, culture/nature and good/bad are not, however, construed as equal partners as they are in, say, the semiological structuralism of Saussure. Rather, they exist, for Derrida, in a series of hierarchical relationships with the first term normally occupying a superior position. Derrida defines the relationship between such oppositional terms using the neologism difference. This refers to the realization that in any statement, oppositional terms differ from each other (for instance, the difference between rationality and irrationality is constructed through oppositional usage), and at the same time, a hierarchical relationship is maintained by the deference of one term to the other (in the positing of rationality over irrationality, for instance). It is this latter point which is perhaps the key to understanding Derrida's approach to deconstruction.

The author continues to construct on the idea he has introduced at the start of the paragraph. He has introduced a new idea—that of differance between the two terms in a linguistic dualism.

For the fact that at any given time one term must defer to its oppositional 'other', means that the two terms are constantly in a state of interdependence. The presence of one is dependent upon the absence or 'absent-presence' of the 'other', such as in the case of good and evil, whereby to understand the nature of one, we must constantly relate it to the absent term in order to grasp its meaning.

Extends the idea introduced towards the end of the previous paragraph.

That is, to do good, we must understand that our act is not evil, for without that comparison the term becomes meaningless. Put simply, deconstruction represents an attempt to demonstrate the absent-presence of this oppositional 'other', to show that what we say or write is in itself not expressive simply of what is present, but also of what is absent. Thus, deconstruction seeks to reveal the interdependence of apparently dichotomous terms and their meanings relative to their textual context; that is, within the linguistic power relations which structure dichotomous terms hierarchically. In Derrida' s own words, a deconstructive reading "must always aim at a certain relationship, unperceived by the writer, between what he commands and what he does not command of the patterns of a language that he uses ... [It] attempts to make the not-seen accessible to sight."

Explanatory details that need to be read fast. However, these can be read fast only if you have connected with the author's idea structure throughout.

Meaning, then, is never fixed or stable, whatever the intention of the author of a text. For Derrida, language is a system of relations that are dynamic, in that all meanings we ascribe to the world are dependent not only on what we believe to be present but also on what is absent. Thus, any act of interpretation must refer not only to what the author of a text intends, but also to what is absent from his or her intention. This insight leads, once again, to Derrida' s further rejection of the idea of the definitive authority of the intentional agent or subject. The subject is decentred; it is conceived as the outcome of relations of difference. As author of its own biography, the subject thus becomes the ideological fiction of modernity and its logocentric philosophy, one that depends upon the formation of hierarchical dualisms, which repress and deny the presence of the absent 'other'. No meaning can, therefore, ever be definitive, but is merely an outcome of a particular interpretation.

This is the concluding idea in the passage. You need to grasp this paragraph well to complete your interpretation of the author's idea structure. Take your time to understand clearly what it says—It is extremely heavy in its ideas.

5. According to the passage, Derrida believes that the system of binary opposition
   (a) represents a prioritization or hierarchy.

This is not the correct option, since the system contains a hierarchy, but is not a representation of it.

   (b) reconciles contradictions and dualities.

Irrelevant as compared to the idea structure of the author.

   (c) weakens the process of marginalization and ordering of truth.
   (d) deconstructs reality.

This is the central idea of the passage. Hence, this has to be correct.

6. According to the passage, Derrida believes that:
   (a) Reality can be construed only through the use of rational analysis.

This option goes against what the passage is talking about—that reality can be better understood by deconstructing it through language.

   (b) Language limits our construction of reality.

Language helps us deconstruct reality. Constructing reality is an irrelevant concept.

   (c) A universal language will facilitate a common understanding of reality.

Derrida believes the opposite.

   (d) We need to uncover the hidden meaning in a system of relations expressed by language.

This is one of the main ideas conveyed by the author in the last two paragraphs.

7. Derrida rejects the idea of 'definitive authority of the subject' because
   (a) interpretation of the text may not make the unseen visible.
   (b) the meaning of the text is based on binary opposites.
   (c) the implicit power relationship is often ignored.
   (d) any act of interpretation must refer to what the author intends.

This is against what the author is trying to say. He is saying the opposite—that interpretation should not be limited to what the author intends.

8. To Derrida, logocentrism does not imply:
   (a) A totalitarian impulse.

It does imply a totalitarian impulse. Hence, this is not the answer.

   (b) A domain of representative language.

Logocentrism has a tendency to try to define one representative language. Hence, this cannot be the answer.

   (c) Interdependence of the meanings of dichotomous terms.

This is what is implied by deconstruction—which differs from logocentrism. Hence, this is the answer.

   (d) A strategy that seeks to suppress hidden meanings in a text.

PASSAGE VIII

Crinoline and croquet are out. As yet, no political activists have thrown themselves in front of the royal horse on Derby Day. Even so, some historians can spot the parallels. It is a time of rapid technological change. It is a period when the dominance of the world's superpower is coming under threat. It is an epoch when prosperity masks underlying economic strain. And, crucially, it is a time when policy-makers are confident that all is for the best in the best of all possible worlds. Welcome to the Edwardian Summer of the second age of globalisation.

Spare a moment to take stock of what's been happening in the past few months. Let's start with the oil price, which has rocketed to more than $65 a barrel, more than double its level 18 months ago. The accepted wisdom is that we shouldn't worry our little heads about that, because the incentives are there for business to build new production and refining capacity, which will effortlessly bring demand and supply back into balance and bring crude prices back to $25 a barrel. As Tommy Cooper used to say, 'just like that'.

Then there is the result of the French referendum on the European Constitution, seen as thick-headed luddites railing vainly against the modern world. What the French needed to realise, the argument went, was that there was no alternative to the reforms that would make the country more flexible, more competitive, more dynamic. Just the sort of reforms that allowed Gate Gourmet to sack hundreds of its staff at Heathrow after the sort of ultimatum that used to be handed out by Victorian mill owners. An alternative way of looking at the French "non" is that our neighbours translate "flexibility" as "you're fired".

Finally, take a squint at the United States. Just like Britain a century ago, a period of unquestioned superiority is drawing to a close. China is still a long way from matching America's wealth, but it is growing at a stupendous rate and economic strength brings geo-political clout. Already, there is evidence of a new scramble for Africa as Washington and Beijing compete for oil stocks. Moreover, beneath the surface of the US economy, all is not well. Growth looks healthy enough, but the competition from China and elsewhere has meant the world's biggest economy now imports far more than it exports. The US is living beyond its means, but in this time of studied complacency, a current account deficit worth 6 percent of gross domestic product is seen as a sign of strength, not weakness.

In this new Edwardian summer, comfort is taken from the fact that dearer oil has not had the savage inflationary consequences of 1973-74, when a fourfold increase in the cost of crude brought an abrupt end to a postwar boom that had gone on uninterrupted for a quarter of a century. True, the cost of living has been affected by higher transport costs, but we are talking of inflation at 2.3 per cent and not 27 per cent. Yet, the idea that higher oil prices are of little consequence is fanciful. If people are paying more to fill up their cars, it leaves them with less to spend on everything else, but there is a reluctance to consume less. In the 1970s unions were strong and able to negotiate large, compensatory pay deals that served to intensify inflationary pressure. In 2005, that avenue is pretty much closed off, but the abolition of all the controls on credit that existed in the 1970s means that households are invited to borrow more rather than consume less. The knock-on effects of higher oil prices are thus felt in different ways–through high levels of indebtedness, in inflated asset prices, and in balance of payments deficits.

There are those who point out, rightly, that modern industrial capitalism has proved mightily resilient these past 250 years, and that a sign of the enduring strength of the system has been the way it apparently shrugged off everything–a stock market crash, 9/11, rising oil prices–that have been thrown at it in the half decade since the millennium. Even so, there are at least three reasons for concern. First, we have been here before. In terms of political economy, the first era of globalisation mirrored our own. There was a belief in unfettered capital flows, in free trade, and in the power of the market. It was a time of massive income inequality and unprecedented migration. Eventually, though, there was a backlash, manifested in a struggle between free traders and protectionists, and in rising labour militancy.

Second, the world is traditionally at its most fragile at times when the global balance of power is in flux. By the end of the nineteenth century, Britain's role as the hegemonic power was being challenged by the rise of the United States, Germany, and Japan, while the

Ottoman and Hapsburg empires were clearly in rapid decline. Looking ahead from 2005, it is clear that over the next two or three decades, both China and India–which together account for half the world's population–will flex their muscles.

Finally, there is the question of what rising oil prices tell us. The emergence of China and India means global demand for crude is likely to remain high at a time when experts say production is about to top out. If supply constraints start to bite, any declines in the price are likely to be short-term cyclical affairs, punctuating a long upward trend.

Q9. Which of the following best represents the key argument made by the author?

(a) The rise in oil prices, the flux in the global balance of power and historical precedents should make us question our belief that the global economic prosperity would continue.

(b) The belief that modern industrial capitalism is highly resilient and capable of overcoming shocks will be belied soon.

(c) Widespread prosperity leads to neglect of early signs of underlying economic weakness, manifested in higher oil prices and a flux in the global balance of power.

(d) A crisis is imminent in the West given the growth of countries like China and India and the increase in oil prices.

Q10. What can be inferred about the author's view when he states, 'As Tommy Cooper used to say "just like that"'?

(a) Industry has incentive to build new production and refining capacity and therefore, oil prices would reduce.

(b) There would be a correction in the price levels of oil once new production capacity is added.

(c) The decline in oil prices is likely to be short-term in nature.

(d) It is not necessary that oil prices would go down to earlier levels.

Q11. What, according to the author, has resulted in a widespread belief in the resilience of modern capitalism?

(a) Growth in the economies of Western countries despite shocks in the form of increase in levels of indebtedness and inflated asset prices.

(b) Increase in the prosperity of Western countries and China despite rising oil prices.

(c) Continued growth of Western economies despite a rise in terrorism, an increase in oil prices and other similar shocks.

(d) The success of continued reforms aimed at making Western economies more dynamic, competitive arid efficient.

Q12. By the expression 'Edwardian Summer', the author refers to a period in which there is:

(a) unparalleled luxury and opulence.

(b) a sense of complacency among people because of all-round prosperity.

(c) a culmination of all-round economic prosperity.

(d) an imminent danger lurking behind economic prosperity.

Have you read the above passage and solved its questions?

Then, check your answers with those given below (along with their explanatory notes or author's advice on how they should be read). The passage in *italics* is a reproduction of relevant section from the original passage, and this will be followed by an explanatory note or interpretation on the same.

Crinoline and croquet are out. As yet, no political activists have thrown themselves in front of the royal horse on Derby Day. Even so, some historians can spot the parallels.

There is an idea here somewhere, which you can expect to be unravelled later. There is obviously a talk about some sort of parallel between two time periods.

It is a time of rapid technological change. It is a period when the dominance of the world's superpower is coming under threat. It is an epoch when prosperity masks underlying economic strain. And, crucially, it is a time when policy-makers are confident that all is for the best in the best of all possible worlds.

The author is defining the time in terms of different characteristics that must have been common between the two periods.

Welcome to the Edwardian Summer of the second age of globalisation.

The author can be understood to be talking about two ages of globalisation—the current one and one that could have been described as an Edwardian summer obviously something to do with King Edward's reign.

Spare a moment to take stock of what's been happening in the past few months. Let's start with the oil price, which has rocketed to more than \$65 a barrel, more than double its level 18 months ago. The accepted wisdom is that we shouldn't worry our little heads about that, because the incentives are there for business to build new production and refining capacity, which will effortlessly bring demand and supply back into balance and bring crude prices back to \$25 a barrel. As Tommy Cooper used to say, 'just like that'.

Then there is the result of the French referendum on the European Constitution, seen as thick-headed luddites railing vainly against the modern world. What the French needed to realise, the argument went, was that there was no alternative to the reforms that would make the country more flexible, more competitive, more dynamic. Just the sort of reforms that allowed Gate Gourmet to sack hundreds of its staff at Heathrow after the sort of ultimatum that used to be handed out by Victorian mill owners. An alternative way of looking at the French "non" is that our neighbours translate "flexibility" as "you're fired".

Finally, take a squint at the United States. Just like Britain a century ago, a period of unquestioned superiority is drawing to a close. China is still a long way from matching America's wealth, but it is growing at a stupendous rate and economic strength brings geo-political clout. Already, there is evidence of a new scramble for Africa as Washington and Beijing compete for oil stocks. Moreover, beneath the surface of the US economy, all is not well. Growth looks healthy enough, but the competition from China and elsewhere has meant the world's biggest economy now imports far more than it exports. The US is living beyond its means, but in this time of studied complacency, a current account deficit worth 6 percent of gross domestic product is seen as a sign of strength, not weakness.

The author has used these three examples—of oil Prices, the French referendum and the United States—in order to lead up to his point which you can anticipate will come in the last two paragraphs.

In this new Edwardian summer, comfort is taken from the fact that dearer oil has not had the savage inflationary consequences of 1973-74, when a fourfold increase in the cost of crude brought an abrupt end to a postwar boom that had gone on uninterrupted for a quarter of a century. True, the cost of living has been affected by higher transport costs, but we are talking of inflation at 2.3 per cent and not 27 per cent. Yet, the idea that higher oil prices are of little consequence is fanciful. If people are paying more to fill up their cars, it leaves them with less to spend on everything else, but there is a reluctance to consume less. In the 1970s unions were strong and able to negotiate large, compensatory pay deals that served to intensify inflationary pressure. In 2005, that avenue is pretty much closed off, but the abolition of all the controls on credit that existed in the 1970s means that households are invited to borrow more rather than consume less. The knock-on effects of higher oil prices are thus felt in different ways– through high levels of indebtedness, in inflated asset prices, and in balance of payments deficits.

There is clearly a negative point of view about the casualness exhibited by the world that the author is trying to convey. Notice that in each of the points above, the author gives his opinion by negating the reasons the world is using for being relaxed about its current problems. The author's opinion clearly is that the false security we are living under is not real.)

There are those who point out, rightly, that modern industrial capitalism has proved mightily resilient these past 250 years, and that a sign of the enduring strength of the system has been the way it apparently shrugged off everything–a stock market crash, 9/11, rising oil prices–that have been thrown at it in the half decade since the millennium. *Even so, there are at least three reasons for concern.*

This sentence signals three upcoming reasons for concern. It is clearly an opinion based sentence. Up until this point, he has not explicitly stated his opinion/s, only hinting at them through his three examples in the last three paragraphs. We will get to finally see the author's opinion in these reasons.

First, we have been here before. In terms of political economy, the first era of globalisation mirrored our own. There was a belief in unfettered capital flows, in free trade, and in the power of the market. It was a time of massive income inequality and unprecedented migration. Eventually, though, there was a backlash, manifested in a struggle between free traders and protectionists, and in rising labour militancy.

Second, the world is traditionally at its most fragile at times when the global balance of power is in flux. By the end of the nineteenth century, Britain's role as the hegemonic power was being challenged by the rise of the United States, Germany, and Japan, while the Ottoman and Hapsburg empires were clearly in rapid decline. Looking ahead from 2005, it is clear that over the next two or three decades, both China and India–which together account for half the world's population–will flex their muscles.

Finally, there is the question of what rising oil prices tell us. The emergence of China and India means global demand for crude is likely to remain high at a time when experts say production is about to top out. If supply constraints start to bite, any declines in the price are likely to be short-term cyclical affairs, punctuating a long upward trend.

These last three passages give the heart of the author's opinion. He has drawn up parallels between the Edwardian era—which he refers to as the first era of globalisation—and the current era of globalisation. He has clearly enumerated three reasons which should cause concern.

9. Which of the following best represents the key argument made by the author?
   (a) The rise in oil prices, the flux in the global balance of power and historical precedents should make

us question our belief that the global economic prosperity would continue.

This is indeed the key argument that the author is making.

(b) The belief that modern industrial capitalism is highly resilient and capable of overcoming shocks will be belied soon.

This option is extremely close and confusing. However, what you should realise is that the option goes further than what the author is saying. The author has just mentioned that we should be concerned—he does not go on to predict that our beliefs will be belied. Hence, this cannot be the answer.

(c) Widespread prosperity leads to neglect of early signs of underlying economic weakness, manifested in higher oil prices and a flux in the global balance of power.

This is the premise, not the argument.

(d) A crisis is imminent in the West given the growth of countries like China and India and the increase in oil prices.

Irrelevant answer.

10. What can be inferred about the author's view when he states, 'As Tommy Cooper used to say "just like that"'?

This question is clearly asking about an inference, hence, you need to understand the author's unstated opinion behind using this phrase.

(a) Industry has incentive to build new production and refining capacity and therefore oil prices would reduce.

This is a clearly stated cause and effect fact. Hence, cannot be an inference about the author's opinion. Thus, this is not the correct answer.

(b) There would be a correction in the price levels of oil once new production capacity is added.

(c) The decline in oil prices is likely to be short-term in nature.

This is indeed the author's opinion. This can be deduced from: firstly, the author's writing style: Throughout the passage, he has adopted a strategy of stating the reasons for being complacent with respect to some facts and then he goes on to ask us not to be so complacent. Further, the opinion the author holds about the oil prices, is clearly stated in the last paragraph's last sentence. The sentence '*If supply constraints start to bite, any declines in the price are likely to be short-term cyclical affairs, punctuating a long upward trend*' clearly shows his opinion about what he expects to happen to oil prices.

(d) It is not necessary that oil prices would go down to earlier levels.

11. What, according to the author, has resulted in a widespread belief in the resilience of modern capitalism?

(a) Growth in the economies of Western countries despite shocks in the form of increase in levels of indebtedness and inflated asset prices.

This option uses a connection between 'growth in western economies' and 'shocks of increased indebtedness and inflated asset prices'. There is no logical connection defined in the passage between these two factors.

(b) Increase in the prosperity of Western countries and China despite rising oil prices.

Irrelevant choice.

(c) Continued growth of Western economies despite a rise in terrorism, an increase in oil prices and other similar shocks.

This is the correct choice, since this according to the author, is what has led to the belief. Clearly stated in the fourth last paragraph.

(d) The success of continued reforms aimed at making Western economies more dynamic, competitive arid efficient.

Irrelevant option.

12. By the expression 'Edwardian Summer', the author refers to a period in which there is

(a) unparalleled luxury and opulence.

The author has never referred to unparalleled luxury and opulence.

(b) a sense of complacency among people because of all-round prosperity.

Throughout the passage, the author has explained the term 'Edwardian Summer'. explaining the complacency that has set into the people due to all round prosperity. Perhaps, you also need to understand that the author is British – since he calls the French his neighbours, refers to Derby day etc., and summer to the British is a time of brightness, happiness and joy, before the onset of the dull, dreary and depressing winter.

(c) a culmination of all-round economic prosperity.

culmination? improbable option.

(d) an imminent danger lurking behind economic prosperity.

Does not fit in with the term Edwardian.

SECTION 2: LOD Exercises

Having gone through the various skills involved in improving your reading skills and your reading comprehension solving skills, you are now in a position to test your abilities in solving reading comprehension questions at various levels of difficulty.

This section comprises two exercises at:

- **Level of Difficulty–I**
- **Level of Difficulty–II**

These exercises have been created to help you go through a structured solving and learning experience and get you ready to solve real-life CAT passages at any level of difficulty.

CHAPTER

5 Level of Difficulty—I

Instruction: Read the passages and answer the questions attached below each passage.

TEST 1

Passage 1

On 7 September 1940, southern England suffered what was then the biggest air raid the world had ever seen.

Over the previous three months, the aircraft of Germany's Luftwaffe had tried to break the resistance of Britain's Royal Air Force (RAF). Already severely depleted from the heavy fighting during the invasion of France, the RAF had buckled several times under the strain. A particularly brutal offensive against its airfields and the factories producing its fighter planes over the weeks before had left it dangerously close to running out of both planes and pilots.

If the attacks had carried on with the same intensity for a few more weeks, the RAF might have collapsed completely. German invasion barges were waiting on the other side of the channel for just such a moment.

But the Germans then turned their attention–mystifyingly–to Britain's cities, hoping that indiscriminate bombing would cause widespread panic and force Britain to surrender. The Luftwaffe decided to throw every available aircraft into the offensive. It started on 7 September.

During the early afternoon, British radar observers hunched over their screens started seeing something massive taking shape. From airfields across France, wave after wave of German bombers and fighters took to the air, forming up into one enormous formation over the English Channel. It was so large–nearly 1,100 planes–that it covered 800 square miles (2,072 sq. km). The last time a force this powerful had threatened England was the Spanish Armada, 500 years before.

The aircraft defending London that day were spearheaded by the Supermarine Spitfire, an iconic single-seat fighter plane which had only entered service a few months before the start of World War Two. The Spitfire was fast, sleek and very agile–but it was outnumbered two to one by another fighter, one often ignored in the popular retelling of the battle. It was the Hawker Hurricane, and most of the RAF squadrons flying over London that day were equipped with it.

It was an aircraft that not only helped turn the tide of a war, but whose legacy can be found today in a wide range of modern life–from aviation to medicine. This year marks the 85th anniversary of the Hawker Hurricane's first flight.

Q1. Which of the following statements would the author agree with?

A. The Spitfire was a better aircraft for the second world war than the Hurricane.

B. The spitfire was very sleek, fast and newly designed.

C. The Hurricane changed the course of the second world war.

(a) Only A and B
(b) Only B and C
(c) Only A and C
(d) Only B

Q2. The word "mystifyingly" is used in the passage in what context?

(a) Meaning to say a sudden change in the course
(b) Meaning to say a surprising and sudden change in the course of action

(c) Meaning to say a magic that they did

(d) Meaning to say the occult they believed in

Q3. The legacy of which one of the following is attributed to have changed a lot of things according to the passage?

(a) The Hurricane

(b) The Spitfire

(c) The RAF

(d) The Luftwaffe

Passage 2

In many countries, formal education starts at four. The thinking often goes that starting early gives children more time to learn and excel. The result, however, can be an "education arms race," with parents trying to give their child early advantages at school through private coaching and teaching, and some parents even paying for children as young as four to have additional private tutoring.

Compare that to the more play-based early education of several decades ago, and you can see a huge change in policy, based on very different ideas of what our children need in order to get ahead. In the United States, this urgency sped up with policy changes such as the 2001 "no child left behind" act, which promoted standardised testing as a way to measure educational performance and progress. In the UK, children are tested in their second year of school (age 5-6) to check they are reaching the expected reading standard. Critics warn that early testing like this can put children off reading, while proponents say it helps to identify those who need additional support.

However, many studies show little benefit from an early overly academic environment. One 2015 US report says that society's expectations of what children should achieve in kindergarten has changed, which is leading to "inappropriate classroom practices," such as reducing play-based learning.

How children learn and the quality of the environment is hugely important. "Young children learning to read is one of the most important things primary education does. It's fundamental to children making progress in life," says Dominic Wyse, a professor of primary education at University College London, in the UK. He, alongside sociology professor Alice Bradbury, also at UCL, has published research proposing that the way we teach literacy really matters.

In a 2022 report, they state that English school system's intense focus on phonics–a method that involves matching the sound of a spoken word or letter, with individual written letters, through a process called "sounding out"–could be failing some children.

A reason for this, says Bradbury, is that the "schoolification of early years" has resulted in more formal learning earlier on. But the tests used to assess that early learning may have little to do with the skills actually needed to read and enjoy books or other meaningful texts.

For example, the tests may ask pupils to "sound out" and spell nonsense words, to prevent them from simply guessing, or recognising familiar words. Since nonsense words are not meaningful language, children may find the task difficult and puzzling. Bradbury found that the pressure to gain these decoding skills–and pass reading tests–also means that some three-year-olds are already being exposed to phonics.

"It doesn't end up being meaningful, it ends up being memorising rather than understanding context," says Bradbury. She also worries that the books used are not particularly engaging.

Language in all its richness–written, spoken, sung or read aloud–plays a crucial role in our early development

Neither Wyse nor Bradbury make the case for later learning per se, but rather highlight that we should rethink the way children are taught literacy. The priority, they say, should be to encourage an interest in and familiarity with words, using storybooks, songs and poems, all of which help the child pick up the sounds of words, as well as expanding their vocabulary.

This idea is backed up by studies that show that the academic benefits of preschool fade away later on. Children who attend intensive preschools do not have higher academic abilities in later grades than those who did not attend such preschools, several studies now show. Early education can however have a positive impact on social development–which in turn feeds into the likelihood of graduation from school and university as well as being associated with lower crime rates. In short, attending preschool can have positive effects on later achievement in life, but not necessary on academic skills.

Too much academic pressure may even cause problems in the long run. A study published in January 2022 suggested that those who attended a state-funded preschool with a strong academic emphasis, showed lower academic achievements a few years later, compared to those who had not gained a place.

This chimes with research on the importance of play-based learning in the early years. Child-led play-based preschools have better outcomes than more academically focussed preschools, for example.

One 2002 study found that "children's later school success appears to have been enhanced by more active, child-initiated early learning experiences," and that overly formalised learning could have slowed progress. The study concluded that "pushing children too soon may actually backfire when children move into the later elementary school grade."

Q4. Which of the following will the author support?

A. Play-based learning is superior to academic learning in elementary levels.
B. Academic learning is important because of the policy of "no child left behind."
C. Early education and learnings can have a good impact on social skills later on.

(a) Only A
(b) Only A and B
(c) Only C
(d) Only A and C

Q5. Why is Bradbury not appreciative of exposing 3 year olds to "phonics"?

(a) Pushing children too soon may actually backfire when children move into the later elementary school grade.
(b) Children who attend intensive preschools do not have higher academic abilities in later grades.
(c) This kind of learning is not meaningful for the child and the student ends of memorising rather than understanding the context.
(d) Too much academic pressure may even cause problems in the long run.

Q6. What could be "inappropriate classroom practices" according to the passage?

A. Less play based learning
B. More games based on virtual practices
C. More emphasis on writing skills
D. More emphasis on speaking skills

(a) Only C and D
(b) Only B
(c) Only A
(d) only A and B

Passage 3

D. H. Lawrence (1885–1930): The Supreme Triumph For man, the vast marvel is to be alive. For man as for flower and beast and bird, the supreme triumph is to be most vividly, most perfectly alive. Whatever the unborn and the dead may know, they cannot know the beauty, the marvel of being alive in the flesh. The dead may look after the afterwards. But the magnificent here and now of life in the flesh is ours, and ours alone, and ours only for a time. We ought to dance with rapture, that we should be alive and in the flesh, and part of the living, incarnate cosmos. I am part of the sun as my eye is the part of me. That I am part of the earth my feet below know the perfectly, and my blood is part of the sea. My soul knows that I am a part of the human race, my soul is an inorganic part of the great human soul, as my spirit is a part of my nation. In my own very self, I am part of my family. There is nothing of me that is alone and absolute except my mind, and we shall find that the mind has no existence by itself, it is only the glitter of the sun on the surface of the waters. - Apocalypse, 1931.

Q7. By triumph the author means:

(a) Sin
(b) Loss
(c) Sorrow
(d) Victory

Q8. When the dead look after the afterwards the living should look at life:

(a) Forever
(b) For some months
(c) For only a short while
(d) In the past

Q9. By rapture the author means an emotion involving great:

(a) Trepidation
(b) Thrill
(c) Fear
(d) Joy

Q10. By the last line, "It .... waters," the author means that the mind is only:

(a) A mirage
(b) An illusion
(c) Magic
(d) A reflection

Q11. The tone of this passage is:

(a) Social
(b) Moral
(c) Reflective
(d) Philosophical

Q12. The most suitable title for this passage would be:

(a) The Surface of the Waters
(b) My Mind
(c) The Human Race
(d) Alive and Kicking

TEST 2

PASSAGE 1

I am in passport control. I can see my face on a screen. The technology recognises me and lets me through. I scan codes showing my vaccination status and recent COVID test results. The machines assess the data regarding my health and microbiology. Through into the waiting room, people are staring into little screens. A strangely large number have the camera flipped, and are capturing their faces at different angles, as if they've forgotten what they look like. I open my laptop and join in. I give my details to a company to enter the digital realm. Adverts tailored to my personality pop up. They know me better than I know myself.

This is 2022. And 2022 is a Philip K. Dick novel.

Writers of science fiction often feel more prescient than others. Whether it's the threat to women's rights in the work of Margaret Atwood, the architectural and social dystopias of J. G. Ballard's novels, or the Internet-predicting world of E. M. Forster's *The Machine Stops* (1909), the genre is replete with prophetic writers dealing with ever more familiar issues.

Out of all such writers, few seem a more unlikely seer of our times than the US author Philip K Dick, who died 40 years ago today at the age of 53. In a remarkably prolific 30-year period of work, Dick authored 44 novels and countless short stories, adaptations of which went on to redefine science fiction on screen–in particular Ridley Scott's Blade Runner (1982), which was based on Dick's story *Do Androids Dream of Electric Sheep?* and Paul Verhoeven's *Total Recall* (1990), which took his 1966 short story *We Can Remember It for You Wholesale* as its source material. More recently Dick's novel *The Man in the High Castle* (1962) has been turned into a hit Amazon series.

Dick was not simply an effective writer of strange fictions, but an unusual person in his own right. Burdened by deteriorating mental health, visions, and what he alleged were all manner of paranormal experiences–many of which were woven into his expansive oeuvre–Dick had a troubled and fragmented relationship with reality. In the 1970s, the author began to experience two parallel timelines of his own life, his thoughts invaded in 1974 by what he told interviewer Charles Platt was a "transcendentally rational mind," something he had many names for, but chiefly VALIS; an acronym for Vast Active Living Intelligence System. It became the subject of one of his late semi-autobiographical works, the 1981 novel VALIS, published not long before his death.

Whether his visions were medical or supernatural, one thing is clear: Dick had a startling ability to foreshadow the modern world. Celebrated science-fiction and fantasy author Stan Nicholls suggests Dick's work is prescient because it explored the future through the then-present. "His stories posited the ubiquitousness of the Internet, virtual reality, facial recognition software, driverless cars and 3D printing," Nicholls tells BBC Culture–while also pointing out that "it's a misconception that prediction is the primary purpose of science fiction; the genre's hit rate is actually not very good in that respect. Like all the best science fiction, his stories weren't really about the future, they were about the here and now." Indeed Dick's incorporation of everyday aspects of post-War America into his futures has meant that his worlds possessed a surreal familiarity.

Nevertheless, the way he also anticipated particular technological and societal developments remains striking. "He had a lot of scientific images of the way the future would work," says Anthony Peake, author of the biography *A Life of Philip K Dick: The Man Who Remembered the Future* (2013). "For instance, he had a concept that you would be able to communicate advertising to people directly, that you'd be able to know them so well that you could target the marketing precisely to their anticipations. And this is exactly what is happening online." In the 1954 short story Sales Pitch, for example, the idea of aggressive yet unnervingly personalised advertising finds fruition in a demented machine that constantly markets itself at the story's protagonist. In the 1964 novel, *The Simulacra*, on the other hand, advertising is embodied by a mechanical fly-like creature. As he writes in the novel, the "commercial, fly-sized, began to buzz out its message as soon as it managed to force entry. 'Say! Haven't you sometimes said to yourself, I'll bet other people in restaurants can see me!'." It's a physical equivalent of spam or tailored adverts popping up on social media.

Dick's work often had a political dimension, too. The Man in the High Castle, for example, imagines an alternative history in which the Nazis won World War two. In lesser-known works such as *Eye in the Sky* (1957), this politics is more of its period. In the novel, a group of people become stuck in various different worlds conjured by each individual, thanks to a malfunctioning particle accelerator. The narrative focuses especially on a world dreamed up by a communist member of the group who has been dismissed from the laboratory for holding such beliefs. The twist is that the world conjured with obvious over-the-top Marxist leanings is, in fact, the product of the lab security chief who is also a communist but in secret. The book showed that Dick's politics could not be simplified into a straightforward description of left or right, as he was biting in his attacks on both the McCarthy-esque witch hunts of the period as well as the more evangelical leanings of communism.

Q1. The lines, "I give my details to a company to enter the digital realm. Adverts tailored to my personality pop up" signify which of the following?

(a) Today's reality which we are experiencing in the world
(b) An excerpt from the novel "2022" by Philip.K.Dick
(c) A normal day in today's world which is portrayed accurately in the novel "2022" by Philip.K.Dick
(d) Cannot be determined

Q2. What can be said about Dick's political ideology?

(a) He was a supporter of the right wing politics.
(b) He was a supporter of the left wing politics.
(c) His political affiliations were not straightjacket and could not be compartmentalised.
(d) He was very aligned toward his own political thoughts which had a strange combination of past and present.

Q3. One line which could aptly describe Philip K. Dick according to what is mentioned in the passage could be?

(a) The man who foretold the future.
(b) The man who witnessed the future.
(c) The man who predicted the future.
(d) The man who linked the future to the past.

Passage 2

In 2006, an ordinary-looking pair of spectacles went on sale at Christie's, the London auction house. They were expected to fetch up to £3,000 ($4,088). In fact, they sold for £6,600 ($8,994), and the buyer had bought a little piece of movie history.

The spectacles were worn by Michael Caine when he played Harry Palmer in the 1965 espionage thriller *The Ipcress File.* Palmer, a former soldier, is introduced in a scene in which he is woken by his alarm clock, and reaches for his glasses before he gets out of bed. He's as blind as a bat without them–just one way in which he was not your typical action hero, certainly not back in the 60s.

In a nod to the movie, the very first shot of the new television adaptation of *The Ipcress File* shows Palmer's thick-rimmed spectacles. This time, Joe Cole (perhaps best known for his role in Peaky Blinders) plays the chippy working-class spy who loves culture, cooking and women but who doesn't have a lot of time for the posh public school boys who run British intelligence.

Like the film before it, the ITV series is based on the 1962 bestseller by the great spy novelist Len Deighton, which was published shortly after the cinema release of Dr No, the first instalment in the James Bond film franchise. Deighton's hero–unnamed in the novel but christened Harry Palmer for the screen–was quickly identified by critics and fans as being the anti-Bond.

James Watkins, director of the six-part adaptation, explains the differences between Ian Fleming's creation and Deighton's agent. "Bond is a superhero," he tells BBC Culture. "He kills without thinking or caring. He is establishment. He went to Eton. He uses his fists and his weapons more than his brain; gadgets, rather than real life."

"Harry is short sighted. Working class. Haunted by killing in Korea. A reluctant spy. Blackmailed into working for the establishment, insolent Harry is a constant thorn in their side. Trying to make his way in a world that is stacked against him. Always facing a class barrier. He's so much more relatable than the dinosaur Bond."

Deighton, the London-born son of a chauffeur and a cook, wrote The Ipcress File, his first novel, on vacation in the Dordogne, France. It was, he writes in an afterword in the Penguin Modern Classics edition, a "holiday diversion". He was a commercial artist, trained at St Martin's School of Art and the Royal College of Art. He had worked for ad agencies and publishers, and knew Soho like the back of his hand. He had also seen a fair bit of the world, having completed two and a half years of national service with the RAF, and worked as a flight attendant with British Overseas Airways.

For The Ipcress File, he also reveals in the afterword, Deighton drew on his experiences at a smart ad agency where he had mixed with "highly educated, witty young men who had been at Eton together." He had actually enjoyed it, especially the barbed banter, and it informed his depiction of the intelligence service offices.

Nevertheless Deighton, who is now 93-years old and retired from writing, has strong views on class and education. "I would do everything I can to prevent my children being educated in England," he told an interviewer on Thames TV's Afternoon Plus in 1983 (his children were at a small village school in France), "because the moment you step across the threshold of any school in England, you've put on a uniform for the class war. Everyone educated in England has been assigned rank badges for the class war."

He would later acknowledge another key influence on his work. His mother sometimes cooked for Anna Wolkoff, a White Russian emigre and Nazi sympathiser who lived near to the Deighton family. In 1940, the 11-year-old Len witnessed her arrest by a group of nondescript Special Branch officers who arrived in unmarked cars. Wolkoff was subsequently imprisoned for spying activities: the incident stayed with Deighton, and made him aware that there was a secret world of espionage in which people might not be what they seemed.

The complicated plot of Ipcress involves the brainwashing of British scientists by foreign powers but it was the tone, characterisation and sardonic style that impressed readers.

"I think the appeal of the [Harry Palmer] books and the films in the 60s were partly that the character was downbeat and relatively unglamorous, and made a contrast with the high fantasy of the Bond films," Duns tells BBC Culture. "I think Deighton was following in the footsteps of the Angry Young Men [writers of the 1950s], and you can see a lot of the same preoccupations, rebellion against authority being the most notable, but also these were 'kitchen sink' spy stories: you literally saw Michael Caine in the kitchen making an omelette (though his hands were, famously, Len Deighton's in that scene)."

Director James Watkins says: "In our modern world where the social mobility promised in the 60s seems to have vanished, Harry is perhaps more relevant than ever: a true working-class hero."

Q4. Harry Palmer the character of *Ipcress files* movie was:

(a) Named in the movie but was not christened in the original novel on which the movie was adapted.

(b) Harry was taken from the book and later adapted into the famous movie, his character was iconic.

(c) The character was in muddied waters and that added to his charm although he might not have been identified by many.

(d) His character was very downbeat and mundane like a common man but he had his own glamorous style which many people identified with.

Q5. Deighton was inspired for the Ipcress files by:

(a) His life experiences and how he had struggled as a child.

(b) His experiences at an ad agency where he had mixed with "highly educated, smart, intelligent young men who had been at Eton together."

(c) By the character of James Bond and he wanted to create a hero who was better than Bond.

(d) All of the above options.

Q6. The hero making omelette in the movie is special because of which of the following?

(a) It was called the kitchen sink series.

(b) The omelette was a symbolic thing in the story.

(c) The actual hands of the author making it were filmed instead of the hero.

(d) None of these.

Q7. Which of the following will the author least agree with?

(a) Bond was more agreeable to the masses than Harry.

(b) Bond was iconic and glamorous, whereas Harry was the person next door

(c) Bond was legendary and Harry made a sharp contrast to his character.

(d) Harry was a rebellion with authority whereas Bond was very straitjacketed in his approach.

PASSAGE 3

Fragrant with steam
were the days
and the nights red
with many braziers
in the beloved house of my father, my mother.

Q8. Which of the following options is the closest expression of the poet's feeling?

(a) The house was located in beautiful settings probably surrounded by flowers in the mountains.

(b) The ancestral home was probably the most important house in the community.

(c) The poet fondly recalls the pleasant climate enjoyed day and night.

(d) The poet misses the braziers and steam she had enjoyed during her childhood.

(e) Everything about the house felt special because of her parents love for her.

TEST 3

PASSAGE 1

On first appearances, Bolzano in the far north of Italy is just like any other alpine town. Nestled in a valley lined by steep green hills peppered with castles, barns and churches, and terraced with vineyards, the city is a whimsical snow globe of winding streets, pastel-coloured houses and Baroque taverns.

But cross the Talfer river on the western edge of town, and suddenly it's a different story. The cosy streets are replaced by wide avenues and large, solemn squares overlooked by austere, grey buildings. The architecture is linear, monotonous and domineering, with porticoes of tall, rectangular columns and strange, looping arches that gallop across the avenues like viaducts to nowhere.

Amidst this gloomy ensemble, two structures stand out. The first is the city's tax office, a hulking grey block adorned with a gigantic bas-relief depicting–across 57 sculpted panels–the unassailable rise of Italian Fascism, from the March on Rome to the colonial conquests in Africa. In its centre is a depiction of Mussolini on horseback, his right arm outstretched in a Roman salute. It's a remarkable piece of fascist agitprop architecture–awe-inspiring, odious and perplexing all at once.

The second is the Bolzano Victory Monument, a striking arch made of white marble, with columns sculpted to resemble *fasces*, the bundle of sticks that symbolised the fascist movement. It has an ethereal, almost ghostly presence, rising like a mirage out of the grey apartment buildings and green trees that surround it. Along its frieze, an inscription in Latin reads: "Here at the border of the fatherland set down the banner. From this point on we educated the others with language, law and culture."

Yet today these two pieces of fascist architectural propaganda are the centrepiece of a bold artistic experiment in addressing the debate around contested monuments, one which offers a template for other communities divided over whether to tear down or keep up monuments with racist, imperialist or fascist connotations.

As a border town with a mostly non-Italian population, it was subject to a policy of intense Italianisation under Mussolini. Place names were changed, Tyrolean cultural institutions were closed, and German–the native language of 90 per cent of the province–was effectively banned.

A huge new city quarter and industrial zone were built across the river from Bolzano, and thousands of Italians were encouraged to settle. The new town was festooned with numerous monuments and buildings dedicated to the "glory" of fascism.

After the War, the Italian government attempted to atone for the fascist policies by granting the inhabitants of South Tyrol a high level of autonomy. Cultural and linguistic rights would be respected, public service jobs would be allocated proportionally based on language, and 90 per cent of tax revenue would remain inside the region.

In 2014, a cross-communal group of historians and artists in Bolzano convened to discuss how to resolve what was becoming an increasingly fractious and emotionally charged dispute. The social dynamics of the city had turned the buildings into contested spaces, creating a necessity and a sense of urgency that a solution be found.

"The binary choice was either to destroy the monuments or leave them up," says Hannes Obermair, professor of contemporary history at the University of Innsbruck and one of the experts tasked with finding a solution to the Bolzano issue. "But if you remove the monuments, you remove the evidence, and avoid dealing with the complex layers of history and identity which drive this dispute. Alternatively, keeping the monuments up without challenging them simply normalises their fascist rhetoric."

In the end, a creative solution was found, one that managed to unite the city and defuse the tension between the two communities. The solution was to "recontextualise" the monuments, maintaining their artistic integrity and historical importance, while simultaneously neutralising and subverting their fascist rhetoric.

First up the Victory Monument, which elicited strong emotions on both sides. It is explicitly fascist, extolling the conquest and colonisation of South Tyrol and the alleged superiority of the Latin civilisation. But through a complex palimpsest of ideologies and symbols, it is also seen as a celebration of Italian victory in World War One and a memorial to the fallen Italian soldiers of the war.

The monument also has significant historical value–as the first fascist monument anywhere in the world–and artistic merit, being an eminent example of Italian Rationalism, a movement now seen as important to the development of modern architecture as French Art Deco and German Bauhaus. Some of the most important Italian architects and artists of the time worked on the monument, including Marcello Piacentini and Adolfo Wildt.

Next came the bas-relief. The task fell to two local artists, Arnold Holzknecht and Michele Bernardi. Their idea was simple: to take a building with explicitly fascist rhetoric, and recontextualise it as an anti-fascist monument.

The artists decided to emblazon the Hannah Arendt quote "Nobody has the right to obey" across the frieze in German, Italian and Ladin–the region's three official languages. The quote is even more subversive when you remember that the building currently houses the city's tax office.

Obermair is enthusiastic that the Bolzano model could be successfully replicated in other parts of Italy, as well as in other countries struggling with divisive and complex fascist legacies, such as Spain. The model also offers a solution to the debate over statues in the UK and US. "Of course the social context in Bolzano is important, and each community needs to imagine its own artistic intervention," says Obermair. "But the basic idea, that we shouldn't destroy monuments but radically transform them, is a powerful one. It provides people with the tools to reflect on history, question ideology and critically examine the built environment around them. No architecture is neutral. Ultimately it is we, not the monuments, who should have the final word."

Q1. According to the passage "recontextualisation" of the controversial monuments was done in order to:

A. To maintain their artistic integrity and historical importance.

B. To reduce the fascist overload which it portrayed.

C. To find a creative solution to reduce the tension between the two opposing communities.

(a) Only A and B
(b) Only B and C
(c) Only A and C
(d) All of the above

Q2. What is the purpose of the passage?

(a) To inform about how people deal with historical structures of the past which are controversial, yet with a historical lineage.

(b) To argue how controversial historical structures inflame even the present masses even if they are decades old.

(c) To propose a unilateral solution for controversial structures which might be making the people agitated.

(d) To entertain people from a past and present perspective of controversial historical structures.

Q3. How does the transformation of the controversial monuments help, as mentioned by Obermair?

A. It helps people to come to terms with reality even though it has bad memories of the ancient times.

B. It helps people to think about history and question different ideals and analyse the environment around them.

C. It helps to preserve monuments which would become a reason for warfare.

(a) Only A

(b) Only B

(c) Only C

(d) Both A and C

Passage 2

Directions for questions 1-4: The passage given below is followed by a set of four questions. Choose the most appropriate option out of the given four options.

There's no emotion we ought to think harder and more clearly about than anger. Anger greets most of us every day–in our personal relationships, in the workplace, on the highway, on airline trips- and, often, in our political lives as well. Anger is both poisonous and popular. Even when people acknowledge its destructive tendencies, they still so often cling to it, seeing it as a strong emotion, connected to self respect and manliness (or, for women, to the vindication of equality). If you react to insults and wrongs without anger you'll be seen as spineless and downtrodden. When people wrong you, says conventional wisdom, you should use justified rage to put them in their place, exact a penalty. We could call this football politics, but we'd have to acknowledge right away those athletes, whatever their rhetoric, have to be disciplined people who know how to transcend anger in pursuit of a team goal.

If we think closely about anger, we can begin to see why it is a stupid way to run one's life. A good place to begin is Aristotle's definition: not perfect, but useful, and a starting point for a long Western tradition of reflection. Aristotle says that anger is a response to a significant damage to something or someone one cares about, and a damage that the angry person believes to have been wrongfully inflicted. He adds that although anger is painful, it also contains within itself a hope for payback. So: significant damage, pertaining to one's own values or circle of cares, and wrongfulness. All this seems both true and uncontroversial. More controversial, perhaps, is his idea (in which, however, all Western philosophers who write about anger concur) that the angry person wants some type of payback, and that this is a conceptual part of what anger is. In other words, if you don't want some type of payback, your emotion is something else (grief, perhaps), but not really anger.

Is this really right? (think so. We should understand that the wish for payback can be a very subtle wish: the angry person doesn't need to wish to take revenge herself.) She may simply want the law to do so; or even some type of divine justice. Or she may more subtly simply want the wrongdoer's life to go badly in future, hoping, for example, that the second marriage of her betraying spouse turns out really badly. (think if we understand the wish in this broad way, Aristotle is right: anger does contain a sort of strike-back tendency.) Contemporary psychologists who study anger empirically agree with Aristotle in seeing this double movement in it, from pain to hope.

The central puzzle is this: the payback idea does not make sense. Whatever the wrongful act was–a murder, a rape, a betrayal- inflicting pain on the wrongdoer does not help restore the thing that was lost. We think about payback all the time, and it is a deeply human tendency to think that proportionality between punishment and offence somehow makes good the offence. Only it doesn't. It's an empirical matter. And usually people do not treat it as an empirical matter: they are in the grip of an idea of cosmic fitness that makes them think that blood for blood, pain for pain is the right way to go. The payback idea is deeply human, but fatally flawed as a way of making sense of the world.

Q4. As understood from the passage, Aristotle defines anger as:

(a) an emotion one believes in when something or someone has been wronged.

(b) the reaction to a wrongfully inflicted damage to someone or something that one cares about.

(c) a significant damage pertaining to one's own value or circle of cases.

(d) none of the above.

Q5. According to the writer what is the most dominant feeling in an angry person?

(a) The person feels he has been insulted.

(b) Justified rage must exact a similar rage.

(c) The angry person expects some sort of strike back.

(d) The anger is turned inwards and it's transcended.

Q6. The word "empirical" as used in the passage means:

(a) Based on experience
(b) Logical reasoning
(c) A primitive form
(d) A popular belief

Q7. Which of the following statements, with reference to the passage, is/are false?

A. Women's idea of anger may be in vindication of equality.
B. Western philosophy advocates payback completing the cycle of emotions.
C. The payback idea is completely fatal and flawed.

(a) Only A
(b) Only B
(c) Both A and B
(d) Only C

Passage 3

Invisible atoms coming together
Revealing themselves in visible forms
Seeds are hugged by the earth
Which renders them as gardens in bloom
And yonder stars, are they not pearls
Floating on teeming seas?
Scattered, yet strung together in orderly constellations
Love binding them lo one another
And each is perpetually seeking it's like?

Q8. Which of the following options best captures the spirit of the above stanza?

(a) Stars and seas are similar.
(b) All rivers flow into the ocean.
(c) United we stand, divided we fall.
(d) Love dissolves all religious differences.
(e) Something invisible binds disparate objects

TEST 4

Passage 1

One of the most successful commercial products ever launched is said to have come about as the result of a mistake. In 1896, Jacob's Pharmacy in Atlanta, Georgia, was selling a nerve tonic known as "French Wine Cola–Ideal Nerve Tonic." By accidentally adding fizzy water instead of still water to the recipe, a pharmacist called John S. Pemberton invented what has today become the most popular soft drink in the world: Coca Cola. Along with its closest rival–Pepsi–which appeared on the market three years later, Coke has enjoyed phenomenal success worldwide, particularly in the past 50 years. Indeed, old Coke bottles and "limited edition" cans can often fetch considerable sums from collectors, and there are even stores which deal exclusively in Coke products and memorabilia.

What could possibly account for the amazing success of Coca Cola? How has this combination of carbonated water, sugar, acid and flavourings come to symbolise the American way of life for most of the world? After all, even the manufacturers could hardly describe Coke as a healthy product since it contains relatively high amounts of sugar (admittedly not the case with Diet Coke which contains artificial sweeteners instead of sugar) and phosphoric acid, both of which are known to damage teeth.

One explanation may be found in the name. The original recipe included a flavouring from the coca plant and probably included small amounts of cocaine (an addictive substance), but since the early part of this century, all traces of cocaine have been removed. However, Coke (like all cola drinks) also includes a flavouring from the cola tree; cola extract contains caffeine, which is a stimulant, and the Coca Cola company adds extra caffeine for good measure. While caffeine is not thought to be an addictive substance in itself, there is considerable evidence that over a period of time, the consumption of caffeine has to be increased in order for its stimulating effect to be maintained, and so sales of Coke perhaps benefit as a result.

A more likely reason for the enduring popularity of Coke may, however, be found in the company's enviable marketing strategies. Over the years, it has come up with some of the most memorable commercials, tunes, slogans and sponsorship in the world of advertising, variously emphasising international harmony, youthfulness and a carefree lifestyle. Few other companies (arguably including Pepsi) have been able to match such marketing ploys so consistently or effectively. As suggested earlier, the influences of American culture are evident just about everywhere, and Coca Cola has somehow come to represent a vision of the United States that much of the rest of the world dreams about and aspires to. Perhaps drinking Coke brings people that little bit closer to the dream.

Q1. According to the paragraph, "cans can often fetch considerable sums" means the same as:

(a) Coke is quite expensive in some parts of the world.
(b) Collectors consider carefully how much they are paying for a can of Coke.
(c) Old Coke cans have a lot of value.

(d) Some collectors will only drink Coke in exclusive stores.

(e) Certain Coke cans are worth a lot of money as collectable items.

Q2. According to the paragraph, the author uses "for good measure" to emphasise the fact that:

(a) There is a lot of caffeine in Coke.

(b) The amount of caffeine in Coke is carefully measured.

(c) The extra caffeine improves the taste of Coke.

(d) The extra caffeine balances the amount found naturally in the cola extract.

(e) The extra caffeine is healthy for the drinkers of Coke.

Q3. According to the paragraph, "Coke has enjoyed phenomenal success" suggests that the author:

(a) Thinks that the success of Coke is very strange.

(b) Believes that the success of Coke has been impressive.

(c) Thinks that the success of Coke is beyond explanation.

(d) Rather disapproves of the success of Coke.

(e) Considers the success of Coke to be undeserved.

Q4. Describing Coke's marketing strategies as "enviable" in the paragraph, the author means that:

(a) The strategies are based on envy.

(b) Coke's marketing staff is encouraged to be envious of each other's ideas.

(c) People are persuaded to buy Coke because they are envious of others.

(d) Rivals are envious of the Coke Company's successful methods of marketing.

(e) Coke's marketing strategies are enviable.

Q5. It can be inferred from the last sentence of the passage that:

(a) Most people would like to live in America.

(b) Many people wish for a lifestyle like they imagine most Americans have.

(c) Drinking Coke reminds a lot of people of visiting America.

(d) Living in the United States is a bit like living in a dream.

(e) Drinking Coke is part of the American dream.

Q6. According to the paragraph, all of the following are not true, except:

(a) Cocaine and caffeine are addictive substances.

(b) At least one of the ingredients of Coke is addictive.

(c) The stimulating effect of caffeine is reduced over time unless consumption of it is increased.

(d) The Coca Cola company has gradually increased the amount of caffeine it puts in Coke.

(e) All of the above are not true.

PASSAGE 2

Writing is both my vocation and my avocation: that's all I do.

You may wonder why I should write a genealogy. Well, to begin with my story is interesting. And, next, I am a mystery more so than a tree or a sunset or even a flash of lightning. But, sadly, I am taken for granted by those who use me, as if I were a mere incident and without background. This supercilious altitude relegates me to the level of the commonplace. This is a species of the grievous error in which mankind cannot too long persist without peril. For, as a wise man, G. K. Chesterton observed, "We are perishing for want of wonder, not for want of wonders."

I, simple though I appear to be, merit your wonder and awe, a claim I shall attempt to prove. In fact, if you can understand me-no, that's too much to ask of anyone–if you can become aware of the miraculousness that I symbolise, you can help save the freedom mankind is so unhappily losing. I have a profound lesson to teach. And I can teach this lesson better than an automobile or on airplane or a mechanical dishwasher because–well, because I am seemingly so simple.

Simple? Yes not a single person on the face of this earth knows how to make me. This sounds fantastic, doesn't it? Especially when you realise that there are about one and–a half billion of my kind produced in the U.S. each year.

Pick me up and look me over. What do you see? Not much meets the eye–there's some wood, lacquer, the printed labelling, graphite lead, a bit of metal, and an eraser.

Q7. "I" in the passage, most likely, refers to:

(a) The author of the passage

(b) A geometry box

(c) A study table

(d) A pencil

(e) The evolution of a book

Q8. A "supercilious attitude" in this passage implies:

(a) Failure to perceive the mystery of the sunset.

(b) Arrogance of treating all simple things as trivial

(c) Lack of curiosity in seeking the mystery behind the lightning.

(d) A tendency to break down intricacies of creation into its simple parts.

(e) Prosaic attitude immune to the mysteries world

Passage 3

A few years ago, I was on ray boat with one of my employees, a great guy named Keenon; I was supposed to be giving him pep talk and performance review.

"When I think of what we do, I describe it as uncovering the riptide," I said.

"Uncovering the riptide," Keenon said.

"Yes, the idea is that we–you and I and everyone here–have the skills to identify the psychological forces that are pulling us away from shore and use them to get somewhere more productive."

"Somewhere more productive," Keenon said.

"Exactly," I said. "To a place where we can..."

We had talked for about 45 minutes when my son Brandon, who runs operations for the Black Swan Group, broke out laughing.

"I can't take it anymore! Don't you see? Really, Dad, don't you see?" I blinked. Did I see what? I asked him.

"All Keenon is doing is mirroring you. And he's been doing it for almost an hour"

"Oh," I said, my face going red as Keenon began to laugh.

He was totally right. Keenon had been playing with me the entire Time, using the psychological tool that works most effectively with assertive guys like me: the mirror.

Your personal negotiation style–and that of your counterpart–is formed through childhood, schooling, family, culture and a million other factors; by recognising it you can identify your negotiating strengths and weaknesses (and those of your counterpart) and adjust your mind-set and strategies accordingly.

Negotiation style is a crucial variable in bargaining. If you don't know what instinct will tell you or the other side to do in various circumstances, you'll have massive trouble gaming out effective strategies and tactics. You and your counterpart have habits of mind and behaviour, and once you identify them you can leverage them in a strategic manner.

Just like Keenon did.

There's an entire library unto itself of research into the archetypes and behavioural profiles of all the possible people you're bound to meet at the negotiating table. It's flat-out overwhelming, so much so that it loses its utility. Over the last few years, in an effort primarily led by my son Brandon, we've consolidated and simplified all that research, cross-referencing it with our experiences in the field and the case studies of our business school students, and found that people fall into three broad categories. Some people are Accommodators; others–like me–are basically Assertive; and the rest are data-loving Analysts.

Accommodators think that as long as there is a free-flowing continuous exchange of information time is being well spent. They will yield a concession to appease or acquiesce and hope the other side reciprocates. The Assertive type believes time is money. For them, potting the solution perfect isn't as important as getting it done. Assertives are fiery people who love winning above all else, often at the expense of others. Analysts are methodical and diligent. They are not in a big rush. Instead, they believe that as long as they are working towards the best result in a thorough and systematic way, time is of little consequence. Their self-image is linked to minimising mistakes.

Their motto is: As much time as it takes to get it right

A study of American lawyer-negotiators found that 65 per cent of attorneys from two major U.S. cities used a cooperative style while only 24 per cent were truly assertive. And when these lawyers were graded for effectiveness, more than 75 per cent of the effective group came from the cooperative type; only 12 per cent were Assertive. So, if you're not Assertive, don't despair. Blunt assertion is actually counterproductive most of the time.

Remember, your personal negotiating style is not a straitjacket. No one is exclusively one style. Most of us have the capacity to throttle up our non-dominant styles should the situation call for it. But there is one basic truth about a successful bargaining style: To be good, you have to learn to be yourself at the bargaining table. To be great you have to add to your strengths, not replace them.

Q9. "Even wasted minute is a wasted dollar" is best associated with:

(a) The Analysts
(b) The Accommodators
(c) The Assertives
(d) None of the options

Q10. With respect to the passage, identify which of the following statement is correct:

(a) One's personal negotiation style and that of one's counterpart is genetically transmitted
(b) Bargaining style is the outcome of interaction between a person and his/her counterpart
(c) Successful negotiators are good at "mirroring" others
(d) To negotiate effectively, one has to understand his/her counterpart's "normal".

Q11. Select the most appropriate title for this passage:

(a) Hard Bargaining Tactics
(b) What Type of a Negotiator Are You?
(c) Punching Back: Using Assertion Without Getting Used
(d) The Three Types of Leverage

Q12. Finishing the negotiation is more important than "getting it right" for:

(a) The Assertives
(b) The Accommodators
(c) The Analysts
(d) None of the options

TEST 5

PASSAGE 1

Last year, Rotterdam-based design student Kirsten Spruit created a mixed media installation titled *A Space for Lingering*. Visitors are invited to lie down on an expansive black mattress, slip on headphones that play resonant soundscapes, and do nothing. An accompanying film using slow textual iterations ("I feel like I did nothing today") encouraged thoughts on passivity. Spruit reflects: "A Space For Lingering stems from a research around the feeling of restlessness, of always needing to be productive and efficient, that seems to dominate the lives of many, especially among my generation."

Is this what rest has become? An exhibit in a gallery, as if it's a relic of a halcyon past? Something we can do only when invited to as part of an art event? Apparently, yes. According to Claudia Hammond, presenter of BBC Radio 4's All in the Mind and author of The Art of Rest: "Busy-ness has become a badge of honour. It's become something we expect of ourselves and other people. Unfortunately, evidence shows that we do think busy people are better. Even rest has, in some ways, been commercialised. Look at the wellness movement. There's this idea you should be doing things that are good for you."

The result is taking its toll: we feel guilty when we rest so we don't do it enough. Earlier this year, research revealed that Americans between the ages of 45 and 65 are more stressed today than people their age in the 1990s. The World Health Organisation has classified stress as the "health epidemic of the 21st Century."

No wonder. The pandemic has meant that we are simultaneously frenetic with worry, often housebound, and denied access to many of life's most restorative activities. If global emergencies are showing us anything, it's that old ways of living aren't working–for ourselves, for other people, for the planet. We need a reassessment, not simply of our own behaviours, but of society. One of the best ways to do this may be to just stop."[We are seeing a] gradual backlash against productivity and self-enhancement and a move towards practical boredom, introspection and opting-out," Holly Friend, senior foresight writer at The Future Laboratory, tells BBC Culture, "With no option but to stay home and recalibrate, consumers are finding themselves experiencing a new pace of life that will impact our daily routines for years to come. This period is giving [people] a chance to get comfortable in missing out and doing nothing, activities that were once shrouded in stigma and Millennial guilt."

Instead, we should allow ourselves to feel bored or lonely, or to take pleasure in simpler, slower, more natural activities, thereby addressing compulsive behaviours that may, in contrast to the way they're portrayed, be simply making us more unhappy.

"A nap, meditation or just a pause without a screen, stepping out of the web of sales, stories and dictums we're constantly fed, allows us to be in a more truthful reality," she adds. "Rest is an act of quiet rebellion, allowing us into new ways of being and seeing the world."

Holly Friend adds, "Taking a step back, pausing, and re-evaluating the stressors of our lives is necessary to achieving skills that we need more than ever–such as resilience. Amid a year that has blindsided us, we have come to realise that as humans we need to be ready to adapt and shift priorities at a moment's notice. Rest is becoming integral to this. In order to deal with such extremities of the world, we need to feel calm, collected and focused." The next time you want to take 40 winks and friends and family tut disapprovingly? Just tell them you're rebelling.

Q1. "Halcyon past" mentioned in the passage is in reference to what?

(a) Something related to peace and tranquillity and belonging as a part of the past not as a thing of today.
(b) Peace and quiet which are important parts of a routine lifestyle.
(c) Peace and quiet which we should strive for but we are also looking at work which needs to be done.
(d) Work versus rest and the daily humdrum of life which makes us forget the importance of other things.

Q2. Why is stress called as the "health epidemic" in the passage?

(a) Because taking rest is an important thing and people are willing to leave their jobs and go in for restful activities.
(b) Resting in today's world is a luxury many cannot afford hence they are worried that they may never catch up with their lives.
(c) Resting is something which is associated with guilt nowadays, hence people are deprived of it and end up getting stressed.
(d) Stress and rest are two sides of the same coin and hence we should be getting more rest and less stress.

Q3. What kinds of things were shrouded in stigma and millennial guilt according to the passage?

(a) The basic pleasures of life like resting, eating, having fun and indulging on a holiday.

(b) The stress buster activities like a get together with friends and a little bit of me time.

(c) The family time which COVID redefined for us and the time to rest and rejuvenate.

(d) The time to just rest and do nothing and the so called missing out on activities.

PASSAGE 2

"The word death is not pronounced in New York, in Paris, in London, because it burns the lips,"

Western culture has developed multiple mechanisms for shielding us from the reality of our mortality, our children, and we shunt the elderly away in care homes out of sight and out of mind.

We must learn to confront the terror of death and develop the courage to explore how awareness of our mortality can help us navigate the now. Just think of Frida Kahlo's self-portrait Thinking About Death, which has a macabre skull plastered on her forehead. Or consider the pithy wisdom of Albert Camus: "Come to terms with death. Thereafter anything is possible." But coming to terms with death is easier said than done. One of the secrets for doing so is not to spend hours contemplating visions of the Grim Reaper, but to reimagine our relationship with time itself. Here are three ideas for doing so that offer the unexpected prospect of existential sustenance.

In Leo Tolstoy's 1886 novella, *The Death of Ivan Ilyich,* a St Petersburg judicial prosecutor who has dedicated his career to rising through the legal ranks and helping his family achieve a respectable place in bourgeois society lies on his deathbed, aged just 45, wondering if he has wasted his life on superficial pursuits. "What if my whole life has really been wrong?" he reflects bitterly.

Imagine yourself at a dinner party in the afterlife. Also present are all the other "yous" who you could have been if you had made different choices. The you who studied harder for exams. The you who walked out on your first job and followed your dream. The you who became an alcoholic, and another you who nearly died in a car accident. The you who put more time into making your marriage work.

You then look around at these alternative selves. Some of them are impressive, while others seem smug and annoying. A few make you feel inadequate and lazy. So which of them are you curious to meet and talk to? Which would you rather avoid? Which do you envy? Out of these many yous, is there one who you would rather be–or become?

Another way to make sense of our existence is to draw on the wisdom of indigenous cultures whose worldviews dissolve the barriers between life and death, offering a sense of transcendence. There is an inspiring Māori concept known as whakapapa, which is their word for "lineage" or "genealogy". It is the idea that we are all connected in a great chain of life that links the present back to the generations of the past and forward to all the generations going on into the future.

It so happens that the light is shining on this moment, here and now, and the idea of whakapapa helps us shine the light more broadly, so we can see everyone throughout the landscape of time. It allows us to recognise that the living, the dead and the unborn are all here in the room with us. And we need to respect their interests as much as our own. Making this imaginative leap is challenging, especially for those of us immersed in a highly individualistic Western consumer culture.

But we can begin to do so with help from another thought experiment that involves journeying through time. Think of a child you know and care about–perhaps a godchild, a niece, or one of your own children or grandchildren. Now imagine them at their 90th birthday party, surrounded by family and friends.

This kind of thought experiment can help us transcend the limits of our own lifespan and get in touch with the wisdom of whakapapa. We are all part of the great chain of life. And by recognising our place in it, we start extending our sense of what constitutes "the now," shifting from a now of seconds and minutes and hours to a longer now of decades, centuries and even millennia. A now that gives us a sense of responsibility for the legacies we leave for the generations of tomorrow, while respecting the generations of the past.

We can also rethink our relationship with death by taking the perspective of "deep time," recognising that humankind, and our own lives, are just an eyeblink in the cosmic story.

But remember, too, that just as there is deep time behind us, there is also deep time ahead. Any creatures that might still exist in five billion years when our sun dies will be as different from us as we are from the first single-celled bacteria.

Don't we have a responsibility to preserve the life-giving potential of the Earth for the generations to come? At the same time, situating ourselves in the grand expanse of time helps put our mortality in perspective. We are just a passing moment in a far bigger, longer narrative.

Q4. "The dinner party of afterlife" signifies what according to the passage?

(a) We are just a passing moment in a far bigger, longer narrative.

(b) A pilgrimage to an ancient tree and experience life "at the speed of wood."

(c) Reflections can alter how we choose to act in the here and now.
(d) None of the above.

Q5. What is the importance of the "concept known as *whakapapa*"?

(a) "The word death is not pronounced in some cultures because it burns the lips".
(b) While deep time is elusive, its wonders are within our grasp.
(c) Situating ourselves in the grand expanse of time helps put our mortality in perspective.
(d) None of these.

Q6. What are the important keynote points of the passage?

A. Journeys into deep time
B. The great chain of life
C. The dinner party of the afterlife

(a) only A and B
(b) only B and C
(c) only C and A
(d) all three A, B and C

PASSAGE 3

As the climate in the Middle East changed beginning around 7000 BCE, conditions emerged that were conducive to a more complex and advanced form of civilisation in both Egypt and Mesopotamia. The process began when the swampy valleys of the Nile in Egypt and of the Tigris and Euphrates Rivers in Mesopotamia became drier, producing riverine lands that were both habitable and fertile, and attracting settlers armed with the newly developed techniques of agriculture. This migration was further encouraged by the gradual transformation of the once-hospitable grasslands of these regions into deserts. Human population became increasingly concentrated into pockets of settlement scattered along the banks of the great rivers.

These rivers profoundly shaped the way of life along their banks. In Mesopotamia, the management of water in conditions of unpredictable drought, flood and storm became the central economic and social challenge. Villagers began early to build simple earthworks, dikes, canals, and ditches to control the waters and reduce the opposing dangers of drought during the dry season (usually the spring) and flooding at harvest time.

Such efforts required a degree of cooperation among large numbers of people that had not previously existed. The individual village, containing only a dozen or so houses and families, was economically vulnerable; but when several villages, probably under the direction of a council of elders, learned to share their human resources in the building of a coordinated network of water-control systems, the safety, stability, and prosperity of all improved. In this new cooperation, the seeds of the great Mesopotamian civilisations were being sown.

Technological and mathematical invention, too, were stimulated by life along rivers. Such devices as the noria (a primitive waterwheel) and the Archimedean screw (a device for raising water from the low riverbanks to the high ground where it was needed), two forerunners of many more varied and complex machines, were first developed here for use in irrigation systems. Similarly, the earliest methods of measurement and computation and the first developments in geometry were stimulated by the need to keep track of land holdings and boundaries in fields that were periodically inundated.

The rivers served as high roads of the earliest commerce. Traders used boats made of bundles of rushes to transport grains, fruits, nuts, fibres, and textiles from one village to another, transforming the rivers into the central spines of nascent commercial kingdoms. Trade expanded surprisingly widely; we have evidence suggesting that, even before the establishment of the first Egyptian dynasty, goods were being exchanged between villagers in Egypt and others as far away as Iran.

Similar developments were occurring at much the same time along the great river valleys in other parts of the world–for example, along the Indus in India and the Hwang Ho in China. The history of early civilisation has been shaped to a remarkable degree by the relation of humans and rivers.

Q7. This passage basically explains:

(a) The similarities and differences among several ancient societies
(b) The influence of river settlements on the growth of early civilisations
(c) How climatic changes led to the founding of the earliest recorded cities.
(d) The development of primitive technologies in the ancient Middle East.

Q8. According to the passage, the increasing aridity of formally fertile grasslands in Egypt and Mesopotamia caused the settlement patterns in those regions to become.

(a) Less nomadic
(b) Less stable
(c) More concentrated
(d) More sparse

Q9. The passage implies that the earliest geometry was practiced primarily by:

(a) Farmworkers
(b) Landowners
(c) Traders and merchants
(d) Mechanical artisans

Q10. The passage indicates that the social effects of the unpredictability of water supplies in Mesopotamia was:

(a) To encourage cooperation in the creation of water management systems
(b) To drive farmers to settle in fertile grasslands far from the uncontrollable rivers
(c) To cause warfare over water rights among rival villages
(d) None of these

Q11. By referring to emerging civilisations in India & China, the author wants to emphasise the:

(a) Relatively advanced position enjoyed by the Middle East in comparison to other regions
(b) Rapidity with which social systems developed in the Middle East spread to other places
(c) Crucial role played by rivers in the development of human cultures around the world
(d) Importance of water transportation in the growth of early trade

Answer Key

Test 1

Passage 1

1. (b) **2.** (b) **3.** (a)

Passage 2

4. (d) **5.** (c) **6.** (c)

Passage 3

7. (d) **8.** (c) **9.** (d)
10. (d) **11.** (d) **12.** (d)

Test 2

Passage 1

1. (c) **2.** (c) **3.** (b)

Passage 2

4. (a) **5.** (b) **6.** (c)
7. (a)

Passage 3

8. (e)

Test 3

Passage 1

1. (d) **2.** (a) **3.** (b)

Passage 2

4. (b) **5.** (c) **6.** (a)
7. (b)

Passage 3

8. (e)

Test 4

Passage 1

1. (e) **2.** (a) **3.** (b)
4. (d) **5.** (b) **6.** (c)

Passage 2

7. (d) **8.** (b)

Passage 3

9. (c) **10.** (d) **11.** (b)
12. (a)

Test 5

Passage 1

1. (a) **2.** (c) **3.** (d)

Passage 2

4. (d) **5.** (d) **6.** (d)

Passage 3

7. (b) **8.** (c) **9.** (b)
10. (a) **11.** (c)

Explanations

Test 1

Passage 1

1. If we see the last paragraph and the following lines: "The Spitfire was fast, sleek and very agile–but it was outnumbered two to one by another fighter, one often ignored in the popular retelling of the battle. It was the Hawker Hurricane, and most of the RAF squadrons flying over London that day were equipped with it. It was an aircraft that not only helped turn the tide of a war," we see that the Hurricane changed the tide of the war, hence statement C is correct. It is also mentioned that the Spitfire was a new, agile and sleek machine so statement B is also correct. But A is not correct because Spitfire for this particular war was not better than the Hurricane.
   Option b is the right answer. [Both B and C]
2. Since it was a sudden and surprising strategy that the Germans used to start bombing the civil areas of Britain hence option b is correct. The following lines from the passage support it, "But the Germans then turned their attention–mystifyingly–to Britain's cities, hoping that indiscriminate bombing would cause widespread panic and force Britain to surrender."
3. The hurricane changed the tide of the war and its legacy is found in many aspects as is mentioned in the last few lines of the passage.
   Hence, option (a) is correct.

Passage 2

4. Statement B is incorrect as it was not mentioned by the Author, rather it was just an opinion in the passage. Statements A and B are both directly and indirectly supported by the author in the passage. Refer to these lines from the passage, "Early education can however have a positive impact on social development."
5. Refer to the following lines in the passage which make option c the correct choice:
   "Bradbury found that the pressure to gain these decoding skills–and pass reading tests–also means that some three year-olds are already being exposed to phonics." It doesn't end up being meaningful, it ends up being memorising rather than understanding context, "says Bradbury." The other options are not mentioned in the context of "phonetics."
6. Since statements (b), (c) and (d) are not mentioned or hinted in the passage, hence options (a), (b) and (d) are incorrect. Only statement A is mentioned in the passage, hence, option (c) is correct.

Passage 3

7. The only meaning which can be derived of the word triumph is victory and hence, option (d) is the answer.
8. "But the magnificent here and now of life in the flesh is ours, and ours alone, and ours only for a time." Hence, "living beings" life is temporary. Therefore, option (c) is the correct answer.
9. The word rapture has been used as a positive word and means joy, hence, option (d) is the correct answer.
10. The sentence indicates towards the reflection of sunlight on the waters which creates a glitter on the surface of waters. Mind has no existence by itself, it is only the glitter of the sun on the surface of the waters, which clearly shows that mind is a reflection.
    Therefore, option (d) is the answer.
11. The author is talking about the importance and philosophy of being alive and how it's important. Hence, the tone is philosophical.
12. Option (d) is the best option and that the passage talks about being alive and how one should live it and hence, option (d) is the correct answer.

Test 2

Passage 1

1. Whether the lines are actually taken from the novel or not is not clear but they definitely portray the lives of our times as mentioned in the novel 2022. Hence, option (c) is the correct answer.
2. The last paragraph clearly says that it is difficult to demarcate Disk's political ideology into left wing or light wing. Hence, option c is correct and option d is not hinted or mentioned anywhere in the passage as he was seeing the future, not the past.
3. "Anthony Peake, author of the biography *A Life of Philip K Dick: The Man Who Remembered the Future* (2013)." These lines from the passage talk about his biography as someone who remembered

the future, then definitely it can be inferred that he saw or witnessed the future and therefore he remembered it.

Passage 2

4. According to the passage, the character was never named in the novel but was called harry in the movie, hence, option (a) is the correct answer. The other options have errors as option (b) talks about him being called Harry in the book which was incorrect. Option (c) talks about him not being identified by many which was opposite to the facts mentioned. Option (d) mentions him as glamorous which was again mentioned otherwise in the passage.
5. Option (b) is directly mentioned in the passage, (c) is incorrect as it is not mentioned or hinted in the passage. Option (a) is very generic whereas option (b) is the specific option we were looking for.
6. The following lines from the passage prove that option (c) as correct "but also these were 'kitchen sink' spy stories: you literally saw Michael Caine in the kitchen making an omelette (though his hands were, famously, Len Deighton's in that scene)."
   Option (a) is not the main reason why the omelette scene was iconic.
7. In the passage, the character of Harry is shown as more agreeable and identifiable to the masses than Bond. Options (b), (c) and (d) are more or less hinted or mentioned in the passage; hence, the author will agree to them. Option (a) is opposite, hence, the author is least likely to agree with that.

Passage 3

8. These lines clearly point towards the feeling of nostalgia and how this feeling has been linked to the childhood memories of the author's ancestral home. Only option (e) is in sync with this idea and hence, is the correct option.

Test 3

Passage 1

1. The following lines mentioned in the passage show that all the statements A, B and C are correct. "In the end, a creative solution was found, one that managed to unite the city and defuse the tension between the two communities. The solution was to "recontextualise" the monuments, maintaining their artistic integrity and historical importance, while simultaneously neutralising and subverting their fascist rhetoric."
2. The author is not putting up any arguments hence option (b) is incorrect. He is not trying to entertain or give an only one of a kind solution, hence, both (c) and (d) are also wrong. He is definitely trying to inform about what is mentioned in option (a). Hence, option (a) is correct.
3. The following lines from the passage: .... "says Obermair. But the basic idea, that we shouldn't destroy monuments but radically transform them, is a powerful one. It provides people with the tools to reflect on history, question ideology and critically examine the built environment around them. No architecture is neutral. Ultimately it is we, not the monuments, who should have the final word." ... shows us that option (b) is the correct answer.

Passage 2

4. Upon reading what Aristotle thinks of anger as an emotion in paragraph 2, we can understand that he believes anger is a reaction to something which a person believes has been wrongly inflicted. Aristotle says that anger is a response to a significant damage to something or someone one cares about, and a damage that the angry person believes to have been wrongfully inflicted. Option (b) expresses this the best way and hence, is the correct answer.
5. The author clearly explains that if there is no strike back or payback feeling, then the emotion is something else, not really anger, the payback is the very concept of anger. Hence, the only choice (c) validates this point.
6. Based on the experiments or experience rather than ideas or theories is what empirical signifies, then the contextual meaning is experience based. Hence, option (a) is correct.
7. The only choice that fits is option (b) as it is clearly stated that Western philosophers have elaborated [meaning that they have explained it] on this fact, not advocated it. Hence, it is false.

Passage 3

8. The above lines state that each different entity is bound together with a force unseen. The only possible options are either option (c) or (e) out of which (e) is a better option since nothing is talked about to explain, "divided we fall". Hence, option (e) is a better option.

Test 4

Passage 1

1. The correct answer is option (e), as is clearly mentioned in the fourth sentence of the first paragraph of the passage that coke cans which are a collector's item fetch a good amount of money.
2. The correct answer is option (a). It is clearly mentioned in the third paragraph of the passage that Coke contains a lot of caffeine, here "for good measure" has nothing to do with the taste or quality of the product, it just signifies that the amount of caffeine added is a lot.
3. Mentioned in the first paragraph of the passage, option (b) is correct. Phenomenal success would signify a significant achievement which could translate as impressive.
4. Enviable marketing strategies can be from the viewpoint of the rivals, thus option (d) is correct.
5. An American lifestyle might be an aspiration for many people and drinking coke makes them similar to that in one way at least, thus option (b) is the best answer. So it is living like an American that is their wish rather than living in America itself, which makes the other options incorrect.
6. In the answer options, we have to find the correct answer. Options (a), (b), (d) and (e) are incorrect. Only option (c) is correct. It is clearly mentioned in the last sentence of the third paragraph of the passage.

Passage 2

7. Look at the last lines of the passage, graphite lead, metal and eraser–all point towards a pencil. Hence, option (d) is the answer.
8. A supercilious attitude is one which is demeaning or meant to look down at someone–in other words, an arrogant attitude. Therefore, option (b) is the correct answer.

Passage 3

9. The author in the passage describes three types of people: the accommodators, the assertives and the analysts. On reading each of their definitions, it is clear that the "Time is Money" aspect is in the nature of the Assertives. Hence, option (c) is the answer.
10. Option (a) is factually incorrect as the negotiation style is not genetically transmitted. Hence, (a) can be ruled out. (c) is also eliminated as this case is true only in the example of the Assertives which is clearly stated in lines of the passage. Option (d) can be inferred from the passage as the crux of the passage is that to negotiate effectively, a person has to understand the other person's strengths and weaknesses and use them to negotiate with the counterpart. Hence, option (d) is the answer.
11. The best title that fits the passage is option (b). Option (a) is a generalised title, (c) specifically talks about assertion while the passage has included two other types of personalities and (d) talks about leverage which is irrelevant with respect to the content of the passage.
12. The correct answer is option (a), the assertives. In the definition for the assertives, it is stated that for them, time is money and finding the solution isn't as important as getting it done. Hence, option (a) is the answer.

Test 5

Passage 1

1. Halcyon refers to peace and tranquillity. In the lines of the passage it is mentioned as the relic of the past, meaning something which was a part of the past but not of today. Hence option a is the correct choice which covers all the points. Options (b), (c) and (d) have distorted the original message, hence are not correct.
2. The lines from the passage, "The result is taking its toll: we feel guilty when we rest so we don't do it enough. Earlier this year, research revealed that Americans between the ages of 45 and 65 are more stressed today than people their age in the 1990s. The World Health Organisation has classified stress as the 'health epidemic of the 21st Century'."
   These lines clearly show option (c) as the correct answer.
   Option (a) is incorrect in this specific question as people are not resting. Option (b) is taking the message in another direction which it was not meant to convey. Option (d) is an irrelevant option and not mentioned in the passage.
3. The line, "This period is giving [people] a chance to get comfortable in missing out and doing nothing, activities that were once shrouded in stigma and Millennial guilt," show us that option (d)

is the perfect answer. The other options have extra information which is not mentioned in that context in the passage.

Passage 2

4. The dinner party of afterlife is clear from the following lines of the passage:
"My favourite approach to making this temporal journey to the end of our lives is a visioning exercise I call 'The dinner party of the afterlife'. Imagine yourself at a dinner party in the afterlife. Also present are all the other 'yous' who you could have been if you had made different choices. The you who studied harder for exams. The you who walked out on your first job and followed your dream. The you who became an alcoholic, and another you who nearly died in a car accident. The you who put more time into making your marriage work. You then look around at these alternative selves. Some of them are impressive, while others seem smug and annoying. A few make you feel inadequate and lazy. So which of them are you curious to meet and talk to? Which would you rather avoid? Which do you envy? Out of these many yous, is there one who you would rather be–or become?" None of these points are covered in options (a), (b) and (c). Hence, option (d) is the correct answer.
5. The following lines from the passage explain what the concept of "Whakapapa" means "There is an inspiring Māori concept known as whakapapa, which is their word for 'lineage' or 'genealogy'. It is the idea that we are all connected in a great chain of life that links the present back to the generations of the past and forward to all the generations going on into the future. It so happens that the light is shining on this moment, here and now, and the idea of whakapapa helps us shine the light more broadly, so we can see everyone throughout the landscape of time. It allows us to recognise that the living, the dead and the unborn are all here in the room with us. And we need to respect their interests as much as our own. Making this imaginative leap is challenging, especially for those of us immersed in a highly individualistic Western consumer culture." None of the options, (a), (b) and (c) cover the actual concept. Thus, the correct answer is option (d).
6. The passage talks about three important points and goes on to explain it as a solution or the way of life. The following lines from the passage explain the start of the three points.... "But coming to terms with death is easier said than done. One of the secrets for doing so is not to spend hours contemplating visions of the Grim Reaper, but to reimagine our relationship with time itself. Here are three ideas for doing so that offer the unexpected prospect of existential sustenance..."

Passage 3

7. The passage totally focuses on the influence of river settlements, hence option (b) is correct. Options (d) and (c) are just mentioned without so much importance hence they are not the main theme. Option (a) talks about similarities and differences which are not mentioned in the passage.
8. "This migration was further encouraged by the gradual transformation of the once-hospitable grasslands of these regions into deserts. Human population became increasingly concentrated into pockets of settlement scattered along the banks of the great rivers." These lines from the passage show that option (c) is correct.
9. "Similarly, the earliest methods of measurement and computation and the first developments in geometry were stimulated by the need to keep track of land holdings and boundaries in fields that were periodically inundated." These lines from the passage show that option (b) is correct.
10. The passage states that to overcome the crisis of the water people cooperated and worked together to create dams, etc. and other water management systems. Hence, option (a) is correct.
11. "Similar developments were occurring at much the same time along the great river valleys in other parts of the world–for example, along the Indus in India and the Hwang Ho in China. The history of early civilisation has been shaped to a remarkable degree by the relation of humans and rivers."... these lines from the passage show that river systems played an important role in the development of civilisations. Hence, option (c) is correct. Option (d) is not correct because water transportation has not been mentioned and it would include other sea routes etc. which is out of the context of the passage.

CHAPTER 6 Level of Difficulty—II

PART I

TEST 1

Passage 1

Q 1-5. Read the following passage and answer the questions that follow.

There are a growing number of Marxists today. By which I mean followers of Groucho, not Karl. "Whatever it is, I'm against it," Marx sang in his 1932 film, Horse Feathers. "I don't know what they have to say/It makes no difference anyway."

What was satire then is ideology today: Cynicism–the belief that people are generally morally bankrupt and behave treacherously in order to maximize self-interest–dominates the American culture. Since 1964, the percentage of Americans who say they trust the government to do what is right "just about always" or "most of the time" has fallen 53 points from 77 to 24 per cent. Sentiments about other institutions in society follow similar patterns.

Whether cynicism is more warranted now than ever is yours to decide. But it won't change the fact that the modern cynical outlook on life is terrible for your well-being. It makes you less healthy, less happy, less successful, and less respected by others.

The problem isn't cynicism per se; it's that modern people have lost the original meaning of cynicism. Instead of assuming that everyone and everything sucks, we should all live like the ancient Greek cynics, who rebelled against convention in a search for truth and enlightenment.

The original cynicism was a philosophical movement likely founded by Antisthenes, a student of Socrates, and popularized by Diogenes of Sinope around the fifth century B.C. It was based on a refusal to accept the assumptions and habits that discourage people from questioning conventional dogmas, and thus hold us back from the search for deep wisdom and happiness. Whereas a modern cynic might say, for instance, that the president is an idiot and thus his policies aren't worth considering, the ancient cynic would examine each policy impartially.

The modern cynic rejects things out of hand ("This is stupid"), while the ancient cynic simply withholds judgment ("This may be right or wrong"). "Modern cynicism [has] come to describe something antithetical to its previous meanings, a psychological state hardened against both moral reflection and intellectual persuasion," the University of Houston's David Mazella wrote in The Making of Modern Cynicism.

There were no happiness surveys in Antisthenes's times, so we can't compare the ancient cynics' life satisfaction with that of those around them who did not share their philosophy. We can most definitely conclude, however, that modern cynicism is detrimental. In one 2009 study, researchers examining negative cynical attitudes found that people who scored high in this characteristic on a personality test were roughly five times more likely to suffer from depression later in life. In other words, that smirking 25-year-old is at elevated risk of turning into a depressed 44-year-old.

Modern cynics also suffer poorer health than others. In 1991, researchers studying middle-aged men found that a cynical outlook significantly increased the odds of death from both cancer and heart disease–possibly because the cynics consumed more alcohol and tobacco than the non-cynics. In one 2017 study on middle-aged Finnish men, high cynicism also predicted premature mortality. (Although both of these studies involved only men, nothing suggests that the results are gender-specific.)

Adding insult to injury, people tend not to respect cynics. Writing in the Journal of *Experimental Psychology: General in 2020*, psychologists found that cynical attitudes lead to being treated disrespectfully–possibly because cynics tend to show disrespect to others, leading to a vicious cycle. You won't be surprised to hear, then, that cynical people also earn less than others. Scholars writing in 2015 found that, even after correcting for gender, education, and age, the least cynical people saw an average monthly increase in income of about $300 over nine years. The most cynical saw no significant income increase at all. The authors explain this pattern by noting that cynics "are more likely to forgo valuable opportunities for cooperation and consequently less likely to reap the benefits of joint efforts and mutual help." In other words, being a misanthrope is costly.

Q1. What does the author imply by "What was satire then is ideology today"?

(a) The author implies that ancient ideas are becoming more mainstream in the modern world.
(b) The author implies that cynicism has become a "way of life" rather than a philosophical idea in the modern world.
(c) The author implies that people are becoming more and more cynical in the modern world.
(d) The author implies that cynicism is supposed to be a satire and not a "way of life."

Q2. What is the main issue being addressed in the passage?

(a) The author is trying to show how cynicism brings more harm than benefits in the modern world.
(b) The author is trying to show how the understanding of cynicism has changed over time.
(c) The author is trying to urge people to be less cynical and more cooperative.
(d) The author is trying to show how ancient people understood real meaning of cynicism.

Q3. Which of the following, if proven to be true, would align with author's thought process?

(a) Ancient cynics actually used cynicism to refuse conventional rules and question them.
(b) Cynicism evolved over time as a more refined concept.
(c) Cynical people tend to be more cautious than the less cynical ones.
(d) Modern day cynicism can be fruitful at times.

Q4. The author is most likely to agree with which of the following?

(a) Modern day cynics tend to embrace the non biased side of the concept of cynicism.
(b) Modern day cynics tend to be more suave in their approach of analysing philosophies.
(c) It is better to analyze policies and give it a thought, rather than rejecting them outright.
(d) Modern day cynics tend to learn a lot from their ancient counterparts.

Q5. The author is LEAST likely to say which of the following?

(a) Cynicism is definitely warranted in the modern world.
(b) Cynical people tend to hurt those around them.
(c) Cynicism is a wrongly interpreted concept in the modern world.
(d) Cynical people bring harm upon themselves too.

PASSAGE 2

Q 6-10. Read the following passage and answer the questions that follow.

MY DAD, when asked about his emotional state, is likely to say "hungry" or "cold," maybe "tired." Once, frustrated after being gently mocked for this kind of response, he asked–in all seriousness–if there was some list of feelings he could consult. This request has led, to his even greater frustration, to yet more gentle mocking. But he is far from alone in his wish for a catalog of emotions.

Perhaps the most famous emotional taxonomy is Paul Ekman's list of "universal basic emotions". Beginning in the 1960s, Ekman, a research psychologist, conducted cross-cultural studies aimed at demonstrating that certain emotions are universal–that is, that they are inborn rather than learned, consistent across cultures and contexts. His work built on Charles Darwin's 1872 book, The Expression of Emotions in Man and Animals, which argued that emotional expressions were vestiges of once-useful evolutionary behaviors (scowling when angry, for instance, may be a vestige of the impulse to curl the lips and bare fangs).

Ekman's most famous experiments involved showing people from different cultures photos of faces and asking the participants to match each facial expression to an emotion. Based on this research, he argued that there are six distinct universal basic emotions–anger, surprise, disgust, happiness, fear and sadness. (Ekman has sometimes suggested that there are seven basic emotions, adding contempt, and many who support his general framework have suggested that there are five, removing surprise; other groups of researchers building on his initial research have proposed that there are as many as 15 or 27). In the popular imagination–and with Ekman's encouragement–these six so-called "basic emotions" have often been interpreted as representing the entirety of emotional experience.

Ekman's work was controversial from the start. In an essay on his trajectory as a researcher, he recounts that during a presentation of his research at the American Anthropological Association in the late 1960s, a colleague shouted that he was a fascist. His research, many argue, does not make space for the role of cultural differences and learned behavior, and it leans too heavily on the idea of biology as destiny; his suggestion that interior states can be easily read through the face has traces of phrenology. Worryingly, this latter concern has affected Ekman's work with the TSA, the Department of Defense, and other institutions, where his theory is incorporated into AI models and surveillance techniques–many of which have demonstrable racial biases. His research has also been criticized on methodological grounds: his studies adopted a forced-choice paradigm, where participants were given limited words and limited photos to match. The photos used were the ones Ekman personally felt best displayed each of his "basic emotions" while more ambiguous expressions were excluded, and these images were of simulated emotional expressions rather than authentic emotional experience.

More recently, the Museum of Contemporary Emotions–a project of the Finnish government's Finland Forward pandemic communications initiative–picked up Ekman's work as its scaffolding. The Museum, really an interactive website, is a kind of digital archive of experience during the Covid-19 pandemic, styled with the sans-serif aesthetics of a direct-to-consumer startup and the haunting, echoing soundtrack of a post-apocalyptic Catholic Mass. The events of the pandemic are positioned on a timeline–the discovery of the virus, the toilet paper panic, the ban on events, and so on–and a click on any one of them leads to recorded testimony from Finns about the emotions they experienced at that time, along with data visualizations and quick facts (for instance: "oven-baked dishes were popular during the pandemic"). Each event is also assigned a "dominant fundamental feeling" drawn from Ekman's six. Remote work is identified with surprise. Coronavirus testing: fear. An anti-racism rally: joy.

The Museum's vision of emotional life is one in which, at any moment, an individual has a "dominant fundamental feeling" of joy, sadness, fear, anger, surprise, or disgust. This model permits some minimal nuance–the Museum allows that, for instance, "when your dominant fundamental feeling is anger, you may feel betrayed, critical, belittling, irritated, humiliated, jealous, or bitter." But the framing makes clear that it is ultimately (and often nonsensically–is "humiliated," for instance, more angry than sad? Was the dominant feeling of the anti-racism protests really joy?) dedicated to the idea that all emotional experiences can be distilled down to one of a finite number of basic emotions.

Q6. What is the author trying to bring out via the line "MY DAD, when asked about his emotional state, is likely to say "hungry" or "cold," maybe "tired."?

(a) The author is trying to bring out how limited human are in their way of expressing their emotions.

(b) The author is trying to show how humans find it almost impossible to express their emotions.

(c) The author is trying to bring out how difficult it is to understand someone's emotional state.

(d) The author is trying to shed light on emotional state of modern humans.

Q7. Ekman is most likely to AGREE with which of the following?

A. Emotions are more of a learned state than an inborn characteristic.

B. Emotions came to humans as a part of the process of evolution.

C. Emotions are universal across the globe.

(a) A and B

(b) B and C

(c) A and C

(d) A, B and C

Q8. Which of the following can be DEFINITELY inferred from the passage?

(a) Ekman's concepts have not been regularly criticized by his contemporaries.

(b) Ekman's theories may be controversial but are widely accepted.

(c) Ekman's theories are yet to be accepted by the larger scientist community.

(d) Ekman was only a widely renowned researcher.

Q9. Which of the following is NOT TRUE regarding Ekman's theories?

(a) Ekman tended to bring out the universality of human emotions.

(b) Ekman's experiments were more from his own perspective rather than different perspectives.

(c) Ekman's theories do not incorporate racism.

(d) Ekman has sometimes suggested that there are seven basic emotions.

Q10. The source of the passage is most likely:

(a) A research journal

(b) A personal blog

(c) An article from a magazine

(d) A book on scientific discoveries

Passage 3

Q 11-15. Read the following passage and answer the questions that follow.

WE ARE IN the throes of a pandemic. Not the pandemic that requires masks to cover our mouths, mind you, but the pandemic that requires masks to cover our motives. According to a recent headline in The Hill, a "Pandemic of Hyper-Hypocrisy is Infecting American Politics." This is hardly surprising when headlines either announce "Hypocrisy, thy name is GOP" or affirm that "Democrats' hypocrisy is Now Impossible to Ignore."

While statistics help us measure the magnitude of the coronavirus pandemic, they are less able to gauge our current outbreak of hypocrisy. Nevertheless, if public trust is the first casualty of the hypocrisy, we have reason to worry. Since the late 1950s, when three-quarters of Americans trusted the government, the percentage has cratered: under one quarter of Americans still expect our elected officials to do the right thing. Another casualty is political moderation, a position that many in both camps see as at best complacent and at worst complicit. Whereas compromise was once considered a civic value, most Americans now value it only when the compromises come entirely from the other side.

While our predicament seems dire, it is not particularly new. Indeed, it would appear déjà vu to Jean-Baptiste Poquelin, an actor (in every sense of the word) in an earlier age of equally great political extremes.

Today, France is celebrating Poquelin's 400th anniversary. Christened in Paris on January 15, 1622, he is known to the world by his pen and stage name, Molière. One of France's greatest playwrights, Molière is best known for his many comedies, which are replete with characters who embody the same foibles we spend our lives tripping over today: vanity, envy, misanthropy, and, yes, hypocrisy.

During his lifetime, Molière's most controversial and most successful comedy was Tartuffe, or The Impostor. The eponymous villain, Tartuffe, is the most scurrilous of scammers. Unburdened by true Christian faith, he nevertheless makes himself indispensable to Orgon, a wealthy and pious Parisian, by pretending to be a dévot: a member of an extremist and ultra-Catholic movement whose prominence and power reached as far as the court of Louis XIV. The problem with the dévots is that they harbored not just true believers, who sought to impose their faith on others, but also phony true believers, who rode the movement for social and financial gain.

The vrai and faux true believers made life difficult not just for the young and untried king, but also for Molière, as both learned when Tartuffe was first performed in 1664. In high dudgeon, both the religious fanatics and phonies forced Louis to annul its public opening. It was only after Molière's petition to Louis, in which he denounced the "tartuffes [who] have underhandedly had the cunning to get themselves into Your Majesty's good graces," that the king allowed the show to go on five years later.

Perhaps Louis saw himself in the character of Orgon. Tartuffe's con is obvious to everyone in Orgon's household – his brother-in-law Cléante, his wife Elmire, his children Damis and Mariane, and his servant Dorine – except to Orgon's mother and the wealthy Orgon himself. Blinded by Tartuffe's act, he insists, in Richard Wilbur's nonpareil translation, that there has "been no loftier soul since time began./He is a man who ... a man who ... an excellent man./To keep his precepts is to be reborn,/And view this dunghill of a world with scorn."

As with most dupes, so too with Orgon: if he's in for a dime, he's in for a dollar. All of his dollars: Orgon promises Tartuffe not just the hand and dowry of his daughter Mariane, but also his entire estate. While Mariane is left wordless, not so Cléante. "There's a vast difference, so it seems to me," he tells Orgon, "Between true piety and hypocrisy." When Orgon remains unmoved, Cléante pleads, "How do you fail to see it, may I ask?/Is not a face quite different from a mask?"

But to no avail. Tartuffe is too skilled a wearer of masks, Orgon too ripe a sucker. Of course, Cléante is outraged by Tartuffe's success, but so are we. Why? How is it that la tartufferie – a term now used interchangeably with hypocrisy – makes us bristle so?

Q11. "Perhaps Louis saw himself in the character of Orgon." Why would Louis do so?

(a) Because Louis had been punished by people close to him.

(b) Because Louis could identify himself only with the wealthy Orgon rather than other poor characters of the play.

(c) Because Moliere had made Louis believe so and Louis felt that he might have been tricked.

(d) Because Louis admired Orgon's character the most.

Q12. The author would AGREE with which of the following?

(a) People have become more double faced and masked in the present day world as compared to 1900s.

(b) Moliere was the best known comedian of his time.

(c) Louis could not stand against popular public opinion.

(d) Poquelin was the best known comedian of his time.

Q13. Which of the following aptly describes the author's attitude towards Poquelin?

(a) He admires Poquelin for his understanding of societal evils.

(b) He admires Poquelin for being a great playwright.

(c) He condones Poquelin for his interpretation of societal evils.

(d) Nothing can be definitely concluded on the basis of the passage.

Q14. Which of the following, if falsified, is in line with author's views?

(a) People tend to trust their elected leaders more as they have been continuously for their well-being.
(b) Hypocrisy has become a widely accepted phenomenon.
(c) People have become more and more aware of their hypocritical nature.
(d) People tend to not to compromise while expecting others to compromise for them.

Q15. Choose a suitable title for the passage.

(a) The Era of Hypocrisy
(b) "Is Not a Face Quite Different from a Mask?": Molière at 400
(c) The excellence of Moliere
(d) Story of Orgon and Tartuffe

TEST 2

PASSAGE 1

Q 1-5. Read the following passage and answer the questions that follow.

When it comes to texting, the period, full stop, point - whatever you call it - has been getting a lot of attention. People have begun noticing slight changes to the way our smallest punctuation mark is deployed, from declarations that it's going out of style to claims that it's becoming angry.

What they're actually noticing is written language becoming more flexible, with texting possessing its own set of stylistic norms (sometimes informally called "textspeak" or "textese").

The period is merely one example of this shift, a change that has opened up new possibilities for communicating with written language. Just as we have different styles of speaking in different situations, so do we have context-dependent styles of writing.

Though periods can still signal the end of a sentence in a text message, many users will omit them (especially if the message is only one sentence long). This tendency now subtly influences how we interpret them.

Because text messaging is a conversation that involves a lot of back-and-forth, people add fillers as a way to mimic spoken language. We see this with the increased use of ellipses, which can invite the recipient to continue the conversation. The period is the opposite of that - a definitive stop that signals, as linguistics professor Mark Liberman has explained, "This is final, this is the end of the discussion." For some, this can appear angry or standoffish.

Earlier this year, psychologist Danielle Gunraj tested how people perceived one-sentence text messages that used a period at the end of the sentence. Participants thought these text messages were more insincere than those that didn't have a period. But when the researchers then tested the same messages in handwritten notes, they found that the use of a period didn't influence how the messages were perceived.

In a 2007 study by linguists Naomi Baron and Rich Ling, multi-sentence text messages often had punctuation to indicate where the sentences stopped, but only 29 percent of these texts had punctuation at the very end of the message. The reason, Baron and Ling explain, is that "the act of sending a message coincides with sentence-final punctuation." But of all the things to feel when seeing a period at the end of a text message - why insincerity?

The answer could have something to do with a term used by linguist John J. Gumperz: "situational code-switching," which is when we change how we talk depending on where we are, who we're talking to or how we're communicating.

A common example is the way we talk in a job interview versus at a bar with friends. Typically, a speaker will use much more formal language in an interview than when hanging out with peers. If you talked to your friends the same way you talked during a job interview, it would probably give a stilted, distant feeling to the conversation.

Scholars originally investigated situational code-switching in spoken language because spoken language was used in both casual and formal settings. In the past, written language was almost always tinged with a level of formality because it was associated with permanence in books and written documents.

However, now that text messaging and social media have given their users an outlet for casual written language, differences between writing styles can be seen.

The use of the period is one example of situational code-switching: When using one in a text message, it's perceived as overly formal. So when you end your text with a period, it can come across as insincere or awkward, just like using formal spoken language in a casual setting like a bar.

Another example of language change in casual written forms is the repetition of letters. Communication scholar Erika Darics has observed that the repetition of letters or punctuation marks adds intensity to messages ("stopppp!!!"). She writes that this creates "a display of informality through using a relaxed writing style."

Linguist Deborah Tannen described a similar phenomenon, noting that repeated exclamation points in a message can convey a sincere tone, like in the following text message:

"JACKIE I AM SO SO SO SORRY! I thought you were behind us in the cab and then I saw you weren't!!!!! I feel soooooooo bad! Catch another cab and ill pay for it for youuuuu".

Q1. What is "situational code-switching" as per the passage?

(a) Different interpretations of the same text in different mediums.
(b) Different interpretations of the same text as the writing style changes.
(c) Different interpretations of text according to change in punctuations.
(d) Different interpretations of the same text by different people.

Q2. Which of the following is TRUE as per the passage?

(a) People tend to use punctuations only when writing formal texts.
(b) Written language is now a days always tinged with formality.
(c) Ellipses indicate that the sender wants to continue the conversation.
(d) Both (b) and (c).

Q3. It can be inferred from the passage that:

(a) Text language is becoming very similar to how we speak.
(b) A distant friend would definitely use formal language with friends.
(c) Period at the end of a sentence always indicates insincerity.
(d) Using repetitive letters may not be sincere.

Q4. What is the main idea of the passage?

(a) To comment on the sudden popularity of "textspeak".
(b) To comment on changing written language especially in the context of texting.
(c) To comment on the changing style of spoken language.
(d) Both (b) and (c).

Q5. Which of the following situations is most likely to happen as per the passage?

(a) Someone writing single sentence texts is being formal.
(b) Someone who writes multiple sentences in a text is being formal.
(c) Someone writing single sentence in a text is being insincere.
(d) Cannot be determined from the passage

PASSAGE 2

Q 6-10. Read the following passage and answer the questions that follow:

There is a recognizable arc to the type of literary career that most interested the public in the days when art was king, and books and magazines were primary means of distributing new fashions, fads, and ideas. First, a blaze of youthful fame, which contained equal portions of originality, promise, and messiness/failure. Second, the construction of a persona around the work, one that could be drawn with clear-enough cartoonlike lines to launch a recognizable character. Third, the deployment of that character in public controversies and soap operas, through the manipulative efforts of bored editors and needy feature writers, with the connivance of the author himself or herself. Fourth, the use of the public stage to launch works that might appeal to a large, global audience, and whose success or failure would themselves create a kind of news; draw attention to a new style, fad, or cause; or possibly launch a television series or an Oscar-winning film from Miramax. Fifth, death by drug overdose, or heart attack, or diabetes, or marriage to a famous musician, guru, movie star, or chef; those who survive this passage can look forward to the cratering of their inflated reputations under the accumulated weight of negative reviews generated by decades of extra-literary distraction, or by the resentments of their less talented peers. Sixth, the realization, impelled by surviving one of the preceding events, that life is short, that all that really matters is the work on the page; for good or for ill, the years spent moving through stages 1-5 of the fame cycle are gone forever. Seventh, a redevotion to the art of one's youth, which is either made deeper or more complicated and difficult by the fact that one is no longer young or even recognizably the same person. Eighth, death, followed by disappearance from the shelves of all but the most remote bookstores and libraries while awaiting the final judgment of the Gods.

It's fun to make lists like this. Yet the main point here in America is that the world depicted above no longer exists except as a parody of something that was once real and can now be sold to trust-fund suckers and crazed midlevel careerists who aren't yet in on the joke, or never got the joke. People, there is no such thing as "the New York literary scene"; no actual writers under the age of 75 can afford to live in New York City, nor do they have any desire to live there. The secret of real achievement in the arts, as someone wise once told me in my youth, is low overhead.

Politics, public boredom, the destruction of gatekeeper institutions, and the bad-faith gamification, expansion, and radical toxification and dumbing-down of the so-called public sphere have put an end to the arts in America, at least for now. What's left is a gigantic, out-of-touch, stale bureaucracy, staffed by people who might, in a different age, have worked at the U.S. Department of Agriculture or in a provincial department store. No one actually gives a crap about the latest novels of Jonathan Lethem and Jonathan Franzen; they're white men on the public dole who are scared to death of being canceled. The last time anyone wrote a "novel that mattered" was 2001. Writers are people who teach in "creative writing" departments; their racket is to sell the coffin odors of the New York literary scene of 40 and 50 years ago to bright-eyed provincials and the children of new immigrants whose parents can somehow afford to pay $60,000 or $70,000 a year. The magazines that once introduced Vladimir Nabokov, J.D. Salinger, and V.S. Naipaul to the world are simply broke; no one reads them or advertises in them; their subscribers are mostly dead; they are ghost ships for trust-fund kids and suckers on starvation wages, the type of people who might buy a steamboat ticket to Paris to see Josephine Baker dance. They would never dream of publishing right-wing cranks like Joan Didion. The anti-woke racket is nearly as depressing, in its muddled thinking, pleas for elite approval, careerist maneuverings, and the neglect of aesthetics. Unless you are Ibram Kendi, there is no such thing as a "literary career" in America anymore.

Which brings me to my friend Bernard-Henri Lévy, otherwise known to his admirers and detractors by his stage-name BHL. Of all my friends, Bernard-Henri has the greatest appetite for fame, and the least interest in himself. BHL is a character that he created, using intelligence, cunning, and art. It is a warrior's mask containing elements of himself, and other elements drawn from films, books, and childhood fantasies.

Bernard-Henri–the creator of the famous BHL–has survived the various stages of the fame cycle, finding himself now somewhat reluctantly posed between stages 6 and 7. He is not as devastatingly handsome in a plain white shirt as he once was, but his facilities are remarkably intact. In his early 70s, he is like a character in a modern version of an Albert Cohen novel co-authored perhaps by Michel Houellebecq.

Q6. What does the first paragraph, "There is a recognizable arc...." define?

(a) It defines the life of a famous artist who belonged to New York.
(b) It defines the life of almost all artists belonging to New York.
(c) It defines the perception of an artist's life and career in New York as was in earlier times.
(d) It defines the perception of an artist's life.

Q7. What is the tone of the author in the passage?

(a) Descriptive
(b) Cynical
(c) Sarcastic
(d) Frustrated

Q8. Which of the following can be definitely understood from the passage?

A. Modern day artists cannot afford staying in New York.
B. Actual writers and artists are busy making a living rather than focussing on the art.
C. Inflation has caused a huge dent in creative New York.

(a) A and B
(b) B and C
(c) A and C
(d) A, B and C

Q9. Which of the following, if proven to be true, would go against author's beliefs?

(a) A recent survey found that majority of America's young artists stay in cities near New York but not in actual New York city.
(b) Modern day artists are less likely to be known for their name but more for their art.
(c) Modern day artists are more likely to be known for their name but less for their art.
(d) Young artists are very well supported by the government of USA.

Q10. What is the main issue being addressed in the passage?

(a) To bring out the state of literature and art in New York and USA at large.
(b) To bring out the career arc of an artist in New York.
(c) To comment on the relevance of New York in USA's literary landscape.
(d) To bring out the genius of Bernard-Henri Lévy.

PASSAGE 3

Q 11-14. Read the following passage and answer the questions that follow.

In Philip K Dick's classic science fiction novel *Ubik*, one of the main characters, Runciter, is in charge of assembling a team of individuals called "inertials." The hope is that they will counteract the power of "precogs" and "telepaths," recruited by corporations to carry out espionage and other nefarious activities. Each inertial is a superstar with a unique talent - but Runciter's concern is their collective power.

Interest in collective behaviour is not new. It's been the research subject of organisation scholars, anthropologists, economists, ethologists studying group-living animals and evolutionary biologists interested in the evolution of cooperation. And, of course, it's the chief occupation of coaches and managers building teams across a wide range of sports. Although many of us believe a team is more than just the sum of its outstanding individual performers, this kind of simple-minded thinking still dominates recruitment and team assembly in sports, finance, academia and other settings.

Part of the reason why recruiters and others resort to going after the best players rather than building the best team is that it remains unclear what other factors contribute to team greatness, and how to quantify them. Moreover, simply recruiting the best players is fairly straightforward, and some analyses suggest this approach might even be the most reliable: as the sociologist Duncan Watts and colleagues argued, overall talent level is often the single best predictor of team performance. Yet we shouldn't be lured into thinking overall talent is the best predictor because it is the most important factor. It might be the best predictor because we're not yet good at capturing the nuance of collective dynamics. Hints that this could be the case come from studies such as that of the management scholar Satyam Mukherjee and colleagues, in which they found that prior shared success can predict performance above and beyond what would be expected from the group's composition and talent.

These seemingly at-odds results raise the question: how does a collective work exactly? When is it more than the sum of its parts? The increasing availability of data on individual decision-making across the social sciences, coupled with how complexity science is improving our understanding of the mechanics of group performance, are changing what's possible. Some of the questions that can now be answered include how a team synchronises, when contributions are synergistic as opposed to additive, and whether it's the players' skill or the strategies they use that's more important. Before we get to promising future directions, though, it's worth considering the existing space of ideas about what makes a good team, as well as some scenarios suggesting greater nuance is required.

In his book *The Captain Class* (2017), Sam Walker - deputy editor for enterprise at The Wall Street Journal - argues that a key to team performance is leadership, defined not by charisma but by the ability to resolve conflict and improve morale behind the scenes. The anthropologist Ruth Benedict proposed culture as a factor in human performance, writing in *Patterns of Culture* (1934):

No individual can arrive even at the threshold of his potentialities without a culture in which he participates. Conversely, no civilisation has in it any element which in the last analysis is not the contribution of an individual.

Michael Lombardi, a former executive at the US National Football League, echoes Benedict's point in his book *Gridiron Genius* (2018). Lombardi proposes that the New England Patriots' dynasty, and the success of their quarterback Tom Brady and coach Bill Belichick, are due in large part to meticulous micromanagement of every detail of recruitment, scheduling, training and play. In the case of the Patriots and other football dynasties such as Nick Saban's Alabama teams, this focus on institutions and process is so pronounced as to give the impression that players could be swapped in or out, with little change to outcomes.

Emphasis on leadership, culture, process over outcome, and attention to detail at all scales might seem obvious. Yet these strategies for optimising team performance depart strongly from the common assumption that the key to making a great team is assembling the best players. What is it about team performance that makes it so hard to reconcile these positions?

Q11. Choose a suitable summary for the passage.

(a) A team with talented players is a super -team.

(b) A team is more than just the sum of talents of its players.

(c) It's the synergy which is important and not the individuals.

(d) It is the individual who is important and not synergy.

Q12. If the author would be recruiting for a team, he would look for:

A. Talents of the individual

B. Behavioral similarity of individuals

C. Prior shared success

(a) A and B

(b) B and C

(c) A and C

(d) A, B and C

Q13. Which of the following is TRUE as per the passage?

(a) Recruiters look at the combined talent of the team rather than that of an individual.

(b) It is difficult to quantify synergy in team members.

(c) Prior shared success is not a useful indicator for forecasting future success

(d) Both (a) and (b).

Q14. Which of the following, if proven to be false, would be against the author's views?

(a) It has been found in a study that team with more star players are more likely to win important championships.

(b) It has been found in a study that team with more star players are less likely to win important championships.

(c) It has been found in a study that team with less star players more likely to win important championships.

(d) None of the above.

TEST 3

PASSAGE 1

Q 1-5. Read the following passage and answer the questions that follow.

On 4 July, the vice-chancellor and the executive council of Jadavpur University (JU), Kolkata, voted to do away with the existing Faculty of Arts admission tests, and replace them with a marks-based admission system. They also stated that they felt JU's teachers should not be involved in the admission process in any capacity.

They failed to answer questions as to why they thought so, or whether any wrongdoing had been discovered in the existing process. This was after they had advertised the test dates for this year on the website and collected fees from over 17,000 candidates. They also failed to answer why they think school-leaving marks are a better yardstick of merit than a free and fair admission test.

What kind of disciplines are the humanities? What are they for? How should their insights and data be used, by whom and for whose benefit? All over the world, State-funded humanities research and teaching are being shut down. We saw the research go, and now the teaching is breaking down as well.

The tide of multiple choice questions, test paper 'patterns', optical machine recognition and quantitative evaluation has overwhelmed most spaces where people can teach youngsters how to see context and nuance. Humanities teachers are no longer rewarded, or even praised, for giving students the skills they need to access the human fabric of knowledge, the terrain of the imagination that constructs the narratives with which we make sense of the world. And those narratives include everything from our deepest personal memories of love and happiness to the most advanced theories of quantum mechanics.

So, why is there an agenda to devalue humanities education? Who benefits from such an agenda? Who loses when the State-funded system scraps the humanities altogether to churn out tech students with practical skills and no understanding of the context in which they are employed, or the resource flows of the world they inhabit?

If state-funded education abandons the humanities, as the JU case seems to indicate, then meritorious students who come from weaker backgrounds will no longer have access to the theories and data that make sense of the human world. They will not be taught how societies are constituted and controlled, how the human mind functions, how people make choices, and how those choices affect their lives, how institutions are set up and managed, and what effect they have on people's bodies and souls. They will not know what constitutes gender or class, or how these ideas relate to their own lives. Furthermore, they will be taught not to care about these questions. All this, while we utter homilies about a "knowledge economy" and "demographic dividend."

Like other teachers, I have watched the slow crumble of humanities education under the pressures of "modernisation." I have seen senior academics having to justify themselves before committees because they write one book every three years, not 60 articles every year. I have seen syllabi torn apart because they were too 'hard' for their target studentship, although, in fact, they were just inconvenient for the operators of tutorial homes.

I have seen perfectly good academic procedures thrown in the dustbin because they did not please the people in power. And now I'm seeing the hope taken away from a generation of brilliant oddballs whom I will now never get a chance to meet, let alone teach.

Q1. What is the main concern of the author in the passage?

(a) To highlight the deficiencies in Indian education system.
(b) To highlight how the emphasis on analytical mindset is crushing a creative mindset.
(c) To highlight the importance of humanities.
(d) To bring out the impact of deficiencies of Indian education system.

Q2. Which of the following can be inferred from the passage?

(a) The author considers marks scored in classes before college to be irrelevant.
(b) The author thinks that technical mindset is not important.
(c) The author thinks that we need to understand our environment, society and midset.
(d) The author considers that marks are not at all a useful parameter to judge anyone at all.

Q3. Which of the following is TRUE as per the passage?

A. Frequency of published work has become more important than the content of published work.
B. Academics are asked to be flexible according to the needs of the student and private tutors.
C. Private tuitions are not very prevalent.

(a) Only A
(b) A and B
(c) B and C
(d) A, B and C

Q4. As per the passage, Faculty of Arts is concerned with teaching:

A. Students how to be great artists
B. Students about their environment/surroundings that make sense of the human world
C. Students the theories of data management

(a) Only A
(b) Only B
(c) A and B
(d) B and C

Q5. Choose a suitable title for the passage.
(a) Rise of Technology
(b) Fall of Humanities
(c) Loss of Knowledge of self
(d) Where are we headed?

PASSAGE 2

Q 6-10. Read the following passage and answer the questions that follow.

Of all the attempts to pinpoint the origin of modernity–an exercise of which modernity never tires–my favorite begins with medieval monks. According to this account, it was the Benedictines who came up with the idea that it was possible to do the same thing, at the same time, every day. Although time was still widely regarded as fluid and coterminous with eternity, the monastery was governed by the rhythms of that most modern instrument: the clock. The monks rose together, ate together, and prayed together, starting and stopping each task at the appointed canonical hour. In time, their obsession with order seeped into the world at large. The tradesmen and merchants in town heard the monastery bells ring out eight times a day and began to synchronize their daily tasks to their rhythm. The butcher picked up his cleaver at Prime and set it down for lunch at None. Clerks hustled to finish their work by Vespers. Time became currency, something that could be spent or saved, and people increasingly turned to machines to make life more efficient. By the dawn of the Industrial Revolution, the religious impulse behind these regimens had been long forgotten. The monastery gave way to the factory. Ritual dissolved into routine.

This is, at any rate, the story that Lewis Mumford tells in his 1934 book Technics and Civilization, which argues that monasteries "helped to give human enterprise the regular collective beat and rhythm of the machine." Contemporary medievalists have come to doubt this tidy account, but I have always liked the picture it paints, as though the life of that era were an enormous astronomical clock with its automaton figures (the friar, the cobbler, the weaver) clicking along their tracks to the same relentless metronome. I've thought of it more than once while plodding along my own daily course, rising at six to prepare the same breakfast every morning (oatmeal, coffee), leaving at seven to embark on the route I have walked for the past ten years, one that winds around the lake and is timed precisely (fifty minutes) so that I can sit down at my desk by eight. I work from home, so I have no co-workers or time card to register my punctuality–though I suppose you could look at my browsing history, which bears the record of a life so deeply routinized that even my screen time falls into a discernible pattern: the email log-in at the top of each hour, the thirty minutes allotted to social media during lunch.

Repetition is a component of all ascetic traditions, and I like to think that my own habits constitute something like a spiritual discipline. My nature bends toward listlessness and disorder. Resolving to do the same thing each day, at the same time, has given my life a center, insulating me from the siren song of novelty and distraction that has caused me so much unhappiness in the past. I live a monotonous life, which is not to say a tedious one. (I believe, with Rilke, that those who find life dull are not poet enough to call forth its riches.) And I imagine that these tightly circumscribed days are radiating, with each turn of the circle, into widening arcs, amounting to a life whose ties are deeper, whose direction is more certain.

But perhaps this is merely so much self-justification. It does not escape me that what I've been describing as a spiritual discipline bears an uncomfortable resemblance to the cruder ethos of "life hacking." Perhaps I am no different from those data fetishists in Silicon Valley who refer to Benjamin Franklin as a "productivity master," and speak of free time as a "release valve". It is difficult today to avoid the thought that we are becoming as rigid and inflexible as the machines that structure our lives. The New York Times columnist Kevin Roose calls this process "machine drift," arguing that it's degrading our humanity and making us professionally obsolete. "For years, the conventional wisdom has been that if machines were the future, we needed to become more like machines ourselves," he writes in his recent book *Futureproof: 9 Rules for Humans in the Age of Automation.* This wisdom, a relic of the Industrial Revolution, persists in our efforts to streamline and quantify our lives (tallying our steps, tracking our REM cycles), and is reinforced by our reliance on algorithms that corral us into making the same choices we've made in the past. The writer George Monbiot similarly considers repetition "dehumanizing," arguing that schools, with their rigid lessons and classroom regimes, are senselessly preparing children for life in a nineteenth-century factory. "In the future, if you want a job, you must be as unlike a machine as possible," he writes in the Guardian. In striving to be more efficient, these critics argue, we are ceding our true advantage over the artificial intelligence systems that are encroaching on so many lines of work. Instead of succumbing to repetitive habits, we should cultivate those qualities that make us most human–our flexibility and spontaneity, our ability to respond to surprises and learn new skills.

Q6. What does the poet imply by "I believe, with Rilke, that those who find life dull are not poet enough to call forth its riches"?

(a) Poets are able to find meaning in the mundaneness of routine life.
(b) Routine in life has its own advantages and does not bring boredom as is normally imagined by people who can't look beyond it.
(c) Only a few can enjoy a routine life.
(d) Poets make it easy for one to enjoy routine life.

Q7. What is "machine drift" as per the passage?

(a) It refers to the act of humans relying a lot on data science to "hack" their life.
(b) It refers to the act of humans relying a lot on machines to "hack" their life.
(c) It refers to the act of humans working in a routine manner and becoming more like "machines."
(d) It refers to the act of humans being professionally obsolete.

Q8. Which of the following is NOT a disadvantage of "machine drift" as per the passage?

(a) It makes humans more efficient.
(b) It makes us rigid.
(c) It makes humans less spontaneous.
(d) It makes humans less prone to surprises.

Q9. Which of the following is TRUE as per the passage?

A. It is widely accepted that monasteries led to the origin of "time" as a concept.
B. The author enjoys his "routine" life.
C. Machine drift is leading to a phenomenon of "dehumanizing."

(a) A and B
(b) B and C
(c) A and C
(d) A, B and C

Q10. The source of the passage most likely is:

(a) Personal blog
(b) Newspaper report
(c) Fiction book
(d) Travelogue

PASSAGE 3

Q 11-14. Read the following passage and answer the questions that follow.

"Wussies and pussies" - those are the only kinds of people who care about plagiarism, according to Bob Dylan. That was his response to an interviewer who asked him about some rather suspicious similarities between lyrics on his 2001 album Love and Theft (pun intended, perhaps?) and a Japanese true-crime book from the '90s. And it's not just the lyrics: a side-by-side comparison makes clear that the music of many of the songs on that record, and other Dylan albums, is nearly identical to that of some old blues numbers (and that's far from the only kind of plagiarism of which Dylan has been accused).

This kind of thing is "part of the folk tradition," Dylan said. "We all do it." And he's right, in a sense: art, and culture more generally, is a big, complex soup of ideas, any of which can be seized on at any time and amplified, altered or improved.

But musicians do still get in hot water for plagiarism - from other artists and their lawyers, if not the public (Dylan's lifting of musical ideas from long-dead bluesmen might explain why it's never been a big deal for him). George Harrison, Dylan's sometime collaborator, ended up embroiled in decades-long legal proceedings and paid damages of $2m in today's money after he accidentally borrowed the backbone of his song "My Sweet Lord" from "He's So Fine" by The Chiffons. There are similar examples from artists as throwaway as Robin Thicke (for plagiarising Marvin Gaye) or as acclaimed as Radiohead (plagiarising The Hollies) and Lana del Rey (plagiarising that same plagiarised Radiohead song).

So culture is both a freewheeling world where anyone steals anything from anyone - everything is a remix - and it has rules about who can copy what: there's a maddening inconsistency between what counts as plagiarism versus "quotation" or "influence" or "tribute," depending on the context (and let's not even get into the complicated world of musical sampling rights).

This is all rather different from my own field, academia. There's no "folk tradition" in universities, nor any ambiguity: you have to cite your sources, and if you don't you're in big trouble. Not only do professors put major efforts into deterring their students from copying each other's work, they themselves are under major pressure not to plagiarise in their published papers. A glance at the website Retraction Watch will show you that plagiarism frequently causes academic papers to be retracted from the literature, with the authors' reputations ruined. According to the University of Kentucky law professor Brian Frye:

A plagiarist is an academic pariah, a transgressor of the highest law of the profession, the embodiment of the "great deceiver," who leads everyone astray. [...] Plagiarism tarnishes the scholarship itself and leaves it forever suspect. If the purpose of scholarship is dowsing for truth, then the plagiarist is a liar who poisons the well from which everyone draws.

Although many would agree, you might have detected a tinge of sarcastic hyperbole - and indeed, in the quoted paper, Frye makes the contrarian argument that academics should stop caring at all about plagiarism. They shouldn't mind if people use their ideas, or even their exact words, without citing them; rules against plagiarism do the reader no favours and exist merely to shore up the ego of the author. "Academic plagiarism norms," Frye writes, "are primarily an inefficient and illegitimate form of extra-legal academic rent-seeking that should be ignored." And although he doesn't quite call those who disagree with him "wussies and pussies," he does disparagingly refer to the "plagiarism police," which includes anyone who tries to identify academic plagiarism and somehow punish the plagiarist.

You've got to respect the boldness of a position like this - an appeal to give academia its own Dylanesque borrowing tradition - even if you disagree. I do disagree, but before I tell you why, let me add another couple of pro-plagiarism arguments to buttress Frye's.

The first is that a more relaxed attitude to plagiarism is all part of the direction in which science is moving. These days, research increasingly emphasizes collaboration and teamwork (think Large Hadron Collider) and is far less a story of the lone genius making big discoveries in their secret lab. Some have even argued against the awarding of Nobel Prizes for science, since they can only be given to a small number of people, perpetuating the wrong idea of modern research. On this view, a focus on the individual ownership of ideas is an anachronism; a relic of how science used to be done.

Not only that, but there's a whole movement that's focused on wresting scientific findings from the grip of flawed, ego-driven academics and sharing them with the world - namely, the Open Science movement. The movement pushes for Open Data (sharing datasets online for anyone to use) and Open Access (making scientific papers accessible to all for free) - so we might wonder why it doesn't take a step further and argue for a system where concepts and theories, and even their verbal expressions, can be shared without worrying too much about who came up with them.

Q11. What is the issue being raised by the author in the passage?

(a) The author is differentiating between academic plagiarism and plagiarism in musical industry.
(b) The author is making a case for allowing plagiarim in academic arena and other domains.
(c) The author is is showing how plagiarism can be negative in certain fields.
(d) The author is showing how musical "inspiration" is actually a form of plagiarism.

Q12. Which of the following, if proven to be true, would jeopardize author's claim that plagiarism rules do more harm than less favor to academic field?

(a) It has been observed that people tend to research better when they can brainstorm together.
(b) It has been observed that one of the major motivation for top class research is having one's name associated to it.
(c) It has been observed that those who work alone tend to bring out average research results.
(d) It has been observed that there has been rampant plagiarim in medical journals in past few years.

Q13. Which of the following can be inferred regarding Frye in the passage?

(a) He is a well-known researcher in the academic arena.
(b) He is a man of contradicting views.
(c) The author is highly influenced by Frye's views.
(d) Frye may actually not be against plagiarism of academic ideas.

Q14. Which of the following is TRUE as per the passage?

(a) It is easy to plagiarise music of a dead musician.
(b) Musical plagiarism has little to no consequences.
(c) Musical plagiarism is a thing of the past.
(d) Academic plagiarism is very difficult to detect.

TEST 4

PASSAGE 1

Q 1-4. Read the following passage and answer the questions that follow.

To be on the internet today is to confront unsettling images–of war, climate change, humanitarian crises. Weird visuals crop up too. A YouTube algorithm provides me, for instance, with videos of a pimple-popping bonanza, or a series of videos in which young men eat glue. If disquieting sensory experiences abound in daily life, why go and seek more out? That question might be put to visitors of the Metropolitan Museum of Art's "Surrealism Beyond Borders" exhibition, a show filled with grotesque representations of political upheaval and private horror, but also with thrillingly odd and beautiful demonstrations of imagination.

The Met's exhibition aims to show a nonchronological and nongeographical view of surrealism, which became a transnational aesthetic phenomenon after being formally established in Paris in 1924 and spreading globally throughout the 20th century. Its founder, André Breton, defined surrealism as pure "psychic automatism"–in which the whims of the artist's unconscious direct their art making. Artists deployed surrealist techniques to process demons, both internal and external, but also to challenge conventional thinking (is a pipe really a pipe, as René Magritte famously queried?) and to express fantasies of artistic or political liberation. The Freudian-influenced idea was that by unlocking the unconscious, artists could assert the independence of their and their viewers' interior worlds. Radical nonconformism was a central tenet, which led some artists to use the form to challenge the pressures and constraints of oppressive regimes.

The Mozambican artist Malangatana Ngwenya (known professionally as Malangatana) adapted surrealist tradition in this very way. Through the '60s, as Malangatana participated in Mozambique's protracted war for independence from Portugal, the surrealist touch was vital–it allowed his images to be legibly brutal without being (perhaps incriminatingly) specific. At the Met, an untitled work from 1967 features a compressed pack of bright and feral, phantasmagoric beasts. The center figure is being eaten alive, blood dripping down his chest, his eyes wide in horror. Sounds of a feeding frenzy seem to buzz forth. The figures appear to be in a hellish prisonscape–fitting, as Malangatana himself was arrested only four years prior for revolutionary activities.

Like all good art, though, the image is broad in implication. It could suggest the exploitative ferocity of the Portuguese colonizers, ruthlessly thirsting for power, or the psychological state of Mozambicans, who were pushed into war with their oppressors (as Malangatana shared in a 2007 interview, during the fight for independence, Mozambicans had no way out). The varied readings of these wild figures add to the work's surreality. The pain in the painting transcends the specifics of its time and place. It rises to the level of archetype, representing a broader spectrum of violence and unease. If one feels an uncanny kinship with these demons, that is the exact kind of pact surrealism allows.

The form, however, can charm even as it unnerves, as is the case in the Puerto Rican artist Frances del Valle's Guerrero y Esfinge ("Warrior and Sphinx"), on view near the Malangatana. Del Valle's 1957 painting makes me laugh. In it, a huge, sphinxy figure kneels not just a little sexually on what appears to be a postapocalyptic Egyptian vista. The sphinx puppets a crouched, contorted warrior who has, apparently, just been made to pulverize his own head. The image is baffling, oddly divine. Its shapes are compellingly fluid. The massive sphinx looks both fetal and futuristic, and the warrior's ravaged head–a cluster of bright pink–resembles a knotted placenta. But the horrific is made gentle through del Valle's thick, luminescent paint. Pearly limbs recall unicorns, fairies. The softness of these textures, paired with the tyrannical posture of the sphinx, turns the painting into a cryptic yet alluring riddle. Del Valle reveals the perverse appeal in confronting the confounding.

Perhaps the most perplexing and amusing image in surrealism is Magritte's 1934 painting Le Viol ("The Rape"), housed permanently in Houston's Menil Collection. Like Malagatana's Untitled, it has the power to disturb, and yet, like del Valle's work, it evokes a strange sense of mirth as well. Le Viol is a figurative portrait of sorts–except with bare breasts in place of eyes, a belly button in place of a nose, and a frothily haired crotch where the mouth would be. Rendered in Magritte's careful hand, these parts become so expressive that the nipples seem to squint, the belly button seems to breathe, the sex seems to smile. If a viewer laughs, they laugh not just at the sudden liveliness of these features. Instead, they may also be responding to a dissonant synthesis: the absurdity of the image paired with the declarative violence of the title, and the utter seriousness of the painting method. In Le Viol, each brushstroke is made with painstaking deliberation, resulting in a weighty stillness that calls to mind the Mona Lisa.

Q1. What is the "main idea" of the passage?

(a) The passage highlights how "surrealism" has changed over time.
(b) The passage highlights how "surrealism" brings out grotesque art work.
(c) The passage brings out how "surrealism" has produced unnerving and disturbing but appealing work.
(d) The passage brings out how artists use "surrealism" as an excuse to make grotesque work.

Q2. Which of the following is NOT a characteristic of "surreal" art?

A. It allows the artists to truly express their vices as well.
B. It is grotesquely attractive.
C. It allows the artist to appeal to the political heads for their mistakes.

(a) A and B
(b) B and C
(c) Only C
(d) Only B

Q3. What does the author imply by "If one feels an uncanny kinship with these demons, that is the exact kind of pact surrealism allows."?

(a) Surrealism allows one to address one's own inner demons.
(b) Surrealism allows only the artists to address their internal and external demons.
(c) Surrealism allows the world to see the true "ugly" face it has.
(d) Surrealism allows the artists to show the ugly face of the world.

Q4. What is the tone of the author in the passage?

(a) Descriptive
(b) Analytical
(c) Cynical
(d) Admiring

Passage 2

Q 5-8. Read the following passage and answer the questions that follow.

Isaac Newton apocryphally discovered his second law - the one about gravity - after an apple fell on his head. Much experimentation and data analysis later, he realised there was a fundamental relationship between force, mass and acceleration. He formulated a theory to describe that relationship - one that could be expressed as an equation, F = ma - and used it to predict the behaviour of objects other than apples. His predictions turned out to be right (if not always precise enough for those who came later).

Contrast how science is increasingly done today. Facebook's machine learning tools predict your preferences better than any psychologist. AlphaFold, a program built by DeepMind, has produced the most accurate predictions yet of protein structures based on the amino acids they contain. Both are completely silent on why they work: why you prefer this or that information; why this sequence generates that structure.

You can't lift a curtain and peer into the mechanism. They offer up no explanation, no set of rules for converting this into that - no theory, in a word. They just work and do so well. We witness the social effects of Facebook's predictions daily. AlphaFold has yet to make its impact felt, but many are convinced it will change medicine.

Somewhere between Newton and Mark Zuckerberg, theory took a back seat. In 2008, Chris Anderson, the then editor-in-chief of Wired magazine, predicted its demise. So much data had accumulated, he argued, and computers were already so much better than us at finding relationships within it, that our theories were being exposed for what they were - oversimplifications of reality. Soon, the old scientific method - hypothesise, predict, test - would be relegated to the dustbin of history. We'd stop looking for the causes of things and be satisfied with correlations.

With the benefit of hindsight, we can say that what Anderson saw is true (he wasn't alone). The complexity that this wealth of data has revealed to us cannot be captured by theory as traditionally understood. "We have leapfrogged over our ability to even write the theories that are going to be useful for description," says computational neuroscientist Peter Dayan, director of the Max Planck Institute for Biological Cybernetics in Tübingen, Germany. "We don't even know what they would look like."

But Anderson's prediction of the end of theory looks to have been premature - or maybe his thesis was itself an oversimplification. There are several reasons why theory refuses to die, despite the successes of such theory-free prediction engines as Facebook and AlphaFold. All are illuminating, because they force us to ask: what's the best way to acquire knowledge and where does science go from here?

The first reason is that we've realised that artificial intelligences (AIs), particularly a form of machine learning called neural networks, which learn from data without having to be fed explicit instructions, are themselves fallible. Think of the prejudice that has been documented in Google's search engines and Amazon's hiring tools.

The second is that humans turn out to be deeply uncomfortable with theory-free science. We don't like dealing with a black box - we want to know why.

And third, there may still be plenty of theory of the traditional kind - that is, graspable by humans - that usefully explains much but has yet to be uncovered.

So theory isn't dead, yet, but it is changing - perhaps beyond recognition. "The theories that make sense when you have huge amounts of data look quite different from those that make sense when you have small amounts," says Tom Griffiths, a psychologist at Princeton University.

Griffiths has been using neural nets to help him improve on existing theories in his domain, which is human decision-making. A popular theory of how people make decisions when economic risk is involved is prospect theory, which was formulated by behavioural economists Daniel Kahneman and Amos Tversky in the 1970s (it later won Kahneman a Nobel prize). The idea at its core is that people are sometimes, but not always, rational.

In Science last June, Griffiths's group described how they trained a neural net on a vast dataset of decisions people took in 10,000 risky choice scenarios, then compared how accurately it predicted further decisions with respect to prospect theory. They found that prospect theory did pretty well, but the neural net showed its worth in highlighting where the theory broke down, that is, where its predictions failed.

These counter-examples were highly informative, Griffiths says, because they revealed more of the complexity that exists in real life. For example, humans are constantly weighing up probabilities based on incoming information, as prospect theory describes. But when there are too many competing probabilities for the brain to compute, they might switch to a different strategy - being guided by a rule of thumb, say - and a stockbroker's rule of thumb might not be the same as that of a teenage bitcoin trader, since it is drawn from different experiences.

Q5. Which of the following can be said about modern scientific methods according to the passage?

(a) They focus more on explaining "what is" than "why it is."

(b) They focus on explaining "what is" and "why it is."

(c) They draw from the past hypothesis and test them to bring accurate theories.

(d) Modern methods are definitely better than the old traditional methods.

Q6. What does the author imply by "Think of the prejudice that has been documented in Google's search engines and Amazon's hiring tools."?

(a) The author implies that almost all MNCs are using AI in their day to day operations.

(b) The author is highlighting that even AI is not always correct and has shortcomings.

(c) The author is highlighting how pervasive AI has become.

(d) The author is highlighting the edge AI has over old traditional methods.

Q7. Which of the following is correct according to the passage?

(a) The theory of science is dead.

(b) The theory of science is not considered the portal of knowledge.

(c) The theory of science is not dead, but it is changing beyond recognition.

(d) None of the above.

Q8. Choose a suitable title for the passage?

(a) Are we witnessing dawn of post-theory science?

(b) Dawn of post-material science

(c) Post-theory science

(d) The new science

PASSAGE 3

Q 9-12. Read the following passage and answer the questions that follow.

Back in the mid-1980s, long before the internet and low-cost flights shrunk the globe, travel writing was on a high. Legendary globetrotting scribes – Bruce Chatwin, Jan Morris, Redmond O'Hanlon, Dervla Murphy, Norman Lewis, Jonathan Raban among many others – were shifting copies in suitcase-fulls as readers devoured stories from across the globe first scribbled in battered old notebooks.

It was a bright, exciting time for the genre, with jet planes opening-up horizons and literary-minded travellers setting forth with eyes wide open in seek of adventure, encounters and stories, often in remote landscapes few back home would, in those days, dream of visiting. Off they went in search of tales to tell, returning with gripping accounts, be it of Chatwin's wanderings in the Australian Outback, Morris's meanderings across Europe, or Lewis's investigations in India and southeast Asia. In his review of Lewis's The Missionaries (1988) the novelist Graham Greene described Lewis, one of the highest flying travel writing stars, as "one of the best writers, not of any particular decade, but of our century."

It was during this heady period, when travel book sales were soaring, that the literary magazine Granta cannily published an issue dedicated to travel writing with contributions from most of the names mentioned above, with Gabriel Garcia Marquez, Paul Theroux, Colin Thubron, Saul Bellow, Martha Gellhorn and others thrown in. This issue of the magazine, Granta 10, edited by Bill Buford, seemed to capture the zeitgeist of enjoyment of this form of writing – of well-told despatches from dusty places with the sense of a narrator with a pen and the detached position of an outsider coming to the fore.

In his introduction, Buford tried to put his finger on why the public was so fascinated by these literary travel jaunts, suggesting that during a period of economic hardship, as there was in the early 1980s, "their tales of the exotic could be seen to bear the same value as that of books and film, say, during the depression: they provide arm-chair emancipation." What he was looking for from his contributors – whom he had to track down diligently as most were not at home (and it was not so easy to contact folk back then without the internet) – was "the sheer glee of story-telling, a narrative eloquence that situates them, with wonderful ambiguity, somewhere between fiction and fact."

This frank note of caution, as to the precise veracity of the stories told, added to the attraction rather than lessen it. Buford believed travel writing to be "the beggar of literary forms: it borrows from the memoir, reportage and, most important, the novel. It is, however, pre-eminently a narrative told in the first person, authenticated by lived experience."

Fast forward 37 years, and it is clear the genre that was once so widely admired and, even, fashionable – inspiring readers' trips and receiving warm widespread reviews – has plummeted in general appreciation. Travel sections in bookshops, as the academic and travel writing enthusiast Tim Hannigan recently noted in his book about the decline of this literary form, The Travel Writing Tribe, have been reduced to "three feet of guidebooks and celebrity jaunts." Meanwhile, travel books struggle to make the literary review sections of papers, the genre often being completely overlooked in the annual Christmas round-ups, for example.

What has happened? Because clearly something has. Ben Macintyre, The Times columnist, wrote in 2011, on the death of the travel scribe Patrick Leigh Fermor (whom Buford could not trace to commission for Granta 10 as he was uncontactable overseas), that he believed the simplicity and affordability of jetting round the globe has meant that old-style travel writing adventures have become outdated. "The world is simply too small, too fast, too well-trodden to admit of such leisurely, civilised wandering," he writes.

"The jumbo jet enabled any traveller to reach the four corners quickly and cheaply. The internet brought the world to your room. There are no spaces on the map to be filled in, no place that Google Earth has not seen already. The empty quarters and forbidden cities are full of tourists, and open to all."

A feeling of hopelessness about the whole place of travel writing in the literary landscape – with billions of people posting pictures of their cheap-and-cheerful travels on social media and, as Macintyre points out, the internet covering just about everywhere – seems to have descended. Instagram stars with iPhones and thousands of followers have replaced correspondents in crumpled jackets clutching dusty Moleskin notebooks. Live webcams stream shots of mountain tops, beaches and the African plains. Who needs a travel writer to tell you how things are?

Of course, there has been another factor, too. In The Travel Writing Tribe, Hannigan refers to a perceived "cultural appropriation" of privileged Westerners, often "very male, very white" and expensively educated turning up in countries and asking questions. The academic Charles Sugnet goes a step further, accusing the Chatwins and Therouxs of being "a highbrow version of the Banana Republic catalog... their baggage full of portable shards of colonialist discourse."

Q9. Why does Buford call travel writing "the beggar of literary forms"?

(a) Because he felt that travel writing could not follow a single genre.

(b) Because he felt that travel writing had qualities of fiction and fact as it borrowed its stories from various sources.

(c) Because he felt that travel writing lacked the substance that it should have.

(d) Because he felt that travel writing was difficult to check their accuracy.

Q10. Which of the following is NOT a reason for the decline in popularity of travel books?

(a) Increased accesibilty to far away places due to improved means of transportation.

(b) Availability of information on internet

(c) Excursions of people to far away places for "travel information."

(d) Lack of fascinating stories in the travel books.

Q11. Which of the following can be inferred regarding readers from the passage?

(a) People tend to relate more to fiction if some facts are stated.

(b) People tend to read about what they fantasize and don't have.

(c) People tend to relate more to fiction over facts.

(d) People avoid reading about what they fantasize and don't have.

Q12. The author of the passage is most likely:

(a) A poet

(b) A journalist

(c) A researcher

(d) Cannot be determined

TEST 5

PASSAGE 1

Q 1-4. Read the following passage and answer the questions that follow.

When I first saw 2001: A Space Odyssey (in 1968), the year 2001 seemed impossibly far out into the future. Now it's more than 2 decades in the past–back in the bygone neoliberal era. This recollection got me thinking about the new field of "progress studies."

It seems to me that human progress is very uneven:

Technology: Very rapid progress

Science: Rapid Progress

Public morals: Slow progress

Sports: Slow progress

Human personalities: No progress

Art: No progress

Ex ante, this is not what one might have expected. The human body doesn't change much from one generation to the next, but athletes are clearly better today than a few decades ago, and much better than a century ago.

On the other hand, art might have been expected to progress, as artists built on the achievements of their predecessors. And yet, as Tyler Cowen recently pointed out, the golden age of music was during the time of Bach, Mozart and Beethoven.

Tyler is much better informed on music than I am, and as you might expect his post contains a number of interesting explanations for historical trends in "classical" music. Nonetheless, I see a big flaw in Tyler's post. Tyler focuses on explanations specific to music, whereas it seems to me that the evolution of highbrow music is quite similar to the evolution of the other forms of art. I know more about the visual arts, so I'll focus there.

Just as the best music was created in earlier centuries, the same is true of the best paintings. And that's despite a huge increase in the global population, and a far greater increase in the number of humans with the economic resources to engage in painting as an art form. Why aren't there hundreds of great painters today? One response is that there are lots of great painters; it's just that we don't see it. After all, artistic taste is subjective.

But that merely pushes the question back one step. Why are composers like Mozart, Beethoven and Bach widely regarded as the greatest of all time? Why is it that in a 1985 survey of art experts by the Illustrated London News, only 2 of the 20 greatest paintings of all time were from the 20th century, one from the 18th century, and none at all from the 19th century? Yes, it can take a while to appreciate new art, but surely by now we can fully appreciate the art of the 18th century.

It also seems to me that art has changed in similar ways in a wide variety of fields. In some sense, modern art seems simpler and more idea-driven than the classics of the past, whereas older art involves a high level of craftsmanship. Doesn't Andy Warhol compare to Titian in much the same way that Philip Glass compares to Beethoven?

My preferred theory is that the field of art involves discovery, and those who arrive first have the greatest opportunity to make major discoveries. If Thomas Edison were born today, he'd have trouble inventing so many new home appliances. Instead, he might have gone into software or biotech. A talented young artist born in the 20th century might have decided that painting and photography were exhausted, and gone into filmmaking. (Kubrick is one such example; he started as a photographer.)

Filmmaking is a newer art form, and its golden age in the West and Japan was roughly 1920-1980 (and perhaps 1985-2005 in the rest of Asia.) Even poetry seems to be in decline. In 1820, Wordsworth, Coleridge, Keats, Shelley and Blake were all writing poetry. Are there 5 comparable living British poets?

So what does all of this mean? Are things getting better? I'm sort of agnostic on that question. I'd put about a 40 per cent probability on the hypothesis that utility is rising due to improvements in technology and public morality, and about a 60 per cent probability on the hypothesis that utility is not rising over time because people have the same sort of personality flaws, they had 100 years ago or 1000 years ago. I'm frequently surprised by the extent to which people can be depressed despite living conditions that are objectively far superior to those in the past. And I'm also surprised by the extent that (from a psychological perspective), life as portrayed in old novels seems very much like life as experienced today. In my own life, a huge increase in economic wellbeing doesn't seem to have made me happier than when I was younger. And young people today don't seem to be happier than I recall young people being in the 1960s.

Nonetheless, because there is a non-trivial probability that progress is making us happier (say 40 per cent), we should continue to strive for improvements in technology and public morals. I recall the pre-novocaine era, and I don't wish to go back even if hedonic set point considerations prevent the drug from making me happier. I also don't wish to go back to the pre-civil rights era.

Q1. What is the main issue that the author is trying to address via the passage?

(a) The author is trying to summarize the various aspects of progress that mankind has made.
(b) The author is trying to raise the issue of slow progress in art.
(c) The author is trying to compare the progress of science vis-à-vis art.
(d) The author is trying to criticize modern day art.

Q2. The author of the passage is most likely to AGREE with which of the following?

(a) The world of art is getting better with the progress.
(b) Different eras can have different forms of art.
(c) Progress always helps mankind live a better life.
(d) Modern forms of art are not as intriguing as were of 18th century.

Q3. Which of the following, if falsified, will jeopardize the author's claim that poetry is on a decline as an art form?

(a) As per the latest survey, the percentage of students enrolling for humanities has been on a rise.
(b) As per an observation, more poetry events took place this year in New York as compared to last year.
(c) A recent survey found that number of published poetry books and new poets are on a decline.
(d) A recent survey found that more and more poets are coming up in New York.

Q4. What is the tone of the author in the passage?

(a) Analytical
(b) Cynical
(c) Praiseworthy
(d) Sarcastic

Passage 2

Q 5-8. Read the following passage and answer the questions that follow.

A couple of years ago, at a massive conference of neuroscientists – 35,000 attendees, scores of sessions going at any given time – I wandered into a talk that I thought would be about consciousness but proved (wrong room) to be about grasshoppers and locusts. At the front of the room, a bug-obsessed neuroscientist named Steve Rogers was describing these two creatures – one elegant, modest, and well-mannered, the other a soccer hooligan.

The grasshopper, he noted, sports long legs and wings, walks low and slow, and dines discreetly in solitude. The locust scurries hurriedly and hoggishly on short, crooked legs and joins hungrily with others to form swarms that darken the sky and descend to chew the farmer's fields bare.

Related, yes, just as grasshoppers and crickets are. But even someone as insect-ignorant as I could see that the hopper and the locust were radically different animals – different species, doubtless, possibly different genera. So I was quite amazed when Rogers told us that grasshopper and locust are in fact the same species, even the same animal, and that, as Jekyll is Hyde, one can morph into the other at alarmingly short notice.

Not all grasshopper species, he explained (there are some 11,000), possess this morphing power; some always remain grasshoppers. But every locust was, and technically still is, a grasshopper – not a different species or subspecies, but a sort of hopper gone mad. If faced with clues that food might be scarce, such as hunger or crowding, certain grasshopper species can transform within days or even hours from their solitudinous hopper states to become part of a maniacally social locust scourge. They can also return quickly to their original form.

In the most infamous species, Schistocerca gregaria, the desert locust of Africa, the Middle East and Asia, these phase changes (as this morphing process is called) occur when crowding spurs a temporary spike in serotonin levels, which causes changes in gene expression so widespread and powerful they alter not just the hopper's behaviour but its appearance and form. Legs and wings shrink. Subtle camo colouring turns conspicuously garish. The brain grows to manage the animal's newly complicated social world, which includes the fact that, if a locust moves too slowly amid its million cousins, the cousins directly behind might eat it.

How does this happen? Does something happen to their genes? Yes, but – and here was the point of Rogers's talk – their genes don't actually change. That is, they don't mutate or in any way alter the genetic sequence or DNA. Nothing gets rewritten. Instead, this bug's DNA – the genetic book with millions of letters that form the instructions for building and operating a grasshopper – gets reread so that the very same book becomes the instructions for operating a locust. Even as one animal becomes the other, as Jekyll becomes Hyde, its genome stays unchanged. Same genome, same individual, but, I think we can all agree, quite a different beast.

Q5. A grasshopper changes into locust when:

A. It goes manic
B. It feels that there is not enough food around
C. The place of living becomes crowded.

(a) A and B
(b) B and C
(c) A and C
(d) A, B and C

Q6. What is the key difference between a grasshopper and locust?

(a) Locust tend to eat their own species whereas grasshoppers do not.
(b) Anatomy and behaviour of both the species is a bit different.
(c) Change in genetic material.
(d) One is more evolved than the other.

Q7. A locust generally has:

A. A grasshopper as its ancestor.
B. It has a color for camouflage.
C. Its legs and wings are smaller than that of a grasshopper.

(a) A and B
(b) B and C
(c) A and C
(d) A, B and C

Q8. Which of the following is TRUE as per the passage?

(a) Locusts stay clear of their species to prevent the danger of becoming a prey.
(b) All grasshoppers are destined to become locusts later.
(c) A locust may go back to becoming a grasshopper.
(d) There are more than 100,000 species of morphing grasshoppers.

Passage 3

Q 9-12. Read the following passage and answer the questions that follow.

What does it take to overthrow a dictator? Reflecting on this question in exile, Leon Trotsky wrote in *History of the Russian Revolution* (1930):

There is no doubt that the fate of every revolution at a certain point is decided by a break in the disposition of the army ... Thus in the streets and squares, by the bridges, at the barrack gates, is waged a ceaseless struggle - now dramatic, now unnoticeable - but always a desperate struggle, for the heart of the soldier.

However solitary the power of an authoritarian leader might seem, dictators never rule alone. When enforcers shirk duty or rebel, the regime collapses. When they stay loyal, the regime stands. Mass protests alone are never enough.

During the Tunisian revolution, the mutiny that ultimately led to the president Zine el Abidine Ben Ali's flight from power on 14 January 2011 started in an elite police unit exceptionally deployed to protect the Ministry of Interior against the biggest demonstration to date. When protesters marched on to the presidential palace, disobedience spread to the other security forces, and Ben Ali was forced to flee hours later. When police turned, the regime fell. But *why* military and police forces decide to follow one course of action over another is poorly understood. Prevailing explanations of military defection during revolutionary uprisings emphasise personal or corporate interests. In this logic, grievances spur to action rebel officers, who hope for a better deal in a new political system. Loyalists, for their part, seek to preserve their material advantages.

Behind this hard-nosed Hobbesian realism, the argument rests on a simple, common sense account: people do what is most advantageous to them. The claim is appealing when made from a distance and with the benefit of hindsight. But it struggles to explain why men who have dedicated their career to the service of a government and who have forged their professional identity on a bedrock of discipline would come to turn around and commit insubordination. The argument gives us no account of how members of the armed and security forces come to change their understanding of their interests when facing a mass unrest. The decision to rebel is a far cry from the execution of obvious and well-understood material interests. It is also easy to overlook how profound an ethical dilemma mass repression can pose to professional soldiers and policemen. Consider a country in the midst of a full-scale uprising. Tens or hundreds of thousands of demonstrators fill the streets of its capital city. The authoritarian ruler can no longer rely on his secret police and riot-response units. He must mobilise reserve forces, who typically carry live ammunition and have no training or experience in dealing with crowds. These men face a stark choice. Defending the regime comes at the price of massive bloodshed. Shirking duty or rebelling carry the threat of court martial and death.

Even for those with experience in repression, being made to kill tens or hundreds of innocents is often a deeply unpleasant prospect. The dilemma is first ethical and individual: it betrays a stark choice between serving one's government and serving one's country. But it quickly becomes collective. When an officer becomes aware that he's not alone in his conundrum, he begins to wonder whether his colleagues will follow orders. From this doubt emerges the possibility of his own disobedience.

Military and police mutinies rarely break out in the face of small demonstrations, but reliably occur when revolutionary uprisings reach a critical mass, making unconscionable largescale killing the government's only survival option.

Q9. What is Hobbesian realism?

(a) Military rebels when they are not satisfied with the dictator.

(b) People take position which is most advantageous to them.

(c) Military rebels when they feel the masses are right.

(d) Loyalists never betray the dictator.

Q10. "The dilemma is first ethical and individual." What is the dilemma?

(a) To follow the dictator or not.

(b) To look for individual gain or collective gain.

(c) To follow individual decision or collective decision.

(d) To protect the regime or the country.

Q11. Which of the following can be inferred from the passage?

(a) It is the dictator who rules alone.

(b) It is the loyalty of the military which keeps the regime going.

(c) The loyalists never rebel against the dictator.

(d) Common masses can stir the life of a dictator hugely.

Q12. Choose a title for the passage?

(a) Military vs. the dictator

(b) Mass uprising Vs. the dictator

(c) Why regimes fall

(d) How to save the regime

TEST 6

Passage 1

Q 1-3. Read the following passage and answer the questions that follow.

In her book *Mother of Invention: How Good Ideas Get Ignored in an Economy Built for Men* (2021), the writer Katrine Marçal argues that many useful innovations have failed to catch on because they are deemed 'too feminine' by marketers. A classic example is the wheeled suitcase. The wheel was invented in ancient Mesopotamia, however the possibility of attaching it to a case went against the whole idea of men showing off their strength by lugging heavy objects around, which is why wheeled suitcases weren't a thing until 1972. As Marçal wrote in The Guardian: 'Gender answers the riddle of why it took 5,000 years for us to put wheels on suitcases.'

Quantum is the scientific equivalent of suitcase wheels. The reason this useful innovation hasn't caught on, or been rolled out, more generally in areas such as economics isn't because it's impractical or too hard - it's because it's too feminine. Or rather, too Female, in a sense to be defined below.

Now, that assertion will seem ridiculous to many readers for a number of reasons - beginning with the idea that quantum has somehow been ignored or repressed. Quantum physics is widely recognised as being a huge success, and is lauded for its ability to predict and explain the bizarre behaviour of tiny subatomic particles. For example, quantum physics says that subatomic entities can be in more than one place at the same time (superposition) and show both particle-like behaviours and wave-like behaviours including interference (they can cancel each other out). Something like the position of a particle is inherently indeterminate, and only takes on a definite value when measured through a poorly understood process of wave function collapse. Particles can also become mysteriously entangled, so that a measurement on one tells us something about an entangled partner, even if it is at the far end of the Universe. The ability to make sense of all this is rightly regarded as one of the triumphs of science.

Everyone also knows that quantum mechanics is both hard and highly counterintuitive, which is why only university graduates in physics and mathematics are typically exposed to it. As one university website once reassured its audience: 'It's OK to be a bit baffled by these concepts, since we don't experience them in our day-to-day lives. It's only when you look at the tiniest quantum particles - atoms, electrons, photons and the like - that you see intriguing things like superposition and entanglement.'

In this view, if quantum ideas haven't reached a broader audience, that is a good thing, because they would be misunderstood and therefore ripe for abuse. As the physicist Sean Carroll stated in his portentously titled book The Big Picture: On the Origins of Life, Meaning, and the Universe Itself (2016): 'No theory in the history of science has been more misused and abused by cranks and charlatans - and misunderstood by people struggling in good faith with difficult ideas - than quantum mechanics.' The philosopher Slavoj Žižek similarly warned of 'New Age obscurantist appropriations of today's "hard" sciences which, in order to legitimise their position, invoke the authority of science itself.' Stand back, social scientists, and leave the heavy lifting to the experts.

Quantum economics in particular sounds like 'physics envy' taken to its logical conclusion. Indeed, the assertion that quantum ideas - developed for tiny particles - could have anything to do with human systems such as the economy will seem patently absurd to most physicists. It is well known in physics that quantum effects wash out at larger scales, where classical behaviour dominates.

Finally, quantum mechanics isn't commonly perceived as being feminine. For one thing, it is the ultimate example of a 'hard' reductionist science - it even has 'mechanics' in the name. Its 'founding fathers' were mostly young men in their 20s. In the postwar era it gained much of its funding and prestige from its association with nuclear weapons, which are pretty butch (and are one place where quantum effects don't wash out). And anyway, science cares about objective results - not things such as gender. Indeed, the whole notion of gender is highly contested and the idea that entire scientific disciplines can be assigned gender labels is just unreconstructed, unsophisticated, reductionist nonsense that will offend and repel scientists, feminists and anyone with a brain.

So how on earth can it make sense in the electronic pages of this magazine to say that quantum hasn't caught on because it is too girly?

Q1. What does the author imply by "Quantum economics in particular sounds like 'physics envy' taken to its logical conclusion"?

(a) The author is trying to show that concepts of quantum physics are also being used in economics and how it is a good thing.

(b) The author is trying to justify the claim that 'quantum' concept is a highly misused concept.

(c) The author is trying to show relation of physics with economics and everything else.

(d) The author is trying to supprt the case for using concepts of quantum physics are also being used in economics for the betterment of the subject.

Q2. The author of the passage is most likely to AGREE that:

(a) A concept has to be "easy and economical" to understand in order for it to become popular.

(b) Quantum economics is a "girly" concept despite being hard.

(c) A concept cannot be popular if it is counterintuitive.

(d) People are expected to understand what they are generally exposed to in their day to day lives.

Q3. What is the main topic of the passage?

(a) To show how a few concepts are not readily accepted despite being useful.

(b) To show how misunderstood the concept of physics is.

(c) To show how physics' concepts can be useful in economics.

(d) To urge people not to think of quantum physics as "feminine."

Passage 2

Q 4-6. Read the following passage and answer the questions that follow.

At the end of the 17th century, Madrid started to be populated, especially around Calle de Postas and Plaza Mayor, by kiosks, stores and street vendors selling chocolate. Individual licenses were granted every year, but several street vendors profited from the curiosity towards the exotic drink by selling a dark beverage made less of cocoa and more from almonds, pine nuts, flour, acorns, coffee, bread and cookie crumbs, pieces of orange rind and even soil.

Trying to put a stop to the proliferation of competitors, in 1723 a group of professional chocolate makers made their request to form a guild, claiming it was time to protect public health from the threats of adulteration. The request was denied as superfluous, but the molenderos (from the Spanish for 'to grind') did not surrender. Twenty-five years later, in 1748, they tried again and found a more favourable response from the city authorities - finally interested in curbing the loss of revenue due to adulteration - but not from their colleagues. Many workers opposed to forming a guild because they were poor, and adulterating chocolate remained the simplest way for them to profit from its sale.

Stories similar to that of the Madrilenian chocolate-makers guild occurred in many other Spanish cities, as well as in the colonies. Indeed, tension between chocolate makers, informal vendors, consumers and authorities both followed and fueled chocolate's passage from being an exotic curiosity to a widespread commodity between the 17th and 18th century.

Greatly valued in Amerindian societies, chocolate had spread among Spanish settlers in New Spain by the 16th century. The great and immediate success of chocolate fascinates today's scholars and novelists as much as it frightened contemporaries, who worried that 'addiction' and 'greed' - in the words of the Jesuit missionary José de Acosta in 1589 - would corrupt the bodies and souls of Spanish settlers. Indeed, as shown by the historian Rebecca Earle, the power of diet to create or dilute bodily differences destabilised borders between colonisers and colonised peoples, at the same time as it fuelled the fear of any Indigenous religious practices persisting.

The drink rapidly popularised to become an everyday reality for all strata of the Novohispanic population, consumed - as observed by a contemporary - 'among Spaniards, as well as among indigenous and mestizos, mulattos, negros and other people, [drunk] during fasting days, Lent and vigils, in the morning as well as in the afternoon, at night and at many times of the day.' In Ciudad de México, until the first half of the 17th century, chocolate could be acquired directly from natives on the street (until the latter were pushed out of its trade by Spanish and mestizo vendors) as cocoa paste in lozenge form, to which consumers could add what they pleased. Preparations ranged from the simplest one with water to more complex procedures with the addition of several spices and flowers, but the most popular way to consume it was hot with atole (a corn dough).

Unfortunately, the decline of the Indigenous population and the impoverishment of the soil that followed the conquest caused the collapse of cocoa's production in the area, making it impossible to satisfy the growing demand. The insatiable Novohispanic market encouraged the cultivation of different qualities of cocoa in the regions of Guayaquil (in today's Ecuador) and Caracas (in today's Venezuela), where cocoa plants had been discovered by Juan López de Velasco as early as 1570. Guayaquil and Caracas quickly established themselves as the most important cocoa-growing areas, laying the foundations for an interregional market in the overseas colonies. The sweeter criollo cocoa from Caracas was more valued and appreciated than the very high-yield forastero cocoa produced in Guayaquil, therefore Caracas remained the main supplier of New Spain until the beginning of the 18th century. For its part, Guayaquil managed to overcome the existing prohibition to export its cocoa, and, thanks to its lower price (due also to the larger quantities of sugar employed for its preparation), became an increasingly successful competitor among the lower classes in the well-differentiated Novohispanic market.

Q4. Choose a suitable summary for the passage.

(a) The passage talks about the popularity of chocolate and how it was used in various forms.

(b) The passage talks about the popularity of chocolate and how it led to evolution of different qualities of cocoa over time.

(c) The passage talks about the popularity of chocolate and the intense competition that it brewed.

(d) The passage talks about the competition for chocolate and how that led to its evolution.

Q5. Who were "molenderos"?

(a) Poor people who benefitted by adulterating the chocolate.

(b) Chocolate vendors who sold chocolate with license.

(c) Chocolate vendors who sold chocolate without license.

(d) Chocolate makers who wanted to form a guild in the chocolate trade.

Q6. Which of the following can be definitely inferred from the passage?

(a) The trade of chocolate was initially done by natives and then taken over by others in Mexico.

(b) Paste of cocoa was the only form in which chocolate was sold.

(c) Caracas served premium quality chocolate as compared to Guayaquil.

(d) Chocolate became popular in Spain in as early as 15th century.

Passage 3

Q 7-10. Read the following passage and answer the questions that follow.

Last fall, hoping to draw weary crowds back to the multiplex, AMC Theatres enlisted Nicole Kidman in what it dubbed "the biggest advertising campaign any theatre chain has ever made." Solemn to the point of absurdity, the ad finds Kidman extolling the cinema as a temple of catharsis, where we go "to laugh, to cry, to care. Because we need that, all of us." At the movies, she says, trying to emote through features stiffened by cosmetic work, we are "not just entertained, but somehow reborn together." But there is no "together": Kidman sits alone, flanked by empty rows of leatherette seats and lit by the flicker of Jurassic World. Here, she tells us, "our heroes feel like the best part of us," and "heartbreak feels good."

As Kidman mused on the transformative power of the cinema, did her thoughts alight, however briefly, on Nicolas Cage? It's possible. They co-starred in Trespass, a home-invasion thriller derided as one of 2011's worst movies, and, ironically, one of the first marquee-name films to be released on streaming services at the same time it debuted in theaters: a harbinger of the silver screen's decline. Or maybe she remembered a moment in 2013, when she and Cage received top honors at Tianxia Yingcai Cultural Media Co.'s Huading Awards, appearing personally in Macau to accept their Best Global Actor and Actress trophies–heralding the rise of a Chinese box office that altered Hollywood. More than anything, Cage should have come to mind because he embodies the tradition that Kidman and AMC both aspire to, at least in theory. If moviegoing is an act of ritual purgation, Cage must be its high priest, his performances a kind of ecstatic self-flagellation through which we're cleansed–or, to use Kidman's term, reborn.

As befits a Best Global Actor, Cage has, for forty years onscreen, delivered performances of such furious spectacle that they transcend the humanity they represent. To see him react is to wonder if you've ever really felt, or could feel, anything so deeply, and if you'd want to. Anger? He sells it by the avalanche. Watch in Matchstick Men as he butts in line at the pharmacy. His "inner trembling," as Roger Ebert called it, turns to outright spasms as he faces down a man who dares to question him: "Have you ever been dragged to the sidewalk and beaten until you–pissed–blood?!" Passion? Look no further than Wild at Heart, where, reminiscing in a smoky barroom, Cage caresses his chin and says, "Man, I had a boner with a capital O." Sadness? See him in Vampire's Kiss, hands clasped, face pursed, wailing that most literal of lachrymose words: "Boo-hoo! Boo-hoo!" Yes, this is why we go to the movies, to see a grown man disfigured by emotion and emotion disfigured by a grown man. Cage has played many a hero, and if, as Kidman maintains, such heroes "feel like the best part of us," we have some soul-searching to do. Can it be that this blubbering, boorish caricature is among the better angels of our nature?

I'll offer an emphatic yes. There's something stalwart, commendable, even comforting about Cage's presence, something that reaches past entertainment toward tangled questions of talent and excess. His acting is too much, not just in tenor but in sheer volume. Since 1986, he has appeared in at least one film a year and sometimes up to six, bringing his total to well over one hundred. This ubiquity, combined with his trademark intensity, can make him seem like a permanently erupting volcano. At this point, it would be more disturbing if he went dormant. His increased output has brought what's often called a cult audience, a euphemism suggesting that his fans are mere ironists, feigning love for the objectively unlovable. Can anyone truly admire an actor who has been attached, in the span of a few years, to such obvious paint-by-numbers fare as Rage, Dark, Primal, and Outcast? Sure, he's won an Oscar–for Leaving Las Vegas, a movie derived from a novel that also became a Sheryl Crow song–but that was almost three decades ago.

Cage's detractors find poetic justice in the fact that much of his recent work has gone straight to video on demand, with no theatrical release. An actor coasting on his larger-than-life performances has been denied the chance to appear larger than life. The shift from theaters to at-home streaming has launched a thousand Norma Desmond references ("I am big, it's the pictures that got small"), but in Cage's case the line is frighteningly apropos, and he's all but quoted it himself. "I want movies to be an event," he said in 2011. "I don't want [them] to get smaller and smaller." And yet here we are: a bona fide star who believes in absolution on the big screen is all but shut out of AMC Theatres.

Q7. Why does the author call Trespass "a harbinger of the silver screen's decline" in the passage?

(a) Because it was one of the worst movies of the year.

(b) Because it streamed simultaneously on streaming platforms and in theatres.

(c) Because it could not garner as much popularity as it was expected to.

(d) Because it did not serve the purpose of bringing back the audience back to theatre.

Q8. Which of the following can be inferred regarding the author from the passage?

(a) He is appreciative of Nicolas Cage.

(b) He is a huge critic of Cage's movies.

(c) He is a movie buff.

(d) He believes that Cage contributed to the career of Nicole.

Q9. What does the author imply by "His increased output has brought what's often called a cult audience, a euphemism suggesting that his fans are mere ironists, feigning love for the objectively unlovable"?

(a) The term "cult" defines the audience of movies in an ironic way.

(b) The author is highlighting the popularity of Nicolas Cage.

(c) The author is showing how Nicolas cage has only "blind" followers for his cult.

(d) The author is showing how he is a part of the "cult."

Q10. Which of the following is FALSE as per the passage?

(a) Nicolas Cage might have lost his popularity and fame in the recent times.

(b) Nicolas Cage was a true theatre star who was never featured on streaming services.

(c) Nicolas Cage wants to see movies as an event.

(d) Nicolas Cage has starred in more than 100 movies.

TEST 7

Passage 1

Q 1-3. Read the following passage and answer the questions that follow.

Sigmund Freud was an ambivalent man, especially when it came to politics. He often held conflicting views of political ideologies: for example, he expressed sympathies for socialism ("anyone who has tasted the miseries of poverty," he wrote, can understand why fighting "against the inequality of wealth" was necessary), only to reject it elsewhere as antithetical to human nature. He similarly supported Zionism (even serving on the founding board of the Hebrew University) while simultaneously criticizing it as "baseless fanaticism." Few works embodied this ambivalence better than *Civilization and Its Discontents* (1930), Freud's most all-encompassing reflection on social matters. Discussing everything from religion to technology to bodily odors, he provocatively concluded that life in society is destined to be tragic: Whatever people gain from their social web, from safety to a sense of belonging, always comes at the price of unhappiness. Even his hair-raising escape from the Nazis, who in 1938 occupied Freud's home country of Austria, evoked mixed feelings. "The triumphant feeling of liberation," he wrote in a letter from exile, "is mingled too strongly with mourning for one had loved the prison from which one has been released."

Civilization and Its Discontents became an instant classic, and over the decades, a wide range of readers–from Marxists and feminists to Christian conservatives–have debated Freud's lessons for their own times. We now have an opportunity to do so for our own catastrophe-stricken world: In a new edition from Norton, the historian Samuel Moyn offers a new introduction, helpful notations, and a selection of short texts that explore the various ways that artists, philosophers, and social theorists have interpreted the book over the years. Moyn, who is also a frequent commentator on contemporary affairs, claims that while Freud's environment in interwar Vienna may be different from ours, his ideas are still invaluable. They urge us to recognize the complicated relationship between psychology and politics, particularly how our arguments about economics, power, and social hierarchies are always shaped by our unconscious impulses. For Moyn, Freud's approach is indispensable in the effort to tackle the most pressing dilemmas in contemporary society. It is only by understanding the psychological forces that foster oppression and conflict that we can hope to "make progress" and change our "war-torn and unequal world".

It is tempting to harness Civilization and Its Discontents as a guide to our contemporary political morass, but doing so may obscure its most valuable message. While Freud does help us to better understand the entanglement of politics and psychologies, we can also read him as making an even more unsettling and relevant claim, one that goes far beyond politics: that human life is always dominated by ambiguity, uncertainty, and inconsistency, and that there's no escape from the haunting torment that this entails. Even Freud's unique writing style radiates with ambivalence. Instead of making arguments in an orderly progression, the book repeatedly digresses, openly questions its own assumptions, and flat-out contradicts itself. Civilization and Its Discontents is worth revisiting, not to make sense of our contemporary politics but because it captures our growing, and often overwhelming, sense of disorientation–over the pandemic, climate change, or other unprecedented crises–and explains why it is likely never to go away.

Q1. Sigmund Freud is most likely to AGREE with which of the following statements?

(a) Politics is irrelevant to human society which is always tormented by ambiguity and uncertainty.

(b) That human life is always dominated by ambiguity, uncertainty, and inconsistency.

(c) Human race can attain complete happiness if it can get rid of ambiguity.
(d) Cannot be determined from the information provided in passage.

Q2. Which of the following can be interpreted regarding Moyn from the passage?

A. He has been a student of Sigmund Freud.
B. He is highly influenced by the theories and ideologies of Sigmund Freud.
C. He is a psychologist trying to understand the structure of human race.

(a) A and B
(b) B and C
(c) Only B
(d) Only C

Q3. Which of the following is FALSE regarding "Civilizations and Discontent"?

(a) It was well received by almost all groups of the society.
(b) It was written in an non- argumentative manner.
(c) It acts only as a guide for several new thinkers and historians.
(d) It provides a detailed view of Freud's thoughts.

PASSAGE 2

Q 4-6. Read the following passage and answer the questions that follow.

Commonplace notions of biology and sex continue to influence what we take as natural and given, including the belief that men don't get pregnant. A question I often ask my students in a class on gender and science is this: how many effective and widely available new forms of birth control have been developed in the past 100 years for men? It's a safe assumption that my captive audience is in the first years of learning about and utilizing contraception. Why had so few considered this situation unfair and overly burdensome on women? Why was there still no easily accessible kind of artificial birth control for men other than the condom, which after all has been around in one form or another for at least hundreds of years?

They knew why, because we all know why: no matter how much we talk about gender equality, the implicit assumption often ends up being that men and women are, deep down, different. Only people with female reproductive organs get pregnant, and somehow this has come to mean that women should be more responsible for contraception. Or at least that's the unspoken belief of many, despite the fact that no one with female reproductive organs ever got pregnant without help from someone with male reproductive organs.

We still live in an age of the gender binary, but it's also a time of mass gender confusion, debate and renegotiation disputing the gender binary. And that's a great thing. Assumptions and shibboleths about gender (and sex and sexuality) are being defended and challenged, and language is being recast - think about the sudden transformations of pronouns people are using to refer to themselves. Language matters, and with respect to gender and sexuality I have come to the conclusion that we need to be very careful indeed when we make unwarranted comparisons about common 'male' and 'female' traits among humans and nonhuman animals. Among other things, there is a whole lot of exaggerated anthropomorphism that tickles our curiosities and satisfies our quixotic yearnings but reinforces erroneous stereotypes about male and female.

Q4. As per the author, which of the following will be supported by him?

(a) No matter how much people try, there will always be only two genders on paper.
(b) People are ignorant to the woes of people who do not identify themselves as either male or female.
(c) People are accepting more than two genders and with time, things will change for the good.
(d) Non-binary gender system is just a scam to rip off the system.

Q5. What does author mean by 'mass gender confusion' in the passage?

(a) There is a confusion related to how many genders there are and how to define them.
(b) Because of make-up and new unisex clothing styles, it is confusing to identify the gender of the person.
(c) Since homo-sexual relationships are allowed in certain countries, identifying oneself got tough.
(d) People are unwilling to disclose their genders as they can form the basis for discrimination against them at work or in life, leading to confusion among the masses.

Q6. As per author, why are there more birth control methods directed towards women?

(a) Contraceptives for men have severe side-effects.
(b) The society assumes that since only women can get pregnant, hence it is their responsibility primarily to think about birth control.
(c) It is not possible to make contraceptives for men.
(d) Women are more accepting and thus are more likely to agree to take contraceptives.

PASSAGE 3

Q 7-9. Read the following passage and answer the questions that follow.

Psychology is not solely the science of the mind. It's a form of knowledge enmeshed with our mythical understanding of deeper questions of significance. In our secular age, many people no longer turn to sacred books to understand who and what they are. Psychology is where many find meaning. Indeed, the stories we tell ourselves through psychology fulfil many of the same functions served in the traditional belief practices of mythology. Falling somewhere between a social science, a natural science and a human science, it isn't simple to determine which type of knowledge the study of the mind is supposed to pursue. Psychology aspires to the status of the physical sciences, but it tries to explain much more, and ends up revealing much less.

Today, the term 'mythology' connotes uncorroborated legend. But that's not entirely accurate. Mythology is really a set of beliefs buttressed by practices, or rituals, that together console our desire for explanation. As the Romanian theorist Mircea Eliade wrote in 1957: 'Myth never quite disappears from the present world of the psyche ... it only changes its aspect.' And in our time its aspect is to be found in psychology.

Mythology remains important in Western culture. Take, for instance, the role model of the hero, of Hercules and Aeneas, of contemporary revolutionaries, martyrs and dictators. These ideal figures exemplify models of human achievement. Similarly, notions of salvation, progress and ethics are so constitutive of our notions of reality that they're often communicated through the format of mythology. There's a surfeit of cultural products that fulfil the function of myth whereby characters and stories give us the means to understand the world we live in. In the imaginary world we enter through novels, to the weightless experience of desire that's consumerism, we inhabit the broad spaces of meaning-construction. Through superhero comic books, to the obscure immanence of modern art, from visions of paradisiacal vacations, to computer games and the self-mythologising of social media production, we seek a higher ground beyond the banal and the profane. We've even replaced the effervescent experience of sacred rites, not in blood sacrifice or vision quests, but in our engagement with art, drugs, cinema, rock music and all-night dance parties. Lastly, individuals have developed their own ways to create self-narratives that include mythical transitions in pilgrimages or personal quests to their ancestral lands. Likewise, some seek inner spaces wherein faith and meaning can be transformed into experience.

To prepare for our exploration of contemporary mythology, we can look back at civilisations and consider the function of the stories they told. The story of the flood, for example, recurs in early urban societies, marking a crisis in human-divine relations and man's experience of gradual self-reliance and separation from nature. Whereas during the Axial Age (800-200 BCE), faith developed in an environment of early trade economies, at which time we observe a concern with individual conscience, morality, compassion and a tendency to look within. According to Karen Armstrong's *A Short History of Myth* (2005), these Axial myths of interiority indicate that people felt they no longer shared the same nature as the gods, and that the supreme reality had become impossibly difficult to access. These myths were a response to the loss of previous notions of social order, cosmology and human good, and represented ways to portray these social transformations in macrocosmic stories. Just as we consider how the myth of the flood or myths of interiority were reflections of how people tried to make sense of their rapidly changing world, our dependence on psychology can be understood as a result of shifts in modes of life and knowledge practices in the 19th and 20th centuries.

What constitutes a mythology? It's an organised canon of beliefs that explains the state of the world. It also delivers an origin story - such as the Hindu Laws of Manu or the Biblical creation story - that creates a setting for how we experience the world. In fact, for Eliade, all myths provided an explanation of the world by virtue of giving an account of where things came from. If all mythologies are origin stories in this sense, what are the origin stories suggested by psychology? Two original elements of human nature are explained in its lore: the story of personhood - that is, what it means to be an individual and have an identity - and, secondly, the story of our physical constitution in the brain. The humanist vision of individualism, of the dignity of a person as a political subject articulates the former notion of what it means to be a person. Neuroscience, meanwhile, offers the latter ontological foundation of our materiality.

Contemporary psychology is a form of mythology insofar as it is an attempt to succour our need to believe in stories that provide a sense of value and signification in the context of secular modernity. The ways in which psychology is used - for example in experiments or self-help literature or personality tests or brain scans - are means of providing rituals to enact the myths of personhood and materialism.

Q7. What is the main purpose of the passage?

(a) To explain what psychology is.

(b) To show the relationship between psysiology and mythology.

(c) To explain contemporary psychology and its relationship with mythology.

(d) To explain the role of mythology and history in evolution of psychology.

Q8. Which of the following is TRUE as per the passage?

A. Modern forms of entertainment have replaced traditional methods of finding salvation.

B. There has always been a divide between humans since ancient times about mythology and science.

C. Cosmology is a part of neuroscience.

(a) Only A
(b) Only B
(c) Only C
(d) A and C

Q9. Why does the author say "Today, the term 'mythology' connotes uncorroborated legend. But that's not entirely accurate."?

(a) Because the tales of mythology are proven to be true.
(b) Because mythology is formed on the basis of a set of beliefs.
(c) Because mythology consists of only meaningful rituals.
(d) Because mythology helps bring out the relevance of psychology.

TEST 8

Poem 1

Read the poem given below and answer the question (1-2) that follows it:

Black lake, black boat, two black, cut-paper people.
Where do the black trees go that drink here?
Their shadows must cover Canada.

A little light is filtering from the water flowers
Their leaves do not wish us to hurry:
They are round and flat and full of dark advice.

Cold words shake from the oar.
The spirit of blackness is in us, it is in the fishes.
A snag is lifting a valedictory, pale hand;
Stars opening among the lilies.
Are you not blinded by such expressionless sirens?
This is the silence of abandoned souls.

Q1. Which of the following options best explains the effect of the images in Line 1?

(a) The black lake lacks regenerative potential; 'black boat' connotes the funerary boat; cut-paper people are unreal.
(b) The images are suffused with an overpowering sense of rebellion.
(c) The first line encapsulates the theme of the poem.
(d) The atmosphere indicates a cyclical nature of life and death.
(e) The repeated use of black suggests evil.

Q2. Which of the following options presents a convincing evaluation of the line, 'Stars opening among the lilies'?

(a) The mirror images, the worlds above and overlap.
(b) The spirit of blackness does not hinder the appearance of beauty in nature which is symbolic of hope blossoming in the soul.
(c) The ethereal light of the stars gets reflected among the lilies.
(d) Lilies purify the 'dark' into 'light' as symbolized in and by stars.
(e) The stars are flowers in the sky and the flowers in the lake are stars in water.

Poem 2

Read the following poem and answer the questions (3-4) that follow:

A spirit that lives in this world and does not wear the shirt of love, such an existence in a deep disgrace. Be foolish in love, because love is all there is.

There is no way into presence except through love exchange.

If someone asks, But what is love? Answer, dissolving the will.

True freedom comes to those who have escaped the question of freewill and fate.

Love is an emperor. The two worlds play across him. He barely notices their tumbling game.

Love and lover live in eternity. Other desires are substitute for that way of being.

How long do you lay embracing a corpse? Love rather the soul, which cannot be held.

Anything born in spring dies in the fall, but love is not seasonal.

With wine pressed from grapes, expect a hangover.

But this love path has no expectations. You are uneasy riding the body?

Dismount, travel lighter. Wings will be given.

Be clear like mirror holding nothing.

Be clean of pictures and the worry that comes with images.

Gaze into what is not ashamed or afraid of any truth.

Contain all human faces in your own without any judgment of them.

Be pure emptiness. What is inside of that? You ask. Silence is all I can say.

Lovers have some secrets they keep.

Q3. How are the words "freewill," "fate" and "will" used in the poem above?

(a) All the three words are opposites of love.
(b) These words are used as a hallmark of an intelligent person.
(c) Freewill and will connote self-determination while fate connotes loss of control.
(d) These are used as something that corpses do not possess.
(e) Freewill and will are synonymous while fate is an antonym to both.

Q4. Which of the following is the closest interpretation of "lovers have some secrets that they keep"?

(a) The secret refers to profundity of knowledge.
(b) The secret is not to have any secret.
(c) The secret refers to freedom from emptiness.
(d) The secret refers to being a fine judge of human quality.
(e) The secret is about loving someone as much as you love yourself.

Poem 3

Read the poem below and answer the two associated questions:

Some say the world will end in fire,
Some say in ice.
From what I've tasted of desire
I hold with those who favor fire.
But, if it had to perish twice,
I think I know enough of hate
To know that for destruction ice
Is also great
And would suffice.

Q5. Which of the following statements will the poet agree with the MOST?

(a) Desire overpowers hatred to control humans.
(b) Greed can destroy one's world.
(c) Ambition is more powerful than envy.
(d) Both desire and hate can create self-doubt.
(e) Hatred destroys what desire cannot.

Q6. Which is the MOST UNSUITABLE title of the poem?

(a) Love and Detest- A Tale of Destruction
(b) The Annihilation Hypothesis
(c) Emotional Destruction of the World
(d) Destruction by Fire and Ice
(e) How the World Ends

PART II

ACCORDING TO THE LATEST CAT COMPREHENSION PASSAGES

TEST 1

Passage 1

Aeschylus was only the first of the great classic Greek dramatists. The generation that followed brought several other talented and powerful tragic playwrights. The most famous of these were Sophocles and Euripides. Both writers did much to expand the traditionally simple expectations of characters in plays. Sophocles' plays feature incredibly strong-willed, modern characters who struggle with serious moral concerns, and Euripides wrote some of the most chilling psychological dramas of classical Greece.

Comic theatre also had its hero. A generation younger than Sophocles and Euripides, the comic playwright Aristophanes is today regarded as the best of the classic comic playwrights. His sometimes absurd and sometimes elegant plays demonstrate a great skill in mixing comedy with honest and sincere ideas. Aristophanes' plays certainly contain many wild and vulgar jokes, yet they also discuss serious concerns of his time, such as politics, art and education. His work provides modern readers with some of the clearest images of the life and daily affairs of the fifth-century Greeks. This literary revolution in the early part of the fifth century was not limited to the stage. The world of philosophy also experienced an awakening. Skills such as oration, logic and rhetoric were polished, and the study of mathematics and the sciences was encouraged. Philosophers such as Socrates became famous for wandering about the city of Athens, engaging students and scholars in lively academic debates about morality and politics. Socrates' most famous pupil, Plato, wrote a number of books and dialogues in which he explains the philosophy and thoughts of his teacher and goes on to develop the ideas further. His work - which deals with a wide range of theoretical concerns, such as politics, ethics and the importance of friendship - is invaluable for modern scholars who wish to understand the ancient Greek mindset.

Another very well-known philosopher of the time was Aristotle. Aristotle was, in his turn, a pupil of Plato's, and is best known for his numerous texts dealing with the natural sciences. Interested in almost every conceivable topic, Aristotle left behind texts detailing his thoughts and questions on physics and astronomy, as well as meteorology, sleep patterns, raising animals and numerous other subjects.

The age of classical Greece drew to a close with the end of the fourth century BC. Yet through its literature, classical Greece still has an enormous effect on modern Western thought and traditions. Almost all Western literature, from histories to romance novels, from thrillers to poetry, is rooted in classical Greek traditions. Many of the themes present in those ancient plays and poems are in fact still popular in modern literature. And even those plays that deal with uniquely modern themes still owe much in the way of technique and style to the golden age of Greece.

Q1. How did Euripides contribute to the development of tragic theatre?

1. He wrote chilling stories about strong-willed, modern characters.
2. He expanded the expectations of characters in plays.
3. He wrote very disturbing plays.

(a) Only 1 and 2
(b) Only 2
(c) Both 2 and 3
(d) Only 1

Q2. Which of the following best describes the plays written by Aristophanes?

1. Funny and light-hearted, yet without purpose
2. Serious and intellectual, discussing political ideas of the day
3. Humorous while still putting across serious ideas

(a) Only 1
(b) Only 2
(c) Only 3
(d) Both 2 and 3

Q3. Which of the following best describes the subjects that Aristotle wrote about?

(a) Meteorology
(b) Sleep disorders
(c) Astronomy
(d) All kinds of natural sciences and more

PASSAGE 2

Up at the League, says a friend, there had been one night a brisk conversational discussion, as to what would happen on the Morrow of the Revolution, finally shading off into a vigorous statement by various friends of their views on the future of the fully developed new society.

Says our friend: Considering the subject, the discussion was good-tempered; for those present being used to public meetings and after-lecture debates, if they did not listen to each other's opinions (which could scarcely be expected of them), at all events did not always attempt to speak all together, as is the custom of people in ordinary polite society when conversing on a subject which interests them. For the rest, there were six persons present, and consequently six sections of the party were represented, four of which had strong but divergent anarchist opinions. One of the sections, says our friend, a man whom he knows very well indeed, sat almost silent at the beginning of the discussion, but at last got drawn into it and finished by roaring out very loud, and damning all the rest for fools; after which befell a period of noise, and then a lull, during which the aforesaid section, having said goodnight very amicably, took his way home by himself to a western suburb, using the means of travelling which civilisation has forced upon us like a habit. As he sat in that vapour-bath of hurried and discontented humanity, a carriage of the underground railway, he, like others, stewed discontentedly, while in self-reproachful mood he turned over the many excellent and conclusive arguments which, though they lay at his fingers' ends, he had forgotten in the just past discussion. But this frame of mind he was so used to, that it didn't last him long, and after a brief discomfort, caused by disgust with himself for having lost his temper (which he was also well used to), he found himself musing on the subject matter of discussion, but still discontentedly and unhappily. 'If I could but see a day of it', he said to himself; 'if I could but see it!'

Q4. The man in the carriage was:

1. Upset with himself at having lost his temper.
2. Angry because he had forgotten to mention so many important points which would have provided buttress to his argument.
3. Thinking about the topic of discussion.

(a) Both 1 and 2
(b) 1, 2 and 3
(c) Both 2 and 3
(d) Only 3

Q5. The person in the discussion who damned everyone:

1. Parted happily.
2. Parted after saying a friendly goodbye
3. Parted after cursing and walked away angrily.

(a) Only 1
(b) Only 2
(c) Only 3
(d) Only 1 and 2

PASSAGE 3

What is an Assembly? It is a structure that brings the people of an entire community into a systematic relationship with one another for the purpose of solving individual and community problems. It is the organisation of a community in such a manner that if a great many people wanted to do a particular thing, they could do it. It is a means - through its formal structure and logical, systematic organisation - of connecting masses of people; a means, through such systematic organisation, of establishing a channel of communication between the Assembly's elected leadership and every last man and woman in the community; a means by which large numbers of people may engage in a common effort.

The Assembly follows certain rules of logic: in order for masses of people to enter into collective decision-making they must be organised prior to any decisions having been made. This means that for an anti-poverty effort to succeed, structure must be established prior to the creation of any program; otherwise it is likely that programs will be designed and controlled by persons outside the community.

We go into a community, and we divide it into Conferences of manageable size. Each Conference meets on a regular basis, and each sends a Representative to a central decision-making body called the Assembly. Within the Assembly, each county or city is organised like a country, but instead of unwieldy Congressional districts there are districts of 50 people - or in cities, 50 households. These districts are called Conferences.

The representational dimension of the Assembly enables it to function community-wide. Each Conference elects one Representative to the Assembly. Thus, if there are 5,000 adults (in cities, 5,000 households) in a given community, there will be 100 Representatives for 100 groups of 50 people (in cities, 50 households). If there are 10,000 adults (or households), there will be 200 Representatives and so forth. Representatives meet at a community-wide Assembly to discuss problems.

Communication is the key to success. Each Representative is in touch with 50 members through seven committee-persons, each of whom in turn communicates with six other members. And it works! What we've done is transform entire communities.

The conference provides a setting in which citizens can bring problems to the group for discussion and creative problem-solving. Problems range from disparities in government services to the need for job training to how to file for Social Security benefits to school problems confronted by a member's children. Community members can fill out a problem sheet to address individual concerns. The sheet is given to their representative. If the representative cannot solve the problem, it is passed on to the Executive Council, which is made up of a dozen chairpersons assigned to areas such as employment, social services, housing, etc.

The Assembly is the heart of the NASP approach to community transformation. It grapples with issues affecting the county as a whole. Its actions often result in new and expanded educational programs; low-income housing projects; improved county facilities such as all-weather roads and modern sanitation systems; and enhanced health, welfare and recreational services.

Q6. Which of the following questions would you ask the author of this piece?

1. Why is the conference a systemic organisation?
2. Why is the Assembly a systematic organisation?
3. Why does the action of the conference affect the county as a whole?

(a) Only 1
(b) Only 2
(c) Only 3
(d) Both 1 and 2

Q7. Which of the following is correct according to the passage?

1. The conference aims at creative problem-solving.
2. The conference transforms the communities.
3. The communities are the districts of the Assembly.

(a) Only 1
(b) Only 2
(c) Only 3
(d) Both 1 and 2

Q8. Which of the following logics applies to the working of the Assembly?

(a) The masses of people can solve the problem once they have identified the problem, picked out the process of problem-solving and then organised themselves into groups.
(b) Before a collective decision is made, the masses of people have to be organised into a structure.
(c) The programs are controlled by people from outside the community.
(d) The Assembly grapples with the problems of the community as a whole.

TEST 2

PASSAGE 1

It was the best of times,
It was the worst of times,
It was the age of wisdom,

It was the age of foolishness,
It was the epoch of belief,
It was the epoch of incredulity,
It was the season of Light,
It was the season of Darkness,
It was the spring of hope,
It was the winter of despair,
We had everything before us,
We had nothing before us,
We were all going direct to Heaven,
We were all going direct the other way -

In short, the period was so far like the present period, that some of its noisiest authorities insisted on its being received, for good or for evil, in the superlative degree of comparison only.

There were a king with a large jaw and a queen with a plain face, on the throne of England; there were a king with a large jaw and a queen with a fair face, on the throne of France. In both countries it was clearer than crystal to the lords of the state preserves of loaves and fishes, that things in general were settled for ever.

It was the year of Our Lord 1775.

Spiritual revelations were conceded to England at that favoured period, as at this. Mrs Southcott had recently attained her five-and-twentieth blessed birthday, of whom a prophetic private in the Life Guards had heralded the sublime appearance by announcing that arrangements were made for the swallowing up of London and Westminster. Even the Cock-lane ghost had been laid only a round dozen of years, after rapping out its messages, as the spirits of this very year last past (supernaturally deficient in originality) rapped out theirs. Mere messages in the earthly order of events had lately come to the English Crown and People, from a congress of British subjects in America: which, strange to relate, have proved more important to the human race than any communications yet received through any of the chickens of the Cock-lane brood.

France, less favoured on the whole as to matters spiritual than her sister of the shield and trident, rolled with exceeding smoothness downhill, making paper money and spending it. Under the guidance of her Christian pastors, she entertained herself, besides, with such humane achievements as sentencing a youth to have his hands cut off, his tongue torn out with pincers and his body burned alive because he had not kneeled down in the rain to do honour to a dirty procession of monks which passed within his view, at a distance of some 50 or 60 yards. It is likely enough that, rooted in the woods of France and Norway, there were growing trees, when that sufferer was put to death, already marked by the Woodman, Fate, to come down and be sawn into boards, to make a certain movable framework with a sack and a knife in it, terrible in history. It is likely enough that in the rough outhouses of some tillers of the heavy lands adjacent to Paris, there were sheltered from the weather that very day, rude carts, bespattered with rustic mire, snuffed about by pigs and roosted in by poultry, which the Farmer, Death, had already set apart to be his tumbrils of the Revolution. But that Woodman and that Farmer, though they work unceasingly, work silently, and no one heard them as they went about with muffled tread: the rather, for as much as to entertain any suspicion that they were awake, was to be atheistical and traitorous.

Q1. What is the tone of the passage?

(a) Argumentative
(b) Nostalgic
(c) Ironical
(d) Aesthetical

Q2. Which one of the following options is correct according to the passage?

1. The author tries to use opposing pairs to highlight how they were equal in their struggle.
2. The author tries to show how Britain was superior to France.
3. The author tries to show how it was going to be the end of the world with things so mismatched as they had never been before.

(a) Only 1
(b) Only 2
(c) Only 3
(d) None of these

Q3. The 'humane achievements' mentioned in the passage refer to:

1. The humane values which were upheld in those times.
2. A sarcastic comment on the system which had become totally 'inhuman' as opposed to 'humane'.
3. The punishments and trials given to people were most humane and would be counted as an achievement.

(a) Only 1
(b) Only 2
(c) Only 3
(d) Both 2 and 3

PASSAGE 2

Egoism can be held as a descriptive or a normative theory and Hobbes seems to have held both versions. As an empirical theory about human motivation generally termed psychological egoism, it holds that persons are always motivated by and act on the basis of what they perceive to be their self-interest and their good. As an ethical or normative theory it holds that all persons have a basic obligation to act to promote their own interests even to the detriment of others. Although Hobbes states in some of his writings that not all helping others is irrational, he does claim that sacrificing one's life is always irrational. Virtues, for Hobbes, have no intrinsic value but only as a means to power.

An essential component of Hobbes theory of human nature is his belief in human equality. This equality is a physical and intellectual equality in that, as Hobbes puts it, the weakest, under the right circumstances, can kill the strongest. Since all persons are equal in this sense, all have an endless desire for power to satisfy their desires, and given a scarcity of power and the goods necessary to satisfy desires, competition for power and conflict are inevitable. In addition to the competition for power, the other major causes of conflict are fear of death and injury and the desire for glory. Given such an analysis of human nature a condition without government has some clear implications for Hobbes.

The condition without a common power or authority Hobbes terms the 'state of nature'. Hobbes does not claim that there was ever such a state throughout the world, but he does believe it is still in existence among the independent nations of the world who have no power over them. He also believed that Native Americans were still in such a circumstance.

Given the infinite desire for power, the state of nature is, for Hobbes, necessarily a state of constant war and threat of war 'of every man against every man'. In such a condition, there is no industry, agriculture, private property or civilisation at all. Hobbes reinforces his claim that war is the natural state of mankind in some ordinary observations of human behaviour.

He notes that all take precautions against robbery and violence even in society by locking their doors and other measures for self-protection.

The state of nature Hobbes describes is far starker than in most contract theories being a state without any morality or justice and permeated by a constant power struggle. In this harsh state of nature there are no moral or legal limits to anything and every person has a right to everything even another's life. Life is reduced to such a primitive, violent and crude level that Hobbes calls it 'solitary, poor, nasty, brutish and short'.

Human beings are, according to Hobbes, rational creatures with an inborn desire for life and pleasure and, as such, seek a way to escape the amoral, lawless and chaotic state of nature they find themselves in. At this point in his argument Hobbes introduces the idea of the 'laws of nature' as immutable laws which exist in the state of nature and which are not fundamental moral rules necessary for social order as understood by Aquinas and Locke, among others, but rather precepts of prudential reason promoting survival and motivating humans to move to a more secure and comfortable life. The laws of nature give humanity what Hobbes calls the 'natural right' to self-preservation. By 'right' Hobbes does not mean a moral or legal notion but simply the natural liberty to act in one's own enlightened interest.

For Hobbes, the desire for power is a basic human drive since power is the necessary means for happiness and getting what humans desire.

Consequently, the more power one has, the more likely one will achieve one's desires. Our desires are, for Hobbes, endless and so is the human need for power, which only ends in death.

Hobbes explains that individuals in the state of nature are in a state of war and so see the need to escape that turbulent state by forming some kind of central power or government. They decide to 'confer all their power and strength upon one man or upon one assembly' and so make that person or group the authority to act for each person of the society. Later Hobbes qualifies this by noting that no one can or should give up the right to survival; this then is the only limit to the contract. The actual words of the contract or covenant 'I authorise and give up my right of governing myself to this man or to this assembly of men on this condition, that you give up your right to him and authorise all his actions in like manner'. However, this agreement need not be unanimous but only a majority decision. If some refuse to consent to the contract, they would be destroyed since they would then be in a state of nature with respect to the others. This agreement creates a 'sovereign', a common political power, and what Hobbes calls a 'commonwealth' which he also calls the 'leviathan'. A sovereign created by agreement Hobbes calls sovereignty by 'institution'.

However, a sovereign can also be created by conquest where one commonwealth overpowers another. For Hobbes, a contract is nothing without the power of enforcement or 'covenants without the sword are but words'. Words cannot keep a contract effective but two ways are effective, the fear of the consequences of breaking the contract and the 'glory' of not breaking it or needing to break it. Hence, the sovereign must have all the necessary power to enforce the contract and the people keep their contract strictly out of fear of punishment and death.

Q4. Which of the following courses of action would Hobbes be most likely to disagree with?

(a) A soldier defending the borders of his country from the belligerent neighbour's surprise attack has to decide whether to take on an individual manoeuvre on the attackers. He knows his actions would buy his country's forces a lot of time and possibly save many lives. He is torn between going forward and retreating as he thinks of his wife and newborn daughter. He decides to withdraw and convene with the others as he rationalises that there must be some other way out.

(b) On the way to an important meeting, a man witnesses a severe accident between a two-wheeler and a car. Both parties are severely injured and there is a large crowd gathering at the scene of the accident. He hears someone call out to him help transport the injured victims to the nearby hospital. The man pretends not have heard and drives away quickly, thinking there would be several others to come to the rescue of the victims and he could not afford to be late to the meeting.

(c) A mother takes the blame for an act of theft on the behalf of her son in order to prevent him from being punished, as she believes he is too young and was under the bad influence of his friends.

(d) A country concludes an entente with its long-standing bitter rival neighbouring country due to mutual strategic advantages that the alliances offer them.

Q5. According to the passage, which of the following are not characteristics of human beings?

(a) A strong urge to acquire might, glory and precedence over others.

(b) The desire to escape conflict, chaos and the fear of death.

(c) A predilection for selfless action and sacrifice.

(d) The capacity for critical reasoning.

Q6. According to Hobbes' formulation of the pre-societal, what are the main disadvantages of the state of nature?

1. No sense of security and a fear for one's life.
2. Absence of law and order and endless power struggle.
3. Equality of all with every other member of the state of nature.
4. There is great possibility of progress and development of mankind.

(a) 1, 2 and 3

(b) Only 2

(c) Both 3 and 4

(d) Both 1 and 2

Q7. In the context of the passage, the word 'covenant' means which of the following:

(a) A decree

(b) An order

(c) A pact

(d) An undertaking

Passage 3

Back in 1991, India was the world's greatest aid recipient, a patently uncompetitive giant begging for alms. Economic reforms from 1991 onwards gradually made India highly competitive, enabled it to touch 9 per cent GDP growth, and to be called a potential superpower.

Those days are gone. GDP growth has halved to 4.5 per cent. India has become uncompetitive in several ways. Worse, the Indian political class has stopped even trying to compete globally. It focuses on subsidies, reservations and special measures for sundry vote banks, regardless of the implications for competitiveness. This will ultimately lead to bankruptcy, not inclusive growth (as claimed by Congress spin-masters).

When India went bust in 1991, drastic measures over several years were needed to restore competitiveness. The rupee was devalued hugely; industrial licencing and MRTP clearance were abolished; trade was liberalised; import duties were gradually slashed from 300 per cent to around 10 per cent by 2005. Public sector monopolies like telecom and oil refining were opened up to the private sector, enabling the creation of the world's fastest growing and cheapest telecom service, and the world's biggest export-oriented refineries. Liberal foreign investment converted India into a global small car hub; many multinationals like GE came in and made India an R&D hub. A liberalised private sector created the software/BPO revolution.

Merchandise exports rose from 5 per cent of GDP to 15 per cent. Service exports rose even faster, and India became a world leader in software. The rupee strengthened from ₹50 per dollar in 2002 to ₹40 per dollar by 2008. India's rising competitiveness made it a potential superpower. That's suddenly gone. In the last 3 years, GDP growth has plummeted, industry and exports have stagnated, the current account deficit has widened dramatically and the rupee has crashed. A year ago this finally persuaded the government to embark on some reforms, but these have failed to revive the old dynamism.

Why? Because the new measures do not change the political mind-set of constantly ignoring competitiveness in formulating new policies and regulations. Politicians take competitiveness for granted, and just want to divide up the spoils of growth. Alas, neglect of competitiveness has meant a collapse of growth, and hence of the spoils too.

India certainly needs new rules to safeguard the environment and tribals. But in formulating new rules and regulations, did anybody check whether our rules compared with those in competing countries? Alas no. We need a fairer land acquisition policy. But our new law mandates a social impact assessment and expert group clearance before any acquisition. Do competing nations have such time-consuming rules? Do they insist on 80 per cent of land-owners consenting to acquisitions? Do they give workers, suppliers and other non-owners of land veto powers? Do they put the burden of rehabilitation on industries or the government?

Activist courts and NGOs have worsened matters, despite good intentions. The green tribunal has banned sand mining without environmental clearance. The result is a huge shortage of legal sand, which simply encourages illegal mining. A similar outcome is evident after ill-formulated bans on rock quarrying. It now takes 12 years to open a new coal mine. Not just illegal but even legal iron ore mining has been banned in some states. Do other Asian competitors have bans of this sort? If not, how does it affect India's competitiveness?

Neither the courts, NGOs nor the politicians seem to care. A profusion of new rules and regulations are constantly churned out without any cost-benefit exercise to judge the impact on competitiveness. The latest *Doing Business 2013* report of the World Bank says India has slipped from 131st to 134th position in ease of doing business. It stands 177th in ease of starting a business; 183rd in getting a construction permit; and 186th in enforcing contracts. Yet this damning expose of our uncompetitiveness produces no political will to change. We have a deep structural problem that is not even recognised, let alone redressed. Will India have to go bust again to concentrate the minds of politicians?

Q8. Identify the false statement:

(a) India's rules and regulations are inefficient in comparison to other countries and have led to time wastage, extra costs and put extra burden on the government.

(b) India has consistently been ranked as one of the more favourable nations in the world in terms of doing business and starting a business.

(c) India is headed towards a crisis similar to that of the years preceding 1991.

(d) India's political class allows irrelevant political concerns to come in the way of good economic decisions.

Q9. According to the author, competitiveness is enhanced by:

(a) Reducing the requirement for industrial licencing and clearances.

(b) By promoting the creation of public sector monopolies.

(c) By creating newer fair and comprehensive policies.

(d) By creating effective filters for foreign investment into the country.

Q10. If you were to ask the author a question on his views on the role of competitiveness in a nation's growth, which of the following would you choose?

(a) In your opinion, is it unnecessary for the incumbent government to consider and protect the interests of the underprivileged while formulating policies?

(b) Should India revert to the pre-liberalisation conditions, given that despite the reforms of 1991, it is still not experiencing the kind of growth that had been envisioned and promised?

(c) What are the key structural changes that should come about in the India system so as to enhance competitiveness and speed up development?

(d) Are over-enthusiastic activism and petitioning solely responsible for the current bleak economic scenario?

TEST 3

Passage 1

After intense negotiations between Iran and the world powers (chiefly among them the US), 24 November saw a historic breakthrough. In a 6-month interim agreement, Tehran has committed itself to a substantial freezing of its nuclear program in return for 'modest relief' - according to the US President Barack Obama - in sanctions. The agreement will be a first step towards achieving a comprehensive solution, with which the peaceful nature of Iran's nuclear program will be ensured while all sanctions against the country would be lifted.

Now, there has been much speculation over the degree in which the decade-long transatlantic Iran strategy of coercive diplomacy was responsible for reaching this diplomatic victory. Was it the permanent threats of war or the increasingly crippling sanctions which, in the eyes of many Western observers, that led Iran to 'give in'?

Arguably, it rather was a shift away from that policy of threats and pressure, and towards serious diplomacy aiming at a reconciliation of interests (especially during the month of November), which rendered the deal possible. But yes, without any doubt the sanctions did have an impact.

The sanctions have severely deepened Iran's economic *malaise*, considerably harmed a variety of social groups, while part of the power elite quite comfortably adjusted to the situation. Consequently, the power gap separating the state and (civil) society was even boosted.

Yet, the immense damage that sanctions have done to society does not bear much relevance for policy-makers. However, what has gone largely unnoticed by supporters of the sanctions policy is the *realpolitik* fact that, contrary to their stated goal, the escalation of sanctions was accompanied by an increase in Iran's nuclear program. When Obama entered the White House, there were not even 1,000 centrifuges spinning in Iran; today, the figure stands at almost 19,000.

The reason for this is that the West views sanctions through the cost-benefit lens, according to which it can only be a matter of time until the sanctioned party will give in. In contrast, Tehran sees sanctions as an illegitimate form of coercion, which ought to be resisted, for the alternative would be nothing less than capitulation.

Nonetheless, many commentators sardonically insist on praising the sanctions' alleged effectiveness for aiding diplomacy. This is not only a sign of analytical short-sightedness, but also constitutes the not-so-covert attempt to shed a positive light on the coercive diplomacy that was pursued so far.

In reality, Iran's willingness to offer concessions is rooted within a wider context.

Firstly, Iran already demonstrated its readiness to compromise over the last 3 years, which the Obama administration did not dare to accept due to domestic political issues (i.e. his re-election).

Secondly, and this is likely to have been crucial for achieving the agreement in Geneva, Iran's current foreign policy is primarily not a result of pressure through sanctions. Instead, it is embedded into a specific foreign-policy school of thought which is characterised by realism and a policy of *détente*.

Notably, with Hassan Rouhani's election, the 'defensive realist' school of thought reasserted power, which had already been leading during Akbar Hashemi Rafsanjani's and Mohammad Khatami's administrations. Their prime objective was a policy of *détente* and rapprochement, especially with the West but also with neighbouring Arab states - namely, Iran's geopolitical adversary, Saudi Arabia.

In contrast to the 'offensive realists' who were taking the lead under the Ahmadinejad administration, 'defensive realists' do not view foreign policy as a zero-sum game but instead as an arena where win-win situations ought to be explored - especially with the US. Another pivotal difference between these schools of thought is their estimation of the US power.

While 'offensive realists' see the superpower's power-projection capabilities rapidly declining, the 'defensive' camp rightly acknowledges that even the US in relative decline can inflict substantial damage on weaker countries like Iran. The historically unprecedented Iran sanctions regime is a prime example for the veracity of the latter view.

Ultimately, the nuclear agreement in its core has to be seen as an American-Iranian one, which expresses the will of both sides to secure their interests in a rapidly changing regional landscape. To what extent this will affect Washington's traditional regional allies in Tel Aviv and Riyadh will be highly interesting to watch.

Q1. Which of the following is the closest meaning of 'realpolitik'?

(a) A kind of politico-economic system.
(b) The actual consequences of political manoeuvres.
(c) A political strategy focused on practical and material factors.
(d) The idea that politics and reality are interlinked and should not be focused upon ideological things.

Q2. What according to the author is the real reason for Iran 'giving in'?

(a) The inability to contain the debilitating effects of economic coercion.
(b) The overall current direction of its general policy being that of reconciliation and peace-making and strategic reasoning.
(c) A new flavour in foreign policy of appeasement and capitulation.
(d) A failure of top political machinery in protecting the nation's pride.

Q3. What is the key point of divergence between the offensive realists and the defensive realists?

(a) The former argues for a state's active pursuit of power and the latter that states are best served by signalling restraint rather than aggression.
(b) Offensive realists don't believe in peaceful resolution of conflict while defensive realists do.
(c) Offensive realism is a strategy of the power elite while the latter belongs to civil society.
(d) Offensive realists believe in the effectiveness of economic sanctions while the latter condemn them.

Q4. The author would most likely agree with which of the following?

(a) Iran's nuclear deal with the US is a sign of its weakness and the effectiveness of the American economic sanctions.
(b) The US has emerged triumphant in the long tussle between Tehran and Washington DC.
(c) Iran has displayed short-sightedness in pandering to the demands of the US and compromised its own interests in the process.
(d) Iran has key political insight and has displayed restraint that will yield invaluable future gains.

PASSAGE 2

Manto was in Bombay when he heard the news about Pakistan: the British, quitting India at last, had decided in their haste to let the Muslim-majority regions in the east and west become a separate country. To a man like Manto - a Muslim who grew up in Sikhism's holiest city, who derived his livelihood from the cosmopolitan film business and had many Hindu friends - this religious designation of a landmass must have seemed unreal. 'Where were they going to Inter the bones that had been stripped of the flesh of religion by vultures and birds of prey?' Manto would ask later, and not wholly rhetorically, recalling the plunder and flag-waving and killing that had broken out all around him. 'Now that we were free, had subjection ceased to exist? Who would be our slaves? Thousands of Hindus and Muslims were dying all around us. Why were they dying?'

The answers were distressingly near. Even in Bombay, now a part of 'secular' India, 'the communal atmosphere was becoming more vicious by the day'. At the Bombay Talkies film studio where Manto was employed, Hindu staffers began sending anonymous letters to the management, demanding the removal of Muslims from high posts and threatening 'everything from murder to the destruction of the studio'. Manto, suddenly a Muslim among Hindus, panicked. He 'stopped going to Bombay Talkies'. He 'began to drink heavily' and 'all day long' would 'lie on [his] sofa in a sort of daze'.

Much has been made of Manto's decision in that difficult hour to flee to Pakistan. His friend Ismat Chughtai, herself a Muslim writer and self-avowed progressive who stayed on in India, saw in it a proof of Manto's opportunism. She quotes him as saying that 'the future looks beautiful in Pakistan' because Muslim migrants could now 'get the houses of people who've fled from there'. But once in Lahore, now Pakistan, Manto was inconsolable. 'Despite my best efforts', he writes, 'I could not dissociate India from Pakistan and Pakistan from India'. What was such a writer - one who saw maddening continuities where borders had been drawn - to do?

He could begin by putting down his most immediate impressions of the partition violence. *Siyah Hashiye* (*Black Margins*), published in October 1948, is a collection of 'sketches', some as short as a paragraph: in *Jelly*, a murdered ice vendor's blood has merged on the road with ice melted from his pushcart, and a child who drives past it in a horse-carriage mistakes it for jelly. In 'warning', a rich man is dragged out of his house by a mob and kicked to the ground. The mob is about to kill him when the man gets up, removes the dust from his clothes 'with great dignity' and 'wagging a finger at the rioters' says, 'You can kill me, but I am warning you, don't you dare touch my money!' In 'The Garland', another mob, this one in Lahore, frantically descends on the statue of a Hindu philanthropist (Hindus began to flee Lahore as soon as it was 'given' to Pakistan). One of the rioters is about to place a garland of shoes around the statue's neck when he is shot by police and taken to the hospital - a hospital built by the same Hindu philanthropist. And this is what happens in 'modesty':

The rioters brought the train to a stop. Those who belonged to the other religion were methodically picked out and slaughtered. After it was all over, those who remained were treated to a feast of milk, custard pies and fresh fruit.

Before the train moved off, the leader of the assassins made a small farewell speech: 'Dear brothers and sisters, since we were not sure about the time of your train's arrival, regretfully we were not able to offer you anything better than this most modest hospitality. We would have liked to have done more'.

That is all there is: murder - methodical and quick - followed by a feast and an ingratiating speech. Note the withholding of tags: we don't know the location of the massacre or the religion of the killers. All we have is a spurt of base instincts. (Including false modesty, present even in carnage.) Though 'Modesty' is unrelated in plot or sequence to the other sketches in *Siyah Hashiye*, it fits in the whole - like a snapshot in a slide show. Taken one at a time, these sketches enact the speed, randomness and anonymity of the partition violence; cumulatively they expose the partition - the coming-into-being of two flag-waving nation-states - as little more than an orgy of loot and blood. Manto's eye for irony here is sharp as ever. And the fragmented feel of his 'sketches' represents a formal breakthrough - Manto has blasted away the conventions of the short story and arrived at a jagged approximation of the partition trauma.

But the timing of *Siyah Hashiye* was off. The literary scene in Pakistan had already broken down into factions: on one side were the progressive writers, now taking cues from the Soviet Union and calling for a socialist reform of the new state, which was the project of 'a few reactionaries, capitalists and feudal landlords'; and on the other side were 'liberal' writers who disdained 'Art for the sake of the Party' and were more inclined to peddle the idea of a fragile and imperilled new state in need of 'nation-building'. In such a fight, of what use were Manto's writings, which offered Pakistan neither a Communist cure nor a patriotic facelift?

He was punished. The progressives called *Siyah Hashiye* reactionary; Manto responded by saying that he didn't 'care at all about "progressivism"'. His next story about the partition, titled *Thanda Gosht* (*Cold Flesh*), was even more unmindful of the literary temperature: Ishwar Singh, a Sikh recently returned from a round of partition killing, can't bring himself to make love to his mistress. The mistress suspects him of infidelity - why else can't he get it up? In a fit of jealousy she stabs Ishwar Singh with his own dagger.

Bleeding to death, Ishwar Singh admits that he tried to rape an unconscious Muslim girl, only to find her already dead (the 'cold flesh' of the title). While it makes some literary stabs (death as contagion, etc.), *Thanda Gosht* is, ultimately, a racy little thing, relying on that last shocking detail for effect - and may well live up to a charge of sensationalism.

But in Pakistan the charge brought against *Thanda Gosht* was much more serious. A local bureaucrat named Chaudhry Muhammad Hussain, 'one of Manto's old tormentors', took the story to mean that 'we Muslims are so utterly without a sense of honour that Sikhs can rape even our dead daughters'.

Manto was back in the dock.

A protracted court trial in Lahore had him worrying about the punishment, which came to 3 years in jail and a fine of 300 rupees. Manto appealed the verdict. Eventually, after a lot of worrying (and drinking), he was let off the hook by a judge who wore a conspicuously Islamic beard. ('If I sentence Saadat Hassan Manto', the judge had said with a Manto-esque smile, 'he will go around telling everyone that he was sentenced by a man with a beard'.)

Manto now found himself in the singularly unfortunate position of being branded a 'progressive' by the state and a 'reactionary' by the progressives. In an essay written at this time and addressed to his readers, Manto admits to feeling 'a strange melancholy'. He had 'rebelled against the great upheaval that the partition of the country caused' and recovered from that 'sea of blood' some 'pearls of regret'. (He means his partition stories.) But these pearls had found no place in Pakistan. Manto the writer had suffered, but so had Manto the man: 'My present life is full of hardship. After working day and night, I barely make enough to fulfil my daily needs. The fear that keeps gnawing at me is that were I to die suddenly who will look after my wife and three little daughters?'

Q5. What does the sentence, '*Manto, suddenly a Muslim among Hindus, panicked*', mean?

(a) Manto had developed strong vitriolic feelings towards Hindus.

(b) Manto did not identify with his Hindu counterparts anymore.

(c) Manto had not changed, but the circumstances around him had changed throwing his religion into sharp relief.

(d) Manto suddenly saw the clear distinction that existed between Hinduism and Islam.

Q6. Which of the following can be said to be true of the bureaucrat's misinterpretation of the premise of *Thanda Ghost*?

1. Manto was a progressive and therefore everything he wrote was reactionary.
2. The bureaucrat believed Manto was trying to dishonour Islam and bring shame to the community.
3. The bureaucrat deliberately missed the real point of the story which aimed to highlight the human elements of the partition and unfairly charged Manto of attacking Islam.
4. The bureaucrat followed Manto's work and looked for opportunities to disparage him.

(a) 1 and 4

(b) 1, 2, 3 and 4

(c) 2, 3 and 4

(d) 3 and 4

Q7. With reference to the passage, what did Manto's writing not offer the reader?

(a) Irony and romanticism

(b) Sensationalism

(c) Satire

(d) Political solutions

Q8. According to the passage, it can be inferred that:

(a) Manto was apathetic to the fate of Pakistan.

(b) The writings of Manto reflected his anguish at the partition as well as his helplessness.

(c) Manto gladly left India for Pakistan.

(d) Manto's work deserved the criticism levelled at it from all ends.

PASSAGE 3

Scientists have found the oldest DNA evidence of humans' biological history. However, instead of clarifying human evolution, the finding is adding new mysteries, NYT reports. Analysis of a DNA test of a 400,000-year-old human thighbone found in a cave in northern Spain known as the 'Pit of Bones' shows an unexpected evolutionary twist, German scientists report.

The fossil found in Spain had previously seemed to many experts to belong to a forerunner of Neanderthals and as the early hominins looked a little like Neanderthals, researchers expected their DNA to share a common ancestor. When Dr Meyer and his colleagues drilled into the femur, they found ancient human DNA inside, just as they had hoped. However, after analysing mitochondrial DNA extracted from the bone, it was found that early Europeans share a common ancestor with another mysterious species - eastern Eurasian sister group to the Neanderthals, the Denisovans. 'Our expectation was that it would be a very early Neanderthal', Dr Meyer said.

First discovered in Siberia in 2010, the Denisovans were a genetically different group of people who are known only by a pinkie bone and a tooth. 'Everybody had a hard time believing it at first', Dr Meyer said. 'So we generated more and more data to nail it down'. Until now, Denisovans were known only from DNA retrieved from 80,000-year-old remains in Siberia, 4,000 miles east of where the new DNA was found.

'Right now, we've basically generated a big question mark', said Matthias Meyer, a geneticist at the Max Planck Institute for Evolutionary Anthropology in Leipzig, Germany, and a co-author of the new study.

The mismatch between the anatomical and genetic evidence surprised the scientists, who are now rethinking human evolution over the past few hundred thousand years.

Finding such ancient human DNA was a major advance, said David Reich, a geneticist at Harvard Medical School. 'That's an amazing, game-changing thing', he said.

'This would not have been possible even a year ago', said Juan Luis Arsuaga, a palaeoanthropologist at Universidad Complutense de Madrid and a co-author of the paper.

Since the 1970s, Spanish scientists have excavated 28 nearly complete skeletons of humans from the cave. Based on the anatomy of the fossils, Dr. Arsuaga has argued that they belonged to ancestors of Neanderthals, which lived in western Asia and Europe from about 2,00,000 to 30,000 years ago but the new finding gives a totally different picture of human evolution especially as Denisovans were believed to be limited to East Asia, and they were not thought to look so Neanderthal-like.

As *The New York Times* writes, based on previously discovered ancient DNA and fossil evidence, scientists generally agreed that humans' direct ancestors shared a common ancestor with Neanderthals and Denisovans that lived about half a million years ago in Africa. In 2006, a team of French and Belgian researchers obtained a fragment of Neanderthal DNA dating back 1,00,000 years, which until now was the oldest human DNA ever found, ScienceDirect says.

Around the same time as that discovery, Russian scientists sent the Max Planck team 80,000-year-old Denisovans' fossils they had found in a cave in Siberia. When the German scientists sequenced the entire genome from the finger bone of a girl, it turned out to be neither human nor Neanderthal.

This made the scientists assume that their shared ancestors split off from humans' lineage and left Africa, then split further into the Denisovans and Neanderthals about 3,00,000 years ago. The evidence suggested that Neanderthals headed west, towards Europe, and that the Denisovans moved east. Humans' ancestors, meanwhile, stayed in Africa, giving rise to *Homo sapiens* about 2,00,000 years ago. Humans then expanded from Africa into Asia and Europe about 60,000 years ago. They then interbred not only with Neanderthals, but with Denisovans, too. Later, both the Denisovans and Neanderthals became extinct.

Dr. Arsuaga doubts that Denisovans were spread out across so much of the Old World, from Spain to Siberia, so one alternative explanation could be that the humans of Sima de los Huesos were not true Neanderthals, but belonged to the ancestors of both Denisovans and Neanderthals.

It is also possible that the newly discovered DNA was passed to both Neanderthals and Denisovans, but eventually disappeared from Neanderthals, replaced by other variants.

Beth Shapiro, an expert on ancient DNA at the University of California, Santa Cruz, assumes that the humans of Sima de los Huesos belong to another branch of humans, which might have been a species called *Homo erectus* and have originated about 1.8 million years ago having become extinct within the last few hundred thousand years.

'The more we learn from the DNA extracted from these fossils, the more complicated the story becomes', Dr Shapiro said. This new genetic link has baffled experts from around the world. Thus, Professor Chris Stringer from London's Natural History Museum says it shattered the previous record of 1,00,000-year-old DNA. 'With the DNA from the rest of the genome, we really can build up a very full story of these earlier stages of human evolution which so far we haven't been able to do', he said.

Q9. Which of the following can be concluded about the Neanderthal DNA?

(a) They were discovered 80, 000 years ago in Siberia.
(b) They could be identified by only a pinkie bone and a tooth and were not very human-like.
(c) They have been found to be unrelated to the newly discovered DNA found in the Pit of Bones.
(d) It was more concentrated in the West than in the East.

Q10. Identify the true statement:

(a) The Denisovans are the ancestors of Eastern civilisations and the Neanderthals of Western civilisations.
(b) The new DNA could have been passed onto both the Denisovans and the Neanderthals.
(c) Finding the new DNA was a one-off chance discovery that won't be possible again.
(d) Dr. Arsuaga is of the opinion that the humans of Sima de los Huesos belonged to another branch of humans called the *Homo erectus*.

Q11. Which of the following is the most startling revelation as a result of the new finding?

(a) The revelation that human biological history may go back further than 1,00,000 years to 4,00,000 years.
(b) That the DNA was related to the Denisovans, thus far believed to have been limited to the 'Old World'.

(c) That the Denisovans were not as genetically different as was previously believed.

(d) That technology that can gauge the age of DNA this old exists.

TEST 4

Passage 1

The 'Right to Protect' (R2P or RtoP) doctrine developed as a direct result of conflict in the former Yugoslavia and Rwanda in the 1990s, beginning with a re-evaluation of both the obligations and role of the international community in times of conflict. In the International Commission on Intervention and State Sovereignty's (ICISS) groundbreaking report of 2001 entitled *Responsibility to Protect*, it was argued that states have a duty to protect their population from four types of crimes: genocide, war crimes, ethnic cleansing and crimes against humanity.

When states were either unable or unwilling to meet this responsibility, the responsibility shifted then to the international community. In this sense, R2P consisted of three consistent sets of responsibilities: to prevent, react and rebuild. In 2005, world leaders at the World Summit collectively endorsed R2P and the Summit's outcome document was later adopted as a resolution of the General Assembly. R2P was further reaffirmed by UN Security Council (UNSC) Resolutions 1674 (2006) and 1894 (2009), respectively. In just a short time, R2P became a concept with significant weight in the international community.

Irrespective of its positive start, R2P had problems moving from a theoretical concept to one firmly recognised in policy. The situation in Dafur was often seen to be a 'test case' for R2P, one which was widely judged to have failed. In 2007, after the Kenyan elections, some 1,500 people were killed as a result of ethnic and tribal violence, yet through a diplomatic effort understood directly in R2P terms, both sides settled on a power-sharing agreement - demonstrating R2P's capacity to facilitate the prevention of crimes through peaceful measures.

Moreover, R2P has been applied to circumstances it was not originally intended for, the slow response of Myanmar to requests for humanitarian access after Cyclone Nargis and the Russian invasion of Georgia both in 2008. In both cases the international community rejected claims of the application of R2P, further clarifying the limitations of R2P's remit. In 2009, in the midst of a situation between Sri Lankan government forces and Tamil Tigers (LTTE) in the Wanni region, the UN country team withdrew its entire staff and remained silent on potential violations of both humanitarian law and international human rights law by the state. In an Internal Review Panel of 2012, it was ruled that this outcome was a 'grave failure' by the UN, in contradiction of its core responsibilities and principles. All of the different interpretations of when R2P comes into effect illustrates that state sovereignty remains a strong international norm that can undermine action.

The different actions of the UNSC in both Libya and Syria shed some light on the current effectiveness of R2P. In 2011, in response to the violence in Libya, the UNSC passed Resolution 1970, under Chapter VII of the UN Charter. With the Qaddafi regime's failure to comply to UNSC demands, the UNSC authorised Resolution 1973, which consented the use of force in order to protect civilians from danger, enforced a no-fly zone over Libya and implemented an arms embargo. This was the first instance where the UNSC had permitted the use of force against a Member State in the name of protecting civilians.

In Syria, the UNSC initially failed to gain consensus on the conflict. There were several attempts to pass UNSC Resolutions, yet all were in vain because of vetoes by both Russia and China. For other actors, namely Russia, the experience of Libya has compelled it to openly criticise Western pressure on Syria as it might have opened the door to an undesirable regime change. The UNSC then authorised the deployment of the UN Supervision Mission in Syria (UNSMIS) during 2012, where only after a couple of months its failure to influence the conflict resulted in an embarrassing withdrawal.

R2P as a concept offers much potential but remains far from perfect. With the 'success' in Libya and bigger failure in Syria, it could be said that the end of R2P is quite close, simply because it is so selectively applied and in the current international framework does not allow much flexibility (such as the sheer difficulty of authorising humanitarian intervention). If it is the end of R2P, one wonders how then intervention will be framed in the future.

Q1. Which of the following is not a weakness of the R2P?

(a) Due to the wide room for interpretation, it is susceptible to misuse.

(b) It falls prey to selective and impartial implementation.

(c) Human rights remain a flexible concept and more so internationally.

(d) There are not enough policy mechanisms or organisations to implement the R2P.

Q2. With reference to the passage, select the option that involves the application of a component of the R2P:

(a) Nearly all states in the world have maintained active defence forces and a slew of international civil servants responsible for international diplomacy.

(b) Some states such as The Peoples' Republic of China engage in repression and contraction of basic liberties like freedom of expression, that all human beings are entitled to.

(c) In many nations of the world women are not yet entitled to the same privileges as men and suffer atrocities at their hands.

(d) In some countries, the government is monarchical, and citizens assume the role of passive subjects instead of active participants.

Q3. With regard to the implementation of R2P, which statement is not justified?

(a) Diplomatic efforts in Kenya in order to bring both the sides to power-sharing agreement show the influence of R2P. Although it missed on the timeliness part, prior implementation could have avoided the genocide that took place just after the elections.

(b) R2P as a concept failed to be implemented in Syria and not in Libya because of the interventions of Russia and China at the right time, seeing the result from the Libyan case. It does reflect the political grasp of superpowers on implementations of UN policies.

(c) Withdrawal of UN forces from Sri Lanka shows the incompetency of the UN organisation for not being able to implement its responsibilities properly and not the weakness of the policy of R2P.

(d) Though theoretically R2P is a strong concept, implementation is difficult because of the difference in interpretation among the nations across the world.

Q4. The author's tone towards the R2P is.

(a) Critical
(b) Sceptical
(c) Neutral
(d) Specious

PASSAGE 2

JFK has often been criticised for his lack of tangible political success in the US yet his domestic record is far from poor. Civil rights formed one of the cornerstones of Kennedy's domestic programme as both the President and the Attorney General, Robert Kennedy strove to improve the living and working conditions of African-Americans in the US. The CEEO (Commission on Equal Employment Opportunity) was created to ensure that all federal government employees were subject to the same employment rights and 40 African-Americans were appointed to senior federal posts under his administration.

While these figures may seem paltry by today's standards, these actions inspired momentum in the movement for racial equality. On 11 June 1963 in his address to the nation, Kennedy became the first president since the much-revered Abraham Lincoln to publically promote the moral necessity for racial equality. In August 1963, despite initial fears about the Civil Rights March on Washington, Kennedy gave it his full backing; Martin Luther King Jr did the rest.

Kennedy's New Frontier essentially centred on breaking down long-held beliefs that had made discrimination and exploitation the norm. During his time in office, the minimum wage was increased to $1.25 and coverage was extended to 4.3 million people. At the same time, the Commission on the Status of Women was created in 1961 to ensure greater standards of equality for women - particularly in the work place. Kennedy's approach to promoting sexual equality as part of his domestic programme was something that even FDR's New Deal had overlooked.

The Peace Corps, created by Kennedy to expand the US influence abroad while also providing the American youth with the opportunity to experience different cultures and ways of life, operated under a $375M budget in 2012. This serves to highlight the longevity of JFK's ideals which would not have stood the test of time had his policies been lacking in substance.

Foreign policy was Kennedy's biggest strength and asset, despite early failings with the Bay of Pigs debacle and the Vienna Conference. While it was Eisenhower who had planned the invasion of Cuba, it was Kennedy who authorised the invasion and was rightly criticised for its failure. In Vienna in 1961, the young Kennedy was no match for his more experienced Soviet counterpart. Khrushchev left Austria thinking Kennedy to be naïve and weak.

These thoughts were quickly dispelled the following year during the Cuban Missile Crisis when Kennedy displayed strong, decisive leadership in the face of an international crisis. Despite intense pressure from leading military figures within ExComm to go to war over the placement of Soviet missiles in Cuba, Kennedy stuck to his guns and gave the Soviet Union every opportunity to withdraw missiles from Cuba without provoking military action. The naval blockade and the covert methods of negotiation he employed ultimately proved successful as he reached his goal, which in his words was 'not the victory of might, but the vindication of right'.

Under the spectre of nuclear war, JFK's leadership was measured. His behaviour not only eased the fears of the American people but also ensured the immediate withdrawal of Soviet missiles, thus handing his administration a significant boost both at home and abroad. Not only was war avoided, but JFK also enabled the Soviets to pull out without losing face at home by agreeing to withdraw outdated US missiles from Turkey.

His actions displayed a deeply held moral belief in the pursuit of peace.

JFK's style has never been called into question. His approach to politics was fresh and he exuded a personable charm that was distinctly lacking in many of his contemporaries.

Q5. Which quality of Kennedy from the following, do you think is not true as per the passage?

(a) His hold on the domestic front by the implementation of the movement against Racial Discrimination.

(b) His methods were different from conventional politicians. He was always up against the rival nations and created shadows of war. This inculcated a feeling of fear not only among the Americans, but brought him criticism throughout the world.

(c) His ability to learn from his mistakes and failures allowed him to achieve success in the later stages of his career.

(d) He not only proved his mettle as a successful strategist and a leader, but also a combination of fresh ideas made him stand apart from his contemporaries.

Q6. The author would agree with which of the following judgements about the style and character of JFK's politics and personality?

(a) He was a misfit in the world of politics, with little relevant experience and lacked foresight.

(b) He was an asset to American polity and was crucial to the success of many civil rights' movements and initiatives in the country.

(c) Kennedy was faultless and always authorised the best possible courses of action.

(d) Kennedy was considered a political hero and there are no questions as to his contributions to the American political system.

Passage 3

China's leaders have now agreed to relax the country's decades-old 'one-child' policy. Couples now will be permitted to have two children if one parent is an only child (previously, both parents had to be only children), making the new rule applicable to most of the post-1980s generation that grew up in urban areas. But, while the potential social consequences are obvious, the likely economic impact is less apparent.

When the one-child policy was implemented in 1979 - in an effort to alleviate social, economic and environmental pressures following the population boom in the 1950s and 1960s - the fertility rate plummeted from three children per household in 1970 to 1.2 per cent in 1982. The household saving rate subsequently soared, from 10.4 per cent in 1983 to a staggering 30.5 per cent in 2011. Could the one-child policy have fuelled this rise? If so, will the modified policy precipitate a reversal in this trend and, in turn, a consumption boom in the coming decade?

Rising fertility rates can lower the household saving rate in two main ways. First, children demand increased household expenditure - especially on education, which, for only children aged 15-22, accounts for 15-25 per cent of total Chinese household expenditures. Second, with more children to support them in their old age, parents feel less pressure to save for retirement.

An examination of the spending and saving patterns of households with twins born under the one-child policy suggests that these changes could lead to a drop of 8-9 percentage points in China's household savings rate - to around 22 per cent - in the coming decades. Because the birth of twins is arguably an exogenous occurrence (unrelated to factors like income and education that affect parents' decision to have multiple children), comparing households with an only child to those with twins can reveal some of the effects that an additional child has on saving.

From 2002 to 2009, the average saving rate for an only-child household was 21.3 per cent, compared to 12.8 per cent for a household with twins - a difference that holds across all income groups. Regression analysis of all urban households in the 1992-2009 period shows that an additional child reduced the saving rate by about 6-7 percentage points. One additional child increased education expenditure (as a percentage of household income) by an average of 7 percentage points, food expenditure by 2.5 percentage points and other spending by roughly 2.7 percentage points.

Intergenerational support - whereby children provide for parents in old age - is not only a social norm; in China, it is stipulated by law. More than half of elderly people's income derives from family support, which includes financial transfers and in-kind benefits like cohabitation. And the total amount of transfers that parents receive rises with the number of children.

The added security offered by additional offspring means that loosening the one-child policy will probably lead parents to save less on their own, and possibly even to make the kind of risky investments that would be unwise for only-child families. In fact, the one-child policy could be an important reason why, in recent decades, Chinese households have gravitated towards riskless assets. If parents view having a second child as doubling their 'safe assets', they may decide to allocate more of their portfolio towards riskier assets.

It follows that parents of multiple children may also feel secure enough to consume more. On average, the share of household income spent by parents of multiple children on non-child-related consumption in later stages of life is about 8 percentage points higher than it is for parents of only children.

The coming demographic shift will also affect national saving. The share of young dependents/borrowers will rise relative to the middle-aged working population. Reducing the proportion of high savers in the economy will tend to lower the aggregate saving rate. The share of elderly people in the population, however, will not change until a generation later.

Though the change to the one-child policy may cause a moderate consumption boom, it could also reverse a positive trend: the acceleration of human-capital accumulation. The typical only child receives significantly more educational investment than the average twin and is 40 per cent more likely to pursue higher education (as opposed to a vocational school). This can likely be explained, in part, by a quantity-quality trade-off.

Q7. Out of the following points which are in sync with the author's thinking about the new policy:

1. The removal of 'one-child policy' will increase the support to the elders in the family, thereby safeguarding their savings and support in the older age.
2. Chinese households will have increased consumption and savings rate will decline, which in turn will make the parents to invest more in assets that are riskier to increase the returns.
3. Rising fertility rates will cause more of social concerns and economic impact will be lesser.
4. The removal of such a policy will soon decrease the average age of China, thus it will add to the national savings.

(a) Only 1 and 3

(b) 1, 2 and 4

(c) 2 and 3

(d) 2, 3 and 4

Q8. Which of the following will NOT be a consequence of the relaxation of the one-child policy:

(a) The Chinese will begin showing less risk-averse behaviour and adopt more unconventional investment practices.

(b) The quality of education per child is likely to suffer.

(c) The economy will contract as household turn towards greater savings.

(d) The fertility rate of household will show a marked jump and the share of elderly people in the population will ascend slowly.

Q9. Identify the correct inference of the author's intent in the passage:

(a) To insinuate that the Chinese consider their offspring as mere assets.

(b) To analyse the socio-economic impact of the revocation of the old one-child policy in China.

(c) To describe the successes and failures of the one-child policy.

(d) To depict the recent changes and patterns in the Chinese society and economy.

TEST 5

Passage 1

Implicit in the freedoms we cherish in our democracy is our right to offend. That is the cornerstone of all free thought and its expression. In a country as beautiful and complex as ours, it is our inalienable right to offend that makes us the nation we are. Of course I also recognise the fact that this right attaches to itself many risks, including the risk of being targeted. But as long as these risks are within reasonable, well-defined limits, most people will take them in their stride. I am ready to defend my right to offend in any debate or a court of law. But it's not fine when mobs come to lynch you. It's not right, when they vandalise your home or burn your books or art or stop you from showing your film or, what's becoming more frequent, hire thugs to kill you. Authors, journalists, painters and now even activists and rationalists are being openly attacked and murdered.

It's a constant challenge to walk the tightrope; to know exactly where to draw the line when you write, paint, speak. The funny thing is truth has no limits, no frontiers. When you want to say something you strongly believe in, there is no point where you can stop. The truth is always whole. When you draw a line, as discretion suggests, you encourage half-truths and falsehoods being foisted on others, you subvert your conscience. In some cases it's not even possible to draw a line. A campaigner against corruption can never stop midway through his campaign even though he knows exactly at which point the truth invites danger, extreme danger. Yet India is a brave nation and there are many common people, ordinary citizens with hardly any resources and no one to protect them who are ready to go out on a limb and say it as it is. They are the ones who keep our democracy burning bright.

Every few days you read about a journalist killed. About RTI activists murdered for exposing what is in the public interest. You read about people campaigning for a cause (like Narendra Dabholkar, who fought against superstitions, human sacrifices, babas and tantriks) being gunned down in cold blood. Even before the police can start investigations, the crime is invariably politicised. Issues of religion, caste, community, political affiliation are dragged in only to complicate (read obfuscate) the crime and, before you know it, the story dies because some other, even more ugly crime is committed somewhere else and draws away the headlines and your attention. And when that happens, criminals get away. We are today an attention deficit nation because there's so much happening everywhere, all pretty awful stuff, that it's impossible for anyone to stay focused.

Even fame and success can't protect you. Dr Dabholkar was a renowned rationalist, a man of immaculate credentials. Yet he was gunned down by fanatics who thought he was endangering their trade in cheating poor and gullible people. Husain was our greatest living painter. He was forced into exile in his 1980s because zealots refused to let him live and work in peace here. They vandalised his art; hunted down his shows; ransacked them. Yet Husain, as I knew him, was as ardent a Hindu as anyone else. His paintings on the Mahabharata are the stuff legends are made of. A pusillanimous government lacked the will to intervene.

When we deny ourselves the right to offend, we deny ourselves the possibility of change. That's how societies become brutal, moribund, disgustingly boring. Is this what you want? If the answer is No and you want to stay a free citizen, insist on your right to offend. If enough people do that, change is not just inevitable. It's assured. And change is what defines a living culture.

Q1. The author is in agreement with which of the following?

1. The right to offend is worth preserving and an essential component of a democratic set up. It allows one to put his/her point upfront when it's the need of hour.
2. The absence of the right to offend would lead to a destruction of cultural freedom and society would degenerate into a lacklustre, homogenous constant.
3. The right to offend should be absolutely limitless to safeguard us against the atrocities that are brought down upon us by the zealots, who will always prevail in the society.
4. The right to offend is responsible for many injustices such as the murder of Narendra Dabholkar and the vandalism against Hussain's paintings.

(a) 1
(b) 1, 2 and 3
(c) 1 and 2
(d) 3 and 4

Q2. If you were to paraphrase the word 'pusillanimous', which of the following would you choose to use:

(a) Complacent
(b) Ineffective
(c) Timid
(d) Sensible

Q3. Why is the right to offend a right worth preserving?

(a) It empowers a select few in enforcing their opinions on others regardless of their acceptance or agreement.
(b) The right to express oneself is essential for individual development and allows for cultural advancement.
(c) To offend is to deny another of his/her right.
(d) The right to offend is a partial representation of the truth, and the truth must be expressed in public.

PASSAGE 2

Simon Murden writes, '*The Clash of Civilisations* may not have told the whole story of what was happening in the post-Cold War world, but it told part of it'. The claims he made shaped the contours of the international realm in a manner which was largely ignored in an age dominated by ideological leanings. The post-Cold War dynamics have been captured by Huntington by elevating the importance of cultural variables. The fervour of the text is decidedly realist; however, Huntington in an interview clarified that he was aware of the views which branded his work as the 'latest version of billiard ball realism' but he also asserted that the difference lay in the replacement of nation-state as a primary actor to civilisations as the movers' history. In essence the Cold War paradigm now came to be replaced by a new paradigm with culture occupying the central role. The problem of binaries was evident as the shifting power equations gave way to identities being defined not in ideological terms rather they were now defined in civilisational terms which he believed was, 'culture writ large'.

Huntington's contribution lay in generating a new paradigm. Gideon Rose argued that his work was directed at the major practical and theoretical questions of the day. Herein lay his brilliance. However, it has also been argued that his methodology was anecdotal in nature and it catered to few specific situations to arrive at a grand theory. His approach many believe can lead to situation-based convenient explanations and arguments. Huntington was aware of this and he acknowledged the need to situating certain issues in time and space. He was never much concerned about the method, as much as he was about arriving at empirical generalisations and this encouraged him to draw comparisons. He identified the emergence of western universalism and the backlash against it which assumed various forms. It ranged from emergence of religious fundamentalism to challenges in the form of assertion of Asian Values which gained salience owing to Japan's emergence as a major economic power.

The notion of power is central to his work. This is evident in his treatment of civilisational differences as a major source of conflict in the post-Cold War era. In this sense he recognised culture as acquiring a political dimension. The issue of identity defined by religion which was obscured by the Cold War obsession with ideologies gained renewed importance. The understanding of the 'other' was weighed against their 'own constructed identities'. Huntington warns against insistence on equating westernization and modernisation. This he argues strengthens indigenising forces and often initiates a violent opposition to the west.

Samuel Huntington's book provides a powerful and compelling analysis of a de-ideologised world in which he writes, 'The velvet curtain of culture has replaced the iron curtain of ideology as the most significant dividing line in Europe'. On the one hand was Francis Fukuyama who was proclaiming that the collapse of the Soviet Union signalled the end of history as liberal values triumphed, and on the other hand was Huntington who evidently was uncomfortable with such a Universalist claim. Huntington writes that, 'western belief in universality of western culture suffers from three problems: it is false; it is immoral; and it is dangerous'.

He recognised the pitfalls of viewing the neoliberal concepts of interdependence largely in terms of the west and acknowledged the need for 'universalism at home and multiculturalism abroad'. The 'Clash of Civilisations thesis' despite its misinterpretations became conventional wisdom when much of the conflicts and wars in the world could be articulated in terms of being a conflict between different cultures. The 9/11 incident signalled the potency of cultural differences. The borders of civilisations for Huntington became sacrosanct. To the extent that many have argued, he ignored the cross-cultural interactions which shaped these civilisations and the internal schisms characteristic of many of them.

Q4. Which of the following is NOT a conclusion applicable to Huntington's work or style?

(a) Huntington's work had a distinctively realist flavour with a stand opposite to the neoliberal world's generalised universality.

(b) Huntington employed an anecdotal methodology to arrive at grand theories.

(c) Huntington was essentially a universalist who used empirical generalisations to justify his deductions.

(d) Huntington was a critic of the neoliberal school of thought and believed that the curtain of ideology was being replaced by the curtain of culture.

Q5. If you were to ask Samuel Huntington a follow-up question based on your reading of this passage, which of the following would be the LEAST FAVOURABLE option?

(a) What are the disadvantages of viewing the world through the Universalist prism?

(b) Can culture be prevented from taking on political dimensions such as in the West, or this inevitable? Again, is it necessary?

(c) In what ways can cross-cultural interactions shape entire civilisations?

(d) Is ideology completely irrelevant in the age of the curtain of culture?

Q6. In the context of the passage, the best replacement (that would not alter the meaning of the sentence) for the phrase 'internal schisms' would be:

(a) Internal estrangements

(b) Internal detachments

(c) Internal rifts

(d) Internal dissension

Passage 3

A country under foreign domination seeks escape from the present in dreams of a vanished age and finds consolation in visions of past greatness. That is a foolish and dangerous pastime in which many of us indulge. An equally questionable practice for us in India is to imagine that we are still spiritually great though we have come down in the world in other respects. Spiritual or any other greatness cannot be founded on lack of freedom and opportunity, or on starvation and misery. Many western writers have encouraged that notion that Indians are other-worldly. I suppose the poor and unfortunate in every country become to some extent other-worldly, unless they become revolutionaries, for this world is evidently not meant for them. So also subject peoples.

As a man grows to maturity he is not entirely engrossed in, or satisfied with, the external objective world. He seeks also some inner meaning, some psychological and physical satisfaction. So also with people and civilisations as they mature and grow adult. Every civilisation and every people exhibit these parallel streams of an external life and an internal life. Where they meet or keep close to each other, there is an equilibrium and stability. When they diverge conflict arises and the crises that torture the mind and spirit.

Q7. The passage mentions that '*this world is evidently not meant for them*'. It refers to people who

1. Seek freedom from foreign domination.
2. Live in starvation and misery.
3. Become revolutionaries.

Which of the statements given above is/are correct?

(a) 1 and 2
(b) 2 only
(c) 2 and 3
(d) 3 only

Q8. Consider the following assumptions:

1. A country under foreign domination cannot indulge in spiritual pursuit.
2. Poverty is an impediment in the spiritual pursuit.
3. Subject peoples may become other-worldly.

With reference to the passage, which of the above assumptions is/are valid?

(a) 1 and 2
(b) 2 only
(c) 2 and 3
(d) 3 only

Q9. The passage thematically centres on

(a) The state of mind of oppressed people.
(b) Starvation and misery.
(c) The growth of civilisation.
(d) Body, mind and spirit of people in general.

Q10. According to the passage, the torture of the mind and spirit is caused

(a) By the impact of foreign domination.
(b) By the desire to escape from foreign domination and find consolation in visions of past greatness.
(c) Due to lack of equilibrium between an external life and an internal life.
(d) Due to one's inability to be either revolutionary or other-worldly.

TEST 6

Passage 1

The concept of 'creative society' refers to a phase of development of a society in which a large number of potential contradictions become articulate and active. This is most evident when oppressed social groups get politically mobilised and demand their rights. The upsurge of the peasants and tribals, the movements for regional autonomy and self-determination, the environmental movements and the women's movements in the developing countries are signs of emergence of creative society in the contemporary times. The forms of social movements and their intensity may vary from country to country and place to place within a country. But the very presence of movements for social transformation in various spheres of a society indicates the emergence of a creative society in a country.

Q1. What does the author imply by 'creative society'?

1. A society where diverse art forms and literary writings seek incentive.
2. A society where social inequalities are accepted as the norm.
3. A society where a large number of contradictions are recognised.
4. A society where the exploited and the oppressed groups grow conscious of their human rights and upliftment.

Select the correct answer using the codes given below:

(a) 1, 2 and 3
(b) 4 only
(c) 3 and 4
(d) 2 and 4

Q2. What according to the passage are the manifestations of social movements?

1. Aggressiveness and being incendiary.
2. Instigation by external forces.
3. Quest for social equality and individual freedom.
4. Urge for granting privileges and self-respect to disparaged sections of the society.

Select the correct answer using the codes given below:

(a) 1 and 3 only
(b) 2 and 4 only
(c) 3 and 4 only
(d) 1, 2, 3 and 4

Q3. With reference to the passage, consider the following statements:

1. To be a creative society, it is essential to have a variety of social movements.
2. To be a creative society, it is imperative to have potential contradictions and conflicts.

Which of the statements given above is/are correct?

(a) 1 only
(b) 2 Only
(c) Both 1 and 2
(d) Neither 1 nor 2

Passage 2

Ecosystems provide people with a variety of goods and services: food, clean water, clean air, flood control, soil stabilisation, pollination, climate regulation, spiritual fulfilment and aesthetic enjoyment, to name just a few. Most of these benefits either are irreplaceable or the technology necessary to replace them is prohibitively expensive. For example, potable fresh water can be provided by desalinating sea-water, but only at great cost.

The rapidly expanding human population has greatly modified the Earth's ecosystems to meet their increased requirements of some of the goods and services, particularly food, fresh water, timbre, fibre and fuel. These modifications save contributed substantially to human well-being and economic development. The benefits have not been equally distributed. Some people have actually been harmed by these changes. Moreover, short-term increases in some ecosystem goods and services have come at the cost of the long-term degradation of others. For example, efforts to increase the production of food and fibre have decreased the ability of some ecosystems to provide clean water, regulate flooding and support biodiversity.

Q4. With reference to the passage, consider the following statements.

Expanding human population has an adverse effect on:

1. Spiritual fulfilment
2. Aesthetic enjoyment
3. Potable fresh water
4. Production of food and fibre
5. Biodiversity

Which of the statements given above are correct?

(a) 1, 2 and 3 only
(b) 2, 4 and 5 only
(c) 3 and 5 only
(d) 1, 2, 3, 4 and 5

Q5. The passage mentions that 'some people have actually been harmed by these changes'. What does it imply?

1. The rapid expansion of population has adversely affected some people.
2. Sufficient efforts have not been made to increase the production of food and fibre.
3. In the short term some people may be harmed, but in the long term everyone will benefit from modifications in the Earth's ecosystems.

Which of the statements given above is/are correct?

(a) 1 only
(b) 2 only
(c) 1 and 3
(d) None of the statements given above

Q6. With reference to the passage, consider the following statements:

1. It is imperative to modify the Earth's ecosystems for the well-being of mankind.
2. Technology can never replace all the goods and services provided by ecosystems.

Which of the statements given above is/are correct?

(a) 1 only
(b) 2 only
(c) Both 1 and 2
(d) Neither 1 nor 2

PASSAGE 3

For achieving inclusive growth there is a critical need to rethink the role of the State. The early debate among economists about the size of the Government can be misleading. The need of the hour is to have an enabling Government. India is too large and complex a nation for the State to be able to deliver all that is needed. Asking the Government to produce all the essential goods, create all the necessary jobs and keep a curb on the prices of all goods is to lead to a large cumbersome bureaucracy and widespread corruption.

The aim must be to stay with the objective of inclusive growth that was laid down by the founding fathers of the nation and also to take a more modern view of what the state can realistically deliver.

This is what leads to the idea of an enabling state, that is, a government that does not try to directly deliver to the citizens everything that they need. Instead, it (1) creates an enabling ethos for the market so that individual enterprise can flourish and citizens can, for the most part, provide for the needs of one another, and (2) steps in to help those who do not manage to do well for themselves, for there will always be individuals, no matter what the system, who need support and help. Hence we need a government that, when it comes to the market, sets effective, incentive-compatible rules and remains on the sidelines with minimal interference, and, at the same time, plays an important role in directly helping the poor by ensuring that they get basic education and health services and receive adequate nutrition and food.

Q7. According to the passage:

1. The objective of inclusive growth was laid down by the founding fathers of the nation.
2. Need of the hour is to have an enabling Government.
3. The Government should engage in maximum interference in market processes.
4. There is a need to change the size of the Government.

Which of the statements given above are correct?

(a) 1 and 2 only
(b) 2 and 3 only
(c) 1 and 4 only
(d) 1, 2, 3 and 4

Q8. According to the passage, the strategy of inclusive growth can be effected by focusing on

(a) Meeting all the needs of every citizen in the country.
(b) Increasing the regulations over the manufacturing sector.
(c) Controlling the distribution of manufactured goods.
(d) Delivery of the basic services to the deprived sections of the society.

Q9. What constitutes Government an enabling?

1. A large bureaucracy.
2. Implementation of welfare programmes through representatives.
3. Creating an ethos that helps individual enterprise.
4. Providing resources to those who are underprivileged.
5. Offering direct help to the poor regarding basic services.

Select the correct answer from the codes given below:

(a) 1, 2 and 3 only
(b) 4 and 5 only
(c) 3, 4 and 5 only
(d) 1, 2, 3, 4 and 5

Q10. Why is the State unable to deliver 'all that is needed'?

1. It does not have sufficient bureaucracy.
2. It does not promote inclusive growth.

Select the correct answer from the codes given below:

(a) 1 only
(b) 2 only
(c) Both 1 and 2
(d) Neither 1 nor 2

Q11. What is the essential message being conveyed by the author of the passage?

(a) The objectives of inclusive growth laid down by the founding fathers of the nation should be remembered.
(b) The Government needs to make available more schools and health services.
(c) The Government needs to establish markets and industries to meet the needs of the poor strata of the society.
(d) There is a need to rethink the role of the State in achieving inclusive growth.

TEST 7

Passage 1

Now India's children have a right to receive at least 8 years of education, the gnawing question is whether it will remain on paper or become a reality. One hardly needs a reminder that this right is different from the others enshrined in the Constitution, that the beneficiary - a 6-year-old child cannot demand it, nor can she or he fight a legal battle when the right is denied or violated. In all cases, it is the adult society which must act on behalf of the child's right to education when denied, no compensation offered later can be adequate or relevant. This is so because childhood does not last. If a legal battle fought on behalf of a child is eventually won, it may be little use to the boy or girl because the opportunity missed at school during childhood cannot serve the same purpose later in life. This may be painfully true for girls because our society permits them only a short childhood, if at all. The Right to Education (RTE) has become law at a point in India's history when the ghastly practice of female infanticide has resurfaced in the form of foeticide. This is 'symptomatic of a deeper turmoil' in society which is compounding the traditional obstacles to the education of girls. Tenacious prejudice against the intellectual potential of girls runs across our cultural diversity and the system of education has not been able to address it.

Q1. With reference to the passage, consider the following statements:

1. When children are denied education, adult society does not act on behalf of them.
2. Right to Education as a law cannot be enforced in the country.

Which of the statements given above is/are correct?

(a) 1 only
(b) 2 only
(c) Both 1 and 2
(d) Neither 1 nor 2

Q2. According to the passage, what could be the traditional obstacle to the education of girls?

1. Inability of parents to fight a legal battle when the Right to Education is denied to their children.
2. The traditional way of thinking about girls' role in society.
3. The prejudice against the intellectual 'potential of girls'.
4. Improper system of education.

Select the correct answer from the codes given below:

(a) 1 and 2 only
(b) 2, 3 and 4 only
(c) 1, 3 and 4 only
(d) 1, 2, 3 and 4

Q3. On the basis of the passage, consider the following statements:

1. Right to Education is a legal right and not a fundamental right.
2. For realising the goal of universal education, the education system in the country must be made identical to that of developed countries.

Which of the statements given above is/are correct?

(a) 1 only
(b) 2 only
(c) Both 1 and 2
(d) Neither 1 nor 2

Q4. Which one of the following statements conveys the key message of the passage?

(a) India has declared that education is compulsory for its children.
(b) Adult society is not keen on implementing the Right to Education.
(c) The Right to Education, particularly of a girl child, needs to be safeguarded.
(d) The system of education should address the issue of Right to Education.

Q5. Which one of the following statements conveys the inference of the passage?

(a) The society has a tenacious prejudice against the intellectual potential of girls.
(b) Adults cannot be relied upon to fight on behalf of children for their Right to Education.
(c) The legal fight to get education for children is often protracted and prohibitive.
(d) There is no sufficient substitute for education received in childhood.

Passage 2

A species that exerts an influence out of proportion to its abundance in an ecosystem is called a keystone species. The keystone species may influence both the species richness of communities and the flow of energy and materials through ecosystems. The sea star *Pisaster ochraceus* which lives in rocky intertidal ecosystems on the Pacific coast of North America is also an example of a keystone species. Its preferred prey is the mussel *Mytilus californianus*. In the absence of sea stars, these mussels crowd out other competitors in a broad belt of the intertidal zone. By consuming mussels, sea star creates bare spaces that are taken over by a variety of other species.

A study at the University of Washington demonstrated the influence of *Pisaster* on species richness by removing sea stars from selected parts of the intertidal zone repeatedly over a period of 5 years. Two major changes occurred in the area from which sea stars were removed. First, the lower edge of the mussel bed extended farther down into the intertidal zone, showing that sea stars are able to eliminate mussels completely where they are covered with water most of the time. Second, and more dramatically, 28 species of animals and algae disappeared from the sea star removal zone. Eventually only *Mytilus*, the dominant competitor, occupied the entire substratum. Through its effect on competitive relationships, predation by *Pisaster* largely determines which species live in these rocky intertidal ecosystems.

Q6. What is the crux of the passage?

(a) Sea star has a preferred prey.
(b) A preferred prey determines the survival of a keystone species.
(c) Keystone species ensures species diversity.
(d) Sea star is the only keystone species on the Pacific coast of North America.

Q7. With reference to the passage, consider the following statements:

1. Mussels are generally the dominant species in intertidal ecosystems.
2. The survival of sea stars generally determined abundance of mussels.

Which of the statements given above is/are correct?

(a) 1 only
(b) 2 only
(c) Both 1 and 2
(d) Neither 1 nor 2

Q8. Which of the following is/are implied by the passage?

1. Mussels are always hard competitors for sea stars.
2. Sea stars of the Pacific coast have reached the climax of their evolution.
3. Sea stars constitute an important component in the energy flow in intertidal ecosystem.

Which of the statements given above is/are correct?

(a) 1 and 2
(b) 2 only
(c) 1 and 3
(d) 3 only

Q9. Consider the following assumptions:

1. The food chains/food web in an ecosystem is influenced by keystone species.
2. The presence of keystone species is a specific characteristic of aquatic ecosystems.
3. If the keystone species is completely removed from an ecosystem, it will lead to the collapse of the ecosystem:

With reference to the passage, which of the above assumptions is/are valid?

(a) 1 only
(b) 2 and 3 only
(c) 1 and 3 only
(d) 1, 2 and 3

Q10. Which is the most dominant competitor in the absence of the Pisaster?

(a) The mussels
(b) The sea oyster
(c) The sea star
(d) The sea urchin

PASSAGE 3

A moral act must be our own act; must spring from our own will. If we act mechanically, there is no moral content in our act. Such action would be moral, if we think it proper to act like a machine and do so. For, in doing so, we use our discrimination. We should bear in mind the distinction between acting mechanically and acting intentionally. It may be moral of a king to pardon a culprit. But the messenger carrying out the order of pardon plays only a mechanical part in the king's moral act. But if the messenger were to carry out the king's order considering it to be his duty, his action would be a moral one. How can a man understand morality who does not use his own intelligence and power of thought, but lets himself be swept along like a log of wood by a current? Sometimes a man defies convention and acts on his own with a view to absolute good.

Q11. Which of the following statements best describe/ describes the thought of the writer?

1. A moral act calls for using our discretion.
2. Man should react to a situation immediately.
3. Man must do his duty.
4. Man should be able to defy convention in order to be moral.

Select the correct answer from the codes given below

(a) 1 only
(b) 1 and 3
(c) 2 and 3
(d) 1 and 4

Q12. Which of the following statements is the nearest definition of moral action, according to the writer?

(a) It is a mechanical action based on official orders from superiors.
(b) It is an action based on our sense of discretion.
(c) It is a clever action based on the clarity of purpose.
(d) It is a religious action based on understanding.

Q13. The passage contains a statement *'lets himself be swept along like a log of wood by a current'*. Among the following statements, which is/are nearest in meaning to this?

1. A person does not use his own reason.
2. He is susceptible to influence/pressure.
3. He cannot withstand difficulties/challenges.
4. He is like a log of wood.

Select the correct answer using the codes given below:

(a) 1 only
(b) 1 and 2
(c) 2 and 3
(d) 1 and 4

Answer Key

PART I

TEST 1

PASSAGE 1

1. (b)	2. (a)	3. (a)	4. (c)	5. (a)

PASSAGE 2

6. (a)	7. (b)	8. (b)	9. (c)	10. (c)

PASSAGE 3

11. (c)	12. (a)	13. (b)	14. (a)	15. (b)

TEST 2

PASSAGE 1

1. (a)	2. (c)	3. (a)	4. (b)	5. (d)

PASSAGE 2

6. (c)	7. (c)	8. (d)	9. (d)	10. (a)

Passage 3

11. (b) **12.** (c) **13.** (b) **14.** (a)

Test 3

Passage 1

1. (b) **2.** (c) **3.** (b) **4.** (b) **5.** (b)

Passage 2

6. (b) **7.** (c) **8.** (a) **9.** (b) **10.** (a)

Passage 3

11. (b) **12.** (b) **13.** (d) **14.** (a)

Test 4

Passage 1

1. (c) **2.** (c) **3.** (a) **4.** (b)

Passage 2

5. (a) **6.** (b) **7.** (c) **8.** (a)

Passage 3

9. (b) **10.** (d) **11.** (b) **12.** (d)

Test 5

Passage 1

1. (a) **2.** (b) **3.** (c) **4.** (a)

Passage 2

5. (b) **6.** (b) **7.** (c) **8.** (c)

Passage 3

9. (b) **10.** (d) **11.** (b) **12.** (c)

Test 6

Passage 1

1. (b) **2.** (d) **3.** (a)

Passage 2

4. (b) **5.** (d) **6.** (a)

Passage 3

7. (b) **8.** (a) **9.** (b) **10.** (b)

Test 7

Passage 1

1. (b) **2.** (c) **3.** (c)

Passage 2

4. (c) **5.** (a) **6.** (b)

Passage 3

7. (c) **8.** (a) **9.** (b)

Test 8

Poem 1

1. (a) **2.** (b)

Poem 2

3. (a) **4.** (b)

Poem 3

5. (b) **6.** (c)

PART II

ACCORDING TO THE LATEST CAT COMPREHENSION PASSAGES

Test 1

Passage 1

1. (b) **2.** (c) **3.** (d)

Passage 2

4. (b) **5.** (b)

Passage 3

6. (b) **7.** (a) **8.** (b)

TEST 2

Passage 1

1. (c) **2.** (a) **3.** (b)

Passage 2

4. (c) **5.** (c) **6.** (d) **7.** (c)

Passage 3

8. (b) **9.** (a) **10.** (c)

TEST 3

Passage 1

1. (c) **2.** (b) **3.** (a) **4.** (d)

Passage 2

5. (c) **6.** (d) **7.** (d) **8.** (b)

Passage 3

9. (d) **10.** (b) **11.** (a)

TEST 4

Passage 1

1. (d) **2.** (a) **3.** (b) **4.** (c)

Passage 2

5. (b) **6.** (b)

Passage 3

7. (c) **8.** (c) **9.** (b)

TEST 5

Passage 1

1. (c) **2.** (c) **3.** (b)

Passage 2

4. (c) **5.** (c) **6.** (c)

Passage 3

7. (b) **8.** (d) **9.** (a) **10.** (c)

TEST 6

Passage 1

1. (c) **2.** (c) **3.** (b)

Passage 2

4. (c) **5.** (a) **6.** (b)

Passage 3

7. (a) **8.** (d) **9.** (c) **10.** (d) **11.** (d)

TEST 7

Passage 1

1. (d) **2.** (b) **3.** (a) **4.** (c) **5.** (d)

Passage 2

6. (c) **7.** (b) **8.** (d) **9.** (a) **10.** (a)

Passage 3

11. (a) **12.** (b) **13.** (b)

Explanations

PART I

Test 1

Passage 1

1. Option (b) is correct. Read the lines, "What was satire then is ideology today: cynicism–the belief that people are morally bankrupt and behave treacherously in order to maximize self-interest–dominates American culture. Since 1964, the percentage of Americans who say they trust the government to do what is right 'just about always' or 'most of the time' has fallen 53 points, from 77 to 24 per cent. Sentiments about other institutions in society follow similar patterns. The original cynicism was a philosophical movement likely founded by Antisthenes, a student of Socrates, and popularized by Diogenes of Sinope around the fifth century BC. It was based on a refusal to accept the assumptions and habits that discourage people from questioning conventional dogmas, and thus hold us back from the search for deep wisdom and happiness. Whereas a modern cynic might say, for instance, that the president is an idiot and thus his policies aren't worth considering, the ancient cynic would examine each policy impartially."
   Option (a) is too generic a sentence and can be negated.
   Option (c) does not cover how cynicism was a "satire" in the past.
   Option (d) takes more of literal meaning of the line rather than the actual meaning.
2. Option (a) is correct. Read the lines, "What was satire then is ideology today: Cynicism–the belief that people are generally morally bankrupt and behave treacherously in order to maximize self-interest–dominates American culture. Since 1964, the percentage of Americans who say they trust the government to do what is right "just about always" or "most of the time" has fallen 53 points, from 77 to 24 per cent percent. Sentiments about other institutions in society follow similar patterns.

   Whether cynicism is more warranted now than ever is yours to decide. But it won't change the fact that the modern cynical outlook on life is terrible for your well-being. It makes you less healthy, less happy, less successful, and less respected by others." The author then goes on to define the harmful aspects of cynicism.

   Option (b) is a sub theme of the passage used to show how it has become harmful over time. Similarly, option (d) is also a sub theme. Option (c) cannot be inferred from the passage at all.
3. Option (a) is correct. Read the lines, "The original cynicism was a philosophical movement likely founded by Antisthenes, a student of Socrates, and popularized by Diogenes of Sinope around the fifth century B.C. It was based on a refusal to accept the assumptions and habits that discourage people from questioning conventional dogmas, and thus hold us back from the search for deep wisdom and happiness. Whereas a modern cynic might say, for instance, that the president is an idiot and thus his policies aren't worth considering, the ancient cynic would examine each policy impartially.

   The modern cynic rejects things out of hand ('This is stupid'), while the ancient cynic simply withholds judgment ('This may be right or wrong'). 'Modern cynicism [has] come to describe something antithetical to its previous meanings, a psychological state hardened against both moral reflection and intellectual persuasion,' the University of Houston's David Mazella wrote in The Making of Modern Cynicism."
   Options (b), (c) and (d) can be negated on the basis of the lines "The original cynicism was a philosophical movement likely founded by Antisthenes, a student of Socrates, and popularized by Diogenes of Sinope around the fifth century BC. It was based on a refusal to accept the assumptions and habits that discourage people from questioning conventional dogmas, and thus hold us back from the search for deep wisdom and happiness. Whereas a modern cynic might say, for instance, that the president is an idiot and thus his policies aren't worth considering, the ancient cynic would examine each policy impartially."
4. Option (c) is correct. Read the lines, "The modern cynic rejects things out of hand ('This is stupid'), while the ancient cynic simply withholds judgment ('This may be right or wrong'). 'Modern cynicism [has] come to describe something antithetical to its previous meanings, a psychological state hardened against both moral reflection and intellectual persuasion,' the University of Houston's David Mazella wrote in The Making of Modern Cynicism."

   Options (a), (b) and (d) can be negated on the basis of above-mentioned lines.
5. Option (a) is correct. Read the lines, "Whether cynicism is more warranted now than ever is yours to decide. But it won't change the fact that the modern cynical outlook on life is terrible for your well-being.

It makes you less healthy, less happy, less successful, and less respected by others."

Options (b) and (d) are author's opinions as per above-mentioned lines.

Option (c) is the opinion of the author as per the lines: "The problem isn't cynicism per se; it's that modern people have lost the original meaning of cynicism. Instead of assuming that everyone and everything sucks, we should all live like the ancient Greek cynics, who rebelled against convention in a search for truth and enlightenment."

Passage 2

6. Option (a) is correct. Read the lines, "MY DAD, when asked about his emotional state, is likely to say "hungry" or "cold," maybe "tired". Once, frustrated after being gently mocked for this kind of response, he asked–in all seriousness–if there was some list of feelings he could consult. This request has led, to his even greater frustration, to yet more gentle mocking. But he is far from alone in his wish for a catalog of emotions.

   Ekman's most famous experiments involved showing people from different cultures photos of faces and asking the participants to match each facial expression to an emotion. Based on this research, he argued that there are six distinct universal basic emotions–anger, surprise, disgust, happiness, fear, and sadness. (Ekman has sometimes suggested that there are seven basic emotions, adding contempt, and many who support his general framework have suggested that there are five, removing surprise; other groups of researchers building on his initial research have proposed that there are as many as fifteen or twenty-seven). In the popular imagination–and with Ekman's encouragement–these six so-called "basic emotions" have often been interpreted as representing the entirety of emotional experience."

   Options (b) and (c) are not mentioned in the passage.

   Option (d) is too generic a choice.

7. Option (b) is correct. Read the lines, "Perhaps the most famous emotional taxonomy is Paul Ekman's list of "universal basic emotions". Beginning in the 1960s, Ekman, a research psychologist, conducted cross-cultural studies aimed at demonstrating that certain emotions are universal–that is, that they are inborn rather than learned, consistent across cultures and contexts. His work built on Charles Darwin's 1872 book, *The Expression of Emotions in Man and Animals,* which argued that emotional expressions were vestiges of once-useful evolutionary behaviors (scowling when angry, for instance, may be a vestige of the impulse to curl the lips and bare fangs)."

   Statements B and C are true as per above-mentioned lines. (a) can also be negated on similar basis.

8. Option (b) is correct. Read the lines, "Ekman's work was controversial from the start. In an essay on his trajectory as a researcher, he recounts that during a presentation of his research at the American Anthropological Association in the late 1960s, a colleague shouted that he was a fascist. His research, many argue, does not make space for the role of cultural differences and learned behavior, and it leans too heavily on the idea of biology as destiny; his suggestion that interior states can be easily read through the face has traces of phrenology. Worryingly, this latter concern has affected Ekman's work with the TSA, the Department of Defense, and other institutions, where his theory is incorporated into AI models and surveillance techniques–many of which have demonstrable racial biases. His research has also been criticized on methodological grounds: his studies adopted a forced-choice paradigm, where participants were given limited words and limited photos to match. The photos used were the ones Ekman personally felt best displayed each of his 'basic emotions' while more ambiguous expressions were excluded, and these images were of simulated emotional expressions rather than authentic emotional experience.

   More recently, the Museum of Contemporary Emotions–a project of the Finnish government's Finland Forward pandemic communications initiative–picked up Ekman's work as its scaffolding."

   Option (a) can be negated on the basis of above-mentioned lines.

   Option (c) is exaggerated because of mention of "larger scientist community."

   Option (d) cannot be inferred from the passage definitely.

9. Option (c) is correct. Read the lines, "His research, many argue, does not make space for the role of cultural differences and learned behavior, and it leans too heavily on the idea of biology as destiny; his suggestion that interior states can be easily read through the face has traces of phrenology. Worryingly, this latter concern has affected Ekman's work with the TSA, the Department of Defense, and other institutions, where his theory is incorporated into AI models and surveillance techniques–many of which have demonstrable racial biases. His research has also been criticized on methodological grounds: his studies adopted a forced-choice paradigm, where participants were given limited words and limited photos to match. The photos used were the ones Ekman personally felt best displayed each of his "basic emotions" while more ambiguous expressions were excluded, and these images were of simulated

emotional expressions rather than authentic emotional experience."

Options (a), (b), and (d) are true as per above-mentioned lines and through the passage.

10. Option (c) is correct as it comments on Ekman's theories and connects it to present day actions being taken on the same.

Options (a) and (d) would focus only on the scientific aspects. Option (b) would focus more on personal comments of the author and not on stating others' opinions.

Passage 3

11. Option (c) is correct. Read the lines, "It was only after Molière's petition to Louis, in which he denounced the "tartuffes [who] have underhandedly had the cunning to get themselves into Your Majesty's good graces," that the king allowed the show to go on five years later.

Perhaps Louis saw himself in the character of Orgon. Tartuffe's con is obvious to everyone in Orgon's household – his brother-in-law Cléante, his wife Elmire, his children Damis and Mariane, and his servant Dorine – except to Orgon's mother and the wealthy Orgon himself."

All other options are not mentioned in the passage at all.

12. Option (a) is correct. Read the lines, "While statistics help us measure the magnitude of the coronavirus pandemic, they are less able to gauge our current outbreak of hypocrisy. Nevertheless, if public trust is the first casualty of the hypocrisy, we have reason to worry. Since the late 1950s, when three-quarters of Americans trusted the government, the percentage has cratered: under one quarter of Americans still expect our elected officials to do the right thing. Another casualty is political moderation, a position that many in both camps see as at best complacent and at worst complicit. Whereas compromise was once considered a civic value, most Americans now value it only when the compromises come entirely from the other side."

Option (c) can be negated on the basis of the lines, "The vrai and faux true believers made life difficult not just for the young and untried king, but also for Molière, as both learned when Tartuffe was first performed in 1664. In high dudgeon, both the religious fanatics and phonies forced Louis to annul its public opening. It was only after Molière's petition to Louis, in which he denounced the 'tartuffes [who] have underhandedly had the cunning to get themselves into Your Majesty's good graces,' that the king allowed the show to go on five years later."

Options (b) and (d) are not mentioned in the passage at all.

13. Option (b) is correct. Read the lines, "While our predicament seems dire, it is not particularly new. Indeed, it would appear déjà vu to Jean-Baptiste Poquelin, an actor (in every sense of the word) in an earlier age of equally great political extremes.

Today, France is celebrating Poquelin's 400th anniversary. Christened in Paris on January 15, 1622, he is known to the world by his pen and stage name, Molière. One of France's greatest playwrights, Molière is best known for his many comedies, which are replete with characters who embody the same foibles we spend our lives tripping over today: vanity, envy, misanthropy, and, yes, hypocrisy."

All other options can be negated on the basis of above-mentioned lines.

14. Option (a) is correct. Falsifying option (a) would mean, people do no tend to trust their elected leaders. It is in line with author's views as per the lines, "Since the late 1950s, when three-quarters of Americans trusted the government, the percentage has cratered: under one quarter of Americans still expect our elected officials to do the right thing. Another casualty is political moderation, a position that many in both camps see as at best complacent and at worst complicit. Whereas compromise was once considered a civic value, most Americans now value it only when the compromises come entirely from the other side."

Falsifying option (d) would mean that people tend to compromise which can be negated on the basis of above-mentioned lines.

Falsifying option (b) would mean hypocrisy is not widely accepted which is not true as per the lines "Not the pandemic that requires masks to cover our mouths, mind you, but the pandemic that requires masks to cover our motives. According to a recent headline in The Hill, a 'Pandemic of Hyper-Hypocrisy is Infecting American Politics.' This is hardly surprising when headlines either announce 'Hypocrisy, thy name is GOP' or affirm that 'Democrats' hypocrisy is Now Impossible to Ignore."

Falsifying option (c) would mean people are not aware of their hypocritical nature. There is no comment on the same in the passage.

15. Option (b) is correct. The passage talks about hypocrisy and then talks about Moliere and his play. Option (b) encompasses both the themes properly. Option (a) ignores Moliere whereas options (c) and (d) ignore the concept of hypocrisy.

Test 2

Passage 1

1. Option (a) is correct. Read the lines, "The answer could have something to do with a term used by linguist John J. Gumperz: 'situational code-switching,' which is when we change how we talk depending on where we are, who we're talking to or how we're communicating."
Options (b), (c) and (d) can be negated on the basis of above-mentioned lines.
2. Option (c) is correct. The passage states that people use "period" in sentences and how it is interpreted. It does not mention usage of punctuations in "formal texts" specifically. So, option (a) is not true.
Read the line "In the past, written language was almost always tinged with a level of formality because it was associated with permanence in books and written documents." So, option (b) is not true.
C can be inferred from "We see this with the increased use of ellipses, which can invite the recipient to continue the conversation."
3. Option (a) is correct. Read the lines, "Because text messaging is a conversation that involves a lot of back-and-forth, people add fillers as a way to mimic spoken language."
Option (b) can be negated because of the usage of "definitely." Passage states that a distant friend is likely to use formal language but usage of "definitely" makes it extreme.
Similarly, Option (c) can be negated because of the usage of "always."
Option (d) can be negated on the basis of the lines, "Linguist Deborah Tannen described a similar phenomenon, noting that repeated exclamation points in a message can convey a sincere tone, like in the following text message:
"JACKIE I AM SO SO SO SORRY! I thought you were behind us in the cab and then I saw you weren't!!!!! I feel soooooooo bad! Catch another cab and ill pay for it for youuuuu."
4. Option (b) is correct as the passage specifically comments on the usage of punctuation in text messages and how it is interpreted differently.
5. Option (d) is correct as the passage gives interpretation of "period" as being formal or insincere but the options do not mention it.

Passage 2

6. Option (c) is correct. Read the lines, "There is a recognizable arc to the type of literary career that most interested the public in the days when art was king, and books and magazines were primary means of distributing new fashions, fads, and ideas. First, a blaze of youthful fame, which contained equal portions of originality, promise, and messiness/failure. Second, the construction of a persona around the work, one that could be drawn with clear-enough cartoonlike lines to launch a recognizable character.
It's fun to make lists like this. Yet the main point here in America is that the world depicted above no longer exists except as a parody of something that was once real and can now be sold to trust-fund suckers and crazed midlevel careerists who aren't yet in on the joke, or never got the joke. **People, there is no such thing as "the New York literary scene"; no actual writers under the age of 75 can afford to live in New York City, nor do they have any desire to live there. The secret of real achievement in the arts, as someone wise once told me in my youth, is low overhead."**
All other options can be negated on the basis of the above-mentioned lines.
7. Option (c) is correct. Read the lines, "Yet the main point here in America is that the world depicted above no longer exists except as a parody of something that was once real and can now be sold to trust-fund suckers and crazed midlevel careerists who aren't yet in on the joke, or never got the joke. People, there is no such thing as 'the New York literary scene'; no actual writers under the age of 75 can afford to live in New York City, nor do they have any desire to live there. The secret of real achievement in the arts, as someone wise once told me in my youth, is low overhead.
Politics, public boredom, the destruction of gatekeeper institutions, and the bad-faith gamification, expansion, and radical toxification and dumbing-down of the so-called public sphere have put an end to the arts in America, at least for now. What's left is a gigantic, out-of-touch, stale bureaucracy, staffed by people who might, in a different age, have worked at the U.S. Department of Agriculture or in a provincial department store. No one actually gives a crap about the latest novels of Jonathan Lethem and Jonathan Franzen; they're white men on the public dole who are scared to death of being canceled."
The author is criticizing the literary scene of New York by being sarcastic. He is not just stating the negative. Thus, he is not cynical or frustrated. He is not just stating the facts. So, he is not just descriptive.
8. Option (d) is correct. Read the lines, "Politics, public boredom, the destruction of gatekeeper institutions,

and the bad-faith gamification, expansion, and radical toxification and dumbing-down of the so-called public sphere have put an end to the arts in America, at least for now. What's left is a gigantic, out-of-touch, stale bureaucracy, staffed by people who might, in a different age, have worked at the U.S. Department of Agriculture or in a provincial department store. No one actually gives a crap about the latest novels of Jonathan Lethem and Jonathan Franzen; they're white men on the public dole who are scared to death of being canceled. The last time anyone wrote a 'novel that mattered' was 2001. Writers are people who teach in 'creative writing' departments; their racket is to sell the coffin odors of the New York literary scene of 40 and 50 years ago to bright-eyed provincials and the children of new immigrants whose parents can somehow afford to pay $60,000 or $70,000 a year. The magazines that once introduced Vladimir Nabokov, J.D. Salinger, and V.S. Naipaul to the world are simply broke; no one reads them or advertises in them; their subscribers are mostly dead; they are ghost ships for trust-fund kids and suckers on starvation wages, the type of people who might buy a steamboat ticket to Paris to see Josephine Baker dance."

All the statements are true as per the above-mentioned lines.

9. Option (d) is correct as others would go against the belief that artists find it difficult to survive on their art's income.

   Options (b) and (c) can be negated as the author has not compared the artists' popularity with their art, hence they are out of context.
   Option (a) actually supports author's belief that modern artists cannot afford to stay in New York.

10. Option (a) is correct as the passage brings out the life of an artist in New York and how it has changed over time.

    Option (b) ignores the present day status of literature and art in New York.
    Option (c) ignores art and just mentions literature.
    Option (d) is just a sub-theme of the passage.

Passage 3

11. Option (b) is correct as the passage states that along with individual talents of a team, how the teams synchronize together plays a vital role in efficient functioning of the team.

    Options (a) and (d) negate the synergy of players whereas (c) negates individual talent of players.

12. Option (c) is correct. Read the lines, "Moreover, simply recruiting the best players is fairly straightforward, and some analyses suggest this approach might even be the most reliable: as the sociologist Duncan Watts and colleagues argued, overall talent level is often the single best predictor of team performance. Yet we shouldn't be lured into thinking overall talent is the best predictor because it is the most important factor. It might be the best predictor because we're not yet good at capturing the nuance of collective dynamics. Hints that this could be the case come from studies such as that of the management scholar Satyam Mukherjee and colleagues, in which they found that prior shared success can predict performance above and beyond what would be expected from the group's composition and talent."

13. Option (b) is true. Read the line, "Part of the reason why recruiters and others resort to going after the best players rather than building the best team is that it remains unclear what other factors contribute to team greatness, and how to quantify them." (a) and (c) can be negated on the basis of the passage.

14. Option (a) is correct. Falsifying option (a) would mean that more star players does not mean more wins. Read the lines "Part of the reason why recruiters and others resort to going after the best players rather than building the best team is that it remains unclear what other factors contribute to team greatness, and how to quantify them. Moreover, simply recruiting the best players is fairly straightforward, and some analyses suggest this approach might even be the most reliable: as the sociologist Duncan Watts and colleagues argued, overall talent level is often the single best predictor of team performance."

    Falsifying option (b) would mean that star players are likely to contribute more to team's win which is in line with author's views.
    Falsifying option (c) would mean that team with less star players are not more likely to win which is in line with authors views.

Test 3

Passage 1

1. Option (b) is correct as the author is pointing out that the funding of humanities (which helps in creating a creative mindset) is being scrapped to support other courses and forming tests which focus on quantitative techniques. Option (b) summarizes it well.

Options (a) and (d) are too generic and option (c) is only partially correct.

2. Option (c) is correct. Read the lines, "If State-funded education abandons the humanities, as the JU case seems to indicate, then meritorious students who come from weaker backgrounds will no longer have access to the theories and data that make sense of the human world. They will not be taught how societies are constituted and controlled, how the human mind functions, how people make choices, and how those choices affect their lives, how institutions are set up and managed, and what effect they have on people's bodies and souls. They will not know what constitutes gender or class, or how these ideas relate to their own lives. Furthermore, they will be taught not to care about these questions. All this, while we utter homilies about a 'knowledge economy' and 'demographic dividend'." The author advocates for humanities but does not undermine importance of science in her comments.

   Options (a), (d) and (b) cannot be definitely inferred from the passage.

3. Option (b) is correct. Read the lines, "Like other teachers, I have watched the slow crumble of humanities education under the pressures of 'modernisation'. I have seen senior academics having to justify themselves before committees because they write one book every three years, not 60 articles every year. I have seen syllabi torn apart because they were too 'hard' for their target studentship, although, in fact, they were just inconvenient for the operators of tutorial homes."

4. Option (b) is correct. Read the lines, "If state-funded education abandons the humanities, as the JU case seems to indicate, then meritorious students who come from weaker backgrounds will no longer have access to the theories and data that make sense of the human world. They will not be taught how societies are constituted and controlled, how the human mind functions, how people make choices, and how those choices affect their lives, how institutions are set up and managed, and what effect they have on people's bodies and souls. They will not know what constitutes gender or class, or how these ideas relate to their own lives. Furthermore, they will be taught not to care about these questions."

5. Option (b) is correct as throughout the passage the author is highlighting how scrapping of funding from humanities will affect the education.

Passage 2

6. Option (b) is correct. Read the lines, "Repetition is a component of all ascetic traditions, and I like to think that my own habits constitute something like a spiritual discipline. My nature bends toward listlessness and disorder. **Resolving to do the same thing each day, at the same time, has given my life a center, insulating me from the siren song of novelty and distraction that has caused me so much unhappiness in the past**. I live a monotonous life, which is not to say a tedious one. (I believe, with Rilke, that those who find life dull are not poet enough to call forth its riches.) And I imagine that these tightly circumscribed days are radiating, with each turn of the circle, into widening arcs, amounting to a life whose ties are deeper, whose direction is more certain."

   Option (a) and (d) take the role of a poet quite literally. Option (c) does not relate to the context at all.

7. Option (c) is correct. Read the lines, "Perhaps I am no different from those data fetishists in Silicon Valley who refer to Benjamin Franklin as a "productivity master," and speak of free time as a "release valve." It is difficult today to avoid the thought that we are becoming as rigid and inflexible as the machines that structure our lives. The New York Times columnist Kevin Roose calls this process "machine drift," arguing that it's degrading our humanity and making us professionally obsolete. "For years, the conventional wisdom has been that if machines were the future, we needed to become more like machines ourselves," he writes in his recent book Futureproof."

   Option (a) and (b) can be negated on the basis of above-mentioned lines. Option (d) is a consequence of "machine drift."

8. Option (a) is correct. Machine drift here refers to the "routine life". Read the lines, "In striving to be more efficient, these critics argue, we are ceding our true advantage over the artificial intelligence systems that are encroaching on so many lines of work. Instead of succumbing to repetitive habits, we should cultivate those qualities that make us most human–our flexibility and spontaneity, our ability to respond to surprises and learn new skills:

   All other options are the disadvantages as mentioned in above lines.

9. Option (b) is correct. Statement (b) is true as per the lines "Repetition is a component of all ascetic traditions, and I like to think that my own habits constitute something like a spiritual discipline. My nature bends toward listlessness and disorder. Resolving to do the same thing each day, at the same time, has given my life a center, insulating me from the siren song of novelty and distraction that has caused me so much unhappiness in the past. I live a monotonous life, which is not to say a tedious one."

   Statement (c) is true as per lines, "The writer George Monbiot similarly considers repetition "dehumanizing," arguing that schools, with their rigid lessons and classroom regimes, are senselessly preparing children for life in a nineteenth-century factory. "In the future, if you want a job, you must be as unlike a machine as possible," he writes in the Guardian."

   Statement (a) is incorrect as per lines "This is, at any rate, the story that Lewis Mumford tells in his 1934 book Technics and Civilization, which argues that monasteries "helped to give human enterprise the regular collective beat and rhythm of the machine." Contemporary medievalists have come to doubt this tidy account, but I have always liked the picture it paints, as though the life of that era were an enormous astronomical clock with its automaton figures (the friar, the cobbler, the weaver) clicking along their tracks to the same relentless metronome."

10. Option (a) is correct as the author has stated his personal views for a large part of the passage. A newspaper would focus on facts. There are no travel stories for (d) to be correct. (a) is a better choice than (c) because of personal opinion and fact mentioned.

PASSAGE 3

11. Option (b) is correct. Read the lines, "I do disagree, but before I tell you why, let me add another couple of pro-plagiarism arguments to buttress Frye's.

    The first is that a more relaxed attitude to plagiarism is all part of the direction in which science is moving. These days, research increasingly emphasizes collaboration and teamwork (think Large Hadron Collider) and is far less a story of the lone genius making big discoveries in their secret lab. Some have even argued against the awarding of Nobel Prizes for science, since they can only be given to a small number of people, perpetuating the wrong idea of modern research. On this view, a focus on the individual ownership of ideas is an anachronism; a relic of how science used to be done.

    Not only that, but there's a whole movement that's focused on wresting scientific findings from the grip of flawed, ego-driven academics and sharing them with the world - namely, the Open Science movement. The movement pushes for Open Data (sharing datasets online for anyone to use) and Open Access (making scientific papers accessible to all for free) - so we might wonder why it doesn't take a step further and argue for a system where concepts and theories, and even their verbal expressions, can be shared without worrying too much about who came up with them."

    Option (a) and (d) are just a sub theme of the passage. Option (c) is not mentioned.

12. Option (b) is correct as it goes against the idea of "lending one's idea freely" or Open Data as has been propagated by the author in the passage.

    Option (a) actually supports author's claims as per the last paragraph.

    Option (c) does not relate to "plagiarisms.

    "Similarly, option (d) supports author's claims that the rules are inefficient.

13. Option (d) is correct. Read the lines, "According to the **University of Kentucky law professor Brian Frye:**

    A plagiarist is an academic pariah, a transgressor of the highest law of the profession, the embodiment of the "great deceiver," who leads everyone astray. [...] Plagiarism tarnishes the scholarship itself and leaves it forever suspect. If the purpose of scholarship is dowsing for truth, then the plagiarist is a liar who poisons the well from which everyone draws.

    Although many would agree, you might have detected a tinge of sarcastic hyperbole - and indeed, in the quoted paper, Frye makes the contrarian argument that academics should stop caring at all about plagiarism. They shouldn't mind if people use their ideas, or even their exact words, without citing them; rules against plagiarism do the reader no favours and exist merely to shore up the ego of the author. **"Academic plagiarism norms," Frye writes, "are primarily an inefficient and illegitimate form of extra-legal academic rent-seeking that should be ignored." And although he doesn't quite call those who disagree with him "wussies and pussies," he does disparagingly refer to the "plagiarism police," which includes anyone who tries to identify academic plagiarism and somehow punish the plagiarist."**

    Options (a) and (c) cannot be inferred from the passage at all.

    Option (b) is not true as it was Frye's university that condemned plagiarism.

14. Option (a) is correct. Read the lines, "But musicians do still get in hot water for plagiarism - from other artists and their lawyers, if not the public (**Dylan's lifting of musical ideas from long-dead bluesmen might explain why it's never been a big deal for him**). George Harrison, Dylan's sometime collaborator, ended up embroiled in decades-long legal proceedings and paid damages of $2m in today's money after he accidentally borrowed the backbone of his song "My Sweet Lord" from "He's So Fine" by The Chiffons."

    Option (b) can be negated on the basis of above-mentioned lines.
    Option (c) can be negated as it is not mentioned."
    There is no comment on option (d) in the passage.

Test 4

Passage 1

1. Option (c) is correct as throughout the passage, the author has shown how artists make "surreal" artwork that can be disturbing yet appeals to its audience.
   Option (a) is negated as there is no such comparison in the passage.
   Option (b) is negated as it leaves the "appealing" part.
   Option (d) is an exaggerated choice and should be avoided.
2. Option (c) is correct as the passage mentions that the art questions political upheavals and liberations. However, political heads are not specifically mentioned.

   A is negated on the basis of the lines "Artists deployed surrealist techniques to process demons, both internal and external, but also to challenge conventional thinking (is a pipe really a pipe, as René Magritte famously queried?) and to express fantasies of artistic or political liberation. The Freudian-influenced idea was that by unlocking the unconscious, artists could assert the independence of their and their viewers' interior worlds. Radical nonconformism was a central tenet, which led some artists to use the form to challenge the pressures and constraints of oppressive regimes."
   Option (b) is negated on the basis of the lines "That question might be put to visitors of the Metropolitan Museum of Art's "Surrealism Beyond Borders" exhibition, a show filled with grotesque representations of political upheaval and private horror, but also with thrillingly odd and beautiful demonstrations of imagination."
3. Option (a) is correct. Read the lines, "The varied readings of these wild figures add to the work's surreality. The pain in the painting transcends the specifics of its time and place. It rises to the level of archetype, representing a broader spectrum of violence and unease. If one feels an uncanny kinship with these demons, that is the exact kind of pact surrealism allows."

   Hence, the lines do not comment only on the artists. So, (b) and (d) can be negated. It is more about understanding one's own emotions than looking at world's picture. So, (a) is a better choice than (c).
4. Option (b) is correct. Read the lines, "If disquieting sensory experiences abound in daily life, why go and seek more out? That question might be put to visitors of the Metropolitan Museum of Art's "Surrealism Beyond Borders" exhibition, a show filled with grotesque representations of political upheaval and private horror, but also with thrillingly odd and beautiful demonstrations of imagination."

   The author has shown his views via analysis of the concept throughout the passage. He is not being cynical as he is not just picturing the "grotesque" side but the beautiful side.

Passage 2

5. Option (a) is correct. Read the lines, "Somewhere between Newton and Mark Zuckerberg, theory took a back seat. In 2008, Chris Anderson, the then editor-in-chief of Wired magazine, predicted its demise. So much data had accumulated, he argued, and computers were already so much better than us at finding relationships within it, that our theories were being exposed for what they were - oversimplifications of reality. Soon, the old scientific method - hypothesise, predict, test - would be relegated to the dustbin of history. We'd stop looking for the causes of things and be satisfied with correlations.

   With the benefit of hindsight, we can say that what Anderson saw is true (he wasn't alone). The complexity that this wealth of data has revealed to us cannot be captured by theory as traditionally understood. "We have leapfrogged over our ability to even write the theories that are going to be useful for description," says computational neuroscientist Peter Dayan, director of the Max Planck Institute for Biological Cybernetics in Tübingen, Germany. "We don't even know what they would look like."

Option (b) can be negated on the basis of above-mentioned lines.
Option (c) may be true for Prospect theory but cannot be generalized to all scientific theories.
Option (d) is negated as the passage does not compare the 2.

6. Option (b) is correct. Read the lines, "But Anderson's prediction of the end of theory looks to have been premature - or maybe his thesis was itself an oversimplification. There are several reasons why theory refuses to die, despite the successes of such theory-free prediction engines as Facebook and AlphaFold. All are illuminating, because they force us to ask: what's the best way to acquire knowledge and where does science go from here?

   The first reason is that we've realised that artificial intelligences (AIs), particularly a form of machine learning called neural networks, which learn from data without having to be fed explicit instructions, are themselves fallible. Think of the prejudice that has been documented in Google's search engines and Amazon's hiring tools."
   All other options can be negated on the basis of the passage.

7. Option (c) is correct. Refer to the following lines .... 'So theory isn't dead, yet, but it is changing - perhaps beyond recognition. "The theories that make sense when you have huge amounts of data look quite different from those that make sense when you have small amounts," says Tom Griffiths, a psychologist at Princeton University.'... these lines prove that option (c) is correct and options (a) and (b) are irrelevant.

8. Option (a) is correct as the author has stated that theoretical science is not totally out of the scenario. Hence, it should be a question.

   Option (b) is changing the information.
   Option (c) shows that theoretical science has stopped to exist and should be negated.
   Option (d) is too generic.

Passage 3

9. Option (b) is correct. Read the lines, "In his introduction, Buford tried to put his finger on why the public was so fascinated by these literary travel jaunts, suggesting that during a period of economic hardship, as there was in the early 1980s, "their tales of the exotic could be seen to bear the same value as that of books and film, say, during the depression: they provide arm-chair emancipation." What he was looking for from his contributors – whom he had to track down diligently as most were not at home (and it was not so easy to contact folk back then without the internet) – was "the sheer glee of story-telling, a narrative eloquence that situates them, with wonderful ambiguity, somewhere between fiction and fact."

   This frank note of caution, as to the precise veracity of the stories told, added to the attraction rather than lessen it. Buford believed travel writing to be "the beggar of literary forms: it borrows from the memoir, reportage and, most important, the novel. It is, however, pre-eminently a narrative told in the first person, authenticated by lived experience. "Bufford stated it in a positive connotation. So, Option (a) should be negated.
   Option (c) is not stated in the passage and option (d) does not relate to the given statement.

10. Option (d) is correct. (a), (b) and (c) are stated in the lines ""The world is simply too small, too fast, too well-trodden to admit of such leisurely, civilised wandering," he writes. "The jumbo jet enabled any traveller to reach the four corners quickly and cheaply. The internet brought the world to your room. There are no spaces on the map to be filled in, no place that Google Earth has not seen already. The empty quarters and forbidden cities are full of tourists, and open to all."

    A feeling of hopelessness about the whole place of travel writing in the literary landscape – with billions of people posting pictures of their cheap-and-cheerful travels on social media and, as Macintyre points out, the internet covering just about everywhere – seems to have descended. Instagram stars with iPhones and thousands of followers have replaced correspondents in crumpled jackets clutching dusty Moleskin notebooks. Live webcams stream shots of mountain tops, beaches and the African plains. Who needs a travel writer to tell you how things are?

    Of course, there has been another factor, too. In The Travel Writing Tribe, Hannigan refers to a perceived "cultural appropriation" of privileged Westerners, often "very male, very white" and expensively educated turning up in countries and asking questions."

11. Option (b) is correct. Read the lines, "In his introduction, Buford tried to put his finger on why the public was so fascinated by these literary travel jaunts, suggesting that during a period of economic hardship, as there was in the early 1980s, "their tales of the exotic could be seen to bear the same value as that of books and film, say, during the depression: they provide arm-chair emancipation." What he was

looking for from his contributors – whom he had to track down diligently as most were not at home (and it was not so easy to contact folk back then without the internet) – was "the sheer glee of story-telling, a narrative eloquence that situates them, with wonderful ambiguity, somewhere between fiction and fact."

Options (a) and (c) cannot be definitely inferred as there is no such direct comparison.
Options (d) is the exact opposite of option (b) and can be negated.

12. Option (d) is correct given that there is no hint in the passage about the author himself. Options (a), (b) and (c) are highly unlikely to write so deeply about literature genre. Option (b) would also be not so concerned with the type of writing.

Test 5

Passage 1

1. Option (a) is correct as can be read in the last 2 paragraphs of the passage.
Options (b) and (c) are just sub themes in the passage.
Option (d) is not stated in the passage at all.
2. Option (b) is correct. Read the lines, "My preferred theory is that the field of art involves discovery, and those who arrive first have the greatest opportunity to make major discoveries. If Thomas Edison were born today, he'd have trouble inventing so many new home appliances. Instead, he might have gone into software or biotech. A talented young artist born in the 20th century might have decided that painting and photography were exhausted, and gone into filmmaking. (Kubrick is one such example; he started as a photographer.)

Filmmaking is a newer art form, and its golden age in the West and Japan was roughly 1920-1980 (and perhaps 1985-2005 in the rest of Asia.) Even poetry seems to be in decline. In 1820, Wordsworth, Coleridge, Keats, Shelley and Blake were all writing poetry. Are there 5 comparable living British poets? So what does all of this mean? Are things getting better? I'm sort of agnostic on that question. I'd put about a 40 per cent probability on the hypothesis that utility is rising due to improvements in technology and public morality, and about a 60 per cent probability on the hypothesis that utility is not rising over time because people have the same sort of personality flaws they had 100 years ago or 1000 years ago."

Option (a) can be negated on the basis of above-mentioned lines.
Option (c) can be negated on the basis of last paragraph of the passage.
Option (d) is not mentioned in the passage at all.

3. Option (c) is correct. Falsifying (a) would mean that percentage of students is not on a rise. It does not affect the author's claim at all.

Falsifying (b) would mean that less poetry events took place this year which supports the author's claims.
Falsifying (c) would mean that number of published books and poets are not on a decline. This jeopardizes the author's claim.
Falsifying (d) would mean that poets are not coming to New York. This supports author's claims.

4. Option (a) is correct as the author has defined and analysed how art and science have changed over time. There is no negative connotation. So, option (b) can be negated. The author has stated negatives as well as positives. So, option (c) can be negated. Option (a) is a better choice than (d).

Passage 2

5. Option (b) is correct. Read the lines, "If faced with clues that food might be scarce, such as hunger or crowding, certain grasshopper species can transform within days or even hours from their solitudinous hopper states to become part of a maniacally social locust scourge. They can also return quickly to their original form."

It becomes manic after becoming locust and does not become locust because it is manic.

6. Option (b) is correct. Read the lines, "these phase changes (as this morphing process is called) occur when crowding spurs a temporary spike in serotonin levels, which causes changes in gene expression so widespread and powerful they alter not just the hopper's behaviour but its appearance and form. Legs and wings shrink. Subtle camo colouring turns conspicuously garish. The brain grows to manage the animal's newly complicated social world, which includes the fact that, if a locust moves too slowly amid its million cousins, the cousins directly behind might eat it."

The key focus here is on explaining the bodily changes which is the anatomy of the hopper to become a locust.

7. Option (c) is correct. Read the lines, "But every locust was, and technically still is, a grasshopper

– not a different species or subspecies, but a sort of hopper gone mad. Legs and wings shrink. Subtle camo colouring turns conspicuously garish. The brain grows to manage the animal's newly complicated social world, which includes the fact that, if a locust moves too slowly amid its million cousins, the cousins directly behind might eat it."

So hoppers have camouflage colouring which turns to garish when it becomes locust.

8. Option (c) is correct. It can be inferred from, "But every locust was, and technically still is, a grasshopper – not a different species or subspecies, but a sort of hopper gone mad. If faced with clues that food might be scarce, such as hunger or crowding, certain grasshopper species can transform within days or even hours from their solitudinous hopper states to become part of a maniacally social locust scourge. They can also return quickly to their original form."

Option (a) can be negated on the basis of "The locust scurries hurriedly and hoggishly on short, crooked legs and joins hungrily with others to form swarms that darken the sky and descend to chew the farmer's fields bare."

Options (b) and (d) can be negated on the basis of "Not all grasshopper species, he explained (there are some 11,000), possess this morphing power; some always remain grasshoppers."

Passage 3

9. Option (b) is correct. Read the lines, "Prevailing explanations of military defection during revolutionary uprisings emphasise personal or corporate interests. In this logic, grievances spur to action rebel officers, who hope for a better deal in a new political system. Loyalists, for their part, seek to preserve their material advantages.

Behind this hard-nosed Hobbesian realism, the argument rests on a simple, commonsense account: people do what is most advantageous to them."

All other options can be negated on the basis of above-mentioned lines.

10. Option (d) is correct. Read the lines, "The dilemma is first ethical and individual: it betrays a stark choice between serving one's government and serving one's country. But it quickly becomes collective. When an officer becomes aware that he's not alone in his conundrum, he begins to wonder whether his colleagues will follow orders. From this doubt emerges the possibility of his own disobedience."

11. Option (b) is correct as the whole passage explains how regimes fall when military turns against the dictator and the reasons for the same.

12. Option (c) is correct. Option (a) may seem tempting but the focus is on why and how regimes fall rather than just the rivalry of the dictator and the military. They may or may not be rivals.

Test 6

Passage 1

1. Option (b) is correct. Read the lines "As the physicist Sean Carroll stated in his portentously titled book The Big Picture: On the Origins of Life, Meaning, and the Universe Itself (2016): 'No theory in the history of science has been more misused and abused by cranks and charlatans – and misunderstood by people struggling in good faith with difficult ideas – than quantum mechanics.' The philosopher Slavoj Žižek similarly warned of 'New Age obscurantist appropriations of today's "hard" sciences which, in order to legitimise their position, invoke the authority of science itself.' Stand back, social scientists, and leave the heavy lifting to the experts.

Quantum economics in particular sounds like 'physics envy' taken to its logical conclusion. Indeed, the assertion that quantum ideas – developed for tiny particles – could have anything to do with human systems such as the economy will seem patently absurd to most physicists. It is well known in physics that quantum effects wash out at larger scales, where classical behaviour dominates."

Options (a), (c) and (d) are not stated in the passage at all.

2. Option (d) is correct. Read the lines "Everyone also knows that quantum mechanics is both hard and highly counterintuitive, which is why only university graduates in physics and mathematics are typically exposed to it. As one university website once reassured its audience: 'It's OK to be a bit baffled by these concepts, since we don't experience them in our day-to-day lives. It's only when you look at the tiniest quantum particles – atoms, electrons, photons and the like – that you see intriguing things like superposition and entanglement.'"

Option (a) is negated as quantum physics is popular despite being "hard."

Option (b) is twisted. Author says so for "quantum physics."

Option (c) is negated as quantum physics is counterintuitive.

3. Option (a) is correct. Read the lines, "In her book Mother of Invention: How Good Ideas Get Ignored in an Economy Built for Men (2021), the writer Katrine Marçal argues that many useful innovations have failed to catch on because they are deemed 'too feminine' by marketers. A classic example is the wheeled suitcase. The wheel was invented in ancient Mesopotamia, however the possibility of attaching it to a case went against the whole idea of men showing off their strength by lugging heavy objects around, which is why wheeled suitcases weren't a thing until 1972. As Marçal wrote in The Guardian: 'Gender answers the riddle of why it took 5,000 years for us to put wheels on suitcases.'

   Quantum is the scientific equivalent of suitcase wheels. The reason this useful innovation hasn't caught on, or been rolled out, more generally in areas such as economics isn't because it's impractical or too hard - it's because it's too feminine. Or rather, too Female, in a sense to be defined below."
   Option (b) is a sub theme of quantum physics not overall physics supporting the above stated idea. Options (c) and (d) are not stated in the passage at all.

Passage 2

4. Option (b) is correct. The whole passage talks about how chocolate became popular. Last paragraph talks about how it led to the growth of different types of cocoa. All other options leave the cocoa part and hence should be negated.

5. Option (d) is correct. Read the lines, "Trying to put a stop to the proliferation of competitors, in 1723 a group of professional chocolate makers made their request to form a guild, claiming it was time to protect public health from the threats of adulteration. The request was denied as superfluous, but the molenderos (from the Spanish for 'to grind') did not surrender. Twenty-five years later, in 1748, they tried again and found a more favourable response from the city authorities - finally interested in curbing the loss of revenue due to adulteration - but not from their colleagues. Many workers opposed to forming a guild because they were poor, and adulterating chocolate remained the simplest way for them to profit from its sale."

   All other options can be negated on the basis of above-mentioned lines.

6. Option (a) is correct. Read the lines, "In Ciudad de México, until the first half of the 17th century, chocolate could be acquired directly from natives on the street (until the latter were pushed out of its trade by Spanish and mestizo vendors) as cocoa paste in lozenge form, to which consumers could add what they pleased. Preparations ranged from the simplest one with water to more complex procedures with the addition of several spices and flowers, but the most popular way to consume it was hot with atole (a corn dough)."

   Option (b) can be negated on the basis of above-mentioned lines.
   Option (c) and (d) are not stated in the passage at all.

Passage 3

7. Option (b) is correct. Read the lines, "They co-starred in Trespass, a home-invasion thriller derided as one of 2011's worst movies, and, ironically, one of the first marquee-name films to be released on streaming services at the same time it debuted in theaters: a harbinger of the silver screen's decline. Or maybe she remembered a moment in 2013, when she and Cage received top honors at Tianxia Yingcai Cultural Media Co.'s Huading Awards, appearing personally in Macau to accept their Best Global Actor and Actress trophies–heralding the rise of a Chinese box office that altered Hollywood."

   As the movie streamed on streaming services along with theatres, it marked the reduction in importance of theatres or silver screens.
   Options (c) and (d) are not stated in the passage. Option (a) would cause less popularity for the movie and not for the theatres.

8. Option (a) is correct. Read the lines, "More than anything, Cage should have come to mind because he embodies the tradition that Kidman and AMC both aspire to, at least in theory. If moviegoing is an act of ritual purgation, Cage must be its high priest, his performances a kind of ecstatic self-flagellation through which we're cleansed–or, to use Kidman's term, reborn.

   As befits a Best Global Actor, Cage has, for forty years onscreen, delivered performances of such furious spectacle that they transcend the humanity they represent. To see him react is to wonder if you've ever really felt, or could feel, anything so deeply, and if you'd want to. Anger? He sells it by the avalanche. Watch in Matchstick Men as he butts in line at the pharmacy."

Option (b) can be negated on the basis of above-mentioned lines.
Options (c) and (d) are not stated in the passage.

9. Option (b) is correct. Read the lines, "I'll offer an emphatic yes. There's something stalwart, commendable, even comforting about Cage's presence, something that reaches past entertainment toward tangled questions of talent and excess. His acting is too much, not just in tenor but in sheer volume. Since 1986, he has appeared in at least one film a year and sometimes up to six, bringing his total to well over one hundred. This ubiquity, combined with his trademark intensity, can make him seem like a permanently erupting volcano. At this point, it would be more disturbing if he went dormant. His increased output has brought what's often called a cult audience, a euphemism suggesting that his fans are mere ironists, feigning love for the objectively unlovable. Can anyone truly admire an actor who has been attached, in the span of a few years, to such obvious paint-by-numbers fare as Rage, Dark, Primal, and Outcast? Sure, he's won an Oscar–for Leaving Las Vegas, a movie derived from a novel that also became a Sheryl Crow song–but that was almost three decades ago."

Option (a) is very generic about movies and is incorrect.
Option (c) has negative connotation and should be negated.
Option (d) is not stated in the passage at all.

10. Option (b) is correct. Read the lines, "Cage's detractors find poetic justice in the fact that much of his recent work has gone straight to video on demand, with no theatrical release. An actor coasting on his larger-than-life performances has been denied the chance to appear larger than life. The shift from theaters to at-home streaming has launched a thousand Norma Desmond references ("I am big, it's the pictures that got small"), but in Cage's case the line is frighteningly apropos, and he's all but quoted it himself. "I want movies to be an event," he said in 2011. "I don't want [them] to get smaller and smaller." And yet here we are: a bona fide star who believes in absolution on the big screen is all but shut out of AMC Theatres."

Video on demand here refers to streaming services.
Options (a) and (c) are true as per the above-mentioned lines.
Option (d) is true as per the lines "Since 1986, he has appeared in at least one film a year and sometimes up to six, bringing his total to well over one hundred."

Test 7

Passage 1

1. Option (b) is correct. Option (a) can be negated as Sigmund was "ambivalent" towards politics and did not discard it outright.
Option (c) is negated on the basis of the lines "While Freud does help us to better understand the entanglement of politics and psychologies, we can also read him as making an even more unsettling and relevant claim, one that goes far beyond politics: that human life is always dominated by ambiguity, uncertainty, and inconsistency, and that there's no escape from the haunting torment that this entails."
These lines make option (b) correct.

2. Option (c) is correct. Read the lines, "In a new edition from Norton, the historian Samuel Moyn offers a new introduction, helpful notations, and a selection of short texts that explore the various ways that artists, philosophers, and social theorists have interpreted the book over the years. Moyn, who is also a frequent commentator on contemporary affairs, claims that while Freud's environment in interwar Vienna may be different from ours, his ideas are still invaluable. They urge us to recognize the complicated relationship between psychology and politics, particularly how our arguments about economics, power, and social hierarchies are always shaped by our unconscious impulses. For Moyn, Freud's approach is indispensable in the effort to tackle the most pressing dilemmas in contemporary society. It is only by understanding the psychological forces that foster oppression and conflict that we can hope to "make progress" and change our "war-torn and unequal world."

Statement C can be negated on the basis of above-mentioned lines.
Statement A is not stated in the passage at all.

3. Option (c) is correct. Read the lines, "**Civilization and Its Discontents became an instant classic, and over the decades, a wide range of readers–from Marxists and feminists to Christian conservatives–have debated Freud's lessons for their own times**. We now have an opportunity to do so for our own catastrophe-stricken world: In a new edition from Norton, the historian Samuel Moyn offers a new introduction, helpful notations, and a selection of short texts that explore the various ways that artists, philosophers, and social theorists have

interpreted the book over the years. Moyn, who is also a frequent commentator on contemporary affairs, claims that while Freud's environment in interwar Vienna may be different from ours, his ideas are still invaluable. They urge us to recognize the complicated relationship between psychology and politics, particularly how our arguments about economics, power, and social hierarchies are always shaped by our unconscious impulses. For Moyn, Freud's approach is indispensable in the effort to tackle the most pressing dilemmas in contemporary society. It is only by understanding the psychological forces that foster oppression and conflict that we can hope to "make progress" and change our "war-torn and unequal world."

It is tempting to harness Civilization and Its Discontents as a guide to our contemporary political morass, but doing so may obscure its most valuable message. While Freud does help us to better understand the entanglement of politics and psychologies, we can also read him as making an even more unsettling and relevant claim, one that goes far beyond politics: that human life is always dominated by ambiguity, uncertainty, and inconsistency, and that there's no escape from the haunting torment that this entails. **Even Freud's unique writing style radiates with ambivalence. Instead of making arguments in an orderly progression, the book repeatedly digresses, openly questions its own assumptions, and flat-out contradicts itself**."

Option (c) is not true as per the above-mentioned lines. All other options are mentioned in the passage.

Passage 2

4. Option (c) is correct. Author mentions how we are still in the age of binary gender system and highlighted gender inequality as well. But author also talks about the changes which are brewing and is positive about the fact that change is inevitable. Thus, option (c) covers this aptly.

5. Option (a) is correct. Options (b), (c) and (d) are nowhere mentioned in the passage. Option (a) can be inferred from the lines- 'but it's also a time of mass gender confusion, debate and renegotiation disputing the gender binary. And that's a great thing. Assumptions and shibboleths about gender (and sex and sexuality) are being defended and challenged, and language is being recast - think about the sudden transformations of pronouns people are using to refer to themselves.'

6. Option (b) is correct. It can be inferred from the lines-'They knew why, because we all know why: no matter how much we talk about gender equality, the implicit assumption often ends up being that men and women are, deep down, different. Only people with female reproductive organs get pregnant, and somehow this has come to mean that women should be more responsible for contraception.'

Passage 3

7. Option (c) is correct. The author begins with what is psychology but then focusses on modern day psychology or contemporary psychology.

   Options (b) and (d) are negated as they do not mention "contemporary psychology."

8. Option (a) is correct. Read the lines, "Similarly, notions of salvation, progress and ethics are so constitutive of our notions of reality that they're often communicated through the format of mythology. There's a surfeit of cultural products that fulfil the function of myth whereby characters and stories give us the means to understand the world we live in. In the imaginary world we enter through novels, to the weightless experience of desire that's consumerism, we inhabit the broad spaces of meaning-construction. Through superhero comic books, to the obscure immanence of modern art, from visions of paradisiacal vacations, to computer games and the self-mythologising of social media production, we seek a higher ground beyond the banal and the profane. We've even replaced the effervescent experience of sacred rites, not in blood sacrifice or vision quests, but in our engagement with art, drugs, cinema, rock music and all-night dance parties. Lastly, individuals have developed their own ways to create self-narratives that include mythical transitions in pilgrimages or personal quests to their ancestral lands. Likewise, some seek inner spaces wherein faith and meaning can be transformed into experience." All other options can be negated on the basis of the passage.

   Options (b) and (c) are not mentioned in the passage.

9. Option (b) is correct. Read the lines, "Today, the term 'mythology' connotes uncorroborated legend. But that's not entirely accurate. Mythology is really a set of beliefs buttressed by practices, or rituals, that together console our desire for explanation. As the Romanian theorist Mircea Eliade wrote in 1957: 'Myth never quite disappears from the present world of the psyche ... it only changes its aspect.' And in our time its aspect is to be found in psychology."

Test 8

Poem 1

1. On reading the lines of the poem, we tend to get an image of darkness and evil and is also conveyed by the last line of the poem 'this is the silence of departed souls' which points towards death. The poem hence, has an atmosphere of darkness and gloominess along with death and despair. Options (c) and (d) do not reflect the exact depiction of the poem. Rebellion has not been talked about and thus (b) is also neglected. Out of (a) and (e), (a) is in sync with the idea of the poem and hence, is the answer.
2. Nothing related to lilies purifying the darkness is mentioned even implicitly in the poem and is ruled out. (e) and (a) are out of context. On reading the lines of the 2nd paragraph, we get a hint that even though the lilies are surrounded by darkness and despair, it still seems to radiate a sense of beauty and hope in the dull and gloomy atmosphere. This idea is best encapsulated by option (b) and hence is the answer.

Poem 2

3. When we read the first few lines of the poem, the poet answers the question "what is love?" to which he says that once you dissolve the will and fate, freedom comes to you. In other words, to attain love, you have to let go of will. Hence, if you let go of one thing to attain the other, both tend to be opposite to each other. For example, to attain peace you need to let go of anger. Hence, (a) is the correct answer.
4. Read the line of the poem which states "be clear like a mirror holding nothing." Also, in reading the poem, we understand that lovers dissolve their will to attain the freedom and become pure emptiness. The crux of these lines then becomes than the lovers hold nothing inside of them and that, is their secret- to have no secret at all. All other options go against the essence of the poem and hence are irrelevant.

Poem 3

5. Fire has been conceptualised metaphorically in the form of desire which translates to greed, therefore option (b) matches closely with the poet's interpretation.
6. Option (c) is the best answer as is it not suited for the title and as the other titles can somewhat be suited to fit the title of the poem. The option (c) is chosen because it could be destruction by emotions and here it is written emotional destruction, since the world does not have emotions of its own hence the answer is incorrect.

PART II

SOLUTIONS ACCORDING TO THE LATEST CAT COMPREHENSION PASSAGES

TEST 1

Passage 1

1. Mentioned in the fourth sentence of the first paragraph.
2. The answer is evident from the following lines from the passage, 'His sometimes absurd and sometimes elegant plays demonstrate a great skill in mixing comedy with honest and sincere ideas. Aristophanes' plays certainly contain many wild and vulgar jokes, yet they also discuss serious concerns of his time, such as politics, art and education'.
3. Clear from the following sentence of the passage, 'Aristotle left behind texts detailing his thoughts and questions on physics and astronomy, as well as meteorology, sleep patterns, raising animals and numerous other subjects'.

Passage 2

4. In the last 5-6 lines of the last paragraph all the three points have been clearly mentioned.
5. The following lines clarify the answer choice, 'having said goodnight very amicably, took his way home by himself to a western suburb'.

Passage 3

6. The assembly is the most important issue; it is the topic of the passage so the question has to be related to it.
7. This is given in the lines from the passage 'The Conference provides a setting in which citizens can bring problems to the group for discussion and creative problem-solving'.

8. The answer is clearly mentioned in the following lines, 'The Assembly follows certain rules of logic: in order for masses of people to enter into collective decision-making they must be organised prior to any decisions having been made'.

TEST 2

Passage 1

1. The tone is clearly ironical as it talks about so many paradoxes that were prevalent in those times, with a tinge of mockery and sadness.
2. The writing style here uses contrasts to show how equal and opposing forces were pitted against each other in the struggle.
3. It is mentioned as a negative remark, a taunt in the case of France, in the last paragraph of the passage.

Passage 2

4. Hobbes espoused psychological egoism, or the belief that human beings are obligated to act in their own self-interest, even to the detriment of others. In all of the above, the protagonist has an option between saving himself/herself or doing good for others. It is only in option (c) that the mother acting to save her own son compromises self-interest. This is the course of action that Hobbes is thus most likely to reject.
5. Hobbes held a pessimistic view of the nature of human beings in that he believed them to be egotistical, power-seeking and rational beings. Selfless action and the spirit of sacrifice were alien to this conception. Thus option (c) is not a characteristic of human beings, as Hobbes saw it.
6. The state of nature is described by Hobbes as an extremely unsafe place where all human beings are equal, but fear for their own lives. It is characterised by a lack of safety, suspicion and each man being against every other. While option (c) describes a characteristic of the state of nature, it does not particularly indicate a disadvantage. It is (a) and (b) together that describe the nature of life in the state of nature.
7. 'Covenant' here signifies the agreement that members of the state of nature enter into, in order to escape it. It is neither a decree nor an order. A close option is 'undertaking' but this does not convey the fact that it is a collective decision. Thus (c) is the correct answer.

Passage 3

8. B is the false statement as it is mentioned in the passage that India in the World Bank's *Doing Business Report 2013* has slipped from 131st to 134th position.
9. In the third paragraph of the passage, the author describes the measures that were undertaken to 'restore competitiveness' to India, which involved industrial licencing and clearances abolishment. This is definitely one of the ways of enhancing competitiveness, which makes option (a), by default, the correct answer. We don't even have to check to the other options, but if we did, we'd find them to be incorrect with respect to given question.
10. The author is opposed to the suggestions in questions (a) and (b), as these are detrimental to the growth of the nation. Option (d) is not correct because it involves an exaggerated suggestion that is not consonant with the theme of the passage. The third passage correctly summarises what has been said in the entire passage, that key structural changes are necessary for enhancing growth and correcting the present order in the country. Hence, this is the correct answer.

TEST 3

Passage 1

1. It is politics or diplomacy based primarily on power and on practical and material factors and considerations, rather than explicit ideological notions or moral or ethical premises.
2. The author mentions in the passage that Iran had thought out its decision to conclude a nuclear deal with the US, and had a strategy behind doing so. Thus, it was not a coerced, confused or hapless move, as is suggested by options (a), (c) and (d). Thus (b) is the correct answer.
3. The 'offensive realists' as their name suggests propose more aggressive and spontaneous measures than their counterparts, the 'defensive realists', who believe in passive defensive techniques. This is best expressed in option (a), while (b), (c) and (d) deal with irrelevant or incomplete.
4. Since the author believes that Iran's move was a tactical and calculated one, which was based on key political considerations and concerns, he would not agree with the view that the US had triumphed over or defeated Iran as is suggested by options (a), (b) and (c). Option (d) is the best answer.

Passage 2

5. The author here wants to suggest that India's partition changed the lives of people, without really changing them at all. They were all still the same people, but suddenly circumstances around them had changed, causing Manto to suddenly feel conscious of his religion among Hindus.
6. The author's suggestion that the bureaucrat was a constant critic of Manto's work would imply that he deliberately chose to ignore the merit that Manto's writing deserved, and instead castigated Manto for faults he perhaps didn't even have. Options (c) and (d) capture this idea the best, and hence (d) is the correct answer.
7. It is said by the author that Manto's work was a misfit in its time, when if writing didn't offer a 'communist cure' or a 'patriotic facelift', it was considered useless. Thus (d), which refers to political ideologising, is what Manto's work did not attempt to provide.
8. The entire passage attempts to delineate Manto's predicament upon the partition of his nation and his subsequent attempts to deal with the same through his written work. His body of work based on the partition suggests that he was deeply moved by it. Nor was he glad to leave his home for Pakistan. Manto's work did indeed receive a huge amount of criticism. Thus option (b) is the correct answer.

Passage 3

9. 'The evidence suggested that Neanderthals headed west, towards Europe, and that the Denisovans moved east'. This line of the passage can make us safely conclude that option (d) is the answer.
10. The author includes Dr. Arsuaga's view that both Denisovans and Neanderthals could have possessed the gene. Thus option (b) is the correct answer.
11. The concluding paragraph of the passage provides the clue as to the most important revelation of the new finding, which is that human biological history may extend beyond 100,000 years ago. This is mentioned in option (a), which is the answer.

TEST 4

Passage 1

1. The first three options can all be regarded as weaknesses of the R2P as it is mentioned in the passage that it is an open, flexible, differently interpreted concept that has been on occasion used by nations to further interests other than human rights. The fourth option is clearly false as the ICISS and UNSC resolutions are mentioned in the passage and there are references to the role of the international community in debate and diplomacy.
2. The Responsibility to Protect involves three components of government action: prevention, reaction and rebuilding efforts in situations that inhibit human rights. Only the first option describes anything that even remotely resembles such government action. The other three options on the other hand involve abuse of human rights.
3. Answer is (b) because author has clearly mentioned that the results of the Libyan war had compelled the countries like Russia and China to draft vetoes. No justification whatsoever can be provided for the political grasp of super powers on the implementation of UN policies, the US being the spearhead of all. Still it was not able to take any corrective measures.
4. The author is both critical and sceptical of the R2P, but he also mentions its achievements, however many they may be. He ends by saying 'R2P as a concept offers much potential but remains far from perfect' and also 'If it is the end of R2P, one wonders how then intervention will be framed in the future', indicating his appreciation of its viability, however limited. The fourth option is a red herring, meant to throw the student because it has no relevance to the author's tone ('specious' meaning: circumspect).

   Therefore the third option is the best answer.

Passage 2

5. The answer is (b) because his way of handling the situations, ability to bounce back from failures, fresh skills as a politician and a successful administrator had made the Americans to have confidence in his leadership skills, thereby easing their fear.
6. The author mentions that although he has been criticised for his lack of political success, Kennedy's domestic record is 'far from poor'. This rules out options (a) and (d) which state these exact extremes. Option (c) is also negated because Kennedy's failure in the Bay of Pigs is mentioned. Therefore, option (b), describing his efforts towards breaking down discriminatory attitudes and practices, is the right answer.

PASSAGE 3

7. Rise in the number of children will cause the savings to fall down, increase in consumption which has been clearly mentioned by the author in the passage. Although number of youngsters will increase, but since the 'One-Child' policy has been running from quite a long time, it would take another generation to change the average age for China. Author has clearly mentioned that more of social concerns will arise instead of economic impacts. Parents will feel their children as 'Safe asset' so will in turn invest more in riskier assets. So the answer is (c).
8. The entire passage focuses on a single theme: that household in China will be encouraged to save less and spend more as a consequence of the relaxation of the old policy. Thus option (c) is clearly not a consequence.
9. Option (b) is the best option of all as it correctly summarises the entire passage. Option (a) is wrong as the author makes no such judgement and makes an objective outline of the policy and its revocation. Option (c) is wrong as the author makes a wider study of the policy than just its successes and failures. Option (d) is wrong as it throws a net too far that includes other analyses that the author in this passage does not cover.

TEST 5

PASSAGE 1

1. Option (c) is the correct answer as the author believes the right to offend (within certain limits) is an essential part of a democratic, vibrant societal set up. Options (c) and (d) are in direct violation of these principles.
2. The meaning of the word is 'lacking in courage'. Timid is the best option in the given context.
3. Option (b) is the best answer as it accurately summarises the sentiment of the author who is in clear support of absolute freedom of expression. The other options are not clear representations of this sentiment, while (c) is in direct contradiction. Thus, option (b) is appropriate.

PASSAGE 2

4. The author categorically mentions that Huntington was uncomfortable with the Universalist claim of Francis Fukuyama in predicting the end of history with the collapse of the Soviet Union. This is clearly not a characteristic of Huntington or his writing.
5. The question in option (c) is one the author is unlikely to entertain as he is believed to have ignored cross-cultural interactions in his study of civilisations. This makes this question the least favourable one to ask him.
6. As the passage speaks of the divisions between different cultures that create separate identities for each of them, option (c), which most nearly means 'divisions', is the best answer.

PASSAGE 3

7. This is evident from the passage because it talks about the poor and the suffering and how they are not able to survive in this world unless they become revolutionaries. Here the thought process of the author goes in the manner that these poor people are not able to live a normal comfortable life, due to which the world is not a place where they could live in a manner every normal person would want to. It is out of their reach and hence it is said that the world is not meant for them. In other words it is a place meant for people who have the means and power to survive.
8. The last line of the first paragraph clearly talks about subject peoples; hence statement 3 is correct.
9. This is the central theme or basis of the whole passage, since it is written from their view point.
10. Mentioned in the last two lines of the passage.

TEST 6

PASSAGE 1

1. Clearly mentioned in paragraphs 1 and 2 of the passage.
2. The urge for social equality and self respect which are the points mentioned in the statements 3 and 4 show the manifestations of a social movement according to the passage. Hence option (c) is correct.
3. A creative society is mostly characterised by political contradictions. Hence option (b) is correct.

PASSAGE 2

4. Mentioned in the last three lines of the passage.

5. Means that the changes have caused harm to some people or affected them negatively.
6. Statement 1 is totally wrong; hence only the second statement is valid.

Passage 3

7. Social movements are the second step, but not the essential part, thus only statement 2 is absolutely correct.
8. Delivery of the basic services to the deprived sections of the society. [Last paragraph of the passage]
9. Mentioned in points 1 and 2 in the passage which talks about the role of the enabling government.
10. Because the government has to be enabling and thereby promote inclusive growth not mentioned in both the statements.
11. The first line of the first paragraph hints towards this; option (a) gets included in option (d), thus option (d) is a superior option.

TEST 7

Passage 1

1. Both the statements are not mentioned in this context in the passage hence both are invalid.
2. The last four lines of the passage mention these points.
3. Mentioned at the start of the passage.
4. Clearly one of the key points of the passage, mentioned as an important fact in the last few lines.
5. Since it is an inferential question, thus the answer cannot be directly stated in the passage and has to be inferred, thus option (d) is the correct choice which is easily inferred whereas option (a) is directly stated, hence not the correct answer.

Passage 2

6. This is the central theme of the passage.
7. It is clearly stated in the passage that the quantity of mussels in an area is determined by the presence or absence of its predators, the sea stars. Statement 1 is incorrect as mussels are controlled by sea stars, hence cannot be termed as the dominant species, and are rather called the competitive species.
8. Clearly mentioned in the passage, in the first paragraph.
9. Statement 1 is definitely true, whereas statement 3 is not true because removal of the keystone species does not devastate or collapse the ecosystem, rather it changes it.
10. The mussel is the most dominant competitor in the absence of the Pisaster, and is clearly mentioned in the first few lines of the passage.

Passage 3

11. A moral act must be our own act; must spring from our own will. Hence statement 1 is correct, although statement 4 is also mentioned but it says sometimes so it is not the usual but a rarity, thus only 1 is the best option.
12. A moral act must be our own act; must spring from our own will. Hence, option (b) is the right option.
13. It means that he is not using his own mind but is influenced or obeys orders blindly. Thus both statements 1 and 2 are relevant.

CHAPTER 7

Previous Years' Questions from CAT*

Given below are a set of original reading comprehension questions from previous years' CAT papers. Readers are advised to attempt on these papers only after going through the theory portion of the book.

I

Directions for the questions (1-30): Each of the six passages given below is followed by questions. Choose the best answers for each question.

PASSAGE 1 (TOTAL WORDS—632) (CAT 2001)

The union government's present position vis-à-vis the upcoming United Nations conference on racial and related discrimination world-wide seems to be the following: discuss race please, not caste; caste is our very own and not at all bad as you think. The gross hypocrisy of that position has been lucidly underscored by *Kancha Ilaiah.* Explicitly, the world community is to be cheated out of considering the matter on the technicality that caste is not, as a concept, tantamount to a racial category. Internally, however, allowing the issue to be put on agenda at the said conference would, we are patriotically admonished, damage the country's image. Somehow, India's virtual beliefs elbow out concrete actualities. Inverted representations, as we know, have often been deployed in human histories as balm for the forsaken–religion being the most persistent of such inversions. Yet, we would humbly submit that if globalizing our markets are thought good for the 'national' pocket, globalizing our social inequities might not be so bad for the mass of our people. After all, racism was uniquely institutionalized in South Africa as caste discrimination has been with in our society: why then can't we permit the world community to express itself on the latter with a fraction of the zeal with which, through the years, we pronounced on the former?

As to the technicality about whether or not caste is admissible into an agenda about race (that the conference is also about 'related discriminations' tends to be forgotten), a reputed sociologist has recently argued that where race is a 'biological' construct, caste is a 'social' one. Having earlier fiercely opposed implementation of the Mandal Commission Report, the said sociologist is at least to be complemented now for admitting, however tangentially, that caste discrimination is a reality, although, in his view, incompatible with racial discrimination. One would like quickly to offer the hypothesis that biology, in important ways that affect the lives of many millions, is in itself perhaps a social construction. But let us look at the matter in another way.

If it is agreed–as per the position today at which anthropological and allied scientific determinations rest–that the entire race of *homo sapiens* derived from an originary black African female (called 'Eve') then one is hard put to understand how, on some subsequent ground, ontological distinctions are to be drawn either between races or castes. Let us also underline the distinction between the supposition that we are all god's children and

* The questions in this section have been compiled from CAT papers till 2005. The original CAT papers from 2017 to 2021 with detailed solutions have been added as a separate section at the end of the book.

the rather more substantiated argument about our descent from 'Eve', lest both positions are thought to be equally diversionary. It then stands to reason that all subsequent distinctions are, in modern parlance, 'constructed' ones, and, like all ideological constructions, attributable to changing equations between knowledge and power among human communities through contested histories here, there, and elsewhere.

This line of thought receives, thankfully, extremely consequential buttress from the findings of the Human Genome project. Contrary to earlier (chiefly 19th century colonial) persuasions on the subject of race, as well as, one might add, the somewhat infamous Jensen offerings in the 20th century from America, those findings deny genetic difference between 'races'. If anything, they suggest that environmental factors impinge on gene-function, as dialectic seems to unfold between nature and culture. It would thus seem that 'biology' as the constitution of pigmentation enters the picture first only as a part of that dialectic. Taken together, the originary mother stipulation and the Genome findings ought indeed to furnish ground for human equality across the board, as well as yield policy initiatives towards equitable material dispensations aimed at building a global order where, in Hegel's stirring formulation, only the rational constitutes the right. Such, sadly, is not the case as everyday, fresh arbitrary grounds for discrimination are constructed in the interests of sectional dominance.

Q1. When the author writes 'globalizing our social inequities", the reference is to:

(a) going beyond an internal deliberation of social inequity.

(b) dealing with internal poverty through the economic benefits of globalization.

(c) going beyond an internal delimitation of social inequity.

(d) achieving disadvantaged people's empowerment, globally.

Q2. According to the author, 'inverted representations as balm for the forsaken;

(a) is good for the forsaken and often deployed in human histories.

(b) is good for the forsaken, but not often deployed historically for the oppressed.

(c) occurs often as a means of keeping people oppressed.

(d) occurs often to invert the status quo.

Q3. Based on the passage, which broad areas unambiguously fall under the purview of the UN conference being discussed?

(A) Racial prejudice

(B) Racial pride

(C) Discrimination, racial or otherwise

(D) Caste-related discrimination

(E) Race-related discrimination

(a) A, E

(b) C, E

(c) A, C, E

(d) B, C, D

Q4. According to the author, the sociologist who argued that race is a 'biological' construct and caste is a 'social' one:

(a) generally shares the same orientation as the author's on many of the central issues discussed.

(b) tangentially admits to the existence of "caste" as a category.

(c) admits the incompatibility between the people of different race and caste.

(d) admits indirectly, that both caste-based prejudice and racial discrimination exist.

Q5. An important message in the passage, if one accepts a dialectic between nature and culture, is that:

(a) the results of the Human Genome Project reinforces racial differences.

(b) race is at least partially, a social construct.

(c) discrimination is at lest partially, a social construct.

(d) caste is at least partially, a social construct.

PASSAGE 2 (TOTAL WORD—652) (CAT 2001)

Studies of the factors governing reading development in young children have achieved remarkable degree of consensus over the past two decades. This consensus concerns the casual role of phonological skills in young children's reading progress. Children, who have good phonological skills, or good "phonological awareness", become good readers and good spellers. Children with poor phonological skills progress more poorly. In particular, those who have a specific phonological deficit are likely to be classified as dyslexic by the time that they are 9 or 10 years old.

Phonological skills in young children can be measured at a number of different levels. The term phonological awareness is a global one, and refers to a deficit in recognizing smaller units of sound within spoken words. Development work has shown that this deficit can be at the level of syllables, of onsets and rimes, or of phonemes.

For example, a 4-year old child might have difficulty in recognizing that a word like valentine has three syllables, suggesting a lack of syllabic awareness. A 5-years old might have difficulty in recognizing that the odd word out in the set of words fan, cat, hat, mat is fan. This task requires an awareness of the sub-syllabic units of the onset and the rime. The onset corresponds to any initial consonants in a syllable, and the rime corresponds to the vowel and to any following consonants. Rimes correspond to rhyme in single-syllable words, and so the rime in fan differs from the rime in cat, hat and mat. In longer words, rime and rhyme may differ. The onsets in val: en: tine are/v/and/t/, and the rimes correspond to the spelling patterns 'al', 'en', and 'ine'.

A 6-year-old might have difficulty in recognizing that plea and pray begin with the same initial sound. This is a phonemic judgment. Although the initial phoneme /P/ is shared between the two words, in plea it is part of the onset 'pl', and in pray it is part of the onset 'pr'. Until children can segment the onset (or the rime), such phonemic judgments are difficult for them to make. In fact, a recent survey of different developmental studies has shown that the different levels of phonological awareness appear to emerge sequentially. The awareness of syllables, onsets, and rimes appears to emerge at around the ages of 3 and 4, long before most children go to school. The awareness of phonemes, on the other hand, usually emerges at around the age of 5 or 6, when children have been taught to read for about a year. An awareness of onsets and rimes thus appears to be a precursor of reading, whereas an awareness of phonemes at every serial position in a word, only appears to develop as reading is taught. The onset-rime and phonemic levels of phonological structure, however, are not distinct. Many onsets in English are single phonemes, and so are some rimes (for example, sea, go, zoo).

The early availability of onsets and rimes is supported by studies that have compared the development of phonological awareness of onsets, rimes, and phonemes in the same subjects using the same phonological awareness tasks. For example, a study by Treiman and Zudowski used a same/different judgment task based on the beginning or the end sounds of words. In the beginning sound task, the words either began with the same onset, as in plea and plank, or shared only the initial phoneme, as in plea and pray. In the end sound task, the words either shared the entire rime, as in spit and wit, or shared only the final phoneme, as in rat and wit. Treiman and Zudowski showed that 4-and 5-year old children found the onset-rime version of the same/different task significantly easier than the version based on phonemes. Only the 6-year old, who had been learning to read for about a year, were able to perform both versions of the tasks with equal levels of success.

Q6. From the following statements, pick out the true statement according to the passage:

(a) A mono-syllabic word can have only one onset.
(b) A mono-syllabic word can have only one rhyme but more than one rime.
(c) A mono-syllabic word can have only one phoneme.
(d) All of the above.

Q7. Which one of the following is likely to emerge last in the cognitive development of a child?

(a) Rhyme
(b) Rime
(c) Onset
(d) Phoneme

Q8. A phonological deficit in which of the following is likely to be classified as dyslexia?

(a) Phonemic judgment
(b) Onset judgment
(c) Rime judgment
(d) Any one or more of the above.

Q9. The Treiman and Zudowski experiment found evidence to support the following:

(a) At age 6, reading instruction helps children perform both, the same-different judgment task.
(b) The development of onset-rime awareness precedes the development of an awareness of phonemes.
(c) At age 4–5, children find the onset-rime version of the same/different task significantly easier.
(d) The development of onset-time awareness is a necessary and sufficient condition for the development of an awareness of phonemes.

Q10. The single-syllable words Rhyme and Rime are constituted by the exact same set of:

I. Rime(s)
II. Onset(s)
III. Rhyme(s)
IV. Phonemes(s)

(a) I, II
(b) I, III
(c) I, II, III
(d) II, III, IV

PASSAGE 3 (TOTAL WORDS—653) (CAT 2001)

Billie Holiday died a few weeks ago. I have been unable until now to write about her, but since she will survive many who receive longer obituaries, a short delay in one small appreciation will not harm her or us. When she died we–the musicians, critics, all who were ever transfixed by the most heart-rending voice of the past generation–grieved bitterly. There was no reason to. Few people pursued self-destruction more whole-heartedly than she, and when the pursuit was at an end, at the age of forty-four, she had turned herself into a physical and artistic wreck. Some of us tried gallantly to pretend otherwise, taking comfort in the occasional moments when she still sounded like a ravaged echo of her greatness. Others had not even the heart to see and listen any more. We preferred to stay home and, if old and lucky enough to own the incomparable records of her heyday from 1937 to 1946, many of which are not even available on British LP, to recreate those coarse-textured, sinuous, sensual and unbearable sad noises which gave her a sure corner of immortality. Her physical death called, if anything, for relief rather than sorrow. What sort of middle age would she have faced without the voice to earn money for her drinks and fixes, without the looks–and in her day she was hauntingly beautiful–to attract the men she needed, without business sense, without anything but the disinterested worship of ageing men who had heard and seen her in her glory?

And yet, irrational though it is, our grief expressed Billie Holiday's art–that of a woman for whom one must be sorry. The great blues singers, to whom she may be justly compared, played their game from strength. Lionesses, though often wounded or at bay (did not Bessie Smith call herself 'a tiger, ready to jump'?), their tragic equivalents were Cleopatra and Phaedra; Holiday's was an embittered Ophelia. She was the Puccini heroine among blues singers, or rather among jazz singers. For though she sang a cabaret version of the blues incomparably, her natural idiom was the op song. Her unique achievement was to have twisted this into a genuine expression of the major passions by means of a total disregard of its sugary tunes, or indeed of any tune other than her own few delicately crying elongated notes, phrased like Bessie Smith or Louis Armstrong in sackcloth, sung in a thin, gritty, haunting voice whose natural mood was an unresigned and voluptuous welcome for the pains of love. Nobody has sung, or will sing, Bess's songs from porgy as she did. It was this combination of bitterness and physical submission, as of someone lying still while watching his legs being amputated, which give such a blood-curdling quality to her Strange Fruit, the anti-lynching poem which she turned into an unforgettable art song. Suffering was her profession; but she did not accept it.

Little need be said about her horrifying life, which she described with emotional, though hardly with factual, truth in her autobiography Lady sings the Blues. After an adolescence in which self-respect was measured by a girl's insistence on picking up the coins thrown to her by clients with her hands, she was plainly beyond help. She did not lack it, for she had the flair and scrupulous honesty of John Hammond to launch her, the best musicians of the 1930s to accompany her–notably Teddy Wilson, Frankie Newton and Lester Young–the boundless devotion of all serious connoisseurs, and much public success. It was too late to arrest a career of systematic embittered self-immolation. But, while she destroyed herself, she sang, unmelodious, profound and heartbreaking. It is impossible not to weep for her, or not to hate the world, which made her what she was.

Q11. Why will Billie Holiday survive many who receive longer obituaries?

(a) Because of her blues creations.

(b) Because she was not as self-destructive as some other blues exponents.

(c) Because of her smooth and mellow voice.

(d) Because of the expressions of anger in her songs.

Q12. According to the author, if Billie Holiday had not died in her middle age:

(a) she would have gone on to make a further mark.

(b) she would have become even richer than she was when she died.

(c) she would have led a rather ravaged existence.

(d) she would have led a rather comfortable existence.

Q13. Which of the following statements is not representative of the author's opinion?

(a) Billie Holiday had her unique brand of melody.

(b) Billie Holiday's voice can be compared to other singers in certain ways.

(c) Billie Holiday's voice had a ring of profound sorrow.

(d) Billie Holiday welcomed suffering in her profession and in her life.

Q14. According to the passage, Billie Holiday was fortunate in all but one of the following ways:

(a) she was fortunate to have been picked up young by an honest producer.

(b) she was fortunate to have the likes of Louis Armstrong and Bessie Smith accompany her.

(c) she was fortunate to possess the looks.

(d) she enjoyed success among the public and the connoisseurs.

Passage 4 (Total Words—880) (CAT 2001)

The narrative of Dersu Uzala is divided into two major sections, set in 1902 and 1907 that deal with separate expeditions, which Arseniev conducts into the Ussuri region. In addition, a third time frame forms a prologue to the film. Each of the temporal frames has a different focus, and by shifting them, Kurosawa is able to describe the encroachment of settlements upon the wilderness and the consequent erosion of Dersu's way of life. As the film opens, that erosion has already begun. The first image is a long shot of a huge forest; the trees piled upon one another by the effects of the telephoto lens so that the landscape becomes an abstraction and appears like a huge curtain of green. A title informs us that the year is 1910. This is as late into the century as Kurosawa will go. After this prologue, the events of the film will transpire even further back in time and will be presented as Arseniev's recollections. The character of Dersu Uzala is heart of the film, his life the example that Kurosawa wishes to affirm. Yet the formal organization of the film works to contain, to close, to circumscribe that life by erecting a series of obstacles around it. The film itself is circular, opening and closing by Dersu's grave, thus sealing off the character from the modern world to which Kurosawa once so desperately wanted to speak. The multiple time frames also work to maintain a separation between Dersu and the contemporary world. We must go back farther even than 1910 to discover who he was. But this narrative structure has yet another implication. It safeguards Dersu's example, inoculates it from contamination with history, and protects it from contact with the industrialized, urban world. Time is organized by the narrative into a series of barriers, which enclose Dersu in a kind of vacuum chamber, protecting him from the social and historical dialectics that destroyed the other Kurosawa heroes. Within the film, Dersu does die. But the narrative structure attempts to immortalize him and his example, as Dersu passes from history into myth.

We see all this at work in the enormously evocative prologue. The camera tilts down to reveal felled trees littering the landscape and an abundance of construction. Roads and houses outline the settlement that is being built. Kurosawa cuts to a medium shot of Arseniev standing in the midst of the clearing, looking uncomfortable and disoriented. A man passing in a wagon asks him what he is doing, and the explorer says he is looking for a grave. The driver replies that no one has died here, the settlement is too recent. These words enunciate the temporal rupture that the film studies. It is the beginning of things (industrial society) and the end of things (the forest), the commencement of one world so young that no one has had time yet to die and the eclipse of another, in which Dersu has died. It is his grave for which the explorer searches. His passing symbolizes the new order, the development that now surrounds Arseniev. The explorer says he buried his friend three years ago, next to huge cedar and fir trees, but now they are all gone. The man on the wagon replies they were probably chopped down when the settlement was built, and he drives off. Arseniev walks to a barren, treeless spot next to a pile of bricks. As he moves, the camera tracks and pans to follow, revealing a line of freshly built houses and a woman hanging her laundry to dry. A distant train whistle is heard, and the sounds of construction in the clearing vie with the cries of birds and the rustle of wind in the trees. Arseniev pauses, looks around for the grave that 1902, and the first section of the film commences, which describes Arseniev's meeting with Dersu and their friendship.

Kurosawa defines the world of the film initially upon a void, a missing presence. The grave is gone, brushed aside by a world rushing into modernism, and now the hunter exists only in Arseniev's memories. The hallucinatory dreams and visions of Dodeskaden are succeeded by nostalgic, melancholy ruminations. Yet by exploring these ruminations, the film celebrates the timelessness of Dersu's wisdom. The first section of the film has two purposes: to describe the magnificence and inhuman vastness of nature and to delineate the code of ethics by which Dersu lives and which permits him to survive in these conditions. When Dersu first appears, the other soldiers treat him with condescension and laughter, but Arseniev watches him closely and does not share their derisive response. Unlike them, he is capable of immediately grasping Dersu's extraordinary qualities. In camp, Kurosawa frames Arseniev by himself, sitting on the other side of the fire from his soldiers. While they sleep or joke among themselves, he writes in his diary and Kurosawa cuts in several point-of-view shots from his perspective of trees that appear animated and sinister as the fire light dances across their gnarled, leafless outlines. This reflective dimension, this sensitivity of the spirituality of nature, distinguishes him from the other and forms the basis of his receptivity to Dersu and their friendship. It makes him a fit pupil for the hunter.

Q15. How is Kurosawa able to show the erosion of Dersu's way of life?

(a) By documenting the ebb and flow of modernization.

(b) By going back farther and farther in time.

(c) By using three different time frames and shifting them.

(d) Through his death in a distant time.

Q16. Arseniev's search for Dersu's grave:

(a) is part of the beginning of the film.

(b) symbolises the end of industrial society.

(c) is misguided since the settlement is too new.

(d) symbolises the rediscovery of modernity.

Q17. The film celebrates Dersu's wisdom:

(a) by exhibiting the moral vacuum of the pre-modern world.

(b) by turning him into a mythical figure.

(c) through hallucinatory dreams and visions.
(d) through Arseniev's nostalgic, melancholy ruminations.

Q18. According to the author, the selection of the film following the prologue:
(a) serves to highlight the difficulties that Dersu faces that eventually kills him.
(b) shows the difference in thinking between Arseniev and Dersu.
(c) shows the code by which Dersu lives that allows him to survive his surroundings.
(d) serves to criticize the lack of understanding of nature in the pre-modern era.

Q19. In the film, Kurosawa hints at Arseniev's reflective and sensitive nature:
(a) by showing him as not being derisive towards Dersu, unlike other soldiers.
(b) by showing him as being aloof from other soldiers.
(c) through shots of Arseniev writing his diary, framed by trees.
(d) All of the above.

Q20. According to the author, which of these statements about the film are correct?
(a) The film makes its arguments circuitously.
(b) The film highlights the insularity of Arseniev.
(c) The film begins with the absence of its main protagonist.
(d) None of these.

PASSAGE 5 (TOTAL WORDS—925) (CAT 2001)

Democracy rests on a tension between two different principles. There is, on the one hand, the principle of equality before the law, or, more generally, of equality, and, on the other, what may be described as the leadership principle. The first gives priority to rules and the second to persons. No matter how skillfully we contrive our schemes; there is a point beyond which the one principle cannot be promoted without some sacrifice of the other.

Alexis de Tocqueville, the great nineteenth century writer on democracy, maintained that the age of democracy, whose birth he was witnessing, would be the age of mediocrity: in saying this he was thinking primarily of a regime of equality governed by impersonal rules. Despite his strong attachment to democracy, he took great pains to point out what he believed to be its negative side: a dead level plane of achievement in practically every sphere of life. The age of democracy would, in his view, be an unheroic age; there would not be room in it for either heroes or hero-worshippers.

But modern democracies have not been able to do without heroes: this too was foreseen, with much misgiving, by Tocqueville. Tocqueville viewed this with misgiving because he believed, rightly or wrongly, that unlike in aristocratic societies, there was no proper place in a democracy for heroes and, hence, when they arose, they would sooner or later turn into despots. Whether they require heroes or not, democracies certainly require leaders, and, in the contemporary age, breed them in great profusion; the problem is to know what to do with them.

In a world preoccupied with scientific rationality, the advantages of a system based on an impersonal rule of law should be a recommendation with everybody. There is something orderly and predictable about such a system. When life is lived mainly in small, self-contained communities, men are able to take finer personal distinctions into account in dealing with their fellow men. They're unable to do this in a large and amorphous society, and organized living would be impossible here without a system of impersonal rules. Above all, such a system guarantees a kind of equality to the extent that everybody, no matter in what station of life, is bound by the same explicit, often written, rules, and nobody is above them.

But a system governed solely by impersonal rules can at best ensure order and stability; it cannot create any shining vision of a future in which mere formal equality will be replaced by real equality and fellowship. A world governed by impersonal rules cannot easily change itself, or when it does, the change is so gradual as to make the basic and fundamental feature of society appear unchanged. For any kind of basic or fundamental change, a push is needed from within, a kind of individual initiative which will create new rules, new terms and conditions of file.

The issue of leadership thus acquired crucial significance in the context of change. If the modern age is preoccupied with scientific rationality, it is no less preoccupied with change. To accept what exists on its terms is traditional, not modern, and it may be all very well to appreciate tradition in music, dance and drama, but for society as a whole, the choice has already been made in favour of modernization and development. Moreover, in some countries, the gap between ideal and reality has become so great that the argument of development and change is now irresistible.

In these countries no argument for development has greater appeal or urgency than the one which shows development to be the condition for the mitigation, it not the elimination, of inequality. There is something contradictory about the very presence of large inequalities in a society which professes to be democratic. It does not take people too long to realize that democracy by itself can guarantee only formal equality; beyond this, it can only whet people's appetite for real or substantive equality. From this arises continued preoccupation with plans and schemes that will help to bridge the gap between the ideal of equality and the reality which is so contrary to it.

When pre-existing rules give no clear directions of change, leadership comes into its own. Every democracy invests its leadership with a measure of charisma, and expects from it a corresponding measure of energy and vitality. Now, the greater the urge for change in a society, the stronger the appeal of a dynamic leadership in it. A dynamic leadership seeks to free itself from the constraints of existing rules; in a sense that is the test of its dynamism. In this process, it may take a turn at which it ceases to regard itself as being bound by these rules, placing itself above them. There is always a tension between 'charisma' and 'discipline' and in the case of a democratic leadership, puts forward revolutionary claims, the tension tends to be resolved at the expense of discipline.

Characteristically, the legitimacy of such a leadership rests on its claim to be able to abolish or at least substantially reduce the existing inequalities in society. From the argument that formal equality or equality before the law is but a limited good, it is often one short step to the argument that it is a hindrance or an obstacle to the establishment of real or substantive equality. The conflict between a 'progressive' executive and a 'conservative' judiciary is but one aspect of this larger problem. This conflict naturally acquires added piquancy when the executive is elected and the judiciary appointed.

Q21. Dynamic leaders are needed in democracies because:

(a) they have adopted the principles of 'formal' equality rather than 'substantive' equality.
(b) 'formal' equality whets people's appetite for 'substantive' equality.
(c) systems that rely on the impersonal rules of 'formal' equality lose their ability to make large changes.
(d) of the conflict between a 'progressive' executive and a 'conservative' judiciary.

Q22. What possible factor would a dynamic leader consider a 'hindrance' in achieving the development goals of a nation?

(a) Principle of equality before the law.
(b) Judicial activism.
(c) A conservative judiciary.
(d) Need for discipline.

Q23. Which of the following four statements can be inferred from the above passage?

I. Scientific rationality is an essential feature of modernity.
II. Scientific rationality results in the development of impersonal rules.
III. Modernisation and development have been chosen over traditional music, dance and drama.
IV. Democracies aspire to achieve substantive equality.

(a) I, II, IV but not III
(b) I, IV but not II, III
(c) I, II but not III, IV
(d) I, II, III but not IV

Q24. Tocqueville believed that the age of democracy would be an un-heroic age because:

(a) Democratic principles do not encourage heroes.
(b) There is no urgency for development in democratic countries.
(c) Heroes that emerged in democracies would become despots.
(d) Aristocratic society has a greater ability to produce heroes.

Q25. A key argument the author is making is that:

(a) in the context of extreme inequality, the issue of leadership has limited significance.
(b) democracy is incapable of eradicating inequality.
(c) formal equality facilitates development and change.
(d) impersonal rules are good for avoiding instability but fall short of achieving real equality.

Q26. Which of the following four statements can be inferred from the above passage?

I. There is conflict between the pursuit of equality and individuality.
II. The disadvantages of impersonal rules can be overcome in small communities.
III. Despite limitations, impersonal rules are essential in large systems.
IV. Inspired leadership, rather than plans and schemes, is more effective in bridging inequality.

(a) II, IV but not I, III
(b) I, II but not III, IV
(c) I, IV but not II, III
(d) I, IV but not II, IV

Passage 6 (Total Words—620) (CAT 2001)

In the modern scientific story, light was created not once but twice. The first time was in the Big Bang, when the universe began its existence as a glowing, expanding fireball, which cooled off into darkness after a few million years. The second time was hundreds of millions of years later, when the cold material condensed into dense nuggets under the influence of gravity, and ignited to become the first stars.

Sir Martin Rees, Britain's astronomer royal, named the longer interval between these two enlightenments, the cosmic "Dark Age". The name describes not only the poorly lit conditions, but also the ignorance of astronomers about that period. Nobody knows exactly when the first stars formed, or how they organized themselves into galaxies–or even whether stars were the first luminous objects. They may have been preceded by quasars, which are mysterious, bright spots found at the centers of some galaxies.

Now, two independent groups of astronomers, one led by Robert Becker of the University of California, Davis, and the other by George Djorgovski of the Caltech, claim to have peered far enough into space with their telescopes (and therefore backwards enough in time) to observe the closing days of the Dark Age.

The main problem that plagued previous efforts to study the Dark Age was not the lack of suitable telescopes, but rather the lack of suitable things at which to point them. Because these events took place over 13 billion years ago, if astronomers are to have any hope of unraveling them, they must study objects that are at least 13 billion light years away. The best prospectuses are quasars, because they are so bright and compact that they can be seen across vast stretches of space. The energy source that powers a quasar is unknown, although it is suspected to be the intense gravity of a giant black hole. However, at the distances required for the study of Dark Age, even quasars are extremely rare and faint.

Recently, some members of Dr. Becker's team announced their discovery of the four most distant quasars known. All the new quasars are terribly faint, a challenge that both teams overcame by peering at them through one of the twin Keck telescopes in Hawaii. These are the world's largest, and can therefore collect the most light. Dr. Becker's team analysed the light from all four quasars. Three of them appeared to be similar to ordinary, less distant quasars. However, the fourth and most distant, unlike any other quasar ever seen, showed unmistakable signs of being shrouded in a fog of hydrogen gas. This gas is leftover material from the Big Bang that did not condense into stars or quasars. It acts like fog because new born stars and quasars emit mainly ultraviolet light, and hydrogen gas is opaque to ultravioletlight. Seeing this fog had been the goal of would-be Dark Age astronomers since 1965, when James Gunn and Bruce Peterson spelled out the technique for using quasars as backlighting beacons to observe the fog's ultraviolet shadow.

The fog prolonged the period of darkness until the heat from the first stars and quasars had the chance to ionize hydrogen (breaking it into its constituent parts, protons and electrons). Ionised hydrogen is transparent to ultraviolet radiation, so at that moment the fog lifted and the universe became the well-lit place it is today. For this reason, the end of the Dark Age is called the "Epoch of Re-ionisation". Because the ultraviolet shadow is visible only in the most distant of the four quasars, Dr. Becker's team concluded that the fog had dissipated completely by the time the universe was about 900 million years old, and one-seventh of its current size.

Q27. In the passage, the Dark Age refers to:

(a) the period when the universe became cold after the Big Bang.
(b) a period about which astronomers know very little.
(c) the medieval period when cultural activity seemed to have come to an end.
(d) the time that the universe took to heat up after the Big Bang.

Q28. Astronomers find it difficult to study the Dark Age because:

(a) suitable telescopes are few.
(b) the associated events took place aeons ago.
(c) the energy source that powers a quasar is unknown.
(d) their best chance is to study quasars, which are faint objects to begin with.

Q29. The four most distant quasars discovered recently:

(a) could only be seen with the help of large telescopes.
(b) appear to be similar to other, ordinary quasars.
(c) appear to be shrouded in a fog of hydrogen gas.
(d) have been sought to be discovered by Dark Age astronomers since 1965.

Q30. The fog of hydrogen gas seen through the telescopes:

(a) is transparent to hydrogen radiation from stars and quasars in all states.
(b) was lifted after heat from stars and quasars ionised it.
(c) is material which eventually becomes stars and quasars.
(d) is broken into constituent elements when stars and quasars are formed.

II

PASSAGE 1 (TOTAL WORDS—884) (CAT 1999)

The World Trade Organisation (WTO) was created in the early 1990s as a component of the Uruguay Round negotiation. However; it could have been negotiated as part of the Tokyo Round of the 1970s, since that negotiation was an attempt at a 'constitutional reform' of the General Agreement on Tariffs and Trade (GATT). Or it could have been put off to the future, as the US government wanted. What factors led to the creation of the WTO in the early 1990s?

One factor was the pattern of multilateral bargaining that developed late in the Uruguay Round. Like all complex international agreements, the WTO was a product of a series of trade-offs between the principal actors and groups. For the United States, which did not want a new organization, the dispute settlement part of the WTO package achieved its longstanding goal of a more effective and more legal dispute settlement system. For the Europeans, who by the 1990s had come to view GATT dispute settlement less in political terms and more as a regime of legal obligations, the WTO package was acceptable as a means to discipline the resort to unilateral measures by the United States. Countries like Canada and other middle and smaller trading partners were attracted by the expansion of a rules-based system and by the symbolic value of a trade organization, both of which inherently support the weak against the strong. The developing countries were attracted due to the provisions banning unilateral measures. Finally, and perhaps most important, many countries at the Uruguay Round came to put a higher priority on the export gains than on the import losses that the negotiation would produce, and they came to associate the WTO and a rules-based system with those gains. This reasoning–replicated in many countries–was contained in U.S. Ambassador Kantor's defence of the WTO, and it amounted to a recognition that international trade and its benefits cannot be enjoyed unless trading nations accept the discipline of a negotiated rules-based environment.

A second factor in the creation of the WTO was pressure from lawyers and the legal process. The dispute settlement system of the WTO was seen as a victory of legalists over pragmatists but the matter went deeper than that. The GATT and the WTO, are contract organizations based on rules, and it is inevitable that an organization created to further rules will in turn be influenced by the legal process. Robert Hudec has written of the 'momentum of legal development', but what is this precisely? Legal development can be defined as promotion of the technical legal values of consistency, clarity (or, certainty) and effectiveness; these are values that those responsible for administering any legal system will seek to maximize. As it played out in the WTO, consistency meant integrating under one roof, the whole lot of separate agreements signed under GATT auspices; clarity meant removing ambiguities about the powers of contracting parties to make certain decisions or to undertake waivers; and effectiveness meant eliminating exceptions arising out of grandfather rights and resolving defects in dispute settlement procedures and institutional provisions. Concern for these values is inherent in any rules-based system of co-operation, since without these values, rules would be meaningless in the first place. Rules, therefore, create their own incentive for fulfillment.

The momentum of legal development has occurred in other institutions besides the GATT, most notably in the European Union (E.U). Over the past two decades, the European Court of Justice (ECJ) has consistently rendered decisions that have expanded incrementally the EU's internal market, in which the doctrine of 'mutual recognition' handed down in the case Cassis de Dijon in 1979 was a key turning point. The Court is now widely recognized as a major player in European integration, even though arguably, such a strong role was not originally envisaged in the Treaty of Rome, which initiated the current European Union. One means the Court used to expand integration was the 'teleological method of interpretation', whereby the actions of member states were evaluated against 'the accomplishment of the most elementary community goals set forth in the Preamble to the [Rome] treaty'. The teleological method represents an effort to keep current policies consistent with stated goals, and it is analogous to the effort in GATT to keep contracting party trade practices consistent with stated rules. In both cases, legal concerns and procedures are an independent force for further co-operation.

In large part, the WTO was an exercise in consolidation. In the context of a trade negotiation that created a near-revolutionary expansion of international trade rules, the formation of the WTO was a deeply conservative act needed to ensure that the benefits of the new rules would not be lost. The WTO was all about institutional structure and dispute settlement; these are the concerns of conservatives and not revolutionaries, which is why lawyers and legalists took the lead on these issues. The WTO codified the GATT institutional practice that had developed by custom over three decades, and it incorporated a new dispute settlement system that was necessary to keep both old and new rules from becoming a sham. Both the international structure and the dispute settlement system were necessary to preserve and enhance the integrity of the multilateral trade regime that had been built incrementally from the 1940s to the 1990s.

Q1. What could be the closest reason why WTO was not formed in the 1970s?

(a) The US government did not like it.

(b) Important players did not find it in their best interest to do so.

(c) Lawyers did not work for the dispute settlement system.

(d) The Tokyo Round negotiation was an attempt at constitutional reform.

Q2. The most likely reason for the acceptance of the WTO package by nations was that:

(a) it had the means to prevent the US from taking unilateral measures.

(b) they recognized the need for a rule-based environment to protect the benefits of increased trade.

(c) it settles disputes more legally and more effectively.

(d) its rule-based system leads to export gains.

Q3. According to the passage, WTO promoted the technical legal values partly through:

(a) integrating under one roof, the agreements signed under GATT.

(b) rules that create their own incentive for fulfillment.

(c) grandfather-rights, exceptions and defects in dispute settlement procedures.

(d) ambiguities about the powers of contracting parties to make certain decisions.

Q4. In the method of interpretation of the European Court of Justice:

(a) current policies need to be consistent with stated goals.

(b) contracting party trade practices needed to be consistent with stated rules.

(c) enunciation of the most elementary community goals needed to be emphasized.

(d) actions of member states needed to be evaluated against the stated community goals.

Q5. In the statement ".... It amounted to a recognition that international trade and its benefits cannot be enjoyed unless trading nations accept the discipline of a negotiated rules-based environment.", 'it' refers to:

(a) Ambassador Cantor's defence of the WTO.

(b) The higher priority on export gains placed by many countries at the Uruguay Round.

(c) The export gains many countries came to associate with a rule-based system.

(d) The provision of a rule-based system by the WTO.

Q6. The importance of Cassis de Dijon is that it:

(a) gave a new impetus to the momentum of legal development at the European Court of Justice.

(b) resulted in a decision that expanded incrementally, the EU's internal market.

(c) strengthened the role of the court beyond what was envisaged in the Treaty of Rome.

(d) led to a doctrine that was a key turning point in European integration.

PASSAGE 2 (TOTAL WORDS—855) (CAT 1999)

Have you ever come across a painting, by Picasso, Mondrain, Miro, or any other modern abstract painter of this century, and found yourself engulfed in a brightly coloured canvas, which your senses cannot interpret? Many people would tend to denounce abstractionism as senseless trash. These people are disoriented by Miro's bright, fanciful creatures and two-dimensional canvases. They click their tongues and shake their heads at Mondrain's grid works, declaring the poor guy played too many scrabble games. They silently shake their heads in sympathy for Picasso; whose gruesome, distorted figures must be a reflection of his mental health. Then, standing in front of a work by Charlie Russell, the famous Western artist, they'll declare it a work of God. People feel more comfortable with something they can relate to and understand immediately without too much thought. This is the case with the work of Charlie Russell. Being able to recognize the elements in his paintings–trees, horses and cowboys–gives people a safety line to their world of "reality". There are some who would disagree when I say abstract art requires more creativity and artistic talent to produce a good piece than does representational art, but there are many weaknesses in their arguments.

People who look down on abstract art have several major arguments to support their beliefs. They feel that artists turn abstract because they are not capable of the technical drafting skills that appear in a Russell; therefore, such artists create an art form that anyone is capable of and that is less time consuming, and then parade it as artistic progress. Secondly, they feel that the purpose of art is to create something of beauty in an orderly, logical composition. Russell's compositions are balanced and rational; everything sits calmly on the canvas, leaving the viewer satisfied that he has seen all there is to see. The modern abstractionists, on the other hand, seem to compose their pieces irrationally. For example, upon seeing Picasso's Guernica, a friend of mine asked me. "What's the point?" Finally, many people feel that art should portray the ideal and real. The exactness of detail in Charlie Russell's work is an example of this. He has been called a great historian because his pieces depict the life style, dress, and events of the times. His subject matter is derived from his own experiences on the trail, reproduced to the smallest detail. I agree in part with many of these arguments, and at one time, even endorsed them. But now, I believe differently. Firstly, I object to the argument that abstract artists are not capable of drafting.

Many abstract artists, such as Picasso, are excellent draftsmen. As his work matured, Picasso became more abstract in order to increase the expressive quality of his work. Guernica was meant as a protest against the bombing of that city by the Germans. To express the terror and suffering of the victims more vividly, he distorted the figures and presented them in a black and white journalistic manner. If he had used representational images and colour, much of the emotional content would have been lost and the piece would not have caused the demand for justice that it did. Secondly, I do not think that a piece must be logical and aesthetically pleasing to be art. The message it conveys to its viewers is more important. It should reflect the ideals and issues of its time and be true to itself, not just a flowery, glossy surface. For example, through his work, Mondrain was trying to present a system of simplicity, logic and rational order. As a result, his pieces did end up looking like a scrabble board. Miro created powerful, surrealistic images from his dreams and subconscious. These artists were trying to evoke a response from society through an expressionistic manner. Finally, abstract artists and representational artists maintain different ideas about 'reality'. To the abstract artist, reality is what he feels about what his eyes see. This is the reality he interprets on canvas. This can be illustrated by Mondrain's Trees series. You can actually see the progression from the early recognizable, though abstracted, Trees, to his final solution, the grid system.

A cycle of abstract and representational art began with the first scratching of prehistoric man. From the abstractions of ancient Egypt to representational, classical Rome, returning to abstractionism in early Christian art and so up to the present day, the cycle has been going on. But this day and age may witness its death through the camera. With film, there is no need to produce finely detailed, historical records manually; the camera does this for us more efficiently. May be, representational art would cease to exist. With abstractionism as the victor of the first battle, may be a different kind of cycle will be touched off. Possibly, some time in the distant future, thousands of years from now, art itself will be physically non-existent. Some artists today believe that once they have planned and constructed a piece in their mind, there is no sense in finishing it with their hands; it has already been done and can never be duplicated.

Q7. The author argues that many people look down upon abstract art because they feel that:

(a) Modern abstract art does not portray what is ideal and real.

(b) Abstract artists are unskilled in matters of technical drafting.

(c) Abstractionists compose irrationally.

(d) All of the above.

Q8. The author believes that people feel comfortable with representational art because:

(a) they are not engulfed in brightly colored canvases.

(b) they do not have to click their tongues and shake their heads in sympathy.

(c) they understand the art without having to put too much strain on their minds.

(d) Paintings like Guernica do not have a point.

Q9. In the author's opinion, Picasso's Guernica created a strong demand for justice since:

(a) it was a protest against the German bombing of Guernica.

(b) Picasso managed to express the emotional content well with his abstract depiction.

(c) it depicts the terror and suffering of the victims in a distorted manner.

(d) it was a mature work of Picasso's, painted when the artist's drafting skills were excellent.

Q10. The author acknowledges that Mondrain's pieces may have ended up looking like a scrabble board because:

(a) many people declared the poor guy played too many scrabble games.

(b) Mondrain believed in the 'grid-work' approach to abstractionist painting.

(c) Mondrain was trying to convey the message of simplicity and rational order.

(d) Mondrain learned from his Trees series to evolve a grid system.

Q11. The main difference between the abstract artist and the representational artist in matters of the 'ideal' and the 'real' according to the author is:

(a) how each chooses to deal with 'reality' on his or her canvas.

(b) the superiority of interpretation of reality over reproduction of reality.

(c) the different values attached by each to being a historian.

(d) the varying levels of drafting skills and logical thinking abilities.

PASSAGE 3 (TOTAL WORDS—1006) (CAT 1999)

Each one has his reasons; for one, art is a flight: for another, a means of conquering. But one can flee into a hermitage, into madness, into death. One can conquer by arms. Why does it have to be Writing, why does one have to manage his escapes and conquests by Writing? Because, behind the various aims of authors, there is a deeper and more immediate choice which is common to all of us. We shall try to elucidate this choice, and we shall see whether it is not in the name of this very choice of writing that the engagement of writers must be required.

Each of our perceptions is accompanied by the consciousness that human reality is a 'revealer', that is, it is through human reality that 'there is' being, or, to put it differently, that man is the means by which things are manifested. It is our presence in the world which multiples relations. It is we who set up a relationship between this tree and that bit of sky. Thanks to us, that star which has been dead for millennia, that quarter moon, and that dark river are disclosed in the unity of a landscape. It is the speed of our auto and our airplane, which organizes the great masses of the earth. With each of our acts, the world reveals to us a new face. But, if we know that we are the directors of being, we also know that we are not its producers. If we turn away from this landscape, it will sink back into its dark permanence. At least, it will sink back; there is no one mad enough to think that it is going to be annihilated. It is we who shall be annihilated, and the earth will remain in its lethargy until another consciousness comes along to awaken it. Thus, to our inner certainty of being 'revealers' is added that of being inessential in relation to the thing revealed.

One of the chief motives of artistic creation is certainly the need of feeling that we are essential in relationship to the world. If I fix on canvas or in writing, a certain aspect of the fields or the sea or a look on someone's face which I have disclosed, I am conscious of having produced them by condensing relationships. By introducing order where there was none, by imposing the unity of mind on the diversity of things. That is, I think myself essential in relation to my creation. But this time, it is the created object which escapes me; I cannot reveal and produce at the same time. The creation becomes inessential in relation to the creative activity. First of all, even if it appears to others as definitive, the created object always seems to us in a state of suspension; we can always change this line, that shade, that word. Thus, it never forces itself. A novice painter asked his teacher. 'When should I consider my painting finished?' And the teacher answered. 'When you can look at it in amazement and say to yourself "I' m the one who did that!"

Which amounts to saying never. For it is virtually considering one's work with someone else's eyes and revealing what has been created. But it is self evident that we are proportionally less conscious of the thing produced and more conscious of our productive activity. When it is a matter of poetry or carpentry, we work according to traditional norms. With tools whose usage is codified, it is Heidegger's famous 'they' who are working with our hands. In this case, the result can seem to us sufficiently strange to preserve its objectivity in our eyes. But if we ourselves produce the rules of production, the measure, the criteria, and if our creative drive comes from the very depth of out heart, then we never find anything but ourselves in our work. It is we who have invented the laws by which we judge it. It is our history, our love, our gaiety that we recognize in it. Even if we should regard it without touching it any further, we never receive from it that gaiety or love. We put them into it. The results which we have obtained on canvas or paper never seem to us objective. We are too familiar with the processes of which they are the effects. These processes remain a subjective discovery; they are ourselves, our inspiration, our ruse, and when we seek to perceive our work, we create it again, we repeat mentally the operations which produced each of its aspects appears as a result. Thus, in the perception, the object is given as the essential thing and the subject as the inessential. The latter seeks essentiality in the creation and obtains it, but then it is the object which becomes the inessential.

The dialectic is nowhere more apparent than in the art of writing, for the literary object is a peculiar top, which exists only in movement. To make it come into view, a concrete act called reading is necessary, and it lasts only as long as this act can last. Beyond that, there are only black marks on paper. Now, the writer cannot read what he writes. Whereas the shoemaker can put on the shoes he has just made if they are to his size, and the architect can live in the house he has built. In reading, one foresees; one waits. He foresees the end of the sentence, the following sentence, the next page. He waits for them, to confirm, or disappoint his foresights. The reading is composed of a host of hypotheses, followed by awakenings, of hopes and deceptions. Readers are always ahead of the sentence they are reading in a merely probable future, which partly collapses and partly comes together in proportion as they progress, which withdraws from one page to the next and forms the moving horizon of the literary object. Without waiting, without a future, without ignorance, there is no objectivity.

Q12. The author holds that:

(a) There is an objective reality and a subjective reality.

(b) Nature is the sum total of disparate elements.

(c) It is human action that reveals the various facets of nature.

(d) Apparently disconnected elements in nature are unified in a fundamental sense.

Q13. It is the author's contention that:

(a) Artistic creations are results of human consciousness.

(b) The very act of artistic creation leads to the escape of the created object.
(c) Man can produce and reveal at the same time.
(d) An act of creation forces itself on our consciousness, leaving us full of amazement.

Q14. The passage makes a distinction between perception and creation in terms of:

(a) Objectivity and subjectivity.
(b) Revelation and action.
(c) Objective reality and perceived reality.
(d) Essentiality and non-essentiality of objects and subject.

Q15. The art of writing manifests the dialectic of perception and creation because:

(a) reading reveals the writing till the act of reading lasts.
(b) writing to be meaningful, needs the concrete act of reading.
(c) this art is anticipated and progresses on a series of hypotheses.
(d) this literary object has a moving horizon brought about by the very act of creation.

Q16. A writer, as an artist,

(a) reveals the essentiality of revelation.
(b) makes us feel essential vis-à-vis nature.
(c) creates reality.
(d) reveals nature in its permanence

Passage 4 (Total Words—921) (CAT 1999)

Since World War II, the nation-state has been regarded with approval by every political system and every ideology. In the name of modernization in the West, of socialism in the Eastern bloc, and of development in the Third World, it was expected to guarantee the happiness of individuals as citizens and of peoples as societies. However, the state today appears to have broken down in many parts of the world. It has failed to guarantee either security or social justice, and has been unable to prevent either international wars or civil wars. Disturbed by the claims of communities within it, the nation-state tries to repress their demands and to proclaim itself as the only guarantor of security of all. In the name of national unity, territorial integrity, equality of all its citizens and non-partisan secularism, the state can use its powerful resources to reject the demands of the communities; it may even go so far as genocide to ensure that order prevails.

As one observes the awakening of communities in different parts of the world, one cannot ignore the context in which identity issues arise. It is no longer a context of sealed frontiers and isolated regions, but is one of integrated global systems. In a reaction to this trend towards globalisation, individuals and communities everywhere are voicing their desire to exist, to use their power of creation and to play an active part in national and international life.

There are two ways in which the current upsurge in demands for the recognition of identities can be looked at. On the positive side, the efforts by certain population groups to assert their identity can be regarded as "liberation movements", challenging oppression and injustice. What these groups are doing–proclaiming that they are different, rediscovering the roots of their culture or strengthening group solidarity–may accordingly be seen as legitimate attempts to escape from their state of subjugation and enjoy a certain measure of dignity. On the downside, however, militant action for recognition tends to make such groups more deeply entrenched in their attitude and to make their cultural compartments even more watertight. The assertion of identity then starts turning into self-absorption and isolation, and is liable to slide into intolerance of others and towards ideas of "ethnic cleansing", xenophobia and violence.

Whereas continuous variations among peoples prevent drawing of clear dividing lines between the groups, those militating for recognition of their group's identity arbitrarily choose a limited number of criteria such as religion, language, skin colour; and place or origin so that their members recognise themselves primarily in terms of the labels attached to the group whose existence is being asserted. This distinction between the group in question and other groups is established by simplifying the feature selected. Simplification also works by transforming groups into essences, abstractions endowed with the capacity to remain unchanged through time. In some cases, people actually act as though the group has remained unchanged and talk, for example, about the history of nations and communities as if these entities survived for centuries without changing, with the same ways of acting and thinking, the same desires, anxieties, and aspirations.

Paradoxically, precisely because identity represents a simplifying fiction, creating uniform groups out of disparate people, that identity performs a cognitive function. It enables us to put names to ourselves and others, form some idea of who we are and who others are, and ascertain the place we occupy along with the others in the world and society. The current upsurge to assert the identity of groups can thus be partly explained by the cognitive function performed by identity. However, that said, people would not go along as they do, often in large numbers, with the propositions put to them, in spite of the sacrifices they entail, if there was not a very strong feeling of need for identity, a need to take stock of things and know who we are where we come from and where we are going.

Identity is thus a necessity in a constantly changing world, but it can also be a potent source of violence and disruption. How can these two contradictory aspects of identity be reconciled? First, we must bear the arbitrary nature of identity categories in mind, not with a view to eliminating all forms of identification–which would be unrealistic since identity is a cognitive necessity–but simply to remind ourselves that each of us has several identities at the same time. Second, since tears of nostalgia are being shed over the past, we recognize that culture is constantly being recreated by cobbling together fresh and original elements and counter-cultures. There are in our own country, a large number of syncretic cults wherein modern elements are blended with traditional values or people of different communities venerate saints or divinities of particular faiths. Such cults and movements are characterized by a continual inflow and outflow of members which prevent them from taking on a self-perpetuating existence of their own and hold out hope for the future, indeed perhaps for the only possible future. Finally, the nation-state must respond to the identity urges of its constituent communities and to their legitimate quest for security and social justice. It must do so by inventing what the French philosopher and sociologist, Raymond Aron, called peace through law. That would guarantee justice both to the state as a whole and its parts, and respect the claims of both reason and emotions. The problem is one of reconciling nationalist demands with the exercise of democracy.

Q17. According to the author, happiness of individuals was expected to be guaranteed in the name of:

(a) Development in the Third World.
(b) Socialism in the Third World.
(c) Development in the West.
(d) Modernisation in the Eastern Bloc.

Q18. Demands for recognition of identities can be viewed:

(a) positively and negatively.
(b) as liberation movements and militant action.
(c) as efforts to rediscover cultural roots which can slide towards intolerance of others.
(d) All of the above.

Q19. Going by the author's exposition of the nature of identity, which of the following statements is untrue?

(a) Identity represents creating uniform groups out of disparate people.
(b) Identity is a necessity in the changing world.
(c) Identity is a cognitive necessity.
(d) None of the above.

Q20. According to the author, the nation-state:

(a) has fulfilled its potential.
(b) is willing to do anything to preserve order.
(c) generates security for all its citizens.
(d) has been a major force in preventing civil and international wars.

Q21. Which of the following views of the nation-state cannot be attributed to the author?

(a) It has not guaranteed peace and security.
(b) It may go as far as genocide for self-preservation.
(c) It represents the demands of communities within it.
(d) It is unable to prevent international wars.

Passage 5 (Total Words—1460) (CAT 1999)

The persistent patterns in the way nations fight reflect their cultural and historical traditions and deeply rooted attitudes that collectively make up their strategic culture. These patterns provide insights that go beyond what can be learnt just by comparing armaments and divisions. In the Vietnam War, the strategic tradition of the United States called for forcing the enemy to fight a massed battle in an open area, where superior American weapons would prevail. The United States was trying to fight World War II in the jungles of Southeast Asia, against an enemy with no intention of doing so.

Some British military historians describe the Asian way of war as one of indirect attacks, avoiding frontal attacks meant to overpower an opponent. This traces back to Asian history and geography: the great distances and harsh terrain have often made it difficult to execute the sort of open field clashes allowed by the flat terrain and relatively compact size of Europe. A very different strategic tradition arose in Asia.

The bow and arrow were metaphors for an Eastern way of war: By its nature, the arrow is an indirect weapon. Fired from a distance of hundreds of yards, it does not necessitate immediate physical contact with the enemy. Thus, it can be fired from hidden positions. When fired from behind a bridge, the barrage seems to come out of nowhere, taking the enemy by surprise. The tradition of this kind of fighting is captured in the classical strategic writings of the East. The 2,000 years' worth of Chinese writings on war constitutes the subtlest writings on the subject in any language. Not until Clausewitz did the West produce a strategic theorist to match the sophistication of Sun-tzu, whose Art of War was written 2,300 years earlier.

In Sun-tzu and other Chinese writings, the highest achievement of arms is to defeat an adversary;

without fighting. He wrote. "To win one hundred victories in one hundred battles is not the acme of skill. To subdue the enemy without fighting is the supreme excellence." Actual combat is just one among many means towards the goal of subduing an adversary. War contains too many surprises to be a first resort. It can lead to ruinous losses, as has been seen time and again. It can have the unwanted effect of inspiring heroic efforts in an enemy, as the United States learned in Vietnam, and as the Japanese found out after Pearl Harbor.

Aware of the uncertainties of a military campaign, Sun-tzu advocated war only after the most thorough preparations. Even then, it should be quick and clean. Ideally, the army is just an instrument to deal the final blow to an enemy already weakened by isolation, poor morale, and disunity. Ever since Sun-tzu, the Chinese have been seen as masters of subtlety, who take measured actions to manipulate an adversary without his knowledge. The dividing line between war and peace can be obscure. Low level violence often is the backdrop to a larger strategic campaign. The unwitting victim, focused on the day-to-day events, never realizes what's happening to him until it's too late. History holds many examples. The Viet Cong lured French and U.S. infantry deep into the jungle, weakening their morale over several years. The mobile army of the United States was designed to fight on the plains of Europe, where it could quickly move unhindered from one spot to the next. The jungle did more than make quick movement impossible; broken down into smaller units and scattered in isolated bases, US forces were deprived of the feeling of support and protection that ordinarily comes from being part of a big army.

The isolation of U.S. troops in Vietnam was not just a logistical detail, something that could be overcome by, for instance, bringing in reinforcements by helicopter. In a big army reinforcements are readily available. It was Napoleon who realized the extraordinary effects on morale that come from being part of a larger formation. Just the knowledge of it lowers the soldier's fear and increases his aggressiveness. In the jungle and on isolated bases, this feeling was removed. The thick vegetation slowed down the reinforcements and made it difficult to find stranded units. Soldiers felt they were on their own.

More important, by altering the way the war was fought, the Viet Cong stripped the United States of its belief in the inevitability of victory, as it had done to the French before them. Morale was high when these armies first went to Vietnam. Only after many years of debilitating and demoralizing fighting did Hanoi launch its decisive attacks, at Dienbienphu in 1954 and against Saigon in 1975. It should be recalled that in the final push to victory, the North Vietnamese abandoned their jungle guerrilla tactics completely, committing their entire army of twenty divisions to pushing the South Vietnamese into collapse. The final battle, with the enemy's army all in one place, was the one that the United States had desperately wanted to fight in 1965. When it did come out into the open in 1975, Washington had already withdrawn its forces and there was no possibility of re-intervention.

The Japanese early in World War II, used a modern form of the indirect attack, one that relied on stealth and surprise for its effect. At Pearl Harbor, in the Philippines, and in Southeast Asia, stealth and surprise were attained by sailing under radio silence so that the navy's movements could not be tracked. Moving troops aboard ships into Southeast Asia made it appear that the Japanese army was also "invisible". Attacks against Hawaii and Singapore seemed, to the American and British defenders, to come from nowhere. In Indonesia and the Philippines, the Japanese attack was even faster than the German blitz against France in the West. The greatest military surprises in American history have all been in Asia. Surely, there is something going on here beyond the purely technical difficulties of detecting enemy movements. Pearl Harbor, the Chinese intervention in Korea, and the Tet offensive in Vietnam, all came out of a tradition of surprise and stealth. U.S. technical intelligence–the location of enemy units and their movements–was greatly improved after each surprise, but with no noticeable improvement in the American ability to foresee or prepare what would happen next. There is a cultural divide here, not just a technical one. Even when it was possible to track an army with intelligence satellites, as when Iraq invaded Kuwait or when Syria and Egypt attacked Israel, surprise was achieved. The United States was stunned by Iraq's attack on Kuwait even though it had satellite pictures of Iraqi troops massing at the border.

The exception that proves the point that cultural differences obscure the West's understanding of Asian behavior was the Soviet Union's 1979 invasion of Afghanistan. This was fully anticipated and understood in advance. There was no surprise because the United States understood Moscow's world view and thinking. It could anticipate Soviet action almost as well as the Soviets themselves, because the Soviet Union was really a Western country.

The difference between the Eastern and the Western way of war is striking. The West's great strategic writer, Clausewitz, linked war to politics, as did Sun-tzu. Both were opponents of militarism, of turning war over to the generals. But there all similarity ends. Clausewitz wrote that the way to achieve a larger political purpose is through destruction of the enemy's army. After observing Napolean conquer Europe by smashing enemy armies to bits, Clausewitz made his famous remark in On War (1932) that combat is the continuation of politics by violent means. Morale and unity are important, but they should be harnessed for the ultimate battle. If the Eastern way of war is embodied by the stealthy archer, the metaphorical Western counterpart is the swordsman charging forward, seeking a decisive showdown, eager to administer the blow that will obliterate the enemy once and for all. In this view, war proceeds along a fixed course and occupies a finite extent of time, like a play in three acts with a beginning, a middle, and an end. The end, the final scene, decides the issue for good.

When things don't work out quite this way, the Western military mind feels tremendous frustration. Sun-tzu's great disciples, Mao Zedong and Ho Chi Minh, are respected in Asia for their clever use of indirection and deception to achieve an advantage over stronger adversaries. But in the West, their approach is seen as underhanded and devious. To the American strategic mind, the Viet Cong guerrilla did not fight fairly. He should have come out into the open and fought like a man, instead of hiding in the jungle and sneaking around like a cat in the night.

Q22. According to the author; the main reason for the U.S losing the Vietnam war was:

(a) the Vietnamese understood the local terrain better.
(b) the lack of support for the war from the American people.
(c) the failure of the U.S. to mobilize its military strength.
(d) their inability to fight a war on terms other than those they understood well.

Q23. Which of the following statements does not describe the 'Asian' way of war?

(a) Indirect attacks without frontal attacks.
(b) The swordsman charging forward to obliterate the enemy once and for all.
(c) Manipulation of an adversary without his knowledge.
(d) Subduing an enemy without fighting.

Q24. Which of the following is not one of Sun-tzu's deans?

(a) Actual combat is the principal means of subduing an adversary.
(b) War should be undertaken only after thorough preparation.
(c) War is linked to politics.
(d) War should not be left to the generals alone.

Q25. The difference in the concepts of war of Clausewitz and Sun-tzu is best characterized by:

(a) Clausewitz's support for militarism as against Sun-tzu's opposition to it.
(b) Their relative degrees of sophistication.
(c) Their attitude to guerilla warfare.
(d) Their differing conceptions of the structure, time and sequence of war.

Q26. To the Americans, the approach of the Viet Cong seemed devious because:

(a) the Viet Cong did not fight like men out in the open.
(b) the Viet Cong allied with America's enemies.
(c) the Viet Cong used bows and arrows rather than conventional weapons.
(d) None of these

Q27. According to the author, the greatest military surprises in American history have been in Asia because:

(a) The Americans failed to implement their military strategies many miles away from their own country.
(b) The Americans were unable to use their technologies like intelligence satellites effectively to detect enemy movements.
(c) The Americans failed to understand the Asian culture of war that was based on stealth and surprise.
(d) Clausewitz is inferior to Sun-tzu.

III

Passage 1 (Total Words—1233) (CAT 2000)

The current debate on intellectual property rights (IPRs) raises a number of important issues concerning the strategy and policies for building a more dynamic national agricultural research system, the relative roles of public and private sectors, and the role of agribusiness multinational corporations (MNCs). This debate has been stimulated by the international agreement on Trade Related Intellectual Property Rights (TRIPs), negotiated as part of the Uruguay Round. TRIPs, for the first time, seeks to bring innovations in agricultural technology under a new world wide IPR regime. The agribusiness MNCs (along with pharmaceutical companies) played a leading part in lobbying for such a regime during the Uruguay Round negotiations. The argument was that incentives are necessary to stimulate innovations, and that this calls for a system of patents which gives innovators the sole right to use (or sell/ lease the right to use) their innovations for a specified period and protects them against unauthorized copying or use. With strong support of their national governments, they were influential in shaping the agreement on TRIPs, which eventually emerged from the Uruguay Round.

The current debate on TRIPs in India–as indeed elsewhere–echoes wider concerns about 'privations' of research and allowing a free field for MNCs in the sphere of biotechnology and agriculture. The agribusiness corporations and those with unbounded faith in the power of science to overcome all likely problems; point to the vast potential that new technology holds for solving the problems of hunger, malnutrition and poverty in the world. The exploitation of this potential should be encouraged and this is best done by the private sector for which patents are essential. Some, who do not necessarily accept this optimism, argue that fears of MNC domination are exaggerated and that farmers will accept their products only if they decisively outperform the available alternatives. Those who argue against agreeing to introduce an IPR regime in agriculture and encouraging private sector research are apprehensive that this will work to the disadvantage of farmers by making them more and more dependent on monopolistic MNCs. A different, though related apprehension is that extensive use of hybrids and genetically engineered new varieties might increase the vulnerability of agriculture to outbreaks of pest and disease. The larger, longer-term consequences of reduced biodiversity that may follow from the use of specially bred varieties are also another cause for concern. Moreover; corporations, driven by the profit motive, will necessarily tend to underplay, if not ignore, potential adverse consequences, especially those which are unknown and which may manifest themselves only over a relatively long period. On the other hand, high-pressure advertising and aggressive sales campaigns by private companies can seduce farmers into accepting varieties without being aware of potential adverse effects and the possibility of disastrous consequences for their livelihood if these varieties happen to fail. There is no provision under the laws, as they now exist, for compensating users against such eventualities. Excessive preoccupation with seeds and seed material has obscured other important issues involved in reviewing the research policy. We need to remind ourselves that improved varieties by themselves are not sufficient for sustained growth of yields. In our own experience, some of the early high yielding varieties (HYVs) of rice and wheat were found susceptible to widespread pest attacks; and some had problems of grain quality. Further research was necessary to solve these problems. This largely successful research was almost entirely done in public research institutions. Of course, it could in principle have been done by private companies, but whether they choose to do so depends crucially on the extent of the loss in market for their original introductions on account of the above factors and whether the companies are financially strong enough to absorb the losses, invest in research to correct the deficiencies and recover the lost market. Public research, which is not driven by profit, is better placed to take corrective action. Research for improving common pool resource management, maintaining ecological health and ensuring sustainability is both critical and also demanding in terms of technological challenge and resource requirements. As such research is crucial to impact new varities, chemicals and equipment in the farmer's field, private companies should be interested in such research. But their primary interest is in the sale of seed material, chemicals, equipments and other inputs produced by them. Knowledge and techniques for resource management are not 'marketable' in the same way as those inputs. Their applications to land, water and forests has a long gestation and their efficacy depends on resolving difficult problems such as designing institutions for proper and equitable management of common pool resources. Public or quasi-public research institutions informed by broader; long-term concerns can only do such work.

The public sector must therefore continue to play a major role in the national research system. It is both wrong and misleading to pose the problem in terms of public sector versus private sector or of privatization of research. We need to address problems likely to arise on account of the public-private sector complementarity, and ensure that the public research system performs efficiently. Complementarity between various elements of research raises several issues in implementing an IPR regime. Private companies do not produce new varieties and inputs entirely as result of their own research. Almost all-technological improvement is based on knowledge and experience accumulated from the past. And the results of basic and applied research in public and quasi-public institutions (universities, research organization). Moreover, as is increasingly recognized, accumulated stock of knowledge does not reside only in the scientific community and its academic publications, but is also widely diffused in traditions and folk knowledge of local communities all over.

The deciphering of the structure and functioning of DNA forms the basis of much of modern biotechnology. But this fundamental breakthrough is a 'public good' freely accessible in the public domain and usable free of any charge. Varieties/ techniques developed using that knowledge can however be, and are, patented for private profit. Similarly, private corporations draw extensively, and without any charge, on germ plasma available in varieties of plants species (neem and turmeric are by now famous examples). Publicly funded gene banks as well as new varieties bred by public sector research stations can also be used freely by private enterprises for developing their own varieties and seek patent protection for them. Should private breeders be allowed free use of basic scientific discoveries? Should the repositories of traditional knowledge and germ plasma be collected which are maintained and improved by publicly funded institutions? Or should users be made to pay for such use? If they are to pay, what should be the basis of compensation? Should the compensation be for individuals of for communities/ institutions to which they belong? Should individuals/institutions be given the right of patenting their innovations?

These are some of the important issues that deserve more attention than they now get and need serious detailed study to evolve reasonably satisfactory, fair and workable solutions. Finally, the tendency to equate the public sector with the government is wrong. The public state is much wider than government departments and includes co-operatives, universities, public trusts and a variety of non-government organizations. Giving greater autonomy to research organizations from government control and giving non-government public institutions the space and resources to play a larger, more effective role in research, is therefore an issue of direct relevance in restructuring the public system.

Q1. Which one of the following statements describes an important issue or important issues, not being raised in the context of the current debate on IPRs?

(a) The role of MNCs in the sphere of biotechnology and agriculture.
(b) The strategy and policies for establishing an IPR regime for Indian agriculture.
(c) The relative roles of public and private sectors.
(d) Wider concerns about 'privatization' of research.

Q2. The fundamental breakthrough in deciphering the structure and functioning of DNA has become a public good. This means that:

(a) Breakthroughs in fundamental research on DNA are accessible by all, without any monetary considerations.
(b) The fundamental research on DNA has the characteristic of having beneficial effects for the public at large.
(c) Due to the large scale of fundamental research on DNA, it falls in the domain of public sector research institutions.
(d) The public and other companies must have free access to such fundamental breakthroughs in research.

Q3. In debating the respective roles of the public and private sectors in the national research system, it is important to recognize:

(a) that private companies do not produce new varieties and inputs entirely on their own research.
(b) that almost all technological improvements are based on knowledge and experience accumulated from the past.
(c) the complementary role of public and private sector research.
(d) that knowledge repositories are primarily the scientific community and its academic publications.

Q4. Which one of the following may provide incentives to address the problem of potential adverse consequences of biotechnology?

(a) Include IPR issue in the TRIPs agreement.
(b) Nationalise MNCs engaged in private research in biotechnology.
(c) Encourage domestic firms to patent their innovation.
(d) Make provision in the law for user compensation against failure of newly developed varieties.

Q5. Which of the following statements is not a likely consequence of emerging technology in agriculture?

(a) Development of newer and newer varieties will lead to increase in biodiversity.
(b) MNCs may underplay the negative consequences of the newer technology on environment.
(c) Newer varieties of seeds may increase vulnerability of crops to pest and diseases.
(d) Reforms in patent laws and user compensation against crop failures would be needed to address new technology problems.

Q6. The TRIPs agreement emerged from the Uruguay Round to:

(a) address the problem of adverse consequences of genetically engineered new varieties of grain.
(b) fulfill the WTO requirement to have an agreement on trade related property rights.
(c) provide innovators a way of protecting their intellectual property.
(d) give credibility to the innovations made by MNCs in the field of pharmaceuticals and agriculture.

Q7. Public or quasi-public research institutions are more likely than private companies to address the negative consequences of new technologies, because of which of the following reason/s?

(a) Public research is not driven by profit motive.
(b) Private companies may not be able to absorb losses arising out of the negative effects of the new technologies.
(c) Unlike new technology, product knowledge and techniques for resource management are not amenable to simple market transactions.
(d) All of the above.

Q8. While developing a strategy and policies for building a more dynamic national agricultural research system, which one of the following statements needs to be considered?

(a) Public and quasi-public institutions are not interested in making profits.

(b) Public and quasi-public institutions have a broader and longer-term outlook than private companies.

(c) Private companies are incapable of building products based on traditional and folk knowledge.

(d) Traditional and folk knowledge cannot be protected by patents.

Passage 2 (Total Words—1195) (CAT 2000)

One of the criteria by which we judge the vitality of a style of painting is its ability to renew itself–its responsiveness to the changing nature and quality of experience, the degree of conceptual and formal innovation that it exhibits. By this criterion, it would appear that the practice of abstractionism has failed to engage creatively with the radical change in human experience in recent decades. It has, seemingly, been unwilling to re-invent itself in relation to the system of artistic expression and viewers' expectations that have developed under the impact of the mass media.

The judgment that abstractionism has slipped into 'inertia gear' is gaining endorsement, not only among discerning viewers and practitioners of other art forms, but also among abstract painters themselves. Like their companions elsewhere in the world, abstractionists in India are asking themselves an overwhelming question today. Does abstractionism have a future? The major crisis that abstractionists face is that of revitalizing their picture surface; few have improvised many solutions beyond the ones that were exhausted by the 1970s. Like all revolutions, whether in politics or in art, abstractionism must now confront its moment of truth: having begun life as a new and radical pictorial approach to experience, it has become an entrenched orthodoxy itself. Indeed, when viewed against a historical situation in which a variety of subversive, interactive and richly hybrid forms are available to the art practitioner, abstractionism assumes the remote and defiant air of an aristocracy that has outlived its age; trammeled by formulaic conventions, yet buttressed by a rhetoric of sacred mystery, it seems condemned to being the last citadel of the self-regarding 'fine-art' tradition, the last hurrah of painting for painting's sake.

The situation is further complicated in India by the circumstances in which an indigenous abstractionism came into prominence here during the 1960s. From the beginning it was propelled by the dialectic between two motives, one revolutionary and the other conservative–it was inaugurated as an act of emancipation from the dogmas of the nascent Indian nation state, when art was officially viewed as an indulgence at worst, and at best, as an instrument for the celebration of the republic's hopes and aspirations. Having rejected these dogmas, the pioneering abstractionists also went on to reject the various figurative styles associated with the Shantiniketan circle and others. In such a situation, abstractionism was a revolutionary move. It led art towards the exploration of the subconscious mind, the spiritual quest and the possible expansion of consciousness. Indian painting entered into a phase of self-inquiry, meditative inner space where cosmic symbols and non-representational images ruled. Often, the transition from figurative idioms to abstractionist ones took place within the same artist.

At the same time, Indian abstractionists have rarely committed themselves wholeheartedly to a non-representational idiom. They have been preoccupied with the fundamentally metaphysical project of aspiring to the mystical-holy without altogether renouncing the symbolic. This has been sustained by a hereditary reluctance to give up the murti, the inviolable iconic form, which explains why abstractionism is marked by the conservative tendency to operate with images from the sacred repertoire of the past. Abstractionism thus entered India as a double-edged device in a complex cultural transaction. Ideologically, it served as an internationalist legitimization of the emerging revolutionary local trends. However, on entry, it was conscripted to serve local artistic preoccupations–a survey of indigenous abstractionism will show that its most obvious points of affinity with European and American abstract art were with the more mystically oriented of the major sources of abstractionist philosophy and practice, for instance, the Kandinsky-Klee, school. There have been no takers for Malevich's Supermatism, which militantly rejected both the artistic forms of the past and the world of appearances, privileging the new-minted geometric symbol as an autonomous sign of the desire for infinity.

Against this backdrop, we can identify three major abstractionist idioms in Indian art. The first develops from a love of earth, and assumes the form of a celebration of the self's dissolution in the cosmic panorama; the landscape is no longer a realistic transcription of the scene, but is transformed into a visionary occasion for contemplating cycles of decay and regeneration. The second idiom phrases its departures from symbolic and archetypal devices as invitations to heightened planes of awareness. Abstractionism begins with the establishment or dissolution of the motif, which can be drawn from diverse sources, including the hieroglyphic tablet, the Sufi meditation dance or Tantric diagram. The third idiom is based on the lyric play of forms guided by gesture or allied with formal improvisations like the assemblage. Here, sometimes, the line dividing abstract image from patterned design or quasi-random expressive marking may blur. The flux of forms can also be regimented through the poetics of pure colour arrangements, vector-diagrammatic spaces and gestural design.

In this genealogy, some pure lines of descent follow their logic to the inevitable point of extinction, others engage in cross-fertilization, and yet others undergo mutation to maintain their energy. However, this genealogical survey demonstrates the wave at its crest, those points where the metaphysical and the painterly have been fused in images of abiding potency, ideas sensuously ordained rather than fabricated programmatically to a concept. It is equally possible to enumerate the troughs where the two principles do not come together; thus arriving at a very different account. Uncharitable as it may sound, the history of Indian abstractionism records a series of attempts to avoid the risks of abstraction by resorting to an overt and near-generic symbolism, which many Indian abstractionists embrace when they find themselves bereft of the imaginative energy to negotiate the union of metaphysics and painterliness. Such symbolism falls into a dual trap: it succumbs to the pompous vacuity of pure metaphysics when the burden of intention is passed off as justification: or then it is desiccated by the arid formalism of pure painterliness. With delight in the measure of change or pattern guiding the execution of a painting, the ensuing conflict of purpose stalls the progress of abstractionism in an impasse. The remarkable Indian abstractionists are precisely those who have overcome this and addressed themselves to the basic elements of their art with a decisive sense of independence from prior models. In their recent work, we see the logic of Indian abstractionism pushed almost to the furthest it can be taken. Beyond such artists stands a lost generation of abstractionism whose work invokes a wistful, delicate beauty, but stops there.

Abstractionism is not a universal language; it is an art that points up the loss of a shared language of signs in society. And yet, it affirms the possibility of its recovery through the effort of awareness. While its rhetoric has always emphasized a call for new forms of attention, abstractionists' practice has tended to fall into a complacent pride in its own incomprehensibility; fatal in an ethos where vibrant new idioms compete for viewers' attention. Indian abstractionists ought to really return to basics, to reformulate and replenish their understanding of the nature of the relationship between the painted image and the world around it. But can they abandon their favourite conceptual habits and formal conventions, if this becomes necessary?

Q9. Which one of the following is not stated by the author as a reason for abstractionism losing its vitality?

(a) Abstractionism has failed to reorient itself in the context of changing human experience.

(b) Abstractionism has not considered the developments in artistic expression that have taken place in recent times.

(c) Abstractionism has not followed the path taken by all revolutions, whether in politics or art.

(d) The impact of mass media on viewers' expectation has not been assessed, and responded to, by abstractionism.

Q10. Which one of the following, according to the author; is the role that abstractionism plays in a society?

(a) It provides an idiom that can be understood by most members in a society.

(b) It highlights the absence of a shared language of meaningful symbols, which can be recreated through greater awareness.

(c) It highlights the contradictory artistic trends of revolution and conservation that any society needs to move forward.

(d) It helps abstractionists invoke the wistful, delicate beauty that may exist in society.

Q11. According to the author, which one of the following characterizes the crisis faced by abstractionism?

(a) Abstractionists appear to be unable to transcend the solutions tried out earlier.

(b) Abstractionism has allowed itself to be confined by set forms and practices.

(c) Abstractionists have been unable to use the multiplicity of forms now becoming available to an artist.

(d) All of the above.

Q12. According to the author; the introduction of abstraction was revolutionary because it:

(a) celebrated the hopes and aspirations of a newly independent nation.

(b) provided a new direction to Indian art, towards self-inquiry and non-representational images.

(c) managed to obtain international support for the abstractionist agenda.

(d) was emancipation from the dogmas of the nascent nation state.

Q13. Which one of the following is not part of the author's characterization of the conservative trend in Indian abstractionism?

(a) An exploration of the subconscious mind.

(b) A lack of full commitment to non-representational symbols.

(c) An adherence to the symbolic while aspiring to the mystical.
(d) Usage of the images of gods or similar symbols.

Q14. Given the author's delineation of the three abstractionist idioms in Indian art, the third idiom can be best distinguished from the other two idioms through its:

(a) depiction of nature's cyclical renewal.
(b) use of non-representational images.
(c) emphasis on arrangement of forms.
(d) limited reliance on original models.

Q15. According to the author; the attraction of the Kandinsky-Klee School for Indian abstractionists can be explained by which one of the following?

(a) The conservative tendency to aspire to the mystical without a complete renunciation of the symbolic.
(b) The discomfort of Indian abstractionists with Malevich's supermatism.
(c) The easy identification of Obvious points of affinity with European and American abstract art, of which the Kandinsky-Klee School is an example.
(d) The double-edged nature of abstractionism which enabled identification with mystically-oriented schools.

Q16. Which one of the following, according to the author, is the most important reason for the stalling of abstractionism's progress in an impasse?

(a) Some artists have followed their abstractionist logic to the point of extinction.
(b) Some artists have allowed chance or pattern to dominate the execution of their paintings.
(c) Many artists have avoided the trap of a near generic and an open symbolism.
(d) Many artists have found it difficult to fuse the twin principles of the metaphysical and the painterly.

PASSAGE 3 (TOTAL WORDS—1244) (CAT 2000)

In a modern computer, electronic and magnetic storage technologies play complementary roles. Electronic memory chips are fast but volatile (their contents are lost when the computer is unplugged). Magnetic tapes and hard disks are slower; but have the advantage that they are non-volatile, so that they can be used to store software and documents even when the power is off.

In laboratories around the world, however; researchers are hoping to achieve the best of both worlds. They are trying to build magnetic memory chips that could be used in place of today's electronic ones. These magnetic memories would be non-volatile; but they would also be faster, would consume less power, and would be able to stand up to hazardous environments more easily. Such chips would have obvious applications in storage cards for digital cameras and music-players; they would enable handheld and laptop computers to boot up more quickly and to operate for longer; they would allow desktop computers to run faster; they would doubtless have military and space-faring advantages too. But although the theory behind them looks solid, there are tricky practical problems that need to be overcome. Two different approaches, based on different magnetic phenomena are being pursued. The first, being investigated by Gary Prinz and his colleagues at the Naval Research Laboratory (NRL) in Washington, D.C., exploits the fact that the electrical resistance of some materials changes in the presence of a magnetic field–a phenomenon known as magneto-resistance. For some multi-layered materials this effect is particularly powerful and is, accordingly, called "giant" magneto-resistance (GMR). Since 1997, the exploitation of GMR has made cheap multi-gigabyte hard disks commonplace. The magnetic orientations of the magnetized spots on the surface of a spinning disk are detected by measuring the changes they induce in the resistance of a tiny sensor. This technique is so sensitive that it means the spots can be made smaller and packed closer together than was previously possible, thus increasing the capacity and reducing the size and cost of a disk drive.

Dr. Prinz and his colleagues are now exploiting the same phenomenon on the surface of memory chips, rather than spinning disks. In a conventional memory chip, each binary digit (bit) of data is represented using a capacitor–reservoir of electrical charge that is either empty or full–to represent a zero or a one. In the NRL's magnetic design, by contrast, each bit is stored in a magnetic element in the form of a vertical pillar of magnetized material, either clockwise or anticlockwise to represent zero or one. Another set of wires allows current to pass through any particular element. By measuring an element's resistance you can determine its magnetic orientation, and hence, whether it is storing a zero or a one. Since the elements retain their magnetic orientation even when the power is off, the result is nonvolatile memory. Unlike the elements of an electronic memory, a magnetic memory's elements are not easily disrupted by radiation. And compared with electronic memories, whose capacitors need constant topping up, magnetic memories are simpler and consume less power. The NRL researchers plan to commercialise their device through a company called Non-Volatile Electronics, which recently began work on the necessary processing and fabrication techniques. But it will be some years before the first chips toll off the production line.

Most attention in the field is focused on an alternative approach based on magnetic tunnel-junctions (MTJs), which are being investigated by researchers at chipmakers such as IBM, Motorola, Siemens and Hewlett-Packard. IBM's research team, led by Stuart Parkin, has already created a 500-element working prototype that operates at 20 times the speed of conventional memory chips and consumes 1 per cent of the power: Each element consists of a sandwich of two layers of magnetable material separated by a barrier of aluminum oxide just four or five atoms thick. The polarization of lower magnetable layer is fixed in one direction, but that of the upper layer can be set (again by passing a current through a matrix of control wires) either to the left or to the right, to store a zero or a one. The polarizations of the two layers are then in either the same or opposite directions.

Although the aluminium-oxide barrier is an electrical insulator, it is so thin that electrons are able to jump across it via a quantum-mechanical effect called tunneling. It turns out that such tunneling is easier when the two magnetic layers are polarized in the same direction than when they are polarized in opposite directions, so, by measuring the current that flows through the sandwich, it is possible to determine the alignment of the topmost layer; and hence, whether it is storing a zero or a one.

To build a full-scale memory chip based on MTJs is, however, no easy matter. According to Paulo Freitas, an expert on chip manufacturing at the Technical University of Lisbon, magnetic memory elements will have to become far smaller and more reliable than current prototypes if they are to compete with electronic memory. At the same time, they will have to be sensitive enough to respond when the appropriate wires in the control matrix are switched on, but not so sensitive that they respond when a neighboring element is changed. Despite these difficulties, the general consensus is that MTJs are the more promising ideas. Dr. Parkin says his group evaluated the GMR approach and decided not to pursue it, despite the fact that IBM pioneered GMR in hard disks. Dr. Prinz, however, contends that his plan will eventually offer higher storage densities and lower production costs.

Not content with shaking up the multi-billion-dollar market for computer memory, some researchers have even more ambitious plans for magnetic computing. In a paper published last month in science, Russell Cowburn and Mark Welland of Cambridge University outlined research that could form the basis of a magnetic microprocessor–a chip capable of manipulating (rather than merely storing) information magnetically. In place of conducting wires, a magnetic processor would have rows of magnetic dots, each of which could be polarized in one of two directions. Individual bits of information would travel down the rows as magnetic pulses, changing the orientation of the dots as they went. Dr. Cowhurn and Dr. Welland have demonstrated how a logic gate (the basic element of a microprocessor) could work in such a scheme. In their experiment, they fed a signal in at one end of the chain of dots and used a second signal to control whether it propagated along the chain.

It is, admittedly, a long way from a single logic gate to a full microprocessor, but this was true also when the transistor was first invented. Dr. Cowburn, who is now searching for backers to help commercialise the technology, says he believes it will be at least ten years before the first magnetic microprocessor is constructed. But other researchers in the field agree that such a chip is the next logical step. Dr. Prinz says that once magnetic memory is sorted out "the target is to go after the logic circuits." Whether all magnetic computers will ever be able to compete with other contenders that are jostling to knock electronics off its perch–such as optical, biological and quantum computing–remains to be seen. Dr. Cowburn suggests that the future lies with hybrid machines that use different technologies. But computing with magnetism evidently has an attraction all its own.

Q17. In developing magnetic memory chips to replace the electronic ones, two alternative research paths are being pursued. These are approaches based on:

(a) Volatile and non-volatile memories.

(b) Magneto-resistance and magnetic tunnel junctions.

(c) Radiation-disruption and radiation-neutral effects.

(d) Orientation of magnetised spots on the surface of a spinning disk and alignment of magnetic dots on the surface of a conventional memory chip.

Q18. A binary digit or bit is represented in the magneto-resistance based magnetic chip using:

(a) a layer of aluminium oxide.

(b) a capacitor.

(c) a vertical pillar of magnetised material.

(d) a matrix of wires.

Q19. In the magnetic tunnel-junctions (MTJs), tunneling is easier when:

(a) two magnetic layers are polarised in the same direction.

(b) two magnetic layers are polorised in the opposite directions.

(c) two aluminium-oxide barriers are polarized in the same direction.

(d) two aluminium-oxide barriers are polarized in opposite directions.

Q20. A major barrier on the way to build a full-scale memory chip based on MTJs is:

(a) The low sensitivity of the magnetic memory elements.

(b) The thickness of aluminium oxide barriers.

(c) The need to develop more reliable and far smaller magnetic memory chips.

(d) All of the above.

Q21. In the MTJs approach, it is possible to identify whether the topmost layer of the magnetised memory elements is storing a zero or one by:

(a) Measuring an element's resistance and thus determining its magnetic orientation.

(b) Measuring the degree of disruption caused by radiation in the elements of the magnetic memory.

(c) Magnetising the elements either clockwise or anti-clockwise.

(d) Measuring the current that flows through the sandwich.

Q22. A line of research which is trying to build a magnetic chip that can both store and manipulate information, is being pursued by:

(a) Paul Freitas.

(b) Stuart Parkin.

(c) Gary Prinz.

(d) None of the above.

Q23. Experimental research currently underway, using rows of magnetic dots, each of which could be polarized in one of the two directions, has led to the demonstration of:

(a) Working of a microprocessor.

(b) Working of a logic gate.

(c) Working of a magneto-resistance based chip.

(d) Working of a magneto tunneling-junction (MTJs) based chip.

Q24. From the passage, which of the following cannot be inferred?

(a) Electronic memory chips are faster and non-volatile.

(b) Electronic and magnetic storage technologies play a complementary role.

(c) MTJs are the more promising idea, compared to the magneto-resistance approach.

(d) Non-volatile Electronics is the company set up to commercialise the GMR chips.

Passage 4 (Total Words—1256) (CAT 2000)

The story begins as the European pioneers crossed the Alleghenies and started to settle in the Midwest. The land they found was covered with forests. With incredible effort they felled the trees, pulled the stumps and planted their crops in the rich, loamy soil. When they finally reached the western edge of the place we now call Indiana, the forest stopped and ahead lay a thousand miles of the great grass prairie. The Europeans were puzzled by this new environment. Some even called it the "Great Desert". It seemed untellable. The earth was often very wet and it was covered with centuries of tangled and matted grasses. With their cast iron plows, the settlers found that the prairie sod could not be cut and the wet earth struck to their plowshares. Even a team of the best oxen bogged down after a few years of tugging. The iron plow was a useless tool to farm the prairie soil. The pioneers were stymied for nearly two decades. Their western march was halted and they filled in the eastern regions of the Midwest.

In 1837, a blacksmith in the town of Grand detour, Illinois, invented a new tool. His name was John Deere and the tool was a plow made of steel. It was sharp enough to cut through matted grasses and smooth enough to cast off the mud. It was a simple tool, the "sod buster" that took the great prairies to agricultural development. Sauk Country, Wisconsin is the part of that prairie where I have a home. It is named after the Sauk Indians. In 1673, father Marquette was the first European to lay his eyes upon their land. He found a village laid out in regular patterns on a plain beside the Wisconsin River. He called the place Prairie Dusac. The village was surrounded by fields that had provided maize, beans and squash for the Sauk People for generations reaching back into the unrecorded time.

When the European settlers arrived at the Sauk prairie in 1837, the government forced the native Sauk people west of the Mississippi River. The settlers came with John Deere's new invention and used the tool to open the area to a new kind of agriculture. They ignored the traditional ways of the Sauk Indian and used their sod-busting tool for planting wheat. Initially, the soil was generous and the farmers thrived. However, each year the soil lost more of its nurturing power. It was only thirty years after the Europeans arrived with their new technology that the land was depleted. Wheat farming became uneconomic and tens of thousands of farmers left Wisconsin seeking new land with sod to bust.

It took the Europeans and their new technology just one generation to make their homeland into a desert. The Sauk Indians who knew how to sustain themselves on the Sauk prairie land were banished to another kind of desert called a reservation. And they even forgot about the techniques and tools that had sustained them on the prairie for generations unrecorded. And that is how it was that three deserts were created–Wisconsin, the reservation and the memories of a people. A century later, the land of the Sauks is now populated by the children of a second wave of European farmers who learned to replenish the soil through the regenerative powers of dairying, ground cover crops and animal manures. These third and fourth generation farmers and townspeople do not realize, however; that a new settler is coming soon with an invention as powerful as John Deere's plow.

The new technology is called 'bereavement counseling'. It is a tool forged at the great state university, an innovative technique to meet the needs of those experiencing the death of a loved one, a tool that can "process" the grief of the people who now live on the Prairie of the Sauk. As one can imagine the final days of the village of the Sauk Indians before the arrival of the settlers with John Deere's plow, one can also imagine these final days before the arrival of the first bereavement counsellor at Prairie Du Sac. In these final days, the farmers and the townspeople mourn at the death of a mother, brother, son or friend. Neighbours join the bereaved and kin, they meet grief together in lamentation, prayer and song, they call upon the words of the clergy and surround themselves in community.

It is in these ways that they grieve and then go on with life. Through their mourning, they are assured of the bonds between them and renewed in the knowledge that this death is a part of the Prairie of the Sauk. Their grief is common property, an anguish from which the community draws strength and gives the bereaved the courage to move ahead.

It is into this prairie community that the bereavement counselor arrives with the new grief technology. The counselor calls the invention a service and assures the prairie folk of its effectiveness and superiority by invoking the name of the great university while displaying a diploma and certificate. At first, we can imagine that the local people will be puzzled by the bereavement counsellor's claim. However, the counselor will tell a few of them that the new technique is merely to assist the bereaved's community at the time of death. To some other prairie folk who are isolated or forgotten, the counselor will approach the Country Board and advocate the right to treatment for these unfortunate souls. This right will be guaranteed by Board's decision to reimburse those too poor to pay for counseling services. There will be others, schooled to believe in the innovative new tools certified by universities and medical centers, who will seek to the bereavement counselor by force of habit. And one of these people will tell a bereaved neighbour who is unschooled that unless his grief is processed by a counselor, he will probably have major psychological problems in later life, several people will begin to use the bereavement counselor because, since the Country Board now taxes them to insure access to the technology, they will feel that to fail to be counseled is to waste their money, and to be denied a benefit, or even a right.

Finally, one day, an aged father of a Sauk woman will die. And the next-door neighbour will not drop by because he doesn't want to interrupt the bereavement counselor. The woman's kin will stay home because they will have learned that only the bereavement counselor knows how to process grief the proper way. The local clergy will seek technical assistance from the bereavement counselor to learn the correct form of service to deal with guilt and grief. And the grieving daughter will know that it is the bereavement counselor who really cares for her because only the bereavement counselor comes when death visits this family on the Prairie of the Sauk.

It will be only one generation between the bereavement counselor arrives and the community of mourners disappears. The counsellor's new tool will cut through the social fabric. Throwing aside kinship, care, neighbourly obligations and community ways of coming together and going on. Like John Deere's plow, the tools of bereavement counseling will create a desert where a community once flourished. And finally, even the bereavement counselor will see the impossibility of restoring hope in clients once they are genuinely alone with nothing but a service for consolation. In the inevitable failure of the service, the bereavement counsellor will find the deserts even in herself.

Q25. Which one of the following best describes the approach of the author?

(a) Comparing experiences with two innovations tried, in order to illustrate the failure of both.

(b) Presenting community perspectives on two technologies, which have negative effects on people.

(c) Using the negative outcomes of one innovation to illustrate how 'deserts' have arisen.

(d) Contrasting two contexts separated in time, to illustrate how 'deserts' have arisen.

Q26. According to the passage, bereavement handling traditionally involves.

(a) The community bereavement counselor working with the bereaved to help him/her overcome grief.

(b) The neighbours and kin joining the bereaved and meeting grief together in mourning and prayer.

(c) Using techniques developed systematically in formal institutions of learning, a trained counselor helping the bereaved cope with grief.

(d) The Sauk Indian Chief leading the community with rituals and rites to help lessen the grief of the bereaved.

Q27. Due to which of the following reasons, according to the author, will the bereavement counselor find the desert even in herself?

(a) Over a period of time, working with Sauk Indians who have lost their kinship and relationships, she becomes one of them.

(b) She is working in an environment where the disappearance of community mourners makes her work place a social desert.

(c) Her efforts at grief processing with the bereaved will fail as no amount of professional service can make up for the loss due to the disappearance of community mourners.

(d) She has been working with people who have settled for a long time in the Great Desert.

Q28. According to the author, the bereavement counsellor is:

(a) A friend of the bereaved helping him or her handle grief.

(b) An advocate of the right to treatment for the community.

(c) A kin of the bereaved helping the bereaved handle grief.

(d) A formally trained person helping the bereaved handle grief.

Q29. The Prairie was a great puzzlement for the European pioneers because:

(a) It was covered with thick, untellable layers of grass over a vast stretch.

(b) It was a large desert immediately next to lush forests.

(c) It was rich cultivable land left fallow for centuries.

(d) It could be easily tilled with iron plows.

Q30. Which of the following does the 'desert' in the passage refer to?

(a) Prairie soil depleted by cultivation of wheat.

(b) Reservations in which native Indians were resettled.

(c) Absence of, and emptiness in, community kinship and relationships.

(d) All of the above.

Q31. According to the author, people will begin to utilize the service of the bereavement counselor because:

(a) New Country regulations will make them feel it is a right, and if they don't use it, it would be a loss.

(b) The bereaved in the community would find her a helpful friend.

(c) She will fight for subsistence allowance from the Country Board for the poor among the bereaved,

(d) Grief processing needs tools certified by universities and medical centers.

Q32. Which one of the following parallels between the plow and bereavement counseling is not claimed by the author?

(a) Both are innovative technologies.

(b) Both result in migration of the communities into which the innovations are introduced.

(c) Both lead to deserts in the space of only one generation.

(d) Both are tools introduced by outsiders entering existing communities.

PASSAGE 5 (TOTAL WORDS—1028) (CAT 2000)

The teaching and transmission of North Indian classical music is, and long has been, achieved by largely oral means. The raga and its structure, the often breathtaking intricacies of tala or rhythm, and the incarnation of raga and tala as bandish or composition, are passed thus, between guru and Shishya by word of mouth and direct demonstration, with no printed sheet of notated music, as it were, acting as a go-between. Saussure's conception of language as a communication between addresser and addressee is given, in this model, a further instance, and a new, exotic complexity and glamour.

These days, especially with the middle class having entered the domain of classical music and playing not a small part in ensuring the continuation of this ancient tradition, the tape recorder serves as a handy technological slave and preserves, from oblivion, the vanishing, elusive moment of oral transmission. Hoary gurus, too, have seen the advantage of this device, and increasingly use it as an aid to instructing their pupils; in place of the shawls and other traditional objects that used to pass from shishya to guru in the past, as a token of the regard of the former for the latter, it is not unusual, today, to see cassettes changing hands.

Part of my education in North Indian classical music was conducted via this rather ugly but beneficial rectangle of plastic, which I carried with me to England when

I was an undergraduate. One cassette had stored in it various talas played upon the tabla, at various tempos, by my music teacher's brother-in-law, Hazarilalji, who was a teacher of Kathak dance, as well as a singer and a tabla player. This was a work of great patience and prescience, a one-and-a-half hour performance without any immediate point or purpose, but intended for some delayed future moment when I'd practice the talas solitarily.

This repeated playing out of the rhythmic cycles on the tabla was inflected by the noises - an irate auto driver blowing a horn; the sound of overbearing pigeons that were such a nuisance on the banister; even the cry of a kulfi seller in a summer–entering from the balcony of the third floor flat we occupied in those days, in a lane in a Bombay suburb, before we left the city for good. These sounds, in turn, would invade, hesitantly, the ebb and flow of silence inside the artificially heated room, in a borough of west London, in which I used to live as an undergraduate. There, in the trapped dust, silence and heat, the theka of the tabla, qualified by the imminent but intermittent presence of the Bombay suburb, would come to life again. A few years later, the tabla and, in the background, the pigeons and the itinerant kulfi seller, would inhabit a small graduate room in oxford.

The tape recorder, though, remains an extension of the oral transmission of music, rather than a replacement of it. And the oral transmission of North Indian classical music remains, almost uniquely, a testament to the fact that the human brain can absorb, remember and reproduce structures of great complexity and sophistication without the help of the hieroglyph or written mark or a system of notation. I remember my surprise on discovering that Hazarilalji–who has mastered Kathak dance, tala and North Indian classical music, and who used to narrate to me, occasionally, compositions meant for dance that were grand and intricate in their verbal prosody, architecture and rhythmic complexity–was near illiterate and had barely learnt to write his name in large and clumsy letters.

Of course, attempts have been made, throughout the 20th century, to formally codify and even notate this music, and institutions set up and degrees created, specifically to educate students in this "scientific" and codified manner. Paradoxically, however, this style of teaching has produced no noteworthy student or performer; the most creative musicians still emerge from the guru-shishya relationship, their understanding of music developed by oral communication.

The fact that North Indian classical music emanates from, and evolved through, oral culture, means that this music has a significantly different aesthetic, and that this aesthetic, has a different politics, from that of Western classical music. A piece of music in the Western tradition, at least in its most characteristic and popular conception, originates in its composer, and the connection between the two, between composer and the piece of music, is relatively unambiguous precisely because the composer writes down, in notation, his composition, as a poet might write down and publish his poem. However far the notion of property remains at the heart of the Western conception of "genius", which derives from the Latin gignere or 'to beget'.

The genius in Western classical music is, then, the originator, begetter and owner of his work–the printed, notated sheet testifying to his authority over his product and his power, not only of expression or imagination, but of origination. The conductor is a custodian and guardian of this property. Is it an accident that Mandelstam, in his notebooks, compares–celebratorily–the conductor's baton to a policeman's saying all the music of the orchestra lies mute within it, waiting for its first movement to release it into the auditorium. The raga-transmitted through oral means is, in a sense, no one's property; it is not easy to pin down its source, or to know exactly where its provenance or origin lies. Unlike the Western classical tradition, where the composer begets his piece, notates it and stamps it with his ownership and remains, in effect, larger than, or the father of, his work, in the North Indian classical tradition, the raga–unconfined to a single incarnation, composer or performer–remains necessarily greater than the artiste who invokes it.

This leads to a very different politics of interpretation and valuation, to an aesthetic that privileges the evanescent moment of performance and invocation over the controlling authority of genius and the permanent record. It is a tradition, thus, that would appear to value the performer, as medium, more highly than the composer who presumes to originate what, effectively, couldn't be originated in a single person, because the raga is the inheritance of a culture.

Q33. The author's contention that the notion of property lies at the western conception of genius is best indicated by which one of the following?

(a) The creative output of a genius is invariably written down and recorded.

(b) The link between the creator and his output is unambiguous.

(c) The word "genius" is derived from a Latin word which means, "to beget".

(d) The music composer notates his music and thus becomes the "father" of a particular piece of music.

Q34. Saussure's conception of language as a communication between addresser and addressee, according to the author, is exemplified by the:

(a) Teaching of North Indian classical music by word of mouth and direct demonstration.

(b) Use of the recorded cassette as a transmission medium between the music teacher and the trainee.

(c) Written down notation sheets of musical compositions.

(d) Conductor's baton and the orchestra.

Q35. The author holds that the "rather ugly but beneficial rectangle of plastic" has proved to be a "handy technological slave" in:

(a) Storing the talas played upon the tabla, at various tempos.

(b) Ensuring the continuance of an ancient tradition.

(c) Transporting North Indian classical music across geographical borders.

(d) Capturing the transient moment of oral transmission.

Q36. The oral transmission of North Indian classical music is an almost unique testament of the:

(a) Efficacy of the guru-shishya tradition.

(b) Learning impact of direct demonstration.

(c) Brain's ability to reproduce complex structures without the help of written marks.

(d) Ability of an illiterate person to narrate grand and intricate musical compositions.

Q37. According to the passage, in the North Indian classical tradition, the raga remains greater than the artiste who invokes it. This implies an aesthetic which:

(a) Emphasises performance and invocation over the authority of genius and permanent record.

(b) Makes the music no one's property.

(c) Values the composer more highly than the performer.

(d) Supports oral transmission of traditional music.

Q38. From the author's explanation of the notion that in the Western tradition, music originates in its composer, which one of the following cannot be inferred?

(a) It is easy to transfer a piece of Western classical music to a distant place.

(b) The conductor in the Western tradition, as a custodian, can modify the music, since it 'lies mute' in his baton.'

(c) The authority of the Western classical music composer over his music product is unambiguous.

(d) The power of the Western classical music composer extends to the expression of his music.

Q39. According to the author; the inadequacy of teaching North Indian classical music through a codified, notation based system is best illustrated by:

(a) A loss of the structural beauty of the ragas.

(b) A fusion of two opposing approaches creating mundane music.

(c) The conversion of free-flowing ragas into a stilted set piece.

(d) Its failure to produce any noteworthy student or performer:

Q40. Which of the following statements best conveys the overall idea of the passage?

(a) North Indian and Western classical music are structurally different.

(b) Western music is the intellectual property of the genius while the North Indian raga is the inheritance of a culture.

(c) Creation as well as performance are important in the North Indian classical tradition.

(d) North Indian classical music is orally transmitted while Western classical music depends on written down notations.

IV

Passage 1 (Total Words—435) (CAT 1998)

Emile Durkheim, the first person to be formally recognized as a sociologist and the most scientific of the pioneers, conducted a study that stands as a research model for sociologists today. His investigation of suicide was, in fact, the first sociological study to use statistics. In 'Suicide' (1964, originally published in 1897) Durkheim documented his contention that some aspects of human behaviour–even something as allegedly individualistic as suicide–can be explained without reference to individuals.

Like all of Durkheim's work, suicide must be viewed within the context of his concern for social integration. Durkheim wanted to see if suicide rates within a social entity (for example a group, organization, or society) are related to the degree to which individuals are socially involved (integrated and regulated). Durkheim described three types of suicide; egoistic, anomic, and altruistic. Egoistic suicide is promoted when individuals do not have sufficient social ties. Since single (never married) adults, for example, are not heavily involved with family life, they are more likely to commit suicide than are married adults. Altruistic suicide on the other hand, is more likely to occur when social integration is too strong. The ritual suicide of Hindu widows on their husband's funeral pyres is one example. Military personnel, trained to lay down their lives for their country, provide another illustration.

Durkheim's third type of suicide–anomic suicide–increases when the social regulation of individuals is disrupted. For example, suicide rates increase during economic depressions. People who suddenly find themselves without a job or without hope of finding one are more prone to kill themselves. Suicides may also increase during periods of prosperity. People may loosen their social ties by taking new jobs, moving to new communities, or finding new mates.

Using data from the government population reports of several countries (much of it from the French Government Statistical Office), Durkheim found strong support for his line of reasoning. Suicide rates were higher among single than married people, among military personnel than civilians, among divorced than married people, and among people involved in nationwide economic crises.

It is important to realize that Durkheim's primary interest was not in the empirical (observable) indicators he used such as suicide rates among military personnel, married people and so forth. Rather, Durkheim used the following indicators to support several of his contentions: (1) social behaviour can be explained by social rather than psychological factors: (2) suicide is affected by the degree of integration and regulation within social entities; and (3) since society can be studied scientifically, sociology is worthy of recognition in the academic world. Durkheim was successful on all three counts.

Q1. In his study of suicide, Durkheim's main purpose was:

(a) to document that suicide can be explained without reference to the individual.
(b) to provide an explanation of the variation in the rate of suicide across societies.
(c) to categorise various types of suicides.
(d) to document that social behaviour can be explained by social rather than psychological factors.

Q2. According to Durkheim, suicide rates within a social entity can be explained in terms of:

(a) absence of social ties.
(b) disruption of social regulation.
(c) nature of social integration.
(d) all of the above.

Q3. Since single adults are not heavily involved with family life they are more likely to commit suicide, which Durkheim categorized as:

(a) anomic suicide.
(b) altruistic suicide.
(c) egoistic suicide.
(d) (b) and (c).

Q4. Higher suicide rates during rapid progress in a society is a manifestation of:

(a) altruistic suicide.
(b) anomic suicide.
(c) egoistic suicide.
(d) None of the above.

Q5. Ritual suicide of Hindu widows on their husband's funeral pyres was:

(a) a manifestation of strong social integration.
(b) an example of brutality against women.
(c) an example of anomic suicide.
(d) an example of egoistic suicide.

Q6. Increase in the suicide rate during economic depression is an example of:

(a) altruistic suicide.
(b) anomic suicide.
(c) egoistic suicide.
(d) both (a) and (c).

Q7. According to Durkheim, altruistic suicide is more likely among:

(a) military personnel than among civilians.
(b) single people than among married people.
(c) divorcees than among married people.
(d) people involved in nationwide economic crises.

Q8. To support his contentions, Durkheim relied on the following indicators:

(a) Social behaviour is explicable predominantly through social factors.
(b) Suicide is contingent upon the degree of regulation and interaction.
(c) Recognising sociology to acknowledge that society is susceptible to scientific investigation.
(d) All of the above.

Q9. Basing himself on his own indicators, Durkheim was:

(a) Right on some counts, not others.
(b) Vindicated on all counts.
(c) Wrong but did not realize that he was right.
(d) Substantially correct but formally wrong.

PASSAGE 2 (TOTAL WORDS—813) (CAT 1998)

How quickly things change in the technology business! A decade ago, IBM was the awesome and undisputed king of the computer trade, universally feared and respected.

A decade ago, two little companies called Intel and Microsoft were mere blips on the radar screen of the industry, upstart startups that had signed on to make the chips and software for IBM's new line of personal computers. Though their products soon became industry standards, the two companies remained protected children of the market leader.

What has happened since is a startling reversal of fortune. IBM is being ravaged by the worst crisis in the company's 79-year history. It is undergoing its fifth restructuring in the past seven years as well as seemingly endless rounds of job cuts and firings that have eliminated 100,000 jobs since 1985. Last week, IBM announced to its shell-shocked investors that it lost $4.97 billion last year–the biggest loss in American corporate history.

And just when IBM is losing ground in one market after another, Intel and Microsoft have emerged as the computer industry's most fearsome pair of competitors. The numbers on Wall Street tell a stunning story. Ten years ago, the market value of the stock of Intel and Microsoft combined amounted to about a tenth of IBM's. Last week, with IBM's stock at an 11 year low, Microsoft's value surpassed its old mentor's for the first time ever ($26.76 billion to $26.48 billion), and Intel ($24.3 billion) is not far behind. While IBM is posting losses, Intel's profits jumped 30 per cent and Microsoft's rose 44 per cent.

Both Intel, the world's largest supplier of computer chips, and Microsoft, the world's largest supplier of computer software, have assumed the role long played by Big Blue as the industry's pacesetter. What is taking place is a generational shift unprecedented in the information age– one that recalls transition in the U.S. auto industry 70 years ago, when Alfred Sloan's upstart General Motors surpassed Ford Motors as America's No. 1 car maker. The transition also reflects the decline of computer manufacturers such as IBM, Wang and Unisys, and the rise of companies like Microsoft, Intel and AT&T that create the chips and software to make the computers work. Just like Dr. Frankenstein, IBM created these two monster competitors, says Richard Shaffer, publisher of the Computer Letter. Now, even IBM is in danger of being trampled by the creations it unleashed.

Although Intel and Microsoft still have close relationships with Big Blue, there is little love lost between IBM and its potent progeny. IBM had an ugly falling-out with former partner Microsoft over the future of personal-computer software. Microsoft developed the now famous disk operating system for the IBM-PC called DOS–and later created the operating software for the next generation of IBM personal computers, the Personal System/2. When PS/2 and its operating system, OS/3, failed to catch on, a feud erupted over how the two companies would upgrade the system. Although they publicly patched things up, the partnership was tattered. IBM developed its own version of OS/3, which has so far failed to capture the industry's imagination, Microsoft's competing version, dubbed New Technology, or NT, will debut in a few months and will incorporate Microsoft's highly successful Windows program, which lets users juggle several programs at once. Windows NT however, will offer more new features, such as the ability to link many computers together in a network and to safeguard them against unauthorized use.

IBM and Intel have also been parting company. After relying almost exclusively on the Santa Clara, California company for the silicon chips that serve as computer brains, IBM has moved to reduce its dependence on Intel by turning to competing vendors. In Europe, IBM began selling a low-cost line of PCs called Ambra, which runs on chips made by Intel rival Advanced Micro Devices. IBM also demonstrated a sample PC using a chip made by another Intel enemy, Cyrix. And last October, IBM said it would begin selling the company's own chips to outsiders, in direct competition with Intel.

IBM clearly feels threatened. And the wounded giant still poses the biggest threat to any future dominance by Intel and Microsoft. Last year, it teamed up with both companies' most bitter rivals–Apple Computers and Motorola–to develop advanced software and microprocessors for a new generation of desktop computers. In selecting Apple and Motorola, IBM bypassed its longtime partners. Just as Microsoft's standard operations system runs only on computers built around Intel's computer chips, Apple's software runs only on Motorola's chips. Although IBM has pledged that the new system will eventually run on a variety of machines, it will initially run only computer programs written for Apple's Macintosh or IBM's OS/2. Its competitive juices now flowing, IBM last week announced that it and Apple Computer will deliver the operating system in 1994–a year ahead of schedule.

Q10. As a result of greater competition in the US Computer industry:

(a) Some computer companies are expanding while others are contracting.
(b) Employment in the industry is going down.
(c) The industry is becoming more monopolized.
(d) The share value of IBM is going up relative to that of Intel and Microsoft.

Q11. Why is something that happened 70 years ago in the US auto industry being mentioned here?

(a) General Motors broke away from Ford Motors.
(b) A new company went ahead of an established market leader.

(c) Like Dr. Frankenstein, Ford Motor created a monster in General Motors.

(d) Microsoft, Intel and AT&T were originally created by IBM.

Q12. Who is mentioned as the principal supplier of silicon chips to IBM?

(a) AT&T

(b) Microsoft

(c) Cyrix

(d) Intel

Q13. The personal computer called Ambra is marketed by:

(a) Cyrix

(b) IBM

(c) Intel

(d) Microsoft

Q14. What was the original reason for the feud between IBM and Microsoft?

(a) The two companies developed competing softwares.

(b) Microsoft and Intel teamed up against IBM.

(c) IBM began to purchase microchips from Intel instead of Microsoft.

(d) IBM made losses while Microsoft made profits.

Q15. Which of the following statements is not implied by the passage?

(a) The makers of microchips and softwares are becoming leaders in the computer industry.

(b) Wang and Unisys are primarily manufacturers of computers.

(c) IBM laying off workers is the biggest job cut in American corporate history.

(d) Intel is based in California.

Q16. Which of the following statements is true?

(a) IBM plans to introduce a new system that will run on a variety of machines.

(b) IBM's new generation desk top computers will run only on Motorola's chips.

(c) IBM is working out a joint strategy with Apple to force Motorola to supply chips at a lower price.

(d) IBM is going to sell its own chips to Apple and Motorola.

Q17. Many computers would be linked together through a network in a system developed by:

(a) IBM

(b) Apple

(c) Microsoft

(d) None of the above.

Q18. One possible conclusion from the passage is that:

(a) Share prices are not a good indicator of a company's performance.

(b) Firing workers restore a company's health.

(c) All companies ultimately regret being a Dr. Frankenstein to some other company.

(c) Consumers gain as a result of competition among producers.

PASSAGE 3 (TOTAL WORDS—1284) (CAT 1998)

Environmental protection and management is deservedly attracting a lot of attention these days. This is a desirable development in the face of the alarming rate of natural resource degradation which greatly hampers their optimal utilization. When waste waters emanating from municipal sewage, industrial effluent, agricultural and land runoffs, find their way either to ground water reservoirs or other surface water sources, the quality of water deteriorates, rendering it unfit for use. The natural balance is disturbed when concentrated discharges of waste water is not controlled. This is because the cleansing forces of nature cannot do their job in proportion to the production of filthy matter.

According to the National Environment Engineering and Research Institute (NEERI), a staggering 70 per cent of water available in the country is polluted. According to the Planning Commission, "From the Dal lake in the North to the Periyar and Chaliyar rivers in the South, from Damodar and Hoogly in the East to the Thane creek in the West, the picture of water pollution is uniformly gloomy. Even our large perennial rivers, like the Ganga, are today heavily polluted."

According to one study, all the 14 major rivers of India are highly polluted. Besides the Ganga, these rivers include the Yamuna, Narmada, Godavari, Krishna and Cauvery. These rivers carry 85 percent of the surface runoff and their drainage basins cover 73 percent of the country. The pollution of the much revered Ganga is due in particular to municipal sewage that accounts for $3/4^{th}$ of its pollution load. Despite India having legislation on water pollution [The water (Prevention and Control of Pollution) Act, 1974] and various water pollution control boards, rivers have today become synonymous with drains and sewers.

Untreated community wastes discharged into water courses from human settlements account for four times as much waste water as industrial effluent. Out of India's 3,119 towns and cities, only 217 have partial (209) or full (8) sewerage treatment facilities and cover less than a third of the urban population, Statistics from a report of the Central Board for Prevention and Control of Water Pollution reveal that 1,700 of 2,700 water using industries in India, are polluting the water around their factories. Only 160 industries have waste water treatment plants.

One estimate suggests that the volume of waste water of industrial origin will be comparable to that of domestic sewage in India by 2000 A.D. Discharges from agricultural fields, which carry fertilizing ingredients of nitrogen, phosphorus and pesticides are expected to be three times as much as domestic sewage. By that date, thermal pollution generated by discharges from thermal power plants will be the largest in volume.

Toxic effluents deplete the level of oxygen in the rivers, endanger all aquatic life and render water absolutely unfit for human consumption, apart from affecting industrial production. Sometimes, these effects have been disastrous. A recent study reveals that the water of the Ganga, Yamuna, Kali and Hindon rivers have considerable concentration of heavy metals due to inflow of industrial wastes, which pose a serious health hazard to the millions living on their bands. Similarly, the Cauvery and Kapila rivers in Karnataka have been found to contain metal pollution which threatens the health of people in riverine towns. The Periyar, the largest river of Kerala, receives extremely toxic effluent that result in high incidence of skin problems and fish kills. The Godavari of Andhra Pradesh and the Damodar and Hoogly in West Bengal receive untreated industrial toxic wastes. A high level of pollution has been found in the Yamuna, while the Chambal of Rajasthan is considered the most polluted river in Rajasthan. Even in industrially backward Orissa, the Rushikula river is extremely polluted. The fate of the Krishna in Andhra Pradesh, the Tungabhadra in Karnataka, the Chaliyar in Kerala, the Gomati in U.P., the Narmada in M.P. and the Sone and the Subarnarekha rivers in Bihar is no different.

According to the W.H.O., eighty percent of diseases prevalent in India are water-borne; many of them assume epidemic proportions. The prevalence of these diseases heighten under conditions of drought. It is also estimated that India loses as many as 73 million man days every year due to water borne diseases, costing Rs. 600 crore by way of treatment expenditure and production losses. Management of water resources with respect to their quality also assumes greater importance especially when the country can no more afford to waste water.

The recent Clean-the-Ganga Project, with an action plan estimated to cost the exchequer Rs. 250 crore (which has been accorded top priority) is a trend setter in achieving this goal. The action plan evoked such great interest that offers of assistance have been received from France, U.K., U.S. and the Netherlands, as also from the World Bank. This is indeed laudable. Poland too has now joined this list.

The very fact that these countries have volunteered themselves to contribute their mite is a healthy reflection of global concern over growing environmental degradation and the readiness of the international community to participate in what is a truly formidable task. It may be recalled that the task of cleansing the Ganga along the Rishikesh-Hardwar stretch under the first phase of the Ganga Action Plan, has been completed and the results are reported to be encouraging.

The crisis of drinking water is deepening because water resources are drying up and the lowering of ground water through over pumping, this is compounded by the pollution of water resources. All these factors increase the magnitude of the problem. An assessment of the progress achieved by the end of March 1985, on completion of the first phase of the International Drinking Water Supply and Sanitation Decade (1981-91), reveals that drinking water has been made available to 73 percent of the urban population and 56 percent of the rural population only. This means that nearly half the country's rural population has to get drinking water facilities. This needs to be urgently geared up especially when considered against the Government's professed objective of providing safe drinking water and sanitation to all by the end of the International Drinking Water Supply and Sanitation Decade, i.e., March 1991. The foremost action in this would be to clean up our water resources.

As per surveys conducted by the NEERI, per capita drinking water losses in different cities in the country range between 11,000 to 31,000 liters annually. This indicates a waste level of 20-35 percent of the total flow of water in the distribution system, primarily due to leaks in mains and household service pipes. Preventive maintenance programme would substantially reduce losses/wastages and would certainly go a long way in solving the problem.

According to the Union Ministry of Works and Housing, out of 2.31 lakh problem villages identified in 1980, 1.92 lakh (83 percent) villages have been provided with at least one source of drinking water as of March 1986. The balance (38,748) villages are expected to be covered during the seventh plan. A time-bound national policy on drinking water is being formulated by Government, wherein the task is proposed to be completed by the end of the seventh plan. An outlay of Rs. 6,522.47 crores has been allotted for the water supply and sanitation sector in the seventh plan period, against an outlay of Rs. 3,922.02 crores in the sixth plan. Of this, outlay for rural water supply sector is Rs. 3,454.47 crores. It is expected that this outlay would help to cover about 86.4 percent of the urban and 82.2 percent of the rural population with safe drinking water facilities by March 1991. Hygienic sanitation facilities would be provided to 44.7 per cent and 1.8 percent of the urban and rural population respectively within, the same period.

Q19. The degradation of natural resources will necessarily lead to:

(a) poor economic utilization of resources.
(b) contamination of water from municipal sewage.

(c) water unfit for human consumption.
(d) None of the above.

Q20. According to NEERI:

(a) the extent of water pollution in the Dal Lake is grim.
(b) seventy percent of total water available in the country is polluted.
(c) only 217 out of 3119 towns and cities have sewage treatment facilities.
(d) all the 14 major rivers of India are highly polluted.

Q21. Municipal sewage pollutants account for:

(a) the lowest percentage of water pollution.
(b) seventy five percent of the Ganga's water pollution load.
(c) twice the volume of the waste water of industrial origin.
(d) three times as much as the discharge from agricultural fields.

Q22. Which of the following statements is correct?

(a) The river Periyar is in South India.
(b) The river Periyar is the largest river of Kerala.
(c) The river Gomti is also extremely polluted.
(d) All of the above are correct.

Q23. The cost of the Clean-the-Ganga Pollution Project Action Plan is likely to be sourced from:

(a) The Indian Exchequer.
(b) France, U.K., U.S and the Netherlands.
(c) The World Bank, Poland, U.K.
(d) The U.S., U.K., Netherlands, Poland, France, the World Bank and India.

Q24. Which of the following statements made by the WHO is correct?

(a) Water-borne diseases account for eighty per cent of all diseases prevalent in India.
(b) Water-borne diseases in India create a loss of Rs. 600 crores every year.
(c) Both (a) and (b) are correct.
(d) None of the above.

Q25. Considerable amounts of metal pollutants are found in the river(s):

(a) Chambal of Rajasthan.
(b) Rushikula in Orissa.
(c) Damodar, Hoogly,, Krishna and Gomti.
(d) Ganga, Yamuna, Kali, Hindon, Cauvery and Kapila.

Q26. The crisis of drinking water is caused chiefly by:

(a) the green house effect.
(b) water pollution caused by industrial development.
(c) drying up of water sources and over- pumping.
(d) increasing urbanization.

Q27. The best remedy for water shortage lies in:

(a) putting up more pumps in rural areas.
(b) cleaning up polluted water.
(c) reducing the waste level of 25-30 per cent of the total flow of water.
(d) constructing large-sized dams.

Q28. Out of the total outlay for water supply and sanitation in the seventh plan, rural water supply sector would receive:

(a) about 53 percent.
(b) over 80 percent.
(c) between 65 and 80 per cent.
(d) equal to 44.7 percent.

PASSAGE 4 (TOTAL WORDS—843) (CAT 1998)

To teach is to create a space in which obedience to truth is practiced. Space may sound like a vague, poetic metaphor until we realize that it describes experiences of everyday life. We know what it means to be in a green and open field; we know what it means to be on a crowded rush hour bus. These experiences of physical space have parallels in our relations with others. On our jobs, we know what it is to be pressed and crowded, our working space diminished by the urgency of deadlines and competitiveness of colleagues.

But then there are times when deadlines disappear and colleagues cooperate, when everyone has space to move, invent and produce with energy and enthusiasm. With family and friends, we know how it feels to have unreasonable demands placed upon us, to be boxed in the expectations of those nearest to us. But then there are times when we feel accepted for who we are (or forgiven for who we are not), times when a spouse or a child or a friend gives us the space both to be and to become.

Similar experiences of crowding and space are found in education. To sit in a class where the teacher stuffs our minds with information, organizes it with finality, insists on having the answers while being utterly uninterested in our views, and forces us into a grim competition for grades–to sit in such a class is to experience a lack of space for learning. But to study with a teacher who not only speaks but also listens, who not only gives answers but asks questions and welcomes our insights, who provides information and theories that do not close doors but open new ones, who encourages students to help each other learn–to study with such a teacher is to know the power of a learning space.

A learning space has three essential dimensions: openness, boundaries and an air of hospitality. To create open learning space is to remove the impediments to learning that we find around and within us: we often create them ourselves to evade the challenge of truth and transformation. One source of such impediments is our fear of appearing ignorant to others or to ourselves. The openness of a space is created by the firmness of its boundaries. A learning space cannot extend indefinitely; if it did, it would not be a structure for learning but an invitation for confusion and chaos. When space boundaries are violated, the quality of space suffers. The teacher who wants to create an open learning space must define and defend its boundaries with care, because the pursuit of truth can often be painful and discomforting, the learning space must be hospitable. Hospitality means receiving each other, our struggles, our new-born ideas with openness and care. It means creating an ethos in which the community of truth can form and the pain of its transformation be borne. A learning space needs to be hospitable not to make learning painless, but to make painful things possible, things without which no learning can occur–things like exposing ignorance, testing tentative hypotheses, challenging false or partial information, and mutual criticism of thought.

The task of creating learning space with qualities of openness, boundaries and hospitality can be approached at several levels. The most basic level is the physical arrangement of the classroom. Consider the traditional classroom setting with row upon row of chairs facing the lectern where learning space is confined to the narrow alley of attention between each student and teacher. In this space, there is no community of truth, hospitality or room for students to relate to the thoughts of each other. Contrast it with the chairs placed in a circular arrangement, creating an open space within which learners can interconnect. At another level, the teacher can create conceptual space–with words, in two ways. One is through assigned reading; the other is through lecturing. Assigned reading, not in the form of speed reading several hundred pages, but contemplative reading which opens, not fills, our learning space. A teacher can also create a learning space by means of lectures. By providing critical information and a framework of interpretation, a lecturer can lay down the boundaries within which learning occurs.

We also create learning space through the kind of speech we utter and the silence from which true speech emanates. Speech is a precious gift and a vital tool, but too often our speaking is an evasion of truth, a way of buttressing our self-serving reconstructions of reality. Silence must therefore be an integral part of learning space. In silence, more than in arguments, our mind-made world falls away and must also create emotional space in the classroom, space that allow feeling to arise and be dealt with because submerged feelings can undermine learning. In an emotionally honest learning space, one created by a teacher who does not fear dealing with feelings, the community of truth can flourish between us and we can flourish in it.

Q29. Which of the following statements best describes the author's conception of learning space?

(a) Where the teacher is friendly.
(b) Where there is no grim competition for grades.
(c) Where the students are encouraged to learn about space.
(d) Where the teacher provides information and theories which open new doors and encourages students to help each other learn.

Q30. The statements 'the openness of a space is created by the firmness of its boundaries' appears contradictory. Which of the following statements provides the best justification for the proposition?

(a) We cannot have a space without boundaries.
(b) Bounded space is highly structured.
(c) When space boundaries are violated, the quality of space suffers.
(d) A teacher can effectively defend a learning space without boundaries.

Q31. According to the author, learning is a painful process because:

(a) It exposes our ignorance.
(b) Our views and hypotheses are challenged.
(c) It involves criticizing the views of others.
(d) Of all of the above reasons.

Q32. The task of creating learning space with qualities of openness, boundaries and hospitality is multidimensional. It involves operating at:

(a) Psychological and conceptual levels.
(b) Physical, perceptual and behavioral levels.
(c) Physical, conceptual and emotional levels.
(d) Conceptual, verbal and sensitive levels.

Q33. According to the author, silence must be an integral part of learning space because:

(a) Silence helps to unite us with others to create a community of truth.
(b) Silent contemplation prepares us to construct our mind-made world.
(c) Speaking is too often an exercise in the evasion of truth.
(d) Speaking is too often a way of buttressing our self-serving reconstruction of reality.

Q34. According to the author, an effective teacher does not allow:

(a) feelings to arise within the learning space.
(b) silence to become an integral part of the learning space.
(c) learning space to be filled by speed reading of several hundred pages of assigned reading.
(d) violation of learning space boundaries.

Q35. Understanding the notion of space in our relations with others is:

(a) To acknowledge the beauty of poetic metaphor.
(b) Exclusively rooted in our experiences of physical space.
(c) To accept a spiritual dimension in our dealings with our peers.
(d) To extend the parallel of physical space to our experiences in daily life.

Q36. Another way of describing the author's notion of learning space can be summarized in the following manner.

(a) It is vital that learning be accompanied by unlearning.
(b) Learning encompasses such elements as courage, dignity and endeavor.
(c) An effective teacher recognizes the value of empathy.
(d) Encourage good learners, discourage indifferent ones.

Q37. Conceptual space with words can be created by:

(a) Assigned reading and lecturing.
(b) Speed reading and written comprehension.
(c) Gentle persuasion and deliberate action.
(d) Creative extrapolation and illustrations.

Q38. An emotionally honest learning space can only be created by:

(a) A teacher committed to join the community.
(b) A teacher who is not afraid of confronting feelings.
(c) A teacher who takes care not to undermine the learning process.
(d) A teacher who worships critical silence.

Passage 5 (Total Words—602) (CAT 1998)

Management education gained new academic stature within US Universities and greater respect from outside during the 1960s and 1970s. Some observers attribute the competitive superiority of US corporations to the quality of business education. In 1978, a management professor, Herbert A. Simon of Carnegie Mellon University, won the Nobel Prize in economics for his work in decision theory. And the popularity of business education continued to grow since 1960's and the MBA has become known as the passport to the good life.

By the 1980s, however, US business schools faced critics who charged that learning had little relevance to real business problems. Some went so far as to blame business schools for the decline in US competitiveness.

Amidst the criticisms, four distinct arguments may be discerned. The first is that business schools must be either unnecessary or deleterious because Japan does so well without them. Underlying these arguments is the idea that management ability cannot be taught–one is either born with it or must acquire it over years of practical experience. A second argument is that business schools are overly academic and theoretical. They teach quantitative models that have little application to real world problems. Third, they give inadequate attention to shop floor issues, to production processes and to management resources. Finally, it is argued that they encourage undesirable attitudes in students, such as placing value in the short term, on bottom line targets, while neglecting longer term developmental criteria. In summary, some business executives complain that MBA's are incapable of making day-to-day peritoneal decisions, unable to communicate and to motivate people, and unwilling to accept responsibility for following through implementation plans. We shall analyze these criticisms after having reviewed experiences in other countries.

In contrast to be the expansion and development of business education in the United States and more recently in Europe, Japanese business schools graduate no more than two hundred MBA's each year. The Keio Business School (KBS) was the only graduate school of management in the entire country until the mid 1970s and it still boasts the only two-year masters programme. The absence of business schools in Japan would appear in contradiction with the high priority placed upon learning by its Confucian culture. Confucian colleges taught administrative skills as early as 1630 and Japan wholeheartedly accepted Western learning following the Meiji restoration of 1868 when hundreds of students were dispatched to universities in the U.S.A., Germany, England and France, to learn the secrets of western technology and modernization. Moreover, the Japanese educational system is highly developed and intensely competitive and can be credited for raising the literary and mathematical abilities of the Japanese to the highest level in the world.

Until recently, Japanese corporations have not been interested in using either local or foreign business schools for the development of their future executives.

Their in-company-training programmers have sought the socialization of newcomers, the younger the better. The training is highly specific and those who receive it, have neither the capacity nor the incentive to quit. The prevailing belief says Imai, is that management should be borne out of experience and many years of effort and not learnt from educational institutions. A 1960 survey of Japanese senior executives confirmed that a majority (54 per cent) believed that managerial capabilities can be attained only on the job and not in universities.

However, this view seems to be changing, the same survey revealed that even as early as 1960, 37 per cent of senior executives felt that the universities should teach integrate professional management. In the 1980s, a combination of increased competitive pressures and greater multi-nationalisation of Japanese business are making the Japanese take a fresh look at Management Education.

Q39. The 1960s and 1970s can best be described as a period:

(a) when quality business education contributed to the superiority of US corporations.
(b) when the number of MBA's rose from under 5,000 to over 50,000.
(c) when management education gained new academic stature and greater respect.
(d) when the MBA became more disreputable.

Q40. According to the passage,

(a) learning, which was useful in the 1960s and 1970's became irrelevant in the 1980s.
(b) management education faced criticisms in the 1980s.
(c) business schools are insensitive to the needs of industry.
(d) by the 1980s, business schools contributed to the decline in US competitiveness.

Q41. The growth in the popularity of business schools among students was most probably due to:

(a) Herber A. Simon, a management professor winning the Nobel Prize in economics.
(b) the gain in academic stature.
(c) the large number of MBA degrees awarded.
(d) a perception that it was a 'passport to the good life'.

Q42. A criticism that management education did not face was that:

(a) it imparted poor quantitative skills to MBAs.
(b) it was unnecessary and deleterious.
(c) it was irrevocably irrelevant.
(d) it inculcated undesirable attitudes in students.

Q43. US business schools faced criticism in the 1980s because:

(a) of the decline in Japanese competitiveness.
(b) many critics felt that learning had little relevance to business problems.
(c) people realised that management ability cannot be taught.
(d) MBAs were unwilling to accept responsibility for implementation on the shop floor.

Q44. The absence of business schools in Japan:

(a) is due to the prevalent belief that management ability can only be acquired over years of practical experience.
(b) was due to the high priority placed on learning as opposed to doing in Confucian culture.
(c) is hard to explain for the proponents of business education.
(d) contributed a great deal to their success in international trade and business.

Q45. The Japanese were initially able to do without business schools as a result of:

(a) their highly developed and intensively competitive education system.
(b) dispatching hundreds of students to learn the secrets of western technology and modernisation.
(c) their highly specific in-company training programmes.
(d) prevailing beliefs regarding educational institutions.

Q46. The Japanese modified their views on management education because of:

(a) greater exposure to U.S. MBA programmes.
(b) the need to develop worldwide contacts and become Americanised.
(c) the outstanding success of business schools in the U.S. during the 1960's and 1970s.
(d) a combination of increased competitive pressures and greater multinationalisation of Japanese business.

Q47. Training programmes in Japanese corporations have:

(a) been based upon Confucian culture.
(b) sought the socialisation of newcomers.
(c) been targeted at people who have neither the capacity nor the incentive to quit.
(d) been teaching people to do menial tasks.

Q48. The author argues that:

(a) Japanese do not do without business schools as is generally perceived.

(b) Japanese corporations do not hire MBAs because of traditions of universal and rigorous academic education, life long employment and strong group identification.

(c) Placing MBAs in operational and menial tasks is a major factor in Japanese business success.

(d) U.S. corporations should emulate the Japanese and change the way new recruits are inducted.

Q49. The main difference between U.S. and Japanese corporations is:

(a) that one employs MBAs, the other does not.

(b) that U.S. corporations do not employ Japanese people.

(c) the U.S. corporations pay more to fresh recruits.

(d) in the process of selecting and orienting new recruits.

Q50. The author argues that the Japanese system:

(a) is better that the American system

(b) is highly productive and gives corporate leadership a long term view as a result of its strong traditions.

(c) is slowly becoming Americanised.

(d) succeeds without business schools, whereas the U.S. system fails because of it.

V

Passage 1 (Total Words—675)

This industry preys on pestilence for profits. As the primary sector thrives under the benevolent gaze of the rain gods, according to the CMIE forecast for Business Today, the production of food grains will touch 187 million tons in 1994-95–up from 182 million tons in 1993-94–pesticides are likely to be a key input in the country's race for a quantum jump in agricultural productivity.

That's because a not-insignificant 30 per cent of the production of food grains in the country is destroyed by insects, pests, plant pathogens, rodents, and birds every year. And even though the per capita consumption of pesticides is currently low–which is also a pointer to the industry's potential - this country is still the world's third largest consumer of pesticides.

Classified by target species, pesticides can be divided into four broad categories. Insecticides–like monocrotophos and fenvalerate–are used for killing insects. Herbicides–such as butachlor and anilophos - remove weeds and unwanted plants. Fungicides–like nickel chloride–kill fungi. And fumigants and rodenticides–such as zinc and aluminium phosphide–are used to kill rodents.

At present, insecticides contribute to almost 75 per cent of the turnover of the pesticides industry in value terms and 85 per cent in terms of volume. This is at variance with the trend in the West, where insecticides account for just 32 per cent of pesticides consumption: it is herbicides and fungicides which account for the largest share of consumption in those countries.

In terms of manufacturing technology, the production of pesticides can be classified into two main categories; technical-grade materials and formulations. Technical-grade-material–the basic chemical of high purity–is manufactured in organized units, with the top 10 units accounting for more than 80 percent of production. Most of them have a dominant market share in one or two key products.

However, most pesticides are used as formulations, which are produced by the processing of technical grade materials and are manufactured by both large and small-scale units. In fact, the Insecticides Act of 1968 stipulates that 50 per cent of the production of technical-grade pesticides must be supplied by every manufacturer to non-associated formulators.

While the stipulation aims at ensuring the sale of pesticides at cheaper prices, arbitrary control has led to a conflict of interests. Formulators complain that technical-grade manufacturers operate a cartel. The latter, however, claim that rising input costs–raw materials constitute 60 percent of the selling price of pesticides–are forcing hikes in selling prices.

The pesticides industry has over 80 registered technical-grade manufacturers and about 800 registered formulators. About 160 formulators are associated with technical-grade manufactures and boast of the advantage of being able to obtain raw materials easily, even during the peak consumption season.

As the level of technology required is relatively low, formulators have low fixed investment per unit of output. At 35 percent, the pesticides industry's average capacity utilization is rather low. And this, notwithstanding the 1974 ban imposed by the government on the addition of formulation capacity. However, firms can expand their formulation capacities so long as such expansions are linked to the increased production of technical-grade material.

One of the main reasons for low capacity utilization in this industry is the seasonal nature of the demand for pesticides. The maximum amount of sales is recorded between July and November, which is reflected in the high inventories that are built up in the first quarter of the year. As the active ingredient deteriorates over time, a large number of formulations have a limited shelf-life.

At another level, the industry is characterized by the practice of credit sales to the trade. These credits–which are typically for 60 to 90 days–coupled with the high level of inventories–to cope with demand fluctuations–contribute to the working capital-intensive nature of the industry. That's why most manufacturers have diversified, the most common diversification being pharmaceuticals. An analysis of pesticides sales as a percentage of the total sales of the major players confirms that most pesticides makers are well-diversified.

Q1. The growth in the production of food grains in 1994-95 over 1993-94 is predicted to be roughly:

(a) 187 million tons.
(b) 2 percent.
(c) 3 percent.
(d) 182 million tons.

Q2. This country is the third largest consumer of pesticides in spite of:

(a) a low per capita consumption of pesticides.
(b) 30 percent of production being destroyed by insects.
(c) our dependence on monsoons.
(d) food grain production being insignificant.

Q3. The market for technical-grade pesticides in India is dominated by:

(a) insecticide manufacturers.
(b) small scale sector.
(c) just ten units.
(d) large scale sector.

Q4. The relationship between formulators and producers of technical-grade material:

(a) is determined by the market.
(b) is rather strong in India.
(c) depends on their end-use.
(d) is partly governed by law.

Q5. The hike in selling prices:

(a) is blamed by formulators on manufacturers.
(b) is the consequence of administered pricing.
(c) is caused by the Act of 1968.
(d) is because there is no cartel of manufacturers.

Q6. The percentage of formulators who can boast of being able to obtain raw materials easily is:

(a) 60
(b) 10
(c) 50
(d) 20

Q7. High inventories are built up during:

(a) October, November, December.
(b) April, May, June.
(c) July, August, September.
(d) None of these.

Q8. The pesticides industry is characterized by credit sales, the typical credit is:

(a) 30 percent of sales.
(b) 2 to 3 months.
(c) to the customers of technical-grade material.
(d) 100 percent of sale.

Q9. That the pesticides makers are well diversified is indicated by the:

(a) dominance of pesticides sales in the total sales.
(b) reduction in pesticides production.
(c) analysis of pesticides sales as a percentage of total sales.
(d) hike in prices of pesticides.

Q10. Capacity utilization in the pesticides industry is low because of:

(a) a ban on expansion.
(b) the seasonal nature of demand.
(c) poor technology.
(d) low per capita consumption.

PASSAGE 2 (TOTAL WORDS—719)

Why can you not tickle yourself? And what does that have to do with artificial consciousness? Quite a lot, according to Rodney Cotterill, a physicist at the Danish Technical University in Lyngby.

After years of pondering over the workings of the brain, Dr. Cotterill believes he has found the quintessence of consciousness for good measure, he has also applied for a patent covering circuit design for conscious computers, and is discussing with several companies.

The nature of consciousness is shrouded in controversy. Theologians, philosophers, biologists, and computer scientists all have their pet theories. So, to understand how Dr. Cotterill's computers might work, it is necessary to understand his views of consciousness.

His is a classical outlook that can be traced to the philosophers and scientists of the first half of this century, who saw muscular movement as the key to understanding consciousness.

They believed that a person's main source of information about the world comes from movement. Even vision depends on the tiny scanning movements that the eye makes to keep the photosensitive cells of the retina refreshed with new information, So, the theory goes, consciousness must be intimately related to muscles.

Like many of his fellow physicists, Dr. Cotterill is intrigued by how artificial neural networks–the vast arrays of interconnected electronic processes–might mimic the real networks of nerve cells of the brain. But whereas many neural-network enthusiasts hope that consciousness will emerge automatically if their machines become sufficiently complex, Dr. Cotterill thinks that something fundamental is missing in such machines. That something is linked to the particular way in which brains communicate with muscles.

Consider what happens when you reach for a glass. Signals to the brain from the eyes and fingers (called afference in the biological jargon) keep it informed about how the task is progressing. Signals from the brain to the fingers and eyes (called efference) make the necessary adjustments to avoid an accident. But at the same time, another type of signal, called an efference copy, is sent out to other parts of the brain. In simple terms, the efference copy warns the brain's sensory-receptor areas about what the muscles are about to do. Hence, since it is anticipated, self-tickling is not very stimulating.

Certain nerve cells in the brain are activated only if they receive efference copy and related afference within about two-tenths of a second of each other.

This seems to be a way of discriminating between events that the brain has caused in the environment and those over which it has no control, and thus distinguishing self and non-self, a central aspect of consciousness.

It is the efference copy that Dr. Cotterill believes is the crucial ingredient of consciousness. Without it, all there is, is a computer-controlled robot. With it, a computer robot becomes aware that it is in control of itself. Efference copy can be produced by a brain even when no muscles move. According to Dr. Cotterill, thought itself may be efference copy looping round and round in a way that allows the brain to simulate vision, speech and other faculties without actually moving a muscle. Such simulations can lead to new associations of muscular movements–associations which are more commonly known as ideas.

Dr. Cotterill's arguments, which have just been published in the Journal of Consciousness Studies, are unlikely to be endorsed universally. But having identified a loop in the brain which he thinks others have overlooked, he is already toying with a host of possible applications of computers containing an artificial version of it. Video games and stock market analysis are two areas where he sees a big potential.

The key to such applications will be for the computer to probe its environment in an electronic analogy of motion and, at the same time, warn itself of what it is doing by sending itself artificial efference copy - thus keeping constant track of the relationship between its own actions and the reactions of the environment.

Dr. Cotterill does not expect the first computer of this sort to soliloquise spontaneously. But they should show rudimentary signs of consciousness, such as hesitancy and the ability to change their minds.

Such traits are absent for most forms of artificial intelligence. Their presence, hopes Dr. Cotterill, will make computer games more fun, and financial forecasting more lucrative.

Q11. Dr. Cotterill's conceptualization of consciousness is based on:

(a) Observation and understanding of muscular movements.

(b) A similar belief shared by theologians and philosophers.

(c) Theory of neural networks

(d) Individual sensory skills.

Q12. The term *efference copy* refers to:

(a) Keeping the brain informed about what is happening to the muscular system.

(b) An early warning system, which informs the brain about proposed muscle movements.

(c) The signal from senses to brain which helps to avoid accidents.

(d) One of the signals exchanged between the brain and senses.

Q13. According to the passage, Dr. Cotterill differs from the neural network scientists because:

(a) Other scientists are mathematicians while Dr. Cotterill is a physicist.

(b) Dr. Cotterill believes that the human mind can be mimicked using neural networks.

(c) Dr. Cotterill believes that complex machines automatically replicate the brain while many other scientists refuse to do so.

(d) Dr. Cotterill considers the linkages between brain and the muscles while developing neural networks.

Q14. Robots with consciousness differ from those without it because:

(a) Such robots are aware of self-control.

(b) Such robots have better control over movements.

(c) Such robots can interact with each other.

(d) Such robots are patented by Dr. Cotterill.

Q15. Computers with built-in consciousness will be able to:

(a) Spew out Shakespeare.

(b) Maintain a constant watch over the mutual relationship between its actions and the environment's reactions.

(c) Communicate with ease.
(d) Replicate the signals from brain to muscle, thus making them more user friendly.

Q16. According to the passage, ideas:
(a) Are the outcome of thinking process, accompanied by sensory action.
(b) Originate in the absence of muscle movements.
(c) Stem from the simulation of senses, without accompanying muscle movement.
(d) Reflect the result of efference copy produced by muscle movements.

Q17. It is difficult to tickle oneself because:
(a) A signal warns the brain to anticipate tickling.
(b) A signal makes the muscles tighten up.
(c) Such signals are not acknowledged by the brain.
(d) None of these.

PASSAGE 3 (TOTAL WORDS—1212)

Many surprises lie in store for an academic who strays into the real world. The first such surprise to come my way during a stint as a university administrator, related to the photocopying machines within my jurisdiction. I discovered that paper for the machines plus contractual maintenance cost substantially more than photocopies in the private market. This took no account of the other costs of the photocopiers ink, spare part, the space occupied by the machine, the interest and depreciation on it, the wages of the machine operator, the loss of time when the machine broke down or the operator absented himself.

The university–and indeed the entire educational system–was in a financial crisis. Here was a situation calling for a quick and painless execution of all white elephants, or so I thought. I proposed that we stop using the photocopying machines and get our photocopies made by a private operator who had rented space from our institution. Further, we could reduce our costs well below the market price through an agreement with the private operator which would let him run our surplus machines in exchange for a price concession.

I had expected my proposal to be eagerly embraced by an impoverished university. Instead, it created a furore. In a progressive institution like ours, how could I have the temerity to suggest handing over university assets to the private sector? Perhaps I was in the pay of the private operator. Friends and well-wishers emphasized the necessity of immediately distancing myself from any plan that may conceivably benefit a private entrepreneur–even if it should concurrently benefit the university. That, I gathered, was the essence of financial rectitude.

Abashed, I repented my indiscretion. The photocopying machines were of course no longer used, but neither were they transferred to the enemy in the private sector. We got our photocopying done privately at market prices, not the concessional rates I had proposed. The university lost money, but the family silver was saved from the private enemy. After a decently long period gathering dust and cobwebs, it could be sold as scrap, but that would not be during my tenure.

The story of the photocopying machines is repeated in many different guises throughout our public and semi-public institutions. The public sector is replete with unproductive assets, their sterile purity jealously protected from the seductive influences of private enterprise. There are the pathetic load factors in our power plants. There are fleets of public buses lying in idle disrepair in our state transport depots. There is the fertilizer plant which has never produced even a gram of fertilizer because, after its executive had scoured the wide world in search of the cheapest possible parts, they found that the specifications of these parts did not match each other. There are the 80 gas guzzling staff cars boasted of by a north Indian university which has little else to boast about.

Perhaps the most spectacular instances of unproductive government assets relate to land. Five years ago, the then minister for Surface Transport, Jagdish Tytler, suggested a plan for developing the vast tracts of unused land in the Delhi Transport Corporation's bus depots. He argued, entirely credibly, that by leasing out this land for commercial purposes, the DTC could not only cover its chronic and massive deficit, but achieve a substantial surplus. The proposal was never implemented; the defiltration of the private sector into DTC depots was heroically resisted by various government departments and the corporation continued its relentless plunge deeper into the red. All other examples of public extravagance however, pale into insignificance alongside the astronomical wastefulness perpetrated by the New Delhi Municipal Committee and the design of Edwin Lutyen's Delhi. Delhi unlike all other major cities of the world has a hollow center–the density of population at the heart of town is negligible. In design, it is no modern metropolis but a medieval imperial capital like the Baghdad of the Abbasid Caliphate. The very center of the city is entirely occupied by the almost empty places of the mighty, while hoi polloi throng the periphery and travel long distances daily to serve their masters.

Within the charmed circle of inner New Delhi, Ministers and Members of parliament, the top military brass and the bureaucratic and the judicial elite of the country luxuriate in sprawling bungalows nestling amidst lush greenery in almost sylvan surroundings. The total land area occupied by these bungalows is one of the best kept official secrets. The ministry of urban development keeps no count of aggregates; but it appears that there are about 600 bungalows with areas varying from one to 10 acres. A not implausible estimate of the total area is about 10 million square yards.

A conservative estimate of the value of land in central New Delhi is Rs. 1,00,000 per square yard. Six hundred families of VIPs are occupying real estate worth about Rs. 1,000 billion; at an interest rate of 12 per cent, this sum would yield an annual income of Rs. 120 billion. This amounts to more than one percent of the gross domestic product.

If the government were to move these six hundreds families to the outskirts of the town and lease this land out, say for multi-storied residential construction–subject, of course, to environmental restrictions that would protect the existing greenery–the primary deficit of India would be wiped out.

What is more, rents would drop all over the city and the housing problem of Delhi would be solved, if not fully, at least in substantial measure. Further, there would be a major inward shift of population reducing transport requirements, and making it more lucrative for public transport to ply through inner Delhi. The removal of the six hundred would, at one stroke, relieve the accommodation and transport problems of Delhi as well as the budget deficit of the country. But who would bell the cat? Would the government do it, considering that the 600 are the government?

Public interest litigation has of late highlighted a relatively minor aspect of the VIP housing issue: the abuse of ministerial discretion in making out of turn allotments. This focuses attention on the question of a fair distribution between the members of the elite of the fruits of power. In the process, unfortunately, a question of infinitely larger import has been conveniently consigned to oblivion. Doesn't the entire scheme of VIP housing in New Delhi imply organized plunder of the citizenry on a scale quite unprecedented and totally incompatible with the principles of a democratic society?

Strangely enough, this matter has entirely eluded the searchlight of public attention. Political parties, the media, public interest litigants, grass root people's movements have all maintained a resounding of reticence on the issue. When the excesses perpetrated in the name of VIP security provoked public protest, the prime minister desired that VIP security should be made unobtrusive. VIP housing, however, is an entirely unobtrusive burden on the public, but a burden of quite mind boggling proportions. Perhaps it is the silent character of this infliction that has made it so easy to impose. Or perhaps centuries of colonial rule have made habitual slaves of us: a mere 50 years of democracy cannot erase our, habit of obsequiousness to the imperial state and its rulers.

Q18. According to the passage, when a public system suffers from financial crisis, the situation calls for:

(a) Tightening the belt all around.
(b) Handing over unproductive assets to private parties.
(c) Contracting our maintenance of assets to less efficient private parties.
(d) Painless and quick execution of all white elephants.

Q19. One proposal made by the author to reduce the cost of photocopying well below the market price, was to:

(a) Stop using owned photocopying machines and get photocopies done by private operators in the market.
(b) Stop using owned photocopying machines and get photocopies done by a private operator who had rented space from the institution.
(c) Have an agreement with the private operator allowing him to use the owned surplus machines in exchange for a price concession.
(d) Put the photocopy operating employees on a piece rate basis.

Q20. The author's experience taught him that the essence of financial rectitude involved:

(a) Dissociating from any plan which benefits a private entrepreneur even if it concurrently benefits a public institution.
(b) Supporting any plan which benefits a public institution while benefiting a private entrepreneur.
(c) Dissociating from any plan which benefits a private entrepreneur at the cost of a public institution.
(d) Supporting any plan which benefits a public institution at the cost of a private entrepreneur.

Q21. The practice of getting the photocopies done privately at market prices was acceptable because:

(a) It saved money for the university.
(b) It lost money for the university.
(c) It saved the family silver from the private enemy.
(d) Though it lost money for the university, it saved the family silver from the private enemy.

Q22. "...their sterile purity jealously protected from the seductive advances of private enterprise"–the author here is referring to:

(a) The family silver of the public institutions.
(b) The productive assets of the public institutions
(c) The rigid financial practices of the public institutions.
(d) None of the above.

Q23. The Delhi Transport Corporation's relentless plunge deeper into the red continued because according to the passage:

(a) Disposing off 80 gas guzzling staff cars was resisted.
(b) Fleets of buses in idle disrepair were not allowed to be sold as scrap.
(c) Leasing out unused land for commercial use was strongly resisted.
(d) Selling off surplus land to private parties was strongly resisted.

Q24. An estimate of the total land area occupied by the sprawling bungalows in inner New Delhi is:
(a) 600 acres
(b) 6000 acres
(c) 10 million square yards
(d) 3000 acres

Q25. The author's proposal to lease out the land occupied by bungalows for multi-storied residential construction would:
(a) Spoil the ecology of inner New Delhi.
(b) Wipe out the primary deficit of India.
(c) Create a surplus of Rs. 120 billion for the Municipal Committee.
(d) Enhance the greenery of the inner city.

Q26. The author contends that shifting 600 elite families of the government from the inner city to the periphery would solve the problem(s) of:
(a) Accommodation and transportation.
(b) Transportation and the country's budget deficit.
(c) Accommodation and the country's budget deficit.
(d) Accommodation, transportation and the country's budget deficit.

Q27. When the author talks about an unobtrusive public burden of mind- boggling proportions, he is referring to the issue of:
(a) VIP security
(b) VIP housing.
(c) Out of turn allotment of housing to VIPs
(d) Unproductive public assets.

PASSAGE 4 (TOTAL WORDS—926)

Every lover of words knows that these little symbolic units of meaning can be as contradictory as subatomic particles sometimes are. This may well be nature's quixotic way of laughing at our desperate need to explain everything. It gives us a full stop, but watches helplessly, as we expand it into three dots and continue to search.

Although the measurement of the velocity of sub-atomic particles precludes the measurement of their position and vice versa, it hasn't stopped nuclear physicists from trying from searching, from attempting to pin down, to explain. And it is important.

In a book on quantum physics called 'In search of Schrodinger's Cat', John Gribbin says something very fascinating. If a mythical god with a magical pair of infinitesimally small pliers started the task of removing one atom from a molecule of hydrogen (if I remember correctly) every second from the time of the Big Bang... today, it would take another million years for him or her to complete the task. Phew!

But it is still important to try. Why? If everything is so small and the now proved quantum world is essentially indefinable, why do we go on trying to define? Because we must. It is as important to be rigorous and empirical as to accept the indefinable. Lest we forget, it is through absorption in the act of definition that we first encountered the indefinable. And it is still found there more easily than anywhere else.

But for the effort to define, how would we find the indefinable? But for the setting of limits, would the notion of the limitless have ever arisen? Didn't William Blake once remind us that we never know what is enough; unless we have known what is more than enough.

So, when we analyse words, they are paradoxical, as anything self-referential is. Whether it is the language of mathematics or the language of words, self reference engenders paradox. But one wonders why this is a cause of concern for some people, who would prefer no shades of grey.

Paradox is delightful. It is a rich and fertile ground that nourishes and nurtures what we want to communicate, which often has a nasty habit of falling in between any two given words available to describe it. Words are very close to what Planck called "quanta" though they are not literally packets of meaning; they are the paradoxical verbal equivalent, receptacles of meaning. Little drawers if you like, into which we can insert fresh meanings that expand, limit or even contradict the accepted meaning of the word or phrase.

When we say, I'll believe you! For instance, we mean the exact opposite. As, indeed, when we say something is 'bad' in Black American language, because it means, good.

The original meaning of the word is like a reference point on a matrix. Good, if we use its definition as a working hypothesis. But very dangerous, if we take it as a full and final, irrevocable statement of what it sets out to describe.

Why, one may ask, give the word a meaning at all, if accepting it is suspect? And why embark on the act of definition at all if the result of the definition is insignificant?

Like many wonderful and rewarding things in this mysterious world, it is not either/or but and/plus. It is like asking why we learnt to crawl, if all we are going to do is unlearning it to walk? And further, when on occasion, we are required to crawl in later life, are we regressing?

Learning is a process, not a thing. If we must look at it as a thing, we must look at it as lying-sitting-standing-crawling-walking-running.

To define words, and define them exactly, is very important at the outset. When one is learning a language and even through the process of getting familiar with it, definitions and boundaries are crucial, just as following a broad road to a place is critical before we know our way there. Once we do, the rules aren't important; once we have found a dozen shorter or pleasanter ways to the place, the highway may be of little use to us.

Like a protective cage around a little sapling, definitions protect us in our fledgling days, from the predators of license and ambiguity. And they are important. In its place, everything is important.

Once we have a certain command of the language, however, rules are meant to be broken. Particularly, if we are riding the crazy roller coaster of the English language. It is then what we thought was a packet turns out to be a receptacle. In the clearer light of day, when there is less confusion and obscurity, what appeared to be a serpent in the dusty light, is now quite clearly a rope.

In Alice in Wonderland, Humpty-Dumpty says it quite brilliantly:

"I don't know what you mean by 'glory'", Alice said.

Humpty Dumpty smiled contemptuously.

"Of course you don't–till I tell you. I meant there's a nice knock-down argument for you!"

"But 'glory' doesn't mean a nice knock-down argument" Alice objected.

"When I use a word", Humpty Dumpty said, in a rather sorrowful tone, "it means just what I choose it to mean–neither more not less."

"The question is", said Alice, "whether you can make words mean so many different things."

"The question is", said Humpty Dumpty, "Which is to be the master–that's all."

Be that as it may, a word in your ear before the words stop. Can you ever have a nice knock-down argument?

Q28. According to the passage:

(a) Anything delightful is paradoxical.
(b) Anything self-referential is paradoxical.
(c) Anything in shades of grey is paradoxical.
(d) Anything in a rich and fertile ground is paradoxical.

Q29. From the passage, it can be inferred that:

(a) To understand a system, we should investigate within its boundaries.
(b) To understand a system, we should investigate beyond its boundaries.
(c) To understand a system, we should be rigorous and empirical.
(d) To understand a system, we should investigate both within and beyond its boundaries.

Q30. According to Humpty Dumpty:

(a) Alice does not know what 'glory' means.
(b) He is Alice's master.
(c) He imparts to a word the meaning he intends.
(d) His words are ambiguous.

Q31. According to the passage:

(a) When some people say 'bad', they mean the opposite.
(b) God will complete the removal of all atoms from the hydrogen molecule in a million years.
(c) One can simultaneously measure both the velocity and position of sub-atomic particles.
(d) Planck called words 'quanta'.

VI

Passage 1 (CAT 2004)

Recently, I spent several hours sitting under a tree in my garden with the social anthropologist William Ury, a Harvard University professor who specializes in the art of negotiation and wrote the best-selling book, *Getting to Yes*. He captivated me with his theory that tribalism protects people from their fear of rapid change. He explained that the pillars of tribalism that humans rely on for security would always counter any significant cultural or social change. In this way, he said, change is never allowed to happen too fast. Technology, for example, is a pillar of society. Ury believes that every time technology moves in a new or radical direction, another pillar such as religion or nationalism will grow stronger–in effect, the traditional and familiar will assume greater importance to compensate for the new and untested. In this manner, human tribes avoid rapid change that leaves people insecure and frightened.

But we have all heard that nothing is as permanent as change. Nothing is guaranteed. Pithy expressions, to be sure, but no more than cliches. As Ury says, people don't live that way from day-to-day. On the contrary, they actively seek certainty and stability. They want to know they will be safe.

Even so, we scare ourselves constantly with the idea of change. An IBM CEO once said: 'We only re-structure for a good reason, and if we haven't re-structured in a while, that's a good reason.' We are scared that competitors, technology and the consumer will put us out of business–so we have to change all the time just to stay alive. But if we asked our fathers and grandfathers, would they have said that they lived in a period of little change? Structure may not have changed much. It may just be the speed with which we do things.

Change is over-rated, anyway. Consider the automobile. It's an especially valuable example, because the auto industry has spent tens of billions of dollars on research and product development in the last 100 years. Henry Ford's first car had a metal chassis with an internal combustion, gasoline-powered engine, four wheels with rubber tyres, a foot operated clutch assembly and brake system, a steering wheel, and four seats, and it could safely do 18 miles per hour. A hundred years and tens of thousands of research hours later, we drive cars with a metal chassis with an internal combustion, gasoline-powered engine, four wheels with rubber tyres, a foot operated clutch assembly and brake system, a steering wheel, four seats–and the average speed in London in 2001 was 17.5 miles per hour!

That's not a hell of a lot of return for the money. Ford evidently doesn't have much to teach us about change. The fact that they're still manufacturing cars is not proof that Ford Motor Co. is a sound organization, just proof that it takes very large companies to make cars in great quantities–making for an almost impregnable entry barrier.

Fifty years after the development of the jet engine, planes are also little changed. They've grown bigger, wider and can carry more people. But those are incremental, largely cosmetic changes.

Taken together, this lack of real change has come to mean that in travel–whether driving or flying–time and technology have not combined to make things much better. The safety and design have of course accompanied the times and the new volume of cars and flights, but nothing of any significance has changed in the basic assumptions of the final product.

At the same time, moving around in cars or aeroplanes becomes less and less efficient all the time. Not only has there been no great change, but also both forms of transport have deteriorated as more people clamour to use them. The same is true for telephones, which took over hundred years to become mobile, or photographic film, which also required an entire century to change.

The only explanation for this is anthropological. Once established in calcified organizations, humans do two things: sabotage changes that might render people dispensable, and ensure industry-wide emulation. In the 1960s, German auto companies developed plans to scrap the entire combustion engine for an electrical design. (The same existed in the 1970s in Japan, and in the 1980s in France.) So for 40 years we might have been free of the wasteful and ludicrous dependence on fossil fuels. Why didn't it go anywhere? Because auto executives understood pistons and carburettors, and would be loath to cannibalize their expertise, along with most of their factories.

Q1. According to the passage, which of the following statements is true?

(a) Executives of automobile companies are inefficient and ludicrous.

(b) The speed at which an automobile is driven in a city has not changed much in a century.

(c) Anthropological factors have fostered innovation in automobiles by promoting use of new technologies.

(d) Further innovation in jet engines has been more than incremental.

Q2. Which of the following views does the author fully support in the passage?

(a) Nothing is as permanent as change.

(b) Change is always rapid.

(c) More money spent on innovation leads to more rapid change.

(d) Over decades, structural change has been incremental.

Q3. Which of the following best describes one of the main ideas discussed in the passage?

(a) Rapid change is usually welcomed in society.

(b) Industry is not as innovative as it is made out to be.

(c) We should have less change than what we have now.

(d) Competition spurs companies into radical innovation.

Q4. According to the passage, the reason why we continued to be dependent on fossil fuels is that:

(a) Auto executives did not wish to change.

(b) No alternative fuels were discovered.

(c) Change in technology was not easily possible.

(d) German, Japanese and French companies could not come up with new technologies.

Passage 2 (CAT 2004)

The painter is now free to paint anything he chooses. There are scarcely any forbidden subjects, and today, everybody is prepared to admit that a painting of some fruit can be as important as a painting of a hero dying. The Impressionists did as much as anybody to win this previously unheard of freedom for the artist. Yet, by the next generation, painters began to abandon the subject altogether, and began to paint abstract pictures. Today, the majority of pictures painted are abstract.

Is there a connection between these two developments? Has art gone abstract because the artist is embarrassed by his freedom? Is it that, because he is free to paint anything, he doesn't know what to paint? Apologists for abstract art often talk of it as the art of maximum freedom. But could this be the freedom of the desert island? It would take too long to answer these questions properly. I believe there is a connection. Many things have encouraged the development of abstract art. Among them has been the artists' wish to avoid the difficulties of finding subjects when all subjects are equally possible.

I raise the matter now because I want to draw attention to the fact that the painter's choice of a subject is a far more complicated question than it would at first seem. A subject does not start with what is put in front of the easel or with something which the painter happens to remember. A subject starts with the painter deciding he would like to paint such-and-such because for some reason or other he finds it meaningful. A subject begins when the artist selects something for *special mention*. (What makes it special or meaningful may seem to the artist to be purely visual–its colours or its form.) When the subject has been selected, the function of the painting itself is to communicate and justify the significance of that selection.

It is often said today that subject matter is unimportant. But this is only a reaction against the excessively literary and moralistic interpretation of subject matter in the nineteenth century. In truth, the subject is literally the beginning and end of a painting. The painting begins with a selection (I will paint this and not everything else in the world); it is finished when that selection is justified (now you can see all that I saw and felt in this and how it is more than merely itself).

Thus, for a painting to succeed, it is essential that the painter and his public agree about what is significant. The subject may have a personal meaning for the painter or individual spectator; but there must also be the possibility of their agreement on its general meaning. It is at this point that the culture of the society and period in question precedes the artist and his art. Renaissance art would have meant nothing to the Aztecs, and vice versa. If, to some extent, a few intellectuals can appreciate them both today, it is because their culture is an historical one: its inspiration is history and therefore, it can include within itself, in principle if not in every particular, all known developments to date.

When a culture is secure and certain of its values, it presents its artists with subjects. The general agreement about what is significant is so well established that the significance of a particular subject accrues and becomes traditional. This is true, for instance, of reeds and water in China, of the nude body in Renaissance, of the animal in Africa. Furthermore, in such cultures, the artist is unlikely to be a free agent: he will be employed for *the sake of particular subjects*, and the problem, as we have just described it, will not occur to him.

When a culture is in a state of disintegration or transition, the freedom of the artist increases–but the question of a subject matter becomes problematic for him: he, himself, has to choose for society. This was at the basis of all the increasing crises in European art during the nineteenth century. It is too often forgotten how many of the art scandals of that time were provoked by the choice of subject (Gericault, Courbet, Daumier, Degas, Lautrec, Van Gogh, etc.).

By the end of the nineteenth century there were, roughly speaking, two ways in which the painter could meet this challenge of deciding what to paint and so choosing for society. Either he identified himself with the people and so allowed their lives to dictate his subjects to him; or he had to find his subjects within himself as painter. By *people* I mean everybody except the bourgeoisie. Many painters did of course work for the bourgeoisie according to their copy-book of approved subjects, but all of them, filling the Salon and the Royal Academy year after year, are now forgotten, buried under the hypocrisy of those they served so sincerely.

Q5. When a culture is insecure, the painter chooses his subject on the basis of:

(a) The prevalent style in the society of his time.
(b) Its meaningfulness to the painter.
(c) What is put in front of the easel
(d) Past experience and memory of the painter.

Q6. In the sentence, "I believe there is a connection" (second paragraph), what two developments is the author referring to?

(a) Painters using a dying hero and using a fruit as a subject of painting.
(b) Growing success of painters and an increase in abstract forms.
(c) Artists gaining freedom to choose subjects and abandoning subjects altogether.
(d) Rise of Impressionists and an increase in abstract forms.

Q7. Which of the following is NOT necessarily among the attributes needed for a painter to succeed:

(a) The painter and his public agree on what is significant.

(b) The painting is able to communicate and justify the significance of its subject selection.
(c) The subject has a personal meaning for the painter.
(d) The painting of subjects is inspired by historical developments.

Q8. In the context of the passage, which of the following statements would NOT be true?
(a) Painters decided subjects based on what they remembered from their own lives.
(b) Painters of reeds and water in China faced no serious problem of choosing a subject.
(c) The choice of subject was a source of scandals in nineteenth century European art.
(d) Agreement on the general meaning of a painting is influenced by culture and historical context.

Q9. Which of the following views is taken by the author?
(a) The more insecure a culture, the greater the freedom of the artist.
(b) The more secure a culture, the greater the freedom of the artist.
(c) The more secure a culture, more difficult the choice of subject.
(d) The more insecure a culture, the less significant the choice of the subject.

Passage 3 (CAT 2004)

The viability of the multinational corporate system depends upon the degree to which people will tolerate the unevenness it creates. It is well to remember that the 'New Imperialism' which began after 1870 in a spirit of Capitalism Triumphant, soon became seriously troubled and after 1914, was characterized by war, depression, breakdown of the international economic system and war again, rather than Free Trade, Pax Britannica and Material Improvement. A major reason was Britain's inability to cope with the by-products of its own rapid accumulation of capital; i.e., a class-conscious labour force at home; a middle class in the hinterland; and rival centres of capital on the Continent and in America. Britain's policy tended to be atavistic and defensive rather than progressive–more concerned with warding off new threats than creating new areas of expansion. Ironically, Edwardian England revived the paraphernalia of the landed aristocracy it had just destroyed. Instead of embarking on a 'big push' to develop the vast hinterland of the Empire, colonial administrators often adopted policies to arrest the development of either a native capitalist class or a native proletariat which could overthrow them.

As time went on, the centre had to devote an increasing share of government activity to military and other unproductive expenditures; they had to rely on alliances with an inefficient class of landlords, officials and soldiers in the hinterland to maintain stability at the cost of development. A great part of the surplus extracted from the population was thus wasted locally.

The New Mercantilism (as the Multinational Corporate System of special alliances and privileges, aid and tariff concessions is sometimes called) faces similar problems of internal and external division. The centre is troubled: excluded groups revolt and even some of the affluent are dissatisfied with the roles. Nationalistic rivalry between major capitalist countries remains an important divisive factor. Finally, there is the threat presented by the middle classes and the excluded groups of the underdeveloped countries. The national middle classes in the underdeveloped countries came to power when the centre weakened but could not, through their policy of import substitution manufacturing, establish a viable basis for sustained growth. They now face a foreign exchange crisis and an unemployment (or population) crisis–the first indicating their inability to function in the international economy and the second indicating their alienation from the people they are supposed to lead. In the immediate future, these national middle classes will gain a new lease of life as they take advantage of the spaces created by the rivalry between American and non-American oligopolists striving to establish global market positions.

The native capitalists will again become the champions of national independence as they bargain with multinational corporations. But the conflict at this level is more apparent than real, for in the end, the fervent nationalism of the middle class asks only for promotion within the corporate structure and not for a break with that structure. In the last analysis, their power derives from the metropolis and they cannot easily afford to challenge the international system. They do not command the loyalty of their own population and cannot really compete with the large, powerful, aggregate capitals from the centre. They are prisoners of the taste patterns and consumption standards set at the centre.

The main threat comes from the excluded groups. It is not unusual in underdeveloped countries for the top 5 per cent to obtain between 30 and 40 per cent of the total national income, and for the top one-third to obtain anywhere from 60 to 70 per cent. At most, one-third of the population can be said to benefit in some sense from the dualistic growth that characterizes development in the hinterland. The remaining two-thirds, who together get only one-third of the income, are outsiders, not because they do not contribute to the economy, but because they do not share in the benefits. They provide a source of cheap labour which helps keep exports to the developed world at a low price and which has financed the urban-biased growth of recent years. In fact, it is difficult to see how the system in most underdeveloped countries could survive without cheap labour since removing it (for example diverting it to public works projects as is done in socialist countries) would raise consumption costs to capitalists and professional elites.

Q10. The author is in a position to draw parallels between New Imperialism and New Mercantilism because:

(a) both originated in the developed Western capitalist countries.

(b) New Mercantilism was a logical sequel to New Imperialism.

(c) they create the same set of outputs - a labour force, middle classes and rival centres of capital.

(d) both have comparable uneven and divisive effects.

Q11. According to the author, the British policy during the 'New Imperialism' period tended to be defensive because:

(a) it was unable to deal with the fallouts of a sharp increase in capital.

(b) its cumulative capital had undesirable side-effects.

(c) its policies favoured developing the vast hinterland.

(d) it prevented the growth of a set-up which could have been capitalistic in nature.

Q12. In the sentence, "They are prisoners of the taste patterns and consumption standards set at the centre." (fourth paragraph), what is the meaning of 'centre'?

(a) National government.

(b) Native capitalists.

(c) New capitalists.

(d) None of the above.

Q13. Under New Mercantilism, the fervent nationalism of the native middle classes does not create conflict with the multinational corporations because they (the middle classes):

(a) negotiate with the multinational corporations.

(b) are dependent on the international system for their continued prosperity.

(c) are not in a position to challenge the status quo.

(d) do not enjoy popular support.

PASSAGE 4 (CAT 2004)

Throughout human, history the leading causes of death have been infection and trauma. Modern medicine has scored significant victories against both, and the major causes of ill health and death are now the chronic degenerative diseases, such as coronary artery disease, arthritis, osteoporosis, Alzheimer's, macular degeneration, cataract and cancer. These have a long latency period before symptoms appear and a diagnosis is made. It follows that the majority of apparently healthy people are pre-ill.

But are these conditions inevitably degenerative? A truly preventive medicine that focused on the pre-ill, analyzing the metabolic errors which lead to clinical illness, might be able to correct them before the first symptom. Genetic risk factors are known for all the chronic degenerative diseases, and are important to the individuals who possess them. At the population level, however, migration studies confirm that these illnesses are linked for the most part, to lifestyle factors–exercise, smoking and nutrition. Nutrition is the easiest of these to change, and the most versatile tool for affecting the metabolic changes needed to tilt the balance away from disease.

Many national surveys reveal that malnutrition is common in developed countries. This is not the calorie and/or micronutrient deficiency associated with developing nations (Type A malnutrition); but multiple micronutrient depletion, usually combined with calorific balance or excess (Type B malnutrition). The incidence and severity of Type B malnutrition will be shown to be worse if newer micronutrient groups such as the essential fatty acids, xanthophylls and flavonoids are included in the surveys. Commonly ingested levels of these micronutrients seem to be far too low in many developed countries.

There is now considerable evidence that Type B malnutrition is a major cause of chronic degenerative diseases. If this is the case, then it is logical to treat such diseases not with drugs but with multiple micronutrient repletion, or 'pharmaco-nutrition'. This can take the form of pills and 'capsules-nutraceuticals', or food formats known as 'functional foods'. This approach has been neglected hitherto because it is relatively unprofitable for drug' companies–the products are hard to patent–and it is a strategy which does not sit easily with modern medical interventionism. Over the last 100 years, the drug industry has invested huge sums in developing a range of subtle and powerful drugs to treat the many diseases we are subject to. Medical training is couched in pharmaceutical terms and this approach has provided us with an exceptional range of therapeutic tools in the treatment of disease and in acute medical emergencies. However, the pharmaceutical model has also created an unhealthy dependency culture, in which relatively few of us accept responsibility for maintaining our own health. Instead, we have handed over this responsibility to health professionals who know very little about health maintenance, or disease prevention.

One problem for supporters of this argument is lack of the right kind of hard evidence. We have a wealth of epidemiological data linking dietary factors to health profiles/disease risks and a great deal of information on mechanism: how food factors interact with our biochemistry. But almost all intervention studies with micronutrients, with the notable exception of the omega 3 fatty acids, have so far produced conflicting or negative results. In other words, our science appears to have no predictive value. Does this invalidate the science? Or are we simply asking the wrong questions?

Based on pharmaceutical thinking, most intervention studies have attempted to measure the impact of a single micronutrient on the incidence of disease. The classical approach says that if you give a compound formula to test, subjects and obtain positive results, you cannot know which ingredient is exerting the benefit, so you must test each ingredient individually. But in the field of nutrition, this does not work. Each intervention on its own will hardly make enough difference to be measured. The best therapeutic response must therefore combine micronutrients to normalize our internal physiology. So, do we need to analyse each individual's nutritional status and then tailor a formula specifically for him or her? While we do not have the resources to analyse millions of individual cases, there is no need to do so. The vast majority of people are consuming suboptimal amounts of most micronutrients, and most of the micronutrients concerned are very safe. Accordingly, a comprehensive and universal program of micronutrient support is probably the most cost-effective and safest way of improving the general health of the nation.

Q14. Type-B malnutrition is a serious concern in developed countries because:

(a) developing countries mainly suffer from Type-A malnutrition.

(b) it is a major contributor to illness and death.

(c) pharmaceutical companies are not producing drugs to treat this condition.

(d) national surveys on malnutrition do not include newer micronutrient groups.

Q15. Why are a large number of apparently healthy people deemed pre-ill?

(a) They may have chronic degenerative diseases.

(b) They do not know their own genetic risk factors which predispose them to diseases.

(c) They suffer from Type-B malnutrition.

(d) There is a lengthy latency period associated with chronically degenerative diseases.

Q16. The author recommends micronutrient-repletion for large-scale treatment of chronic degenerative diseases because:

(a) it is relatively easy to manage.

(b) micronutrient deficiency is the cause of these diseases.

(c) it can overcome genetic risk factors.

(d) it can compensate for other lifestyle factors.

Q17. Tailoring micronutrient-based treatment plans to suit individual deficiency profiles is not necessary because:

(a) it very likely to give inconsistent or negative results.

(b) it is a classic pharmaceutical approach not suited to micronutrients.

(c) most people are consuming suboptimal amounts of safe-to-consume micronutrients.

(d) it is not cost effective to do so.

Passage 5 (CAT 2004)

Fifty feet away, three male lions lay by the road. They didn't appear to have a hair on their heads. Noting the color of their noses (leonine noses darken as they age, from pink to black), Craig estimated that they were six years old-young adults. "This is wonderful!" he said, after staring at them for several moments. "This is what we came to see. They really are maneless." Craig, a professor at the University of Minnesota, is arguably the leading expert on the majestic Serengeti lion, whose head is mantled, in long, thick hair. He and Peyton West, a doctoral student who has been working with him in Tanzania, had never seen the Tsavo lions that live some 200 miles east of the Serengeti. The scientists had partly suspected that the maneless males were adolescents mistaken for adults by amateur observers. Now they knew better.

The Tsavo research expedition was mostly Peyton's show. She had spent several years in Tanzania, compiling the data she needed to answer a question that ought to have been answered long ago: Why do lions have manes? It's the only cat, wild or domestic, that displays such ornamentation. In Tsavo, she was attacking the riddle from the opposite angle. Why do its lions not have manes? Some "maneless" lions in Tsavo East do have partial manes, but they rarely attain the regal glory of the Serengeti lions. Does environmental adaptation account for the trait? Are the lions of Tsavo, as some people believe, a distinct subspecies of their Serengeti cousins?

The Serengeti lions have been under continuous observation for more than 35 years, beginning with George Schaller's pioneering work in the 1960s. But the lions in Tsavo, Kenya's oldest and largest protected ecosystem, have hardly been studied. Consequently, legends have grown up around them. Not only do they look different, according to the myths, they *behave* differently, displaying greater cunning and aggressiveness. "Remember too," *Kenya: The Rough Guide* warns, "Tsavo's lions have a reputation of ferocity." Their fearsome image became well-known in 1898, when two males stalled construction of what is now Kenya Railways by allegedly killing and eating 135 Indian and African laborers. A British Army officer in charge of building a railroad bridge over the Tsavo River, Lt. Col. J. H. Patterson, spent nine months pursuing the pair before he brought them to bay and killed them. Stuffed and mounted, they now glare at visitors to the Field Museum in Chicago. Patterson's account of the leonine reign of terror, The *Man-Eaters of Tsavo,* was an international best-seller when published in 1907. Still in print, the book has made Tsavo's lions notorious. That annoys some scientists. "People don't want to give up on mythology," Dennis King told me one day. The zoologist has been working in Tsavo off and on for four years. "I am so sick of this man-eater business. Patterson made a helluva lot of money off that story, but Tsavo's lions are no more likely to turn man-eater than lions from elsewhere."

But tales of their savagery and wiliness don't all come from sensationalist authors looking to make a buck. Tsavo lions are generally larger than lions elsewhere, enabling them to take down the predominant prey animal in Tsavo, the Cape buffalo, one of the strongest, most aggressive animals of Earth. The buffalo don't give up easily: They often kill or severely injure an attacking lion, and a wounded lion might be more likely to turn to cattle and humans for food.

And other prey is less abundant in Tsavo than in other traditional lion haunts. A hungry lion is more likely to attack humans. Safari guides and Kenya Wildlife Service rangers tell of lions attacking Land Rovers, raiding camps, stalking tourists. Tsavo is a tough neighborhood, they say, and it breeds tougher lions.

But are they really tougher? And if so, is there any connection between their manelessness and their ferocity? An intriguing hypothesis was advanced two years ago by Gnoske and Peterhans: Tsavo lions may be similar to the unmaned cave lions of the Pleistocene. The Serengeti variety is among the most evolved of the species–the latest model, so to speak–while certain morphological differences in Tsavo lions (bigger bodies, smaller skulls, and maybe even lack of a mane) suggest that they are closer to the primitive ancestor of all lions. Craig and Peyton had serious doubts about this idea, but admitted that Tsavo lions pose a mystery to science.

Q18. The book *Man-Eaters of Tsavo* annoys some scientists because:

(a) it revealed that Tsavo lions are ferocious.
(b) Patterson made a helluva lot of money from the book by sensationalism.
(c) it perpetuated the bad name Tsavo lions had.
(d) it narrated how two male Tsavo lions were killed.

Q19. According to the passage, which of the following has not contributed to the popular image of Tsavo lions as savage creatures?

(a) Tsavo lions have been observed to bring down one of the strongest and most aggressive animals–the Cape buffaloes.
(b) In contrast to the situation in traditional lion haunts, scarcity of non-buffalo prey in the Tsavo makes the Tsavo lions more aggressive.
(c) The Tsavo lion is considered to be less evolved than the Serengeti variety.
(d) Tsavo lions have been observed to attack vehicles as well as humans.

Q20. The sentence which concludes the first paragraph, "Now they knew better", implies that:

(a) The two scientists were struck by wonder on seeing maneless lions for the first time.
(b) Though Craig was an expert on the Serengeti lion, now he also knew about the Tsavo lions.
(c) Earlier, Craig and West thought that amateur observers had been mistaken.
(d) Craig was now able to confirm that darkening of the noses as lions aged applied to Tsavo lions as well.

Q21. Which of the following, if true, would weaken the hypothesis advanced by Gnoske and Peterhans most?

(a) Craig and Peyton develop even more serious doubts about the idea that Tsavo lions are primitive.
(b) The maneless Tsavo East lions are shown to be closer to the cave lions.
(c) Pleistocene cave lions are shown to be far less violent than believed.
(d) The morphological variations in body and skull size between the cave and Tsavo lions are found to be insignificant.

VII

Directions for the questions (1-25): Each of the five passages given below is followed by questions. Choose the best answer for each question.

PASSAGE 1 (CAT 2002)

The production of histories of India has become very frequent in recent years and may well call for some explanation. Why so many and why this one in particular? The reason is a twofold one: changes in the Indian scene requiring a re-interpretation of the facts and changes in attitudes of historians about the essential elements of Indian history. These two considerations are in addition to the normal fact of fresh information, whether in the form of archeological discoveries throwing fresh light on an obscure period or culture, or the revelations caused by the opening of archives or the release of private papers. The changes in the Indian scene are too obvious to need emphasis. Only two generations ago, British rule seemed to most Indian as well as British observers, likely to extend into an indefinite future; now there is a teenage generation which knows nothing of it. Changes in the attitudes of historians have occurred everywhere, changes in attitudes to the content of the subject as well as to particular countries, but in India, there have been some special features. Prior to the British, Indian historiographers were mostly Muslims, who relied, as in the case of Sayyid Ghulam Hussain, on their own recollection of events and on information from friends and men of affairs. Only a few like Abu'l Fazl had access to official papers. These were personal narratives of events, varying in value with the nature of the writer. The early British writers were officials. In the eighteenth century, they were concerned with some aspect of Company policy, or, like Robert Orme in his *Military Transactions,* gave a straight narrative in what was essentially a continuation of the Muslim tradition. In the early nineteenth century, the writers were still, with two notable exceptions, officials, but they were now engaged in chronicling, in varying moods of zest, pride, and awe, the rise of the British power in India to supremacy. The two exceptions were James Mill, with his critical attitude to the Company and John Marchman, the Baptist missionary. But they, like the officials, were anglo-centric in their attitude, so that the history of modem India in their hands came to be the history of the rise of the British in India.

The official school dominated the writing of Indian history until we get the *first* professional historian's approach, Ramsay Muir and P.E. Roberts in England and H. H. Dodwell in India. Then Indian historians trained in the English school joined in, of whom the most distinguished was Sir Jadunath Sarkar and the other notable writers: Surendranath Sen, Dr. Radhakumud Mukerji, and Professor Nilakanta Sastri. They, it may be said, restored India to Indian history, but their bias was mainly political. Finally have come the nationalists who range from those who can find nothing good or true in the British to sophisticated historical philosophers like K.M. Panikker.

Along with types of historians with their varying biases, have gone changes in the attitude to the content of Indian history. Here, Indian historians have been influenced both by their local situation and by changes of thought elsewhere. It is in this field that this work can claim some attention since it seeks to break new ground, or perhaps to deepen a freshly turned furrow in the field of Indian history. The early official historians were content with the glamour and drama of political history from Plassey to the Mutiny, from Dupleix to the Sikhs. But when the *raj* was settled down, glamour departed from politics, and they turned to the less glorious but more solid ground of administration. Not how India was conquered but how it was governed was the theme of this school of historians. It found its archpriest in H.H. Dodwell, its priestess in Dame Lilian Penson, and its chief shrine in the Volume VI of the *Cambridge History of India.* Meanwhile in Britain, other currents were moving, which led historical study into the economic and social fields. R.C. Dutt entered the first of these currents with his *Economic History of India,* to be followed more recently by the whole group of Indian economic historians. W.E. Moreland extended these studies to the Mughal Period. Social history is now being increasingly studied and there is also of course, a school of nationalist historians; who see modern Indian history in terms of the rise and the fulfillment of the national movement.

All these approaches have value, but all share in the quality of being compartmental. It is not enough to remove political history from its pedestal of being the only kind of history worth having if it is merely to put other types of history in its place. Too exclusive an attention to economic, social, or administrative history can be as sterile and misleading as too much concentration on politics. A whole subject needs a whole treatment for understanding. A historian must dissect his subject into its elements and then fuse them together again into an integrated whole.

The true history of a country must contain all the features just cited, but must present them as parts of a single consistent theme.

Q1. Which of the following may be the closest in meaning to the statement "restored India to Indian history"?

(a) Indian historians began writing Indian history.
(b) Trained historians began writing Indian history.
(c) Writing India-centric Indian history began.
(d) Indian history began to be written in India.

Q2. Which of the following is the closest implication of the statement "to break new ground, or perhaps to deepen a freshly turned furrow"?

(a) Dig afresh or dig deeper.
(b) Start a new stream of thought or help establish a recently emerged perspective.
(c) Begin or conduct further work on existing archeological sites to unearth new evidence.
(d) Begin writing a history free of any biases.

Q3. Historians moved from writing political history to writing administrative history because:

(a) attitudes of the historians changed.
(b) the *raj* was settled down.

(c) politics did not retain its past glamour.
(d) administrative history was based on solid ground.

Q4. According to the author, which of the following is **not** among the attitudes of Indian historians of Indian origin?

(a) Writing history as personal narratives.
(b) Writing history with political bias.
(c) Writing non-political history due to lack of glamour.
(d) Writing history by dissecting elements and integrating them again.

Q5. In the table given below, match the historians to the approaches taken by them:

A. Administrative	E. Robert Orme
B. Political	F. H. H. Dodwell
C. Narrative	G. Radha Kumud Mukherji
D. Economic	H. R. C. Dutt

(a)	(b)	(c)	(d)
A → F	A → G	A → E	A → F
B → G	B → F	B → F	B → H
C → E	C → E	C → G	C → E
D → H	D → H	D → H	D → G

PASSAGE 2 (CAT 2002)

There are a seemingly endless variety of laws, restrictions, customs and traditions that affect the practice of abortion around the world. Globally, abortion is probably the single most controversial issue in the whole area of women's rights and family matters. It is an issue that inflames women's right groups, religious institutions, and the self-proclaimed "guardians" of public morality. The growing worldwide belief is that the right to control one's fertility is a basic human right. This has resulted in a worldwide trend towards liberalization of abortion laws. Forty percent of the world's population live in countries where induced abortion is permitted on request. An additional 25 percent live in countries where it is allowed if the women's life would be endangered if she went to full term with her pregnancy. The estimate is that between 26 and 31 million legal abortions were performed in 1987. However, there were also between 10 and 22 million illegal abortions performed in that year.

Feminists have viewed the patriarchal control of women's bodies as one of the prime issues facing the contemporary women's movement. They observe that the definition and control of women's reproductive freedom have always been the province of men. Patriarchal religion, as manifest in Islamic fundamentalism, traditionalist Hindu practice, orthodox Judaism, and Roman Catholicism, has been an important historical contributory factor for this and continues to be an important presence in contemporary societies. In recent times, governments, usually controlled by men, have "given" women the right to contraceptive use and abortion access when their countries were perceived to have an overpopulation problem. When these countries are perceived to be underpopulated, that right has been absent. Until the nineteenth century, a woman's rights to an abortion followed English common law; it could only be legally challenged if there was a "quickening", when the first movements of the foetus could be felt. In 1800, drugs to induce abortions were widely advertised in local newspapers. By 1900, abortion was banned in every state except to save the life of the mother. The change was strongly influenced by the medical profession, which focussed its campaign ostensibly on health and safety issues for pregnant women and the sanctity of life. Its position was also a means of control of non licensed medical practitioners such as midwives and women healers who practiced abortion.

The anti-abortion campaign was also influenced by political considerations. The large influx of eastern and southern European immigrants with their large families was seen as a threat to the population balance of the future United States. Middle and upper class Protestants were advocates of abortion as a form of birth control. By supporting abortion prohibitions, the hope was that these Americans would have more children and thus, prevent the tide of immigrant babies from overwhelming the demographic characteristics of Protestant America.

The anti-abortion legislative position remained in effect in the United States through the first sixty-five years of the twentieth century. In the early 1960s, even when it was widely known that the drug thalidomide taken during pregnancy to alleviate anxiety was shown to contribute to the formation of deformed "flipper-like" hands or legs of children, abortion was illegal in the United States. A second health tragedy was the severe outbreak of rubella during the same time period, which also resulted in major birth defects. These tragedies combined with a change of attitude towards a woman's right to privacy lead a number of states to pass abortion-permitting legislation.

On one side of the controversy are those who call themselves "pro-life". They view the foetus as a human life rather than as an unformed complex of cells; therefore, they hold to the belief that abortion is essentially murder of an unborn child. These groups cite both legal and religious reasons for their opposition to abortion. Pro-lifers point to the rise in legalized abortion figures and see this as morally intolerable. On the other side of the issue are those who call themselves "pro-choice". They believe that women, not legislators or judges, should have the right to decide whether and under what circumstances they will bear children. Pro-choicers are of the opinion that laws will not prevent women from having abortions and cite the horror stories of the past when many women died at the hands of "backroom" abortionists and in desperate attempts to self-abort. They also observe that legalized abortion is especially important for rape victims and incest victims who became pregnant. They stress physical and mental health reasons why women should not have unwanted children.

To get a better understanding of the current abortion controversy, let us examine a very important work by Kristin Luker, titled Abortion and The Politics of Motherhood. Luker argues that female pro-choice and pro-life activists hold different world views regarding gender, sex, and the meaning of parenthood. Moral positions on abortions are seen to be tied intimately to views on sexual behaviour, the care of children, family life, technology, and the importance of the individual. Luker identifies "pro-choice" women as educated, affluent, and liberal. Their contrasting counterparts, "pro-life" women, support traditional concepts of women as wives and mothers. It would be instructive to sketch out the differences in the world views of these two sets of women. Luker examines California, with its liberalized abortion law, as a case history. Public documents and newspaper accounts over a twenty-year period were analyzed and over 200 interviews were held with both pro-life and pro-choice activists.

Luker found that pro-life and pro-choice activists have intrinsically different views with respect to gender. Pro-life women have a notion of public and private life. The proper place for men is in the public sphere of work; for women, it is the private sphere of the home. Men benefit through the nurturance of women; women benefit through the protection of men. Children are seen to be the ultimate beneficiaries of this arrangement by having the mother as a full-time loving parent and by having clear role models. Pro-choice advocates reject the view of separate spheres. They object to the notion of the home being the "women's sphere". Women's reproductive and family roles are seen as potential barriers to full equality. Motherhood is seen as a voluntary, not a mandatory or "natural" role.

In summarizing her findings, Luker believes that women become activists in either of the two movements as the end result of lives that center around different conceptualizations of motherhood. Their beliefs and values are rooted to the concrete circumstances of their lives, their educations, incomes, occupations, and the different marital and family choices that they have made. They represent two different world views of women's roles in contemporary society and as such, the abortion issue represents the battleground for the justification of their respective views.

Q6. According to your understanding of the author's arguments, which countries are more likely to allow abortion?

(a) India and China.
(b) Australia and Mongolia.
(c) Cannot be inferred from the passage.
(d) Both (a) and (b).

Q7. Which amongst these was not a reason for banning of abortions by 1900?

(a) Medical professionals stressing the health and safety of women.
(b) Influx of eastern and southern European immigrants.
(c) Control of unlicensed medical practitioners.
(d) A tradition of matriarchal control.

Q8. A pro-life woman would advocate abortion if:

(a) the mother of an unborn child is suicidal.
(b) bearing a child conflicts with a woman's career prospects.
(b) the mother becomes pregnant accidentally.
(c) none of the above.

Q9. Pro-choice women object to the notion of the home being the "women's sphere" because they believe:

(a) that the home is a "joint sphere" shared between men and women.
(b) that reproduction is a matter of choice for women.
(c) that men and women are equal.
(d) both (b) and (c).

Q10. Two health tragedies affecting U.S. society in the 1960s led to:

(a) a change in attitude to women's right to privacy.
(b) retaining the anti-abortion laws with some exceptions.
(c) scrapping of anti-abortion laws.
(d) strengthening of the pro-life lobby.

Q11. Historically, the pro-choice movement has got support from, among others,:

(a) major patriarchal religions.
(b) countries with low population density.
(c) medical profession.
(d) none of the above.

PASSAGE 3 (CAT 2002)

The conceptions of life and the world which we call 'philosophical' are a product of two factors: one, inherited religious and ethical conceptions; the other, the sort of investigation which may be called 'scientific', using this word in its broadest sense. Individual philosophers have differed widely in regard to the proportions in which these two factors entered into their systems, but it is the presence of both, in some degree, that characterizes philosophy.

'Philosophy' is a word which has been used in many ways, some wider, some narrower. I propose to use it in a very wide sense, which I will now try to explain.

Philosophy, as I shall understand the word, is something intermediate between theology and science. Like theology, it consists of speculations on matters as to which definite knowledge has, so far, been unascertainable; but like science, it appeals to human reason rather than to authority, whether that of tradition or that of revelation. All definite knowledge–so I should contend–belongs to science; all dogma as to what surpasses definite knowledge belongs to theology. But between theology and science, there is a 'No Man's Land', exposed to attack from both sides; this 'No Man's Land' is philosophy. Almost all the questions of most interest to speculative minds are such as science cannot answer, and the confident answers of theologians no longer seem so convincing as they did in former centuries. Is the world divided into mind and matter, and if so, what is mind and what is matter? Is mind subject to matter, or is it possessed of independent powers? Has the universe any unity or purpose? Is it evolving towards some goal? Are there really laws of nature, or do we believe in them only because of our innate love of order? Is man what he seems to the astronomer, a tiny lump of carbon and water impotently crawling on a small and unimportant planet? Or is he what he appears to Hamlet? Is he perhaps both at once? Is there a way of living that is noble and another that is base, or are all ways of living merely futile? If there is a way of living that is noble, in what does it consist, and how shall we achieve it? Must the good be eternal in order to deserve to be valued, or is it worth seeking even if the universe is inexorably moving towards death? Is there such a thing as wisdom, or is what seems such merely the ultimate refinement of folly? To such questions; no answer can be found in the laboratory. Theologies have professed to give answers, all too definite; but their definiteness causes modern minds to view them with suspicion. The studying of these questions, if not the answering of them, is the business of philosophy.

Why, then, you may ask, waste time on such insoluble problems? To this, one may answer as a historian, or an individual facing the terror of cosmic loneliness.

The answer of the historian, in so far as I am capable of giving it, will appear in the course of this work. Ever since men became capable of free speculation, their actions in innumerable important respects, have depended upon their theories as to the world and human life, as to what is good and what is evil. This is as true in the present day as at any former time. To understand an age or a nation, we must understand its philosophy, and to understand its philosophy, we must ourselves be in some degree philosophers. There is here a reciprocal causation: the circumstances of men's lives do much to determine their philosophy, but, conversely, their philosophy does much to determine their circumstances.

There is also, however, a more personal answer. Science tells us what we can know, but what we can know is little, and if we forget how much we cannot know, we may become insensitive to many things of very great importance. Theology, on the other hand, induces a dogmatic belief that we have knowledge, where in fact, we have ignorance, and by doing, so generates a kind of impertinent insolence towards the universe. Uncertainty, in the presence of vivid hopes and fears, is painful, but must be endured if we wish to live without the support of comforting fairy tales. It is not good either to forget the questions that philosophy asks, or to persuade ourselves that we have found indubitable answers to them. To teach how to live without certainty, and yet without being paralyzed by hesitation, is perhaps the chief thing that philosophy, in our age, can still do for those who study it.

Q12. The purpose of philosophy is to:

(a) reduce uncertainty and chaos.
(b) help us to cope with uncertainty and ambiguity.
(c) help us to find explanations for uncertainty.
(d) reduce the terror of cosmic loneliness.

Q13. Based on this passage, what can be concluded about the relation between philosophy and science?

(a) The two are antagonistic.
(b) The two are complementary.
(c) There is no relation between the two.
(d) Philosophy derives from science.

Q14. From reading the passage, what can be concluded about the profession of the author? He is most likely to be a:

(a) historian.
(b) philosopher.
(c) scientist.
(d) theologian.

Q15. According to the author, which of the following statements about the nature of the universe must be definitely true?

(a) The universe has unity.
(b) The universe has a purpose.
(c) The universe is evolving towards a goal.
(d) None of the above.

PASSAGE 4 (CAT 2002)

Cells are the ultimate multitaskers: they can switch on genes and carry out their orders, talk to each other, divide in two, and much more, all at the same time. But they couldn't do any of these tricks without a power source to generate movement. The inside of a cell bustles with more traffic than Delhi roads, and, like all vehicles, the cell's moving parts need engines. Physicists and biologists have looked "under the hood" of the cell–and laid out the nuts and bolts of molecular engines.

The ability of such engines to convert chemical energy into motion is the envy of nanotechnology researchers looking for ways to power molecule-sized devices. Medical researchers also want to understand how these engines work. Because these molecules are essential for cell division, scientists hope to shut down the rampant growth of cancer cells by deactivating certain motors. Improving motor-driven transport in nerve cells may also be helpful for treating diseases such as Alzheimer's, Parkinson's or ALS, also known as Lou Gehrig's disease.

We wouldn't make it far in life without motor proteins. Our muscles wouldn't contract. We couldn't grow, because the growth process requires cells to duplicate their machinery and pull the copies apart. And our genes would be silent without the services of messenger RNA, which carries genetic instructions over to the cell's protein-making factories. The movements that make these cellular activities possible, occur along a complex network of threadlike fibers, or polymers, along which bundles of molecules travel like trams. The engines that power the cell's freight are three families of proteins, called myosin, kinesin and dynein. For fuel, these proteins burn molecules of ATP, which cells make when they break down the carbohydrates and fats from the foods we eat. The energy from burning ATP causes changes in the proteins' shape that allow them to heave themselves along the polymer track. The results are impressive: In one second, these molecules can travel between 50 and 100 times their own diameter. If a car with a 5-foot-wide engine were as efficient, it would travel 170 to 340 kmph.

Ronald Vale, a researcher at the Howard Hughes Medical Institute and the University of California at San Francisco, and Ronald Milligan of the Scripps Research Institute have realized a long-awaited goal by reconstructing the process by which myosin and kinesin move, almost down to the atom. The dynein motor, on the other hand, is still poorly understood. Myosin molecules, best known for their role in muscle contraction, form chains that lie between filaments of another protein called actin. Each myosin molecule has a tiny head that pokes out from the chain like oars from a canoe. Just as rowers propel their boat by stroking their oars through the water, the myosin molecules stick their heads into the actin and hoist themselves forward along the filament. While myosin moves along in short strokes, its cousin kinesin walks steadily along a different type of filament called a microtubule. Instead of using a projecting head as a lever, kinesin walks on two "legs." Based on these differences, researchers used to think that myosin and kinesin were virtually unrelated. But newly discovered similarities in the motors' ATP-processing machinery now suggest that they share a common ancestor–molecule. At this point, scientists can only speculate as to what type of primitive cell-like structure this ancestor occupied as it learned to burn ATP and use the energy to change shape. "We'll never really know, because we can't dig up the remains of ancient proteins, but that was probably a big evolutionary leap," says Vale.

On a slightly larger scale, loner cells like sperm or infectious bacteria are prime movers that resolutely push their way through to other cells. As L. Mahadevan and Paul Matsudaira of the Massachusetts Institute of Technology explain, the engines in this case are springs or ratchets that are clusters of molecules, rather than single proteins like myosin and kinesin. Researchers don't yet fully understand these engines' fueling process or the details of how they move, but the result is a force to be reckoned with. For example, one such engine is a spring like stalk connecting a single-celled organism called a vorticellid to the leaf fragment it calls home. When exposed to calcium, the spring contracts, yanking the vorticellid down at speeds approaching 3 inches (8 centimeters) per second.

Springs like this are coiled bundles of filaments that expand or contract in response to chemical cues. A wave of positively charged calcium ions, for example, neutralizes the negative charges that keep the filaments extended. Some sperm use spring like engines made of actin filaments to shoot out a barb that penetrates the layers that surround an egg. And certain viruses use a similar apparatus to shoot their DNA into the host's cell. Ratchets are also useful for moving whole cells, including some other sperm and pathogens. These engines are filaments that simply grow at one end, attracting chemical building blocks from nearby. Because the other end is anchored in place, the growing end pushes against any barrier that gets in its way.

Both springs and ratchets are made up of small units that each move just slightly, but collectively produce a powerful movement. Ultimately, Mahadevan and Matsudaira hope to better understand just how these particles create an effect that seems to be so much more than the sum of its parts. Might such an understanding provide inspiration for ways to power artificial nano-sized devices in the future? "The short answer is absolutely," says Mahadevan. "Biology has had a lot more time to evolve enormous richness in design for different organisms. Hopefully, studying these structures will not only improve our understanding of the biological world, it will also enable us to copy them, take apart their components and re-create them for other purposes."

Q16. According to the author, research on the power source of movement in cells can contribute to:

(a) control over the movement of genes within human systems.
(b) the understanding of nanotechnology.
(c) arresting the growth of cancer in a human being.
(d) the development of cures for a variety of diseases.

Q17. The author has used several analogies to illustrate his arguments in the article. Which of the following pairs of words are examples of the analogies used?

I. Cell activity and vehicular traffic.
II. Polymers and tram tracks.
III. Genes and canoes.
IV. Vorticellids and ratchets.

(a) I and II
(b) II and III
(c) I and IV
(d) I and III

Q18. Read the five statements below: I, II, III, IV, and V. From the options given, select the one which includes statement that are **not** representative of an argument presented in the passage.

I. Sperms use spring like engines made of actin filament.
II. Myosin and kinesin are unrelated.
III. Nanotechnology researchers look for ways to power molecule-sized devices.
IV. Motor proteins help muscle contraction.
V. The dynein motor is still poorly understood.

(a) I, II and III
(b) III, IV and V
(c) I, IV and V
(d) I, III and IV

Q19. Read the four statements below: I, II, III, and IV. From the options given, select the one which includes only statement(s) that are representative of arguments presented in the passage.

I. Protein motors help growth processes.
II. Improved transport in nerve cells will help arrest tuberculosis and cancer.
III. Cells, together, generate more power than the sum of power generated by them separately.
IV. Vorticellid and the leaf fragment are connected by a calcium engine.

(a) I and II but not III
(b) I and III but not IV
(c) I and IV but not II
(d) III and IV but not II

Q20. Read the four statements below: I, II, III, and IV. From the options given, select the one which include statement(s) that are representative of arguments presented in the passage.

I. Myosin, kinesin and actin are three types of protein.
II. Growth processes involve a routine in a cell that duplicates their machinery and pulls the copies apart.
III. Myosin molecules can generate vibrations in muscles.
IV. Ronald and Mahadevan are researchers at Massachusetts Institute of Technology.

(a) I and II but not III and IV
(b) II and III but not I
(c) II and IV but not I and III
(d) I, II and III but not IV

Passage 5 (CAT 2002)

If translated into English, most of the ways economists talk among themselves would sound plausible enough to poets, journalists, businesspeople, and other thoughtful though *noneconomical* folk. Like serious talk anywhere–among boat designers and baseball fans, say–the talk is hard to follow when one has not made a habit of listening to it for a while. The culture of the conversation makes the words arcane. But the people in the unfamiliar conversation are not Martians. Underneath it all (the economist's favorite phrase), conversational habits are similar. Economics uses mathematical models and statistical tests and market arguments, all of which look alien to the literary eye. But looked at closely, they are not so alien. They may be seen as figures of speech-metaphors, analogies, and appeals to authority.

Figures of speech are not mere frills. They think for us. Someone who thinks of a market as an "invisible hand" and the organization of work as a "production function" and his coefficients as being "significant," as an economist does, is giving the language a lot of responsibility. It seems a good idea to look hard at his language.

If the economic conversation were found to depend a lot on its verbal forms, this would not mean that economics would be not a science, or just a matter of opinion, or some sort of confidence game. Good poets, though not scientists, are serious thinkers about symbols; good historians, though not scientists, are serious thinkers about data. Good scientists also use language. What is more (though it remains to be shown) they use the cunning of language, without particularly meaning to. The language used is a social object, and using language is a social act. It requires cunning (or, if you prefer, consideration) attention to the other minds present when one speaks.

The paying of attention to one's audience is called "rhetoric," a word that I later exercise hard. One uses rhetoric, of course, to warn of a fire in a theatre or to arouse the xenophobia of the electorate. This sort of yelling is the vulgar meaning of the word, like the president's "heated rhetoric" in a press conference or the "mere rhetoric" to which our enemies stoop. Since the Greek flame was lit, though, the word has been used also in a broader and more amiable sense, to mean the study of all the ways of accomplishing things with language: inciting a mob to lynch the accused, to be sure, but also persuading readers of a novel that its characters breathe, or bringing scholars to accept the better argument and reject the worse.

The question is whether the scholar–who usually fancies himself an announcer of "results" or a stator of "conclusions" free of rhetoric–speaks rhetorically. Does he try to persuade? It would seem so. Language, I just said, is not a solitary accomplishment. The scholar doesn't speak into the void, or to himself. He speaks to a community of voices. He desires to be heeded, praised, published, imitated, honored, en-Nobeled. These are the desires. The devices of language are the means.

Rhetoric is the proportioning of means to desires in speech. Rhetoric is an economics of language, the study of how scarce means are allocated to the insatiable desires of people to be heard. It seems on the face of it a reasonable hypothesis that economists are like other people in being talkers, who desire listeners when they go to the library or the laboratory as much as when they go to the office on the polls. The purpose here is to see if this is true, and to see if it is useful: to study the rhetoric of economic scholarship.

The subject is scholarship. It is not the economy, or the adequacy of economic theory as a description of the economy, or even mainly the economist's role in the economy. The subject is the conversation economists have among themselves, for purposes of persuading each other that the interest elasticity of demand for investment is zero or that the money supply is controlled by the Federal Reserve.

Unfortunately, though, the conclusions are of more than academic interest. The conversations of classicists or of astronomers rarely affect the lives of other people. Those of economists do so on a large scale. A well known joke describes a May Day parade through Red Square with the usual mass of soldiers, guided missiles, rocket launchers. At last come rank upon rank of people in gray business suits. A bystander asks, "Who are those?" "Aha!" comes the reply, "those are economists: you have no idea what damage they can do!" Their conversations do it.

Q21. According to the passage, which of the following is the best set of reasons for which one needs to "look hard" at an economist's language?

I. Economists accomplish a great deal through their language.
II. Economics is an opinion-based subject.
III. Economics has a great impact on other's lives.
IV. Economics is damaging.

(a) I and II
(b) III and IV
(c) I and III
(d) II and IV

Q22. In the light of the definition of rhetoric given in the passage, which of the following will have the least element of rhetoric?

(a) An election speech.
(b) An advertisement jingle.
(c) Dialogues in a play.
(d) Commands given by army officers.

Q23. As used in the passage, which of the following is the closest meaning to the statement "The culture of the conversation makes the words arcane"?

(a) Economists belong to a different culture.
(b) Only mathematicians can understand economists.
(c) Economists tend to use terms unfamiliar to the lay person, but depend on familiar linguistic forms.
(d) Economists use similes and adjectives in their analysis.

Q24. As used in the passage, which of the following is the closest alternative to the word 'arcane'?

(a) Mysterious
(b) Secret
(c) Covert
(d) Perfidious

Q25. Based on your understanding of the passage, which of the following conclusions would you agree with?

(a) The geocentric and the heliocentric views of the solar system are equally tenable.
(b) The heliocentric view is superior because of better rhetoric.
(c) Both views use rhetoric to persuade.
(d) Scientists should not use rhetoric.

VIII

Passage 1 [CAT 2003 (cancelled)]

At the heart of the enormous boom in wine consumption that has taken place in the English-speaking world over the last two decades or so, is a fascinating, happy paradox. In the days when wine was exclusively the preserve of a narrow cultural elite, bought either at auctions or from gentleman wine merchants in wing collars and bow-ties, to be stored in rambling cellars and decanted to order by one's butler, the ordinary drinker didn't get a look-in. Wine was considered a highly technical subject, in which anybody without the necessary ability could only fall flat on his or her face in embarrassment. It wasn't just that you needed a refined aesthetic sensibility for the stuff if it wasn't to be hopelessly wasted on you. It required an intimate knowledge of what came from where, and what it was supposed to taste like.

Those were times, however, when wine appreciation essentially meant a familiarity with the great French classics, with perhaps a smattering of other wines–like sherry and port. That was what the wine trade dealt in. These days, wine is bought daily in supermarkets and high-street chains to be consumed that evening, hardly anybody has a cellar to store it in and most don't even possess a decanter. Above all, the wines of literally dozens of countries are available on our market. When a supermarket offers its customers a couple of fruity little numbers from Brazil, we scarcely raise an eyebrow.

It seems, in other words, that the commercial jungle that wine has now become has not in the slightest deterred people from plunging adventurously into the thickets in order to taste and see. Consumers are no longer intimidated by the thought of needing to know their Pouilly-Fume from their Pouilly-Fuisse just at the very moment when there is more to know than ever before.

The reason for this new mood of confidence is not hard to find. It is on every wine label from Australia, New Zealand, South Africa and the United States: the name of the grape from which the wine is made. At one time, that might have sounded like a fairly technical approach in itself. Why should native English-speakers know what Cabernet Sauvignon or Chardonnay were? The answer lies in the popularity that wines made from those grape varieties now enjoy. Consumers effectively recognize them as brand names, and have acquired a basic lexicon of wine that can serve them even when confronted with those Brazilian upstarts.

In the wine heartlands of France, they are scared to death of that trend–not because they think their wine isn't as good as the best from California or South Australia (what French winemaker will ever admit that?) but because they don't traditionally call their wines Cabernet Sauvignon or Chardonnay. They call them Chateau Ducru- Beaucillou or Corton-Charlemagne, and they aren't about to change. Some areas, in the middle of southern France, have now produced a generation of growers using the varietal names on their labels and are tempting consumers back to French wine. It will be an uphill struggle, but there is probably no other way if France is to avoid simply becoming a specialty source of old-fashioned wines for old-fashioned connoisseurs.

Wine consumption was also given a significant boost in the early 1990s by the works of Dr. Serge Renaud, who has spent many years investigating the reasons for the uncannily low incidence of coronary heart disease in the south of France. One of his major findings is that the fat-derived cholesterol that build up the arteries and can eventually lead to the heart trouble, can be dispersed by the tannins in wine. Tannin is derived from the skin of grapes, and is therefore, present in higher level in red wines, because they have to be infused with their skin to attain the red colour. That news caused a huge upsurge in red wine consumption in United States. It has not been accorded the prominence it deserves in the UK, largely because the medical profession still sees all alcohol as a menace to health, and is constantly calling for it to be made prohibitively expensive. Certainly, the manufacturers of anticoagulant drugs might have something to lose if we all got the message that we would do just as well for our hearts by taking half a bottle of red wine every day!

Q1. The tone that the author uses while asking "What French winemaker will ever admit that?" is best described as:

(a) caustic
(b) satirical
(c) critical
(d) hypocritical

Q2. Which one of the following CANNOT be reasonably attributed to the labeling strategy followed by wine producers in English-speaking countries?

(a) Consumers buy wines on the basis of their familiarity with a grape variety's name.
(b) Even ordinary customers now have more access to technical knowledge about wine.
(c) Consumers are able to appreciate better quality wines.
(d) Some non-English speaking countries like Brazil indicate grape variety names on their labels.

Q3. Which one of the following, if true, would provide most support for Dr. Renaud's findings about the "effect of tannins"?

(a) A survey showed that film celebrities based in France have a low incidence of coronary heart disease.
(b) Measurements carried out in southern France showed red wine drinkers had significantly higher levels of coronary heart incidence than white wine drinkers did.
(c) Data showed a positive association between sales of red wine and incidence of coronary heart disease.
(d) Long-term surveys in southern France showed that the incidence of coronary heart disease was significantly lower in red wine drinkers than in those who did not drink red wine.

Q4. The development which has created fear among winemakers in the wine heartlands of France is the:
(a) tendency not to name wines after the grape varieties that are used in the wines.
(b) 'education' that consumers have derived from wine labels from English speaking countries.
(c) new generation of local winegrowers who use labels that show names of grape varieties.
(d) ability of consumers to understand a wine's qualities when confronted with "Brazilian upstarts'.

Q5. What according to the author should the French do to avoid becoming a producer of merely old-fashioned wines?
(a) Follow the labelling strategy of the English-speaking countries.
(b) Give their wines English names.
(c) Introduce fruity wines as Brazil has done.
(d) Produce the wines that have become popular in the English-speaking world.

PASSAGE 2 [CAT 2003 (CANCELLED)]

Right through history, imperial powers have clung to their possessions to death. Why, then, did Britain in 1947, give up the jewel in its crown, India? For many reasons. The independence struggle exposed the hollowness of the white man's burden. Provincial self-rule since 1935 paved the way for full self rule. Churchill resisted independence, but the Labour government of Atlee was anti-imperialist by ideology. Finally, the Royal Indian Navy mutiny in 1946 raised fears of a second Sepoy mutiny, and convinced British waverers that it was safer to withdraw gracefully. But politico-military explanations are not enough. The basis of empire was always money.

The end of empire had much to do with the fact that British imperialism had ceased to be profitable. World War II left Britain victorious but deeply indebted, needing Marshall Aid and loans from the World Bank. This constituted a strong financial case for ending the no-longer-profitable empire.

Empire building is expensive. The US is spending one billion dollars a day in operations in Iraq that fall well short of full-scale imperialism. Through the centuries, empire building was costly, yet constantly undertaken because it promised high returns. The investment was in armies and conquest. The returns came through plunder and taxes from the conquered.

No immorality was attached to imperial loot and plunder. The biggest conquerors were typically revered (hence, titles like Alexander the Great, Akbar the Great, and Peter the Great). The bigger and richer the empire, the more the plunderer was admired. This mindset gradually changed with the rise of new ideas about equality and governing for the public good, ideas that culminated in the French and American revolutions. Robert Clive was impeached for making a little money on the side, and so was Warren Hastings. The white man's burden came up as a new moral rationale for conquest: It was supposedly for the good of the conquered. This led to much muddled hypocrisy. On the one hand, the empire needed to be profitable. On the other hand, the white man's burden made brazen loot impossible.

An additional factor deterring loot was the 1857 Sepoy Mutiny. Though crushed, it reminded the British vividly that they were a tiny ethnic group who could not rule a gigantic subcontinent without the support of important locals. After 1857, the British stopped annexing one princely state after another, and instead treated the princes as allies. Land revenue was fixed in absolute terms, partly to prevent local unrest and partly to promote the notion of the white man's burden. The empire proclaimed itself to be a protector of the Indian peasant against exploitation by Indian elites. This was denounced as hypocrisy by nationalists like Dadabhoy Naoroji in the 19th century, who complained that land taxes led to an enormous drain from India to Britain.

Objective calculations by historians like Adams Maddison suggest a drain of perhaps 1.6 percent of Indian Gross National Product in the 19th century. But land revenue was more or less fixed by the Raj in absolute terms and so its real value diminished rapidly with inflation in the 20th century. By World War II, India had ceased to be a profit centre for the British Empire.

Historically, conquered nations paid taxes to finance fresh wars of the conqueror. India itself was asked to pay a large sum at the end of World War I to help repair Britain's finances. But, as shown by historian Indivar

Kamtekar, the independence movement led by Gandhiji changed the political landscape, and made mass taxation of India increasingly difficult. By World War II, this had become politically impossible. Far from taxing India to pay for World War II, Britain actually began paying India for its contribution of men and goods. Troops from white dominions like Australia, Canada and New Zealand were paid for entirely by these countries, but Indian costs were shared by the British government. Britain paid in the form of non-convertible sterling balances, which mounted swiftly. The conqueror was paying the conquered, undercutting the profitability on which all empire is funded. Churchill opposed this, and wanted to tax India rather than owe it money. But he was overruled by India hands who said India would resist payment, and paralyze the war effort. Leo Amery, Secretary of State for India, said that when you are driving in a taxi to the station to catch a life-or-death train, you do not loudly announce that you have doubts whether to pay the fare. Thus, World War II converted India from a debtor to a creditor with *over* one billion pounds in sterling balances. Britain, meanwhile, became the biggest debtor in the world. It's not worth ruling over people you are afraid to tax.

Q6. Which one of the following best expresses the main purpose of the author?

(a) To present the various reasons that can lead to the collapse of an empire and the granting of independence to the subjects of an empire.

(b) To point out the critical role played by the 'white man's burden' in making a colonizing power give up its claims to native possessions.

(c) To highlight the contradictory impulse underpinning empire building which is a costly business but very attractive at the same time.

(d) To illustrate how erosion of the financial basis of an empire supports the granting of independence to an empire's constituents

Q7. Which of the following was not a reason for the emergence of the 'white man's burden' as a new rationale for empire building in India?

(a) The emergence of the idea of the public good as an element of governance.

(b) The decreasing returns from imperial loot and increasing costs of conquest.

(c) The weakening of the immorality attached to an emperor's looting behaviour.

(d) A growing awareness of the idea of equality among peoples.

Q8. Which of the following best captures the meaning of the 'white man's burden', as it is used by the author?

(a) British claim to a civilizing mission directed at ensuring the good of the natives.

(b) Inspiration for the French and American revolutions.

(c) Resource drain that had to be borne by the home country's white population.

(d) Imperative that made open looting of resources impossible.

Q9. What was the main lesson the British learned from the Sepoy Mutiny of 1857?

(a) That the local princes were allies, not foes.

(b) That the land revenue from India would decline dramatically.

(c) That the British were a small ethnic group.

(d) That India would be increasingly difficult to rule.

Q10. Why didn't Britain tax India to finance its World War II efforts?

(a) Australia Canada and New Zealand had offered to pay for Indian troops.

(b) India had already paid a sufficiently large sum during World War I.

(c) It was afraid that if India refused to pay, Britain's war efforts would be jeopardized.

(d) The British empire was built on the premise that the conqueror pays the conquered.

PASSAGE 3 [CAT 2003 (CANCELLED)]

The controversy over genetically modified food continues unabated in the West. Genetic modification (GM) is the science by which the genetic material of a plant is altered, perhaps to make it more resistant to pests or killer weeds, or to enhance its nutritional value. Many food biotechnologists claim that GM will be a major contribution of science to mankind in the 21st century. On the other hand, large numbers of opponents, mainly in Europe claim that the benefits of GM are a myth propagated by multinational corporations to increase their profits, that they pose a health hazard, and have therefore, called for governments to ban the sale of genetically-modified food.

The anti-GM campaign has been quite effective in Europe, with several European Union member countries imposing a virtual ban for five years over genetically modified food imports. Since the genetically-modified food industry is particularly strong in the United States of America, the controversy also constitutes another chapter in the US-Europe skirmishes which have become particularly acerbic after the US invasion of Iraq.

To a large extent, the GM controversy has been ignored in the Indian media, although Indian biotechnologists have been quite active in GM research. Several groups of Indian biotechnologists have been working on various issues connected with crops grown in India. One concrete achievement, which has recently figured in the news is that of a team led by the former vice-chancellor of Jawaharlal Nehru University, Asis Datta—it has successfully added an extra gene to potatoes to enhance the protein content of the tuber by at least 30 percent. Not surprisingly, the new potato has been called the protato. The protato is now in its third year of field trials. It is quite likely that the GM controversy will soon hit the headlines in India since a spokesperson of the Indian Central government has recently announced that the government may use the protato in its midday meal programme for schools as early as next year.

Why should 'scientific progress", with huge potential benefits to the poor and malnourished, be so controversial'? The anti-GM lobby contends that pernicious propaganda has vastly exaggerated the benefits of GM and completely evaded the costs which will have to be incurred if the genetically-modified food industry is allowed to grow unchecked. In particular, they allude to different types of costs.

This group contends that the most important potential cost is that the widespread distribution and growth of genetically modified food will enable the corporate world (alias the multinational corporations–MNCs) completely capture the food chain. A "small" group of biotech companies will patent the transferred genes as well as the technology associated with them. They will then buy up the competing seed merchants and seed-breeding centres, thereby controlling the production of food at every possible level. Independent farmers, big and small, will be completely wiped out of the food industry. At best, they will be reduced to the status of being subcontractors.

This line of argument goes on to claim that the control of the food chain will be disastrous for the poor since the MNCs , guided by the profit motive, will only focus on the high-value food items demanded by the affluent in the long run, the production of basic staples which constitute the food basket of the poor will taper.

However, this vastly overestimates the power of the MNCs. Even if the research promoted by them does focus on the high-value food items, much of biotechnology research is also funded by governments in both developing and developed countries. Indeed, the protato is a by-product of this type of research. If the protato passes the field trials, there is no reason to believe that it cannot be marketed in the global potato market. And this type of success story can be repeated with other basic food items.

The second type of cost associated with the genetically-modified food industry is environmental damage. The most common type of "genetic engineering" involves gene modification in plants designed to make them resistant to applications of weed-killers. This then enables farmers to use massive dosages of weed-killers so as to destroy or wipe out all competing varieties of plants in their fields. However, some weeds through genetically-modified pollen contamination, may acquire resistance to a variety of weed-killers. The only way to destroy these weeds is through the use of ever-stronger herbicides which are poisonous and linger on in the environment.

Q11. Using the clues in the passage, which of the following countries would *you* expect to be in the forefront of the anti-GM campaign?

(a) USA and Spain
(b) India and Iraq
(c) Germany and France
(d) Australia and New Zealand.

Q12. The author doubts the anti-GM lobby's contention that MNC control of the food chain will be disastrous for the poor because:

(a) MNCs will focus on high-value food items.
(b) MNCs are driven by the motive of profit maximization.
(c) MNCs are not the only group of actors in genetically-modified food research.
(d) economic development will help the poor buy MNC-produced food.

Q13. Which of the following about the Indian media's coverage of scientific research does the passage seem to suggest?

(a) Indian media generally covers a subject of scientific importance when its mass application is likely.
(b) Indian media's coverage of scientific research is generally dependent on MNCs' interests.
(c) Indian media, in partnership with the government, is actively involved in publicizing the results of scientific research.
(d) Indian media only highlights scientific research which is funded by the government.

Q14. Genetic modification makes plants more resistant to killer weeds. However, this can lead to environmental damage by:

(a) wiping out competing varieties of plants which now fall prey to killer-weeds.
(b) forcing application of stronger herbicides to kill weeds which have become resistant to weak herbicides.

(c) forcing application of stronger herbicides to keep the competing plants weed-free.
(d) not allowing growth of any weeds, thus reducing soil fertility.

Q15. According to the passage, biotechnology research:
(a) Is of utility only for high value food items.
(b) Is funded only by multinational corporations.
(c) allows multinational corporations to control the food basket of the poor.
(d) Addresses the concerns of rich and poor countries.

PASSAGE 4 [CAT 2003 (CANCELLED)]

Modern science, exclusive of geometry, is a comparatively recent creation and can be said to have originated with Galileo and Newton. Galileo was the first scientist to recognize clearly that the only way to further our understanding of the physical world was to resort to experiment. However obvious Galileo's contention may appear in the light of our present knowledge, it remains a fact that the Greeks, in spite of their proficiency in geometry, never seem to have realized the importance of experiment. To a certain extent, this may be attributed to the crudeness of their instruments of measurement. Still, an excuse of this sort can scarcely be put forward when the elementary nature of Galileo's experiments and observations is recalled. Watching a lamp oscillate in the cathedral of Pisa, dropping bodies from the leaning tower of Pisa, rolling balls down inclined planes, noticing the magnifying effect of water in a spherical glass vase, such was the nature of Galileo's experiments and observations. As can be seen, they might just as well have been performed by the Greeks. At any rate, it was thanks to such experiments that Galileo discovered the fundamental law of dynamics, according to which the acceleration imparted to a body is proportional to the force acting upon it.

The next advance was due to Newton, the greatest scientist of all time if account be taken of his joint contributions to mathematics and physics. As a physicist, he was of course an ardent adherent of the empirical method, but his greatest title to fame lies in another direction. Prior to Newton, mathematics, chiefly in the form of geometry, had been studied as a fine art without any view to its physical applications, other than in very trivial cases. But with Newton, all the resources of mathematics were turned to advantage in the solution of physical problems. Thenceforth, mathematics appeared as an instrument of discovery, the most powerful one known to man, multiplying the power of thought just as in the mechanical domain, the lever multiplied our physical action. It is this application of mathematics to the solution of physical problems, this combination of two separate fields of investigation, which constitutes the essential characteristic of the Newtonian method. Thus, problems of physics were metamorphosed into problems of mathematics.

But in Newton's day, the mathematical instrument was still in a very backward state of development. In this field again, Newton showed the mark of genius by inventing the integral calculus. As a result of this remarkable discovery, problems, which would have baffled Archimedes, were solved with ease. We know that in Newton's hands, this new departure in scientific method led to the discovery of the law of gravitation. But here again the real significance of Newton's achievement lay not so much in the exact quantitative formulation of the law of attraction, as in his having established the presence of law and order at least in one important realm of nature, namely, in the motions of heavenly bodies. Nature thus exhibited rationality and was not mere blind chaos and uncertainty. To be sure, Newton's investigations had been concerned with but a small group of natural phenomena, but it appeared unlikely that this mathematical law and order should turn out to be restricted to certain special phenomena; and the feeling was general that all the physical processes of nature would prove to be unfolding themselves according to rigorous mathematical laws.

When Einstein, in 1905, published his celebrated paper on the electrodynamics of moving bodies, he remarked that the difficulties, which surrounded the equations of electrodynamics, together with the negative experiments of Michelson and others, would be obviated if we extended the validity of the Newtonian principle of relativity to the Galilean motion, which applied solely to mechanical phenomena, so as to include all manner of phenomena: electrodynamics, optical, etc. When extended in this way, the Newtonian principle of relativity became Einstein's special principle of relativity. Its significance lay in its assertion that absolute Galilean motion or absolute velocity must ever escape all experimental detection. Henceforth, absolute velocity should be conceived of as physically meaningless, not only in the particular realm of mechanics, as in Newton's day but in the entire realm of physical phenomena. Einstein's special principle, by adding increased emphasis to this relativity of velocity, making absolute velocity metaphysically meaningless, created a still more profound distinction between velocity and accelerated or rotational motion. This latter type of motion remained absolute and real as before. It is most important to understand this point and to realize that Einstein's special principle is merely an extension of the validity of the classical Newtonian principle to all classes of phenomena.

Q16. According to the author, why did the Greeks NOT conduct experiments to understand the physical world?

(a) Apparently they did not think it necessary to experiment.
(b) They focused exclusively on geometry.
(c) Their instruments of measurement were very crude.
(d) The Greeks considered the application of geometry to the physical world more important.

Q17. Newton may be considered one of the greatest scientists of all time because he:
(a) discovered the law of gravitation.
(b) married physics with mathematics.
(c) invented integral calculus.
(d) started the use of the empirical method in science.

Q18. The statement "nature thus exhibited rationality and was not mere blind chaos and uncertainty" suggests that:
(a) problems that had baffled scientists like Archimedes were not really problems.
(b) only a small group of natural phenomena was chaotic.
(c) physical phenomena conformed to mathematical laws.
(d) natural phenomena were evolving towards a less chaotic future.

Q19. The significant implication of Einstein's special principle of relativity is that:
(a) absolute velocity was meaningless in the realm of all physical phenomena.
(b) Newton's principle of relativity needs to be modified.
(c) there are limits to which experimentation can be used to understand some physical phenomena.
(d) it is meaningless to try to understand the distinction between velocity and accelerated or rotational motion.

Q20. Which of the following statements about modern science best captures the theme of the passage?
(a) Modern science rests firmly on the platform built by the Greeks.
(b) We need to go back to the method of enquiry used by the Greeks to better understand the laws of dynamics.
(c) Disciplines like Mathematics and Physics function best when integrated into one.
(d) New knowledge about natural phenomena builds on existing knowledge.

Directions for the questions (21-25): The poem given below is followed by five questions. Choose the best answer to each question.

As you set out for Ithaka
hope the journey is a long one,
full of adventure, full of discovery.
Laistrygonians and Cyclops,
angry Poseidon–don't be afraid of them:
you'll never find things like that on your way.
as long as you keep your thoughts raised high,
as long as a rare excitement
stirs your spirit and your body.
Laistrygonians and Cyclops,
wild Poseidon–you won't encounter them
unless you bring them along inside your soul,
unless your soul sets them up in front of you.
Hope the voyage is a long one,
may there be many a summer morning when
with what pleasure, what joy,
you come into harbours seen for the first time;
may you stop at Phoenician trading stations
mother of pearl and coral, amber and ebony
sensual perfume of every kind
as many sensual perfumes as you can;
and may you visit many Egyptian cities
to gather stores of knowledge from their scholars.

Keep Ithaka always in your mind.

Arriving there is what you are destined for.
But do not hurry the journey at all.
Better if it lasts for years.
so you are old by the time you reach the island,
wealthy with all you have gained on the way,
not expecting Ithaka to make you rich.
Ithaka gave you a marvelous journey,
without her you would not have set out.
She has nothing left to give you now.

And if you find her poor, Ithaka won't have fooled you
Wise as you will have become, so full of experience,
you will have understood by then what these Ithakas mean.

Q21. Which of the following best reflects the central theme of this poem?
(a) If you don't have high expectations, you will not be disappointed.

(b) Don't rush to your goal; the journey is what enriches you.
(c) The longer the journey, the greater the experiences you gather.
(d) You cannot reach Ithaka without visiting Egyptian ports.

Q22. The poet recommends a long journey. Which of the following is the most comprehensive reason for it?
(a) You can gain knowledge as well as sensual experience.
(b) You can visit new cities and harbours.
(c) You can experience the full range of sensuality.
(d) You can buy a variety of fine things.

Q23. In the poem, Ithaka is a symbol of:
(a) the divine mother
(b) your inner self
(c) the path to wisdom
(d) life's distant goal

Q24. What does the poet mean by 'Laistrygonians' and 'Cyclops'?
(a) Creatures which, along with Poseidon, one finds during a journey.
(b) Mythological characters that one should not be afraid of.
(c) Intra-personal obstacles that hinder one's journey.
(d) Problems that one has to face to derive the most from one's journey

Q25. Which of the following best reflects the tone of the poem?
(a) Prescribing
(b) Exhorting
(c) Pleading
(d) Consoling

Answer Key

I

Passage 1

1. (a) **2.** (c) **3.** (a) **4.** (d) **5.** (b)

Passage 2

6. (a) **7.** (d) **8.** (d) **9.** (b) **10.** (b)

Passage 3

11. (a) **12.** (c) **13.** (d) **14.** (b)

Passage 4

15. (c) **16.** (a) **17.** (d) **18.** (c) **19.** (d) **20.** (c)

Passage 5

21. (c) **22.** (c) **23.** (a) **24.** (a) **25.** (d) **26.** (b)

Passage 6

27. (b) **28.** (b) **29.** (a) **30.** (b)

II

Passage 1

1. (b) **2.** (b) **3.** (a) **4.** (d) **5.** (b) **6.** (d)

Passage 2

7. (d) **8.** (c) **9.** (b) **10.** (c) **11.** (a)

Passage 3

12. (d) **13.** (b) **14.** (d) **15.** (a) **16.** (b)

Passage 4

17. (a) **18.** (d) **19.** (d) **20.** (b) **21.** (c)

Passage 5

22. (d) **23.** (b) **24.** (a) **25.** (d) **26.** (a) **27.** (c)

III

Passage 1

1. (b) **2.** (a) **3.** (c) **4.** (d) **5.** (a) **6.** (c) **7.** (d) **8.** (b)

Passage 2

9. (c) 10. (b) 11. (d) 12. (b) 13. (a)
14. (c) 15. (a) 16. (d)

Passage 3

17. (b) 18. (c) 19. (a) 20. (c) 21. (d)
22. (d) 23. (b) 24. (a)

Passage 4

25. (c) 26. (b) 27. (c) 28. (d) 29. (a)
30. (d) 31. (a) 32. (b)

Passage 5

33. (c) 34. (a) 35. (d) 36. (c) 37. (a)
38. (b) 39. (d) 40. (b)

IV

Passage 1

1. (a) 2. (d) 3. (c) 4. (b) 5. (a)
6. (b) 7. (a) 8. (d) 9. (b)

Passage 2

10. (a) 11. (b) 12. (d) 13. (b) 14. (a)
15. (c) 16. (a) 17. (c) 18. (c)

Passage 3

19. (a) 20. (b) 21. (b) 22. (d) 23. (d)
24. (c) 25. (d) 26. (c) 27. (b) 28. (a)

Passage 4

29. (d) 30. (c) 31. (d) 32. (c) 33. (a)
34. (c) 35. (d) 36. (c) 37. (a) 38. (b)

Passage 5

39. (c) 40. (b) 41. (b) 42. (c) 43. (b)
44. (a) 45. (a) 46. (d) 47. (b) 48. (a)
49. (d) 50. (b)

V

Passage 1

1. (c) 2. (a) 3. (c) 4. (d) 5. (a)
6. (d) 7. (b) 8. (b) 9. (c) 10. (b)

Passage 2

11. (a) 12. (b) 13. (d) 14. (a) 15. (b)
16. (c) 17. (a)

Passage 3

18. (b) 19. (c) 20. (a) 21. (c) 22. (d)
23. (c) 24. (c) 25. (a) 26. (a) 27. (b)

Passage 4

28. (b) 29. (c) 30. (c) 31. (a)

VI

Passage 1

1. (b) 2. (d) 3. (b) 4. (a)

Passage 2

5. (b) 6. (c) 7. (d) 8. (a) 9. (a)

Passage 3

10. (d) 11. (a) 12. (d) 13. (b)

Passage 4

14. (b) 15. (d) 16. (b) 17. (c)

Passage 5

18. (c) 19. (c) 20. (c) 21. (c)

VII

PASSAGE 1

1. (c) 2. (b) 3. (c) 4. (d) 5. (a)

PASSAGE 2

6. (a) 7. (d) 8. (d) 9. (d) 10. (b) 11. (d)

PASSAGE 3

12. (b) 13. (b) 14. (d) 15. (d)

PASSAGE 4

16. (d) 17. (a) 18. (a) 19. (b) 20. (a)

PASSAGE 5

21. (c) 22. (d) 23. (c) 24. (a) 25. (c)

VIII

PASSAGE 1

1. (b) 2. (d) 3. (d) 4. (b) 5. (a)

PASSAGE 2

6. (d) 7. (a) 8. (d) 9. (c) 10. (c)

PASSAGE 3

11. (c) 12. (c) 13. (a) 14. (b) 15. (a)

PASSAGE 4

16. (a) 17. (b) 18. (c) 19. (a) 20. (d)

PASSAGE 5

21. (b) 22. (a) 23. (d) 24. (c) 25. (b)

PART 2 Verbal Ability

The chapters in this part will help you to hone your language skills in the following ways:

- Helping you to identify and use words of varying frequency levels as have been seen in CAT and other MBA entrance exams as well as in normal usage in English.
- Making you understand important roots, prefixes and suffixes and foreign words used in the English language.
- Helping you understand words that are often confused with each other. (Note: This is very crucial in CAT and all other exams over the past few years.)

Key Components of this part:

- **Words of different difficulty levels**
- **Bit-by-bit explanation of words in English language**
- **Theoretical inputs and level of Difficulty based exercises from the areas of**
  - **Fill in the Blanks**
  - **Paragraph Jumbles**
  - **Sentence Corrections**
  - **Phrasal Verbs**
  - **Paragraph Completion/ Last Sentence of the Paragraph**
  - **Irrelevant Statement**
  - **Summary of the Paragraph**

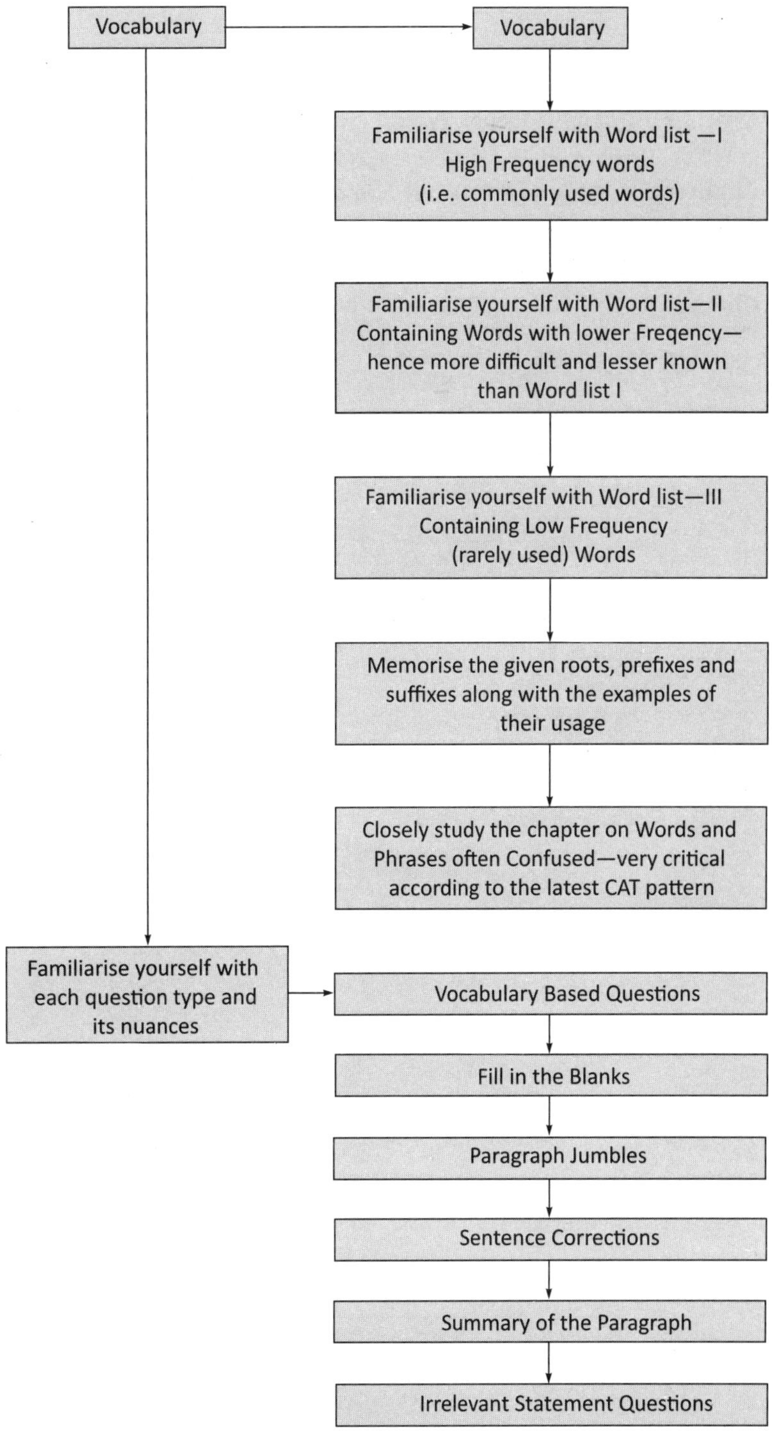

In This Part

Section 1: **Vocabulary**
Section 2: **Vocabulary-Based Questions**
Section 3: **Fill in the Blanks**
Section 4: **Paragraph Jumbles**
Section 5: **Sentence Correction**
Section 6: **New Verbal Question Types in CAT**

SECTION 1: Vocabulary

This section is divided into following five chapters.

Chapter 1 (High Frequency Words) gives you a list of words which you can expect to see in your day to day newspaper reading.

Chapter 2 (Medium Frequency Words) and **Chapter 3** (Low Frequency Words) gives you a list of progressively difficult words that you can expect in more complicated reading.

Chapter 4 gives you a comprehensive listing of roots, prefixes, suffixes and words of foreign origin.

Chapter 5 gives you a unique list of words and phrases which are often confused.

CHAPTER 1

Word List I—High Frequency Words

In this chapter, we will discuss words that are frequently asked in CAT examinations. The treatment has been done in such a manner that the meaning is given first, followed by the synonym (denoted by the letter *S*) and antonym (denoted by the letter *A*).

No.	Word	Definition
		A
1.	**abandon**	*to give up* *S: Desert, Forsake, Leave* *A: Retain unrestrained activity*
2.	**abase**	*to humiliate* *S: Scorn, Belittle, Degrade* *A: Exalt, Cherish*
3.	**abate**	*to lessen; to subside*
4.	**abbreviate**	*to shorten* *S: Abridge, Condense* *A: Expand, Prolong*
5.	**abdicate**	*to give up formally* *S: Resign, Renounce* *A: Retain, Uphold*
6.	**abdication**	*giving up control, authority*
7.	**aberration**	*straying away from what is normal*
8.	**abet**	*to assist (normally a crime)* *S: Conspire, Connive* *A: Dissuade, Deter*
9.	**abhor**	*to hate; to detest*
10.	**abide**	*be faithful; to endure*
11.	**abjure**	*promise or swear to give up*
12.	**ablution**	*washing*
13.	**abridgement**	*a short summary* *S: Outline, Abbreviation, Summary, Abstract* *A: Enlargement, Expansion*
14.	**abscond**	*to go away suddenly (to avoid arrest)*
15.	**abstruse**	*difficult to comprehend; obscure*
16.	**abysmal**	*extremely bad*
17.	**abyss**	*a bottomless pit, anything too deep to measure* *S: Chasm.* *A: Summit, Elevation*
18.	**accede**	*agree to* *S: Assent, Concur* *A: Refuse, Dissent*
19.	**acclaimed**	*welcomed with shouts and approval*
20.	**accolade**	*praise; approval*
21.	**accost**	*to approach and speak to* *S: Greet* *A: Shun, Avoid*
22.	**accredit**	*to approve, certify*
23.	**accomplice**	*a partner in crime*
24.	**acquaint**	*to inform, to make familiar*
25.	**acquit**	*to clear (a person) of a charge*
26.	**acrid**	*sharp (as in speech)*
27.	**acrimony**	*bitterness or harshness of speech or manner*
28.	**acronym**	*word formed from the initial letters of a group of words.*
29.	**acumen**	*Keenness of mind, Insight*
30.	**adage**	*An old saying, Proverb*
31.	**adamant**	*inflexible*
32.	**addle**	*to become rotten; to become confused*

33. **adduce** *to offer as example, reason or proof*
34. **adjudicate** *to settle judicially*
35. **adjure** *to beg; appeal*
36. **admonish** *to warn, reprove mildly*
S: Censure, Rebuke
A: Applaud, Praise, Compliment
37. **admonitory** *containing warning*
38. **ado** *fuss, trouble*
S: Bustle, Commotion
39. **adorn** *add beauty; decorate*
40. **adroit** *skilful and clever*
S: Proficient, Dextrous
A: Awkward, Dull
41. **adulteration** *making impure, poorer in quality*
42. **advent** *an arrival, coming*
43. **adventitious** *coming from another source and not innate*
44. **adversary** *enemy, opponent*
45. **adversity** *misfortune, troubled state*
S: Distress, Ill luck
A: Fortune
46. **advert** *to call attention to, refer to*
47. **aeon** *eternity, immeasurable period*
48. **affable** *polite and friendly*
49. **affinity** *close connection, relationship*
50. **affirm** *to declare positively, to confirm*
S: Assert, Declare, Assure
51. **agape** *the mouth open wide with surprise*
52. **aggravate** *make worse; irritate*
53. **agile** *active; quick-moving*
54. **agog** *eager; excited*
55. **ail** *trouble; be ill*
56. **alacrity** *eager and cheerful readiness*
57. **alcove** *recess; partially enclosed place*
58. **alienate** *cause to make unfriendly, to distance oneself.*
S: Estrange
A: Familiarise
59. **allay** *to calm, quieten*
S: Soothe, Pacify
A: Agitate, Kindle
60. **allegiance** *duty; support; loyalty*
61. **alleviate** *make (pain) easier to bear*
62. **allocate** *to set apart for a specific purpose*
63. **alloy** *mixture of two or more metals*
64. **allure** *to tempt with something desirable*
S: Lure, Inveigle
A: Repel, Deter, Discourage
65. **aloof** *reserved; indifferent*
66. **amalgamate** *mix, combine, unite*
67. **ambient** *Surround on all sides*
68. **ambiguous** *doubtful; uncertain*
69. **amble** *leisurely walk*
70. **amiable** *good natured*
S: Gentle, Pleasing, Charming
A: Sullen, Churlish, quarrelsome
71. **amicable** *friendly, peaceful*
A: Warlike, Argumentative
72. **amnesia** *partial or total loss of memory*
73. **amorphous** *without definite form*
S: Undefinable
A: Crystalline, definite
74. **analogy** *similarity in some way*
75. **anarchy** *absence of government, political disorder*
A: Order, Discipline
76. **ancillary** *helping, subordinate*
77. **anguish** *severe suffering*
78. **animosity** *feeling of strong dislike*
S: Enmity, Hostility, Rancour, Animus
A: Amiability, Friendliness
79. **annihilate** *to destroy completely*
80. **annuity** *a fixed sum paid every year*
81. **annul** *to do away with*
A: Enforce
82. **anoint** *to put oil on as part of a ceremony*
83. **anomaly** *departure from the usual*
S: Abnormality
A: Normality
84. **anon** *soon*
A: Normality
85. **antidote** *medicine used against a poison or a disease*
86. **apiary** *a place where bees are kept*
87. **appease** *make quiet or calm*
88. **appraise** *to assess the value, evaluate*
S: Assess
89. **apprehensive** *unhappy feeling about future; anxious*
90. **apprise** *give notice; to inform*
91. **arcade** *a covered passage (especially lined with shops)*
92. **arcane** *secret, mysterious*
93. **archaic** *ancient, old-fashioned*
94. **archives** *collection of the historical records or documents of a government or organisation*
95. **arid** *dry and barren, dull*
S: Parched, Dry, Bare
A: Lush, Fertile
96. **arrogance** *proud superior manner of behaviour*
97. **articulate** *to express oneself in words clearly*
98. **articulate** *speak distinctly; connect by joints*
99. **artefact** *a hand-made object*
100. **ascend** *go or come up*
101. **ascendancy** *dominance*
102. **ascertain** *get to know*

103. **ashen** *deadly pale*
104. **asterisk** *the star-shaped symbol (*)*
105. **astringent** *substance that shrinks*
106. **atheism** *the belief that there is no god*
107. **atonement** *repayment, death of Jesus, make amends*
108. **attune** *bring into harmony*
109. **audacious** *daring; foolishly bold; impudent*
110. **august** *majestic; venerable*
111. **auspicious** *favorable; successful; prosperous*
112. **austere** *severely moral and strict; simple and plain*
113. **auxiliary** *helping; supporting*
114. **aver** *affirm; assert; prove; justify*
115. **aversion** *strong dislike*
116. **avid** *eager; greedy*
117. **avow** *admit; declare openly*

B

118. **babble** *to talk foolishly or like a small child.*
S: Prattle, Chatter, Palaver
A: Wisdom, Wit, Prudence
119. **bacchanalia** *orgy, wild-drunken party*
120. **backlog** *an accumulation or reserve*
121. **badger** *to nag, annoy, an animal*
122. **bait** *to persecute; piece of food put in a trap to attract*
123. **baleful** *harmful; ominous; causing evil*
124. **balk** *obstacle; purposely to get on the way of*
125. **banal** *trite, commonplace*
S: Inane, Vapid
A: Fresh, Original, New
126. **barbaric** *Primitive, Uncivilised, Cruel*
S: Savage, Inhuman, Tyrannical
A: Civilised, Humane, Cultured
127. **barrage** *heavy attack*
128. **barrage** *artificial obstacle built across a river*
129. **barren** *not good enough; unable to have young ones, without value*
130. **bashful** *easily embarrassed*
S: Shy, Diffident
A: Bold, Adventurous, Arrogant
131. **bask** *enjoy warmth and light*
132. **beacon** *a light used for warning or guiding*
133. **benediction** *something that promotes goodness or well-being*
134. **benefactor** *person who has given help*
135. **benevolence** *wish or activity in doing good*
136. **benign** *kind and gentle; mild (climate)*
137. **berate** *scold sharply*
138. **bereave** *to leave in a sad or lonely state, as by death*
139. **bereft** *rob or dispossess of something (material)*
140. **berserk** *in or into a violent rage or frenzy*
S: Wild, Frenzied
A: Calm, Tranquil
141. **besiege** *to overwhelm, surround*
142. **besotted** *made silly or stupid by love*
143. **bestial** *like a beast*
S: Brutish, Savage, Barbaric
A: Civilised, Cultured, Learned
144. **bewilder** *puzzle; confuse*
145. **bigot** *stubborn; narrow-minded person*
146. **bizarre** *odd, grotesque*
S: Eccentric, Unexpected
A: Plain, Commonplace
147. **bland** *uninteresting*
148. **blast** *explosion; gust of wind*
149. **blatant** *boldly conspicuous or obtrusive*
A: Obscure, Subtle, Hidden
150. **blatant** *noisy and rough*
151. **blemish** *to mar or spoil, a defect*
S: Flaw, Imperfection
A: Embellishment
152. **bogus** *sham; counterfeit; not genuine*
153. **boisterous** *loud; noisy; rough; lacking restraint*
154. **bolster** *give greatly needed support*
155. **boorish** *crude; offensive; rude*
156. **brainchild** *a person's own idea*
157. **brash** *hasty; rush; cheeky; saucy*
158. **brass** *an alloy of copper and zinc*
159. **bravado** *pretended courage or feigned confidence*
A: Cowardice
160. **bravura** *boldness, dashing style*
161. **brazen** *shameless, bold*
S: Daring
A: Submissive, Humble
162. **breach** *a violation, gap; opening; broken place; breaking*
163. **brittle** *easily broken*
164. **broach** *bring up; announce; begin to talk about*

C

165. **cacophony** *harsh sound*
166. **cajole** *use flattery or deceit; to persuade*
167. **callous** *hardened, unyielding*
S: Obdurate, Insensible
A: Compassionate, Sympathetic
168. **camaraderie** *friendship*
169. **camouflage** *a disguise in order to conceal*
170. **candid** *frank; straightforward*
171. **canon** *a basic law or principle by which something is judged.*

172. **cant**	*insincere talk; tilt; overturn*
173. **canvass**	*discuss thoroughly; sort of touting; try to get votes or support*
174. **cardinal**	*principal, chief, most important* *S: Fundamental, Vital* *A: Insignificant, Negligible, Minor*
175. **caricature**	*an exaggerated imitation of a person* *S: Exaggeration, Parody, and Mimicry* *A: Reality*
176. **catalyst**	*substance that causes speeding up*
177. **cataract**	*a large waterfall; an eye disease*
178. **catholic**	*comprehensive; universal*
179. **caustic**	*biting; sarcastic*
180. **cede/cession**	*to surrender possession of, especially by treaty*
181. **celerity**	*rapidity of motion or action*
182. **celestial**	*of the heavens and sky* *S: Heavenly, Divine* *A: Mortal, Earthly, Terrestrial*
183. **celibacy**	*complete sexual abstinence, the state of being unmarried* *A: Matrimony*
184. **censure**	*expression of blame or disapproval; a rebuke*
185. **chaff**	*to tease good-naturedly; grain husk*
186. **charismatic**	*possessing spiritual grace, inspiring* *A: Uninspiring*
187. **chisel**	*steel tool for shaping materials*
188. **chromatic**	*of colour*
189. **circumscribe**	*to draw line around; to limit*
190. **clamor**	*shout; complain with a lot of noise*
191. **clerical**	*of the clergy or clerk*
192. **clientele**	*customers*
193. **clinch**	*settle conclusively*
194. **cling**	*to resist separation; hold tightly*
195. **clot**	*half-solid lump formed from liquid*
196. **coax**	*get somebody to do something by kindness*
197. **coerce**	*compel or force to make obedient*
198. **cognizant**	*being fully aware of*
199. **collusion**	*secret agreement for a deceitful purpose*
200. **comatose**	*of, like or in a coma, lethargic* *S: Unconscious* *A: Alert*
201. **combustion**	*process of burning*
202. **comely**	*attractive*
203. **commuter**	*person who travels regularly*
204. **compatible**	*getting along or going together* *A: Opposite, Intolerant*
205. **conceal**	*hide; keep secret*
206. **concede**	*to admit as true, accept* *S: Surrender, Admit, Own* *A: Deny, Refuse, Disagree*
207. **conceited**	*having an excessively high opinion of oneself*
208. **concise**	*brief and to the point* *S: Compact, Short, Terse* *A: Diffuse, Repetitive, Wordy*
209. **concord**	*agreement or harmony*
210. **concur**	*agree in opinion; happen to-gether*
211. **condense**	*increase in density, strength; make short*
212. **condone**	*forgive*
213. **conduct**	*manage, to lead* *S: To direct, To transmit or convey, Guide* *A: Desert, Abandon, Forego*
214. **congenial**	*kindred, compatible*
215. **conjure**	*to summon as if by magic*
216. **connive**	*to pretend not to look (at crime, etc.), Assist.*
217. **conspicuous**	*easily seen; remarkable*
218. **constrain**	*compel*
219. **constrict**	*make tight or smaller*
220. **construe**	*to interpret, to analyse* *S: Translate, Explain*
221. **consume**	*get to the end of; eat*
222. **conviction**	*firm belief*
223. **cordial**	*warm and sincere*
224. **correlate**	*have a mutual relation*
225. **corroboration**	*additional strengthening evidence*
226. **countenance**	*to favor or approve of*
227. **counterfeit**	*forgery*
228. **covetous**	*eagerly desirous*
229. **cower**	*crouch; shrink back*
230. **coy**	*shy, modest (esp of a girl)*
231. **crass**	*stupid*
232. **crease**	*line made by crushing white line on the ground in cricket; crush*
233. **cringe**	*to behave in an excessively servile way; flinch*
234. **cryptic**	*secret; with a hidden meaning*
235. **cumbersome**	*burdensome; heavy and awkward to carry*
236. **cupidity**	*greed; lust*
237. **curriculum**	*course of study*
238. **cursory**	*quick, hurried*
239. **curtail**	*make shorter than was planned*

D

240. **dabble**	*to play in water as with hands*
241. **daft**	*silly, inane* *S: Idiotic, Foolish* *A: Profound, Wise, Intelligent*
242. **dainty**	*pretty, delicate (food); difficult to please*
243. **dally**	*to deal carelessly (with), trifle*

244. **dearth** *shortage*
245. **debacle** *a breakup; overthrow; sudden disaster*
246. **debutante** *a girl making her social debut*
247. **deciduous** *ephemeral; of a tree shedding its leaves annually*
248. **decisive** *that settles a dispute*
A: Indecisive
249. **declaim/ declamation** *to speak pompously or bombastically; protest loudly*
250. **decorum** *propriety; properness*
251. **decree** *order given by authority*
252. **decry** *disapprove of*
253. **defer** *to postpone; to yield due to respect*
S: Delay, Adjourn
A: Expedite, hasten, Quicken
254. **defiance** *open disobedience or resistance*
255. **defile** *to pollute, to corrupt*
A: Glorify
256. **definitive** *conclusive, final*
S: Precise
A: Vague, Confused
257. **deft** *skilful*
S: Adept, Dexterous, Agile
A: Awkward, Clumsy, Inept
258. **demean** *to degrade*
S: Humble
A: Honour, Revere
259. **demur** *to hesitate; raise objections*
260. **demure** *decorous, modest*
S: Coy, Shy
A: Brazen, Impudent, Shameless
261. **denizen** *an inhabitant or frequenter of a particular place*
S: Citizen
A: Alien, Foreigner
262. **denounce** *condemn publicly*
263. **deplete** *use until none remains*
264. **depreciate** *to lessen in value*
S: Undervalue, Lower, Decry
A: Boost, Raise, Praise
265. **derivative** *unoriginal; obtained from another source*
266. **derogatory** *insulting; tending to damage*
267. **desiccant** *substance used to absorb moisture*
268. **despicable** *deserving scorn*
S: Low, Mean, Cowardly
A: High, Noble, Exalted
269. **despot** *An absolute ruler*
S: Tyrant
A: Democrat
270. **deter** *discourage; hinder*
271. **detraction** *slandering; verbal attack; aspersion*
272. **detriment** *damage*
S: Harm, Hurt, Injury
A: Advantage, Gain, Interest
273. **deviance** *being different in moral standards (from normal)*
274. **devious** *not direct, roundabout, Not honest*
S: cunning, Underhand
A: Straightforward, Honest
275. **dexterity** *skill (esp. in handling)*
276. **diffidence** *shyness*
277. **dilapidated** *falling to pieces (due to a severe earthquake)*
278. **dilate** *speak comprehensively; become wider, large*
279. **dilatory** *intended to delay*
280. **disabuse** *to free from error*
281. **disallow** *refuse to allow or accept as correct*
282. **discern** *see with an effort but clearly*
283. **discomfit** *confuse; embarrass*
284. **discompose** *to destroy the composure of*
285. **discord** *disagreement, quarrel, lack of harmony between musical notes*
286. **discourse** *speech; lecture*
287. **discredit** *refuse to believe*
288. **discreet** *careful, prudent*
289. **discrete** *individually distinct*
290. **discretion** *the freedom to make decisions*
291. **disdain** *look on with contempt*
292. **disinter** *dig up from the earth; reveal*
293. **dislodge** *remove from the place occupied*
294. **dismal** *sad; gloomy; miserable*
295. **disparate** *essentially different*
296. **disproof** *proof to the contrary*
297. **dissemble** *speak or behave so as to hide something (in mind)*
298. **dissent** *have a different opinion; refuse to assent*
299. **dissipate** *waste or squander*
300. **dissolute** *marked by indulgence in vices*
301. **dissolution** *disintegration; looseness in morals*
302. **distraught** *distracted violently; upset in mind*
303. **divergence** *getting farther apart from a point*
304. **divulge** *make known something secret*
305. **dogmatic** *positive; certain; arbitrary; without room for discussion*
306. **dolt** *stupid fellow*
307. **dormant** *in a state of inactivity but awaiting development*
308. **dote** *show much fondness; center one's attention*
309. **drawl** *slow way of speaking*
310. **drone** *male bee; person who isn't self-employed*
311. **drowsiness** *feeling sleepy; half asleep*
312. **drudge** *to do hard, menial or monotonous work*

313. **dubious** *feeling doubt or causing doubt*
314. **dud** *useless person; something that fails*
315. **dupe** *cheat; make a fool of*
316. **duplicity** *deliberate deception*
317. **dwarf** *person or somebody much below the usual size*
318. **dynamo** *a generator; something that produces electric current*

E

319. **earthenware** *dishes made of baked clay*
320. **earthy** *coarse, unrefined behaviour, of the earth*
    A: Cultured, Refined
321. **eddy** *circular or spiral movement (for example, of wind), a current*
322. **edible** *fit to be eaten; not poisonous*
323. **efficacy** *production of a desired result*
324. **egoism** *selfishness*
    A: Asceticism
325. **egotism** *excessive reference to oneself in speaking or writing*
    S: Egoism, Conceit
    A: Humility
326. **egress** *way out; exit*
327. **elaborate** *worked out with much care, in great detail*
328. **elan** *spirited self-assurance*
    S: Vivacity, Enthusiasm, Exuberance
    A: Sobriety, Depression
329. **elegiac** *Sad, Mournful*
    A: Happy
330. **elegy** *a lament; a melancholy composition*
331. **elicit** *draw out*
332. **eloquence** *fluent speaking; skillful use of language*
333. **emaciate** *make thin and weak*
334. **emanate** *to come forth, Issue, as from a source*
    S: Emerge, Originate
    A: Stop
335. **embark** *Begin a journey or endeavor*
336. **embellish** *make beautiful*
337. **embezzle** *use in a wrong way for one's own benefit*
338. **emend** *To make scholarly corrections in a text*
    S: Correct, Revise, Rectify
    A: Corrupt, Debase, Spoil
339. **emote** *stir up; excite*
340. **emulate** *to try to equal or surpass; copy*
341. **encapsulate** *enclose in capsule*
342. **encumbrance** *burden, things that get in the way of*
343. **endearing** *making dear or liked*
344. **endorse** *write one's name on the back of*
345. **enduring** *lasting*
346. **engrave** *impress deeply, carve*
347. **engrossing** *taken up all the time or attention; writing in large or formal way*
348. **engulf** *swallow up*
349. **enmity** *hatred; being an enemy*
350. **ennui** *boredom*
351. **enormity** *of great size, number, etc. huge; a serious crime*
    S: Vast, Immense
    A: Smallness, Insignificance
352. **ensign** *flag; badge*
353. **entangle** *put into difficulties; involve as in a tangle*
354. **enthrall** *please greatly; enslave (fig.)*
355. **entice** *tempt or persuade*
356. **entreat** *ask earnestly*
357. **enunciate** *pronounce (words); express a theory*
358. **enzyme** *catalyst*
359. **eon** *an extremely long, indefinite period of time*
360. **epitome** *representative example; a typical model*
361. **equable** *steady; regular*
362. **equilibrium** *state of being balanced*
363. **eradicate** *get rid of; pull up by the roots*
364. **erratic** *irregular in behaviour or opinion*
365. **erudite** *learned; scholarly*
366. **espouse** *marry; give one's support to*
367. **etiquette** *the forms, manners, etc. conventionally acceptable or required in society, profession, etc.*
368. **eulogy** *formal praise; panegyric*
369. **euphoria** *elation; state of pleasant excitement*
370. **euthanasia** *easy and painless death*
371. **evasive** *tending to evade*
372. **evoke** *call up; bring out*
373. **exasperate** *to irritate*
    S: Exacerbate, Provoke
    A: Mollify, Placate, Conciliate
374. **excerpt** *a passage or extract from a book, film or piece of music*
375. **exhaustive** *complete; thorough*
376. **exigency** *emergency; an urgent situation*
377. **exorbitant** *much too high or great*
378. **expedient** *likely to be useful for a purpose*
379. **exploit** *brilliant achievement; develop, use selfishly*
380. **extempore** *without previous thought or preparation*
381. **extinct** *no longer active*
382. **extinguish** *end the existence of; wipe or put out*

383. **extol**	*praise highly*
384. **extort**	*obtain by threats, violence*
385. **extrovert**	*cheerful person*

F

386. **fallacious**	*based on error*
387. **falter**	*waver; move in an uncertain manner*
388. **fanciful**	*imaginary*
389. **fawn**	*young deer; try to win some-body's favor*
390. **feign**	*to pretend* *S: sham, dissemble, simulate, counterfeit*
391. **felon**	*person guilty of murder*
392. **femur**	*thighbone, longlegs bone extending from the pelvis to the knee*
393. **ferment**	*undergo fermentation; become excited, commotion*
394. **ferocity**	*savage cruelty*
395. **fervor**	*warmth of feelings; earnestness*
396. **feud**	*bitter quarrel over a long period of time*
397. **fidelity**	*loyalty; accuracy*
398. **fidget**	*move restlessly; make nervous*
399. **figurehead**	*carved image on the brow of a ship; nominal leader*
400. **finesse**	*delicate way of dealing with a situation*
401. **finical**	*too fussy about food, clothing, etc.*
402. **finicky**	*finical*
403. **fission**	*splitting or division (esp. of cells)*
404. **fixate**	*stare at*
405. **flak**	*criticism; anti-aircraft guns*
406. **flamboyant**	*brightly colored; florid*
407. **flaunting**	*show off complacently*
408. **flax**	*pale; yellow (hair); a plant*
409. **fleet**	*number of ships; quick-moving*
410. **flop**	*fail; move; fall clumsily*
411. **florid**	*very much ornamented; naturally red (for example, of face)*
412. **flout**	*reject, mock; to go against (as in going against tradition)*
413. **fluke**	*lucky stroke*
414. **fluster**	*make nervous or confused*
415. **foil**	*prevent from carrying out; contrast*
416. **foment**	*put something warm (to lessen the pain)*
417. **foolproof**	*incapable of failure or error*
418. **forbear**	*refrain from; be patient; ancestor*
419. **forbearance**	*patience; willingness to wait*
420. **forensic**	*belonging to courts of judicature*
421. **forerunner**	*a sign that tells or warns of something to follow* *S: Herald, Harbinger, Predecessor* *A: Successor, Offspring*
422. **forfeit**	*suffer the loss of something*
423. **forge**	*workshop for the shaping of metal; to shape metal lead*
424. **forgery**	*counterfeit*
425. **forte**	*that which one does particularly well*
426. **forthright**	*direct and frank* *S: Outspoken, Straightforward* *A: Obscure, Veiled*
427. **foster**	*nurture; care for*
428. **fragile**	*easily injured, broken or destroyed*
429. **frantic**	*wildly excited with joy; anxiety*
430. **fraternal**	*brotherly*
431. **fraudulent**	*based on or using fraud* *S: Cheating, Deceitful* *A: Honest*
432. **fray**	*to wear out by use, cloth etc.* *S: frazzle, tatter*
433. **frenzied**	*wildly, insanely, excited* *S: wild, frantic, hysterical*
434. **fret**	*worry; irritation; wear away*
435. **fringe**	*edge; ornamental border; part of hair over the forehead*
436. **frolicsome**	*light-hearted, gay* *S: playful, pranks*
437. **frugal**	*careful; economical*
438. **futile**	*useless* *S: Trifling, Trivial, Vain* *A: Effective, Satisfactory, Fruitful*

G

439. **gala**	*a festivity, celebration, commemoration*
440. **gale**	*cyclone, hurricane, storm, tempest*
441. **gallant**	*brave, noble, attentive to ladies, amorous*
442. **gallivant**	*(derogatory) to go about from one place to another in search of pleasure*
443. **galvanise**	*to stimulate*
444. **gambol**	*frolic, play*
445. **gamut**	*the entire range or extent* *S: Range, Scope, Purview*
446. **gape**	*to stare with open mouth, to be wide open* *S: Gawk, ogle, peer*
447. **garish**	*gaudy* *S: Ostentatious* *A: Sober, Modest*
448. **garment**	*article of clothing*
449. **garnish**	*to decorate* *S: Embellish, Adorn, Beautify* *A: Spoil, Disfigure, Impair*

450. **gasket** *a layer of packing material like a sheet of asbestos, etc. used for making gas-tight joints*
451. **gasp** *to gape for breath*
452. **gawk** *to stare stupidly*
453. **gawky** *clumsy*
S: Awkward, Ungainly
A: Elegant
454. **generic** *of a whole class, kind or group*
S: Typical, Characteristic, Common
A: Individual, Particular
455. **genteel** *polite or well bred*
S: Polished, Refined, Cultured
A: Rough, Coarse, Ill-bred
456. **gentry** *people of the upper class*
457. **gesticulate** *to make lively gestures*
S: Signal, Pantomime
458. **gibe** *An insulting remark*
S: Scoff, Sneer, Mock
A: Praise, Exalt, Applaud
459. **gild** *to cover with gold or gold-like substance; gift*
460. **girth** *circumferential measure of thickness*
461. **gist** *the point; general sense*
462. **gleam** *to glow or shine, to flash*
463. **glib** *ready and smooth but not sincere*
464. **glimmer** *weak, unsteady light, twinkle*
465. **gloss** *brightness, polish, radiance, luster, shine*
466. **gnarled** *contorted, twisted, weather-beaten, knotty*
467. **gnaw** *waste away; bite steadily*
468. **goad** *something urging a person to action*
469. **gorge** *eat greedily; narrow opening with a stream*
470. **gouge** *tool for cutting grooves in wood; scoop out*
471. **grave** *serious; requiring consideration*
472. **gravel** *an assemblage of stones*
473. **graze** *touch or scrape lightly in passing, feed on grass*
474. **grievous** *causing grief or pain; serious*
475. **grimace** *make a distorted face*
476. **grit** *persistence, stamina, pluck, determination*
477. **grovel** *crawl; humble oneself*
478. **grueling** *exhausting*
479. **grumpy** *peevish*
S: Morose, Irritable, Surly
A: Amicable, Gentle
480. **guild** *an association for mutual aid/help*
481. **guise** *external appearance, manner, behaviour, dress*
482. **gullible** *easily tricked*
483. **gush** *burst out suddenly; talk ardently*
484. **gust** *outburst of feeling; sudden rain, wind, fire, etc.*
485. **gyrate** *To move in a circular or spiral path*
S: Spin, Whirl, Rotate

H

486. **hack** *cut roughly; hired horse*
487. **hardihood** *resolute; courage and fortitude*
488. **harmonious** *having parts arranged in an orderly, pleasing way*
S: Agreeable, Concordant, Congruous
A: Dissonant, Opposed, Incompatible
489. **haughty** *arrogant; conceited*
490. **heady** *intoxicating*
491. **heed** *attention; give notice to*
492. **heinous** *odious (of crime)*
493. **hematology** *the study of blood and its diseases*
494. **hereditary** *of, or passed down by inheritance from an ancestor*
S: Inherited, Congenital
495. **heresy** *belief contrary to what is generally accepted*
496. **hermaphrodite** *a person, animal or plant with sexual organs of both male and female*
497. **heterogeneous** *made up of different kinds*
498. **heyday** *the time of greater vigor, prosperity etc.*
499. **hibernate** *to spend the winter in a dormant state (of animals), to be inactive*
500. **highbrow** *(person) with superior tastes*
501. **hinder** *to keep back, stop*
S: Impede, Obstruct, Prevent
A: Help, Assist, Further
502. **hinterland** *The land away from a river*
503. **hirsute** *hairy; shaggy*
504. **hoax** *mischievous trick played on somebody for a joke*
505. **hobnob** *To be on close terms (with the government)*
A: Alienate, Estrange
506. **homicide** *the killing of one person by another*
507. **hone** *stone used for sharpening tools, sharpen*
508. **hoodwink** *trick; mislead*
509. **hospitable** *to give hospitality, welcoming to guests*
510. **hush** *make or become silent*
511. **husk** *worthless outside part of anything (seed, fruit, etc.)*
512. **hypocrisy** *falsely making oneself appear to be good*

I

513. **icon**	*an image, figure, statue*
514. **idealism**	*behaviour or thought based on a conception of things as one thinks they should be*
515. **ignoramus**	*an ignorant person* *S: Dunce, Dolt, Dope* *A: Genius, Prodigy, Scholar*
516. **illegible**	*hard or impossible to read because badly written or printed* *S: Unreadable, Indecipherable* *A: Legible, Readable, Decipherable*
517. **illicit**	*unlawful; forbidden*
518. **illusion**	*an unreal or misleading appearance or image* *S: Fantasy, Image* *A: Reality, Fact*
519. **immaculate**	*pure; faultless*
520. **imminent**	*likely to come or happen soon*
521. **immune**	*exempt from or protected against something harmful* *S: Exculpate, Reprieve* *A: Condemn, Convict, Blame*
522. **impair**	*worsen; diminish in value*
523. **impassioned**	*filled with passion or zeal*
524. **impassive**	*unmoved feeling; no sign of passion*
525. **impeach**	*to accuse; to charge with a crime*
526. **impede**	*hinder; get in the way of*
527. **impending**	*imminent; being about to happen; expected*
528. **imperative**	*urgent; essential*
529. **impermeable**	*that cannot be permeated*
530. **impertinent**	*given to insolent rudeness*
531. **imperturbable**	*calm; not capable of being excited*
532. **impervious**	*not allowing to pass through (of materials)*
533. **implacable**	*incapable of being placated; unpleasable*
534. **implicit**	*implied though not plainly expressed*
535. **improvise**	*to compose and perform without preparation* *S: Extemporise, Invent, Compose*
536. **impudent**	*rash; indiscreet*
537. **inane**	*silly; senseless*
538. **inasmuch**	*since; because*
539. **incandescent**	*white, glowing or luminous with intense heat*
540. **incarcerate**	*to put in prison; to confine*
541. **incense**	*make angry*
542. **inception**	*Act of beginning, Start* *S: inauguration, Beginning, Origin* *A: Termination, End, Finish*
543. **incessant**	*often repeated; continual*
544. **incise**	*engrave; make a cut in*
545. **incite**	*stir up; rouse*
546. **incoherent**	*Not logically connected, Disjointed* *S: Confused* *A: Clear, Vivid*
547. **incongruous**	*out of place; not in harmony or agreement*
548. **incredible**	*seeming too unusual to be possible*
549. **inculcate**	*fix firmly by repetition*
550. **indeterminate**	*indefinite* *A: Definite, Clear*
551. **indignant**	*feeling or expressing anger especially at unjust or mean action* *S: Anger, Wrath, Scorn* *A: Calm Cool, Patient*
552. **indiscreet**	*to open in what one says or does* *S: Brash, Rash, Reckless* *A: Wise*
553. **indistinct**	*not easily heard, seen*
554. **indolence**	*laziness*
555. **indomitable**	*not easily discouraged or subdued*
556. **induct**	*to place formally in an office, a society, etc.* *S: Install, Initiate*
557. **indulge**	*gratify; give way to; satisfy; allow oneself*
558. **indulgent**	*inclined to indulge*
559. **inebriated**	*intoxicated* *S: Drunk, Tipsy* *A: Sober, Teetotal*
560. **inept**	*unskillful; said or done at the wrong time*
561. **ineptitude**	*quality of being unskillful*
562. **infirm**	*Weak from age* *S: Weak, Languid, Feeble* *A: Strong, Powerful, Tough*
563. **inflammatory**	*rousing excitement, anger, etc.* *S: Incendiary, Infuriating* *A: Reconciling. Mitigating*
564. **inflict**	*to cause (wounds, pain etc.) suffering*
565. **infringe**	*To break (a law or pact)* *S: Transgress, Violate, Trespass*
566. **infuriate**	*fill with fury or rage*
567. **infuse**	*put; pour; fill*
568. **ingenious**	*clever, resourceful* *S: Skillful, Inventive* *A: Unskilled, Awkward, Dull*
569. **ingest**	*take in by swallowing*
570. **ingress**	*the act of entering; entrance*
571. **inhibition**	*restraint, reserve* *S: Repression, Ban, Opposition* *A: Approval, Permission, Accordance*

572. **inimitable** *defying imitation; unmatchable*
573. **insane** *mentally ill or deranged, Not sane S: Mad, Delirious, Frenzied A: Sound, Sane, Normal*
574. **insensible** *unconscious; unresponsive; unaffected*
575. **insignia** *distinguishing marks as emblems of rank S: Sign*
576. **insipid** *without taste or flavor*
577. **insolent** *boldly disrespectful, rude S: Impudent, Impertinent, Offensive*
578. **insolvent** *unable to pay debts; impoverished*
579. **interim** *as an installment, provisional*
580. **intimate** *to announce; to suggest or hint, close to (as in relations)*
581. **intractable** *not easily managed or controlled; unruly*
582. **inundate** *flood; cover by overflowing*
583. **irate** *angry*
584. **ire** *anger*
585. **irksome** *tiresome*
586. **irresolute** *hesitating; undecided*

J

587. **jab** *sneer, taunt, belittle*
588. **jabber** *To talk quickly and incoherently*
589. **jabber** *talk excitedly; utter rapidly*
590. **jacuzzi** *a special type of bath mechanism where water is agitated to give extra invigoration*
591. **jaded** *bored, satiated, dulled S: inferior, wearied, listless, exhausted A: refreshed, strengthened*
592. **jagged** *uneven, rough edged, notched*
593. **jeer** *to make fun of, deride; scoff; mock*
594. **jerk** *a spasmodic muscle movement;*
595. **jester** *clown; buffoon*
596. **jibe** *gibe; make fun of*
597. **jittery** *jumpy; nervous; shaky; anxious*
598. **jockey** *to manoeuvre, to position of advantage; horse rider*
599. **jocular** *meant as a joke*
600. **jolt** *to shake with a sudden jerk; startle*
601. **jostle** *to hustle; to elbow*
602. **jovial** *joyous; full of geniality*
603. **jubilant** *shouting with joy; rejoicing*
604. **jubilation** *celebration; elation; euphoria; exultation*
605. **judicious** *sound in judgment; wise*
606. **junk** *rubbish; garbage; trivia; trash*
607. **junta** *a group of men united for some secret intrigue*
608. **jurisdiction** *legal authority; extent of power*
609. **juvenile** *young; childish; youthful; immature*

K

610. **keen** *intense, sharp, vivid, acute*
611. **keep-sake** *gift, usually small and often not very costly, that is kept in memory of the giver*
612. **kennel** *house for dogs, a pack of hounds*
613. **keynote** *(i) The basic idea or Ruling principle S: Theme, Nub (ii) Musical Note*
614. **killjoy** *One who destroys or lessens other people's enjoyment*
615. **kiln** *a furnace or oven for drying, burning or baking bricks, pottery, etc.*
616. **kimono** *a traditional dress of Japan*
617. **kin** *relative, family related as by blood*
618. **kindergarten** *school for infants*
619. **kindle** *to set fire to S: light, inflame, ignite A: extinguish, discourage, snuff out*
620. **kingpin** *chief, don, boss*
621. **kiosk** *a small stall for the sale of newspapers, etc.*
622. **kit** *apparatus, gear, outfit*
623. **kith** *kith and kin; friends and relations*
624. **kitty** *pool of money to be played for*
625. **knack** *dexterity, talent, proficiency, ability*
626. **knit** *draw together; unite firmly*
627. **kudos** *credit for achievement, glory, fame*

L

628. **lacklustre** *(of eyes) dull*
629. **lag** *(i) To fall behind, Not keep pace, Move slowly (ii) Imprison, Arrest (iii) A piece of non-conductive cover of a boiler to prevent heat transfer*
630. **lament** *show, feel great sorrow*
631. **languish** *To become weak, Droop, Be unhappy*
632. **languid** *without vigour or vitality S: Pensive, Drooping, Lethargic A: Brisk, Lively, Vivacious*
633. **languor** *Lack of vigour or vitality*
634. **latent** *present but not visible or active; the latent force of an atomic bomb S: dormant, potential*
635. **lavish** *giving or producing freely, liberally or generously*
636. **legacy** *something handed down from ancestors*

637. **lethal** *causing death*
S: Deadly, Fatal
A: Harmless

638. **lewd** *pertaining to lust, indecent*
S: Obscene, Lustful, Licentious
A: Pure, Chaste

639. **liberality** *free giving; generosity*

640. **limp** *lacking strength; walking unevenly*

641. **limpid** *transparent; absolutely serene and untroubled*

642. **lingo** *a dialect, jargon etc., that one is not familiar with*

643. **listless** *characterised by lack of interest, energy or spirit*

644. **lithe** *bending, twisting*

645. **litigate** *to contest in a lawsuit*

646. **livid** *(i) Discoloured by a bruise, Black and blue (ii) Furiously angry*
S: Discoloured, Angry

647. **loathe** *To feel intense dislike or disgust for*
S: Detest, Abhor, Abominate

648. **loll** *rest; to sit or stand in a lazy way; hang (dog's tongue)*

649. **lucid** *clear, readily understood*
S: Clear, Intelligible
A: incomprehensible, irrational, Illegible

650. **lull** *become quiet or less active*

651. **lumber** *move in a clumsy, noisy way*

652. **luminary** *star; light-giving body*

653. **lurk** *be out of view, ready to attack*

654. **lustrous** *being bright, polished*

M

655. **machination** *plot; scheme (esp. evil)*

656. **maestro** *a master in an art, especially a great conductor or composer of music*

657. **magnanimous** *generous*
A: Selfish, Mean, Miserly

658. **magnate** *important person in any field*

659. **malady** *disease, Illness*
S: Illness, Disorder, Ailment

660. **malice** *active ill will, desire to harm another*
S: Spite, Grudge, Hatred
A: Benevolence, Goodwill

661. **malign** *injurious; speak ill of somebody; tell lie*

662. **malinger** *to fake illness or injury in order to shirk a duty*

663. **malleable** *yielding easily; can be moulded; adapting*

664. **malodorous** *producing a bad odour, stinking*
S: foul, Noxious
A: fragrant

665. **mandatory** *authoritatively commanded*
S: Compulsory

666. **massacre** *cruel killing of a large number of people*

667. **matriculation** *be admitted, enter a university as a student*

668. **maul** *hurt by rough handling*

669. **mediocre** *ordinary, Average*

670. **melancholy** *very sad and depressed state*
S: Dispirited, Sorrowful
A: Happy, Merry

671. **mendacity** *dishonesty*

672. **mendicant** *a beggar*

673. **mercurial** *quick, changeable in character; fleeting*

674. **mesmerise** *hypnotise*

675. **metamorphosis** *transformation*
S: Conversion, Change

676. **meticulous** *giving great attention to details*

677. **mettle** *quality of endurance or courage*

678. **mettlesome** *courageous; high-spirited*

679. **mince** *pronounce or speak affectedly; euphemise; pound to a pulp*

680. **mischievous** *harmful; causing mischief*

681. **miscreant** *heretical; villainous*

682. **miser** *person who loves wealth and spends little; frugal*

683. **missive** *letter*

684. **moderation** *quality of being limited; not extreme*

685. **mollify** *make calmer or quieter*

686. **molt** *moult; lose hair, feathers before new growing*

687. **morbid** *diseased; unhealthy (for example, about ideas)*

688. **mordant** *biting and caustic; incisive*

689. **morose** *ill-tempered, unsocial*

690. **muffler** *cloth worn round the neck; silencer*

691. **multifarious** *varied; motley; greatly diversified*

692. **mundane** *worldly as opposed to spiritual; commonplace; everyday*

693. **myriad** *very great number*

N

694. **nadir** *lowest, weakest point*

695. **nag** *to find fault with*

696. **naive** *Unaffectedly simple*
S: Artless, Innocent, Unsophisticated,
A: Cunning, Shrewd, Sly

697. **narcotic** *a drug such as morphine, used to relieve pain and induce sleep*
S: Dope, Opiate, Drug
A: Stimulant

698. **nascent** *coming into existence; emerging*

699. **natal** *of or relating to one's birth*
A: Mortal

700. **nautical** *of sailors, ships or navigation*

701. **negligent** *taking too little care*

702. **nervy** *bold or brash; nervous*

703. **neurotic** *having neurosis (a functional derangement caused by disorder of the nervous system)*
A: Sane, Poised, Rational

704. **nexus** *a connection, tie or link*

705. **nibble** *take little bites*

706. **nocturnal** *of or in the night*

707. **nomenclature** *the system of naming used in a science, etc.*
S: Terminology

708. **nonentity** *a person or thing of little or no importance*

709. **notorious** *widely known especially unfavourably*
S: ill-famed, Infamous, Dis-honourable
A: Good, Virtuous, Honest

710. **noxious** *harmful*

711. **nuptial** *of marriage or wedding*

O

712. **obese** *corpulent, fat*

713. **oblivious** *unaware; having no memory*

714. **obnoxious** *odiously or disgustingly objectionable*

715. **obstinate** *determined to have one's own way, Stubborn*
S: Head-Strong
A: Obliging, Yielding, Flexible

716. **obtain** *to be established; accepted or customary*

717. **obtrusive** *projecting; prominent; undesirably noticeable*

718. **obtuse** *blunt; stupid*

719. **occluded** *blocked up*

720. **octogenarian** *a person between the ages of eighty and ninety*

721. **odious** *repulsive; hateful*

722. **odium** *contempt; dislike; aversion*

723. **odor** *smell; favor; reputation*

724. **offal** *waste or by-product of a process; rubbish*

725. **ogle** *to keep looking at flirtatiously*

726. **ominous** *threatening*

727. **onus** *a burden, unpleasant duty etc.*

728. **opaqueness** *dullness; not allowing light to pass through*

729. **opinionated** *holding obstinately to one's opinions*
S: Obstinate, Dogmatic
A: Open-minded

730. **opportune** *suitable, said of time*
S: Appropriate
A: Untimely, Unsuitable, Inappropriate

731. **opulent** *Having much wealth. rich*
S: Affluence, Wealth
A: Poverty, Penury, Frugality

732. **outlandish** *very odd or strange*
S: Strange, Odd, Peculiar
A: Normal, Well mannered

733. **overhaul** *examine thoroughly; to learn about the condition*

P

734. **palate** *roof of the mouth; sense of taste*

735. **palatial** *magnificent*

736. **palliate** *lessen the severity of*

737. **palpability** *can be felt, touched, understood*

738. **paradigm** *a model; example or pattern*

739. **paraphrase** *express meaning in different words*

740. **parasol** *umbrella used as a sunshade, especially by women*

741. **pariah** *an outcast; a rejected and despised person*

742. **partisan** *one-sided; committed to a party; biased or prejudiced*

743. **pathos** *emotion of sympathetic pity*

744. **patron** *regular customer; person who gives support*

745. **paucity** *scarcity; a lacking of*

746. **pedestrian** *commonplace; trite; unremarkable, person who walks*

747. **peevish** *bad-tempered; irritable*

748. **penchant** *strong inclination; a liking*

749. **penitent** *feeling or showing regret*

750. **penurious** *poor; stingy*

751. **penury** *extreme poverty*

752. **perilous** *dangerous*

753. **perish** *be destroyed; decay*

754. **perky** *cheerful and lively*

755. **permeate** *spread into every part of*

756. **pernicious** *harmful; injurious*

757. **perpetrate** *be guilty; commit (a crime)*

758. **perquisite** *gratuity or tip*

759. **personable** *pleasing in appearance; attractive*

760. **pertain** *belong as a part; have reference*

761. **pervade** *diffuse*

762. **pest**	*destructive thing or a person who is a nuisance*
763. **petrified**	*power (to think, feel, act) taken away, scared*
764. **petrify**	*to make hard, rocklike; frighten*
765. **phoney**	*not genuine*
766. **piety**	*the quality of being religious*
767. **pinch**	*be too tight; take between the thumb and finger*
768. **pine**	*waste away through sorrow or illness*
769. **pious**	*dutiful to parents; devoted to religion*
770. **pitfall**	*covered hole as a trap; unsuspected danger*
771. **pith**	*essential part; soft liquid substance; inner core of stems in plants.*
772. **pivotal**	*of great importance (others depend on it)*
773. **placate**	*soothe; pacify; calm*
774. **placid**	*serenely free of interruption or disturbance*
775. **plaintive**	*mournful melancholy; sorrowful*
776. **plaque**	*flat metal on a wall as a memorial*
777. **plea**	*request*
778. **plead**	*address a court of law as an advocate*
779. **plethora**	*excess*
780. **pliant**	*pliable; easily bent, shaped or twisted*
781. **plod**	*continue doing something without resting*
782. **pluck**	*pull the feathers off; pick (for example, flowers)*
783. **plunge**	*move quickly, suddenly and with force*
784. **poncho**	*large piece of cloth*
785. **portent**	*omen; marvellous; threatening*
786. **postulate**	*to claim; to assume as true, existent or necessary*
787. **prattle**	*chatter; to utter or make meaningless sounds*
788. **precarious**	*uncertain; risky; dangerous*
789. **precipitous**	*steep*
790. **précis**	*concise summary*
791. **precursory**	*preliminary; anticipating*
792. **predominate**	*have more power than others*
793. **preen**	*tidy; show self-satisfaction*
794. **premature**	*doing or happening of something before the right time*
795. **preponderance**	*greatness in number, strength, weight*
796. **prevalent**	*common*
797. **prim**	*neat; formal*
798. **pristine**	*primitive; unspoiled; pure as in earlier times*
799. **procrastination**	*to keep putting off*
800. **prodigal**	*wasteful; reckless with money*
801. **prodigy**	*a person with a special talent*
802. **profuse**	*abundant; lavish*
803. **progeny/ progenitor**	*descendants; children*
804. **prone**	*prostrate; inclined to (undesirable things)*
805. **propagation**	*increasing the number; spreading; extending*
806. **provident**	*frugal; looking to the future*
807. **provisional**	*of the present time only*
808. **provoke**	*make angry*
809. **prudence**	*careful; forethought*
810. **prudish**	*easily shocked; excessively modest*
811. **prune**	*dried plum; silly person, shorten*
812. **pry**	*inquire too curiously*
813. **pseudonym**	*a false name*
814. **pummel**	*to pound or beat*
815. **pungency**	*sharpness; stinging quality*
816. **pungent**	*marked by a sharp incisive quality; caustic*
817. **punitive**	*inflicting, involving or aiming at punishment*
818. **pyre**	*large pile of wood for burning*

Q

819. **quack**	*person dishonestly claiming*
820. **quaff**	*drink deeply*
821. **qualm**	*feeling of doubt; temporary feeling of sickness*
822. **quash**	*to annul, cancel, smother*
823. **queer**	*odd, strange, bizarre, erratic*
824. **quell**	*suppress; subdue*
825. **quench**	*satisfy, satiate, allay*
826. **quilt**	*banquet cover, warmer*
827. **quip**	*A witty or sarcastic remark* *S: Sally, Retort, Jest*
828. **quirk**	*habit or action peculiar to somebody or something*
829. **quorum**	*minimum number of people who have to be present to make the vote valid*

R

830. **rabble**	*mob; crowd; the lower classes of populace*
831. **racket**	*a noisy confusion* *S: Noise, Clamour, Commotion* *A: Peace, Quietude, Harmony*

832. **racy** *full of zest or vigor; piquant*
833. **rake** *dissolute person; libertine , sweep, an instrument to gather leaves, etc.*
834. **rally** *(i) To come together to support (ii) Give new strength (iii) Gathering or assembly (iv) A contest of motor vehicle endurance*
835. **ramble** *to move aimlessly from place to place*
836. **rampant** *widespread, raging*
837. **rancid** *having the bad smell or taste of stale fats or oils, Spoiled*
S: Stinking, Offensive, Decaying
A: Sweet, Fresh, Fragrant
838. **ransack** *to plunder, Pillage*
S: Rummage
A: Restore, Compensate, Redress
839. **rant** *use extravagant language*
840. **rapport** *sympathetic relationship, Harmony*
S: Accord
A: Hatred, Enmity, Animosity
841. **rarefy** *to make thin, less dense; to purify or refine*
842. **ratify** *to approve and sanction formally*
843. **rave** *act with excessive enthusiasm*
844. **reactionary** *opposing progress*
845. **rebuff** *snub*
846. **recast** *cast or fashion anew*
847. **reciprocity** *granting of privileges in return for similar*
848. **recitals** *a number or performance of music*
849. **recluse** *person who lives alone and avoids people*
850. **reconcile** *settle a quarrel; restore peace*
851. **recourse** *turning to someone or something for help*
852. **redeem** *get back by payment; compensate*
853. **refine** *make or become pure, cultured*
854. **regale** *to delight or entertain; to feast*
855. **rehabilitate** *to put back to useful life*
S: Restore, Cure
A: Ruin, Destroy
856. **rejoinder** *An answer especially to a reply,*
S: Answer, Retort, Reply
857. **rejuvenation** *becoming young in nature or appearance*
858. **relapse** *fall back again*
859. **reluctant** *unwilling, disinclined*
S: Unenthusiastic, Opposed
A: Willing, Eager, Ready
860. **render** *deliver; provide; represent*
861. **renovate** *restore something to better condition*
862. **renowned** *celebrated; famous*
863. **repast** *meal*
864. **repel** *refuse to accept; cause dislike*
865. **reproach** *scold; upbraid*
866. **repulsive** *causing a feeling of disgust*
867. **resigned** *unresisting; submissive*
868. **resort** *to frequently visit*
869. **retard** *check; hinder*
870. **revere** *have deep respect for*
871. **reverent** *feeling or showing deep respect*
872. **riddle** *puzzling person or thing*
873. **rift** *split; crack; dissension*
874. **roll** *call; calling of names*
875. **ruffian** *violent, cruel man*

S

876. **sadism** *Seeking pleasure from hurting others*
877. **salient** *Conspicuous, Prominent*
S: Outstanding
A: Hidden
878. **sallow** *of a grayish greenish yellow color*
879. **salutary** *remedial; causing improvement*
880. **sanction** *approval (by authority); penalty*
881. **sanctuary** *a holy place or a place of refuge or protection*
882. **sanity** *health of mind; soundness of judgement*
883. **sardonic** *disdainfully or skeptically humorous; sarcastic*
884. **sash** *long strip worn round the waist*
885. **satiate** *satisfy fully*
886. **saucy** *rude, impudent*
S: Insolent
A: Modest, Humble
887. **savor** *taste, flavor something*
888. **sawdust** *tiny bits of wood*
889. **scent** *smell (esp. pleasant)*
890. **scorch** *become discolored; dry up; go at high speed; to burn*
891. **scribble** *write hastily*
892. **scurvy** *disease due to deficiency of vitamic C*
893. **secede/ secession** *to withdraw from an organisation*
894. **secular** *material (not spiritual); living outside monasteries; worldly*
895. **sedate** *sober, serious and unemotional; calm and composed*
S: Serene
A: Mercurial, Frivolous
896. **sedentary** *marked by much sitting*
A: Peripatetic

897. **sediment**	*matter that settles to the bottom of liquid*
898. **seduce**	*to tempt into wrong-doing* *S: Allure, Inveigle, Entice* *A: Protect, Guide, Discourage*
899. **self-contained**	*complete within itself*
900. **semblance**	*outward appearance* *S: likeness, Form*
901. **sequence**	*succession; connected line of*
902. **sermon**	*reproving a person for his faults*
903. **serrated**	*having a toothed edge*
904. **servile**	*like a slave; lacking independence*
905. **sever**	*break off*
906. **severance**	*severing*
907. **shallow**	*little depth; not earnest*
908. **shambles**	*a scene of great destruction or disorder* *S: Mess, Muddle* *A: Order*
909. **sheath**	*cover for the blade of a weapon or a tool*
910. **shrewd**	*astute; showing sound judgement*
911. **shrill**	*sharp; piercing*
912. **shun**	*keep away from; avoid*
913. **shunt**	*send from one track to another; lay aside*
914. **sidestep**	*step to one side, dodge*
915. **silt**	*a fine-grained sandy sediment carried or deposited by water*
916. **skeptic**	*one who habitually questions matters generally accepted*
917. **sketchy**	*Rough or rapid*
918. **skit**	*short piece of humorous writing*
919. **slack**	*sluggish; dull; not tight*
920. **slate**	*kind of blue-grey stone; propose; criticize*
921. **slither**	*to sleep, slide or glide along*
922. **sluggard**	*lazy, slow-moving person*
923. **slur**	*join sounds, words (indistinct)*
924. **smirk**	*to smile in a conceited and complacent way*
925. **smoulder**	*burn slowly without flame*
926. **smug**	*annoyingly self-satisfied or complacent,* *S: Self-satisfied*
927. **snare**	*trap*
928. **snide**	*slyly malicious or derisive* *S: Sneer, Slyness* *A: Praising, Eulogising*
929. **snub**	*treat with contempt*
930. **soar**	*rise; fly high*
931. **sober**	*self-controlled*
932. **sobriety**	*quality or condition of being sober*
933. **soggy**	*heavy with water*
934. **solitude**	*being solitary or alone, seclusion* *S: Loneliness* *A: Society*
935. **solvent**	*of the power of forming a solution*
936. **somatic**	*of the body, physical*
937. **soot**	*black powder in smoke*
938. **sophisticated**	*complex; subtle; refined*
939. **spartan**	*hardy, warlike, disciplined*
940. **spleen**	*feelings of anger or ill will; often suppressed*
941. **sponge**	*porous rubber for washing; live at other's expense*
942. **sporadic**	*happening or appearing in isolated instances* *S: infrequent* *A: Constant, Prevalent, Continue*
943. **spruce**	*neat and in a smart way* *S: Neat* *A: Untidy, Slovenly*
944. **spurious**	*counterfeit*
945. **spurn**	*have nothing to do; reject or refuse*
946. **squabble**	*to quarrel noisily over a small matter* *S: Wrangle, Dispute, Quarrel*
947. **squander**	*spend wastefully*
948. **squat**	*crouch; settle without permission*
949. **staid**	*sober, sedate* *S: Serious* *A: Excited*
950. **standing**	*status or reputation (figurative)*
951. **stationary**	*still, motionless*
952. **stationery**	*writing material*
953. **steeply**	*rising or falling sharply*
954. **stigma**	*mark of shame or disgrace*
955. **stigmatise**	*describe somebody scornfully*
956. **stilted**	*artificially formal or dignified* *S: Stiff, Unnatural* *A: Casual, Informal*
957. **sting**	*something sharp*
958. **stingy**	*spending, using unwillingly*
959. **stint**	*to be thrifty; to set limits*
960. **stray**	*wander; lose one's way*
961. **streak**	*long; thin; move very fast*
962. **stride**	*walk with long steps*
963. **strut**	*a supporting bar; swagger*
964. **subdue**	*overcome; bring under control*
965. **subjugate**	*to conquer; to subdue*
966. **sublime**	*extreme; astounding*
967. **submerge**	*put under water, liquid; sink out of sight*
968. **suffice**	*be enough*

969. **suffocate** *cause or have difficulty in breathing*
970. **suffrage** *short prayer usually in a series; right of voting*
971. **sullied** *to be stained or discredited*
972. **summarily** *briefly; without delay*
973. **summary** *done without delay or formality*
974. **sundry** *various; miscellaneous; separate*
975. **superannuate** *to become retired; to become obsolete*
976. **supercilious** *disdainful; characterised by haughty scorn*
977. **superfluous** *more than is needed or wanted*
978. **superimpose** *put something on the top*
979. **supersede** *take the place of*
980. **suppress** *prevent from being known; put an end to*
981. **surcharge** *additional load; charge*
982. **surveillance** *watch kept over a person, especially a suspect*
S: Supervision, Invigilation
983. **sustenance** *nourishment, support*
984. **swagger** *To walk with a bold, arrogant stride*
985. **swerve** *change direction suddenly*
986. **symbiosis** *the living together of two kinds of organisms to their mutual advantage*
987. **syndrome** *a set of symptoms characterising a disease or condition*
988. **synopsis** *summary or outline*

T

989. **taboo** *any social restriction*
S: Forbidden
A: Permit, Allow, License
990. **tacit** *unspoken, silently understood*
A: Explicit, Verbal
991. **tactile** *perceptible by touch*
992. **tadpole** *form of a frog when it leaves the egg*
993. **talisman** *a ring, stone, etc. bearing engraved figures supposed to bring good luck, avert evil, etc.*
994. **tamper** *interfere with*
995. **tangential** *suddenly changeable*
996. **tantrum** *a violent outburst of rage etc.*
997. **tarnished** *lost brightness*
998. **tassel** *bunch of threads*
999. **taunt** *contemptuous reproach; hurtful remark*
1000. **taut** *tightly stretched*
1001. **tawdry** *cheap; gaudy; showy; tacky*
1002. **tawny** *brownish-yellow, tan*
1003. **tedious** *Long and dull*
S: Slow, Wearisome, Fatiguing
A: Light, Hearty, Cheerful
1004. **teem** *to be prolific, abound, swarm*
1005. **teetotal** *opposed to alcohol*
1006. **temperate** *showing self-control*
1007. **tentative** *done as a test, not final*
A: Established, Certain
1008. **tepid** *lukewarm*
1009. **theatrical** *designed for effect, Show, Unnatural*
S: Dramatic
1010. **therapeutic** *serving to cure or heal or to preserve health*
1011. **thesaurus** *a book of synonyms and antonyms*
1012. **thespian** *(i) Having to do with drama*
(ii) An actor
1013. **thickset** *Thick in body, stocky*
1014. **threshold** *the beginning point*
S: Beginning, Start
A: End
1015. **thrift** *care; economy; thriving; prosperous*
1016. **thwart** *obstruct; frustrate*
1017. **timid** *shy; easily frightened*
1018. **titanic** *of great size, strength or power*
S: Gigantic, Immense
A: Tiny, Small
1019. **tonic** *something giving strength or energy*
1020. **topple** *be unsteady and overturn*
1021. **torment** *severe pain or suffering*
1022. **tortuous** *devious; not straightforward*
1023. **totalitarian** *designating or of a government in which one political group maintains complete control, especially under a dictator*
1024. **tout** *person who worries others to buy something, to use his service*
1025. **traumatic** *an emotional shock having a lasting psychic effect*
S: Unpleasant, Agonising
A: Titillating
1026. **tremor** *trembling*
S: Shaking, Fearful
A: Brave
1027. **trickle** *flow in drops*
1028. **trifling** *unimportant*
1029. **troupe** *a group especially of actors, singers etc.*
1030. **truant** *one who shirks his duties*
S: Vagrant, idler, Shirker
1031. **trustworthy** *Worthy of trust, Reliable*
S: Dependable, Honest
A: Vacillating, Undependable
1032. **turbulence** *being uncontrolled; violent*
1033. **turgid** *excessively ornate; swollen or bloated*

1034. **turmoil**	*state of extreme confusion, agitation or commotion*
1035. **turmoil**	*trouble; disturbance*
1036. **turquoise**	*greenish-blue precious stone*

U

1037. **ulterior**	*situated beyond*
1038. **ultimatum**	*a final offer or demand as in negotiations*
1039. **uncanny**	*mysterious, astonishing, strange, bizarre*
1040. **uncouth**	*rough; awkward*
1041. **underbid**	*make a lower bid than somebody else*
1042. **undermine**	*weaken gradually at the base*
1043. **undertone**	*quiet voice, murmur, whisper*
1044. **undo**	*loosen, open, unfasten*
1045. **unearth**	*discover and bring to light*
1046. **unexceptionable**	*not open to objection or criticism*
1047. **unexceptional**	*dull, commonplace, typical, ordinary* *A: Exceptional*
1048. **unfeigned**	*not pretended; sincere*
1049. **unilateral**	*of occurring on, or affecting one side only*
1050. **unison**	*agreement, Harmony* *S: Accord* *A: Discord, Enmity*
1051. **unprecedented**	*never having happened, not known before*
1052. **unrivalled**	*With no equal, unmatched*
1053. **unruffled**	*Calm, not anxious*
1054. **unruly**	*wild, with no discipline, defiant, indomitable*
1055. **unscathed**	*unharmed; unhurt*
1056. **unseemly**	*inappropriate; indecorous*
1057. **untoward**	*unfortunate; inconvenient*
1058. **upheaval**	*A sudden, violent change*
1059. **uphill**	*(i) Up a slope (ii) Laborious, Tiring* *S: Arduous, Difficult* *A: Easy*
1060. **uprising**	*a revolt against the rulers,* *S: Insurrection* *A: Submission*
1061. **uproar**	*Violent* *S: Confusing, Chaos* *A: Peace, Calm, Tranquility*
1062. **upsurge**	*an increase, rise*
1063. **urbane**	*elegant; refined in manners*
1064. **urchin**	*a mischievous child*
1065. **usurp**	*to take possession by force*
1066. **utopia**	*an imaginary ideal place*

V

1067. **vacillation**	*being uncertain; hesitating*
1068. **vain**	*without use, result; conceited*
1069. **valiant**	*brave*
1070. **vamp**	*Flirtatious woman, coquette, seductress, temptress*
1071. **vandal**	*person who destroys property for the pleasure of destruction*
1072. **vanity**	*pride, disdain, narcissism*
1073. **varnish**	*Adornment, decoration, polish, display*
1074. **vat**	*a large vessel*
1075. **veer**	*change direction*
1076. **vendetta**	*private quarrel between families*
1077. **venom**	*poison, toxin, bane, acrimony, ill will, malice*
1078. **veracity**	*truth*
1079. **verdant**	*fresh and green*
1080. **verdict**	*judgement, decision, ruling*
1081. **verve**	*spirit; vigor; enthusiasm*
1082. **vestige**	*trace or sign*
1083. **veterinary**	*Referring to treatment of sick animals*
1084. **vex**	*annoy; distress; trouble*
1085. **vice**	*evil, iniquity, sin, wickedness, depravity* *S: foible, dishonesty*
1086. **vicious**	*evil, wild, violent, fierce*
1087. **vigilance**	*watchfulness; self-appointed group that maintains order*
1088. **vigilant**	*member of a vigilance committee, alert, watchful*
1089. **vigorous**	*strong; energetic*
1090. **vile**	*extremely unpleasant, wicked, wretched*
1091. **vilify**	*slander; say evil things*
1092. **vindicate**	*to free from allegation or blame; to justify*
1093. **vindictive**	*having a desire to revenge*
1094. **vintage**	*old, ancient, antique, Collecting of grapes to make wine*
1095. **virile**	*manly, masculine, stalwart*
1096. **visceral**	*of the internal organs of the body*
1097. **viscous**	*sticky; semi-fluid*
1098. **vitiate**	*lower the quality; weaken the strength*
1099. **vivacious**	*lively; high-spirited*
1100. **volatile**	*changeable; inconstant*
1101. **volition**	*power of choosing or determining*
1102. **voluptuous**	*full of pleasure to the senses*

W

1103. **wag** *merry person*
1104. **warmonger** *person who stirs up war*
1105. **warrant** *authority; written order; guarantee*
1106. **wean** *to turn away (from a habit)*
1107. **whimsical** *full of odd and fanciful ideas*
1108. **wince** *show bodily or mental pain*
1109. **woo** *try to win*
1110. **wrangle** *to dispute angrily or peevishly*
1111. **writ** *written order*

Y

1112. **Yarn** *tale, story, fibers for knitting*

Z

1113. **zeal** *intense enthusiasm, ardour, fervour*
S: Easements
A: Apathy, Indifference
1114. **zenith** *the highest point*
S: Pinnacle, Summit
A: Base, Nadir
1115. **zest** *(i) keen enjoyment (ii) stimulating quality*
S: Gusto
A: Depression, Despondency

CHAPTER 2

Word List II—Medium Frequency Words

In this chapter, words that have a medium frequency (to be clear, words that are regularly appearing in CAT examinations, but not as frequent as those in Chapter 1) are being discussed. Even here the treatment has been done in such a manner that the meaning is given first, followed by the synonym (denoted by the letter *S*) and antonym (denoted by the letter *A*).

No.	Word	Definition
	A	
1.	**abashed**	*embarrassed*
2.	**abeyance**	*suspended action, not being used*
3.	**abject**	*miserable* *S: Pitiful, Despicable* *A: Noble, Lofty*
4.	**abnegation**	*self-denial*
5.	**abominate**	*to detest, to dislike strongly*
6.	**abrogate**	*repeal or annul by authority*
7.	**absolve**	*to free from guilt or duty* *S: Pardon, Exonerate* *A: Accuse, Inculpate*
8.	**abstemious**	*restraint, especially of food and alcohol*
9.	**abstinence**	*keeping away from all food, liquor, etc.* *S: Moderation, Temperance* *A: Excess, Wantonness*
10.	**abut**	*border on, next to*
11.	**acarpous**	*effete; no longer fertile; worn out*
12.	**accentuate**	*emphasise* *S: Stress, Highlight, Underline* *A: De-emphasise, Hide*
13.	**acclimate**	*to adapt, get used to*
14.	**accretion**	*growing of different things into one*
15.	**acoustics**	*branch of physics dealing with sound*
16.	**acrophobia**	*an abnormal fear of being in high places*
17.	**ad infinitum**	*forever, endlessly*
18.	**addendum**	*something added as a supplement*
19.	**ad hoc**	*for a specific purpose, especially arranged for a purpose*
20.	**adjunct**	*something added; assistant*
21.	**ad-lib**	*Improvise* *S: Spontaneous, Extemporised* *A: Rehearsed, Deliberate* *(ii) Do as one pleases*
22.	**adumbrate**	*to suggest or hint; overshadow*
23.	**ad-valorem**	*in proportion to the estimated value of goods*
24.	**aegis**	*Shield, Protection*
25.	**aestival**	*appearing in summer*
26.	**affectation**	*artificial, behaviour* *S: Pretence, Artificiality, Unnaturalness* *A: Simplicity, Naivete*
27.	**afforest**	*convert into forest* *A: Deforest, Denude*
28.	**affray**	*fight in a public place, battle* *S: Conflict, fight* *A: Tranquillity, Peace*
29.	**affront**	*insult openly* *S: Provoke, Humiliate* *A: Placate, Please*
30.	**aggrandise**	*to make greater, more powerful, richer*

S: Exalt, Advance
A: Degrade, Debase

31. **agnostic** *one who believes that it is impossible to know if God exists*
A: Theist
32. **agnostic** *non-committal*
33. **akimbo** *with hands on hips and elbows bent outwards*
34. **albeit** *although*
35. **alchemy** *chemistry of the middle ages with the chief aim of changing base metals to gold*
36. **algorithm** *a special way of solving a mathematical problem*
37. **allegory** *a story in which people, things, events have a symbolic meaning*
38. **allude** *to refer indirectly*
39. **alter ego** *one's other self, a constant companion*
A: Enemy
40. **altercate** *to dispute angrily or noisily*
41. **ambidextrous** *able to use the left hand or the right equally well*
42. **ambivalent** *having both of two contrary meanings*
43. **ameliorate** *improve; to make or become better*
S: Improve
A: Worsen
44. **amnesty** *a general pardon (especially for political offences)*
A: Punishment
45. **amortise** *end (a debt) by setting aside money*
46. **anachronism** *anything out of its proper historical time*
47. **anagram** *a word made by rearranging letters*
48. **anamnesis** *recollection (especially of previous existence)*
49. **anathema** *something loathed; curse*
50. **anchorite** *a religious recluse, hermit*
51. **androgynous** *hermaphrodite, having characteristics of both sexes*
52. **anecdote** *a short entertaining account of a real event or person*
53. **anodyne** *dull, Unlikely to cause offence, that relieves pain (Drug)*
54. **antagonism** *opposition or hostility*
S: Antipathy, Enmity
A: Harmony, Accord, Agreement
55. **antecedent** *that which goes before something else*
56. **anthology** *collection of literary works*
57. **antipathy** *strong dislike*
S: Hatred, Repugnance, Abhorrence
A: Honour, Admiration, Love, Esteem
58. **antithesis** *a contrast of position (especially of ideas)*
59. **antithetical** *direct opposing*
60. **apartheid** *brutal racial discrimination*
61. **apathy** *lack of emotion*
S: Indifference, Passiveness
A: Care, Sympathy
62. **aphasia** *loss of the power to use or comprehend words*
63. **aplomb** *self-confidence*
64. **apogee** *a point farthest from a heavenly body, the earth, powerful position*
65. **apologue** *moral fable especially one in which animals speak*
66. **apparition** *a ghost*
67. **appendage** *thing added to something larger or a natural part of a large thing*
S: Adjunct, Addition
68. **approbation** *approval*
69. **appurtenance** *a minor possession or piece of property*
70. **apropos** *appropriate to the situation; apt*
71. **archetype** *an original model, Prototype, ideal model which is not changed*
72. **ardour** *enthusiasm*
73. **arduous** *steep; difficult; ascent; laborious*
74. **argot** *jargon; slang*
75. **arrant** *in the highest degree, total*
76. **artifice** *skill or ingenuity, Trickery*
S: Wile, Guile, Fraud, Cunning
A: Innocence, Candour, Honesty
77. **ascribe** *consider to be the origin of or belonging to*
78. **aseptic** *surgically clean*
79. **asinine** *stupid, foolish*
S: Silly
A: Learned, Knowledgeable
80. **askance** *to look with suspicion*
81. **askew** *not in a straight or level position*
S: Awry, Crooked
82. **asperity** *roughness; harshness; ill temper; irritability*
83. **asseverate** *to state positively, Assert*
84. **assuage** *make something (pain, desire) less*
85. **astute** *clever, quick at seeing to get an advantage*
86. **asunder** *into pieces*
S: Apart
A: United, Harmonious
87. **athwart** *lying across, side-wise*
S: Across, Against, Crosswise
88. **atrophy** *wasting away or failure to grow (especially of body tissue)*
89. **attenuate** *make thin; weaken; enervate*
90. **attrition** *wearing away by or as by friction*

91. **atypical** *not typical*
S: Abnormal
A: Typical, Normal

92. **augury** *omen; sign*

B

93. **babel** *a scene of confusion of noises, sounds, etc.*
S: Confusion
A: Distinctness

94. **badinage** *Playful talk*
S: Banter
A: Discourse

95. **bagatelle** *thing of little value, trifle, game*

96. **bauble** *a trinket, worthless thing*

97. **balderdash** *odd mixture, nonsense*
S: Drivel, Gibberish
A: Wisdom, Logic

98. **baneful** *causing harm or ruin; pernicious; destructive*

99. **banter** *playful teasing*

100. **baritone** *the range of a male voice between tenor and bass*

101. **bastion** *any strong defence*

102. **bathos** *anticlimax*
A: Decent

103. **baulk** *stumbling block (N), To hinder (V)*
S: Hindrance
A: Gratify, Fulfil

104. **bawdy** *indecent, obscene*
A: Decent

105. **beatify** *to bless; make happy or ascribe a virtue to*

106. **beatitude** *perfect blessedness or happiness*
A: Curse, Condemnation

107. **bedlam** *any place or situation with noise and confusion*

108. **bedraggle** *to make wet, limp or dirty*
S: Wet, Dirty
A: Clean, spotless

109. **befuddle** *to confuse, perplex*

110. **begrudge** *to resent another's success*

111. **beguile** *to mislead or deprive of; to delight*

112. **behest** *a command or earnest request*

113. **belabor** *beat hard*

114. **beleaguer** *to besiege by encircling, to harass*

115. **bellicose** *belligerent; pugnacious; warlike*

116. **belligerent** *(person, nation) waging war*

117. **benison** *blessing*
A: Curse

118. **bequeath** *to leave to another by one's will*

119. **bequest** *arrangement to give something at death*

120. **besmirch** *to soil, to damage the reputation*
S: Defile, Sully

121. **bibliography** *a list of writings on a given subject*

122. **bibliophile** *one who loves or collects books*

123. **bilious** *bad-tempered*
S: Peevish, Pessimistic
A: Optimistic, Lively

124. **bilk** *to cheat*

125. **blasphemy** *profane, abuse of God or sacred things*

126. **bleary** *Dim or blurred*

127. **blithe** *cheerful; casual; carefree*

128. **bluster** *to talk or act with noisy swaggering threats*

129. **bounteous** *generous, abundant*
S: Benevolent, Liberal, Generous
A: Miserly

130. **bourgeois** *middle class*

131. **bovine** *of an ox or cow, slow and stupid*
A: Sharp, Intelligent, Sprightly

132. **braggart** *An offensively boastful person*

133. **brevity** *Brief*
S: Brief, Short, Terse, Concise
A: Lengthy, Elaborate

134. **broach** *To start a discussion of*

135. **brook** *not allow; a small stream*

136. **browbeat** *to intimidate*
S: Force
A: Coax, Cajole

137. **brusque** *rough and abrupt in manner of speech*
S: Curt, Blunt
A: Rambling

138. **bucolic** *rural, rustic*
A: Urban

139. **bulbous** *swollen, shaped like a bulb*

140. **bulwark** *a defence*

141. **buoyant** *able to float; light-hearted*

142. **burnish** *to polish, rub to a shine*

143. **buttress** *a strong Support*
S: Bolster, Prop-up

C

144. **cabal** *a scheme or plot; a group of plotters*

145. **cadaverous** *of or like a cadaver (Corpse)*
S: Pale, Ghastly
A: Cheerful, Youthful

146. **cadence** *rhythmic modulation of sound*

147. **cadge** *to beg or get by begging*

148. **calligraphy** *art of producing beautiful handwriting*

149. **callow** *immature, inexperienced*
S: Raw, Unfledged, Inexperienced
A: Mature, Wise, Sagacious

150. **calumny** *slander; aspersion*
151. **canard** *a false especially malicious report*
S: Hide/Hoax
A: Expose
152. **canker** *a spreading sore*
153. **canonise** *to glorify, to declare (a dead person) a saint*
154. **canorous** *melodious, Resonant*
S: Melodious
A: Harsh, Discordant
155. **capacious** *Roomy*
S: Spacious
A: Narrow, Limited, Confined
156. **capitulate** *surrender*
157. **capricious** *subject to caprices (Eccentricities), erratic*
S: Fanciful, Odd, Whimsical
A: Staid, Steadfast
158. **captious** *Critical*
159. **carmine** *a red or purplish red colour*
160. **carnage** *extensive slaughter, Massacre*
S: Butchery, Destruction
161. **carnal** *of the flesh*
S: Sensual, Lustful, Concupiscent
A: Spiritual, Ethereal
162. **carp** *to find fault or complain querulously*
163. **carrion** *decaying flesh of a dead body*
164. **cartel** *an association of business firms etc. establishing a national or international monopoly*
165. **catastrophe** *any sudden, great disaster*
S: Calamity, Cataclysm
A: Blessing
166. **catatonic** *immobile*
167. **catechise** *to question searchingly*
168. **caucus** *a meeting of a party or faction (Usually derogatory)*
169. **cavalcade** *A procession, Sequence of events*
170. **cavil** *to raise trivial and frivolous objection*
171. **centurion** *leader of a unit of 100 soldiers*
172. **cerebrate** *to think*
173. **charlatan** *quack or fraud*
174. **chary** *cautious; wary*
175. **chastisement** *punishment*
176. **chauvinist** *a blindly devoted patriot*
177. **chequered** *Marked by vicissitudes*
178. **chivy** *to tease or annoy with persistent petty attacks*
179. **choleric** *irritable; bad-tempered*
180. **churl** *bad-tempered person*
181. **closure** *closing device (in Parliament) to end a debate by voting*
182. **coagulation** *change to a thick and solid state*
183. **coalescing** *coming together and uniting into one substance*
184. **coddle** *treat with care and tenderness*
185. **coeval** *of the same period; coexisting*
186. **cogent** *strong; convincing*
187. **cognomen** *surname, last name*
188. **coherent** *sticking together, logically connected*
S: Unity,
A: Separation
189. **collateral** *a) Parallel or corresponding*
S: Secondary, Parallel, Concurrent
b) Security towards a loan
190. **comity** *courtesy*
S: Friendly
A: Hostility
191. **commemorate** *keep the memory of*
192. **commodious** *having plenty of space for what is needed*
193. **complaisance** *tending to comply; obliging willingness to please*
194. **complement** *the amount needed to fill or complete*
195. **compliment** *a formal act of courtesy, praise*
S: Flatter, Felicitate
A: Disparage, Censure, Blame
196. **conciliatory** *reconciling; soothing; comforting; mollifying*
197. **concomitant** *accompanying*
198. **condescend** *to deal with others patronisingly, do something below one's dignity; comedown*
199. **congeal** *make or become stiff and solid*
200. **congenital** *existing from birth; inherent*
201. **conjecture** *inferring or predicting from incomplete evidence*
S: Guesswork
A: Affirmation
202. **connoisseur** *a person with good judgement (for example in art)*
203. **connotation** *suggestion in addition to*
204. **connubial** *Of marriage, Conjugal*
S: Matrimonial
205. **conscientious** *governed by one's conscience*
S: Scrupulous, Painstaking
206. **console** *give comfort or sympathy to*
207. **conspectus** *a general view*
S: Summary
208. **consternation** *surprise and fear; dismay*
209. **consummate** *perfect; make perfect, complete*
210. **condemn** *to scorn or despise*
211. **contemptible** *deserving contempt, scorn*
S: Despicable, Mean, Cowardly
A: Good, Worthy, Brave

212. **contemptuous** *full of contempt, scornful*
213. **contentious** *argumentative; pugnacious; combative; quarrelsome*
214. **contiguous** *touching; neighboring*
215. **contingent** *a) a group of people sharing particular characteristics b) dependent c) troops part of a larger force*
216. **convivial** *fond of feasting, drinking and good company*
217. **convoluted** *complicated; coiled; twisted*
218. **cordon** *line (of police acting as a guard)*
219. **corporeal** *physical of or for the body*
220. **corpulent** *having a large bulky body*
221. **countervail** *counterbalance*
222. **covert** *disguised*
223. **cozen** *to cheat*
224. **cravat** *piece of linen worn as a necktie*
225. **craven** *cowardly*
226. **credulous** *ready to believe things*
227. **crotchet** *highly individual and usually eccentric opinion*

D

228. **dank** *disagreeably damp*
S: Moist, Soggy, Wet
229. **dapper** *small and active*
S: Trim, Neat
A: Awkward, Untidy
230. **dastard** *coward*
231. **daunt** *intimidate; make fearful*
232. **dawdler** *person who is slow; waste of time*
233. **debauch** *to corrupt*
S: Corrupt, Debase, Defile
234. **debilitate** *to make weak*
S: Enervate
A: Strengthen, Invigorate
235. **debonair** *dashing, Courteous*
236. **decadence** *A process, condition or period of decline as in morals, art, etc.*
237. **decant** *Pour off*
238. **decimate** *To destroy or kill a large part of*
239. **defalcate** *to steal or misuse funds entrusted to one*
S: Embezzle
240. **deferential** *showing respect*
241. **defray** *to pay*
S: Settle, Adjust
A: Decamp, Repudiate, Disown
242. **defunct** *no longer existing*
S: Extinct, Dead
A: Alive, Fashionable
243. **deify** *to look upon as a God*
244. **deign** *to condescend; to give*
245. **delineate** *to portray, depict, sketch out*
246. **deluge** *great flood; heavy rush of water*
247. **delusion** *a false belief, the act of deluding*
S: Hallucination, Illusion, Error
A: Certainty, Reality, Fact
248. **demeanour** *outward Behaviour*
S: Behaviour, Manner, Conduct
249. **denigrate** *blacken; belittle; defame*
250. **deposition** *dethronement; depositing*
251. **deprave** *make morally bad, corrupt*
252. **deprecate** *protest against; express disapproval of*
253. **depredation** *damage caused by an attack or an accident*
254. **deride** *to ridicule*
S: Taunt, Mock, Scorn
A: Encourage, Cheer, Incite
255. **derision** *ridicule; mockery; deriding*
256. **descry** *catch sight of; see something in the distance*
257. **desecrate** *to violate the sacredness of*
S: Profane, Misuse, Pollute
A: Sanctify, Purify, cleanse
258. **desperado** *dangerous criminal*
259. **despondency** *dejection*
S: Melancholy, Depression
A: Buoyancy, Elation
260. **desultory** *aimless; haphazard; digressing at random*
261. **detention** *detaining*
262. **devolve** *to pass on to another, said of duties, responsibilities etc.*
263. **diacritic** *distinguishing*
264. **diaphanous** *transparent; gauzy*
265. **diatribe** *bitter and violent attack in words*
266. **dichotomy** *division into two parts*
267. **diligent** *hardworking*
S: Perseverance, Earnest
A: Lazy, Careless, Lethargic
268. **dirge** *A song, poem, etc., of grief or mourning*
269. **disconcert** *upset the self-possession of*
270. **disconsolate** *cheerless; dejected*
271. **discursive** *wandering from one topic to another*
272. **disenchanted** *disillusioned; Having lost one's good opinion of something*
273. **disencumber** *free from encumbrance*
274. **disgorge** *to pour or let out people or things in a mass*
275. **disheveled** *untidy*
276. **disingenuous** *sophisticated; artful; trying to deceive; cunning*

277. **disparage** *to Discredit*
A: Praise, Eulogise
278. **disport** *to play*
279. **disquiet** *to take away the peace or tranquility*
280. **disquisition** *a long or elaborate spoken or written report*
281. **disseminate** *distribute (esp. ideas)*
282. **distend** *to swell, to expand*
283. **divestiture** *taking off; getting rid of; giving up*
284. **doggerel** *trivial, poorly constructed verse*
285. **dolorous** *marked by misery or grief*
286. **droll** *jesting*
287. **dulcet** *melodious; harmonious*
288. **duress** *threats to compel somebody*

E

289. **ebullience** *exuberance; outburst of feeling*
290. **ebullient** *overflowing with enthusiasm; showing excitement*
291. **eclat** *brilliant success*
292. **efface** *to make indistinct*
293. **effeminate** *show qualities attributed to a woman such as delicacy, weakness, etc.*
S: Womanly, Feminine, Unmanly
A: Manly, Masculine, Virile
294. **effervesce** *to be lively*
S: Buoyant, Gleeful
A: Staid, Sober, Sedate
295. **effete** *infertile; worn out; weak*
296. **effrontery** *boldness; impudence; arrogance*
297. **effusion** *unrestrained expression in speaking or writing; Heavy flow*
A: Reticence
298. **egalitarian** *advocating full political and social equality for all people*
A: Fanatic
299. **egregious** *flagrant*
300. **elision** *leaving out a sound or part of a word in pronunciation as in Don't, Let's*
301. **elucidate** *to make something clear*
S: Explain, Illustrate, Clarify
A: Obscure, Confuse, Disorder
302. **emancipate** *to set free (a slave etc.)*
S: Liberate, Release
A: Suppress, Hold, Restrain
303. **emasculate** *to weaken*
304. **embargo** *any legal restriction of commerce*
305. **emollient** *soothing to the skin; mollifying*
306. **empathy** *intellectual or emotional identification with another*
S: Understanding, Sensitivity
A: Insensitivity
307. **empirical** *relying on experiment*
308. **encomium** *warm or glowing praise; eulogy; panegyric*
309. **endemic** *prevalent in or restricted to a particular locality*
A: Pandemic
310. **enervate** *to deprive of strength, vigour etc.*
S: Weaken, Enfeeble, Devitalise
A: Strengthen, Energise
311. **enfeeble** *weaken; deprive of strength; attenuate*
312. **enigma** *something that is puzzling*
313. **ensconce** *to place or settle snugly or securely*
A: Estrange, Alienate
314. **entourage** *A group of personal attendants*
315. **epicurean** *devoted to pleasure (sensuous enjoyment)*
316. **epigram** *terse or witty and often paradoxical saying*
317. **epistle** *letter*
318. **equanimity** *calmness of temperament*
319. **equestrian** *of horses or horsemanship*
320. **equipoise** *equal distribution of weight; equilibrium*
321. **equitable** *Fair*
S: Impartial, Fair, Just
A: Prejudiced, Partial
322. **equivocal** *having a double or doubtful meaning; suspicious*
323. **equivocate** *try to deceive by equivocal language*
324. **erroneous** *containing an error*
S: False, Inaccurate, Erring
A: Accurate, Genuine, Factual
325. **escapade** *Reckless adventure*
326. **eschew** *avoid*
327. **esoteric** *abstruse; intended only for a small circle of people*
328. **estrange** *to turn from an affectionate attitude to an indifferent or unfriendly one*
S: Alienate, Withdraw, Disagree
A: Unite, Conjoin, Harmonise
329. **ethos** *the characteristic attitude, habits etc. of an individual or group*
330. **euphemism** *the use of a less direct word or phrase instead of an unpleasant one*
331. **evince** *to show clearly; to indicate*
332. **exacerbate** *to make more violent, bitter or severe*
333. **exacting** *making severe demands, Strict*
334. **exactitude** *The quality of being exact*

335. **exalt** *to praise, glorify, to raise in rank*
A: Degrade, Condemn, Despise
336. **excision** *pruning*
337. **excruciating** *intensely painful*
S: Agonising, Intense, Severe
A: Soothing
338. **exegesis** *interpretation of a word, passage, etc. in the Bible*
339. **exemplary** *serving as a model or example*
S: Model, Pattern
340. **exhort** *to urge earnestly*
S: Urge, Advise
A: Deter, Prevent, Oppose
341. **exiguous** *scanty*
S: Meagre, Small
A: Huge, Enormous
342. **exoneration** *set somebody clear, free (for example, from blame)*
343. **exorcise** *to expel (an evil spirit) by incantations, etc.*
A: Bedevil
344. **expansive** *effusive, open*
S: Unreserved, Broad, Demonstrative
A: Laconic, Cantankerous
345. **expatiate** *to roam; wander freely*
346. **expiation** *ending; expiring*
347. **expostulate** *argue earnestly; to dissuade, correct or protest*
348. **expurgate** *to remove obscenity, purify, censor*
349. **extant** *still in existence*
350. **extenuate** *reduce the strength; lessen seriousness; partially excuse*
351. **extirpate** *to destroy; exterminate*
352. **extralegal** *outside the law*
353. **extraneous** *extrinsic; not forming an essential part*
354. **extricable** *that can be freed*
355. **exuberance** *state of growing vigorously; being full of life*

F

356. **facetious** *humorous; funny; jocular*
357. **facile** *easily done*
358. **fait accompli** *foreign phrase, thing done beyond recall, accomplished fact*
359. **fallow** *left without seeding after being ploughed to make fertile*
360. **fatuous** *without sense; foolish self-satisfaction*
361. **feckless** *lacking purpose or vitality; ineffective*
362. **fecund** *fertile*
363. **feint** *pretend*
364. **ferret** *discover by searching; search*
365. **fervid** *showing earnest feeling*
366. **fervour** *enthusiasm*
S: zeal, ardour, passion, fervent
A: coolness, indifference, impassiveness
367. **fetid** *stinking*
368. **fetter** *to shackle; put in chains*
369. **filch** *steal slyly in small amounts*
S: Snitch, swipe, pilfer, purloin
370. **filial** *befitting a son or daughter*
371. **firmament** *sky*
372. **flay** *to skin; to excoriate*
373. **fledged** *able to fly; trained, experienced*
374. **flinch** *draw; move back; wince*
375. **flippancy** *lack of seriousness*
S: levity, pertness, impudence
376. **flounder** *to struggle to move; to proceed clumsily*
377. **foible** *defect of character (a person is wrongly proud)*
378. **foppish** *like a man who pays too much attention to his clothes*
379. **forage** *food for horses and cattle*
380. **ford** *shallow place in a river (to cross)*
381. **forebode** *to foretell or predict*
382. **forestall** *prevent by taking action in advance, preempt*
383. **foretoken** *premonitory sign*
384. **forswear** *renounce; disallow; repudiate*
385. **fortitude** *courage*
S: Heroism, Spirited
A: Cowardice, Shyness
386. **fortuitous** *happening by chance*
S: Incidental, Adventitious, Accidental
A: Deliberate, planned
387. **fragrant** *sweet-smelling*
388. **frenetic** *frantic, frenzied*
389. **fresco** *art of painting on a plaster surface especially when the surface is moist*
390. **fritter** *to waste (money, time, etc.)*
391. **frivolous** *of little value, Trivial, Silly*
S: Petty, Worthless, Futile
A: Serious, Important
392. **fulsome** *disgusting; offensive due to excessiveness, insincere praise*
393. **furore** *a widespread commotion or uproar*
394. **furtive** *done secretly*
S: stealthy, clandestine
A: open, apparent
395. **fusillade** *simultaneous discharge of many firearms*
S: volley, salvo, broadside
396. **fusty** *musty; rigidly old-fashioned or reactionary*

G

397. **gabble** *to talk or utter rapidly, or incoherently*
S: Chatter, Babble, Jabber
398. **gaff** *a large hook on a pole for landing fish*
399. **gaffe** *a blunder*
400. **gainsay** *to deny; to oppose*
401. **galore** *in abundance, plentiful*
S: ample, bounteous, prodigal
A: Scarce, deficient
402. **gambit** *an action intended to gain an advantage*
403. **garner** *to gather and save to store up*
404. **garrulity** *talkativeness*
405. **garrulous** *too talkative*
406. **gastronomy** *the art of cooking and eating good food*
407. **gazebo** *An open structure with an enjoyable view*
408. **genealogy** *recorded history of one's ancestry*
409. **genesis** *origin*
410. **genitor** *a father/parent*
411. **genuflect** *to bend the knee as in worship*
412. **gibber** *to speak rapidly and incoherently*
A: Enunciate
413. **gizmo** *a gadget, device, mechanism*
414. **glean** *gather facts in small quantities*
415. **glitch** *a small hurdle or problem*
416. **gloat** *look at with selfish delight*
417. **glut** *supply too much; fill to excess*
418. **glutino** *sticky*
S: Viscous
A: Dry
419. **gnome** *A dwarf (like an old man) living in a cave*
420. **gnomic** *characterised by aphorism*
421. **graffiti** *a crude inscription or drawing on a wall or other public surface*
422. **grandiose** *impressive, Showy*
423. **grapple** *to seize, to hold tightly*
424. **gravid** *pregnant*
425. **gregarious** *living in societies; liking the company*
426. **grisly** *terrifying*
S: Horrible, Terrible, Ghastly
A: Attractive, Charming, Dainty
427. **grizzle** *of a grey colour*
428. **grouch** *to grumble, grouse*
429. **guffaw** *to laugh loudly*
430. **guile** *deceit, wile, cunning, jugglery*
431. **gumption** *initiative and courage*
S: Commonsense, Sagacity, Acumen
A: Apathy, Indifference
432. **gustatory** *of the sense of taste*
433. **gusto** *zest, enjoyment*
S: Relish, Pleasure, Enthusiasm
A: Apathy
434. **guttural** *pertaining to the throat, formed in the throat*

H

435. **habitué** *one who frequents a certain place*
436. **hackneyed** *made trite by overuse*
S: stereotyped Commonplace,
437. **haggard** *having a wild, wasted, worn look,*
S: Gaunt, Tired, weary
A: strong, Robust, Exuberant
438. **hallow** *to make holy; consecrate*
439. **hapless** *unfortunate*
S: Luckless, Unlucky
A: Fortunate, Successful, Happy
440. **harangue** *a long passionate speech*
441. **harbinger** *something or somebody that foretells the coming of*
442. **harrow** *to distress; create stress or torment*
443. **harrowing** *upsetting*
444. **heckle** *to harass, (a speaker) with questions or taunts*
445. **heckle** *to harass with questions, challenges or gibes*
446. **hedonism** *the doctrine that pleasure is the principal good*
S: Epicureanism, Sensualism, debauchery
A: Slavery, Servility
447. **herculean** *calling for great strength, size and courage*
S: Rugged, Enduring, Steadfast
448. **hermetic** *sealed by fusion, a closed group*
449. **heterodox** *opposed to the usual beliefs especially in religion*
S: Unorthodox
A: Orthodox
450. **hew** *make by hard work cut (by striking)*
451. **hiatus** *a gap or break as where a part is missing*
452. **histrionic** *of acting*
453. **hoary** *Very old and well known; Grey or white (of hair) with age*
454. **hobgoblin** *Something that causes fear, A frightening apparition*
455. **hogwash** *insincere talk, writing, etc.*
456. **holster** *leather case for a pistol*
457. **homonym** *a word with the same pronunciation and spelling as another but with a different meaning, origin*
458. **honorific** *conferring or conveying honor*

459. **horology** *the science of measuring time or making time pieces*

460. **horrendous** *horrible*
S: Frightful, Horrifying, Fearful
A: Appealing, Pleasant, Charming

461. **hubbub** *noise; confusion*

462. **hyperbole** *extravagant exaggeration*

I

463. **iconoclast** *person who attacks popular beliefs*

464. **ides** *in ancient Roman calendar, 15th day of May, March, July or October or 13th of the other months*

465. **idiosyncrasy** *personal mannerism*

466. **idolatry** *excessive admiration of*

467. **idyll** *a carefree episode or experience*

468. **igneous** *of fire, fiery, type of rock*

469. **ignoble** *dishonorable; common; undignified*

470. **imbecile** *a person with abnormally low intelligence*
S: Weak-minded, Deranged, Childish
A: Strong-minded, Intellectual, Genius

471. **imbroglio** *complicated and embarrassing situation*

472. **imbue** *to permeate with ideas, feelings etc.*
S: Pervade, Suffuse, Inspire
A: Discourage, Condemn

473. **immanent** *operating within, Inherent*
S: Indwelling
A: Transcendent

474. **immutable** *that cannot be changed*

475. **impale** *to pierce with a sharp stake through the body*

476. **impalpable** *not perceptible to touch*
S: Intangible, Vague
A: Material, Solid, Definite

477. **impeccable** *Flawless*
S: Immaculate, Faultless, Perfect
A: Defective, Rowdy

478. **imperil** *To put in danger*
S: Endanger, Hazard, Jeopardise
A: Safeguard, Protect, Preserve

479. **imperious** *commanding; haughty; arrogant*

480. **imperviousness** *not permeable; not moved easily*

481. **impetuous** *having sudden energy; impulsive*

482. **impiety** *lack of reverence or dutifulness*

483. **impinge** *to strike, hit, etc. (on or upon)*
S: Strike, Hit

484. **implicate** *show that somebody has a share*

485. **implosion** *collapse; bursting inward*

486. **impromptu** *without preparation*

487. **impropriety** *being improper*

488. **impugned** *challenged; to be doubted*

489. **impunity** *exemption from punishment, harm or loss*

490. **impute** *to attribute; to a cause or source; ascribe*

491. **inchoate** *not yet fully formed; rudimentary; elementary*

492. **incipient** *beginning*

493. **incognito** *disguised under an assumed name, rank, etc.*
S: Unidentified

494. **incorrigibility** *cannot be cured or corrected*

495. **incredulous** *skeptical; unwilling to believe*

496. **incubus** *A nightmare*

497. **incumbents** *official duties*

498. **incursion** *a raid; a sudden attack*

499. **indict** *to charge with a crime*
S: Accuse, Incriminate

500. **indigenous** *native*

501. **indite** *to compose and write*
S: Compose

502. **indubitable** *too evident to be doubted*

503. **ineffable** *too great to be described in words*

504. **inferno** *hell, large fire*

505. **infinitesimal** *Too small to be measured*

506. **infraction** *a violating of a law or pact*
S: Violation, Infringement
A: Compliance, Submission

507. **ingenuous** *naïve; young; artless; frank*

508. **inimical** *harmful*

509. **inkling** *a hint*
S: Intimation, Idea

510. **innate** *Inborn, Natural (an innate sense of style)*
S: Intrinsic
A: Extrinsic, Alien

511. **innocuous** *causing no harm*

512. **inordinate** *exceeding reasonable limits*

513. **insatiable** *that cannot be satisfied*
S: Unquenchable, Greedy, Un-appeasable
A: Appeasable, Quenchable

514. **inscrutable** *not easily understood*
S: Incomprehensible, Baffling, Mysterious
A: Obvious, Plain, Evident

515. **inscrutable** *incapable of being discovered or understood*

516. **insouciant** *unconcerned; carefree*

517. **insularity** *narrow-mindedness; isolated*

518. **insurrection** *rising of people to open resistance to*

519. **interpose** *to come between*

520. **intersperse** *place here and there*

521. **intransigence** *unwillingness to compromise; stubbornness; intractability*

522. **intransigent** *uncompromising*
523. **intrepid** *fearless; brave; undaunted*
524. **introspection** *examining one's own thoughts and feelings*
525. **inured** *accustomed to, adapted*
526. **inveigh** *to attack verbally; denounce; deprecate*
527. **invincible** *too strong to be defeated*
528. **involute** *complex*
529. **irascible** *irritable; easily angered*
530. **irrevocable** *final and unalterable*
531. **itinerate** *to travel from place to place; to peregrinate*

J

532. **jackass** *a fool, a blockhead*
533. **jalopy** *a battered old car*
534. **janitor** *Attendant, caretaker, doorkeeper*
535. **jargon** *The terminology of a specific group or profession*
A: confused talk, chatter
536. **jaunt** *an excursion, jaunt, to make a short journey*
537. **jaunty** *Having a sprightly manner*
S: cheerful, Confident, vivacious
A: gloomy, listless, dull
538. **jeopardy** *danger, insecurity, peril, hazard*
539. **jettison** *to get rid of as superfluous or encumbering*
540. **jinx** *a person or thing supposed to bring bad luck*
541. **jocose** *full of jokes, merry, playful, jocular*
542. **jocund** *playful, pleasant, cheerful, merry, jovial*
543. **john bull** *a person who brings bad luck; a typical Englishman*
544. **jovian** *of the planet Jupiter*
545. **judas** *a traitor*
546. **judicature** *jurisdiction, power of dispensing justice by legal trial*
547. **jugular** *Pertaining to the neck veins*
548. **junket** *a picnic, an outing, a spree, a feast, a paid excursion*
549. **jurassic** *the Jurassic period, very old period*
550. **jurisprudence** *science of laws*

K

551. **Kaiser** *a German emperor*
552. **kaleidoscope** *an optical toy showing a changing variety of forms*
553. **kaleidoscopic** *constantly changing*
554. **kaput** *Rendered useless; unable to function*
555. **kickback** *percentage given back to a person who has enabled one to make money*
556. **kilt** *pleated knee-length skirt of tartan wool, worn by men as part of Scottish costume*
557. **kindred** *related, congruous, akin*
558. **kinetic** *related to motion, not static*
559. **kink** *a whim, a mental twist, imperfection*
560. **kleptomania** *an abnormal, persistent impulse to steal*
561. **knap-sack** *a rucksack, a case/bag strapped onto the shoulders*
562. **knave (nave)** *A false/deceitful fellow, a serving boy*
563. **knead** *press and stretch with the hands to form a firm smooth paste; knead the dough*
564. **knell** *to ring slowly, toll (omen of death, failure, etc.)*
565. **knick-knack** *a small trifling toy, plaything, amusement, trinket*
566. **kurd** *one of the people of Kurdistan*

L

567. **labyrinthine** *to entangle; the state of affairs*
568. **lacuna** *a blank space, especially a missing portion in a text, etc.*
S: Gap
569. **laggard** *A slow person, especially one who falls behind*
S: Slowpoke, Dawdler
570. **lapidary** *(i) Concerned with stone, Engravings on stone (ii) A cutter or polisher of precious stones*
571. **lascivious** *characterised by or expressing lust*
S: Immoral, Lustful, Lecherous
A: Pure, Chaste, virtuous
572. **lassitude** *weariness; tiredness*
573. **laudatory** *expressing or giving praise*
574. **leer** *A sly, sidelong look showing lust, malicious triumph*
575. **levee** *formal reception; embankment*
576. **levitation** *the power of raising a body in the air (against gravity) with no support*
577. **levity** *lack of seriousness*
578. **libertine** *immoral person*
579. **licentious** *morally unrestrained.*
S: Wanton, Lustful
A: Continent, Chaste
580. **lien** *legal claim until a debt on it is repaid*
581. **limber** *easily bent, flexible, to exercise in preparation for a sport*

582. **limbo** — *in an uncertain state*
583. **lionise** — *treat as a famous person*
584. **logistics** — *the military science of procuring, maintaining and transporting material and personnel*
585. **lope** — *move along with long strides*
586. **loquacious** — *talkative; garrulous*
587. **lucre** — *riches, money, used chiefly in a derogatory sense*
588. **ludicrous** — *causing laughter because it is absurd or ridiculous*
S: Absurd, Laughable, Preposterous
589. **lurid** — *shocking, Sensational, Violent*
A: Bright, Pleasant, highly coloured

M

590. **macabre** — *gruesome; suggesting death*
591. **maladroit** — *tactless; clumsy*
592. **malaise** — *A vague feeling of physical discomfort or of uneasiness*
593. **malediction** — *curse; execration*
594. **malefaction** — *evil deed; crime*
595. **malefactor** — *An evil doer or criminal*
S: Wrong doer
596. **maleficent** — *baleful*
597. **malevolence** — *wishing to do evil*
598. **mammoth** — *Huge, Enormous*
599. **maraud** — *To raid, Plunder*
600. **martinet** — *Strict disciplinarian*
601. **masquerade** — *disguise*
602. **maudlin** — *sentimental in a silly or tearful way*
603. **maunder** — *To talk or move in a confused, aimless way*
604. **maverick** — *rebel; nonconformist*
605. **mawkish** — *sickly or puerilely sentimental*
606. **mayhem** — *Any violent destruction or disorder.*
S: Havoc, Chaos
A: Peace, Tranquility
607. **megalomania** — *A mental disorder characterised by delusions of power, grandeur etc.*
608. **melee** — *A confused fight, Confused crowd of people*
S: Scuffle, Brawl, Affray
A: Order
609. **mellifluous** — *sweetly flowing, sweet sounding*
610. **menage** — *a household*
611. **mercenary** — *working or done for payment only*
S: Venal, Pecuniary, Avaricious
A: Altruistic
612. **meretricious** — *attractive on the surface but of little value*
613. **mete** — *distribute in portions*
614. **meteoric** — *momentarily brilliant*
S: Rapid, Transient
A: Gradual, Dull, Slow
615. **miasma** — *vaporous exhalation causing disease*
616. **microcosm** — *a miniature representation of a whole*
S: Portion
A: Macrocosm
617. **middling** — *fairly good but not very good*
618. **milieu** — *environment, especially a social setting,*
S: Background, Atmosphere
619. **minatory** — *menacing; threatening*
620. **misogynist** — *one who hates women, females*
621. **monomania** — *excessive concentration on a single object or idea*
622. **mottle** — *surface having colored spots or blotches*
623. **munificent** — *characterised by great liberality or generosity*

N

624. **narcissistic** — *conceited, vain*
625. **natation** — *act or art of swimming*
626. **nebulous** — *cloud-like; hazy; vague*
627. **necromancy** — *magic, especially that practiced by a witch*
628. **nefarious** — *very wicked*
S: Unlawful, Villainous
A: Virtuous, Innocent
629. **nemesis** — *(i) Just punishment, Deserved fate*
(ii) Goddess of vengeance
630. **neologism** — *new use of a word*
631. **neophyte** — *person who has been converted to a belief*
632. **nepotism** — *favouritism shown by a person in high position to relatives especially in securing jobs,*
A: Impartiality
633. **nescient** — *ignorant*
A: Knowledgeable
634. **nettle** — *to sting, annoy, bother, exasperate*
635. **niggard** — *a stingy person, miser*
S: Stingy
A: Generous, Spendthrift, Bounteous
636. **nimbus** — *a halo, aura, cloud*
637. **nincompoop** — *a stupid, silly person, Fool*
S: Simpleton, Stupid, Fool
A: Genius
638. **nit-picking** — *carping, fault-finding*
639. **noisome** — *injurious to health*
640. **noisome** — *offensive; disgusting (smell)*
641. **nonchalant** — *not having interest*
642. **nondescript** — *belonging to no definite class or type*
643. **nonpareil** — *unequaled*
S: Unrivaled, Peerless
A: Commonplace

644. **nonplus** *confuse*
645. **nonplussed** *greatly surprised*
646. **nostalgia** *a longing for something far away or long ago*
647. **noveau riche** *a newly rich person of poor tastes*
648. **novitiate** *period of being a novice; house where novices are trained*
649. **nuance** *A slight variation in tone, colour, meaning etc.*
650. **nugatory** *trifling; worthless*
651. **numskull** *stupid, fool*

O

652. **obdurate** *hardened and unrepentant; stubborn; inflexible*
653. **obeisance** *a gesture of respect*
 S: deep bow, Homage, Reverence, Deference
 A: Irreverence, Impudence
654. **oblation** *An offering or sacrifice to God*
655. **obliterate** *to blot out, to erase,*
 S: Delete, Raze
 A: Preserve, Build
656. **oblivion** *Forgetfulness*
 S: Obscurity
657. **obloquy** *abusively detractive language; sharp criticism*
658. **obviate** *to make unnecessary; get rid of*
659. **occult** *(i) Hidden, mysterious*
 (ii) Supernatural, Magical
660. **ocular** *of, for, or like the eye*
661. **odoriferous** *giving off an odour, especially a fragrant one*
 S: Fragrant, Sweet-smelling
 A: Malodorous
662. **officious** *too eager or ready to help; offer advice*
663. **ogre** *in fairy tales and folklore, a man-eating giant*
 S: Monster, Demon
664. **olfactory** *of the sense of smell*
665. **oligarchy** *a government in which a few persons have the ruling power*
666. **omnipotent** *having unlimited power or authority,*
 S: All-powerful
 A: Weak, Powerless
667. **omnipresent** *present at all places at all times*
668. **onerous** *needing effort; burdensome*
669. **opiate** *anything quieting*
670. **oracle** *the revelation by a medium or priest*
671. **ornithology** *the branch of zoology dealing with the study of birds*
672. **ossify** *to turn to bone; to settle rigidly into an idea*
673. **ostensible** *seeming; appearing as such; professed*
674. **ostracism** *shut out from society; refuse to meet, talk*
675. **overweening** *presumptuously arrogant; being a jerk*

P

676. **palpitate** *tremble; beat rapidly and irregularly*
677. **paltry** *very small*
678. **panegyric** *formal praise; eulogy*
679. **panorama** *perspective, land*
680. **paper tiger** *a person or thing that is threatening but is actually weak*
681. **parry** *block*
682. **parsimonious** *too economical; miserly*
683. **pedantic** *bookish; showing off learning*
684. **pellucid** *transparent; easy to understand*
685. **per se** *by itself*
686. **perambulate** *to travel over or through (esp. on foot)*
687. **percipient** *capable of perception; discerning*
688. **peripatetic** *wandering*
689. **perspicacity** *quick judging and understanding*
690. **pestilent** *deadly*
691. **petrous** *like a rock, hard, stony*
692. **phalanx** *a group of similar things standing close*
693. **pied** *of mixed colors*
694. **piffle** *nonsense*
695. **pillage** *rob or steal with violence*
696. **piquant** *agreeably pungent; stimulating*
697. **plaintiff** *a person who brings a case against another in the court*
698. **platitude** *a trite or banal statement; unoriginality*
699. **plumb** *get to the root of*
700. **plummet** *fall; plunge steeply*
701. **poignant** *deeply moving; keen*
702. **pollster** *a person who takes opinion polls*
703. **ponderous** *heavy; bulky; dull*
704. **posit** *to postulate; to suggest*
705. **potentate** *ruler; one who wields great power or sway*
706. **prate** *to talk long and idly*
707. **precepts** *rules establishing standards of conduct*
708. **preclude** *prevent; make impossible*
709. **predilection** *special liking; mental preference*
710. **premonition** *a feeling that something bad is about to happen*
711. **presage** *warning sign*
712. **presumption** *arrogance*
713. **preternatural** *not normal or usual*

714. **primp** *to dress or arrange in a careful or finicky manner*
715. **probity** *uprightness; incorruptibility*
716. **prodigious** *enormous; wonderful*
717. **profane** *worldly; having contempt for God*
718. **profligacy** *shameless immorality*
719. **profligate** *wasteful; prodigal; extravagant*
720. **prognosticate** *to foretell from signs or symptoms; presage*
721. **prolix** *tiring because too long*
722. **promiscuous** *having many brief sexual relationships*
723. **prosaic** *everyday; mundane; commonplace*
724. **proscribe** *denounce as dangerous*
725. **protracted** *prolonged*
726. **pucker** *wrinkle*
727. **pugnacious** *fond of, in the habit of fighting*
728. **puissance** *strength*
729. **pundit** *pedant; authority on a subject*
730. **purvey** *provide supply*

Q

731. **quadruped** *an animal with four legs*
732. **quadruple** *multiply four times*
733. **quail** *lose courage; turn frightened*
734. **quaintness** *Pleasing, odd and old fashioned*
S: Freakish
A: Modern
735. **quandary** *state of doubt or perplexity*
736. **quarry** *(i) An animal etc. being hunted down (ii) To extract laboriously from books (iii) Excavation made by removing stone*
737. **quart** *measure of capacity for liquids*
738. **quartz** *any of various types of hard metals*
739. **quaver** *To shake or tremble (of voice or sound)*
740. **quay** *landing place*
741. **queasy** *Squeamish, Easily nauseated*
742. **querulous** *habitually complaining*
743. **quick-silver** *very quickly, like lightning, mercury*
744. **quintuple** *multiply five times*
745. **quittance** *Discharge from a debt*
746. **quiver** *skate slightly, holder for arrows*
747. **quixotic** *generous; unselfish*
748. **quizzical** *amused*

R

749. **rabid** *Violent, Intense*
S: Frantic, Fanatical
A: Sober, Sane, Rational
750. **raffish** *low; vulgar*
751. **ragamuffin** *ragged; often disreputable person*
752. **rakish** *(i) Gay and dashing, Carefree (ii) Looking smart and as if built for speed*
753. **ramify** *to be divided or subdivided; to branch out*
754. **ramshackle** *loose and rickety, Likely to fall to pieces*
S: Shaky
755. **rancorous** *feeling bitterness; spitefulness*
756. **rapacious** *greedy (esp. for money)*
757. **raucous** *hoarse, Irritating*
758. **ravenous** *greedy, very hungry*
S: Voracious
A: Assuaged, Full
759. **recant** *take back as being false; give up*
760. **recapitulate** *To repeat, To summarise*
761. **recompense** *make payment to reward; punish*
762. **recondite** *little known; abstruse*
763. **recumbent** *lying down, reclining*
764. **recuperate** *become strong after illness, loss, exhaustion*
765. **redoubtable** *formidable; causing fear*
766. **refractory** *stubborn; unmanageable; intractable*
767. **refurbish** *to freshen or polish again*
768. **regression** *The act of going back,*
S: Reversion, Retrogression
A: Progress, Advancement
769. **reiterate** *say or do again several times*
770. **relegate** *to consign or assign especially to an inferior position*
771. **reminiscence** *remembrance*
772. **remiss** *careless*
S: Negligent, Unmindful
A: Careful, Scrupulous, Mindful
773. **remonstrate** *to protest, object*
774. **renaissance** *rebirth or revival*
775. **reprisal** *recurrence, renewal or resumption of an action*
776. **reprobate** *person hardened in sin; one devoid of decency*
777. **repudiate** *disown; refuse to accept or pay*
778. **resilience** *quality of quickly recovering the original shape*
779. **restive** *refusing to move; reluctant to be controlled*
780. **resuscitation** *coming back to consciousness*
781. **reticent** *reserved; untalkative*
782. **ribald** *crude; characterised by coarse indecent humor*
783. **rivet** *fix; take up; secure metal pin*
784. **rotund** *rich and deep; plump and round*
785. **rumple** *make rough*
S: Latent, Mysterious, Secretive
A: Plain, Clear, Evident, Worldly

S

786. **sacrosanct** *most sacred or holy; immune from criticism or violation*
787. **sagacious** *having sound judgment; perceptive; wise like a sage*
788. **sally** *(i) Sudden breaking out by soldiers surrounded by enemy*
(ii) lively, witty remark
789. **salubrious** *healthful*
790. **sanguine** *cheerful; confident; optimistic*
791. **scruple** *minute part or quantity; qualm*
792. **scrupulous** *having moral integrity; punctiliously exact*
793. **seamy** *Unpleasant or sordid*
A: Pleasant, Decent
794. **sedulous** *persevering*
795. **seminal** *like a seed; constituting a source; originative*
796. **sere** *make hard and without feeling*
797. **shard** *piece of broken earthenware*
798. **shibboleth** *any phrase, custom etc., peculiar to a certain class, faction etc., a slogan*
799. **shiftless** *lacking in resourcefulness; lacking in ambition*
800. **shrew** *ill-tempered, scolding woman*
801. **sidereal** *of or expressed in reference to the stars*
S: Starry, Astral
802. **simper** *(give a) silly, self-conscious smile*
803. **simulate** *to give a false appearance, Feign*
S: Pretend, Imitate, Feign
804. **sinew** *power; chief supporting force*
805. **sinuous** *winding, undulating, serpentine*
806. **sire** *a father or forefather*
807. **skiff** *small boat*
808. **skinflint** *miser*
S: Niggard
A: Spendthrift
809. **skittish** *Lively, Playful*
810. **slake** *to assuage*
811. **sleight** *skill with the hands, especially in deceiving onlookers as in magic*
812. **sobriquet** *a nickname*
813. **sodden** *soaked; saturated*
814. **solicitude** *being solicitous, care, concern*
S: Anxiety
A: Apathy, Indifference
815. **sop** *something given to appease*
816. **soporific** *producing sleep*
817. **sordid** *wretched; comfortless*
818. **sot** *A habitual drunkard*
A: Teetotaler
819. **sphinx** *enigmatic or mysterious person*
820. **squalid** *foul; filthy*
821. **squeamish** *easily upset; having strong moral views, Stale*
A: Original, Fresh, Novel
822. **stentorian** *extremely loud and powerful*
823. **sterling** *excellent*
S: Genuine, Valuable
A: Spurious, Trivial
824. **stickler** *person who insists on importance of something*
825. **stipulate** *state or put forward as a necessary condition*
826. **stodgy** *dull, Uninteresting*
A: Interesting, Attractive, Magnetic
827. **stoical** *showing indifference to joy, grief pain, etc.*
S: Insensitive
A: Sensitive
828. **stolid** *showing no emotion; impassive*
829. **strait-laced** *narrowly strict in behaviour or moral views*
830. **striated** *striped; grooved or banded*
831. **stricture** *something that limits; adverse criticism*
832. **stupefy** *to amaze, stun*
833. **stupendous** *astonishing*
S: Amazing, Prodigious
A: Minuscule, Meager
834. **suborn** *induce by bribery; to commit perjury*
835. **subpoena** *written order requiring a person to appear in a law court*
836. **succinct** *clear and brief, terse*
S: Concise
A: Circumlocutory
837. **succor** *assistance, relief in time of distress*
838. **sumptuous** *magnificent*
839. **supernal** *Celestial, Heavenly*
S: Divine
A: Earthy
840. **supernumerary** *an extra person or thing*
841. **supervene** *to come or happen, a something additional or unexpected*
842. **supine** *lying on the back; slow to act; passive*
843. **suppliant** *asking humbly; beseeching*
844. **supplicate** *make a humble petition to*
845. **surcease** *an end or cessation*
S: Ceasing
846. **surfeit** *satiate; feed to fulness or to excess*
847. **surmise** *to guess*
S: Assume
A: Certainty
848. **surrogate** *a substitute or deputy*
849. **susceptibility** *sensitiveness*

850. **swill** *to drink greedily*
851. **sylvan** *Rural, Rustic*
852. **synchronism** *to cause to happen at the same time or rate*

T

853. **taciturn** *untalkative, silent*
854. **talon** *claw of a bird of prey*
855. **tamp** *tap or drive down by repeated light blows*
856. **tantamount** *equal in value, effect etc.*
857. **tardy** *(i) Late, Delayed, Dilatory (ii) Slow moving*
A: Prompt, Punctual, Ready
858. **tautology** *a repetition, redundancy*
859. **taxidermy** *the art of preparing, stuffing, etc. the skins of animals to make them appear lifelike*
860. **teeny-bopper** *a faddish young teenager, especially a girl of the 1960s*
861. **temerity** *boldness; brashness; intrepidness*
862. **temperance** *abstinence from alcohol; self-control; moderation*
863. **tempestuous** *of or like a tempest, violent*
S: Stormy
A: Sedate, Calm, Peaceful
864. **temporal** *of time*
865. **temporise** *to give temporary compliance, evade decision*
866. **tenacity** *firmness; persistency*
867. **tendentious** *biased*
868. **terse** *brief and to the point*
869. **tete-a-tete** *a private conversation between two people*
870. **thrall** *enslave*
871. **timorous** *fearful; timid*
872. **tincture** *a light colour, tinge*
873. **tinsel** *superficial adornment*
874. **titillate** *to excite pleasurably*
S: Stimulate, Excite
A: Repulse, Disgust, Annoy
875. **toady** *obsequious flatterer*
876. **topography** *description of surface features of a region on maps and charts*
877. **torpid** *sleeping; sluggish; lethargic; dormant*
878. **torpor** *dullness, lack of energy*
S: Inactivity
A: Enthusiasm, Involvement
879. **torque** *twisting force causing rotation*
880. **tractable** *easily controlled or guided*
881. **transfigure** *to transform so as to glorify.*
A: Mutilate, Destroy
882. **transfix** *to make motionless as if impaled*
S: Petrify, Paralyse
A: Animate, Rejuvenate
883. **transient** *temporary; fleeting*
884. **transitory** *brief*
885. **transvestite** *a person who gets sexual pleasure from dressing in clothes of the opposite sex*
886. **travail** *(i) very hard work, laborious effort (ii) Pains of child birth*
887. **traverse** *A farcical imitation in ridicule*
888. **travesty** *parody; imitation, bad representation*
889. **trite** *not new, much used*
890. **truce** *(agreement) stop of fighting for a time*
891. **trudge** *walk heavily*
892. **truism** *a statement, the truth of which is obvious*
893. **truncate** *to cut off a part or top*
894. **tryst** *a secret meeting*
895. **tumid** *swollen, bulging,*
S: Distended,
A: Shrunken, Reduced, Concise
896. **turbid** *muddy; having the sediment stirred up*
897. **tutelage** *guardianship, care, instruction*
898. **tyro** *tiro; beginner*

U

899. **ubiquitous** *present everywhere*
900. **ululate** *to howl, hoot or wail loudly*
901. **umbra** *A shadow from a planet or satellite on the side opposite the sun*
902. **umbrage** *offense; resentment*
903. **undulate** *to move in wavelike fashion; fluctuate*
904. **unencumbered** *easy-going; trifle*
905. **unequivocal** *having one meaning, Clear*
S: Plain, Clear
A: Ambiguous, Confusing, Vague
906. **unfounded** *without any basis in truth*
907. **unhinge** *mentally unstable*
S: Unsettled
A: Sane, Rational, Calm
908. **unmitigated** *absolute*
S: Complete
909. **unpalatable** *not pleasant to the taste, sickening*
910. **unsavoury** *disgusting, unpleasant, disagreeable, notorious*
911. **unscrupulous** *not restrained by moral scruples*
S: unprincipled
A: Scrupulous, Conscientious
912. **unversed** *with no experience*
913. **unwary** *who does not take care, careless person*
914. **unwieldy** *large and awkward*
915. **upbraid** *to scold, censure, rebuke*
916. **upbraid** *scold; reproach*

917. **upheaval** *great change, cataclysm*
918. **usurer** *a person who lends money at high interest*
919. **utilitarian** *practical, accessible, within reach*
920. **uxorious** *submissively fond of a wife*

V

921. **vacuous** *with no meaning, silly, vacant*
922. **vagary** *strange act or idea*
923. **vagrant** *wandering, gypsy, nomadic*
924. **valorous** *brave*
925. **vanquish** *conquer*
926. **vantage point** *place from where you can see well*
927. **vapid** *dull, absentminded, silly*
928. **vasectomy** *operation on a man to cut the tube through which sperms flow to make him sterile*
929. **vaunt** *to boast*
930. **vehemence** *forceful way (adj.: vehement = fierce, furious)*
931. **venal** *ready to do something dishonest*
932. **veneer** *surface appearance covering the true nature*
933. **veneration** *regard with deep respect*
934. **venial** *excusable*
935. **verbatim** *word for word, exactly same words*
936. **verbiage** *lot of useless words*
937. **verbose** *using more words than necessary*
938. **veritable** *real; rightly named*
939. **vertigo** *dizziness caused by heights*
940. **vestibule** *entrance hall, doorway, approach*
941. **viaduct** *bridge, overpass*
942. **vibes** *sensation*
943. **vicarious** *felt through imagining what other person feels, indirectly felt*
944. **viraginous** *of a virago*
945. **virago** *a loud domineering woman; a scold or nag*
946. **virology** *study of viruses*
947. **virtuoso** *person skilled in an art, expert, master*
948. **virulence** *great strength (adj.: virulent)*
949. **volubility** *fluency; verbosity; easy use of spoken language*
950. **voluble** *fluent*
951. **vouchsafe** *to grant (often in a gracious manner)*

W

952. **waffle** *talk vaguely and without much result*
953. **waft** *scent; waving movement; carry lightly through*
954. **wallop** *to beat or defeat soundly*
S: Thrash
955. **wallow** *to indulge oneself fully in something sensual*
956. **warlock** *male equivalent or a witch*
957. **waspish** *bad-tempered, Snappish*
S: Irritable
A: Affectionate
958. **waylay** *to wait for and attack by surprise*
S: Accost
959. **welter** *turmoil; a bewildering jumble*
960. **wend** *to go, proceed*

Y

961. **yahoo** *a rude or violent person*
962. **yokel** *a person from the country, bumpkin*
963. **yule** *Christmas*

Z

964. **zany** *a clown or buffoon, a half-witted person*
965. **zephyr** *a gentle breeze*

CHAPTER 3

Word List III—Low Frequency Words

In this chapter, we will discuss the low-frequency words–in other words, words that are not regularly appearing in the vocabulary part of the CAT. Even here the treatment has been done in such a manner that the meaning is given first, followed by the synonym (noted by the letter *S*) and antonym (noted by the letter *A*).

No.	Word	Definition
	A	
1.	**accolade**	*honor, award*
2.	**accoutrement**	*equipment*
3.	**acephalous**	*headless, having no leader*
4.	**acolyte**	*assistant, beginner*
5.	**adscititious**	*supplemental, adopted form*
6.	**afflatus**	*inspiration, divine revelation*
7.	**affusion**	*pouring on (Particularly of water)*
8.	**aficionado**	*devotee or fanatic of any sport/past time*
9.	**agnate**	*(One who is) descended by male links from same male ancestor*
10.	**ala-mode**	*fashionable (of clothes and ideas)*
11.	**allegro**	*rapid, Quick*
12.	**altruism**	*unselfish concern for the welfare of others* *S: Unselfishness* *A: Egocentricity, Selfishness*
13.	**amanuensis**	*a secretary, Literary assistant*
14.	**amazon**	*a female warrior, tall, strong or athletic women*
15.	**anagnorisis**	*recognition*
16.	**animadvert**	*to comment adversely* *S: Criticise, Censure* *A: Praise, Eulogise, Approbate*
17.	**antebellum**	*existing before a war*
18.	**antediluvian**	*made a long time ago*
19.	**anthropomorphic**	*having human characteristics*
20.	**antiquary**	*student or collector of antiques*
21.	**aperitif**	*an alcoholic drink taken before a meal*
22.	**aphorism**	*concise statement of a principle*
23.	**apocalypse**	*revelation of the future*
24.	**apocryphal**	*of doubtful authenticity* *S: Spurious, counterfeit,* *A: Authentic, Original*
25.	**apologist**	*one who defends or attempts to justify a doctrine, faith, action, etc.*
26.	**apostasy**	*abandoning of what one believed in*
27.	**apostasy**	*renunciation of a religion*
28.	**apothecary**	*A person who prepares and sells medicines*
29.	**apotheosis**	*most perfect development of something, A declaration that a person has become a god* *S: Consecration, Glorification, Deification* *A: Desecration*
30.	**apotheosis**	*deification; glorification to godliness*
31.	**appellation**	*identifying name or title*
32.	**apposite**	*appropriate, fitting* *A: Irrelevant*
33.	**arabesque**	*a complex ornate design*
34.	**arboreal**	*of or connected with trees*
35.	**arraign**	*to bring before a law court to answer charges, to call to account* *S: Accuse, Charge* *A: Excuse, Condone, Acquit*
36.	**arrogate**	*to clinch or seize without right* *A: Abdicate, Surrender*

37. **arroyo** *a gully*
38. **aspersion** *slander*
39. **assiduous** *diligent; hard-working; sedulous*
40. **atavism** *resemblance to remote ancestors*
41. **atelier** *artist's workroom*
42. **atrabilious** *ill-tempered*
A: Happy, Good-tempered
43. **atticism** *extreme elegance of speech*

B

44. **bacchanalian** *drunken revelry*
45. **bailiff** *A law officer who collects property of those who cannot pay debts; A person employed as the manager of an estate, An official who keeps order in a court*
46. **bairn** *a child*
47. **banns** *proclamation made in church of an intended marriage*
48. **barmecide** *giver of benefits that are imaginary, Illusory*
49. **baroque** *having elaborate style, fashionable in architecture*
50. **behemoth** *any huge or powerful animal*
51. **betrothed** *engaged, Pledged to marry*
52. **bibulous** *addicted to or fond of alcoholic liquor*
53. **billingsgate** *foul, vulgar, abusive talk*
54. **bionic** *very strong, skilful*
A: Weak, Imbecile
55. **bivouac** *a temporary encampment in the open*
56. **blandishment** *flattery, coaxing*
57. **bludgeon** *(N) A short club with a heavy end (V) To bully or coerce*
58. **bluestocking** *a woman pretending to have literary taste*
59. **bodkin** *a thick, blunt needle*
60. **bonmot** *a clever or witty remark*
61. **buccaneer** *Pirate*
62. **bugbear** *Source of annoyance or fear*
S: Bugaboo
63. **bumptious** *disagreeably conceited*
A: Humble, Polite, Modest
64. **burgeon** *grow forth; send out buds*
65. **burgess** *citizen broadly comic*
66. **burlesque** *any satirical invitation*
S: Parody

C

67. **caboodle** *whole group*
68. **cachet** *respect or admiration, prestige, Seat of approval, complete acceptance*
69. **cadge** *to beg; to get by begging*
70. **callisthenics** *athletic exercises*
71. **canaille** *mob, Multitude*
72. **cantankerous** *bad-tempered; quarrelsome*
73. **carapace** *Protective covering*
74. **carousal** *A noisy drinking party*
S: Revelry, Saturnalia, Debauchery
A: Austerity, Sobriety
75. **carouse** *to drink alcohol freely*
76. **carte blanche** *full discretionary power*
77. **castigation** *severe punishment*
78. **casuistry** *Subtle but false reasoning especially, about moral issues*
S: Evasion, Sophistry
79. **cataclysm** *Any sudden, violent, change*
S: Catastrophe, Upheaval, Calamity
A: Blessing
80. **caveat** *Warning, Proviso*
81. **certitude** *Sureness*
S: Certainty, Inevitability
A: Uncertain, Unsure
82. **chagrin** *Embarrassment due to disappointment*
S: Failure, Annoyance, Shame
A: Delight, Glorification
83. **chicanery** *legal trickery; false argument*
84. **chimera** *illusion or fabrication of the mind*
85. **chutzpah** *nerve; gall*
86. **coda** *passage that completes a piece of music*
87. **cogitate** *think deeply; mediate*
88. **comestibles** *food*
89. **commiserate** *to feel or show pity for*
S: Condole, Sympathise
90. **compunction** *feeling of regret for one's action*
91. **concatenate** *Link together*
92. **concussion** *Impaired functioning especially of brain caused by a violent blow*
93. **conjoin** *to join together*
94. **conscript** *to enroll for compulsory service in armed forces*
95. **consecrate** *to bring something into religious use by a special ceremony*
96. **contretemps** *confusing, embarrassing or awkward occurrence*
A: Good fortune, Good luck
97. **contrite** *filled with deep sorrow for wrongdoing*
98. **contumacious** *insubordinate; rebellious*
99. **conundrum** *a riddle; dilemma; enigma*
100. **convalesce** *to recover health gradually after sickness*
101. **convoke** *call together; summon*
102. **cornucopia** *abundant supply*
103. **curmudgeon** *bad-tempered person*

D

104. **dastardly**	*mean, cowardly*
105. **decapitate**	*to behead*
106. **declivity**	*downward inclination*
107. **decrepit**	*Broken down or worn out by old age or long use* *S: Weak, Aged* *A: Robust, Agile*
108. **delectation**	*delight, enjoyment*
109. **deleterious**	*harmful*
110. **delinquent**	*said of young people showing a tendency to commit crimes*
111. **delirium**	*A temporary mental disturbance as during a fever, marked by confused speech and hallucination* *S: Mania, Frenzy, Insanity* *A: Sanity, Normality*
112. **demagogue**	*person appealing not to reasons*
113. **denouement**	*an outcome or solution; the unraveling of a plot*
114. **dereliction**	*deserting and leaving; to fall into ruins*
115. **dereliction**	*forsaking of* *S: Neglect (of duty)* *A: Restoration*
116. **descant**	*a tune usually sung or played at the same time as the main tune*
117. **desideratum**	*something needed and wanted*
118. **desuetude**	*cessation of use; disuse*
119. **détente**	*lessening of tension, especially between nations*
120. **detumescence**	*diminishing or lessening of swelling*
121. **didactic**	*intended to teach; preachy*
122. **dilettante**	*one who is not an expert*
123. **discountenance**	*refuse to approve of*
124. **dissimulate**	*to hide one's feelings*
125. **dissonance**	*discord*

E

126. **ecclesiastical**	*of the church or the clergy*
127. **echelon**	*a level of authority or responsibility; A formation of troops or ships*
128. **ecumenical**	*representing the whole Christian world*
129. **edacious**	*voracious; devouring*
130. **effluvia**	*outflow in a stream of particles; a noxious odor or vapor*
131. **egocentric**	*selfish* *S: Self centred* *A: Altruistic*
132. **elysian**	*Blissful, Heavenly*
133. **emeritus**	*having retired but keeping title as an honour*
134. **emetic**	*causing Vomiting*
135. **empyrean**	*the highest heaven*
136. **encomium**	*high praise* *S: Praise, Laudatory, Glorification* *A: Denunciation, Blame, Censure*
137. **entente**	*an understanding or agreement as between nations* *S: Cordiality, Amiability* *A: Enmity, Hatred*
138. **entree**	*right to enter*
139. **ephemeral**	*short-lived* *S: Fleeting, Momentary* *A: Lasting*
140. **epithet**	*adjective*
141. **ersatz**	*substitute or synthetic and inferior*
142. **escutcheon**	*a shield on which a coat of arms is displayed; reputation*
143. **ethereal**	*spiritual*
144. **etymology**	*study of the origin and development of words*
145. **eugenics**	*the movement devoted to improving the human species by controlling heredity*
146. **evanescent**	*tending to fade from sight* *S: Transient, Fleeting, Ephemeral* *A: Immortal, Eternal*
147. **eviscerate**	*to remove the internal organs of a body*
148. **excoriate**	*to take out harshly* *S: Flay, Abrade, Chafe* *A: Laud, Eulogise*
149. **excoriation**	*severe criticism*
150. **exculpate**	*to clear from a charge of guilt*
151. **excursive**	*digressive* *S: Rambling, Diverse* *A: Similar, Uniform*
152. **execrate**	*to denounce; to detest utterly*
153. **exordium**	*introductory part* *S: Beginning, Preface, Prologue* *A: Epilogue*
154. **exscind**	*to cut out; cut away*

F

155. **felicitous**	*apt; suitably expressed; well chosen*
156. **filibuster**	*time consuming legislative tactics, long speeches*
157. **fracas**	*noisy quarrel*
158. **fractious**	*quarrelsome; irritable*
159. **froward**	*intractable; not willing to yield or comply; stubborn*
160. **frowzy**	*Dirty and Untidy* *S: Ill-smelling, Musty, Dingy* *A: Natty, Sweet-smelling, pleasant*
161. **fulmination**	*bitter protest*
162. **furbish**	*to renovate*

G

163. **gamin**	*a homeless child who roams the streets*
164. **gangling**	*tall and awkward*
165. **garble**	*make unfair selection from facts*
166. **gargantuan**	*Colossal, huge, very big, enormous, prodigious*
167. **gasconade**	*boastful behaviour* *A: Reticence, Taciturnity*
168. **gestalt**	*Pattern, form, shape*
169. **gauche**	*lacking social grace* *S: Inept, Awkward, Clumsy* *A: Adroit, Skillful, Dexterous*
170. **gaucherie**	*socially awkward, tactless behavior*
171. **gauntlet**	*a knight's arm glove (A challenge)*
172. **gelid**	*extremely cold*
173. **gendarme**	*A policeman* *S: police, authorities, bobbies, cops, troopers*
174. **geodesy**	*Earth measurement on a large scale*
175. **germane**	*relevant, pertinent to*
176. **gerrymander**	*To rearrange voting districts to suit the interests of a party; to manipulate facts*
177. **gewgaw**	*a toy, a bauble, knickknack*
178. **ghetto**	*Residential area inhabited by a poor, racial group*
179. **gormandize**	*to eat like a glutton* *S: Devour* *A: Starve*
180. **gossamer**	*soft light; delicate material*
181. **gourmand**	*One who likes good food and drink, often to excess*
182. **grandiloquent**	*using pompous words*
183. **gratis**	*Free of charge*
184. **gratuitous**	*given free of charge, of no use and given in excess, not necessary*
185. **grotesque**	*distorted in appearance, shape etc.* *S: Bizarre* *A: Normal, Usual, Customary*
186. **gubernatorial**	*pertaining to the governor*
187. **gung-ho**	*enthusiastic, eager, zealous*

H

188. **habiliment**	*clothing, attire* *S: Garb, Dress, Apparel*
189. **halcyon**	*calm and peaceful*
190. **hallucination**	*the apparent perception of sights, sounds etc. that are not actually, present* *S: Delusion, Illusion, Mirage*
191. **harlequin**	*A clown*
192. **harridan**	*A disreputable able shrewish old woman*
193. **hauteur**	*disdainful pride* *S: Snobbishness, Haughtiness* *A: Meekness, Modesty*
194. **hebdomadal**	*weekly*
195. **hector**	*to bully*
196. **hieroglyphic**	*a picture or symbol representing a word sound, etc.*
197. **highfalutin**	*pompous*
198. **hoi polloi**	*the common people* *S: Masses, Crowd, Riffraff* *A: Elite, Society*
199. **holocaust**	*great destruction of life, especially by fire* *S: Conflagration, Devastation, Ruin*
200. **homiletics**	*act of preaching*
201. **hors d'oeuvre**	*an appetizer, as Olives, canapes etc. served before a meal*
202. **hors de combat**	*unable to take part in activity sport due to injury*
203. **hortatory**	*exhorting, advising* *S: Inciting, Urging*
204. **hubris**	*arrogant pride*

I

205. **ignominious**	*shameful; dishonorable; undignified; disgraceful*
206. **immure**	*To shut oneself in a place alone* *S: Imprison* *A: Wander, Loiter*
207. **impecunious**	*having little or no money*
208. **importune**	*beg urgently; solicit (of a prostitute)*
209. **imprecation**	*an invocation of evil; a curse*
210. **inadvertent**	*not paying proper attention*
211. **incertitude**	*Doubt* *S: Uncertainty* *A: Certainty*
212. **inchoate**	*just begun, rudimentary* *S: Elementary, Incipient, Undeveloped* *A: Mature*
213. **incinerate**	*to burn to ashes*
214. **inclement**	*Stormy, Unfavourable* *A: Mild. Fair*
215. **indefatigability**	*not easily exhaustible; tirelessness*
216. **indelible**	*that cannot be erased, blotted out, etc.* *A: Erasable*
217. **indelible**	*that cannot be rubbed out*
218. **indemnify**	*To insure against damage etc.* *S: Recompense, Repay, Compensate*
219. **indigence**	*poverty*
220. **ineluctable**	*certain; inevitable*
221. **ingrate**	*an ungrateful person*
222. **innuendo**	*a hint or indirect reference, usually derogatory* *S: Insinuation, Intimation, Allusion*

223. **insidious** *characterized by treachery or slyness*
S: Crafty, Treacherous, Tricky
A: Open, Fair, Candid
224. **insinuate** *suggest unpleasantly; make a way for something gently*
225. **insuperable** *incapable of being surmounted or solved*
226. **inter** *to entomb or bury*
227. **interdict** *prohibit; forbid*
228. **interloper** *to encroach; to intrude*
229. **interregnum** *lapse in a continuous series*
230. **invective** *abusive language; curses*
231. **inveterate** *deep-rooted; long-established*
232. **invidious** *of an unpleasant or objectionable nature*

J

233. **jackanapes** *impertinent fellow, mischievous child*
234. **jamboree** *A boisterous frolic, a spree*
235. **janus faced** *Deceitful*
236. **jape** *Joke played on somebody*
237. **jejune** *lacking nutritive value; dull; juvenile*
238. **jeremiad** *A tale of woe: in allusions to the lamentations of Jeremiad*
S: Grief
A: Happiness
239. **jingoist** *a person boasting and demanding an aggressive foreign policy*
240. **joie de vivre** *the joy of living*
241. **juggernaut** *a massive object, a belief*
242. **jung** *Swiss psychologist Kari Gustav Jung*
243. **juxtaposition** *placing close together*

K

244. **kangaroo court** *An improperly constituted court with no legal standing*
245. **ken** *(i) (Out of or beyond) Range of sight or knowledge*
(ii) Recognise at sight, Know -
S: Knowledge, Range, Purview
246. **kerfuffle** *fuss; noise; excitement*
247. **ketch** *small sailing-boat with two masts*
248. **keystone** *Essential Part*
249. **khmer** *a member of a people inhabiting Cambodia*
250. **kitsch** *Pretentious (especially in art, design etc.)*
251. **knoll** *a small hillock, top of a hill*
252. **kow-tow** *to act in an obsequious way, bow, kneel, genuflect*

L

253. **lacerate** *to tear roughly*
S: Mangle
A: Restore, Placate, Sympathize
254. **lachrymose** *causing tears; tearful*
255. **lackadaisical** *showing lack of interest or spirit*
S: Languishing, Indolent, Apathetic
A: Energetic, Lively
256. **laconic** *terse in expression, using few words, concise*
S: Brief, Pithy
A: Profuse, Wordy, Discursive
257. **lagniappe** *a present given to a customer with a purchase*
S: Gratuity, Bonus, Tip
258. **laissez-faire** *Policy of non interference, absence of government control over industry and business*
259. **lambent** *playing lightly over a surface; often said of aflame*
S: Radiant, Brilliant
A: Dull, lackluster
260. **larceny** *the unlawful taking of another's property*
S: Theft, Robbery, Plunder
A: Restoration, Compensation, Atonement
261. **largess** *generous giving*
262. **lenitive** *lessening pain or distress, Merciful*
263. **leviathan** *a sea monster; Any huge thing*
264. **lexicon** *Dictionary (Esp. of Greek, Latin or Hebrew)*
265. **libel** *statement that damages reputation*
266. **libidinous** *lascivious, lustful*
S: Lewd
A: Pure, Chaste
267. **licentious** *lacking legal or moral restraints*
268. **limn** *paint; portray*
269. **lucubrate** *write in scholarly fashion*
270. **luculent** *easily understood; lucid; clear*
271. **lugubrious** *mournful; excessively sad*
272. **lummox** *a clumsy, stupid person*

M

273. **ma'jor-do'mo** *a man in charge of a great household*
274. **macerate** *make or become soft by soaking in water*
275. **machiavellian** *crafty, deceitful*
S: Intriguing, Cunning, Unscrupulous
A: Honest, Straightforward, Open
276. **macrocosm** *the universe*
277. **maelstrom** *powerful, violent whirlpool*
278. **malapropism** *misuse of a word (for one that resembles it)*

279. **manacle** *chains for the hands or feet*
280. **mandarin** *An influential person*
281. **misanthrope** *person who hates mankind*
282. **mulish** *unreasonably and inflexibly obstinate*

N

283. **nabob** *a wealthy and powerful person*
284. **narcolepsy** *short attacks of drowsiness*
285. **namby-pamby** *sentimentally childish in behaviour*
286. **napalm** *Highly inflammable material*
287. **neurasthenia** *debility or weakness of the nerves*
288. **nihilism** *The general rejection of customary beliefs in morality religion, etc.*
289. **nom de plume** *a writer's assumed name, pseudonym*
290. **non sequitur** *An irrelevant conclusion*
291. **nostrum** *a quack, remedy; an untested cure*
292. **nota bene** *take notice*
293. **numismatics** *the study or collection of coins, medals, paper money, etc.*

O

294. **obfuscate** *to darken; make obscure; muddle*
295. **obsequious** *too eager to obey or serve*
296. **obstreperous** *noisy; loud*
297. **occident** *west-Europe and countries of the American continents*
S: West
A: Orient, East
298. **oenophile** *connoisseur of wines*
299. **opprobrious** *showing scorn or reproach*
300. **orotund** *sonorous; bombastic*
301. **osculate** *to kiss*
302. **ostentation** *display to obtain admiration or envy*

P

303. **paean** *song of praise or triumph*
304. **panoply** *Something forming a protective covering; impressive array*
305. **paroxysm** *sudden outburst*
306. **peccadillo** *small sin; small weakness in one's character*
307. **pedagogue** *a teacher*
308. **pedant** *a person concerned with minor detail*
309. **pejorative** *expressing contempt*
310. **penitentiary** *a prison*
311. **peregrination** *traveling about; wandering*
312. **peremptory** *urgent; imperative*
313. **perfidious** *treacherous; faithless*
314. **perfunctory** *done as a duty, without care*
315. **persona non grata** *a person who is not acceptable*
316. **pertinacious** *stubbornly unyielding or tenacious*
317. **petulant** *unreasonably impatient*
318. **philistine** *a smug, ignorant person; one who lacks knowledge*
319. **phlegmatic** *calm sluggish temperament; unemotional*
320. **picaresque** *involving clever rogues or adventurers*
321. **piccaninny** *a small black child*
322. **pince-nez** *a pair of glasses with nose clips*
323. **pique** *hurt the pride or self-respect; stir (curiosity)*
324. **pluperfect** *referring to an action that was completed in the past*
325. **poisoned chalice** *something which seems attractive but may be harmful to the person receiving it*
326. **polemic** *aggressive attack on opinions of another; disputant*
327. **prevaricate** *to equivocate; to stray from the truth*
328. **prima donna** *the chief female singer in an opera*
329. **pro tem** *for the time being*
330. **proclivity** *inclination*
331. **profundity** *depth*
332. **proliferate** *grow, reproduce by rapid multiplication*
333. **propinquity** *nearness in time or place; affinity of nature*
334. **propitiatory** *conciliatory; appeasing; mitigating*
335. **propitious** *auspicious; presenting favorable circumstances*
336. **protean** *displaying great diversity or variety; versatile*
337. **pulchritude** *physical beauty*
338. **punctilious** *precise; paying attention to trivialities*
339. **pusillanimous** *cowardly; craven*
340. **putative** *commonly accepted or supposed*
341. **putrefaction** *becoming rotten*

Q

342. **quadraphonic** *sound which is reproduced through four loudspeakers*
343. **quadrennial** *happening every four years*
344. **quagmire** *Swamp, area of dangerous marsh*
345. **quandary** *Dilemma, enigma, puzzle, predicament*
346. **quarantine** *period of time when patients are kept secluded to prevent spread of infection*
S: exile, isolation

347. **quatrain** *Stanza of poetry with four lines*
348. **quibble** *try to avoid by sophistication*
349. **quid pro quo** *Thing given in return for something else*
350. **quiescence** *state of being passive, motionless*
351. **quiescent** *at rest; dormant; torpid*
352. **quietude** *a state of being quiet*
S: Repose, tranquility
353. **quietus** *Finishing strike, Any thing that ends an activity*
354. **quinquennial** *happening every five years*
355. **quinsy** *inflammation of the throat due to abscess on the tonsils*
356. **quintessence** *the pure essence or perfect*
357. **quisling** *person who betrays his country*
358. **qui vive** *Watching for something to happen, alert, watchful*
359. **quod** *prison*
360. **quoit** *ring made of metal, rubber that is thrown on an upright peg as a game*
361. **quotidian** *banal; everyday*

R

362. **raconteur** *a person skilled at telling stories or anecdotes*
363. **ragamuffin** *a dirty, ragged person especially a child*
364. **rambunctious** *disorderly, boisterous, unruly*
365. **ramification** *A result, Consequence*
A: branch
S: Subdivisions
366. **rankle** *to fester, To cause irritation*
367. **recalcitrant** *disobedient*
368. **recension** *a revision of the text based on a study of sources*
369. **recherche** *too unusual or obscure to be easily understood*
370. **recidivism** *relapse into antisocial or criminal behavior*
371. **reconnoiter** *to survey a region especially for obtaining military information of the enemy*
S: Survey
372. **recreancy** *cowardice; cowardly giving up*
373. **recreant** *coward; apostate or deserter*
374. **recrimination** *to answer an accuser by accusing him in return, counter charge*
375. **recrudescence** *the appearance of something unpleasant*
376. **rectitude** *the quality of being straight; righteousness*
377. **redact** *to edit*
378. **redound** *to contribute to somebody's reputation*
S: Promote
379. **refection** *A light meal*
380. **refectory** *dining hall as in a monastery*
381. **refulgent** *shining; brilliant*
382. **regicide** *crime of killing a king*
383. **regnant** *Ruling, Predominant, Prevalent*
S: Reigning
384. **renascent** *rising again into being or vigor*
385. **renegade** *deserter; unconventional or unlawful person*
386. **renege** *to deny; to renounce; to go back on a promise*
387. **requiem** *mass for the dead; solemn chant for the dead*
388. **requite** *repay; give in return*
389. **rescind** *repeal; annul; cancel*
390. **retrograde** *tending toward a worse or previous state*

S

391. **sable** *small animal valued for its black fur; dark, African antelope; black, gloomy*
392. **sacerdotal** *of priests or office of priest*
S: Priestly; System of government in which priests dominate
393. **salacious** *obscene*
394. **sanctimony** *self-righteousness; hypocritical*
395. **sanguinary** *bloody*
396. **sartorial** *concerned with clothes and tailoring*
397. **saturnine** *gloomy; dark; morose*
398. **savant** *person of great learning*
399. **scabbard** *sheath for the blade*
400. **scepter** *a staff held by a ruler as a symbol of sovereignty*
401. **schism** *a split (esp. in a church) because of difference of opinion, doctrine, etc.*
402. **scintilla** *a speck, a tiny amount*
403. **sclerosis** *an abnormal hardening of soft body tissues*
404. **scrimmage** *a confused struggle*
S: Tussle
405. **scurrilous** *given to coarse language*
406. **sententious** *short and pithy; full of maxims, proverbs*
407. **sentient** *of or capable of feeling, conscious*
408. **serendipity** *phenomenon of finding valuable things not sought for*
409. **serried** *placed close together*
410. **sesquicentennial** *a period of 150 years*
411. **shilly-shally** *to be irresolute, vacillate especially over trifles*

	S: Vacillation, Irresolution, Indecision *A: Determination. Obstinacy*
412. **sibylline**	*a prophetess of ancient Greece or Rome*
413. **sinecure**	*any position that brings profit without involving much work*
414. **slattern**	*a slovenly or sluttish women*
415. **smithereens**	*fragments* *S: Pieces* *A: Whole*
416. **sodality**	*a society of Roman Catholic church numbers for religious or charitable purposes*
417. **solecism**	*a violation in the conventional usage, grammar, etc. of a language*
418. **somnolent**	*likely to induce sleep; inclined to sleep*
419. **sophistry**	*fallacious reasoning; faulty logic*
420. **sophomoric**	*self-assured though immature*
421. **specious**	*illogical or questionable truth or merit*
422. **splenetic**	*bad-tempered; irritable*
423. **splice**	*join (two ends)*
424. **spoonerism**	*the accidental interchange of the initial sound of words*
425. **staccato**	*Music with distinct breaks between successive tones*
426. **stanch**	*to stop the flow of a fluid*
427. **stertorous**	*characterised by raspy, laboured breathing*
428. **stevedore**	*A person employed for loading and unloading ships*
429. **stipple**	*paint with dots*
430. **strident**	*characterised by harsh and discordant sound*
431. **stultify**	*to cause to appear or be foolish*
432. **stygian**	*dark, gloomy*
433. **stymie**	*to hinder, obstruct or block*
434. **subliminal**	*below the threshold of conscious awareness*
435. **subrosa**	*secretly, privately*
436. **substantiation**	*giving facts to support (statement)*
437. **subsume**	*include under a rule*
438. **subterfuge**	*deception*
439. **supererogation**	*doing more than is needed*
440. **surrealism**	*modern movement in arts trying to depict the workings of the subconscious mind*
441. **surreptitious**	*done, got, acting, etc. in a stealthy way* *S: Clandestine* *A: Open, Frank*
442. **suture**	*the stitching together of the two edges of a wound* *S: Stitch*
443. **suzerain**	*A state in relation to another over which it has some political control*
444. **sybarite**	*voluptuary*
445. **sycophant**	*person who flatters the rich and powerful*
446. **syncopated**	*abbreviated; stressing the weak beat*

T

447. **tatterdemalion**	*a person in ragged clothing*
448. **tautology**	*needless repetition of an idea, using a redundant word, phrase, etc.* *S: Redundancy*
449. **tenterhooks**	*anxious suspense*
450. **tenuous**	*insubstantial, flimsy, weak*
451. **termagant**	*shrew*
452. **testiness**	*witness; evidence*
453. **theocracy**	*a government by priests claiming to rule with divine authority*
454. **threadbare**	*exhausted of interest or freshness; trite*
455. **threnody**	*a song of lamentation, Dirge*
456. **tintinnabulation**	*the ringing sound of bells* *S: Tinkling*
457. **tracery**	*ornamental work of interlacing or branching lines*
458. **traduce**	*to malign; to violate*
459. **trammel**	*something that confines or restrains* *S: Hinder, Hamper* *A: Encourage, Help*
460. **transcendental**	*(i) Supernatural, Not based on human experience or reason* *A: Natural (ii) Vague, Not clear to ordinary minds*
461. **transgress**	*break; go beyond (a limit)*
462. **tremulous**	*characterised by trembling; affected with timidity*
463. **trenchant**	*forceful; effective; vigorous*
464. **trepidation**	*alarm; excited state of mind*
465. **tribulation**	*Great misery or distress* *S: Trouble, Grief, Trail*
466. **troglodyte**	*any of the prehistoric people who lived in caves*
467. **trojan**	*a strong, hard-working, determined person* *S: Brave* *A: Coward*
468. **trollop**	*A prostitute*
469. **truckle**	*to act in a subservient manner*
470. **truculence**	*aggressiveness; ferocity*
471. **trumpery**	*Something which is showy but worthless*
472. **turpitude**	*wickedness; shamefulness*
473. **twaddle**	*foolish empty talk or writing, nonsense*
474. **tyrannicide**	*slaying of a tyrant*

U

475.	**ukase**	*an official decree, Arbitrary order*
476.	**unbosom**	*to tell or reveal (feelings or secrets)*
477.	**unconscionable**	*not guided or restrained by conscience; excessive* *S: Inordinate, Unreasonable* *A: Conscientious*
478.	**unction**	*flattery, Pretended and insincere smoothness in speech, Insincerity* *S: Flattery*
479.	**unctuous**	*Characterised by smooth pretence of fervour or earnestness, Too suave or oily* *S: Flattering* *A: Blunt, Straightforward, Frank*
480.	**unflappable**	*imperturbable, never upset in a crisis* *S: Calm, Composed* *A: Agitated, Excited*
481.	**unguent**	*A salve or ointment* *S: Ointment, Lubricant*

V

482.	**vagabond**	*who has no home and wanders about*
483.	**valedictory**	*of an act of bidding farewell*
484.	**valetudinarian**	*person who likes to feel he is an invalid*
485.	**ventriloquist**	*person who can make his voice appear to come from a different source*
486.	**verisimilitude**	*appearing true or real*
487.	**vicissitude**	*variation in luck*
488.	**vignette**	*small sketch, headline, article, story*
489.	**vituperate**	*curse; abuse in words*

W

490.	**wangle**	*to get or cause by persuasion, manipulation*
491.	**warren**	*any crowded building or buildings*
492.	**wassail**	*festive occasion of drinking and merry making*
493.	**welter**	*a confused mixture of things or people*
494.	**wharf**	*a structure on a shore, at which ships are moored for loading or unloading*
495.	**wheedle**	*to influence or entice by soft words or flattery*

X

496.	**xanthippe**	*shrewish woman*

Z

497.	**zymurgy**	*the chemistry of fermentation as applied in brewing*

CHAPTER 4 Roots, Prefixes, Suffixes and Foreign Words

Every word in the English language has a history. In this section, you will find that words can be understood in a better manner if you can break them down to their roots and relate them to their core meanings. Therefore, when you come across words using the same roots/prefixes or suffixes, you can relate them, thus understanding the words and the text in a more structured manner.

Besides, knowing the origins of important words often gives us clues to interpret the meaning of an entire family of words derived from them.

For example, in Latin the word for 'other' is 'alter', and a number of important words in English are built on its Latin root.

We will begin with a list of root words and their meanings and go on to the words derived from these roots.

Many a time, knowing root words helps us in guessing the probable meaning of a word. This chapter lists out root words in detail to help you hone this skill further.

GREEK ROOTS

I. Root = 'Chron'

The Greek root 'Chron' means or denotes 'time'. Some of the words derived from this root are:-

Word	Meaning
1. **Chronology**	*arrangement of events in order of occurrence*
2. **Chronicle**	*historical record*
3. **Chronograph**	*a stop watch, that records time with great accuracy*
4. **Chronic**	*lasting a long time (of illness)*
5. **Chronometer**	*time piece*
6. **Asynchronous**	*occurrence of two or more processes at different times*

II. Root = 'Macro, Mega'

Greek root 'macro/mega', which means 'large' or 'big'.

Word	Meaning
1. **Macroscopic**	*visible to the naked eye*
2. **Megalith**	*huge stone*
3. **Mega star**	*very great*
4. **Megahertz**	*one million hertz*
5. **Megaphone**	*instrument needed to amplify voice*
6. **Megalopolis**	*universe, very large city containing many cities.*

III. Root = 'Micro'

Greek root 'micro' means 'small'.

Word	Meaning
1. **Microbe**	*tiny organism*
2. **Microcosm**	*miniature representation of something*
3. **Microfilm**	*miniature record of documents or a film*
4. **Microlight**	*very small, light aircraft with large wings*

IV. Root = 'Morph'

The Greek root 'morph' means 'form'.

Word	Meaning
1. **Morphology**	*form and structure of an organism; study of the form*

2. **Metamorphosis**	*change of form*
3. **Morphogenesis**	*development of species of an organism*

V. Root = 'poly'

Greek root 'poly' means 'many'.

Word	Meaning
1. **Polyglot**	*competent in many languages*
2. **Polygon**	*a geometrical plane figure with three or more straight lines*
3. **Polynomial**	*used to describe a mathematical expression with more than two terms*
4. **Polymath**	*knowledgeable in a variety of subjects*

VI. Root = 'pan'

Greek root 'pan' means 'all'.

Word	Meaning
1. **Panhuman**	*for all humanity*
2. **Pantheism**	*belief that God is everything*
3. **Panorama**	*an all-round view*
4. **Pantropic**	*found throughout the tropics*

VII. Root = 'meter'

Greek root 'meter' means 'measure'.

Word	Meaning
1. **Ammeter**	*device used to measure current*
2. **Voltmeter**	*device used to measure voltage*
3. **Altimeter**	*device that measures altitude*
4. **Pedometer**	*instrument used to measure distance covered by walking*
5. **Meteorology**	*scientific study of earth's atmosphere*

VIII. Root = 'neo'

Greek root 'neo' means 'new'.

Word	Meaning
1. **Neophyte**	*beginner, recent convert*
2. **Neologism**	*new word or meaning, newly coined word*
3. **Neonate**	*a newborn child*

IX. Root = 'andr/gyn'

Greek root 'andr' means 'man'.

Greek root 'gyn' means 'woman'.

Word	Meaning
1. **Androgen**	*male hormone*
2. **Gynecoid**	*characteristic of a woman*
3. **Polyandry**	*having multiple husbands*

X. Root = 'pyr'

Greek root 'pyr' means 'fire'.

Word	Meaning
1. **Pyre**	*pile of burning material*
2. **Pyrogenic**	*producing heat*
3. **Pyromaniac**	*person who sets fire to things*
4. **Pyrotechnics**	*relating to fireworks.*

XI. Root = 'astro'

Greek root 'astro' means 'star'.

Word	Meaning
1. **Astronomy**	*science of stars*
2. **Astrologer**	*person who practices and studies astrology*
3. **Astronaut**	*space traveler*

XII. Root = 'ped'

Greek root 'ped' means 'child'.

Word	Meaning
1. **Pediatrician**	*doctor who treats children*
2. **Pedodontics**	*concerned with dental care and treatment of children*
3. **Pedology**	*study of physical and mental development of children*

XIII. Root = 'soma'

Greek root 'soma' means 'body'.

Word	Meaning
1. **Somato type**	*body type*
2. **Somatic**	*of body*
3. **Psychosomatic**	*physical illness which is mentally induced*
4. **Somatology**	*study of physiology and anatomy of body*

XIV. Root = 'ideo'

Greek root 'ideo' means 'idea'.

Word	Meaning
1. **Ideology**	*system of social beliefs*
2. **Ideologue**	*an ideologist*
3. **Ideography**	*use of graphical symbols to convey ideas.*

XV. Root = 'gam'

Greek root 'gam' means 'marriage'.

	Word	Meaning
1.	**Monogamy**	*married to one person*
2.	**Bigamy**	*married to two people*
3.	**Polygamy**	*married to many*
4.	**Gamete**	*a specialised male or female cell*

XVI. Root = 'theo'

Greek root 'theo' means 'God'.

	Word	Meaning
1.	**Theology**	*study of God or religion*
2.	**Theocracy**	*government by Gods*
3.	**Theomachy**	*battle among Gods*

XVII. Root = 'onym'

Greek root 'onym" means 'name'.

	Word	Meaning
1.	**Pseudonym**	*pen name*
2.	**Antonym**	*word opposite in meaning*
3.	**Synonym**	*word similar in meaning*
4.	**Toponym**	*word derived from name of place*
5.	**Homonym**	*word with same spelling or sound*

XVIII. Root ='path'

Greek root 'path' means 'feeling'.

	Word	Meaning
1.	**Sympathy**	*compassion for someone else's pain*
2.	**Empathy**	*feel someone else's pain and sympathise*
3.	**Apathy**	*indifference, lack of interest or enthusiasm*

XIX. Root = 'biblio'

Greek root 'biblio' means 'book'.

	Word	Meaning
1.	**Bibliopole**	*book seller*
2.	**Bibliophile**	*lover of books or collector of books*
3.	**Bibliography**	*a list of books and articles consulted, book sources*
4.	**Bibliomania**	*extreme fondness or obsession for books*

XX. Root = 'soph'

Greek root 'soph' means 'wisdom'.

	Word	Meaning
1.	**Philosophy**	*love of wisdom*
2.	**Sophist**	*ancient Greek philosopher*
3.	**Sophisticated**	*urbane, classy, complex*

XXI. Root = 'Misein'

The root 'misein' is a Greek root which means 'to hate'.

	Word	Meaning
1.	**Misanthropist**	*one who hates mankind*
2.	**Misogynist**	*one who hates women*
3.	**Misogamist**	*one who hates marriage*

XXII. Root = 'Anthropos'

The root 'anthropos' is a Greek word meaning 'mankind'.

	Word	Meaning
1.	**Anthropology**	*study of development of human race*
2.	**Philanthropist**	*one who loves mankind*

XXIII. Root = 'Phil'

The Greek root 'phil' means 'to love'.

	Word	Meaning
1.	**Philology**	*love of language /words*
2.	**Philosophy**	*love of wisdom*
3.	**Philanthropy**	*love of mankind*
4.	**Philadelphia**	*city of brotherly love*
5.	**Philharmonic**	*love of music/harmony*
6.	**Bibliophile**	*lover of books*
7.	**Anglophile**	*admirer of British culture, people, etc.*
8.	**Philatelist**	*one who collects or studies stamps*

XXIV. Root = 'logy'

The Greek root 'logy' means 'study of'.

	Word	Meaning
1.	**Anthropology**	*study of human race*
2.	**Biology**	*study of living things*
3.	**Astrology**	*study of the sun, moon and other planets*
4.	**Archaeology**	*study of the buildings, graves, etc. of the past*
5.	**Climatology**	*study of general weather conditions*
6.	**Psychology**	*study of human mind and behaviour*
7.	**Graphology**	*study of handwriting*
8.	**Gerontology**	*study of problems of the elderly*

XXV. Root = 'psyche'

The Greek root 'psyche' means 'mind, spirit, soul'.

	Word	Meaning
1.	**Psychosis**	*a mental disorder*

2. **Psychiatrist**	*a mind-healer*
3. **Psychotic**	*one who loses touch with reality*
4. **Psychedelic**	*that which causes effect on mind*
5. **Psychic**	*having special mental (knowing) ability*
6. **Psycho kinesis**	*change the physical state or position of a physical object by the power of the mind*

XXVI. Root = 'archy'/'cracy'

The Greek root 'archy/cracy' means 'rule by'.

Some of the words derived from this root, depicting different types of rules by people, are as follows:

Word	Meaning
1. **Monarchy**	*rule by one king/queen*
2. **Autocracy**	*government by a single person/ single group*
3. **Democracy**	*where power is held by elected representatives*
4. **Aristocracy**	*rule by people of high social class, for example, royalty*
5. **Theocracy**	*rule of gods*
6. **Plutocracy**	*rule by the rich*
7. **Anarchy**	*state of nature where there is no government*
8. **Diarchy**	*dual rule*
9. **Oligarchy**	*rule by few powerful people*
10. **Patriarchy**	*oldest male of a family is the head*

LATIN ROOTS

I. Root = 'cede', 'ceed' and 'cess'

All the three Latin roots mean 'go' or 'movement'.

Word	Meaning
1. **Precede**	*come before*
2. **Proceeding**	*course of action*
3. **Process**	*method of doing something*
4. **Succeed**	*go ahead, be successful*
5. **Proceed**	*go before*
6. **Exceed**	*go ahead of*
7. **Recede**	*go back*
8. **Recession**	*depression in economic activity*

II. Root = 'scribe'

Latin root 'scribe' means 'to write'.

Word	Meaning
1. **Prescribe**	*order the use of, esp. used in the context of medication*
2. **Inscribe**	*to write or engrave words on a surface*
3. **Scribble**	*write illegibly*
4. **Describe**	*write in detail*
5. **Proscribe**	*to prohibit or ban something*

III. Root = 'brev'

Latin root 'brev' means 'short'.

Word	Meaning
1. **Abbreviation**	*short end form*
2. **Brevity**	*briefness*
3. **Breviary**	*summary, abridgement*

IV. Root = 'centr'

Latin root 'centr' means 'center'.

Word	Meaning
1. **Centrist**	*one with moderate views*
2. **Centrifugal**	*away from center*
3. **Centripetal**	*towards center*
4. **Egocentric**	*selfish*
5. **Eccentric**	*unconventional in a whimsical way.*
6. **Heliocentric**	*with the sun at the centre*

V. Root = 'later'

Latin root 'later' means 'side'.

Word	Meaning
1. **Bilateral**	*two-sided*
2. **Unilateral**	*one-sided*
3. **Multilateral**	*many-sided*
4. **Lateralisation**	*the localisation of a control centre for a particular function.*
5. **Lateral**	*at the side*

VI. Root = 'magni'

Latin root 'magni' means 'large'.

Word	Meaning
1. **Magnify**	*make larger*
2. **Magnitude**	*greatness of size*
3. **Magniloquent**	*employing impressive words while speaking*
4. **Magnificent**	*impressive, splendid*
5. **Magnanimous**	*very generous, large hearted*

VII. Root = 'nihil'

Latin root 'nihil' means 'nothing'.

Word	Meaning
1. **Annihilate**	*kill, reduce to nothing*

2. **Nihilism**	*rejection or opposition to all authority*

VIII. Root = 'omni'

Latin root 'omni' means 'all'.

Word	Meaning
1. **Omniscient**	*all knowing*
2. **Omnipotent**	*all powerful*
3. **Omnipresent**	*present everywhere*
4. **Omnibus**	*a single book containing separate works as a collection*
5. **Omnificent**	*with unlimited power to create*

IX. Root = 'rect'

Latin root 'rect' means 'straight'.

Word	Meaning
1. **Rectify**	*straighten or to correct*
2. **Rectitude**	*righteousness*
3. **Rectilinear**	*straight line*

X. Root = 'cide'

The Latin root 'cide' means 'to kill' or 'cut'.

Word	Meaning
1. **Ceticide**	*killing of whales*
2. **Mariticide**	*killing of husband*
3. **Parricide**	*killing of parent (either father or mother)*
4. **Filicide**	*killing of children*
5. **Fratricide**	*killing of brother*
6. **Patricide**	*killing of father*
7. **Fungicide**	*killing of fungi*
8. **Insecticide**	*killing of insects*
9. **Uxoricide**	*killing of wife*
10. **Tyrannicide**	*killing of tyrants*
11. **Suicide**	*killing of oneself*
12. **Sororicide**	*killing of sister*
13. **Genocide**	*killing of races*
14. **Homicide**	*killing of people*
15. **Infanticide**	*killing of babies*
16. **Lapicide**	*killing of pets*

XI. Root = 'mort', 'necro'

Latin root, which means 'death'.

Word	Meaning
1. **Mortal**	*subject of death*
2. **Mortuary**	*place for dead bodies*
3. **Necrology**	*list of the dead, obituary*
4. **Necromancy**	*prediction using spirits*
5. **Necropolis**	*city of dead, cemetery*
6. **Necropsy**	*autopsy*
7. **Mortification**	*deep shame and humiliation*

XII. Root = 'dorm', 'somn'

Latin roots which mean 'to sleep'.

Word	Meaning
1. **Dormant**	*asleep*
2. **Insomnia**	*inability to sleep*
3. **Somnambulist**	*walks in his sleep*
4. **Somnambulism**	*sleep walking*
5. **Somnolent**	*feeling sleepy*

XIII. Root = 'aqu'

Latin root 'aqu' means 'water'.

Word	Meaning
1. **Aquatic**	*of the water*
2. **Aquarium**	*container for fish*
3. **Aquaculture**	*farming of fish and aquatic plants*

XIV. Root = 'mar'

Latin root 'mar' means 'sea'.

Word	Meaning
1. **Marine**	*of sea*
2. **Marina**	*small harbor*
3. **Maritime**	*of the sea*
4. **Mariner**	*one who sails or navigates vessels at sea*

XV. Root = 'doc'

Latin root 'doc' means 'to teach'.

Word	Meaning
1. **Indoctrinate**	*instruct one in basics*
2. **Doctrine**	*rule or principle*
3. **Doctor**	*medically qualified*
4. **Doctrinaire**	*determined to use a theory*

XVI. Root = 'luc'

Latin root 'luc' means 'light'.

Word	Meaning
1. **Elucidate**	*make clear*

2. **Lucid**	*clear/ transparent*
3. **Pellucid**	*transparent*

XVII. Root = 'flect/flex'

Latin root 'flect/flex' means 'to bend'.

Word	Meaning
1. **Inflect**	*turn*
2. **Influx**	*inward flow*
3. **Flexible**	*adaptable*
4. **Flexography**	*printing using a flexible plate*
5. **Genuflect**	*bend in a gesture of respect*

XVIII. Root = 'fract'/'frag'

Latin root means 'break'.

Word	Meaning
1. **Fracture**	*break*
2. **Fragile**	*easily broken*
3. **Fragment**	*break into small pieces*
4. **Infraction**	*failure to obey a law or contract*

XIX. Root = 'tract/tang'

Latin root means 'touch'.

Word	Meaning
1. **Intact**	*untouched*
2. **Tangible**	*real/can be touched*
3. **Intangible**	*cannot be seen or touched*
4. **Tactile**	*of touch*

XX. Root = 'Loqu/locut'

Latin root meaning 'to speak'.

Word	Meaning
1. **Circumlocution**	*evasive speech*
2. **Soliloquy**	*speaking alone*
3. **Eloquence**	*persuasive speech*
4. **Interlocution**	*conversation*
5. **Somniloquy**	*speak in sleep*
6. **Elocution**	*public speaking*
7. **Grandiloquence**	*speech*
8. **Colloquiality**	*informal speaking*
9. **Allocution**	*formal speaking*
10. **Magniloquence**	*bombastic speech*
11. **Colloquium**	*scholarly conference*

XXI. Root = 'bene, bone'

Latin root meaning 'good'.

Word	Meaning
1. **Beneficial**	*good for*
2. **Bonus**	*premium*
3. **Benefit**	*advantage*
4. **Benevolent**	*kind*
5. **Benefactor**	*somebody who helps or aids a cause*
6. **Benediction**	*blessing, expression of approval*
7. **Benign**	*harmless*

XXII. Root = 'mal'

Latin root means 'bad'.

Word	Meaning
1. **Malevolent**	*harmful, wanting to cause harm*
2. **Malnutrition**	*lack of healthy food in a diet*
3. **Malignant**	*evil, full of evil*
4. **Malady**	*illness, disease*
5. **Malinger**	*to pretend illness especially to avoid work*
6. **Malediction**	*curse, to utter a curse*

XXIII. Root = 'cred'

Latin root means 'believe'.

Word	Meaning
1. **Credible**	*believable*
2. **Incredulous**	*skeptical*
3. **Incredible**	*astonishing, hard to believe*
4. **Credential**	*proof to ability or trust worthiness, a certificate*
5. **Credulous**	*ready to believe*

XXIV. Root = 'sens', 'sent'

Latin root means 'feeling'.

Word	Meaning
1. **Sensible**	*reasonable*
2. **Sentiment**	*emotion*
3. **Sensory**	*relating to sensation or sense organs*
4. **Sensitive**	*acutely perceptive*
5. **Sentient**	*conscious, capable of feeling*
6. **Sensibilia**	*things that can be felt or sensed*
7. **Sensitise**	*make sensitive*

XXV. Root = 'bel'

Latin root means 'war'.

Word	Meaning
1. **Belligerent**	*warring*
2. **Bellicose**	*warlike*
3. **Antebellum**	*preceding a war*

XXVI. Root = 'cogn', 'sci'

Latin roots meaning 'know able to understand'.

Word	Meaning
1. **Recognize**	*understand*

2. **Science**	*factual knowledge*
3. **Unconscionable**	*morally unacceptable*
4. **Conscious**	*able to understand*
5. **Unconscious**	*experiencing loss of senses*

XXVII. Root = 'vore'

Latin root 'vore' means 'eat'.

Word	Meaning
1. **Carnivore**	*flesh eater*
2. **Herbivore**	*plant eater*
3. **Frugivore**	*fruit eater*
4. **Omnivore**	*who eats everything*
5. **Nectarivore**	*nectar eater*
6. **Insectivore**	*insect eater*
7. **Graminivore**	*grass eater*
8. **Granivore**	*grain eater*

XXVIII. Quasi.

The combining form 'Quasi' of Latin origin, is used to combine words. It means 'resembling' 'or very similar to but not the real thing'. Some words of this form are–

Word	Meaning
1. **Quasi-judicial**	*semi-judicial powers resembling to those of judges or courts*
2. **Quasi-dictatorship**	*a dictatorship hiding under another form*
3. **Quasi-scientific**	*supposedly scientific but not backed by fact*
4. **Quasi-periodic**	*something that is almost predictable*

XXIX. Root = 'Alter'

The root 'alter' in Latin means 'other'.

Word	Meaning
1. **Altruism**	*the philosophy practiced by altruists*
2. **Alternate**	*skip one and take the other*
3. **Alternative**	*the other choice*
4. **Alteration**	*change*
5. **Altercation**	*a verbal dispute*
6. **Alter ego**	*other self*
7. **Altruistic**	*interested in the welfare of others*

XXX. Root = 'Ego'

The root word 'ego' is a Latin root, which means 'I'.

Word	Meaning
1. **Egoist**	*excessively high opinion of oneself*
2. **Egocentric**	*one who is excessively fixated upon his own needs, desires, etc.*
3. **Egomaniac**	*morbidly, excessively wrapped up in oneself.*

XXXI. Root = 'Vert'

The root 'Vert' is a Latin verb which means 'to turn'.

Word	Meaning
1. **Introvert**	*to turn your thoughts inwards*
2. **Extrovert**	*to turn your thoughts outward*
3. **Ambivert**	*to turn your thoughts in both directions*

MANIAS AND PHOBIAS

The Greek root 'Phobia' means 'fear' and the Greek root 'mania' means a 'compulsion' or ' preoccupation for'. Some of the manias and phobias as follows–

Word (mania)	Meaning (Preoccupation with)
1. **Philopatridomania**	*extreme home sickness*
2. **Mythomania**	*lies*
3. **Oinomania**	*wine*
4. **Gamo mania**	*marriage*
5. **Klepto mania**	*stealing*
6. **Megalomania**	*self-greatness*
7. **Gynecomania**	*woman*
8. **Zoo mania**	*animals*
9. **Xenomania**	*foreigners*
10. **Phagomania**	*eating*
11. **Pyromania**	*fire*
12. **Pluto mania**	*wealth*

Word (Phobia)	Meaning (Fear of ____)
1. **Thermophobia**	*heat*
2. **Pedophobia**	*children*
3. **Acrophobia**	*heights*
4. **Chronophobia**	*time*
5. **Nyctophobia**	*night*
6. **Theophobia**	*God*
7. **Arachibutyrophobia**	*peanut butter*
8. **Demophobia**	*people*
9. **Entomophobia**	*insects*
10. **Ergophobia**	*work*
11. **Gerontophobia**	*old people*
12. **Necrophobia**	*corpses*
13. **Hematophobia**	*blood*
14. **Arachnophobia**	*spiders*
15. **Triskaidekaphobia**	*fear of the number thirteen*

We now move on to Prefixes and Suffixes.

PREFIXES

Prefixes are fixed before a word or a root to convey a modified version of the word or the root.

Some important Greek and Latin prefixes with a set of illustrative words are as follows:–

(1) Prefix = 'ante'

Latin prefix which means 'before'.

Word	Meaning
1. **Antecedent**	*preceding*
2. **Antediluvian**	*before the flood; ancient*
3. **Antenatal**	*of care before birth (during pregnancy)*
4. **Anterior**	*to the front; before*
5. **Ante meridiem**	*before noon*

(2) Prefix = 'dia'

Greek prefix which means 'across'.

Word	Meaning
1. **Diagonal**	*connecting line*
2. **Diaspora**	*the breaking up and scattering of a people; people settled far from their ancestral homelands*
3. **Dialectic**	*art of arguing*
4. **Dialect**	*local variety of language*
5. **Diameter**	*straight line from side to side of figure*

(3) Prefix = 'ultra'

Latin prefix 'ultra' means 'beyond'.

Word	Meaning
1. **Ultramarine**	*very deep in blue*
2. **Ultra modern**	*very modern*
3. **Ultraviolet**	*beyond violet; at the violet end of spectrum*
4. **Ultrasonic**	*sound waves beyond the range of human ear*

(4) Prefix = 'trans'

Latin prefix which means 'over, across'.

Word	Meaning
1. **Transcend**	*go beyond*
2. **Transverse**	*eyeing across; at right angles*
3. **Transgress**	*break (law)*
4. **Transient**	*fleeting, not permanent*

(5) Prefix = 'super'

Latin prefix which means 'over, beyond'.

Word	Meaning
1. **Superior**	*of greater rank*
2. **Supercilious**	*displaying arrogant pride*
3. **Supernumerary**	*in excess of normal number*
4. **Supersede**	*take the place of; set aside*
5. **Supervise**	*oversee; direct; inspect*
6. **Superlative**	*in/of highest degree or quantity*

(6) Prefix = 'Epi'

Greek prefix, which means 'over, on, of'.

Word	Meaning
1. **Epiderm**	*outer skin layer*
2. **Epiphany**	*festival of the announcement of Christ's coming.*
3. **Epigraph**	*inscription*
4. **Epicentre**	*focus of earthquake*

(7) Prefix = 'Hypo'

Greek prefix, which means 'under, below'.

Word	Meaning
1. **Hypocrisy**	*false virtue*
2. **Hypodermic**	*below the skin*
3. **Hypothesis**	*suggested explanation of something*
4. **Hypogastric**	*of or related to lower median region of the abdomen*
5. **Hypochondria**	*morbid depression without reason about one's own health, extreme depression of mind or spirits often centered on imaginary physical ailments*

(8) Prefix = 'Hyper'

Greek prefix, which means 'over/above/excessive/abnormally high'.

Word	Meaning
1. **Hyperactivity**	*too much activity*
2. **Hyperesthesia**	*excessive sensory feeling*
3. **Hyperbole**	*person prone to exaggerated speaking*
4. **Hyperkinesis**	*excessive amount of spasms*
5. **Hyperventilation**	*excessive breathing*
6. **Hyper baric**	*greater than normal pressure*
7. **Hyperacid**	*the condition of containing more than the normal amount of acid*

(9) Prefix = 'ab'

Latin prefix, which means 'from/away'.

Word	Meaning
1. **Absent**	*not present*
2. **Abstemious**	*sparing in food and drink*
3. **Abstraction**	*preoccupation*
4. **Abnegate**	*give up, renounce*
5. **Abolish**	*do away with*
6. **Abrade**	*scrape away*

(10) Prefix = 'ad'

Latin prefix, which means 'to towards'.

Word	Meaning
1. **Adhere**	*stick to*
2. **Adumbration**	*to suggest or disclose partially, give a vague indication*
3. **Ad hoc**	*for a particular purpose only*
4. **Ad infinitum**	*endlessly*
5. **Ad interim**	*for the mean time*
6. **Adjunct**	*added, joined*
7. **Adjudge**	*decide, declare*
8. **Adlib**	*improvise and speak spontaneously*
9. **Adjourn**	*postpone temporarily*
10. **Ad rem**	*to the point*
11. **Ad valorem**	*according to the value*
12. **Advert**	*turn the mind or attention towards*
13. **Adulterate**	*make impasse by adding*
14. **Adumbrate**	*give outline of, indicate*

(11) Prefix = 'Ambi'

Latin prefix, which means 'both sides'.

Word	Meaning
1. **Ambient**	*on all sides*
2. **Ambiguity**	*obscure*
3. **Ambivalent**	*simultaneous existence of two different opinions*
4. **Ambidextrous**	*able to use both sides*

(12) Prefix = 'Peri'

Greek prefix, which means 'around, about'.

Word	Meaning
1. **Peripatetic**	*walking around*
2. **Periphery**	*circumference*
3. **Perimeter**	*outer boundary*
4. **Perihelion**	*point in orbit of planet or comet nearest to sun.*

(13) Prefix = 're'/'retro'

Latin prefix, which means 'back'.

Word	Meaning
1. **Return**	*go back*
2. **Retrospect**	*look back*
3. **Retroflex**	*curved backwards*
4. **Retrograde**	*going backwards, reverting*
5. **Retard**	*make slow*
6. **Retort**	*retaliate, reply*

(14) Prefix = 'circum'

Latin prefix, which means a 'path' or 'orbit'.

Word	Meaning
1. **Circumpolar**	*circles around the polar region*
2. **Circumsolar**	*circles around the Sun.*
3. **Circumspect**	*circles around the fences*
4. **Circumlocution**	*round about or evasive speech*

(15) Prefix = 'a'/'an'

Greek prefix, which means 'without'.

Word	Meaning
1. **Anaemia**	*blood deficiency*
2. **Amoral**	*not moral*
3. **Anaesthetic**	*causing loss of sensation*
4. **Achromatic**	*without colour*
5. **Anachronism**	*mistake of time*

(16) Prefix = 'anti'

Greek prefix, which means 'against'.

Word	Meaning
1. **Antidote**	*remedy*
2. **Antipathy**	*dislike, aversion*
3. **Antipyretic**	*effective against fever*
4. **Antiseptic**	*preventing infection*
5. **Antigen**	*substance stimulating production of antibodies in the world*

(17) Prefix = 'counter', 'contra'

Latin prefix, which means 'against'.

Word	Meaning
1. **Counterfeiter**	*forger*
2. **Contrary**	*opposite*
3. **Constrain**	*force, compel*
4. **Contraband**	*illegal, smuggled goods*

(18) Prefix = 'dys'

Greek prefix, which means 'bad'.

Word	Meaning
1. **Dysfunctional**	*badly functioning*
2. **Dyspepsia**	*indigestion*
3. **Dyslexia**	*impaired ability to read*

(19) Prefix = 'eu'

Greek prefix, which means 'good, well'.

Word	Meaning
1. **Euphony**	*sweet sounding*
2. **Eulogy**	*speech or writing in praise of*
3. **Euphoria**	*sense of well-being or elation*

(20) Prefix = 'inter'

Latin prefix, which means 'between'.

Word	Meaning
1. **Interloper**	*intruder*
2. **Interlude**	*interval*
3. **Intermediate**	*coming between*

(21) Prefix = 'meta'

Greek prefix, means 'besides/with'.

Word	Meaning
1. **Metamorphose**	*transform*
2. **Metathesis**	*transposition*
3. **Metaphorical**	*figurative*

(22) Prefix = 'Sym/syn'

Greek prefix, which means 'together'.

Word	Meaning
1. **Synergy**	*unified action*
2. **Symmetrical**	*balanced*
3. **Synchronise**	*happen at the same time*
4. **Symbiotic**	*living together for mutual benefit*
5. **Symphony**	*harmony of sounds*

(23) Prefix = 'be'

Germanic prefix, which means 'around/on'.

Word	Meaning
1. **Beside**	*by side of*
2. **Bespatter**	*to splash with*
3. **Besiege**	*to surround on all sides*

(24) Prefix = 'for'

Germanic prefix, which means 'apart/away'.

Word	Meaning
1. **Forbid**	*prohibit*
2. **Forbear**	*cease, refrain*
3. **Forlorn**	*forsaken, desperate*

(25) Prefix = 'mis'

Germanic prefix, means 'bad/wrong'.

Word	Meaning
1. **Mistake**	*error*
2. **Misnomer**	*wrong name*
3. **Mishap**	*minor accident*
4. **Misfit**	*not a suitable person*

(26) Prefix = 'fore'

Germanic prefix, which means 'before'

Word	Meaning
1. **Foresee**	*indication in advance, predict*
2. **Forestall**	*prevent*

SUFFIXES

Suffixes are added to the end of a word or a root and can sometimes lead to a difference in the meaning of the original word or root. Some of the common suffixes of Greek, Latin and German origin are discussed below:

A. Latin Suffixes

(1) Suffix = 'age'

Latin suffix, which means 'place/collection'.

Word	Meaning
1. **Personage**	*minister's house*
2. **Steerage**	*cheapest accommodation on a ship*
3. **Peerage**	*bodies or group of peers*

(2) Suffix = 'arium'/'ary'

Latin Suffix, which means 'place'.

Word	Meaning
1. **Aquarium**	*place for keeping live fish*
2. **Library**	*place for storing books*
3. **Sanatorium**	*hospital for chronically ill*
4. **Seminary**	*college for priests*
5. **Apiary**	*place where bees are kept*

Some Important Words derived from common Suffixes

(1) Suffix = 'ist'

It is a Greek Suffix, which denotes people who perform certain actions, are experts in certain fields or are adherents to specific beliefs.

Word	Specialist in
1. **Verbalist**	*words*
2. **Purist**	*traditions*
3. **Geneticist**	*heredity*
4. **Arborist**	*Tree care*
5. **Agronomist**	*crop production*
6. **Entomologist**	*insects*
7. **Numismatist**	*coins*
8. **Philatelist**	*stamps*
9. **Toxicologist**	*poison*
10. **Semanticist**	*word meanings*
11. **Meteorologist**	*weather*

(2) Suffix = 'Sis'

It is a Greek Suffix, which means a 'state of/process'.

Word	Meaning
1. **Synthesis**	*formation of whole from different parts*
2. **Osmosis**	*diffusion of fluids through a membrane*
3. **Prognosis**	*forecasted recovery from illness*
4. **Necrosis**	*death of live tissue*
5. **Dialysis**	*separation of substances in a solution*
6. **Hypnosis**	*physically induced sleeplike condition*
7. **Metastasis**	*spread of disease in the body*

(3) Suffix = 'ancy'

Latin Suffix, which means 'state, action or process', and is frequently used in words which describe ways to foretell the future.

Word	Meaning
1. **Bibliomancy**	*forecasting future through biblical books*
2. **Anthropomancy**	*forecasting through studying human entrails*
3. **Cubomancy**	*forecasting through use of dice*
4. **Osteomancy**	*forecasting through observing bones.*
5. **Cheiromancy**	*forecasting by reading the palms.*
6. **Graphomancy**	*forecasting through observing handwriting*

(4) Suffix = 'oid'

Greek Suffix, which means 'like/ shape of".

Word	Meaning
1. **Hypsiloid**	*letter 'v'*
2. **Xiphoid**	*sword*
3. **Scaphoid**	*boat*
4. **Sigmoid**	*letter 'c'*
5. **Schizoid**	*split*
6. **Cuboid**	*cube*
7. **Actinoid**	*star*
8. **Belonoid**	*needle*
9. **Pemphigoid**	*bubble*
10. **Ovoid**	*egg*
11. **Helicoid**	*screw*
12. **Beloid**	*arrow*

(5) Suffix = 'ent'

Latin Suffix, which means 'being/manifesting/possessing'.

Word	Meaning
1. **Truculent**	*aggression*
2. **Imminent**	*pending danger*
3. **Flocculent**	*woolliness*
4. **Innocent**	*purity*
5. **Indigent**	*need/poverty*
6. **Intransigent**	*stubbornness*
7. **Diligent**	*earnestness*
8. **Effulgent**	*radiance*
9. **Plangent**	*expressive sound*
10. **Nocent**	*harm*
11. **Continent**	*restraint*
12. **Ambivalent**	*uncertainty*
13. **Prudent**	*Wisdom/judiciousness*

B. Germanic Suffixes

Some important Germanic suffixes illustrated with examples, are as follows:-

(1) Suffix = 'dom'

Germanic Suffix, which means 'state/quality'.

Word	Meaning
1. **Freedom**	*liberty*
2. **Kingdom**	*state ruled by king*
3. **Officialdom**	*state ruled by officials*
4. **Dukedom**	*state ruled by duke*

(2) Suffix = 'ard'

Germanic Suffix, which means 'one who/characteristic of'.

Word	Meaning
1. **Dullard**	*stupid person*
2. **Pollard**	*horn less animal*

(3) Suffix = 'hood'

Germanic Suffix, which means 'state/quality'.

Word	Meaning
1. **Brotherhood**	*alliance*
2. **Widowhood**	*state of being a widow*

(4) Suffix = 'ling'

Germanic Suffix, which means 'having the characteristic of/minor'.

Word	Meaning
1. **Yearling**	*year old animal*
2. **Fingerling**	*baby fish*

(5) Suffix = 'ness'

Germanic Suffix, which means 'condition/state'.

Word	Meaning
1. **Goodness**	*decency*
2. **Populousness**	*state of large population*
3. **Business**	*occupation*
4. **Wickedness**	*being bad*

(6) Suffix = 'ship'

Germanic Suffix, which means 'state /rank/skill'.

Word	Meaning
1. **Penmanship**	*art of writing*
2. **Craftsmanship**	*art of making crafts*
3. **Township**	*unit of local government*
4. **Musicianship**	*skill of a musician*

(7) Suffix = 'ful'

Germanic Suffix, which means 'full of/providing'.

Word	Meaning
1. **Healthful**	*promoting health*
2. **Plentiful**	*having plenty*
3. **Earful**	*lot of information*

(8) Suffix = 'fold'

Germanic Suffix, which means 'increased by'.

Word	Meaning
1. **Tenfold**	*multiplied by ten*
2. **Manifold**	*many times*

(9) Suffix = 'ish'

Germanic Suffix, which means 'somewhat like'.

Word	Meaning
1. **Childish**	*child like*
2. **Churlish**	*ill-bred, rustic*
3. **Impish**	*imp-like, naughty*

(10) Suffix = 'wise'

Germanic Suffix, which means 'in the manner of/with regard to'.

Word	Meaning
1. **Dollarwise**	*with respect to dollars*
2. **Weatherwise**	*with regard to weather*
3. **Moneywise**	*with regard to money*
4. **Healthwise**	*with respect to health*

Let us now move on to words with foreign origins.

ENGLISH WORDS OF FOREIGN ORIGIN

In addition to the study of word components and roots, the diversity and complexity of English can be seen in the thousands of borrowed and intended words used today. Some of the important words borrowed from different languages are listed in this chapter.

German Words

Some important English words, which have been taken from German are as follows:

Word	Meaning
1. **Pumpernickel**	*a dark, dense, sour bread.*
2. **Kindergarten**	*a school or class for young children.*
3. **Hoodlum**	*a petty criminal*
4. **Delicatessen**	*prepared food sold in a shop serving*
5. **Loafers**	*casual leather slip-on shoe;/ imported or unusual foods; such a shop*
6. **Glitch**	*minor hitch, lazy person*
7. **Glisten**	*to shine*

Dutch Words

Some important English words, which have been taken from Dutch are as follows:

Word	Meaning
1. **Landscape**	*scenery*

Word	Meaning
2. **Holster**	*leather case for firearm*
3. **Sleigh**	*sledge*
4. **Caboose**	*rail guard's van*
5. **Coleslaw**	*salad made with mayonnaise dressing.*
6. **Boss**	*senior or person in charge of*
7. **Cookie**	*biscuit*
8. **Freight**	*commercial transport esp. railways or ship*
9. **Snoop**	*meddle, spy on*
10. **Skipper**	*captain of ship or team*
11. **Bumpkin**	*rustic*
12. **Bed spread**	*bed cover, decorative covering on bed*

Japanese Words

Some important English words, which have been taken from Japanese are as follows:

Word	Meaning
1. **Tsunami**	*large destructive ocean wave*
2. **Hibachi**	*a portable barbeque*
3. **Tycoon**	*powerful and wealthy businessman*
4. **Bonsai**	*art of growing miniature trees*
5. **Bonzai**	*a patriotic battle cry or shout*
6. **Origami**	*Japanese art of paper folding*
7. **Samurai**	*former Japanese warrior class*
8. **Karate**	*traditional Japanese form of unarmed combat*
9. **Shogun**	*any hereditary military commands in feudal Japan*
10. **Kimono**	*traditional Japanese garment*

African Languages

Some important English words, which have been taken from African languages are as follows:

Word	Meaning
1. **Banana**	*tropical plant and its fruit*
2. **Dashiki**	*clothes*
3. **Chimpanzee**	*an ape*
4. **Samba**	*a Brazilian dance of African origin*
5. **Yam**	*a root vegetable*
6. **Okra**	*lady finger plant, a vegetable*
7. **Tse-tse**	*two-winged biting fly*

Spanish Words

Some important English words, which have been taken from Spanish are as follows:

Word	Meaning
1. **Bolero**	*Spanish dance*
2. **Fiesta**	*religious festival or celebration*
3. **Primero**	*card game played in 16th and 17th century*
4. **Tango**	*Latin-American or Spanish dance*
5. **Ombre**	*card game popular in 18th century*
6. **Domino**	*board game*
7. **Quadrille**	*card game for four players; a French dance*
8. **Spade**	*digging tool*
9. **Monte**	*betting game played with cards*
10. **Castanets**	*wooden or plastic device that makes a clicking sound when pressed by palm of hand*
11. **Embargo**	*restricting commerce*
12. **Pronto**	*fast*
13. **Galleon**	*large sailing vessel*
14. **Grenade**	*small bomb*
15. **Guerrilla**	*independent soldiers*
16. **Flotilla**	*group of ships*
17. **Garrote**	*strangulation*
18. **Junta**	*ruling group*
19. **Intransigent**	*inflexible*
20. **Machete**	*large, heavy knife*
21. **Parade**	*large public procession*
22. **Anchovy**	*small savoury fish*
23. **Sherry**	*fortified wine*
24. **Tortilla**	*thin Mexican pan cake or chips*
25. **Marinade**	*seasoned, flavoured liquid used to soak meat*
26. **Sarsaparilla**	*drink made from root of plant*
27. **Bravado**	*bluster*
28. **Barbecue**	*an open grill or fireplace*
29. **Sassafras**	*aromatic tree whose bark has medicinal value*
30. **Adobe**	*sun dried brick*
31. **Canyon**	*deep valley with steep sides*
32. **Arroyo**	*gulch*
33. **Toreador**	*bull fighter*
34. **Senorita**	*Miss.*
35. **Senora**	*Mrs.*
36. **Senor**	*Mr.*
37. **Matador**	*Bull fighter*
38. **Renegade**	*deserter*
39. **Don**	*lord or gentleman*
40. **Dona**	*title of respect for a married woman*
41. **Desperado**	*bold, reckless criminal*
42. **Albino**	*person deficient in pigmentation*
43. **Patio**	*courtyard*
44. **Pueblo**	*adobe house*
45. **Hacienda**	*landed estate*
46. **Sierra**	*chain of hills or mountains*
47. **Vega**	*grassy plain*
48. **Plaza**	*open space or square; complex of shops*
49. **Esplanade**	*level space*
50. **El Dorado**	*fictitious country rich in gold*
51. **Rodeo**	*showing of cowboy skills*

52. **Lariat**	*long, noosed rope for catching horses*
53. **Bronco**	*untamed horse*
54. **Lasso**	*long, noosed rope, lariat*
55. **Gaucho**	*cowboy of South American Pampas.*

Celtic Words

Some important English words, which have been taken from Celtic are as follows:

Word	Meaning
1. **Banshee**	*Irish fairy with a wail portending death*
2. **Plaid**	*long cloak or shawl*
3. **Shamrock**	*clover leaf, esp. an Irish emblem*
4. **Vassal**	*dependent*
5. **Gravel**	*small stones; coarse sand*
6. **Truant**	*one absent without a leave*
7. **Galore**	*in plenty*
8. **Colleen**	*young Irish girl*
9. **Blarney**	*flattering talk*
10. **Bog**	*soft, wet ground*
11. **Brogue**	*stout shoe; Irish accent*
12. **Lawn**	*stretch of grass in garden; fine linen*
13. **Crag**	*steep, rugged rock*
14. **Quay**	*dock*
15. **Loch**	*lake*
16. **Gull**	*aquatic bird*
17. **Javelin**	*light spear*
18. **Tory**	*member of conservative party in England*
19. **Clan**	*group of families*
20. **Glengarry**	*a small brimless hat*

Arabic Words

Some important English words, which have been taken from Arabic are as follows:

Word	Meaning
1. **Camphor**	*strong smelling ketone*
2. **Alchemy**	*magic, art of converting metal into gold*
3. **Garble**	*mix-up*
4. **Henna**	*dye*
5. **Tarragon**	*spice*
6. **Saffron**	*orange/ yellow spice*
7. **Lute**	*stringed instrument*
8. **Bedouin**	*member of nomadic Arab race*
9. **Fakir**	*member of Islamic religious order, ascetic*
10. **Sequin**	*small ornamental stars to be stitched on clothes*
11. **Sherbet**	*flavoured drink*
12. **Sultan**	*ruler of Muslim kingdom*
13. **Zenith**	*highest point*
14. **Nadir**	*lowest point*
15. **Muezzin**	*crier, who summons Muslims to prayer*
16. **Minaret**	*tall, slender tower of Mosque*
17. **Almanac**	*yearly calendar*
18. **Amber**	*yellowish, translucent fossil resin*
19. **Alcove**	*recess*
20. **Algebra**	*method of calculating*
21. **Carafe**	*decanter*
22. **Harem**	*women's dwelling, one man's wives*
23. **Carat**	*small weight used to measure gold, etc.*
24. **Cipher**	*secret writing*
25. **Civet**	*strong, musky perfume*
26. **Emir**	*an independent Islamic ruler*
27. **Cotton**	*thread or cloth made from this plant's seed*
28. **Elixir**	*medicine or remedy, used by alchemists*
29. **Monsoon**	*heavy rainfall season, rainy season*
30. **Ream**	*large bundles of paper*

Indian Words

Some important English words, which have been taken from India are as follows:

Word	Meaning
1. **Yoga**	*Hindu system of physical and mental exercise*
2. **Tantra**	*religious writing*
3. **Tonga**	*horse-drawn carriage*
4. **Wallah**	*somebody in-charge of a certain thing*
5. **Dhoti**	*Indian male unstitched garment wrapped on waist*
6. **Avatar**	*incarnation*
7. **Gunny**	*jute bag, sack*
8. **Nawab**	*Indian nobleman in Mughal Empire*
9. **Sahib**	*respectful form of address for men*
10. **Pundit**	*Expert, authority, priest*
11. **Guru**	*teacher, wise leader*
12. **Sandal**	*type of wood*
13. **Chutney**	*sweet and sour sauce*
14. **Pachisi**	*board game*
15. **Nirvana**	*heaven, freedom*
16. **Myna**	*bird*
17. **Karma**	*fate*
18. **Dharma**	*code of conduct of Hindus*
19. **Ginger**	*spice*
20. **Stupa**	*dome-shaped structure where ashes are kept*

French Words

Some important English words, which have been taken from French are as follows:

	Word	Meaning
1.	**Bouillon**	*Thin soup*
2.	**Praline**	*nut candy*
3.	**Potage**	*thick coup*
4.	**Absinthe**	*green, flavoured liqueur*
5.	**Cuisine**	*style of cooking*
6.	**Casserole**	*covered baking dish*
7.	**Nougat**	*type of candy*
8.	**Croquette**	*patty of cooked meat or fish*
9.	**Flambe**	*pour alcoholic drink on food and ignite*
10.	**Liqueur**	*flavoured alcoholic liquid*
11.	**Tureen**	*serving dish for soup*
12.	**Gourmet**	*connoisseur of wine, food, etc.*
13.	**Gourmand**	*glutton*
14.	**Blancmange**	*jelly-like dessert made with milk*
15.	**Serviette**	*table-napkin*
16.	**Burlesque**	*ludicrous parody*
17.	**Marquee**	*Sign used in a theater*
18.	**Roulette**	*game of chance*
19.	**Pirouette**	*to whirl on one foot*
20.	**Silhouette**	*outline of object against light*
21.	**Nuance**	*delicate shade of differences*
22.	**Precis**	*abstract, summary*
23.	**Vignette**	*design on a book page*
24.	**Critique**	*critical essay*
25.	**Coterie**	*social clique, exclusive group*
26.	**Connoisseur**	*critical expert of matters of art*
27.	**Belles-letters**	*aesthetic writings*
28.	**Memories**	*reward of events, autobiography*
29.	**Bon mot**	*clever saying*
30.	**Repartee**	*witty talk*
31.	**rapport**	*harmony*
32.	**Idee fixe**	*obsession*
33.	**Bourgeois**	*middle class*
34.	**Charlatan**	*faker, quack*
35.	**Faux pas**	*social blunder*
36.	**Genteel**	*element refined*
37.	**Largesse**	*generosity*
38.	**Gauche**	*socially inept*
39.	**Nonchalance**	*indifferent*
40.	**Raconteur**	*expert storyteller*
41.	**Avant-garde**	*in advance*
42.	**Milieu**	*environment*
43.	**Tete-a-tete**	*private conversation*
44.	**Vis-à-vis**	*regarding, in relation to*
45.	**Outre**	*bizarre*
46.	**Passe**	*out of date*
47.	**Liaison**	*connection*
48.	**Rendezvous**	*meeting place, appointment*
49.	**Joie de vivre**	*enjoyment of life*
50.	**Eclat**	*success*
51.	**Savoir**	*fair*
52.	**Boulevard**	*broad avenue in a city*
53.	**Salon**	*a shop of fashion, drawing room*
54.	**Chateau**	*castle*
55.	**Façade**	*front of a building*
56.	**Chaise**	*light, open carriage*
57.	**Bureau**	*office disk*
58.	**Concierge**	*doorman*
59.	**Melee**	*a mixed fight or crowd*
60.	**Terrain**	*area of ground*
61.	**Saboteur**	*damage closer (esp. secretly)*
62.	**Aide-de-camp**	*a military officer personality assisting their superior*
63.	**Chasseur**	*driver*
64.	**Espionage**	*use of spice*
65.	**Ricochet**	*rebound (of bullet)*
66.	**Envoy**	*official representative*
67.	**Bivouac**	*temporary camp of soldiers*
68.	**Espirit de corps**	*feelings of pride in belonging to a group*
69.	**Despot**	*a tyrant or absolute ruler*
70.	**Commandant**	*officer in command*

Italian Words

Some important English words, which have been taken from Italian are as follows:

	Word	Meaning
1.	**Prima donna**	*principle female singer in an opera*
2.	**Soprano**	*highest singing voice*
3.	**Crescendo**	*gradual increase in volume or force*
4.	**Bravo**	*well done*
5.	**Quartet**	*group of four musicians*
6.	**Maestro**	*famous conductor*
7.	**Mandolin**	*stringed musical instrument*
8.	**Finale**	*the last piece*
9.	**Duet**	*a composition for two singers*
10.	**Forte**	*to play loudly*
11.	**Libretto**	*text of long musical piece*
12.	**Allegro**	*at a quick and lively tempo; quickly*
13.	**Presto**	*to be played very fast*
14.	**Falsetto**	*high-pitched singing method*
15.	**Virtuoso**	*exceptional performer*
16.	**Diva**	*women opera singer, famous lady*
17.	**Dilettante**	*dabbler in art or knowledge*
18.	**Bravura**	*great skill*
19.	**Tempo**	*music's speed*
20.	**Opera**	*musical drama*
21.	**Piccolo**	*a very small flute-like musical instrument*

22. **Coda** *final section of musical piece*
23. **Concerto** *musical composition for soloist and orchestra*
24. **Madrigal** *a song with parts*
25. **Balcony** *a gallery*
26. **Villa** *country, estate*
27. **Arcade** *arched passageway, shops*
28. **Catacomb** *tomb*
29. **mezzanine** *lowest balcony*
30. **Portico** *porch*
31. **Piozza** *plaza*
32. **Grotto** *cave*
33. **Corridor** *hallway*
34. **Pedestal** *a base or support*
35. **Alfresco** *in the open air*
36. **Lotto** *game of chance*
37. **Tarot** *fortune telling cards*
38. **Valise** *small piece of luggage*
39. **Garb** *dress*
40. **Gondola** *venetian canal boat*
41. **Lagoon** *area which is sand banked, saltwater lake*
42. **Gala** *festive occasion, show*
43. **Casino** *place for gambling*
44. **Cascade** *waterfall, anything like a waterfall*
45. **Gazette** *official newspaper for announcements*
46. **Incognito** *assumed identity*
47. **Parasol** *sunshade, umbrella*
48. **Regatta** *meeting for yacht or boat races*
49. **Battalion** *an army group*
50. **Fracas** *uproar*
51. **Citadel** *fortress*
52. **Bandit** *robber*
53. **Salvo** *a round of artillery*
54. **Vendetta** *a private feud*
55. **Stiletto** *a small dagger with a thin blade, a heel of female shoe*
56. **Cartel** *alliance of political parties or business houses*
57. **Tirade** *long angry speech*
58. **Partisan** *prejudiced, adherent of a party, biased*
59. **Cavalcade** *procession of riders, fleet of cars*
60. **Panache** *dashing style*
61. **Manifesto** *declaration of policy by a political party*
62. **Squadron** *an army, navy or air force unit*
63. **Ducat** *a gold coin*
64. **Mercantile** *trade*
65. **Parmesan** *type of cheese*
66. **Contra band** *smuggled goods*
67. **Porcelain** *fine china, earthenware*
68. **Frigate** *old warship, corresponding to modern cruiser*
69. **Skiff** *small flat-bottomed boat*
70. **Milliner** *maker or dealer in women's hat*
71. **Settee** *comfortable seat for two people*
72. **Bankrupt** *financially insolvent*

Yiddish Words

Some important English words, which have been taken from Yiddish are as follows:

	Word	***Meaning***
1.	**Schnapps**	*brandy, alcoholic drink*
2.	**Challah**	*soft egg bread*
3.	**Bagel**	*chewy roll with a hole in the middle*
4.	**Matzoth**	*unleavened bread*
5.	**Nosh**	*food, eat*
6.	**Kosher**	*permitted, clean, good (as of food)*
7.	**Yenta**	*gossip*
8.	**Boychik**	*little boy*
9.	**Shmo**	*butt of a joke*
10.	**Nudnick**	*bore*
11.	**noodge**	*nag*
12.	**Shiksa**	*non-jewish woman*
13.	**Maven**	*expert*
14.	**Klutz**	*clumsy person*
15.	**Chai**	*life*
16.	**Broche**	*blessing*
17.	**Mazel tov**	*congratulations*
18.	**Gesundheit**	*Good health*
19.	**Chutzpah**	*boldness, self confidence*
20.	**Bummer**	*annoying thing*
21.	**Kvetch**	*to grumble or complain*
22.	**Kibitzer**	*one who interferes*
23.	**Golem**	*creature of clay brought to life by magic as in legend*
24.	**Naches**	*proud pleasure*
25.	**Mitzva**	*a good deed*
26.	**Kine-abhora**	*Magical phrase to ward off evil*
27.	**Fen**	*expression of disgust*
28.	**Boo-boo**	*mistake*
29.	**plotz**	*explode*
30.	**Gehenna**	*hell*
31.	**Mish-mosh**	*confusion*
32.	**Bupkes**	*nothing*
33.	**Mishegoss**	*nonsense*
34.	**Phooey**	*expression of disgust, contempt*

CHAPTER 5

Words and Phrases often Confused

INTRODUCTION

In this chapter, we will discuss words that are often confused with each other because they are:

1. similar in spelling and different in usage; or
2. similar in spelling and different in pronunciation; or
3. similar in pronunciation but different in usage and spelling; or
4. similar in spelling but different in meaning; or
5. slightly different in spelling but might have similar usage; or
6. words whose usage is commonly mistaken by the non native speaker.

If we analyse the CAT examination questions of 2007 and 2008, we find that these confusing words have found a place in the CAT in the two consecutive years. Although most of the words which had come in CAT 2007 and 2008 have been covered in the vocabulary section of this book, the recurrence of this question type makes it obligatory to devote a full chapter to it. This question type is some times appearing in the exam since CAT went online in 2009 and thus still remains an important chapter.

In linguistics, a homonym is one or a group of words that share the same spelling and the same pronunciation but have different meanings, usually as a result of the two words having different origins.

Some books only require that homonyms share the same spelling or pronunciation (in addition to having different meanings), but these are the definitions most other sources give for *homographs* and *homophones* respectively.

Examples of homonyms are:

- stalk (which as a noun can mean part of a plant, and as a verb to follow/harass a person),
- *bear* (animal to and carry something), *leaf* (part of a plant or page of a book).

Some sources state that homonym meanings must be unrelated in origin (rather than just different). Thus *right* (correct) and *right* (opposed to left) would be polysemous (see below) and not homonyms.

Capitonyms are words that share the same spelling but have different meanings when capitalised (and may or may not have different pronunciations). Such words include polish (to make shiny) and Polish (from Poland).

The word 'homonym' comes from the conjunction of the *Greek* prefix homo- (όμο-), meaning 'same', and suffix-*ǒnimus* (-wvuino), meaning 'name'. Thus, it refers to two or more distinct concepts sharing the 'same name' or signifier.

Several similar linguistic concepts are related to homonymy. The terms *homograph* and *homophone* are, however, usually defined the same way as meaning 'same spelling' and 'same sound' respectively, and **heteronym** and **homonym** can be seen as respective subclasses of these.

- **Homographs** are words that share the same spelling regardless of how they are pronounced. Homographs may be pronounced the same, in which case they are also homophones - for example, *ball* (toy) and *ball* (form of dance). Alternatively they may be pronounced differently, in which case they are also heteronyms - for example, *bow* (the front of a ship) and *bow* (a type of knot).

- **Homophone** can be called as words that share the same pronunciation regardless of how they are spelled. Homophones may be spelled the same (in which case they are also homographs) or spelled differently.
- **Polysemes** are words with the same spelling and distinct but *related* meanings. The distinction between polysemy and homonymy is often subtle and subjective, and not all sources consider polysemous words to be homonyms. So they can be treated differently also. Words such as 'mouth', meaning either the orifice on one's face, or the opening of a cave or river, are polysemous and may or may not be considered homonyms.

Examples below illustrate the above given concept:

- bough–a branch on a tree.
- bow–to bend forward at the waist in respect
- bow–the front of the ship
- bow–the weapon which shoots arrows
- bow–a kind of tied ribbon
- bow–to bend outward at the sides
- bo–a long staff, usually made of tapered hard wood or bamboo
- beau–a male paramour

In derivation, ***homograph*** means 'same writing', ***homophone*** means 'same sound', ***heteronym*** means 'different name', and ***heterophone*** means 'different sound'.

A

1. **Abdicate/Abrogate**
   - We *abandon* things when *abdicating*.
   - We *abrogate* things when we abolish them.
2. a**ccede**/ex**ceed**
   - *Accede* means 'to agree' or ' to allow
   - *Exceed* means 'to go beyond' or 'to surpass' as in
   - 'Drivers who exceed the speed limit are asking for hefty fines.'
3. **Accept** (receive)/**Except** (leave out)
   - To *accept* is 'to agree to something or to receive something willingly
   - To *except* is 'to exclude or omit.'
4. **Access** (approach)/**Excess** (too much)
5. **Adapt** (change)/a**dept** (skill)/**Adopt** (choose)
   - *Adapt* means 'to adjust'
   - *adept* means 'skilled' and
   - *adopt* means 'to take as your own'
6. **Adverse/Averse**
   - *Adverse* means 'inauspicious' or 'hostile'
   - *averse* means 'disinclined' or 'repelled'
7. **Advice** (suggestion)/**Advise** (to recommend)
   Advice is the noun and *advise* the verb.
   - You advise someone.
   - What you give that person is advice.
8. **Affluence/Effluence**
   - *Affluence* is wealth;
   - *Effluence* is waste or useless product
9. **Aisle/Isle**
   - An *aisle* is a narrow passageway, especially in a church or store;
   - An *isle* is an island
10. **Aisle** (space, between rows)/**Advise** (to recommend)
11. **All right/Alright**
    - *All right* is the correct form;
    - *alright* is grammatically incorrect.
    The misspelling 'alright' is nonstandard usage. The two words are separate.
12. **Allot** (assign, distribute)/**A lot** (a large amount)
13. **Allude** (suggest)/**Elude** (escape)
14. **Allusion** (suggestion)/**Illusion** (deception, fantasy)
    - *Allusion* is a reference to something literary or historical with which the reader is presumably familiar.
    - An *illusion* is a false, misleading, idea.
15. **Aloud/Allowed**
    - *Aloud* means 'out loud' or 'speaking so that someone else can hear you'.
    - *Allowed* means 'permitted'.
16. **Already** (previously)/**All ready** (completely prepared)
    - *Already* means 'by this time'
    - *all ready* means 'prepared'
17. **Altar** (church table)/**Alter** (change)
    - *Altar*: I was married at the altar of my church.
18. **Altogether** (entirely)/**All together** (complete group)
    - Altogether means 'wholly'.
    - *all together* means 'everybody in a group'
19. **Always** (at all times)/**All ways** (all methods)
    - *All ways* means 'by every way or method'.
    - *Always* means 'all the time, forever.'
20. **Among/Between**
    - *Between* expresses the joining or separation of two people or things.
    - *Among* refers to a group of three or more.
21. **Amoral/Immoral**
    - 'Amoral' is a rather technical word meaning 'unrelated to morality.'

- When you mean to denounce someone's behavior, call it 'immoral.'

22. **Amount/Number**
    - Write 'number' when things can be counted.
    - When things are lumped together write 'amount'.
23. **Annual/Annul**
    - *Annual* means 'yearly'
    - *Annul* means to 'make void or invalid'
24. **Anxious/Eager**
    - 'Anxiety' is unpleasant.
    - 'Eagerness' is joyous. They are not synonyms.
25. **Anyone/Any one**
    This is quite tricky.
    - *Anyone* means 'anybody, any person at all'
    - *Any one* means 'any one person' and is followed by 'of'.
26. **Appraise/Apprise**
    - *Appraise* is 'to assess or estimate'.
    - *Apprise* is 'to inform or notify'.
27. **Ascent** (climb)/**Assent** (agree)
    - *Ascent* is an upward movement;
    - *Assent* means 'agreement'.
28. **Ascribe/Subscribe**
    - If you agree with a theory or belief, you *ascribe* to it, just as you
    - subscribe to a magazine.
29. **Assistance/Assistants**
    - *Assistance* means 'help' or 'aid'
    - *Assistants* is the plural of assistant which means 'one who gives help'
30. **Assume/Presume**
    - We 'assume' things in the absence of evidence.
    - We 'presume' things when it is reasonable to do so and there is no evidence to the contrary.
31. **Assure/Ensure/Insure**
    - *Assure* means 'to guarantee'
    - *Ensure* means 'to make sure'
    - *Insure* means 'to protect against loss or damage'.
32. **Attain/Obtain**
    - *Attain* means 'reach';
    - *Obtain* means 'get.'
33. **Auger/Augur**
    - *Auger* is a tool;
    - *Augur* means 'to predict' 'or 'a sort of an omen.'
34. **Affect** (influence)/**Effect** (result)
    - *Affect* is a verb meaning either 'to influence' or 'to pretend.'
    - *Effect* as a verb means 'to accomplish or to produce as a result' as a noun, *effect* means 'result.'
    - *Affect* is a verb; effect is more usually a noun.
    - When used as a verb it means 'to achieve'or 'fulfil' or 'realise'
35. **Aid/Aide**
    - We *aid* people when we help them.
    - An *aide* is a special assistant.

B

1. **Bail/Bale**
    - You *bail* the boat and *bale* the hay.
    - The expression 'bail out' meanings 'to abandon a position or situation', and ***bale*** is a bundle.
2. **Baited/Bated**
    - *Baited* usually refers to traps or snares.
    - When the reference is to someone who is hardly daring to breathe, the correct word is always *'bated'*.
3. **Ball/Bawl**
    - To 'bawl' is to cry out loudly;
    - *ball* is a toy or a plaything.
4. **Bare** (uncovered)/**Bear** (carry; the animal)
5. **Bazaar** (market)/**Bizarre** (weird)
6. **Been/Gone**
    - *Been* is the past participle of *'be,'* gone is the past participle of *'go'*.
    - *Been* is used to describe completed visits, gone does not specify the return or completion of the visit.
7. **Bemuse/Amuse**
    When you *bemuse* someone, you confuse them, and not necessarily in an entertaining way. Don't confuse this word with 'amuse.'
8. **Benefactor/Beneficiary**
    - *Benefactors* give benefits;
    - *Beneficiaries* receive them
9. **Beside/Besides**
    - *Beside* means 'at the side of'.
    - *Besides* means 'in addition to.'
10. **Biannual/Biennial**
    These two are really tricky!
    - *Biannual* means happening twice a year;
    - *Biennial* means every two years.
11. **Birth** (childbearing)/**Berth** (place of rest)
    - *Berth* is a place to sleep on a boat or ship or train;
    - *Birth* is the beginning (usually of life).

12. **Blonde/Blond**
- Because these are borrowed from French, there is a feminine and masculine form. *Blonde* is feminine and *blond* is masculine.

13. **Blunt/Brunt**
- Some people mistakenly substitute the adjective 'blunt' for the noun 'brunt' in standard expressions like 'bear the brunt'.
- *Brunt* means 'main force.'

14. **Board** (plank; food)/**Bored** (drilled; uninterested)
- *Board* is a long sheet of wood, also a group of people as in 'Board of Directors', and as a verb means to go onto a ship, plane or other form of public transport;
- *Bored* means 'not interested'.

15. **Bore/Boar/Boor**
- *Bore* as a noun is a boring or tiresome person, or something that you don't like doing;
- Bore as a verb is 'to drill'.
- *Boar* is a male pig;
- *Boor* is a vulgar person.

16. **Born** (given birth to, beginning of life)/**Borne** (carried)

17. **Bought/Brought**

Bought is the past tense of 'buy', *brought* is the past tense of 'bring'. So, I *bought* (paid for) a load of topsoil, and a truck driver *brought* (delivered) it to my home.

18. **Braise/Braze**
- *Braise* means 'to cook slowly in liquid (usually meat)'.
- *braze* most commonly means 'to solder with an alloy of copper and zinc'.

19. **Breach/Breech**

Breach is to break and *breeches* are worn by horse riders on their legs.

20. **Break** (smash, split)/**Brake** (stopping device)

21. **Breath/Breathe**
- When you need to *breathe*, you take a *breath.*
- 'Breathe' is the verb, 'breath' the noun.

22. **Bridal/Bridle**
- *Bridal* has to do with brides and weddings;
- *bridle* as a noun means a halter or restraint and as a verb it means to restrain or to draw oneself up in anger.

23. **Broach/Brooch**
- A decorative pin is a 'brooch' even though it sounds like 'broach'–a quite different word.
- To broach means 'to touch upon or start especially a topic'.

24. **By/Buy/Bye**
- *By* is a preposition meaning 'next to';
- *buy* means 'purchase'; *bye* means 'farewell' or 'goodbye'.

C

1. **Cache/Cachet**
- 'Cache' comes from the French verb *'cacher,'* meaning 'to hide,' and in English is pronounced exactly like the word 'cash.'
- But speaking of a *cache* (hidden hoard of weapons, drugs, etc.)
- Often mispronounced to sound like *cachet* is a word with a very different meaning: it was originally a seal affixed to a document but now it refers to the quality attributed to anything with authority or prestige.

2. **Callous/Callused**
- Calling someone *callous* is a way of metaphorically suggesting a lack of feeling similar to that caused by calluses on the skin; but if you are speaking literally of the tough build-up on a person's hand or feet, the word you need is 'callused.'

3. **Can/May**
- *Can* refers to one's ability.
- *May* concerns whether one has permission.

4. **Canon/Cannon**
- 'Canon' is used for principles or rules and 'cannon' refers to a large piece of artillery.

5. **Canvas** (fabric)/**Canvass** (examine, campaign for election)

6. **Capital** (city; wealth)/**Capitol** (building)

7. **Carat/Caret/Carrot/Karat**

'Carrots' are those crunchy orange vegetables, but this spelling gets misused for the less familiar words which are pronounced the same but have very different meanings.
- Precious stones like diamonds are weighed in *carats.* The same word is used to express the proportion of pure gold in an alloy, though in this usage it is sometimes spelled 'karat' (hence the abbreviation '20K gold').
- A *caret* is a proofreader's mark showing where something needs to be inserted, shaped like a tiny pitched roof. It looks rather like a French circumflex, but is usually distinct from it on modern computer keyboards.
- *Carets* are extensively used in computer programming.

8. **Career/Careen**

Careening down the road is swerving from side to side, whereas *career* relates to your future, job, etc.

9. **Censor** (prohibit)/**Sensor** (measuring device)

- To *censure* someone, however, is to officially denounce an offender

10. **Cereal/Serial**

- *Cereal* is something you might eat for breakfast, such as porridge.
- *Serial* is something in a series; something that continues one after another.

11. **Choose** (to select)/**Chose** (past tense of choose)

12. **Chunk/Chuck**

- *Chunk* is a big piece, whereas *chuck* means 'to throw'.

13. **Cite/Site/Sight**

- *Cite* means 'to indicate'.
- A *site* is a place.
- *Sight* is vision.

14. **Click/Clique**

- To *click* is to push a button, or switch; to emit or make a slight, sharp sound, or series of such sounds; and *clique* is a small exclusive group of friends or associates.

15. **Coarse** (rough)/**Course** (way, path)

16. **Collaborate/Corroborate**

- *Collaborate* means 'to work with someone';
- *Corroborate* means 'to establish the truth of something'.

17. **Collage/College**

You can paste together bits of paper to make a *collage*, but the institution of higher education is a *college*.

18. **Come over/Overcome**

- *Come over* is a phrasal verb, that can mean several things. It can mean 'to move from one place to another' or 'move towards someone'.
- *Overcome* is a verb, which means 'to defeat or succeed in controlling or dealing with something'.

19. **Compare/Contrast**

- You *compare* like objects for both similarities and differences.
- You *contrast* any two things (like or unlike) by identifying dissimilarities.

20. **Complement** (make complete, to supplement)/ **Compliment** (praise)

21. **Concentrate/Concentrated**

- When you *concentrate* (verb) you direct all your efforts towards a particular activity, subject or problem. If something is *concentrated* (asiective) it means it has had some liquid removed.

Note: The simple past of 'to concentrate' is 'concentrated' and this is where the confusion may arise.

22. **Connote/Denote**

The literal meaning of a word is its *denotation;* the broader associations we have with a word are its *connotations.*

23. **Conscience** (moral sense)/**Conscious** (aware)

24. **Conscience/Conscious/Consciousness**

- Your *conscience* makes you feel guilty when you do bad things.
- *Consciousness* is your awareness.
- If you are awake, you are *conscious.*

25. **Consul/Council/Councilor/Counsel/Counselor**

- *Consul* is a diplomat to a foreign country.
- *Council* refers to a group to discuss and take action on official matters.
- A *councilor* is a member of such a group.
- *Counsel* is advice or to advise.
- A *counselor* is an adviser.

26. **Continual/Continuous**

Continual means 'something that happens' frequently, with breaks between the occurrences. *Continuous* means 'something that happens without stopping'.

27. **Convince/Persuade**

- We *persuade* people to act.
- We *convince* when using proof to accept a belief. Hence, we usually are *'convinced'* something is true, but others try to *'persuade'* us to do something.

28. **Cooperation/Corporation**

- *Cooperation* '(usually spelt without the hyphen in US English)' means working together;
- *Corporation* is a business organisation.

29. **Copyright/Copywrite**

- *Copyright* is the legal ownership of a book, film, play, piece of artwork, musical composition, etc. or the right to print, publish, film, record or perform them.
- *Copywrite* is something you do if you are creating advertising or publicity material.

30. **Core/Corps/Corpse**

- Apples have *cores.*
- A *corps* is an organisation, like the Peace *Corps.* A *corpse* is a dead body, a carcass.

31. **Correspondence/Correspondents**

Correspondence is written communication; *correspondents* are those who write it.

32. **Creak/Creek**

- *Creak* is both a noun and a verb and means 'squeak or groan' (for instance, rusty hinges and loose floorboards creak);
- *Creek* is a noun and means a 'waterway' or 'stream'.

33. **Credible/Creditable**

- *Credible* means 'believable';
- *Creditable* means 'praiseworthy' or 'deserving credit.'

34. **Credible/Credulous**

- 'Credible' means 'believable or trustworthy.' It is also used in a more abstract sense, meaning something like 'worthy'.
- Don't confuse 'credible' with 'credulous,' a much rarer word which means 'gullible.'

35. **Crevice/Crevasse**

- *Crevices* are by definition tiny, like that little
- *crevice* between your teeth where the popcorn hulls always get caught.
- A huge crack in a glacier is given the French spelling, *crevasse.*

36. **Criteria/Criterion**

Criterion is singular; *criteria* is plural.

Criterion is in the case of a single specification.

Criteria is in the case of more than one specification.

37. **Cue/Queue**

'Cue' has a variety of meanings like a clue or a play instrument as in a game of billiard, but all uses of 'queue' relate to its original French meaning of 'tail,' which becomes a metaphor for a line.

38. **Curb/Kerb**

Curb means 'to control' as in 'curb your temper', while *kerb* is the edge of a footpath or sidewalk.

39. **Currant/Current**

Currant is a fruit, usually dried.

- *Current* as an adjective which means 'contemporary', or 'fashionable'; as a noun it means 'stream,' or 'flow'.

40. **Cursor** (computer marker)/**Curser** (swearer)

D

1. **Dairy** (milk-producing farm)/**Diary** (daily book)
2. **Data/Datum**

- The dictionaries treat *data* as a group noun meaning information, especially facts or numbers, collected for examination and consideration.
- Strictly speaking *datum* is the singular form of *data* which is the the plural form.

3. **Dateline/Deadline**

The word 'dateline' is used today mainly to label the bit of text at the top of a printed news story that indicates where and–often, but not always–when it was written.

- *Deadline* is most often the date by which something must be accomplished.

4. **Decent/Descent**

- *Decent* is an adjective meaning 'socially acceptable' or 'good.'
- Descent is a noun which means a 'movement downwards' or 'your ancestry.'

5. **Definite/Definitive**

- 'Definite' means 'certain (a word you can do without since it adds redundant stress).
- 'Definitive' means 'conclusive and unamendable.'

6. **Defuse/Diffuse**

You *defuse* a dangerous situation by treating it like a bomb and removing its fuse.

- To *diffuse,* in contrast, is to spread something out.

7. **Depreciate/Deprecate**

To *depreciate* something is to actually make it worse, whereas to *deprecate* something is simply to speak or think of it in a manner that demonstrates your low opinion of it.

8. **Dessert** (sweet food)/**Desert** (dry land) Dessert

- A *desert* (pronounced des¢ ert) is a dry region.
- To *desert* (pronounced desert¢) is to leave.
- The *dessert* is the last part of a meal.

9. **Device** (a mechanism)/**Devise** (to arrange)

- *Device* is a noun, meaning a 'gadget' or (particularly in writing terms) an 'invention;
- *devise* is a verb, meaning to 'invent' or 'plot'.

10. **Different from/Different than**

- Although both ***different from*** and *different than* are common American usages, the preferred idiom is *different from.*

11. **Dilemma/Difficulty**

A *dilemma* is a difficult choice, not just any *difficulty* or problem.

12. **Disburse/Disperse**

You ***disburse*** money by taking it out of your purse (French 'bourse') and distributing it.

- ***Disperse*** means 'to scatter.'

13. **Discreet, discrete**
    - *Discreet* means 'respectful,' or ' prudent;'
    - *Discrete* means 'separate' or 'detached from others.'
14. **Disinterested/Uninterested**
    - *Uninteresting* people are bored, but *disinterested* people are impartial. We are tried by 'a *disinterested* jury of our peers.'
15. **Don't have to/mustn't**
    - We have to use
    - *(or do not have to)* to say that there is no obligation or necessity to do something.
    - *Mustn't/must not* is a modal verb used to show that something is not allowed. When you use *mustn't* you are telling people not to do things.
16. **Downside/ Underside**
    - *Downside* is a noun that means 'the disadvantage of a situation'.
    - *Underside* is a noun that means 'the side of something that is usually nearest the ground'.
17. **Draft/ Draught**
    - *Draft* refers to the first writing of your novel or story (or any other document). You can also be *drafted* (enlisted or recruited) into the army, navy, etc.
    - Draught is an air movement, a drink (as in 'draught of ale')
18. **Dredge/ Drudge/ Trudge**
    - You use machinery to scoop stuff up from underwater called a *dredge*, to *dredge* up junk or debris from the bottom of a river or lake.
    - To *drudge* is to do hard, annoying work; and a person who does such work can also be called a *drudge*.
    - When you slog laboriously up a hill, you *trudge* up it.
19. **Dribble/Drivel**
    - *Dribble* means 'to drool'.
    - When you mean to criticise someone else's speech as stupid or pointless, the word you want is *drivel*.
20. **Dual** (having two parts)/**Duel** (fight between two people)
21. **Dye** (color)/**Die** (perish)

E

1. **Ecology/Environment**

   Ecology is the study of living things in relationship to their *environment*.
2. **Elicit** (draw forth)/**Illicit** (improper)
3. **Emigrant/Immigrant**
    - An *emigrant* is a person who moves out of a country;
    - An *immigrant* is one who moves into a country.
    - A similar distinction holds for the verbs *emigrate* and *immigrate*.
4. **Eminent** (noteworthy)/**Immanent** (inherent)/ **Imminent** (impending)
    - *Eminent* means 'distinguished;' or 'famous;'
    - *Imminent* means 'near', or 'close at hand'.
    - The rarest of the three is *immanent*, used by philosophers to mean 'inherent' and by theologians to mean 'present throughout the universe.'
5. **Empathy/Sympathy**
    - If you think you feel just like another person, you are feeling *empathy*.
    - If you just feel sorry for another person, you're feeling *sympathy*.
6. **Endemic/Epidemic**
    - An *endemic* condition is one characteristic of a particular region, population, or environment: a condition need not affect a majority or even a very large number of people in a population to be *endemic*. In biology, an endemic disease is one that is maintained locally without the need for outside influence.
    - An *epidemic* condition is widespread,or rampant.
7. **Enormous/Enormity**
    - Big things are *enormous*.
    - A heinous or atrocious thing has *enormity*.
8. **Ensure** (make certain)/**Insure** (indemnify)
9. **Envelop/ Envelope**
    - To wrap something up in a covering is to *envelop* it.
    - The specific wrapping you put around a letter is an *envelope*.
10. **Envious/Jealous**

    Although these are often treated as synonyms, there is a difference.
    - You are *envious* of what others have that you lack.
    - *Jealousy*, on the other hand, involves wanting to hold on to what you do have
11. **Epic/Epochs**
    - An *epoch* is a long period of time, like the Pleistocene Epoch.
    - An *epic* is a lengthy narrative poem, ordinarily concerning a serious subject containing details of heroic deeds and events

12. **Epigram/Epigraph/Epithet**
    - An *epigram* is a pithy saying, usually humorous.
    - An *epigraph* is a brief quotation used to introduce a piece of writing or the inscription on a statue or building.
    - An *epitaph* is the inscription on a tombstone or some other tribute to a dead person.
    - In literature, an *epithet* is a term that replaces or is added to the name of a person. You are more likely to encounter the term in its negative sense, as a term of insult or abuse: 'the people hurled *epithets* at the police who had arrested her.'
13. **Etymology/Entomology**
    - 'Etymology' is the study of the origins of words. 'Entomology' is the study of insects.
14. **Everyday** (ordinary)/**Every day (**each day)
15. **Everyone/Every one**
    - *Everyone* means 'every person in a group'.
    - *Every one* means 'each person' and is always followed by 'of'
16. **Evoke/Invoke**
    - The action of 'invoking' is usually more direct and active. It originally involved calling upon or summoning up a god or spirit. An invocation calls upon whatever is invoked to do something or serve a function. *Invoke* now can also be used to mean 'to appeal to,'or ' to cite'.
    - *Evoke* is usually less purposefully active, more indirect, often used to mean 'suggest.'
17. **Exalt/Exult**
    - When you celebrate joyfully, you *exult*.
    - When you raise something high (even if only in your opinion), you *exalt* it.
18. **Exasperate/Exacerbate**

    People get *exasperated* (irritated); situations get *exacerbated* (made worse).
19. **Exercise** (activity)/**Exorcise** (drive out)

F

1. **Fair** (just)/**Fare** (food; fee)
    - *Fair* means 'average', 'good-looking', 'pale', 'unbiased' (what a lot of meanings for one little word!);
    - *fare* is the money you pay to go somewhere by bus, train, plane, etc.
2. **Fatal/Fateful**
    - A *fatal* event is a deadly one;
    - A *fateful* one is determined by fate.
3. **Faze** (disturb)/**Phase** (stage)

    To *faze* someone is to fluster or confuse them, whereas *phase* is mostly used in reference to a stage in someone's life–though it can be a stage in almost anything else.
4. **Fearful/Fearsome**
    - To be *fearful* is to be afraid.
    - To be *fearsome* is to cause fear in others.
    - Remember that someone who is fierce is fearsome rather than fearful.
5. **Feel/Believe**

    You can *feel* tired, *feel* happy, or *feel* angry, but a belief describes your assessment of a proposition. One way to tell if you are dealing with true feelings is this test: Restate the sentence and substitute the word 'am' for the word 'feel.' If the sentence makes sense, you have isolated a feeling. If not, substitute the word 'belief'.
6. **Feint/Faint**
    - A *feint*, whether in chess or on the battlefield, is a maneuver designed to divert the opponent's attention from the real center of attack.
    - A *feint* is a daring move. It might also mean to make a false show of; simulate.
    - While 'faint of heart' (or 'faint at heart'), implies timidity or to *faint* means 'to lose consciousness'.
7. **Fewer/Less**
    - *Fewer* is used to describe things that can be counted.
    - *Less* refers to quantity or degree.
8. **Fiancé/Fiancée**
    - Your *fiance* is the man you plan to marry.
    - Your *fiancee* is the woman you plan to marry.
9. **Flammable/Inflammable**

    The prefix 'in' does not indicate negation here; it comes from the word 'inflame.' *Flammable* and *inflammable* both mean 'easy to catch on fire'.
10. **Flare/Flair**
    - *Flare* means 'to flash' or 'blaze'and '(as a noun) is a pyrotechnic device;/it also means to spread gradually outward, as the end of a trumpet, the bottom of a wide skirt, or the sides of a ship.;
    - *Flair* means 'ability' or 'skill.'
11. **Flaunt/Flout**
    - When you show off something or boast about it, you *flaunt* it.
    - When you *flout* something you show your contempt for it.

- In passing, it might be noted that a flautist also is one who plays the flute and in Middle English 'to *flout*' meant to play the flute.

12. **Flounder/Founder**
    - When something thrashes about, it *flounders*. When it fails completely, it *founders*.
13. **For/Since**
    - The prepositions *for* and *since* are often used with time expressions.
    - *For* indicates a period of time.
    - *Since* indicates a point in time.
14. **Forbear/Forebear**
    - *Forbear* means 'to refrain from';
    - *Forebear* is an ancestor or forefather.
15. **Forego/Forgo**
    - The 'e' in 'forego' tells you it has to do with going before. It occurs mainly in the expression 'foregone conclusion,' a conclusion arrived at in advance.
    - *Forgo* means 'to abstain from or do without'.
16. **Foreword/Forward**
    - *Foreword* is the preface in a book, usually written by someone who is not the author.
    - *Forward* means 'ahead, near the front.'
17. **Formerly** (at an earlier time)/**Formally** (according to a pattern, formal)
18. **Forth/Fourth**
    - *Forth* means 'forward';
    - *Fourth* is after 'third'.
19. **Fortunate/Fortuitous**
    - If something *fortunate* happens, we got lucky.
    - If it happened by chance, it is *fortuitous*.
20. **Foul/Fowl**
    - *Foul* can mean 'dishonourable' (by foul means), 'disgusting' (a foul smell), 'entangle' (rubbish dumped in the river can foul fishing lines);
    - *Fowl* is a bird.
21. **Found/Founded**
    - *Found* is the past tense of find;
    - *founded* means 'started'.
22. ***Full/Fulsome***
    - When things are *full* they contain abundant supplies of something.
    - When things are *fulsome* they are fat, excessive, and offensive to good taste.
23. **Furthest/Farthest**

    Generally, in good usage, *farther* is used for comparisons of distance and *further* for anything else. *Farther* is used for physical distance; *further* for non-physical.

G

1. **Gaff/Gaffe**

   Gaffe is a French word meaning 'embarrassing mistake', and should not be mixed up with *gaff*: a large hook.
2. **Gamut/Gantlet/Gauntlet**
   - A *gamut* is a full range or scope of things.
   - A *gantlet* is a form of punishment in which people run between rows of people who attempt to beat them.
   - A *gauntlet* is a glove thrown down when a person is challenged to a duel.
3. **Gender/Sex**
   - Do not substitute the word 'gender' to avoid embarrassment. People and animals differ by sex. Words differ by gender. Thus, unless a study involves gender classifications of words, it is a study of *sex* differences.
4. **Gibe/Jibe**
   - *Gibe* means 'to taunt';
   - *jibe* means 'to agree, correspond or tally'; in boating it means to shift the sails.
5. **Gig/Jig**
   - To *jig* is to move with a quick, jerky motion or hop; or bob. 'The jig is up' is an old slang expression meaning 'the game is over–we're caught.'
   - A musician's job is a *gig;* also, a gig is a light, two-wheeled one-horse carriage.
6. **Gild/Guild**
   - You *gild* an object by covering it with gold;
   - a *guild* is a group or an organisation of people doing similar things.
7. **Good/Well**
   - *Good* is an adjective. Do not use it to modify a verb.
   - *Well* is an adverb except in three uses:

     (i) when used to mean 'healthy,'

     (ii) when used to mean 'neatly groomed' or 'attractively dressed,' and

     (iii) when used to mean 'satisfactory.'
8. **Gorilla** (ape)/**Guerilla** (fighter)
9. **Grisly/Grizzly**
   - *Grisly* means 'horrible';
   - A *grizzly* is a bear.

H

1. **Hail/Hale**
   - *Hail* means 'to greet or to come from'; and as a noun it is frozen raindrops;
   - *hale* means 'healthy or (as a verb) to haul.'
2. **Hanged/Hung**
   - A criminal is always *hanged;*
   - A picture is *hung.*
3. **Hard/Hardly**
   - *Hard* is an adjective. It can mean 'solid', 'industrious', or 'difficult'.
   - *Hardly* is an adverb and means only just or certainly not.
4. **Hardy/Hearty**
   - *Hardy* is durable, whereas hearty is healthy or happy as in 'hale and *hearty.*'
5. **Hear** (perceive)/**Here** (in this place)
6. **Hear/Listen**
   - *Hear* is a verb that means 'to receive or become aware of a sound using your ears, so you don't have to make an effort in order to just hear something.'
   - *Listen* is a verb that means 'to give attention to someone or something in order to hear them, so you make an make an effort in order to hear something properly.'
7. **Heard** (perceived)/**Herd** (group of animals)
8. **Heel** (part of foot)/**Heal** (to make better)
9. **Heroin** (drug)/**Heroine** (principle female character)
10. **He's/His**
    - *He's* is the short form of 'he is' or 'he has'.
    - *His* is a possesive pronoun, it is used to show something belonging to or connected with a man, boy or male animal that has just been mentioned.
11. **Historic/Historical**

    An event is *historic,* whereas a place is *historical.*
12. **Hoard/Horde**
    - *Hoard* means 'to stockpile' and as a noun it is a cache of stockpiled stuff;
    - *Horde* is a large group.
13. **Hole** (opening)/**Whole** (entire)
14. **Holiday/Weekend**
    - A *holiday* (noun), refers to time, often one or two weeks, when someone does not go to work or school but is free to do what he/she wants, such as travel or relax. You usually have to book your holiday with your boss.
    - The *weekend* (noun) refers to the time from Saturday and Sunday, or Friday evening until Sunday night. It's the part of the week in which most paid workers living in the West do not go to work. It is a time for leisure and recreation, and/or for religious activities.
15. **Holy** (sacred)/**Wholly** (entirely)
16. **Home/Hone**
    - *Home* is your house or abode.
    - *Hone* means to sharpen.
17. **Homework/Housework**
    - *Homework* (noun) refers to tasks assigned to students by teachers to be completed mostly outside of class, and derives its name from the fact that most students do the majority of such work at home.
    - *Housework* (noun) refers to domestic household chores such as cleaning and cooking.
18. **'How do you do?'/'How are you?'/'How do you do?'**

    This is not a question. It is another, very formal way of saying 'Hello'. It is also very British. We only really use it the first time we meet someone.

    How are you? This is a question.
19. **Human** (of people)/**Humane** (merciful)

I

1. **I/me**

   Usually we choose the correct form by instinct.
   - *I* like tea.
   - Give *me* my tea.

   There are other times when people make mistakes with these two pronouns. *I/me* is difficult when it is coupled with another pronoun or with a noun. This is when you have to think about the subject/object in a sentence.
2. **Idea/Ideal**

   Any thought can be an *idea,* but only the best ideas worth pursuing are *ideals.*
3. **If/Whether**
   - Use *whether* when alternatives are involved ('I do not know whether I should complain or remain silent').
   - Otherwise *if* is acceptable ('I do not know if I should reconsider my decision').
4. **Illude/Elude**

   Illude is a very rare word, most of whose former meanings are obsolete, but which can mean 'to deceive' or 'lead astray.' But *elude* means to 'escape' or 'evade'.

5. **Illusion/Delusion**
   - *Illusions* are images of nonexistent things.
   - *Delusions* are misguided beliefs people hold despite evidence to the contrary. Thus, 'Daydreams can be enjoyable *illusions*, but *delusions* of grandeur come from self deceit or mental imbalance.'
6. **Immemorial/Immortal**
   - *Immemorial* means ancient beyond memory (as in the cliché 'since time immemorial');
   - *immortal* means 'deathless' or 'eternal.'
7. **Immigrate** (come in)/**Emigrate** (leave)
8. **Imply/Infer**
   - *Imply* means 'to suggest something'.
   - *Infer* means 'to derive a certain meaning from a remark or an action'. We *imply* things when we suggest them without actually saying so.
   - We *infer* conclusions from evidence by reasoning from data to claims.
9. **In/Into**
   - *In* means 'inside something.'
   - *Into* tells of motion from the outside to the inside of something.
10. **Incredulous/Incredible**

    Use *incredible* in the casual sense of 'unbelievably good' and use *incredulous* to mean 'unbelieving' or 'skeptical', which is the only standard usage for this word.
11. **Inside of/Outside of**
    - *Inside* of and *outside* of generally should not be used as Compound prepositions.
    - *Inside of* is acceptable in most formal writing when it means 'in less than'. The more formal term is within.
    - Both *inside of* and *outside of* are appropriate when *inside* or *outside* is a noun followed by a phrase.
12. **Insight/Incite**
    - An *insight* is something you have: an understanding of something, a bright idea about something.
    - To *incite* is to do something: to stimulate some action or other to be taken.
13. **Install/Instill**

    You *install* equipment and you *instill* feelings or attitudes.
14. **Interested/Interesting**
    - *Interested* is a past participle. When used as an adjective it says how someone feels.
    - *Interesting* is a present participle. When used as an adjective it describes the people or things that cause the feelings.
15. **Intolerable/Intolerant**
    - *Intolerable* means 'tiring, onerous, crushing.' Someone cannot be intolerable of another's beliefs.
    - *intolerant* means 'biased' or 'prejudiced.'
16. **Intricate/Integral**
    - An *integral* part of a machine, organisation, or idea is a necessary, inseparable part of it.
    - Whereas *intricate* means small or complex.
17. **Irregardless/Regardless**

    There is no such word as *irregardless;* the correct word is *regardless.*
18. **Its** (possessive of it)/**It's** (contraction of it is)

    This is confusing because possessives normally have an apostrophe, but in this case *it's* is short for it is and *its* is possessive–*always.*

K

1. **Knew/New**
   - *Knew* is the past tense of know;
   - *new* is the opposite of old.
2. **Know** (be aware)/**No** (negative, not yet)

L

1. **Later** (subsequently)/**Latter** (last thing mentioned)
   - *Later* means 'afterwards';
   - *latter* is the second of two things.
2. **Laudable/Laudatory**
   - Something *laudable* is worth praising.
   - *Laudatory* activity is the expression of such praise.
3. **Lay down/Lie down**
   - *Lay down* has several different meanings.
   - If you *lay* something *down,* it can mean you officially establish a rule, or officially state the way in which something should be done.
   - If you *lay down* your weapons, it means you stop fighting.
   - If you *lay* wine *down,* it means you are storing it for drinking in the future.
   - *Lie down* means to move into a position in which your body is flat, usually in order to sleep or rest.
4. **Lay/Lie**
   - *Lay* is an irregular transitive verb (lay/laid/laid - laying). It needs a direct object. It means 'to put something or someone down' (often in a horizontal postion).

- *Lie* is an irregular intransitive verb (lie/lay/lain - lying). It does not take a direct object. It means 'to rest in a horizontal position' or 'to be located somewhere.'
- *Lie* also means 'to say something that isn't true'; it takes the following form (lie/lied/lying).

5. **Leach/Leech**

Water *leaches* chemicals out of soil or colour out of cloth, while *leech* is a bloodsucking creature.

6. **Lead/Led/Lead**

- *Lead* (pronounced leed) means 'to go first'.
- *Led* is the past tense of *lead*.
- *Lead* is a heavy metal; also the graphite in a pencil.

7. **Least/Lest**

There are uses of old word *lest* in phrases like *'lest* we forget,' referring to something to be avoided or prevented.

- *Least* means something that is very less; it is the opposite of most.

8. **Legend/Myth**

Myths are generally considered to be traditional stories whose importance lies in their significance, whereas *legends* can be merely famous deeds.

9. **Lend/Loan**

- *Lend* is a verb meaning 'to give something temporarily to someone'.
- *Loan* is a noun, meaning the temporary transfer of something to someone else. So, 'Dad, can you loan me a few dollars until pay day?'

10. **Lesson** (instruction)/**Lessen** (reduce)

- *Lessen* means 'to make less'.
- *Lesson* is something you learn.

11. **Liable/Libel**

- *Liable* means 'subject to' or 'answerable for' or 'likely';
- *Libel* is written (as opposed to spoken) untruths about someone, for which you may be taken to court.

12. **Licence/License**

In British usage, *licence* is always the noun and *license* the verb.

13. **Lie/Lay**

- *Lie* means 'to recline'. When you recline, you ***lie*** down. If you tell someone you will ***lay*** down, you may risk embarrassment. For reclining, the past tense is *lay* and the past participle is *'lain.'*
- *Lay* means 'to put or place something'.
- Thus, you may say 'I have lain on my bed for half an hour,' but you cannot write 'I have laid on the lounge chair for half an hour.' On the other hand, you may 'lay the plate on the table,' in which case all past tense forms are the word 'laid.' By the way, once you 'lay' the plate on the table, it **lies** there until moved.

14. **Lightening/Lightning**

- *Lightening* means making 'lighter' or 'brighter';
- *Lightning* (which is always a noun) is what comes out of the sky, usually followed by a crack of thunder.

15. **Like/As/As if**

While the use of *like* as a conjunction is common in speaking, its use *as* a conjunction is not fully established in writing. *Like* is better used as a preposition.

16. **Look at/Watch**

- In this context, *look* is usually followed by the preposition *at*. When you *look at* someone or something you are interested in the appearance. Generally we *look at* things that are static.
- *Watch* is a verb. When you *watch* someone or something you are interested in what happens. Generally we *watch* things that move or change state.

17. **Like/As**

- Do not confuse them. *Like* means that one is drawing a similarity from dissimilar groups. The error is created when one uses 'like' as a conjunction. The person should substitute 'as' for 'like'.

18. **Literally/Figuratively**

- Do not confuse these words.
- *Literally* means that one's words describe what actually occurred. Most of the time, the word is tossed into sentences in which it is unnecessary.
- The word 'figuratively' means that one is using language metaphorically.

19. **Look after/Look for**

- To *look after* means 'to take care of' or 'be in charge of something or someone.'
- To *look for* means 'to try to find something or someone.'

20. **Look over/Overlook**

- *Look over* is a phrasal verb. When you *look over* something or someone you quickly examine it or them.
- *Overlook* is a verb. When you *overlook* someone or something, you fail to notice or consider it or them.

Note: If you *look forward/forwards*, it simply means you are looking ahead of you. *Look forward to* is a phrasal verb. When you *look forward to* something, you feel happy and excited about something that is going to happen.

21. **Loose** (not snug)/**Lose** (to misplace, fail to win)
    - *Loose* means 'to be free, not close together'.
    - To *lose* means 'to suffer loss.'
    - *Lose* always means 'mislaying or dropping something and not being able to find it', while *loose* means 'slack' or 'free'.
    - *Loose* is an adjective. If something isn't fixed properly or it doesn't fit, because it's too large, or because its not tight enough, it's loose.
    - *Lose* is a verb that means 'to no longer possess something because you do not know where it is, or because it has been taken away from you.'
22. **Luxurious/Luxuriant**
    - *Luxurious* living means that you enjoy luxuries.
    - *Luxuriant* means that something (such as a plant) is growing abundantly.

M

1. **Madding/Maddening**
    - 'A *madding* crowd' is a group of people who can drive you insane.
    - 'A *maddening* crowd' is a group of people who make you angry.

    Hardy's novel is *Far from the Madding Crowd.*
2. **Mantel/Mantle**
    - *Mantel* is the shelf above a fireplace, or the fireplace surrounding;
    - *Mantle* is a cloak or blanket.
3. **Manufacture/Manufacturer**

    When your company makes stuff, it *manufactures* it; but the company itself is a *manufacturer.*
4. **Marshal/Marshall**
    - *Marshal* is a military officer or a sheriff;
    - *marshall* is a verb, as in marshalling yard.
5. **Maybe** (perhaps)/**May be** (could be)
6. **Me/My**
    - As between *I and me* we usually choose the correct form by instinct.
    - *Me* is used as the object of a verb or preposition. You use *me* to refer to yourself.

      In short answers, we usually use this form.
    - *My* is a possessive adjective.
7. **Meat** (food)/**meet** (encounter)
8. **Medal/Metal/Meddle/Mettle**
    - A person who proves his or her *mettle* displays courage or stamina.
    - The word *mettle* is seldom used outside of this expression. *Metals* are nouns like silver, gold, etc.
    - *Medal* is a prize given and *meddle* means 'to interfere'.
9. **Media/Medium/Median**
    - 'Media' is a plural word. One mass *media* form is a medium.
    - *Medium* is also a size between large and small;
    - *median* is the mid point.
10. **Meet/Mete/Meat**

    The two more often confused are *meet* and *mete.*
    - *Meet* means 'to encounter' (and can also mean fit or suitable); *mete* means 'to allot, apportion or distribute'; *meat* refers to flesh as food.
11. **Militate/Mitigate**
    - *Militate* is usually followed by 'against' in a phrase that means 'works against'.
    - *Mitigate* means almost the opposite: 'to make easier' or 'to moderate'. It should not be followed by 'against.'
12. **Miner** (excavator)/**Minor** (person under a given age)

    Children are *minors* (unless they are violating child-labour laws, and) those who work in mines are *miners.*
13. **Minimal/Minimum**
    - A *minimal* amount is the minimum in a data set.
    - *'Minimal'* is an adjective and *'minimum'* may be used either as a noun or an adjective.
14. **Moral/Morale**
    - *Moral* means good ; it is also a lesson on conduct.
    - *Morale* is a mental condition, spirit ('The team's morale was low?').
15. **Most/Almost**
    - *Almost* is an adverb meaning 'nearly.'
    - *Most* is an adjective meaning 'the greater part.'
16. **Mucus/Mucous**
    - *Mucous* membranes secrete *mucus.*
    - *Mucus* is the noun and *mucous* is the adjective.
17. **Mute/Moot**
    - *Mute* as a verb means 'to silence or quieten down'; as a noun it's a little gadget used by string players to soften the sound from their instruments; as an adjective, it means dumb

or making no sound (as in 'He looked at me in mute appeal'.)

- *Moot* means 'debatable'. So, it's a 'moot point'.

18. **Most/the Most**
- *Most* without an article is usually used as an adjective, which means 'almost all'.
- *The most* is usually used to form the superlative of many adjectives and adverbs.

19. **Mutual/common**
- *Mutual* refers to two people who share the same emotion, as in ' 'My friend and I have *mutual respect'*.
- *Common* refers to something shared by at least two people, such as *'a common goal'* or 'a common point of departure'.

N

1. **Naïve/Knave**
- A *knave* is an unprincipled, untrustworthy, or dishonest person, whereas *naïve* means 'having or showing unaffected simplicity of nature or absence of artificiality' or 'unsophisticated or ingenuous'.

2. **Naval/Navel**
- Your belly button is your *navel,* and 'navel oranges' look like they have one;
- all terms having to do with ships and sailing require *naval.*

3. **No/Know**

Strange that these two should get confused, but they do.
- *No* is always the opposite of 'yes';
- to *Know* is to be certain.

O

1. **Once/Ones**
- *Once* always has to do with time and answers the questions, 'how many times?' or 'when?'
- In contrast, *ones* have to do with things.

2. **Oppress/Repress**

Dictators commonly *oppress* their citizens and *repress* dissent, but these words don't mean exactly the same thing.
- *Repress* just means 'keep under control.' Sometimes *repression* is a good thing.
- *Oppression* is always bad, and implies serious persecution.

2. **Oral/Verbal**
- Some people insist that *verbal* refers to anything expressed in words, whether written or spoken, while *oral* refers exclusively to speech;but in common usage *verbal* has become widely accepted for the latter meaning.
- However, in case of a legal context, an unwritten agreement is still an *'oral contract,'* not a *'verbal contract.'*

3. **Oriental/Asian**
- *Oriental* is generally considered old-fashioned now, and many find it offensive.
- *Asian* is preferred for telling about Asia.

  It baffles me that people get these mixed up, but they do.

4. **Overdo/Overdue**
- *Overdo* means 'to exaggerate' or 'carry to something too far';
- *overdue* is what your bills are, when you forget to pay them!

5. **Overtake vs Takeover/Take over**
- *Overtake* is a verb. It can mean to go beyond something by being better, or if you're driving to come from behind another vehicle or a person and move in front of it.
- *Takeover* as a noun is used when one organisation gains control of a company by buying most of its shares.

P

1. **Pair** (two)/**Pare** (peel; reduce)

2. **Palate/Palette/Pallet/Pellet**
- Your *palate* is the roof of your mouth, and by extension, your sense of taste.
- A *palette* is the flat board an artist mixes paint on (or by extension, a range of colours).
- A *pallet* is either a bed (now rare) or a flat platform onto which goods are loaded.
- A *pellet* is a bullet.

3. **Parameter/Perimeter**
- A *parameter* is a number that describes a population or, metaphorically, a distinctive characteristic of a population of events.
- A *perimeter* is a boundary.

4. **Paramount/Tantamount**
- *Paramount* means 'best' or 'top.'
- *Tantamount* means 'equivalent'.

5. **Partake/Participate**
- *Participate* means 'take part'.

- The main modern meaning of *partake* is 'consume,' especially in relation to food.

6. **Past** (an earlier time)/**Passed** (went by)

7. **Patience/Patients**
   - *Patience* means 'forbearance';
   - *patients* are people under medical care.

8. **Peasant/ Pheasant**

   pheasant is a favorite game bird whereas *peasants* are rural people or farm workers.

9. **Pedalled/Peddled**
   - *Pedalled* is the past tense of 'pedal', which as a *verb* means to use your feet to turn the pedals on something, such as a bicycle, to make it move; or to operate the pedals on a piano, or the lower keys on an organ;
   - *peddled* is the past tense of 'peddle', which means 'to sell'.

10. **Peek / Pique/Peak**
    - *Pique* means 'to excite or irritate';
    - *peek* means 'to peep or snoop';
    - *peak* as a *noun* means the summit or tip, and as a *verb* means 'to climax'.

11. **Peer/Pier**
    - *Peer* as a noun means 'a person who is your equal' and as a verb it means to squint or look obliquely at something;
    - *pier* is a type of wharf or dock.
    - Two other words that sound similar are pear (a fruit) and pare (to peel).

12. ***Percent / Percentage***
    - Use *percent* when identifying a particular number.
    - Use *percentage* when there is no definite figure.

13. **Perfect /perfectly**
    - *Perfect* is as singular as it gets.
    - *Perfectly* is an adverb used to emphasie another concept.

14. ***Precedence/ Precedents***
    - Things have *precedence* over others if they are given preference.
    - *Precedents* are events that serve as standards.

15. **Persecute/Prosecute**
    - When you *persecute* someone, you're treating them badly, whether they deserve it or not;
    - but only legal officers can *prosecute* someone for a crime.

16. **Personal** (private)/**Personnel** (staff)
    - *Personal* means 'of a person': 'a personal opinion,' 'a personal matter.'
    - *Personnel* refers to the people in an organisation, especially employees.

17. **Persons/ People**

    Use *'people'* if you can. *Persons* usually involves a collection of *people* who are counted or numbered. *People* can refer to a large group of *people*, usually unnumbered. Thus, *people* often can be substituted for *persons*, but *persons* cannot be substituted for *people*.

18. **Perspective** (angle of view)/**Prospective** (in the future)

19. **Phenomenon /Phenomena**

    One *phenomenon* or many *phenomena* may exist.

20. **Piece** (part, portion)/**Peace** (absence of war)

21. **Plain** (simple; flat land)/**Plane** (flat surface; smooth off)

22. **Podium /Lectern**
    - Strictly speaking, a *podium* is a raised platform on which you stand to give a speech;
    - the piece of furniture on which you place your notes and behind which you stand is a *lectern*.

23. **Pole/Poll**
    - A *pole* is a long stick.
    - You could take a *poll* (survey or ballot).

24. **Pour/Pore**

    You *pour* sauces, gravies, etc., over your dinner, while *pore* means to study something–so, *'pore* over the book', not *'pour* over the book'.

25. **Practice/Practise**

    In usage, *practice* is always the *noun* and *practise*, the *verb*.

26. **Pray** (ask, implore)/**Prey** (hunt down; what is hunted)

27. **Perpetuate/Perpetrate**
    - *Perpetrate* is something criminals do –they *perpetrate* a crime.
    - When you seek to continue something, you are trying to *perpetuate* it.

28. **Premiere/Premier/ Debut**
    - An actor makes a *debut*, whereas a movie has a *premiere*.

    The prime minister of a parliamentary government is known as a *premier*.
    - The opening night of a film or play is its *premiere*.

29. **Premise/Premises**

    Premise usually means 'assumption' or 'supposition' while *premises* means 'an apartment, house or building and its grounds'.

30. **Presence/Presents**
- *Presence* means 'being near at hand';
- *Presents* are gifts.

31. ***Pretty/Very***
- Do not use *pretty* as a synonym for *very*.

32. **Principle** (rule)/**Principal** (chief, chief person; sum of money)

33. **proceed/precede**
- To *proceed* is to 'go forward';
- to *precede* means 'to go ahead of'.

34. **Prodigy/ Progeny/Protege**
- Your *progeny* are your kids.
- If your child is a brilliantly outstanding person he or she may be a child *prodigy*. In fact, anything amazingly admirable can be a *prodigy*.
- But a person that you take under your wing in order to help promote his or her career is your *protégé*.

35. **Profit/Prophet**
- *Profit* means 'gain', 'earnings', 'advantage', and is usually associated with business.
- A *prophet* is a seer, a diviner.

36. **Prophecy** (noun)/**Prophesy** (verb)

37. **Purposely/Purposefully**
- Actions are done *purposely* if they are intended.
- Actions are done *purposefully* if the person doing them is very determined.

Q

1. **Quiet** (silent)/**Quite** (really, positively, very much)

2. **Quotation/Quote**
- *Quote* is a *verb;*
- *Quotation* is a *noun.*
- You *quote* people, but you read *quotations*.

R

1. **Rain/Reign/Rein**
- *Rain* is the water that comes down from clouds;
- *Reign* means 'to rule';
- *Rein* is a strap, usually leather, for controlling an animal, especially a horse.

2. **Raise/Raze**

These two are exact opposites. *Raise* means 'to lift' or 'build up' and *raze* means 'to pull down'.

3. **Rapt/Rapped/Wrapped**
- *Rapt* means 'enchanted' or 'engrossesd';
- *rapped* is the past tense of 'rap', which means 'to hit' or 'criticise';
- *wrapped* is the past tense of wrap, to coat or enfold.

4. **Rational/Rationale**
- *Rational* is an adjective meaning 'reasonable' or 'logical'.
- *Rationale* is a *noun* which most often means underlying reason.

5. **Reality/Realty**
- *Reality* is real life.
- *Realty* is real estate.

6. **Rebut/Refute**
- When you *rebut* someone's argument you argue against it.
- To *refute* someone's argument is to prove it incorrect.

7. **Refer back/look back**
- A confusion between 'look back' and 'refer'. This usage is objected to in formal writing on the ground that since the re- of refer means 'back,' 'refer back' is redundant. *Refer back* is acceptable when it means 'refer again' .

8. **Reference/Reverence**

Reference is something referred to, *reverence* means 'respect'.

9. **Refute/ Reject**
- To *refute* someone's argument is to prove it incorrect.
- If you attempt no such proof but simply disagree with an argument, the word you want is *reject*.

10. **Regimen/ Regiment**
- *Regimen* is a *noun* and is mostly used to refer to a prescribed way of life, or diet or exercise. It is also the action of governing.
- *Regiment* as a *verb* means 'to direct' or 'to command'; as a *noun* it refers to a military unit.

11. **Remember/Remind**
- To *remember* means 'to be able to bring back a piece of information into your mind', or 'to keep a piece of information in your memory.'
- To *remind* means 'to make someone aware of something they have forgotten or might have forgotten'.

12. **Replete/Complete**
- *Replete* usually means 'stuffed,' 'full to overflowing.'
- *Complete* means 'finished or total.'

13. **Residence/Residents**
    - *Residence* is a house;
    - *Residents* are the people who live there.
14. **Respectfully/Respectively**
    - *Respectfully* means 'politely';
    - *Respectively* means 'in the order stated.'
15. **Retch/Wretch**
    - *Retch* means 'to gag' or 'try to vomit';
    - *Wretch* is a grovelling person, a creep.
16. **Rifle/Riffle**
    - *Rifle* (apart from being a firearm) means 'to steal';
    - *Riffle* means 'to leaf through or browse.'
17. **Right** (proper, entitlement)/**Rite** (ceremony)
18. **Right/Rite/Write**
    - *Right* means 'correct';
    - *Rite* is a ceremony, usually religious;
    - *write* means 'to make words'.
19. **Risky/Risque**

    French-derived word *'risque'* means 'slightly indecent' whereas *risky* is dangerous.
19. **Road** (path)/**Rode** (past of ride)
    - *Road* is a long surface for cars and other vehicles;
    - *rode* is the past tense of ride.
20. **Role/Roll**
    - *Role* is a part in a play or film.
    - *Roll* as a *noun* is a document or something that is cylindrical in shape and as a *verb*, it means to make something into a cylindrical shape, to turn or spin.
21. **Root/Rout/Route**

    You can 'root' for your team (cheer them on) and hope that they utterly smash their opponents–*rout*, then come back in triumph on the straight *Route* (a road).
22. **Rye/Wry**
    - *Wry* means 'bent' or 'twisted.' Even if you don't have a wry sense of humor you may crack a wry smile.
    - A *rye* is the seed or grain of this plant.

S

1. **Sacred/Scared**
    - Gods are *sacred.*
    - The damned in Hell are *scared* (afraid).
2. **Sail/Sale/Sell**
    - You *sail* a boat which has a *sail* of canvas. (*Sail* is part of a ship or boat.)
    - You *sell* your old pot at a yard sale.
    - *Sale* is either offering something for purchase ('for sale') or offering it at a special price ('on sale').
3. **Salsa Sauce/Salsa**
    - *Salsa* is Spanish for 'sauce,' so 'salsa sauce' is redundant.
    - *Salsa* is also a type of dance.
4. **Sarcastic/Ironic**
    - Not all ironic comments are *sarcastic.* Sarcasm is meant to mock or wound.
    - *Irony* has an element of sadness.
5. **say/said *vs* tell/told**
    - *Said* (verb) is the past simple and past participle of 'to say'. It can be used in direct speech: It can be used in indirect (reported) speech (followed by that).
    - *Said* (adjective) is used before the name of a person or thing you have already mentioned
    - *Told* (verb) is the past simple and past participle of 'to tell'. It is normally used in reported speech, i.e. it is used to talk about what people say (followed by an object + 'that'). When *told* has the meaning of 'instruct', it can be followed by an object and an infinitive.
6. **Scene**(setting, stage setting)/**Seen** (perceived)
    - *Scene* is the place where something happens.
    - *Seen* is the past participle of 'see'.
7. **Scone/Sconce**
    - A jam or cream filled biscuit is a *scone.*
    - If you are describing a wall-mounted light fixture, the word is 'sconce'.
8. **Seam/Seem**
    - *Seam* is most often used to refer to the joining of two pieces of fabric with thread, but it can refer to other types of joints.
    - *Seem* means 'appear'.
9. **Sell/Cell**
    - *Sell* means 'to exchange for money'.
    - *Cell* is a small room (invariably lacking in comfort). *Cell* is also an organism (as in 'stem cells'). *Cell* is also used to refer to the small divisions in something large such as a container or a table in a web page or word-processed document.
10. **Sense** (perception)/**Since** (from that time)
11. **Sensual/Sensuous**
    - *Sensual* usually relates to physical desires and experiences, and often means 'sexy.'

- *Sensuous* is more often used for aesthetic pleasures, like 'sensuous music.'

12. **Serf/Surf**
    - *Serf* means slave or servant.
    - *Surf* is a wave and as a verb is also the action of riding the waves on a board or using a computer to find something on the Internet.
13. **Set** (to put)/**Sit** (to be seated)
14. **Sever/Severe**
    - *Sever* means 'to separate' or 'detach'.
    - *Severe* means 'grim' or 'stern'.
15. **Shear/Sheer**
    - *Shear* means 'to cut or clip'.
    - *Sheer* means 'transparent' (as in 'sheer nylon hosiery') or 'steep' (as in 'a sheer drop') or 'total' or 'absolute' (as in 'sheer stupidity').
16. **Sheath/Sheaf**
    - If you take your knife out of its *sheath* (case) you can use it to cut a *sheaf* (bundle) of paper.
17. **Shone** (past of shine)/Shown (displayed)
18. **Shore/Sure**
    - *Shore* as verb means 'to brace or support' and as a noun, it is usually a beach but can also be 'a support' or 'a brace'.
    - *Sure* means 'certain' or 'confident'.
    - So you do not *sure up* a company by borrowing more capital; you *shore it up.*
19. **Shortage/Shortness**
    - *Shortage* is a noun meaning when there is not enough of something.
    - *Shortness* is a also a noun meaning the condition of being short spatially (in length).
20. **sick/ill**
    - Use 'sick' when you mean a person is nauseated.
    - Use 'ill' when the person is not well but not necessarily nauseated.
21. **Silicon/Silicone**
    - *Silicon* is a chemical element, the basic stuff of which microchips are made. Sand is largely silicon.
    - *Silicones* are plastics and other materials containing silicon.
22. **Singly/Singularly**
    - *Singly* means 'individually' or 'one-by-one'.
    - *Singularly* means 'strangely' or 'uniquely'.
23. **Site/Sight/Cite**
    - *Site* always refers to location or place–building site, archaeology site, etc.
    - *Sight* always refers to vision, as in the cliché 'a sight for sore eyes'.
    - *Cite* means 'to summon' or 'to refer to a source'.
24. **Slither/Sliver**
    - *Slither* means 'to slip' or 'to slide'.
    - *Sliver* is a noun, meaning a thin piece, such as a flake, paring or chip.
25. **So/Such**
    - *So* when used as in front of an adjective or an adverb means 'very'.
    - *Such* when used as a determiner can be used in front of a noun or an adjective and a noun to show extremes, you can't use it in front of adverbs.
    - Remember that without the noun you need to use 'so'.
26. **Soar/Sore**
    - *Sore* refers to aches, pains and wounds - sore feet, sore backs, and sores on your skin.
    - The more unusual word used to describe the act of gliding through the air or swooping up in the sky is *soar.*
27. **Sojourn/Journey**
    - A *sojourn* is actually a temporary stay in one place.
    - If you're constantly on the move, then it is a *journey.*
28. **Sole/Soul**
    - *Sole* as an adjective means 'single' and as a noun it is a type of fish and the under part of a foot or a shoe.
    - *Soul* generally refers to the invisible part of you that lives on after you die; it also refers to heart or mind or a human being.
29. **Some time/Sometime**
    - This is a common confusion. *Some time* is a period of time and *sometime* means at some time which is not specified.
30. **Specially/Especially**
    - When something is *special,* it is not ordinary.
    - *Especially* refers to things that are pre-eminent or primary.
31. **Stand/Stance**
    - When you courageously resist opposing forces, you take a *stand.*
    - Your *stance,* on the other hand, is just your position–literal or figurative–which may not be particularly militant.
32. **Stationary/Stationery**
    - *Stationary* means 'standing still'.

- *Stationery* refers to writing paper.

33. **statue/statute/stature**
    - *Statue* is a carved or moulded likeness.
    - *Statute* is law.
    - *Stature* means 'height' or 'status'.
34. **Stint/Stent**
    - When the time to work comes, you've got to do your 'stint'.
    - The medical device installed to keep an artery open is a 'stent'.
35. **Straight** (not curved)/**Strait** (narrow place)
    - *Straight* means 'without bends'.
    - *Strait* is a passage of water.
36. **Suit/Suite**
    - Your bedroom *suite* consists of the bed, the nightstand, and whatever other furniture goes with it.
    - *Suit* is your formal dress.
37. **Sulking/Skulking**
    - That guy sneaking furtively around the neighborhood is *skulking* around.
    - *Sulking* is related to your not being in a good mood.
38. **To see/To watch**
    - *To see* means to be aware of what is around you by using your eyes.
    - *To watch* means to look at something for a period of time, especially something that is changing or moving. We *watch* things that move, such as TV, a film, sport, etc. while we *look* at static things, such as a photograph, a painting, the stars, etc.

T

1. **Tack** (angle of approach)/**Tact** (sensitivity, diplomacy)
2. **Taken Back/Taken Aback**
    - When you're startled by something, you're *taken aback* by it.
    - When you're reminded of something from your past, you're *taken back* to that time.
3. **Taut/Taught/Taunt**
    - *Taut* means 'tight' or 'firm'.
    - *Taught* is the past tense of teach.
    - *Taunt* means 'jeer' or 'insult'.
4. **Tenant/Tenet**
    - *Tenant* is one who rents a property.
    - *Tenet* is a principle or belief.
5. **Than** (word of comparison)/**Then** (at that time)
6. **That/Which/Who**
    - *That* refers to persons or things,
    - *which* refers to things, and
    - *who* refers to persons.
7. **There/Their/They're**
    - *There* is a location.
    - *Their* is the possessive form of 'they'.
    - *They're* the short form of 'they are'.
8. **Threw** (past of throw)/**Through** (by way of)
9. **Throes/Throws**
    - *Throes* are violent spasms or painful struggles, though not always physical. *Throes* can also mean the 'midst of'.
    - *Throws* means 'to hurl' or 'to toss'. As a noun, it means blankets or other types of covering.
10. **Throne/Thrown**
    - A *throne* is a chair for a king to sit on.
    - *Thrown* is the past participle of 'throw'.
11. **Tic/Tick**
    - The word for a spasmodic twitch or habitual quirk of speech or behaviour is spelled the French way: 'tic.'
    - Tick, as a noun, is a parasitic insect and, as a verb, it is 'a mark'.
12. **Timber/Timbre**
    - *Timber* is a type of wood.
    - The quality which distinguishes the sound produced by one instrument or voice from others is *timbre.*
13. **To**(in the direction of)/**Too**(also)/**Two**(the number)
    - *To* is a preposition meaning 'towards'.
    - *Too* means 'also' or 'extremely' (as in 'You are walking too fast for me').
    - *Two* is the number after one.
14. **Trainee/Trainer**
    - A *trainee* is a person who is learning and practising the skills of a particular job.
    - A *trainer* is a person who teaches skills for a particular job, activity or sport.
15. **Troop/Troupe**
    - A group of performers is a *troupe.*
    - Any other group of people, military or otherwise, is a *troop.*
16. **Tussle/Tousled**
    - *Tussle* is a struggle, fight or scuffle
    - *Tousled* means 'messed up'.

U

1. **Unchartered/Uncharted**
   - *Unchartered* means 'lacking a charter' whereas
   - *uncharted* means 'unmapped' or 'unexplored.
2. **Undo/Undue**
   - The verb 'undo' is the opposite of 'do.' *Undo* means 'to erase or remove something that was done'.
   - The adjective 'undue' is the opposite of 'due' and means 'unwarranted' or 'improper.' It is used in phrases like 'undue advantage'.
3. **Unique/Uncommon**
   - The formal meaning of unique is 'sole' or 'only' or 'being the only one of its kind'.
   - The meaning of 'uncommon' is 'rare' or 'unusual'.
4. **Upmost/Utmost**
   - *Upmost* means 'uppermost' referring to something on top.
   - *Utmost* means 'extreme or greatest or maximum'.
5. **Used to/Used to do**
   - *Used to* can be used as an adjective and we use it to talk about things that have become familiar, and are no longer strange or new. You can also be used to doing something.
   - *Used to do*–If we say something *used to* happen we are talking about repeated events and actions in the past, usually things that happened a long time ago and are now finished.

V

1. **Vane/Vain/Vein**
   - *Vane* is an instrument that shows from which direction the wind is blowing; it also means the sail of a windmill, the flat part on either side of the *shaft of a feather, a revolving fan or flywheel.*
   - *Vain* means too concerned about how one looks or being too conceited and also means useless as in 'a vain attempt'.
   - *Vein* is a blood vessel, a channel.
2. **Vary/Very**
   - *Vary* means 'to change'.
   - *Very* describes an extreme form of anything like 'very nice','very bad', etc.
3. **Venal/Venial**
   - *Venal* means 'dishonest' or 'dishonourable'.
   - *Venial* means 'forgivable' or 'unimportant' (as in 'venial sins').
4. **Veracious/Voracious**
   - *Veracious* means 'truthful, honest'. A truthful person has 'veracity'.
   - *Voracity* means 'extreme appetite' and *voracious* means 'insatiable' or 'ravenous'.
5. **Verses/Versus**
   - *Verses* are the plural of verse, something a poet writes.
   - *Versus* means 'against' or 'in comparison with'.
6. **Viable/Vie/Workable**
   - Something that is *viable* is capable of living (from the Latin vita or 'life').
   - *Vie* means 'compete for'.
   - *Workable* means 'feasible'.
7. **Vicious/Viscous**
   - *Vicious* means 'savage' or 'cruel'.
   - *Viscous* means 'thick and gummy'.

W

1. **Wail/Whale**
   - One informal meaning of 'whale' is 'to beat.' Whale also is a large mammal (fish-like).
   - To 'wail' means 'to cry loudly'.
2. **Waist** (middle of torso)**/Waste** (squander)
   - *Waist* is that part of your body around which you fasten your belt.
   - *Waste* as a noun mostly refers to stuff that's thrown away and as a verb it usually means 'to squander'.
3. **Wander/Wonder**
   - *Wander* (verb) means 'to travel aimlessly'.
   - *Wonder* (verb) means 'to consider or question or think about some issue'. *Wonder* (noun) means 'the feeling aroused by something strange and surprising'.
4. **Wary/Weary**
   - *Wary* means 'careful'.
   - *Weary* means 'tired'.
5. **Wave/Waive**
   - *Wave* means 'to flap your hand in farewell' as a verb. As a noun, it is also a breaker on the beach.
   - *Waive* means 'to give up one's rights or claim'.
6. **Waver/Waiver**
   - *Waver* means 'to be undecided'.
   - *Waiver* means 'the giving up of rights or claims'.

7. **Ways/Way**
   - Use 'way' when referring to distance.
   - Use 'ways' when referring to methods
8. **Weak** (feeble)/**week** (seven days)
9. **Wear** (carry on the body)/**where** (in what place)
10. **Weather** (atmospheric conditions)/**Whether** (if, in case)
    - Use *whether* as in the phrase 'whether or not'.
    - Use *weather* when referring to atmospheric or climatic conditions.
11. **Wet/Whet**
    - *Wet* as a verb means strictly to pour liquid on something.
    - *Whet* means 'to sharpen or stimulate'.
12. **Which** (what one, one of a group)/**Witch** (sorceress)
13. **Who/Whom**
    - *Who* is the nominative case ('He is the one who will be elected'), while
    - *whom* is the objective case ('He is the one whom you have been seeking').
14. **Whole/Hole**
    - *Whole* means 'entire' ('He ate the whole pie'), while
    - a *hole* is an empty hollow ('My dog dug a hole in my yard').
15. **Whose** (possessive of who)/**Who's** (contraction of who is)
16. **Wont/Won't**
    - *Wont* means 'accustomed'.
    - *Won't* is short form for 'will not'.
17. **Write/Right/Rite**
    - *Write* means 'to scrawl' or 'to pen' or 'to put thoughts into readable format'.
    - *Right* means 'correct'.
    - A *rite* is a 'ceremony'.

Y

1. **Yoke/Yolk**
   - The yellow center of an egg is its *yolk.*
   - The link that holds two oxen together is a *yoke;* they are yoked.
2. **Your** (possessive of you)/**You're** (contraction of you are)

SECTION 2: Vocabulary-Based Questions

This section will help you in the following ways:

- In the chapter on Synonyms, you would get to tackle question types related to words with similar meanings.
- In the chapter on Antonyms, you would get to tackle question types related to words that are opposite in meanings.
- In the chapter on Odd Man Out, you would get to tackle questions which are situation based and which require you to choose out of a group of words one which does not belong to the group.
- In the chapter on Analogies, you would get to tackle questions which are relationship based and are very commonly used in exams like MAT, IRMA, CET Maharashtra, etc. In this chapter you would learn to identify the various types of relationships that are used in Analogies.

CHAPTER

6 Synonyms

Directions for Exercise (1-2): *Choose the option closest in meaning to the word given.*

EXERCISE 1

1. **Low-Key**
   (a) official (b) secret
   (c) subdued (d) complicated
2. **Stipulation**
   (a) imitation (b) signal
   (c) excitement (d) requirement
3. **Antithesis**
   (a) fixed dislike (b) musical reponse
   (c) lack of feeling (d) direct opposite
4. **Transitory**
   (a) short-lived (b) idle
   (c) unexpected (d) clear
5. **Entrenched**
   (a) filled up (b) fortified
   (c) followed by (d) kept down
6. **Lot**
   (a) right (b) folly
   (c) fate (d) oath
7. **Apprehension**
   (a) gratitude (b) apology
   (c) dread (d) punishment
8. **Amenable**
   (a) religious (b) masculine
   (c) proud (d) agreeable
9. **Affluent**
   (a) neutral (b) sentimental
   (c) wealthy (d) handsome
10. **Counterpart**
   (a) hindrance (b) peace offering
   (c) password (d) complementary
11. **Superficial**
   (a) shallow (b) unusually fine
   (c) proud (d) aged
12. **Disparage**
   (a) separate (b) compare
   (c) refuse (d) belittle
13. **Protagonist**
   (a) prophet (b) explorer
   (c) talented child (d) leading character
14. **Ludicrous**
   (a) profitable (b) excessive
   (c) disordered (d) ridiculous
15. **Intrepid**
   (a) middle (b) tolerant
   (c) fearless (d) rude
16. **Sage**
   (a) wise man (b) tale
   (c) era (d) fool
17. **Admonish**
   (a) warn (b) escape
   (c) worship (d) distribute

18. **Beset**
    (a) plead (b) assail
    (c) pertain to (d) deny
19. **Figment**
    (a) perfume (b) undeveloped fruit
    (c) statuette (d) invention
20. **Glib**
    (a) dull (b) thin
    (c) weak (d) fluent

EXERCISE 2

1. **Grandiose**
   (a) imposing (b) unpretentious
   (c) boring (d) lanky
2. **Parley**
   (a) fraud (b) paraphrase
   (c) conclave (d) spectacle
3. **Lassitude**
   (a) lethargy (b) puritan
   (c) energy (d) meeting
4. **Ruse**
   (a) break (b) stratagem
   (c) maudlin (d) guru
5. **Aphorism**
   (a) prune (b) wither
   (c) aphis (d) proverb
6. **Hybrid**
   (a) pure (b) benefactor
   (c) partisan (d) crossbreed
7. **Passé**
   (a) rude (b) old-fashioned
   (c) modern (d) chic
8. **Louse**
   (a) lukewarm (b) beast
   (c) parasitic insect (d) infant
9. **Scuttle**
   (a) rumor (b) priority
   (c) run hurriedly (d) solemn
10. **Utopia**
    (a) holiday home (b) music
    (c) vacant (d) perfect state
11. **Idiocy**
    (a) brilliancy (b) privilege
    (c) dogma (d) absurdity
12. **Spry**
    (a) doubtful (b) nimble
    (c) prognosticate (d) leave
13. **Harbinger**
    (a) forerunner (b) reel
    (c) epic (d) footstool
14. **Simpleton**
    (a) dunce (b) tattler
    (c) genius (d) quack
15. **Brevity**
    (a) corporal (b) shortness
    (c) moisture (d) valour

Directions for Exercise 3: *Select the word having the same meaning as the given word.*

EXERCISE 3

1. **Vituperation**
   (a) moisture (b) parallel
   (c) malediction (d) recover
2. **Repeal**
   (a) sharp (b) applaud
   (c) acceptance (d) abrogation
3. **Foreclose**
   (a) shut out (b) nearby
   (c) liberty (d) indicate
4. **Qualm**
   (a) concavity (b) amplitude
   (c) misgiving (d) repute
5. **Controversial**
   (a) pulse (b) polemic
   (c) record (d) integrity
6. **Elation**
   (a) happiness (b) naturalize
   (c) poverty (d) parsimony
7. **Apportionment**
   (a) coexist (b) period
   (c) appoint (d) dispensation

8. **Vaunt**
   (a) lack (b) sufferance
   (c) resign (d) boast
9. **Equivocal**
   (a) questionable (b) resistance
   (c) actual (d) fall apart
10. **Fetid**
   (a) comical (b) ornament
   (c) stinking (d) regular

Directions for Exercises (4-5): *Choose the word which is* not *a synonym for the given word.*

EXERCISE 4

1. **Stingy**
   (a) amicable (b) penurious
   (c) parsimonious (d) frugal
2. **Persistence**
   (a) perilous (b) sedulity
   (c) pertinacity (d) plodding
3. **Untrue**
   (a) spurious (b) false
   (c) meretricious (d) chaste
4. **Relax**
   (a) rest (b) unwind
   (c) ease (d) relegate
5. **Accumulation**
   (a) collection (b) conglomeration
   (c) assemblage (d) collagen
6. **Sleep Inducing**
   (a) soporific (b) sedative
   (c) somnolent (d) hygroscopic
7. **Swelling**
   (a) turgidity (b) distention
   (c) inflammation (d) flaccidity
8. **Incline**
   (a) trenchant (b) slope
   (c) acclivity (d) gradient
9. **Shining**
   (a) indolent (b) dazzling
   (c) gleaming (d) glistening
10. **Loafer**
   (a) vagrant (b) lounger
   (c) bantam (d) idler

EXERCISE 5

1. **Emigrate**
   (a) depart (b) elude
   (c) relocate (d) resettle
2. **Eloquent**
   (a) elusive (b) articulate
   (c) fluent (d) expressive
3. **Defendant**
   (a) accused (b) appellant
   (c) offender (d) defoliant
4. **Abase**
   (a) adjourn (b) degrade
   (c) humiliate (d) mortify
5. **Aplomb**
   (a) ease (b) ribald
   (c) repose (d) serenity
6. **Porcelain**
   (a) ceramics (b) pottery
   (c) earthenware (d) mirror
7. **Eccentric**
   (a) aberrant (b) atypical
   (c) facile (d) bizarre
8. **Quagmire**
   (a) fen (b) morass
   (c) swamp (d) palisade
9. **Stockade**
   (a) rampart (b) fence
   (c) paling (d) shuttle
10. **Bestial**
   (a) feral (b) feminine
   (c) fiendish (d) savage
11. **Revelry**
   (a) jollity (b) slough
   (c) conviviality (d) feasting
12. **Fester**
   (a) putrefy (b) ulcerate
   (c) rot (d) retrieve

13. **Jiggle**
(a) squirm (b) fret
(c) flighty (d) twitch

14. **Paddock**
(a) filament (b) glebe
(c) pasture (d) mead

15. **Flake**
(a) scurf (b) sliver
(c) chip (d) bunting

16. **Canyon**
(a) ravine (b) gorge
(c) pass (d) kayak

17. **Capsule**
(a) lozenge (b) mantle
(c) pill (d) tablet

18. **Heresy**
(a) parole (b) blasphemy
(c) dissent (d) non-conformity

19. **Anchorite**
(a) eremite (b) recluse
(c) infirm (d) hermit

20. **Dither**
(a) dilly-dally (b) falter
(c) hum and haw (d) doughty

21. **Abandon**
(a) cast away (b) forsake
(c) butch (d) maroon

22. **Negotiate**
(a) mediate (b) milliner
(c) intercede (d) liaise

23. **Itinerant**
(a) peripatetic (b) nomadic
(c) wayfaring (d) sprightly

24. **Nimble**
(a) adroit (b) patrician
(c) nippy (d) dexterous

25. **Clamorous**
(a) raucous (b) blaring
(c) dissonant (d) stately

26. **Oracular**
(a) clairvoyant (b) soothsayer
(c) lineage (d) sibyl

27. **Clannish**
(a) cliquish (b) close-knit
(c) insular (d) clanger

28. **Hook**
(a) brooch (b) claque
(c) hasp (d) buckle

29. **Masterpiece**
(a) classic (b) archetypal
(c) urbane (d) copybook

30. **Escort**
(a) convoy (b) chattel
(c) entourage (d) retinue

31. **Opening**
(a) ingress (b) turnstile
(c) vestibule (d) wheedle

32. **Entrails**
(a) viscera (b) Eocene
(c) guts (d) bowels

33. **Tawdry**
(a) gimmick (b) gimcrack
(c) shoddy (d) worthless

34. **Introverted**
(a) reserved (b) contemplative
(c) introspective (d) intrusive

35. **Jailer**
(a) warder (b) jalousie
(c) gaoler (d) guard

36. **Jargon**
(a) argot (b) patois
(c) cant (d) screw

37. **Container**
(a) amphora (b) carafe
(c) chaff (d) jar

38. **Clown**
(a) comedian (b) jester
(c) buffoon (d) Creole

39. **Quay**
(a) jetty (b) lurch
(c) wharf (d) breakwater

40. **Spray**
(a) squirt (b) spurt
(c) gush (d) jewry

41. **Election**
(a) poll (b) plebiscite
(c) bandwagon (d) referendum

42. **Bandage**
(a) gauze (b) plaster
(c) lint (d) bandy

43. **Highwayman**
(a) bandit (b) marauder
(c) bandanna (d) brigand

44. **Symbol**
(a) design (b) pattern
(c) motif (d) scrap

45. **Morose**
(a) churlish (b) sullen
(c) humble (d) taciturn

46. **Motionless**
(a) morel (b) inanimate
(c) immobile (d) paralysed

47. **Temporal**
(a) transient (b) ephemeral
(c) mortal (d) melancholy

48. **Speckled**
(a) blotchy (b) rocky
(c) flecked (d) mottled

49. **Motto**
(a) maxim (b) sculpt
(c) aphorism (d) precept

50. **Hilly**
(a) craggy (b) rocky
(c) mountainous (d) mounted

51. **Mouthful**
(a) gobbet (b) morsel
(c) bite (d) muzzle

52. **Portable**
(a) movable (b) immovable
(c) mobile (d) transferable

53. **Dirt**
(a) mire (b) muck
(c) mud (d) muff

54. **Hush**
(a) stifle (b) mugger
(c) muffle (d) quieten

55. **Pageant**
(a) spectacle (b) ceremony
(c) show (d) verso

56. **Essential**
(a) requisite (b) mandatory
(c) imperative (d) repugnant

57. **Rescue**
(a) liberation (b) reredos
(c) salvage (d) emancipate

58. **Optimistic**
(a) sanguine (b) vitriolic
(c) buoyant (d) hopeful

59. **Sarcasm**
(a) contumely (b) acerbity
(c) derision (d) sapphic

60. **Satanic**
(a) diabolical (b) mephistophelean
(c) burlesque (d) demonic

61. **Pan**
(a) skillet (b) cauldron
(c) saucepan (d) souse

62. **Compact**
(a) brief (b) succinct
(c) indict (d) condensed

63. **Stones**
(a) pebbles (b) yokel
(c) gravel (d) cobbles

64. **Graft**
(a) join (b) gram
(c) splice (d) implant

65. **Framework**
(a) grid (b) mesh
(c) lattice (d) leeway

66. **Larva**
(a) maggot (b) grub
(c) lard (d) caterpillar

67. **Flail**
(a) whip (b) lash
(c) flog (d) trellis

68. **Knock**
(a) rap (b) tap
(c) thump (d) stud

69. **Mindful**
(a) heedful (b) attentive
(c) frantic (d) observant

70. **Neglectful**
(a) oblivious (b) temperate
(c) reckless (d) heedless

71. **Hallowed**
(a) blessed (b) phlegmatic
(c) consecrated (d) holy

72. **Enchant**
(a) raze (b) bewitch
(c) ravish (d) entrance

73. **Titular**
(a) nominal (b) official
(c) putative (d) causative

74. **Vicarious**
(a) surrogate (b) second-hand
(c) atrocious (d) indirect

75. **Wordy**
(a) loquacious (b) phrasing
(c) pleonastic (d) garrulous

76. **Lament**
(a) dirge (b) elegy
(c) lackey (d) monody

77. **Fuzzy**
(a) frizzy (b) fuffy
(c) furry (d) fleecy

78. **Hinder**
(a) stoke (b) inhibit
(c) foil (d) impede

79. **Jittery**
(a) fretful (b) petulant
(c) anxious (d) testy

80. **Freight**
(a) cargo (b) consignment
(c) chafing (d) shipment

81. **Astern**
(a) aft (b) abaft
(c) behind (d) apt

82. **Ashamed**
(a) bashful (b) venerable
(c) sheepish (d) shy

83. **Attire**
(a) array (b) raiment
(c) apparel (d) assail

84. **Assert**
(a) engross (b) vindicate
(c) aver (d) insist

85. **Asperse**
(a) calumniate (b) traduce
(c) slander (d) disconcert

86. **Diligent**
(a) assiduous (b) appendage
(c) industrious (d) persevering

87. **Asylum**
(a) shelter (b) refuge
(c) sanctuary (d) presage

88. **Majestic**
(a) august (b) heinous
(c) stately (d) grand

89. **Aureate**
(a) brilliant (b) gilded
(c) resplendent (d) archaic

90. **Greed**
(a) avarice (b) expiation
(c) rapacity (d) cupidity

91. **Bamboozle**
(a) hoax (b) mystify
(c) cheat (d) gabble

92. **Bastille**
(a) fortress (b) prison
(c) jail (d) fop

93. **Blench**
(a) flinch (b) prate
(c) wince (d) quail

94. **Deprive**
(a) rob (b) bereave
(c) reprove (d) dispossess

95. **Cabal**
(a) plot (b) machination
(c) conspiracy (d) portend

96. **Melodious**
(a) musical (b) canorous
(c) sprightly (d) resonant

97. **Raw**
(a) unfledged (b) callous
(c) inexperienced (d) callow

98. **Caprice**
(a) whim (b) fancy
(c) quirk (d) brace

99. **Critical**
(a) carping (b) censorious
(c) cardinal (d) captious

100. **Gallant**
(a) quixotic (b) chivalrous
(c) prudent (d) honorable

101. **Cherish**
(a) tend (b) foster
(c) nurture (d) vouch

Directions for Exercise 6: *Choose the option which is a synonym or closest in meaning to the word in capitals:*

Exercise 6

1. **Pandemonium**
(a) lock (b) instrumental
(c) garment (d) uproar

2. **Manoeuvre**
(a) upset (b) inflict
(c) scheme (d) slow

3. **Relinquish**
(a) abandon (b) relish
(c) proceed (d) defeat

4. **Tumid**
(a) humid (b) revolting
(c) mean (d) inflated

5. **Veritable**
(a) obedient (b) approval
(c) genuine (d) false

6. **Canard**
(a) a bird (b) spare
(c) offensive (d) hoax

7. **Idolatry**
(a) admiration (b) sadness
(c) corruption (d) faithless

8. **Gratuitous**
(a) correct (b) unkind
(c) absurd (d) given freely

9. **Sagacious**
(a) appealing (b) placid
(c) wise (d) shaky

10. **Lethal**
(a) conventional (b) deadly
(c) averse (d) demonstrative

11. **Feint**
(a) religious (b) digress
(c) pretense (d) swoon

12. **Perambulate**
(a) withdraw (b) obstruct
(c) retail (d) walk

13. **Admonish**
(a) give (b) warn
(c) accustom (d) forgive

14. **Jettison**
(a) throw (b) travel
(c) collect (d) sympathize

15. **Expurgate**
(a) enjoy (b) clear
(c) display (d) harbour

16. **Surmount**
(a) climb (b) dwindle
(c) conquer (d) repair

17. **Nettle**
(a) knit (b) vessel
(c) irritate (d) restore

18. **Intercept**
(a) display (b) arrest
(c) allot (d) amaze

19. **Desultory**
(a) changeable (b) result
(c) hazardous (d) rivalry

20. **Salient**
(a) skillful (b) seasonal
(c) prominent (d) solitary

21. **Pester**
(a) irritate (b) illuminate
(c) challenge (d) choice

22. **Salutary**
(a) honest (b) obedient
(c) dishonest (d) beneficial

23. **Turbulent**
(a) unbiased (b) agitated
(c) orderly (d) shiny

24. **Credence**
(a) corrupt (b) incredible
(c) virtue (d) belief

25. **Imbibe**
(a) emit (b) absorb
(c) imitate (d) convince

26. **Baneful**
(a) fever (b) quiet
(c) harmful (d) over

27. **Eloquent**
(a) rhetoric (b) legal
(c) edible (d) feeble

28. **Explicit**
(a) clear (b) obvious
(c) cautious (d) exorbitant

29. **Putrid**
(a) pure (b) decayed
(c) shallow (d) sweet

30. **Flagrant**
(a) aroma (b) fuming
(c) scandalous (d) spreading

31. **Rectify**
(a) tip (b) release
(c) compromise (d) remedy

32. **Graphic**
(a) vivid (b) fancy
(c) vague (d) great

33. **Cadence**
(a) rhythm (b) retreat
(c) fix (d) final

34. **Duress**
(a) step (b) constraint
(c) relapse (d) credit

35. **Fumigate**
(a) upset (b) submit
(c) disinfect (d) rankle

36. **Bedraggle**
(a) reduce (b) soiled
(c) hypnotize (d) sell

37. **Penchant**
(a) liking (b) hatred
(c) naughty (d) good

38. **Scathing**
(a) tossing (b) damaging
(c) hating (d) fat

39. **Hilarious**
(a) hopeless (b) comic
(c) hideous (d) gloomy

40. **Taint**
(a) corrupt (b) paint
(c) polish (d) publish

41. **Absolve**
(a) accuse (b) acquit
(c) bind (d) colour

42. **Coalesce**
(a) fuel (b) fiery
(c) amalgamate (d) relate

43. **Switch**
(a) current (b) swap
(c) circuit (d) egress

44. **Rapier**
(a) svelte (b) sabre
(c) wood (d) wound

45. **Sycophantic**
(a) circular (b) symmetrical
(c) servile (d) fertile

46. **Syllabus**
(a) cutlass (b) curriculum
(c) arboreal (d) sylvan

Answer Key

Exercise 1

1. (c)	**2.** (d)	**3.** (d)	**4.** (a)	**5.** (b)
6. (c)	**7.** (c)	**8.** (d)	**9.** (c)	**10.** (d)
11. (a)	**12.** (d)	**13.** (d)	**14.** (d)	**15.** (c)
16. (a)	**17.** (a)	**18.** (b)	**19.** (d)	**20.** (d)

EXERCISE 2

1. (a)	2. (c)	3. (a)	4. (b)	5. (d)
6. (d)	7. (b)	8. (c)	9. (c)	10. (d)
11. (d)	12. (b)	13. (a)	14. (a)	15. (b)

EXERCISE 3

1. (c)	2. (d)	3. (a)	4. (c)	5. (b)
6. (a)	7. (d)	8. (d)	9. (a)	10. (c)

EXERCISE 4

1. (a)	2. (a)	3. (d)	4. (d)	5. (d)
6. (d)	7. (d)	8. (a)	9. (a)	10. (c)

EXERCISE 5

1. (b)	2. (a)	3. (d)	4. (a)	5. (b)
6. (d)	7. (c)	8. (d)	9. (d)	10. (b)
11. (b)	12. (d)	13. (c)	14. (a)	15. (d)
16. (d)	17. (b)	18. (a)	19. (c)	20. (d)
21. (c)	22. (b)	23. (d)	24. (b)	25. (d)
26. (c)	27. (d)	28. (b)	29. (c)	30. (b)
31. (d)	32. (b)	33. (a)	34. (d)	35. (b)
36. (d)	37. (c)	38. (d)	39. (b)	40. (d)
41. (c)	42. (d)	43. (c)	44. (d)	45. (c)
46. (a)	47. (d)	48. (b)	49. (b)	50. (d)
51. (d)	52. (b)	53. (d)	54. (b)	55. (d)
56. (d)	57. (b)	58. (b)	59. (d)	60. (c)
61. (d)	62. (c)	63. (b)	64. (b)	65. (d)
66. (c)	67. (d)	68. (d)	69. (c)	70. (b)
71. (b)	72. (a)	73. (d)	74. (c)	75. (b)
76. (c)	77. (b)	78. (a)	79. (d)	80. (c)
81. (d)	82. (b)	83. (d)	84. (a)	85. (d)
86. (b)	87. (d)	88. (b)	89. (d)	90. (b)
91. (d)	92. (d)	93. (b)	94. (c)	95. (d)
96. (c)	97. (b)	98. (d)	99. (c)	100. (c)
101. (d)				

EXERCISE 6

1. (d)	2. (c)	3. (a)	4. (d)	5. (c)
6. (d)	7. (a)	8. (d)	9. (c)	10. (b)
11. (c)	12. (d)	13. (b)	14. (a)	15. (b)
16. (c)	17. (c)	18. (b)	19. (a)	20. (c)
21. (a)	22. (d)	23. (b)	24. (d)	25. (b)
26. (c)	27. (a)	28. (a)	29. (b)	30. (c)
31. (d)	32. (a)	33. (a)	34. (b)	35. (c)
36. (b)	37. (a)	38. (b)	39. (b)	40. (a)
41. (b)	42. (c)	43. (b)	44. (b)	45. (c)
46. (b)				

CHAPTER

7 Antonyms

Directions for Questions 1-200: *Choose the option which is the antonym of the given word.*

1. **Amusing**
(a) silent (b) later
(c) boring (d) nice

2. **Egoism**
(a) familial (b) altruism
(c) fabianism (d) marxism

3. **Separate**
(a) amalgamate (b) lonely
(c) operate (d) none of these

4. **Professional**
(a) conservative (b) liberal
(c) amateur (d) legal

5. **Ambiguity**
(a) lucidity (b) basal
(c) lovable (d) necessity

6. **Ancestor**
(a) peer (b) seer
(c) descendant (d) genetic

7. **Omega**
(a) beta (b) gamma
(c) delta (d) alpha

8. **Amass**
(a) demote (b) remote
(c) scatter (d) better

9. **Amplification**
(a) abbreviation (b) operation
(c) observation (d) application

10. **Hurry**
(a) worry (b) amble
(c) sorry (d) enable

11. **Hostile**
(a) alluvial (b) able
(c) amicable (d) alterable

12. **Ameliorate**
(a) mar (b) west
(c) stuff (d) fade

13. **Amnesty**
(a) loyalty (b) punishment
(c) depth (d) dearth

14. **Scanty**
(a) ample (b) sample
(c) adore (d) afore

15. **Anabolism**
(a) metabolism (b) catabolism
(c) quantity (d) autism

16. **Order**
(a) anarchy (b) endarch
(c) mesarch (d) none of these

17. **Angelical**
(a) magnanimous (b) diabolical
(c) benevolent (d) critical

18. **Ecstacy**
(a) anguish (b) appeal
(c) amenable (d) lucidity

19. **Antidote**
(a) medicine (b) poison
(c) anodyne (d) amity

20. **Apex**
(a) base (b) zenith
(c) meridian (d) median

21. **Haughtiness**
(a) unskilled (b) affability
(c) adduce (d) abject

22. **Ally**
(a) aide (b) opponent
(c) amor (d) rely

23. **Alcoholic**
(a) drunk (b) addict
(c) teetotaler (d) venom

24. **Apocryphal**
(a) apocalypse (b) authentic
(c) amusing (d) disgusting

25. **Hidden**
(a) appealing (b) apparent
(c) apparel (d) none of these

26. **Appeasable**
(a) antecedent (b) incident
(c) unrelenting (d) unloved

27. **Applaud**
(a) placate (b) denounce
(c) order (d) conserve

28. **Stinking**
(a) smelly (b) apathy
(c) aromatic (d) acrobatic

29. **Mislead**
(a) alter (b) separate
(c) malady (d) apprise

30. **Aristocrat**
(a) plutarchy (b) commoner
(c) royalty (d) none of these

31. **Coloured**
(a) troubled (b) anfractuous
(c) ashen (d) complexion

32. **Disarray**
(a) disorder (b) order
(c) bore (d) store

33. **Assumption**
(a) aspersion (b) aspiration
(c) proof (d) prediction

34. **Denial**
(a) disturb (b) avowal
(c) astern (d) atonement

35. **Democrat**
(a) royalty (b) anarchy
(c) autocrat (d) plutocrat

36. **Awry**
(a) austere (b) offend
(c) asthenia (d) straight

37. **Silence**
(a) attune (b) babble
(c) achromatic (d) aurora

38. **Badger**
(a) bad (b) sober
(c) pacify (d) assure

39. **Bane**
(a) ban (b) band
(c) boon (d) bloom

40. **Civilised**
(a) palpable (b) civic
(c) incongruent (d) barbarian

41. **Audacious**
(a) silent (b) polite
(c) astute (d) avarice

42. **Barefaced**
(a) babel (b) baffle
(c) concealed (d) chaste

43. **Befoul**
(a) flounder (b) cleanse
(c) buoyant (d) flambé

44. **Unsuitable**
(a) sudorific (b) soporific
(c) befitting (d) bawdy

45. **Benign**
(a) benevolent (b) malevolent
(c) blessing (d) curse

46. **Peaceful**
(a) beatific (b) belligerent
(c) belie (d) belle

47. **Bellow**
(a) whisper (b) tout
(c) stupor (d) above

48. **Usual**
(a) bigotry (b) bizarre
(c) bewail (d) biased

49. **Blasphemous**
(a) irreligious (b) inferior
(c) reverent (d) blarney

50. **Darken**
(a) rejoice (b) bleach
(c) inculpate (d) corolla

51. **Lengthen**
(a) elongate (b) evacuate
(c) abbreviate (d) encompass

52. **Abhorrent**
(a) obnoxious (b) attractive
(c) abeyance (d) ablution

53. **Abrupt**
(a) brusque (b) precipitous
(c) terse (d) gradual

54. **Abstruse**
(a) esoteric (b) obvious
(c) complex (d) enigmatic

55. **Paradoxical**
(a) rational (b) crazy
(c) daft (d) zany

56. **Accepted**
(a) indisputable (b) controversial
(c) accede (d) axiomatic

57. **Proletariat**
(a) rationalist (b) evangelist
(c) bourgeoisie (d) Marxist

58. **Boundless**
(a) further (b) astute
(c) abutting (d) finite

59. **Braggart**
(a) modest (b) harangue
(c) adept (d) competent

60. **Brevity**
(a) prolixity (b) niggardly
(c) reconciliation (d) smoldering

61. **Bury**
(a) bristle (b) exhume
(c) consume (d) bombast

62. **Callow**
(a) mature (b) oppose
(c) bustle (d) burly

63. **Euphony**
(a) concord (b) symphony
(c) cacophony (d) sync

64. **Fortune**
(a) blessing (b) calamity
(c) cabal (d) blasphemy

65. **Calumniate**
(a) eulogise (b) callous
(c) enervate (d) temperate

66. **Truth**
(a) carnage (b) canaille
(c) canard (d) candid

67. **Candour**
(a) frankness (b) cunning
(c) ingenuous (d) sincere

68. **Capricious**
(a) lozenge (b) acquiesce
(c) erratic (d) steady

69. **Disgust**
(a) duress (b) captivate
(c) repel (d) rebel

70. **Anxious**
(a) crafty (b) métier
(c) carefree (d) slapdash

71. **Manikin**
(a) dwarf (b) giant
(c) figure (d) statue

72. **Retreat**
(a) haven (b) shelter
(c) advance (d) egress

73. **Affluence**
(a) poverty (b) influence
(c) affinity (d) prosperity

74. **Diffidence**
(a) ascent (b) confidence
(c) penchant (d) prescription

75. **Detraction**
(a) contraction (b) flattery
(c) cannery (d) deacon

76. **Inequity**
(a) law (b) illegal
(c) slander (d) libel

77. **Hope**
(a) beatitude (b) platitude
(c) despair (d) deign

78. **Oblivion**
(a) memory (b) comely
(c) comfrey (d) bijou

79. **Plaintiff**
(a) bigot (b) defendant
(c) decoy (d) frond

80. **Folly**
(a) wisdom (b) antidote
(c) humility (d) blame

81. **Affirmative**
(a) positive (b) negative
(c) derogatory (d) affiliate

82. **Carnal**
(a) infernal (b) internal
(c) spiritual (d) egoist

83. **Diffuse**
(a) concise (b) incise
(c) temporal (d) opulent

84. **Flaccid**
(a) exotic (b) turgid
(c) insipid (d) fresco

85. **Industrious**
(a) idle (b) compatible
(c) buoyant (d) adversity

86. **Immanent**
(a) impatient (b) amiable
(c) transcendent (d) diffident

87. **Profane**
(a) sacred (b) denounce
(c) announce (d) penance

88. **Figurative**
(a) literal (b) liberal
(c) perennial (d) annual

89. **Sprightly**
(a) bright (b) effulgent
(c) indulgent (d) dull

90. **Vigorous**
(a) feeble (b) regal
(c) frugal (d) immortal

91. **Condemn**
(a) convict (b) acquit
(c) accuse (d) enervate

92. **Repudiate**
(a) discharge (b) disagree
(c) admit (d) reject

93. **Expedite**
(a) extract (b) distract
(c) delay (d) defend

94. **Lament**
(a) languish (b) anguish
(c) rejoice (d) languor

95. **Absurd**
(a) funny (b) expedient
(c) sensible (d) gallant

96. **Augment**
(a) increase (b) argument
(c) diminish (d) delay

97. **Censure**
(a) appreciate (b) reprimand
(c) apprehend (d) comprehend

98. **Impertinent**
(a) blunder (b) excuse
(c) polite (d) insolent

99. **Commend**
(a) criticize (b) comment
(c) forsake (d) dexterity

100. **Obligatory**
(a) derogatory (b) optional
(c) compulsion (d) repulsion

101. **Ignore**
(a) adjudicate (b) infallible
(c) anarchy (d) infidel

102. **Agnostic**
(a) euphoric (b) putrid
(c) evangelical (d) abhor

103. **Blessing**
(a) malediction (b) catholic
(c) engaging (d) incredible

104. **Cleave**
(a) disjunction (b) separate
(c) adjunct (d) revoke

105. **Loose**
(a) lax (b) vitiate
(c) astringent (d) frigid

106. **Erase**
(a) arcane (b) inscribe
(c) infallible (d) invalidate

107. **Customary**
(a) aberrant (b) harsh
(c) common (d) ratify

108. **Gratuitous**
(a) unwarranted (b) restrained
(c) anomalous (d) viable

109. **Tremulous**
(a) fearful (b) intrepid
(c) supplant (d) whimsical

110. **Feeble**
(a) omniscient (b) omnipotent
(c) heathen (d) corporate

111. **Prevaricate**
(a) truth (b) abate
(c) restrained (d) tactful

112. **Multifarious**
(a) nonentity (b) singular
(c) gallant (d) invidious

113. **Circuitous**
(a) roundabout (b) manifold
(c) rectilinear (d) mechanical

114. **Overrule**
(a) ratify (b) countermand
(c) sedge (d) anomalies

115. **Humane**
(a) charitable (b) philanthropic
(c) perturb (d) callous

116. **Consanguinity**
(a) affinity (b) corpulent
(c) estrangement (d) anarchy

117. **Volatile**
(a) explosive (b) immutable
(c) sedulous (d) secretive

118. **Naive**
(a) sanctimonious (b) ingenuous
(c) artless (d) affable

119. **Impenetrable**
(a) translucent (b) sinister
(c) queasy (d) impede

120. **Glorification**
(a) exaltation (b) aspersion
(c) vitreous (d) sententious

121. **Dishearten**
(a) construe (b) solace
(c) absolve (d) attribute

122. **Unquestionable**
(a) veritable (b) spurious
(c) temporal (d) penultimate

123. **Revitalize**
(a) debilitate (b) animate
(c) quicken (d) feign

124. **Vapid**
(a) insipid (b) prosaic
(c) pithy (d) relieve

125. **Ally**
(a) epitome (b) cleanse
(c) split (d) comely

126. **Foster**
(a) interrogate (b) satiate
(c) travesty (d) impede

127. **Persevere**
(a) tenacity (b) capitulate
(c) tawdry (d) ululate

128. **Cosmopolitan**
(a) worldly (b) sophisticated
(c) insular (d) chic

129. **Master**
(a) tyrant (b) tyro
(c) rodeo (d) toreador

130. **Antagonistic**
(a) congenial (b) neophyte
(c) vex (d) menacing

131. **Preclude**
(a) obviate (b) prevent
(c) augment (d) segment

132. **Contemptible**
(a) venerable (b) barbarous
(c) jocose (d) sickening

133. **Inclination**
(a) propensity (b) aversion
(c) liking (d) attenuated

134. **Uninspired**
(a) pedestrian (b) common
(c) stellar (d) approbation

135. **Atrocious**
(a) grievous (b) serious
(c) good (d) tirade

136. **Garrulous**
(a) loquacious (b) talkative
(c) quiet (d) weary

137. **Kindly**
(a) comely (b) homely
(c) sparse (d) harsh

138. **Vital**
(a) inanimate (b) alive
(c) strength (d) excite

139. **Gluttonous**
(a) estrange (b) abstemious
(c) sanctimonious (d) contingency

140. **Impetuous**
(a) rash (b) harsh
(c) cautious (d) flighty

141. **Anathema**
(a) contravene (b) love
(c) masquerade (d) identify

142. **Admonish**
(a) censure (b) censor
(c) approve (d) prudent

143. **Diligent**
(a) indolent (b) assiduous
(c) assimilate (d) apprehend

144. **Indigent**
(a) opulent (b) poor
(c) indomitable (d) abatement

145. **Lampoon**
(a) mock (b) satirize
(c) exalt (d) energize

146. **Ennoble**
(a) eulogize (b) dishonor
(c) salutary (d) morbid

147. **Impromptu**
(a) intuitive (b) deliberate
(c) portent (d) bucolic

148. **Ephemeral**
(a) eternal (b) internal
(c) inanimate (d) sedate

149. **Familiar**
(a) nostalgic (b) noxious
(c) foreign (d) native

150. **Sullen**
(a) cynical (b) blissful
(c) hopeless (d) genuine

151. **Delay**
(a) curb (b) advancement
(c) waylay (d) warren

152. **Deride**
(a) scoff (b) sedate
(c) laud (d) deluge

153. **Sanguine**
(a) pessimistic (b) mitigate
(c) exhibitionist (d) modest

154. **Servile**
(a) accommodating (b) indomitable
(c) demoralized (d) hail

155. **Reticent**
(a) brazen (b) reserved
(c) apathetic (d) dull

156. **Perfunctory**
(a) careless (b) thorough
(c) bold (d) lazy

157. **Tranquilise**
(a) anesthetic (b) energise
(c) atoll (d) guzzle

158. **Inveigh**
(a) insinuate (b) embezzle
(c) praise (d) scold

159. **Necessary**
(a) exacerbate (b) burgeon
(c) raconteur (d) superfluous

160. **Guileless**
(a) hermit (b) deceitful
(c) nebulous (d) amorphous

161. **Tarnish**
(a) inchoate (b) squander
(c) deride (d) polish

162. **Subordination**
(a) stipulation (b) cimmerian
(c) autonomy (d) desalinize

163. **Contumacious**
(a) willful (b) pliable
(c) mercurial (d) temperamental

164. **Pernicious**
(a) drone (b) travesty
(c) benign (d) false

165. **Rampant**
(a) raging (b) wanton
(c) quiescent (d) apocryphal

166. **Bellicose**
(a) militant (b) demagogue
(c) champion (d) congenial

167. **Cantankerous**
(a) belligerent (b) thimble
(c) gregarious (d) cathartic

168. **Quixotic**
(a) exotic (b) ruse
(c) pragmatic (d) romantic

169. **Jingoistic**
(a) satisfied (b) contemplative
(c) noncommittal (d) zealous

170. **Strutting**
(a) cowering (b) smocking
(c) confident (d) dissipating

171. **Histrionic**
(a) dramatic (b) sincere
(c) hermetic (d) optic

172. **Deference**
(a) sequester (b) deadpan
(c) sauciness (d) entreaty

173. **Sardonic**
(a) cheeky (b) pleasing
(c) impetuous (d) ironic

174. **Pandemonium**
(a) confusion (b) uproar
(c) laxity (d) equanimity

175. **Hermetic**
(a) opulent (b) airy
(c) confined (d) refined

176. **Evanescent**
(a) convoluted (b) fleeting
(c) enigma (d) perpetual

177. **Blithe**
(a) puzzling (b) uniform
(c) disconsolate (d) vivacious

178. **Comity**
(a) argot (b) dialect
(c) gracious (d) curt

179. **Commend**
(a) please (b) chastise
(c) discern (d) famish

180. **Jaded**
(a) excited (b) deployed
(c) employed (d) exploit

181. **Repine**
(a) master (b) delight
(c) innocent (d) simplify

182. **Quell**
(a) subdue (b) allay
(c) inflame (d) deflate

183. **Enshroud**
(a) apprise (b) incense
(c) wallow (d) camp

184. **Odium**
(a) abhorrence (b) approbation
(c) induce (d) assimilate

185. **Dispassionate**
(a) essence (b) innocent
(c) encoded (d) torrid

186. **Fearless**
(a) intrepid (b) craven
(c) vacillate (d) oscillate

187. **Refractory**
(a) obstinate (b) averse
(c) assess (d) impressionable

188. **Listless**
(a) phlegmatic (b) discredit
(c) spirited (d) inanimate

189. **Garrote**
(a) strangle (b) emancipate
(c) industrious (d) impudent

190. **Minatory**
(a) inspiring (b) menacing
(c) infuriated (d) opaque

191. **Creative**
(a) seminal (b) far-reaching
(c) stifling (d) flinging

192. **Desiccated**
(a) flaccid (b) sodden
(c) arid (d) crushed

193. **Facile**
(a) burdensome (b) effortless
(c) worthless (d) opulent

194. **Nullify**
(a) void (b) legitimize
(c) repose (d) indomitable

195. **Fierce**
(a) pitiless (b) generous
(c) augment (d) cleanse

196. **Indenture**
(a) manumit (b) enslave
(c) affix (d) pungent

197. **Pursue**
(a) foster (b) eschew
(c) judgmental (d) debate

198. **Dark**
(a) vitreous (b) obscure
(c) scarce (d) devout

199. **Conclusive**
(a) definitive (b) wanting
(c) singular (d) distinguished

200. **Defamation**
(a) apotheosis (b) obloquy
(c) limpid (d) parochial

Answer Key

1. (c)	**2.** (b)	**3.** (a)	**4.** (c)	**5.** (a)
6. (c)	**7.** (d)	**8.** (c)	**9.** (a)	**10.** (b)
11. (c)	**12.** (a)	**13.** (b)	**14.** (a)	**15.** (b)
16. (a)	**17.** (b)	**18.** (a)	**19.** (b)	**20.** (a)
21. (b)	**22.** (b)	**23.** (c)	**24.** (b)	**25.** (b)
26. (c)	**27.** (b)	**28.** (c)	**29.** (d)	**30.** (b)
31. (c)	**32.** (b)	**33.** (c)	**34.** (b)	**35.** (c)
36. (d)	**37.** (b)	**38.** (c)	**39.** (c)	**40.** (d)
41. (b)	**42.** (c)	**43.** (b)	**44.** (c)	**45.** (b)
46. (b)	**47.** (a)	**48.** (b)	**49.** (c)	**50.** (b)
51. (c)	**52.** (b)	**53.** (d)	**54.** (b)	**55.** (a)
56. (b)	**57.** (c)	**58.** (d)	**59.** (a)	**60.** (a)
61. (b)	**62.** (a)	**63.** (c)	**64.** (b)	**65.** (a)
66. (c)	**67.** (b)	**68.** (d)	**69.** (b)	**70.** (c)
71. (b)	**72.** (c)	**73.** (a)	**74.** (b)	**75.** (b)
76. (a)	**77.** (c)	**78.** (a)	**79.** (b)	**80.** (a)
81. (b)	**82.** (c)	**83.** (a)	**84.** (b)	**85.** (a)
86. (c)	**87.** (a)	**88.** (a)	**89.** (d)	**90.** (a)
91. (b)	**92.** (c)	**93.** (c)	**94.** (c)	**95.** (c)
96. (c)	**97.** (a)	**98.** (c)	**99.** (a)	**100.** (b)
101. (a)	**102.** (c)	**103.** (a)	**104.** (c)	**105.** (c)
106. (b)	**107.** (a)	**108.** (b)	**109.** (b)	**110.** (b)
111. (a)	**112.** (b)	**113.** (c)	**114.** (a)	**115.** (d)
116. (c)	**117.** (b)	**118.** (a)	**119.** (a)	**120.** (b)
121. (b)	**122.** (b)	**123.** (a)	**124.** (c)	**125.** (c)
126. (d)	**127.** (b)	**128.** (c)	**129.** (b)	**130.** (a)
131. (c)	**132.** (a)	**133.** (b)	**134.** (c)	**135.** (c)
136. (c)	**137.** (d)	**138.** (a)	**139.** (b)	**140.** (c)
141. (b)	**142.** (c)	**143.** (a)	**144.** (a)	**145.** (c)
146. (b)	**147.** (b)	**148.** (a)	**149.** (c)	**150.** (b)
151. (b)	**152.** (c)	**153.** (a)	**154.** (b)	**155.** (a)
156. (b)	**157.** (b)	**158.** (c)	**159.** (d)	**160.** (b)
161. (d)	**162.** (c)	**163.** (b)	**164.** (c)	**165.** (c)
166. (d)	**167.** (c)	**168.** (c)	**169.** (c)	**170.** (a)
171. (b)	**172.** (c)	**173.** (b)	**174.** (d)	**175.** (b)
176. (d)	**177.** (c)	**178.** (d)	**179.** (b)	**180.** (a)
181. (b)	**182.** (c)	**183.** (a)	**184.** (b)	**185.** (d)
186. (b)	**187.** (d)	**188.** (c)	**189.** (b)	**190.** (a)
191. (c)	**192.** (b)	**193.** (a)	**194.** (b)	**195.** (b)
196. (a)	**197.** (b)	**198.** (a)	**199.** (b)	**200.** (a)

CHAPTER 8

Odd Man Out

Directions for Exercises (1-5): *Pick the odd man out from the options.*

EXERCISE 1

1. (a) Haughty (b) Reticent (c) Sociable (d) Aloof
2. (a) Mitigate (b) Aggravate (c) Ameliorate (d) Assuage
3. (a) Consortium (b) Guild (c) Bloc (d) Dole out
4. (a) Flabbergast (b) Stupefy (c) Dumbfound (d) Zeal
5. (a) Disconcert (b) Equivocal (c) Ambivalent (d) Ambiguous
6. (a) Amorous (b) Carnal (c) Ardent (d) Loathe
7. (a) Ampersand (b) Amperage (c) Ammeter (d) Current
8. (a) Happy (b) Gladden (c) Anaemic (d) Mirth
9. (a) Pollard (b) Truncate (c) Amputate (d) Capacious
10. (a) Munificent (b) Ambulate (c) Copious (d) Voluminous
11. (a) Engross (b) Pasty (c) Sallow (d) Wan
12. (a) Vexation (b) Rancour (c) Choler (d) Metaphor
13. (a) Bedlam (b) Anarchy (c) Anatomize (d) Insurrection
14. (a) Archangel (b) Genealogy (c) Progenitor (d) Ancestry
15. (a) Antediluvian (b) Superannuated (c) Venerable (d) Beatific
16. (a) Grate (b) Badger (c) Pique (d) Elucidate
17. (a) Embrocate (b) Anoint (c) Umbrage (d) Smear
18. (a) Colt (b) Filly (c) Steed (d) Bull
19. (a) Aviator (b) Bull (c) Matador (d) Toreador
20. (a) Purloin (b) Usurp (c) Appropriate (d) Anodyne

Exercise 2

1. (a) Augury (b) Aural
   (c) Portent (d) Omen
2. (a) Propitious (b) Abstemious
   (c) Parsimonious (d) Exacting
3. (a) Avocado (b) Papaya
   (c) Mulberry (d) Eucalyptus
4. (a) Awning (b) Tarpaulin
   (c) Canopy (d) Endow
5. (a) Hatchet (b) Cleaver
   (c) Axe (d) Spindle
6. (a) Eliminate (b) Animate
   (c) Stimulate (d) Kindle
7. (a) Truss (b) Bale
   (c) Bundle (d) Stark
8. (a) Balaclava (b) Bonnet
   (c) Beret (d) Bagatelle
9. (a) Pushpin (b) Tetris
   (c) Blocks (d) Cushions
10. (a) Chevron (b) Bagpipes
    (c) Crest (d) Emblem
11. (a) Haversack (b) Reticule
    (c) Racquet (d) Holdall
12. (a) Banshee (b) Churl
    (c) Heathen (d) Vandal
13. (a) Putt (b) Birdie
    (c) Eagle (d) Puck
14. (a) Halloween (b) Mistletoe
    (c) Bunting (d) Santa Claus
15. (a) Incandescent (b) Smouldering
    (c) Ablaze (d) Bursting
16. (a) Burrow (b) Nest
    (c) Rodent (d) Rat
17. (a) Parody (b) Satire
    (c) Burdock (d) Burlesque
18. (a) Play (b) Pantomime
    (c) Opera (d) Banquet
19. (a) Abbey (b) Chasm
    (c) Abyss (d) Crater
20. (a) Tornado (b) Twister
    (c) Cyclone (d) Volcano

Exercise 3

1. (a) Breach (b) Canny
   (c) Fissure (d) Cranny
2. (a) Astute (b) Guileful
   (c) Machiavellian (d) Atavistic
3. (a) Fiend (b) Fecund
   (c) Ingenious (d) Fertile
4. (a) Cube (b) Cubicle
   (c) Cuboid (d) Cubic
5. (a) Cryptic (b) Esoteric
   (c) Recondite (d) Crust
6. (a) Limousine (b) Sedan
   (c) Concorde (d) Hatchback
7. (a) Masticate (b) Scrunch
   (c) Pulverize (d) Sepulchre
8. (a) Cuirass (b) Cudgel
   (c) Bludgeon (d) Cosh
9. (a) Ford (b) Boeing
   (c) Toyota (d) General Motors
10. (a) Lufthansa (b) Cathay Pacific
    (c) Eurail (d) Biman
11. (a) Bolster (b) Hassock
    (c) Duvet (d) Pillow
12. (a) Pierce (b) Precis
    (c) Bowdlerize (d) Censor
13. (a) Misanthropic (b) Cynosure
    (c) Incredulous (d) Cynical
14. (a) Cymbal (b) Harp
    (c) Bonito (d) Bongo
15. (a) Tuna (b) Octopus
    (c) Electric ray (d) Salmon
16. (a) Phantom (b) Diana
    (c) Rex (d) Mandrake

17. (a) Crown (b) Enamel
(c) Dentine (d) Dendrite
18. (a) Downgrade (b) Abnegation
(c) Repudiation (d) Contradiction
19. (a) Plummet (b) Plunge
(c) Plume (d) Sink
20. (a) Cradle (b) Crib
(c) Cot (d) Croft

EXERCISE 4

1. (a) Frugivore (b) Carnivore
(c) Herbivore (d) Graminivore
2. (a) Miscreant (b) Defendant
(c) Accused (d) Plaintiff
3. (a) Assault (b) Extortion
(c) Attorney (d) Battery
4. (a) Accelerometer (b) Ammeter
(c) Galvanometer (d) Voltmeter
5. (a) COBOL (b) DOS
(c) C+ (d) Fortran
6. (a) Armada (b) Corvette
(c) Flotilla (d) Machete
7. (a) Lasso (b) Rodeo
(c) Desperado (d) Lariat
8. (a) Constable (b) Bobby
(c) Policeman (d) Major
9. (a) Barrister (b) Attorney
(c) Juror (d) Advocate
10. (a) Azure (b) Turquoise
(c) Indigo (d) Magenta
11. (a) Leotard (b) Boots
(c) Galoshes (d) Wellingtons
12. (a) Cardigan (b) Pullover
(c) Tuxedo (d) Sweater
13. (a) Croissant (b) Croquet
(c) Crouton (d) Croquette
14. (a) Cower (b) Crouch
(c) Cringe (d) Croup
15. (a) Dactyl (b) Potter
(c) Paddle (d) Dabble
16. (a) Stiletto (b) Bayonet
(c) Blade (d) Dacha
17. (a) Curdle (b) Coagulate
(c) Clot (d) Clout
18. (a) Flecked (b) Blotchy
(c) Dingy (d) Dotted
19. (a) Squalid (b) Gauze
(c) Membrane (d) Mesh
20. (a) Flavour (b) Carrion
(c) Savour (d) Taste

EXERCISE 5

1. (a) Circumvent (b) Thwart
(c) Foil (d) Foist
2. (a) Wary (b) Gullible
(c) Credulous (d) Naïve
3. (a) Gusto (b) Verve
(c) Burst (d) Zest
4. (a) Diatribe (b) Beatific
(c) Blithe (d) Ecstatic
5. (a) Assonance (b) Euphony
(c) Cacophonous (d) Consonance
6. (a) Quirk (b) Idiosyncracy
(c) Malingerer (d) Peculiarity
7. (a) Plasma (b) Pixel
(c) Flat (d) Projection
8. (a) Fetish (b) Phobia
(c) Mania (d) Moribund
9. (a) Trappings (b) Orifice
(c) Egress (d) Vent
10. (a) Cache (b) Reservoir
(c) Stockpile (d) House-in
11. (a) Sleet (b) Brook
(c) Rivulet (d) Stream
12. (a) Smog (b) Marsh
(c) Haze (d) Mist

13. (a) Blackjack (b) Flash
(c) Roulette (d) Bridge
14. (a) Cloak (b) Robe
(c) Shawl (d) Jacket
15. (a) Coal (b) Humus
(c) Loam (d) Clay
16. (a) Spectre (b) Apparition
(c) Hoodlum (d) Phantom
17. (a) Ruminate (b) Chew
(c) Ponder (d) Wager
18. (a) Swim (b) Swill
(c) Ablution (d) Bathe
19. (a) Quack (b) Imposter
(c) Knave (d) Naïve
20. (a) Coalescence (b) Fission
(c) Amalgamation (d) Fusion

Answer Key

Exercise 1

1. (c)	**2.** (b)	**3.** (d)	**4.** (d)	**5.** (a)
6. (d)	**7.** (a)	**8.** (c)	**9.** (d)	**10.** (b)
11. (a)	**12.** (d)	**13.** (c)	**14.** (a)	**15.** (d)
16. (d)	**17.** (c)	**18.** (d)	**19.** (a)	**20.** (d)

Exercise 2

1. (b)	**2.** (a)	**3.** (d)	**4.** (d)	**5.** (d)
6. (a)	**7.** (d)	**8.** (d)	**9.** (d)	**10.** (b)
11. (c)	**12.** (a)	**13.** (d)	**14.** (a)	**15.** (d)
16. (b)	**17.** (c)	**18.** (d)	**19.** (a)	**20.** (d)

Exercise 3

1. (b)	**2.** (d)	**3.** (a)	**4.** (b)	**5.** (d)
6. (c)	**7.** (d)	**8.** (a)	**9.** (b)	**10.** (c)
11. (c)	**12.** (a)	**13.** (b)	**14.** (c)	**15.** (b)
16. (d)	**17.** (d)	**18.** (a)	**19.** (c)	**20.** (d)

Exercise 4

1. (b)	**2.** (d)	**3.** (c)	**4.** (a)	**5.** (b)
6. (d)	**7.** (c)	**8.** (d)	**9.** (c)	**10.** (d)
11. (a)	**12.** (c)	**13.** (b)	**14.** (d)	**15.** (a)
16. (d)	**17.** (d)	**18.** (c)	**19.** (a)	**20.** (b)

Exercise 5

1. (d)	**2.** (a)	**3.** (c)	**4.** (a)	**5.** (c)
6. (c)	**7.** (b)	**8.** (d)	**9.** (a)	**10.** (d)
11. (a)	**12.** (b)	**13.** (c)	**14.** (d)	**15.** (a)
16. (c)	**17.** (d)	**18.** (a)	**19.** (d)	**20.** (b)

CHAPTER

9 Analogies

INTRODUCTION AND BASIC STRATEGY

The analogy question type is one of the common types of questions that appears in all exams of this nature. Normally, there would be around 5 questions on this in the CAT (although there have been years when analogies were missing from the CAT paper altogether.)

In this question type you are asked to identify and assess the logical relationship between a given pair of words (in the question). You then must choose a pair of words from the options given that exhibit the same logical relationship as the original pair in the question. Thus it can be said that the analogy question tests not only your vocabulary skills, but also your ability to identify the relationship between words. You are given four pairs of words from which to choose. Let's start off by looking at an extremely simple example.

Artist : Painting ::

A) driver : car
B) composer : symphony
C) surgeon : operation
D) novel : author

What are we asked to do? To tackle analogy questions, first read the initial pair of words, substituting words for the colons. The first colon (:) is translated "is to" and the two colons (::) are translated "as". So for this example, we read the question as "artist is to painting as..." Next, we need to define the relationship between this pair of words. What is the relationship between an artist and a painting? An artist creates a painting. So, the relationship between the words is that the second word of the pair is created by the first. Because analogy problems require us to look for a pair of words that have the same relationship that the initial two words had, we are looking for a pair in which the second word of the pair is the creation of the first. Once you have determined the relationship between the given pair of words and stated it in your mind in sentence form (an artist creates a painting OR a painting is created by an artist), read through the answer choices substituting the possible pairs into the same sentence you have created to describe the initial pair. Let's work through the answer choices. Is a car created by a driver? No, this does not make sense. The relationship for this pair is a driver drives a car. Is a symphony created by a composer? Yes, this makes sense, but let's still look at the remaining choices to be sure. Is an operation created by a surgeon? No, a surgeon performs an operation, but is not the creator of an operation. Is an author created by a novel? No, but the reverse is true, i.e., a novel is created by an author. However, you need to be careful here as this is not the correct answer since it does not fit into the original sentence we created.

Hence, the correct answer is (B). Just as an artist creates a painting, a composer, creates a symphony.

Let's look at another example:

Puppy : Dog ::

A) sheep : flock
B) mare : goose
C) kitten : cat
D) child : adult

Again, read the initial pair of words, substituting words for the colons. So for this example, we read the question as "Puppy is to dog as..." Next, we need to define the relationship between this pair of words. What is the relationship between a puppy and a dog? A puppy is a young dog. So, the relationship between the words is that the first word of the pair is the name for the young of the second word. Because we are looking for a pair of words that have the same relationship as the initial pair, we are looking for a pair in which the first word of the pair is the name for the young of the second word. Once you have determined the relationship, between the given pair of words and stated it in your mind in a sentence form (a puppy is a young dog), read through the answer choices substituting the possible pairs into the same sentence you have created to describe the initial pair. Let's work through the answer choices. Is a sheep a young flock? No, this does not make sense. The relationship for this pair is that a group of sheep is called a flock. Is a mare a young goose? No, these are different animals. Is a kitten a young cat? Yes, this makes sense, but let's still look at the remaining choice to be sure. Is a child a young adult? Now this one may seem a little tricky, because a child will eventually age to become an adult, but we are not looking for the relationship of young to old, we are instead looking for the relationship of young of some kind of animal to that animal. If instead, the answer choice was child: human, then this relationship would be similar to that of kitten: cat, since child is the young of humans, and we would need to consider this choice further. In this case, however, the pair of words that exhibits the most similar logical relationship is choice C, giving us the completed analogy, puppy is to dog as kitten is to cat.

Note: It is extremely important to substitute the pairs of words into your sentence in the same order in which they are given. For example, if the answer choice was cat: kitten, we would substitute this into our original sentence as: a cat is a young kitten, and this would not make sense. Maintaining the same order for the two words in a pair when substituting into your sentence for checking an option's relationship is a very critical point. You need to remember this when solving analogies.

Critical Points

There are seven critical points that the reader should keep in mind while solving analogy questions.

(1) The study of analogy falls into nice neat patterns. Hence, it is one of the most learnable areas of the test. Once you gain familiarity with these patterns and learn to identify the traps, you will be able to increasingly develop your ability to solve analogy questions.

(2) Always make it a point to create a short sentence that expresses the relationship between the two words of the question. This should be done before looking at the answer choices.

(3) While defining the logical relationship between the component parts of a question, remember that analogies involve an exactness and precision to their solving.

In order to avoid errors you need to specify as exact a relationship as possible between the words in the question. The logical relationship between the given pair of words is sometimes obvious, but at other times, it may be more obscure, requiring you to be able to discern subtleties of meaning. The best sentence will explain the logical relationship explicitly and precisely. The more precise your sentence, the easier it will be to select the correct option that has the most similar logical relationship. On the other hand, if your sentence is too general, it is possible that more than one of the options would fit into that sentence.

In such a case, go back to the original pair of words again and make your sentence more specific. Let's look at an example.

Carpenter : Hammer

A) painter : paint

B) pilot : airplane

C) philosopher : books

D) plumber : wrench

We are trying to create a sentence that describes a relationship between the words carpenter and hammer. Let's say, we use the sentence, "A carpenter uses a hammer." Now let's look at the answer choices. Does a painter use paint? Yes. Does a pilot use an airplane? Well, a pilot flies an airplane, so maybe this could be thought of as a type of use. Does a philosopher use books? Well, a philosopher might read books, so this might be a use. Does a plumber use a wrench? Yes. You see that by using an imprecise sentence to describe our original pair of words, we have not been very successful in eliminating incorrect word pairs. If we go back to the original word pair, we can make our sentence more precise as, "A carpenter uses a hammer as a tool." Now if we work through the answer choices, substituting each word pair into our new sentence, we see that the only pair that can be substituted is choice D, a plumber uses a wrench as a tool. Thus, our analogy becomes carpenter is to hammer as plumber is to wrench.

This is especially important in case more than one answer choice fits in the logical relationship you may have defined. In such cases, you need to become more specific in your logical relationship defining sentence.

Let us look at an example:

Racket : Tennis

A) ball : football
B) glove : cricket
C) board : chess
D) bat : cricket

If you define the logical relationship here as: A racket is used to play tennis, it will not eliminate any of the four answer choices. However, if you say that a racket is used to strike a ball in the game of tennis, then D becomes the obvious answer, since a bat is used to strike a ball in the game of cricket.

(4) For analogies involving verbs, use the infinitive form of the verb to define the logical relationship. The structure you use in such analogies would be:

To ___ is to ___.

For example, sprint: run → To sprint is to run quickly.

Or skim: read → to skim is to read fast.

(5) Often, you might need to reverse the order of the words while stating the logical relationship. Be extra cautious about options that might have the same relationship as the original pair of words–but in the opposite order.

(6) In all problems of analogies, the parts of speech are consistent between the question and the correct answer. Hence, if the given pair is a noun and an adjective, the answer pair will also be a noun and an adjective in that order.

(7) Often, questions are formed in such a manner, that they contain an option that might remind you of the original pair, but might have a totally different relationship. For instance:

Democracy : Monarchy

A) anarchy : government
B) laptop : desktop

The second word in the option A (government) reminds one of the capitalized pair. However, what you need to be mindful of is that Democracy and Monarchy are different forms of government and hence, the relationship is not maintained in this option. However, option B here is correct since the logical relationship is maintained (laptop and desktop are both types of computers.)

Such distracting options can be termed as eye washers, since they have a tendency to confuse the student.

However, as a thumb rule, remember that normally, eye washers will almost never be the correct option (especially in tough problems).

The Cream of the Piece

Summary of general strategy for solving analogy problems

1. Read the initial pair of words, substituting words for the colons. The first colon (:) is translated as "is to" and the two colons (::) are translated as "as".
2. Define the logical relationship between the pair of words in the form of a sentence.
3. Go through the options, substituting the possible pairs into the sentence you created to describe the initial pair in the question.
4. In case the answer is unclear after looking at the options, and you are confused between two or more options, since more than one option fits into the sentence you have created, make your sentence describing the logical relationship between the initial pair of words more precise and work through the options again.

STRATEGIES FOR SOLVING THE PROBLEM WHEN THE MEANING OF THE WORDS ARE NOT KNOWN*

This does not mean the end of the problem. There are a few strategies elucidated below, which you could try to use in case you are unsure of the meanings of some of the words in the problem. The broad strategies are:

STRATEGY 1: PUT THE UNKNOWN WORD/S INTO A CONTEXT

In normal circumstances, we always come across words in some context. Hence, most of the times, we fill in the meaning of the word on the basis of the overall context and the context of the specific sentence in which the word is used. Due to this, many a time, we are unable to understand standalone words (even though we might be able to understand the same word in case it comes in some context.) Hence, in case you are not able to understand the word in isolation, it might not be a bad idea to try to put it into a natural sentence to try to guess the meaning.

*The strategies explained here will also apply in the questions of antonyms, synonyms, odd man out as well as other vocabulary based questions.

This will be clear from the following examples:

1. Whet

   This word will be better understood in the context of 'whetting one's appetite'.

2. Gumption

   This will be better understood in the context of 'grit and gumption'.

3. Gormandize

   This will be better understood in the context of 'gormandizing one's food'.

4. Eerie

   This will be better understood in the context of 'an eerie feeling'.

5. Gruesome

   This will be better understood in the context of 'a gruesome murder'.

6. Obeisance

   This will be better understood in the context of 'Paying obeisance'.

7. Gory

   This will be better understood in the context of 'a gory battle'.

8. Prudent

   This will be better understood in the context of 'a prudent decision'.

9. Agog

   This will be better understood in the context of 'agog with expectations'.

10. Retrograde

    This will be better understood in the context of 'a retrograde step'.

11. Hackneyed

    This will be better understood in the context of 'a hackneyed plot or a hackneyed path'.

12. Kick Start

    This will be better understood in the context of 'Kick starting an event'.

13. Choc-a-Bloc

    This will be better understood in the context of 'choc-a-bloc with vehicles'.

14. Hunky dory

    This will be better understood in the context of 'a hunky dory situation'.

As you can clearly see in the above examples, words that you might have read in some context somewhere in your normal reading tasks and which you fail to recollect in isolation can be understood more clearly if you are able to recollect even vaguely, some of the contexts in which you have come across the word. This is a very important strategy to be used in the case of familiar words whose meaning you might not remember exactly.

Strategy 2: Change the Word into a More Common Form

Some words are by nature, more used in one form and hence, more familiar in that form. However, its appearance in another form results in the creation of confusion in the mind of the student solving the question. In such cases, it is often a good idea to try to change the form in which the word appears into a more common and used form. This has an effect of reducing the difficulty level of the word since we have converted it from an uncommon word to a common word. This might help us in deducing the meaning of the uncommon word. Let us look at a few uncommon words.

1. Tyranny

   This can be understood through the more common word 'tyrant'.

2. Perturbation

   This can be understood through the more common word 'perturbed'.

3. Tempestuous

   This can be understood through the more common word 'tempest' or even through the very common 'temper'.

4. Voluminous

   This can be understood through the very common word 'volume'.

5. Abstemious

   This can be understood through the more common word 'abstain'.

6. Virulent

   This can be understood through the more common word 'virus'.

7. Ornate

   This can be understood through the more common word 'ornament'.

8. Bejeweled

   This can be understood through the very common words 'jewel or Jewelry.

9. Applicatory

   This can be understood through the very common word Apply.

Strategy 3: Use the roots (both prefixes and suffixes within the word)

A lot of times, the meaning of a word can be guessed through the roots in the form of prefixes and suffixes. Common roots and their meanings are given in detail in the section of vocabulary in this book. You are advised to look up these roots and consign them to your memory.

Strategy 4: Test words for positive and negative connotations

Many a time, words having negative or positive connotations can be identified. This will help in understanding the meaning of the word better. This strategy is an extension of the third strategy of looking for roots of the words – since negative or positive connotations in a word normally emerge out of prefixes and/or suffixes that are attached to a word.

Hence, for example, you would normally (but not always) associate negative connotations with words having the following prefixes:

(a) Mal (for example, malevolence, meaning bad intent or malice, maladroit: meaning clumsy, malicious: meaning spiteful, malediction: meaning a curse, malapropism: meaning the comical misuse of a word, malaise: meaning a feeling of uneasiness or illness, malady: meaning illness, malign: meaning to defame etc.)

(b) De (for example, delimitation: meaning removal of limits, devastate: meaning to lay waste, demerit: meaning a flaw, depletion: meaning exhaustion, decry: meaning to castigate, despot: meaning tyrant, deprivation: meaning scarcity, demean: meaning to degrade, demoralize: meaning to dishearten, denigrate: meaning to defame, denounce: meaning to condemn, derogatory: meaning degrading, deplore: meaning to condemn, depravity: meaning immorality, depredation: meaning plunder or preying on, deracinate: meaning to uproot, derelict: meaning negligent, etc.)

(c) Dis (for example, disarray: meaning disorder, disdain: meaning contempt, disfigure: meaning mar or ruin, disheveled: meaning disordered or untidy, disparage: meaning to belittle, dismal: meaning gloomy, etc.)

(d) Anti (for example, antediluvian: meaning ancient or obsolete, antiquity: meaning ancient times, antithesis: meaning the opposite point of view, antibody: meaning proteins which destroy bacteria, anticlimax: meaning a disappointing conclusion to a series of events, antipathy: meaning dislike or hostility, antipyretic: meaning a drug that reduces fever, etc.)

(e) A (for example, achromatic: meaning the removal of colour, atypical: meaning not typical, etc.)

(f) Re (for example, repudiate: meaning to disavow, repugnant: meaning distasteful, reprove: meaning to rebuke or to scold sternly, restive: meaning nervous or uneasy, reproach: meaning to blame, repress: meaning to suppress, reprobate: meaning a miscreant, etc.)

Other negative prefixes and suffixes include dys, hypo, less, un, non, etc.[1] Similarly, you should associate positive connotations with words containing the following prefixes:

(a) Bene (for example, benevolent: meaning kind, benediction: meaning blessing, benefactor: meaning a patron, etc.)

(b) Sym (for example, symbiotic: meaning mutually beneficial, symmetrical: meaning harmonious, etc.)

(c) Omni (for example, omnipotent: meaning having unlimited power, omniscient: meaning all knowing, omnipresent: meaning present everywhere, omnivorous: meaning eating all kinds of food, etc.)[2]

Strategy 5: Be alert to secondary (often rarer) meanings of the original word

Many a times, a word in the problem might have more than one meaning. In some cases, the problem might be framed on the basis of a rare meaning of the word than the more commonly understood and used meaning. In case, you are not being able to get a hold on the question by interpreting the words in the problem in their most common form, it might pay off to think of the more uncommon meaning of the word/s. Sometimes, this might give us the solution.

[1] For more negative prefixes and suffixes, the student is advised to go to the relevant part of the vocabulary section.

[2] For more positive prefixes and suffixes, the student is advised to go to the relevant part of the vocabulary section.

The following examples will make the above point clear:

The word **Champion** might be used in the context of 'Championing a cause', which is not as common as its normal usage.

The word **Twilight** might be used in the context of 'twilight of one's career' where it means the fag end of one's career. This usage of the word is not as common as its normal usage.

The word **Air** might be used in the context of 'airing one's feelings' where it means to discuss publicly, which is not as common as its normal usage.

The word **Engage** might be used in the context of 'engaging an employee' where it means to hire someone as an employee, which is not as common as its normal usage of engagement or being busy.

The word **Franchise** might be used in the context of 'exercising one's franchise' where it means to vote. This meaning of the word is not as common as its normal usage.

The word **Admission** might be used in the context of 'admission of one's guilt' where it means to own up to one's guilt, which is different and less common than its normal usage of admission meaning entry.

COMMON RELATIONSHIPS

One of the advantages of questions on analogies is that the logical relationships between words are all clear-cut, common sense relationships that can be easily deduced (given, of course, that you know the definitions of the words contained in the question.) We now go ahead and look at some of the typical and common logical relationships that appear often in the analogy section of the CAT and other multiple choice tests. Detailed examples are given for the important types of relationships, while others are mentioned in brief.

Type 1: Synonyms

Synonyms, as you are already aware, are words that have same or similar meanings. When you recognise the capitalised pair as a pair of synonyms, you will then look for a pair of words that also have the same or similar meanings. For example, polite: courteous are synonyms and so are engagement: betrothal.

Extemporaneous : Impromptu

A) reputable : elusive
B) antiquated : modern
C) depressed : ecstatic
D) morose : saturnine

Extemporaneous and impromptu are synonyms. Option A does not have any obvious relationship between its two words, while options B and C are both in the form of antonyms. Option D has to be the answer since morose describes someone who is gloomy or melancholy and saturnine is synonymous with morose.

Type 2: Antonyms

Antonyms as we have already seen earlier in the chapter dedicated to the same, are words that have opposite meanings. In the context of an analogy question, if the two words in the initial pair are antonyms, you are looking for an option that contains a pair of words that are opposite in meaning to each other. Consider the following example:

Zealous : Indifferent

A) diligent : hard working
B) perplexing : explicable
C) incorrigible : instantaneous
D) mysterious : exclusive

A zealous person is one who cares very strongly about something, while someone who is indifferent does not care about things. Option B contains an antonym since something that is perplexing is difficult to explain or inexplicable, while explicable describes something that can be explained. Thus, these two words are antonyms. The words in option A are synonyms while those in options C and D are irrelevant.

Type 3: Degree of Intensity

In this type of problem, the question contains a pair of words that are similar in meaning (similar to synonyms), however the two words vary in their intensity as one is more intense than the other. For example, in the pair jog: sprint, both words describe running, but a jog is a very slow run, while a sprint is a full-speed, extremely fast run. A similar relationship exists between sip and gulp, eat and hog, good and fantastic, etc.

Enthusiastic : Fanatical

A) frugal : miserly
B) faithful : kind
C) admonish : warn
D) virtuous : wholesome

Fanatical is an extreme form of being enthusiastic while miserly describes a person who is extremely frugal. Options C and D are synonyms; while the relationship between the words in option B is unclear.

Type 4: Part to Whole

In this type of analogy, the first word is part of the second word (or vice versa). For example, in the word pair star: constellation, a group of stars makes up a constellation. Similarly, a toe is a part of a foot.

Consider the following example:

Paragraph : Essay

A) scene : play
B) cast : actor
C) symphony : orchestra
D) dictator : oppressed

An essay (whole) is composed of a series of paragraphs(part). Likewise, a series of scenes (part) makes up a dramatic play (whole). Option B is close but the relationship is in the reverse direction. The relationship between cast and actor is one of part to whole, but a cast is composed of actors (this is whole : part). The other word pairs in options choices C and D are not related by the part to whole structure.

Type 5: Actor to Action

The relationship used in this kind of problem is that of a person or object with the action they commonly perform. In most cases, this includes professions, and the jobs that people in those professions perform. For example, in the word pair teacher : educate, a teacher's job is to educate, while in the word pair tailor : sew, the tailor's job is to sew. Remember when working analogies of this type that you are looking for the word pair in which the action most explicitly describes the major activity of the actor. This point will be amply illustrated through the example below:

Arbitrator : Judge

A) mechanic : repair
B) direction : orient
C) lawyer : legislate
D) musician : orchestra

An arbitrator judges or decides when there is a dispute while a mechanic works to repair things that are broken. If we consider option C, although you could envision circumstances in which a lawyer might work to legislate, but this would not be the primary action of a lawyer.

Type 6: Cause and Effect

In this type of problems, one of the words describes a condition or action (which is a cause), while the other word describes a response to that action or condition (which is the effect). For instance, the following word pairs describe cause and effect relationships (bacteria: infection, accident: injury, cold: fever, etc.) Remember to be careful of the direction of the relationship in such word pairs. Thus, if the original pair of words has the cause first and the effect later, the correct answer will also follow the same order. Consider the following example:

Tremble : Fear

A) shiver : cold
B) stifle : sneeze
C) itch : scratch
D) irritate : nettle

While a tremble is a response to fear, a shiver is a response to cold. Option C is also a cause and effect but in the reverse order.

Type 7: Member and Class

In this type of problem on analogy, one of the words in the pair is an element of a class that the other word in the pair describes. For example, frog : amphibian means that frog is a kind of amphibian. An appropriate matching pair might be tuna : fish, since tuna is a kind of fish. (tragedy : drama and cow : mammal are other examples of the same.)

Ballet : Dance

A) book : novel
B) theater : play
C) sonnet : poem
D) artist : sculptor

Ballet is one form of dance while sonnet is a kind of poem.

Type 8: Definition

In this type of problem, one of the words in the pair can be used to define the other word. For instance, someone who is frivolous is silly, someone who is careless is casual. Consider, the following example:

Philanthropist : Altruism

A) nationalist : orthodoxy
B) ascetic : self-denial
C) writer : publication
D) general : soldier

A philanthropist practices altruism while an ascetic is one who practices self-denial. The other options do not fit into this structure and hence the answer is B.

Type 9: Function

In this type of analogy, the relationship between the two words is a functional one. For example, in the word pair gloves : hands, the gloves serve to protect the hands. Similarly in the word pair feet: walk, the two words are connected to each other through the relationship of function.

Training : Skill

A) neurological : brain
B) auspicious : event
C) speech : lesson
D) mnemonic : memory

Training can be used to improve skill just as a mnemonic is something that can be used to improve memory.

Type 10: Symbol and Representation

In this type of problem structure, one of the words in the pair is the representation of the concept or thing denoted by the other. Common symbols include punctuation marks. For example, comma : pause :: period : stop. Other examples are objects that now represent actions or events, such as a white flag indicating surrender or hawk indicating warlike or a dove representing peace.

Laurel Wreath : Victory ::

A) honor : pride
B) olive branch : peace
C) parentheses : continuous
D) light : darkness

An olive branch is a symbol of peace while a laurel wreath is a symbol of victory.

Type 11: Defining Characteristic

Stable : Horse :: Fire Station : Fire Engine

The defining characteristic of a stable is a horse while that of a fire station is a fire engine.

Type 12: Manner

Strut : Walk :: Yodel : Sing.

Strut is a type or manner of walking just as yodel is a type of singing.

Type 13: Articles Made by A Worker

Artist : Painting :: Carpenter : Table.

Just as an artist creates a painting, a carpenter makes a table.

Type 14: The Worker and his Tools

Artist : Paintbrush :: Programmer : Computer.

An artist uses a paintbrush while a programmer uses a computer.

Type 15: The Worker and his Task

Teacher : Teaches :: Driver : Drives.

A teacher teaches while a driver drives.

Type 16: The Worker and the Work Place

Teller : Bank :: Sergeant : Post.

A teller works in the bank while a sergeant works on his post.

Type 17: The Tool and the Object

Scissors : Paper :: Hammer : Nail.

Scissors are used on paper just as a hammer is used on a nail.

Type 18: The Tool and the Action

Scissors : Cut :: Screwdriver : Screw.

Scissors cut while a screwdriver screws.

Type 19: Actions and their Significance

Smile : Pleasure :: Frown : Displeasure.

A smile conveys pleasure while a frown conveys displeasure.

Type 20: Sequence of Time

Beginning : End :: Opening : Closing

Type 21: Gender

Duke : Duchess :: Prince : Princess

Type 22: Age

Calf : Cow :: Tadpole : Frog.

The calf is the young of the cow, while the tadpole is the young of a frog.

Practice Exercises

Exercise 1

1. Saturated : Wet ::
   (a) acrid : acidic
   (b) distant : faraway
   (c) damp : drenched
   (d) arid : dry
2. Cacophonous : Harmonious ::
   (a) bellicose : pacific
   (b) beauty : peace
   (c) tempestuous : stormy
   (d) considerate : sympathetic
3. Kangaroo : Joey ::
   (a) lion : pride
   (b) goose : gosling
   (c) bevy : beauties
   (d) foal : horse
4. Capricious : Fixed ::
   (a) laughter : joy
   (b) agitated : uneasy
   (c) fickle : decisive
   (d) biased : judgmental
5. Unhappy : Miserable ::
   (a) vocal : quiet
   (b) mournful : oblivious
   (c) passionate : appreciative
   (d) content : euphoric
6. East : Oriental ::
   (a) west : occidental
   (b) global : universal
   (c) forest : jungle
   (d) west : east
7. Yeast : Leavening ::
   (a) antibiotic : microorganisms
   (b) water : valve
   (c) illness : cure
   (d) fertilizer : growth
8. Botany : Plants ::
   (a) geology : earth
   (b) stars: astronomy
   (c) teacher : class
   (d) disease : etiology
9. Snake : Reptile ::
   (a) snake : cobra
   (b) bird : mammal
   (c) wasp : insect
   (d) lion : amphibian
10. Illiterate : Education ::
    (a) naive : experience
    (b) well-mannered : rude
    (c) miserly : money
    (d) pristine : elegance
11. Eat : Gorge ::
    (a) drink : guzzle
    (b) saunter : walk
    (c) expel : admit
    (d) advanced : primitive
12. Loneliness : Privacy ::
    (a) passion : apathy
    (b) composure : equanimity
    (c) destiny : fateful
    (d) illusory : unpredictable
13. Fake : Genuineness ::
    (a) flawless : perfection
    (b) nebulous : definition
    (c) deceitful : intent
    (d) amoral : wicked
14. Opaque : Light ::
    (a) absorbent : liquid
    (b) desert : sand
    (c) autoclave : germ-free
    (d) hermetic : air

15. Rude : Boorish ::
    (a) deadly : pernicious
    (b) suspicious : pernicious
    (c) patronise : support
    (d) daring : daredevilry
16. Mosaic : Tile ::
    (a) fabric : tapestry
    (b) portrait : paint
    (c) document : author
    (d) coverlet : cloth
17. Glass : Shard ::
    (a) wood : splinter
    (b) rock : stone
    (c) soil : earth
    (d) wood : tree
18. Scale : Tone ::
    (a) dark : light
    (b) wave : amplitude
    (c) spectrum : colour
    (d) rainbow : shower
19. Skin : Dermatologist ::
    (a) physician : medicine
    (b) conductor : orchestra
    (c) bone : osteopath
    (d) ventriloquist : throat
20. Saunter : Stroll ::
    (a) perambulate : walk
    (b) gyrate : twist
    (c) amble : path
    (d) baby carriage : walk
21. Nightly : Daily ::
    (a) nocturnal : diurnal
    (b) black : white
    (c) sunset : sunrise
    (d) opalescent : iridescent
22. Physician : Surgeon ::
    (a) nurse : doctor
    (b) optometrist : ophthalmologist
    (c) urologist : gynecologist
    (d) optician : obstetrician
23. Bull : Buys ::
    (a) Wolf : Defrauds
    (b) Lion : Brokers
    (c) Tiger : Speculates
    (d) Bear : Sells
24. Cacophony : Euphony ::
    (a) belligerent : soothing
    (b) loveliness : peace
    (c) tempestuous : Atlantic
    (d) horrific : sympathetic
25. Feather : Bird ::
    (a) snake : scale
    (b) bark : tree
    (c) human: epidermis
    (d) hump : camel
26. Rebellious : Conformist ::
    (a) accepting : taking
    (b) courtesan : rude
    (c) acquiescent : rebel
    (d) darkness : lamp
27. Author : Manuscript ::
    (a) architect : blueprint
    (d) engineer : bridge
    (c) optician : spectacles
    (d) doctor : stethoscope
28. Pencil : Graphite ::
    (a) pen : refill
    (b) house : bricks
    (c) car : steel
    (d) dress : wool
29. Fickle : Stable ::
    (a) laughter : barn
    (b) equine : horse
    (c) impulsive : considered
    (d) fundamental : elemental
30. Feeble : Potent ::
    (a) borrow : give
    (b) file : classify
    (c) stroke : feel
    (d) fertile : barren
31. Manipulate : Control ::
    (a) exacerbate : cure
    (b) inanimate : dead
    (c) distinguish : change
    (d) articulate : speak
32. Sound : Decibel ::
    (a) earthquake : tremors
    (b) noise : intensity
    (c) light : radiance
    (d) length : meters

33. Word : Dictionary ::
    (a) roe : fish
    (b) cell : body
    (c) teeth : mouth
    (d) hair : scalp
34. Vertigo : Height ::
    (a) xenophobia : fear
    (b) triskaidekaphobia : spiders
    (c) agoraphobia : space
    (d) claustrophobia : darkness
35. Pupil : Eye ::
    (a) elbow : wrist
    (b) teeth : mouth
    (c) arm : leg
    (d) fist : hand
36. Matriarchal : Women ::
    (a) patriarchal : men
    (b) virago : female
    (c) oligarchy : dictator
    (d) patriotic : country
37. Ascetic : Luxury ::
    (a) teacher : classroom
    (b) capitalist : communist
    (c) misogynist : women
    (d) musician : composition
38. Slander : Reputation ::
    (a) deceit : hope
    (b) indiscretion : secrecy
    (c) hypocrite : praise
    (d) vandalism : property
39. Christmas : Christianity ::
    (a) Holi : Jews
    (b) Sabbath : Hindus
    (c) Eid : Parsis
    (d) Diwali : Hindus
40. Suave : Blunt ::
    (a) refined : cultured
    (b) pure : adulterated
    (c) severe : intense
    (d) eligible : qualify
41. Unriddle : Mystery ::
    (a) deactivate : bomb
    (b) fish : anemone
    (c) strike : harder
    (d) crack : glass
42. Artist : Painting ::
    (a) driver : car
    (b) pedestrian : road
    (c) composer : symphony
    (d) surgeon : operation
43. Stable : Horse ::
    (a) hotel : guest
    (b) sty : pig
    (c) teacher : school
    (d) kennel : cat
44. Rock : Marble ::
    (a) ebony : ivory
    (b) woods : mahogany
    (c) scissors : glue
    (d) tusk : elephant
45. Mammal : Cow ::
    (a) woods : tree
    (b) school : fish
    (c) reptile : snake
    (d) wings : bird
46. Change : Immutable ::
    (a) constancy : unsteady
    (b) mobile : movement
    (c) implicit : notions
    (d) impossible : plausible
47. Libertine : Immorality ::
    (a) altruist : selflessness
    (b) miser : selfishness
    (c) victim : depravation
    (d) policeman : law
48. Authorisation : Warrant ::
    (a) warrant : arrest
    (b) subpoena : summons
    (c) permission : license
    (d) indignation : protest
49. Scabbard : Sword ::
    (a) gamble : cards
    (b) cup : beverage
    (c) wish : intuition
    (d) foot : shoe
50. Uncle : Avuncular ::
    (a) mother : maternity
    (b) father : patricide
    (c) brother : fraternal
    (d) sister : sorority

EXERCISE 2

1. Necromancer : Witchcraft ::
   (a) puritan : excellence
   (b) gourmand : starvation
   (c) swindler : knavery
   (d) lawyer : graft
2. Extract : Tooth ::
   (a) cut : nail
   (b) uproot : stump
   (c) pull out : pin
   (d) cut : wood
3. Hug : Affection ::
   (a) dour : humous
   (b) nod : assent
   (c) virus : influenza
   (d) feet : walk
4. Island : Archipelago ::
   (a) shoulder : arm
   (b) stomach : intestine
   (c) shoe : laces
   (d) toe : foot
5. Codicil : Will ::
   (a) book : chapter
   (b) outhouse : premises
   (c) annexure : book
   (d) limb : extremity
6. Gets On : Bus ::
   (a) hopes : fear
   (b) enters : account book
   (c) disembarks : airplane
   (d) boards : rowboat
7. Mumble : Indistinct ::
   (a) scribble : illegible
   (b) screech : gentle
   (c) swagger : timid
   (d) sneeze : deliberate
8. Football : Sport ::
   (a) rhythm : poetry
   (b) verse : literature
   (c) dancing : ballet
   (d) research : biology
9. Sailor : Lighthouse ::
   (a) snake : hiss
   (b) air raid : siren
   (c) car horn : driver
   (d) sleeper : smoke alarm
10. Simmer : Boil ::
    (a) glide : drift
    (b) gambol : play
    (c) drizzle : downpour
    (d) stagnate : flow
11. Mitigate : Punishment ::
    (a) change : order
    (b) place : placement
    (c) monotonous : change
    (d) alleviate : pain
12. Sapling : Tree ::
    (a) puppy : dog
    (b) canine : feline
    (c) cat : lion
    (d) poodle : terrier
13. Tyre : Rubber ::
    (a) oasis : desert
    (b) house : roof
    (c) paper : wood
    (d) pebble : boulder
14. Angler : Bait ::
    (a) mouse : mousetrap
    (b) hunter : decoy
    (c) language : code
    (d) treasure : map
15. Bacterium : Colony ::
    (a) microbe : disease
    (b) whale : school
    (c) shoal : fish
    (d) virus : immunization
16. Childish : Maturity ::
    (a) pungent : poignancy
    (b) profuse : extravagance
    (c) obscure : clarity
    (d) poised : serenity
17. Tiny : Huge ::
    (a) chaotic : confuse
    (b) sad : gloomy

(c) great : grand
(d) weak : strong

18. Optimistic : Hope ::
(a) indecisive : idea
(b) impulsive : whim
(c) parsimonious : poverty
(d) garrulous : talk

19. Wardrobe : Clothes ::
(a) newspaper : headlines
(b) record : label
(c) album : stamps
(d) almanac : dates

20. Deluge : Water ::
(a) igloo : ice
(b) landslide : earth
(c) sleet : hail
(d) dew : rain

21. Cobbler : Boot ::
(a) potter : kiln
(b) banker : deposit
(c) carpenter : cabinet
(d) musician : clarinet

22. Seethe : Anger ::
(a) chortle : distress
(b) fidget : uneasiness
(c) snarl : confusion
(d) waddle : embarrassment

23. Merciless : Sympathy ::
(a) needless : intelligence
(b) belligerent : detachment
(c) pathetic : pity
(d) frank : reticence

24. Disagreement : Harmony ::
(a) predictability : routine
(b) predicament : dilemma
(c) advantage : agreement
(d) impartiality : prejudice

25. Key : Ignition ::
(a) helmet : motorcycle
(b) switch : light
(c) boot : saddle
(d) pad : helicopter

26. Bucket : Water ::
(a) milk : quart
(b) eggs : dozen
(c) shaker : salt
(d) river : ocean

27. Humans : Sotonny ::
(a) kinsfolk : family
(b) spectators : game
(c) animals : jungle
(d) rivals : team

28. Caterpillar : Leaves ::
(a) moth : wool
(b) silkworm : silk
(c) oyster : shell
(d) anthracite : coal

29. Tally : Votes ::
(a) census : population
(b) taxation : revenue
(c) government : laws
(d) team : athletes

30. Lull : Storm ::
(a) marriage : divorce
(b) battery : missiles
(c) recess : business
(d) bonfire : kindling

31. Grape : Raisin ::
(a) corn : flake
(b) flesh : bone
(c) cane : sugar
(d) jaggery : cane

32. Library : Books ::
(a) hotel : children
(b) zoo : animals
(c) office : sales
(d) park : car

33. Smell : Nose ::
(a) calligraphy : eye
(b) piquancy : taste
(c) noise : ear
(d) tracheotomy : throat

34. Slander : Disparagement ::
(a) sorrow : death
(b) commendation : praise

(c) paean : anger
(d) reproof : confirmation

35. Outpace : Speed ::
(a) outwit : cunning
(b) outline : thought
(c) outrage : wrath
(d) outreach : charity

36. See : Look ::
(a) feel : touch
(b) giggle : laugh
(c) sprint : lift
(d) drive : do

37. Imperil : Danger ::
(a) emulate : model
(b) entangle : conflict
(c) chafe : restriction
(d) embarrass : pride

38. Motel : Lodging ::
(a) godown : storage
(b) closet : linen
(c) hangar : plane
(d) desk : typing

39. Bracelet : Wrist ::
(a) frame : picture
(b) bat : glove
(c) hat : head
(d) foot : shoes

40. Wooden : Rigid ::
(a) fractious : whole
(b) mild : strident
(c) illegal : inconsiderate
(d) obstinate : stubborn

41. Satin : Soft ::
(a) polyester : expensive
(b) iron : hard
(c) soft : cotton
(d) wood : colored

42. Century : Years ::
(a) rupees : paise
(b) yard : inches
(c) week : days
(d) centimeter : millimeters

43. Axle : Steer ::
(a) tire : ride
(b) awl : puncture
(c) plane : soar
(d) knife : slice

44. Infertile : Desert ::
(a) delicious : fruit
(b) diligent : worker
(c) verdant : jungle
(d) hot : weather

45. Foot : Sore ::
(a) tree : cut
(b) skin : wrinkle
(c) toe : crushed
(d) hand : gnarled

46. Top : Spins ::
(a) earth : rotates
(b) car: accelerates
(c) moon : glows
(d) toy : plays

47. Milk : Spoil ::
(a) metal : bend
(b) water : filter
(c) flower : wilt
(d) fish : swim

48. Munificent : Generosity ::
(a) vivacious : happiness
(b) domineering : timidity
(c) indisputable : doubt
(d) fortunate : haplessness

49. Ship : Disembark ::
(a) train : board
(b) fail : arrest
(c) discharge : job
(d) horse : dismount

50. Retreating : Advancing ::
(a) oblique : indirect
(b) red : crimson
(c) dorsal : ventral
(d) snowy : windy

EXERCISE 3

1. Teacher : Instruction ::
(a) police : law
(b) army : soldier
(c) nurse : medicine
(d) sentinel : protection

2. Usher : Theater ::
   (a) anchor : show
   (b) driver : truck
   (c) conductor : train
   (d) fiancee : girl
3. Exercise : Strength ::
   (a) business : resource
   (b) practice : skill
   (c) defeat : gain
   (d) games : contest
4. Pipe : Water ::
   (a) sofa : furniture
   (b) fan : air
   (c) door : look
   (d) chimney : smoke
5. Damage : Demolish ::
   (a) construct : make
   (b) yap : howl
   (c) alleged : punished
   (d) action : plan
6. Stammer : Talk ::
   (a) anxious : analyze
   (b) stagger : walk
   (c) trip : fall
   (d) walk : run
7. Fret : Relax ::
   (a) sad : avoid
   (b) sob : cry
   (c) resist : surrender
   (d) giggle : laugh
8. Joey : Kangaroo ::
   (a) fern : plant
   (b) grain : wheat
   (c) kitten : cat
   (d) seed : fruit
9. Skate : Rink ::
   (a) park : bench
   (b) play : stadium
   (c) paint : picture
   (d) build : column
10. Lord : Serf ::
   (a) police : officer
   (b) slave : misery
   (c) capital : punishment
   (d) ruler : subject
11. Wheel : Spoke ::
   (a) tea : sugar
   (b) pen : cap
   (c) ladder : rung
   (d) lever : balance
12. Gaggle : Geese ::
   (a) tail : dog
   (b) goat : bleat
   (c) lion : roar
   (d) bevy : bees
13. Scales : Fish ::
   (a) paws : tiger
   (b) wings : butterfly
   (c) feathers : bird
   (d) tail : monkey
14. Shovel : Tool ::
   (a) cargo : hold
   (b) brake : automobile
   (c) car : means of transportation
   (d) squadron : plane
15. Godown : Goods ::
   (a) penitentiary : guards
   (b) arsenal : weapons
   (c) courthouse : laws
   (d) bank : mortgages
16. Mutineer : Rebellion ::
   (a) sluggard : haste
   (b) hypocrite : condemnation
   (c) renegade : accusation
   (d) terrorist : terror
17. Deferential : Obsequious ::
   (a) strong : sturdy
   (b) loyal : optimistic
   (c) reckless : daring
   (d) astute : perceptive
18. Triangle : Prism ::
   (a) circle : cylinder
   (b) square : rhomboid
   (c) sphere : earth
   (d) polygon : diamond
19. Hand : Arm ::
   (a) nose : head
   (b) foot : toe
   (c) eye : lid
   (d) wrist : finger

20. Parrot : Crow ::
    (a) eagle : ant
    (b) goldfish : trout
    (c) goat : butterfly
    (d) sheep : mouse
21. Trough : Animals ::
    (a) carton : eggs
    (b) den : bears
    (c) manger : cattle
    (d) flock : sheep
22. Sugar : Sweeten ::
    (a) cinnamon : prepare
    (b) pepper : season
    (c) celery : plant
    (d) accent : cook
23. Murmur : Shriek ::
    (a) merge : break
    (b) run : hover
    (c) crack : smash
    (d) play : work
24. Baldness : Hair ::
    (a) curly : wig
    (b) aridity : rain
    (c) cooked : egg
    (d) skin : rough
25. Ruffle : Equanimity ::
    (a) flounce : turmoil
    (b) flourish : prosperity
    (c) provoke : discussion
    (d) disturb : balance
26. Unveiling : Statue ::
    (a) premiere : movie
    (b) rookie : football
    (c) debutante : teenager
    (d) ruler : subject
27. Decrepitude : Renovation ::
    (a) doctor : consultation
    (b) estrangement : reconciliation
    (c) credulity : fury
    (d) reproof : confirmation
28. Braggart : Modest ::
    (a) dilettante : amateurish
    (b) visionary : practical
    (c) insurgent : revolutionary
    (d) expert : refined
29. Doggerel : Poet ::
    (a) symphony : composer
    (b) easel : painter
    (c) caption : cartoonist
    (d) potboiler : novelist
30. Bone : Ligament ::
    (a) knee : joint
    (b) nails : finger
    (c) fat : tissues
    (d) muscle : sinew
31. Gymnast : Agile ::
    (a) craftsman : dexterous
    (b) actress : beautiful
    (c) athlete : tall
    (d) clown : fat
32. Recipe : Chef ::
    (a) jury : trial
    (b) novel : novelist
    (c) soloist : music
    (d) pattern : dressmaker
33. Sound : Homonym ::
    (a) ideas : acronym
    (b) fake : pseudonym
    (c) meaning : synonym
    (d) confusion : antonym
34. Whale : Fish ::
    (a) hound : dog
    (b) bat : bird
    (c) alligator : crocodile
    (d) fly : worm
35. Dancer : Spectators ::
    (a) king : country
    (b) yardstick : dimension
    (c) barometer : weather
    (d) singer : audience
36. Gloves : Hands ::
    (a) tyre : wheel
    (b) hood : vehicle
    (c) nail : screw
    (d) socks : legs
37. Protein : Meat ::
    (a) cream : calories
    (b) salt : salty
    (c) starch : potatoes
    (d) diet : cyclamates

38. Praise : Extol ::
 (a) hurry : run
 (b) stuff : cram
 (c) insure : rely
 (d) dislike : loathe
39. Glass : Water
 (a) ship : fuel
 (b) car : petrol
 (c) plate : food
 (d) cup : sugar
40. Smell : Olfactory ::
 (a) touch : tactile
 (b) feel : sense
 (c) misnomer : word
 (d) pleasant : jovial
41. Suave : Sophisticated ::
 (a) attitude : conduct
 (b) adage : language
 (c) calmness : placidity
 (d) ally : foe
42. Vixen : Fox ::
 (a) mare : horse
 (b) kitten : cat
 (c) mouse : rat
 (d) puma : cheetah
43. Sluggish : Inert ::
 (a) axis : pivot
 (b) fission : fusion
 (c) bad : evil
 (d) affect : effect
44. Bovine : Herbivorous ::
 (a) ovine : omnivorous
 (b) simian : monkey
 (c) leonine : carnivorous
 (d) masculine : portentous
45. Buzz : Hum ::
 (a) whisper : noise
 (b) echo : sound
 (c) crack : whip
 (d) chime: ring
46. Deer : Venison ::
 (a) pig : hog
 (b) cous : mutton
 (c) pig : pork
 (d) steer : steak
47. Synagogue : Religion ::
 (a) court : law
 (b) hospital : illness
 (c) asylum : lunacy
 (d) prison : crime
48. Insipid : Piquant ::
 (a) tasty : bland
 (b) relish : spice
 (c) sweet : dessert
 (d) flat : spicy
49. Tipsy : Drunken ::
 (a) intelligent : dumb
 (b) generous : cheerful
 (c) sensible : lively
 (d) pleased : thrilled
50. Spasm : Pain ::
 (a) touch : delicate
 (b) flash : light
 (c) hurt : agony
 (d) love : hate

EXERCISE 4

From the choices given below, select the pair of words which exhibits the same relationship between each other as the given capitalised pair of words.

1. Writing : Plagiarism ::
 (a) confidence : deception
 (b) money : misappropriation
 (c) gold : theft
 (d) germ : disease
2. Lorry : Truck ::
 (a) torch : light
 (b) motor : car
 (c) coal : coke
 (d) petrol : gasoline
3. Waiter : Tip ::
 (a) professor : tenure
 (b) pharmacist : prescription
 (c) bank teller : interest
 (d) sales person : commission
4. Whelp : Dog ::
 (a) child : teenager
 (b) herd : ship
 (c) pup : seal
 (d) student : teacher

5. Condensation : Refrigerate ::
   (a) evaporation : heat
   (b) consumption : cook
   (c) oration : listen
   (d) exhaustion : buy
6. Eye : Socket ::
   (a) heart : aorta
   (b) chest : ribs
   (c) bone : joint
   (d) tooth : gum
7. Man : Handcuff ::
   (a) cat : mousetrap
   (b) dog : kennel
   (c) monkey : trick
   (d) cow : tether
8. Illness : Health ::
   (a) minotaur : nose
   (b) sequela : heart
   (c) halitosis : breath
   (d) aphasia : memory
9. Drabble : Dirty ::
   (a) goof : wise
   (b) cuesta : valley
   (c) drench : wet
   (d) furphy : freebooter
10. Onset : Expiration ::
   (a) desires : aspirations
   (b) drama : scene
   (c) proposal : final
   (d) tempo : time
11. Shower : Inundation ::
   (a) inception : perception
   (b) history : portent
   (c) imagine : sight
   (d) criticism : vilification
12. Bewilderment : Confusion ::
   (a) bursa : sack
   (b) bewitched : alliteration
   (c) fantod : nervousness
   (d) coracle : lodestar
13. Jingoism : War ::
   (a) antagonism : support
   (b) puritanism : austerity
   (c) arianism : doctrine
   (d) schism : unity
14. Agnostic : Atheist ::
   (a) misanthrope : misogynist
   (b) agglomerate : accumulate
   (c) philanthropic : patronizing
   (d) agrophobia : agnosia
15. Ridicule : Lampoon ::
   (a) knell : death
   (b) canard : rumour
   (c) jibe : remark
   (d) derision : fact
16. Jog : Fatigue ::
   (a) sing : voice
   (b) fast : hunger
   (c) tight : choke
   (d) camp : fire
17. Lumen : Light ::
   (a) weight : mineral
   (b) decibel : sound
   (c) gallon : water
   (d) band : signal
18. Take : Steal ::
   (a) leave : abscond
   (b) interest : astound
   (c) build : renovate
   (d) evacuate : flee
19. Lampoon : Satirize ::
   (a) ode : criticize
   (b) tirade : entertain
   (c) panegyric : eulogize
   (d) ballad : stigmatize
20. Jester : Clowning ::
   (a) coquette : flirtation
   (b) neophyte : mentoring
   (c) termagant : encomium
   (d) precocious : innocuous
21. Preamble : Statute ::
   (a) prologue : novel
   (b) movement : sympathy
   (c) sketch : drawing
   (d) index : book
22. Farmer : Field ::
   (a) ring : finger
   (b) cricket : pitch
   (c) wrestler : arena
   (d) workshop : carpenter

23. Mural : Painting ::
(a) symphony : dance
(b) editorial : journal
(c) preface : book
(d) ode : poetry

24. Hammer : Ironsmith ::
(a) car : driver
(b) seeds : farmer
(c) axe : woodcutter
(d) medicine : doctor

25. Beautiful : Ugly ::
(a) morose : dull
(b) priest : gangster
(c) good : bad
(d) criminal : padre

26. Animal : Fire ::
(a) child : work
(b) misogynist : women
(c) child : eating
(d) vegetarian : meat

27. Host : Gracious ::
(a) car : flies
(b) cheat : cunning
(c) doctor : handy
(d) blade : barber

28. Prude : Modesty ::
(a) enemy : friendly
(b) blunt : politician
(c) pedant : erudition
(d) diplomat : tactful

29. Perform : Entertain ::
(a) virus : prevent
(b) heuristic : teach
(c) pedant : construct
(d) parable : obfuscate

30. Hyphen : Join ::
(a) dash : shorten
(b) colon : introduce
(c) comma : possess
(d) semicolon : transfer

31. Extortion : Intimidating ::
(a) in extremis : early
(b) non sequitur : vital
(c) redundant : useless
(d) caveat emptor : trivial

32. Tree : Maple ::
(a) barter : guid pro guo
(b) medicine : profession
(c) building : construction
(d) vehicle : passenger car

33. Chimera : Authenticity ::
(a) melodrama : subtlety
(b) parody : wit
(c) brief : abstract
(d) war : strategy

34. Air Craft: Jet ::
(a) climate : rain
(b) instrument : calibration
(c) atmosphere : stratosphere
(d) nimbus : cloud

35. Nitty : Gritty ::
(a) nuts : bolts
(b) naked : clothed
(c) hard : soft
(d) bare : feet

36. Frosting : Cake ::
(a) lace: gown
(b) tie : shoe
(c) zipper : coat
(d) paint : enamel

37. Squander : Money ::
(a) shirk : task
(b) dally : time
(c) achieve : victory
(d) trespass : land

38. Admonishment : Castigation ::
(a) anxiety : fear
(b) perjury : corruption
(c) provocation : instigation
(d) peccadillo : sin

39. Deforestation : Trees ::
(a) inoculation : vaccine
(b) defamation : enemies
(c) amnesty : deserters
(d) sterilization : microorganism

40. Interpret : Examine ::
(a) foresee : perform
(b) plan : scheme
(c) interest : inveigle
(d) evaluate : suggest

41. Termination : Closure ::
    (a) hospitalization : sickness
    (b) majority : concession
    (c) amendment : constitution
    (d) quorum : filibuster
42. Resistance : Adversary ::
    (a) dilettantism : connoisseur
    (b) dogmatism : scholar
    (c) espionage : felon
    (d) humility : supplicant
43. Furniture : Chair ::
    (a) landscape : tree
    (b) apple : pear
    (c) animal : cat
    (d) club : player
44. Prattle : Succinct ::
    (a) tirade : critical
    (b) circumlocution : direct
    (c) bombast : pompous
    (d) prose : economical
45. Prodigal : Spend ::
    (a) treacherous : trust
    (b) querulous : complain
    (c) laconic : talk
    (d) humble : fawn
46. Bile : Liver ::
    (a) insulin : pancreas
    (b) oxygen : heart
    (c) honey : bee
    (d) menthol : eucalyptus
47. Hint : Suggestion ::
    (a) shade : spectrum
    (b) trace : existence
    (c) nuance : distinction
    (d) remnant : preservation
48. Anaesthetic : Insensibility ::
    (a) astringent : insensibility
    (b) coagulant : euphoria
    (c) stimulant : drowsiness
    (d) analgesic : painlessness

For the following question, mark as your answer the option that represents a relationship with the third word that is opposite to the first pair of words:

49. Philistine : Uncultured :: Precocious :
    (a) clever
    (b) mature
    (c) doltish
    (d) intelligent

For the following question, mark your answer as the option that represents a relationship not similar to the one exhibited by the given capitalized question pair of word.

50. Lugubrious : Lachrymose :: Salutary:
    (a) remedial
    (b) consistent
    (c) wholesome
    (d) curative

Answer Key

Exercise 1

1. (d)	2. (a)	3. (b)	4. (c)	5. (d)
6. (a)	7. (d)	8. (a)	9. (c)	10. (a)
11. (a)	12. (b)	13. (b)	14. (d)	15. (a)
16. (d)	17. (a)	18. (c)	19. (c)	20. (a)
21. (a)	22. (b)	23. (d)	24. (a)	25. (b)
26. (c)	27. (a)	28. (a)	29. (c)	30. (d)
31. (d)	32. (d)	33. (b)	34. (c)	35. (b)
36. (a)	37. (c)	38. (d)	39. (d)	40. (b)
41. (a)	42. (c)	43. (b)	44. (b)	45. (c)
46. (a)	47. (a)	48. (c)	49. (b)	50. (c)

Exercise 2

1. (c)	2. (b)	3. (b)	4. (d)	5. (c)
6. (d)	7. (a)	8. (b)	9. (d)	10. (c)
11. (d)	12. (a)	13. (c)	14. (b)	15. (b)
16. (c)	17. (d)	18. (b)	19. (c)	20. (b)
21. (c)	22. (b)	23. (d)	24. (d)	25. (b)
26. (c)	27. (c)	28. (a)	29. (a)	30. (c)
31. (c)	32. (b)	33. (c)	34. (b)	35. (a)
36. (a)	37. (b)	38. (a)	39. (c)	40. (d)
41. (b)	42. (a)	43. (d)	44. (c)	45. (b)
46. (a)	47. (c)	48. (a)	49. (d)	50. (c)

Exercise 3

1. (d)	2. (c)	3. (b)	4. (d)	5. (b)
6. (b)	7. (c)	8. (c)	9. (b)	10. (d)

11. (c)	12. (d)	13. (c)	14. (c)	15. (b)
16. (d)	17. (c)	18. (a)	19. (a)	20. (b)
21. (c)	22. (b)	23. (c)	24. (b)	25. (d)
26. (a)	27. (b)	28. (b)	29. (d)	30. (d)
31. (a)	32. (d)	33. (c)	34. (b)	35. (d)
36. (d)	37. (c)	38. (d)	39. (c)	40. (a)
41. (c)	42. (a)	43. (c)	44. (c)	45. (d)
46. (c)	47. (a)	48. (a)	49. (d)	50. (c)

Exercise 4

1. (b)	2. (d)	3. (d)	4. (b)	5. (a)
6. (d)	7. (d)	8. (c)	9. (c)	10. (c)
11. (d)	12. (c)	13. (b)	14. (a)	15. (b)
16. (b)	17. (b)	18. (a)	19. (c)	20. (a)
21. (a)	22. (c)	23. (d)	24. (c)	25. (c)
26. (b)	27. (b)	28. (d)	29. (b)	30. (b)
31. (c)	32. (d)	33. (a)	34. (c)	35. (a)
36. (a)	37. (b)	38. (d)	39. (d)	40. (b)
41. (a)	42. (d)	43. (c)	44. (b)	45. (b)
46. (a)	47. (c)	48. (d)	49. (c)	50. (b)

Explanations

Exercise 1

1. The relationship between arid and dry is one of degree of intensity. Aridity is an intense form of dryness, and saturated is an intense form of wetness. The correct choice is (d).
2. The relationship here is one of antonyms. Cacophonous and harmonious are opposites of each other, which is also the relationship between bellicose which means war-like, and pacific which means peace-loving.
3. The correct answer is (b). The relationship here is one of parent to offspring–a kangaroo's baby is a joey. While option (d) also contains two words that have the parent-offspring relationship, the words are reversed. A foal is the offspring of a horse rather than the other way around (as in the original pair).
4. Something or someone who is fickle is not decisive, which is the relationship between something that is capricious and fixed.
5. This problem is based on degree of intensity. Someone who is miserable is extremely unhappy while someone who is euphoric is extremely content.
6. This is an analogy based on definition since oriental describes the east, just as occidental describes the west.
7. Fertilizer is used to stimulate growth, just as yeast is used for stimulating leavening (rising).
8. Botany is the study of plants, just as geology is the study of the earth. In option B and D, the same relationship holds but in the reverse order. Etiology is the study of disease and astronomy is the study of stars.
9. The relationship here is of member and class. A wasp is a kind of insect, as a snake is a kind of reptile.
10. This is a definitional type of analogy. Someone who is illiterate lacks an education, while someone who is naïve lacks experience.
11. This is a degree of intensity analogy. To guzzle is to drink a lot, rapidly. Likewise, to gorge is to eat intensely.
12. Just as loneliness and privacy are synonyms, describing the state of being alone or separate from others, composure and equanimity are synonyms describing a calm or peaceful state of mind.
13. Something that is fake is lacking in genuineness. Similarly, something that is nebulous is hazy or vague, lacking in definition.
14. Something that is opaque blocks light completely. Likewise, something that is hermetic is completely sealed against the escape or entry of air. (d) is the answer.
15. Deadly and pernicious are synonyms as are rude and boorish.
16. A coverlet is made up of many pieces of cloth, just as mosaic is made up of many pieces of tile.
17. A splinter is a sharp piece of wood, while a shard is a sharp piece of glass.
18. This problem contains a part to whole analogy. A musical scale is a series of tones in a particular arrangement; similarly a spectrum is made up of a series of colours in a particular order.
19. The relationship here is person to tool (specialist to body part treated); the correct choice is (c) since a dermatologist treats the skin and an osteopath treats the bones.
20. The relationship between the two words here is that of intensity. A saunter is a leisurely stroll and a perambulate is a leisurely walk. Thus, the correct choice is (a).
21. The relationship here is that of opposite portions of the day. Nocturnal means nightly; diurnal means daily. Thus, (a) is the answer.

22. While the physician can diagnose and treat a patient with drugs, the surgeon treats a patient through an operation. The same relationship works in the case of an optometrist and an ophthalmologist.
23. The relationship here is one of action. A bull is a person who buys on the stock market, while a bear is one who sells on the stock market.
24. This is a problem based on antonyms. Just as cacophony (sound) is the opposite of euphony (pleasant sound), so also belligerent is the opposite of soothing.
25. This is a part to whole problem. The bird is covered by its feathers completely, just as a tree is covered completely by its bark. Neither (a) nor (c) can be correct since the order is reverse.
26. A conformist is one who is not rebellious, while a rebel is one who is not acquiescent.
27. The relationship is that just as an author creates a manuscript, an architect creates a blueprint.
28. The relationship here is one of tool to the product that makes it work. Thus, the answer is (a). A house does not work with bricks, and a car does not work with steel in order to run.
29. The answer is (c). The relationship here is one of opposites. Although the word pair fundamental : elemental is also opposite, it does not also show the idea of something that changes and something that is fixed.
30. Another question based on opposites. Feeble and potent are opposites, just as fertile and barren are opposites of each other.
31. The answer is (d). The relationship here is one of degree.
32. Sound is measured in decibels just as length is measured in meters.
33. The relationship here is one of part to whole.
34. The answer is (c). The relationship here is that of'Fear of'. So, Vertigo is the fear of heights while agoraphobia is the fear of spaces. The other options are using inaccurate definitions.
35. Just as the pupil is a part of the eye, so also the teeth are part of the mouth.
36. The obvious answer is (a).
37. An ascetic is defined as one who denounces luxury just as a misogynist is one who denounces women. Option (b) is incorrect since it is too broad. A capitalist might not like a communist, but that is in no way a defining characteristic.
38. Vandalism is the desecration of property just as slander is the desecration of a reputation.
39. Based on celebration. Option (d) is the best curser.
40. Based on opposites. Option (b) expresses a relationship of opposites just as the capitalized pair.
41. The answer is (a). One unriddles a mystery in thesame way that one deactivates a bomb.
42. An artist creates a painting just as a composer creates a symphony.
43. The relationship here can be described as: Horses stay in a stable, just as pigs stay in a sty.

Exercise 2

1. A necromancer is one who practices witchcraft, while a swindler practices knavery.
2. Just as you extract a tooth, you uproot a stump.
4. Islands are parts of an archipelago, just as a toe is a part of a foot. (A part to whole analogy)
5. A codicil is an addition to a will, just like an annexure is an addition to a book.
6. We get on a bus, just as we board a rowboat.
7. A mumble is indistinct, while a scribble is illegible.
8. Football is a type of sport, just as verse is a type of literature.
9. A sailor is warned by a light house, just as a person who is sleeping is warned by a smoke alarm.
10. This is a degree of intensity analogy. Simmer is a milder form of boiling just as a drizzle is a milder form of a downpour.
11. Just as we mitigate (lessen) punishment, we alleviate (lessen) pain.
12. A sapling is a baby tree, just as a puppy is a baby dog.
13. A tyre is made from rubber, while paper is made out of wood. In other words, rubber is a raw material for tyre as wood is a raw material for paper.
14. An angler uses a bait to attract fish, as a hunter uses a decoy.
15. A colony of bacterium, as a school of whales.
16. Opposites. Both the capitalized pair and option (c) represent opposite meanings.
17. Opposites. Both the capitalized pair and option (d) represent opposite meanings.
18. An optimistic person operates on hope, while an impulsive person operates on his will.
19. An album is a book designed to keep a collection of stamps just as a wardrobe is a locker designed to keep a collection of clothes.

20. A deluge is a sudden great or overwhelming rush of water just as a landslide is a sudden great or overwhelming rush of earth.
21. A carpenter constructs a cabinet just as a cobbler constructs a boot.
22. To fidget is to show uneasiness (mental or physical uneasiness). To seethe is to show anger.
23. Someone frank and candid lacks reticence just as someone merciless lacks sympathy.
24. Disagreement is characterized by a lack of harmony. Similarly, impartiality is characterized by a lack of prejudice.
25. A key turns on an ignition. A switch turns on a light.
26. A bucket holds water and water can be poured from a bucket. A shaker holds salt and salt can be poured from a shaker.
27. Humans live in town as animals live in a jungle.
28. A caterpillar feeds on leaves, while a moth feeds on wool.
29. A tally is a recorded account of votes. A census is a recorded account of population.
30. A lull is a temporary halt in storm. A recess is a temporary halt in business.
31. Raisins are made from grapes, just as sugar is made out of cane.
32. Just as a library is a place for books, a zoo is a place for animals.
33. Noise is heard through the ear just as one smells through the nose.
34. A commendation is an expression of praise. A slander is an expression of disparagement.
35. To outpace someone is to surpass that person in speed, to outwit someone is to surpass that person in cunning.
36. When you look at something, you see it. Similarly, when you touch something, you feel it.
37. To imperil someone is to involve him in danger. To entangle someone is to involve him in conflict.
38. The purpose of a godown is storage of goods. The purpose of a motel is lodging people.

    Answer (b) is incorrect. It is a trap; although linen is stored in a closet, you cannot say that "the purpose of a closet is linen".

    Answer (c) is also incorrect. It is also a trap; although a hangar is where you store a plane, you can't say, "the purpose of a hangar is a plane".
39. A bracelet is worn on the wrist just as a hat is worn on the head.
40. Wooden is used as a synonym of rigid here. Similarly, obstinate is the synonym of stubborn.
41. The feel of satin is soft, while the feel of iron is hard.
42. One-hundred paise make a rupee, just as a hundred years make a century.
43. An axle is used to steer a vehicle, just as a knife is used to slice things.
44. A desert is infertile, just as a jungle is verdant (green).
45. Sores represent damage to feet, just as wrinkles represent damage to skin.
46. Just as a top spins, the earth rotates.
47. Milk gets destroyed when it gets spoilt and a flower gets destroyed when it wilts.
48. Munificence represents generosity, just as vivaciousness represents happiness.
49. To get off a ship one disembarks. To get off a horse, one dismounts from it.
50. Retreating and advancing are opposite actions. Similarly, dorsal and ventral are adjectives which refer to the back and front of an animal's body. All other choices are synonyms in nature.

EXERCISE 3

1. A teacher gives instruction and a sentinel gives protection.
2. An usher shows people to their seats in a theater. A conductor shows people to their seats on a train.
3. Practice builds skill just as exercise builds strength.
4. This is a functional analogy. A chimney is used to conduct smoke, just as a pipe is used to conduct water.
5. This is a degree of intensity based analogy. Damage is a less intense degree of destruction than demolish. Similarly, yapping is much less intense than howling.
6. To stammer impedes talking, to stagger impedes walking.
7. The analogy is based on the relationship of opposites. Just as fret is the opposite of relax, resist is the opposite of surrender.
8. A joey is a young kangaroo, just as a kitten is a young cat.
9. A rink is a place to skate, just as a stadium is a place to play. Alternately, we skate in a rink, just as we play in a stadium.

10. A serf is bound to the bidding of his or her lord just as a subject is bound to the bidding of his or her ruler.
11. There are several spokes in a wheel just as there are several rungs in a ladder.
12. A gaggle is a group of geese. A bevy is a group of bees.
13. Scales cover the body of fish, just as feathers cover the body of birds. (a), (b), (d)–don't make sense when the relation is applied. Each is a filler.
14. A car is a kind of means of transportation just as a shovel is a kind of tool.
15. One stores goods in a godown just as one stores weapons in an arsenal.
16. A terrorist is someone who spreads terror just as a mutineer is someone who spreads a mutiny.
17. Reckless is the negative extreme of daring just as obsequious is the negative extreme of being deferential.
18. Just as a prism is a solid figure which is triangular, a cylinder is a solid figure that is circular.
19. The nose is a part of the head just as the hand is a part of the arm.
20. A goldfish and a trout are two different sorts of fish just as a parrot and a sparrow are two different sorts of birds.
21. A manger is a feeding bin for cattle just as a trough is a feeding bin for animals.
22. Sugar is added to food to sweeten it, while pepper is added to food to season it.
23. The relationship here is one of degree of intensity. To smash something is to do much greater damage than merely to crack it, just as shrieking has a much greater intensity than murmuring.
24. Baldness is the lack of hair, just as aridity is the lack of rain.
25. Equanimity is ruffled (when it is affected negatively) just as balance is disturbed.
26. A statue is unveiled just as a movie is premiered.
27. Renovation removes decrepitude, just as reconciliation removes estrangement.
28. A braggart (boaster) is not modest just as a visionary (dreamer) is not practical.
29. A potboiler is a trivial or inferior literary work produced by a novelist just as a doggerel is a trivial verse produced by a poet.
30. Ligaments connect bones just as sinews connect muscles.
31. It is necessary for a craftsman to be dexterous just as it is essential for a gymnast to be agile.
32. Just as a chef uses a recipe to make a particular meal, a dressmaker uses a pattern to enable the making of an article of clothing.
33. Meaning determines whether two words are synonyms. Sound determines whether two words are homonyms.
34. A bat is a mammal that is mistakenly thought to be a bird. A whale is a mammal that is mistakenly thought to be a fish.
35. A dancer performs to spectators just as a singer performs to an audience.
36. Gloves are worn in the hands, just as socks are worn on the legs.
37. Meat contains protein just as potatoes contain starch.
38. An analogy based on degree of intensity. Both praise and extol mean the same thing, however extol means praise very greatly. Similar is the case with dislike and loathe, since loathe is to dislike intensely.
40. Olfactory relates to the sense of smell, as tactile relates to the sense of smell.
41. Suave and sophisticated are synonyms of each other.
42. The vixen is the female of a fox, just as the mare is the female of the horse.
43. Sluggish and inert are synonyms of each other. So are bad and evil.
44. Something that is bovine (cow like) is herbivorous, just as something that is leonine (lion like) is carnivorous.
45. Buzz and hum are synonyms, just as chime and ring.
46. Venison is deer meat, while pork is pig meat.
47. A synagogue is a place of religion, just as a court is a place of law.
48. Relation of opposites.
49. A degree of intensity based analogy. Tipsy means slightly drunk, as pleased means slightly thrilled.
50. A cause and effect based analogy. Just as a spasm causes pain, hurt causes agony.

SECTION 3: Fill in the Blanks

This section will help you in the following ways:

- In the chapter on Sentence Completion (fill in the blanks), you would get exposed to questions having single blanks, double blanks and multiple blanks in a paragraph. Single and double blank questions are a constant nowadays in the CAT, XAT and all other MBA entrance examinations.
- Besides the exercises at various levels of difficulty as also original CAT questions of this type would give you an opportunity to practise and benchmark your skills in Sentence Completion.

BLOCK 1: Theory

In this block, through the theory of sentence completion you will learn:

1. The difference between reactive and proactive solving of sentence completion questions.
2. The various steps you should go through when you are reading the sentence completion questions for the first time.
3. To identify the types of sentence structures and the process of identification of the key words.

Sentence structures you would learn to recognise and anticipate include:

(a) Cause and Effect
(b) Parallelism and Reiteration
(c) Similarity of Support
(d) Contrast

You are advised to go through the theory closely and use it to extend your basic understanding of language in all your reading activity.

In This Block	*Chapter 10* **Sentence Completion**

BLOCK 2: LODs and CAT Questions

Having seen and understood the theory and process of solving sentence-completion questions, it is now time for you to work on applying what you have learnt.

The following chapters (11 to 13) contain Exercises on Sentence Completion on varying Levels of Difficulty (LODs).

- Chapter 11 contains LOD I questions
- Chapter 12 contains LOD II questions
- Chapter 13 contains Previous Years' Questions on Sentence

Completion that have been asked in the CAT

You are required to solve each level of difficulty and try to find out the major sources of error for you -

Is it due to your lack of vocabulary

Or

Due to your inability to understand the language and the relationships within the sentence?

Based on this analysis, you would need to work on improving your ability to solve such questions - either by working on your vocabulary or by working towards improving your ability to comprehend sentences.

In This Block	*Chapter 11* **Level of Difficulty—I**
	Chapter 12 **Level of Difficulty—II**
	Chapter 13 **Previous Years' Questions from CAT**

CHAPTER 10

Sentence Completion

WHAT ARE SENTENCE COMPLETION QUESTIONS?

Sentence completion questions test your vocabulary skills as well as your reading ability. These problems contain a single sentence expressing a complete idea that can be understood without any additional information. This is quite unlike the reading comprehension questions, which require you to read long passages. Each sentence contains one, two or three blanks, which need to be filled up appropriately. These questions typically contain four options to fill in the blanks in the sentence. From these choices, you need to select the words or phrases that fit into the blanks to best complete the sentence.

This question type tests the student's ability to understand the main idea of the sentence and the logical structure of the sentence. It also tests the ability of the student to anticipate what idea conveyed by a particular word will most aptly fit into the blank provided. Besides, your vocabulary is also tested because there is not much you can do if you are unaware of the word/s contained in the question or in the options. Your knowledge of roots, prefixes and suffixes will come in handy.

In order to successfully solve the sentence completion section, the student should have a strong understanding of the relationships within the sentence. These relationships might include the use of equivalents, analogies, parallel sets, contrasts and word clusters. Solving the sentence completion section will draw on your adeptness and facility with antonyms and synonyms, your understanding of parallel sets, and the breadth and depth of your general vocabulary.

The Cream of the Piece

Needless to say, having a good vocabulary helps in doing better at this question type. The student is hence advised to work on his/her vocabulary simultaneously in order to improve his/her ability at this type of question. However, even if you are caught short in your vocabulary by a particular question, you can still try to solve it by following a few rules which are enumerated below.

REACTIVE SOLVING VERSUS PROACTIVE SOLVING

In our observation, a critical mistake that students end up committing while solving questions of sentence completion is trying to solve these questions by going through the options and trying to fit the options in the sentence.

We call this reactive solving and this process leads to students committing avoidable errors. Instead, the student should consciously follow proactive solving, which is explained below.

Proactive Solving

As a conscious strategy, the student is advised to use their anticipation by following the following three-step process while solving sentence completion exercises:

Step 1 Understand the Message and the tone of the author In simple language this implies understanding what he is trying to say (message) and how he is trying to say it (tone).

(a) Understanding the message While doing this, the student should focus on identifying the principal subject/idea of the sentence–about what or whom the sentence is trying to talk. Note here that many a time, there might be more than one idea in the sentence. In such cases, the key is to understand how the two ideas are connected to each other.

While doing this, one should also try to identify the key words which the author has used to convey his message. Briefly, key words include words such as therefore, because, similarly, although, in contrast, etc.

(b) Identify the logical structure of the sentence While doing this, look for whether the sentence has one or more parts, i.e., whether it is a simple sentence or it is a complex sentence having more than one part(s), which are connected to each other through a sentence connector.

(c) Understanding the tone Ask yourself questions like whether the author is talking about the subject in a positive, neutral or negative way. Also, try to identify the degree to which the author is positive or negative about the subject.

Step 2. Anticipating words This implies anticipating the meaning of the word/s that will fill in the blanks appropriately and in particular, that it should be in sync with what the author's message and tone are.

Step 3. Scanning Scan the choices to see if the word/s you have thought of figure(s) in these choices. If not, look for a synonym/s of the word/s. However, do look through all the choices before you actually select one. Try each answer choice in the blank to see which one suits the best.

Step 4. The Final Answer Reread the sentence with your answer choice and make your assessments about the smoothness of the flow of the idea. If you find that everything matches, then you have got the correct answer to the question.

Let's look at an example of how to apply this process to reach the correct answer.

Because scientific research and the consequential assessments of whether or not global warming is occurring have been __, it has been difficult to convince the public that this phenomenon is a critical problem that needs to be addressed.

Step 1) What are the ideas in this sentence?

The *first idea* in the sentence describes the 'research and the consequential assessments of the occurrence of global warming'.

From this part of the sentence, we are getting no clue about the nature of these assessments. Hence, we get no clue about the nature of the word to be used in the blank in the sentence (that is whether it is a positive word, a negative word or a neutral word.)

The *second part* of the sentence talks about the difficulty in convincing the public about the importance of global warming. How are these two parts of the sentence connected? Essentially, both the parts of the sentence are dealing with the issue of global warming. The kind of connecting/key words used in the sentence will help us further determine the nature of the connection between the ideas contained in the two parts of the sentence.

The first word is 'because'. What does this tell us? It tells us that the information in the second part of the sentence in some way, is caused by the first part of the sentence. (As we will see later on in this chapter, this is one of the four common structures of sentence completion problems: cause-effect.)

Step 2) Think of a word that would make sense in the blank

Without even looking at the answer choices, use the information you have learned from the ideas and key words in the sentence, to guess at a possible choice of word to fill the blank. While doing this, just allow your instincts to run freely and simply react to the sentence–assuming you were the author of the same and try to fit in word/s with the most appropriate meanings into the blank/s.

If there are two blanks, think of a set of two words that would make sense for each one.

In our example, the presence of the word "because" tells us that the second idea is caused by the first idea. We know that some factor about the scientific research and the consequential assessments of global warming has made it difficult to convince the public that it is a problem.

What type of scientific research and assessments must these be?

They must not be convincing/believable or in some way, must be lacking in credibility, otherwise the public would know that this issue was important. Therefore, some appropriate words that might make sense in the blank would be words that describe the scientific studies as lacking in some way: unpersuasive, not credible, deficient, or unbelievable. If we again read the sentence with one of these words substituted into the blank, the sentence makes sense.

Step 3) Scan the choices

Let us suppose that the options given to us were:

(A) well-designed
(B) inconclusive
(C) substantial
(D) irrefutable

We are looking for an answer choice that is similar in meaning to not credible, deficient, or unbelievable. Something that will make the public unconvinced about the gravity of the problem.

Well-designed is opposite to the idea we need; if the assessments were well-designed, it would be easy to convince the public.

Inconclusive seems to be similar to the idea we were looking for, so we can hold onto that one. The last two choices, substantial and irrefutable are again more opposite in meaning to our guess word, so we can eliminate these two.

Note: Even though inconclusive fits our idea in the first place, make it a habit to check out all the options. Very often, more than one word will have the same general meaning as your guess word, and you will need to narrow it down and then choose the best-fitting word.

It is quite common in these problem types to find words opposite in meaning to your guess word among the answer choices.

Step 4) The Final Answers

If you have narrowed down to a particular answer choice that reflects the idea of your guess word, reread the sentence to see if the logic follows when you substitute that word into the blank. If you have only narrowed down your choices to a few, read the sentence with each of the possible choices. For problems with two blanks, it is often the case that you will be able to eliminate some of the choices because the first word does not fit well into the blank and others because the second word doesn't fit. Together, you can eliminate more of the incorrect answer choices and narrow it down to the correct choice.

TYPES OF SENTENCE STRUCTURES AND KEY WORDS

Having seen the process applied to one particular problem, let us now look at the four common types of sentence structures and some key words, which are the basis of the basic problem types, viz: Cause & Effect, Reiteration, Similarities/Parallelisms & Contrast.

TYPE I. CAUSE AND EFFECT

As seen in the solved example above, a common sentence structure seen in the CAT is one that contains two ideas, where one causes the other. In other words, one is the cause of the other (which then becomes the effect). Needless to say, the two ideas have to be related to the same principal topic.

Key words that may indicate cause and effect include: because, as a result, thus, resulting from, hence, therefore, consequently, causes, leading to, due to.

The Cream of the Piece

The typical sentence structures of cause and effect are as follows. In the following notations, imagine two ideas related to the same principal topic. Let A be the effect of B, which is the cause of A i.e. B $\rightarrow$ A.

(i) A **Because** B,
(ii) **Because** B, **Hence** A
(iii) A **as a result of** B,
(iv) B **thus** A,
(v) B **therefore** A,
(vi) B **causes** A,
(vii) A **due to** B,
(viii) B **consequently** A
(ix) B **leading to** A

Let's look at an example:

Because of Jim Carrey's reputation as a comic actor, suited best for playing hilarious roles, the director was ___ considering him for the more serious role of the solemn monk.

(A) discouraged from (B) encouraged to
(C) irrelevant to (D) ambivalent of

The sentence structure here is:

Because A, hence B.

Note here that the 'hence' is silent in this sentence and its meaning is implied.

The key word 'because' should indicate to you that this is a cause and effect sentence. The first part of the sentence gives us the cause–Jim Carrey's reputation as an actor playing comic roles. What impact would this history have on the suitability of the actor to play a more serious role? It is most likely, to cause some doubts in the director's mind, and he might be unwilling or reluctant to cast him in this new role. Looking through the answer choices, the correct answer is A, **discouraged from**.

Many a times, the effect is a chronological follow up of the cause, i.e., the effect comes later in time to the cause. Here's an example:

The mass release of greenhouse gases causes a detrimental effect on the environment of the whole world.

Today, advanced computer technology can _____ information from a number of sources, then automatically ___ the data and draw conclusions from the same.

(A) collate...analyse
(B) extrapolate...assemble
(C) adjudicate...assemble
(D) research...expand

The first part of the sentence deals with something that computer technology can do; the second part deals with the next part of a two-part process. First, guess at a word that would fill the first blank and look through the answer choices.

One possible guess would be that computers "collect" or "compare" information. Choice A, collate, means to compare or examine, so this is a reasonable choice. Choice B–extrapolate–means to use existing data to make predictions. Although this does not fit with our guess word, this seems a reasonable thing to do with information, so let's keep this choice for now. Choice C–adjudicate–means to settle a dispute; this can be eliminated since it does not make sense in this situation. Choice D–research–can also be eliminated since computers are tools of research and cannot do research themselves.

Now move on to the second blank. Remember, the first part of the sentence describes something that must be done before what is done in the second part of the sentence (we know this because of the 'then'). Can we select between choices A and B now? Choice A makes sense: information is collated and then analysed to draw conclusions. Choice B does not make sense in terms of cause and effect. Extrapolation is done from existing information, and an assembly would not be a consequence. Hence, choice A is the correct answer.

Type II. Reiteration or Restatement/Parallelisms

Sentences of this type again, will usually have two ideas, one of which clarifies or further supports the other. The ideas will have the same general meaning, but will be restated in a slightly more explanatory way. Sometimes, such sentences will also have the reiteration in the form of an explanatory example.

The Cream of the Piece

Key words to identify reiteration type sentences are: in fact, in other words, surely, to be sure, and, namely, that is, furthermore and likewise.

The typical sentence structure is (A and B are ideas):

(i) A **in fact** B, (ii) A **in other words** B,
(iii) A **and** B, (iv) A **likewise** B,
(v) A **that is** B, (vi) A **namely** B,
(vii) A **surely** B

Here is an example:

He was the most __ person he had ever met; in fact, his magnanimity knew no limits.

(A) charitable (B) miserly
(C) reclusive (D) prolific

Looking for the key words in the sentence, we notice the in fact connecting the two ideas contained in the two parts of the sentence. Hence, you should be able to identify the sentence as one wherein the two ideas are reiterations of one another. Hence, the second idea reiterates or supports the first idea. In this case, the second idea is complete in itself, describing the magnanimity of the person. The first part of the sentence has to be parallel to this part. Hence, the blank has to be filled in with a synonym for magnanimity. When we read the answer choices, we can see that the best match to our requirement is Option A.

Let's look at another example:

The Age of Enlightenment, acknowledged as one of the greatest periods of history for intellectual activity, exhibited a proclivity for literalism and______ argumentation.

(A) credible
(B) specious
(C) pensive
(D) congruous

The key word here is and, which shows that this sentence has a reiteration element in it. The two ideas should be parallel to each other and hence, should be reiterations of each other. The first part of the sentence describes that the kind of intellectual activity that occurred during the age of Enlightenment showed a proclivity for literalism. Now, if you don't know what literalism means, you will have difficulty in determining which of the choices is synonymous with it and will successfully complete the sentence. Literalism describes an argument that sounds plausible, but is actually misleading or fallacious. Since this is a negative comment, the second part of the sentence must also be negative. Option A and D are basically positive and can be eliminated. Choice B is negative; this turns out to be the correct answer as specious argumentation is synonymous with literalism. Choice C can be eliminated as it has no relevance in the current sentence (we are looking for an adjective to describe argumentation and there is nothing called pensive argumentation).

Type III. Similarity or Support

Sentences of this type compare distinct but similar ideas. When choosing a word to fill the blank, you must look for a word that allows the two ideas of the sentence to be similar in meaning.

The Cream of the Piece

Key words for similarity sentence completions are: likewise, in the same way, for instance, similarly, furthermore, as, same, just as, specifically, such as, as an example, resembles, like and also.

Examples of sentence structures used for similarities are (A and B are ideas):

(i) A **likewise** B, (ii) **Just as** A, **similarly** B, (iii) A **like** B

Just as television surpassed radio as the major source of entertainment and information for the world, it seems destined that the Internet will eventually ___ television.

(A) invigorate (B) alter
(C) eliminate (D) supplant

The key words here are 'just as,' and they suggest that this is a sentence based on the similarity of the argument. Hence, we should look for a word that will allow the two ideas of the sentence to be similar. The defining word in the first idea is surpassed. Since we need a word that will convey the same meaning as the first idea, we are looking for a word similar to surpass. If we work through the options, we can eliminate all but C and D. Both might make sense in the context of the sentence, but D, supplant, is more similar to the original idea of surpassing, rather than eliminating, which is too drastic in the context of the question.

It is characteristic of old age to sap a man's ebullience and rob him of his natural___.

(A) senility (B) vigor
(C) maturity (D) insensibility

The key connector here is 'and' which hints at the similarity of the ideas. The first part of the sentence describes a negative fact about old age, namely, that a man starts to lose his ebullience. Since the two parts of the sentence are joined by 'and', the second idea contained in the sentence must also state something negative related to aging. Just as a man's ebullience is lost with old age, we are looking for a positive attribute that is lost with aging. Option A and D can be directly eliminated in this context since senility and insensibility are both negative attributes (in fact, senility generally arrives with old age and not the other way round.) Option C, maturity can also be eliminated since it is a positive that arrives with old age and does not go away. That leaves us with option B, vigor, which is a positive attribute that goes away with old age. As a further insurance of the answer, always make it a habit to reread the complete sentence with the selected option. Here, it makes complete sense.

Type IV. Contras

Contrast sentences contain ideas that are opposite to one another or are dissimilar to each other.

The Cream of the Piece

Key words indicating a contrast in the ideas of the sentence include:

Although, but, despite, in spite of, however, as against, as opposed to, whereas, on the contrary, yet, on the other hand, On the one hand.... On the other, surprisingly, unlike, in contrast, rather, and Even though.

Examples of sentence structures used for contrast (A and B are ideas).

(i) A **although** B, (ii) A **yet** B, (iii) A **on the contrary** B, (iv) **On the one hand** A, (v) **On the other** B (vi) A **unlike** B (vii) A **in contrast to** B

In a large group of people consisting of strangers, Aishwarya often seemed ___ and aloof, although among her friends and family she was quite ___.

(A) reticent...convivial
(B) gregarious...outgoing
(C) detrimental...multifarious
(D) unattainable.... taciturn

The "although" tells us that this is a sentence that contains a contrast in its ideas, so the two parts of the sentence should contain opposite ideas. Since both the parts describe Aishwarya's behavior, the two words should logically describe opposite behaviors. Hence, the description of Aishwarya's behavior in a large group of people should be different from her behavior when she is with her friends and family. (If we look through our answer choices, choices B and D can be removed immediately since they contain synonyms, not antonyms.)

What else do we know about the words that will best fit the blanks? Notice the use of the conjunction **'and'** used to connect the word in the first blank and aloof. The use of and between two descriptive adjectives describing behaviors can only mean that the two should be similar to each other and should mean the same thing. Of our answer choices, which of the first words in the pair is most similar to aloof? Both reticent and unattainable are reasonable choices. Gregarious and detrimental don't seem to make a lot of sense, so we can exclude those. Once you have narrowed down your options as much as possible on the basis of the first word, look at the second word, which has to be opposite in meaning to the first word. Between A and D, option A is the best choice.

The Cream of the Piece

Summary of basic strategy for sentence completion problems

Read the sentence and determine the principal idea/s to which the sentence is related. Learn the four main types of sentence completion problems and look for these problems in the exam.

Look for key words. Again, knowing the key words for each of the four major types of sentence completion problems will enable you to recognize the type of sentence and quickly know what kind of word you need to complete the logic of the sentence.

Think of a word that would make sense in the blank. Do this before even looking at the answer choices.

Look at the option choices that give you the closest fit to your guess word. Re-read the sentence with the filled in option to see the coherence of the sentence with the word before marking the answer.

CHAPTER 11

Level of Difficulty—I

EXERCISE 1

Directions: Fill in the blanks with the appropriate words from the options given below. Do not use the same word twice.

Options: abolished, abated, abdicated, abandoned, able, rebates, capable, abridged, banished, capacious, abbreviation, about, bear, exile, bared, sale, war, barter, battle, above.

1. Lord Buddha .... his kingship and became a hermit.
2. The Indian government .... slavery.
3. The residents .... the haunted house.
4. The rain .... after some time.
5. The shops offer .... in the off season.
6. Our government is .... to confront any type of situation.
7. He is .... of solving this problem.
8. Confucius possessed a .... mind.
9. B.A. is an .... of 'Bachelor of Arts'.
10. .... versions of classics are easier to read than the original versions.
11. It was .... ten in the night when we reached home.
12. The painting was hung .... the window.
13. The Shah of Iraq was .... from his country.
14. Prospero, a character of Shakespeare's play 'The Tempest', was living in ....
15. The patient .... his chest when the doctor examined him.
16. We have to .... our own burdens.
17. Napoleon was killed in the .... of Waterloo.
18. The world is on the verge of a third world ....
19. .... is an economic transaction involving exchange of articles.
20. This premises is for ....

EXERCISE 2

Directions: Fill in the blanks with the appropriate words from the options given below. Do not use the same word twice:

Options: bend, calamity, bow, captivated, dainty, elect, captured, careful, deduced, select, catastrophe, tragedy, cautious, character, conduct, decimated, delicate, delicious, destroy, fascinating.

1. can .... my head till my toes.
2. Lord Rama had to break Shiva's .... in order to marry Sita.
3. Alexander the Great .... many kingdoms.
4. The movie Sholay .... whosoever saw it.
5. The Niagara Falls is a .... place to visit.
6. Sita had to give a test of her .... after coming back from the clutches of Ravana.
7. The codes of .... are specified in every job.
8. We .... our clothes from the choices that we have.
9. We .... our own representatives.
10. The floods are a natural ....
11. The movie Titanic was a ....
12. The atom bomb dropped on Hiroshima and Nagasaki resulted in a ....
13. We should be .... of wild animals when we are walking through a forest.

14. We should be .... to speak the right thing at the right time.
15. The daisy is a .... flower.
16. Porcelain statues are very ....
17. Lucknow is very famous for its .... kebabs.
18. The Tsunami incident .... a large number of people.
19. Sometimes one has to .... to recreate.
20. This theory has been .... from the observed data.

EXERCISE 3

Options: absolute, efficacious, anxious, ballad, curious, ballet, decrease, differs, reduce, diminishes, eagerly, effective, bail, effectual, elder, guarantee, older, deferred, efficient.

1. We should try to .... our wants.
2. The payment was ....
3. Coke .... from coffee in taste and flavour.
4. There is a .... in the sale of geysers in the summer.
5. With age, the physical beauty of every person ....
6. The students .... wait for the exams to end.
7. Children, by nature, are a .... lot.
8. Akhil is .... about the results of his examinations.
9. Lord Krishna's advice to Arjuna proved ....
10. Rajeev used .... methods to convince his students.
11. Sunil is an .... worker.
12. The treatment given by the doctor to the patient was ....
13. Ram was Lakshman's .... brother.
14. Balram was much .... than Krishna.
15. A .... is necessary to get the accused released from custody.
16. Nowadays, all companies give a .... of their products.
17. A .... is a type of traditional song, conveying a story.
18. The .... dancers have to get initiated.
19. The .... power in a democracy is in the hands of the common people.

EXERCISE 4

Options: accepted, quiet, accomplished, achievement, gathers, acquaintances, acquitted, incident, agreed, amassing, applauded, attaining, discharged, accident, factual, acclaimed, familiarity, obsolete, quite, accumulate,

1. The usage of a word like thou is .... in common conversation.
2. The coffee is .... good.
3. It was very .... in the church.
4. Rahul .... the offer given to him.
5. The teacher .... to arrange for extra classes for weak students.
6. The boy was injured when he met with an ....
7. The tsunami .... left a great impact on anyone who even remotely heard about it.
8. Amitabh is widely .... as a great actor.
9. The mayor .... the efforts of the citizens to protect the environment.
10. If dusting is not done regularly, wooden furniture has a tendency to .... dust.
11. The politicians are only concerned with ...... wealth.
12. It has been truly said that a rolling stone .... no moss.
13. For India, to get a permanent place in the UN Security Council will be a great ....
14. For management students, ... the position of the C.E.O of a big company is the final goal.
15. Our first President, Dr. Rajendra Prasad was an .... scholar.
16. All our .... cannot become our friends.
17. The proverb that .... breeds contempt holds true for all relationships.
18. Innocent people who have been falsely charged with a crime should be .... as soon as they are proved not guilty.
19. The patient was .... from the hospital.
20. He gave a .... account of the accident.

EXERCISE 5

Options: accentuate, congenial, action, bow, actuate, adjoining, congenital, adjourned, diffused, auction, bend, benefactor, beneficiaries, benefits, bough, defusing, intrusive, pestilent, postponed, urge.

1. Every .... has an equal and opposite reaction.
2. The sword of Tipu Sultan was recently bought at an .... by an Indian.
3. The vitamins .... the human body to fight against diseases.
4. We should .... the right words while reciting poetry.
5. Sometimes, even the most honest people have to .... the rules to do the right things.
6. We .... before God to show our reverence.

7. The word .... has been replaced by the word branch in common conversation.
8. The greatest .... of all is God.
9. Adversity has its .... too.
10. The areas ....river banks are generally fertile as they are rich in alluvial soil.
11. The parliament is .... at the end of each session.
12. The exams when .... create problems for the students.
13. .... should be thankful to their benefactors.
14. .... lighting creates a pleasant ambience.
15. .... a bomb requires skill as well as courage.
16. Some diseases are .... and cannot be cured.
17. The atmosphere was .... in the new workplace, so Shyam did not feel uneasy.
18. The online popup advertising is very .... and distracts the surfer.
19. Sleeping sickness is caused by the bite of the .... tse-tse fly.
20. An .... can also be described as a strong inclination.

EXERCISE 6

Directions: Choose the best option.

1. This is a .... on his character.
   (a) blot (b) blur
   (c) slur (d) spot
   (e) mark
2. This is a good .... for a picnic.
   (a) plot (b) spot
   (c) scene (d) landscape
3. The .... of the state is efficient.
   (a) administration (b) democracy
   (c) policy (d) autocracy
   (e) plutocracy
4. The .... of private limited companies is in the hands of its directors.
   (a) managers (b) administrators
   (c) management (d) department
   (e) society
5. Ram the prince of Ayodhya .... his siblings.
   (a) adorned (b) adored
   (c) vitiated (d) endangered
   (e) abhored
6. The Christmas tree was .... with stars and other decorative items.
   (a) adorned (b) endowed
   (c) encased (d) enticed
   (e) encompassed
7. There is no place for .... in an accountant's job.
   (a) assets (b) asserts
   (c) errors (d) duffers
8. A wise person is one who learns from his ....
   (a) errors (b) mistakes
   (c) falsities (d) lies
   (e) bad manners
9. Many companies ask their employees to sign a .... of secrecy.
   (a) agreement (b) bond
   (c) bondage (d) espionage
   (e) treaty
10. Slaves were freed from .... only after they died.
    (a) ablution (b) pilferage
    (c) agreement (d) bondage
    (e) abolition
11. Before the .... of the Europeans in India, India was a free country.
    (a) entry (b) amalgamation
    (c) emigration (d) advent
    (e) immigration
12. Duryodhana was the main .... of the Pandavas.
    (a) enmity (b) adversary
    (c) effrontery (d) adversity
    (e) disparage
13. Gandhi .... the cause of the untouchables.
    (a) blessed (b) held
    (c) advocated (d) argued
    (e) confronted
14. All citizens should be ready to .... their country.
    (a) defend (b) uphold
    (c) nurture (d) assert
    (e) convoy
15. Smoking .... health.
    (a) effects (b) kills
    (c) affects (d) rejects
    (e) underestimates
16. The theory of cause and .... explains many mysteries of the universe.
    (a) affect (b) effect
    (c) reasons (d) concept
    (e) conquer
17. It is difficult to drink from a cup which is full to the ....
    (a) top (b) edge
    (c) brim (d) circumference
    (e) topmost

18. .... and ecstasy are two sides of a puzzle called life.
    (a) pain (b) penury
    (c) agony (d) anguish
    (e) elation
19. Leo experienced great .... when his pet dog died.
    (a) pain (b) anguish
    (c) losses (d) serendipity
    (e) mourning
20. A .... of fresh air relaxes a tense mind.
    (a) breathe (b) volley
    (c) gulp (d) breath
    (e) brush
21. Pollution causes a lot of .... problems.
    (a) breath (b) breathe
    (c) breather (d) breathing
    (e) brethren
22. If a rider doesn't hold the .... correctly, he can fall.
    (a) bridle (b) bridal
    (c) whip (d) saddle
    (e) pedal
23. Ali's horse is of an excellent ....
    (a) brood (b) steed
    (c) breed (d) stood
    (e) quality
24. Her complaints .... with the complaints we have received from others.
    (a) agree (b) similar
    (c) identical (d) tally
    (e) accord
25. His opinion .... with the general opinion of the experts on this matter.
    (a) concurs (b) tally
    (c) assert (d) assimilate
    (e) simulate
26. The ruling party found itself in full .... with the opposition.
    (a) opinion (b) accord
    (c) record (d) discordant
    (e) swing
27. The jury's views .... with those of the lawyer on the issues of crime and punishment.
    (a) coincided (b) ally
    (c) approve (d) apprise
    (e) assert
28. Her ideas do not .... to the general definition of civilization.
    (a) review (b) conform
    (c) opine (d) confirm
    (e) contrite
29. The committee .... of all the changes in the report.
    (a) dissent (b) assented
    (c) approved (d) argued
    (e) accorded
30. The political .... of the1980s and 90s resulted in a civil war.
    (a) accord (b) discord
    (c) contentment (d) discretion
    (e) descent
31. The president has .... to the demands to release secret documents related to the army.
    (a) acceded (b) refused
    (c) endorsed (d) vetoed
    (e) incited
32. The leading newspaper has revealed that the PM had .... in the secret decision to sell arms to the dictator.
    (a) countenance (b) acquiesced
    (c) forewarned (d) accede
    (e) espionaged
33. The King has .... to a proposal to enhance the powers of the council of ministers.
    (a) coincided (b) allied
    (c) assented (d) opined
    (e) identified
34. The disciplinary committee has .... the use of detention after classes as a punishment for bad behaviour.
    (a) extended (b) authorised
    (c) clamped (d) embargo
    (e) intended
35. The judge .... the use of capital punishment for serious crimes.
    (a) franchised (b) endorse
    (c) agreed (d) condoned
    (e) endured
36. The committee was in favour of the proposal but the president .... it.
    (a) vetoed (b) countenance
    (c) sanctioned (d) condoned
    (e) assented
37. The cabinet has .... a proposal to change the way private educational institutions are funded and managed.
    (a) acceded (b) actualize
    (c) endorsed (d) approve
    (e) franchised
38. The generals from the opposing armies declared a/an ....
    (a) armistice (b) treaty
    (c) parley (d) accord
    (e) summit

39. The two sides in the civil war signed a peace ....
(a) truce (b) accord
(c) partey (d) pretext
(e) review

40. Tony offered his most heartfelt .... for having offended everyone.
(a) sorry (b) pardon
(c) excuse (d) apology
(e) application

41. Wearing a safety helmet is .... in this area.
(a) obligatory (b) option
(c) compulsion (d) resolved
(e) contented

42. Some courses are optional but Maths and English are ....
(a) compulsion (b) compulsory
(c) essential (d) referential
(e) important

43. Jess caused her parents a lot of .... when she was a teenager.
(a) problem (b) yearning
(c) anxiety (d) vex
(e) compulsion

44. In all .... Hursh will get the job.
(a) likelihood (b) odds
(c) options (d) candidates
(e) evens

45. At first there were some .... with the software, but it's okay now.
(a) pitfalls (b) impediments
(c) ordeal (d) snags

46. The only .... with the proposal is that it is a little expensive.
(a) glitch (b) blunder
(c) hardship (d) dilemma
(e) snag

47. To use a sporting ...., middle age is like half-time at a hockey match.
(a) device (b) analogy
(c) antonym (d) synonym
(e) acronym

48. Jaya knew that to apologise would be .... to admitting she had failed.
(a) equate (b) assumed
(c) tantamount (d) abrogate
(e) about

49. Mr. Sharma's shop was .... from all the others in the street.
(a) indistinguishable (b) inalienable
(c) akin (d) disreputable
(e) impregnable

50. There are several .... categories of nouns in the English language.
(a) various (b) disparate
(c) discrete (d) divergent
(e) types

Answer Key

Exercise 1

1. abdicated	**2.** abolished	**3.** abandoned
4. abated	**5.** rebates	**6.** able
7. capable	**8.** capacious	**9.** abbreviation
10. abridged	**11.** about	**12.** above
13. banished	**14.** exile	**15.** bared
16. bear	**17.** battle	**18.** war
19. barter	**20.** sale	

Exercise 2

1. bend	**2.** bow	**3.** captured
4. captivated	**5.** fascinating	**6.** character
7. conduct	**8.** select	**9.** elect
10. calamity	**11.** tragedy	**12.** catastrophe
13. cautious	**14.** careful	**15.** dainty
16. delicate	**17.** delicious	**18.** decimated
19. destroy	**20.** deduced	

Exercise 3

1. reduce	**2.** deferred	**3.** differs
4. decrease	**5.** diminishes	**6.** eagerly
7. curious	**8.** anxious	**9.** effective
10. efficacious	**11.** efficient	**12.** effectual
13. elder	**14.** older	**15.** bail
16. guarantee	**17.** ballad	**18.** ballet
19. absolute		

Exercise 4

1. obsolete	**2.** quite	**3.** quiet
4. accepted	**5.** agreed	**6.** accident
7. incident	**8.** acclaimed	**9.** applauded
10. accumulate	**11.** amassing	**12.** gathers
13. achievement	**14.** attaining	**15.** accomplished
16. acquaintances	**17.** familiarity	**18.** acquitted
19. discharged	**20.** factual	

EXERCISE 5

1. action	**2.** auction	**3.** actuate
4. accentuate	**5.** bend	**6.** bow
7. bough	**8.** benefactor	**9.** benefits
10. adjoining	**11.** adjourned	**12.** postponed
13. beneficiaries	**14.** diffused	**15.** defusing
16. congenital	**17.** congenial	**18.** intrusive
19. pestilent	**20.** urge	

EXERCISE 6

1. (c)	**2.** (b)	**3.** (a)	**4.** (c)	**5.** (b)
6. (a)	**7.** (c)	**8.** (b)	**9.** (b)	**10.** (d)
11. (d)	**12.** (b)	**13.** (c)	**14.** (a)	**15.** (c)
16. (b)	**17.** (c)	**18.** (c)	**19.** (b)	**20.** (d)
21. (d)	**22.** (a)	**23.** (c)	**24.** (d)	**25.** (a)
26. (b)	**27.** (a)	**28.** (b)	**29.** (c)	**30.** (b)
31. (a)	**32.** (b)	**33.** (c)	**34.** (b)	**35.** (d)
36. (a)	**37.** (c)	**38.** (a)	**39.** (b)	**40.** (d)
41. (a)	**42.** (b)	**43.** (c)	**44.** (a)	**45.** (d)
46. (a)	**47.** (b)	**48.** (c)	**49.** (a)	**50.** (c)

CHAPTER 12 Level of Difficulty—II

Exercise 1

Directions: Choose the correct option.

1. George Bernard Shaw said that the contemporary social values could be flippant and .... at some times.
   (a) important (b) profound
   (c) inane (d) riveting
   (e) absurd
2. .... the general had been told by the field staff that continuing warfare would be .... to his soldiers, he insisted on deploying more battle tanks.
   (a) Although, detrimental
   (b) Because, instrumental
   (c) Although, formidable
   (d) Because, immediate
   (e) Because, incremental
3. The Senate warned the Prime Minister that if he did not accept their advice, the differences between the Legislative and the Executive arms of the Government would be ....
   (a) eliminated (b) eroded
   (c) exacerbated (d) exemplified
   (e) exasperated
4. Most journalistic writing could do with .... of paragraphs to make the prose more ....
   (a) suppression, legible
   (b) removal, argumentative
   (c) simplification, abstruse
   (d) deletion, succinct
   (e) exemplification, incoherent
5. Varun was accused of murdering his wife, and though he was never ...., he never recovered from the shame and the scandal.
   (a) charged (b) booked
   (c) indicted (d) acquitted
   (e) applauded
6. The earthquake warnings and the fragility of our houses make us certain that disaster is ....
   (a) available (b) imminent
   (c) forthcoming (d) catastrophic
7. The television serials are characterized by an .... story line and .... plots and sub-plots.
   (a) unending, convoluted
   (b) infantile, simple
   (c) uniform, emotional
   (d) extempore, routine
   (e) erratic, forthcoming
8. The .... transformation of the former Soviet Union or Russia, as it was popularly known, remains one of the biggest stories of the decade.
   (a) smooth (b) singular
   (c) tumultuous (d) prophetic
   (e) traumatic
9. If mankind has to survive for long, it must .... and deliberately renounce the fruits of .... and whirling technology.
   (a) wilfully, wild (b) honestly, responsible
   (c) sincerely, labor (d) effectively, sliding
   (e) knowingly, impending

10. Although similar to moths in many ways, butterflies may be .... moths by the beauty of their wings.
(a) akin to (b) in comparison with
(c) listed as (d) distinguished from
(e) equal to the

11. Renu saw no .... in the exercises that had been set for her and worked at them in a .... manner.
(a) reason, organised (b) point, desultory
(c) strength, careless (d) meaning, dutiful
(e) sense, painful

12. Mother Teresa was .... about her achievements and unwilling to .... them before anyone.
(a) modest, discuss (b) proud, promote
(c) unsure, reveal (d) ignorant, eulogise
(e) immodest, play

13. Martin Luther strived for justice and fought against attempts to .... ignorant peasants in the medieval ages.
(a) influence (b) change
(c) exploit (d) corrupt
(e) discharge

14. The instruction manual that came with the computer is no masterpiece of .... prose because its instructions are so .... that we still do not know how to set up the computer.
(a) clear, garbled
(b) valuable, intelligent
(c) worthless, clear
(d) confused, varied
(e) worth, muffled

15. The strike will not end because both the management and the workers are ....
(a) insipid (b) intransigent
(c) intricate (d) inexplicable
(e) saddened

16. Book lovers who think of *Gone With The Wind* as a Southern romance miss its underlying .... import.
(a) democratic (b) novelistic
(c) thematic (d) exceptional
(e) argumentative

17. The professors at Lucknow University have a permanent .... on their positions and do not have to look for more secure ....
(a) fixture, jobs (b) tenure, employment
(c) security, means (d) right, employees
(e) eye, seats

18. It is very difficult to overcome the .... of habits such as smoking and taking drugs.
(a) stupidity (b) tenacity
(c) insecurity (d) insistence
(e) ravages

19. The .... and .... happenings in many talk shows annoy many viewers.
(a) aggravating, irritating
(b) trite, predictable
(c) happy, playful
(d) dramatic, eventful
(e) ranting, jocular

20. Slander and libel laws stand as a protection of a person's reputation against the .... dissemination of falsehood.
(a) inferential (b) inevitable
(c) incontestable (d) irresponsible
(e) semblance

21. Most of the settlements that grew up near the logging camps were .... affairs, thrown together in a hurry because people needed to live on the job.
(a) nomadic (b) protracted
(c) unobtrusive (d) rickety
(e) uncouth

22. Pipes are not a safer .... to cigarettes because, though pipe smokers do not inhale, they are still .... higher rates of lung and mouth cancers than nonsmokers.
(a) preference, free from
(b) answer, responsible for
(c) alternative, subject to
(d) rejoinder, involved in
(e) offer, involved with

23. Author Anjali Agarwal was a rare phenomenon, a single woman who maintained and even .... a respectable reputation while earning a living by her pen.
(a) impaired (b) decimated
(c) avoided (d) enhanced
(e) evacuated

24. Because Sherry is so ...., we can never predict what he will do at any moment.
(a) old (b) immature
(c) capricious (d) lazy
(e) dormant

25. Paper money is merely a representation of wealth; therefore unlike gold or any other precious metal, it has no .... value.
(a) financial (b) fiscal
(c) inveterate (d) intrinsically
(e) intrinsic

26. The law cannot and should not pardon such .... act of violence.
(a) a flagrant (b) a lavish
(c) a cautious (d) a dull
(e) condemn

27. As many students know, a/(an) .... response, if skillfully worded, can imply at least a superficial .... of knowledge about the subject.
(a) ambiguous, veneer (b) garbled, ignorance
(c) inarticulate, piece (d) elegant, lack
(e) wrong, lack

28. There are too many .... and not enough serious students.
(a) dilettantes (b) hunky dory
(c) lay-men (d) novices
(e) nascent

29. Her parents were .... when, despite losing the first three games, Sandy .... to win the set by a 6-3 score.
(a) surprised, failed (b) relieved, came back
(c) puzzled, refused (d) alarmed, attempted
(e) shocked, failed

30. The reviews of Deepak Chopra's latest literary work were enjoyed by many of his readers, but the subjects of his analysis dreaded Mr. Chopra's comments; he was scathing, bitter, irritating and never ....
(a) illogical (b) constructive
(c) uncharitable (d) controversial
(e) acidic

31. In poor and under developed countries, trucks are the only means of getting about town, the public transportation being virtually ....
(a) indecipherable (b) ubiquitous
(c) inadequate (d) nonexistent
(e) negligent

32. Given the .... state of published evidence, we cannot conclude here that exposure to low-level microwave energy is either hazardous or safe.
(a) inconclusive (b) indulging
(c) descriptive (d) immaculate
(e) descriptive

33. The clothes Nafees, the famous designer, designs for men are conservative, but her fashions for women are more ....
(a) subtle (b) flamboyant
(c) tasteful (d) expensive
(e) open

34. The equipments that were being used in the survey were ...., and because of the below-zero temperature, it was feared they would freeze and ....
(a) icy, capsize (b) frosty, shide
(c) fragile, shatter (d) frozen, dehydrate
(e) useless, capsize

35. Because of its tendency to ...., most Indian art is .... Japanese art, where symbols have been minimized and meaning has been conveyed by using the method of the merest suggestion.
(a) imitate, superior to
(b) understate, reminiscent of
(c) overdraw, similar to
(d) sentimentalise, supportive of
(e) synergise, half

36. Irony can sometimes become a mode of escape: to laugh at the terrors of life is, in a way, to .... them.
(a) bolster (b) approve
(c) evade (d) foster
(e) avail

37. The negotiations for the deal were often surprisingly ...., deteriorating at times into a volley of accusations and counter-accusations.
(a) insouciant (b) sedate
(c) acrimonious (d) propitious
(e) adequate

38. A .... student is unlikely to gain admission to a top-level institution.
(a) mediocre (b) putative
(c) mendacious (d) vicarious
(e) commerce

39. Either Japanese dishes are ...., or the one I had was a poor example.
(a) delicious
(b) overrated
(c) underestimated
(d) unpopular
(e) horrible

40. A person who is .... is slow to adapt to a new way of life.
(a) intractable (b) furious
(c) insolent (d) valiant
(e) constructive

41. Amit, who refrained from excesses in his personal life, differed markedly from Nirmal, who .... notorious drinking bouts with his buddies.
(a) minimised (b) indulged in
(c) shunned (d) compensated for
(e) specialised

42. The library incharge proposed a new schedule of fines for overdue books with the ...., if not the outright encouragement, of the faculty library committee.
(a) cynosure (b) acquiescence
(c) scorn (d) applause
(e) management

43. Maya's remarks were so .... that Arun could not decide which possible meaning was correct.
(a) congruent (b) impalpable
(c) ambiguous (d) facetious
(e) incorrigible

44. By nature, Rahul was ...., given to striking up casual conversations with strangers he encountered at bus stops or check-out stands.
(a) gregarious (b) reticent
(c) casual (d) diffident
(e) indulgent

45. In the absence of native predators, to stop the spread of their population, the imported goats .... to such an inordinate degree that they over grazed the country side and .... the native vegetation.
(a) propagated, cultivated
(b) suffered, abandoned
(c) thrived, threatened
(d) dwindled, eliminated
(e) outnumbered, cultivated

46. Jayashree was habitually so docile and .... that her friends could not understand her sudden .... her employers.
(a) accommodating, outburst against
(b) erratic, envy of
(c) truculent, virulence toward
(d) hasty, annoyance toward
(e) apologetic, hostile

47. That Amitabh's newest film is No. 1 at the box office this week is a testament to the star's .... power and not the reviews, which were .... at best.
(a) increasing, matchless
(b) ongoing, glowing
(c) drawing, modest
(d) waning, indifferent
(e) super, dismal

48. The .... background music hinted of the dangers threatening the movie's protagonist.
(a) loud (b) sardonic
(c) ebullient (d) portentous
(e) icy

49. In order to ensure that she passed the exam, Asha .... outlined every chapter of her course book, painstakingly noting the most obscure points.
(a) carefully (b) playfully
(c) jokingly (d) superficially
(e) cursory

50. Mr. Purty hastily .... all the warnings of his friends. And now, he finds it difficult to complete the task within its time and budget ....
(a) accepted, amounts
(b) ignored, amounts
(c) listened to, problems
(d) disregarded, constraints
(e) acknowledged, schedule

51. Lacking confidence in his skills in English, Pervez was .... when called on to speak in class.
(a) horrified (b) reticent
(c) impolite (d) sartorial
(e) shocked

52. The castle has been ....; we cannot even be sure exactly where it stood.
(a) obliterated (b) burned down
(c) ruined (d) debilitated
(e) spoilt

53. Being a bit hesitant about .... the man as the complete fraud he suspected him to be, Bill chose to attack the weaker points of his theory, ... them one by one.
(a) denouncing, debunking
(b) ridiculing, proving
(c) castigating, strengthening
(d) mocking, destroying
(e) mistrusting, telling

54. The analysis of the coach's report was anything but ...., but those of us who have learned to discount such dismal .... are optimistic.
(a) pessimistic, confusion
(b) sanguinary, traps
(c) malicious, benefits
(d) pleasant, prognostications
(e) sugary, performances

55. Angered by the bureaucrat's .... comments; the reporter insisted for a more .... response.
(a) redundant, repetitive
(b) tactless, immediate
(c) phlegmatic, lackadaisical
(d) circumlocutious, direct
(e) Sarcastic, beneficial

56. Raman's .... record collection included everything from Bach to rock.
(a) comprehensive
(b) rhapsodic
(c) eclectic
(d) inherent
(e) refulgent

57. My grandparents were such .... followers of the soap opera that they taped every episode.
(a) avid (b) skillful
(c) flagrant (d) retentive
(e) hopeless

58. .... the finer points of etiquette in high society, Devesh simply watched his host and followed his actions.
(a) Arguing for
(b) Unaware
(c) Ignorant of
(d) Saddened by
(e) Looking at

59. This book of Covey creates a mood of ...., a(n) .... of tranquility and calm.
(a) sombreness, atmosphere
(b) serenity, ambience
(c) melancholy, oasis
(d) formality, feeling
(e) tranquility, sea

60. Although they seem amateurish, primitive art has become more sophisticated as its creator becomes increasingly ....
(a) infamous (b) aged
(c) jaded (d) impotent
(e) ignorant

61. Though a .... of four campaigns, Bush had never seen such demonstrations.
(a) watchman (b) veteran
(c) volunteer (d) witness
(e) follower

62. Carried away by the .... effects of the experimental medication, the patient ...._ his desire to continue as a subject for as long as he could.
(a) supplementary, announced
(b) noxious, proclaimed
(c) frantic, repeated
(d) salutary, reiterated
(e) painful, undermined

63. Confused and.........., Hogwart fumbled to make sense of seemingly inconsistent statements, ... the impatience of his listeners.
(a) prostrate, listening to
(b) muddled, aware of
(c) philosophical, overlooking
(d) incoherent, oblivious to
(e) agitated, following

64. One of the most productive research .... in contemporary neuroscience is devoted to .... maps of human consciousness.
(a) trajectories; reconnoitering
(b) designs; enunciating
(c) paradigms; elucidating
(d) declensions; obfuscating
(e) terminologies, newal

65. Today computers can .... information from a number of sources, then automatically create a picture of their data manipulations.
(a) collate
(b) inculcate
(c) extrapolate
(d) adjudicate
(e) execute

66. Just as a highway automobile accident leaves lasting marks of spilled coolant, ... and oil, the smashing together of gigantic land masses releases and redirects fluids that flow, heat, ... and deposit, leaving an enduring record of their presence.
(a) petrol, disappear
(b) fuel, evaporate
(c) paint, mark
(d) anti-freeze, drip
(e) gases, electric

67. Although publicity has been .... the film itself is intelligent, well-acted, handsomely produced and altogether ....
   (a) tasteless, respectable
   (b) extensive, moderate
   (c) sophisticated, amateur
   (d) perfect, spectacular
   (e) useless, entraneous

68. Ironically, his normally .... speaker became shy and .... when confronted with the approbatory stares of her eager audience.
   (a) quiet, passionate
   (b) garrulous, reticent
   (c) dispassionate, passionate
   (d) humble, supercilious
   (e) soft, remorseful

69. Although the whole team acted in unison, each member was .... for a(n) .... of the production process.
   (a) reliable, source (b) responsible, element
   (c) appointed, article (d) agreeable, felony
   (e) agreeable, amount

70. The studies of the children were .... and .... was the result of it.
   (a) neglected, ignorance
   (b) interrupted, incongruence
   (c) off tracked, alienation
   (d) instructed, genius
   (e) ignored, negligence

71. The US has shown little .... to go after the terrorist or help India get him.
   (a) inclination (b) urgency
   (c) importance (d) alacrity
   (e) endeavour

72. Most young children are highly conformist and will .... a classmate whose appearance or manners are ....
   (a) ostracise, conventional
   (b) emulate, different
   (c) shun, unusual
   (d) deride, ordinary
   (e) choose, deriding

73. The royal astrologers had to determine the most .... date for the coronation ceremony.
   (a) propitious (b) sacred
   (c) approximate (d) resplendent
   (e) expected

74. A satirical poem is often venom-filled, ... with scorn.
   (a) contained (b) filled up
   (c) dripping (d) sardonic
   (e) acidic

75. The .... rites of the Black Magic cult were kept secret by the members and were never .... to outsiders.
   (a) eclectic, delegated
   (b) esoteric, divulged
   (c) inscrutable, introduced
   (d) elusive, prescribed
   (e) exclusive, delegated

76. Mr. Sharma, the critic, was .... enough to praise an author he detested.
   (a) magnanimous (b) loquacious
   (c) parsimonious (d) surreptitious
   (e) verbose

77. The goodwill of its clients is a genuine .... asset for any business.
   (a) redolent (b) dismissive
   (c) intangible (d) vigilant
   (e) indolent

78. Though the law's .... purpose is to curtail false advertising, its actual result is to .... free speech.
   (a) erroneous, eschew
   (b) ostensible, repress
   (c) illicit, reconcile
   (d) recalcitrant, characterise
   (e) elusive, contain

79. .... by her children, Radha Devi ultimately agreed to sell the house.
   (a) Decimated (b) Importuned
   (c) Interpolated (d) Designated
   (e) Apportioned

80. There was a .... all about the palace, and the .... concerned the security guards.
   (a) gift, distribution (b) silence, quiet
   (c) tranquil, temper (d) feast, circulation
   (e) commotion, quiet

81. Guilliano Benetton .... a small neighborhood business into a worldwide chain of stores.
   (a) renovated (b) infused
   (c) parlayed (d) blessed
   (e) decimated

82. The football team was once .... by injuries; of 11 members, only 5 were fit to play.
(a) decimated (b) isolated
(c) boycotted (d) heckled
(e) ambushed

83. Displeased with the .... of the novel, the writer abandoned the idea of a film to be made on his writings.
(a) adaptation (c) transfer
(d) transfusion (b) resurgence
(e) imagination

84. Because of his indecisive nature, Mr Bhushan has a reputation for ....
(a) impartiality (b) tenacity
(c) prevarication (d) vacillation
(e) wandering

85. The conspirators met .... in order to plot a(n) .... against the oppressive governance of Julius Ceaser.
(a) clandestinely, revolt
(b) wickedly, invocation
(c) craftily, referendum
(d) wittily, ban
(e) aggressively, crime

86. Vinay is much too .... in his writings: he writes a paragraph when a sentence should suffice.
(a) benevolent (b) skilled
(c) verbose (d) lucid
(e) crafted

87. With one .... motion, Rakesh disarmed his assailant.
(a) swift (b) ponderous
(c) superficial (d) boisterous
(e) levitational

88. The patient put up with the pain ...., neither wincing nor whimpering when the surgeon made an incision to drain the pus of his abscess.
(a) surprisingly (b) miserably
(c) logically (d) stoically
(e) enduringly

89. In relation to the interrelationships among a number of the Indo-Pakistani stalwarts treated in this compilation, there is surely a certain amount of .... in some of the essays presented here.
(a) overlap (b) indulgences
(c) exaggerating (d) objectivity
(e) obligation

90. Being an advocate of consumer rights, Sharad has spent much of his career trying to .... the fraudulent claims of the businessmen of his hometown Patna.
(a) reprove (b) debunk
(c) immortalise (d) import
(e) improve

91. The report was .... since the information on which it was based was erroneous, but it was brilliantly presented.
(a) intelligent (b) wonderful
(c) worthless (d) verbose
(e) elegant

92. Pretending not to notice the toys in the shop, Aryan the small boy acted in a .... manner.
(a) doleful
(b) nonchalant
(c) convincing
(d) ordinary
(e) indulgent

93. As several shops have .... across the street, the old directory is ....
(a) relocated, obsolete
(b) reversed, enticing
(c) transferred, dismantled
(d) vanished, beautiful
(e) transferred, upto date

94. The .... room in this apartment has not been used for a long time.
(a) derelict (b) contractual
(c) bereaved (d) crowded
(e) interpolated

95. Salman the superstar felt that certain incidents in his life were too .... to be divulged.
(a) intriguing
(b) derivative
(c) private
(d) rudimentary
(e) incremental

96. Distressed at an increasing .... for books, Amrita, the famous novelist has turned to painting.
(a) disregard (b) imagination
(c) panacea (d) prominence
(e) derelict

97. The bank is negotiating with Group 4 security to devise a system to provide .... security to account holders.
(a) accurate (b) prompt
(c) reliable (d) tough
(e) proactive

98. As the rate of life expectancy has increased due to tremendous progress in medical science, the overpopulation problem has ....
(a) aggravated (b) minimised
(c) distorted (d) encouraged
(e) unfazed

99. The story of the novel, *The Deranged*, is very .... It shows how a man cut off from the world for a long time becomes a mad man.
(a) absorbing (b) irritating
(c) controversial (d) useless
(e) derived

100. Although Agatha is arguably as good a mystery writer as Grundy, she is clearly far less .... than Grundy, having written only six books in comparison to Grundy's sixty.
(a) prolific
(b) equivocal
(c) verbose
(d) gripping
(e) astronomical

101. Being cynical, Ashish was reluctant to .... the .... of any kind act until he had ruled out all possible secret, uncharitable motives.
(a) acknowledge, wisdom
(b) accept, unselfishness
(c) endure, loss
(d) witness, outcome
(e) uncover, outcome

102. A golden rule which should always be followed by an investor is that: never invest on sentiment or on a tip; look for stocks with promising .... potential for growth.
(a) fast (b) long-term
(c) higher (d) quick
(e) string

103. At the world's finest educational institutes, only students with the .... to succeed are selected.
(a) luck (b) drive
(c) resources (d) experience
(e) reliable

104. Jamshedji Tata, the founder of the Tata Group in India, knew that only dedication and .... could ensure that the customer gets the very best.
(a) commitment (b) money
(c) perception (d) supervision
(e) doubt

105. Parveen fascinated the world with her beauty and her charm, and her life mixed public spectacle with private anguish; her tragic death .... a flood of grief on every continent.
(a) brought (b) prompted
(c) called (d) managed
(e) revoked

106. As Shyam .... retirement, he became more intelligent and active.
(a) awarded (b) withdrew
(c) derived (d) neared
(e) recollected

107. As a steadfast .... of our right to liberty time, Mishra had few ....
(a) defender, equals (b) opponent, enemies
(c) follower, enemies (d) advocate, defenders
(e) leader, unequals

108. A careful .... of the premises revealed some useful clues.
(a) autopsy (b) incarceration
(c) examination (d) incineration
(e) emphases

109. Almost everyone was .... by the cheerful, lively sound of the dance music.
(a) revived (b) tired
(c) fired (d) bored
(e) withdrawn

110. The .... of the aircrash could have been avoided if more safety .... had been taken.
(a) sad event, preservers
(b) disaster, reservations
(c) scientist, measures
(d) tragedy, precautions
(e) aftermath, steps

111. They were disappointed to see the armed guards. It .... them from doing anything disruptive.
(a) inspired (b) prevented
(c) encouraged (d) irritated
(e) enraged

112. The .... politician thought that all bureaucrats should be polite to him.
(a) insolent (b) merciless
(c) civilised (d) docile
(e) amateur

113. The newspaper accused the politician of .... for making promises he knew he could not ....
(a) revulsion, condone
(b) liability, improve
(c) impunity, reprise
(d) hypocrisy, fulfill
(e) forgery, overcome

114. Paula was .... as a child, accepting without a question, everything she was told.
(a) reticent
(b) taciturn
(c) recalcitrant
(d) credulous
(e) impatient

115. Cautioned by an anonymous phone call that an explosion was ...., the anti-bomb police squad .... the building immediately.
(a) expected, filled
(b) ubiquitous, purged
(c) imminent, evacuated
(d) eminent, checked
(e) eminent, entered

116. The route between the two cities has always been known to wind its .... way through steep mountain passes and coarse terrain.
(a) easy (b) smooth
(c) elusive (d) tortuous
(e) trajectory

117. As there were not enough seats to .... so many people at the venue of the address, they had to put up a big tent outside.
(a) entertain
(b) ascertain
(c) welcome
(d) accommodate

118. This .... old stone farmhouse has been a landmark since before the Independence.
(a) fragile (b) sturdy
(c) ramshackle (d) flimsy
(e) rickety

119. The Chief Minister was .... in his commitment to .... the rise of crime and unemployment among his constituents.
(a) uncertain, staunch (b) headstrong, stem
(c) faltering, identity (d) firm, uphold
(e) sturdy, counter

120. Sahil's clear .... of the situation kept the meeting from breaking up into ....
(a) idea, humor (b) notion, anarchy
(c) understanding, chaos (d) wit, tumult
(e) report, tumult

121. In the past, the coach had always viewed Kapil's ideas with ...., but today he surprised the team by enthusiastically .... his proposal.
(a) disdain, rejecting
(b) empathy, considering
(c) objectivity, forgetting
(d) skepticism, adopting
(e) temerity, dissuading

122. The embarrassed host felt that the uninvited guest's rude comments and offensive jokes were ....
(a) steadfast (b) reactionary
(c) intolerable (d) partisan
(e) alarming

123. The celebrated trainer's .... for helping his trainees to learn and achieve their goals was highly ....
(a) propensity, commendable
(b) distinction, enigmatic
(c) predilection, reprehensible
(d) derision, admissible
(e) decisiveness, desired

124. A few decades ago, ... about gender roles made it somewhat difficult for a woman to study veterinary science, but today, female veterinarians are quite ....
(a) diatribes, affluent
(b) preconceptions, prevalent
(c) mindsets, poor
(d) lectures, negligent
(e) analysis, prominent

125. Greg Chappell was impressed by the .... of the youthful railways team.
(a) ardor (b) corpulence
(c) languor (d) impertinence
(e) turbulence

126. In the plots of most Bollywood movies, there is/are a character/s with .... intentions, whose primary role is to try to .... the handsome hero in his noble mission.
   (a) furtive, abet
   (b) malevolent, thwart
   (c) unsavory, depict
   (d) inappropriate, derail
   (e) benevolent, obstruct

127. After a natural spring was discovered in the arid region, the family's old, abandoned farm was quickly .... into a profitable private business, centered around a state-of-the-art well that .... valuable water.
   (a) turned, expiates
   (b) configured, manipulates
   (c) transformed, emanates
   (d) expropriated, eradicates
   (e) transpired, exhaled

128. The young boy's .... attempts to explain to his girlfriend why he had failed to show for their movie date did little to ease her .... feelings.
   (a) impassioned, disconsolate
   (b) veracious, vacuous
   (c) unbelievable, gluttonous
   (d) chronic, vicarious
   (e) immeasurable, vacuous

129. For some politicians, charm is a mere .... adopted to get votes and .... criticism.
   (a) prerequisite, distort
   (b) affectation, alleviate
   (c) tool, inflict
   (d) ruse, condone
   (e) contender, earn

130. Although the food in the hostel mess was barely ...., after six months, the residents of the hostel had become .... to it.
   (a) edible, immune (b) edible, inured
   (c) palatable, immune (d) palatable, inured
   (e) affordable, attuned

131. During childhood and adolescence, individuals acquire habits that are .... to good health: which include having a sedentary lifestyle, frequently eating fatty and fast foods, and developing poor sleep patterns.
   (a) perilous (b) harmless
   (c) inimical (d) unsuitable
   (e) despicable

132. Divyansh's disciplined and .... study habits resulted in his earning numerous honors and awards which also included an academic scholarship.
   (a) painstaking (b) sedulous
   (c) unhealthy (d) taciturn
   (e) pecuniary

133. The old miser's .... did him little good when he died without heir or friend, and all his precious money was .... to the state.
   (a) frugality, escheated
   (b) miserliness, ordained
   (c) exemplariness, given
   (d) frugality, ordained
   (e) indulgence, willed

134. To most modern day readers, the language in Shakespeare's plays seems obscure and inaccessible, lacking the .... of modern day authors.
   (a) elegance (b) impertinence
   (c) perspicuity (d) perceptibility
   (e) diligence

135. Unlike the other photojournalists, Rochelle despised the .... nature of the newspaper business because she craved ....
   (a) permutable, habitude
   (b) flexible, chaos
   (c) permutable, chaos
   (d) flexible, stable
   (e) heinous, posterity

Exercise 2

CLOSE TESTS

Test 1

I shall here take leave to 1 a brief argument much 2 at a few years ago when it was still 3 to consider Hegel a greater philosopher than Plato. Abbreviating it, I repeat it, because I believe in it yet today, when Hegel (for causes unconnected with pure right and wrong) has gone somewhat out of 4 for a while.

As the tale, then, is told by Plato, in the tenth book of *The Republic*, one Er, the son of Arminius, a Pamphylian, was slain in 5; and ten days afterwards, when they collected the dead for burial, his body alone showed no 6 of corruption. His relatives, however, bore it off to the 7 pyre; and on the twelfth day, lying there, he returned to life, and he told them what he had seen in the other world. Many wonders he related concerning the dead, for example, with their rewards and 8: but what had impressed him as most wonderful of all was the great spindle of Necessity, reaching up to Heaven, with the planets 9 around it in graduated whorls of width and spread: yet all 10 and so timed that all complete the full circle punctually together. 'The Spindle turns on the knees of Necessity; and on the rim of each 11 sits perched a Siren who goes round with it, hymning a single note; the eight notes together forming one 12.'

Now, as we have the divine word for it – upon two great 13 hang all the law and the prophets, so all religions, all philosophies, hang upon two steadfast and faithful beliefs; the first of which Plato would show by the above 14.

(a) Sneered, (b) Recapitulate,
(c) Parable, (d) Funeral,
(e) Revolving, (f) Punishments,
(g) Fashion, (h) Taint,
(i) Battle, (j) Harmony,
(k) Commandments, (l) Concentric,
(m) Whorl, (n) Fashionable.

Test 2

What sacred 1 did inspire
My 2 in childhood with a hope so strong?
What 3 force moved my desire
To expect new joys beyond the 4, so young?
Felicity I knew
Was out of view,
And being here alone,
I saw that 5 was gone
From me! For this
I thirsted absent bliss,
And thought that sure beyond the seas,
Or else in something 6 at hand –
I knew not yet (since naught did please
I knew) my Bliss did stand.
But little did the 7 dream
That all the treasures of the world were by:
And that 8 was so the cream
And 9 of all which round about did lie.
Yet thus it was: the Gem,
The Diadem,
The Ring enclosing all
That stood upon this earthly ball,
The 10 Eye,
Much wider than the sky,
Wherein they all included were,
The glorious Soul, that was the King
Made to possess them, did appear
A small and little thing!

(a) instinct, (b) soul,
(c) secret, (d) seas,
(e) happiness, (f) near,
(g) infant, (h) himself,
(i) crown, (j) heavenly.

Test 3

Now the other and second great belief is, that the Universe, the 1, cannot be apprehended at all except as its rays converge upon the eye, brain, soul of Man, the 2: on you, on me, on the tiny percipient centre upon which the immense cosmic circle focusses itself as the sun upon a burning-glass – and he is not shrivelled up!

(a) macrocosm, (b) microcosm,

Test 4

Other nations have received their laws from conquerors; some are indebted for a constitution to the suffering of their 1 through revolving centuries. The people of this country, alone, have formally and 2 chosen a government for themselves, and with open and uninfluenced consent, bound themselves into a social compact. Here, no man 3 his birth or wealth as a title to honorable distinction, or to sanctify ignorance and vice, with the name of hereditary authority. He who has most 4 and ability to promote public 5, let him be the servant of the public. This is the only line of distinction drawn by nature. Leave the bird of night to the 6 for which nature intended him, and expect only from the eagle to brush the clouds with his wings and look 7 in the face of the sun.

(a) zeal, (b) boldly,
(c) obscurity, (d) ancestors,
(e) felicity, (f) proclaims,
(g) deliberately.

Test 5

Ye darkeners of counsel, who would make the property, lives, and religion of millions depend on the evasive 1 of 2 parchments; who would send us to antiquated charters of uncertain and 3 meaning, to prove that the present generation are not bound to be victims to cruel and unforgiving 4, tell us whether our pious and generous ancestors 5 to us the miserable privilege of having the 6 of our honesty, industry, the fruits of those fields which they purchased and bled for, wrested from us at the will of men over whom we have no 7. Did they 8 for us that, with 9 arms, we should expect that justice and mercy from brutal and inflamed invaders which have been denied to our supplications at the foot of the throne?

(a) contract, (b) contradictory,
(c) musty, (d) check,

(e) folded, (f) rewards,
(g) despotism, (h) interpretations,
(i) bequeathed.

Test 6

Were we to hear our character as a people 1 with indifference? Did they promise for us that our 2 and patience should be insulted, our coasts harassed, our towns 3 and plundered, and our wives and offspring exposed to nakedness, hunger, and death, without our feeling the resentment of men, and exerting those powers of self-preservation which God has given us?

No man had once a 4 veneration for Englishmen than I entertained. They were dear to me as 5 of the same parental trunk, and 6 of the same religion and laws; I still view with respect the remains of the Constitution as I would a lifeless body which had once been 7 by a great and heroic soul. But when I am aroused by the din of arms; when I 8 legions of foreign assassins paid by Englishmen to imbrue their hands in our blood; when I tread over the 9 bodies of my countrymen, neighbors, and friends; when I see the locks of a 10 father torn by savage hands, and a 11 mother, clasping her infants to her bosom, and on her knees imploring their lives from her own slaves, whom Englishmen have 12 to treachery and murder; when I 13 my country, once the seat of industry, peace, and plenty, changed by Englishmen to a theater of blood and misery, Heaven forgive me if I cannot root out those passions which it has 14 in my bosom, and 15 submission to a people who have either ceased to be human, or have not virtue enough to feel their own 16 and servitude!

(a) behold, (b) greater,
(c) branches, (d) meekness,
(e) demolished, (f) venerable,
(g) wretchedness, (h) ridiculed,
(i) feeble, (j) partakers,
(k) implanted, (l) behold,
(m) allured, (n) feeble,
(o) animated, (p) uncoffined.

Test 7

Men who content themselves with the 1 of truth, and a display of words talk much of our 2 to Great Britain for protection. Had she a single eye to our advantage? A 3 of shopkeepers are very seldom so disinterested. Let us not be so 4 with words! the 5 of her commerce was her object. When she defended our 6, she fought for her 7, and convoyed our ships loaded with wealth, which we had acquired for her by our 8. She has treated us as 9 of burden, whom the lordly masters 10 that they may carry a greater load. Let us inquire also against whom she has protected us? Against her own 11 with whom we had no quarrel, or only on her account, and against whom we always readily exerted our wealth and strength when they were required. Were these Colonies backward in giving assistance to Great Britain, when they were called upon in 1739 to aid the 12 against Cartagena? They at that time, sent three thousand men to join the British army, although the war commenced without their consent.

(a) industry, (b) cherish,
(c) extension, (d) enemies,
(e) nation, (f) customers,
(g) coasts, (h) semblance,
(i) expedition, (j) obligation,
(k) amused, (l) beasts.

Test 8

But the last war, it is said, was purely American. This is a vulgar 1, which, like many others, has gained 2 by being confidently repeated. The 3 between the courts of Great Britain and France related to the limits of Canada and Nova Scotia. The controverted 4 was not claimed by any in the Colonies, but by the crown of Great Britain. It was therefore their own 5. The 6 of a right which England had, by the treaty of Utrecht, of trading in the Indian country of Ohio, was another cause of the war. The French seized large quantities of British manufactures and took possession of a fort which a company of British merchants and factors had erected for the security of their commerce. The war was therefore 7 in defense of lands claimed by the Crown, and for the protection of British 8. The French at that time, had no quarrel with America, and, as appears by letters sent from their 9 to some of the Colonies, wished to remain in peace with us.

(a) commander-in-chief, (b) property,
(c) quarrel, (d) waged,
(e) dispute, (f) infringement,
(g) territory, (h) credit,
(i) error.

Test 9

Sir, there are two 1 which have a powerful influence in the affairs of men. These are ambition and avarice - the love of 2 and the love of 3. Separately, each of these has great force in prompting men to action; but, when united in view of the same object, they have, in many minds, the most 4 effects. Place before the eyes of such men a post of honor, that shall, at the same time, be a place of profit, and they will move 5 and 6 to obtain it. The vast number of such places it is that renders the British government so 7. The struggles for them are the true source of all those 8 which are 9 dividing the nation, distracting its councils, hurrying it sometimes into 10 and mischievous wars, and often compelling a submission to 11 terms of peace.

(a) fruitless, (b) heaven,
(c) factions, (d) earth,
(e) power, (f) violent,
(g) perpetually, (h) money,
(i) tempestuous, (j) passions,
(k) dishonorable.

Test 10

And of what kind are the men that will strive for this profitable 1, through all the bustle of 2, the heat of contention, the infinite mutual abuse of parties, tearing to pieces the best of characters? It will not be the wise and moderate, the lovers of peace and good order, the men fittest for the trust. It will be the bold and the violent, the men of strong passions and 3 activity in their selfish pursuits. These will thrust themselves into your government and be your rulers. And these, too, will be mistaken in the expected happiness of their situation, for their 4 competitors, of the same spirit, and from the same motives, will perpetually be 5 to distress their administration, 6 their measures, and render them odious to the people.

(a) endeavoring, (b) vanquished,
(c) thwart, (d) cabal,
(e) preeminence, (f) indefatigable.

Test 11

WHAT is the sum of 1 science? Compared with the 2 universe and with 3 time, not to speak of infinity and eternity, it is the observation of a mere 4, the experience of an 5. Are we 6 in founding anything upon such data, except that which we are obliged to found upon them - the daily rules and processes 7 for the natural life of man? We call the discoveries of science 8; and truly. But the sublimity belongs not to that which they 9, but to that which they suggest. And that which they suggest is, that through this material glory and beauty, of which we see a little and imagine more, there speaks to us a being whose nature is akin to ours, and who has made our hearts capable of such converse. Astronomy has its practical uses, without which man's 10 would scarcely rouse itself to those speculations; but its greatest result is a 11 of immensity pervaded by one informing mind; and this revelation is made by astronomy only in the same sense in which the 12 reveals the stars to the eye of the astronomer.

Science finds no law for the thoughts which, with her aid, are ministered to man by the starry skies. Science can 13 the hues of sunset, but she cannot tell from what urns of pain and 14 its pensiveness is poured. These things are felt by all men, felt the more in proportion as the mind is higher. They are a part of human nature; and why should they not be as sound a basis for 15 as any other part? But if they are, the solid wall of 16 law melts away, and through the whole order of the material world pours the influence, the personal influence, of a spirit 17 to our own.

If they could not show a Newton as we show an ape, or a Newton's discoveries as we show the feats of apish cunning, it was because Newton was not a mere intellectual power, but a moral being, laboring in the service of his kind, and because his discoveries were the reward, not of sagacity only, but of virtue. We can imagine a mere organ of vision so constructed by omnipotence as to see at a glance infinitely more than could be discovered by all the Newtons, but the animal which possessed that organ would not be higher than the moral being.

Reason, no doubt, is our appointed guide to truth. The limits set to it by each dogmatist, at the point where it comes into conflict with his dogma, are human limits; its providential limits we can learn only by dutifully exerting it to the utmost. Yet, reason must be impartial in the acceptance of data and in the demand of proof. Facts are not the less facts because they are not facts of sense; materialism is not necessarily enlightenment; it is possible to be at once chimerical and gross.

(a) philosophy, (b) instant,
(c) corresponding, (d) comprehensible,
(e) point, (f) telescope,
(g) material, (h) explain,
(i) pleasure, (j) revelation,
(k) intellect, (l) warranted,
(m) sublime, (n) reveal,
(o) physical, (p) necessary,
(q) conceivable.

Answer Key

EXERCISE 1

1. (c)	2. (a)	3. (c)	4. (d)	5. (c)
6. (b)	7. (a)	8. (c)	9. (a)	10. (d)
11. (b)	12. (a)	13. (c)	14. (a)	15. (b)
16. (c)	17. (b)	18. (b)	19. (b)	20. (d)
21. (d)	22. (c)	23. (d)	24. (c)	25. (e)
26. (a)	27. (a)	28. (a)	29. (b)	30. (b)
31. (d)	32. (a)	33. (b)	34. (c)	35. (b)
36. (c)	37. (c)	38. (a)	39. (b)	40. (a)
41. (b)	42. (b)	43. (c)	44. (a)	45. (c)
46. (a)	47. (c)	48. (d)	49. (a)	50. (d)
51. (a)	52. (a)	53. (a)	54. (d)	55. (d)
56. (a)	57. (a)	58. (c)	59. (b)	60. (c)
61. (b)	62. (d)	63. (d)	64. (c)	65. (a)
66. (b)	67. (a)	68. (b)	69. (b)	70. (a)
71. (a)	72. (c)	73. (a)	74. (c)	75. (b)

76. (a)	**77.** (c)	**78.** (b)	**79.** (b)	**80.** (b)
81. (c)	**82.** (a)	**83.** (a)	**84.** (d)	**85.** (a)
86. (c)	**87.** (a)	**88.** (d)	**89.** (a)	**90.** (b)
91. (c)	**92.** (b)	**93.** (a)	**94.** (a)	**95.** (c)
96. (a)	**97.** (c)	**98.** (a)	**99.** (a)	**100.** (a)
101. (b)	**102.** (b)	**103.** (b)	**104.** (a)	**105.** (b)
106. (d)	**107.** (a)	**108.** (c)	**109.** (a)	**110.** (d)
111. (b)	**112.** (a)	**113.** (d)	**114.** (d)	**115.** (c)
116. (d)	**117.** (d)	**118.** (b)	**119.** (b)	**120.** (c)
121. (d)	**122.** (c)	**123.** (a)	**124.** (b)	**125.** (a)
126. (b)	**127.** (c)	**128.** (a)	**129.** (b)	**130.** (d)
131. (c)	**132.** (b)	**133.** (a)	**134.** (c)	**135.** (a)

Exercise 2

Test 1

1. (b)	**2.** (a)	**3.** (n)	**4.** (g)	**5.** (i)
6. (h)	**7.** (d)	**8.** (f)	**9.** (e)	**10.** (l)
11. (m)	**12.** (j)	**13.** (k)	**14.** (c)	

Test 2

1. (a)	**2.** (b)	**3.** (c)	**4.** (d)	**5.** (e)
6. (f)	**7.** (g)	**8.** (h)	**9.** (i)	**10.** (j)

Test 3

1. (a)	**2.** (b)

Test 4

1. (d)	**2.** (g)	**3.** (f)	**4.** (a)	**5.** (e)
6. (c)	**7.** (b)			

Test 5

1. (h)	**2.** (c)	**3.** (b)	**4.** (g)	**5.** (i)
6. (f)	**7.** (d)	**8.** (a)	**9.** (e)	

Test 6

1. (h)	**2.** (d)	**3.** (e)	**4.** (b)	**5.** (c)
6. (j)	**7.** (o)	**8.** (a)	**9.** (p)	**10.** (f)
11. (n)	**12.** (m)	**13.** (l)	**14.** (k)	**15.** (i)
16. (g)				

Test 7

1. (h)	**2.** (j)	**3.** (e)	**4.** (k)	**5.** (c)
6. (g)	**7.** (f)	**8.** (a)	**9.** (l)	**10.** (b)
11. (d)	**12.** (i)			

Test 8

1. (i)	**2.** (h)	**3.** (e)	**4.** (g)	**5.** (c)
6. (f)	**7.** (d)	**8.** (b)	**9.** (a)	

Test 9

1. (j)	**2.** (e)	**3.** (h)	**4.** (f)	**5.** (b)
6. (d)	**7.** (i)	**8.** (c)	**9.** (g)	**10.** (a)
11. (k)				

Test 10

1. (e)	**2.** (d)	**3.** (f)	**4.** (b)	**5.** (a)
6. (c)				

Test 11

1. (o)	**2.** (d)	**3.** (q)	**4.** (e)	**5.** (b)
6. (l)	**7.** (p)	**8.** (m)	**9.** (n)	**10.** (k)
11. (j)	**12.** (f)	**13.** (h)	**14.** (i)	**15.** (a)
16. (g)	**17.** (c)			

CHAPTER 13 Previous Years' Questions from CAT

CAT 1996

Directions for the questions (1-2): In each of the following sentences, a part of the sentence is left unfinished. Beneath each sentence, four different ways of completing the sentence are indicated. Choose the best alternative among the four.

1. ...., the more they remain the same.
   (a) The more the merrier
   (b) The less the dynamism
   (c) The more things change
   (d) The more pronounced the transformation
2. The stock market is probably .... And the way the market has been plunging says a lot about investor's confidence.
   (a) the best barometer to assess the sentiment of the public.
   (b) an ideal indication of the health of public sentiment.
   (c) the least imperfect mechanism for judging the quantity of the sentiment of the public.
   (d) the best indicator of public sentiment.

CAT 1997

1. .... that in this apparent mess, two things need not be interfered with.
   (a) It is important
   (b) It is of cardinal importance
   (c) It should be urgently understood
   (d) It cannot be emphasised
2. The highest reward for a man's toil is not what he gets for it, but what ....
   (a) he makes out of it.
   (b) he gets for others
   (c) he has overcome through it.
   (d) he becomes by it.
3. Wines that yield a good commercial profit .... in the same limited areas of France as now.
   (a) seem to have been produced
   (b) appear to have a remarkable semblance
   (c) bear a significant similarity in terms of production to those grown
   (d) appear to have been similarly produced

CAT 1998

Directions for the questions (1-5): In each of the following sentences, part/parts of the sentence is/are left blank. Beneath each sentence, four different ways of completing the sentence are indicated. Choose the best alternative from among the four.

1. In pursuance of their decision to resist what they saw as anti-labour policies, the company employees' union launched agitation to ....
   (a) show their virility
   (b) reaffirm their commitment to the company
   (c) bring down the government
   (d) demonstrate their strength
2. The safest general characterisation of the European philosophical tradition as it has developed up to now, with all its diverse proponents, is that it consists of a .... Plato.

(a) series of footnotes to
(b) set of prologues to
(c) collection of chapters on
(d) string of commentaries to

3. The interest generated by the soccer World Cup is .... compared to the way cricket .... the nation.
(a) milder, fascinates (b) lukewarm, electrifies
(c) tepid, inspires (d) unusual, grips

4. No doubt, it was our own government but it was being run on borrowed ideas, using .... solutions.
(a) worn out (b) second hand
(c) impractical (d) appropriate

5. The telephone symbolises that awkward .... in all communication technologies; while it .... to bring us together, it keeps us apart.
(a) paradox, needs (b) irony, intends
(c) paradox, tries (d) irony, wishes

CAT 2000

Directions for the questions (1-5): In each of the following sentences, parts of the sentence are left blank. Beneath each sentence, four different ways of completing the sentence are indicated. Choose the best alternative from among the four.

1. Though one eye is kept firmly on the ...., the Company now also promotes .... contemporary art.
(a) present, experimental
(b) future, popular
(c) present, popular
(d) market, popular

2. The law prohibits a person from felling a sandalwood tree even if it grows on one's own land, without prior permission from the government. As poor people cannot deal with the government, this legal provision leads to a rip-roaring business for .... who care neither for the .... nor for the trees.
(a) middlemen, rich
(b) the government, poor
(c) touts, rich
(d) touts, poor

3. It will take some time for many South Koreans to .... the conflicting images of North Korea, let alone to .... what to make of their northern cousins.
(a) reconcile, decide (b) understand, clarify
(c) make out, decide (d) reconcile, understand

4. In these bleak and depressing times of .... prices, non-performing governments and .... crime rates, Sourav Ganguly has given us Indians a lot to cheer about.
(a) escalating, increasing
(b) spiraling, booming
(c) spiraling, soaring
(d) ascending, debilitating

5. The manners and .... of the nouveau riche is a recurrent .... in the literature.
(a) style, motif (b) morals, story
(c) wealth, theme (d) morals, theme

CAT 2002 (I)

Von Neumann and Morgenstern assume a decision framework in which all options are thoroughly considered, each option being independent of the others, with a numerical value derived for the utility of each possible outcome the expected utility. (1) .... such a model reflects major simplifications of the way decisions are made in the real world. Humans are not to process information as quickly and effectively as the model assumes; they tend not to think (2) .... as the model calls for, they often deal with a particular option without really assessing its (3) .... and, when they do assess alternatives, they may be externally nebulous about their criteria of evaluation.

1. (a) Regrettably (b) Firstly
(c) Obviously (d) Apparently
2. (a) Quantitatively (b) Systematically
(c) Scientifically (d) Analytically
3. (a) Implications (b) Disadvantages
(c) Utility (d) Alternatives

CAT 2002 (II)

In a large company, (1) .... people is about as common as using a gun or a switch-blade to (2) .... an argument. As a result, most managers have little or no experience of firing people, and they find it emotionally traumatic; as a result, they often delay the act interminably, much as an unhappy spouse will prolong a bad marriage. And when the firing is done, it's often done clumsily, with far worse side effects than are necessary.

Do the world-class software organizations have a different way of firing people? No; but they do the deed swiftly, humanely and professionally.

The key point here is to view the fired employee as a "failed product" and to ask how the process (3) .... such a phenomenon in the first place.

1. (a) dismissing (b) punishing
   (c) firing (d) admonishing
2. (a) resolve (b) thwart
   (c) defeat (d) close
3. (a) derived (b) engineered
   (c) produced (d) allowed

CAT 2003

1. The Internet is a medium where users have nearly .... choices and .... constraints about where to go and what to do.
   (a) unbalanced, non-existent
   (b) embarrassing, no
   (c) unlimited, minimal
   (d) choking, shocking
2. The best punctuation is that of which the reader is least conscious; for when punctuation, or lack of it, ... itself, it is usually because it ....
   (a) obtrudes, offends (b) enjoins, fails
   (c) conceals, recedes (d) effaces, counts
3. The argument that the need for a looser fiscal policy to ___ demand outweighs the need to .... budget deficits is persuasive.
   (a) assess, minimise (b) outstrip, eliminate
   (c) stimulate, control (d) restrain, conceal
4. The Athenians, on the whole, were peaceful and prosperous; they had .... to sit at home and think about the universe and dispute with Socrates, or to travel abroad and .... the world.
   (a) leisure, explore (b) time, ignore
   (c) ability, suffer (d) temerity, understand
5. This simplified .... to the decision-making process is a must read for anyone .... important real estate, personal or professional decisions.
   (a) primer, maximising
   (b) tract, enacting
   (c) introduction, under
   (d) guide, facing
6. Physicians may soon have .... to help paralysed people move their limbs by bypassing the .... nerves that once controlled their muscles.
   (a) instruments, detrimental
   (b) ways, damaged
   (c) reason, involuntary
   (d) impediments, complex
7. Their achievement in the field of literature is described as ....; sometimes it is even called ....
   (a) magnificent, irresponsible
   (b) insignificant, influential
   (c) significant, paltry
   (d) unimportant, trivial
8. From the time she had put her hair up, every man she had met had groveled before her and she had acquired a mental attitude toward the other sex which was a blend of .... and ....
   (a) admiration, tolerance
   (b) indifference, contempt
   (c) impertinence, temperance
   (d) arrogance, fidelity

CAT 2004

1. Early .... of maladjustment to college culture is .... by the tendency to develop friendship networks outside college which mask signals of maladjustment.
   (a) treatment, compounded
   (b) detection, facilitated
   (c) identification, complicated
   (d) prevention, helped
2. The British retailer, M&S, today formally .... defeat in its attempt to .... King's, its US subsidiary, since no potential purchasers were ready to cough up the necessary cash.
   (a) admitted, acquire (b) conceded, offload
   (c) announced, dispose (d) ratified, auction
3. Companies that try to improve employees' performance by .... rewards encourage negative kinds of behaviour, instead of .... a genuine interest in doing the work well.
   (a) giving, seeking
   (b) bestowing, discouraging
   (c) conferring, discrediting
   (d) withholding, fostering
4. A growing number of these expert professionals .... having to train foreigners as the students end up .... the teachers who have to then unhappily contend with no jobs at all or new jobs with drastically reduced pay packets.
   (a) resent, replacing (b) resist, challenging
   (c) welcome, assisting (d) are, supplanting

5. The .... regions of Spain all have unique cultures, but the .... views within each region make the *issue* of an acceptable common language of instruction an even more contentious one.
   (a) different, discrete (b) distinct, disparate
   (c) divergent, *distinct* (d) different, competing

CAT ARCHIVES

I. At that time, the White House was as serene as a resort hotel out of season. The corridors were [1]. In the various offices, [2] gray men in waistcoats talked to one another in low-pitched voices. The only color, or choler, curiously enough, was provided by President Eisenhower himself. Apparently, his [3] was easily set off; he scowled when he [4] the corridors.

1. (a) striking (b) hollow
   (c) empty (d) white
2. (a) quiet (b) faded
   (c) loud (d) stentorian
3. (a) laughter (b) curiosity
   (c) humour (d) temper
4. (a) paced (b) strolled
   (c) stormed (d) prowled

II. "Between the year 1946 and the year 1955, I did not file any income tax returns." With that [1] statement, Ramesh embarked on an account of his encounter with the Income Tax Department. "I originally owed Rs 20,000 in unpaid taxes. With [2] and [3], the 20,000 became 60,000. The Income Tax Department then went into action and I learned first hand just how much power the Tax Department wields. Royalties and trust funds can be [4]; automobiles may be [5] and auctioned off. Nothing belongs to the [6] until the case is settled."

1. (a) devious (b) blunt
   (c) tactful (d) pretentious
2. (a) interest (b) taxes
   (c) principal (d) returns
3. (a) sanctions (b) refunds
   (c) fees (d) fines
4. (a) closed (b) detached
   (c) attached (d) impounded
5. (a) smashed (b) seized
   (c) dismantled (d) frozen
6. (a) purchaser (b) victim
   (c) investor (d) offender

III. It was [1], and the new sun sparkled gold across the ripples of a gentle sea. A mile from shore, a fishing boat [2] the water, and the word for Breakfast Flock flashed through the air, till a crowd of a thousand seagulls came to [3] the fight for bits of food. It was another busy day [4].

But way off [5], out by himself beyond boat and shore, Jonathan Livingston Seagull was practicing. A hundred feet in the sky, he lowered his webbed feet, lifted his beak, and strained to hold a painful hard twisting curve through his wings. The curve meant that he would fly slowly, and now he slowed until the wind was a whisper in his face, until the ocean stood [6] beneath him. He [7] his eyes in fierce concentration, held his breath, forced one single more inch of curve. Then his feathers ruffled, he stalled and fell.

1. (a) morning (b) twilight
   (c) dawn (d) mendicant
2. (a) meandered (b) chummed
   (c) anchored (d) languished
3. (a) dodge (b) lodge
   (c) nudge (d) vacillate
4. (a) culminating (b) beginning
   (c) practicing (d) gainsaying
5. (a) shore (b) scared
   (c) alone (d) brood
6. (a) deep (b) akimbo
   (c) still (d) conspicuous
7. (a) narrowed (b) widened
   (c) opened (d) decreed

Answer Key

CAT 1996

1. (c) **2.** (d)

CAT 1997

1. (a) **2.** (d) **3.** (a)

CAT 1998

1. (d) **2.** (a) **3.** (b) **4.** (b) **5.** (c)

CAT 2000

1. (b) **2.** (d) **3.** (a) **4.** (c) **5.** (d)

CAT 2002 (I)

1. (c) **2.** (a) **3.** (d)

CAT 2002 (II)

1. (c) **2.** (a) **3.** (d)

CAT 2003

1. (c) **2.** (a) **3.** (c) **4.** (a) **5.** (d)
6. (b) **7.** (d) **8.** (b)

CAT 2004

1. (c) **2.** (b) **3.** (d) **4.** (a) **5.** (d)

CAT ARCHIVES – I

1. (c) **2.** (a) **3.** (d) **4.** (a)

CAT ARCHIVES – II

1. (b) **2.** (a) **3.** (d) **4.** (c) **5.** (b)
6. (d)

CAT ARCHIVES – III

1. (a) **2.** (a) **3.** (a) **4.** (b) **5.** (a)
6. (c) **7.** (a)

SECTION 4: Paragraph Jumbles

This section will help you in the following ways:

- In the chapter on Paragraph Jumbles (PJ), you would learn to identify the 10 types of relationships on the basis of which you can identify the correct sequence of jumbled paragraphs. Along with that you would also get a huge number of practise questions and solved examples on all types of paragraph jumbles. These question types is very important for the CAT examination.
- In the chapter on PJ exercises, you would get a chance to practise two types of PJ questions.
- LODs and CAT paper exercises in Block II would help you to practise sentence completion questions.

BLOCK 1: Theory

In this block through the theory of paragraph jumbles (PJ) you will learn:

1. The standard process of solving paragraph jumbles questions.
2. The nine types of logic structures used in paragraphs.

This is followed by an exercise of solved examples actually illustrating this entire process through step-by-step explanations of high-quality PJ questions.

You are advised to go through the theory closely and use it to extend your basic understanding of language in all your reading activity.

Chapter 15 contains a practise exercise of 25 questions on this topic as a precursor to the solving of the exercises on the various difficulty levels on this topic. Take it as a test and see what kind of score you are getting in it to decipher how much basic work you need to do.

In This Block	*Chapter 14* **Paragraph Jumbles**

BLOCK 2: LODs and CAT Questions

The following chapters contain exercises on Paragraph Sentence Completion on varying levels of difficulty.

You are required to solve each level of difficulty and try to find out the major sources of error for you–

Is it due to your lack of understanding the information contained in an individual sentence?

Or

Is it due to your inability to understand the relationships between various sentences within a paragraph?

Based on this analysis, you would need to get back to the drawing board and work on improving your ability to solve such questions–either by working on your ability to comprehend sentences or your ability to identify relationships between sentences and within paragraph – something that can be called your paragraph comprehension ability.

In This Block	
	Chapter 15 **Level of Difficulty—I**
	Chapter 16 **Level of Difficulty—II**
	Chapter 17 **New TITA Type CAT Level Para Jumble Questions**
	Chapter 18 **Type I and II Exercises on Paragraph Jumbles**
	Chapter 19 **Previous Years' Questions from CAT**

CHAPTER

14 Paragraph Jumbles

Paragraph jumbles (PJ), as the name itself suggests consist of sentences not arranged in a logical sequence. A choice of arrangement of the sentences is given from which the candidate has to choose the most logical sequence which would be the most appropriate for conveying the message of the passage. This is a test of the student's logical ability, his/her language interpretation ability, and depth in vocabulary. It also tests the student's comprehension abilities since the solving of a para jumble involves very often, the grasping of diverse messages from a wide range of topics.

Before you go through the specific theory of this chapter, make sure that you have completed the 'Ten Step Approach to Improving your Reading Skills' explained in Part I of this book.

Solving a question of this nature is both an art and a science. Art because it requires the specific usage of skills under various conditions and science because there are certain thumb rules that exist, which can be used effectively to improve one's ability to solve paragraph jumbles.

Needless to say, it helps if the student is an avid reader of various kinds of books and magazines. In general, the more diverse the exposure to different texts of varied nature in terms of subjects, authors, writing styles, etc. the better will be your ability to solve paragraph jumble questions. The student is advised to develop his reading habits in such a way that he incorporates varied subjects like philosophy, psychology, sciences, medicine, astronomy, metaphysics, management, finance, marketing, etc. Please re-read the portion about the process of improving reading habits given in the reading comprehension section of the book. This is a very important activity if you want to do well at paragraph jumbles. Before we move ahead, let us illustrate to you the importance of having wide reading habits. Consider the following example. Arrange the given sentences in the correct sequence:

A. He rung the doorbell.

B. Ramu's school bell rung at precisely 1:35 p.m.

C. He rushed home as he was very excited about the present waiting for him at home.

D. His mother opened the door.

E. He reached home at 5 minutes past two.

What is your answer?

Is it BCEAD? Most people reading this question will get it right. The reason–the topic described in the passage is so simple and the exposure to something like this so common that there is no strain on the mind. Most readers will be able to logically structure the sequence of events described in the paragraph jumble above. Hence, the chances of error will be remote, and will arise only if you were not focused enough while solving the passage.

Now consider this example:

1. This book has grown out of an attempt to harmonize two different tendencies, one in psychology, the other in physics, with both of which I find myself in sympathy, although at first sight, they might seem inconsistent,

A. They make psychology increasingly dependent on physiology and external observation, and tend to think matter as something much more solid and indubitable than mind.

B. Their world consists of 'events,' from which 'matter' is derived by a logical construction. Whoever reads, for example, Professor

Eddington's 'Space, Time and Gravitation' (Cambridge University Press, 1920), will see that an old-fashioned materialism can receive no support from modern physics.

C. On the one hand, many psychologists, especially those of the behaviourist school, tend to adopt what is essentially a materialistic position, as a matter of method if not of meta-physics.

D. Meanwhile the physicists, especially Einstein and other exponents of the theory of relativity, have been making 'matter' less and less material.

E. I think that what has permanent value in the outlook of the behaviourists is the feeling that physics is the most fundamental science at present in existence.

7. But this position cannot be called materialistic, if, as seems to be the case, physics does not assume the existence of matter.

1. BECAD 2. DBECA
3. ADBCE 4. CADBE

Getting this correct will be a different kettle of fish. The reason–the topic is one where your exposure is much lower and this makes the structuring of the idea much more difficult. In the CAT and other aptitude tests, this is more likely to be the level of complexity of paragraph jumbles that you are likely to encounter. In case you are not exposed to ideas and writing of this level, you are likely to face a lot of difficulties while solving questions of this level.

Another important way through which diverse reading habits help is that it enhances the skills of finding clues and links within sentences–a skill which is very important to solve paragraph jumbles.

In order to understand the science of solving paragraph jumble questions, we need to first understand the reasons for the creation of paragraphs:

The Cream of the Piece

A paragraph is a collection of sentences and normally, is used to convey a concise idea within a larger idea structure of a passage. In general, paragraphs can be either top heavy or bottom heavy. A top heavy paragraph is one which conveys its main idea at the start of the passage–and then it tapers off in its content; while a bottom heavy paragraph has its main idea towards the end of the paragraph with the start of the paragraph being usually light in content. In our experience, top heavy paragraphs are much more common than bottom heavy paragraphs in general English writing.

STANDARD PROCESS FOR SOLVING PARAGRAPH JUMBLE QUESTIONS

A PJ question has to be solved using the following four step process, which occur automatically one after the other. One step leads to the next and so on, as given below in (Fig 14.1):

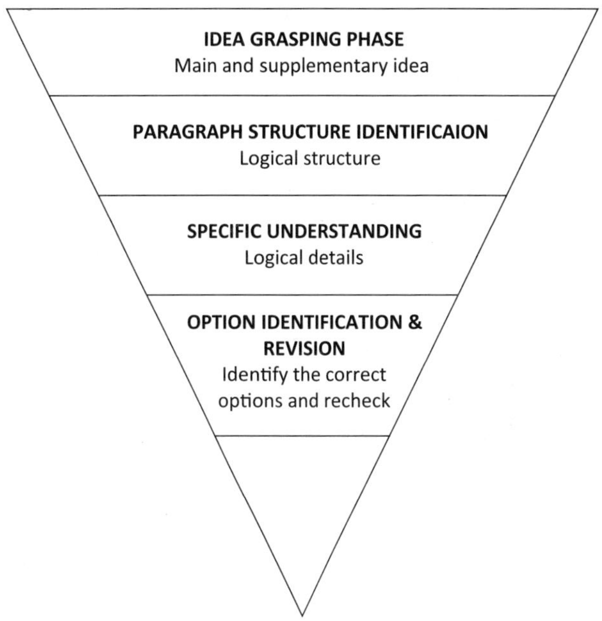

Fig. 14.1 The Inverted Triangle Method

Step 1: Idea Grasping Phase

In the **idea grasping phase,** the focus has to be on identifying the main and supplementary ideas which constitute the message being conveyed by the paragraph. This gives us a clear picture of the main and the supplementary themes running through the paragraph.

Step 2: Paragraph Structure Identification Phase

In the **paragraph structure identification phase,** try to identify the logical structure used in the paragraph. The seven structures of a paragraph are detailed below. Perhaps, this is the most critical phase of the solving process. A correct identification of the logical structure of the paragraph will ensure that you look for the correct clues in the next two phases of the solving process. During this phase, try to develop an inkling about the author's tone and style of writing and try to discover the structure and style which the author uses to present his/her ideas.

Step 3: Specifics Understanding Phase

In the **specifics understanding phase,** we try to fit into the logical structure identified above, the minor details of the key words used. Identify the logical sequence of the sentences and also try to fill in the minor gaps in your understanding of the jumbled sequence.

Step 4: Incorporation Phase

Finally, in the **incorporation stage,** integrate the ideas presented in the sentences in your own thought process and try to apply them in a structured logical string to test whether the chosen sequence conveys the idea or theme accurately to the reader.

Analyzing a sentence jumble to understand how it should be correctly constructed can be compared to dismantling a machine to understand how it was built. We may stop occasionally and reassemble parts of it to review what we just did and then proceed again to dismantle and assemble more of it. During this process, the understanding proceeds from the specific to the generic and vice versa. The inverted triangle method aptly represents what we have just tried to explain.

WHAT TO LOOK FOR WHEN YOU SOLVE PARAGRAPH JUMBLES

The Nine Types of Structures used in Standard Writing within Paragraphs

There are certain standard structures used for the writing of paragraphs (in fact for the presentation of ideas). The following being the standard structures of paragraphs, they are also usually the dominant ideas or clues to look for in various types of paragraph jumble questions. (What you need to be clear about at the outset is that a single paragraph might use one or more of these types of writing.) These are:

(1) Cause & Effect

(2) Generic to Specific

(3) Contrast

(4) Parallelisms

(5) Idea–Explanation/Elaboration

(6) Chronological (based on the time dimension)

(7) Action Sequence

(8) Idea Transformation

(9) Idea Reiteration

The Cream of the Piece

Notice the similarity between the theory of Paragraph Jumbles and that of Reading Skills development in the first part of the book. Isn't it to be expected that these are almost the same categories as those given under the heading 'Idea Organization' under the reading skills development part of Part I of this book? It further goes to emphasize our constant advice–that the entire English section (VA and RC) is based on your ability and skillfulness at reading. Hence, the best way to improve your scores in this section is to improve your reading skills.

A paragraph jumble question will normally exhibit one or more of the above types of writing within the paragraph.

Let us now take a closer look at each of the above types. While doing so, please take care to remember that these rules of paragraph jumbling are at best, thumb rules, i.e., they have to be applied flexibly. You will have to correlate multiple rules while trying to solve a single question. One of the most common reasons for mistakes is that students have a tendency of solving a question on the basis of one or two rules, where more apply. Just because one of these rules fits in, it does not mean that what it points to will be the answer. Typically, in a PJ question, the correct answer will be supported by more than one thumb rule. Let us now explore the different types of structures listed above, one by one:

Type 1: The Cause & Effect structure As the name itself suggests, the cause and effect paragraph consists of two parts–the cause, leading to the effect.

The typical structure of this paragraph is:

A, hence B or A causes B (where A and B are ideas such that A is the cause and B is the effect.) Paragraphs of this nature will normally contain defining words like: hence, because, causes, leads to (for more key words refer to the chapter of sentence completion, where cause and effect is explained in the context of a single sentence.) These words will segregate the effect from the cause.

The Cream of the Piece

In cause-effect paragraphs, you will see the effect following the cause in most cases.

In other words, the cause precedes the effect. (Again, remember this is only a thumb rule and is not a rigid one. You will have to apply it using your own discretion and in the context of the overall writing style of the author.) Let us look at a few examples.

1. The governance of the Ashoka dynasty was amongst the most efficient of its time. **(Cause)**
2. It led to the elimination of crime and created a general feeling of security in the masses. **(Effect)**

Type 2: Generic to Specific In this structure of paragraph, the author talks about a generic idea and then backs it up with specific examples of the same. The flow of this type of paragraph is always from the general to the specific–the idea to the example.

1. Economic justice demands a diminution, if not a total abolition, of the proportion of the national income which goes to the recipients of rent and interest. **(generic statement)**
2. But when the holders of railway shares are given government stock to replace their shares, they are given the prospect of an income in perpetuity equal to what they might reasonably expect to have derived from their shares. **(Specific example)**

Type 3: Contrast As the name itself suggests, this is based on the contrast or opposite of one idea against another. In such presentations of ideas, there is a transformation from one point of view, to the opposite point of view. Typically, both the points of view are presented with equal force and the author does not give away his/her biases towards either of the opposite points of view.

This type of paragraph is often signified by a turnaround point between two parts of a paragraph. The turnaround point is signaled by words such as: but, on the other hand, as against, however, although, etc. These indicate a transformation from one point of view to the other.

1. In the late 90s, Brian Lara strode the cricket field like a colossus–an all conquering batsman who had few equals in the history of the game.
2. However, his presence was not enough to inspire his West Indian team mates, resulting in one of the worst periods of West Indian cricket coinciding with Lara's extraordinary artistry at the crease.

Type 4: Parallelisms In such kind of writing, you will come across two parallel points of view presented one after the other. Normally, you would find key words such as: likewise, similarly, just as, equally, in the same manner, etc.

1. The investigators directly assessed relations between racial attitudes and values and argued in favor of linkages to two clusters of values.
2. One of these clusters, individualism, corresponds to the Protestant ethic values emphasized in discussions of symbolic racism.
3. The other cluster, communalism, which emphasizes concern about community and the well being of others, has been neglected by theorists of symbolic racism, as has the idea that these values' conflicting implications for racial attitudes produce ambivalence on the part of white Americans.

(In the above sentence sequence, statements 2 & 3 are talking about parallel concepts, one after the other.)

Type 5: Idea-Explanation/Elaboration/Completion One sentence will present an idea and then it is either explained in detail or elaborated (expanded) or completed in the subsequent sentence/s.

I. (a) I was lucky.
   (b) The bus driver applied the brakes a meter or two away from my car.

II. (a) The theory of the legitimate use of force in human affairs, where a government exists, seems clear.
   (b) Force should only be used against those who use force against others, or against those who will not respect the law in cases where a common decision is necessary and a minority are opposed to the action of the majority.

Type 6: Chronological (based on the time dimension) As the name itself suggests, successive sentences will be demarcated on the basis of the time dimension. Normally, successive sentences will take you further along in time (although you might also have paragraphs which go back and forth in time). All action sequences have chronological sequences involved. However, chronology is not just used to illustrate action sequences.

1. Sigmund Freud, the oldest child of a second marriage of Jacob Freud, the Jewish owner of a small cloth mill in the little Austrian town of Freiberg, was born on 6 May 1856.
2. Owing to the changes brought about in weaving by the industrial revolution, in 1860, Jacob Freud moved to Vienna and there set up as a cloth merchant.

Type 7: Action Sequence Action sequences depict a set of actions, logically connected to each other. (The example used above where Ramu goes back home from school, would qualify as a typical action sequence.) Note, that in normal circumstances, the action sequence will have a chronological sequence involved.

Type 8: Idea Transformation In this presentation, a concept is introduced in the first sentence and the following sentence draws from that concept (in fact it directly refers to it) and presents a new dimension associated with the concept. Note, that the key difference between this type and the idea-elaboration type is that the latter elaborates and explains the idea introduced in the initial part of the sequence, while this type uses the idea presented in the start of the sentence sequence and portrays a totally different dimension to it.

Considered the following examples. The 'component parts' referred to are used in two different contexts.

1. If this sense of humanity came into being in the course of evolutionary history, then it must have component parts, and they, in turn, must be identifiable.
2. It is my conviction that we are beginning to identify these components, that we can see the gradual emergence of humanness in our evolutionary history.

Type 9: Idea Reiteration Sentence sequences which use this structure of argumentation will start off by giving a point of view, followed by one or more sentences reiterating the fact. Consider, the following example:

I. (a) Sachin was one of the best batsmen of his time.
   (b) In fact, he was so good that his team hardly ever lost a match.

II. (a) By definition, any model necessarily abstracts from and simplifies reality.
   (b) But the model of competitive equilibrium is a travesty of reality.

Type 10: Question–Answer As the name itself suggests, in such sentence sequences, the answer to a question follows the question.

1. What was this dreadful little book?
2. Its name in Italian is Il Principe, in English, The Prince.

Now go through the following real life Paragraph Jumble questions to get a feel of how to apply the above principles in real-time problem-solving. These examples will illustrate to you the above points in ample details.

SOLVED EXAMPLES

Directions: The sentences given in each question, when properly sequenced, form a coherent paragraph. Each sentence is labelled with a letter. Choose the most logical order of sentences from among the given choices to construct a coherent paragraph.

1. In the twentieth century, John Maynard Keynes has been the most important scholar working in the tradition of the classical political economists.

A. But his interest, like theirs, was in the analysis of the great issues of his day, the greatest of which in the inter-war period was not growth but unemployment, a problem so acute at the time that in desperation, the Germans turned to Hitler and to fascism.

B. The very future of Western democracies was placed at risk.

C. Keynes was concerned not just to understand unemployment intellectually, but to put forward practical suggestions as to how the problem could be solved.

D. This does not mean that he agreed with everything they wrote.

6. He believed fervently that, for all its faults, Western liberal democracy offered the best hope for the world, and he saw himself working to save it.

1. DCBA 2. BACD
3. BCDA 4. DABC

In the above paragraph, the starting sentence is already defined. The sentence sequence 1DA is using a double contrast–a kind of flip flop argument. Statement D opposes (contrasts) the idea of 1, while statement A again contrasts the opposition of D. In this question, recognizing this structure is sufficient to get to the correct answer, which is 4.

A similar structure of argumentation (**using a double contrast**) can be used in diverse situations. Consider the following examples:

I. 1. In the 1990s, Sachin, one of the greatest batsmen of all time, dominated cricket like never before.
   2. This does not mean that he always performed in every innings of his.
   3. But his mere presence was enough to strike fear and awe in the minds of all bowlers in the opposition.

II. 1. The Indian economy is on a growth path never experienced before.
   2. This does not mean that all the problems inherent to the Indian economy over the past half century have been eradicated.
   3. But, there is a definite movement towards alleviating these problems.

In fact, as a student trying to improve your language ability, you should recognize that all language used today operates on standard structures such as these. Having as wide an exposure to these nuances

will help you develop an internal instinct towards identifying these structures. You should try to develop your perception on these dimensions as you develop your reading habits.

Coming back to the question above, the sentence sequence AB is using a cause and effect structure. The effect of the future of Western democracies being placed at risk was caused by the Germans turning to Hitler and fascism.

A. A transplant from my younger brother, Philip, effectively gave me a second life.

B. Feeling that whatever years I now had ahead of me were a bonus, I initiated the exploration of the western shore of Lake Turkana.

C. I was lucky.

D. Following our first tentative prospecting came remarkable finds, some of them technically stunning, some emotionally thrilling.

E. The discoveries were worth waiting for, as I shall recount.

1. EDCAB 2. ABDCE
3. BCDEA 4. CABED

In the above question, the sentence sequence CA uses an idea-elaboration structure, while from A to B it is a cause and effect sentence sequence. Sentence sequence ED is also in the form of an idea elaboration, where E introduces the idea of the discoveries, while D elaborates the same.

1. For centuries, philosophers have dealt with aspects of humanness, of humanity. But, surprisingly, there is no agreed-upon definition of the quality of humanness.

A. It is my conviction that we are beginning to identify these components, that we can see the gradual emergence of humanness in our evolutionary history.

B. But if this sense of humanity came into being in the course of evolutionary history, then it must have component parts, and they, in turn, must be identifiable.

C. Those who tried to define humanness found themselves moulding Jell-O: it kept slipping through the fingers.

D. It hardly seemed necessary, partly because it appeared so obvious: humanness is what we feel about ourselves.

6. I am therefore perplexed by, and impatient with, a popular alternative view that is championed by several scholars.

1. ABCD 2. DCBA
3. BCDA 4. CBDA

In the above question, the key sentence sequence is the BA sequence, which is in the form of an idea transformation, since B introduces the concept of the component parts, while A refers to these components in a different context altogether. Hence, the correct answer is 2.

A. Economists see the world as a machine.

B. A very complicated one perhaps, but nevertheless a machine, whose workings can be understood by putting together carefully and meticulously, its component parts.

C. A lever pulled in a certain part of the machine with certain strength will have regular and predictable outcomes elsewhere in the machine.

D. The behaviour of the system as a whole can be deducted from a simple aggregation of these components.

1. ABDC 2. ABCD
3. ACBD 4. ADBC

The sentence sequence AB is in the form of an **idea elaboration**, while the sentence sequence DC is in the form of **generic to specific**. Hence, the correct answer is 1.

1. The benefits of growth are plain to see.

A. But in recent decades, some people have begun to question the foundations of classical and orthodox economics on the question of growth, asking whether its benefits are being wisely used and distributed and, at a more fundamental level, whether its costs, particularly in environmental terms, do not outweigh the benefits.

B. What may be termed the Green critique of growth is powerful.

C. More precisely, the word 'critique' should appear in the plural, for there are a number of quite different dimensions to it.

D. No single source of intellectual authority exists within the movement, and environmentalism embraces many different strands of opinion.

6. All of them require, in different ways and with different degrees of intensity, alterations in behaviour and in the priorities which as a society, we attach to the various outcomes.

1. ABCD 2. BCDA
3. CDAB 4. DBCA

The sentence sequence 1A represents a contrast while the sentence sequence BCD represents an idea elaboration. Hence, the correct answer is 1.

1. 'We have many bones to show you,' promised Kamoya as we unpacked the belly of the plane.

A. I joked, and we all laughed at the improbable prospect.

B. 'You will like the hominids.'

C. I knew I would.

D. 'Skeletons?'

6. With evening upon us, we drank beer by the mess tent; the darkness fell quickly, as it always does this close to the equator.

1. BCDA 2. BDCA
3. BACD 4. BCAD

The joke referred to in A is obviously referring to the question 'Skeletons?' The structure used in DA is an idea completion. Hence, DA is one sentence sequence. Although that is enough to give us an answer, the sentence sequence BC is another one in the idea completion format. Option (1) is correct.

A. Competitive advantage is not something which falls from the skies like manna from Heaven.

B. However, according to orthodox economic theory, this should not happen, since if any single firm were able to gain an advantage at any point in time, competitive forces would rapidly ensure that this state of affairs would be purely temporary.

C. It has to be created and earned, but once earned, it can be used to ensure a position of enduring dominance.

D. Economic competition between companies, particularly large ones, bears a strong resemblance to this military world.

1. ABDC 2. BCDA
3. BCAD 4. DACB

The sentence sequence AC is one where the idea (competitive advantage) is elaborated, while CB uses a structure of a contrast. The sentence D can only come before the sequence ACB, since it is an introduction sentence, drawing a parallel from the military world (which must have been talked about before this sentence sequence). Hence, option (4) is correct.

A. Contemporary orthodox economics is isolated.

B. And its methodology, despite the pretensions of many of its practitioners, is isolated from that of the physical sciences, to whose status it none the less aspires.

C. It is isolated from its roots in the late eighteenth and early nineteenth centuries, when economists were by no means afraid to theorise, but did so purely to illustrate and understand the great practical issues of the day.

D. Its method of analysis is isolated from the wider context of society, in which the economy operates, and which Adam Smith believed to be of great importance.

1. ADCB 2. BDCA
3. CDBA 4. ACDB

The sentence sequence ACDB is an obvious case of idea elaboration. Hence 4.

A. Fear of destitution is not a motive out of which free creative life can grow, yet it is the chief motive which inspires the daily work of most wage-earners.

B. The hope of possessing more wealth and power than any man ought to have, which is the corresponding motive of the rich, is quite as bad in its effects; it compels men to close their minds against justice, and to prevent themselves from thinking honestly on social questions, while in the depths of their hearts they uneasily feel that their pleasures are bought by the miseries of others.

C. Then a great fear would be removed from the lives of the many, and hope would have to take on a better form in the lives of the few.

D. The injustice of destitution and wealth alike, ought to be rendered impossible.

1. ABCD 2. BDAC
3. BCDA 4. ABDC

The sentence sequence AB uses a parallelism between the two motives of working ('Fear of destitution' for the poor and 'the hope of possessing more wealth and power than any man ought to have' for the rich). DC uses a cause and effect structure, where C is the effect of the cause of rendering impossible the injustice of destitution and wealth. Hence, the answer will be 4.

A. Few men seem to realise how many of the evils from which we suffer are wholly unnecessary, and they could be abolished by a united effort within a few years.

B. With goodwill, generosity, intelligence, these things could be brought about.

C. If a majority in every civilised country so desired, we could, within twenty years, abolish all abject poverty, quite half the illness in the world, the whole economic slavery which binds down nine tenths of our population; we could fill the world with beauty and joy, and secure the reign of universal peace.

D. It is only because imagination is sluggish, and what always has been is regarded as what always must be.

1. CDBA 2. ACDB
3. BCDA 4. BDCA

The sentence sequence AC uses an idea elaboration structure. B obviously has to come later than C in the paragraph since the 'these things' referred to in it are defined in sentence C. (Note: 'These things' in sentence C refer to the abolition of poverty, and of half the illnesses in the world, removal of economic slavery and the consequential filling of the world with beauty and joy.) The sentence D does not quite fit in, however, its placement becomes a non issue due to the options available. The correct answer is obviously option 2.

A. Thus, while not in any way seeking to deny the existence of serious poverty and hardship in many developing economies, present accounting conventions underestimate their per capita incomes precisely because they do not take account of economic activity which takes place outside the market.

B. In a subsistence economy, a great deal of food production, for example, will never be bought and sold in the market, but is consumed by the community in which it is produced.

C. Its value is therefore, not reflected in the national accounts of these economies.

D. In developing economies, a far higher proportion of total transactions takes place within the household compared to those in the money economy.

1. DBCA 2. DBAC
3. DCAB 4. DABC

Sentence D introduces the idea, while BC is an example of the idea. Hence, the idea example structure operates in DBC. Further, A is an idea completion sentence, completing the sentence sequence in DBCA.

A. But this point is so obvious that it needs no elaboration.

B. I am not prepared to maintain that economic justice requires an exactly equal income for everybody.

C. It would be utterly absurd to maintain that the men who inherit great wealth deserve better of the community than those who have to work for their living.

D. Economic injustice is perhaps the most obvious evil of our present system.

E. Some kinds of work require a larger income for efficiency than others do; but there is economic injustice as soon as a man has more than his share, unless it is because his efficiency in his work requires it, or as a reward for some definite service.

1. ABCDE 2. DCBEA
3. CDBAE 4. BACDE

In the above question we see a mixture of two levels of idea elaboration (as seen in the sentence sequence DC as also in BE). Further, the sentence sequence BE follows up the idea introduced and elaborated in DC. Thus, the correct option is 2.

The Cream of the Piece

Tips for solving PJ questions

The following techniques would be of further help to you in focussing on:

1. **Finding the starting sentence:** One of the keys to solving a question correctly is the location of the starting sentence. Very often, a paragraph jumble question will get solved only by identifying the starting sentence. In the context of the types of sentence sequences used in writing paragraphs, the starting sentence can be identified as the first part of one of the ten types. (For example, the cause will mostly be the starting sentence in a typical cause and effect sentence structure. Similarly, the starting idea in a sentence sequence involving a contrast is likely to be the starting sentence of the paragraph.)
2. **Locating the 'topic sentence':** Mostly, one of the sentences in a paragraph will introduce the main topic of the paragraph. This sentence will give us the key to the entire paragraph. Very often, the topic sentence might be the clue to the first sentence of the passage, but that is not an absolute rule.
3. **Finding the general theme:** Finding the general theme or main idea from the jumbled sentences may require some skill, but careful reading can reveal which idea is the central or the main one, and can be found if it is most frequently used or when most of the other sentences relate to it.
4. **Finding logical relationships:** Once you have found the general theme, you should relate the ideas and opinions found in the sentences and place them in a logical sequence. You can look for the interrelation of ideas in the sentences to form a whole. Supporting facts, words or phrases that signal emphasis or a shift in thought, and the relation of one idea to another– for example, the cause and effect relationship, help in finding the logical relationship and thus give clues about the structure of the paragraph.
5. **Finding the concluding sentence:** The concluding sentence will normally wind up the argument, without leaving any loose ends.

A PRACTICAL GUIDE TO PARAGRAPH JUMBLES PROBLEM-SOLVING

Let us now analyze all the above points with the help of the following solved CAT questions, to make the whole theory very clear.

Consider the following question:

1. What does the state do in a country where tax morality is very low?
   A. It tries to spy upon the tax payers.
   B. It investigates income sources and spending patterns.
   C. Exactly what the tax authorities tries to do now even if inconsistently.
   D. It could also encourage people to denounce to the tax authorities, any conspicuously prosperous neighbours who may be suspected of not paying their taxes properly.
6. The ultimate solution would be an Orwellian system.

(a) BACD (b) DBAC
(c) ABCD (d) DCBA

As is seen in the above question, we know that the government here is seeking to solve the problem of tax evasion & looking at the options available for doing so. So the first thing to look for in this jumble is either the starting or the finishing sentence, as we know that the general theme is tax evasion.

Keeping that in mind, the sentence 'D', starting with 'it could also..............', shows that this sentence is not the first as it talks of other options of solving the problem before it. The use of the word 'also' here shows that there are other sentences before it. Similarly the sentence 'C', starting with the word 'Exactly', also illustrates that it is trying to corroborate a fact previously talked about. So that leaves us with only 'A' or 'B' as the starting sentences. Since spying is the aim of the government and the sentence 'B' directly extends the answer given in 'A', it is the more logical option as the first sentence in the paragraph. This is followed by sentence 'B', which is just an illustrative restatement of statement 'A' and which is corroborated by sentence 'C', finally ending with sentence 'D', which has to be the last sentence since the paragraph ends with the mention of the 'Orwellian system' which was largely about people supplying information to the authorities about others. So ABCD is the correct answer.

Here, it is important to note that if you had good reading habits, you might have been aware of the Orwellian system and would have thus been able to logically solve the jumble faster and more accurately due to your prior knowledge of the subject than a student who has not been reading widely. This again strengthens our previous emphasis on varied reading and its usefulness.

CHAPTER 15

Level of Difficulty—I

1. (A) God has managed the amazing feat of being worshipped and invisible at the same time.
   (B) Millions of people might describe him as a white bearded father figure sitting on a throne in the sky, but none could claim to be an eyewitness.
   (C) Although it doesn't seem possible to offer a single fact about the Almighty that would hold up in a court of law, somehow the vast majority of people believe in God–as many as 96 percent, according to some polls.
   (D) This reveals a huge gap between belief and what we call everyday reality.
   (E) We need to heal this gap.
   (a) ABCDE (b) BCDEA
   (c) ABDEC (d) CABDE
   (e) BADCE
2. (A) This result was all the more astonishing when it was discovered that the person doing the praying didn't have to know the patient personally, or even know their names.
   (B) Seriously ill patients in hospitals were divided into groups, some being prayed for, while others were not.
   (C) A striking example that there is a reachable place beyond material reality, and that is prayer.
   (D) In all cases, best medical care was still given, yet it became evident that the prayed-for group seemed to recover better.
   (E) Beginning more than twenty years ago, researchers devised experiments to try to verify whether prayer had any efficacy.
   (a) ECBAD (b) CEBDA
   (c) EADCB (d) CBEDA
   (e) ABCDE
3. (A) A snail's neurons pick up signals from the outside worlds so slowly, for example, that events any faster than three seconds would not be perceived.
   (B) In other words, if a snail was looking at an apple, and I quickly reached in and snatched it away, the snail would not be able to detect my hand.
   (C) It would 'see' the apple disappear before its very eyes.
   (D) In the animal kingdom some nervous systems are much faster than ours and others much slower.
   (E) In the same way, quantum flashes are millions of time too rapid for us to register, so our brains play a trick on us by 'seeing' solid objects that are continuous in time and space, the same way that a movie seems continuous.
   (a) DABCE (b) DEABC
   (c) DACBE (d) EDABC
   (e) ACBDE
4. (A) A person is neither the product of just their environment nor just their genetic make up.
   (B) Let me give an example.
   (C) A child is born with a talent for music, which then gets nurtured through continuous training in a conducive atmosphere.
   (D) The transactional model of child development helps to resolve the split between nature and nurture.

(E) Rather it is the complex interaction between the two that is key.
(a) BCDAE (b) DAEBC
(c) ADBCE (d) ADEBC
(e) EABCD

5. (A) At first, you think of it as just a matter of growing bigger.
(B) There is nothing in the world more fascinating than watching a child grow and develop.
(C) Then, as the infant begins to do things, you may think of it as 'learning tricks'.
(D) In some ways, the development of each child retraces the whole history of the human race, physically and spiritually, step by step.
(E) But, it's really more complicated and full of meaning than that.
(a) BACED (b) DABCE
(c) ACBDE (d) DACBE
(e) ABCDE

6. (A) On the one hand, we can trivialize the word by applying it to virtually any human activity.
(B) On the other hand, we can ignore or reject the significance of the original meaning of the term and replace it with a technical definition, such as 'conceptual analysis' or 'the methodology of science'.
(C) Like all expressions, however it is subject to two kinds of distortion.
(D) The word 'philosophy' is of Greek origin and means literally, 'love of or friendship for wisdom.'
(E) This simple linguistic fact shows us at once that philosophy is an intrinsic expression of human nature.
(a) CABDE (b) ABCDE
(c) DCABE (d) DECAB
(e) ACBDE

7. (A) Some books, nevertheless, offer 'inside stuff' or 'tricks' which they claim will enable you to beat the test.
(B) This is not to say that the CAT is 'beatable'.
(C) Although the CAT is a difficult test, it is a very learnable test.
(D) You probably have already realized this.
(E) There is no bag of tricks that will show you how to master it overnight.
(a) ABCDE (b) CBEDA
(c) CABED (d) BACED
(e) ADBCE

8. (A) Its aim was to remove from dance, any external associations, so that the dancers could concentrate on pure movement and pure pattern.
(B) Abstract dance was the name of a specific style of ballet, devised in the 1920s and developed at the bahaus.
(C) Ballroom dancing, for example, is concerned with the pleasure the movement and pattern-making give to the dancers, and not with some external 'programme'.
(D) In the wider sense, a great deal of dance is 'abstract'.
(a) DBAC (b) BADC
(c) BDCA (d) BDAC
(e) ABCD

9. (A) In those countries where the ideals of liberty and equality have received the greatest devotion, and particularly in America, the political constitution has been framed with the precise object of making impossible too great a concentration of power.
(B) A philosophy that emphasizes the likeness of all men will be averse from recognizing those exceptional qualities in any individual which place him so clearly above his fellows that he may justly claim to lead and influence them.
(C) A different though related strand of thought is equalitarian.
(D) Further, when circumstances make it necessary for a particular individual to display qualities of leadership in a very high degree, his position is under constant and bitter attack on the score of dictatorship, and it is necessary for him to conceal his qualities, consciously, behind a façade of 'ordinariness'.
(a) CBAD (b) CABD
(c) CDAB (d) DCAB
(e) DCBA

10. (A) It has removed many of the material obstacles to the pursuit of the good life from the majority of mankind in those countries at a high level of technical development.
(B) But it has exposed us to new dangers, not the obvious dangers of new weapons of destruction, but the much more serious ones of a purely materialist view of life.
(C) The growth of science and technology has conferred obvious and immense benefits upon the community.
(D) It has also, as we too often forget, made possible new and daring adventures of the mind.

(a) CADB (b) ABDC
(c) ACBD (d) CDBA
(e) ABCD

11. (A) There are manifest dangers in the persuasive aspect of leadership.
(B) It is alarming, for example, to reflect how great a part the power to speak well has acquired in an age of broadcasting.
(C) It is quite possible for men to feel that they are freely giving their allegiance to a leader, when actually they are simply slaves of his techniques of propaganda.
(D) At its lowest, the technique of persuasion may involve all those devices of suggestion and propaganda which are so freely available to the unscrupulous in a scientific age.
(a) ABDC (b) ACBD
(c) CDBA (d) ADBC
(e) DABC

12. (A) The leader should possess high intelligence.
(B) The reasons for this frequent neglect of intelligence as a prerequisite of leadership are complex.
(C) It is certainly true to say that this is more commonly underrated than any other aspect of leadership.
(D) There is first, a very general misunderstanding of such a phrase as 'of very high intelligence.'
(a) ABCD (b) ACBD
(c) DABC (d) DBAC
(e) CABD

13. (A) As with everybody else, the guard was ordered to go through the metal detector.
(B) Before doing so, he handed his M-16 rifle to security personnel, along with other items such as handcuffs and a torch.
(C) The guard shift was rotating, and a guard in full uniform, was in line in front of him.
(D) When returning from a business trip, my father approached a security checkpoint at the airport.
(E) When the guard went through the machine, an alarm went off and he was inspected with a hand-held wand which detected a Swiss army knife inside one of his pockets.
(a) DCABE (b) DBCAE
(c) DCAEB (d) BCAED
(e) ABCDE

14. (A) He required, for instance, that all cars be parked 'about a meter' away from the others cars.
(B) I had a very organized commanding officer when I was in the army.
(C) Once he called me over and pointed out a car that was parked less than 'about a meter' away from the other cars.
(D) I told him that the vehicle in question was owned by Captain Jorge, well known for his ill temper and feared by those above and below him in rank.
(E) The commander thought for a few minutes and ordered: 'Tell everyone to align their cars according to Captain Jorge's'.
(a) ABDCE (b) BACDE
(c) DCABE (d) EBADC
(e) ABCDE

15. (A) She had made her last trip to Canada.
(B) Five years later, she surprised me when she phoned to say she had booked a flight and was coming to visit.
(C) My mother, who lives in Germany, visited my family in Canada every year.
(D) But at age 80, she informed us that the 16 hours of travelling was too much for her.
(E) I asked her what, at age 85, had made her change her mind
(a) CDBAE (b) CDABE
(c) CEDAB (d) ABECD
(e) DACBE

16. (A) On one of our walks, three lads cycled past.
(B) I am short and stocky with grey hair and beard
(C) My dog was also short and stocky and had grey hair.
(D) I heard one of them say, 'That's a strange one.'
(E) The second boy agreed, exclaiming, 'Yes–It's all grey and fluffy.'
(a) ADCEB (b) CADEB
(c) BCADE (d) DCABE
(e) BCDAE

17. (A) Easy or not, etiquette is important.
(B) There's a reason for doing things the way we do them–we just have no idea what it is.
(C) I had to interrupt my cell phone call to tell him off.
(D) I was trying to explain this the other night to my children–Matt, 15, and Becky, 11–who, I'm ashamed to say, have been allowed to develop less-than perfect manners, especially at the table.
(E) At this particular family dinner, I caught Matt buttering his baked potato with his finger.
(a) ABCDE (b) ABDEC
(c) BCDAE (d) BDACE
(e) ABECD

18. (A) Not a plastic tray or all-you-can-eat dessert bar in sight.
    (B) Becky, whose idea of great dining is to graze the free sample aisle at cafes, immediately had questions.
    (C) The Restaurant was amazing.
    (D) A distinguished-looking waiter with an elegant accent presented our menus.
    (E) 'How can they charge this much for food?'
    (a) CDABE (b) ADCBE
    (c) EDBCA (d) CADEB
    (e) ABCDE
19. (A) A trainee was standing guard inside a room when he heard a pounding on the door and the order 'Let men in!'
    (B) Through the window, he saw the uniform of an officer and immediately opened the door.
    (C) He quickly realized his mistake when the officer yelled, 'Airman! Why didn't you check for my authority to enter?'
    (D) Guards in air force basic training must check all IDs.
    (E) Thinking fast, the airman replied, 'Sir, you'd have got in anyway.'
    (a) DABCE (b) DBACE
    (c) DBECA (d) DAEBC
    (e) DCABE
20. (A) Peggy Conlon was 15 when her mum, dad and 14 siblings moved to a big house in Adelanto, a tiny town in California's high southern desert.
    (B) School lunches were packed assembly-line style; baths taken in shifts in the bathroom–younger kids before bed, older kids in the morning.
    (C) Life was all about directing traffic and as the oldest child, Peggy was the chief traffic monitor.
    (D) In addition to the Conlon brood, there were cats, dogs, chickens, rabbits and a pony.
    (E) Dinner was set on a 3.5 metre long dining table her father had made from a church door.
    (a) ADEBC (b) AEBCD
    (c) DAECB (d) CABDE
    (e) ABCDE
21. (A) There in the soap-scented air and the glare of neon, they sorted, washed, dried, and folded up to 20 loads of clothes.
    (B) That's when Mary would talk to her daughter about helping others and her dreams for the future.
    (C) Every Friday night, from the time she was eight, Peggy and her mother, Mary, loaded the family station wagon with dirty clothes and drove to a Laundromat.
    (D) When they were finally done at about 1 am, they'd head to an all night coffee shop for hot fudge sundaes and a rare quiet time together.
    (E) Diapers were always a big item.
    (a) CADEB (b) CBDAE
    (c) CAEDB (d) BCADE
    (e) BACDE
22. (A) I lived with my grandparents until I left home at 16.
    (B) She worked and did very well, but she still needed the support her parents provided, and we lived with them in New York for many years.
    (C) So all three of them, my mum, Ondrea Smith, and my grandparents Eugene and Ellen Griffith–raised me.
    (D) Don't get me wrong; my mum was around too,
    (E) But she was a single parent and had me when she was just 21.
    (a) AEDCB (b) ADEBC
    (c) CADEB (d) ACDED
    (e) ABCDE
23. (A) He had been a paramedic in the army in World War II, and when I lived with him, he worked for the post office.
    (B) He was from a west Indian family, and people from the west Indies are known for their frugality–like the work 300 jobs and spend no money.
    (C) I'd see him leave every morning, go to work and come home at night.
    (D) Then he'd do things like fix his own car. And instead of relaxing, he'd be out patrolling the neighborhood, making sure it was safe for his family.
    (E) My grandfather looked like a big Buddha, and his overall vibe was jolly, like Santa.
    (a) EBCAD (b) ECBAD
    (c) EBACD (d) CDABE
    (e) EABCD
24. (A) When I say tough, I mean she was the kind of person that didn't want to be kissed or hugged, but she would show you all the love in the world.
    (B) My grandmother–she was generous, but she was tough.
    (C) They let the employees have certain stuff, damaged goods.

(D) She used to bring little race cars and other toys home to me every day.
(E) Talk about a kid being blessed, and God has been looking out for me from the beginning: My grand mother worked in a toy factory!
(a) EDCAB (b) BAECD
(c) BCAED (d) EDABC
(e) BDAEC

25. (A) The man shook his head and pointed to a stage close to my wife, where the pianist was sitting at a grand piano, cheerfully playing away.
(B) As the negotiations were completely new to her, she had to focus her full attention on the discussion.
(C) She was invited by some customers to discuss business in a well-known tavern.
(D) The background music bothered her greatly, so when the waiter was passing her table, she asked if he could turn the music down.
(E) My wife had just been appointed bank manager of a local branch.
(a) ECBDA (b) EBCDA
(c) BCDAE (d) BCDEA
(e) DAEBC

26. (A) He insisted we check again, and again the deckhand found nothing out of order.
(B) When the man called a third time, I sent the deckhand directly to his cabin.
(C) I sent a deckhand to check the lifeboat and called the guest back to say nothing had been found.
(D) During my work, handling the front desk of a cruise ship, a passenger called to say he'd spotted a stowaway in a lifeboat when he'd glanced out of his cabin window.
(E) The deckhand soon called to assure me there was no need for alarm: The guest had been reporting on his own reflection in the window.
(a) EBACD (b) DCBAE
(c) DCABE (d) DBACE
(e) EABCD

27. (A) Their son, Matthew, a Navy meteorologist, was assigned there.
(B) Michael Flocco veered into the driveway of his home and dashed from his truck.
(C) The stocky sheet-metal worker had rushed back from a construction site nearby to join his wife, Sheila, after learning of the terrorist attack on the Pentagon.
(D) Michael found Sheila sitting on the couch sobbing.
(E) It was almost 10:30 am on Tuesday, September 11, 2001.
(a) BECAD (b) BDECA
(c) BEDCA (d) DACEB
(e) BAECD

28. (A) Handsome in his tuxedo.
(B) Lanky at his high school prom.
(C) Matthew with the striped kitten–had he been five?
(D) At ten–smiling in his yellow soccer jersey.
(E) Throughout the TV replays of the collapsing Trade Towers, Michael's glance shifted from one framed photo to the next.
(a) ECDBA (b) ABCDE
(c) ECBDA (d) DABCE
(e) DAEBC

29. (A) Matthew was always the kid with his head in the clouds, the stars, the sky.
(B) With high marks, and great moves on the sports field, his dream had been an athletic scholarship, but an injured elbow and a bad rotator cuff got in the way.
(C) So Matthew enlisted in the Navy.
(D) By fourth standard, Matthew was bored with cartoons on TV, and his dad often returned from work to find him lying on the floor, absorbed in the blue and red curves of the cold fronts and low-pressure systems swirling across the weather channel maps.
(E) He hoped to go to college, even though the family's savings would not stretch far.
(a) DABEC (b) DACEB
(c) DBCEA (d) DAEBC
(e) EABDC

30. (A) The couple have diametrically opposite approaches to investing.
(B) Lynn, 58, is a believer in mutual funds and has 'a bit of a gambler's streak' that's made her a successful investor.
(C) That could have been the case for Lynn and George Wick.
(D) According to financial planner Michael Banwell, antagonism can arise when couples have different investing styles, especially when there are concerns there won't be enough money to retire with.
(E) George, 12 years her senior, has always put cash into FDs and left it there.
(a) DACBE (b) DCABE
(c) EBADC (d) ECABD
(e) ABCDE

31. (A) With her friends crowded round, she opened a package to find ...a dictionary and a thesaurus.
(B) 'She was forever looking for a dictionary and didn't have one,' he says, 'but it was obvious I didn't get it right.'
(C) On her 25th birthday, Maria Nicozzi got a gift from her boy friend, Thomas that she'll never forget.
(D) For his part, Thomas, who went on to become Maria's husband despite the gift, had carefully considered what to get her.
(E) 'I felt it should have been something more substantial and romantic.' She says.
(a) CDBEA (b) CAEDB
(c) CBAED (d) CEABD
(e) DCABE

32. (A) Once it was installed, however, I realized that the new chair's enormous flowers, so playful in the furniture store, overwhelmed the muted stripes of our downstairs wallpaper.
(B) 'It's a little loud, isn't it?' my husband asked cautiously.
(C) While I was expecting our fifth child, I chose a chair at a discount furniture store to replace a dog-eared, stuffing-spitting relic.
(D) In fact, the sight of the chair in the living room made my teeth hurt.
(E) 'It's shouting,' I agreed glumly.
(a) ABECD (b) BAECD
(c) CABED (d) CBAED
(e) ABCDE

33. (A) You can't change public perception by force.
(B) So we start making films where violence is not the only solution, like Hero and the next film I plan to make.
(C) When you get older, you start to think, What can we give to the younger audience.
(D) But we are so used to watching heroes use violence to stop violence.
(E) When I was young, I didn't know if the violence was bad or good, so I just did the action – good guy kills bad guy.
(a) ECBDA (b) BDAEC
(c) ECDBA (d) EDCBA
(e) EABCD

34. (A) I really did quit once when I was nine years old
(B) My coach came to my home every week and just cut my hair, brought a book or food and didn't talk about training.
(C) He tried to make me feel guilty.
(D) Children think of quitting many times.
(E) My foot was broken, and I trained for three days before I decided I didn't want to.
(a) DABCE (b) DBACE
(c) DAEBC (d) AEBCD
(e) BACDE

35. (A) In obstructive sleep apnea, tissue in the throat relaxes during sleep, collapsing–and closing off–the airway.
(B) Worse, he routinely stopped breathing. Tests at a sleep clinic yielded a quick diagnosis: sleep apnea.
(C) Then his weight ballooned and his blood pressure soared.
(D) Along with the weight gain, Currie, a 55-year-old radio announcer, developed a snoring problem, his wife informed him.
(E) Roger Currie quit smoking ten years ago.
(a) EDCBA (b) ECBDA
(c) ECDBA (d) EABDC
(e) EBCDA

36. (A) The result: an epidemic of fatigue that's ratcheting up stress at work and road rage among motorists, and is literally aging us before our time.
(B) Some of us may need the attention of professionals; others have to make more time for sleep in their schedules.
(C) People are sleeping less today and snoring more, tossing and turning and eyeing the clock, praying for dawn.
(D) Either way, quality sleep should be a priority.
(E) It's a shame, since scientists have made great strides in treating almost every type of sleep disorder often without medication and with great rates of success.
(a) EBDCA (b) EBDAC
(c) CAEBD (d) CADEB
(e) ACBED

37. (A) Van Cauter then tested the volunteers on insulin resistance, a measure of how well the body processes blood sugar.
(B) Van Cauter recently monitored 27 sleepers between the ages of 23 and 42 in their homes.
(C) One group slept just over five hours on weeknights; the other eight.
(D) The greater one's resistance, the greatest his risk of diabetes.
(E) The results were astonishing. The shorter sleepers had 50 per cent more insulin resistance than the longer sleepers.
(a) BACDE (b) BCADE
(c) CADBE (d) CADEB
(e) BDACE

38. (A) 'Mum's been murdered,' his brother said in a shaky voice.
(B) It was a burglary gone awry.
(C) On New Year's Day, 1996, psychologist Everett Worthington's phone rang.
(D) Two youths had broken in, and she had surprised them.
(E) She was killed with a crowbar.
(a) CABDE (b) CDBAE
(c) ABDEC (d) CDBEA
(e) ABCDE

39. (A) The role of Western values in contemporary Indian society is a subject on which I have pondered for years.
(B) Moreover, various stakeholders of our company–employees, investors, customers and vendors–come from across the globe.
(C) An organization is representative of society, and some of the lessons that I have learnt from the West regarding values are, I think, applicable to us as a nation.
(D) I come from a company that is built on strong values.
(E) In dealing with them over the years, I have come to appreciate several aspects of the West's value system.
(a) ABDEC (b) ADBEC
(c) DBECA (d) DBCAE
(e) ABCDE

40. (A) Indian culture has deep-rooted family values.
(B) Unfortunately, our attitude towards the community is very different from our attitude towards the family.
(C) Although we keep our homes spotlessly clean, when we go out we do not think twice before littering.
(D) Parents make enormous sacrifices for their children; children consider it their duty to take care of aged parents.
(E) And marriage is held to be a sacred union with husband and wife bonded for life.
(a) AEBCD (b) ACBED
(c) DEBCA (d) ADEBC
(e) DABCE

41. (A) 'To play great music,' he said, 'you must keep your eyes on a distant star.'
(B) Eleven years old, I was taking a violin lesson with Georges Enesco, my teacher, in his Paris studio.
(C) At the time, I took this to mean, simply, 'Give your very best to every piece.'
(D) A deep-chested, powerful man with a rugged, gentle face, Enesco looked at me across the violin he held under his chin, and shook his bow.
(a) BACD (b) BDAC
(c) DACB (d) DACB
(e) ACBD

42. (A) I felt the truth of it when I visited Rock-feller Institute.
(B) They were as dedicated as monks in a 14th century monastery, yet their lives were being fulfilled because their eyes were on the star.
(C) Here a scientist worked with quite absorption developing antibiotics; there, another investigated a possible cure for tuberculosis; a third studied the effects of too much sugar in the blood.
(D) You don't have to be a musician to benefit from my teacher's wisdom.
(a) CBAD (b) ACDB
(c) DACB (d) DABC
(e) ABCD

43. (A) They learned that if they brought the kid in, they could get another $5.
(B) The first time I went onstage with my father, I was five years old, and we were at a hotel in New York.
(C) My mother was being paid $5 as his pianist, and he got $15 to perform comedy and sing.
(D) I sang, 'Brother, Can You Spare a Dime?'
(a) DCBA (b) ADBC
(c) BCAD (d) BADC
(e) DABC

44. (A) I did everything–conducting the orchestra, monologue, mime, audience participation, playing instruments, dancing, singing, production numbers, incredible bits and pieces and wild physicality.
(B) My mum and dad came back to the dressing room, and I said, 'How was it, Dad?'
(C) Whew! I did a show in Vegas years later, in 1980, the best two hours and 20 minutes I ever had onstage.
(D) He said, 'It wasn't bad for an amateur.'
(a) DBAC (b) BCDA
(c) CABD (d) BDCA
(e) BADC

45. (A) When a man is his son's hero, it's about the best thing that God gave us on this planet.
(B) I can see it now with my son Anthony, who's been traveling with me and documenting my work.

(C) I was doing a lecture recently.
(D) And he was out in the audience with a camera, and I caught his face, that twinkles for a second, where his eyes said to me, that's my dad.
(a) ABCD (b) ACBD
(c) BACD (d) CBAD
(e) DABC

46. (A) On the one hand, I want very much for someone else to clean our house, as neither I nor my husband, Ed, has shown any aptitude for it.
(B) No one but me, for instance, should have to clean up the dental floss heaped like spaghetti near the wastebasket where I toss it each night, never catching on that floss is not something that can be thrown with a high degree of accuracy.
(C) On the other hand, I'd feel guilt inflicting such distasteful drudgery on another human being.
(D) Have always wanted and not wanted a cleaning person.
(a) DACB (b) CBAD
(c) CABD (d) ABDC
(e) BADC

47. (A) 'Are you all right?' I asked, as I helped her to her seat. 'That turbulence was as bad as it gets.'
(B) Flying in the summer in the US means one thing: turbulence.
(C) I was working as a flight attendant when we hit a patch of very rough air just after a young teenager, obviously on her first flight, had entered the bathroom.
(D) After the bumps had subsided, she exited the bathroom, a look of sheer terror etched on her face.
(E) 'So that's what it was,' she said, 'I thought I'd pushed the wrong button.'
(a) DAEBC (b) BCDAE
(c) AEBDC (d) CADBE
(e) ABCDE

48. (A) And when it happens on rare occasions that we 'cheat' death, we believe just for a moment, in immorality.
(B) Today scientists are tempting fate in ways never before imagined, as they demystify the secrets of longevity.
(C) We human beings are the only animals capable of contemplating our own demise.
(D) We mourn, we memorialize, we philosophize and we pray.
(a) DACB (b) DCBA
(c) CDAB (d) ABCD
(e) ABCD

49. (A) An expert in the genetics of aging, she believes that altering genes to extend life span may not be far off.
(B) Campisi is a senior molecular biologist at one of America's top research centers.
(C) Piles of papers rise from the floor like unsteady chimneys, some nearly as tall as four-foot ten scientists.
(D) In her basement office, Judith Campisi sits on the edge of a chair and speaks with wide-eyed enthusiasm, usually reserved for first-year graduate students.
(a) DCBA (b) DBCA
(c) BCAD (d) BDAC
(e) ABCD

50. (A) Paying the cable bill had been on my to-do list, but somehow it hadn't been paid in well, let's just say a number of months.
(B) As I handed over the cheque, I mumbled my apologies and berated myself for my oversight.
(C) I was packing the paper into my briefcase when the doorbell rang.
(D) It was a bill collector from the local cable-TV company.
(E) Shouldn't have been home that afternoon eight years ago, but I had forgotten a term paper and was close to missing the 3pm deadline.
(F) After all, I was a student of library science, and keeping track of papers was supposed to be my specialty.
(a) ECDBAF (b) CDBAFE
(c) ECDABF (d) CDBFEA
(e) CBADEF

51. (A) If you're like me, your toughest decisions will come in your reference files.
(B) My personal rule of thumb is that if I haven't used a piece of information for two years, I get rid of it.
(C) Of course, it's a law of nature that whenever you finally get rid of something, you will always need it the very next day.
(D) I recommend going through your files once a year, discarding information that is old or out-of-date.
(a) DBAC (b) DABC
(c) CBAD (d) ACBD
(e) ABCD

52. (A) I placed my new treadmill in the middle of our family room to encourage myself to use it.
(B) 'No one,' Julia replied in her most convincing tone. 'Not even my mum.'
(C) My children knew they were not to touch it, but their friends often gravitated to it.

(D) Months after I bought the treadmill, I knew I had been remiss in my fitness plan but didn't realize how much until my five-years-old daughter Julia had her friend Makenzie over to play.

(E) From a nearby room I heard Julia say, 'That's Mummy's treadmill, and no one is allowed to use it.'

(F) 'No one?' asked her friend.

(a) ACDFBE (b) ACDBFE
(c) ACDEFB (d) DCAFBE
(e) ABCDEF

53. (A) Wasting little time, he started T.T. Pond Company and began commercially marketing the product.

(B) A druggist by profession and a businessman in the making, he was amazed by the curative powers of an extract made using the witch hazel shrub.

(C) 1907 proved to be a major turning point, with the addition of Ponds Cold Cream, legendary classic even today.

(D) T.T. Pond did not imagine the success his little trip during 1846 to a remote Indian settlement in upstate New York would create.

(E) It was called thus because of the cooling effect evaporation caused on the skin.

(a) DBACE (b) DBCEA
(c) ABCDE (d) ACBDE
(e) ADBCE

54. (A) Nunes is taking me down Transpanteneria Highway, a 150-kilometer ribbon of red dirt and 127 plank bridges, that runs south form Pocone to Porto Jofre.

(B) They used soil from alongside the highway, leaving trenches filled with water and fish that attract other animals in abundance.

(C) As a result, the Transpantaneira Highway may offer the greatest wildlife show on earth.

(D) The engineers who built this raised the surface about four meters from then surrounding terrain to keep it dry during the rainy season.

(a) DBAC (b) DBCA
(c) ADBC (d) BCAD
(e) BACD

55. (A) Strutting and vaguely comic, two female rheas head for nests where their two males guard the eggs with menacing looks.

(B) My host, cattle rancher Jose Tocqueville de Carvalho Neta, says that the rheas will occasionally rearrange the eggs in the nest.

(C) The Ostrich-like birds are here in front of the Campo Neta Lodge, a five-room Mexican farm house in the middle of the Pantanal.

(D) 'This happens so they will not take the sun in only one position.'

(a) ABCD (b) ACBD
(c) ADCB (d) ABDC
(e) CABD

56. (A) But, transportation is difficult and the Pantanal is little known outside of Brazil.

(B) The people who live here have their fingers crossed.

(C) Because if ecotourism doesn't work, an alternative is waiting.

(D) There are now some 60-tourist facilities here, most of them small and locally owned

(E) Worldwide, the jury is still out on the idea of ecotourism and the Pantanal has become a testing ground

(a) EDABC (b) DAEBC
(c) ECBAD (d) EDCBA
(e) ABCDE

57. (A) Carolina Coelho sits up in her saddle, turns 90 degrees and points to a stately umbauba tree.

(B) 'Toucans feed on the eggs and nestling of other birds,' my guide says.

(C) 'So they make a lot of enemies'

(D) Shading my eyes with my hand, I still can't see the creature until it flies off with a dozen smaller birds in pursuit.

(E) 'Toucan,' she says.

(a) ADBCE (b) AEDBC
(c) ACDEB (d) ADECB
(e) ABCDE

58. (A) The subject has two half ping-pong balls taped over his eyes and wears headphones that emit a roar of static–he is in a sensory cocoon, a uniform field of light and sound.

(B) This is so he can pick up psychic signals without distraction.

(C) On the top floor of the psychology department building at Edinburgh University, Professor Robert Morris and his team are performing an experiment.

(D) You read that right: psychic signals.

(a) CABD (b) BCDA
(c) ABCD (d) DABC
(e) ADBC

59. (A) On a cold day in Tornato I meet Professor James Alcock at York University, one of the most widely respected skeptics.

(B) 'I have a lot of respect for the leading parapsychologist I know personally,' he says.
(C) Alcock has spent decades analyzing the procedures used by parapsychologists and advising on how to make them watertight.
(D) 'In a few cases, we've gone through the same research report and independently come up with the same flaws, usually statistical errors.'
(a) ABCD (b) ACBD
(c) DCBA (d) DCAB
(e) ADBC

60. (A) He has set up the James Randi Educational Foundation to challenge believers to prove their statements about paranormal abilities.
(B) If someone chases will-o'-the-wisps like speaking with the dead, it subverts them from things that could really help them.
(C) So if the paranormal consists of nothing more than occasionally being able to sense that someone is staring at us, does it matter if science accept the parapsychologists' results or not.
(D) Randi is adamant it does.
(a) BACD (b) ACDB
(c) DCBA (d) BCDA
(e) ABCD

61. (A) Four-year-old Evan Petropoulos has a serious infection.
(B) So it might be tough to comprehend why the little guy is giggling like a maniac.
(C) The infection has swollen Evan's right eye shut and put him in considerable pain.
(D) He's in the hospital with an IV in his arm.
(a) BACD (b) CBAD
(c) BDAC (d) ADCB
(e) DABC

62. (A) Using humour to ease pain and help healing is no laughing matter to a growing number of doctors, nurses and health care workers.
(B) We all know that it feels great to engage in a good laugh, but a small yet significant body of research suggests that the ability to see life from the lighter side may be medicinal.
(C) And even help diabetics control their blood sugar.
(D) Studies have hinted that humour can alleviate allergy symptoms, increase pain tolerance, bolster the disease-fighting immune system, reduce the risk of stroke and heart attack.
(a) ADCB (b) ADBC
(c) ABDC (d) DACB
(e) ABCD

63. (A) That's where Jennifer Lopez, the daughter of Puerto Rican immigrants, got her start, singing and dancing in neighborhood shows in New York City.
(B) She's dressed all in white–squeaky-clean running shoes and velour track suit she designed herself, with a 'J. Lo' insignia over the breast.
(C) She's come a long way from the Kips Bay Boys & Girls Club.
(D) Today she's in Vancouver, filming *An Unfinished Life*, in which she teams up with Robert Redford.
(a) DBCA (b) ADBC
(c) CDAB (d) CADB
(e) ABCD

64. (A) Wandering along the streets of New York city, my daughters and I stop at shoe stores wherever we happen to be.
(B) This is their choice, these women who as little girls teetered around the house balancing like cranes in my mother's high heels.
(C) I sit on a bench and wait while they try on shoe after shoe, readjusting their positions in the mirror, eyes down cast, considering their feet.
(D) 'So?' one of them will ask me. 'What do you think of these?'
(a) ADBC (b) DBCA
(c) ABCD (d) DCBA
(e) CABD

65. (A) And long before anyone in my class had heard of ballroom dancing, my mother played swing music on the gramophone in the living room, took me in her arms and taught me how.
(B) By age 12, after a series of operations, I could walk unaided.
(C) By the time I was seven, my mother had moved on to tennis, which she decided I could play while wearing black galoshes over my brown orthopedic shoes.
(D) When I turned 15, she signed me up for dancing school with boys.
(a) CABD (b) BACD
(c) CDAB (d) ABCD
(e) CDBA

66. (A) If my husband, Ed, had his way, you could pop by our place any given night and see me sitting in bed, struggling to hold my head up under the weight of a night-vision headset.
(B) Ed is an early-to-sleep sort of chap, who'll announce around 8 pm 'just going to change into my pajamas and read for a while.'
(C) Once he becomes horizontal, however, it's pretty much over.

(D) This makes it difficult for yours truly, for I really do read in bed, including the part where you turn the page and read a second one and then a third one.
(a) BACD (b) ACBD
(c) BCAD (d) ABCD
(e) ADBC

67. (A) We call it Pillow Mountain.
(B) I roll over in the middle of the night and find myself suffocating against a towering mound of goose down.
(C) I offered to stop eating in bed if Ed would agree to wean himself from his need for multiple pillows.
(D) A married couple can best be defined as a unit of people whose sleep habits are carefully engineered to keep each other awake.
(a) DABC (b) DCBA
(c) ABCD (d) ACBD
(e) ADBC

68. (A) It's that rare state when it seems you can do no wrong.
(B) You know the feeling.
(C) Maybe you're playing tennis and every shot is landing right where you aim it.
(D) Or perhaps solutions to those gnarly work problems are coming to you so easily that you wonder why they seemed insurmountable before.
(E) Why is it that sometimes you fire on all cylinders and at other times you can't even start the engine?
(F) For most of us, these moments of visions and high performance are too rare.
(G) The answer may be this: You're at your best when you get your mind out of the way.
(a) BACDFEG (b) FEGBAC
(c) CDEGFBA (d) AFEGDCB
(e) ABCDEFG

69. (A) Every bit of his well-muscled arms is covered with tattoos.
(B) Today Kent Lindahl is the father of two children, has finished college, and is working towards a degree in psychotherapy.
(C) Yet fragments of his past will always haunt him.
(D) With his intelligent eyes, neatly trimmed beard and wire-rimmed glasses, Lindahl looks like a professor–until he rolls up his sleeves.
(a) BDCA (b) BCDA
(c) DCBA (d) DBCA
(e) ABCD

70. (A) Amberry teaches professional basketball players how to shoot free throws and has produced an instructional book and video.
(B) The key, he says, is to become mentally absorbed in a physical routine, which clears the head of negative ideas, such as missing the shot.
(C) 'You can't have an extraneous thought in your mind when you make that free throw,' says Amberry.
(D) Refocusing the mind to eliminate the buzz and the static of everyday thought, according to a new book by Dr Herbert Benson, has powers beyond the basketball court.
(a) ACBD (b) ABCD
(c) CABD (d) CBDA
(e) BACD

71. (A) So she took her dog, Elsie Mae, for a stroll on the beach near her home in California.
(B) Of course, some people seem to know intuitively that the best way to cope with a problem can be to walk away from it.
(C) Artist and graphic designer Lisa Gizara, 43, was struggling to come up with a fresh advertising idea for one of her clients, a computer company.
(D) She took a few more steps, and saw an image: Michelangelo's 'Creations of Adam,' which features the famous detail of God's and Adam's fingers nearly touching.
(E) As they tromped across the sand, suddenly a phrase popped into Gizara's head: 'Get connected.'
(a) DACEB (b) EDCBA
(c) CDAEB (d) BCAED
(e) ABCDE

72. (A) Benson believes that when you 'break the train of everyday thought'–a phrase he repeats like a mantra–your body increases production of a gas molecule called nitric oxide (not to be confused with nitrous oxide, or laughing gas).
(B) Scientists once thought nitric oxide, or NO, was merely a toxin.
(C) It's a component of cigarette smoke, for example.
(D) But in the late 1980s, researchers learned that the gas is made in the human body and plays a role in a range of physiological processes, such as controlling blood pressure.
(a) ACBD (b) ABCD
(c) BDCA (d) BCDA
(e) DABC

73. (A) Many of his colleagues told him he was wasting his time and would ruin his career.

(B) But Benson went on to become a pioneer in the now-nourishing field known as mind-body medicine, which explores how our thoughts and feelings contribute to disease.
(C) Benson has grown accustomed to skepticism about his work.
(D) Trained as a cardiologist at Harvard Medical School, Benson began in the 1960s to study how stress affects physical well being, then considered a radical idea.
(a) CDAB (b) CBAD
(c) CDBA (d) CABD
(e) BACD

74. (A) To the soundtrack of cicadas and the wind in the leaves, Abrams repeated the motions, over and over, until her brain and body went on autopilot.
(B) 'It's a very Zen kind of thing.'
(C) She would sit in the night air for hours, slowly rocking the treadle of a spinning wheel with her feet and guiding the fibres with sweeping motions of her arm.
(D) Consider Charlene Abrams, who spent every free evening in the summer of 1994 on the front step of her home, spinning yarn.
(E) 'You get into this almost altered state,' says Abrams, 43, a software engineer.
(F) 'Sitting there spinning, my mind wanders and goes wherever it needs to go.'
(a) ABCDEF (b) ACFBED
(c) DCABEF (d) DACBEF
(e) FABEDC

75. (A) And then suppose you pushed the 'Reverse' button and took a trip in the opposite direction–journeying into the dim recesses of the past.
(B) Just suppose you could clamber aboard a Time Machine and press the 'Forward' button.
(C) You might just land right into your favorite period of history.
(D) Z..a.Ap..Would you hurtle forward through a blinding flash of days and nights, months and years–even long centuries–perhaps, to land into an alien world of the future...?
(E) A world that will be a marvel of technology.
(a) CDABE (b) CBADE
(c) BDEAC (d) BDECA
(e) DABCE

76. (A) Could you think of a world without time?
(B) It all sounds too good to be true, or even practical for that matter, does it not?
(C) To be able to play on endlessly without being told that it was time to go home...
(D) For a world without time would probably be a totally chaotic place to live in, where everything happened all at once–a kind of topsy-turvy land!
(E) Imagine what it would be like not to have to tumble out of bed to the shrill buzz of the morning alarm and to hurry to catch the school bus!
(a) AECBD (b) AECDB
(c) CDBAE (d) ECBDA
(e) DECBA

77. (A) It covers 1,86,000 miles per second.
(B) This means you would zoom more than seven times around the world in one second!
(C) Light travels at an enormous speed, faster than anything else we know.
(D) The distance will be about 58,80,000,000,000 miles. This distance is called a light year.
(E) It has a speed more than 5,00,000 times faster than the Concorde. Now calculate how far light will travel in a year.
(a) CEABD (b) CEDAB
(c) CABDE (d) CABED
(e) CBADE

78. (A) Small distance, such as the length and breadth of this book, are measured in centimeters or inches.
(B) Even millions or billions of miles would not be enough to express these immense distances. We need an altogether different unit for measuring them.
(C) However, sizes and distance in the universe are too vast to be measured in terms of any of these units.
(D) Bigger distances are measured in meters or feet, while still bigger distances are measured in terms of any of these units.
(E) The stars of our galaxy whirl together in space in a gigantic spiral, so vast that ordinary words for describing hugeness just cannot describe this.
(a) ABCDE (b) ADBEC
(c) ADCBE (d) ADCEB
(e) AEBCD

79. (A) In ancient times, man had a very simple picture of the universe.
(B) He believed that the sun, moon, stars, and planets were small objects that moved round the earth.
(C) The universe was taken to be a great dome overhead having glittering lights.

(D) Below, in the centre of all creation, lay the vast, flat, immovable earth, around which everything else moved.

(a) ABCD (b) ABDC
(c) ACBD (d) ACDB
(e) CABD

80. (A) Then the earth turned green and joyful, the birds sang and flowers bloomed. And then came the blazing, hot summer when the earth became parched and dry, and everything dried up.
(B) The cold, windy winter when man huddled before a fire to keep himself warm was followed by spring.
(C) The monsoons provided some solace from the heat. And leaves fell off the trees in autumn before winter came once again.
(D) This cycle of seasons covered about 365 days or a whole year.
(E) It is likely that the change in seasons gave birth to the idea of the year.

(a) EBACD (b) BACDE
(c) EDBAC (d) CABED
(e) ABCDE

81. (A) At night it disappears altogether from our sight.
(B) It is *we* who have moved!
(C) Just as it appeared to our ancestors, the sun seems to us to rise in the east and journey across the vast archway of the sky before setting in the west.
(D) This movement does not actually happen, but appears to do so.
(E) The sun at night is in exactly the same place as it was during the day.

(a) CEABD (b) CADBE
(c) CABED (d) CADEB
(e) BCEAD

82. (A) The shadow clock was a clever invention, although not a very accurate timekeeper.
(B) It was a fairly simple device, consisting of a straight base placed in an east to west direction, on which stood a crosspiece.
(C) This crosspiece was placed at the east end of the base in the morning, and shifted to the west end in the afternoon.
(D) As the sun's rays fell on the crosspiece, it cast its shadow on the base.
(E) This was marked by a scale of six time divisions, so intervals of time could be measured.

(a) ABCDE (b) ABECD
(c) ABCED (d) CABED
(e) DACBE

83. (A) If the water level fell to the next mark, it showed that the clock had run for two hours.
(B) In this way, as marks were exposed, the time could be read.
(C) To start the clock, the vessel was filled to the brim with water. As the water ran out through the hole in the bottom, the level of water in the vessel kept falling.
(D) The water-clock was actually a basin shaped, stone vessel with a small hole at the bottom. Its inner walls were marked with divisions to show the hours, so the 'clock' was easy to read.
(E) When the water level dropped to the first mark on the walls, it indicated that the clock had been running for one hour.

(a) DEACB (b) DECAB
(c) DCBEA (d) DCEAB
(e) DBCEA

84. (A) The ancient Greek philosopher Plato invented an ingenious alarm clock by fitting a siphon (a bent tube used to transfer liquids from one vessel to another) to a water-clock.
(B) Plato effectively used this device to summon his pupils for classes at the unearthly hour of 4 a.m.
(C) Since this had to be set six hours beforehand, Plato probably did not get much sleep himself as he set about adjusting it!
(D) As soon as the water was level with the top of the siphon, it ran down a tube into a vessel below so quickly that the air in it was compressed, and escaped through a pipe with a piercing whistle.
(E) It is not likely that they could have continued to sleep once their alarm clock went off.

(a) ABDEC (b) ADBEC
(c) ABCDE (d) ADBCE
(e) ACBED

85. (A) When the sand has run through from one glass vessel to the other, the egg is hardboiled.
(B) Today, if you want to boil an egg for three minutes and you have an egg-timer or three minute sandglass, you cannot really go wrong.
(C) Start the sand 'clock' as soon as you have dropped the egg into boiling water in the fire.
(D) But if you are impatient and do not wait for the sand to run right through, you will have to eat a rather 'gooey' egg.
(E) If, on the other hand, the egg keeps boiling after the sandglass has run through, you will have to chew a very hard-boiled egg indeed!

(a) BAECD (b) BECAD
(c) BCADE (d) BADCE
(e) BACED

86. (A) It was taken from the French word *Cloche* which means a bell.
(B) French was widely spoken by the English upper classes, and many English words were 'borrowed' from it.
(C) In fact, even before mechanical clocks existed, churches and monasteries rang bells to tell the common folk that it was time for prayers.
(D) Bells were, therefore, associated with clocks in those early days of mechanical timekeeping.
(E) The word 'clock' or 'cloch' as it was called in Middle English, goes back to this time.
(a) EABDC (b) BACDE
(c) EABCD (d) EACDB
(e) CABDE

87. (A) With the twentieth century, time had to be much more exact.
(B) After all, it had to keep pace with the new science and technology that was sweeping the modern world.
(C) Even one-hundredth of a second mattered in fields like astronomy.
(D) Accuracy no longer meant keeping time to the half minute or even second.
(a) ABDC (b) ABCD
(c) DCBA (d) DCAB
(e) DABC

88. (A) These were really our earliest calendars.
(B) They simply used sticks with crude notches in them to count the days, or strings with knots in them to keep a record of so many full moons or even seasons.
(C) In those far-off days, there were no fancy calendars like the one you have hung up in your room to keep track of the year.
(D) They probably called a number of days so many 'dawns' or 'suns'.
(E) Ancient tribes used a dawn-to-dawn reckoning to count the days.
(a) EDCAB (b) EDCBA
(c) CEDBA (c) CAEDB
(e) ABCDE

89. (A) Every calendar welcomes the first day of the year as the 'NEW YEAR'. This is one of the oldest and gayest customs of mankind, and is celebrated the world over.
(B) New Year's day is a great time for parties and reunions that ring out the old year and ring in the new one.
(C) It is a time to make New Year 'resolutions' as well, though these are soon forgotten!
(D) In the bigger cities of the world, many people collect in a big square to welcome the New Year. They greet each other and embrace each other.
(E) In London, Trafalgar Square is the traditional gathering place, while Times Square is popular in New York.
(a) ABCED (b) ADECB
(c) ABCDE (d) BCDEA
(e) AEBCD

90. (A) At sixteen, Mamie was something of a knockout.
(B) She had wide blue eyes, a pert nose, soft brown hair worn long with a dip over her high forehead, and one of the most infectious smiles around.
(C) As the prettiest Doud girl, she drew many young men to the house on Saturday afternoons and Sunday evenings, when they would gather around the piano to sing.
(D) All this was coupled with a gaiety of personality, an honesty and a directness that were most appealing.
(a) DCBA (b) ACDB
(c) CDAB (d) ABDC
(e) DABC

91. (A) He was about to receive an honorary degree of Doctor of Laws.
(B) In 1948, he would assume the presidency of Columbia.
(C) Precisely at four o' clock on a snow February afternoon in 1947, Dwight David Eisenhower, in full military uniform, walked down the aisle in the great rotunda of Law Memorial Library at Columbia University in New York City.
(D) In 1945, he had returned in triumph from Europe, where he had served as Supreme Commander of the Allied Expeditionary Forces.
(a) CDAB (b) BDAC
(c) ACBD (d) CABD
(e) ABCD

92. (A) After all, he was only a soldier and a poor boy, and everybody felt he was marrying above his 'class'.
(B) and...people felt she could have done a good deal better.
(C) 'The Douds were well off financially,'
(D) When the engagement of Dwight David Eisenhower and Mamie Doud was announced in Denver, neighbours were astounded at Mamie's choice.

(a) ABDC (b) DCBA
(c) ACBD (d) CBDA
(e) ABCD

93. (A) At the end of their lives, it could truly be said that they loved each other more than on the day they first met.
(B) Yet the steadfast devotion and mutual respect of the general and his lady carried them through the travails of World War II and on to the triumphs of the White House.
(C) Ike and Mamie had no such misgivings as they took their vows–or throughout their warm and loving marriage of almost fifty-three years.
(D) Innumerable army-ordered separations, the tragic loss of their first son, and the rumors on two continents of Ike's involvement with another woman were almost devastating.
(E) The way was not always smooth.
(a) ABECD (b) CEDBA
(c) CDEBA (d) BCADE
(e) ABCDE

94. (A) Mother Morag not only saw them, she deliberately came up to her cell to watch them–her window overlooked the road–but this was not Dilbury, England, not the mists and freshness of the downs.
(B) There, the first sound was the bird chorus, especially larks; here, the first sound was cawing of crows.
(C) Early every morning of each racing season, Mother Morag, Reverend Mother of the Sisters of our lady of poverty, saw the string go by, a line of horses, brown, bay, chestnut–worst of all colors–in the heat; now and again a roan, or a dappled gray.
(D) In winter, there was mist, but it swirled above arid dust, because this was Calcutta, India, and the string was not Michael Traherne's– Michael, friend of royalty and other famous owners–it was John Quillan's, he who had defiantly chosen to drop out.
(a) CBAD (b) ABDC
(c) BACD (d) CABD
(e) ABCD

95. (A) They had to wait in the outer kitchens, among squalid washing up, shouting, horseplay.
(B) The night round was hard, not only on the sisters but on Solomon and Gulab.
(C) Solomon often had to stand for half an hour-some restaurants seemed to take pleasure in keeping the sisters waiting–and in the cold-weather months, Solomon and Gulab shivered.
(D) The sisters, too, often met with contempt.
(a) BCAD (b) ADCB
(c) DCBA (d) BADC
(e) ABCD

96. (A) Ted raised his head.
(B) He was sitting where he had sat for most of the last two days, at the desk in the darkest corner of the darkened room.
(C) He had kept the shutters closed.
(D) There was nothing on the desk now; the photograph of him and Ella in her 'lace curtain' had been shut away in the drawer, as had been the framed form of his new license.
(a) ADBC (b) BCAD
(c) ABCD (d) DACB
(e) CABD

97. (A) My sense of direction wasn't clear, and at first, I didn't know where we were going.
(B) We left the car in the almost empty parking area and walked once more into a world of perfect beauty and harmony.
(C) Beside me, Rick was quiet, though tension showed in his hands on the wheel.
(D) Not until I saw the lighted bell tower of Tlaquepaque did I realize where we were.
(a) ACDB (b) DCAB
(c) CBDA (d) ADCB
(e) BACD

98. (A) Without a pause he rushed outside to search the vicinity.
(B) When Rick came back, I started, as though I'd been in a trance.
(C) I followed him into the shop, and just when we stepped inside, a sound came back from the back, as if something had been knocked over in the darkness.
(D) It was a while before he returned, his effort futile.
(E) He ran into the rear rooms, and I waited tensely among the counters, remembering the desecrated blue cloth upstairs.
(F) Rick flicked switches, and the shop blazed with light.
(a) CFEBAD (b) CEFABD
(c) BACEFA (d) CBFEDA
(e) BDCEAF

99. (A) The boy looked puzzled and disappointed.
(B) As he walked down the path, a park Service ranger heard him blurt out to his mother, 'But it looks just like Grandma's house!'
(C) It does, and it did.

(D) In 1980, when the Eisenhower Gettysburg farm was opened to the public, a young boy and his mother emerged after a tour of the stone and brick house on the edge of the Civil War battlefield.

(a) ACDB (b) DACB
(c) CBDA (d) DABC
(e) ABDC

100. (A) 'Johnny, how do you keep so lean?'
(B) Mr. Leventine did not lunch there either–anyone thinking of inviting him would have been quietly persuaded not to by the club secretary, 'as they would with me,' John could have said, for a different reason.'
(C) Mr. Leventine had once lamented. John gritted his teeth.
(D) The Bengal club had the best food east of Suez and a renowned wine cellar.
(E) 'Sweat,' said John, 'and I don't lunch at the Bengal Club.'
(F) He detested the nickname.

(a) EFBDCA (b) ACFEDB
(c) CFAEDB (d) DEAFBC
(e) ABCDEF

101. (A) He was arriving tomorrow and she hadn't finished her programme.
(B) The school inspector.
(C) Too late.
(D) She snuggled down in her bed, hoping to push the worry away for a little longer.
(E) She knew there was something unpleasant in her memory and that it would be in her consciousness in seconds.
(F) Sally Jones opened her eyes at seven a.m. that May 8 and looked at the rust stain on the ceiling.

(a) FEBCDA (b) EBADCF
(c) FEDCBA (d) DCFEBA
(e) EFABCD

102. (A) It was the school inspector and another person, unknown to them.
(B) A car pulled up, and two men got out and walked toward the little group.
(C) Sally was reading aloud.
(D) Magpies called from the pepper tree and, high above, an eagle circled, watching for prey, barely moving its wings.
(E) Later that day, the children and their teacher were sitting on the grass in the warm winter sun.

(a) EDCBA (b) ABEDC
(c) EDABC (d) DCEAB
(e) ABCDE

103. (A) Gabrielle Lord published her first novel, *Fortress*, to instant acclaim in her native Australia.
(B) The eldest of six children, she grew up in Sydney and attended the University of New England, in Armidle, New South Wales.
(C) Success did not come easily, however.
(D) Writing appealed to her even as a child–she was composing stories at nine.
(E) But it wasn't until she was thirty that she completed her first book, a literary novel that was rejected by every publishing firm to which it was sent.

(a) ADBCE (b) CDEBA
(c) ACBDE (d) DEBAC
(e) ABCDE

104. (A) I can still hear Mother calling from the staircase landing, 'Mary, is your light out?'
(B) Then I would set the alarm so that in the morning I could get up early, fix a cup of hot cocoa and snuggle back in bed for a blissful hour with my current book.
(C) Yes, it was–but the streetlight in front of my window threw a very satisfactory beam on my pillow, and most evenings I would manage to sneak in a little extra reading.
(D) It was heaven!

(a) ABCD (b) DABC
(c) BCAD (d) ACBD
(e) CABD

105. (A) From halfway up that hill, one can see on the clear autumn day most of the majesty that is Washington.
(B) Across the muddy Potomac from the Lincoln Memorial a gentle slope rises gradually to what was once the home of Robert E. Lee.
(C) The three marble monuments and memorials—to the men who forged in the Presidency an instrument of power and compassion–remind a grateful nation that it has been blessed in its gravest trials with its greatest leaders.
(D) In the distance, the dome of the capital covers a milieu of wisdom and folly, Presidential ambitions and antagonisms, political ideals and ideologies.

(a) CABD (b) BACD
(c) BCAD (d) DABC
(e) ABCD

106. (A) The senator never wore a ring, a diamond stickpin or any jewellery other than an ordinary watch and tie clasp.
(B) But he was not ashamed of the fact that his father's wealth had enabled him to present himself for public office without being financially dependent on powerful pressure groups.
(C) His political campaigns, while costly, avoided the kind of lavish display (such as billboards, full-page advertisements or telethons) that might provoke charges of excess.
(D) All his government salaries–as Congressman, Senator and President–he donated to charity, roughly half a million dollars.
(a) ADCB (b) CDBA
(c) BADC (d) BCAD
(e) DABC

107. (A) Despite many similarities, each of the Kennedys differed from the Senator and from each other.
(B) But they were bound by ties of genuine filial and fraternal affection, ties that were strengthened by family tragedy and pride.
(C) But when it came to competing with the rest of the world, the warmth of their solidarity strengthened Jack and awed his adversaries.
(D) They were all intensely competitive and at home, vied with each other.
(a) CDAB (b) ABDC
(c) CDBA (d) DCAB
(e) DABC

108. (A) Ever interested in history, he asked Senator Hayden what changes, if any, had occurred in that time, and the reply was: 'New members did not speak in those days.'
(B) He was too young, too liberal and too out spoken.
(C) Senator Kennedy was never a full-fledged member of the Senate's inner circle, the 'club' whose influence has been exaggerated by both its defenders and its detractors.
(D) Early in his first term, his participation in a floor debate caused him to move closer to the front from his seat in the back row, and he found himself temporarily sitting next to Senate 'Dean' Carl Hayden, who had entered Congress more than forty years earlier.
(a) ACDB (b) ABDC
(c) BCDA (d) CBDA
(e) DABC

109. (A) The speech proved to be substantially, and in some ways distressingly prophetic in subsequent years, but it was bitterly criticized at the time in Washington as well as Paris.
(B) A tremendous amount of staff research preceded every Kennedy talk.
(C) He was known in the library of Congress as the heaviest borrower of their reference works.
(D) One of the most carefully researched, widely publicized and officially ignored speeches Senator Kennedy ever delivered was his address in 1957, outlining the interest of America and the west in a negotiated solution of eventual self-determination in Algeria.
(E) His same speech, he later discovered, was hailed throughout North Africa–and an American correspondent who visited the Algerian camp related to the Senator his surprise at being interviewed by weary grimy rebels on Kennedy's chances for the Presidency.
(F) He did not make as many major Senate speeches as some of his more vocal colleagues, nor did he measure his–or their–effectiveness by the publicity a speech was given.
(a) BDEFAC (b) CDEAFB
(c) BCFDAE (d) ADEFBC
(e) ABEDCF

110. (A) The only two other people in the house had been a servant who was drunk and a chauffeur enraged at the servant.
(B) While they chased each other threatening murder, the then Senator sat alone with his crutches in deadly still air, watching nature's fury swirl about him and wondering whether he would survive.
(C) In 1961, he found himself once again in the eye of a hurricane.
(D) John Kennedy once recalled with humor the day at Cape Cod when he sat handicapped by his bad back, in the eye of a New England hurricane.
(a) DABC (b) CDAB
(c) DACB (d) ACDB
(e) CABD

Answer Key

1. (a)	**2.** (b)	**3.** (a)	**4.** (b)	**5.** (a)
6. (d)	**7.** (b)	**8.** (b)	**9.** (a)	**10.** (a)
11. (d)	**12.** (b)	**13.** (a)	**14.** (b)	**15.** (b)
16. (c)	**17.** (b)	**18.** (d)	**19.** (a)	**20.** (a)
21. (c)	**22.** (b)	**23.** (c)	**24.** (b)	**25.** (a)
26. (c)	**27.** (a)	**28.** (a)	**29.** (d)	**30.** (b)
31. (b)	**32.** (c)	**33.** (a)	**34.** (c)	**35.** (c)
36. (c)	**37.** (b)	**38.** (a)	**39.** (b)	**40.** (d)
41. (b)	**42.** (c)	**43.** (c)	**44.** (c)	**45.** (a)
46. (a)	**47.** (b)	**48.** (c)	**49.** (a)	**50.** (c)
51. (b)	**52.** (c)	**53.** (a)	**54.** (c)	**55.** (b)
56. (a)	**57.** (b)	**58.** (a)	**59.** (b)	**60.** (d)
61. (d)	**62.** (c)	**63.** (d)	**64.** (c)	**65.** (a)
66. (d)	**67.** (b)	**68.** (a)	**69.** (b)	**70.** (b)
71. (d)	**72.** (b)	**73.** (a)	**74.** (c)	**75.** (c)
76. (a)	**77.** (d)	**78.** (d)	**79.** (a)	**80.** (a)
81. (d)	**82.** (a)	**83.** (d)	**84.** (b)	**85.** (c)
86. (a)	**87.** (a)	**88.** (b)	**89.** (c)	**90.** (d)
91. (d)	**92.** (b)	**93.** (b)	**94.** (d)	**95.** (a)
96. (c)	**97.** (d)	**98.** (a)	**99.** (d)	**100.** (b)
101. (c)	**102.** (a)	**103.** (c)	**104.** (d)	**105.** (b)
106. (a)	**107.** (b)	**108.** (d)	**109.** (c)	**110.** (a)

CHAPTER 16 Level of Difficulty—II

1. (A) Aristotle begins his treatise on metaphysics with the assertion that all human beings have the desire to acquire knowledge.
   (B) As evidence, Aristotle cites the delight that we take in sense perception, and in particular, in vision.
   (C) By this, he means that we value knowledge for its own sake, entirely apart from its utility.
   (D) His teacher, Plato, expressed the delight in vision in a still more radical way in the *Symposium* by attributing it to a demonic force, Eros.
   (E) The sense that discriminates the largest number of intelligible forms.
   (a) ABCDE (b) ACBED
   (c) ABCED (d) ADBCE
   (e) ADBEC
2. (A) There is so much disagreement about the correct sense of Holy Scripture that the claim that this sense is manifest is itself an interpretation, and so subject to rejection.
   (B) Prophets, preachers, and scholars alike, all attempt to derive the genuine will of God from the revealed text.
   (C) The commands of God, that is, the contents of divine revelation, are sufficiently ambiguous that they require interpretation.
   (D) But this distinction cannot be unambiguously preserved, for a very simple reason.
   (E) We seem to have arrived at a sharp distinction between philosophy and religion.
   (a) ABCED (b) CEDAB
   (c) EDCAB (d) CABED
   (e) DABCE
3. (A) Everything that we experience as material reality, is born in an invisible realm beyond space and time, a realm revealed by science to consist of energy and information.
   (B) What would the facts be like if we had them? They would be as follows.
   (C) This invisible source of all that exists is not an empty void, but the womb of creation itself.
   (D) Something creates and organizes this energy.
   (E) It turns the chaos of quantum soup into stars, galaxies, rain forests, human beings, and our own thoughts, emotions, memories and desires.
   (a) ACEDB (b) BACED
   (c) ADCEB (d) BCDEA
   (e) CABDE
4. (A) The experience of God feels like flying.
   (B) It feels as if I'm walking above the ground with such equibrium that nothing can sway me from my path.
   (C) It's like being the eye of the storm.
   (D) I see without judgment or opinion.
   (E) It's just as everything passes in and out of my awareness like clouds.
   (a) ABEDC (b) ABDCE
   (c) ABCDE (d) ADCEB
   (e) EADCB
5. (A) This is far from true.
   (B) It is typical of modern life to believe that nature is set up to be random and chaotic.
   (C) As one spiritual teacher wisely put it, "The material world is infinite, but it is a boring infinity. The really interesting infinity lies beyond."

(D) Life looks meaningless when you have worn out old responses, old realities, and an old version of God.

(E) To bring God back, we have to follow new, even strange responses wherever they lead us.

(a) DCBEA (b) DCEBA
(c) DECBA (d) BADEC
(e) EABDC

6. (A) The whole universe is as we are, because without the human mind, there would be only quantum soup, billions of random sensory impressions.

(B) He is as real as they are, but just as elusive.

(C) Yet thanks to the mind/brain, we recognize that encoded into the swirling cosmos, are the most valued things in existence: form, meaning, beauty, truth, love.

(D) These are the realities the brain is reaching for when it reaches for God.

(E) The most startling conclusion of our new model is that God is as we are.

(a) EBCDA (b) ADCBE
(c) EACDB (d) AEBCD
(e) DABCE

7. (A) From quarks to quasars, all will be revealed as the old melodramas used to promise.

(B) Is there a place for God in this "everything," or does the Creator get booted out of his own creation?

(C) Some scientists believe we are closer than ever to a "Theory of Everything," or TOE, as the physicists dub it. TOE will explain the beginning of the universe and the end of time, the first and last breaths of cosmic existence.

(D) His fate may be important, but when it is wrapped up with ours, it becomes all-important.

(E) The mystery of God wouldn't exist if the world wasn't also a mystery.

(a) CBADE (b) CBDAE
(c) EDCAB (d) ECABD
(e) DEABC

8. (A) Neurologists have long divided the brain into old and new. The new brain is an organ to be proud of.

(B) When you have a reasoned thought, it is this area of gray matter, primarily the cerebral cortex that comes into play.

(C) Shakespeare was referring to the new brain (and using it) when he had Hamlet utter, "What a piece of work is a man, how noble in reason, how infinite in faculties."

(D) But Hamlet was also wrapped up in a murder case that called for vengeance, and as he dug deeper into the sins of his family, he dug deeper into his own mind.

(E) The old brain wanted its due; this is the part of us that claws for survival and is willing to kill, if need be to protect us.

(a) ACEDB (b) ACDEB
(c) ABCDE (d) ABEDC
(e) ADBEC

9. (A) However, each stage of God must give scope to the whole range of human abilities; even in the worst situations, a person aspires to do more than cope.

(B) In stage one, the limit is set by physical circumstances.

(C) If you are surrounded by threats, to survive is a high aspiration. This would be true in a shipwreck, a war, a famine, or an abusive family.

(D) Every stage of God implies a life challenge, which can be expressed in terms of a higher aspiration.

(E) God exists to inspire us, and we express this through the aspirations we set for ourselves. An aspiration is the limit of the possible.

(a) DEACB (b) DEBCA
(c) EDCAB (d) EDCBA
(e) CDEBA

10. (A) Such as the experiences involved in looking at the cat and the mat.

(B) A statement is a posteriori (Latin, literally 'from the latter') just if it cannot be known to be true or false independently of experience.

(C) 'The cat is on the mat' is a posteriori because it cannot be known to be true or false independently of experience.

(D) One can establish whether it is true or false only by having certain experiences.

(a) BDAC (b) BCAD
(c) BACD (d) BCDA
(e) CABD

11. (A) Philosophers often contrast objective reality and subjective appearances.

(B) How things seem from different points of view and how things really are.

(C) For example, one can contrast how the sand really is, independently of any subjective point of view, and the different ways it appears through a fish's eyes and through human eyes.

(D) In this context, the absolute is usually taken to mean the totality of objective reality, which transcends all subjective points of view upon it.

(a) ABCD (b) ADBC
(c) BCDA (d) BADC
(e) CABD

12. (A) Absolute advantage, in economics, is a concept of trade in which one country can produce a quantity of a product in a more efficient manner (that is, with fewer resources of labour, land and/or capital) than another country.
(B) However, this statistics does not carry the implication that Japan should specialize in steel and the UK should not because Japan might be even better relative to the UK at other things.
(C) For example, in 1981, Japan produced a ton of steel with only 9.4 man-hours at a cost of only \$502, compared with 16.5 man hours and \$622 in the UK
(D) Not only that, but neither absolute nor comparative advantage are necessarily static for all time: Once, UK steel producers were more efficient than the Japanese.
(E) The real guide to specialization and to maximizing the gains from trade is comparative advantage.
(a) EACBD (b) ECBAD
(c) ACBED (d) ACBDE
(e) BACDE

13. (A) It marks off the beginning of mathematics from what went before.
(B) Ever since this discovery, abstraction has been a major theme in the development of mathematics, as those interested in the field have come up with ideas further and further divorced from their basis in the real world, and then sought ways to bring them back to tell us things about the real world which we might otherwise not have known.
(C) The discoverer of abstraction was the person who first realized that numbers are independent of the objects being counted, that two oranges and two apples (for instance) share a property, 'twoness', which is independent of what kinds of fruit they are.
(D) Abstraction, the action of divorcing properties of physical objects from the objects themselves, is a fundamental concept, perhaps the most fundamental concept, in mathematics.
(a) DACB (b) DBCA
(c) CBAD (d) DABC
(e) BACD

14. (A) The aim was to capitalize on the rising status of the artist as the exponent of a liberal art.
(B) Other cities soon followed Florence's example, a notable case being Rome, where the Academy of St Luke was founded in 1593 with Frederico Zuccaro as its president.
(C) Towards the end of the 16th century, groups of European painters and sculptors, dissatisfied with the venality and artisanal aspects of the guild system, joined together into academies of art which sought to promote the intellectual and creative aspects of producing art over that of their craft-based predecessors.
(D) In France, the Academic Royale de Peinture et de Sculpture was founded in 1648 around the ambitious and politically astute Charles Le Brun, who enlisted the royal support which was to make this academy the envy of Europe.
(E) The first artists' academy (as opposed to the gathering of dilettanti, antiquarians and amateurs also called academies), was established in 1563 in Florence by the artist and historiographer Giorgio Varansi, under the patronage of Cosimo de' Medici and with Michelangelo at its head.
(a) CABED (b) EABCD
(c) EADBC (d) CAEBD
(e) ABCDE

15. (A) The accommodation theory, in linguistics, starts from the premise that speech accommodation takes place when people modify their speech so that it conforms more with the way their conversational partner speaks.
(B) For example, the speeed at which people talk, the length of both pauses and utterances, the kind of vocabulary and syntax used, as well as intonation, voice pitch and pronunciation are all subject to the accommodation process.
(C) A wide range of subtle adaptations have been observed, which tend to occur more or less unconsciously.
(D) This kind of convergence is by no means an automatic feature of all conversations, and we can discern certain social contexts in which accommodation can be predicted.
(a) ACBD (b) DABC
(c) BDAC (d) ABCD
(e) CABD

16. (A) Managerial accountability, whether in the public or the private sector, similarly requires that managers be answerable for the tasks which they have contracted to perform, according to agreed standards of competence.
(B) In parliamentary systems, ministers are held to account through oral and written questions–

in some cases through 'interpellation', that is, through requiring them to give a detailed response to a question on policy or administration.

(C) Regimes in which rulers cannot be held to account, either by representatives or by judges, are called arbitrary and authoritarian.

(D) Political accountability is the hallmark of responsible and representative government.

(E) Political accountability requires the actions of politicians, or public officials, whether they be administrative, ethical or financial, to be open to inspection, scrutiny and challenge.

(a) ABCDE (b) EDBCA
(c) CDEBA (d) DEBAC
(e) BACDE

17. (A) Their aim was to write about everyday phenomena, and to use words and images for their primary, stripped-down meanings, without metaphor, clogged syntax or other forms of 'poeticizing'.

(B) The acmeists were particularly opposed to the mysticism and erotic suggestiveness of symbolist writing, and to the experiments of Mayakovsky and the surrealists.

(C) The idea of cleansing language, of using words for words' sake alone, has been a recurring feature of poetry, not least in the 20th century (for example in the work of T.S. Eliot and William Carlos Williams) but the acmeists, in a way characteristic of artists in the 1910s, were the only ones to give it a name and a specific agenda.

(D) Acmeism (from Greek ame, 'point') was a movement in Russian poetry of the 1920s led by the writers Niloai Gumilev and Sergei Gorodetsky, and followed by Anna Akmatova and Osip Mandelstam.

(E) They published a magazine, Apollo, from, 1909-17, and were denounced by the authorities as decadent and 'individualist': socialism demanded realism of a rather different kind.

(a) BDAEC (b) CDBAE
(c) CBDAE (d) DABCE
(e) ABCDE

18. (A) Not all actions are bodily movements, and the causal theory of action also applies to mental actions such as imagining and calculating.

(B) It is not enough for imagining a teddy bear that one has an image as of a teddy bear.

(C) If a hallucinogenic drug causes me to have an image as of a teddy bear, then I have not imagined a teddy bear, since my having the image as of a teddy bear is something that has happened to me, rather than an action of mine.

(D) A mental event is an action only if it is caused by an appropriate intention of the subject's.

(E) Having an image is an action of mine only if it is preceded by my having an appropriate intention. And if, as a matter of complete coincidence, I intended to imagine a toy just before a hallucinogenic drug caused me to have an image as of a teddy bear, then I have not imagined a teddy bear.

(a) ABCED (b) DAEBC
(c) ABECD (d) DABEC
(e) BADCE

19. (A) Fossil evidence suggests that the mammals underwent adaptive radiation to produce the range of mammal types extant today.

(B) Adaptive radiation, in the life sciences, refers to the differentiation (or anagenesis) of one or a few species into many to fill a large number or related ecological niches by adaptation.

(C) Thus the first bird species may have given rise to many more bird species by adaptive radiation.

(D) Typically, a species adapts to colonize a new habitat and, this adaptation opening up a new range of niches, adapts again to fill the new niches which are presented.

(a) BADC (b) BDCA
(c) CBAD (d) CBDA
(e) ABCD

20. (A) It has clearly done much good by bringing many useful inventions, ideas and by-products of major research programmes to a wide number of people.

(B) But to say that this is still all it does would be too superficial.

(C) Advertising is arguably a main vehicle of social communication; and as such, it has become the subject of much critical comment and even concern.

(D) Advertising was conceived essentially as a kind of social, consumer rhetoric: a way of publicly praising goods in order to encourage or persuade the public to use or buy them.

(a) CABD (b) CDBA
(c) DCAB (d) DABC
(e) BDCA

21. (A) The main application of aerodynamics is in aviation.

(B) The concept of flight was established by Leonardo da Vinci, who made sketches of devices similar to the modern helicopter and hang-glider.

(C) Aerodynamic analysis is also used to study the effect that wind will have on such artificial structures as bridges and tower block, on the flow of steam in turbines, or on the operation of wind-power generators.

(D) Although Leonardo's ideas were well ahead of their time, they were doomed to failure, as the principles of aerodynamics were unknown.

(E) Aerodynamics (Greek, 'study of the power of air') is the study of the flow of air or gases in motion.

(a) ABCDE (b) BEDCA
(c) EACBD (d) EBDCA
(e) CABDE

22. (A) In literary criticism, the effective fallacy assumes that works can be read not as independent structures, but in terms of their emotional or other effects on their readers.

(B) In other words, the preconceptions we bring to our reading of any literary work.

(C) Our cultural, emotional and verbal baggage, as well as that of our society and of the author–are part of the 'meaning' of the text as we perceive it, and cannot be dissociated from our perception.

(D) 'Non-affective' reading, by contrast, excludes all such external associations and concentrates solely on what is in the actual text.

(a) ACDB (b) ABCD
(c) ABDC (d) ACBD
(e) CABD

23. (A) The concept of the affluent society, used to describe post-1945 democratic welfare capitalist societies, was pioneered by the Canadian economist, John Kenneth Galbraith.

(B) He argued that a long-term unintended consequence of economic growth in Western democracies was the simultaneous development of 'private affluence' and 'public squalor'.

(C) While very efficient in encouraging the demand for private goods and services, including consumer-durables, liberal-democratic capitalist societies are prone to under-supply public goods, like education, public health, environmental protection and public transport.

(D) Galbraith later embellished this argument: because modern liberal democracies contain satisfied majorities, which have the skills and resources to avoid poverty, a 'culture of contentment' has developed, hostile to active and progressively redistributive big government.

(E) Whereas in the earliest electoral democratic systems, the poor comprised (potential) electoral majorities, affluent or contented societies are likely to be content with tax-cutting conservative administrations.

(a) ACDBE (b) ABCDE
(c) ABDCE (d) ADECB
(e) ADCEB

24. (A) The main application of aleatory techniques is in the performing arts, and particularly in music.

(B) Aleatory music is, in conception, similar to both Far Eastern art music and to jazz and rock, all of which involve improvisation, on an agreed basis, as a feature of the performance.

(C) In art music, 20th century composers as significant as Pierre Boulez, Gyorgi Ligeti, Witold Lutoslawski and Karlheinzz Stockhausen use aleatory techniques as an integral, and entirely accepted, component of their work.

(D) In aleatory music the players are encouraged to choose the sequence of movements, sections or individual chords and notes, or to improvise on a pattern or idea suggested by the composer–for example, in Ligeti's Aventures, on letters of the alphabet, and in Lutoslawski's Preludes and Fugue, on a series of lines, squares and triangles.

(E) Thus, the result differs from player to player and from performer to performer.

(a) BACDE (b) CBADE
(c) ACDEB (d) EBACD
(e) ABCDE

25. (A) In the development of numbers, algebraic numbers come in generality between the rational numbers and the real numbers. A rational number is one that can be expressed in the form p/q, where p and q are integers and q is non-zero.

(B) Suppose that there was a rational number whose square was b. It can be written in its lowest terms as p/q (this means that p and q have no common factors). So, $(p/q)^2 = p^2/q^2 = 2$.

(C) The Greeks discovered the alarming fact (to them) that not all numbers are rational, through a classic use of the technique of proof by contradiction.

(D) So, cancelling by 2, we see that $2 \times r^2 = q^2$, which means that 2 also divides q. So 2 divides both p and q, contradicting that p/q was in its lowest terms. So, the original assumption must be false.

(E) Therefore, $p^2 = 2 \times q^2$, so that 2 divides p^2 and therefore p (this is because 2 is a prime number). So, we write p as $2 \times r$, and, rewriting the original equation, $(2 \times r)^2 = 4 \times r^2 = 2 \times q^2$.

(a) CABDE (b) CBEDA
(c) ABEDC (d) ACBED
(e) DEBCA

26. (A) Religious allegory was especially popular in medieval Europe, when stories of love, descriptions of nature and tales of heroic adventure were all allegorized to have a deeper, Christian meaning.
(B) Allegories may also be philosophical and political.
(C) Allegory is a form of irony; one in which the added meanings are generally more significant than the events from which they are grafted.
(D) Typical examples are versions of the Holy Grail and Parsifal legends, in which knights stand for the beleaguered Christian soul, dragons and wizards for the Devil and his minions, and attainment of the goal is overlaid with images of transfiguration and ascension into heaven.
(a) CADB (b) CBAD
(c) DCBA (d) CDAB
(e) ABCD

27. (A) Trance states can be defined according to the degree of interaction believed to occur between the individual, who is in an altered state, and the spirit realm.
(B) Modern Psychology locates these changes as arising within the psyche, while other cultures explain them in terms of changes in external reality, such as access to a spirit realm or extrahuman power.
(C) Altered States of Consciousness is an umbrella term for describing physical and mental states which are not considered part of ordinary experience.
(D) In states of possession, the spirit is assumed to be in control of the person, who acts as the bodily vehicle by means of which the spirit can communicate.
(E) They occur in many societies in connection with mystical practices, ecstatic and trance states.
(a) ABCDE (b) ABDCE
(c) BECDA (d) CEBAD
(e) EABCD

28. (A) As this fact becomes clearer, governments and individuals have begun to look at different propositions in order to save on energy costs.
(B) With the environmental problems as well as the finite supplies of the four energy sources, more time and research is being spent on alternative sources of energy.
(C) At this present time, the main sources of energy available to the Westernized culture are oil, gas, coal and nuclear power.
(D) It has become apparent over the past thirty years that the total energy from a fuel source has to be maximized to its full potential, in order to save money and mineral resources.
(a) CADB (b) CABD
(c) DBAC (d) DACB
(e) ABCD

29. (A) The statement 'all bachelors are male' is analytically true because it is true solely in virtue of its meaning–'bachelor' means 'unmarried adult male'. The statement 'some spinsters are married' is analytically false because it is false solely in virtue of its meaning–'spinster' means 'unmarried adult female'.
(B) A statement in analytical just if it is true or false solely in virtue of its meaning.
(C) Whether this statement is true or false depends not only on what it means but also on facts about John on whether or not he is married and an adult.
(D) A statement is synthetic just if it is not true or false solely in virtue of its meaning. The statement 'John is a bachelor' is synthetic because it is not true or false solely in virtue of its meaning.
(a) DBAC (b) BADC
(c) BDCA (d) DACB
(e) CABD

30. (A) It was felt that their elders had failed them, and that the values of society should be certainly questioned and probably swept away.
(B) The group included Kingsley Amis, John Osborne, Alan Sillitoe, John Wain and others. Their works attacked the Establishment not merely in thought and utterance, but in a social way (by letting us hear the voice of what one critic disparagingly called 'the bright working class'), and above all, by using techniques of popular culture (notably the routines of stand-up comedy) to subvert such hallowed Establishment forms as the 'novel of ideas' and the 'well-made play'.
(C) This is, perhaps, a common, even healthy, feeling among the young, but it was particularly vehement from the mid-1950s, and was one of the forces that led to the rise, at about the same time, of 'teenage culture'.
(D) In the period following World War II, there was a feeling among younger people in many

western countries that the entire fabric of society was rotten.

(E) In the UK, it was given literary form by a group of writers nicknamed 'the angry young men'.

(a) DACEB (b) EBACD
(c) BDCAE (d) DCAEB
(e) CABDE

31. (A) These are known as the 'supreme feminine figure', what Goethe called the 'Eternal Feminine'.

(B) The anima as the female element in the male unconscious is often symbolized as a hermaphrodite figure.

(C) Myths that illustrate the male need to rescue the female in himself are those where the hero rescues the damsel in distress.

(D) Mistress figures, who guide initiates through spiritual journeys are also symbols of the anima for example, Kwan-yn in Chinese Buddhism, Sophia in Christian Gnostic doctrine or the ancient Greek goddess of wisdom, Pallas Athene.

(a) DBCA (b) DBAC
(c) BCDA (d) BADC
(e) ACBD

32. (A) In Europe, from the 15th century onwards, accounts from travelers about people encountered in distant territories were widely available.

(B) During the Enlightenment, the idea of 'primitive man existing in a simple communal society, became prevalent.

(C) Remote and unfamiliar peoples have been a topic of interest since recorded times.

(D) In 1761, the French philosopher Jean-Jacques Rousseau lauded the 'noble savage' who lived in a communal and dignified state–an ideal that was preferable, he claimed, to the economic iniquity and social deterioration of European societies.

(a) ABDC (b) CABD
(c) BCDA (d) BDCA
(e) ABCD

33. (A) A contemporary example of organized anti-clericalism is the movement in the US to prevent religious fundamentalists winning the right to practise religious activities in state schools.

(B) In the 20th century, political cleavages between clericalists and anti-claricalists shaped electoral support for parties, especially in Italy and France.

(C) Anti-clericalist movements range from having particularist objectives (for example, getting rid of Jesuits) to general opposition to all types of clerical power (for instance, atheist campaigns in USSR in the 1930s).

(D) Anti-clericalism is a liberal or socialist doctrine of opposition to the political authority, power and status of the clergy.

(E) In Europe, the Catholic clergy were the special target of the currents of anti-clericalism which flourished in the post-Enlightenment era and influenced many European nationalist movements, including the French, Spanish Italian and Irish revolutionary nationalist movements of the mid 19th century.

(a) ABCDE (b) DCABE
(c) BDCAE (d) DEBCA
(e) EADBC

34. (A) Anxiety (Greek, 'racking'), that is distress of mind, disquietude and uneasiness, is not generally regarded in psychology as an irrational fear–a suggestion that may come from such common phrases as 'Anxiety was driving him out of his mind'.

(B) Anxiety does not have a clear source, unlike a phobia, but can be traced to unconscious processes (in psychonalysis) and to faulty responses and thinking (cognitive therapy).

(C) Psychoanalysis has focused on the unconscious sources of anxiety.

(D) Originally, it saw anxiety as the outcome of repressed libido.

(E) Freud also thought at one time that anxiety was the result of an unconscious memory of the birth trauma.

(a) CABED (b) CADBE
(c) ABCDE (d) CABDE
(e) DBCAE

35. (A) Apocalyptic writers in general, however, are more concerned with the sequence of dire events, the crumbling of civilization, which precedes that end.

(B) The root thought that gave rise to apocalyptic literature was the Judaeo-Chiristian idea that human life, indeed the life of the universe, is not random, but an ordered progression from the Beginning through to the End.

(C) Some apocalyptic writers, for example William Blake, were particularly concerned with the End, and developed images, ideas and language directly from Revelation, the last book of the

New Testament, which details the final days of the world.

(D) Once such broadening of the idea is allowed, a huge range of writers can be described as apocalyptic, from Swift to George Orwell, from Zola to Wyndham Lewis. Critics have suggested that the apocalyptic imagination is a particular characteristic of 20th century writing, both directly in sf (where writers such as J.G. Ballard, Harry Harrison and George Turner regularly depict the horrors of a future in which present-day problems–the greenhouse effect, over-population, too many cars–are multiplied in geometric progression towards oblivion), or in writers who have used sf ideas and techniques in a wider context, such as John Barth, Alasdair Gray, Thomas Pynchon and Kurt Vonnegut.

(E) Systopian writing of this kind sees the human race as doomed (usually self-doomed). We are trapped like animals, laboratory specimens at the mercy of irresponsible powers; we are too prolific; we are plundering the planet.

(a) AECDB (b) ABCDE
(c) ECBDA (d) BACDE
(e) CABDE

36. (A) This abstraction is then manipulated mathematically, possibly with other assumptions thrown in (for example, Newton assumed that the attraction between the planets varied according to the inverse of the square of the distance between them), to find a mathematical way of describing this data (in Newton's case, that the planets move in elliptical orbits around the sun), which can then be verified by further experimentation (which in this example, had already been done a century before by Kepler).

(B) The whole of physics and much of many other sciences depends on this procedure.

(C) Mathematics began with the abstraction of properties from the real world around us; it proves its usefulness when the results obtained from this abstraction are turned back again to the real world.

(D) This is how science works; scientists abstract the properties they wish to study from experimental evidence (for example, the observations of planetary motion over many years were used to find the positions of the planets).

(E) Applicability is the real strength of mathematics: its relationship to the scientific method is due the fact that it is so successful in explaining the real world.

(a) CABDE (b) EDCAB
(c) ECDAB (d) CAEBD
(e) DABCE

37. (A) Factions of the Ba'athist Party have held power in Iraq under Saddam Hussein, and in Syria, under President Assad. Their dictatorships have not led to Pan-Arabist unity, but rather the converse.

(B) The Arab league was formed in 1945 with the aspiration to create eventual unity, but it has remained committed only to the moderate goals of inter-governmental co-operation.

(C) A short-lived United Arabic Republic (1958–61) of Syria and Egypt created temporary optimism that a broader pan-Arabic ideal could be achieved.

(D) Pan-Arabism seeks a unified state embracing all Arabic speaking peoples.

(E) Like the Pan-Africanist movement was divided between proponents of inter-governmental economic and political co-operation between sovereign Arab states (for example Lebanon), and advocates of the merger of existing Arab states into a single state (such as Syria).

(a) BACED (b) BACDE
(c) DCEAB (d) DEBCA
(e) EABDC

38. (A) He discovered that images occur which are not always part of our own history or personal experience.

(B) He also discovered that these elements, which seemed to be inherited from somewhere else, had a tendency to organize themselves into predetermined patterns or symbols; these he called archetypes.

(C) Freud's analysis of dreams had come up with similar anomalies which he called 'archaic past and biological development, a part of our mind that is close to animals.

(D) Archetypes (Greek, 'originals') were discovered by Jung through the analysis of dreams.

(E) Each of us, in this sense, has an extremely old psyche, a deposit of collective images and primitive motifs.

(a) CABDE (b) DABCE
(c) ECABD (d) DECAB
(e) ABCDE

39. (A) Art Deco design was an amalgam of the changes affecting fine art and design in the interwar years, for example the bold colours of Fauve and Cubist painting and the architecture of modernism.

(B) Populist application of the new Modernism influenced design across the board from cinemas to radios and vacuum cleaners.

(C) Art Deco (derived from the phrase 'art as decoration') was a design style universally popular from late 1920s onwards.

(D) It also led to several important critics and designers criticizing Art Deco as a mere style without the intellectual rigor of hard-line Modern Movement thinking. In this context, the term Moderene was used to suggest the Art Deco style as a much less serious version of Modernism.

(E) It was charactericized by geometric forms, distinctive colour combinations, modern materials like stainless steel and in furniture, smooth wraparound surfaces in luxurious veneers.

(a) CBEAD (b) CEBDA
(c) ADBCE (d) CEABD
(e) BADCE

40. (A) This kind of question is not really answerable in the present state of philosophy and psychology.

(B) For example, it is not possible to answer the question 'Do computers have knowledge of the data they process?' unless you can define the term knowledge. (This question also has consequences in the legal field–can a computer be allowed as a witness in court if it does not really know what it is talking about?)

(C) Thanks to our limited understanding of human thought, it is quite difficult to define what the goal of artificial intelligence actually is.

(D) It is an area in which much research has been done since the end of the World War II, beginning with the theoretical work of Alan Turing (1912-54) in the 1940s.

(E) Artificial Intelligence is the most controversial area of computing today, an area beloved of authors–the duplications of human thought patterns by computer.

(a) EDCBA (b) ECDAB
(c) ECBDA (d) CEDBA
(e) DABCE

41. (A) Essentially, they are communities which grow up around a religious figure.

(B) The Upanishad tradition of sages going to the forest to mediate resulted in communities of disciples and devotees settling around their hut, following their teacher's guidance.

(C) Probably the most famous in modern times are Rabindranath Tagore's community at Shantiniketan, West Bengal, where he conducted his educational and cultural experiments (and which is now recognized as a university, although originally, it was closer to deschooling, non-formal education and arts workshops), and Gandhi's ashram on the banks of the Sabarmati near Ahmedabad, which was a springboard for his independence campaign.

(D) Ashrams are quite different from Buddhist or western-Christian monasteries.

(a) DBAC (b) ACDB
(c) BDAC (d) DABC
(e) CABD

42. (A) Insofar as Marx's and Engels' writings can be decoded and clearly understood, the Asiatic mode of production refers to a system in which the vast majority of the population lives in villages, in which there is no private property, complex division of labour or significant external trade.

(B) The Asiatic mode of production is both the most obscure and controversial of the 'modes of production' (economic systems) mentioned in Karl Marx's writings.

(C) The villages are exploited by a despot and his officials, to whom they pay a combination of rent and taxes.

(D) They were arbitrary, despotic and stagnant, historical culs-de-sac, which could only be transformed by external intervention by more advanced societies.

(E) The Urban population centred on the court aristocracy and the monarchy, are parasitic on the rural population. Marx described such Oriental societies, following in the tradition of British political economy, as incapable of development into more progressive social formations.

(a) BACED (b) ABCDE
(c) BCEDA (d) BCDEA
(e) CABDE

43. (A) Although, in many ancient societies, 'natural' astrology was the nearest thing to what we might nowadays think of as a 'proper' science, and its practitioners were among the most learned and intellectually sophisticated members of the community, two things fatally hampered its development.

(B) First was the lack of instruments to make precise observations of the heavens, and of mathematical systems or devices which would allow any but (in our terms) the crudest calculations.

(C) Second was the interdependence of astrologers with religion.
(D) Because the astrologers dealt with heavenly bodies (which were thought to be under the control of the gods), and because they made predictions, they were thought to have supernatural contracts and abilities denied to less-learned people.
(E) Even in societies as sophisticated as ancient China and ancient Babylon, magic and esoteric Jargon were essential tools of the astrologers, allying them with sibyls, soothsayers and other prophets rather than with surveyors, for instance, or merchants, the other main group skilled in the use of numbers.
(a) AEBDC (b) ADEBC
(c) EABDC (d) ABCDE
(e) DABCE

44. (A) 'The fool says in his heart, there is not God.'
(B) The *Old Testament* verse accurately sums up the attitude to atheism found in the Bible.
(C) Even in the *Book of Job* (4th century BCE), it is not the existence of God which is questioned, but only his justice, mercy and love.
(D) But the question there is only whether one worships and obeys the true God or a false God.
(E) When Job is finally vindicated, his hypocritical friends are said 'not to know' God, meaning that for all their protestations of faith, they understand nothing.
(a) ABCDE (b) CEDAB
(c) ABDCE (d) ADBCE
(e) BADCE

45. (A) As land plants grew larger and more elaborate, they provided another sink for carbon and another source of free oxygen.
(B) The first green plants were the phytoplankton, which lived in the surface waters of the oceans.
(C) Like other green plants, they liberated oxygen through photosynthesis but then reused it in respiration.
(D) However, because they lived in the deep ocean they caused a small net addition to oxygen levels because some of the carbon compounds incorporated in their cells sank to the bottom of the oceans and were locked into sediments which do not decompose because of the cold, dark and oxygen-free conditions.
(a) BACD (b) ABDC
(c) DABC (d) BCDA
(e) CABD

46. (A) Chiristians believe that reconciliation between God and humankind took place through the sacrificial life and death of Jesus Christ.
(B) Humankind being too far sunk in sin and misery, and too restricted by the limitations of the human conditions, to initiate reconciliation from the human side, the death of Christ was necessary to transform human awareness, to jolt humankind out of the consequence of sin, to vanquish death and to assuage God's wrath.
(C) Atonement ('at-one-ment'), originally a legal term for the reconciliation of two parties, has been annexed–almost exclusively for theological use.
(D) In Buddhism and Judaism, atonement is thought to be initiated by the divine party, acting out of compassion and love, and despite the alienation caused by human sin and weakness.
(a) CDAB (b) ABDC
(c) ABCD (d) CABD
(e) BDCA

47. (A) It is an economic system that is totally self-sufficient, producing all that is consumed and importing nothing from outside.
(B) Autarky (Greek, 'self-sufficiency'), in economics, is a Utopian aim.
(C) Others have pursued autarky together with social isolation to maintain the mores and genetic purity of the native population or to maintain the leaders' control.
(D) However, because no country is able to produce the whole range of goods demanded, at competitive prices, in practice, autarky condemns its disciples to inefficiency and relative poverty.
(E) Some countries' leaders have attempted to achieve autarky in order to eliminate any reliance on foreign materials and better to defend the society in time of war.
(a) CABED (b) BECDA
(c) ABCDE (d) BADEC
(e) BDACE

48. (A) In politics, autonomy is a relative concept which refers to the degree of freedom from coercion or outside influence which a state, a region, a group or an individual has over its own actions.
(B) However, in practice, the autonomy of sovereign states is limited by international organizations, like the United Nations, NATO, ASEAN, supranational organizations, like the EC, and multiple forms of economic, cultural and political interdependence between states.

(C) The expression the 'autonomy of the state', when used by historians or political scientists may also refer to the ability of state officials to pursue state interests, rather than simply reflecting or reacting to the interests of dominant groups in society.

(D) Theoretically, all states which are recognised in the world system as sovereign are thought to be autonomous from other states.

(a) DCAB (b) ACDB
(c) CDBA (d) CADB
(e) ABCD

49. (A) International balance of power theories focus on the mechanisms which are used to prevent war or aggression between and among sovereign states, the key idea being that wars are caused by a disruption of the existing balance of power.

(B) Debate among historians and political theorists has centered on whether or not a single hegemony (or dominant power) is necessary to prevent war and whether (and how) deterrence is essential to the preservation of stability in international relations. The relations between the 'great powers' between 1815 and 1945 remain the subject of controversy for balance of power theorists.

(C) Theories which describe conditions of equilibrium in political systems are called 'balance of power' theories.

(D) Internal balance of power theories describe the political process through which certain parties and interest groups influence the allocation of resources or access to political power.

(E) They can be divided into those which describe stability within internal (or domestic) political systems and those which refer to external or international systems.

(a) DCEAB (b) CADEB
(c) CEADB (d) CEDAB
(e) EADBC

50. (A) By the mid-20th century, ballet throughout the world had become an esoteric and extravagant minority interest, exclusive and self-obsessed.

(B) It still has its purist corners, dazzling shrines to decadence–the Japanese court tradition and Bolshoi tradition come to mind.

(C) But elsewhere, the influence of folk dance and popular dance from around the world, and even of athletics and gymnastics, has made ballet one of the most eclectic and dynamic of all performing arts.

(D) But in the latter half of the century, with increased international travel and awareness of other cultures, ballet has been regenerated.

(a) ABCD (b) ADBC
(c) ADCB (d) ACBD
(e) CABD

51. (A) Batteries have come a long way since then and are now used in everything from a watch to powerful fuel cells.

(B) Batteries consist of one or more electric cells which produce electric currents directly from chemical reactions.

(C) The first battery was the Voltaic Pile, named after Alessandro Volta (1745-1827).

(D) Volta discovered that, by using dissimilar metals immersed in water with a little acid added, an electric current was produced.

(a) BCDA (b) ACDB
(c) BACD (d) CDAB
(e) ABCD

52. (A) The rule shows how to handle 'conditional probabilities', ones which show the effect of one event on another.

(B) Bayes's rule is used to find the probability of an event experimentally; the experimenter starts off with a degree of belief in each of his or her hypotheses, and uses Bayes's rule to modify these degrees of belief according to the results of experimentation (for example, an experiment could consist of asking a patient if he or she has back pains). The method is commonly used today by computers, providing 'expert systems' used in medicine, prospecting and fault diagnosis.

(C) We make one event (that the patient claims to have back pains) a condition of the other (that he or she has back trouble). It is usual to write the conditional probability of event *A*, given that event *B* is known to have happened, as p(*A* *B*); Bayes's rule tells us that p(*A*)=p(*AB*) × p(*B*)+p(*A* not *B*) × p(not *B*).

(D) For example, the probability that a patient has back trouble is higher if it is known that he or she claims to have back pains.

(E) Bayes's rule, formulated by Thomas Bayes (1702-61), sparked off a radical new direction in statistics, the application in mathematics of probability theory.

(a) ABCDE (b) BDACE
(c) ABDCE (d) EADCB
(e) CADBE

53. (A) When the future date arrives, the bear expects to buy in at a lower price to deliver the stock that had been sold under the future contract at a higher price.

(B) A market in which prices are falling or are expected to fall is called by economists a bear market.

(C) Likewise, the term bear can be applied to a person who expects stock prices to fall and sells stock that he or she does not have for delivery at a future date.

(D) It is a designation commonly used in securities markets and commodity markets and is the opposite of a bull market.

(a) BACD (b) BCAD
(c) BDCA (d) ACBD
(e) ABCD

54. (A) To some extent, it arises naturally enough from the events of our time.

(B) An age that has seen Fascist states trample down the liberties of a continent, and has heard them hail their leaders with a mindless and horrifying devotion, will understandably view with distrust the whole conception of leadership.

(C) The very word is contaminated by the associations of a fuhrer or a Duce, and, seen in the light of our experiences, the great leader-figures of the past, Napoleon or Fredrick the Great for example, seem unworthy of the respect, still less of the admiration, with which they have sometimes been regarded.

(D) The reasons for the rejection of the idea of leadership are complex.

(a) DABC (b) CDBA
(c) CABD (d) DBAC
(e) ACBD

55. (A) It is sometimes contented that modern war has become so highly technical in character that the role of the army, with its demands for leadership at all levels, has become far less important.

(B) Let us take as an example, exercise of leadership in war, the most obvious field in which it is required–in deed, so obvious that the reactions of many people towards the whole subject are coloured by the picture of the leader as a military commander.

(C) The very fact that many of the problems which arise in a technical world are necessarily very complex in character, sometimes divert attention from the fact that they require leadership to solve them.

(D) But, though the fields in which leadership has to be exercised have changed, most of its essential qualities remain as necessary as ever.

(a) CDBA (b) CADB
(c) ADCB (d) DACB
(e) DABC

56. (A) Leadership in any of the fields in which it is most obvious, in the armed forces, in politics, in commerce, has until quite recently been determined by birth.

(B) The fact that the principle is still obviously followed to some degree in the very different social climate of today reminds us how strong it was, and how unquestioningly it was accepted.

(C) It imposes on us rather a greater obligation to investigate the qualities of good leadership and its recognition by other means, if birth and wealth are no longer to be the criteria of choice.

(D) But the rejection of an elite recruited by birth in the democratic and equalitarian temper of the modern, world does not imply that all leadership can be dispensed with.

(a) ABCD (b) ABDC
(c) CDAB (d) BADC
(e) CABD

57. (A) A belief in equality of opportunity of and in the necessity of recruiting leaders from every class imposes on society an obvious obligation to break down those obstacles as rapidly and as completely as possible.

(B) Others are more peculiar to individual circumstance, and attempts to overcome them by society are less easy to envisage and less likely to succeed.

(C) Some of them are removable by social change; bad housing, inferior education, the limitations on personal development imposed by poverty are all barriers to the emergence of leadership among some sections of the community.

(D) In practice, there are admittedly very great difficulties in the way of realizing the ideal of equality of opportunity.

(a) DCBA (b) DCAB
(c) BACD (d) BADC
(e) DACB

58. (A) At present, many of those most prominent in our national life, particularly in trade unionism, business, and industry, are men who received little formal education.

(B) Among men of the most obvious distinction and holding the most responsible positions, a number can be found who left school at eleven or twelve.

(C) To cite these as examples of the fact that high intellectual capacity is unnecessary for leadership is to make an elementary confusion between ability and educational attainment, quite apart from the fact that many of them have by private study, more than repaired the deficiencies of their formal education.

(D) But, much more important, such an attitude shows a failure to grasp the magnitude of the educational revolution of the past forty years.

(E) With any educational change, there is inevitably a time-lag before its effects become clear in society, but it is nevertheless surprising that the full meaning of the 1902 Act is still only imperfectly realised.

(a) ABCDE (b) ADCBE
(c) ACBDE (d) EABDC
(e) CABDE

59. (A) I have to admit that knowing all the finer points of etiquette is not always easy.

(B) For instance, it is just not civilized to hover over someone's table in a busy coffee shop, eyeing her half finished tea until she finally lets you have her seat.

(C) Loosely defined, the right way to do things is how I do them myself.

(D) The well-bred thing to do is to stand quietly at a discreet distance until the table is vacated and then elbow out of your way anyone who tries to get there first.

(E) As an adult, I have come to see that there is a right and wrong way to do everything.

(a) EDBCA (b) ECDAB
(c) ECBDA (d) CDEBA
(e) DABCE

60. (A) However, Indians were charged 10 per cent extra premium.

(B) Humiliating as it may seem today, it was much more so for self respecting Indians then.

(C) Life insurance, known to India since Vedic times, arrived here from England in its modern form only in the year 1818, to insure Europeans and support their widows.

(D) Under pressure of influential Indians, Insurance Companies that were established later started insuring Indians.

(E) It all began like this..."The Company does not Insure Natives of India" Shocking?!? But this is exactly what our forefathers had to face in their own land in an era much before nationalisation of life insurance in India.

(a) EDCAB (b) EDACB
(c) ECDAB (d) CEDAB
(e) DEACB

61. (A) Did you ever wonder what your long policy number means, and how, among fifteen crore policyholders, your number is unique?

(B) A series of roughly ten crore numbers are allotted to each of the 7 zonal offices of LIC, and further to lower offices.

(C) So your number arises systematically from the series that your issuing branch gets.

(D) Well, the 9-digit number makes a count of one hundred crores (short by one).

(E) And, by the way, did you know that each time you breathe, LIC settles 3 claims. Are you counting?

(a) ABDCE (b) ACBDE
(c) ADBCE (d) DABCE
(e) BACED

62. (A) Everyone has insecurities.

(B) When you show yourself in the world and display your talents, you naturally stir up all kinds of resentment, envy, and other manifestations of insecurity.

(C) This is to be expected. You cannot spend your life worrying about the petty feelings of others.

(D) With those above you, however, you must take a different approach.

(E) When it comes to power, outshining the master is perhaps the worst mistake of all.

(a) EDABC (b) ACBED
(c) ABCDE (d) ABDEC
(e) AECBD

63. (A) They also become spoiled and tyrannical.

(B) But hire a former enemy and he will be more loyal than a friend, because he has more to prove.

(C) If you have no enemies, find a way to make them.

(D) In fact, you have more to fear from friends than from enemies.

(E) Be wary of friends–they will betray you more quickly, for they are easily aroused to envy.

(a) CDBEA (b) CEDAB
(c) ECDAB (d) EABDC
(e) BADCE

64. (A) The problem is that you often do not know your friends as you imagine.

(B) It is natural to want to employ your friends when you find yourself in times of need.

(C) The world is a harsh place, and your friends soften the harshness.
(D) Why depend on a stranger when you have a friend at hand?
(E) Besides, you know them.
(a) ABCDE (b) BCEDA
(c) CBADE (d) CDBEA
(e) EABCD

65. (A) Although it is generally best not to mix work with friendship, there are times when a friend can be used to greater effect than an enemy.
(B) A man of power, for example, often has dirty work that has to be done.
(C) But for the sake of appearances, it is generally preferable to have other people do it for him.
(D) Friends often do this the best, since their affection for him makes them willing to take chances.
(E) Also, if your plans go awry for some reason, you can use a friend as a convenient scapegoat.
(a) ABCDE (b) DCEAB
(c) ADCEB (d) ABDCE
(e) EBACD

66. (A) Do not give them the chance to sense what you are up to:
(B) If at any point in the deception you practice, people have the slightest suspicion as to your intentions, all is lost.
(C) Throw them off the scent by dragging red herrings across the path.
(D) Use false sincerity; send ambiguous signals, set up misleading objects of desire.
(E) Unable to distinguish the genuine from the false, they cannot pick out your real goal.
(a) EACDB (b) ABCDE
(c) BCDEA (d) BACDE
(e) CADBE

67. (A) How and why has the atmosphere changed so much? The earliest atmosphere probably consisted of gases like hydrogen, helium, methane, ammonia and carbon dioxide (CO_2)–gases which occur in the atmospheres of the other planets.
(B) Less well known but much more interesting is the fact that the present-day composition is totally different from that of the primitive.
(C) Hence, the atmosphere for most of the Earth's history, consisted largely of CO_2 with small amounts of nitrogen.
(D) Most of these gases were lost and replaced by atmospheres of gases emitted by volcanoes.
(E) The Earth's atmosphere is made up of 79 per cent nitrogen, 21 per cent oxygen and a small but growing trace of carbon dioxide.
(a) ABECD (b) EBACD
(c) EADCB (d) ADCBE
(e) DEABC

68. (A) That is the Homeric Question which has intrigued classical scholars down the centuries.
(B) One genius who selected, refined, and embellished the material from the countless lays available in those far-off times and bound them together to produce the *Iliad* and the *Odyssey* in their present form.
(C) Modern opinion is overwhelmingly in favour of the view that there was, indeed, one outstanding poet named Homer among the throng of minstrels in Greek-speaking world during the eighth or ninth century before Christ.
(D) Were the early epic masterpieces, the *Iliad* and the *Odyssey*, composed by one hand or by many?
(a) CABD (b) DCBA
(c) DABC (d) BDAC
(e) ABCD

69. (A) But two special themes made certain appeal to an audience nurtured on memories of a magnificent past:
(1) The siege of Troy which was the supreme glory of their heroic ancestry, and (2) the wanderings overseas forced upon their forebears by the all-conquering Dorians.
(B) But such a splendid theme could not be worthily expressed in short lays.
(C) As the art of minstrelsy was passed down from one generation to the next, a repertoire of short lays about the heroic times was built up.
(D) Every well-born Ionian was familiar with the history of the Trojan War and its sequel.
(E) The grandeur of the subject called into being narrative verse which used the traditional saga as raw material but was composed in epic dimensions, magnifying the two favourite themes far beyond historical fact.
(a) CBEAD (b) ADCBE
(c) CADBE (d) BACDE
(e) EABCD

70. (A) The Athenians are revolutionary and their designs are characterised by swiftness alike in conception and execution; you have a genius for keeping what you have got, accompanied by a total want of invention and, when forced to act, you never go far enough.

(B) They are adventurous beyond their power and daring beyond their judgment and in danger, they are sanguine; your way is to attempt less than your power justifies, to mistrust even what your judgement sanctions and to convince yourself that there will be no end to your danger.

(C) They are prompt, you procrastinate; they are never at home, you are never from it; they hope by leaving it to extend their acquisitions, you fear any new enterprise will endanger what you possess.

(D) They are swift to follow up a success and slow to recoil from a reverse; their bodies they spend ungrudgingly in their country's cause; their intellect they jealously husband to be employed in her service.

(a) CADB (b) ABCD
(c) BADC (d) ABDC
(e) DABC

71. (A) We have no black looks or angry words for a neighbour if he enjoys himself in his own way, we abstain from the little act of churlishness which, though they leave no mark, yet cause annoyance to those who notes them.

(B) But our laws secure equal justice for all their private disputes, and our public opinion welcomes and honours talent in every branch of achievement, not for any sectional reason, but on grounds of excellence alone.

(C) And, as we give free play to all in our public life, so we carry the same spirit into our daily relation with one another.

(D) Our constitution is named a democracy because it is in the hands not of the few but of the many.

(a) DBCA (b) CDAB
(c) ADBC (d) DACB
(e) CADB

72. (A) And their story is not graven only on stone over their native earth, but lives on far away, without visible symbol, woven into stuff of other men's lives...

(B) Fix your eyes on the greatness of Athens as you have it before you day by day, fall in love with her, and when you feel her greatness, remember that this greatness was won by men with courage, with knowledge of their duty, and with a sense of honour in action, who, if they failed in any ordeal, disdained to deprive the city of their service, but sacrificed their lives as the best offering on her behalf.

(C) So they gave their bodies to the commonwealth and received, each so for his own memory, praise that will never die, and with it the grandest of all sepulchres, not that in which their mortal bones are laid, but a home in the minds of men where their glory remains fresh to stir to speech or action as the occasion comes by.

(D) For the whole earth is the sepulchre of famous men.

(a) ADCB (b) BCDA
(c) BDCA (d) DCBA
(e) CBDA

73. (A) In early youth, the poet as well as an intellectual, Plato it is believed, was a great wrestler, and he also served as a soldier.

(B) It is through that he adopted the name of Plato, because of his broad shoulders.

(C) He was not only born a free man but an aristocrat, his father's name being Ariston, a descendant of one of the legendary founder of Athens, while on his mother's side, he was related to many wealthy and well-born Athenians.

(D) Plato, the father of Western philosophy, used to say that he thanked the Gods for three things: one, that he was born a free man and not a slave; that he was born a Greek and not Barbarian; and three, that he lived in the days of Socrates.

(a) ACBD (b) CADB
(c) DCBA (d) ACBD
(e) BACD

74. (A) The whole of Plato's philosophy is expressed in dialogues and many of early dialogues preserve an air of having risen from chance conversations in the streets.

(B) He also attacked the Sophists, the new brand of philosophers who, in Athens, were examining everything and teaching the people no longer to respect the old ideas on which the city had been founded and whose brilliant speech and witty paradoxes attracted men to them–and yet Plato himself had all the qualities, and often used them, of these enemies of his.

(C) Plato's philosophy seems to arise directly out of daily life and this is one of its great charms.

(D) For this father and fountain-head of philosophy, unequalled in the breadth of his ideas, is also unmatched for the persuasive beauty of his writing.

(E) Plato is said to have burnt his poems after he met Socrates and he adopted a very severe view of poet in republic–but he could not help being a poet himself.

(a) ACDEB (b) BADCE
(c) ABCDE (d) CDABE
(e) DBCAE

75. (A) Socrates, who always stated that he was only wise because other men thought they knew certain thing for sure while he knew he did not know, went about asking very simple questions and using the language of metaphor of the market place.

(B) It has the many sided attraction of thought at its fullest and most elegant, combined with an intense moral preoccupation, the preoccupation of getting somewhere, of not being satisfied with the most ingenious argument, the most appealing and attractive arrangement of ideas.

(C) The work of Plato can be said to be the simple moral teaching Socrates understood, re-expressed by the most brilliant man of his age who preserved, while being the passionate disciple of Socrates, the quantities of mind he was born with, those of the clever fashionable world.

(D) Socrates was the contrary of Plato–a man of the people, a sort of poor monk whose teaching, based on questioning and cross-questioning, tended to turn to ridicule the poetry, the eloquence and the metaphysics of which the young aristocratic Plato was a master.

(a) CDAB (b) ADCB
(c) DACB (d) BDCA
(e) BACD

76. (A) He was convinced that truth and goodness exist and are inseparable, and that virtue is one thing and is dependent upon knowledge.

(B) On account of this unity of goodness, truth and beauty, Plato considered that the arts–music, literature, poetry, architecture, rhetoric, politics and the practical arts–must be the servant of moral philosophy and only have value in so far as they serve it.

(C) In essence, the doctrine of Plato has many similarities with that of Christianity's.

(D) But it is a doctrine founded on an intellectual view of man and of the soul rather than one based on belief in God and Redeemer of mankind.

(E) There is a false architecture, false music, literature, etc., which takes man away from the pursuit of the perfect and help him to remain ignorant and malformed, and there is the converse.

(F) Plato's foremost place as a philosopher lies in his conception of unity.

(a) FABECD (b) CBEDAF
(c) FACEDB (d) ABFCDE
(e) EFACBD

77. (A) In all his writing on philosophy, whether political or ethical, Aristotle reveals himself as a teleologist, this is attempting the interpretation of things under discussion in terms of purpose or end (Greek *telos*: end).

(B) "Every art and every science," it begins," and in like manner every action and every moral choice, aims, it is thought at some good".

(C) What that good is depends of course on the things concerned: some activities are undertaken only for what they lead to or produce and bring about, while others are engaged in for their own sakes.

(D) So far as man is concerned, this end must be the good of man.

(E) But it is surely clear that there must be something that may be fairly described as the Chief Good, that is, the best thing of all.

(F) This is clearly evidenced from the very first statement of his *Nicomachean Ethics*.

(a) ABEFDC (b) BDCAFE
(c) AFBCED (d) DCBEFA
(e) FAEDCB

78. (A) For some say it is one of those things which are palpable and apparent, as pleasure or wealth or honour; in fact, some one thing, some another; nay, often times the same man gives a different account of it, for when ill, he calls it health, when poor, wealth; and conscious of their own ignorance, men admire those who talk grandly and above their comprehension.

(B) To use the more common form, "happiness (says Aristotle) is what both the multitude and the refined few call it, and 'living well' and 'doing well' they conceive to be the same with 'being happy'; but about the nature of this happiness men dispute, and the multitude do not in their account of it agree with wise."

(C) Now, what is this very special Good?

(D) There is pretty general agreement that is eudaimonia, a Greek word which is usually translated as Happiness, although a possibly better rendering would be Well-being or Welfare.

(a) DBAC (b) CDBA
(c) BCDA (d) ADBC
(e) ABCD

79. (A) After some pages descriptive of the liberal Man, who "will give and spend on proper objects, and in proper proportion, in great things and small alike, and all this with pleasure to himself," we come to a portrait of the Magnificent Man, which is doubtless based on what Aristotle had observed of the great aristocratic, popularity seeking spenders of Athens.
(B) "The expenses of the Magnificent Man are great fitting: such also are his works."
(C) The kind of expenditure which he will incur will be what are called honourable, "such as dedicatory offering to the gods, and furnishing their temples, and sacrifices, and in like manner everything that has reference to the deity, and all such public matters as are objects of honourable ambition, as when men think it is their duty to furnish a chorus for the stage splendidly, or fit out and maintain a three-decker for the navy, or give a great public feast... It is characteristic of the Magnificent Man to do magnificently whatever he is about."
(D) He will consider how a thing may be done most beautifully and fittingly, rather than for how much.
(a) ACBD (b) CDBA
(c) BACD (d) ABDC
(e) DABC

80. (A) Comparisons between Vergil and his great Greek prototype, Homer, are inevitable, although academic admirers of the Latin poet find them odious, arguing that Homer composed for an audience which knew only the epic on the grand scale and that his poetry was meant to be heard, not read.
(B) Nevertheless it can hardly be disputed that poetic merits of the *Aeneid* are far below those of *Iliad*, lacking the unity of purpose and integrity of construction of the earlier work as well as its truth and simplicity.
(C) It is also true that Homer's society was relatively uncomplicated, with a nobility not unlike the barons of England's feudal ages, whereas Vergil's civilisation was complex and he wrote for scholarly and thoroughly educated readers.
(D) Perhaps a model, however masterly, can never quite capture the spontaneous freshness of a glorious original.
(a) DCBA (b) ACBD
(c) CABD (d) ABCD
(e) BACD

81. (A) But later, when scholars had deciphered the cuneiform inscriptions of Babylon and Assyria, the historicity of a large part of the Old Testament was vindicated.
(B) The story of Abraham, for instance, is now to be seen much more than a folk tale, for the discoveries in the 'thirties of the Amorite Kingdom ruled by the smiling-faced Mari kings have unearthed cities such as Harun and Nathor mentioned in the Bablical narrative, but totally unknown till they were unearthed'.
(C) By the end of the century, when the work of geologists and physicists had begun to enlarge man's knowledge about the beginning of the physical world, the *Bible* as history, began to be considered largely as fable or folk-lore; by Christians it was thought divinely inspired but still basically mythical.
(D) To the simple-minded then, as in past centuries, the story of the *Old Testament* appeared as exact, literal history.
(E) When Queen Victoria came to the throne, it was generally believed that the world was created in 4004 BC.
(F) In fifty years or so, when so much has been discovered by archaeology about the Middle East and Egypt, the claim of the whole Old Testament story to be a valuable historical record, has been more and more accepted.
(a) DCAEFB (b) EDCAFB
(c) ACEFDB (d) FCDABE
(e) CABDEF

82. (A) When the Meccans challenged Mohammed to perform a miracle as proof of his Divine mission, he appealed, boldly and confidently, to the book which was taking shape under his supervision.
(B) It was indeed a miracle, the miracle of miracles, this book that had come down from heaven ...
(C) So wonderful a work (he maintained), written in such superlatively beautiful language and expressing the most profound and majestic of religious truths, could surely not have been written by mere man, most certainly not by such an unlettered man as he was himself.
(D) The book in question was *Koran*, as we generally call it, although a more correct rendering is Quran, which is an Arabic word meaning reading, lecture, or recitation, or perhaps that which ought to be read.
(a) ACBD (b) BACD
(c) ABCD (d) CDBA
(e) DCAB

83. (A) Fortunately, the lack of details available about the life of Shakespeare does not apply to Dante,

who is revealed to us as the hero of one of the strangest and most beautiful love stories in the world.

(B) If a limit may be set to the period of medieval literature, Dante's *Divine Comedy* may be said to have brought it to an end in a glorious climax.

(C) Of all the great figures, who embellish the pageant of literature, Dante shares an equal place with Shakespeare.

(D) Here all the greatest and best in thought and work that flowered in the millenium between the fall of Roman Empire and the close of the thirteenth century, is given a new vitality and endowed with poetic passion.

(a) ACDB (b) DBAC
(c) BDCA (d) CDBA
(e) BACD

84. (A) There were numerous religious shrines at home and abroad that attracted the pilgrims hosts, but in England, by far the most popular was Canterbury, where in the great cathedral stood the magnificent tomb of Thomas Beckett–St. Thomas of Canterbury–hard by the spot where in 1170 he had been brutally slain by four of King Henry's knights.

(B) On an April morning, many centuries ago, a band of pilgrims set out from the Tabard inn in Southwark to go to Canterbury.

(C) We should not suppose that the fact that they were pilgrims means that they were specially devout.

(D) Pilgrimages in the Middle Ages–and the year in question is somewhere in the 1380s–were a most welcome break in the monotonous round of daily existence, an occasion for seeing the sight and meeting fresh people and exchanging gossip and tales of high life, and of low.

(a) DBAC (b) ACDB
(c) BADC (d) BCDA
(e) CADB

85. (A) It was invented by More, and is a reminder of the fact that it was one of the most famous figures of revivals of Learning that was inspired by the rediscovery of the ancient classical civilisation of Greece and Rome after the long night of middle ages.

(B) Of all the cities that men have built in the cloudlands, the most famous is the one described in a small book written by the English scholar-statesman, Sir Tomas More, in the beginning of the sixteenth century.

(C) It is called *Utopia*, and so famous it is that ever since, all similar imaginary commonwealths have been referred to as Utopias.

(D) It comes from the Greek words, ou meaning not, and topas, a place, and so means literally, nowhere.

(E) The word is a made-up one.

(a) BCEDA (b) CDBCA
(c) ADCBE (d) EDCAB
(e) ABCDE

86. (A) What an audacious declaration it is, this of Jean-Jacques Rousseau, that "Man is born free; and everywhere he is in chains!".

(B) No matter that the critics in every generation have insisted that the first part of the declaration is untrue, since men come into the world carrying a heavy burden of heredity; and that as for the second part, there are quite a lot of places in the world nowadays where chains have long ceased to form part of the political machinery.

(C) No matter: it has a splendid, fine-sounding ring about it, and our political philosophy would be ever so much duller without it.

(D) When he first spat it out, it shocked and shattered the complacency of the eighteenth century, and it has been an inspiration and encouragement to the young and hopeful ever since.

(a) ADCB (b) CBAD
(c) BADC (d) ADBC
(e) CDBA

87. (A) From them he obtained a mass of information on business matters that came in exceedingly useful in writing his book.

(B) He may well have felt that his career was fixed, but then in 1764, he was invited to accompany the young Duke of Buccleugh on the customary "grand tour" of the continent.

(C) In the middle of the eighteenth century, Glasgow was still a small provincial city, but by 1760 it had supplanted Bristol as the principal tobacco port, and its "tobacco lords" were fine men of business.

(D) Adam Smith cultivated their acquaintance, and felt highly honoured when he was invited to join their weekly dining-club.

(a) DBCA (b) CDAB
(c) DACB (d) BCDA
(e) ABCD

88. (A) Now a few words on the third of the main themes of the Wealth of Nations, the one which is of greatest practical interest and importance–what may be described as his policy or programme of action.
(B) Under the influence of Mercantilist ideas, Adam Smith declared, "nations have been taught that their interest consisted in beggaring all their neighbours... Commerce which ought naturally to be, among nations as among individuals, a bond of union and friendship, has become the most fertile source of discord and animosity."
(C) It will be found for the most part in his fourth book, where we have a lengthy, detailed, and highly critical examination of the "Commercial or Mercantile System" that was the accepted ideology of the principle governments of his time.
(D) The Mercantilists held that wealth consists primarily of money, and mercantilist governments strove to foster home industries and encourage the export of as large an amount of goods as possible, and to import as little possible, when the difference would have to be made up in cash or bullion.
(a) CDAB (b) ACDB
(c) BADC (d) BACD
(e) CADB

89. (A) Mention should be made, too, of the many pithy sayings that ought to find a place in every dictionary of quotations.
(B) For example, "the delightful art" of gardening, "the desire for food is limited by the narrow capacity of the human stomach", "a man is of all sorts of luggage the most difficult to be transported", and "When you have got a little money, it is often easy to get more: the great difficulty is to get that little".
(C) All these things are of secondary importance, however.
(D) The really important thing about Adam Smith is that it was he who mapped out the ground and prepared the way for Economics to become what it is today, one of the most interesting, stimulating and vitally important of the science that are the instruments of human progress.
(a) ABCD (b) DABC
(c) CDBA (d) BCDA
(e) CABD

90. (A) Here, perhaps even more importantly than with any other science, the scientist has created a barrier of terms by which to express thoughts and ideas about matter affecting us all–the origins of knowledge and wisdom–but which effectively cuts off the ordinary man from the thinker, the man who by terming himself philosopher, clearly looks upon himself, as the word implies, as the fount of wisdom.
(B) Unfortunately, as with most sciences, the would-be interpreter of philosophy finds himself becoming involved in almost insoluble complications of expression if he does not use some of the jargon, the special terms by which philosophers convey, in a kind of shorthand, their own particular thoughts to their professional colleagues.
(C) If a really outstanding example of non-communication were ever to be sought, scarcely a better one could be cited than that of philosophy.
(D) The preceding paragraph, simple though it is in philosophical expression, is nevertheless sufficient to show the non-philosophic student that, like all sciences, philosophy has acquired its own particular jargon which only the initiated can understand with ease.
(a) DBAC (b) ACDB
(c) CABD (d) DCAB
(e) BACD

91. (A) All our intuitions have a dual nature; objects appear to be outside ourselves and externally co-existent in space; and they also seem to exist within our own minds, either simultaneously or in succession, and so, in time.
(B) The reason why all our intuitions are bound up with these two forms lies in the manner in which our faculty of imagination receives the impression of objects.
(C) Space and time, then, are pure intuitions, which are present a priori in advance of any real sensation, inherent in the faculty of imagination in our soul, and are thus only necessary ideas a priori, underlying all intuitions.
(D) Thus, space and time are the two forms to which all our intuitions are bound, and as they are ideas directly related to objects, they are themselves intuitions.
(a) BDAC (b) ADBC
(c) BACD (d) CADB
(e) DABC

92. (A) The important place that it occupies in Marx's system is shown by the hundreds of pages that he devotes in Capital to its elucidation and illustration.

(B) But nowhere do we find any indication that Marx had ever been inside a cotton-mill or down a coal-mine, that he had ever visited pottery or ironworks or railway shed; and all the detail with which his pages are filled was what he could collect from seat No.7 in row G in the British Museum reading-room.

(C) Most of his supporting material is drawn from English practice, for the very good reason that it was in England that the capitalized system had mainly originated and had reached its most advanced development.

(D) This theory of surplus value is Marx's special contribution to economic ideology, and it is no wonder that it made a strong appeal to the workers, especially those engaged in factory production in the industrialised countries of Europe and America.

(a) DCAB (b) CADB
(c) BCDA (d) DACB
(e) ABCD

93. (A) Before the modern system of capitalist enterprise could come into existence, there had to be what Marx calls the stage of "primary accumulation", which he defines as "the historical process whereby the producer was divorced from the means of production."

(B) These were "the idyllic methods of primary accumulation", which cleared the ground for capitalist agriculture and provided urban industry with the requisite number of "masterless proletarians".

(C) This was effected through the spoliation of the property of the Church at the Reformation, the subsequent alienation of the State domains, the transformation of feudal property and the property of the Scottish clans, by a system of ruthless terrorism, into modern private property.

(D) Hard upon their heels came the commercial wars between the great European powers, fought over the whole surface of the globe, of which a recent sequel had been the opium wars against China.

(E) Then followed the discoveries of gold and silver in America, the extirpation or enslavement and entombment of the native, the beginning of the conquest of the East Indies, the transformation of Africa into a source of raw material of the slave trade–these were the incidents that characterised the "rosy dawn of the period of capitalist production".

(a) ACEBD (b) DABCE
(c) ACBED (d) CAEDB
(e) EADCB

94. (A) He had been led to this discovery by applying to dreams, a new method of psychological investigation which had proved of great value in the solution of phobias, obsessions, delusions and so on–namely, psycho-analysis.

(B) Serious-minded people were apt to smile at all this, but one day he was astonished to find that the view of dream which most nearly approached the truth was not the medical one–that dreams are caused entirely by sensory and somatic stimuli–but the popular one.

(C) The methods of interpretation consist in transferring the content of a dream as it is remembered, either by replacing it piecemeal in accordance with a fixed key, or by replacing the dream as a whole by a certain series of symbols.

(D) Having thus set out his problem, and referred to the more recent pronouncements on the nature of dreams by scientists and medical men, Freud points out that popular opinion has taken little heed of scientific judgments in this field, and persists in the belief that dreams have meaning which relates to the prediction of the future and which can be discovered by some process of interpretation of a content which is often confused and puzzling.

(E) An investigation into the significance of dream inquiries, first, into the psychical significance of dreaming, into the relation of dreams to the mental processes and into any biological function dreams may have; while, second, it tries to discover whether dreams can be interpreted, whether the content of individual dreams has a "meaning" such as can be found in other psychical structures.

(a) EDCBA (b) ABEDC
(c) DEBCA (d) DECBA
(e) ABCDE

95. (A) The impression which acts as the dream-instigator may be such an important one that we feel no surprise at being concerned with it in the day-time.

(B) If we unravel dream-displacement by analysis, we obtain what appears to be completely trustworthy information about dream-instigators and the connection of dreams with waking life.

(C) By analysis, we find that every dream without exception, goes back to an impression received during the last few days.

(D) As a rule, however, if a connection is to be found between a dream-content and an impression received the previous day, it is usually so trivial that we can recall it only with difficulty, and dream content seems concerned with trivialities.

(a) DBAC (b) ACDB
(c) BCAD (d) DCAB
(e) ABCD

96. (A) Joe had had trouble falling asleep, and once asleep, he went from one dream to another.
(B) The phone rang.
(C) He was showing a house to a young couple.
(D) He looked at it but could not find it.
(a) ADCB (b) ACBD
(c) BDCA (d) CBAD
(e) ADBC

97. (A) I dressed and fixed breakfast in the small kitchen.
(B) Afterward, I stepped out on the narrow deck to breathe the mountain air.
(C) The answers would come gradually, I told myself.
(D) The next morning, I awakened early and lay quietly, trying to orient myself.
(E) Last night, there had been much that was strange and perplexing.
(a) DECAB (b) ADECB
(c) CABDE (d) ADCEB
(e) BADCE

98. (A) Later that night, as I sat up in bed trying to read the *Book of the Hopi*, my thoughts were melancholy and not the pages.
(B) Mountain silence seemed to press all around the small guesthouse, threatening me.
(C) I was about to put the book aside and attempt to fall asleep when a light tapping sounded on the outside door.
(D) In my present state of mind, the sound was unnerving.
(E) Nevertheless, I drew on my robe and went into the little hallway.
(a) DBCAE (b) ADBCE
(c) ABCDE (d) CAEBD
(e) EDCBA

99. (A) "Who's there?" I called.
(B) I sighed and turned the latch, not at all sure that I could cope with Marilla just then.
(C) "It's me-Marilla. Open the door, Lindsay."
(D) She stood on the flagstones outside, dressed in pajamas and one of her father's sweaters, and holding both hands behind her back.
(E) She smiled at me angelically.
(a) ACBDE (b) BACED
(c) DBCEA (d) CABDE
(e) ECABD

100. (A) I decided to ask her a direct question.
(B) "You've already told me that Sybil came to talk to you about the dinner on the day she disappeared. Was there anything else?"
(C) For a moment, I thought Orva wouldn't answer.
(D) Then she seemed to make a decision.
(a) ACDB (b) BADC
(c) CADB (d) ABCD
(e) DABC

101. (A) A Roman chariot decorated with the figure of Columbia on the front.
(B) On Sunday afternoons John Doud, wearing goggles and a long white coat, took the family for outings in his Stanley Steamer, one in a series of cars that he owned.
(C) Sometimes they would go to City Park, where the Doud girls would wander through the Zoological Gardens or listen to band concerts.
(D) Other times, they went to Elitch Gardens, one of the oldest amusement parks in the country, where Mamie had a favorite seat on the merry-go-round–
(a) DCAB (b) BCDA
(c) CBDA (d) CDAB
(e) ABCD

Answer Key

1. (b)	**2.** (c)	**3.** (b)	**4.** (c)	**5.** (d)
6. (c)	**7.** (d)	**8.** (c)	**9.** (b)	**10.** (d)
11. (a)	**12.** (c)	**13.** (a)	**14.** (d)	**15.** (a)
16. (b)	**17.** (d)	**18.** (a)	**19.** (b)	**20.** (d)
21. (c)	**22.** (b)	**23.** (b)	**24.** (c)	**25.** (d)
26. (a)	**27.** (d)	**28.** (d)	**29.** (b)	**30.** (a)
31. (c)	**32.** (b)	**33.** (d)	**34.** (c)	**35.** (d)
36. (c)	**37.** (d)	**38.** (b)	**39.** (d)	**40.** (a)
41. (d)	**42.** (a)	**43.** (d)	**44.** (c)	**45.** (d)
46. (a)	**47.** (d)	**48.** (b)	**49.** (d)	**50.** (b)
51. (a)	**52.** (d)	**53.** (c)	**54.** (a)	**55.** (a)
56. (b)	**57.** (b)	**58.** (a)	**59.** (c)	**60.** (c)
61. (c)	**62.** (c)	**63.** (d)	**64.** (b)	**65.** (a)
66. (d)	**67.** (b)	**68.** (c)	**69.** (c)	**70.** (b)
71. (a)	**72.** (b)	**73.** (c)	**74.** (a)	**75.** (c)
76. (a)	**77.** (c)	**78.** (b)	**79.** (d)	**80.** (b)
81. (b)	**82.** (a)	**83.** (c)	**84.** (d)	**85.** (a)
86. (d)	**87.** (b)	**88.** (b)	**89.** (a)	**90.** (d)
91. (b)	**92.** (d)	**93.** (c)	**94.** (a)	**95.** (c)
96. (b)	**97.** (a)	**98.** (c)	**99.** (a)	**100.** (d)
101. (b)				

CHAPTER 17

New TITA Type CAT Level Para Jumble Questions

PARA-JUMBLES

EXERCISE 1

Paragraph Jumbles in CAT 2015 to 2021 came without options. Here are some questions to help you be up to date with the latest pattern of the examination.

Also called as TITA question types [Type In The Answer = TITA]

Directions:

Q1–25. Five sentences are given below. Rearrange them to make a meaningful paragraph.

Q1. I. Together, we can gallop up to obstacles standing 8 feet (2.4 metres) high, leave the ground, and fly blind

II. In freestyle dressage events, we dance in place to the rhythm of music, trot sideways across the centre of an arena with huge leg-crossing steps, and canter in pirouettes with the horse's front feet circling her hindquarters.

III. And neither party is able to see over the top until after the leap has been initiated

IV. Horse-and-human teams perform complex manoeuvres in competitions of all sorts.

V. No one disputes the athleticism fuelling these triumphs, but few people comprehend the mutual cross-species interaction that is required to accomplish them.

Q2. I. The bank's website provides an 'idiot's guide' to the economy that explains how 'Supply and demand is a bit like an economist's version of the law of gravity.'

II. It decides how much everything costs: a cup of coffee, a house and even your salary.'

III. The workers are curious why their wages have not increased in the past decade – while the incomes of some, such as footballers, have soared

IV. The Bank of England's website has a reassuring message: 'There is a method to this madness: the economic theory of supply and demand'.

V. The US Federal Reserve Bank provides similar explainers for Americans who want to understand how their country's wealth is created or allocated.

Q3. I. On the other hand, a life well lived requires new experiences, risk and authentic independence, in ways incompatible with a family or partner or job.

II. That's because we sense, the demands of a good life are not merely difficult, sometimes, the demands of a good life actually contradict.

III. On the one hand, a life well lived requires security, safety and regularity.

IV. That might mean a family, a partner, a steady job.

V. Here is a dilemma you may find familiar.

Q4. I. He greeted his audience with a speech calling for the overthrow of Russia's government and, six months later, he made this happen.

II. On 3 April 1917, a crowd gathered to meet a train arriving from Helsinki at Petrograd's Finland Station.

III. Lenin, who had been living outside of Russia for more than a decade, was known as a theorist on the fringe of Russian political society.

IV. The train carried Vladimir Ilyich Lenin.
V. He shaped Marxist thought to support his own theory of change.

Q5. I. Inflation has hit a 30-year high and the average British worker is entering their third drop in real wages in a decade.
II. Next month, the regulator Ofgem announces the maximum price for heating bills and energy company bosses are already warning that they will almost certainly be double last winter's levels.
III. The economic news this week is stark.
IV. But what's really sobering is that the worst is still to come.
V. The new price cap kicks in from April, at just the point that national insurance goes up alongside council tax increases in many boroughs, and there's a stealth rise in income tax.

Q6. I. The advent of peace saw the population rocketing from 540 million to 969 million over the next three decades.
II. These days, most Chinese couples are curtailing their families - or going without - by choice.
III. "Of all things in the world, people are the most precious," Mao Zedong said soon after taking power, believing China needed more soldiers and workers.
IV. Authorities abruptly switched to curbing births and brutally implementing the "one-child" policy.
V. The population now stands at 1.4 billion; a sixth of the global total.

Q7. I. An investigation launched last year by the regulator, Ofwat, and the Environment Agency, is a chance to put things right.
II. English water companies have got used to pumping raw sewage into the sea and rivers.
III. But there are worrying signs that this opportunity to shine a light is in danger of being missed.
IV. That the investigation is happening at all is due to huge efforts by campaigners.
V. The refusal by the Environment Agency to reveal which 2,000 sewage treatment works in England are being looked at, and whether this will lead to delays in dealing with new complaints, raises questions about its commitment to openness.

Q8. I. These days that kind of optimism - along with any sense of unity among progressives - is just a poignant memory.
II. With less than 100 days to go before the first round of the French presidential election, the jockeying for position among the flatlining candidates of the left has become a fractious sideshow.
III. The campaign continues to be dominated by the right.
IV. In better times, the French left used to draw inspiration from the old Popular Front phrase, "les lendemains qui chantent" (the tomorrows that sing).
V. At the weekend, the Socialist former justice minister, Christiane Taubira, became the latest hopeful to formally throw her hat into the ring.

Q9. I. The UK's biggest energy supplier, Centrica, says high gas and electricity prices could last for another two years.
II. The good news is that energy prices will be coming down.
III. The International Energy Agency (IEA) reckons that's too optimistic.
IV. The bad news is nobody knows when for sure.

Q10. I. No one believed that three rounds of talks between the United States, Russia and others would magically resolve the Ukraine crisis.
II. With 100,000 Russian troops massed near the country's borders, the build-up of weaponry and growing sabre rattling from Moscow
III. A week that began with low expectations has ended with a still bleaker mood.
IV. The hope was that the negotiations could help to probe Vladimir Putin's intentions, and perhaps offer him pathways towards an eventual de-escalation.
V. After the NATO discussions and before the Organization for Security and Co-operation in Europe talks concluded, Russian's Deputy Foreign Minister, Sergei Ryabkov said the parties had reached a dead end.

Q11. I. The FM did state that a 'bare minimum' of CPSEs would operate in four strategic sectors and the rest privatised.
II. The finance minister's budget speech was unabashedly bold on strategic sale and privatisation of central public sector enterprises (CPSEs).
III. It will provide resources for developmental purposes and generally redeploy valuable assets earning suboptimal returns.
IV. The welcome divestment strategy makes perfect sense, policy designed as it is to better leverage private sector efficiency.
V. He stated that all CPSEs in non-strategic areas would be privatised.

Q12. I. The military takeover came hours ahead of the swearing in of the newly elected parliament.
II. Democracy requires work and support.
III. India has, along with other countries, expressed its concern at the developments and called

for upholding the rule of law and democratic process.

IV. The military coup in Myanmar curtails democracy, limited and imperfect as it was, in one of the poorest countries.

V. Stronger, more mature democracies must provide support required by newer democracies, without becoming prescriptive.

Q13. I. That's something Al Hirschfeld did so beautifully, especially as his artwork changed during different phases.

II. The more spare it was, I found, the more moved I was.

III. I fight when people ask me to put colour in a picture.

IV. A line with a hand at the end of it can give you just enough to envision an arm.

V. I love colour, but I'm more intrigued by the relationship between black and white and space.

Q14. I. In the 55 countries with food-insecurity crises, 75 million children under the age of five are chronically undernourished.

II. Save the Children is responding to these emergencies.

III. They face higher risks of diarrhoea, pneumonia and other killer diseases that accompany droughts and floods.

IV. Stick a pin in a map of global humanitarian emergencies, and you will most likely land on a crisis that has been caused or aggravated by droughts, floods and storms.

V. In 2019, extreme weather events pushed more than 34 million people into hunger and food insecurity.

Q15. I. Within weeks, the military, under orders issued by Senior General Min Aung Hlaing, had arrested Suu Kyi and other National League for Democracy (NLD) ministers and declared a one-year state of emergency.

II. Following the 1962 putsch and a bloody crackdown on pro-democracy demonstrators in 1988.

III. Myanmar's civilian government, led by Aung San Suu Kyi's National League for Democracy, may not have been perfect, but it had the people's support.

IV. Myanmar has been here before and has endured nearly a half-century of military dictatorship and international isolation

V. In last November's election, the NLD won with a strong majority against the military-backed opposition.

Q16. I. One wallows in loneliness, while the other tries to do away with it altogether.

II. Writing on loneliness often falls into one of the two camps: the overindulgent memoir, or the rational medicalisation that treats loneliness as something to be cured.

III. And this is in part because loneliness is so difficult to communicate.

IV. Both approaches leave the reader a bit cold.

V. As soon as we begin to talk about loneliness, we transform one of the most deeply felt human experiences into an object of contemplation, and a subject of reason.

Q17. I. The problem has understandable roots: the human brain evolved to detect difference, and then to categorise that difference as either threat or non-threat.

II. Plants, being unlikely to attack, are lumped together and treated as background, a green screen against which dramas take place.

III. The term "plant blindness" was coined in 1998 to describe our general tendency, as humans, not to see the plant life that surrounds us.

IV. Many plants, and especially trees, exist on a different timescale to humans

V. Who have spent millennia dividing existence into conscious beings and things, where the former are afforded automatic importance over the latter.

Q18. I. Judge Lewis Kaplan's decision meant that the case would go ahead and there was thus no good option for the Queen's son.

II. Reality has finally caught up with Prince Andrew.

III. His attempt to stop Virginia Giuffre from pursuing her civil damages claim against him was thrown out by a New York judge on Wednesday.

IV. For the prince, it was a day of disgrace. It has been too long coming.

V. On Thursday, Buckingham Palace moved decisively to cut the prince loose, stripping him of his military titles, his royal patronages and his use of 'His Royal Highness'.

Q19. I. Amendments added to the police, crime, sentencing and courts bill by the government late last year would restrict the right to protest beyond the measures already debated by MPs.

II. The new powers granted to the police by these extra clauses, along with sentences of up to a year for offences such as obstructing "nationally significant infrastructure" including roads and airports, are an assault on civil liberties.

III. Checks and balances are built into every democracy.

IV. Freedom of expression, including the freedom of assembly, is central to a liberal democracy.

V. On Monday, the House of Lords has the chance to show how much this matters and why.

Q20. I. In June, the Methodist church became the largest religious denomination in the United Kingdom to allow same-sex marriage.

II. Soon after the Anglican Church in Wales voted to introduce special blessings for same-sex married couples.

III. For LGBT+ Christians, 2021 provided two significant causes for celebration.

IV. Across the border in England, the bishop of Liverpool, the Right Rev Paul Bayes, hailed the Welsh move.

V. He said, "I trust that my own church will follow this creative and gospel-inspired lead, and I hope that this will happen soon."

Q21. I. It is the United Nations' biggest ever appeal for a single country.

II. The Disasters Emergency Committee says that 95 per cent of Afghans do not have enough to eat and one million children are at the risk of dying from malnutrition this winter.

III. But the $5bn (£3.7bn) sought to stave off catastrophe in Afghanistan is dwarfed both by the trillions that were poured into the war, and by the level of current need.

IV. Women and other vulnerable people are especially hard-hit.

V. The money is merely a stopgap, as the UN itself points out.

Q22. I. Property developers and speculators cannot be saddled with all the blame for this.

II. It was a project of successive governments, and notably that led by David Cameron.

III. They removed rules that they saw as making life unnecessarily difficult for construction businesses.

IV. The tragedy of the 2017 Grenfell Tower fire in west London has revealed a house-building industry corrupted by a profits-first and anti-regulation ideology.

V. The dysfunctional system that led to 72 people losing their lives included failures of housing management and safety culture as well as the inappropriate use of flammable cladding.

Q23. I. Recent polls indicate that Italy's technocrat prime minister, appointed last February by the country's president, Sergio Mattarella, basks in stellar approval ratings of about 65 per cent.

II. The explanation for his success lies in the unaccustomed sense of stability and calm that the former head of the European Central Bank has delivered.

III. As honeymoon period go, this one has justified the "Super Mario" hype that accompanied Mr Draghi's installation.

IV. Since taking office, following the mid-Covid implosion of a centre-left coalition government, Mr Draghi has presided with authority over a unity administration that involves every party apart from the far-right Brothers of Italy.

V. No Italian has ever voted for Mario Draghi in an election, but given the opportunity it seems that many might choose to do so.

Q24. I. The television documentary maker Adam Curtis, for example, long ago embraced iPlayer rather than linear television for his films,

II. It's nothing new to note that the rise of streaming services has the potential to unleash the screen artwork from its standard length and form.

III. Because on the streaming platform he would find a home away from the "rigid formats and schedules of network television."

IV. In audio, podcasting has long liberated itself from the tight, clock-regulated schedules of radio.

V. In 2015, his film Bitter Lake, about the banal narratives imposed on a complex world by reductive world leaders, occupied two hours and 20 minutes - more time than he would have been allotted by even the most indulgent channel controller.

Q25. I. This week, Sir Phil Redmond disclosed that he is updating Grange Hill, the greatest school soap of them all, for a one-off movie version set in the present day.

II. Meanwhile, in America, Disney has rebooted the equally admired The Wonder Years.

III. For readers whose formative years were enriched by the after-school teatime TV experience, the revival of two coming-of-age classics may be sparking a sudden rush of nostalgia.

IV. But with the twist that this time it chronicles the vicissitudes of childhood and adolescence through the eyes of a black boy living in Alabama.

V. Bringing these two televisual gems back to life necessarily entails substantial reinterpretation; the impact of social media, for example, will loom large in the Grange Hill of 2022.

PARAGRAPHS JUMBLES WITHOUT OPTIONS (ACCORDING TO NEW CAT PATTERN)

Paragraph Jumbles in CAT 2015 to 2021 came without options. Here are some questions to help you be up to date with the latest pattern of the examination.

Also called as TITA question types [Type In The Answer = TITA]

EXERCISE 1

Rearrange the following sentences in a logical order to form a coherent paragraph.

Q1. I. Let's understand what motivates behavior change. Say you want to create a website or app to help people exercise more, but you're not sure how to motivate users.

II. Rewarding someone for an activity they already inherently enjoy might lead to a short-term increase in behavior but as soon as reward is taken away, the activity is often pursued less than before the reward was given. This phenomenon is called **"over-justification effect"**.

III. A website or app that encourages people to exercise more might offer a reward whenever a user exercises, thus creating extrinsic motivation for the person to show that behavior. The Pact app runs with this idea by allowing users to earn money by reaching their health goals.

IV. In psychology, we distinguish between *extrinsic* and *intrinsic* motivation. This means that someone can be driven to do something either by external factors, like the prospect of receiving a reward, like money, or by internal factors, like enjoyment derived from doing an activity.

V. Research has shown that this approach works well for people who do not enjoy the behavior. However, for people who do enjoy the behavior but would like to improve on it or are not doing it for some reason, giving a reward could actually have a negative effect.

Q2. I. Yet while Francis Crick revealed the hidden secrets of DNA through a model, his attempts at applying similar techniques to neuroanatomy in an exploration of our inner sense of "self" were less successful.

II. "We brought a couple of neuroscientists in to look at them and bafflement was the result of that encounter too," admits Emily Sargent, curator of the Wellcome Collection's latest exhibition *States of Mind.* Nevertheless Crick's wide-ranging work in the field was influential, not least in breaking the taboo of tackling the topic in scientific circles.

III. For these are, in fact, part of a determined effort by a great scientist to explore one of the most curious facets of being: consciousness.

IV. On a crumpled sheet of tin foil in the Wellcome Collection's conservation studio lies an odd assortment of plasticine forms.

V. One looks suspiciously like the footprint of a chicken, another like a deformed pot, while a large, red lump bears more than a passing resemblance to a gammon joint. But the comparisons are hopelessly wide of the mark.

Q3. I. I felt pretty hopeless about my future.

II. When I was in high school I took the ACT, a college aptitude exam used as an admissions criterion by most American universities.

III. That was painful enough but adding insult to injury, the ACT score report informed me that, based on my score, my expected probability of succeeding at my hometown college, the University of Utah, was around 15 per cent. As I remember it, my chance of success at my dream school of Harvard University was less than 3 per cent.

IV. My score was in the lowest third of all students.

V. After all, these stark percentages were endowed with the sober authority of mathematics. Before I took the exam, I had thought that one day I might become a scientist or neurologist, but no–what a silly fantasy that was.

Q4. I. "Some studies indicate that solitary confinement can worsen existing mental illnesses and even trigger new ones."

II. "Research suggests that solitary confinement has the potential to lead to devastating, lasting psychological consequences," Mr. Obama wrote. "It has been linked to depression, alienation, withdrawal, a reduced ability to interact with others and the potential for violent behavior."

III. U.S. President Obama banned the practice of holding juveniles in solitary confinement in federal prisons, saying it could lead to "devastating, lasting psychological consequences."

IV. Mr. Obama on Monday said federal prisons would no longer use solitary confinement for juveniles or for inmates serving time for low-level infractions. He said the change, along with expanded mental health treatment, would affect as many as 10,000 inmates in the federal system, about a tenth of those being held in solitary confinement in the United States, including in state prisons.

V. The move, which Mr. Obama outlined in an op-ed article published by *The Washington Post* on Monday night, adds the weight of the federal government to a growing movement among state prison administrators, who have begun sharply limiting or ending the use of solitary confinement.

Q5. I. Five or 10 or 20 years from now, when all those who care about the basketball team here talk about the gloriously unexpected winning streak that began in October, stretched until mid-January and covered 28 games in six countries, they will talk about the upset in Madrid that started it all.

II. Sikma said: "There was some homeless drifter to it, some mountain man. It was very solid."

III. "He looked like Shaggy from 'Scooby-Doo,' but on steroids," said Luke Sikma, one of three American players on the team. "The hair was everywhere, the beard was everywhere."

IV. Or the late comeback in Germany. Or maybe the overtime game against Bilbao. Then they will talk about the beard.

V. The beard, otherwise known as the unkempt, untamed, unruly thicket of wires located on the cheeks and chin of forward John Shurna, became the unofficial mascot of Valencia's winning streak, a lucky charm that inspired everyone around it but–unlike most other furry mascots–also seemed to grow like virulent kitchen mold.

Q6. I. Ahead of a first-round match pitting Lara Arruabarrena and David Marrero against Andrea Hlavackova and Lukasz Kubot, large amounts of money poured in on what would normally be an obscure contest, said Marco Blume, head of sportsbook at the website, Pinnacle Sports, one of the largest and most influential betting websites in the world.

II. Nearly all of the money, Blume said, came down for Hlavackova and Kubot, which he said was an indication that the match might be fixed.

III. Hlavackova and Kubot won, 6-0, 6-3. The first set lasted only 20 minutes.

IV. A major sports betting website suspended betting on Sunday for a mixed doubles match at the Australian
Open, raising suspicions of match fixing at one of the world's most prestigious tennis tournaments.

V. Arruabarrena, the 33rd-ranked doubles player on the women's tour, and Marrero, ranked 32nd among men, rejected any possibility of fixing in an interview after the match. Marrero, who like Arruabarrena is from Spain, cited a knee injury in explaining their performance.

Q7. I. Now Islamic scholars have added their voice to a crescendo of spiritually-inspired cries for action to conserve the planet.

II. The statement was hailed by Cardinal Peter Turkson, head of the Vatican's council for justice and peace, and by eco-religious groups like the green-minded Franciscans who in common with the pope find inspiration in the nature-respecting, wealth-abjuring example set by Francis of Assisi 800 years ago.

III. "We particularly call on the well-off nations and oil-producing states to lead the way in phasing out greenhouse-gas emissions as early as possible and no later than the middle of the century," it said.

IV. From a meeting in Istanbul attended by senior Muslims from Morocco to Bosnia to Indonesia there came a passionate and impressively detailed appeal for a new global pact at the Paris climate summit in December.

V. When Pope Francis issued his 192-page encyclical on climate change and pollution, this was rightly hailed as a landmark in the history of the papacy, and of environmentalism.

Q8. I. Everyone has gone through a fight where the pilot asks you to tighten your seat belts because of excessive turbulence, but even though it is so important to things like air safety, we just have absolutely no idea how it works.

II. The problem is aggravated by the fact that wherever the need to study turbulence arises–like in jet propulsion–chemical reactions take place alongside the high pressure and extreme conditions, which makes it difficult for researchers to study the exact conditions needed to produce turbulence.

III. If somehow we could figure it out, it could be applied to a variety of uses since turbulence occurs everywhere in nature.

IV. It has even perplexed scientists to such an extent that Einstein once famously said, "Before I die, I hope someone will clarify quantum physics for me. After I die, I hope God will explain turbulence to me."

V. Maybe one day we'd even be able to predict hurricanes or other natural disasters with accuracy, thus minimising the damage and finally scoring one over nature.

Q9. I. Clearly, cuckoos are one species you don't want to mess with.

II. Scientists do believe that cuckoos are able to use a variety of compasses based on the stars and the Earth's magnetic field, but a compass can only guide you–it can't tell you the coordinates of a location you have no idea about.

III. This behavior of migration of birds remains one of the most mysterious animal behaviors known to science, and even though they've been trying hard to solve it for a long time, answers haven't been easy to come by.

IV. We know that birds migrate over really long distances every year to lay eggs or to escape harsh winters. What we don't know is how they do it at all.

V. Consider this: Cuckoos migrate and lay their eggs in other birds' nests, then just fly away to their own business. When the young ones grow up, they make their way to their ancestral lands without any help whatsoever.

Q10. I. As the evil is discovered by experience to be greater than the good, the sufferers, who cannot also be doers, make a compact that they will have neither, and this compact or mean is called justice, but is really the impossibility of doing injustice.

II. No one would observe such a compact if he were not obliged.

III. And he who abstains will be regarded by the world as a fool for his pains.

IV. Let us suppose that the just and unjust have two rings, like that of Gyges in the well-known story, which make them invisible, and then no difference will appear in them, for everyone will do evil if he can.

V. To do injustice is said to be a good; to suffer injustice an evil.

Q11. I. The world is faced yet again with an alarming disease for which we are woefully unprepared to combat: the mosquito-borne Zika virus.

II. But today, there are up to 1.3 million estimated cases in Brazil, and cases have been reported in other countries in South America, Central America, and the Caribbean, as well as in the U.S.

III. Mosquitoes, not just Zika carriers in discussion but generally, kill more humans every year than any other animal.

IV. We know exactly how dangerous they can be, making the frequency with which they catch us off guard all the more disconcerting.

V. Just a few years ago, this virus was not present in the Western hemisphere.

Q12. I. World health leaders have described antibiotic-resistant bacteria as "nightmare bacteria" that "pose a catastrophic threat" to people in every country in the world.

II. Each year in the United States, at least 2 million people become infected with bacteria that are resistant to antibiotics, and at least 23,000 people die each year as a direct result of these infections.

III. In addition, almost 250,000 people who are hospitalised or require hospitalisation get *Clostridium difficile* each year, an infection usually related to antibiotic use. *C. difficile* causes deadly diarrhea and kills at least 14,000 people each year.

IV. Many more people die from other conditions that were complicated by an antibiotic-resistant infection.

V. Antibiotic resistance is a quickly growing, extremely dangerous problem.

Q13. I. The untimely death of Sandra Bland in a rural Texas jail last month has led to many unanswered questions.

II. Lost in the emotion of yet another tragic death of a young African American in police custody is the real possibility that untreated mental illness led to Bland's death.

III. Texas prison authorities say Bland hanged herself with a plastic garbage bag in her cell, a claim her family has questioned. Many suspect that Bland was murdered by corrupt law enforcement officials or correctional officers.

IV. And, while African Americans have lower suicide rates relative to whites, the rate of suicide among African-American males and females has also been climbing each year since 2009.

V. Regardless of what happened in that Texas jail, Centers for Disease Control data tell us that rates of suicide have seen a steady increase each year since 2000. Suicide is now the 10th leading cause of death among all Americans.

Q14. I. The islands–which would become the 50th American state on Aug. 21, 1959–were populated by more than a dozen ethnic groups.

II. Photographer Eliot Elisofon's portraits of the people of Hawaii serve as a visual aid to the magazine's utopian perspective on the territory.

III. In November of 1945, LIFE Magazine declared Hawaii "the world's most successful experiment in mixed breeding, a sociologist's dream of interracial cultures".

IV. A young white girl and a young Chinese girl hold hands as they play together. A white man from Indiana and his Chinese wife pose for a sweet family photo with their two young daughters. A series of attractive young women are presented with captions that describe their racial makeup: "Caucasian-Hawaiian," "Asiatic-Caucasian," "Asiatic-Hawaiian." All are smiling, windswept, a picture of harmony.

V. Intermarriage was common, and from the children produced by those marriages, LIFE declared, "a new race is emerging and stabilizing".

Q15. I. Those, such as the advocates of the revised metaphysical interpretation, interpreting Hegel as basically a metaphysician, typically stress the former, while post-Kantian interpreters typically stress the latter.

II. In short, taking the logic as a category theory opens up two general lines of interpretation: should the categories be understood as primarily ontological categories, as found in Aristotle, or as primarily categories revealing the necessary structure of thought, as in Kant?

III. In this sense it should thereby be thought of as a successor to Kant's "transcendental deduction of the categories" in the Critique of Pure Reason in which Kant attempted to derive a list of those non-empirical concepts, the categories, which he believed to be presupposed by all empirical judgments made by finite, discursive knowers like ourselves.

IV. Others argue that in contrast to the project of formal (or general) logic, it is best understood as a version of what Kant had called "transcendental logic" in the Di Giovanni.

V. Some advocate that Science of Logic be read as a first-order ontological doctrine or as a category theory that simultaneously represents structures of being and thought, and so as having very little to do with what has traditionally been known as logic.

EXERCISE 2

TITA without options

Rearrange the following sentences in a logical order to form a coherent paragraph.

Q16. I. Maybe they could even find life in damp Martian nooks and crannies, areas where the dusty red planet can still fuel microbes.

II. It's tempting to say that the announcement of liquid water on the surface of Mars heralds a new era in Martian exploration.

III. You might think that the first human explorers on Mars will park next to a salty stream and use it to manufacture fresh drinking water.

IV. Finding evidence for flowing water is not the same as finding life.

V. Reality is much more subtle.

Q17. I. One, the gas was stored at the end of the supply chain and contained mercaptans, the odorous additives used to make leak detection easier in homes.

II. Two, EDF and the environmental group Earthworks released infrared footage of the leak that got more than 1 million views on YouTube.

III. Alan Septoff, strategic communications director for Earthworks, says the group was able to acquire its $100,000 camera because of "one very interested and supportive donor."

IV. The footage was made possible with special cameras developed over the past decade that can transform transparent plumes of gas into vivid, dark clouds.

V. There were two key factors that helped highlight the infamous Aliso Canyon leak.

Q18. I. A car that drives itself. A watch that remotely turns lights on or off. A home that produces power for neighbors during a blackout.

II. Yet they still need public acceptance, lawmakers' approval, and enough funding to avoid innovation's often-cited "valleys of death."

III. These three don't belong to a Jetsons-like future.

IV. They've already arrived. They're part of a new tech era in which scientists and entrepreneurs are rapidly trying bold ideas to save energy or provide cleaner alternatives.

V. Their discoveries could help countries meet the goals of this month's historic UN climate accord, aimed at slashing greenhouse gas emissions.

Q19. I. The Mirai, which converts hydrogen into electricity and emits nothing but drops of water, is a Japanese word that means "future"– can go 310 miles on a single tank.

II. Toyota, maker of the Prius–the best-selling first hybrid car–is moving ahead with a mass-production fuel cell sedan in California.

III. That range is greater than any electric car on the market (even Tesla's) or the current hydrogen-powered competitors–the Honda FCX Clarity and the Hyundai Tucson Fuel Cell. Yet the car is pricey, costing at least $57,500 before subsidies.

IV. It has another serious obstacle: lack of stations to dispense compressed hydrogen gas.

V. California has only about a dozen filling locations statewide, creating a chicken-and-egg problem in which customers don't want the car unless stations are available but stations aren't opening without the cars.

Q20. I. Panasonic and SolarCity, the largest residential solar installer in the U.S., debuted new rooftop panels this year that they say are the world's most efficient.

II. Solar is taking off as its prices have plummeted, an estimated 70 per cent since 2009, according to a September report from Lawrence Berkeley National Laboratory.

III. Panels will likely continue to improve. In March, researchers from MIT and Stanford said they developed a new kind of "tandem" solar cell that could boost efficiency and lower cost.

IV. They connected two different layers of photovoltaic material: one with silicon–the basis for most of today's panels–and the other with perovskite, which can absorb higher-energy particles of light. This differential layer concept with 2 unique and cheaply available elements covers the efficiency and low cost part.

V. This plunge occurs as researchers find new ways to make solar not only smaller, see-through, or sticky so it can be used almost anywhere–whether roads, golf courses, or landfills–but also more efficient.

Q21. I. The fine coat of hairs on the ants traps enough air that those on the bottom layer of the raft avoid being completely submerged.

II. The ants move their queen and larvae to the center of the raft, where they stay high and dry on top of the mass of bodies.

III. Worker ants link legs and mouths together, weaving a raft in a process that can take less than two minutes.

IV. Fire ants can survive in a raft up to several weeks, though they must eventually reach dry land if they are to restart their colony.

V. When waters start to food a fire ant colony, they take evasive action.

Q22. I. The once-heralded blood-testing company Theranos received a letter from the Centers for Medicare & Medicaid Services (CMS) this week outlining key areas in which its laboratory fails to meet federal guidelines.

II. The notice comes on the heels of a remarkable downfall for Theranos, whose CEO went from posing for laudatory magazine cover stories to defending her business against a slew of accusations after a series of *Wall Street Journal* investigative reports alleging its pin-prick blood-sampling method is not as effective as promised. "This survey of our Newark, CA lab began months ago and does not reflect the current state of the lab," Theranos said in a statement.

III. The notice, which is dated Monday, requires the company to bring itself into compliance within 10 calendar days of its receipt.

IV. According to the CMS, practices at Theranos' laboratory "pose immediate jeopardy to patient health and safety"–boilerplate language the agency uses when companies are found non-compliant.

V. "As the survey took place we were simultaneously conducting a comprehensive review of our laboratory's systems, processes and procedures to ensure that we have best-in-class quality systems."

Q23. I. First and foremost, as the title page states, the book is "not a medical manual".

II. One of the most revealing elements in Amazon's release, however, is a declarative statement Kristin made in the introduction.

III. Second, it has a lot of pictures.

IV. "For the first time in my life, I know who I am," she writes. "I'm pretty simple."

V. Since Amazon.com released over 50 pages of Kristin Cavallari's forthcoming book *Balancing in Heels* earlier this week, a few things have become clear.

Q24. I. If you don't remember logarithms from school, each number on a logarithmic scale represents a factor of ten, so a magnitude 8 earthquake shows up on a quake-measuring seismometer as ten times larger than a magnitude 7.

II. That's because the earthquake scale-called the Moment Magnitude Scale, which replaced the Richter Scale is logarithmic, rather than arithmetic.

III. Actually, a quake of magnitude 8 releases a million times more energy than a magnitude 4 quake.

IV. When we hear that a magnitude 8 earthquake has struck, we know that's worse than a magnitude 4 earthquake.

V. It sounds like it should be twice as strong, but it's not.

Q25. I. The characters were not dropouts or rebels, but neither were they high-fylers or industry trailblazers.

II. They were just normal. To go to work, the boys just buttoned up the oversized Gap shirts they wore loose over a T-shirt to Central Park, and swapped the jeans for chinos.

III. It was the perfect style formula for an era that championed what the costume designer of Oscar-contender, about-to-be-released *Spotlight*, set in a newspaper office in 2001, calls "unthought about" clothes. Not thinking about clothes was big, in those days.

IV. "Layering" did not mean poring over the Gucci catwalk photos for inspiration for ingenious new color combinations; it just meant wearing a cardigan.

V. We loved *Friends* for making adult life look un-intimidating.

Q26. I. "I ended up shopping vintage or buying oversized dresses two sizes up from Acne, which was a good alternative but I couldn't wear those pieces afterwards." She added.

II. One of the most influential ranges in the subtle maternity movement is Hatch, a U.S. brand that has recently launched in the U.K. through Net-a-Porter.

III. Its founder and CEO Ariane Goldman says she was "shocked by what was out there" while pregnant five years ago.

IV. "I felt ostracized from fashion and from any opportunity to look and feel good" she said.

V. Her solution was to create a brand specialising in voluminous shapes that could be worn during and after pregnancy. This is how Hatch was founded.

Q27. I. Widely recognised as the dean of American climbing literature, Roberts has penned 26 books, including classics like *The Mountain of My Fear* and a memoir entitled *On the Ridge Between Life and Death.*

II. But a lot of people don't realize that, like Honnold, Roberts himself was a pioneering climber.

III. His latest work, *Alone on the Wall,* which he co-wrote with legendary free soloist Alex Honnold, recently spent time on the New York Times Best Sellers List.

IV. If you've ever read a book about mountaineering, there's a good chance it was written by David Roberts.

V. During the 1960s and 1970s he undertook more than a dozen expeditions to remote corners of Alaska, where he made numerous first ascents, including the Wickersham Wall on Denali, the West Rib of Mount Huntington, Kichatna Spire, the East Face of Mount Dickey, and numerous peaks in the Revelation Range.

Q28. I. In 1965, my senior year at Harvard, we made the first ascent of the Harvard Route on Mount Huntington, and one of our team members Ed Bernd was killed on the descent.

II. I wrote the whole book in only nine days–a chapter a day–during summer break in 1968.

III. I was so obsessed with this tragic triumph that I finally sat down and wrote *The Mountain of My Fear*

IV. Yes, this is how I became a writer.

V. That crazy, obsessive, cathartic act of cranking out a book about the most traumatic and disturbing experience of my then young life was key to becoming a writer.

Q29. I. Found only on the islands of Montserrat and Dominica in the east Caribbean Sea, the *Leptodactylus fallax* frog also known as the mountain chicken was once a local delicacy.

II. It is one of the largest frogs in the world and appears on the official seal of Dominica.

III. And what does it taste like? You guessed it: chicken.

IV. But years of overhunting and habitat loss, as well as volcanic eruptions in Montserrat, diminished the mountain chicken population, and the species has been declared extinct in Guadeloup, Antigua, and other islands where it used to live.

V. In 2002, the chytrid fungus (*Batrachochytrium dendrobatidis*) devastated the population in Dominica and in 2009 in Montserrat, researches estimate, it wiped out more than 80 per cent of that island's population.

Q30. I. There was no official policy on this, but government propaganda condemned contraceptives and even banned the import of some.

II. Shortly after the establishment of the People's Republic of China in 1949, Mao Zedong encouraged the population to multiply and create manpower.

III. As a result, the population of China doubled over the next few years.

IV. The nearly 40-year-old restriction on having multiple children isn't the only time the Chinese government stepped into family planning.

V. The success was short lived though. China's food supply was strained and the government had to reverse the campaign against contraceptives.

EXERCISE 3

Rearrange the following sentences in a logical order to form a coherent paragraph.

Q31. I. I'm no different.

II. When I was diagnosed with breast cancer, some years ago, I had surgery several times, and also chemotherapy and radiotherapy.

III. Today now that I have recovered fully, I thank them all to have been there for me and have saved my life. If it were not because of them I would have not been writing this.

IV. The sheer number of individual professionals I encountered was huge–maybe 100, over the years.

V. When you have undergone intensive NHS treatment, it's routine to feel grateful to the NHS staff who saved your life.

Q32. I. To avoid this fate, they grow high up on the central plateau where it is too wet for the flames to take hold.

II. Last week a huge and uncharacteristically dry electrical storm flashed its way across the state, igniting the land.

III. But a desiccating spring and summer has turned even the wettest rainforest dells and high-altitude bogs into tinder.

IV. If burned, they die.
V. Unlike Australia's eucalyptus forests, which use fire to regenerate, Nothofagus trees have not evolved to live within the natural cycle of conflagration and renewal.

Q33. I. By taking a closer look at Camus' life and thought, we may discover that there really is no contradiction here the literary establishment has a constant tendency to lump thinkers together into easily digestible categories.
II. *The Fall* is a work absolutely drenched in Christian, particularly Catholic, symbolism.
III. Yet the novel was written by Albert Camus, a man generally considered a leading light of the atheistic French existentialist movement of the mid-twentieth century.
IV. I believe that Camus was, at least partially, a victim of this lust for simplicity.
V. The title is an obvious reference to the Biblical story of Adam and Eve; the novel's setting of Amsterdam is a stand-in for Dante's Nine Circles of Hell; and the work is structured as an extended confession of the narrator's sins, with the reader playing the role of the priest.

Q34. I. There are many good reasons why women have left little in the way of literary monuments, especially poetry.
II. The main reason is education, or more specifically, the lack of it in most women's lives until well into the twentieth century.
III. This meant she generally produced poetry that was at best imperfect, at worst, frankly bad
IV. In the light of this, what is surprising is not that so few women wrote poetry, but that any women wrote poetry at all.
V. When a woman who had never been to grammar school, never learnt Latin and did not know the rules of syntax, let alone of prosody, set herself to writing lines that rhymed, she was imitating an art that, admire it though she might, she did not understand a male art, a male tradition.

Q35. I. Following a serious health scare, the opportunity to get involved with the family business was something that I didn't want to pass up.
II. Having worked in administration for over 10 years, the decision to pursue a career in farming may perhaps not have seemed the obvious choice for a 28-year-old woman.
III. Left a job that I loved and my life in the city and moved 100 miles away to run a 300-acre mixed arable and livestock farm in a rural area.
IV. But four years ago that is exactly what I did.

Q36. I. Psychologists David Comer Kidd and EmanueleCastano, at the New School for Social Research in New York, have proved that reading literary fiction enhances the ability to detect and understand other people's emotions, a crucial skill in navigating complex social relationships.
II. Have you ever felt that reading a good book makes you better able to connect with your fellow human beings?
III. In a series of five experiments, 1,000 participants were randomly assigned texts to read, either extracts of popular fiction such as bestseller Danielle Steel's *The Sins of the Mother* and *Gone Girl* by Gillian Flynn, or more literary texts, such as Orange-winner *The Tiger's Wife* by TéaObreht, Don DeLillo's *The Runner*, or work by Anton Chekhov.
IV. If so, the results of a new scientific study back you up, but only if your reading material is literary fiction–pulp fiction or non-fiction will not do.
V. Scores were consistently higher for those who had read literary fiction than for those with popular fiction or non-fiction texts.
VI. The pair then used a variety of Theory of Mind techniques to measure how accurately the participants could identify emotions in others.

Q37. I. His view is grounded in the belief that the facts about social life are accessible to anybody interested in them.
II. To whom or to what, if to anything at all, should intellectuals be responsible?
III. The longstanding view of Noam Chomsky is that intellectuals are obliged to tell the truth and to expose the lies of those in positions of authority.
IV. Here "intellectuals" is used broadly to refer to anyone interested in ideas and abstract thought, in cerebration, in theorising.
V. They can be found in documents and case studies, in the alternative press, in policy journals, in the reports of human-rights organisations, the testimony of witnesses to power abroad.

Q38. I. While the World Health Organisation suggests one doctor per 1,000 people, India's ratio is as low as 1:1,428 and then 74 per cent of these doctors serve in urban areas.
II. One of the priority areas for strengthening healthcare in India is dealing with the low doctor to population ratio.
III. These include permitting the establishment of private medical colleges and encouraging

institutions which give training in Ayurveda, Yoga and Naturopathy, Unani, Siddha and Homoeopathy (AYUSH).

IV. The government has tried many measures to increase the number of doctors in the population.

Q39. I. The trip was led by two young women and I thought, "If they can do it, maybe I can", so I applied for a job with the company as soon as I got back.

II. It was a rewarding job and I had great colleagues, but I was always restless.

III. I cried when it finished–the idea had been to cure me of my wanderlust, but it backfired!

IV. The idea that I could do something else came after I took a four-week overland trip to Africa with overland adventure specialist Dragoman. It was the longest time I could get off work and it was amazing.

V. I was a cardiac physiologist working at St Thomas's Hospital in London and had spent seven years working, studying and watching the NHS struggle.

Q40. I. Our children, George, then seven, and Lucy, then four, went to a local school, where we discovered to our consternation that Spanish was not the first language.

II. In 2004, I was a financial controller in manufacturing and Sally, my wife, was customer services manager with a building society.

III. We had not realised until then that Valenciana, a dialect of Catalan, was what was generally spoken

IV. Without any clear plan, we sold our house and moved to Spain, eventually buying a house in a remote mountain community: the Vall de Gallinera, about 40km from Benidorm.

V. Maybe it was a mid-life crisis, but we just could not face the prospect of another 25 years doing the same.

Q41. I. An attempt to trademark the word "react" has ended badly for the YouTube network Fine Brothers Entertainment, with former fans unsubscribing from the group's main channel en masse in protest.

II. In 2010, they launched the series Kids React, which involved the pair showing children videos–initially other popular viral videos–and filming their reactions.

III. The network, which was launched by brothers Benny and Rafi Fine in 2007, is one of the most popular on YouTube, with 14 million subscribers.

IV. In 2014, the quantity of videos had reached a critical mass, which led Fine Bros to spin them off into their own YouTube channel called React.

V. After becoming a hit, the series led to a huge number of spin-offs, including Teens React, Elders React, YouTubers React (featuring other famous YouTubers, some of whom were filmed watching their own videos) and Adults React.

Q42. I. Yet, on a plan that has been placed high on this government's priorities–the Ganga Action Plan or the NamamiGange (Obeisance to the Ganga) as it is now called–the two ministers have had a public spat centred on the trade-off between environment and development.

II. The stand-off between the Union Environment Minister Prakash Javadekar and Water Resources Minister Uma Bharti over the future of six hydroelectric dams on the tributaries of the Ganga River exempli-fes the muddled thinking in this government.

III. And the Ministry of Water Resources is tasked with protecting, conserving and maximising the benefits from the country's water resources.

IV. We know that the environment ministry is supposed to safeguard the environment, or at least ensure that infrastructure and other developmental projects do not lead to irreplaceable environmental damage.

Q43. I. Why is that? Because they have no option but to work outdoor irrespective of the weather conditions. They have no option but to sleep without shelter.

II. Every year winter brings with, especially in the northern states of the country, severe cold and dense fog which spread respiratory diseases, mess up transport and kill numerous people who have inadequate protection against the cold.

III. But who are they? These are those who have escaped from rural destitution and oppression, and provide all forms of labor to the urban economy without having any protection for their body or dignity.

IV. Needless to say, it is the urban homeless and those who are forced to be outdoors for their daily livelihood who are affected the most by it.

Q44. I. U.S. Republican frontrunner Donald Trump is so confident in his support base that he said he could stand on New York's Fifth Avenue "and shoot somebody" and still not lose voters.

II. Also the Register picked Hillary Clinton for the Democrats, nine days from the first nominating contest in Iowa.

III. His typically inflammatory comments came as his Republican rival Marco Rubio won the endorsement this Saturday from Iowa's biggest and most influential newspaper Register.

IV. Speaking in Iowa, Trump claimed he could withstand any attempt by his political rivals to knock him off his top perch.

Q45. I. The Indian government launched a judicial probe into Rohith's death and the prime minister, Narendra Modi, said: "Mother India has lost a son."

II. Copies of his final letter are stuck to every wall at the University of Hyderabad, where the 28-year-old dalit, or untouchable, PhD scholar hanged himself from the ceiling fan of a friend's hostel bedroom, some time during the night of Saturday before last.

III. Rohith Chakravarti Vemula never lost his poetic fair, even when writing his suicide note.

IV. "Never was a man treated as a mind, a glorious thing made up of stardust," he wrote. "Uma Anna, sorry for using your room for this thing".

Answer Key

Para-Jumbles

Exercise 1

1. Correct sequence is IV I III II V
2. Correct sequence is III IV I II V
3. Correct sequence is V III IV I II
4. Correct sequence is II IV I III V
5. Correct sequence is III I IV II V
6. Correct sequence is III I IV II V
7. Correct sequence is II I III V IV
8. Correct sequence is IV I II III V
9. Correct sequence is II IV I III
10. Correct sequence is III I II IV V
11. Correct sequence is II I V IV III
12. Correct sequence is IV I III II V
13. Correct sequence is III V I II IV
14. Correct sequence is IV V I III II
15. Correct sequence is III V I IV II
16. Correct sequence is II IV I III V
17. Correct sequence is III I II IV V
18. Correct sequence is II III I V IV
19. Correct sequence is III V I II IV
20. Correct sequence is III I II IV V
21. Correct sequence is I III II IV V
22. Correct sequence is IV I II III V
23. Correct sequence is V I III II IV
24. Correct sequence is II I III V IV
25. Correct sequence is III I II IV V

Paragraphs Jumbles Without Options (According To New CAT Pattern)

Exercise 1

1. Correct sequence is I IV III V II
2. Correct sequence is IV V III I II
3. Correct sequence is II IV III I V
4. Correct sequence is III V IV II I
5. Correct sequence is I IV V III II
6. Correct sequence is IV I II III V
7. Correct sequence is V I IV III II
8. Correct sequence is I IV II III V
9. Correct sequence is IV III V II I
10. Correct sequence is V I II IV III
11. Correct sequence is I V II III IV
12. Correct sequence is V I II IV III
13. Correct sequence is I III II V IV
14. Correct sequence is III I V II IV
15. Correct sequence is V IV III II I

Exercise 2

16. Correct sequence is II III I V IV
17. Correct sequence is V I II IV III
18. Correct sequence is I III IV V II
19. Correct sequence is II I III IV V
20. Correct sequence is II V I III IV
21. Correct sequence is V III II I IV
22. Correct sequence is I III IV II V
23. Correct sequence is V I III II IV
24. Correct sequence is IV V III II I
25. Correct sequence is V I II IV III
26. Correct sequence is II III IV I V
27. Correct sequence is IV I III II V
28. Correct sequence is I III II V IV
29. Correct sequence is I II III IV V
30. Correct sequence is IV II I III V

Exercise 3

31. Correct sequence is V I II IV III
32. Correct sequence is V IV I III II
33. Correct sequence is II V III I IV
34. Correct sequence is I II IV V III
35. Correct sequence is II IV I III
36. Correct sequence is II IV I III VI V
37. Correct sequence is II IV III I V
38. Correct sequence is II I IV III
39. Correct sequence is V II IV III I
40. Correct sequence is II V IV I III
41. Correct sequence is I III II V IV
42. Correct sequence is II IV III I
43. Correct sequence is II IV I III
44. Correct sequence is I IV III II
45. Correct sequence is III IV II I

Explanations

Para-Jumbles

Exercise 1

1. (IV) introduces the topic of the passage - relation between human and horses. (I) then defines the relation. (III) should follow (I) as the "leap" has been defined in (I). So, (IV) (I) (III) is the correct sequence. (II) then continues defining the relation making (IV) (I) (III) (II) the right sequence. (V) introduces a new topic. So, it should be the last sentence. So, (IV) (I) (III) (II) (V) is the correct sequence.
2. (III) introduces the topic of the passage, i.e., why the workers' salary is not rising. (IV) (I) form a mandatory pair as "the bank" refers to Bank of England. (IV) (I) follows (III) as it mentions why the salaries are not rising. So, (III) (IV) (I) is the right sequence. (II) further builds on the theory. (V) comes after (III) (IV) (I) (II) as "similar explainers" are stated in (IV) (I) (II). So, (III) (IV) (I) (II) (V) is the right sequence.
3. (V) introduces the topic of the passage, i.e., 'the dilemma'. (III) gives first part of the dilemma and (IV) defines that part. So, (V) (III) (IV) is the right sequence. (I) then provided the second part of the dilemma. (II) provides a conclusion to the dilemma. So, (V) (III) (IV) (I) (II) is the right sequence.
4. (II) starts the passage with the introduction of an event taking place on a specific date. (IV) (I) form a mandatory pair going by the rule of full name to the crowd mentioned in (II) and he greeting his audience in statement (I). So, (II) (IV) (I) is the right sequence. (III) then talks about how he had been living outside Russia and was a theorist and then statement (V) comments further on him being a "theorist" as mentioned in (III). So, (II) (IV) (I) (III) (V) is the right sequence.
5. (III) introduces the topic of the passage, i.e., "bad economic news" and (I) provides an example of it. (IV) provides a contradiction to (III) (I). So, (III) (I) (IV) is the right sequence. (II) (V) form a mandatory pair in that sequence as "new price caps" refer to the heating bill prices. (II) (V) should follow (IV) as they give an example of (IV). So, (III) (I) (IV) (II) (V) is the right sequence.
6. (III) (I) form a mandatory pair as (III) gives reason for (I). (IV) then brings us to the present and gives a contradiction to (I). So, (III) (I) (IV) is the right sequence. (II) (V) build on (IV). (V) gives a conclusion to the "population policy" of China. So, (III) (I) (IV) (II) (V) is the right sequence.
7. (II) introduces the topic of the passage, i.e., issue of raw sewage in sea. (I) shows what is being done about it. (III) provides a contradiction to (I). So, (II) (I) (III) is the right sequence. (V) then further elaborates on (III). So, (II) (I) (III) (V) is the correct sequence. (IV) gives a conclusion to (III) (V). So, (II) (I) (III) (V) (IV) is the correct sequence.
8. (IV) (I) form a mandatory pair as "the optimism" is mentioned in (IV). (II) (III) for a mandatory pair as they talk about the French election. (III) gives reason for why is it a "fractious sideshow" mentioned in (II). (V) should be the last sentence as it introduces a new topic. Now, (II) (III) give specific information. Going by the rule of generic to specific, (II) (III) should follow (IV) (I). So, (IV) (I) (II) (III) (V) is the correct sequence.
9. (II) (IV) form a mandatory pair by contradicting each other. (I) (III) form a mandatory pair as "that" mentioned in (III) refers to what is mentioned in (I). Now, going by the rule of generic to specific, (I) (III) should come after (II) (IV). So, (II) (IV) (I) (III) is the correct sequence.
10. (III) begins the paragraph with a general statement. (I) then brings why the week began with "low expectations." So, (III) (I) is the right sequence. (II) (IV) form a mandatory pair talking about Russia's attack on Ukraine and explaining the Ukraine crisis mentioned in (I). So, (III) (I) (II) (IV) is the right sequence. (V) then shows why it ended on a "bleaker" mood. So, (III) (I) (II) (IV) (V) is the right sequence.
11. (II) should start the paragraph as it contains the full form of CPSE which is then discussed in the whole

passage. (I) takes the point made in (II) forward. (I) (V) form a mandatory pair as they combine to form "strategic" and "non-strategic" CPSEs and also the usage of "He." So, (II) (I) (V) is the correct sequence. (IV) should follow (I) (V) as they define the "divestment strategy." (III) completes (IV). So, (II) (I) (V) (IV) (III) is the correct sequence.

12. (IV) (I) form a mandatory part as (I) defines how the coup took place. (III) should follow (IV) (I) as "developments" are defined in (IV) (I) making (IV) (I) (III) the right sequence. (II) (V) form a mandatory pair as (V) defines the support. As India showed the required support, (II) (V) should follow (III) as (II) (V) carry the idea stated in (III) forward.

    So, (IV) (I) (III) (II) (V) is the right sequence.

13. (III) introduces that author does not like much colour in picture. (V) gives the reason why.(I) gives the example of the idea started in (III) (V). (II) and (IV) carry forward the change explained in the artist's work in statement (I). (IV) follows (II) as "a line...it" in (IV) refers to spare space of black and white in (II). So, (III) (V) (I) (II) (IV) form the right sequence.

14. (IV) introduces the topic of the paragraph, i.e., global crisis. (V) (I) (III) then describe the crisis in that order. (V) states the timeline of the crisis and (I) then shows its coverage. "They" in (III) refer to children mentioned in (I). So, (IV) (I) (V) (III) is the right sequence.

    (II) then gives the response to crisis and should follow (V) (I) (III). So, (IV) (V) (I) (III) (II) is the right sequence.

15. (III) introduces the topic i.e. the democratic situation in Myanmar. (V) (I) then define the crisis and (IV) (II) show how the country also faced it in the past. (V) mentions the win of NLD and then (I) defines the actions taken by the opposition. So, (I) follows (V). So, (V) (I) should follow (III) carrying the idea forward. So, (III) (V) (I) is the right sequence. (II) follows (IV) as it completes (IV) and defines the events in a chronological sequence. (IV) (II) should follow (III) (V) (I) following the rule of moving from present to past.

    So, (III) (V) (I) (IV) (II) is the right sequence.

16. (II) introduces the topic, i.e., "writings on loneliness." (IV) should follow (II) as "approaches" are defined in (II). (I) (III) then define what the approaches are. So, (II) (IV) (I) (III) is the right sequence and (V) takes the idea stated in (III) forward. So, (II) (IV) (I) (III) (V) is the right sequence.

17. (III) introduces the topic of the passage, i.e., "plant blindness." (I) (II) then elaborate on it making (III) (I) (II) the right sequence. (IV) (V) form a mandatory pair talking about timescale of plants vs. humans. (IV) (V) should follow (III) (I) (II). So, (III) (I) (II) (IV) (V) is the correct sequence.

18. (II) introduces the topic, i.e., what happened with Prince Andrew. (III) then explains it, making (II) (III) the right sequence. (I) tells about "a New York judge" mentioned in (III). So, (II) (III) (I) is the right sequence. (V) then follows the chronology from Wednesday to Thursday and (IV) gives an ending comment. So, (II) (III) (I) (V) (IV) is the correct sequence.

19. (III) starts the passage with a general statement. (V) should follow (III) as "this" refers to the checks and balances. (I) (II) form a mandatory pair talking about the powers given to police and should follow (III) (V). (IV) then brings the public perspective which is a new topic. Hence, (V) should be the last sentence. So, (III) (V) (I) (II) (IV) is the right answer.

20. (III) introduces the topic of the passage, i.e., "happy news for LGBTQ." (I) (II) form a mandatory pair in that sequence and provide the "good news." So, (III) (I) (II) form the correct sequence. (IV) (V) form a mandatory pair as "He" refers to the bishop of Liverpool. (IV) (V) should follow (III) (I) (II). So, (III) (I) (II) (IV) (V) is the correct sequence.

21. (I) (III) form a mandatory pair as (III) explains the "appeal" mentioned in (I). (II) (IV) form a mandatory pair explaining the plight of people in Afghanistan. (II) (IV) should follow (I) (III) as they explain why the appeal was made. (V) then gives a concluding comment. So, (I) (III) (II) (IV) (V) is the right sequence.

22. (IV) introduces the topic of the passage, i.e., issues with housing industry. (II) (III) form a mandatory pair talking about the actions of the government. (II) (III) also give the reason for (I). So, (I) (II) (III) is the right sequence. (V) gives a conclusion making it the last sentence. So, (IV) (I) (II) (III) (V) is the correct sequence.

23. (V) begins the passage with a general statement. (I) elaborates on (V) as to why it can happen. (III) (II) (IV) form a sequence as (II) (IV) explain the "hype" of Mr. Draghi. Now, (III) (II) (IV) should follow (V) (I). So, (V) (I) (III) (II) (IV) is the right sequence.

24. (II) introduces the topic of the passage, i.e., effect of streaming services. (I) then gives an example of it. (I) (III) form a mandatory pair as (III) explains why Adam did that. So, (II) (I) (III) is the right sequence. (V) builds on the same. (IV) should be the last sentence as it introduces the new topic of audio platforms. So, (II) (I) (III) (V) (IV) is the right sequence.

25. (III) introduces the topic of the passage with a general statement. (I) then gives specific information about it. So, (III) (I) is the right sequence. (II) (IV) form a mandatory pair and should follow as they

provide another example of (III). So, (III) (I) (II) (IV) is the right sequence. (V) acts as the concluding comment making (III) (I) (II) (IV) (V) the correct answer.

Paragraphs Jumbles Without Options (According To New Cat Pattern)

Exercise 1

1. (IV) (III) (V) form a mandatory pair.

   (I) introduces the central idea of author which is an attempt to understand what motivates change in behavior. Also this introduces an example of a website and app that is built to help people exercise more.

   (IV) Paragraph moves on to explaining the raised idea from psychology perspective. Two types of motivations are introduced and defined here: extrinsic and intrinsic.

   (III) Extrinsic motivation is further elaborated with reference to the website and app which is built to help people exercise more. It introduces the idea of rewarding the users for more exercise. Example of Pact app is given.

   (V) Presents the results of research on this idea of rewarding, that it positively motivates people who don't enjoy exercising and on contrary negatively motivates people who already enjoy it.

   (II) Further explains how this is a negative motivation. Te users who already enjoy exercising increase their exercise on a short term basis and as soon as the rewards are taken away they do not enjoy this behavior as much as before now. So they were better off without getting motivated by this extrinsic action.

2. (IV) (V) (III) form a mandatory sequence.

   (IV) best starts the paragraph. It mentions the miscellaneous collection of models/forms made from plasticine (a soft modeling material).

   (V) explains how these models look like. One model is like a footprint of chicken, and many other forms. Further it states that any attempt of comparison would be hopelessly inaccurate.

   (III) because these are determined efforts of a great scientist to explore one of the many sided explanations of "being" viz. consciousness.

   (I) introduces that while Crick revealed these secrets of DNA through modeling using plasticine as mentioned above, the similar attempt to reveal secrets of neuroanatomy of "self " is less successful.

   (II) closes the paragraph well with a conclusion that how much ever unsuccessful this modeling technique has been in this area but it is influential nevertheless.

3. (II) (IV) form a mandatory sequence.

   (I) (V) form a mandatory sequence.

   (II) best introduces the paragraph. Author confesses that when in high school he took a college aptitude exam, named ACT. ACT as an exam is best introduced in this statement.

   (IV) continues that the author scored bad (his position was in the lowest third of all students).

   (III) expresses that the author felt it was painful enough for him to feel sad about it, yet worse was when ACT score report informed him of his probability of getting into 2 universities in U.S.

   (I) expresses hopelessness in the mind of the author.

   (V) expresses hopelessness because of the reasons mentioned in this statement. This statement closes the paragraph with a mention of the author's emphasis on his silly fantasy of becoming a scientist or neurologist which needs a high aptitude. Silly because the score report has a different story to tell about his aptitude.

4. (II) (I) form a mandatory pair.

   (III) starts the paragraph. It introduces Obama as a U.S. President and that he banned the practice which would hold juveniles in solitary confinement.

   (V) mentions "the move"–some move which is already defined or discussed about earlier, in this case the move is banning the practice as mentioned earlier.

   (IV) explains the move of Obama in detail, what it is and how it would affect convicted juveniles.

   (II) and (I) further Obama's justifies move on the basis of research results. The statement also talks about effects of solitary confinement

5. (III) (II) form a mandatory pair. (I) (IV) form a mandatory pair

   (I) introduces the paragraph perfectly. It mentions that years from now all basketball enthusiasts who will remember the unexpected winning streak of the team (not explicitly mentioned here but later can be concluded is Valencia team) will also talk about Upset match in Madrid. Upset is a match in which a low ranked team beats a higher (better) ranked team.

   (IV) continues this further; they talk about the late comeback in Germany or the overtime game. And then they talk about the "beard". Here beard becomes the next idea of passage.

(V) elaborates why the beard will be talked about; introduces a player whose beard has become a rage in conversations now and will be remembered, it's that of forward player John Shurna. Ten the details on his beard are mentioned in the statement.

(III) paragraph goes on to the comment of Luke Sikma on John's beard. Luke is an American player on the team.

(II) continues the comment of Sikma.

6. (I) (II) form a mandatory pair.

(IV) A major sports betting website (not named for now) was suspended. This fits in as the starting statement of the paragraph.

(I) Details of the above made statement are stated here. Names of the team players and the website is finally named–Pinnacle sports.

Also head of a section at this website is referred to by his comments; he is Marco Blume.

(II) continues the dialogue of Blume. Blume is referred to by his second name so he must have been introduced/mentioned some place earlier in the paragraph.

(III) continues the paragraph with emphasis on the strange stats of the game here, for example, that the game lasted for only 20 minutes. To complete the paragraph we can expect the losing team be asked for explanation next.

(V) Losing team interrogated and explanation is given by the team players on what led to their losing in the game with such bad scores.

7. (V) (I) form a mandatory pair

(V) introduces the subject of environmentalism and that Pope Francis issued a 192-page encyclical on it. Encyclical is a circular letter sent to all churches.

(I) talks of how Islamic scholars have added their support to environmentalism.

(IV) further elucidates the details of Muslims meeting on this issue and that they made an appeal.

(III) continues this because "it" mentioned in the made "statement" is the appeal mentioned above.

(II) talks of "the statement" i.e. this statement is mentioned some where above. We see that statement was made in (III) which is referred to here.

8. (I) (IV) form a mandatory pair.

(III) (V) form a mandatory pair.

(I) introduces the idea of turbulence and that we have "absolutely" no idea how it works.

(IV) "It has even perplexed....". "It" here refers to "turbulence" and suggests that the concept of turbulence has even perplexed scientists, this is supported by Einstein's statement about it.

(II) "Te problem...".–now that we have stated and described what the issue is, this statement takes it further. It states that this whole problem of no one/no field knowing about how turbulence works is aggravated by the fact that whenever the need to understand turbulence arises, we see other chemical reactions taking place at those extreme conditions that it gets difficult to study it.

(III) "If somehow we could figure it out....." paragraph now puts forward the need to study turbulence.

(V)–one of such areas where we could use this understanding of turbulence is mentioned viz. that we can predict hurricanes in future.

9. (V) (II) (I) form a mandatory pair.

(IV) best introduces the essence of the paragraph. It is that we know birds migrate long distances but how they do it, we don't know.

(III) further elaborates on how mysterious the behavior of migration of birds is.

(V) "Consider this..." suggests that an idea is stated before and a case/example is going to be taken up next. Example of Cuckoos is being studied.

(II) continues the example of Cuckoos.

(I) "Clearly.." suggests that this statement is a conclusion. It wraps up the idea with a comment that one shouldn't mess with cuckoos, for reasons explained in (V) and (II).

10. (IV) (III) is a mandatory pair.

(V) introduces the concept of good and evil.

(I) concept of good and evil is explained here. It also introduces the concept of "compact".

(II) "such a compact.." suggests that concept of "compact" is mentioned before, this simply continues the concept of compact.

(IV) introduces a new idea of just and unjust like good and evil; and that people will do evil if not obliged. It also takes instance of "Gyges" from some well know story.

(III) follows (IV) because (III) states "And he who abstains...."–abstain from what? This is mentioned in (IV), that he, who abstains from doing evil when he can, will be regarded as a fool by the world.

11. (V) (II) form mandatory pair.

(III) (IV) form mandatory pair.

(I) starts the paragraph stating that the world is facing an alarming disease yet again. It is spread by mosquito-borne Zika virus.

(V) "this virus..." hints at Zika virus mentioned in (I). It also states that few years ago this virus was not in the West.

(II) follows (V). Hint: "But today....”- this follows (V).

(III) introduces a general statement about mosquitoes, not just Zika virus carriers but all. Here Zika virus is stated explicitly, and we have introduced Zika virus before in this paragraph.

(IV) "they" in the statement refers to mosquitoes. This continues the idea that these mosquitoes spread more diseases than any other animal.

12. (II) (IV) (III) form a mandatory sequence.

(V) best starts the paragraph. It introduces the concept of antibiotic resistance.

(I) continues the idea and views of world health leaders on this topic.

(II) presents the statistics of the situation. What number of people got infected and died of these infections.

(IV) "Many more" suggests more number add to the death poll.

(III) "In addition..." suggests an addition of another statistical report, of may be another infection, to this already stated statistics of deaths and infections.

13. (V) (IV) form a mandatory pair.

(I) introduces the case of untimely death of Ms Sandra Bland, which has led to many unanswered questions. What questions? We expect consequent statements to talk about this.

(III) Ms Bland is addressed by her second name, so she has been introduced before this statement. Clearly suggests that the most important of these unanswered questions seems to be: How did she die? It goes on to present 2 theories: One as stated by prison authorities that she hanged herself, other that she was in fact murdered by corrupt officers.

(II) again Ms Bland is addressed by her second name so she has to be introduced before this statement. Also this statement continues the previous one and suggests the real possibility of her death, i.e. she died due to untreated mental illness.

(V) states that whatever happened in this case, suicide rate is on increase in the U.S. (IV) continues this claim.

14. (III) (I) (V) form a mandatory sequence.

(II) (IV) form a mandatory pair.

(III) Follow chronology, "In 1945, LIFE Magazine...." Introduces LIFE magazine and that it declared Hawai as a successful experiment.

(I) "The islands..." Which islands? Hawai, as has already been stated in statement above. Also another hint is Aug 21, 1959, following choronology this would come after 1945. This statement also states that there were many different ethnic groups in Hawai–the idea which would be elaborated in the next statement.

(V) states that because there were many different ethnic groups (as mentioned in statement above), there were interracial marriages.

(II) Photographer Eliot's portraits are talked about and that they serve as a visual aid to the utopian image of the islands. Utopia means a Perfect World.

(IV) Portraits captured by this photographer are discussed about.

15. (II) (I) form a mandatory pair.

(V) best opens the dialogue about how some think about Science of logic. This is either a version or is derived from Aristotle's theory (as would be revealed later in paragraph).

(IV) presents the view of others; hint is "Others argue......". In the previous statement "some" argued, here "others" argue and continue the dialogue. It suggests that this argument is also understood as a version of Kant's theory.

(III) This explains how this other argument is a version of Kant's theory.

(II) briefs the two arguments/theories.

(I) states what audience interprets the Science of Logic–former as also found in Aristotle's or latter as is a version of Kant's

Exercise 2

16. (V) (IV) form mandatory pair.

(III) (I) form mandatory pair.

(II) introduces the scenario about what the announcement of liquid water on Mars would mean.

(III) mentions what you may think that "first human explorers" on Mars would do.

(I) continues. Hint: "they.." in (I) refers to human explorers mentioned above.

(V) A contradiction is introduced that reality is different from what one is expecting.

(VI) continues the idea of what actual reality is, that how it is different.

17. This is an easy one.

(V) introduces that there are 2 factors.

(I) states the 1st factor

(II) states the 2nd factor. It also talks of some footage".

(IV) talks about "the footage" further, that it was shot using some camera.

(III) concludes by stating that this camera that shot the footage was donated by some man Alan.

18. (III) (IV) a form a mandatory pair.

(V) (II) form a mandatory pair.

(I) introduces the idea–an advancement in technology.

(III) states that this advancement is not a far-fetched future.

(IV) advancement is already happening, today. These are part of new tech era where scientists and Entrepreneurs are trying their ideas.

(V) "Their discoveries could..."- refers to Scientists' and Entrepreneurs' discoveries. Mention of "could" suggests that these were capable of meeting some goals as mentioned,

(VI) yet couldn't because of reasons mentioned in this statement.

19. (IV) (V) form a mandatory pair.

(II) (I) (III) form a mandatory sequence.

(II) statement opens up with announcement of a new mass fuel cell sedan in California by Toyota, which is also the maker of Prius. We are expecting the name of this car to be declared next.

(I) declares the name of this car, described above. It is "The Mirai"- which can go 310 miles in one fill.

(III) "That range..." refers to 310 miles in one full tank as mentioned above. However the car has one issue–that it is expensive–one obstacle.

(IV) mentions the other obstacle which is "lack of stations providing compressed H2 gas".

(V) elaborates on the problem of lack of H2 stations in California.

20. (II) (V) form a mandatory pair.

(III) (IV) form a mandatory pair.

(II) mentions the concept of solar power and its price that has soared.

(V) "This plunge.."–refers to the plummeted/soared price as mentioned above. Later this statement talks about efficiency.

(I) rooftop panels by Panasonic and SolarCity cover the efficiency concern as talked about earlier.

(III) not only this, but panels (solar Panels as talked about in (I)) will continue to improve. How? Instance of researchers from MIT and Stanford given, they developed what they claim boosted the efficiency.

(IV) "They connected..."–refers to Researchers from MIT and Stanford. Elaboration on their energy efficient and low cost solar cell done here.

21. (III) (II) is a mandatory pair.

(V) best introduces the paragraph. It talks of "evasive action".

(III) describes what the "evasive action" is for these ants; that they weave a raft.

(II) then these ants move their queen to this newly weaved raft.

(I) gives additional information about the raft and how these ants manage to stay afloat and avoid being submerged.

(IV) continues the paragraph by talking about the surviving ability of these ants and that eventually they have to reach dry land to try colonizing again.

22. (II) (V) form a mandatory pair.

(I) (III) (IV) form a mandatory sequence.

(I) breaks the headlines that a notice is issued to Theranos by CMS.

(III) talks about what the notice requires Theranos to do.

(IV) extends and talks about the claims of CMS further.

(II) introduces the CEO of Theranos and the circumstances under which the notice was issued. He gives a public statement over this issue.

(V) continues his public statement.

23. (II) (IV) form a mandatory pair.

(I) (III) form a mandatory pair.

(V) introduces the paragraph alluding that a few things will be talked about consequently.

(I) talks about the 1st thing.

(III) talks about the 2nd thing.

(II) states that the most important is not amongst the above 2 but this one–it is a declarative statement by Kristin.

(IV) is that declarative statement.

24. (IV) (V) form a mandatory pair.

(IV) introduces the paragraph; that magnitude of 8 of Earthquake is worse than magnitude 4.

(V) states that it sounds like it's double but it's not. It's actually exponential (as would turn up later in the paragraph).

(III) describes what it actually means–a million times more energy and not double the energy.

(II) reasons stated here, because Moment Magnitude Scale is a logarithmic scale.

(I) talks about logarithms, continuing from the logarithmic scale talked about in the previous statement.

25. (I) (II) form a mandatory pair.

(IV) (III) form a mandatory pair.

(V) introduces the paragraph that *Friends* was loved because it made adult life look not scary and intimidating.

(I) "The characters.."–refers to characters from *Friends* as introduced in the previous statement.

(II) "They were..."–refers to the characters talked about above. It also mentions how simple were their clothing.

(IV) elaborates on the simplicity of their clothing.

(III) continues that simplicity of just buttoning up, wearing a cardigan and leaving for work was the perfect style formula for that era.

26. (II) starts the paragraph by introducing the Hatch–a maternity clothing.

(III) "its founder..." refers to Hatch's founder. Hatch is just introduced in the previous statement. She tells how she felt when she herself was pregnant.

(IV) she says that she felt ostracised and secluded from fashion.

(I) continues that, after how she felt she ended up shopping vintage cloths.

(V) concludes by stating that she found a solution to this problem for everyone and founded a clothing brand specialising in large sized clothes that can be worn in and around pregnancy; this is how she ended up founding this company.

27. (IV) (I) form a mandatory pair.

(II) (V) form a mandatory pair.

(IV) best starts the paragraph. Mentions that a book on mountaineering, any, if ever read by the reader, could be of David Roberts. He must be a famous author we can infer. How is/was he?

(I) introduces David Roberts.

(III) "His latest.."–refers to Roberts here. It mentions the book written by him as author.

(II) gives another introduction of Roberts which is of a mountaineer/climber.

(V) describes his climbing/mountaineering experience.

28. (I) (III) (II) form a mandatory sequence.

On careful scrutiny this paragraph clearly looks like an answer to the question–How did you become a writer?

(I) best starts the paragraph. It mentioned of an accident that killed one team member.

(III) "...obsessed with this tragic..."–here "this" suggests the accident that killed a team member. Ten a book named *The Mountain of my Fear* is mentioned.

(II) "I wrote this whole book....."–here "this" refers to the book *The Mountain of my Fear.*

(V) This all crazy act of making a book out of the traumatic accident was the key to becoming a writer.

(IV) concludes the paragraph.

29. (I) best starts the paragraph by introducing the mountain chicken and that it was once a local delicacy in two islands.

(II) "It is one of the...."–"It" refers to the mountain chicken and that it is the largest frog.

(III) "...does it taste..."–refers to mountain chicken, and that it tastes like chicken, hence the name "mountain chicken".

(IV) introduces another idea, that of its extinction and its reasons.

(V) continues the extinction discussion of mountain chicken.

30. (II) (I) make a mandatory pair.

(III) (V) make a mandatory pair.

(IV) introduces the subject birth control policy of China. It says that that this has been imposed once before. When and how? We expect answers in the consequent statements.

(II) mentions when it was imposed last i.e during the rule of People's Republic of China in 1949.

(I) states that there was no official policy on this imposition but other ways were adopted to promote the policy, like condemning and banning contraceptives.

(III) states the success of this policy imposition.

(V) states that this success did not last for long and the government has to reverse the campaign.

Exercise 3

31. (V) introduces the subject–it's routine to feel grateful to NHS staff when someone has undergone NHS treatment.

(I) "I am no different"–to what? Here the author states that he is no different to the above idea and that he felt the same way. We expect the author to tell present facts to support this claim in the next statement.

(II)–the author presents support for his claim that he is no different.

(IV) continues the support.

(V) finally concludes that she is thankful to all these doctors. This concludes the idea presented in the first statement and closes the paragraph.

32. (V) (IV) form a mandatory pair.

(V) best introduces the theme of the paragraph. It's quite clear from this statement that we are going to discuss Nothofagus trees. Also this statement mentions "fire" which can be borne by Eucalyptus and is instead used by it to regenerate, which is unlike Nothofagus trees. How's that?

(IV) that is, not just they not regenerate but instead die when burnt with fire.

(I) " To avoid this fate...."–here "this fate" is the fate of getting burnt which was stated about these trees. So they have adapted to grow on areas where it is too wet to catch fire.

(I) "But..."–introduces a contradiction to the above claim, i.e. even after growing on such areas (high altitude areas) a very dry, desiccating summer and spring makes the wet lands dry like wood. Desiccating means very dry, arid and tinder means dry and flammable like wood which can be burnt easily.

(II) Instance of last week stated when this high altitude land got burnt due to lightning; this concludes the theme.

33. (II) (V) form a mandatory pair.

(I) (IV) form a mandatory pair.

(II) introduces the name of some work which is based on Christian catholic symbolism. Title of this work is "The Fall". This work may be a painting, novel, other artistic work, it is not clear yet. We expect to get that information next.

(V) "The title.."–here refers to the title "The Fall". Also we now know that it is a novel. This statement also mentions that the novel is structured in such a way that the reader while reading takes the role of a priest.

(III) "Yet.." introduces a contradiction. On careful reading we conclude that the priest role though assigned to the reader, the author himself is an atheist which is ironic. The author Albert Camus is introduced.

(I) ".... look at Camus'..."–here Camus is addressed by his first name so he has been introduced before. So this follows (III). Also an idea of easily digestible categories, simple ideas to be used in works is introduced.

(IV) "..... this lust for simplicity.."–here this lust continues the idea of simplicity mentioned in (I).

34. (I) introduces the subject, that there are many reasons.

(II) introduces the first and foremost reason.

(IV) elaborates the above reason using the hint, "In the light of this...". It states what is surprising in this.

(V) further elaborates this.

(III) "This meant..." this concludes the above stated explanation.

35. (II) (IV) form a mandatory pair.

(II) best introduces the main idea that the author has taken or is taking a decision to pursue farming.

(IV) Author did that 4 years ago.

(I) introduces why she took that decision.

(III) explains that she had a job in city and had to displace to take up her family business.

36. (II) (IV) form a mandatory pair.

(II) best opens the paragraph.

(IV) clearly follows. It mentions that the above statement stands true only if you're reading literary fiction and not otherwise.

(I) mentions that the two psychologists have proved the above claim about literary fiction.

(III) explains the experiment.

(VI) continues the details of this experiment.

(V) states the results/scores of this experiment.

37. (IV) (II) form a mandatory pair. This looks tricky but these two form a mandatory pair because (II) introduces intellectuals in his questions and (IV) immediately defines it for the reader before starting to answer.

(II) best states the subject of the paragraph i.e. to what and whom should intellectuals be held responsible?

(IV) defines "intellectuals" for the reader before moving ahead to answer the question. Please note that this definition had to be stated before author can answer the questions he proposed.

(III) goes on to the answer finally.

(I) "His view....." refers to Noam Chomsky's view.

(V) "they can be found..." refers to facts about social life, as mentioned in the previous statement.

38. (IV) (III) form a mandatory pair.

(II) best introduces the subject–areas for strengthening healthcare in India. One way to do that is mentioned viz. to deal with low doctor to population ratio.

(I) mentions the figures that WHO suggests.

(IV) states that the government has tried many measures to deal with it, to increase the no. of doctors.

(III) "These include..."- refers to the measures the government has taken, as mentioned above.

39. (V) (II) form a mandatory pair.

(III) (I) form a mandatory pair.

(V) introduces the speaker/writer. She mentions about her job.

(II) mentions that this job she is into right now, though it was rewarding she'd feel restless at it always. Why? May be the speaker wasn't happy with what she was doing. May be she wanted something else for her life.

(IV) narrows down the conjecture that speaker indeed wanted to do something else, but she realised it as she got back from a trip to Africa.

(III) continues the above idea. "... but it backfired!". How's that? We can safely expect to get the answer to this next.

(I) states the reason how it backfired seeing two women leading the trip on the speaker thought that she can and she should do it too; maybe she would have never imagined doing something like this on her own. She applied to this job once she got back.

40. (II) (V) form a mandatory pair.

(I) (III) form a mandatory pair.

(II) introduces the speaker and his wife, they were working in their respective professions.

(V) They realised that they cannot continue to do what they were doing (as mentioned above) for the rest of their lives.

(IV) So with a vague plan they moved to some place they wanted.

(I) mentions about children whom they admitted in a local school of that area. Living there they realised that Spanish was not the first language at the school but some other was.

(III) "....until then.."–refers to until they discovered that fact about Spanish language.

41. (I) introduces the subject that an attempt to trademark the word "React" has backfired.

(III) follows chronology. In 2007, this concept was introduced.

(II) In 2010, they launched some series.

(V) After becoming a hit, the series led to a huge spin-off.

(IV) Then in 2014 they finally launched their own channel called "react".

42. (II) introduces that there is a stand-off between two ministries of government–Environment and Water resources with environment mentioned first and water resources later. This is over the future of dams on 6 tributaries of river Ganga.

(IV) "We know that..."–begins the explanation. Also in (II), the Environment ministry is mentioned first, so the stand of this ministry is stated first.

(III) "And the....."–states the job of water resources ministry.

(I) After respective jobs of both the ministries is explicitly stated and we all are aware of it, "yet" there is a lag in implementation.

43. (II) best introduces the issue which is of winters and it repercussions.

(IV) mentions who all get affected by it.

(I) "Why is that?..." continues the idea of why these urban homeless are affected by it.

(III) "But who are they?...." completes the paragraph by defining who they are and where they have come from.

44. (I) best starts the paragraph. It introduces Donald Trump as the U.S. Republican frontrunner and that he made a comment to shoot somebody and still get away with it.

(IV) elaborates his above stated comment.

(III) explains why he made such a comment, which is because his political rival won an endorsement in Iowa's most influential newspaper *The Register.*

(II) It mentions "The" with Register, which grammatically means Register must have got introduced before this statement.

45. (III) introduces the idea well. It starts by introducing Rohith (by mentioning his full name). Further it also presents the fact that Rohith never lost his poetic fair even when he wrote his suicide note. (IV) further the above idea establishes mentioning the poetry written by him in his suicide letter.

(II) further elaborates the details on his suicide letter and the suicide incident.

(I) closes the paragraph by mentioning Prime Minister's reaction to this incident.

CHAPTER 18 Type I and II Exercises on Paragraph Jumbles

TYPE I

The first line [A] of each question is fixed. Arrange the other four lines in a logical sequence.

QUESTION 1

A. As the recession deepens, people across the ideological spectrum declare that capitalism has failed.

B. Yet, recessions are not aberrations of capitalism but an intrinsic part of it.

C. A bust is an occasion for cleaning out deadwood and failed experiments, and re-inventing capitalism.

D. Almost every economic news report carries Countries in recession words like 'crisis' and 'disaster'.

E. Markets create boom and bust cycles, arising from human tendencies to swing from euphoria to fear and back.

(a) ECDB (b) EDCB
(c) DBEC (d) BECD
(e) DCEB

QUESTION 2

A. Two decades ago, economist Jerry Muller chronicled never-ending predictions of the demise of capitalism, by its friends as well as foes.

B. The Great Depression of the 1930s provoked further predictions of capitalism's demise.

C. Lenin harboured similar illusions: his 1916 book was titled *Imperialism: the Last Stage of Capitalism.*

D. In the 1850s, Karl Marx claimed capitalism was dying.

E. Rosa Luxemburg wrote in 'The Accumulation of Private Capital' (1913), "Though imperialism is the historical method prolonging the career of capitalism, it is also a sure means of bringing it to a swift conclusion."

(a) DECB (b) CBDE
(c) CDBE (d) DEBC
(e) DCEB

QUESTION 3

A. Building new towns is the key to raising productivity of the Indian economy as well.

B. Expensive real estate makes education and health care costly as well.

C. This jacks up the cost of quality healthcare and education and these higher costs feed into business costs, affecting India's competitiveness in the global marketplace.

D. Right now, artificial shortage of urban land has put a premium on the cost of real estate.

E. Office rentals, hotel accommodation, land for factories, all these cost the earth and add to the cost of the goods and services emerging from these expensive sites of production.

F. Hospitals and schools in urban areas will find that upwards of 50 per cent of their capital cost is accounted for by real estate.

(a) DECBF (b) BCDEF
(c) DCEFB (d) DEBFC
(e) CBEFD

Question 4

A. In other words, instead of more "reservations", with the resentment that breeds, let us make it easier for minorities to join the police.

B. Unless young people from minorities see that the police service offers real career opportunities and a good quality of life in the workplace; they will not overcome their negative perceptions.

C. In India, the promotion of minority police personnel at senior and middle levels and using them as visible symbols of the police force would constitute a powerful model to the minority community.

D. The fact that, in many Western countries, there are several officers from the visible minorities now at senior officer rank, sends a powerful message to these communities.

E. But let's not stop with recruitment; we also need to focus on the retention and progression of minority officers.

(a) EBCD (b) EBDC
(c) DCEB (d) DBCE
(e) ECDB

Question 5

A. So when fear happens, just become totally aware and don't get identified with that thought.

B. You feel insecure because you have a concept of what is security and from that concept you are seeing life.

C. Anything that does not fit that concept makes you insecure.

D. With wordless awareness, just watch.

E. This is called objective watching.

F. This watching will not allow the previous fears to have a snowballing effect.

(a) DFECB (b) DFCBE
(c) DFEBC (d) CDEFB
(e) CDBFE

Question 6

A. I'm a huge fan of Vikas Swarup's novel, one of the most delightful reads I've enjoyed in years.

B. He was rescued by a female lawyer who gets him to tell his life story and explain how he, an uneducated slum kid, knew the answers to such difficult questions.

C. But he has retained the novel's structure and premise, and Danny Boyle has brought its spirit alive in a way that I believe even Swarup would appreciate.

D. Screenwriter Simon has changed pretty much all of Swarup's stories, introduced a romantic element and even re-baptised the hero.

E. It's about an orphan boy called Ram Mohammed Thomas who is about to win a TV quiz show based on *Kaun Banega Crorepati* and is arrested on suspicion of having got that far by cheating.

F. Ram then tells a number of stories, each of which explains how he knew what he happened to know.

(a) EBFDC (b) EDEBC
(c) CEDBF (d) FEBCD
(e) ECDFB

Question 7

A. According to Defence Secretary Gotabaya Rajapaksa, the troops close to PTK, the last remaining LTTE-held town at that time, passed on information about the two aircraft even before the radars detected them.

B. The Tiger Craft flew over Mannar and Wilpattu en route to Colombo. It was their normal route. The troops would have captured the LTTE planes within days, and the LTTE had acted before they lost the craft on the ground."

C. The Defence Ministry said each aircraft was loaded with explosives weighing 215 kg and added that the pilots failed to drop any bomb.

D. He said: "The LTTE may have used a straight road in their last stronghold for taking off as the outfit had lost all the airstrips to the troops during the past few months.

E. There was no explanation as to how the two light-wing aircraft managed to make their way from PTK to the heart of the national capital and come within metres of their purported targets.

(a) CDEB (b) CDBE
(c) DBCE (d) DBEC
(e) CBDE

Question 8

A. Over a span of less than two years, some have been displaced at least a dozen times and are haunted by memories of sleepless nights spent in bunkers, constant bombardment and an uncertain future.

B. The worst nightmare for them was the possibility of forcible recruitment of their young boys and girls by the Tigers as the military began to corner them from mid-2008.

C. Reporters who visited the village heard horror tales of innocent citizens caught in the crossfire.

D. Every one of the 500-odd families in the village has gone through more or less the same trauma.

E. The choice before them was the known devil, the Tigers, and the unknown deep sea, the military.

(a) CEBD (b) CEDB
(c) CBED (d) CDBE
(e) CBDE

QUESTION 9

A. US President Barack Obama made a significant commitment to reversing the previous president's attitude towards combating climate change earlier this week.

B. The California regulations would force automakers to reduce vehicle emissions by a third by 2016, four years before new federal standards take effect.

C. The move would increase fuel efficiency by as much as eight miles per gallon.

D. If, as expected, California receives permission from the EPA to move ahead, it would mean that both US and other automakers would have to produce cars that are more fuel-efficient than current models.

E. He directed the Environmental Protection Agency (EPA) to reconsider allowing the state of California to set stricter fuel-emission standards on vehicles than federal limits.

(a) BCDE (b) EDCB
(c) EDBC (d) ECBD
(e) CDEB

QUESTION 10

A. Under the US Clean Air Act, the state of California is allowed to petition the federal government for a waiver to set its own stricter standards for tailpipe emissions and fuel economy.

B. Thirteen states have joined California in applying to the EPA, while three others have said that they will impose the standards if the waiver is granted.

C. The move has not been popular with American carmakers, who successfully argued to the Bush administration that rising standards would cripple the industry.

D. Other states can choose to adopt California's standards or stick with federal rules.

E. That accounts for nearly half the country's auto market, thus forcing car manufacturers worldwide to conform to stricter standards.

(a) BDCE (b) DBEC
(c) DCBE (d) DBCE
(e) CDBE

QUESTION 11

A. Indians and Pakistanis are the same people.

B. The idea of India is stronger than the Indian, and the idea of Pakistan weaker than the Pakistani.

C. Why then have the two nations moved on such divergent arcs over the last six decades?

D. India has progressed into a modern nation occasionally hampered by backward forces. Pakistan is regressing into a medieval society with a smattering of modern elements.

E. Multi-religious, multi-ethnic, secular, democratic India was an idea that belonged to the future; one-dimensional Pakistan was a concept borrowed from the fears of the past.

(a) CBED (b) CBDE
(c) DECB (d) DBCE
(e) EDCB

QUESTION 12

A. As the country copes with the aftermath of the horrors of Mumbai, the hard work of reconstruction, of rebuilding–of reimagining our country–has begun.

B. The victims of the killers were from every faith, and Indians of every religion have stood united in their anger and determination.

C. And yet it was just the weekend before the attacks that the PM had urged senior police officers not to widen "the fault lines in our society" and to act to "restore the faith of the people–especially those belonging to religious and ethnic minorities and the weaker sections–in the impartiality and effectiveness of the police."

D. One genuine cause of satisfaction must be that there was no demonisation of our Muslim minority, which the terrorists must have hoped to provoke.

E. His words reflected a real conundrum: the general public feels it is not adequately protected against the random violence of terrorists, but every proactive policing effort seriously alienates India's largest minority community.

(a) DCBE (b) DEBC
(c) EDBC (d) DBCE
(e) BCDE

QUESTION 13

A. Instead, we saw the majority of Sikhs stay loyal to their country, as a largely Sikh police force, led by a charismatic Sikh officer, K.P.S. Gill, ably combated the minority of Sikh terrorists, while the Indian state orchestrated a democratic political process which brought elected Sikh leaders to power in Punjab.

B. Obviously, we cannot infuse a significant number of Muslims into these forces overnight.

C. There are well-known historical and sociological reasons that explain why Muslims are under-represented in the country's police forces, the Central Reserve Police and crucial gendarmeries like UP's Provincial Armed Constabulary.

D. There is absolutely no reason why a similar approach cannot work with the Muslim community, the overwhelming majority of whom are proud and loyal Indians.

E. To do so we must start by getting more Muslims into the security forces.

(a) DEBC (b) DECB
(c) EDCB (d) ECBD
(e) CDEB

Question 14

A. The one advantage that people of peace have over war-mongers is numbers.

B. You can be as private or outspoken as you wish.

C. But those around you will know that you are for peace.

D. If enough people turned into peacemakers, war could end.

E. When the time is right and enough people participate, critical mass can change the world.

F. The programme for peacemakers asks you to follow a specific practice every day of the week. It takes only a few minutes.

(a) EDBCF (b) DCBEF
(c) DEBCF (d) DEFBC
(e) BCEFD

Question 15

A. The film will be released in India, both in its original bilingual version and in a version dubbed in Hindi, in January.

B. There is even a scene involving human excrement that is both revolting and hilarious. But this is not, despite all of that, an exercise in the pornography of poverty.

C. Slum life is depicted with integrity and dignity, and with a joie de vivre that transcends its setting.

D. It was filmed in large part with small hand-held digital cameras on location in Dharavi and in the Juhu slums, and the mounds of garbage, the cesspits, and the overflowing drains are all very present.

E. It is easy to see why this movie would appeal to international cinegoers in a way that a bleaker film like *City of Joy* could not.

F. One fair warning to Indian viewers: its depiction of Indian poverty and slum life is searingly real.

(a) FDBEC (b) FDBCE
(c) EFDBC (d) EBDCF
(e) CBEFD

Question 16

A. I saw the film in New York with an audience made up largely of Indian expatriates.

B. Danny Boyle reacted to that charge by pointing out that his Scottish characters in *Trainspotting* were also conniving, unprincipled and ruthless, and that he happened to like to depict people like that.

C. And the film's hero, played by the teenage British Indian actor Dev Patel with a look that combines intensity and expressiveness and yet seems utterly genuine, is as sincere a protagonist as you could hope to find.

D. In the enthusiastic discussion that followed, only one person reacted negatively, saying that the film seemed to show all Indians as conniving, unprincipled and ruthless, and that the only compassionate people in the film were a pair of white tourists who give Jamal some money.

E. Something tells me that most Indian viewers will take this in stride–we live in a land largely devoid of larger-than-life heroes, and we have learned to take human beings as they are, which is to say, as grossly imperfect.

(a) DBEC (b) DCEB
(c) EDCB (d) BCED
(e) EDCB

Question 17

A. She was undergoing treatment for pneumonia at the time when the radiologist had raised an alarm and sent her to a cardiologist.

B. Even in my dazed state, I remember wondering how it was at all possible that a well-built woman like Angel could shrink to half her size within a day of being in hospital.

C. It was absurd, insane.

D. Within an hour, she was in hospital and our carefree, happy little world came crumbling down like a house of cards.

E. The bony woman lying helplessly in that sterile hospital room with strange machines blinking around her wasn't my Angel at all.

(a) DBEC (b) DBCE
(c) DECB (d) DEBC
(e) CBED

Question 18

A. Lead researcher Eden King says that a study has revealed that people, who support diversity programs, have changing attitudes in times of economic strife.

B. "The reality is, diversity programs and disadvantaged groups may be the first to go in times of economic uncertainty.

C. This causes real problems for people of socially disadvantaged groups," she says.

D. King points out that competition for fewer jobs and resources often increases tension among workers, and may especially affect minority groups.

E. The study also suggests that those in hiring positions may be less likely to hire a minority job applicant in an economic downturn, she adds.

(a) EBCD (b) EDBC
(c) DCBE (d) DCEB
(e) CBED

Question 19

A. But the problem is that politics has power; religion has only love, peace and the experience of the divine.

B. Religion has no mundane power like nuclear weapons and atom bombs and guns; its dimension is totally different.

C. It is just like a beautiful rose flower: its beauty, poetry, its dance makes life worth living, gives life meaning and significance.

D. Politics can easily interfere with religion; and it has been interfering all along, to such an extent that it has destroyed many religious values which are absolutely necessary for the survival of humanity and life on this Earth.

E. Religion is not a will to power; religion is a search for truth. And the very search makes the religious man humble, simple and innocent.

(a) EBDC (b) EDCB
(c) DBEC (d) BDEC
(e) DCBE

Question 20

A. Sufism is among the easiest and a unique path to achieve ultimate flowering.

B. The association of the master is satsang, and the world of the master is satnam or the only scripture.

C. Thus, the entire edifice of the Sufi path rests on the Master.

D. It is not a religion but the way... It is the art and science of correct living through a systematic understanding and following of austerities.

E. This path has three pillars which form the basis: Meditation; master and the remembrance; Zikr qulb or repeating the remembrance at the heart centre; tasubbre sheikh or remembrance of the master and marakba or meditation.

(a) DCBE (b) DECB
(c) CEDB (d) DEBC
(e) CBED

Question 21

A. The word 'Master' does not refer to a specific person.

B. As an individual you cannot see beyond your understanding.

C. And as you are, you cannot envision a master.

D. This is the state of spiritual awareness.

E. This is the reason the masters appear from time to time to manifest that state of awareness, the light absolute and the path laid down by other masters.

(a) DBCE (b) DECB
(c) BCDE (d) CBED
(e) CEDB

Question 22

A. As a novelist myself, I wondered about the changes made to the book on its way to the screen.

B. In particular, novels can afford to digress in ways that the attention span of movie audiences cannot accept: a film requires one clear over-arching narrative, fewer characters to keep straight, and a common thread from beginning to end.

C. But some of the changes were arguably unnecessary: I lamented, in particular, the loss of *Ram Mohammed Thomas* and his mongrelised *Amar-Akbar-Anthony* exemplifying of Indianess.

D. But above all, Danny Boyle's *Slumdog Millionaire* is the work of an artist at the peak of his powers.

E. Some I could understand; cinema and novels are distinct art forms, and what works well in one medium does not necessarily translate well into the other.

F. I hope that people will both read the book and see the movie to savour the differing strengths of Swarup's original premise and Danny Boyle's transcreation of it.

(a) EDCBF (b) DCEBF
(c) EBCFD (d) CFEDB
(e) CFBDE

Question 23

A. It was time for Tina's annual art show 'Harmony' and Jaya did the honours of inaugurating the same.

B. Giving Tina all the support she needed was her camera-shy husband Anil, her son Jai and her mother-in-law Kokilaben.

C. And of course, supporting the show and Tina's tireless efforts were a huge number of art lovers and her friends and well-wishers.

D. Reema Jain met Jaya warmly, and the two spent some time talking. Adi Godrej and Harsh Goenka made time out for Tina, and congratulated her on her efforts.

E. Devieka and her mother took a round of the gallery as did the other guests that included Gulshan Grover, Siddharth Jaideep and Seema Mehrotra and Gauri.

F. Joining Jaya was her son Abhishek, looking cool in his crop cut and a black jacket with jeans. But what was cooler was the way he embraced Tina with a warm hug.

(a) FBCDE (b) FCBDE
(c) EDCBF (d) DFEBC
(e) DBCEF

Question 24

A. The space shuttle and its crew of seven blasted off Sunday just as the sun was setting.

B. NASA is thrilled to see Discovery finally on its way.

C. That's because Discovery needs to be gone from the space station before a Russian rocket lifts off to put a fresh crew at the space station March 26.

D. The shuttle is carrying a final set of solar wings for the space station that the astronauts will install.

E. A hydrogen leak on Wednesday scrapped the first launch attempt. Before that, valve concerns kept postponing the flight that was originally scheduled to launch in mid-February.

F. Because of the delays, the mission has been shortened by a day, and one of four spacewalks has been dropped.

(a) BDCEF (b) BDECF
(c) DBEFC (d) DBECF
(e) EDCBF

Question 25

A. However, following the collection of evidence and material used by the attackers, and their subsequent verification by the forensic laboratories, the charge sheet puts down, officially and conclusively, what has been reported in the media and stated by officials in the past three months.

B. In doing so, it debunks conspiracy theories such as the one that Anti-Terrorism Squad chief Hemant Karkare was killed by some "other" groups because of his investigations into the September 29, 2008, Malegaon blast case.

C. Investigating officials said they put together the charge sheet on the basis of the evidence collected from the boat, that the terrorists hijacked the five targeted sites and approximately 150 eyewitness accounts.

D. For instance, it categorically states that the men came from Pakistan, and that it was the LeT that planned and executed the attack.

E. It details the sequence of events and the entire operation in each location.

(a) DECB (b) DEBC
(c) DCEB (d) DBEC
(e) CBDE

TYPE II

The first line [A] and last line [F] of each question are fixed. Arrange the other four lines in a logical sequence.

Question 1

A. The estimate on the number of civilians has been a matter of debate for over six months.

B. The government contested both these figures as vastly exaggerated and estimated the number to be 75,000.

C. Neutral observers are now veering round to the view that the government figure appears more reliable.

D. The United Nations and other international agencies projected a figure of 2.5 lakhs.

E. The LTTE has consistently maintained that the figure is above four lakhs.

F. It is improbable for more than a lakh people to be present in LTTE-controlled territory, which is shrinking with every passing day.

(a) EDCB (b) EDBC
(c) BCED (d) DEBC
(e) BEDC

Question 2

A. First, take five minutes to meditate for peace.

B. Allow them to radiate from your stillness out into your body.

C. Bring into your mind anyone against whom you have a grievance and let it go.

D. Close your eyes.

E. Put your attention on your heart and inwardly repeat the words: peace, harmony, laughter, love.

F. Then introduce the intention of peace in your thoughts. After a few moments of silence, repeat this prayer: let me be loved, happy and peaceful; let my friends, my perceived enemies, all beings in the world be happy, loved, and peaceful too.

(a) CBED (b) CDEB
(c) EBDC (d) DEBC
(e) DBEC

Question 3

A. India is fast losing its low-cost position. In Mumbai, executive compensation levels for the financial sector are higher than in London, rental costs are above those in New York and electricity is dearer than in Tokyo.

B. The software sector will have to aspire to be the poet, not just the scribe. Indian exports of its own software, or licensing of its own intellectual property (IP), amounted to only about $450 million in the year ending March 31, 2007.

C. Increasingly, Indian companies will have to do more with their intellectual resources.

D. As Azim Premji, chairman of Wipro, mentioned, in the crucial IT sector, cost arbitrage is one entry point but the continued growth of the sector will have to be based on quality.

E. Indian companies will need to evolve from their low-cost position.

F. This is a tiny fraction of India's IT service exports. India's IT sector must go beyond "renting out IQ and start creating IP" if it is to compete in the face of ever-rising costs.

(a) BDCE (b) EDCB
(c) DBCE (d) ECDB
(e) BCDE

Question 4

A. The Defence Ministry proudly proclaimed that the two LTTE-improvised, Czech-manufactured Zlin-143 aircraft were brought down by anti-aircraft fire within an hour of their detection.

B. The body of the second pilot was found near the wreckage of the aircraft at Katunayake.

C. The air raids surprised political and diplomatic circles in Colombo, considering that on the day of the air raids the LTTE was confined to an area of less than 100 sq. km.

D. Incidentally, the air raids coincided with the visit of Sir John Holmes, U.N. Under-Secretary-General for Humanitarian Affairs and Emergency Relief Coordinator, for a first-hand assessment of the crisis triggered by the war.

E. The first craft crashed into the rear of the building housing the Inland Revenue Department, opposite the Air Force headquarters, killing the pilot and two persons in the building, three storeys of which were damaged, and injuring 45, including two airmen.

F. In the course of his interaction with the media, Sir John hinted at efforts by neutral parties to reach a settlement between the LTTE and the government for safe passage for the trapped civilians.

(a) EBCD (b) CDEB
(c) BECD (d) EBDC
(e) CDBE

Question 5

A. The political head of the LTTE, B. Nadesan, urged the international community to affect a ceasefire and initiate a political solution as a priority rather than insist that the LTTE lay down arms.

B. There is no evidence to suggest that the LTTE is concerned about the safety and welfare of civilians in the war zone.

C. The government is not prepared on the ground to deal with the internally displaced.

D. In an appeal to the heads of the co-chair countries, he said, "When a permanent political solution is reached for the Tamil people, with the support and the guarantee of the international community, the situation will arise where there will be no need for the arms of the LTTE."

E. The Sri Lankan government dismissed it as "hilarious."

F. Samarasinghe told the Human Rights Council in Geneva on March 3 that over 36,000 people trapped in the Wanni had managed to escape the LTTE and flee the theatre of conflict.

(a) BCDE (b) EDBC
(c) CBED (d) DEBC
(e) DECB

Question 6

A. However, the ground realities are far from satisfactory.

B. However, at the moment only one camp, which can accommodate 500 families, is ready. The rest are housed in schools and other public buildings.

C. To give one example, minutes away from the model village, several hundred people are housed in a school.

D. The government has been talking for months about its preparedness to accommodate the displaced in temporary camps.

E. A group of foreign and local media personnel who were flown in to the government "model village" on the outskirts of Vavuniya returned with the impression that the government was simply not geared to meet the gigantic task.

F. The visiting journalists were taken to the school after they insisted on looking at least one other facility. Each classroom in the school is packed with at least 40 persons. Their belongings are kept on benches along the walls.

(a) BCDE (b) EDBC
(c) BCED (d) DEBC
(e) EDCB

Question 7

A. The government is working on a project close to the model camp to create facilities to accommodate more people.

B. Informed sources suggest that shortage of funds is a serious hurdle.

C. The authorities are not sure how long it will take to complete the facility.

D. There is no clarity at the moment on how long the people will stay in the camps.

E. On paper, the government is gearing up to accommodate 200,000 displaced people.

F. The government's argument is that it will take time to rebuild infrastructure and remove landmines before the people can return to their original places.

(a) BCDE (b) BDCE
(c) CEBD (d) CEDB
(e) CBDE

Question 8

A. Given that the Indian armed forces have an overwhelming dependence on Russian defence equipment, the news that Russia has grounded its entire fleet of MiG-29 aircraft due to structural defects and subsequently found a large percentage unsafe to fly is ominous.

B. And in a larger context, this is the latest in a series of developments over the past few years that suggest it is time for India to diversify its sources of defence equipment.

C. Russia's defence manufacturing base is facing shortfalls in capabilities and capacities, leading to contract deadline overruns and increased costs, as seen repeatedly in the case of the Gorshkov.

D. The immediate implications for India are worrying. The IAF operates over 60 of the aircraft and is in the midst of procuring 45 more to fly off the much-delayed Admiral Gorshkov and indigenous Cochin-built carriers.

E. Poor quality and a lack of spare parts only worsen the situation, as do its moribund R&D facilities which compel it to rely on technology dating back to the 1970s and 1980s

F. India's ambitious plans to upgrade its military technology and the changing profile of its requirements mean that it can no longer afford to persist with a strategy that depends on Russia as its primary supplier.

(a) CEBD (b) DBCE
(c) BDCE (d) CEDB
(e) DBEC

Question 9

A. Obama allows federal funding for stem cell research in the US. The controversy in America over the ethics of using embryonic stem cells to heal the sick hasn't deterred US President Barack Obama from making a new policy announcement.

B. By issuing an executive order on March 9, Obama has reversed George W Bush's policy that no federal funding would be available to promote research in human embryonic stem cells.

C. Stem cells are undefined cells present in adults; they are also found in abundance in embryos and umbilical cord blood.

D. Though all stem cells have the potential to heal–because they can be coaxed to grow into specific kinds of tissues or organs with cloning technology–it is embryonic stem cells that have greater potential on account of their ability to grow into virtually any body part.

E. Will the US Congress now allow taxpayers' money to be used for human embryo experiments involving their creation and destruction, overturning the legislative ban it has been renewing every year since 1996?

F. That's why researchers prefer to work with embryonic stem cells that have greater scope than adult stem cells with their limitations.

(a) BEDC (b) CDBE
(c) EBCD (d) BECD
(e) BCDE

Question 10

A. Embryonic stem cells are controversial because the embryos are discarded once the cells are extracted from them. Critics object to creation of embryos for the purpose of harvesting their cells.

B. Researchers are sourcing these to-be-discarded embryos for stem cells, and not creating new ones for the purpose.

C. The other objection is that the technology could be used in human reproductive cloning.

D. However, given the growth of infertility treatments and with more people opting for assisted reproductive techniques, fertility clinics end up with more embryos than they require.

E. Fears of reproductive cloning–as opposed to therapeutic cloning–are unfounded, too, since the US, like most countries, expressly prohibits it.

F. The Indian Council of Medical Research has laid down guidelines on stem cell research, following a proposal to set up a national apex committee for this purpose.

(a) DBCE (b) BDCE
(c) CEDB (d) CEBD
(e) DBEC

Question 11

A. Giving a new twist to probe into Mumbai attacks, Pakistan is now alleging that there were "elements in India" who helped carry out the strikes and wants its investigators to be provided access to them.

B. In what could further delay the prosecution of Mumbai attackers, the paper said Pakistan is also seeking DNA samples of the terrorists involved in the strikes and more information about contacts made by them through the internet.

C. In its report, Pakistan has sought results of DNA tests on Ajmal Kasab and the nine other attackers killed by Indian security forces so that these could be matched with their family members, if any, in Pakistan, the sources said.

D. "There is a strong realisation in Pakistani security agencies that without the help of elements in India, the Mumbai crime could have not been committed," official sources were quoted as saying by the *Dawn* newspaper on Tuesday.

E. Pakistan's investigation report into the Mumbai attacks, which was reviewed on Monday at a meeting of the Defence Committee of the Cabinet chaired by Prime Minister Yousuf Raza Gilani, would be sent to New Delhi in a couple of days, the paper quoted these officials.

F. Pakistan wants information about weapons used by the terrorists and details of mobile phone calls made by them and taped by Indian security agencies.

(a) BCDE (b) EDCB
(c) DBEC (d) DECB
(e) CBDE

Question 12

A. Pakistan also wants information regarding IP addresses from which emails were sent to attackers by the alleged perpetrators, the sources said.

B. An FIR would be registered in a "couple of days" and this would also make the contents of the Pakistani report public, the paper said quoting sources.

C. It wants India to provide details about people who were reportedly killed by the terrorists when they illegally entered the country's territorial waters.

D. The government has described the information provided by India as "insufficient" to reach a logical conclusion and to bring the perpetrators to justice.

E. The Pakistan government on Monday decided to register a case against the perpetrators of the Mumbai attacks to bring them to justice in accordance with Pakistani laws.

F. An official statement issued on Monday said further queries would soon be sent to India.

(a) CEBD (b) BDEC
(c) CEDB (d) EDBC
(e) CBDE

Question 13

A. This is not the only fallout of switching to bio-fuels.

B. Obama's new energy plan, which backs a greater use of ethanol, could worsen the situation.

C. In the US, government subsidies have ensured that nearly 30 million tonnes of maize have been diverted for the production of ethanol.

D. Many American farmers are also switching to maize production from other crops.

E. Several studies have found evidence of a link between spiraling food prices and increased acreage for crops used to produce bio-fuel.

F. This has led to an increase in global food prices, particularly of wheat.

(a) CDEB (b) EBDC
(c) DCEB (d) EBCD
(e) EDBC

Question 14

A. The current situation does not warrant such large-scale diversion of land and resources to produce bio-fuels.

B. Given the global recession, there is little likelihood of oil prices soaring soon. So there is no immediate need to rush to substitute oil.

C. From a peak of $147 a barrel last year, oil prices are now below $40.

D. The electric car is an innovation that could significantly cut down the world's dependence on oil.

E. Instead the world should be looking at developing long-term replacements for fossil fuels.

F. What we need is more research to make electric cars that can run longer on a single charge and are also competitively priced.

(a) BCDE (b) EDCB
(c) CBED (d) CDEB
(e) BCDE

Question 15

A. But Obama, while acknowledging that Detroit's auto majors would see the move as an added burden on an ailing industry in the short term, made clear that the way forward was to embrace green technology.

B. Such political commitment to fight climate change seems lacking in India. Attempts to set fuel emission standards have been stymied by inter-agency squabbling on exactly how such norms should be set.

C. It was only with the recent intervention of the Prime Minister's Office that a consensus was reached.

D. Fuel economy regulations will go some way in reducing India's import bill since we import 78 per cent of our oil.

E. In doing so, he has sent a clear signal that his administration is prepared to act on climate change even in the face of opposition from interest groups such as the car industry.

F. The government should follow Obama's example and act quickly to fight climate change and cut oil imports.

(a) DEBC (b) EBDC
(c) EBCD (d) DBCE
(e) ECDB

Question 16

A. Why does the institution of the arranged marriage survive in India in this day and age? The India I am talking about in this case includes the educated middle class, where the incidence of arranged marriages continues to be high and more importantly, is accepted without any difficulty as a legitimate way of finding a mate.

B. Twenty years ago, looking at the future, one would have imagined that by now, the numbers of the arranged marriage types would have shrunk and the few remaining stragglers would be looked down upon as belonging to a somewhat primitive tribe.

C. The answer lies partly in the elastic nature of this institution, and indeed most traditional Indian customs that allows it to expand its definition to accommodate the needs of modernity.

D. So today's arranged marriage places individual will at the heart of the process; young men and women are rarely forced to marry someone against their wishes.

E. But this is far from being so.

F. The role of the parents has moved to that of being presiding deities, with one hand raised in blessing and the other hand immersed purposefully in the wallet.

(a) BEDC (b) BECD
(c) CDBE (d) CDEB
(e) CBDE

Question 17

A. The arranged marriage of today is more clearly manufactured but it also offers a more certain outcome.

B. In the West, the curiously antiquated notion that it is the prerogative of the man to propose marriage makes for a situation where the promise of marriage is tantalisingly withheld by one of the concerned parties for an indefinite period of time.

C. Indeed, going by Hollywood movies, it would appear that to mention marriage too early in a relationship is a sure way of scaring off the man.

D. So we have a situation where marriage is a mirage that shimmers on the horizon frequently, but materialises rarely.

E. Online matrimonial sites are full of young professionals seeking matches on their own, knowing that what is on the table here is not a date but the promise of marriage.

F. The mating process becomes a serial hunt with the man doing the pursuing to begin a relationship and the woman taking over the role in trying to convert it into something more lasting.

(a) EBCD (b) CDEB
(c) EBDC (d) DEBC
(e) DBEC

Question 18

A. At a more fundamental level, the idea that romantic love is the most suitable basis for a long-term relationship is not as automatic as it might appear.

B. For a long time, in a lot of cultures, and even now in some, marriage too is a relationship we do not personally control.

C. This view of marriage works best in contexts where the idea of the individual is not fully developed. People live in a sticky collective and individuality is blurred.

D. Marriage is the only significant kinship tie that we enter into by choice.

E. We don't choose our parents, our relatives or our children–these are cards that are dealt out to us.

F. A young Saraswat Brahmin boy, earning in four figures was sufficient as a description and one such person was broadly substitutable with another.

(a) BCDE (b) DBCE
(c) BDEC (d) DEBC
(e) CEDB

Question 19

A. As the role of the individual increases and as dimensions of individuality get fleshed out in ever newer ways, marriage must account for these changes.

B. In contexts where communities fragment and finding mates as a task devolves to individuals, romance becomes a natural agent of marriage.

C. For, the greater emphasis on the individual has also meant that personal needs and personal growth come to occupy a privileged position in every individual's life.

D. The trouble is that while the device works very well in bringing people together, it is not intrinsically equipped to handle these individuals over time.

E. The idea of romance makes the coming together of individuals seem like a natural event. Mutual attraction melts individuals together into a union.

F. Falling in love becomes infinitely easier than staying in it as individuals are no longer defined primarily by the roles they play in marriage.

(a) EBCD (b) EBDC
(c) DCEB (d) ECBD
(e) BCDE

Question 20

A. So we have a situation where people fall in and out of love more often, making the idea of romance as a basis of marriage not as socially productive as it used to be.

B. In a world where our present has become a poor indicator of our future, the idea of arranging marriages continues to hold charm.

C. Of course, the arranged marriage has its own assumptions about what variables make this contract work and these too offer no guarantees.

D. It keeps the headiness of romance at bay, and recognises that romance and the sustenance of a socially constructed long-term contract like marriage do not necessarily converge.

E. Romantic love seeks to extend the present while the arranged marriage aims at securing the future.

F. Whether it is cloaked in tradition as it is in India or in modernity as it is elsewhere, the institution of marriage needs some help.

(a) CBED (b) EDCB
(c) DEBC (d) BCED
(e) EDBC

Question 21

A. The Indian state was founded on equality and equity: political equality through democracy, religious equality through secularism, gender equality, and economic equity

B. India, therefore, saw land reforms and the abolition of zamindari. Pakistan has been unable to enforce land reforms.

C. India and Pakistan were alternative models for a nation-state. Time would determine which idea had the legs to reach a modern horizon.

D. Economic equality is a fantasy, but without an equitable economy that works towards the elimination of poverty there cannot be a sustainable state.

E. The two strands within Pakistan's DNA began to slowly split its personality.

F. The father of the nation, Mohammed Ali Jinnah, thought he had produced a child in his own image, but his secular prescription was soon suppressed.

(a) DBCE (b) BDEC
(c) DBEC (d) BDCE
(e) CBDE

Question 22

A. After some debate, the first Constitution in 1956 proclaimed Pakistan as an "Islamic" state.

B. The principal institutions of state, and the economy, remained largely in the control of the secular tendency until, through racist prejudice, arrogance and awesome military incompetence it was unable to protect the integrity of the nation.

C. No one cared (or dared) to examine what it might mean.

D. The crisis of 1969-1971, and the second partition of the subcontinent, which created a Muslim-majority Bangladesh out of a Muslim-majority Pakistan, forced Pakistan to introspect deeply about its identity.

E. It was an uneasy compromise.

F. Perhaps the last true secularist of this Islamic state was the Western-Oriented-Gentleman Zulfikar Ali Bhutto, who came to power in 1971, preached emancipation from poverty and did not mind a shot of whisky in the evening.

(a) BDEC (b) CEBD
(c) ECBD (d) ECDB
(e) CDBE

Question 23

A. If it had been only a question of an individual's excesses Zia's death could have been a swivel moment for the restoration of the pre-Zia era, particularly since his successor was Benazir Bhutto

B. There are now over 20,000 of them, with perhaps two million students, most (not all) of them controlled by extremists.

C. The children of Gen Zia are now threatening Islamabad. Sometimes a simple fact can illuminate the nature of a society.

D. Worse, prompted by thoughtless advice, Benazir engineered the rise of the Taliban and helped it conquer Kabul.

E. But in the quarter century since his sudden death by mid-air explosion, no one in Islamabad has had the courage to change the curriculum or challenge the spread of the madrassas.

F. During the 2005 earthquake, male students of the Frontier Medical College were stopped by religious fanatics–their elders–from saving girls from the rubble of their school building.

(a) EDCB (b) EBDC
(c) BDEC (d) DCEB
(e) DBCE

Question 24

A. For six decades, power in Pakistan has teetered between military dictatorship and civilian rule.

B. Men like Baitullah Mehsud, Mangal Bagh and Maulana Faziullah are a very different breed from the mullahs who have already been coopted and corrupted by the system.

C. When the credibility of civilians was exhausted the people welcomed the army; when the generals overstayed their welcome, the citizen returned to political parties.

D. How long before the poor and the middle classes turn to the theocrats waiting to take over? The state has already handed over a province like Swat to Islamic rule.

E. Pakistan is facing a dangerous moment, when the credibility of both the military and politicians seems to have ebbed beyond recovery.

F. They have a supplementary query which resonates with the street and the village after 9/11: why is Pakistan's army fighting America's war against fellow Muslims?

(a) DBCE (b) CEBD
(c) DBEC (d) CEDB
(e) BCDE

Question 25

A. We could also take a leaf out of Britain's book in what they do to combat racism within the police, as well as enhance cross-cultural knowledge, offering training courses to white officers that include a 'long weekend' spent living with a minority family.

B. But we must acknowledge the grave risk to the national fabric of any community being alienated from the police.

C. Of course India is not Britain and no foreign ideas can simply be imported wholesale into our country.

D. Britain is far from perfect–as the current discrimination case filed by Deputy Commissioner Tariq Ghafoor suggests–but many Hindu policemen, especially in Gujarat and the suburbs of Mumbai, would benefit immeasurably by spending a few days in a Muslim mohalla.

E. Let's face it: if our police are not properly and continuously trained in minority relations, the current problems will continue.

F. Our police forces must reflect the diversity of India. Such a policy would be the "other side of the coin" to a tough security policy which is indispensable to reassure the common urban resident, terrorised by the bomb blasts, that the Government can keep them safe.

(a) DEBC (b) DECB
(c) CBED (d) BCED
(e) BDEC

Answer Key

Type I

1. (c)	**2.** (a)	**3.** (d)	**4.** (b)	**5.** (c)
6. (a)	**7.** (d)	**8.** (b)	**9.** (c)	**10.** (b)
11. (a)	**12.** (d)	**13.** (b)	**14.** (d)	**15.** (b)
16. (a)	**17.** (d)	**18.** (b)	**19.** (c)	**20.** (d)
21. (a)	**22.** (c)	**23.** (a)	**24.** (c)	**25.** (b)

Type II

1. (b)	**2.** (d)	**3.** (b)	**4.** (a)	**5.** (d)
6. (b)	**7.** (c)	**8.** (b)	**9.** (d)	**10.** (a)
11. (c)	**12.** (a)	**13.** (d)	**14.** (c)	**15.** (c)
16. (b)	**17.** (a)	**18.** (d)	**19.** (b)	**20.** (b)
21. (a)	**22.** (c)	**23.** (b)	**24.** (d)	**25.** (b)

CHAPTER 19 Previous Years' Questions from CAT

CAT 1994

Directions for the questions (1-8): In each question a set of six sentences of a continuous paragraph are provided. The sentence numbered 1 starts the paragraph and the sentence numbered 6 ends it. Arrange statements A, B, C, D between 1 and 6 to form a coherent paragraph.

Q1.

1. What does the state do in a country where tax morality is very low?

(A) It tries to spy upon the taxpayers.

(B) It investigates income sources and spending patterns.

(C) Exactly what the tax authority tries to do now, even if inconsistently.

(D) It could also encourage people to denounce to the tax authorities any conspicuously prosperous neighbours who may be suspected of not paying their taxes properly.

6. The ultimate solution would be an Orwellian system.

(a) BACD (b) DBAC

(c) ABCD (c) DCBA

Q2.

1. The fragile Yugoslav state has an uncertain future.

(A) Thus, there will surely be chaos and uncertainty if the people fail to settle their differences.

(B) Sharp ideological differences already exist in the country.

(C) Ethnic, regional, linguistic and material disparities are profound.

(D) The country will also lose the excellent reputation it enjoyed in the international arena.

6. At worst, it will once more become vulnerable to international conspiracy and intrigue.

(a) BCAD (b) ADCB

(c) ACBD (d) DBCA

Q3.

1. India's experience of industrialization is characteristic of the difficulties faced by a newly independent developing country.

(A) In 1947, India was undoubtedly an under-developed country with one of the lowest per capita incomes in the world.

(B) Indian industrialization was the result of a conscious deliberate policy of growth by an indigenous political elite.

(C) Today India ranks fifth in the international community of nations if measured in terms of purchasing power.

(D) Even today, however, the benefits of Indian industrialization since independence have not reached the masses.

6. Industrialisation in India has thus been a limited success: 'One more example of growth without development'.

(a) CDAB (b) DCBA

(c) CABD (d) BACD

Q4.

1. The new Economic Policy comprises the various policy measures and changes introduced since July 1991.

(A) There is a common thread running through all these measures.

(B) The objective is simple–to improve the efficiency of the system.

(C) The regulatory mechanism involving multitude of controls has fragmented the capacity and reduced competition even in the private sector.

(D) The thrust of the new policy is towards creating a more competitive environment as a means to improving the productivity and efficiency of the economy.

6. This is to be achieved by removing the barriers and restrictions on the entry and growth of firms.

(a) DCAB (b) ABCD
(c) BDAC (d) CDBA

Q5.

1. It is significant that one of the most common objections to competition is that it is blind.

(A) This is important because in a system of free enterprise based on private property, chances are not equal and there is indeed a strong case for reducing that inequality of opportunity.

(B) Rather it is a choice between a system where it is the will of a few persons that decides which is to get what and one where it depends at least partly, on the ability and the enterprise of the people concerned.

(C) Although competition and justice may have little else in common, it is as much a commendation of competition as of justice that it is no respecter of persons.

(D) The choice today is not between a system in which everybody will get what he deserves according to some universal standard and one where individual shares are determined by chance or goodwill.

6. The fact that opportunities open to the poor in a competitive society are much more restricted than those open to the rich, does not make it less true that in such a society, the poor are more free than a person commanding much greater material comfort in a different type of society.

(a) CDBA (b) DCBA
(c) ABCD (c) BADC

Q6.

1. The necessity for regional integration in South Asia is underlined by the very history of the last 45 years since the liquidation of the British Empire in this part of the world.

(A) After the partition of the Indian subcontinent, Pakistan was formed in that very area which the imperial powers had always marked out as the potential base for operations against the Russian power in Central Asia.

(B) Because of the disunity and ill-will among the South Asian neighbours, particularly India and Pakistan, great powers from outside the area could meddle into their affairs and thereby keep neighbours apart.

(C) It needs to be added that it was the bountiful supply of sophisticated arms that emboldened Pakistan to go for warlike bellicosity toward India.

(D) As part of the cold war strategy of the US, Pakistan was sucked into Washington's military alliance spreading over the years.

6. Internally too, it was the massive induction of American arms into Pakistan which empowered the military junta of that country to snuff out the civilian government and destroy democracy in Pakistan.

(a) ACBD (b) ABDC
(c) CBAD (d) DCAB

Q7.

1. Commercial energy consumption shows an increasing trend and poses the major challenge for the future.

(A) The demand, for petroleum, during 1996-97 and 2006-07 is anticipated to be 81 million tonnes and 125 million tonnes respectively.

(B) According to the projections of the 14th Power Survey Committee Report, the electricity generation requirements from utilities will be about 416 billion units by 1996-97 and 824 billion units by 2006-07.

(C) The production of coal should reach 303 million tonnes by 1996-97 to achieve Plan targets and 460 million tonnes by 2006-07.

(D) The demand for petroleum products has already rapidly outstripped indigenous production.

6. Electricity is going to play a major role in the development of infrastructural facilities.

(a) DACB (b) CADB
(c) BADC (d) ABCD

Q8.

1. The success of any unit in a competitive environment depends on prudent management of resources.

(A) In this context, it would have been more appropriate if the concept of accelerated depreciation, together with additional incentives towards capital allowances for recouping a portion of the cost of replacements out of the current generations had been accepted.

(B) Added to this are the negligible retention of profits because of inadequate capital allowances and artificial disallowances of genuine outflows.

(C) One significant cause for the poor generation of surpluses is the high cost of capital and its servicing cost.

(D) The lack of mechanism in Indian tax laws for quick recovery of capital costs has not received its due attention.

6. While this may apparently look costly from the point of view of the exchequer, the ultimate cost to the Government and the community in the form of losses suffered through poor viability will be prohibitive.

(a) ADBC (b) BCDA
(c) CBDA (d) DBAC

Directions for the questions (9-14): A number of sentences are given below which, when properly sequenced, form a coherent paragraph. Each sentence is labeled with a letter. Choose the most logical order of sentences from among the four given choices to construct a coherent paragraph.

Q9. (A) Realists believe that there is an objective reality out there independent of ourselves.
(B) This reality exists solely by virtue of how the world is, and it is in principle discoverable by application of the methods of science.
(C) They believe in the possibility of determining whether or not a theory is indeed really true or false.
(D) I think it is fair to say that this is the position to which most working scientists subscribe.

(a) ABCD (b) CDBA
(c) DCBA (d) BCAD

Q10. (A) There is a strong manufacturing base for a variety of products.
(B) India has come a long way on the technology front.
(C) But the technology adopted has been largely of foreign origin.
(D) There are, however, areas such as atomic energy, space, agriculture and defence where significant strides have been made in evolving relevant technologies within the country.

(a) ADCB (b) DBAC
(c) BACD (d) CBAD

Q11. (A) In emission trading, the government fixes the total amount of pollution that is acceptable to maintain a desired level of air quality.
(B) Economists argue that this approach makes air pollution control more cost effective than the current practice of fixing air pollution standards and expecting all companies to pollute below these standards.
(C) USA uses emission trading to control air pollution.
(D) It then distributes emission permits to all companies in the region, which add up to the overall acceptable level of emission.

(a) BADC (b) ACBD
(c) CADB (d) DBAC

Q12. (A) The individual companies vary in size, from the corner grocery to the industrial giant.
(B) Policies and management methods within firms range from formal, well-planned organizations and controls to slipshod day-to-day operations.
(C) Various industries offer a wide array of products or services through millions of firms largely independent of each other.
(D) Variation in the form of ownership contributes to diversity in capital investment, volume of business, and financial structure.

(a) DBCA (b) CADB
(c) BADC (d) ADCB

Q13. (A) All levels of demand, whether individual, aggregate, local, national, or international are subject to change.
(B) At the same time, science and technology add new dimensions to products, their uses and the methods used to market them.
(C) Aggregate demand fluctuates with changes in the level of business activity, GNP, and national income.
(D) The demand of individuals tend to vary with changing need and rising income.

(a) CBDA (b) DCAB
(c) BCAD (d) ADCB

Q14. (A) Secret persons shall strike with weapons, fire or poison.
(B) Clans, mutually supporting each other, shall be made to strike at the weak points.
(C) He shall destroy their caravans, herds, forests and troop reinforcements.
(D) The conqueror shall cause enemy kingdom to be destroyed by neighbouring kings, jungle tribes, pretenders or unjustly treated princes.

(a) DCBA (b) ABCD
(c) BDCA (d) ADCB

CAT 1995

Directions for the questions (15-17): Arrange the sentences A, B, C and D to form a logical sequence between sentences 1 and 6.

Q15.

1. That was the day that Walter Alva made the boldest decision of his career.

(A) He had believed that somehow the situation would resolve itself.
(B) First, he apologized to his teammates for putting them in danger.

(C) He now encouraged anyone who wished to leave to do so without delay.
(D) Until recently, he explained, his fascination with the tomb had blinded him to the peril of their position.

6. None did.

(a) BACD (b) DBAC
(c) BDAC (d) DCBA

Q16.

1. During this summer, I spent blissfully long days with my friend.

(A) In the afternoons, we would retire to the cottage, and she would talk about her husband–what a fine man he'd been.
(B) I discovered she made the finest shortbread (a kind of biscuit) in the universe.
(C) Once or twice she seemed about to cry and left the room quickly to make more tea.
(D) We could explore Bear Wood, munching happily and discussing the books she had lent me.

6. But she always came back smiling.

(a) BCAD (b) ADCB
(c) ACBD (d) BDAC

Q17.

1. The chainsaw howled as I finished cutting through the branch.

(A) The branch crashed to the ground, taking my spectacles with it.
(B) I almost dropped the saw as I shielded my face from the twigs that brushed by.
(C) Howard retrieved my glasses and handed them up to me.
(D) I pulled the saw away, and my husband tugged against the other end of the rope that I had tied just above the cut.

6. Are you okay? He asked.

(a) BCAD (b) DBAC
(c) DCAB (d) BDAC

Directions for the questions (18-19): Sentences given in each question, when properly sequenced, form a coherent paragraph. Each sentence is labeled with a letter. Choose the most logical order of sentences from among the four given choices to construct a coherent paragraph.

Q18. (A) One reason can be that the total investment allocated to power was deficient.
(B) However, it may also be that the demand for power was based on incorrect information.
(C) The question arises as to why the planning of the power sector in Indian plans turned out to be faulty, as widely alleged.
(D) In that case, obviously the plan was bad even on paper.

(a) DABC (b) CBAD
(c) CADB (d) DBAC

Q19. (A) Children need to be loved, and in a sense they cannot have too much of it.
(B) She herself doesn't want to grow up and attempts to make time stand still.
(C) Fortunately, she cannot succeed.
(D) But it is not because of love that a mother prevents her child from growing up.

(a) ACDB (b) DABC
(c) CADB (d) ADBC

CAT 1996

Directions for the questions (20-22): Arrange the sentences A, B, C and D to form a logical sequence between sentences 1 and 6.

Q20.

1. The market mechanism is the natural coordinator of private sector activities.

(A) It is also linked to the centrality of the notion of a free contract for both the operation of the market mechanism and the safeguarding of private property.
(B) This is linked to the autonomy of the decision maker under the market mechanism.
(C) It is futile to expect the State unit to behave as if it were privately owned.
(D) It is time to get rid of this vain hope once and for all.

6. There is no reason to be astonished by the fact that the State ownership permanently recreates the bureaucracy because it is but an organic part of the bureaucratic hierarchy.

(a) BADC (b) ACDB
(c) DCBA (d) BACD

Q21.

1. A manager is faced with innumerable situations in which he has to make a choice.

(A) These are not the only kind of decisions that managers take.
(B) As a seller, he has to decide what to sell.
(C) As a producer, he has to decide what to produce, how to produce, how much to produce and where to produce.
(D) As a buyer, he has to decide what to buy.

6. They generally face a wide range of situations involving choice.

(a) ABCE (b) DCBA
(c) CDAB (d) BDAC

Q22.

1. Operating a small motel, I tried to avoid answering the doorbell before 6:30 a.m.
   (A) One morning at about five o'clock, the doorbell rang.
   (B) So I had a box put up next to the door and placed a sign on it saying, Deposit keys here.
   (C) But some guests continued to summon me as early as 4:30 a.m.
   (D) Customers were told to leave their keys in the rooms when checking out.
6. When I opened the office door, a smiling guest greeted me with: I just wanted you to know, I put my key in the box.
   (a) DCBA (b) DACD
   (c) BADC (d) ABDC

Directions for the questions (23-27): Sentences given in each question, when properly sequenced, form a coherent paragraph. Each sentence is labeled with a letter: Choose the most logical order of sentences from among the four given to construct a coherent paragraph.

Q23. (A) Widely publicized tables of income levels of all countries indicate that when incomes are higher, the greater is the contribution made by the manufacturing industry.
(B) Countries which have little or no industry are almost invariably poor.
(C) The lesson is clear: to overcome poverty and backwardness, a country must industrialize.
(D) Industrialization is seen as the key to growth and a prerequisite for development.
(a) CBAD (b) DCBA
(c) DABC (d) CABD

Q24. (A) A wife may not be sure that what her husband is saying means the end.
(B) She has found that people's voices often get higher or shriller when they lie, and they are more likely to stumble over words.
(C) According to De Paulo, changes in voice can be significant.
(D) She should listen closely, not only to what he says, but how he says it.
(a) ADCB (b) ACDB
(c) ADBC (d) ABCD

Q25. (A) He pulled popcorn dipped in ketchup out of her mouth with a pair of pliers.
(B) Soon Steven was making horror pictures, using his sisters as victims.
(C) A few years later, Steven borrowed his dad's eight-millimeter movie camera to film 'The Last Train Wreck' using his own electric train set.
(D) In one, he played a dentist, with his sister Ann as the patient.
(a) CBAD (b) DACB
(c) DABC (d) CBDA

Q26. (A) In bulk processing, a set of standard prices typically emerge.
(B) Competing therefore means keeping products flowing, trying to improve quality, getting costs down.
(C) Let us look at the two cultures of competition.
(D) Production tends to be repetitive–much the same from day to day or even from year to year.
(a) CDBA (b) ABDC
(c) CADB (d) DCBA

Q27. (A) A moment later, my prospective fiancée reappeared and shoved a ticket to Jiuquan through the hatch.
(B) The queue gazed at me dumbstruck, then broke into a little ripple of applause.
(C) The station master and clerk retreated into the back room.
(D) I lifted it like a trophy.
(a) CABD (b) ACDB
(c) ACBD (d) CADB

CAT 1997

Directions for the questions (28-30): Arrange the sentences A, B, C and D to form a logical sequence between sentences 1 and 6.

Q28.

1. So now, let's sum it up.
   (A) We can call this the material of knowledge.
   (B) According to Kant, there are two elements that contribute to man's knowledge of the world.
   (C) The other is the internal conditions in man himself.
   (D) One is the external conditions that we cannot know of before we have perceived them through the sense.
6. We can call this the form of knowledge.
   (a) BDAC (b) BADC
   (c) CADB (d) CBDA

Q29.

1. I may have a strong desire for a fresh ripe peach, but no peaches may be available.
   (A) I am about to take a bite when news arrives of an accident injuring someone dear to me.
   (B) The hay fever passes.
   (C) On the other hand, I buy some peaches but a sudden attack of hay fever prevents me from enjoying their fragrance or taste.
   (D) My interest in the peach vanishes.
6. I no longer have any appetite.
   (a) DCBA (b) CBAD
   (c) ABCD (d) ACBD

Q30.

1. A nation, like an individual, has many personalities and many approaches to life.
   (A) If there is a strong organic bond between different personalities, it is well.
   (B) Otherwise, this could lead to disintegration and trouble.
   (C) Normally, some kind of equilibrium is eventually established.
   (D) If normal development is arrested, then conflict arises between different personalities.
6. In the mind and spirit of India, there has been this fundamental conflict due to a long period of arrested growth.
   (a) ABCD (b) BDCA
   (c) CABD (d) DBCA

Directions for the questions (31-33): Sentences given in each question, when properly sequenced, form a coherent paragraph. Each sentence is labeled with a letter. Choose the most logical order of sentences from among the four given choices to construct a coherent paragraph.

Q31. (A) Because negotiations had been delayed until the last moment, he was at a tremendous disadvantage.
(B) Only then did the truth dawn on him.
(C) He broke off talks and returned home.
(D) My friend was under intense pressure to make concessions.
(a) DBAC (b) ACBD
(c) ABCD (d) DBCA

Q32. (A) "Son, why are you reading that sissy magazine?" he asked.
(B) "There's an article that tells women where to meet men," I responded; pointing to the magazine's cover.
(C) "I need to know where I'm supposed to be."
(D) When I was a teenager, my father caught me reading one of my older sister's magazines.
(a) DCAB (b) ADCB
(c) DABC (d) DACB

Q33. (A) "Actually," Ronnie replied, "I asked my wife."
(B) One day, a man named Ronnie answered a difficult one correctly to put the men in front.
(C) Impressed, the host kept Ronnie on the line and asked how he knew the answer to such a tough question.
(D) Occasionally, a local radio station airs "Battle of the Sexes," in which listeners phone in to answer trivial questions.
(a) BCAD (b) ACDB
(c) CABD (d) DBCA

CAT 1998

Directions for the questions (34-36): Arrange the sentences A, B, C and D to form a logical sequence between sentences 1 and 6.

Q34.

1. Why are horses the same?
   (A) It may be old and lame, and in time, it will die.
   (B) A particular horse 'flows', naturally.
   (C) But there is something all horses have in common.
   (D) You probably don't think they are at all.
6. But the 'form' of the horse is eternal and immutable.
   (a) DCAB (b) CABD
   (c) CBDA (d) DCBA

Q35.

1. Buddhism is a way to salvation.
   (A) But Buddhism is more severely analytical.
   (B) In the Christian tradition, there is also a concern for the fate of human society conceived as a whole, rather than merely as a sum or network of individuals.
   (C) Salvation is a property, or achievement, of individuals.
   (D) Not only does it dissolve society into individuals; the individual in turn is dissolved into component parts and instants, a stream of events.
6. In modern terminology, Buddhist doctrine is reductionism.
   (a) BCAD (b) ADBC
   (c) CBAD (d) CDAB

Q36.

1. Matrilineal systems of land inheritance advantaged women in many respects, especially in granting them economic and social security.
   (A) Women, in particular; were profoundly affected by these changes.

(B) The large joint family estates came to be partitioned; there was an increasing penetration of market forces and patriarchal ideologies spread in influence.

(C) These systems, however, did not remain fixed over time.

(D) Interventions by the colonial and post-colonial states, and the processes of social change which these set in motion, eroded customary practices.

6. At the same time, their customary exclusion from major authority in public bodies meant that they were unlikely to be the ones directing the changes.

(a) BDCA (b) CDBA
(c) CDAB (d) CADB

Directions for the questions (37-39): Sentences given in each question, when properly sequenced, form a coherent paragraph, Each sentence is labeled with a letter. Choose the most logical order of sentences from among the four given choices to construct a coherent paragraph.

Q37. (A) However, the real challenge today is unlearning, which is much harder.

(B) But the new world of business behaves differently from the world in which we grew up.

(C) Learning is important for both people and organizations.

(D) Each of us has a 'mental model' that we've used over the years to make sense.

(a) DBCA (b) CADB
(c) DACB (d) CBDA

Q38. (A) A large number of intellectuals believe that the North is using its military and economic powers to force unequal contracts on the South.

(B) The make-believe ethical issue of the sanctity of law camouflages the unethicality of the entire transaction, which is a travesty of the ethical concept of the greatest good for the greatest number.

(C) Once these contracts are made, the North uses the façade of legality and ethics to pin down the South.

(D) Thus, it suffers from the flaw that the law–one of the useful means to implement ethics–has fouled the ethicality of the ends.

(a) DACB (b) CBDA
(c) ACBD (d) BDAC

Q39. (A) The fact that he could find absolutely nothing to substantiate their wild claims made no difference.

(B) We always gave the poor man a cup of tea, and he grew quite fond of some of the animals.

(C) The neighbors, now thoroughly indignant, kept bombarding the local health authorities.

(D) On an average, twice a week, the poor inspector was forced to come up to the house.

(a) DBAC (b) CDAB
(c) ADBC (d) CADB

CAT 1999

Directions for the questions (40-44): Sentences given in each question, when properly sequenced, form a coherent paragraph. Each sentence is labeled with a letter. Choose the most logical order of sentences from among the four given choices to construct a coherent paragraph.

Q40. (A) In rejecting the functionalism in positivist organization theory, either wholly or partially, there is often a move towards a political model of organization theory.

(B) Thus the analysis would shift to the power resources possessed by different groups in the organization and the way they use these resources in actual power plays to shape the organizational structure.

(C) At the extreme, in one set of writings, the growth of administrators in the organization is held to be completely unrelated to the work to be done and to be caused totally by the political pursuit of self-interest.

(D) The political model holds that individual interests are pursued in organizational life through the exercise of power and influence.

(a) ADBC (b) CBAD
(c) DBCA (d) ABDC

Q41. (A) Group decision making, however, does not necessarily fully guard against arbitrariness and anarchy, for individual capriciousness can get substituted by collusion of group members.

(B) Nature itself is an intricate system of checks and balances, meant to preserve the delicate balance between various environmental factors that affect our ecology.

(C) In institutions also, there is a need to have in place a system of checks and balances which inhibits the concentration of power in only some individuals.

(D) When human interventions alter this delicate balance, the outcome have been seen to be disastrous.

(a) CDAB (b) BCAD
(c) CABD (d) BDCA

Q42. (A) He was bone-weary and soul-weary, and found himself muttering, "either I can't manage this place, or it's unmanageable".

(B) To his horror; he realized that he had become the victim of an amorphous, unwitting, unconscious conspiracy to immerse him in routine work that had no significance.

(C) It was one of those nights in the office when the office clock was moving towards four in the morning and Bennis was still not through with the incredible mass of paper stacked before him.

(D) He reached for his calendar and ran his eyes down each hour, half-hour, and quarter hour, to see where his time had gone that day, the day before, the month before.

(a) ABCD (b) CADB
(c) BDCA (d) DCBA

Q43. (A) With that I swallowed the shampoo, and obtained most realistic results almost on the spot.

(B) The man shuffled away into the back regions to make up a prescription, and after a moment, I got through on the shop-telephone to the Consulate, intimating my location.

(C) Then, while the pharmacist was wrapping up a six-ounce bottle of the mixture, I groaned and inquired whether he could give me something for acute gastric cramp.

(D) I intended to stage a sharp gastric attack, and entering an old-fashioned pharmacy, I asked for a popular shampoo mixture, consisting of olive oil and flaked soap.

(a) DCBA (b) DACB
(c) BDAC (d) BCDA

Q44. (A) Since then, intelligence tests have been mostly used to separate dull children in school from average or bright children, so that special education can be provided to the dull.

(B) In other words, intelligence tests give us a norm for each age.

(C) Intelligence is expressed as intelligence quotient, and tests are developed to indicate what an average child of a certain age can do–what a 5-year-old can answer, but a 4-year-old cannot, for instance.

(D) Binet developed the first set of such tests in the early 1900s to find out which children in school needed special attention.

(E) Intelligence can be measured by tests.

(a) CDABE (b) DECAB
(c) EDACB (d) CBADE

Directions for the questions (45-49): Sentences given in each question, when properly sequenced, form a coherent paragraph. The first and last sentences are 1 and 6, and the four in between are labeled A,B, C and D. Choose the most logical order of these four sentences from among the four given choices to construct a coherent paragraph from sentences 1 to 6.

Q45.

1. Security inks exploit the same principle that causes the vivid and constantly changing colours of a film of oil on water.

(A) When two rays of light meet each other after being reflected from these different surfaces, they have each traveled slightly different distances.

(B) The key is that the light is bouncing off two surfaces, that of the oil and that of the water layer below it.

(C) The distance the two rays travel determines which wavelengths, and hence colours, interface constructively and look bright.

(D) Because light is an electromagnetic wave, the peaks and troughs of each ray then interface either constructively, to appear bright, or destructively, to appear dim.

6. Since the distance the rays travel changes with the angle as you look at the surface, different colours look bright from different viewing angles.

(a) ABCD (b) BADC
(c) BDAC (d) DCAB

Q46.

1. Commercially reared chicken can be unusually aggressive, and are often kept in darkened sheds to prevent them pecking at each other:

(A) The birds spent far more of their time–up to a third–pecking at the inanimate objects in the pens, in contrast to birds in other pens which spent a lot of time attacking others.

(B) In low light conditions, they behave less belligerently, but are more prone to ophthalmic disorders and respiratory problems.

(C) In an experiment, aggressive head pecking was all but eliminated among birds in the enriched environment.

(D) Altering the bird's environment, by adding bales of wood–shavings to their pens, can work wonders.

6. Bales could diminish aggressiveness and reduce .injuries; they might even improve productivity, since a happy chicken is a productive chicken.

(a) DCAB (b) CDBA
(c) DBAC (d) BDCA

Q47.

1. The concept of a 'nation-state' assumes a complete correspondence between the boundaries of the

nation and the boundaries of those who live in a specific state.

(A) Then there are members of national collectivities who live in other countries, making a mockery of the concept.

(B) There are always people living in particular states who are not considered to be (and often do not consider themselves to be) members of the hegemonic nation.

(C) Even worse, there are nations which never had a state or which are divided across several states.

(D) This, of course, has been subject to severe criticism and is virtually everywhere, a fiction.

6. However, the nation has been, and continues to be, at the basis of nationalist ideologies.

(a) DBAC (b) ABCD
(c) BACD (d) DACB

Q48.

1. In the sciences, even questionable examples of research fraud are harshly punished.

(A) But no such mechanism exists in the humanities– much of what humanities researchers call research does not lead to results that are replicable by other scholars.

(B) Given the importance of interpretation in historical and literary scholarship, humanities researchers are in a position where they can explain away deliberate and even systematic distortion.

(C) Mere suspicion is enough for funding to be cut off, publicity guarantees that careers can be effectively ended.

(D) Forgeries, which take the form of practices in which the forger intersperses fake and real parts can be defended as mere mistakes or aberrant misreading.

6. Scientists fudging data have no such defenses.

(a) BDCA (b) ABDC
(c) CABD (d) CDBA

Q49.

1. Horses and communism were, on the whole, a poor match.

(A) Fine horses bespoke the nobility the party was supposed to despise.

(B) Communist leaders, when they visited villages, preferred to see cows and pigs.

(C) Although a working horse was just about tolerable, the communists were right to be wary.

(D) Peasants from Poland to the Hungarian Pustza preferred their horses to party dogma.

6. 'A farmer's pride is his horse, his cow may be thin but his horse must be fat,' went a Slovak saying.

(a) ACDB (b) DBCA
(c) ABCD (d) DCBA

Directions for the questions (50-54): The sentences given in each question, when properly sequenced, form a coherent paragraph. Each sentence is labeled with a letter. Choose the most logical order of sentences from among the four given choices to construct a coherent paragraph.

Q50. (A) If caught in the act, they were punished, not for the crime, but for allowing themselves to be caught, with another lash of the whip.

(B) The bellicose Spartans sacrificed all the finer things in life for military expertise.

(C) Those fortunate enough to survive babyhood were taken away from their mothers at the age of seven to undergo rigorous military training.

(D) This consisted mainly of beatings and deprivation of all kinds like going around barefoot in winter, and worse, starvation so that they would be forced to steal food to survive.

(E) Male children were examined at birth by the city council and those deemed too weak to become soldiers were left to die of exposure.

(a) BECDA (b) ECADB
(c) BCDAE (d) ECDAB

Q51. (A) This very insatiability of the photographing eye changes the terms of confinement in the cave, our world.

(B) Humankind lingers unregenerately in Plato's cave, still reveling, its age-old habit, in mere images of truth.

(C) But being educated by photographs is not like being educated by older images drawn by hand; for one thing, there are a great many more images around, claiming our attention.

(D) The inventory started in 1839 and since then, just about everything has been photographed, or so it seems.

(E) In teaching us a new visual code, photographs alter and enlarge our notions of what is worth looking at and what we have a right to observe.

(a) EABCE (b) BDEAC
(c) BCDAE (d) ECDAB

Q52. (A) To be culturally literate is to possess the basic information needed to thrive in the modern world.

(B) Nor is it confined to one social class; quite the contrary.

(C) It is by no means confined to "culture", narrowly understood as an acquaintance with the arts.

(D) Cultural literacy constitutes the only sure avenue of opportunity for disadvantaged children, the only reliable way of combating the social determinism that now condemns them.

(E) The breadth of that information is great, extending over the major domains of human activity from sports to science.

(a) AECBD (b) DECBA
(c) ACBED (d) DBCAE

Q53. (A) Both parties use capital and labour in the struggle to secure property rights.

(B) The thief spends time and money in his attempt to steal (he buys wire cutters) and the legitimate property owner expends resources to prevent the theft (he buys locks).

(C) A social cost of theft is that both the thief and the potential victim use resources to gain or maintain control over property.

(D) These costs may escalate as a type of technological arms race unfolds.

(E) A bank may purchase more and more complicated and sophisticated safes, forcing safecrackers to invest further in safecracking equipment.

(a) ABCDE (b) CABDE
(c) ACBED (d) CBEDA

Q54. (A) The likelihood of an accident is determined by how carefully the motorist drives and how carefully the pedestrian crosses the street.

(B) An accident involving a motorist and a pedestrian is such a case.

(C) Each must decide how much care to exercise without knowing how careful the other is.

(D) The simplest strategic problem arises when two individuals interact with each other and each must decide what to do without knowing what the other is doing.

(a) ABCD (b) ADCB
(c) DBCA (d) DBAC

CAT 2000

Directions for the questions (55–59): Arrange sentences A, B, C and D to form a logical sequence between sentences 1 to 6.

Q55.

1. Making people laugh is tricky.

(A) At times, the intended humour may simply not come off.

(B) Making people laugh while trying to sell them something is a tougher challenge, since the commercial can fall flat on two grounds.

(C) There are many advertisements which do amuse, but do not even begin to set the cash tills ringing.

(D) Again, it is rarely sufficient for an advertiser simply to amuse the target audience in order to reap the sales benefit.

6. There are indications that in substituting the hard sell for a more entertaining approach, some agencies have rather thrown out the baby with the bath water.

(a) CDBA (b) ABCD
(c) BADC (d) DCBA

Q56.

1. Picture a termite colony, occupying a tall mud hump on an African Plain.

(A) Hungry predators often invade the colony and unsettle the balance.

(B) The colony flourishes only if the proportion of soldiers to workers remains roughly the same, so that the queen and workers can be protected by the soldiers, and the queen and soldiers can be serviced by the workers.

(C) But its fortunes are presently restored, because the immobile queen, walled in well below ground level, lays eggs not only in large enough numbers, but also in the varying proportions required.

(D) The hump is alive with worker termites and soldier termites going about their distinct kinds of business.

6. How can we account for her mysterious ability to respond like this to events on the distant surface?

(a) BADC (b) DBAC
(c) ADCB (d) BDCA

Q57.

1. According to recent research, the critical period of developing language skills is between the ages of three and five and a half years.

(A) The read-to child already has a large vocabulary and a sense of grammar and sentence structure.

(B) Children who are read to in these years have a far better chance of reading well in school, indeed, of doing well in all their subjects.

(C) And the reason is actually quite simple.

(D) This correlation is far and away the highest yet found between home influences and school success.

6. Her comprehension of language is therefore very high.

(a) DACB (b) ADCB
(c) ABCD (d) BDCA

Q58.

1. High-powered outboard motors were considered to be one of the major threats to the survival of the Beluga whales.

(A) With these, hunters could approach Belugas within hunting range and profit from its inner skin and blubber.

(B) To escape an approaching motor, Belugas have learned to dive to the ocean bottom and stay there for up to 20 minutes, by which time the confused predator has left.

(C) Today, however; even with much powerful engines, it is difficult to come close, because the whales seem to disappear suddenly just when you thought you had them in your sights.

(D) When the first outboard engines arrived in the early 1930s, one came across 4 and 8HP motors.

6. Belugas seem to have used their well-known sensitivity to noise to evolve an 'avoidance' strategy to outsmart hunters and their powerful technologies,

(a) DACB (b) CDAB
(c) ADBC (d) BDAC

Q59.

1. The reconstruction of history by post-revolutionary science texts involves more than a multiplication of historical misconstructions.

(A) Because they aim quickly to acquaint the student with what the contemporary scientific community thinks it knows, textbooks treat the various experiments, concepts, law and theories of the current normal science as separately and as nearly seriatim as possible.

(B) Those misconstructions render revolutions invisible; the arrangement of the still visible material in science texts implies a process that, if it existed, would deny revolutions a function.

(C) But when combined with the generally unhistorical air of science writing and with the occasional systematic misconstruction, one impression is likely to follow.

(D) As pedagogy, this technique of presentation is unexceptionable.

6. Science has reached its present state by a series of individual discoveries and inventions that, when gathered together, constitute the modern body of technical knowledge.

(a) BADC (b) ADCB
(c) DACB (d) CBDA

CAT 2001

Directions for the questions (60-64): The sentences given in each question, when properly sequenced, form a coherent paragraph. Each sentence is labelled with a letter: Choose the most logical order of sentences from among the given choices to construct a coherent paragraph.

Q60. (A) Although there are large regional variations, it is not infrequent to find a large number of people sitting here and there and doing nothing.

(B) Once in office, they receive friends and relatives who feel free to call any time without prior appointment.

(C) While working, one is struck by the slow and clumsy actions and reactions, indifferent attitudes, procedure rather than outcome orientation, and the lack of consideration for others.

(D) Even those who are employed often come late to the office and leave early, unless they are forced to be punctual.

(E) Work is not intrinsically valued in India.

(F) Quite often, people visit ailing friends and relatives or go out of their way to help them in their personal matters even during office hours.

(a) ECADBF (b) EADCFB
(c) EADBFC (d) ABFCBE

Q61. (A) But in the industrial era, destroying the enemy's productive capacity means bombing the factories which are located in the cities.

(B) So in the agrarian era, if you need to destroy the enemy's productive capacity, what you want to do is burn his fields, or if you're really vicious, salt them.

(C) Now in the information era, destroying the enemy's productive capacity means destroying the information infrastructure.

(D) How do you do battle with your enemy?

(E) The idea is to destroy the enemy's productive capacity, and depending upon the economic foundation, that productive capacity is different in each case.

(F) With regard to defence, the purpose of the military is to defend the nation and be prepared to do battle with its enemy.

(a) FDEBAC (b) FCABED
(c) DEBACF (d) DFEBAC

Q62. (A) Michael Hofman, a poet and translator, accepts this sorry fact without approval or complaint.

(B) But thanklessness and impossibility do not daunt him.

(C) He acknowledges too–in fact he returns to the point often that best translators of poetry always fail at some level.

(D) Hofman feels passionately about his work, and this is clear from his writings.

(E) In terms of the gap between worth and rewards, translators come somewhere near nurses and street-cleaners.

(a) EACDB (b) ADEBC
(c) EACBD (d) DCEAB

Q63. (A) Passivity is not, of course, universal.
(B) In areas where there are no lords or laws, or in frontier zones where all men go armed, the attitude of the peasantry may well be different.
(C) So indeed, it may be on the fringe of the unsubmissive.
(D) However, for most of the soil-bound peasants, the problem is not whether to be normally passive or active, but when to pass from one state to another.
(E) This depends on an assessment of the political situation.
(a) BEDAC (b) CDABE
(c) EDBAC (d) ABCDE

Q64. (A) The situations in which violence occurs and the nature of that violence tends to be clearly defined at least in theory, as in the proverbial Irishman's question: "Is this a private fight or can anyone join in?"
(B) So the actual risk to outsiders, though no doubt higher than our societies, is calculable.
(C) Probably the only uncontrolled applications of force are those of social superiors to social inferiors and even here, there are probably some rules.
(D) However, binding the obligation to kill, members of feuding families engaged in mutual massacre will be genuinely appalled if by some mischance, a bystander or outsider is killed.
(a) DABC (b) ACDB
(c) CBAD (d) DBAC

CAT 2003

Directions for the questions (65-72): The sentences given in each question, when properly sequenced, form a coherent paragraph. Each sentence is labelled with a letter. Choose the most logical order of sentences from among the given choices to construct a coherent paragraph.

Q65. (A) The wall does not simply divide Israel from a putative Palestinian state on the basis of the 1967 borders.
(B) A chilling omission from the road map is the gigantic 'separation wall' now being built in the West Bank by Israel.
(C) It is surrounded by trenches, electric wire and moats; there are watchtowers at regular intervals.
(D) It actually takes in new tracts of Palestinian land, sometimes five or six kilometers at a stretch.
(E) Almost a decade after the end of South African apartheid, this ghastly racist wall is going up with scarcely a peep from Israel's American allies, who are going to pay for most of it.
(a) EBCAD (b) BADCE
(c) AEDCB (d) ECADB

Q66. (A) Luckily, the tide of battle moved elsewhere after the American victory at Midway and an Australian victory over Japan at Milne Bay.
(B) It could have been no more than a delaying tactic.
(C) The Australian military, knowing the position was hopeless, planned to fall back to the south-east in the hope of defending the main cities.
(D) They had captured most of the Solomon Islands and much of New Guinea, and seemed poised for an invasion.
(E) Not many people outside Australia realize how close the Japanese got.
(a) EDCBA (b) ECDAB
(c) ADCBE (d) CDBAE

Q67. (A) Call it the third wave sweeping the Indian media.
(B) Now, they are starring in a new role, as suave dealmakers who are in a hurry to strike alliances and agreements.
(C) Look around and you will find a host of deals that have been inked or are ready to be finalized.
(D) Then the media barons wrested back control from their editors, and turned marketing warriors with the brand as their missile.
(E) The first came with those magnificent men in their mahogany chambers who took on the world with their mighty fountain pens.
(a) ACBED (b) CEBDA
(c) CAEBD (d) AEDBC

Q68. (A) The celebrations of economic recovery in Washington may be as premature as that "Mission Accomplished" banner hung on the USS Abraham Lincoln to hail the end of the Iraq war.
(B) Meanwhile, in the real world, the struggles of families and communities continue unabated.
(C) Washington responded to the favorable turn in economic news with enthusiasm.
(D) The celebrations and high-fives up and down Pennsylvania Avenue are not to be found beyond the Beltway.
(E) When the third quarter GDP showed growth of 7.2 per cent and the monthly unemployment rate dipped to 6 per cent, euphoria gripped the US capital.
(a) ACEDB (b) CEDAB
(c) ECABD (d) ECBDA

Q69. (A) To much of the Labour movement, it symbolises the brutality of the upper classes.

(B) And to everybody watching, the current mess over fox hunting symbolises the government's weakness.

(C) To fox hunting's supporters, Labour's 1991 manifesto commitment to ban it, symbolises the party's metropolitan roots and hostility to the countryside.

(D) Small issues sometimes have large symbolic power.

(E) To those who enjoy thundering across the countryside in red coats after foxes, foxhunting symbolises the ancient roots of rural lives.

(a) DEACB (b) ECDBA
(c) CEADB (d) DBAEC

Q70. (A) In the case of King Merolchazzar's courtship of the Princess of the Outer Isles, there occurs a regrettable hitch.

(B) She acknowledges the gifts, but no word of a meeting date follows.

(C) The monarch, hearing good reports of a neighbouring princess, dispatches messengers with gifts to her court, beseeching an interview.

(D) The princess names a date, and a formal meeting takes place; after that everything buzzes along pretty smoothly.

(E) Royal love affairs in olden days were conducted on the correspondence method.

(a) ACBDE (b) ABCDE
(c) ECDAB (d) ECBAD

Q71. (A) Who can trace to its first beginnings, the love of Damon for Pythias, of David for Jonathan, of Swan for Edgar?

(B) Similarly with men.

(C) There is about great friendships between man and man a certain inevitability that can only be compared with the age-old association of ham and eggs.

(D) One simply feels that it is one of the things that must be so.

(E) No one can say what was the mutual magnetism that brought the deathless partnership of these wholesome and palatable foodstuffs about.

(a) ACBED (b) CEDBA
(c) ACEBD (d) CEABD

Q72. (A) Events intervened, and in the late 1930s and 1940s, Germany suffered from "over-branding".

(B) The British used to be fascinated by the home of Romanticism.

(C) But reunification and the federal government's move to Berlin have prompted Germany to think again about its image.

(D) The first foreign package holiday was a tour of Germany organized by Thomas Cook in 1855.

(E) Since then, Germany has been understandably nervous about promoting itself abroad.

(a) ACEBD (b) DECAB
(c) BDAEC (d) DBAEC

CAT 2004

Directions for the questions (73-77): The sentences given in each question, when properly sequenced, form a coherent paragraph. Each sentence is labeled with a letter. Choose the most logical order of sentences from among the given choices to construct a coherent paragraph.

Q73. (A) He felt justified in bypassing Congress altogether, on a variety of moves.

(B) At times, he was fighting the entire Congress.

(C) Bush felt he had a mission to restore power to the presidency.

(D) Bush was not fighting just the democrats.

(E) Representative democracy is a messy business, and a CEO of the White House does not like a legislature of second guessers and time wasters.

(a) CAEDB (b) DBAEC
(c) CEADB (d) ECDBA

Q74. (A) The two neighbours never fought each other.

(B) Fights involving three male fiddler crabs have been recorded, but the status of the participants was unknown.

(C) They pushed or grappled only with the intruder.

(D) We recorded 17 cases in which a resident that was fighting an intruder, was joined by an immediate neighbour, an ally.

(E) We therefore tracked 268 intruder males until we saw them fighting a resident male.

(a) BEDAC (b) DEBAC
(c) BDCAE (d) BCEDA

Q75. (A) In the west, Allied Forces had fought their way through southern Italy as far as Rome.

(B) In June 1944, Germany's military position in World War Two appeared hopeless.

(C) In Britain, the task of amassing the men and materials for the liberation of northern Europe had been completed.

(D) The Red Army was poised to drive the Nazis back through Poland.

(E) The situation on the eastern front was catastrophic.

(a) EDACB (b) BEDAC
(c) BDECA (d) CEDAB

Q76. (A) But this does not mean that death was the Egyptians' only preoccupation.

(B) Even papyri come mainly from pyramid temples.

(C) Most of our traditional sources of information about the Old Kingdom are monuments of the rich like pyramids and tombs.

(D) Houses in which ordinary Egyptians lived have not been preserved, and when most people died, they were buried in simple graves.

(E) We know infinitely more about the wealthy people of Egypt than we do about the ordinary people, as most monuments were made for the rich.

(a) CDBEA (b) ECDAB
(c) EDCBA (d) DECAB

Q77. (A) Experts such as Larry Burns, head of research at GM, reckon that only such a full hearted leap will allow the world to cope with the mass motorisation that will one day come to China or India.

(B) But once hydrogen is being produced from biomass or extracted from underground coal or made from water, using nuclear or renewable electricity, the way will be open for a huge reduction in carbon emissions from the whole system.

(C) In theory, once all the bugs have been sorted out, fuel cells should deliver better total fuel economy than any existing engines.

(D) That is twice as good as the internal combustion engine, but only five percentage points better than a diesel hybrid.

(E) Allowing for the resources needed to extract hydrogen from hydrocarbon, oil, coal or gas, the fuel cell has an efficiency of 30 per cent.

(a) CEDBA (b) CEBDA
(c) AEDBC (d) ACEBD

Answer Key

CAT 1994

1. (c)	**2.** (a)	**3.** (d)	**4.** (b)	**5.** (a)
6. (b)	**7.** (a)	**8.** (d)	**9.** (a)	**10.** (c)
11. (c)	**12.** (d)	**13.** (d)	**14.** (a)	

CAT 1995

15. (c)	**16.** (d)	**17.** (b)	**18.** (c)	**19.** (d)

CAT 1996

20. (a)	**21.** (b)	**22.** (a)	**23.** (c)	**24.** (a)
25. (d)	**26.** (c)	**27.** (c)		

CAT 1997

28. (a)	**29.** (d)	**30.** (a)	**31.** (b)	**32.** (d)
33. (d)				

CAT 1998

34. (d)	**35.** (c)	**36.** (b)	**37.** (a)	**38.** (c)
39. (b)				

CAT 1999

40. (a)	**41.** (d)	**42.** (b)	**43.** (a)	**44.** (c)
45. (b)	**46.** (d)	**47.** (a)	**48.** (c)	**49.** (c)
50. (a)	**51.** (c)	**52.** (a)	**53.** (b)	**54.** (d)

CAT 2000

55. (c)	**56.** (b)	**57.** (d)	**58.** (a)	**59.** (a)

CAT 2001

60. (c)	**61.** (a)	**62.** (c)	**63.** (d)	**64.** (b)

CAT 2003

65. (b)	**66.** (a)	**67.** (d)	**68.** (d)	**69.** (a)
70. (c)	**71.** (b)	**72.** (c)		

CAT 2004

73. (d)	**74.** (a)	**75.** (b)	**76.** (c)	**77.** (a)

SECTION 5: Sentence Correction

This section will help you in the following ways:

- In the chapter on **'Sentence Correction'**, you would learn what the common grammatical errors are on the basis of which sentence correction questions are framed, as also how to identify these errors. You would also familiarise yourself with the various question types in the exam. This question type is always present in CAT and all other management entrance exams and hence becomes extremely relevant.

CHAPTER 20 Sentence Correction

INTRODUCTION

Questions based on standard written English grammar are very common in the CAT, XAT and most other management entrance examinations. These questions are designed to test your ability to identify written English that is grammatically correct. They also test your ability to understand the essential message being given–and find out the most concise and grammatically correct way of conveying the same.

An analysis of previous papers of various institutes yields that there have been four patterns under which these questions can be segregated. These are:

SENTENCE CORRECTION: QUESTION PATTERN

QUESTION TYPE 1

Each question will begin with sentences, parts of which have been underlined. You are then presented with 4 different options presenting alternative ways of stating the underlined portion of the text. The first answer choice will repeat the text without any changes (meaning that the sentence is clear in meaning, concise as well as grammatically correct as it is written originally).

The other choices will re-write the text. Wrong options are created by any one or more of the following methods:

(1) Introduction of grammatical mistakes. These are explained in greater detail in the later part of this chapter.

(2) By introducing an incorrect sentence structure.

(3) Introducing changes in the message to the reader by changing the intended meaning of the sentence.

(4) Introducing verbosity in the sentence–i.e., writing the same thing in more number of words.

This, however, does not mean that the shortest and most concise answer choice is always the correct answer–but it does mean that if there are no errors (grammatical, sentence structural or in message conveyance) in the option which is the shortest, it is the answer more often than not. Hence, before succumbing to the temptation of marking the shortest option as the correct answer choice, you need to read it carefully in order to make sure that the sentence has no error.

QUESTION TYPE 2

This question type is very similar to Type 1. The only difference between the two is that in this type, the entire sentence has to be tested for its grammar and accuracy.

There is no underlined part of the sentence. Incorrect answer choices are formed on the basis of the same errors as discussed above.

In the context of the above two question types, it is important to note the following:

Do not Waste Time on a Close Reading of Option A. Option A always simply repeats the wording of the original sentence/underlined part of the sentence. Hence, reading it closely again right at the start might entail a waste of time.

However, you should remember that before you mark the correct answer choice, if Option A figures in your shortlist, you should read it closely. This you need to do since you will need to make a comparison between all the options on your shortlist for their correctness of grammar, sentence structure and the lack of verbosity.

On the other hand, if the original sentence looks incorrect straightaway, you will not need to read Option A at all.

Look Out for Multiple Errors in the Sentence: A sentence might contain more than one error. Hence, while reading the original sentence, do not be led into the fallacy that if you have found one error in the sentence, all you will need to do is eliminate it in order to get the correct answer. This is a common error that students make, i.e., they find one error and then quickly choose the answer that corrects that error. They fail to consider whether there are other errors in the sentence that an alternative answer choice might also address.

The correct answer must correct *all* the errors contained in the original sentence.

Question Type 3

This question type consists of 4 sentences, out of which you have to identify the correct sentence/s.

Question Type 4

In this question type, you are given 4 sentences, out of which you are supposed to identify the incorrect sentence/s.

Question Type 5

This question type consists of correct/incorrect usage of words/phrases. It consists of a capitalised word or phrase which is used in four different ways. You have to find out the incorrect usage of the word in the four sentences.

STANDARD SOLVING PROCESS

Elimination Employ the process of elimination. Eliminate any answer choices that are obviously grammatically incorrect. Besides, you can also eliminate any choices that alter the intended meaning of the sentence.

Your first objective should be to come down to a short list of sentences which is as small as possible.

If you are still unsure about how to answer a question even after narrowing your choices down to two, you will fare better by selecting the more concise of the remaining answer choices.

Small/Minute Differences When in doubt, look for small/minute differences among the different answer choices. After you create a short list of options that are not easily eliminated, you will need to examine each of the remaining options closely. Very often, the difference between two of the answer choices will be in a single word/phrase usage. Use your 'feel' for standard usage of these words in the English language.

Spelling Errors Do not worry about spelling or capitalisation errors. Questions do not test you for these two types of errors.

Trust your Ears If you become stuck, 'say' the choices in your head and then select the sentence that sounds best to your ears. This method will be particularly useful if you have a natural feel for the language. If you are used to English, you will have internalised many more grammar rules than you can explicitly identify.

Look for standard errors listed below while reading the question and its options.

IMPORTANT TIPS FOR GRAMMAR AND SENTENCE CORRECTION

There are many grammatical errors that can be made while speaking or writing.

The CAT has a question type called Sentence Correction which tests your ability to spot errors.

To excel in this question type you have to be well versed in the kind of errors that are most common, so that those can be noticed easily while solving this question type.

Let us look at some errors commonly made or the common confusions which lead us to make errors:

1. Countable and Uncountable Nouns: A countable noun has both a singular and a plural form. Countable nouns are the opposite of non-countable nouns and collective nouns.

A non-countable noun does not have a plural form and is similar to a collective noun and it always takes the singular verb in the sentence.

Example:

1. We decided to sell the furniture [non-countable] of the house as it was damaged.
2. Fans (countable) and tubes (countable) are not counted as furniture [non-countable].

Examples of countable nouns: Apple, fruits, river, mountains, boy, girl, humans, animals, etc.

Examples of non-countable nouns: music, art, love, happiness, advice, information, news, electricity, gas, power, money, currency, furniture, luggage, rice, sugar, butter, water, etc.

Exceptions: some nouns can be used as both countable and non-countable nouns, like hair, light and room.

Example: I have few hairs [countable] on my head.

My hair [non-countable] looks unmanageable.

2. Possessive Nouns: When we want to show that something belongs to somebody or something, we usually add ('s)to a singular noun and an apostrophe to a plural noun.

For example:

1. the boy's toy (one boy)
2. the boys' toy (two or more boys)

3. Singular & Plural Pronouns: There are some pronouns which seem to be plural but act as singular, taking singular verbs. The most common of these pronouns is anybody, anything, any, each, either, everyone, everybody, nobody, not one, etc.

These kinds of pronouns must be followed by a singular verb.

Example:

i. Not one of the oranges was (not 'were') ripe.

ii. Everyone has (not 'have') written the application.

4. Comparative and Superlative Adjectives: Comparative adjectives are used when we compare two things, not three or more things. **Example:** Ravi is shorter than Arun.

Superlative adjectives are used to express the extreme or highest degree of an adjective. We use a superlative adjective to describe the extreme quality of one thing in a group of things, **Example:** Mohan is the tallest of all myfriends.

5. Prepositions: A preposition links nouns, pronouns and phrases to other words in a sentence. Some common prepositions are about, above, below, beneath, between, beyond, but, by, despite, down, during, etc.

A preposition is always followed by a 'noun'. It is never followed by a verb. A preposition cannot be followed by a verb. If we want to follow a preposition by a verb, we must use the '-ing' form which is really a gerund or verb in noun form.

Examples: The bag is on the table.

The bag is beneath the table.

The bag is leaning against the table.

The bag is beside the table.

She held the bag over the table.

She opened the bag during class.

6. Conjunctions: Conjunctions are used to link words, phrases, and clauses.

Examples: I ate the sandwich and the cake.

Co-ordinating Conjunctions: You use a co-ordinating conjunction (and, but, or, nor, for, so, yet) to join individual words, phrases, and independent clauses that are grammatically equal.

Example: Apples and oranges are both types of fruits.

A subordinating conjunction introduces a dependent clause and indicates the nature of the relationship among the independent clause(s) and the dependent clause(s). Some subordinating conjunctions are: after, although, as, because, before, how, if, once, since, than, that, though, till, until, when, where, whether, and while.

Example: After she had learnt to cook, Rani felt more confident.

7. Subject, Object and Predicate: A subject is the noun [person or thing], who/which carries out the action of the verb in the sentence. Example: the teacher was teaching the students. Here the teacher was the subject carrying out the action of teaching.

The object is the person or thing upon whom/which the action of the verb is carried out. Example: The students in the above sentence are the object on the action of the verb [teaching] was carried out.

The predicate in a sentence tells us what a person or thing does or did, or what happened to a person or thing. Thus in the above example 'is teaching' is the predicate. Many times the verb is a predicate but all verbs are not predicates and all predicates might not just be verbs. They might be something more.

8. Participles: A participle is a verbal that is used as an adjective and most often ends in -ing or -ed. It has some features of verbs and some of adjectives, but it is most basically a type of adjective. Since it functions as an adjective, participle can only modify nouns or pronouns.

Example: The crying baby had an upset stomach.

9. Punctuation: *Use colon to either introduce a list or to introduce an explanation.

*Use semicolons to connect two independent clauses.

*Never use a semicolon and a conjunction together.

10. Subject-Verb Agreement Rule: A singular verb must take a singular subject and a plural verb must take a plural subject

Example: The boys has finished the job. [incorrect]

The boys have finished the job. [correct]

11. Appositives: Appositives are nouns, pronouns, or noun phrases that are placed next to nouns to further describe them. If there are some parts of a sentence between commas, it would be correct to ignore the part between commas and read the remaining sentence as a whole.

Example: Nuclear energy, one of the best ways to generate energy through fission and fusion, are being misused by countries to make weapons. [incorrect]

Nuclear energy, one of the best ways to generate energy through fission and fusion, is being misused by countries to make weapons. [correct]

The subject here was 'nuclear energy' a singular and we could get confused by ' fission and fusion' which were plural together.

12. Additives: Ram as well as his brother Shyam is/are coming to meet us.

Here the correct usage is 'is'. [Only the word 'and' can make a subject plural, 'as well as' is not included]

These are called as additives which do not make a subject plural.

Some additives are: As well as; in addition to; along with; together with; including.

Exception:

Ex : Soups and salads is a good meal.

[Here, 'is' is correct because meal will in itself constitute a single unit.]

13. Either/or; Neither/nor:

Example:

Neither Sita, nor her friends are coming today. [correct]

Neither Sita's friends nor Sita is coming today. [correct]

The rule is simple, make the verb agree with the subject/ noun closest to it.

The same rule will apply for 'either/or' too.

14. Collective Nouns: These are always singular.

Example: A flock of birds is flying [correct]

15. Each and Every: Each of the students is studying. [correct]

Each is singular.

Some singular subjects often confused are:

Each/Every

Anybody/Everybody/Somebody

Nobody/Nothing/No one

Anyone/Everyone/Someone

Whoever/Whatever

Anything/Everything/Something

Either/Neither (unless accompanied with 'or' in which case refer to previously discussed rule)

16. The Number/A Number: The number is singular where as a number is plural.

*The number of boys is more than the number of girls in the class. [correct]

*A number of boys are participating in the concert.

17. One of the: One of the shirts that belong/ belongs to him is/are torn.

One of the shirts that belong to him is torn. [correct]

One of the noun is always plural.

18. Use of had had and has had:

* Has/Have had - Present perfect of 'to have'

*Had had - Past perfect of 'to have'

19. If ...... Then: This is a conditional statement, If X, then Y.

Example: If I am hungry (then) I will eat food.

Then is not written in the sentence, it is implied.

Present tense: If you eat, [then] you will be satisfied.

Past tense: If you ate, [then] you would be satisfied.

Past perfect tense: If you had eaten, [then] you would have been satisfied.

20. Pronoun Errors: A pronoun is that which replaces a noun. Some common errors related to pronouns are:

(a) Whether the pronoun refers to a specific noun.

Example: Sita and Gita went for a walk and she fell down. [error: who is she referring to?]

(b) The pronoun has to agree in number with the noun it replaces.

You cannot replace a singular noun with a plural pronoun and vice versa.

(c) If the pronoun has an incorrect or no antecedent, it will constitute an error.

These days they have started charging you for baggage at the airports. [not clear who 'they' is referring to]

(d) **That or which:** both of these belong to a small group of words known as relative pronouns, which are used to relate parts of a sentence to one another.

Example: consider the two sentences:

- The fifth bike, which is black in colour, belongs to Mike.
- The fifth bike that is black in colour belongs to Mike.

Are both of these sentences referring to the same bike? Not necessarily.

The first sentence is definitely referring to the fifth bike and we are provided with the additional information that it is black in colour but even without this information we can easily identify the bike because it has to be bike number five.

The second sentence just takes you to the fifth black bike; now this bike could be the fifth bike (in case the first four bikes are also black) or it could be the tenth bike or, it can be at any number as long as it satisfies the criterion of being the fifth black bike.

Rule: 'Which' should always come after a comma.

'Which' must refer to the noun that comes immediately before the comma.

(e) **Who and Whom:** The difference between who and whom is exactly the same as the difference between I and me, he and him, she and her, etc.

Who, like I, he, and she, is a subject–it is the person performing the action.

Whom, like me, him, and her, is an object–it is the person to/about/for whom the action is being done.

Example: Who is going for the play?

Whom is the play about?

If the response to Who/Whom is I, he, she, etc., then the correct word is 'Who' and if the response is me, him, her, etc., then the correct word is 'Whom'.

Whom is also the correct choice after a preposition: with whom, one of whom, etc.

21. Modifiers: A modifier should be placed as close as possible to that which it modifies.

Whenever a sentence begins with a modifying phrase (especially one that starts with an '-ing' word) followed by a comma, the noun or pronoun following the comma should be what the modifier is referring to.

Example:

Only Mina can cook the food.

Mina can only cook the food.

Mina can cook the food only.

The word 'only' which is the modifier will be placed next to what it is modifying. In this case it can be Mina, food or cook.

22. Parallel Structure errors: Whenever you see a sentence that contains a list or series of items or actions separated by commas, you should realise that it has a parallel structure.

Example: Mini can't decide whether she should drink tea, coffee or milk.

Like and As: Since 'Like' is a preposition and 'As' is a conjunction, use 'like' only to compare nouns and 'as' for all other comparisons.

- Whenever comparison is done, it is done with similar articles...apples with apples and oranges with oranges, not apples with oranges.
- The compared things must be grammatically similar.
- When two things are compared, the comparative form is used. [**Example:** better]

When more than two things are compared, then the superlative form is used. [**Example:** best]

23. Idioms, Styles and Phrases: The errors of idioms are very common because they are used incorrectly in sentences.

Some common idioms which are often confused are listed below:

- An instance of: an example of. An instance of confusion.
- A means to: something done to get something else. A means to an end.
- Accused of, not accused for, accused with or accused to
- Ability to, not ability of or ability for
- Act as: to serve in some special capacity
- Act like: behave in a particular manner
- Agree to a proposal and agree with someone or their opinion
- Agree on/upon, a date or time
- Allow for: to give consideration for something.
- Among (a) and (b): evaluating between two options or more than two options.
- Appear to be: seem to be
- Appeal to, not appeal with
- As a result of: due to something
- Approve of/disapprove of
- As a child
- As an adolescent/as a teenager
- As good as: Tea is as good as coffee
- As great as: used for comparison. Example: Is he really as great as he is supposed to be?
- As much/as many: I have got as many clothes as you have.
- Associate with
- Ask for
- Attend to: take care of
- Be afraid of something
- Based on something
- Believe to be: have faith
- Better than, not better of
- Between (a) and (b): used to choose between two things
- Capable of, not capable for
- Care about, care for
- Choose as: select
- Claim that; claim to; claim to be [Ram claims that he knows English. Ram's claim to fame is that he knows English. Ram claims to have been educated in an English medium school.]
- Compare with: used in case of actual comparison.
- Compare to: when only comparing similarities, not an actual comparison.
- Composed of, not composed from
- Concerned with, concerned about, not concerned for.
- Conceive of
- Confirm with: Maya is confirming the plan with Mira.
- Conform to: agree to
- Consequence of, not consequence for
- Connection between a and b
- Contend that: claim
- Contend with: compete

- Continue with: carry on
- Contrast (a) with (b): compare two dissimilar things
- Correlate with, not correlate to
- Count on: depend on
- Credited with, not credited as or credited for
- Date from: to have an origin from a particular time
- Dated at: to show a time period
- Debate about/on/over, not debate for
- Decide on: to take a decision
- Delighted to: be happy
- Defined as
- Dependent on
- Demand that
- Determined by
- Depicted as
- Different/differ from
- Disagree with, not disagree to
- Disclose to, not disclose with
- Agree with a noun and agree to a verb
- Use 'shall' when speaking in the first person and 'will' when speaking in the second or third person.

First Person - I

Second Person - You

Third Person - He, She, etc.

- Use 'will to' refer to some event that will happen in the future in relation to the present and use would to refer to the future in the past.
- Use 'will' to refer to future in the present

  Use 'would' to refer to future in the past

  Use 'should' to denote suggestion or recommendation.

  Never use 'should' along with verbs such as 'recommend', 'suggest', etc.
- Between/among: Use 'between' while evaluating two options and 'among' while evaluating more than two options.
  - Farther/Further: Farther' refers to actual measurable distance whereas 'Further' refers to degree, quantity, time, or some such other quality that cannot or is not being precisely measured.
  - Differ with/Differ from: Use 'differ from' to imply 'unlike' (as in one thing differing from the other) and 'differ with' to imply 'disagreement' (as in differing with a point of view).
  - Rather than/Instead of: 'Rather than' is used to express preference of one thing over another whereas 'instead of' is used to replace one thing with another.
  - Everyday/Every day: Everyday is something commonplace, whereas every day means each day.
  - If/Whether: "If" is used to introduce a conditional idea or an idea that has just one possibility whereas 'Whether' is used to introduce alternative possibilities, usually with 'or not' implied or explicitly stated in the sentence.
  - Where/when: "Where" will always refer to a specific location and "when" will always refer to a specific time period; else their use is wrong.
  - Fewer/Less: Less is used for uncountable nouns, whereas fewer is used for countable nouns.
  - Double negatives should be avoided in a sentence.
  - When contemplating hypothetical or contrary-to-fact situations, always use 'were' and 'would'. Please note that even if the subject is singular you will still use 'were' and not 'was'. Example: I wish I were rich.
  - Verbs such as order, suggest, demand, etc. must be followed by 'that' and the infinitive form of the verb being ordered or suggested, without the "to". Example: The boss demanded that Jane show up for work on time.
  - Style primarily involves the following two variables - Wordiness and Redundancy
  - Discourage from, not discourage about or to.
  - Dispute over, not dispute about.
  - Distinguish between A and B: I cannot distinguish between mocha and latte.
  - Distinguish from A and B: Children cannot distinguish wrong from right.
  - Drawn to something
  - Draw attention to something/somebody
  - Drawn upon: used up
  - Doubt that instead of doubt for.
  - Dream about something or somebody.
  - Dwindle away: The rations dwindled away.
  - Either A or B: Choose between two things
  - Elect as/elected as the President.
  - Elect to the office, instead of elect for office.
  - Emerge as/Emerged as the winner, not emerged to be.
  - Encourage A to B: We encouraged Maya to pursue her interest in cooking.
  - Encourage in: We encouraged Maya in her cooking career.
  - Escape from something, not escape of.
  - Escape notice: something going unnoticed. Example: My earlier mail escaped your notice.
  - Essential to, not essential for. Example: Water is essential to life.
  - Estimated to be worth something.
  - Estimated at: denoting the place where estimation was done.

- Except for: denoting an exception.
- Expect to: The mother was expected to take care of the child.
- Expect from: I am expecting a letter from my sister.
- Expect A of B: I expected better of Mary.
- Explain away: You just cannot explain away all your errors.
- Fail on: The teacher failed the students on the test.
- Fail in: I hope I don't fail in satisfying you.
- Fascinated by something not fascinated with.
- Flee from: run away from something/someplace.
- Flee to: run to something/someplace.
- Forbid A to do B: Ram forbade his assistant to come home.
- From A to B: I shifted from Patna to Lucknow.
- Grow from something
- Grow out of something
- Grow into something
- Identical with, not identical to.
- Contrast to, used in case of a noun.
- Contrast with, used in case of a verb.
- Danger of getting a disease/something.
- Danger to something
- In order to, not in order that.
- Independent from some authority
- Independent of some logic or reason.
- Indicate that: His action indicated that he was no longer interested.
- Indicate to: He indicated his preferences to me.
- Inherit from: Mary inherited her blue eyes from her mother.
- Invest in: I have invested my money in some shares.
- Invest with: The principal was invested with the authority to control the school.
- Isolated from: separated from.
- Just as A, so B: to point out similarities. Example: Just as Ram is a good cook, so is Shyam.
- Lead away: take away from.
- Lead to: take to.
- Less A than B: My pain is less intense than yours.
- Likely to be: The announcement is likely to be made today.
- Localised in, not localised with.
- Mistake A for B, not A as B: Sherry mistook tea for coffee.
- Modelled after: I modelled myself after my sister.
- More than: Ram is more clever than Shyam.
- Much as: Much as Mary needed the money, I had to refuse.
- Native of: used for human beings.
- Native to: used for plants and animals.
- Necessary to: It is necessary to brush your teeth daily.
- Neither A nor B: she could neither eat nor drink anything.
- No less than: Singing is no less than dancing.
- Not only A, but also B: Not only is she pretty, but also very intelligent.
- Not A but rather B: I would have not cola, but rather juice.
- Opinion on something.
- Opinion of somebody.
- Originate in/originate from: Most of my fears originate in my mind. Most of the fears originated from the past beliefs I had about things.
- A is enough to B: The wind is strong enough to cause a storm.
- A instead of B: I will have cake instead of cookies.
- A is attributed to B: The loss has been attributed to bad management of the resources.
- A is to B, what C is to D: You are to me what, she is to her parents.
- Worried about something, not worried of.
- With the aim of achieving something.
- Whether to: Mira is unable to decide whether to go to Mumbai or Delhi.
- View A as B: I view every adversity as an opportunity.
- Used A as B: Sometimes we use pens as painting tools too.
- Try to, not try and: John said that he would try to come to the show.
- Trained to, not trained as: May was trained to become a singer.
- Think of A as B: I always thought of my brother as my friend.
- The more/greater X, the more/greater Y: The more the adversity, the stronger you become.
- Targeted at, not targeted on.
- Subscribe to some thing, not subscribe for.
- Speak for: your actions speak for themselves.
- Speak with: I will speak with my husband about the issue.
- Speak up: Someone has to speak up for the poor.
- Speak from: My mother said that she was speaking from experience.

- So much as means 'but rather', or sometimes 'even': I was not talking to her so much as checking out her clothing.
- So X that Y: Mini is so sweet that you can hardly find fault in her.
- So X as to Y: His grades are so bad as to lead to his expulsion from school.
- Similar to, not similar with: My dress is similar to yours.
- Sequence of something, not sequence for.
- Seem to: The child seemed to be hiding something in his fist.
- Seem like: He seemed like a nice person, when I talked to him.
- Seek after: The police continued to seek after the convict, long after he had run away.
- Seek from: We seek support from our elders.
- Seek out/sought out: Jane sought out a car for herself from the available ones.
- Sacrifice to: I made a lot of sacrifices to finance my trip.
- Sacrifice A for B: Sometimes we have to sacrifice something small for bigger things.
- Result in: lead to
- Result from: We will see what results from your effort.
- Restrictions on something or somebody.
- Responsibility to do something.
- Resemble in: Tea resembles coffee in colour but not in flavour.
- Require to/require X to/require that X
- Require of: I want to know what is required of me in this job.
- Reluctant to do something, not reluctant about.
- Regard as: I have always regarded you as my friend.
- Refer to/referred X to/refers to
- Rates for, not rates of.
- Range over/range from X to Y
- Promise to: Do not make false promises to anyone.
- Potential to, not potential for.
- Prohibit A from B: The landlord has prohibited Jay from calling his friends over.
- Preoccupied with: busy with.
- Prized above: He has prized his child above everything else.
- Prized as: The Encyclopedia has been prized as a collector's item.
- Prized for: Diamonds have been prized for thousands of years.

The above tips will come handy in case of any confusion in choosing the error or a correct sentence.

GRAMMATICAL ERRORS IN SENTENCE CORRECTION QUESTIONS

Essentially, there are six basic kinds of errors in the grammar of a sentence.

Error Type 1: Subject-Verb Agreement Errors

The lack of agreement between the subject and verb is one of the main errors introduced in questions of sentence correction. The basic underlying principle is that–**"Verbs should always agree with their subjects"**.

As per the basic sentence structuring, every sentence has to have a Subject, a Verb and an Object–wherein the subject (noun) does an act (verb) with the object (another noun). The principle clearly is that the conjugation (form of the verb used) of the verb should be in line with the subject to which it is attached. Thus, you need to check whether the form of the verb used agrees with the number and the person of the subject noun.

As is obvious, number refers to whether the noun is singular or plural and person refers to whether the noun is in the first person (I/we), second person (You) or third person (he, she, it, one, they).

While looking out for this error, you are advised to be careful of–

(a) The conjugation of irregular verbs; and

(b) The disguising of the subject by creating a complex sentence structure having multiple messages between the subject and the verb.

The subject and the verb are put far apart from each other, making it more difficult to recognise. In such cases, you will need to correctly identify the subject with which the verb needs to agree.

The depletion of natural resources, in addition to the rapid increase in their utilisation, have/has encouraged many countries to develop new sources of energy.

In the above sentence, the verb 'to have' has a singular subject. Hence, it will take the second person singular form 'has'.

Error Type 2: Errors of Modifiers

Modifiers are words/group of words/phrases in one part of the sentence, which modify (add to the meaning of) another part of the sentence. In correct written English, the modifier has to be kept as close as possible to the word or clause it modifies. Placing the modifiers at the wrong position in a sentence often has the effect of changing the meaning of the sentence. This happens because the modifier modifies the word/clause closest to it.

The following examples will make it clear:

Bruised and battered, Ravi gave his car to the mechanic.

Bruised and battered, the car was given to the mechanic by Ravi.

Notice in the example above, the chances in the use of words bruised and battered.

While solving sentence correction questions, you should try to identify the modifiers used in the sentence and decide which clause it modifies. Then ensure that in the correct answer, the modifier is attached to the correct clause. In order to do this, you will need to make sure that you have understood the intended meaning of the writer.

Error Type 3: Errors in the Usage of Pronouns

Pronouns are defined as any of a small set of words in a language that are used as substitutes for nouns or noun phrases. Their references are named or understood in the context of their usage. The basic principle that needs to be adhered to is that -

"The pronouns used in a sentence should agree with their antecedents."

Besides, in correct written English, there should be no ambiguity about which noun the pronoun is replacing. You will need to consider both these factors while evaluating the pronouns used within a sentence. Consider the following example:

Amit told Ameer that he should take his car to the party.

In the above sentence, it is not clear as to whose car is being referred to. Hence, the sentence will not qualify as standard written English.

Pay special attention to problems involving it-they, he-his, me-mine, they-their, etc.

Error Type 4: Errors in the Tense of Verbs

The sentence should reflect the correct order in which the sequence of events occurs. For this purpose, it is crucial that the verbs used are in the correct tense–be it past, present or future and be it in the normal form, the continuous form or the perfect form. It would be wise of you to review the rules for all these and be especially aware of the various tense forms of irregular verbs.

Pay special attention to the appropriateness of the use of the continuous form, because errors based on incorrect use of the continuous form are very common in sentence correction questions (especially questions of type 1 & type 2).

Remember that: The 'ing' form of a verb is used

(a) Either to emphasise the continuing nature of an action *OR*

(b) To emphasise that two actions are happening simultaneous to each other.

Consider the following example:

If the experiment works, it will represent/will be representing a giant leap forward for human sciences.

In the above sentence, even though will be representing is grammatically correct, it is not appropriate in relation to will represent as it is unnecessary and verbose.

Error Type 5: Errors of Parallel Form

One of the common methods of presenting an idea having multiple facets is by writing sentences in the parallel form. For example:

In India today, an investor might invest his money in stocks, in real estate or in debt based mutual funds.

The last part of the above sentence is in a parallel form, since multiple ideas of the same level and category (investment options in this case) are presented within one part of the sentence.

You need to look out for parallel form problems in:

(a) List of actions/items or series of items/actions.

(b) Expressions using the structures–Both X and Y, Either X or Y or Z, Any of X, Y and Z, etc.

(c) Expressions involving comparisons between two or more things–Prefer X to Y, Y is preferred to X.

Spotting errors in such sentences is easy, since you have to just ensure that the individual parts have to be written in the same form.

Error Type 6: Errors in the Use of Singular Words, Idioms and Phrases

Idioms are defined as expressions in the usage of English (or for that matter any other language), that is peculiar to itself either grammatically (for example, No, it wasn't me) or in having a meaning that cannot be derived from the conjoined meanings of its elements (as Monday week for conveying the meaning that we are referring to 'the Monday a week after next Monday').

The only way to prepare for the errors in idioms is through improved exposure to the English language. In this context, if you are a natural at the language, you should just trust your ear. Trying to reason out on points of grammatical correctness of the idiom used will take you nowhere.

Consider the following sentences for understanding idiomatic usage:

1. The French grand Prix is considered *as/to be* one of the most arduous races.

   The correct idiom is *'to be'*

2. The issue covers such questions *like/as* who should cover the losses borne out of the project.

   The correct idiom is *'as'*.

Apart from those mentioned above, you need to be aware of the following errors.

(a) Proper use of adverbs (they modify verbs);

(b) Proper use of the semicolon; and

(c) Relative use of words like

   (i) 'Among' versus 'between',

   (ii) 'Fewer' versus 'less',

   (iii) 'Who' versus 'whom' and

   (iv) 'Me' versus 'I' versus 'Mine', etc.

Practice Exercises

Type 1

Directions for the questions (1-50): In each of the following sentences, four options are given. You are required to identify the best way of writing the sentence in the context of the correct usage of standard written English. While doing so, you have to ensure that the message being conveyed remains the same in all the cases.

1. If he was to decide to go to college, one would recommend that he plan to go to IIM, Ahmedabad.
   (a) If he was to decide to go to college, one would recommend that he plan to go to IIM, Ahmedabad.
   (b) If he were to decide to go to college, one would recommend that he plan to go to IIM, Ahmedabad.
   (c) Had he decided to go to college, one would recommend that plan to go to IIM, Ahmedabad.
   (d) In the event that he decides to go to college, one would recommend that plan to go to IIM, Ahmedabad.
   (e) Had he decide to go to college, one would recommend that he go to IIM, Ahmedabad.

2. Except for you and I, everyone brought a present for the little birthday boy.
   (a) Except for him and I, everyone brought a present for the little birthday boy.
   (b) With the exception of you and I, everyone brought a present for the little birthday boy.
   (c) Except for you and I, everyone had brought a present for the little birthday boy.
   (d) Except for you and me, everyone brought a present for the little birthday boy.
   (e) Excepting you and I, all brought present for the little boy.

3. When one reads the Hindi literature of the twentieth century, you find a striking contrast between the writings of Munshi Premchand and later day writers of popular Hindi fiction.
   (a) When one reads the Hindi literature of the twentieth century, you find a striking contrast between the writings of Munshi Premchand and later day writers of popular Hindi fiction.
   (b) When you read the Hindi literature of the twentieth century, one finds a striking contrast between the writings of Munshi Premchand and later day writers of popular Hindi fiction.
   (c) When one reads the Hindi literature of the twentieth century, he finds a striking contrast between the writings of Munshi Premchand and later day writers of popular Hindi fiction.
   (d) If one reads the Hindi literature of the twentieth century, you find a striking contrast between the writings of Munshi Premchand and later day writers of popular Hindi fiction.
   (e) When one reads the Hindi Literature of the twentieth century, one finds a striking contrast between the writings of Munshi Premchand and later day writers of popular Hindi fiction.

4. Because of his tennis elbow injury, Limba Ram has not and possibly never will be able to pick up the bat again.
   (a) Because of his tennis elbow injury, Limba Ram has not and possibly never will be able to pick up the bat again.
   (b) Because of his tennis elbow injury, Limba Ram has not and possibly will never be able to pick up the bat again.
   (c) Because of his tennis elbow injury, Limba Ram has not been and possibly never would be able to pick up the bat again.
   (d) Because of his tennis elbow injury, Limba Ram has not been able to and possibly never will be able to pick up the bat again.
   (e) Because of his tennis elbow injury, Limba Ram has not and if possible be never able to pick up the bat again.

5. Had he realised how close he was to failing, he would not have gone to the party.

(a) Had he realised how close he was to failing, he would not have gone to the party.
(b) If he would have realised how close he was to failing, he would not have gone to the party.
(c) Had he had realised how close he was to failing, he would not have gone to the party.
(d) When he realised how close he was to failing, he did not go to the party.
(e) If he would realise how close he was to failing, he should not have gone to the party.

6. The Indian cricket team's winning it's first game of the 2007 World Cup excited the fans of the team.

(a) The Indian cricket team's winning it's first game of the 2007 World Cup excited the fans of the team.
(b) The Indian cricket team having won its first game of the 2007 World Cup, excited the fans of the team.
(c) The Indian cricket team's having won its first game of the 2007 World Cup excited the fans of the team.
(d) The Indian cricket team's winning its first game of the 2007 World Cup excited the fans of the team.
(e) The Indian cricket team's had won its first game of the 2007 World Cup excited the fans of the team.

7. Poor product quality angers Mr. Garbole, who wonders if it is part of a strategy by marketers.

(a) Poor product quality angers Mr. Garbole, who wonders if it is part of a strategy by marketers.
(b) Poor product quality angers Mr. Garbole, who wonders if marketers are part of the strategy.
(c) Poor product quality angers Mr. Garbole, that wonders if it is part of a strategy by marketers.
(d) Poor product quality angers Mr.Garbole, who wonders if they are part of a strategy by marketers.
(e) Poor product quality angers Mr. Garbole, who wonders if it are part of a strategy.

8. Ambikesh noticed the cat's soft hair, sharp paws, and keen sense of hearing.

(a) Ambikesh noticed the cat's soft hair, sharp paws, and keen sense of hearing.
(b) Ambikesh noticed the cat's soft hair, sharp paws, and that his sense of hearing was keen.
(c) Ambikesh noticed the cat's soft hair, that he had sharp paws, and a very keen sense of hearing.
(d) Ambikesh noticed the cat's soft hair, keen sense of hearing and also that it had sharp paws.
(e) Ambikesh as noticed the cat's soft hair, sharp paws and keen sense of hearing.

9. Having bowed our heads, the priest in the temple led us in prayer.

(a) Having bowed our heads, the priest in the temple led us in prayer.
(b) After we bowed our head, the priest in the temple led us in prayer.
(c) After we bowed our heads, the priest in the temple led us in prayer.
(d) After we had bowed our heads, the priest in the temple led us in prayer.
(e) After having bowed our head, the priest in the temple led us in prayer.

10. My grandmother seldom ever wants to try and face the facts.

(a) My grandmother seldom ever wants to try and face the facts.
(b) My grandmother seldom if ever wants to try and face the facts.
(c) My grandmother seldom ever wants to try to face the facts.
(d) My grandmother seldom wants to try to face the facts.
(e) My grandmother seldom want to try face the facts.

11. Anyone interested in flying planes can learn much if you have access to a flight simulation machine.

(a) Anyone interested in flying planes can learn much if you have access to a flight simulation machine.
(b) Anyone interested in flying planes can learn much if he has access to a flight simulation machine.
(c) Anyone interested in flying planes can learn much if access is available to a flight simulation machine.
(d) Anyone interested in flying planes can learn much from access to a flight simulation machine.
(e) Anyone interests in flying planes can learn much if they had access to a flight simulation machine.

12. No officer had ought to be put into a situation where he has to choose between his love for his family and the responsibilities accompanying his duty.

(a) No officer had ought to be put into a situation where he has to choose between his love for his family and the responsibilities accompanying his duty.
(b) No officer had ought to be put into a situation in which he has to choose between his love for his family and the responsibilities accompanying his duty.
(c) No officer should be put into a situation where he has to choose between his love for his family and the responsibilities accompanying his duty.
(d) No officer ought to be put into a situation in which he has to choose between his love for his

family and the responsibilities accompanying his duty.

(e) No officer would be put in a situation where he have to choose between his love for family and the responsibilities accompanying his duty.

13. Being a realist, the detective could not accept the statement of the accused that UFOs had caused the disturbance.

(a) Being a realist, the detective could not accept the statement of the accused that UFOs had caused the disturbance.

(b) Since he was a realist, the detective could not accept the statement of the accused that UFOs had caused the disturbance.

(c) Being that he was a realist, the detective could not accept the statement of the accused that UFOs had caused the disturbance.

(d) Realist that he was, the detective could not accept the statement of the accused that UFOs had caused the disturbance.

(e) Being a realist that he was, the detective could not accept the statement of the accused that UFOs had caused the disturbance.

14. The reason I came late to office today is because my car broke down.

(a) The reason I came late to office today is because my car broke down.

(b) Why I came late to office today is because my car broke down.

(c) The reason I was late to office today is because my car broke down.

(d) The reason I came late to office today is that my car broke down.

(e) The reason I came late to office is since my car broke down.

15. The shopkeeper hadn't hardly any of those kind of goods.

(a) The shopkeeper hadn't hardly any of those kind of goods.

(b) The shopkeeper hadn't hardly any of those kinds of goods.

(c) The shopkeeper had hardly any of those kind of goods.

(d) The shopkeeper had hardly any of those kinds of goods.

(e) The shopkeeper had not hardly any of those kinds of goods.

16. If we cooperate together by dividing up the booty, we shall be able to work together smoothly in the future.

(a) If we cooperate together by dividing up the booty, we shall be able to work together smoothly in the future.

(b) If we cooperate by dividing up the booty, we shall be able to work together smoothly in the future.

(c) If we cooperate by dividing up the booty together, we shall be able to work together smoothly in the future.

(d) If we cooperate with each other by dividing the booty, we shall be able to work together smoothly in the future.

(e) If we cooperate with one other by dividing up the booty, we will be able to work smoothly together in future.

17. The entire cast and crew of the film, enjoyed splashing in the pool, bathing in the ocean, and, particularly, *to* sun bathe on the shore.

(a) The entire cast and crew of the film, enjoyed splashing in the pool, bathing in the ocean, and, particularly, to sun bathe on the shore.

(b) The entire cast and crew of the film, enjoyed splashing in the pool, to have a bath in the ocean, and, particularly to sun bathe on the shore.

(c) The entire cast and crew of the film, enjoyed swimming in the pool to bathe in the ocean, and, particularly sun bathing on the shore.

(d) The entire cast and crew of the film, enjoyed swimming in the pool, bathing in the ocean, and, particularly, sun bathing on the shore.

(e) The entire cast and crew of the film, enjoyed splashing in the pool, bathing in the ocean, particularly to sun bathing on the shore.

18. Crossing the street, a bus almost crushed us to death.

(a) Crossing the street, a bus almost crushed us to death.

(b) A bus almost crushed us, crossing the street.

(c) As we crossed the street, a bus almost crushed us.

(d) A bus, crossing the street, almost crushed us.

(e) While we crossed a street, a bus almost crushed us.

19. The moral of the entire story is how money doesn't make you happy.

(a) The moral of the entire story is how money doesn't make you happy.

(b) The moral of the entire story is that money doesn't make you happy.

(c) In this novel, its moral of the story is how money doesn't make you happy.

(d) That money does not make you happy, is the entire moral of the story.

(e) The moral of the story is that as to how money doesn't make you happy.

20. Entertainment being recognised as an important factor in improving mental and physical health and thereby reducing human misery and poverty.

(a) Entertainment being recognised as an important factor in improving mental and physical health and thereby reducing human misery and poverty.
(b) Recognising entertainment as an important factor in improving mental and physical health and thereby reducing human misery and poverty.
(c) Recognition of it being an important factor in improving mental and physical health entertainment reduces human misery and poverty.
(d) Entertainment is recognised as an important factor in improving mental and physical health and thereby reducing human misery and poverty.
(e) Entertainment while being recognised as an important factor in improving mental and physical health and thereby reducing human misery and poverty.

21. When one travels by Air Lahara, you often find that the prices are high and that the journey experience is extremely poor.

(a) When one travels by Air Lahara, you often find that the prices are high and that the journey experience is extremely poor.
(b) When you travel by Air Lahara, one often finds that the prices are high and that the journey experience is extremely poor.
(c) As you travel by Air Lahara, you often find that the prices are high and that the journey experience is extremely poor.
(d) If you travel by Air Lahara, you often find that the prices are high and that the journey experience is extremely poor.
(e) Whenever you are travelling by Air Lahara, you find the prices are high and the journey experience is extremely poor.

22. Ever since the sting operation, there has been much opposition from they who maintain that it was an unauthorised act.

(a) Ever since the sting operation, there has been much opposition from they who maintain that it was an unauthorised act.
(b) Ever since the sting operation, there has been much opposition from they who maintain that it had been an unauthorised act.
(c) Ever since the sting operation, there has been much opposition from those who maintain that it was an unauthorised act.
(d) Ever since the sting operation, there has been much opposition from those maintaining that it was an unauthorised act.
(e) Ever since the sting operation, there has been much of an opposition from them who maintain that it was an unauthorised act.

23. Having stole the money, the class teacher searched the student's pocket.

(a) Having stole the money, the class teacher searched the student's pocket.
(b) Having stolen the money, the student's pockets were searched by the class teacher.
(c) Having stolen the money, the class teacher searched the student's pockets.
(d) Having stole the money, the class teacher was searched by the student.
(e) While stealing the money, the class teacher had searched the student's pockets.

24. The child is neither encouraged to be critical or to examine all the aspects of his opinion.

(a) The child is neither encouraged to be critical or to examine all the aspects of his opinion.
(b) The child is neither encouraged to be critical nor to examine all the aspects of his opinion.
(c) The child is either encouraged to be critical or to examine all the evidence for his opinion.
(d) None of these
(e) The child is either encouraged to be critical not to examine all the aspects of his opinion.

25. Although I calculate that my girlfriend will be here any minute, I cannot wait much longer for her to arrive.

(a) Although I calculate that my girlfriend will be here any minute, I cannot wait much longer for her to arrive.
(b) Although I reckon that my girlfriend will be here any minute, I cannot wait much longer for her to arrive.
(c) Because I calculate that my girlfriend will be here any minute, I cannot wait much longer for her to arrive.
(d) Although I think that my girlfriend will be here any minute, I cannot wait much longer for her to arrive.
(e) Because I think that my girlfriend will be here any minute, I cannot wait any longer for her to arrive.

26. The process by which the community influences the actions of its members is known as social control.

(a) The process by which the community influences the actions of its members is known as social control.
(b) The process by which the community influence the actions of its members is known as social control.

(c) The process by which the community goes about influencing the actions of its members is known as social control.
(d) The process by which community influences the actions of its members is known as social control.
(e) The process by which the community influences the actions of its members could be known by social control.

27. To be sure, there would be scarcely no time left over for other things if school children would have been expected to have considered all sides of every matter on which they had opinions.

(a) There would be scarcely no time left over for other things if working people would have been expected to have considered all sides of every matter on which they had opinions.
(b) To be sure, there would be scarcely any time left for other things if working people should be expected to have considered all sides of every matter on which they had opinions.
(c) To be sure, there would be scarcely any time left over for other things if school children were expected to consider all sides of every matter on which they had opinions.
(d) To be sure, there would be scarcely no time left over for other things if school children will be expected to have been considering all sides of every matter on which they had opinions.
(e) Sure enough, scarcely there would be any time left for other things if school children were expected to consider all sides of the matters on which they had opinions.

28. Depending on skillful suggestion, argument is seldom used in advertising.

(a) Depending on skillful suggestion, argument is seldom used in advertising.
(b) Argument is seldom used by advertisers, who depend on skillful suggestion instead.
(c) Skillfull suggestion is depended on by advertisers instead of argumentation.
(d) Suggestion, which is skillful, is used in place of argumentation by advertisers.
(e) Suggesting skillfully is what advertisers do apart from argumentation.

29. When this war is over, no kingdom will either be isolated in war or peace.

(a) When this war is over, no kingdom will either be isolated in war or peace.
(b) When this war is over, no kingdom will be either isolated in war or peace.
(c) When this war is over, no kingdom will either be isolated in war or be isolated in peace.
(d) When this war is over, no kingdom will be isolated either in war or peace.
(e) When this war is over, no kingdom will be isolated either in war nor peace.

30. The twelve-hour work day not only has been reduced to one of ten hours but also, in some lines of work, to below eight hours.

(a) The twelve-hour work day not only has been reduced to one of ten hours but also, in some lines of work, to below eight hours.
(b) Not only has the twelve-hour work day been reduced to one of ten hours but also, in some lines of work, to below eight hours.
(c) The twelve-hour work day has not only been reduced to one of ten hours but also, in some lines of work, to below eight hours.
(d) The twelve-hour work day has been reduced not only to one of ten hours but also, in some lines of work, to below eight hours.
(e) The twelve-hour working day has not only been reduced to ten hours but also, in some cases, to less than eight hours.

31. If some Indians look at where they are going, it can be seen that our goal is money.

(a) If some Indians look at where they are going, it can be seen that our goal is money.
(b) If some Indians look back to where they are going, it can be seen that our goal is money.
(c) If some Indians look at where they are going, it can be seen that their goal is money.
(d) If some Indians look at where they are going, they can see that their goal is money.
(e) If they Indians look at where they are going, they can see that their goal is money.

32. Sherry, a little girl with little talent for cooking, enjoys preparing Fried Rice.

(a) Sherry, a little girl with little talent for cooking, enjoys preparing Fried Rice.
(b) Sherry, is a little girl who has little talent for cooking but she enjoys preparing Fried Rice.
(c) Sherry, a little girl who has little cooking talent, enjoys preparing Fried Rice.
(d) Sherry, a girl with little talent for cooking, enjoys preparing Fried Rice.
(e) Sherry, a little girl, having little talent of cooking, still enjoys preparing Fried Rice.

33. Of all the persons I have ever met, Arjit is the most remarkable person.

(a) Of all the persons I have ever met, Arjit is the most remarkable person.
(b) Arjit is the most remarkable person of all the persons I have ever met.

(c) Of all the persons I have ever met, Arjit is the most remarkable person.
(d) Of all the persons I have ever met, Arjit is the most remarkable.
(e) Arjit being the most remarkable person of all I have met.

34. Unless they reverse present policies immediately, the world may suffer irreversible damage from the unregulated use of Bio weapons.

(a) Unless they reverse present policies immediately, the world may suffer irreversible damage from the unregulated use of Bio weapons.
(b) Unless present policies are reversed immediately, the world may suffer irreversible damage from the unregulated use of Bio weapons.
(c) Unless present policies are reversed, the world may suffer irreversible damage by the unregulated use of Bio weapons.
(d) Unless present policies are reversed, the world may suffer irreversible damage through the unregulated use of Bio weapons.
(e) Unless reversal of the present policies happen, the world should suffer irreversible damage from the unregulated use of Bio-weapons.

35. The panel interviewed several candidates who they thought had the experience and qualifications the position at IIM Bangalore required.

(a) The panel interviewed several candidates who they thought had the experience and qualifications the position at IIM Bangalore required.
(b) The panel interviewed several candidates whom they thought had the experience and qualifications the position at IIM Bangalore required.
(c) The panel interviewed several candidates from whom they thought had the experience and qualifications the position at IIM Bangalore required.
(d) The panel interviewed several candidates which he thought had the experience and qualifications the position at IIM Bangalore required.
(e) The panel interviews several candidates who they thought has the experience and qualifications the position at IIM Bangalore required.

36. The trend toward a decrease in the working hours is already evident in the longer weekend given to employees in many multinational organisations.

(a) The trend toward a decrease in the working hours is already evident in the longer weekend given to employees in many multinational organisations.
(b) The trend toward a decrease in the working hours is all ready evident in the longer weekend given to employees in many multinational organisations.
(c) The trend toward a decrease in the working hours is allready evident in the longer weekend given to employees in many multinational organisations.
(d) The trend toward a decrease in the working hours is all in already evident in the longer weekend given to employees in many multinational organisations.
(e) The trend toward a decrease in working hours is already evidently in the longer weekend given to employers in many multinational organisations.

37. Using it wisely, leisure promotes health, long life, efficiency, and happiness.

(a) Using it wisely, leisure promotes health, long life, efficiency, and happiness.
(b) If used wisely, leisure promotes health, long life, efficiency, and happiness.
(c) Having used it wisely, leisure promotes health, long life, efficiency, and happiness.
(d) If it is used wisely, leisure promotes health, long life, efficiency, and happiness.
(e) If, when using wisely, leisure promotes health, long life, efficiency, and happiness.

38. We want the trainer to be him who has the best rapport knowledge about the subject and the most superior communication skills.

(a) We want the trainer to be him who has the best rapport knowledge about the subject and the most superior communication skills.
(b) We want the trainer to be he who has the best rapport knowledge about the subject and the most superior communication skills.
(c) We want him to be the trainer who has the best rapport knowledge about the subject and the most superior communication skills.
(d) We desire that the trainer be him who has the best rapport knowledge about the subject and the most superior communication skills.
(e) We would want the trainer to be him who has the best rapport knowledge about the subject and superior most communications skill.

39. If she were to win the Olympic medal, I for one would be surprised.

(a) If she were to win the Olympic medal, I for one would be surprised.
(b) If she were to go on to win the Olympic medal, I for one would be surprised.
(c) If she becomes the winner of the Olympic medal, I for one would be surprised.
(d) In the event that she would win the Olympic medal, I for one would be surprised.
(e) If she goes to win the Olympic medal, I for one would be surprised.

40. The soldiers were told to take a long arduous hike, pitch their camps, have dinner, and that they should be in bed by 10 p.m.

(a) The soldiers were told to take a long arduous hike, pitch their camps, have dinner, and that they should be in bed by 10 p.m.
(b) The soldiers were told to take an arduous hike, pitch their camps, have dinner, and that they should be in bed by 10 p.m.
(c) The soldiers were told to take a long arduous hike, pitch camp, have dinner, and be in bed by 10 p.m.
(d) The soldiers were told to take a long arduous hike, pitching their camps, have dinner, and be in bed by 10 p.m.
(e) The soldiers was told to take a long arduous hike, pitch camp, having dinner and to be in bed by 10 p.m.

41. The Indian government's failing to keep its pledges will have the effect of earning distrust from all the other nation in the region.

(a) The Indian government's failing to keep its pledges will have the effect of earning distrust from all the other nation in the region.
(b) The Indian government failing to keep it's pledges will have the effect of earning distrust from all the other nations in the region.
(c) The Indian government's failing to keep its pledges will have the effect of earning distrust from all the other nations in the region.
(d) The Indian government failing to keep its pledges will have the effect of earning distrust from all the other nations in the region.
(e) The Indian government's fail to keep its pledges will have the effect of earning distrust of all other nations in the region.

42. Her elder brother along with her grandparents insist that she remain in the same college.

(a) Her elder brother along with her grandparents, insist that she remain in the same college.
(b) Her elder brother along with her grandparents insists that she remain in the same college.
(c) Her elder brother along with her grandparents are insisting that she remain in the same college.
(d) Her brother along with her grandparents have insisted that she remain in the same college.
(e) Her elder brother along with her grandparents insisted on that she remained in the same college.

43. Most students like to read these kind of books for using their spare time.

(a) Most students like to read these kind of books for using their spare time.
(b) Most students like to read these kind of book for using their spare time.
(c) Most students like to read this kind of book for using their spare time.
(d) Most students like to read this kind a book for using their spare time.
(e) Most students like to read this kind of book for using of their spare time.

44. Not only was he competent but also welcoming in nature.

(a) He not only was competent but also friendly in nature.
(b) Not only was he competent but also friendly in nature.
(c) He not only was competent but friendly too in nature.
(d) He was not only competent but also friendly in nature.
(e) He, not only was competent but friendly also in nature.

45. In the normal course, John will graduate from college and enter a Post Graduate course in two years.

(a) In the normal course, John will graduate from college and enter a Post Graduate course in two years.
(b) In the normal course, John will graduate college and enter a Post Graduate course in two years.
(c) In the normal course, John should graduate from college and enter a Post Graduate course in two years.
(d) In the normal course, John will be able to graduate from college and enter a Post Graduate course in two years.
(e) In the normal course, John would graduate of college and enter a Post Graduate course in two years.

46. With the exception of Dipanjan and I, everyone in the class finished the assignment before the teacher came.

(a) With the exception of Dipanjan and I, everyone in the class finished the assignment before the teacher came.
(b) With the exception of Dipanjan and me, everyone in the class finished the assignment before the teacher came.
(c) With the exception of Dipanjan and me, everyone in the class had finished the assignment before the teacher came.
(d) With the exception of Dipanjan and I, everyone in the class had finished the assignment before the bell rang.

(e) With the exception of Dipanjan and I, everyone in the class finished the assignment before the teacher comes.

47. Familiar with the terrain from previous visits, the explorer's search for the Big Monkey's abode was a success.

(a) Familiar with the terrain from previous visits, the explorer's search for the Big Monkey's abode was a success.
(b) Familiar with the terrain from previous visits, the success of the explorer's search for the Big Monkey's abode was a mere formality.
(c) Familiar with the terrain from previous visits, the explorer succeeded in finding the Big Monkey's abode.
(d) Familiar with the terrain from previous visits, the search by the explorer for the Big Monkey's abode was successful.
(e) Familiar of the terrain with previous visits, the explorer succeeded in searching the Big Monkey's abode.

48. Liberalisation has gone hand in hand and has offered incentives for things as personal initiative, ambition, loyalty, hard work, and resourcefulness.

(a) Liberalisation has gone hand in hand and has offered incentives for such things as personal initiative, ambition, loyalty, hard work, and resourcefulness.
(b) Liberalisation has gone hand in hand with and has offered incentives for such things as personal initiative and ambition, loyalty, hard work, and resourcefulness.
(c) Liberalisation has gone hand in hand and is offering incentives for such things as personal initiative ambition, loyalty, hard work, and resourcefulness.
(d) Liberalisation has gone hand in hand while and providing incentives for such things as personal initiative and ambition, loyalty, hard work, and resourcefulness.

49. I am not to eager to go to this movie because it did not get good reviews.

(a) I am not to eager to go to this movie because it did not get good reviews.
(b) Because of its poor reviews, I am not too eager to go to this movie.
(c) I am not too eager to go to this movie because the critics did not give it good reviews.
(d) I am not too eager to go to this movie because of its poor reviews.
(e) I am not too eager to go to these movie because of its poor reviews.

50. May I venture to say that I think this batting performance is the most superior I have ever seen?

(a) May I venture to say that I think this batting performance is the most superior I have ever seen?
(b) May I venture to say that this batting performance is the most superior I have ever seen?
(c) May I say that this batting performance is the most superior I have ever seen?
(d) I think this performance is superior to any I have ever seen.
(e) May I venture to say that this batting performance is more superior to anyone I have ever seen.

Type 2

Directions for the questions (1-25): For each of the following questions, a part or the whole of the original sentence has been underlined. You have to find the best way of writing the underlined part of the sentence.

1. <u>The matter was referred back to the expert committee since the solution to the problem was different from the one proposed earlier.</u>

(a) referred back to the expert committee since the solution to the problem was different from the one proposed earlier.
(b) referred to the expert committee since the solution to the problem was different from the one proposed earlier.
(c) referred back to the expert committee since the solution to the problem was different than the one proposed earlier.
(d) referred to committee since the solution to the problem was different than the one proposed earlier.
(e) referred back to the committee since the solution for problem was different than one proposed earlier.

2. <u>Completing the physical examination, the tonsils were found to be diseased.</u>

(a) Completing the physical examination, the tonsils
(b) Having completed the physical examination, the tonsils
(c) When the physical examination was completed, the tonsils
(d) The physical examination completed, the tonsils
(e) Completion of the physical examination, the tonsils

3. <u>The smaller firms in any industry sell either on a price or quality-of-workmanship basis.</u>

(a) The smaller firms in any industry sell either on a price or quality-of-workmanship basis.
(b) The smaller firms in any industry either sell on a price or quality-of-workmanship basis.
(c) The smaller firms in any industry sell on either a price or a quality-of-workmanship basis.
(d) The smaller firms in any industry sell on either a price or on a quality-of-workmanship basis.
(e) The smaller firms of any industry sell off either on a price or quality-of-workmanship basis.

4. Current economic conditions demand that we not only cut jobs and prices but also reduce the rate of interest on PF deposits.

(a) that we not only cut jobs and prices but also
(b) not only cutting job and prices but also to
(c) not only to cut jobs and prices but also
(d) not only a cut in jobs and prices but also to

5. All rounders in any cricket team, in theory, make good sense; in actuality, however, they are normally difficult to discover.

(a) they are normally
(b) it is normally
(c) such players are normally
(d) it is usually expected that it is
(e) as they are normally difficult to discover.

6. Aamir was sitting with his friends when the Premier, in accompaniment with his only social secretary, entered the garden.

(a) in accompaniment with his only social secretary
(b) accompanying only by his social secretary
(c) accompanied only by his social secretary
(d) only accompanied by his social secretary
(e) is accompanied by only his social secretary

7. Being in the need for a variety of clothing, he founded Azam Lucman, a Bihari tailor in Patna who could produce any type of uniform in a couple of days.

(a) he founded Azam Lucman, a Bihari tailor in Patna who could produce any type of uniform in a couple of days.
(b) a Bihari tailor Azam Lucman found him in Patna who could produce any type of uniform in a couple of days.
(c) a Bihari tailor Azam Lucman was found by him a couple of days later, who could produce any type of uniform.
(d) he founded Azam Lucman tailors, a Bihari tailor in Patna who could produce any type of uniform in a couple of days.
(e) a Bihari tailor Azam Lucman was founded by him in Patna who could produce any type of uniform in a couple of days.

8. Reared in a village where computers and the internet were objects of curiosity, Purty today hardly gives a thought to the immense possibilities that the internet revolution has thrown open to him.

(a) Reared in a village where computers and the internet were objects of curiosity
(b) Curious to know that computers and the internet were objects of curiosity in the village he was reared up
(c) Being reared in the village where the computers and the internet are objects of curiosity
(d) Reared in a village where computers and the internet were an object of curiousness
(e) Rearing in a village where computers and the internet were objects of curiosity

9. In the attempt to destroy them with completeness, the Indian team has launched a coordinated attack on the opposing team.

(a) In the attempt to destroy them with completeness
(b) In attempting to destroy them completely,
(c) In an attempt to destroy them completely,
(d) In the attempt of destroying them completely,
(e) In the attempt to destroy them with completely

10. Balancing a home delivery pizza with one hand and gripping a six-pack carton of Coke with another, the young boy Vijay, paused in front of the guard room of the building.

(a) Balancing a home delivery pizza with one hand and gripping a six-pack carton of Coke with another
(b) Balancing a home delivery pizza with one hand and having gripped a six-pack carton of Coke with another
(c) Having a balance of a home delivery pizza with one hand and gripping a six-pack of carton of Coke with the other
(d) Balancing a home delivery pizza with one hand and gripping a pack of six Cokes with the other
(e) Balancing a home delivery pizza in one hand and gripping a six-packed carton of Coke with another

11. Armed with the talents of a high intellect, an actor with extraordinary gifts and an ingenious criminal, Charles Sobhraj played an overbearing role in the sensationalisation of crime during the later part of the 20th century in the Indian sub continent.

(a) an actor with extraordinary gifts and an ingenious criminal,
(b) an ingenious actor and an extraordinarily gifted criminal,
(c) a gifted actor and an ingeniously criminal,
(d) an extraordinarily gifted actor and an ingenious criminal,

(e) An actor with extraordinary gifts of an ingenious criminal,

12. Dr. Pam Saxena, an Indian specialist in drug rehabilitation medicine, advises against going easy on rehabilitated drug addicts for the fear of their relapsing into addiction.

(a) Dr. Pam Saxena, an Indian specialist in drug rehabilitation medicine, advises against going easy on rehabilitated drug addicts
(b) An Indian specialist in drug rehabilitation medicine, Dr. Pam Saxena, advises against going easy on rehabilitated drug addicts
(c) An Indian specialist in drug rehabilitation medicine, Pam Saxena, is of the opinion that one should not go easy on rehabilitated drug addicts
(d) Dr. Pam Saxena, an Indian specialist in drug rehabilitation medicine, advice against going easy on rehabilitated drug addicts
(e) Dr. Pam Saxena, an Indian specialist in drug rehabilitation medicines advises against easy going of rehabilitated drug addicts

13. In the fall of 1996, the Indian government dispatched samples of the cells of the militants to those four US scientists, who were only the Americans authorised to test them.

(a) dispatched samples of the cells of the militants to those four US scientists, who were only the Americans authorised to test them.
(b) dispatched samples of the militant's cells to those four US scientists, the only Americans authorised to test them.
(c) dispatched samples of the cells of militants to those four US scientists who were authorised to test them.
(d) dispatch the samples of the cells of the militants to those four US scientists, who were the only Americans authorised to test them.
(e) dispatched samples of cells of militants to those four US scientists, of the only Americans authorised to test them.

14. To prepare himself, he subjected himself to two weeks of total abstinence and intensive training in the open fields of the Panipat, climbing the hills nearby 30 times, spend nights in the open and to test to see how long he could hold out without food.

(a) climbing the hills nearby 30 times, spend nights in the open and to test to see
(b) climbed the hills nearby 30 times, spending nights in the open and tested to see
(c) spending nights in the open by climbing the hills nearby 30 times and tested for seeing
(d) climbing the hills nearby 30 times, spending nights in the open and testing to see
(e) climbing the nearby hills 30 times, spend nights in the open and tested to see

15. In November 1984, the Vesuvius volcano, started showing seismic activity, and later beginning belching gases, fumes and water and rumbled with the force of millions of tones of molten rock beneath the earth.

(a) started showing seismic activity, and later beginning belching gases, fumes and water and rumbled with
(b) started showing seismic activity, and later began belching gases, fumes and water and rumbling with
(c) showing some seismic activity, and later began belching gases, fumes and water and rumbled with
(d) had started to show seismic activity, and later began belching gases, fumes and water and began rumbling with
(e) has starting to show some seismic activity, and later began belching gases, fumes and water and rumbled with

16. Many middle-class South Asians find that they cannot obtain good medical attention, despite the fact they need it badly.

(a) they need it badly.
(b) they badly need it.
(c) of they need it badly.
(d) that they need it badly.
(e) they need it that badly.

17. The world today is totally different than, we have seen in the last century.

(a) than, we have seen
(b) from what we have seen
(c) from what we seen
(d) than what we seen
(e) than from that we have seen

18. Start the engine, and then you should press the accelerator.

(a) Start the engine, and then you should press
(b) Start the engine and then press
(c) Start the engine, then go on pressing
(d) Starting the engine, then pressing
(e) Starting the engine go on to pressing

19. He is an asset to the organisation, although he seems to be an eccentric and is a loner.

(a) He is an asset to the organisation, although he seems to be an eccentric and is a loner.
(b) Although he is eccentric, he is an asset to the organisation and wants to be a loner.
(c) Although he is eccentric, he is an asset to the organisation although he wants to be a loner.
(d) Although he is eccentric and wants to be a loner, he is an asset to the organisation.

(e) He is an asset to the organisation, seeming an eccentric and a loner although.

20. During the oil price hike of 2005 caused by the global market conditions, the amount of oil imported by our country decreased markedly.

(a) amount of oil imported by our country decreased markedly.
(b) amount of the oil imported by our country decreased markedly.
(c) amount of oil imported by our country decreased very visibly.
(d) amount of the oil we imported as a country decreased markedly.
(e) amount of oil imports of our country decreases markedly.

21. In rural India, many mango trees are planted at the end of a village or at the border of a district, for providing excellent shade during summer, and shelter during winter.

(a) for providing excellent shade during summer, and shelter during winter.
(b) to provide excellent shade in summer, and shelter in winter.
(c) in order to provide excellent shade in summer, and shelter in winter.
(d) so as to excellently provide shade in summer, and shelter in winter.
(e) for providing excellent shading during summer and shelter in winter.

22. Some of the most gut wrenching images of the previous year 1985 were, the tsunami striking South East Asian countries, the earthquake striking Pakistan, and famine stalking region after region.

(a) the tsunami striking South East Asian countries, the earthquake striking Pakistan, and famine
(b) the tsunami stricken South East Asian countries, the earthquake stricken Pakistan, and famine
(c) the tsunami striking South East Asian countries, the earthquake stricken Pakistan, and famine
(d) the tsunami striking South East Asian countries, the earthquakes striking Pakistan, and the famine
(e) the tsunami striking the South East Asian countries, the earthquake striking the Pakistan, and famine

23. Mental intelligence and common sense are essential for outstanding achievement because they involve your natural ability to comprehend difficult concepts quicker and to analyse them clearly and incisively.

(a) your natural ability to comprehend difficult concepts quicker and to analyse them clearly and incisively.
(b) one's natural ability for the comprehension of difficult concepts quickly and analysing them clearly and incisively.
(c) your natural ability of comprehension of difficult concepts quickly and clear and incisive analysis of it.
(d) one's natural ability to comprehend difficult concepts quickly and to analyse them clearly and incisively.
(e) one has natural ability to comprehension of difficult concepts quickly and to analyse them clearly and incisively.

24. Panchayati Raj institutions are now entrusted upon the execution of all rural upliftment schemes and programs in India.

(a) entrusted upon the execution of all rural upliftment schemes and programs
(b) entrusted with the execution of all rural uplift schemes and programs
(c) entrusted with the execution of all rural upliftment schemes and programs
(d) entrusted within the execution for all rural uplift programs and schemes
(e) entrusted of the execution of all rural upliftment schemes and programs

25. Mr. Singhania was perhaps the single most effective executive within the country, who had succeded without a degree, money and without any logistic support.

(a) who had succeeded without a degree, money and without any logistic support.
(b) without whom, a degree, money or logistic support, succeeded.
(c) who, without a degree, money or logistic support, succeeded.
(d) who, succeeded without a degree, money or logistic support.
(e) who, had succeed without a degree, money and without any logistic support.

Type 3

***Directions for the questions (1-50)*:** In the following questions, you have to identify the correct sentence/s.

For each of the following questions find the sentence/s that are correct.

1. (A) When you look up a word, the main thing that you want to know was its basic meaning.
(B) It's time to winding up the discussion now.

(C) A great many various words in English have more than one meaning.
(D) That wasn't a very fair thing to say!
(a) D only
(b) A and D
(c) A, B and D
(d) All of the above are correct
(e) None of the above

2. (A) She has a fair chance of winning the first prize.
(B) Fair weather is forecasted for tomorrow.
(C) There's a fair on at the park this very week.
(D) Don't forget to wind down your watch.
(a) A only
(b) A and C
(c) A, B and C
(d) None of the above are correct
(e) Only A and B

3. (A) Every language has a lot of different words with similar but slightly differing meanings.
(B) Words are used with each other in fairly fixed ways in every language.
(C) Words do not only have meanings, they also have associations.
(D) At an advanced level of any language, it is important to develop an impression of what connotations certain words have.
(a) A only
(b) A and C
(c) A, B and C
(d) All of the above are correct
(e) Only (b)

4. (A) Make a special note of any special characteristics that a word has had.
(B) The judge Mr. Dhuan increased the sentence of life imprisonment.
(C) We had a lightish dinner.
(D) Raveesh is very good at putting on different accentuals.
(a) A only
(b) A and C
(c) A, B and C
(d) None of the above are correct
(e) Only (b) and (c)

5. (A) I don't like recorded music, I prefer the real thing.
(B) These items are the genuine articles.
(C) You can give a wide summary of something.
(D) You can describe something in minute detail.
(a) A and C (b) A and B
(c) B and D (d) C only
(e) None of these

6. (A) It's something I feel powerfully about.
(B) If I remember perfectly, it happened at about six-thirty.
(C) It is useful to learn which adverbs most typically modify particular types of objectives.
(D) The majority of these adjectives has a negative connotation.
(a) C only (b) B and C
(c) A only (d) None of these
(e) All of these

7. (A) You lift your hand to ask a question.
(B) You can raise a family.
(C) You can go to a website on the world wide web.
(D) You can inspect a hotel inside which you want to stay.
(a) A only (b) C only
(c) B and D (d) B and C
(e) None of these

8. (A) The Seven Horses hotel in Singapore is much great.
(B) He just doesn't live in the genuine world.
(C) This briefcase is made of authentic leather.
(D) She is a very genuine person.
(a) A, B and D (b) B and D
(c) C only (d) D only
(e) A and B only

9. (A) After his death, she went to the hospital to collect his personal affairs.
(B) He made a rather fragile attempt of an apology, but it didn't convince anyone.
(C) Abhijit was a dreadful opponent, and I respected him for that.
(D) I was feeling pretty anxious when she didn't arrive on time.
(a) A only
(b) B only
(c) D only
(d) C only
(e) None of these

10. (A) A brash walk before dinner helps to enforce the appetite.
(B) The death tally in the Pakistan earthquake has now risen to 300,000.
(C) Let's take a sluggish stroll along the beach, shall we?
(D) If you want to stay at home tonight, that's perfectly OK with me.
(a) A only (b) B only
(c) C only (d) D only
(e) A and B only

11. (A) My aunt bereaved Rs. 500,000 in her will to cancer research.

(B) If I remember rightly she had two brothers, both older than her.
(C) If you want information about the publisher of this book, you can accede their website.
(D) Eating all those peanuts has attacked my appetite.
(a) B only (b) B and C
(c) A and C (d) D only
(e) Only A

12. (A) It's only fair that we should share the work equally.
(B) The Patna Book Fair is a very important event for most publishers.
(C) Our house gives us shelter through fair weather or foul.
(D) I've got fair eyelashes, hence my eyes look awful without mascara.
(a) A, B and C (b) C and D
(c) A, C and D (d) All of the above
(e) Only A and B

13. (A) The firefighters managed to save the people trapped in the burning third-floor flat.
(B) The countryside round here is terribly flattened and boring.
(C) To join the Lucknow Golf Club you pay a flattened fee of Rs. 5 lacs.
(D) He was able to erect the child's toy in five minutes flat.
(a) B and C
(b) A only
(c) A and D
(d) None of above
(e) A and B

14. (A) He struck a match box and we slowly began to look around the pitch dark room.
(B) The batsmen of the visiting team were not a matching for any of the home team batsmen.
(C) Their marriage has been called a matching made in heaven.
(D) The tense match between India and Pakistan ended in a draw.
(a) A only
(b) C only
(c) D only
(d) C and D
(e) Only B

15. (A) Rameez's going to be in the saddle while the boss is on the foreign trip.
(B) It's hard to know what to do when the management keeps moving the goalposts.
(C) Starting his own decorating business was just another of his half-baked ideas.
(D) We've had to tighten our belts since our father lost his job.
(a) A only (b) B, C and D
(c) All of the above (d) A, C and D
(e) A and B

16. (A) More unusual and original metaphors are used a great dealing in literature.
(B) All the world's a stage and all the men and women merely players.
(C) The candles of the night are burnt out; and the jocular day stands tiptoe atop the misty mountain tops.
(D) There is a tide in the affairs of men, which, taken at the peak of the flood, leads on to fortunate.
(a) B and C (b) D and C
(c) C only (d) B only
(e) Only A

17. (A) This book threw a great deal of fresh light on the history of the period.
(B) We could save half an hour at least if we went through the wood forest.
(C) Try to keep your cool even if he argues with you.
(D) She spent all her life fighting to get her company recognised and magnificent.
(a) A only (b) B only
(c) C only (d) C and D
(e) A and C

18. (A) She works in a shop that sells lady's clothes.
(B) Do you like the new shades that I've got?
(C) Did you see that documentary about Wales on TV last night?
(D) Have you met Amita's newish boy friend?
(a) C only (b) B only
(c) B and C (d) D only
(e) C and D

19. (A) It was a very bad hotel, with an overpriced menu.
(B) In this program, you can choose to overwrite the existing file or to save it as a new file.
(C) Our garden is overshadowed by the apartment block built next door.
(D) Amit always felt overshadowed by his older, more talented and successful, brother.
(a) All of the above
(b) A, C and D
(c) A, B and D
(d) C and D
(e) None of the above

20. (A) Don't underestimate the time that the work will take.
(B) The company is variously understaffed.
(C) The underlying issue is a very simple one.
(D) Kapil wishes his would not undermine everything that he does.

(a) A and C (b) C and D
(c) B and D (d) A and B
(e) Only B

21. (A) The airline upgraded me to business class.
(B) There has been an upward upturn in the economy.
(C) Cross-border cooperation has led to series of arrests of drug smugglers.
(D) Cross-cultural misunderstandings happen very often in today's world.
(a) C and D (b) B and C
(c) A and B (d) A and D
(e) B and D

22. (A) He was ejected from the restaurants for bad behaviour.
(B) The engine emitted a loud noise and then stopped running.
(C) The building is adjacent of the hotel.
(D) She gave me an annotated edition to Salman Rushdie's works.
(a) A and B (b) B only
(c) B and C (d) D only
(e) All of the above

23. (A) I really think he overstayed his case, and lost a lot of sympathy.
(B) The plane's undercarriage failed to open and it crashed.
(C) A detailed list of the participants in the seminar is given overleaf.
(D) Rajendra has a very overbearing personality.
(a) C and D (b) A and C
(c) A and B (d) D only
(e) Only A

24. (A) The project was underfunded from the outset.
(B) During the cruise, a small cat fell board and drowned.
(C) Cooperation across the fronts has been very good.
(D) Cross-border cooperation has been exemplary good.
(a) A only (b) B only
(c) C and D (d) None of the above
(e) A and B

25. (A) The hotel staff members gave me a luxury room instead of the ordinary one I'd booked.
(B) Would you like to spend the night at the camp site or come back the same day?
(C) The problem that lies under surface is a very serious one.
(D) Misunderstandings between culture, is sadly, extremely frequent.
(a) A and C (b) B and C
(c) B only (d) A and D
(e) A, B and C

26. (A) I think this restaurant charges too much.
(B) The company experienced a rise in popularity since he changed its name.
(C) I felt that what she said was critical of my position and weakened it some well.
(D) It would be a mistake to think Monica was less intelligent than she really would be.
(a) A only (b) B only
(c) C only (d) D only
(e) A and D

27. (A) The weather can't be predictable.
(B) Poisonous snakes can be easily identified.
(C) He thinks so much about his career that he has no time for their family.
(D) The new windscreen designs are supposed to be in the process of being destructible by vandals.
(a) A and D (b) A, B and C
(c) B only (d) C and B
(e) Only C

28. (A) I had to postpone my trip to Kanpur.
(B) She asked the star for his signature on the behind of her table napkin.
(C) She took a degree in the sciences of crime at the Harvard University.
(D) The novel is largely based on the writer's own life story.
(a) A only (b) B only
(c) A and D (d) C only
(e) C and B

29. (A) It's an art exhibition looking back of the artists life and work.
(B) Deepak Chopra believes you can cure yourself into telling yourself that you are cured.
(C) Working at the home site and keeping in contact with the office by phone, fax and electronics is becoming increasingly common.
(D) Some constituencies are now deliberately trying to becoming less backward.
(a) None of Above (b) A only
(c) C only (d) D only
(e) A and C

30. (A) Most of the time modern airplanes fly on autopilot.
(B) The firm makes job applicants do a graphology tests.
(C) Rajat's a technique-wizard!
(D) Is it OK if I post-date this cheque!

(a) A only (b) B only
(c) C only (d) D only
(e) All of the above

31. (A) The company will be committing economics hara-kiri if it agrees to such a proposal.
(B) Most children these days are inoculated against vaccines when they are babies.
(C) I have some lovely pink earrings, they match my pink pendant perfectly.
(D) A weekend at the seaside was just the roster we needed after the long arduous journey.
(a) A only (b) A and B
(c) A and D (d) C only
(e) None of the above

32. (A) Seventeen prisoners have broken out into the high security Ambarka jail.
(B) The disease has broken out of several villages in the north of the country.
(C) Economists are looking out for signs in an end to the recession.
(D) He stood at the corner looking out at passing cars.
(a) A only
(b) C and D
(c) B only
(d) None of the above
(e) A and D

33. (A) There has been a breakout of a high security jail.
(B) There has been an outbreak of the deadly disease in several villages in the south of the state.
(C) The outlook is not gracious as the country's economy seems be stagnant.
(D) He was the overlooker while the others robbed the bank.
(a) A only (b) A and C
(c) B only (d) B and D
(e) Only C

34. (A) I have always maintained a policy of not intervening affairs that are not my business.
(B) The traffic was stationery for a few minutes after the accident, then its begun to move again.
(C) She paid me a nice complement by saying that I was the most intelligent person she had ever worked with.
(D) I am sorry but I wasn't trying to avoid you.
(a) A and C
(b) D only
(c) C and D
(d) A and B
(e) B and C

35. (A) At the entrance there was a big signal saying 'No dogs allowed'.
(B) The coach intervened in order to stop the argument between the two players.
(C) The other benefits I received in the job were complimented by an excellent pension plan.
(D) If you need stationery for your desk at the office, just ask the secretary.
(a) A only (b) B only
(c) C only (d) D only
(e) All of the above

36. (A) Amitesh was continually complaining about something or other.
(B) Amit was fined Rs. 25,900 for avoiding taxes and failing to declare one's income.
(C) The signal changed to green and the train moved away from the station.
(D) You have to press the button continuously until the light comes out.
(a) C and B (b) D only
(c) C only (d) A only
(e) A and C

37. (A) I don't think these sweaters will outlast till the end of the season.
(B) We ended up the table and used it to block the doorway.
(C) The cheetah is such a fast animal that it can even out run the fastest cars.
(D) Binny is always trying to do out everyone.
(a) A only (b) B only
(c) C only (d) D only
(e) B and C

38. (A) The committee held up her complaint, and she was awarded compensation.
(B) The Rolling Stones have out lasted most other music groups of the 1960s in popularity.
(C) We ended up eating in a dingy café on the edge of town.
(D) I'll leave on Monday as I don't want to stay out my welcome.
(a) B only (b) B and A
(c) C and D (d) A and C
(e) A, B and C

39. (A) There has been a violence out break in the old part of the city.
(B) I couldn't go to work since my stomach was bad inside.
(C) He is extremely cheerful and positive about his life.
(D) They fooled him into thinking his car had been set up and stolen, but it hadn't.
(a) A and C (b) D only
(c) C only (d) B only
(e) None of the above

40. (A) I imagine that I would get bored if I had a nine-and five job.
(B) When I arrive in the morning and leave in the evening I use this card to clock out and check in.
(C) I'm very tired as recently I've had a very heavy task.
(D) I don't want an office job because I don't want to spend all day stuck in house.
(a) A only
(b) B and C
(c) None of the above
(d) D only
(e) B only

41. (A) Amitabh can clock in any time between eight and ten and clock out between four and six; he is on flexi-time.
(B) I'd hate to feel trapped in my job and to be stuck inside lift.
(C) Amitabh's not here this evening, he's working nights as he does shifty work.
(D) Amitabh said "I work for different companies at different times as it suits me. I'm flexi-worker."
(a) A only (b) B only
(c) C only (d) D only
(e) All of the above

42. (A) I used to work for a company, but now I'm my own senior boss, I'm free lance.
(B) Ravindra stopped working in the restaurant as it was just a dead shift.
(C) When I was working for Reliance, all I could think of all day was about the evening.
(D) Being a corporate executive is a nice job, but you can't go out much with friends.
(a) A and C (b) C and D
(c) D only (d) A and B
(e) B and D

43. (A) A unique painting will come inside the hammer in at Sotheby's tomorrow.
(B) It's a sensible idea to shop around a bit before buying a computer.
(C) Jimmy has promised me that, if he ever decides to sell his motorbike, I can have refusal on it.
(D) Amisha doesn't mind trying a hard sell on a person who has expressed an interest in her company's products.
(a) B and C (b) A and C
(c) D only (d) B and D
(e) Only B

44. (A) I wasn't sure whether the shoe would fit my son's foot size so I bought it on approval.
(B) If you hope to make a bids for something in an open auction you first have to catch the auctioneer's eyes.
(C) If you work as a receptionist in this industry you spend most of your day on the cold-calling.
(D) They produce special implements for elderly people who like to do yoga and have really captured this very wide market.
(a) A only
(b) B only
(c) C only
(d) D only
(e) Only A and B

45. (A) As they had common business interests, it did not take them very long to come to an agreement on the issues under discussion.
(B) If you want to go into the manufacturing business, you had better be prepared for a lot of bureaucracy and governance.
(C) Sportswear is very profitable business to be in at the peak of the inflation.
(D) Only a small percentage of IIM Graduates have a real talent for the risk-taking of opening new business avenues.
(a) A only (b) B only
(c) C only (d) D only
(e) All of the above

46. (A) Does the customer know that he has many accounts outstanding which have yet to be paid?
(B) Until what date is the employment contract valid to expire?
(C) Please let us know when you receive our payment.
(D) It is very important that you complete your work by the agree time table.
(a) A and B (b) C and D
(c) C only (d) B and D
(e) None of the above

47. (A) Perizaad is working on a very interesting resource project at the moment.
(B) Unfortunately, there's a morale flaw in your reasoning.
(C) What used to be called Personnel in the 1980s is now named Human Resource.
(D) Mr. Mazumdar, the new COO is doing his best to raise the morale in the office.
(a) A only (b) B only
(c) D only (d) A and C
(e) All of the above

48. (A) The top brass of an organisation is often in the habit of rewarding itself, regardless of the performance of the organisation.
(B) It is impossible to be both brainy and beautiful at the same time.
(C) Managers don't pay enough attention to the people who work for them.
(D) Large businesses succeed by destroying small businesses.
(a) All of the above
(b) B, C and D
(c) A, B and D
(d) D only
(e) Only A

49. (A) It's very easy to fall behind your annual targets even if you under perform for a few days every month.
(B) She seemed to just breeze through the exams.
(C) I just can't seem to get hang of my biology subjects.
(D) When I sat down and looked at the exam paper my mind just went black.
(a) A only (b) B only
(c) C and D (d) A and B
(e) D only

50. (A) He is the nicest person you can hope to come across.
(B) Six Indians were awarded the Order of Merit by the foreign dignitary.
(C) You should treat everyone with equal respect.
(D) Man is a severely competent person.
(a) A only (b) B and C only
(c) A and C (d) A, B and C
(e) None of the above

Type 4

Directions for the questions (1-50): In each of the following questions, one or more of the sentences is/are incorrect. You have to identify the incorrect sentence/s:

1. (A) Soaring oil prices have raised the stakes in China's game of brinkmanship over the hotly disputed Spratly islands, with the Philippines this week becoming the first rival claimant to break ranks.
(B) In a separate development, Beijing reacted with unusual restraint to Vietnam's announced plans to begin regular air services to another Spratlys atoll within months, indicating that the feuding neighbours may have reached an accommodation on the issue.
(C) Philippine President Gloria Macapagal-Arroyo and her Chinese counterpart Hu Jintao agreed at talks in Beijing jointly to study potential oil deposits in the South China Sea atolls as part of a three-year research project involving two state energy firms.
(D) A communiqué by the Philippine government went to great pains to emphasise that the pact did not imply that the two countries, whose naval forces have clashed over the contested reefs, would proceed past the drilling stage.
(a) A and B (b) B and D
(c) A, C and D (d) D only
(e) All of the above

2. (A) Salvation was to come from the direction of Central Asia, with Russia shipping 400,000 barrels per day of crude through an overland pipeline to Daqing, in northern China.
(B) However, it is more than a year behind schedule, and dogged by uncertainty.
(C) Suddenly the hundreds of coral atolls have shifted over into focus, even though the documented evidence of oil and gas supplies is at best circumspect.
(D) Diplomatic reports suggest that China may be poised for a decisive push into the region.
(a) A only (b) A and C
(c) C only (d) A, B, C and D
(e) Only B

3. (A) Tokyo, concerned that gas fields on his side of the boundary might be exhausted, sent a survey team to the area in July.
(B) Japan's gas reserves are projected at 200 billion metres, a commercially viable level.
(C) Beijing proposed in June that the gas field be jointly developed, but Tokyo has not responded, reportedly because the extent of the Chinese reserves is unknown and out of concern that the issue might inflame tensions between China and Taiwan.
(D) Further to the east, Petro China has been given the green light to begin drilling for gas near the Nanxia Archipelago, a strategic area contested by Vietnam, Malaysia, Taiwan and the Philippines.
(a) A only (b) B only
(c) A and B (d) A and D
(e) None of the above

4. (A) Think of the merger and acquisition (M&A) game and immediately a lot number of American or European companies come to mind.
(B) Indian firms takes over more than 75 international companies last year.

(C) Among the most publicised deals, Tata Motors, part of Tata Group, India's oldest industrial conglomerate, bought South Korean company Daewoo's truck plant in that country.
(D) Reliance Infocomm, belonging to India's largest privately held business house, Reliance Group, took over Flag International, a major telecom network, for US $211 million.
(a) A and B (b) A, B and C
(c) A only (d) B only
(e) C only

5. (A) In fact, the global ambitions of Indian industrial houses are best illustrated by Aditya Birla Group, which has a presence in 18 countries and overseas revenue of $1.8 billion.
(B) The group employs 12,000 people in 20 countries.
(C) Their manufacturing activities include carbon black, tire cord, viscose staple fibre, metals and chemicals.
(D) Earlier, global operations for an Indian company means plain exports.
(a) A and D (b) A only
(c) D only (d) A, C and D
(e) A, B and C

6. (A) It began with acquisitions in the information technology and related services sector.
(B) In pharmaceuticals, Wockhardt has bought C P Pharma of the United Kingdom for $10.85 million.
(C) Tata Tea has taken over Tetley of the UK, the world's biggest tea bag maker, for $430 million.
(D) With the processes, it has become the world's second largest tea company.
(a) B and D (b) D only
(c) B only (d) A, B and D
(e) A only

7. (A) There are two main reason for that predatory mood.
(B) Having established a domestic presence, the component makers are now looking for an international presence.
(C) Second, having improved their productivity, quality and reliability, Indian companies feel more confident about spreading their wings abroad.
(D) Various other factors are being attributed to this Indian penchant for the takeover game in all sectors.
(a) A only
(b) A and B
(c) B only
(d) none of those
(e) C only

8. (A) Since 1996, it has been regularly been winning GM's "Supplier of the year" award.
(B) It is on the urging of GM that SFL set up its China operations in May 2004 in Hainan province.
(C) A presence aboard means easier reaches to new markets.
(D) This explains why TVS Group has also set up motorcycle plant in China.
(a) A and C
(b) A, C and D
(c) C and D
(d) A and D
(e) All of the above

9. (A) A changing perception as to India has also helped.
(B) India is no longer a backward, third world country.
(C) Helping boost the image are favourable opinions of leading international financial institutions (FI).
(D) India will be the third biggest economy by 2050, just behind China and the US, in that order.
(a) A (b) A and D
(c) B only (d) No error
(e) C only

10. (A) Alfa Laval India, which has plants in three locations, is taking this step to better utilise its reserves.
(B) In the UK alonely, Indian firms have about 440 investments/joint ventures.
(C) There are 1,441 Indian companies operating in Singapore.
(D) Of these more than 450 are technology enterprises.
(a) A (b) B
(c) B and C (d) no error
(e) A and B

11. (A) A print design project communicates a message.
(B) Contrast is a good way to create a noticeable design and layout.
(C) Contrasted can be size, colour, direction, format or the expected versus the unexpected.
(D) Size contrast can involve graphics or type.
(a) B (b) B and C
(c) C (d) A, B and C
(e) A and C

12. (A) I remember seeing a full page-advertisement with a bright background colour.
(B) The only other item on the page was a very small line of type in a lighter shade of the same colour.
(C) Since I can still recall the ad, it must made an impression.
(D) Using colour to impact your design works best when it involves the unexpected or extreme.

(a) B (b) C
(c) D (d) No error
(e) A

13. (A) Moving one by one step away from the expected with graphics and photography can also create reader interest.
(B) Try using a conceptual image or photo to highlight your main message versus very first thing to come to mind when thinking about your product or service.
(C) Another form of contrast is in the actual design.
(D) An unusual fold in a brochure or direct mail piece can add excitement.
(a) A and B
(b) B only
(c) A only
(d) No error
(e) B and D

14. (A) The typeface that you choose for your print project is an important piece of the foremost overall design process.
(B) First, narrow down your choice by selecting the tone you want to present.
(C) Typefaces can convey personality.
(D) For instance, if you are in the banking industry you might choose a classic serif font such as Garamond, to convey dependability.
(a) A only
(b) B only
(c) C only
(d) no error
(e) D only

15. (A) Readability is crucial.
(B) Be sure the font we choose is legible and logical.
(C) With all of the newest and interesting typefaces available today, it is tempting to pick one that you think looks "cool".
(D) This can work if you are going for an edgy look that will appeal to a young audience, but your copy still needs to be easily understood.
(a) A and D (b) B only
(c) C only (d) B and C
(e) A only

16. (A) Words setting and word spacing are another consideration to achieve for your design.
(B) The optimal setting for your body text is flush left, rag right.
(C) This setting allows comfortable readability.
(D) The flush left makes it easier for the reader to find the next line.
(a) B only (b) C only
(c) B and C (d) no error
(e) A only

17. (A) Justified text work best for a lengthy materials such as books or magazine articles.
(B) Centred text will create right and left ragged edges.
(C) This can create a dignified look if treated carefully.
(D) Vary the lines to give the ragged edges an interesting look and try increasing the space between the lines to add readability.
(a) A only (b) A and D
(c) B and D (d) C and D
(e) None of the above

18. (A) The brain is a strange organ.
(B) It works in ways we don't understand and manage to create everything we see.
(C) Working at odds with the rest of the body it performs best when we are not consciously trying.
(D) Creativity will be at the life-blood of every facet of life.
(a) B and D
(b) B only
(c) D only
(d) A and B
(e) A only

19. (A) One easy answer is water colour painting.
(B) The gentle movement of a brush has a relaxing, de-stressing effect which has also been noted in activities such as calligraphy.
(C) Whilst the mix of colours and there application energises parts of the brain which would normally get scanned stimulation.
(D) Couple this to mix this a visual/tactile experience as your painting emerges and presto!
(a) B, C and D (b) C and D
(c) B and D (d) B and C
(e) A, B and C

20. (A) Painting a water colour is a life-affirming thing.
(B) You have an image of the world in your head.
(C) You start getting it down on your art paper and before you know it you have captured a piece of the world around you and it's been through your own efforts.
(D) What could be more satisfying than that?
(a) B only (b) B and D
(c) A and C (d) no error
(e) A and B

21. (A) The rightfully believing that his geniuses in poetry laid in personal utterances, Irish poet

William Butler Yeats recognised that these personal utterances alone could not organise a body of a lyric poetry and drama into the organic structure he hoped to build.

(B) For one thing personal utterances is beset by danger of sentimentality, which leads poetry away from that reality that poetry would deal with various kinds of self-pity and self-deceptions.

(C) He thus has to technique by which the person could some how be objectified, be given the appearance of impersonal 'truth' and yet retained motive force of privately felt belief.

(D) The partial solution was the theory the mask.

(a) A, C and D (b) B, C and D
(c) A, B, C and D (d) A and B
(e) All of the above

22. (A) Those not under the confluence with the mask are much more concerned with the things at hand.

(B) They see no reason of building castles in the air and certainly no reason to go live into them.

(C) They will not dare to dream and will like things to be as they appear or seem to appear.

(D) They do not question and certainly do not venture to know more than what is let known to them by their predecessors.

(a) A and B (b) A, C and D
(c) A, B and C (d) None of these
(e) A only

23. (A) We observe today not a victory of party but a celebration of freedom.

(B) Symbolising an end as well as a beginning.

(C) I have sworn before you and Almighty God the same solemn oath our forbears will prescribed nearly a century and three-quarters ago.

(D) The world was very different now.

(a) A, C and D (b) A and B
(c) A, B and C (d) All of above
(e) B and C

24. (A) Let the world go forth from this time and place would be to friend and foe alike.

(B) The torch has been passed to a new generation of Americans.

(C) Born in this century, tempered by war, disciplined by a hard and bitter peace, proud of which our ancient heritage.

(D) Unwilling to witness or permit the slow undoing of those human rights to which this nation has always been committed.

(a) A and C (b) A, B and C
(c) A, C and D (d) A only
(e) No error

25. (A) In the long history of the world, only a few generations have been granted the role of defending freedom in its hour of maximum danger.

(B) I do not believe that any of us would exchange places with any other people or any other generation.

(C) The energy, the faith, the devotion which we bring to this endeavour will light our country and all who serve it.

(D) The glow from that fire can truly light the world.

(a) A only
(b) B only
(c) C only
(d) no error
(e) D only

26. (A) Finally, television stars had came into their own.

(B) They are big enough to be 'celebrity contestants' on KBC.

(C) Of course, there are also endorsements, charity causes and ribbon-cuttings that were hitherto reserved for the big screen idols.

(D) These gods of Bollywood clutter as the preferred professionals for festivals in Navratri and Diwali melas.

(a) A and D
(b) A, B and C
(c) B and D
(d) A and C
(e) A only

27. (A) "I just reads in a news magazine that TV comprises 67 per cent of the Indian entertainment industry."

(B) Films and other things comprise the other 23 per cent.

(C) Finally, television is at par with the film industry.

(D) A TV actor is a bonafide star now and TV is not a poor cousin of Bollywood anymore.

(a) A and C (b) B only
(c) A, B and C (d) A and D
(e) C only

28. (A) I am probably the world's worst cook.

(B) I am fine when it comes to appreciating this cuisines of great chefs but, left to myself, I couldn't even fry an egg.

(C) It is not that I don't know how to do all this.

(D) I can tell you how a kakori kabab is made, how the flavour of a coq au vin is directly related to the wine you should use.

(a) A only (b) B only
(c) B and D (d) no error
(e) C only

29. (A) The problem is that I am all theory; no practice.
(B) Put me in a kitchen and a look of panic will settle on my face while I clumsily bash around with the pots and pans.
(C) Within the trade, they have a term for this: a bad hand.
(D) A good chef is not somebody who know how the great dishes are made while these days everybody has access to most recipes.
(a) B only
(b) B and D
(c) D only
(d) C and D
(e) A and D

30. (A) The reason I like risotto has nothing to do with taste.
(B) Most rice dishes, pulao for instance–require you to cover the rice with water and then go away and do something else while it cooks.
(C) It requires very constant attention.
(D) Take your eye away from the pan and you will soon have an ex-risotto or a risotto that has failed its exam.
(a) A only (b) C only
(c) B and C (d) D only
(e) B only

31. (A) The whole point of a risotto is that the creaminess comes from the rice's own starch.
(B) You should never wash the rice you use for risotto (to preserve the starch) but should add it straight to the pan.
(C) Then you need to add stock, one ladleful at a time, and stir, stir, stir.
(D) It is the stirring that persuades the grains of rice to surrender to their starch.
(a) A and D (b) B and C
(c) C and D (d) D only
(e) Only A and C

32. (A) A new year is a goodwill time for a reality check on your love life.
(B) If we have attached any much importance to specific days, using those days to take specific decisions is a strategic approach.
(C) Let go of memorabilia from old, failed relationships.
(D) Bring all problems to the table in a spirit of give and take and thrash things out.
(a) A and B (b) B and C
(c) C and A (d) D and B
(e) A and D

33. (A) The phone rang horribly late at night fall but, for reasons I cannot fathom.
(B) Normally the hour and tone of the conversation would undoubtedly have put me off.
(C) I am a regular reader of your column and I notice that you are always criticising everything.
(D) The bold and blunt query took me aback.
(a) A only (b) B only
(c) C only (d) D only
(e) All of the above

34. (A) A reflective calm seemed to have released the earlier impatience.
(B) Why don't you write about what you like about India?
(C) Give me three good reasons on a Sunday morning to feel happy and satisfied.
(D) Instead, you often leave me feeling the opposite other way.
(a) A and C (b) B and D
(c) A and D (d) C and D
(e) Only B

35. (A) When they want to, Indians have an amazing way of telling the truth.
(B) At the most surprising of moments they exactly blurt it out.
(C) It's said without artifice and without care for political correctness.
(D) Unvarnished it no doubt is but it's also refreshingly unalloyed.
(a) A only (b) B only
(c) C only (d) D only
(e) A and D

36. (A) In fact, no other country seems to have this incredible quality.
(B) The Brits are too phlegmatic, the French too loquacious, the Germans far too upright and the Italians simply muddleheaded.
(C) The Americans wouldn't know enough and the Chinese races would be horrified at anything approximates to the blunt truth.
(D) That's not their way of doing things.
(a) A only (b) B only
(c) C only (d) D only
(e) None of these

37. (A) They don't ever care if they end up making a spectacle of themselves.
(B) They do it because they feel they have to.
(C) The passion that moves them cannot be diffused by etiquette or politesse or even lack of opportunity.
(D) So, this morning, I want to compliment my late night interlocutor for helping me appreciate a quality I had not properly think before.

(a) A and B (b) C and D
(c) A, B and D (d) None of these
(e) A and C

38. (A) Do you knew how many illegal Bangladeshi immigrants there are in India?
(B) I ask because this truth is that nobody knows how many illegal Bangladeshi migrants have made India their home.
(C) Every figure you read will be an approximation.
(D) The 30-million figure, for instance, is usually quoted by people who want to claim that the problem of migration has now veered dangerously out of control.
(a) A and B (b) A and C
(c) B, C and D (d) A, B and D
(e) All of the above

39. (A) At an incentive level, however, we do recognise that there are many illegal migrants in India.
(B) The border between India and Bangladesh is porous and there is little that anyone can do to check migration.
(C) Moreover, many people in the border villages do not recognise that an international boundary exists.
(D) It is not uncommon for a man to cycle from a Bangladeshi village to a town in India to buy something–and for him to then cycle back home on the same day.
(a) A only (b) B only
(c) D (d) C and D
(e) C only

40. (A) First of all, there are supposed to be too many of them.
(B) Secondly, there is a danger that some of them will have terrorist links.
(C) There are simply not enough jobs too go around.
(D) If you think about it, no of this makes much sense.
(a) A, C and D (b) B, C and D
(c) C and D (d) A and D
(e) All of the above

41. (A) In my view, the police should have better things to do.
(B) I don't to think it is possible for anybody to support the manner in which alleged Bangladeshis are being deported.
(C) I have been reading a pamphlet produced by the Citizen's Campaign for Preserving Democracy.
(D) Members of this group studied the way in which the police rounded up Bangladeshis.
(a) A only (b) B only
(c) C only (d) D only
(e) B and C

42. (A) In effect, this means that the authorities can decide that anybody is an legal immigrant and can throw him out of the country.
(B) There is nothing a victim can do by way of protest.
(C) There is no appeal at all.
(D) Anybody who does not keep them happy will be deported unless he then pays off the local police.
(a) A only (b) B only
(c) C only (d) D only
(e) None of these

43. (A) For anyone who believes in the law of averages or the notion that whatever goes up must come down, it may well appear that the prospects for 2006 will not be as bright as they were in the last year.
(B) After all, world economy grew at 4 per cent-plus for the second consecutive year in 2005.
(C) Significantly, the biggest contribution to global growth came from Asia.
(D) The Indian economy has grown at nearly 8 per cent in 2005, which is a rare feat considering that agricultural growth were quite ordinary.
(a) A only (b) B only
(c) A and D (d) D only
(e) D and B

44. (A) One of the most telling trends of last year were that news of 8 per cent GDP growth stopped surprising us in India.
(B) The competitiveness-led buoyancy would continue and consolidate further in 2006.
(C) Even if one grants the possibility of some cyclical correction in the global growth momentum or the consumer demand, there is likely to be a compensatory force in the formed of investment demand.
(D) No doubt, with such robust investment activity, it is now going to be increasingly difficult to keep interest rates low.
(a) A and C (b) B and C
(c) A and D (d) C and D
(e) B and D

45. (A) As the growing economy makes increasing demands on infrastructure inputs, these problems could worsen in the coming year.
(B) Therefore, addressing infrastructure gaps needs to doing our topmost priority next year.
(C) The second risk lies in the global macroeconomic imbalances, reflected in the twin deficits of the US and rising surpluses of Asia.
(D) The longer these imbalances have persisted, the greater has become the risk of a disruptive correction.

(a) B only (b) A only
(c) D only (d) C only
(e) None of these

46. (A) Where there are wills there's always a way.
(B) This is an old saying, but so true.
(C) All these years we have been hearing from BCCI officials that if players don't play domestic cricket, they will not be considered for selection to the national team.
(D) That was only talk and nothing else, for most of the top players stayed away from Ranji, Duleep or Challenger Trophy games.
(a) A only (b) A and C
(c) B and A (d) D
(e) B and C

47. (A) The only problem is that the wickets that are on offer for domestic cricket are hardly conducive for batsman.
(B) It is here that BCCI needs to show the same will, as they have shown in making players play domestic cricket.
(C) For years now, pitches have been prepared to suit the home team's strengths and that is fine so long as the pitch is not a lottery.
(D) If one goes by the scores in some of the matches, especially Delhi's games, then it is quite obvious that the pitches prepared are sub-standard and not conducive to a fair contest between bat and ball.
(a) B only (b) A only
(c) D only (d) C only
(e) A and B

48. (A) A day after a controversy broke out over medicines manufactured by the guru, the Health Ministry said that they would put the medicines to the test.
(B) The government will not scrap the Delhi-Mumbai airport modernisation plan.
(C) In the district town, the children told the committee members that they were not consuming the meals served by the schools.
(D) The committee would keep watch on the quality of grain.
(a) B only (b) A only
(c) D only (d) C only
(e) C and D

49. (A) In an economy heady with its success in Information Technology, it is easy to forget that industrially advanced regions like California or countries like France are also leading agriculture producers.
(B) But politicians have not been particularly helpful in the process.
(C) The situation there is almost alarming.
(D) The spread of these activities to the south is a clear matter of worry.
(a) B only (b) A only
(c) D only (d) No error
(e) C only

50. (A) "You are from England? After Israel and America you are our best friends."
(B) The national team floundered thanks to an insistence that players be pious rather than professional.
(C) In Iran, the conservative clergy has no greater foe than soccer.
(D) Now, any Iranian football defeat is laid at their feet.
(a) B only (b) A only
(c) D only (d) No error
(e) B and C

Answer Key

Type 1

1. (b)	**2.** (d)	**3.** (e)	**4.** (d)	**5.** (a)
6. (d)	**7.** (a)	**8.** (a)	**9.** (d)	**10.** (d)
11. (b)	**12.** (c)	**13.** (a)	**14.** (d)	**15.** (d)
16. (d)	**17.** (d)	**18.** (c)	**19.** (b)	**20.** (d)
21. (d)	**22.** (c)	**23.** (b)	**24.** (d)	**25.** (d)
26. (a)	**27.** (c)	**28.** (b)	**29.** (d)	**30.** (d)
31. (d)	**32.** (a)	**33.** (d)	**34.** (b)	**35.** (a)
36. (a)	**37.** (b)	**38.** (b)	**39.** (a)	**40.** (c)
41. (c)	**42.** (b)	**43.** (c)	**44.** (d)	**45.** (a)
46. (c)	**47.** (c)	**48.** (b)	**49.** (d)	**50.** (d)

Type 2

1. (b)	**2.** (b)	**3.** (c)	**4.** (a)	**5.** (a)
6. (c)	**7.** (d)	**8.** (a)	**9.** (c)	**10.** (d)
11. (d)	**12.** (a)	**13.** (b)	**14.** (d)	**15.** (b)
16. (d)	**17.** (b)	**18.** (b)	**19.** (d)	**20.** (a)
21. (b)	**22.** (d)	**23.** (d)	**24.** (c)	**25.** (d)

Type 3

1. (a)	**2.** (a)	**3.** (d)	**4.** (d)	**5.** (b)
6. (d)	**7.** (d)	**8.** (d)	**9.** (c)	**10.** (d)
11. (a)	**12.** (d)	**13.** (c)	**14.** (c)	**15.** (c)
16. (d)	**17.** (c)	**18.** (c)	**19.** (a)	**20.** (a)
21. (d)	**22.** (b)	**23.** (a)	**24.** (d)	**25.** (c)
26. (a)	**27.** (c)	**28.** (a)	**29.** (a)	**30.** (a)
31. (d)	**32.** (d)	**33.** (c)	**34.** (b)	**35.** (b)

36. (c)	37. (c)	38. (a)	39. (c)	40. (c)
41. (a)	42. (b)	43. (d)	44. (a)	45. (a)
46. (c)	47. (c)	48. (a)	49. (d)	50. (d)

Type 4

1. (d)	2. (c)	3. (a)	4. (a)	5. (a)
6. (b)	7. (a)	8. (b)	9. (a)	10. (b)
11. (b)	12. (b)	13. (a)	14. (a)	15. (d)
16. (d)	17. (b)	18. (a)	19. (b)	20. (d)
21. (c)	22. (a)	23. (a)	24. (a)	25. (d)
26. (a)	27. (a)	28. (b)	29. (c)	30. (b)
31. (d)	32. (a)	33. (a)	34. (c)	35. (b)
36. (c)	37. (b)	38. (a)	39. (a)	40. (c)
41. (b)	42. (a)	43. (d)	44. (a)	45. (a)
46. (a)	47. (b)	48. (c)	49. (b)	50. (d)

Explanations

Type 1

1. B is the best way of expressing the idea.
2. D. The correct answer corrects the incorrect use of I in the other sentences.
3. The improper use of the pronouns *one* and *you* is corrected in Choice E.
4. The omission of the past participle *been* is corrected in Choice D.
5. A. There is no error in the original sentence.
6. D. The correct pronoun is *its*.
7. No error. *Poor product quality* is singular, so the singular noun ' it' must also be correct.
8. A. No error. The phrases are all parallel: soft hair sharp paws, and keen sense of hearing
9. D. *Having bowed our heads* is a dangling modifier. Option D is the best way of rephrasing it.
10. Option D is the best way of phrasing the message.
11. B. This corrects the unnecessary switch in the pronouns, *anyone-you*.
12. C. This is the most correct and concise form of the sentence.
13. A. There is no error in the original sentence.
14. D. *The reason is that* is preferable to *The reason is because*.
15. D. This corrects the double negative *(hadn't hardly)* and also uses *those* with *kinds* correctly.
16. D. Both together and up are unnecessary since their meaning is included in the words cooperate and divide.
17. D. Parallel structure requires the use of the verbal noun as the object of the verb enjoyed: Enjoyed what? splashing, bathing; and sun bathing, Enjoy should not be followed by an infinitive construction.
18. C. The other choices have misplaced modifiers.
19. B. The clause that money doesn't make you happy is the predicate nominative of the verb is.
20. D. This is an incomplete sentence since the verb is missing. Option D provides the verb (is *recognised)* and presents the only complete sentence among the options.
21. D. This was an unnecessary shift of pronoun. Do not shift from *you* to *one*. Choice D changes the meaning unnecessarily.
22. C. The demonstrative pronoun *those* is needed here *–from those* (persons).
23. B. This corrects the dangling participle and the misuse of *stole* for *stolen*.
24. D. None of the sentences are correct.
25. D. Do not use calculate or reckon when you mean think.
26. A. This question tests the agreement between subject and verb and pronoun and antecedent are both involved. *Community* (singular) needs a singular verb, *influences*. Also, the pronoun which refers to *community* should be singular *(its)*. Choice B is best.
27. Option C is the correct answer as it is the best way of expressing the idea. All the other options are awkward
28. Option B is the best way of phrasing the answer. The original sentence contains a dangling participle *depending*. The other choices change the emphasis presented by the author.
29. D. Either should precede the two choices offered.
30. D. Since the words *but also* precede a phrase, the words *not only* should precede the previous phrase.
31. Option D is the most appropriate answer. The pronoun *they* has to match with *their*.
32. A. No error. Option D is also correct grammatically, but it changes the message.
33. D. The other options repeat the word 'person' unnecessarily.
34. B. Choice A suffers from the use of the ambiguous pronoun *they*. Choices C and D are correct grammatically but they change the message by dropping the word *immediately*.
35. A. Choice A is correct because the subject of the verb *had* must be *who*, not *whom*. *Which* in Choice E should not be used to refer to a person.
36. A. *Already* is an adverb; *all ready* is an adjectival construction. *Allready* is a misspelling. Choices D and E do not convey the thought of the sentence.

37. B. One way of correcting a dangling participle is to change the participial phrase to a clause. Choices B and D substitute clauses for the phrase. However, choice D changes the meaning of the sentence.

38. B. "He" is the subject of the sentence, which takes who as the relative pronoun.

39. A. No error. Some of the other sentences are also grammatically correct, but are rejected on the grounds that Choice A is more concise than them.

40. C. This choice does not violate the parallel structure, neither does it change the original message.

41. Choice C corrects errors in the possessive form of *government* (needed before a verbal noun) and *it*.

42. B. The agreement should be between *Her elder brother* and *insists*.

43. C. This is also an error in agreement: *Kind* is singular and requires a singular modifier *(this)*.

44. D. This choice eliminates the error in parallel structure.

45. A. The correct idiom is *graduate from*. Choice C changes the meaning of the message.

46. C. This corrects the two errors in this sentence–the error in case *(me* for I) and the error in tense *(had finished* for *finished)*.

47. C. In choices A, B, and D, the modifier *familiar* is dangling. Choice C corrects the error while retaining the original meaning of the sentence and conveying it most concisely.

48. B. The preposition *with* is needed to complete the phrase *has gone hand in hand with*. Choice C unnecessarily loses the parallel structure.

49. D. It is the shortest and most concise form of writing the sentence, while retaining the original idea.

50. D. The correct answer is Option D.

Type 2

1. B. *Referred back* is redundant. The prefix *re* means "back."

2. Option B is the best way to convey the message.

3. C. The *either... or* structure should always be as close as possible to the things that they are attached to.

4. Option A maintains the parallel structure in the best way.

5. A.

6. C.

7. D. The modifier 'Being in the need of a variety of clothing' qualifies for the pronoun 'he'. As a general rule, the modifier must be placed as near to the noun or pronoun it qualifies, as possible. Option D is both, grammatically and structurally correct.

8. A. The 'first principle' of sentence correction questions is, 'never make an unnecessary correction.' There is nothing wrong with the original sentence. The modifier is correctly used and the part also follows 'subject-verb agreement.

9. C. The problem in the original sentence is in the use of the noun (completeness) in place of an adverb (completely). Option C corrects this.

10. D. A question on parallelism. Two 'actions' are being described in the underlined part of the sentence, and both the 'actions' must be in the same form.

11. D. Option A is incorrect as it uses the adjective AFTER the noun it qualifies. Options B and C are eliminated as they change the meaning of the sentence. Hence, the correct option is D.

12. A. The original sentence is correct and needs no change.

13. B. The only problem with the original sentence is its structure. 'cells of the militants' should be replaced with 'the militants cells'. Moreover, the use of the modifier 'only' at the appropriate place can make the sentence correct. Option C changes the meaning of the sentence, and hence it is eliminated.

14. D. A question on parallelism. As the sentence has several 'actions', all the 'actions' must be in the same form. Only option D takes care of it. None of other options follows the rule of parallelism.

15. B. Another question on parallelisms which are only dealt with correctly in option B.

16. D. *Despite* should be used as a preposition, not as a word joining clauses.

17. Option B is the most grammatically correct way of phrasing the message.

18. B. The two verbs should be parallel: *start* and *press*.

19. D. The key idea is that *he is an asset to the organisation*. To create a suspenseful or periodic sentence, the writer should place *he is a genius* at the end of the sentence.

20. A. Never change a correct sentence.

21. B. 'To provide' is the best way to state the idea.

22. D. A sentence that tests the knowledge of 'prepositions' and 'parallelism'. Option D is perfect.

23. D. *One's natural ability* is the best way to phrase the start of the underlined portion. That leaves us with option B & D. Option D is more succinct and correct.

24. C. 'Entrust with' is the correct phrase. This eliminates options A and D. The noun 'upliftment' has to be used instead of the verb 'uplift'.

25. D. A question on parallel structure.

SECTION 6: New Verbal Question Types in CAT

The CAT is a dynamic exam and it keeps changing or altering its pattern from time-to-time. We try our best to keep abreast of the latest pattern of the exam and provide content to you which is up-to-date and relevant from the examination point of view. The CAT has introduced 2-3 different question types in the verbal section like **Phrasal Verbs**, **Summary of the Paragraph and Paragraph Completion/Last Sentence of the Paragraph**, **Missing Sentence of the Paragraph**, **Irrelevant Statement Questions**, **Summary of the Passage Questions**. These new chapters have been included in this section.

The question type "Missing Statement of the Paragraph" appeared in CAT 2022 instead of the Irrelevant Statement question type. But, in CAT 2023 it came back again along with the Irrelevant Statement question type.

The Missing Statement question is a paragraph-level question where one sentence is deleted from a paragraph and there are four places in the paragraph which are given as options where this sentence could be placed. The student has to select the correct location where the given statement could be placed so that the paragraph is completed in the best possible manner.

This question type is a combination of a paragraph-level sentence completion and paragraph completion question type.

The best way to solve this question type is to find the idea of the paragraph and link the given statement with the different sentences of the paragraph. Special attention has to be given to the style of writing, the clues given and the general or specific nature of the paragraph. This question type will require similar linking skills as the ones we use in paragraph jumble and paragraph completion question types. Please revise those chapters from the book and then attempt this question type. We have provided typical CAT-level questions with detailed solutions for your practice. Make sure you solve them twice with a detailed analysis of each question so that you have a good learning experience. Then, you can go ahead and solve these questions in the CAT experience and previous years' CAT papers chapters as well.

CHAPTER

21A Phrasal Verbs

Questions based on the correct usage of **phrasal verbs** have become an integral part of the ***Verbal Ability*** section in the CAT exam since the last seven years. Each year a minimum of two to three questions come in the exam, which test the correct usage of phrasal verbs. Ever since CAT became online and its pattern has assumed consistency, it is seen as an important part of the verbal section.

This chapter aims at providing you with an exhaustive list of phrasal verbs for your preparation. Practice exercises have also been provided according to the questions that come in the CAT exam.

WHAT ARE PHRASAL VERBS?

Phrasal verbs are basic verbs which can combine with different propositions (particles) to make verbs with completely new and often unfathomable meanings.

Phrasal verbs are combinations of ordinary verbs like 'put', 'take', 'come', and 'go' and particles like 'in', 'out', 'on', and 'off'. They are a very important part of everyday English. Every student of English needs a basic understanding of the most common phrasal verbs and also of common nouns and adjectives made from phrasal verbs.

Most phrasal verbs are not informal, slang, or improper for educated speech or formal writing. Exactly the opposite is true–most phrasal verbs are acceptable at all levels of spoken or written English. In fact, for many of the phrasal verbs, there is no alternative to the phrasal verb–there is no other way to say it.

Many verbs in English are followed by an adverb or a preposition (also called a particle), and these two-part verbs, are also called phrasal verbs. The particle that follows the verb changes the meaning of the phrasal verb in idiomatic ways.

PHRASAL VERBS

Verb	Meaning	Example
drop off	decline gradually	The hill dropped off near the river.
drop off(2)	fall asleep	While doing his homework, he dropped off.
drop off(3)	stop and give something	Would you drop this off at the post office to someone?
drop out	cease to participate	After two laps, the runner dropped out.

Some particles can be separated from the verb so that a noun and pronoun can be inserted, and some particles can't be separated from the verb. In addition, some phrases are intransitive, meaning they cannot take a direct object.

Separable	add up (meaning: to add)	Correct: She **added up** the total on her calculator.
		Correct: She **added** it **up** on her calculator.
Inseparable	get around (meaning: to evade)	Correct: She always **gets around** the rules.

		Incorrect: She always **gets** the rules around (This construction makes no sense in English.)
Intransitive	catch on (meaning: to understand)	Correct: After I explained the math problem, she began to **catch on**.
		Incorrect: She began to **catch on** the math problem. (**Catch on** cannot take a direct object in this meaning.)
		Correct: She began to **catch on** to the math problem. (The word **to** makes **the math problem** an indirect object, which is acceptable in this meaning.)

Unfortunately, there is usually no indicator whether an idiomatic phrase is separable, inseparable, or intransitive. In most cases the phrases must simply be memorised. Below is a partial list of each kind of phrase.

PHRASAL VERBS WITH THE LETTER

A

1. **act up** (no object): misbehave (for people); not work properly (for machines).

   "The babysitter had a difficult time. The children **acted up** all evening."

   "I guess I'd better take my car to the garage. It's been **acting up** lately."

2. **act like** (inseparable): behave in a way that's like __ .

   "What's wrong with Bob? He's **acting like** an idiot."

   Note: This phrasal verb is very informal.

3. **add up** (1. no object): logically fit together.

   "His theory is hard to believe, but his research **adds up**."

   Note: This phrasal verb is often negative.

   "His theory seems, at first, to be plausible, but the facts in his research don't **add up**."

4. **add up** (2. separable): find the total.

   "What's the total of those bills? Could you **add** them **up** and see?"

5. **add up to** (inseparable): to total.

   "The bills **add up to** Rs.734.96. That's more than I expected!"

6. **ask out** (separable): ask for a date.

   "Nina has a new boyfriend. James **asked** her **out** last night."

B

7. **back down** (no object): not follow a threat.

   "Timmy was going to call the police when I told him I'd wrecked his car, but he **backed down** when I said I'd pay for the damages."

8. **back up** (1. no object): move backward; move in reverse.

   "You missed the lines in the parking space. You'll have to **back up** and try again."

   "The people waiting in line are too close to the door. We won't be able to open it unless they **back up**."

9. **back up** (2. separable): drive a vehicle backwards (in reverse).

   "You're too close! **Back** your car **up** so I can open the garage door."

10. **back up** (3. separable): confirm a story, facts, or information.

    "If you don't believe me, talk to Dave. He'll **back** me **up**."

11. **back up** (4. separable): make a "protection" copy to use if there are problems with the original.

    "When my computer crashed, I lost many of my files. It's a good thing I **backed** them **up**."

12. **beg off** (no object): decline an invitation; ask to be excused from doing something.

    "At first Lily said she would be at the party. Later she **begged off**."

13. **blow up** (1. separable): inflate.

    "We need lots of balloons for the party. Will you **blow** them **up**?"

    blow up (2. separable): explode; destroy by exploding.

    A: "That old building really came down quickly!"
    B: "That's because the construction company used dynamite to **blow** it **up**."

    blow up (3. no object): suddenly become very angry.

    "When I told Jerry that I'd had an accident with his car, he **blew up**."

14. **bone up on** (inseparable): review/study thoroughly for a short time.

    "If you're going to travel to Peru, you'd better **bone up on** your Spanish."

15. **break down** (1. separable): separate something into component parts.

    "We spent a lot of money at the supermarket. When we **broke** the total cost **down**, we spent more on cleaning supplies than food."

    break down (2. no object): stop working/functioning.

"Sharon will be late for work today. Her car **broke down** on the freeway."

16. **break in** (1. often no object; with an object, **break into**–inseparable): enter by using force (and breaking a lock, window, etc.)

"Jane's apartment was burglarized last night. Someone **broke in** while Jane was at the movies."
"Somebody **broke into** Jane's apartment while she was at the movies.

17. **break in** (2. separable): wear something new until it's/they're comfortable.

"These are nice shoes, but they're too stiff. I hope it doesn't take too long to **break** them **in**."

18. **break in** (3. separable): train; get someone/something accustomed to a new routine.

"I hope I can learn my new job quickly. The manager hasn't scheduled much time for **breaking me in**."

19. **break up** (1. no object): disperse; scatter.

"What time did the party **break up** last night?"

20. **break up** (2. usually no object; with an object, **break up with** [inseparable)]): end a personal relationship.

"Tim and Julie aren't going steady any more. They got really angry with each other and **broke up**."

"Have you heard the news? Julie **broke up with** Tim!"

"I'm sorry to hear that their marriage **broke up**. I'm sure the divorce will be difficult for the children."

21. **bring/take back** (separable): return something.

"Yes, you can borrow my pen, don't forget to **bring** it **back** to me when you're finished."

"This book is due tomorrow. I guess I should **take** it **back** to the library."

22. **bring off** (separable): accomplish something difficult; accomplish something people had considered impossible or unlikely.

"No one thought Jack could get an A in that course, but he **brought** it **off**. "

23. **bring up** (1. separable): mention (as a topic of discussion).

"We planned to discuss overtime pay in the meeting. Why didn't someone **bring** that topic **up**?"

24. **bring up** (2. separable): raise; rear.

"Lily's parents died when she was a baby. Her grandparents **brought** her **up**."

25. **brush up on** (inseparable): review/study thoroughly for a short time.

"If you're going to travel to Peru, you'd better **brush up on** your Spanish."

26. **burn down** (no object): destroyed/consumed by fire.

Note: For upright things-trees, buildings, etc.-only.

"Lightning struck Mr. Kennedy's barn last night. It **burned down** before the fire fighters arrived."

27. **burn up** (1. no object): destroyed/consumed by fire.

Note: For people and non-upright things only.

"All of Mr. Kennedy's hay **burned up** when his barn burned down."

28. **burn up** (2. separable): cause someone to become very angry.

"Did you hear how rudely Fred talked to me? That really **burned** me **up**!"

29. **butt in** (no object): impolitely interrupt (a conversation, an action).

"Hey, you! Don't **butt in**! Wait for your turn!"

30. **butter up** (separable): praise someone excessively with the hope of getting some benefit.

"I guess Marty really wants to be promoted. He's been **buttering** his boss **up** all week."

C

31. **call off** (separable): cancel something that has been scheduled.

"We don't have school today. The mayor **called** classes **off** because of the snow."

32. **call on** (inseparable): ask someone for an answer in class.

"I don't know why the teacher never **calls on** you. You always know the answer."

33. **calm down** (with or without an object; with an object, separable): become calm/less agitated or upset; help someone become calm/less agitated or upset.

"Why are you so upset? Suzie didn't intend to spill orange juice on you. **Calm down**!"

"I know Ralph is upset, but can you **calm** him **down**? He's making so much noise that he's irritating everyone in the office."

34. **(not) care for** (1. inseparable): like; want.

Note: This phrasal verb is usually negative, though it may be used affirmatively in questions.

A: "Would you **care for** something to drink? We have coffee, tea, or orange juice."

B: "Could I have water, please? I don't **care for** coffee, tea, or juice."

35. **care for** (2. inseparable): take care of; supply care to; attend/watch over.

"Amy's father got out of the hospital last week. The family is **caring for** him at home."

36. **catch on** (no object): develop understanding or knowledge of something.

"Bill had never used a computer until he took this class, but he **caught on** very quickly and is now one of the best students."

37. **catch up (with)** (often without an object; with an object, inseparable): stop being behind.

"Terry stopped to rest for a few minutes. He'll **catch up/catch up with** us later."

38. **check in(to)** (inseparable): register for/at a hotel, conference, etc.; let someone know officially that you have arrived.

"My plane will arrive around 5:00 PM. I should be able to **check into** the hotel by 6:00 or 6:30."

"When you arrive at the convention, be sure to **check in** at the registration desk."

39. **check off** (separable): make a mark to indicate that something on a list has been completed.

"Here are the things you need to do. Please **check** each one **off** when you've finished it."

40. **check out (of)** (1. inseparable): follow procedures for leaving (a hotel, etc.)

"Don't forget to take your room key to the front desk when you **check out** (when you **check out of** the hotel)."

41. **check out** (2. separable): follow procedures for borrowing something (usually for a limited period of time).

"I'm sorry, but you can't take that encyclopedia home. The library won't allow you to **check** reference books **out**."

42. **cheer up** (separable): help someone feel less worried/depressed/sad.

"Suzie's brother was depressed about not getting a promotion, so she sent him a funny card to **cheer** him **up**."

43. **chew out** (separable): scold someone severely; berate.

"Tom's father was really angry when Tom didn't come home until 3:00 AM. He **chewed** Tom **out** and then said Tom had to stay at home for two weeks."

44. **chicken out** (no object): lose the courage or confidence to do something–often at the last minute.

"Sam said he was going to ask Lulu for a date, but he **chickened out**."

45. **chip in** (inseparable): contribute/donate (often money) to something done by a group.

"We're going to buy a birthday cake for our boss and I'm collecting donations. Do you want to **chip in**?"

46. **clam up** (inseparable): suddenly become quiet/ refuse to talk about something.

"Lila wouldn't talk about the accident. When I asked her what happened, she **clammed up**."

47. **come across** (inseparable): find (unexpectedly).

"I've lost my extra car keys. If you **come across** them while your're cleaning the room, please put them in a safe place."

48. **come down with** __ (inseparable): become ill with __ .

"George won't be at the office today. He **came down with** the flu over the weekend."

49. **come to** (1. inseparable): total.

"Your charges **come to** `124.38. Will you pay by cheque, in cash, or with a credit card?"

50. **come to** (2. no object): regain consciousness.

"When I told Gina that she'd won a million dollars, she fainted. When she **came to**, I told her it was a joke and she almost hit me!"

51. **count on** (inseparable): depend on; trust that something will happen or that someone will do as expected.

"I'm **counting on** you to wake me up tomorrow. I know I won't hear the alarm."

52. **cross out** (separable): show that something written is wrong or unnecessary by making an X across it.

"We can't afford to buy everything on your shopping list, so I've **crossed** all the unnecessary things **out**."

53. **cut back (on)** (often without an object; with an object, **cut back on** [inseparable]): use less of something.

"You drink too much coffee. You should **cut back**."

"You should **cut back on** the amount of coffee that you drink."

D

54. **do in** (1. separable): cause to become very tired.

"Those three games of tennis yesterday afternoon really **did** me **in**. I slept for ten hours after I got home."

55. **do in** (2. separable): to kill; to murder.

"They said that the murdered man was **done in** between 10 and 11 o'clock last night."

56. **do over** (separable): do something again.

"Oh, no! I forgot to save my report before I turned the computer off! Now I'll have to **do** it **over**!"

57. **drag on** (no object): last much longer than expected or is necessary.

"I thought the meeting would be a short one, but it **dragged on** for more than three hours."

58. draw up (separable): create a formal document.

"The Ajax and Tip-Top Banks have decided to merge. Their lawyers will **draw** all the official documents **up** sometime this month."

59. drop off (separable): deliver something; deliver someone (by giving him/her a ride).

"Yes, I can take those letters to the post office. I'll **drop** them **off** as I go home from work."

"You don't have to take a taxi. You live fairly close to me, so I'll be happy to **drop** you **off**."

60. drop in (on) (inseparable): visit informally (and usually usually without scheduling a specific time).

"If you're in town next month, we'd love to see you. Please try to **drop in**. (Please try to **drop in on** us."

61. drop by (inseparable): visit informally (and usually without scheduling a specific time).

"If you're in town next month, we'd love to see you. Please try to **drop by** the house."

62. drop out (of) (inseparable): stop attending/leave school or an organization.

"No, Paul isn't at the university. He **dropped out**./He **dropped out of** school."

63. draw out (separable): prolong something (usually far beyond the normal limits).

"I thought that speech would never end. The speaker could have said everything important in about five minutes, but he **drew** the speech **out** for over an hour!"

E

64. eat out (no object): have a meal in a restaurant.

"I'm too tired to cook tonight. Why don't we **eat out**?"

65. egg on (separable): urge/encourage greatly toward doing something (usually something negative).

"At first Bob and Chuck were just having a mild argument, but Bob's friends **egged** them **on** until they started fighting."

66. end up (1. no object): finally arrive at; arrive at an unexpected place.

"We got lost last night and **ended up** in the next town."

67. end up (2. no object): arrive somewhere as a result or consequence.

"You're working too hard. If you don't take it easy, you'll **end up** in the hospital!"

F

68. face up to (inseparable): admit to; take responsibility for.

"You can't pretend that you're doing OK in this course, Joe. Sooner or later, you'll have to **face up to** the fact that you're failing it."

69. fall through (no object): not happen. (**Note:** describes something that was planned but didn't happen.)

"We had originally intended to go to Mexico for our vacation, but our trip **fell through** when I got sick."

70. feel up to (inseparable): feel strong enough or comfortable enough to do something.

"I know the accident was a terrible shock. Do you **feel up to** talking about it?"

71. figure out (1. separable): logically find the answer to a problem; solve a problem by thinking about it carefully.

"For a long time I couldn't understand the last problem, but I finally **figured** it **out**."

72. figure out (2. separable): understand why someone behaves the way she/he does.

"I can't **figure** Margie **out**. Sometimes she's very warm and friendly and sometimes she acts as if she doesn't know me."

73. fill in (1. separable): add information to a form.

"The office needs to know your home address and phone number. Could you **fill** them **in** on this form?"

74. fill in (on) (2. separable): supply information that someone doesn't know.

"I wasn't able to attend the meeting yesterday, but I understand that it was important. Could you **fill** me **in**?/Could you **fill** me **in on** what was discussed?"

75. fill in for (inseparable): temporarily do someone else's work; temporarily substitute for another person.

"Professor Newton is in the hospital and won't be able to teach for the rest of the term. Do you know who's going to **fill in for** her?"

76. fill out (1. separable): complete a form by adding required information.

"Of course I completed my application! I **filled** it **out** and mailed it over three weeks ago!"

77. fill out (2. no object): become less thin; gain weight.

"Jerry used to be really skinny, but in the last year he's begun to **fill out**."

78. find out (about) (inseparable): learn/get information (about).

"I'm sorry that you didn't know the meeting had been canceled. I didn't **find out** (**find out about** it) myself until just a few minutes ago."

G

79. get across (separable): make something understood; communicate something understandably.

"Alan is really intelligent but sometimes he has problems **getting** his ideas **across**."

80. get along (with) (inseparable): have a friendly relationship (with); be friendly (toward).

"Why can't you and your sister **get along**? Everyone else **gets along with** her just fine!"

81. get around (1. inseparable): avoid having to do something.

"Teresa **got around** the required math classes by doing well on a math proficiency test."

82. get around (2. no object): move from place to place.

"She doesn't have a car. She **gets around** by bicycle, bus, or taxi."

83. get around to (inseparable): do something eventually.

"I really should wash the dishes, but I don't feel like it. Maybe I'll **get around to** them tomorrow morning."

84. get by (no object): survive, financially, in a difficult situation.

"It's going to be hard to pay the rent now that you've lost your job, but somehow we'll **get by**."

85. get in (1. inseparable): enter a small, closed vehicle.

"I don't know where Carole was going. She just **got in** her car and drove away."

86. get in (2. no object): arrive.

"Do you know what time Fred's plane **gets in**?"

87. get on (inseparable): enter a large, closed vehicle.

"I'm sorry, but you're too late to say goodbye to Angela. She **got on** the plane about 20 minutes ago."

88. get off (1. inseparable): leave a large, closed vehicle.

"When you **get off** the bus, cross the street, turn right on Oak Street, and keep going until you're at the corner of Oak and Lincoln Boulevard."

89. get off (2. separable): be excused (for a period of time) from work, class, or other regularly scheduled activities.

"Some schools **got** President's Day **off** but ours didn't. We had classes as usual."

90. get off (3. separable): make it possible for someone to avoid punishment.

"Everyone knew he was guilty, but his lawyer was clever and **got** him **off**."

91. get out of (1. inseparable): leave a small, closed vehicle.

"There's something wrong with the garage door opener. You'll have to get out of the car and open it by hand."

92. get out of (2. inseparable): escape having to do something.

"Lisa said she had a terrible headache and **got out of** giving her speech today."

93. get over (1. no object): finish. (**Note**: for individual activities, not ones that happen again and again.)

"What time do your classes **get over**?"

94. get over (2. inseparable): recover from an illness or painful experience.

"Katy was really upset when she failed the test. She thought she would never **get over** feeling so stupid."

95. get rid of (1. inseparable): dispose of; give away or throw away.

"That shirt is really ugly. Why don't you **get rid of** it?"

96. get rid of (2. inseparable): dismiss someone; fire someone from a job; cause someone to leave.

"The treasurer of the XYZ company was spending too much money so the company president **got rid of** him."

97. get up (usually no object; with an object, separable): leave bed after sleeping and begin your daily activities.

"You'll have to **get up** much earlier than usual tomorrow. We have to leave by no later than 6:00 AM."

"I know I won't hear the alarm tomorrow morning. Can you **get** me **up** at 6:00 AM?"

98. give up (1. separable): stop doing something (usually a habit).

"He knows smoking isn't good for his health, but he can't **give** it **up**."

99. give up (2. no object): decide not to try (unsuccessfully) to solve a problem.

A: "What's black and white and red all over?"

B: "I **give up**. What?"

A: "An embarrassed zebra!"

100. go out with (inseparable): have a date with.

"You **went out with** Sharon last night, didn't you?"

101. go with (1. no object): look pleasing together. (**Note:** for clothes, furniture, etc.)

"You should buy that shirt. It will **go** well **with** your dark brown suit."

102. go with (2. no object): date regularly and steadily.

"Is Gina **going with** Jim? I see them together all the time."

103. goof off (no object): be lazy; do nothing in particular.

A: "Do you have any special plans for your vacation?"

B: "No. I'm just going to stay home and **goof off**."

104. grow up (1. no object): spend the years between being a child and being an adult.

"Did you know that Frank **grew up** in Malaysia?"

105. grow up (2. no object): behave responsibly; behave as an adult, not a child.

A: "Lee really irritates me sometimes. He's really silly and childish."

B: "I agree. I wish he would **grow up**."

H

106. hand in (separable): submit homework, an assignment, etc.

"You'd better get started on your report. You know that you have to **hand** it **in** at 8:30 tomorrow morning!"

107. hand out (separable): distribute.

"Why don't you have a course description and list of assignments? The teacher **handed** them out on the first day of class."

108. hang up (no object): end a phone conversation by replacing the receiver.

"I'd like to talk longer, but I'd better **hang up**. My sister needs to make a call."

109. have to do with (inseparable): be about.

"This class **has to do with** the behavior of people in groups."

110. hold up (1. separable): raise; lift to a higher-than-normal position.

"The winner of the race proudly **held** his trophy **up** for all to see."

111. hold up (2. separable): delay.

"I'm sorry I'm late. There was an accident on the freeway and traffic **held** me **up**."

112. hold up (3. separable): rob; threaten someone with harm unless he/she gives her/his money or other valuable things.

"Sarah is very upset. When she was walking home last night, two men **held** her **up** and took her purse and jewelry."

I

113. iron out (separable): mutually reach an agreement; mutually resolve difficulties

"Yes, I know we disagree on lots of things, Susan, but we can **iron** them **out**."

J

114. jack up (1. separable): raise/lift by using a jack.

"We'll have to **jack** the back of the car **up** before we can change the tyre."

115. jack up (2. separable): raise (used for prices).

"The car dealer bought my old Ford for $750 and **jacked** the price **up** to $1,500 when they sold it."

116. jump all over (inseparable): severely scold someone; berate someone.

"Arthur is really upset. His boss **jumped all over** him because he's been late for work three times this week."

K

117. keep on (1. inseparable–followed by an -ing verb): continue

"I'm not ready to stop yet. I think I'll **keep on** working for a while."

118. keep on (someone) (2. inseparable): continue to remind someone to do something until he/she does it (even if this irritates her/him).

"Bill's very forgetful. You'll have to **keep on** him or he'll never do all the things you want him to do."

119. kick out (separable): expel; force someone to leave because of his/her poor performance or unacceptable behavior.

"Jim's club **kicked** him **out** because he didn't pay his dues or come to meetings."

120. knock out (separable): make unconscious.

"The boxing match ended when one boxer **knocked** the other one **out**."

"That medicine really **knocked** me **out**. I slept for 14 hours straight!"

121. knock oneself out (separable): work much harder than normal or than what is expected.

"We completed the project on time because of Chuck. He **knocked** himself **out** to be sure we didn't miss the deadline."

L

lay off (separable): dismiss someone from a job because of lack of work or money (not because of poor performance)

"I feel really sorry for Sally's family. Her father was **laid off** yesterday."

123. leave out (separable): forget; omit.

"Oh, no! When I made the list of those who attended the meeting, I **left** your name **out**!"

124. let down (separable): disappoint.

"I know I **let** you **down** when I didn't do what I promised. I'm really sorry."

125. **let up** (no object): become less intense or slower.
"It's been raining hard for a long time. Will it ever **let up**?"

126. **look back on** (inseparable): remember; reflect on/consider something in the past.
"When they **looked back on** their many years together, they realized that their marriage had been a very happy one."

127. **look down on** (inseparable): hold in contempt; regard as inferior.
"It's not surprising that Fred has few friends. He seems to **look down on** anyone who doesn't like the same things that he does."

128. **look forward to** (inseparable): anticipate pleasantly; think about a pleasant thing before it happens
"I'm really **looking forward to** vacation. I can't wait for it to begin!"

129. **look in on** (inseparable): visit in order to check something's/someone's condition.
"My father just came home from the hospital. I plan to **look in on** him today after I finish work."

130. **look into** (inseparable): investigate/get more details about something.
"Someone said there was a meeting at 9:30 but I haven't heard anything about it. Shall I **look into** it?"

131. **look like** (inseparable): resemble (in appearance).
"Does he **look like** his father or his mother?"

132. **look over** (separable): check; review.
"I think I may have some typos in this report. Could you **look** it **over**?"

133. **look up** (1. separable): find something in a reference work.
"I'm sorry, but I don't know what that word means. I'll have to **look** it **up**."

134. **look up** (2. separable): find where someone lives or works and visit him/her.
"Thanks for giving me your brother's address. When I'm in Chicago next month, I'll be sure to **look** him **up**."

135. **look up to** (inseparable): respect.
"Everyone **looks up to** Joyce because she always makes time to help others."

136. **luck out** (no object): be unexpectedly lucky.
"Gloria was worried because she wasn't prepared to give a report at the meeting, but she **lucked out** as the meeting got postponed."

M

137. **make fun of** (inseparable): make jokes about (usually unkindly).
"I agree that Bob looks ridiculous since he shaved his head, but don't **make fun of** him. You'll hurt his feelings."

138. **make up** (1. separable): invent/create (imaginary) information.
"Judy's story is hard to believe. I'm sure she **made** it **up**."

139. **make up** (2. separable): compensate for something missed or not done by doing extra or equivalent work.
"I'm sorry I missed the test. May I **make** it **up**?"

140. **make up (with)** (3. insepárable): re-establish a friendly relationship by admitting guilt.
"Jack and his girlfriend were very angry with each other, but last night they finally **made up**."
"Jack and his girlfriend were very angry with each other, but last night they finally **made up with** each other."

141. **make out** (separable): see / hear something well enough to understand what it means. (**Note:** often negative.)
"Ruth's writing is very small. I almost need a magnify glass to **make** it **out**."
"What were the last two examples that he gave? I couldn't **make** them **out**."

142. **make for** (1. inseparable): go to or toward.
"Her teen-aged children are always hungry. As soon as they arrive home from school, they **make for** the refrigerator."

143. **make for** (2. inseparable): result in; cause.
"Many hands **make for** light work. (If many people work together, there's less work for everyone.)"

144. **mark up** (separable): increase the price (for resale).
"Mrs. White's import shop is profitable because she buys things inexpensively and then **marks** them **up**."

145. **mark down** (separable): reduce the price (as an incentive to buy).
"These shoes were really a bargain! The store **marked** them **down** by 40 per cent!"

146. **mix up** (separable): cause to become confused.
"I didn't complete the assignment because I didn't know how. The directions **mixed** me **up**."

N

147. **nod off** (no object): fall asleep (usually unintentionally).
"The speech was so boring that several people in the audience **nodded off** before it was finished."

P

148. pan out (no object): succeed; happen as expected (for plans). (**Note:** almost always negative when in statements.)

"I'll be here next week after all. My trip to Chicago didn't **pan out**."

149. pass away (no object): die.

"I was very sorry to hear that your grandfather **passed away**."

150. pass out (1. no object): faint; lose consciousness.

"When Ella heard that she'd won a million dollars, she was so shocked that she **passed out**."

151. pass out (2. separable): distribute.

"Everyone in the room needs one of these information sheets. Who will help me **pass** them **out**?"

152. pick out (separable): choose; select.

"Billy's grandmother especially liked her birthday card because Billy had **picked** it **out** himself."

153. pick up (1. separable): lift; take up.

"Those books don't belong on the floor. Will you help me **pick** them **up**?"

154. pick up (2. separable): arrange to meet someone and give her/him a ride.

"Of course we can go there together. What time should I **pick** you **up**?"

155. pick up (3. separable): get; buy.

"The children just drank the last of the milk. Could you **pick** some more **up** on your way home this evening?"

156. pick up (4. separable): refresh; revitalize.

"He was feeling a little tired, so he drank a glass of orange juice. It **picked** him **up** enough to finish his work."

157. pick on (inseparable): bully; intentionally try to make someone upset.

"You should be ashamed of teasing your little brother, Bob! **Pick on** someone your own size!"

158. pitch in (no object): help; join together to accomplish something.

"We'll be finished soon if everyone **pitches in**."

159. pull over (no object): drive a vehicle to the side of the road.

"When the policeman indicated that I should **pull over**, I knew he was going to give me a ticket."

160. put away (separable): return something to the proper place.

"I just took these clothes out of the dryer. Will you help me **put** them **away**?"

161. put off (1. separable): postpone; delay; avoid

"I can't **put** this work **off** any longer. If I don't do it soon, it'll be impossible to finish it in time."

"When will Mr. Smith agree to a meeting? I keep asking for an appointment, but he keeps **putting** me **off**."

162. put on (1. separable): begin to wear; don.

"It's a little bit chilly outside. You'd better **put** a sweater **on**."

163. put on (2. separable): try to make someone believe something that is ridiculous or untrue.

"Don't believe a word of what Jim was saying. He was just **putting** us **on**."

164. put (someone) **out** (separable): inconvenience someone.

"I hate to **put** you **out**, but I need a ride to the train station and hope you can take me."

165. put up (1. separable): return something to the proper place.

"Your toys are all over the floor, Timmy. Please **put** them **up**."

166. put up (2. separable): provide someone with a place to sleep.

"There's no need for you to check into a hotel. I'll be happy to **put** you **up**."

167. put up with (inseparable): tolerate.

"It's really important to come to work on time. The boss won't **put up with** tardiness."

168. put back (separable): return something to the proper place.

"I've finished with these books. Do you want me to **put** them **back** on the shelves?"

R

169. rip off (separable): cheat; take advantage of; charge too much.

"Don't even think about buying a car there. They'll **rip** you **off**."

170. round off (separable): change from a fraction to the nearest whole number.

"**Round** all prices **off** to the closest whole-dollar amounts. For example, **round** $33.73 **off** to $34.00."

171. run into (inseparable): meet by chance.

"Yesterday at the supermarket, Jan **ran into** her former roommate. Before yesterday, they hadn't seen each other for nearly five years."

172. run out of (inseparable): use the last of.

"On the way home from work, Art **ran out of** gas."

S

173. set up (separable): make arrangements for something.

"You'll see Mr. Thomas tomorrow. I've **set** a meeting **up** for 9:30 AM."

174. set back (1. separable): cause a delay in scheduling.

"We've had some problems with the project that have **set** us **back** at least two days . We'll give you a progress report tomorrow."

175. set back (2. separable): cost.

"I wonder how much Bill's new car **set** him **back**?"

176. slip up (no object): make a mistake.

"You **slipped up** here. The amount should be $135.28, not $132.58."

177. stand out (no object): be noticeably better than other similar people or things.

"Good job, Ann! Your work really **stands out**!"

178. stand up (1. no object): rise to a standing position.

"When the Chairperson entered the room, everyone **stood up**."

179. stand up (2. separable): make a date but not keep it.

"Angela was supposed to go to the dance with Fred, but she **stood** him **up** and went with Chuck instead."

180. show up (1. no object): arrive; appear.

"The boss was very upset when you didn't **show up** for the meeting. What happened?"

181. show up (2. separable): do a noticeably better job (often unexpectedly) than someone else.

"Everyone thought Marsha would win, but Jean did. Actually, Jean really **showed** Marsha **up**."

182. stand for (1. no object): represent.

"These letters seem to be an abbreviation. Do you know what they **stand for**?"

183. stand for (2. inseparable): tolerate; permit (usually negative).

"I'm not surprised that Mrs. Johnson rejected your report. She won't **stand for** shoddy work."

T

184. take after (inseparable): resemble; favour (in appearance).

Note: used for people.

"Both my sister and I **take after** our father."

185. take/bring back (separable): return.

"This book is due tomorrow. I guess I should **take** it **back** to the library."

"Yes, you can borrow my pen, but don't forget to **bring** it **back** to me when you're finished."

186. take care of (1. inseparable): provide care for; watch one's health.

"Lois has been **taking care of** her father since he returned home from the hospital."

"You've been working too hard lately. You'd better **take care of** yourself!"

187. take care of (2. ineparable): make arrangements (for something to happen); take responsibility for.

"Will you **take care of** making reservations for our flight to Boston?"

188. take off (1. separable): remove (something you're wearing).

"Please **take** your hat **off** when you go inside a building."

189. take off (2. no object): leave; depart (often suddenly or quickly).

"Was something wrong with Jill? She **took off** without saying goodbye."

"When does your plane **take off**?"

190. take off (3. separable): make arrangements to be absent from work.

"Susan isn't here today. She's **taking** today and tomorrow **off**."

191. take up (separable): begin (a hobby or leisure-time activity).

A: "Do you like to ski?"

B: "I've never been skiing, but I think I'd like to **take** it **up**."

192. tell (someone) **off** (separable): speak to someone bluntly and negatively, saying exactly what she/he did wrong.

"Julie was really angry at Bob; she **told** him **off** in front of all of us."

193. tick off (1. separable): irritate someone; make someone upset or angry.

"It really **ticks** her **off** when someone is late for an appointment."

194. tick off (2. separable): show that something has been completed by putting a tick (check) beside it.

"Here are the things you need to do. **Tick** each one **off** when you finish it."

195. throw away (separable): discard; put in the garbage.

"You shouldn't **throw** those newspapers **away**; they're recyclable."

196. throw out (1. separable): discard; put in the garbage.

"This food smells bad. You'd better **throw** it **out**."

197. throw out (2. separable): forcibly make someone leave (usually because of bad behavior).

"Those people are drunk and making everyone uncomfortable. The manager should **throw** them **out**."

198. throw up (usually no object; with an object, separable): vomit.

"Paul was so nervous about his job interview that he **threw up** just before he left for it."

198. try on (separable): wear something briefly to check its fit, how it looks, etc.

"I'm not sure that the jacket is large enough. May I **try** it **on**?"

199. try out (separable): use a machine briefly to determine how well it works.

"I really like the way this car looks. May I **try** it **out**?"

200. try out (for) (inseparable): try to win a place on a team or other organization.

"I know you want to be on the football team. Are you going to **try out**?"

"If you like to sing, you should **try out for** the choir.

201. turn around (1. usually no object): move so that you are facing the opposite direction.

"Everyone **turned around** and stared when I entered the meeting late."

202. turn around (2. separable): move so that someone/something is facing the opposite direction.

"I don't want this chair facing the window. Will you help me **turn** it **around**?"

203. turn around (3. separable): make changes so that something that was unprofitable is profitable.

"The company was doing poorly until it hired a new president. He **turned** it **around** in about six months and now it's doing quite well."

204. turn down (1. separable): decrease the volume.

"Your music is giving me a headache! Please **turn** it **down** or use your headphones!"

205. turn down (2. separable): refuse.

"I thought I could borrow some money from Joe, but when I asked, he **turned** me **down**."

206. turn in (1. separable): give/deliver/submit to someone.

"I've written my report, but I haven't **turned** it **in**."

207. turn in (2. no object): go to bed.

"I'm pretty tired. I guess I'll **turn in**."

208. turn in (3. separable): report or deliver wrongdoers to the authorities.

"Two days after the robbery, the thieves **turned** themselves **in**."

209. turn off (1. separable): stop by turning a handle or switch.

"I'm cold. Do you mind if I **turn** the air conditioner **off**?"

210. turn off (2. separable): bore; repel (very informal).

"That music **turns** me **off**. Please play something else!"

211. turn on (1. separable): start by turning a handle or switch.

"It's cold in here. I'm going to **turn** the heater **on**"

212. turn on (2. separable): interest very much; excite (very informal).

"What kind of music **turns** you **on**?"

213. turn up (1. separable): increase the volume.

"I can barely hear the TV. Can you **turn** it **up** a little?"

214. turn up (2. no object): appear unexpectedly.

"We were all surprised when Pam **turned up** at the party. We didn't even know she was in town."

W

215. wait on (1. inseparable): serve (usually customers in a restaurant, shop, etc.)

"I want to make a complaint. The person who just **waited on** me was very impolite."

216. wait for (inseparable): wait until someone/something arrives or is finished with something else.

"When will Kenny be finished with work? I've been **waiting for** him for almost an hour!"

"I'm tired of **waiting for** the bus. I guess I'll take a taxi instead."

217. wake up (1. no object): stop sleeping.

"I usually **wake up** around 5:00 AM each day."

218. wake up (2. separable): rouse someone; cause someone to stop sleeping.

"I have an important meeting tomorrow and I'm afraid I won't hear my alarm. Will you **wake** me **up** at 6:00 AM?"

219. watch out for (inseparable): be careful of; beware of.

"There's a school at the end of this block. **Watch out for** children crossing the street."

"If you take that road, **watch out for** ice during the winter."

220. wear out (1. separable): wear something/use something until it can no longer be worn/be used.

"I need a new pencil sharpener. I **wore** this one **out**."

"I suppose I should get some new shoes. I've almost **worn** this pair **out**."

221. wear out (2. separable): cause to become exhausted; cause to become very tired.

"I had four different meetings today. They **wore** me **out**."

"I suppose I should get some new shoes. I've almost **worn** this pair **out**."

222. work out (1. no object): exercise (usually in a gym, etc.) to build muscles, body tone, etc.

"Instead of eating lunch on Monday, Wednesday, and Friday, Sheila goes to the recreation center to **work out**."

223. work out (2. separable): solve a problem/resolve a difficult situation (usually by working together).

"I know we disagree on many points, but I believe we can **work** things **out**."

224. wrap up (1. no object): wear enough clothes to keep warm.

"It's really cold today. Be sure you **wrap up** when you leave the house."

225. wrap up (2. separable): finish something; bring something to a conclusion.

"We've been talking about the problem for nearly three hours. I hope we'll be able to **wrap** the discussion **up** soon."

226. write down (separable): record something in writing.

"Could you tell me your e-mail address again? I want to **write** it **down**."

227. write up (separable): record; report in writing.

"You'll need to make a report on your business meetings. Be sure you **write** them **up** as soon as possible after you return from your trip."

Z

228. zonk out (no object): fall asleep quickly because of exhaustion.

"I intended to go shopping after work, but I was so tired that I **zonked out** as soon as I got home."

CHAPTER

21B Phrasal Verbs

PRACTICE EXERCISES

Directions: In each of the questions, a word has been used in sentences in four different ways. Choose the option corresponding to the sentence in which the usage of the word is incorrect or inappropriate.

Test 1

1. Account
   (a) How will you account of the money you spent?
   (b) He couldn't account for his absence from college.
   (c) How will you account for such a big difference?
   (d) Hari was able to account for his actions.
2. Act
   (a) When you read a story or a poem to your child, act it out with him or her.
   (b) This computer's acting up again
   (c) The children were acting over because their mother wasn't there
   (d) The script itself is well written and well acted out by the cast.
3. Add
   (a) This just doesn't add up
   (b) Slowly add in flour, baking powder and salt. Mix until well blended.
   (c) She added up the bill.
   (d) These are quite expensive though, by the time you've added in border taxes
4. Answer
   (a) Don't answer back to your mother.
   (b) You are answerable for your mistakes
   (c) You have to give me an answer.
   (d) Answer up, or you will be punished.
5. Ask
   (a) The next day, her brother came to ask after her.
   (b) I'll ask around and see if there's a room vacant somewhere
   (c) I'll ask her over in to dinner next weekend.
   (d) This is the third time he's asked me out.
6. Back
   (a) The company only backed in after a worldwide campaign by activists
   (b) He backed out at the last moment.
   (c) We had to back up a long way and try a different route.
   (d) Five witnesses backed him up.
7. Blow
   (a) I don't understand. It's not like her to blow up over a silly little row like that.
   (b) The politician is keeping a low profile until the scandal blow over.
   (c) More volunteers are needed to blow up balloons.
   (d) I blew out the candles and we ate cake.
8. Break
   (a) When he told her he didn't love her anymore, she broke down.
   (b) I was extremely stunned when May and Brad broke off their engagement.

(c) The meeting broken up around 10 o'clock.
(d) The two criminals broke out of prison yesterday.

9. Bring
(a) Looking at the photos brought back a lot of memories of my visit to the place.
(b) It isn't easy to bring up children nowadays.
(c) Madonna is just bringing out a new record.
(d) The early rains will bring a much needed relief from the heat.

10. Call
(a) Can you ask her to call me back, please?
(b) We had to call in a doctor.
(c) It's too late to call off the ceremony now.
(d) Call up me when you get there.

11. Carry
(a) She got carried away in the shop and spent all her money on new dresses
(b) He carried on as if nothing had happened.
(c) It's going to be difficult to carry out that plan.
(d) If things get carried on the way they are, you'll lose your job.

12. Check
(a) I arrived in Lucknow a few days ago and checked into the Taj Hotel.
(b) I will check out of the hotel after breakfast.
(c) You should check out your pockets before you leave home.
(d) Quickly check out of the hotel before they charge you for an additional day.

13. Clear
(a) The boy asked his friends to clear off before his father arrived.
(b) During the night the fog cleared off.
(c) I think this misunderstanding will be cleared up soon.
(d) Clear up the mess before you leave.

14. Come
(a) I had no idea what had happened to me when I came round.
(b) As new jobs come up, we will contact students who have signed the contract.
(c) Ram came up with a very good plan.
(d) When we came together we make things happen.

15. Cut
(a) For years, the country was part of the Soviet Union and was cut off from the rest of Europe.
(b) People with diabetes are usually advised to cut down on sugar.
(c) We will take a cut in our salaries.
(d) The tree was damaged in the storm so they had to cut down it.

16. Die
(a) The rumours will soon die down.
(b) Sadly this tradition died out in the early 1800s.
(c) The strong colour will die out with washing.
(d) As we moved away from the sea, the sound of the waves died down.

17. Do
(a) I spent a month doing up the flat and I think it's quite nice now.
(b) The death penalty has been done away in many countries.
(c) Do your best and leave the rest to God.
(d) When you do something up, you fasten it.

18. Drop
(a) Ben finally dropped off to sleep after midnight.
(b) I thought I'd drop in and say hello.
(c) We will drop you off at the next shop.
(d) The fielder dropped off the catch.

19. Eat
(a) She really enjoys eating out.
(b) Eat out your vegetables!
(c) The journalist had to eat up his words when the true story came out.
(d) We won't eat in tonight.

20. Fall
(a) She felled down and hurt her knees.
(b) It's great to have a friend to fall back on.
(c) Why does he always fall for the wrong women.
(d) The building is falling apart.

21. Help
(a) This syrup will help ease your pain.
(b) I can't help the colour of my skin.
(c) Ranjit may help him with the beer in the fridge.
(d) Do you really expect me to help you in this?

22. Reason
(a) Your stand is beyond all reason.
(b) Has she given you any reason for her resignation?
(c) There is no reason why you should behave like this.
(d) How do you deal with a friend who doesn't listen to a reason?

23. Paper
(a) Your suggestions look great on the paper, but are absolutely impractical.
(b) Do you know how many trees are killed to make a truckload of paper?

(c) So far I have been able to paper over the disagreements among my brothers.
(d) Dr. Malek will read a paper on criminalization of politics.

24. Business
(a) I want to do an MBA before going into business.
(b) My wife runs profitable business in this suburb.
(c) If we advertise we will get twice as much business as we have now.
(d) How you spend your money is as much my business as yours.

25. Bundle
(a) He made a bundle in the share market.
(b) It was sheer luck that brought a bundle of boy-scouts to where I was lying wounded.
(c) The newborn baby was a bundle of joy for the family.
(d) Mobile operators are offering a bundle of additional benefits.

26. Bolt
(a) The shopkeeper showed us a bolt of fine silk.
(b) As he could not move, he made a bolt for the gate.
(c) Could you please bolt the door?
(d) The thief was arrested before he could bolt from the scene of the crime.

27. Near
(a) I got there just after you left - a near miss!
(b) She and her near friend left early.
(c) The war led to a near doubling of oil prices.
(d) They came near to tears seeing the plight of the victims.

28. Hand
(a) I have my hand full, I cannot do it today.
(b) The minister visited the jail to see the breach at first hand.
(c) The situation is getting out of hand here!
(d) When the roof of my house was blown away, he was willing to lend me a hand.

29. For
(a) He has a great eye for detail.
(b) We are waiting for the day.
(c) I can't bear for her to be angry.
(d) It couldn't be done for ever.

30. Run
(a) I must run fast to catch up with him.
(b) Our team scored a goal against the run of play
(c) You can't run over himself like that.
(d) This film is a run-of-the-mill production.

31. Buckle
(a) After the long hike our knees were beginning to buckle.
(b) The horse suddenly broke into a buckle.
(c) Sometimes, an earthquake can make a bridge buckle.
(d) People should learn to buckle up as soon as they get into a car.

32. Hand
(a) He was handing out free tickets for the concert.
(b) The minister handed in his resignation when it was known that he was implicated in the scandal.
(c) Have things changed since the hand over of sovereignty from the British to Koreans?
(d) Hand up your coat and come and join us.

33. Hang
(a) Hang over a minute; I need to talk to you.
(b) Don't hang up; I need to speak to your sister.
(c) You should not allow your son to hang around in the street after dark.
(d) She was hanging on to each word that I was speaking.

34. Fill
(a) She gave me a form and told me to fill it in.
(b) She filled up the kettle with water and made everyone a cup of tea.
(c) The glass was filled to the brim.
(d) Fill out the details of your resume.

35. Get
(a) The boy tried to catch to the butterfly but it got away.
(b) The word got around that she was going to change her job.
(c) How are you getting over with your studies?
(d) I'll tell her when she gets back

Test 2

In each question, the word at the top is used in four different ways, numbered 1 to 4. Choose the option in which the usage of the word is *INCORRECT* or *INAPPROPRIATE.*

1. Break
(a) My boyfriend and I broke up before I moved to America. (end a relationship)
(b) We broke bread during the Thanksgiving dinner.

(c) The prisoners broke out of jail when the guards weren't looking.
(d) I broke up in a rash after our camping trip.

2. Do
(a) Do your best, it always works.
(b) My teacher wants me to do my essay over because she doesn't like my topic.
(c) Do your coat over before you go outside. The snow is falling heavily!
(d) It's time to do away with all of these old tax records.

3. Get
(a) I tried to get my point across to the judge but she wouldn't listen.
(b) We worked so hard this year that we had to get away for a week.
(c) My grandfather can get away fine in his new wheelchair.
(d) This weather is getting me down.

4. Hang
(a) Hang in there. I'm sure you'll find a job very soon.
(b) Hang on while I grab my coat and shoes!
(c) Instead of going to the party we are just going to hang up at my place.
(d) He didn't say goodbye before he hung up.

5. Keep
(a) Keep on stirring until the liquid comes to a boil.
(b) Medicines should always be kept out from children.
(c) Try to keep the wet dog out of the living room.
(d) If you keep those results up you will get into a great college.

6. Cut
(a) The phone company cut off our phone because we didn't pay the bill.
(b) My grandparents cut my father off when he remarried.
(c) The doctors cut down his leg because it was severely injured.
(d) I cut this ad out of the newspaper.

7. Give
(a) My boyfriend didn't want to go to the ballet, but he finally gave up.
(b) They were giving out free perfume samples at the department store.
(c) I am giving up smoking as of January 1st.
(d) My maths homework was too difficult so I gave up.

8. Hand
(a) I handed my old comic books down to my little cousin.
(b) I have to hand out my essay by Friday.
(c) We will hand out the invitations at the door.
(d) The police asked the man to hand over his wallet and his weapons.

9. Turn
(a) Your mother wants you to turn the TV down and come for dinner.
(b) Just turn left at the end of the street and you will reach my house.
(c) Can you turn the music up? This is my favourite song.
(d) Our cat turned up after we put posters up all over the neighbourhood.

10. Hold
(a) A man in a black mask held the bank up this morning.
(b) Hold onto your hat because it's very windy outside.
(c) Please hold on while I transfer you to the Sales Department.
(d) Jamie held on his tears at his grandfather's funeral.

11. Mark
(a) The clerk will mark prices down later in the day.
(b) They can clearly mark the boundaries up with red tape.
(c) The manager will mark up the prices that the clerk marked down.
(d) I will buy a lot more if you mark the prices down.

12. Talk
(a) A good partner can talk you through some tough places.
(b) She was able to talk the young child out of jumping into the pool.
(c) Sit in the driver's seat while I talk you through the controls.
(d) We talked over the problems in our relationships, but couldn't sort things out.

13. Jack
(a) We jacked the car up and changed the tyre.
(b) Don't listen to him – he always jacks people in.
(c) I jacked my job in because my boss refused to give me a raise.
(d) Once the tourists arrive, the restaurants jack up their prices

14. Look
    (a) I have to look after my sick grandmother.
    (b) Ever since we stole that chocolate bar your dad has looked down on me.
    (c) I'm looking into a red dress for the wedding.
    (d) I'm looking forward to the Christmas break.
15. Run
    (a) Let's run through our lines for the school play.
    (b) He runs with a rough crowd, no wonder he ended up in jail.
    (c) The young father ran off from his responsibility and didn't support his family.
    (d) The child ran away because her parents beat her.

TEST 3

In each question, the word at the top is used in four different ways, numbered a-d. Choose the option in which the usage of the word is INCORRECT or INAPPROPRIATE.

1. Follow
    (a) He followed up the meeting with a report.
    (b) The project went wrong when the staff failed to follow through.
    (c) The film follows down the original.
    (d) He left an hour ago and I'll be following on soon.
2. Scout
    (a) We'd better scout up a replacement for her.
    (b) I scouted round for a bargain.
    (c) The researcher spent months scouting for the answer.
    (d) We scouted around to find the best price.
3. Send
    (a) I sent my food back because it was overcooked.
    (b) The police were sent in to quell the riot as the protesters had started burning cars and wrecking shops.
    (c) The football striker was sent off for arguing with the referee's decision.
    (d) They sent for a fact list to all their existing customers.
4. Hang
    (a) You can hang out your jacket in the front closet.
    (b) What are you doing? - I'm just hanging out.
    (c) Don't hang up. I'm going to change phones.
    (d) Maria and Freya usually hang around the beach after school.
5. Hold
    (a) The police held the demonstrators back while the politicians entered the building.
    (b) We should hold back on making dinner until your parents arrive.
    (c) The teacher held Frank back a year, so he couldn't enter fifth grade.
    (d) Mr. Johnson held the dog off while we crossed the yard.
6. Pass
    (a) Jennifer passed on the work to someone else.
    (b) After battling cancer for several years, he finally passed out at the age of 87.
    (c) He tried to pass the fake watch off as a real Rolex.
    (d) We need to pass our exams.
7. Pick
    (a) Diane picked out a lovely dress for the dance.
    (b) What time are you going to pick me up?
    (c) Business is really picking out this quarter.
    (d) It's possible to pick up enough English in two weeks to get by on your trip to Los Angeles.
8. Eat
    (a) The heavy rains ate away at the sandstone cliffs.
    (b) Ken ate on the cookies.
    (c) We usually eat in instead of going out for dinner.
    (d) They eat out once a week.
9. ZIP
    (a) He was being stupid in the meeting, so we told him to zip around.
    (b) We zipped around the supermarket to get the shopping done.
    (c) The motorbike zipped by the cars stuck in the traffic jam.
    (d) He told me to zip it, so I said nothing.
10. Come
    (a) I just knew the manager would come and solve the problem.
    (b) They come up as very rude.
    (c) No one can come up with a good advertisement for the toothpaste.
    (d) Bob has come up with a welding torch and some scrap iron.
11. Stop
    (a) After the terrorist attacks on London, tourists stopped coming for a while.
    (b) I didn't have time to talk so I told him to stop back later when I had some free time.

(c) I stopped behind after the meeting to talk to Bill.
(d) I'm going to stop in Jim's house on the way home.

12. Bang
(a) He banged the door while going out.
(b) He's always banging on the counter.
(c) He's banging on in the kitchen.
(d) She banged the car again.

13. Kick
(a) The budget cuts are starting to kick about and people are struggling.
(b) I'll kick the dog if it comes to bite me.
(c) The police kicked the door down
(d) Children love to kick the ball.

14. Tag
(a) He tagged the clothes with the correct price tags.
(b) You're off to the cinema; can we tag on?
(c) He tagged me in a few comments on facebook.
(d) The post was tagged with keywords.

15. Jump
(a) I'd jump at the chance to go and live in Japan.
(b) He jumped over the hurdle in the race.
(c) The cat jumped off the sofa to catch the mouse.
(d) Everyone jumped at me and tried to kill me when I raised the issue.

16. Tune
(a) I had just tuned in to a TV show when my sister came back home.
(b) I just love this tune.
(c) He's tuned out his car for the race.
(d) Make sure you tune in to next week's show.

17. Blow
(a) My parents blew up when they found me smoking. They were so angry.
(b) I couldn't light the campfire. The wind kept blowing it up.
(c) The wind blew the smoke back down the chimney into the room.
(d) To blow a balloon, you have to blow hard into it.

18. OPT
(a) I opted for an endowment mortgage and lost a lot of money.
(b) I opted for tea because I don't drink coffee.
(c) The US opted out of an arms deal with other countries.
(d) If you want them to notify you of updates, you have to opt out.

19. Ride
(a) Her skirt rode up when she sat down.
(b) They managed to ride off the recession.
(b) They managed to sit through the journey, even though it was a bumpy ride.
(c) She got on her horse and rode off.

20. Rake
(a) She's raking in thousands a day.
(b) It's the only shop in the area and they're raking it in.
(c) The rake is coming in any moment.
(d) Tim keeps raking off the rows we had last year.

21. Mark
(a) His dedication marked him up for great things.
(b) I marked off the items on the list as I finished purchasing them.
(c) They marked out the pitch.
(d) Her speed marks her out from the rest of the group.

22. Roll
(a) They rolled in very drunk at three o'clock in the morning.
(b) The government want to roll back the freedom of the press.
(c) The army rolled by when they came under attack.
(d) Roll on Friday! It's been a dreadful week.

23. Mess
(a) The children were messing about with the TV remote control and broke it.
(b) They messed with the discussions and the contract fell through.
(c) She's been messing with it for hours and it still doesn't work.
(d) They messed up the kitchen.

24. Rush
(a) They rushed away when the police arrived.
(b) Zain rushed out to get to his medical appointment.
(c) They don't want to be rushed into giving an answer and have asked for more time.
(d) They rushed out to catch the first rain of the season.

25. Fasten
(a) Fasten your seatbelts.
(b) We fastened it down to keep the wind from blowing it away.

(c) They have fastened up the speech as a source of inspiration.
(d) He fastened the latch of the door.

26. Wave
(a) They waved at us when they passed by.
(b) Don't wave at people you don't know.
(c) We waved her down at the station.
(d) The accident was bad, but the police waved us on.

27. Leap
(a) The tiger leapt at the deer.
(b) A leap of faith is what it takes.
(c) Look before you leap.
(d) He leaped out the chance to visit America.

28. Act
(a) The police were acting on a tip from an informer and caught the gang red-handed.
(b) The enzyme acts upon certain proteins.
(c) My computer's acting out I think I might have a virus.
(d) They acted out the story on stage.

29. Finish
(a) They finished off all the chocolates and had to go to the all-night store to buy some more.
(b) We went out for dinner and finished out in a club.
(c) We attended some workshops and finished the project.
(d) She finished with him a few months ago.

30. Turn
(a) She turned up an hour late.
(b) Please turn up the music; it's too loud.
(c) Turn off the lights please before you leave.
(d) Hundreds of fans were turned away from the football stadium.

31. Ask
(a) My mother is always asking after you.
(b) I'll ask around and see if anyone has seen your cat.
(c) Let's ask to the teacher our question.
(d) John has asked Mary out several times.

32. Put
(a) Could you put off the light please?
(b) The meeting was put off because of the strike. (Postpone/arrange a later date)
(c) Please don't put yourself out for us. (Go to a lot of trouble/be inconvenienced.)
(d) We put you up if you'd like to come for the week-end.

33. Get
(a) Some people manage to get up early.
(b) It's time to get down to some serious work!
(c) Be quiet and get on with your homework.
(d) Charlie had the 'flu but he got rid of it.

34. Pick
(a) Children are quick to pick up a new language.
(b) Can you pick me out at the station?
(c) Will you help me pick out a handbag to go with my outfit?
(d) The other children were always picking on Charlie because of his red hair.

Answer Key

Test 1

1. (a)	**2.** (c)	**3.** (d)	**4.** (d)	**5.** (c)
6. (a)	**7.** (b)	**8.** (c)	**9.** (c)	**10.** (d)
11. (d)	**12.** (c)	**13.** (a)	**14.** (d)	**15.** (d)
16. (c)	**17.** (b)	**18.** (d)	**19.** (b)	**20.** (a)
21. (c)	**22.** (d)	**23.** (c)	**24.** (b)	**25.** (b)
26. (a)	**27.** (b)	**28.** (a)	**29.** (c)	**30.** (c)
31. (b)	**32.** (d)	**33.** (a)	**34.** (d)	**35.** (c)

Test 2

1. (d)	**2.** (c)	**3.** (c)	**4.** (c)	**5.** (b)
6. (c)	**7.** (a)	**8.** (b)	**9.** (a)	**10.** (d)
11. (b)	**12.** (a)	**13.** (b)	**14.** (c)	**15.** (c)

Test 3

1. (c)	**2.** (c)	**3.** (d)	**4.** (a)	**5.** (b)
6. (b)	**7.** (c)	**8.** (b)	**9.** (a)	**10.** (b)
11. (d)	**12.** (c)	**13.** (a)	**14.** (b)	**15.** (d)
16. (c)	**17.** (b)	**18.** (d)	**19.** (b)	**20.** (d)
21. (a)	**22.** (c)	**23.** (d)	**24.** (b)	**25.** (c)
26. (c)	**27.** (d)	**28.** (c)	**29.** (b)	**30.** (b)
31. (c)	**32.** (a)	**33.** (d)	**34.** (b)	

Explanations

Test 1

1. One does not account of the money spent... one gives account of or accounts for is also acceptable.
2. Children were acting up
3. added on is the correct usage
4. answer up is wrong usage
5. ask her over is correct, no need to add 'in'
6. Company only backed down
7. Scandal blows over
8. The meeting broke up
9. Madonna has just brought out a new record.
10. Call me up when you get there.
11. If things carry on the way they are, you'll lose your job.
12. You should check your pockets before you leave home.
13. Wrong usage as when something clears off or you clear it off, it disappears or is removed.
14. When we get together, we make things happen
15. Cut it down
16. Colours fade and don't die out
17. The death penalty has been done away with in many countries.
18. The fielder dropped the catch.
19. Eat up your vegetables!
20. She fell down and hurt her knees.
21. Help himself to.
22. Who doesn't listen to a reason is wrong usage as it conveys an unclear message.
23. Paper over the disagreements is wrong usage.
24. Runs a profitable business
25. Bundle of boy-scouts is wrong usage.
26. Bolt of fine silk is wrong usage.
27. She and her dear friend
28. Hands full
29. Bear for her is wrong usage.
30. Run over himself is not fitting in this context.
31. Broke into a buckle is wrong usage.
32. Hang your coat and come and join us.
33. Hang on a minute;
34. Fill in the details
35. getting on with your studies

Test 2

1. Option (d) is the answer as to break up means to end a relationship and to start laughing, in an informal way while it is used in the sentence where the speaker wants to tell that he has developed some kind of rash, skin sores or irritation, therefore it should be 'broke out in' and not 'broke up in'.
2. Option (c) is the answer. It should be 'Do your coat up' instead of 'Do your coat over'.
3. Option (c) is the answer. To get away means to go on a vacation, while the intended meaning in the sentence is that the speaker's grandfather can have mobility by getting a new wheel chair. Hence, the correct phrase to be used is 'get around'.
4. Instead of going to the party we are just going to hang out at my place. Hence option (c) is the answer.
5. 'Medicines should be kept away from children.' And not 'kept out'. Hence option (b) is the answer.
6. The correct phrase that should be used in the sentence is: 'cut off' as the phrase 'cut down' means to make something fall to the ground. Option (c) is the answer.
7. The correct phrase should be 'he finally gave in' where the phrase gave in means "to reluctantly stop fighting or arguing". Option (a) is the answer.
8. The answer should be: option (b) where to hand out means to distribute to a group of people. But the speaker wants to tell that he has to submit his essay by Friday therefore the correct phrase should be 'to hand in' instead of 'to hand out'.
9. Option (a) is the answer. The speaker wants the child to switch off the TV as he is been called for dinner where the phrase 'turn down' means to decrease the volume. Hence it should be 'to turn the TV off'.
10. Option (d) is the answer. The correct sentence is: Jamie held back his tears at his grandfather's funeral.
11. Option (b) is the answer. To mark up means to increase while the person has been told to define

the boundaries there therefore the phrase should be - 'to mark out'.

12. Option (a) is the answer. The sentence tells that a good partner can help one to overcome from tough times. Hence the sentence (a) is wrong.

13. Option (b) is the answer. The speaker wants to tell someone that a person always puts other people in trouble. Therefore the correct sentence should be: Don't listen to him- he always jacks people around.

14. Option (c) is the answer as the speaker wants to tell that she wants to wear a red dress on her wedding day. Therefore the correct phrase should be 'looking for' instead of 'looking into'

15. Option (c) is the answer as ran off means to leave quickly while the person left to neglect his responsibilities. Therefore the correct phrase is: 'ran away from'.

Test 3

1. Option (c) is the answer as the sentence is grammatically incorrect; the correct sentence is "The film follows on from the original." The intended meaning of which is to be a part of something i.e. the film is a part of the original version.

2. Option (c) is the answer as it intends to state that the researcher spent too many months searching for the answer, so the correct phrase applied here should be "The researcher spent months scouting out the answer."

3. Option (d) is the answer because Sent for means to call someone and it doesn't fit here as the intended meaning of the sentence is that the company has sent a fact list to all of its existing customers, so the correct phrase to be used is 'sent out' and not 'sent for'.

4. Option (a) is the answer as to hang out means to stay in a place for fun whereas the intended meaning of the sentence is to hang the jacket in front of the closet so the correct phrase to be used here is hang up which means to suspend something somewhere.

5. Option (b) is the answer as the intended meaning of the sentence here is to delay the preparation of the dinner till parents arrive and hold back means to restrain or not allow, which doesn't fit in.

6. Option (b) is the answer. It is incorrect because the intended meaning of the sentence is that after fighting with cancer the person died at age of 87, and for this we use the phrase passed away.

7. Option (c) is the answer; the correct phrase to be used here is 'picking up' which means 'to increase'.

8. Option (b) is the answer because the sentence is grammatically incorrect. The correct sentence is 'Ken ate the cookies up' which means that Ken greedily ate all the cookies.

9. Option (a) is the answer .The phrase used is incorrect as 'zip around' means to move about quickly, so the correct phrase to be used here is 'zip up'.

10. Option (b) is the answer, as to 'come up' means to 'procure or conceive' and the intended meaning of the sentence is that they seem to be very rude for which the phrase 'come across' which means 'appear' should be used.

11. Option (d) is the answer; the correct phrase to be used here is 'stop by'.

12. Option (c) is the answer. The correct phrase which should be used here is 'he's banging about_in the kitchen'.

13. Option (a) is the answer. Kick about means to discuss which does not fits in here. The correct phrase to be used here is Kick in.

14. Option (b) is the answer, the correct phrase is tag along; it means to Accompany someone, especially if they haven't specifically invited you.

15. Option (d) is the answer; the phrase should be jump on, which if written here will mean to attack or to criticise.

16. Option (c) is the answer, The phrase 'tune out' means to ignore or not pay any attention, but here the sentence conveys the idea that the person owing the car prepared his car for the race, so the correct phrase which should be used here is 'tune up' which means to improve the performance of the vehicle.

17. Option (b) is the answer. The intended meaning of sentence (b) seems to be that as the wind was blowing the speaker couldn't light the campfire. The correct phrase which should be used here is 'blow out' and not 'blow up'. As 'to blow out 'means to extinguish a fire or a flame.

18. Option (d) is the answer, to opt out means to choose not to be part of something, but the intended meaning of the sentence here is that the person wants to be notified for getting updates. For this the correct phrase which should be used here is opt

in which means to choose to be part or a member of something.

19. Option (b) is the answer because the phrase ride off means to Go away which doesn't fits here.

20. Option (d) is the answer, 'Rake off' means to cheat someone, here the sentence explains that Tim keeps talking about the rows the speaker had last year, here the phrase should be 'raking over' which means to talk, think, etc, about something negative in the past. "Tim keeps raking over the rows we had last year".

21. The phrase 'mark up' means to increase the price or number of something, Option (a) is the answer, the intended meaning of the sentence here is that his dedication shall lead him to reach great heights so here the phrase to be used should be 'mark out' which means to show promise for the future. "His dedication marked him out for great things."

22. Option (c) is the answer, as to 'roll by' means to pass and it does not fit in here as it is very clear from the sentence that the army moved back when they were attacked. So, the correct phrase which should be used here is "The army rolled back when they came under attack". Here 'roll back' means retreat or to move back.

23. Option (b) is the answer as the intended meaning of the sentence is that because the discussion was spoiled and it didn't work the contract was dropped off. So, the correct phrase which should be used here is 'messed up' which means to spoil or ruin. "They messed up the discussions and the contract fell through".

24. Option (b) is the answer. The intended meaning of the sentence is that Zain went in hurry to get his medical appointment. The correct phrase which should be used here is 'Rush off' which means to depart in hurry.

25. Option (c) is the answer. The sentence here intends to explain that the people have taken the speech as a source of inspiration but the phrase used here is incorrect.

26. Option (c) is the answer. Here the intended meaning of the sentence is that we waved to her to say goodbye.

27. Option (d) is the answer. The intended meaning of the sentence seems to be that the person willingly wanted an opportunity to visit America.

28. Option (c) is the answer, the correct sentence should be "My computer's acting up I think I might have a virus". Here acting up refers to behave badly or strangely.

29. Option (b) is the answer.

30. Option (b) is the answer as to turn up means to raise the volume while it is used in the sentence where the intended meaning is to lower the volume as it is too loud.

31. The sentence is used in correct form with some grammatical errors. While others are correct in every respect. The correct form of option (c) should be: Let's ask the teacher our question.

32. To put off means to postpone or arrange a later date while speaker is asking the person to turn off or switch off the lights. Hence correct choice is option (a).

33. To get rid of means to eliminate.

34. To pick out means to choose or to select. The correct sentence is: Can you pick me up at the station?

CHAPTER 22

Paragraph Completion/Last Sentence of the Paragraph

Select the best concluding statement of a paragraph: In this type of questions, a paragraph is given and four alternative concluding statements are stated for the same. You are required to choose the option that best concludes the paragraph. These questions first made their appearance in the CAT 2005 examination and sparked huge debates amongst the student community about their answers.

The reason for the confusion was that when read normally, each of the four options for the concluding sentence, logically followed the material of the text in the paragraph. However, in these questions the key to deducing the one correct option is the ability to understand the author's opinion (Advanced reading skill 5 from the PART I of this book.). Once you have identified the author's opinion you can evaluate the options for the concluding sentence by trying to fit in the one option that made the most 'concluding sense' in the context of the author's opinion about the topic.

By trying to fit the concluding sense of each option we mean to say that you need to compare how each sentence concludes the argument - i.e. winds up the points made by the author and best conveys the author's opinion about the topic.

Further, the concluding sentence also needs to be a conclusion of the paragraph. It should not leave the scope of further carrying the paragraph's discussion forward.

The following examples will help you understand this type of question:

Example 1

Complete the following paragraph with the most suitable sentence.

In order to boost sales of toys at times other than the peak sale time. Toy manufacturers take recourse to the use of several techniques. Some of these include promoting character toys from Bollywood and Hollywood movies or TV series. All these sets are marketed as "collectibles" for the young consumers. The collections within a family of Collectibles, however, never appear to be complete (especially to the parents). As soon as all the characters are acquired, the child then requires the associated gadgets and gizmos that are bundled into the collectible set. Thus parents go shopping for the "car," the "home," the "mobile home," and even the "airplane" to ensure a happy homely environment for the toys. Ultimately, just as the elusive final piece of the series is attained the manufacturer and promoter release the next series of "collectibles."

The prime aim of the manufacturer and promoter is to ensure that

(a) all children should be happy and no child can be happy without a complete series of toys.

(b) as soon as one set is complete or almost complete, then the next one arrives on the scene.

(c) children should be encouraged to complete their collections of toys.

(d) sales need to be artificially bolstered throughout the year.

The correct answer is (d).

Let us now look at the following examples from the CAT 2005:

Example 2

Federer's fifth grand slam win prompted a reporter to ask whether he was the best ever. Federer is certainly not lacking in confidence, but he wasn't about to proclaim himself the best ever. "The best player of this generation, yes" he said, "But nowhere close to ever. Just look at the records that some guys have. I'm a minnow." _______

(a) His win against Agassi, a genius of the previous generation, contradicts that.
(b) Sampras, the king of an earlier generation, was as humble.
(c) He is more than a minnow to his contemporaries.
(d) The difference between 'the best of this generation' and 'the best ever' is a matter of perception.

The correct answer is (c). You need an answer that concludes the passage. While options (a) and (b) take the paragraph into a new direction, (d) is irrelevant in the context provided - it is too general in nature.

Example 3

Thus the end of knowledge and the closing of the frontier that it symbolizes is not a looming crisis at all, but merely one of many embarrassing fits of hubris in civilizations long industry. In the end, it will pass away and be forgotten. Ours is not the first generation to struggle to understand the organizational laws of the frontier, deceive itself that it has succeeded, and go to its grave having failed. _______

(a) One would be wise to be humble.
(b) But we might be the first generation to actually reach the frontier.
(c) But we might be the first generation to deal with the crisis.
(d) However, this time the success is not illusory.

Options (b) and (d) seem to indicate that we might have reached the frontier. But by its very definition the frontier of knowledge can never be reached. Hence, you can eliminate these answers. Further, if you consider Option c, it talks about dealing with the crisis - which does not exist at all according to the first sentence of the paragraph.

Example 4

Most firms consider expert individuals to be too elitist, temperamental, egocentric, and difficult to work with. Force such people to collaborate on a high stakes project and they just might come to fisticuffs. Even the very notion of managing such a group seems unimaginable. So most organizations will fall into default mode, setting up project teams of people who get along nicely. __________

(a) The result however is disastrous.
(b) The result is mediocrity.
(c) The result is the creation of experts who then become elitists.
(d) Naturally, they drive innovations.

The paragraph clearly states that teams are formed on the basis of people's ability to get along with each other (rather than on their merit with respect to the task at hand.) Obviously, this leads to a compromise in the quality of the work being performed. Hence, Option (d) is eliminated. Option (a) simply does not follow from the previous sentence since the word *however* indicates that the author should be contradicting his previous idea with this sentence. However, if you analyse the ideas in the last sentence of the paragraph and the Option (a), you will clearly see that there is no contrast between the two ideas.

Option (c) talks about an effect that is highly improbable in the context. Option (b) is perfect since you will expect mediocrity when you create a team on the basis of parameters other than ability.

Example 5

The audience for crosswords and sudoku, understandably, overlap greatly, but there are differences, too. A crossword attracts a more literary person, while sudoku appeals to a keenly logical mind. Some crossword enthusiasts turn up their noses at sudoku because they feel it lacks depth. A good crossword requires vocabulary, knowledge, mental flexibility and sometimes even a sense of humor to complete. It touches numerous areas of life and provides an 'Aha!' or two along the way.__________

(a) Sudoku, on the other hand, is just a logical exercise, each one similar to the last.
(b) Sudoku, incidentally, is growing faster in popularity than crosswords even among the literate.
(c) Sudoku, on the other hand, can be attempted and enjoyed even by children.
(d) Sudoku, however, is not exciting in any sense of the term.

In order to solve the above question, you need to understand that you are looking for the option that best 'completes' the paragraph. The structural construct under which we reach the last sentence of the paragraph is that of the comparison of crosswords and sudokus. The author has shown a clear bias towards crosswords - and in fact is in the process of explaining his sentence '*Some crossword enthusiasts turn up their noses at sudoku because they feel it lacks depth.*' So obviously after praising crosswords, he has to talk in a dark light about sudoku. Option (a) has the perfect fit under this structure. Although Option (d) is also negative in its construction, it is unlikely to be the answer because of the fact that it is too crude and direct - something that you cannot associate with the atuhor's style of writing. Options (b) and (c) get eliminated because they are talking positive about sudokus - something that goes against our expectations of what the author is likely to convey.

Practice Exercise 1

The following questions have a paragraph from which the last sentence has been deleted. From the given options, choose the one that completes the paragraph in the most appropriate way.

1. And those newly democratic countries have done relatively well. Elsewhere, the first flowerings of protest in the spring of 2011 brought not freedom but more tyranny and vicious civil strife. When the police in the tiny island kingdom of Bahrain failed to stamp out a raucous pro-democracy mutiny, the ruling family panicked._______
   (a) Not only has Bahrain failed to progress, it has turned the clock back to where it was after a previous bout of sectarian tensions in the 1980s.
   (b) The result is a grim stand-off between the country's embittered two-thirds majority of Shia Muslims and a wary Sunni minority.
   (c) It invited nearby Sunni monarchs to send in troops, which lead to scores of deaths and hundreds of arrests.
   (d) Nowhere, as yet, has the right to vote or greater freedom to speak translated into markedly better government, more jobs or brighter short-term prospects.
2. U.S. secretary of state John Kerry and his Russian counterpart, Sergey Lavrov, affirmed their support for a Geneva peace conference in August 2013, but offered little in the way of a strategy to bring the warring sides to the table. Rebels appear unwilling to consider a plan that does not include Assad's ouster, while Assad is unwilling to go voluntarily.______
   (a) Moreover, neither side seems willing to negotiate from a perceived position of weakness.
   (b) The Assad regime's alleged use of chemical weapons in August has only complicated international discussions of a peace process.
   (c) The Arab League suspended Syria's membership and imposed economic sanctions on Damascus.
   (d) Arab governments, including Gulf states and Jordan, have provided arms and financial and diplomatic support to the opposition.
3. Many voters remember a time when hard work was reliably rewarded with economic security. This was not really true in the 1950s and 60s if you were black or female, but the question still remains: what if Mr Cowen is right? What if the bottom 85 per cent today are mostly doomed to stay there? In a country founded on hope, that would require something like a new social contract.______
   (a) For their part Republican leaders offer long-cherished shrink-the-government schemes, rebranded as plans to save the American Dream.
   (b) In truth, the links between investment and government policy are rarely so neat, and even such a boom might do little for middle-class wage stagnation.
   (c) Politics risks becoming a "zero-sum game where a few do very well while struggling families of every race fight over a shrinking economic pie."
   (d) Politicians cannot duck Mr Cowen's conundrum for ever.
4. Previous studies over the years have suggested that we use one half of our brain more often than the other, playing a part in the type of personality we have.

   While the left side of the brain is usually associated with logical, analytical and detail-oriented behavior, the right side has been connected to creative, thoughtful and subjective thinking.________
   (a) But a new study published in the journal *PLOS ONE*, suggests there is no evidence within brain imaging that proves some people are right-brained or left-brained.
   (b) The research team conducted a two-year study of 1,011 people who were part of the International Neuroimaging Data-Sharing Initiative (INDI), and who were between the ages of 7 and 29.
   (c) All connections in the brain were examined, and all possible combinations of the brain regions were correlated for each brain region that was left-lateralized or right-lateralized.
   (d) However, we just do not see patterns where the whole left-brain network is more connected or the whole right-brain network is more connected in some people.
5. It is not uncommon for an El Niño winter to be followed by a La Niña one - where climate patterns and worldwide effects are, for the most part, the opposite of those produced by El Niño. Where there was flooding there is drought, where winter weather was abnormally mild, it turns abnormally harsh.________
   (a) By the time it had run its course eight months later, the giant El Niño of 1997-98 had deranged weather patterns around the world
   (b) Hundreds of families splashed frantically through the muddy flood to save what they could.
   (c) La Niñas have followed El Niños three times in the past 15 years - after the 1982-83 event and after those of 1986-87 and 1995.

(d) By the time the debris settled and the collective misery was tallied, the devastation had in some respects exceeded even that of the El Niño of 1982–83

6. *Dust Bowl* is "a Ken Burns film" in what might by now be called the traditional sense - that is to say, a beautifully wrought, latitudinous, and, at the very least, aspirationally definitive work of filmic nonfiction, right at home among the documentarian's prior oeuvre. It is a wholly appropriate approach to the terrors of the Dust Bowl. Consider: What do three hundred fifty million tons of airborne dirt, blown up on sixty-mile-an-hour winds and crackling with electricity, look like? How does it feel to watch that cloud roll in? To be caught up in its abrasive, blinding rage?________
   (a) Tapping their childhood memories, Burns's vision of the Dirty Thirties departs ever so slightly from the sense of staid authority that his viewers have come to expect and takes on something of the haunting quality of a remembered nightmare
   (b) Measurements and meteorological data, film and still photographs, even eyewitness reports can only suggest so much - and Burns, deft storyteller that he is, knows it.
   (c) No fact or artifact could make the storm any more visible, any more real, for the viewer than the act of sympathetic imagination that it takes to conjure an image of this mustachioed, older gentleman as a kid, huddled against his praying mom as the dark dirt blasted their home.
   (d) He knows that, of the resources available to him, it's the child's-eye view, a naive and poignant focus on the so-called small picture, the apparently miscellaneous detail that all but magically gives expression to whatever is unfathomable beyond it.

7. New Deal efforts at soil conservation brought back the land. When the rains came back in '39, and dust storms started to settle down, farmers on the Plains turned to the Ogallala Aquifer, the 174,000-square-mile water table beneath them, to satisfy their crops' needs._______
   (a) Wells started cropping up everywhere, some feeding crops that required more moisture than the wheat lost only a decade or two earlier.
   (b) What seemed like a good idea at the time "was the beginning of a bad idea," said one old-timer at the close of the film.
   (c) At the present rate of depletion, the aquifer could, at some point, be pumped dry.
   (d) In a region with so little and such unreliable rainfall, it made sense: All the water that they could ask for was right there, under their feet, and the technology to get at it finally was affordable.

8. But when a tsunami hits Japan, an earthquake crushes Haiti, or an embassy attack leaves foreign servicemen dead, even the most calloused tweeter goes soft inside, and every laptop turns into a small news service all its own._______
   (a) At such moments, the web becomes a nurturing and shining place, and every stiff-jawed critic seems to want to send you forward with hugs and a smile.
   (b) Sarcasm pours down from the loftiest peaks.
   (c) This wasn't disaster porn but a startling flood of goodwill.
   (d) These days, life online has become friendly, well mannered, oversweet.

9. King Herod had a substantial architectural heritage to his name in the Levant by the time of his death in 4th century BCE. As one of Rome's most loyal client kings, he incorporated much Roman-style architecture throughout the lands he ruled. He visited Rome in 40th century BCE and returned two more times, between 19 and 12th century BCE. _________
   (a) Herod's building program in Jerusalem and in other parts of his kingdom rivaled much of what he had seen in Rome.
   (b) Herod's mimicry of things Roman encompassed the public and the monumental as well as the private and domestic.
   (c) The last two trips were during Augustus' building frenzy in Rome, when the emperor famously turned a city of bricks into one of marble.
   (d) He also created Roman-style baths, with various chambers for different temperatures and employed hypocaust technology, which heated water from underneath.

10. On 22 June 2012, for $9,826,500, the Mount Vernon Ladies' Association purchased George Washington's personal bound copy of the Constitution with the Bill of Rights and Acts of Congress. The volume dated from 1789, Washington's first year in office as president of the United States. In its margins, he repeatedly wrote the word "president" to emphasize those sections relating to his official powers and responsibilities. __________
   (a) With his meticulous - some might say pedantic - mind, he carefully measured the dimensions of the presidency as if it were a suit of clothes.
   (b) Washington's approach to leadership emerged from a code of personal conduct that he began developing as a young man.

(c) The deaths of his father and his brother - Lawrence died when George was only twenty - appears to have left him touchy and insecure - a temperament that did not bode well for his future.
(d) Washington looked forward to his first experiences of combat in the French and Indian War, expecting a great adventure that would put the seal on his manhood.

11. And when the words run out, there are numbers. The news that physicists had found the Higgs boson confirmed some of the greatest intellectual work ever carried out. True, the human race may not be able to resolve territorial disputes or run a stable currency bloc but it has established why the universe has structure.__________
(a) In the eurozone crisis, some leaders have now looked properly at the effects of failure.
(b) The world's worst problems can be solved by face-to-face negotiation.
(c) There is only one route through the crisis, much of it unpalatable to voters - and hence to leaders.
(d) We should recognise this at least as progress, and of an astounding kind.

12. Languages are extremely diverse, but they are not arbitrary. Behind the bewildering, contradictory ways in which different tongues conceptualise the world, we can sometimes discern order. Linguists have traditionally assumed that this reflects the hardwired linguistic aptitude of the human bra-in.__________
(a) Yet recent scientific studies propose that language "universals" aren't simply prescribed by genes but that they arise from the interaction between the biology of human perception and the bustle, exchange and negotiation of human culture.
(b) Language has a logical job to do - to convey information - and yet it is riddled with irrationality: irregular verbs, random genders, silent vowels, ambiguous homophones.
(c) You'd think languages would evolve towards an optimal state of concision, but instead they accumulate quirks that hinder learning, not only for foreigners but also for native speakers.
(d) These peculiarities have been explained by linguists by reference to the history of the people who speak it.

13. How liberal democracy will emerge from this process is difficult to imagine. The Syrian people - the driving force of the peaceful protests against Assad's regime - are faced with a "choice" between Assad's brutal dictatorship, and US-sponsored Islamist rebel militants allied with an exiled Muslim Brotherhood-dominated opposition.__________
(a) It is therefore far from clear that the FSA represents the sentiments of Syrian civil society.
(b) But just as the West's Islamist gambit during the Cold War (and after) paved the way for the global acceleration of al-Qaeda's operations, the implications of this ill-conceived strategy will be even more devastating.
(c) They have become unwitting pawns on a geopolitical chessboard in which the principal players - the US, Iran, Russia, and China - are fighting a proxy war for strategic influence.
(d) It is not too late to reverse course. Caught in the midst of a proxy war for strategic influence, UN envoy Kofi Annan's diplomatic efforts never had a chance.

14. In Rwanda, stability has been achieved partly by the drive to stress national, not ethnic identity. Given the genocide, the exhortation that "we are all Rwandans" is understandable. But it is striking how far the government goes to downplay ethnic identities. There is no official recognition of different ethnic groups. While there is an unwritten rule that the prime minister to President Kagame should be a Hutu, officially questions about the balance of Hutus and Tutsis in power do not arise.__________
(a) Political activity is tightly controlled and discussion managed through a system of forums while the country focuses on economic development.
(b) Decades of apparent stability under the rule of Marshal Tito masked antagonisms which, in the right conditions, exploded.
(c) But as any good researcher looking at a twin study will know, you need to look for the differences over the long-term too.
(d) Rwanda is assimilationist and emphasises its citizens are Rwandan, never mind their ethnic identity, more like France, for example.

15. Not that billboards are themselves unusual. What marked these out was that each and every one was either ragged and empty, or else carrying posters so old that the sun had bleached them illegible. If they're selling anything, it's the vivid reality of decline.__________
(a) At least that was how a number of high-profile figures sought to characterise the situation.
(b) Whether a direct symptom of Greece's problems or not, they serve as an eerie reminder of the country's economic plight.

(c) Such interventions have not been welcomed by everyone - many I spoke to here said they felt like an attempt to influence the vote.
(d) No doubt many who voted for the anti-austerity parties will claim that what looks to have been a concerted campaign against the left-wing Syriza party helped their centre-right rivals New Democracy to victory yesterday.

16. At the end of his Digital Life Design talk in January, Thrun confirmed that he had resigned his tenure at Stanford. Instead, he was throwing his energy into a new venture, going live that day, called Udacity. The site would offer "massive online open courses" (MOOCs) free of charge to the global 99 per cent, to the tech-savvy and web-illiterate alike.__________
(a) With student debt at $1 trillion in the United States alone - greater than credit card debt - the current education system, with its barriers, privileges, and vast inequalities, was no longer defensible, he said.
(b) The Grand Challenge called on American university students to build robotic cars and race them, unassisted, across 131 miles of unforgiving desert scrub, over salt flats and down the treacherous Beer Bottle Pass.
(c) As the lab's director, Thrun developed "enhanced reality" glasses worthy of a dystopian sci-fi novel and built a second generation of robotic cars that have since logged thousands of miles on California roads.
(d) By the time classes began, enrolment had swelled to 158,000, with students from every country in the world except North Korea.

17. We're the richest country on earth - four and a half percent of the world's people producing more than twenty percent of the world's wealth. But you wouldn't know from the cheapjack spending squabbles in Congress. We possess more military power than the rest of the planet combined. Though you couldn't tell by the way we're treated by everyone from the impotent Kremlin to the raggedy councils of the Taliban.__________
(a) Witness our foreign policy deliberations, mired in snits about what kind of underachievement to pursue.
(b) Consider our domestic policy debates - a people once proverbial for our risk-taking, our biggest election-year issue is now health insurance.
(c) And we fret ceaselessly over balancing the budget as if the first duty of nationhood is to be a thrifty parent trying to skimp on a country's infrastructure with a box of "Highway Helper."
(d) The earth is ours. We have the might and means to achieve the spectacular - and no intention of doing so.

18. Just as the Indian subcontinental plate has a tendency to constantly rub and push against the Eurasian tectonic plate, causing friction and volatility in the entire Himalayan mountain range, India's bilateral relationship with China is also a subtle, unseen, but ongoing and deeply felt collision, the affects of which have left a convoluted lineage.__________
(a) The relationship is into layers of rivalry, mistrust, and occasional cooperation, not to mention actual geographical disputes.
(b) Several rounds of talks held since 1981 have failed to resolve the disputed claims.
(c) Tensions between the two powers have come to influence everything from their military and security decisionmaking to their economic and diplomatic maneuvering, with implications for wary neighbors and faraway allies alike.
(d) An unsettled border provides China the strategic leverage to keep India uncertain about its intentions, and nervous about its capabilities, while exposing India's vulnerabilities and weaknesses, and encouraging New Delhi's "good behavior" on issues of vital concern.

19. It used to be that people from my ethnicity (Jewish) and my geography (the Northeast) retired to Florida when they reached the age of 65. Sometimes, if they could afford it, they retired at 60 and gave themselves a few extra years in the sun. The East Coast of Florida, whose informal capital is Boca Raton, was the mecca for those who wanted to take it easy after years of hard labor. __________
(a) Most retirees were small merchants and entrepreneurs who'd risen early every morning and come home late every night in order to buy the split level in the suburbs and send their kids to college.
(b) For their children - of which I count myself one - it was hard to understand. Florida seemed so unlike what we thought of as the center of the world: New York City.
(c) They wanted peace and quiet, sunshine and poolside, canasta and golf. Florida was leisurely, pastel-colored, and sun-drenched, not fast, grubby, and overcast. New York was exciting, but they'd had enough of exciting.
(d) It's true that many of the people living in this area of Florida are old, but is that bad? Old people, I've come to feel, are often very interesting people - a fact that becomes increasingly evident as I grow old myself.

Practice Exercise 2

Para-Completion

1. The Assad regime depends on its patrons in Iran and the Iranian-backed Hezbollahmilitia in neighboring Lebanon. The Sunni-led opposition is similarly turning to its regional patrons. These regional players, with their own agendas, will keep pulling Syria apart until a functioning national government can be reestablished.
   (a) The resolution must be political - but grounded in a realistic assessment of the difficulty in putting the pieces of Syria back together.
   (b) The regime has seemed equally bent on division.
   (c) What's happening in Syria isn't an insurgency now but a sectarian civil war.
   (d) The country should enter what is similar to quarantine until it is cured from the sectarian disease.
2. Naseeruddin Shah is undoubtedly one of the best performers on the Indian screen. Despite his atypical looks, he managed to make a mark for himself in both parallel and commercial films, but gives credit to Bollywood megastar Amitabh Bachchan for paving the way for unconventional looking heroes in the Hindi filmdom.
   (a) Naseeruddin's own achievements are no mean feat, but despite three National Awards, international honour and acclaim, the seasoned actor wonders why he isn't seen as a commercially viable artist by filmmakers.
   (b) Nowadays unconventional-looking actors like Nawazuddin Siddiqui and Irrfan among others have raised the bar in filmdom, but Naseeruddin feels the real credit goes to Amitabh Bachchan.
   (c) Mentality has not changed. It's just that the audience has always appreciated good acting.
   (d) But the tendency has not changed. Still the chocolate face is acceptable.
3. Given that all three major parties - Congress, BJP and AAP - have declared that they would not enter into any post-poll alliances, the chances of President's Rule seem higher, especially if the largest party is way short of the majority mark. Since President's Rule cannot last beyond six months,
   (a) Experts, however, also feel a huge voter-turn out usually suggests a decisive and clear mandate.
   (b) However, absence of a formal government can slow down functioning of the departments.
   (c) Experts look at the scenarios as an 'unfortunate' one for the city as it hurts the functioning of the government in a significant way.
   (d) The fresh election to the Delhi assembly may well be held along with the Lok Sabha election in the summer of 2014.
4. Mourn the statesman and the revolutionary and the terrorist and the neoliberal and the ethicist and the pragmatist and the saint and don't you dare try to discard or remove any part of that whole.
   (a) He had a compliment to give to everybody, including my housekeeper and doorman. It was amazing. A gentle giant, he was.
   (b) Celebrate him? Sure, but then make sure you're willing to consider emulating him.
   (c) Mandela faced, the hypocrisy of many who praise his life.
   (d) He showed us how liberating it is to forgive.
5. Freedom of the Press, the Ark of the Covenant of Democracy", as proudly proclaimed by our Supreme Court, is not in good shape. A document published by The Free Speech Hub, an initiative of the Media Foundation, records how journalists in Kashmir have been beaten and shot at by the security forces. Journalist Amulya Pani was assaulted when he went to cover the police firing on villagers in Kalinganagar in Orissa, and journalists Moirangthem Romeo and Atom Lukhoi were arrested by the Imphal East commandos in Jirabam in Manipur, for no apparent reason. Attacks on freedom of the press and journalists are not the monopoly of the security forces. Attacks on and vandalising M F Husain's paintings, threats against writer Arundhati Roy for her article about Maoists and the onslaught on Bollywood film My Name is Khan emanated from intolerant social and political groups.
   (a) We have not learnt to accord freedom to the thought we hate or to a movie of which we disapprove.
   (b) Regrettably, law enforcement authorities look the other way when powerful political personalities and organisations are involved.
   (c) We have not learnt to give freedom to the thought we dislike.
   (d) The root cause is the inability to stomach anything which is unconventional or opposed to one's idea of truth and morality.
6. 1967 Border: At the start of the Six Day War in 1967, Gaza was held by Egypt, the Golan Heights by Syria, and the West Bank by Jordan; after the Six Day War, Israel had pushed its Arab neighbors to the Sinai Peninsula to the West, to the Jordan River to the East, and out of the Golan, and its occupation of these new territories has continued since (except for Gaza, from which Israel withdrew but has since subjected to a military blockade to isolate the Strip's

Hamas-led government). The two-state solution is premised on a Palestinian state established in the Gazan and West Bank territory held by Egypt and Jordan at the start of the Six Day War.

(a) The compromise, then, is to exchange territory - Palestinian negotiators will concede settlement blocs in the West Bank to Israel in exchange for territorial additions to the Palestinian state.
(b) The last round of direct talks fell apart when Palestinian negotiators reportedly would not concede that Israel is a "Jewish state" in exchange for a settlement freeze.
(c) Israeli negotiators have consistently resisted the resettlement of Palestinian refugees to Israel, arguing that it is logistically not feasible and would alter the fundamental identity of the Israeli state.
(d) But those exact borders, Israeli Prime Minister Benjamin Netanyahu has argued, have become indefensible, and Israeli negotiators are pushing to retain settler-held territory in the West Bank.

7. In July this year, Twitter introduced "Promoted Products", a paid service that highlights advertiser's tweets, handles or trends, to India. As it edges ever closer to the traditional model of a content-driven media company through such advertising efforts and new content partnerships, Twitter's India initiatives can be seen as a clear - but cautious - part of a larger, less organic growth strategy for its global future.
(a) Indian brands could also create "promoted tweets", which would also be sold through a cost-per-engagement model.
(b) Twitter hinted that it intended to launch this service in "selected international markets", but did not name India specifically.
(c) There are many people on Twitter who actually take the brand's promotion and do it in their own way.
(d) Twitter was still growing in the US, its home country, but that it already had a larger user base in some other countries.

8. India return to the trajectory of growth? It was not "will" India return, but "when". Underlying this question has been disappointment and hope. There is the perception that India's current economic woes are of its own making. This disappoints, because India did so well to withstand the Great Recession of 2008. There is also the view, however, that these problems can be remedied with stronger leadership.
(a) The hope is that this leadership will be forthcoming and that a resurgent India will counter an ambitious China.
(b) There were, of course, supplementary questions - is corruption an endemic feature of our polity? Who will best whom in the presidential tussle between Narendra Modi and Rahul Gandhi? What is the nature and consequence of the strengthening tide of federalism? - but they all flowed from this interest in the future prospects of the economy.
(c) We focus on the trees and lose sight of the forest. The challenge of responding to interested, non-partisan and well-meaning critics of the India story on foreign soil compels analytical realignment.
(d) Most of us who live in large cities and circle the opinion formers in government, politics and journalism tend to get bogged down in the minutiae of anecdotal analysis.

9. The House of Lords has been replaced by the UK Supreme Court which is now the highest court of appeal in the United Kingdom. It was established by the Constitutional Reform Act 2005. The Court is housed in a building opposite the Big Ben. The atmosphere in Court is genial, not forbidding. The court rooms are spacious and brightly lit. There is pin drop silence in the Court. Counsel respectfully answer occasional polite queries from the Bench without loud interruptions from counsel on the other side. The day I visited the Court it delivered an important judgment in which by a majority of 6 to 3 it ruled that the Human Rights Act 1998 did not apply to British armed forces on foreign soil, viz. Iraq. A noteworthy feature is that a concise press summary outlining the facts of the case, the legal issues involved and the reasons for the judgment is issued at the same time by the registry with the approval of the Court to "assist in understanding the Court's decision". Judgments of the Court are available on the same day.
(a) A shameful blot on our criminal justice system is the phenomenon of undertrials rotting in jails for periods longer than the maximum punishment imposable upon conviction.
(b) If this be judicial activism, it is most welcome because it enforces the right of under-trials to a speedy trial guaranteed by Article 21 of the Constitution.
(c) Adoption of this practice in our Supreme Court is worth consideration.
(d) In this context, the anguished observations of a Bench of the Delhi High Court, comprising Chief Justice Dipak Misra and Justice Manmohan, were most timely.

10. A crisis in Indo-US relations has long been in the making. There is, of course, the massive shift in

perceptions of India that frames the reception of events. India's new economy used to be the darling of The New York Times, now its old society is subject to yawningly relentless indictment. India was the maturing great power, now it has become an infantile wannabe. It had a strong government, now it is flailing.

(a) The case has become a marker of our confusions over our relationship with the US.
(b) Our self-esteem is shaped by what others think of us.
(c) The Ugly Indian and Ugly American have rediscovered each other.
(d) The American liberal establishment has suddenly rediscovered an India that is reactionary, exploitative, deceitful, feudal and incapable of the rule of law.

11. Currently, India has more than 7 lakh teachers who are untrained and teaching in classrooms across the country. A further 5 lakh are expected to be recruited to fill in teacher vacancies. The DIET is able to cater to only 40 per cent of the teachers in the country. In this context, distance education offers an opportunity for large-scale upgradation of teacher skills and qualifications.
(a) Currently, India has more than 7 lakh teachers who are untrained and teaching in classrooms across the country. A further 5 lakh are expected to be recruited to fill in teacher vacancies.
(b) The Government should scale up operations of IGNOU's distance education program for teacher education, which is already collaborating with states to provide pre-service and in-service training to government teachers.
(c) Implementing a work-based curriculum will involve designing a textbook that has activities finely interwoven into the theory.
(d) If distance training is to be provided to all the untrained teachers, the capacity of the current distance education program will have to be increased.

12. It is a vicious circle. Girls are being discriminated against and hence, there are less girls being born. The lesser the number of girls the more in the society the higher the crime against them for sexual desires are not a taboo but a condition that needs to be taken into account in any society. Rapes are the most common occurrence in a society where not each man finds at least one woman for himself. The more the crime, the more women do not want girls to be born to "save" them from this life leading to lesser number of girls. We need to educate and make aware the root cause.
(a) Why I ask in this country, which has in his history held women in high regard, which prays to goddesses for SHAKTI, DHAN and PEACE are we so distant from ground realities of women who live amongst us.
(b) Even when the girls survive, we as a society in India have always given priority to the need of the men and boys in the house.
(c) It's unnerving to think how women can do this to girls. How the educated, learned and aware women can commit such brutality.
(d) Yet rather than understanding the reason all the women who have been subject to these crimes either by family or fate do not want their girls to be born to avoid such a life for them.

13. While several feminists demand death penalty for rapists, even right-wing conservatives would also ask for the same. Why this convergence of interests? Extremist positions seem to create this problem quite frequently. While feminists would base it on the absolute right of a woman over her sexuality, the conservatives come from where a woman's sexual 'purity' or 'impurity' defines her identity and place. Here India and Bharat (if such a demarcation exists) want the same, but one looks forward, while the other is regressive. Legitimacy for an argument drawn from cultural past is always problematic. Culture has, for the most part, evolved in ways in which a group is held inferior through elaborate myths and mythologies, it sustains status quo, it works through complicity of the group held inferior through incentives.
(a) Sacrifice is a woman's test to greatness, not her mental acumen or control of her agency.
(b) So is it worthwhile for a woman to try to achieve the ideal in this scenario?
(c) A rational discussion on human rights requires freedom from the tendency of romanticization of culture, it needs to be peeled, its nuances understood, since it is very clear that an image of glorification of powerful woman does not destroy or even nullify the more horrifying ground realities.
(d) Empowering though it may seem, this cultural representation is not very liberating.

14. The example set forth by Malala has helped bring the world's focus on the very serious issue affecting the people in Malala's country. Going against the odds, Malala had started to voice her defiance against the Taliban for banning girls from going to school much before the world's spotlight came to rest on her. She started blogging about the dismal situation of education for girls around her as early

as in December 2009 and was also interviewed on local news channels. But her leap to international recognition after October 2012 gave her the platform to address the world, and on 12th July 2013 she stood at the UN calling out for worldwide access to education.

(a) Malala, in her show of defiance, has sparked a movement.
(b) She has emerged as a global leader who seems to have every intention to use the pedestal she has acquired for the cause of education.
(c) The words uttered by her during her interview in The Jon Stewart Show, "But then if I hit a Talib with a shoe, then there would be no difference between you and the Talib...." clearly portrays that age isn't a basis to be a leader.
(d) This young girl has started on a path to bring on a much needed change and with the world willing to lend her its support, one can always aspire to see her dream turning into a reality in the near future.

15. Where some Economists argued that the Food security bill would be a huge liability to India and that it was out of India's financial capability to fund this Bill, Amartya Sen responded in a stern way saying that "Sitting in a room with Air Conditioning which is working as a result of subsidized electricity as well as eating food prepared with subsidized cooking gas as well as the fact that rich farmers being able to buy subsidized fertilizers" for their own profit depicted a very selfish act. Economic Growth has to be fairly distributed among the various social strata of society according to their needs and in a country like India where the majority population is under the BPL certain preferences of opportunities, minority security as well as relief funds are to be provided.
(a) Reduction of communal violence, health, education and shelter remain Indian Primary worries and Economic Growth can contribute to them if used judiciously and effectively.
(b) In statements made by certain Economists as well as Global Organizations, Economic Policies and Social Policies are seen to be not incompatible but" bound to be at war with each other "and that Growth is the enemy of social equity.
(c) A very important fact that our world economy misinterprets it, is that both these economic variables are not contradicting each other but have a subtle and important correlation between them.
(d) Hence we can therefore conclude that Economic Growth and Social Welfare are Correlative variables and that with proper channelization of Policies leads to higher social welfare which indirectly leads to more Economic Growth.

16. There is no one *best price* that the government can and should try to find and dictate. Creating conditions for ensuring market prices can be the only best response of the government that will help ensure the most efficient allocation of resources. You cannot stand for making things affordable for the *common man* while at the same time oppose FDI in retail. Competition among various kinds of retailers will help ensure that. Also, strict action against hoarders will not help curb occasional jump in prices of certain commodities. Removing trade barriers will. Howsoever we may like to, we cannot legislate away scarcity. As a *common man* trying to make a living in Delhi, these are some of my areas of concern which I hope you will take note of and find ways to address.
(a) First principles of economics tells us that it is because of the mismatch in demand and supply.
(b) At the very least, you have certainly raised the level of debate in this country and brought some serious competition amongst a field dominated by age-old political parties.
(c) For once, no one wants to identify with a politician with a criminal background.
(d) You have certainly raised the bar of expectations that we as the *common man* have from public offices and for that we thank you.

17. The aim of the youth in politics appears to be not just contesting elections and assuming power, but a larger aim to serve the society and save it from innumerable social-ills. However, to achieve these conceived objectives of progress, development, peace and empowerment, the youth need adequate nurturing. Education must be a mix of theory, case studies and practical exposure, which would make them aware of the realities of the society. Political parties must also focus on the capacity development of the youth who would be the harbingers of change. Development and enhancement of the leadership skills must be focused upon.
(a) Ingrained with rational values, perceptions and ideals, the youth in Indian politics hold the promise that they would not yield to obsolete dogmas and slogans. The mantra that now rings loud is–"If politics determines our future, it is time, we determined our politics".
(b) Youth of such high characters in a civil society make for a more informed citizenry, who have the power to facilitate better awareness, make for better participation in the political realm and articulate the choices of the people at

large, thereby holding the government more accountable.

(c) Elastic as the concept is, politics demands the qualities of the youth, said Robert Kennedy in 1966. Youth is not a time of life, but a state of mind, a temper of the will, a quality of the imagination, predominance of courage over timidity and of the appetite for adventure over the love of ease.

(d) Their activism has shown that their voices cannot be subdued as they belong to the land of Mahatma Gandhi.

18. Legitimacy of a government is one that has been an incessant thorn for the international community. One would assume that the post-Cold War ideology which believes that the best and only form of a legitimate government is the one which is elected through a democratically held election would settle matters easily with election being the only benchmark for determining legitimacy. But then to classify a democratically elected government which refuses its citizenry the most basic of democratic rights as the representatives of its people would be a gross human rights violation.

(a) But the recognition that such government has from the international community is also an important element determining the legitimacy of such government.

(b) This creates a rather meek reality for the many struggling in the Middle East or the other regions for the new government they aim to create would be subject to a more rigorous international diplomatic scrutiny than their tyrannical counterparts they would be replacing.

(c) The moral compass of the nation states whose recognition is sought is a subjective tool and can liberally sway in the direction that favours that nation's own national interest or even soothe the ruling party's vote banks.

(d) Sanction of the citizen which it seeks to represent is an important source for deriving legitimacy for a government.

19. There is no final judgment in the marketplace for ideas since one can never know when the circumstances will lead to a renewed interest for that idea. There was a time when libertarianism was very dormant and now because of excessive government regulation, people looking for answers have re-discovered it. By the author's logic, Copernicus should have conceded defeat to Helios-centric model of solar system, Communists should have conceded defeat after Soviet's fall and Mao's Great Leap Forward. Besides, it is extremely ignorant to call the market place of ideas as free and unfettered given the extent of state sponsored education that almost never showed the nation state's founding philosophy in bad light.

(a) If you believe in the free market, why weren't you willing to accept as final the judgment against libertarianism rendered decades ago in the free and unfettered marketplace of ideas?

(b) History, the repository of ideas has almost always been directed by the State to promote nationalism at the cost of truth.

(c) The author need only read USA's account of Great Depression, Vietnam War, Iraq and Afghanistan War etc. to realize the truth.

(d) Does our libertarian recognize that large corporations are a threat to our freedoms?

20. Taking a bike on to Britain's roads is not as dangerous as it once was. Estimates from the Department for Transport show that, per million miles cycled, the number of cyclists killed or seriously injured has fallen by 33 per cent since the 1990s. But the rate has recently moved up again, even as the number of road accidents in general has fallen sharply.

(a) In London, cyclists made up 22 per cent of all casualties on the roads in 2012, up from just 10 per cent in 2006

(b) Thus, it can be concluded that cyclists are responsible for their own safety, or lack thereof.

(c) Cars, on the other hand, have seen a 7 per cent fall in accidents and have also lower figures for number of casualties in the past two decades, as compared to cycle accidents.

(d) Road accidents are an unnatural phenomenon and no blame can be attached to cyclists for having seen a rise in their contribution towards the same.

21. Mr Modi would face more constraints, and enjoy fewer direct powers, as prime minister of India than he does as chief minister of Gujarat. It is unclear whether he would be good at holding together a coalition (which any BJP-led government would surely be), delegating to others, negotiating on legislation or responding to crises as they arise. But the record from Gujarat suggests he thinks hard about policy, has clear ideas of how he would promote higher economic growth and social development and would prefer to bolster overall wealth creation than promote social welfare schemes. If economics alone mattered, Mr Modi's achievements in Gujarat suggest he is the man best placed to get India moving again. The problem is that political leaders are responsible for more.

(a) For all his crowds of supporters, his failures in 2002, and his refusal since to atone for them leave him a badly compromised candidate with much left to do.

(b) Mr. Modi is a political leader like none other and is sure to become India's next Prime Minister, come May 2014.
(c) And Mr. Modi has chalked out the solution to this problem, in the form of higher economic growth and social development.
(d) Surely, a Chief Minister for a Third Term can be called a political leader, isn't it?

22. It is worth noting that if the political structure of North African countries was characterized by strong and efficient checks and balances, politicians and policy-makers would have less freedom to influence the countries' political economy according to their own interests. Individual economic and social agents would then have less leeway to behave in a manner serving their private interest by exercising disproportionate lobbying influence on politicians.

In the same fashion, the existence of a strong legal and judicial framework that enforces property rights would allow the efficient supervision of international, economic, and financial standards and provide private market participants with the ability to monitor and control economic activities. Levels of corruption would also be brought down and the economic and banking sectors' performance would improve.

(a) The absence of checks and balances facilitated the establishment of what Acemoglu and Robinson called "vicious circles."
(b) The low level of participation, transparency, and information-sharing allowed by the institutional infrastructure in North African countries provide fertile grounds for pressure and lobbying from powerful interest groups pursuing personal interests.
(c) The picture painted by the various economic and financial reforms implemented in the region, however, ignores rooted institutional deficiencies. These are crucial to fully understand the social unrest that has swept the region.
(d) Going beyond mere economic factors, the lack of transparency, symmetrical access to information and practical accountability to the public - as exclusive networks hold power over the political economy structures - represent a significant stumbling block to political transition and make North African economies more prone to economic and social instability.

23. The moral and legal prohibitions on torture and any kind of humiliating and degrading treatment, create an immense moral presumption against such actions. Torture is judged wrong both because of its immediate harmful consequences - the severe pain or suffering, whether physical or mental - as well as its wider adverse consequences. These include the way torture can provide a recruiting sergeant for the terrorists' cause by exposing the gap between liberal values that we proclaim and the illiberal practices we adopt, as Guantanamo Bay demonstrated. But the harmful consequences of torture are only part of the explanation. We also condemn torture because of its internal qualities.

(a) In deciding whether to legalize torture, we need, therefore, ultimately to consider whether, even if torture sometimes works, we want to belong to the kind of society that institutionalizes such a practice, despite its morally corrosive internal and external qualities, affecting all those involved.
(b) To succeed in his craft, the special interrogator needs to become, at best, indifferent to the pain of those whom he is interrogating; and, at worst, adept in the vice of cruelty.
(c) Yet, we need our special interrogators to be - professionally - men or women of vice. In the ticking bomb examples, the torturer arrives by magic just at the moment we need him; and he departs, conveniently, shortly thereafter.
(d) Torture adversely affects the character of those involved in the process: both the torturers and the tortured.

24. Effective foreign policy requires a clarity regarding the nation's interests. It requires focus and will. With no clarity, will or focus, Indian foreign policy is a disaster. Politicians are both uninformed and uninterested in foreign policy. Diplomats of the elite Indian Foreign Service (IFS) care more about cushy assignments in the US and Europe than serving the nation's interests.

(a) India's response has been woefully inadequate - this is in keeping with historical precedent.
(b) India's foreign policy establishment has a reputation for lacking a backbone.
(c) For too long, India tolerated the lack of respect shown to its dignitaries.
(d) Few care about serving in strategically important places such as Afghanistan or Egypt. It is little wonder that India has made little progress in its quest for permanent seat in the United Nations Security Council.

25. Understanding Iran's scientific heritage and respecting it builds the kind of trust that will inevitably be necessary for sustained engagement and reducing insecurities that can lead to counter-productive actions by hardliners. Success in this field can spill over to other crucial areas, such

as the human rights situation in Iran, which has significantly deteriorated over the course of the past years. Time, however, is limited. The political pendulum in Iran will swing back in favor of the hardliners if the Rouhani government has little to show for in the next six to twelve months.

(a) By following through on scientific and technological collaboration, Washington and Brussels can - over time - help fundamentally transform Tehran's relations with the West.
(b) Second chances do not come often. We have a golden opportunity to test win-win proposals and strengthen the positive-sum narrative of the Iranian moderates - not just at the negotiating table, but also through concrete actions that can facilitate a new, cooperative relationship with Iran and its people, void of the painful baggage of the past.
(c) Will the more cooperative, moderate and win-win approach favored by President Hassan Rouhani and the majority of the population take root and prevail?
(d) The human rights situation in Iran, which has significantly deteriorated over the course of the past years.

26. I criticized Adonis because he engaged politically, and placed himself firmly on the side of the government. He himself criticized the revolution, and the people themselves. He can criticize me *personally* as Ali Ferzat, he can criticize *individual* people, but he really cannot criticize the majority or the movement. He also contradicts himself; he supported the [1979] revolution in Iran, which was all about religion, but now he's outspoken against the Syrian revolution, because he says it's coming from the mosques. So you can see the contradiction.
(a) This regime came riding in military tanks - but he hasn't criticized the regime, he's criticized the people whose crime was simply asking for their freedom.
(b) As an artist you need to tackle important issues but not engage in political polemics yourself.
(c) Caricature is on the front line against dictatorship. It is an art form for *all* people - people who may not necessarily understand painting or sculpture, but [who will all] understand caricature.
(d) His position on religion is confused and misleading at the same time.

27. Love affairs are based on opportunism and the fulfillment of some kind of need in the moment without foresight for future consequences of action. They have no substance of loyalty and Qatar is most certainly not monogamous. Qatar's rendezvousing all at once with the Brotherhood among other Islamist groups, Saudi Arabia, Israel, Western powers, Iran and whoever should ascend to power regionally, is highly risky behavior. The Muslim Brotherhood itself is far removed from its original formation in goals and will not lose sight of its most earnest desire for expansionism, power and influence. Given this cocktail mix of relations and conflicting interests, the potential long-term consequences are unfathomable.
(a) However, does this mean the love affair with the Muslim Brotherhood is over?
(b) Having held close ties with the Brotherhood for some time, Qatar's relationship with the movement has only grown stronger in recent years.
(c) But for now, and for some time to come, we have a flourishing Qatar-Muslim Brotherhood love affair.
(d) The Qatari state does not have a clear strategy on how to move forward due to Syria's worsening crisis.

28. As more and more consumers opt to view content via the Internet, the playing field may eventually level, although Netflix and Amazon have a significant head start, Raff adds. For example, HBO could garner similar analytics through its HBO Go app. What's unclear at the moment is whether new outlets for original programming will dilute the market for high-end productions. "Obviously, there isn't room for infinite content, but there is definitely room for multiple providers," says Bradlow, noting that customers have multiple tastes and the mass market has fragmented.
(a) The subscription nature of their businesses and the data collection mechanisms built into their systems means the companies are all in a position to know hourly what customers are watching, how they interact with content and what their preferences are.
(b) In theory, if the online channels can use original content to attract new groups of viewers who wouldn't otherwise subscribe, they can invest the extra money in producing more in-house series and features and recoup those costs over time.
(c) This is a matter of having privileged access to customers and exploiting a fixed cost to do as much business as you can.
(d) The real impact of the company's original content plans will play out in the years to come.

Answer Key

Practice Exercise 1

1. (c)	2. (a)	3. (d)	4. (a)	5. (c)
6. (b)	7. (d)	8. (a)	9. (c)	10. (a)
11. (d)	12. (a)	13. (c)	14. (a)	15. (b)
16. (a)	17. (d)	18. (c)	19. (a)	

Practice Exercise 2

1. (a)	2. (b)	3. (d)	4. (b)	5. (d)
6. (d)	7. (b)	8. (a)	9. (c)	10. (a)
11. (b)	12. (a)	13. (c)	14. (d)	15. (d)
16. (d)	17. (a)	18. (d)	19. (c)	20. (a)
21. (a)	22. (d)	23. (a)	24. (d)	25. (b)
26. (a)	27. (c)	28. (c)		

Explanations

Practice Exercise 1

1. The passage talks about the Arab Spring bringing about more tyranny and civil strife. As the last sentence given, talks about the ruling family of Bahrain panicking, the last sentence of the passage should talk about the result of this panicking. So, option (c) is the correct answer as it completes the paragraph. Options (a) and (d) cannot be the answer. Option (b) could have been the answer, but since option (c) talks about what the royal family did as a result of this panicking, it is the correct answer.
2. The passage talks about the warring sides i.e. the rebels and the Assad government. Option (a) completes the passage as it talks about neither of the sides being willing to negotiate. So, option (a) is the correct answer.
3. The paragraph talks about an idea presented by Mr Cowen and its effects. Option (d) talks about this and completes the paragraph. So, option (d) is the correct answer.
4. The paragraph talks about the different halves of the brain playing a different part in the type of personality people have. Option (a) talks about a journal which talks about people not being left or right brained. Since this sentence takes the idea forward, it is the correct answer. Options (b), (c) and (d) talk about the research related to this idea. So, these options are incorrect.
5. The passage talks about the La Niñas having followed El Niños. So, option (c) is the correct answer. None of the other options talk about this idea.
6. The passage talks about the terrors of the Dust Bowl and option (b) is the sentence that best follows the given paragraph. So, option (b) is the correct answer.
7. The paragraph talks about the farmers on the Plains turning to the Ogallala Aquifer. This idea is best completed by the sentence in option (d), so it is the correct answer.
8. The passage says that at the time of a disaster, it becomes the most talked about topic in the internet world and even the most indifferent internet users tend to talk about it. So, option (a) is the correct answer. None of the other options are correct according to the flow of ideas.
9. The paragraph talks about King Herod who had architectural heritage to his name in the Levant. Since it talks about him returning to Rome two times between 19 and 12 BCE, option (c) is the correct answer because it talks about the last two trips during Augustus' building frenzy. None of the other options make sense according to the flow of the paragraph.
10. The paragraph talks about George Washington's habit of repeatedly writing of the word "president" on his personal bound copy of the Constitution with the Bill of Rights and Acts of Congress to emphasize those sections relating to his official powers and responsibilities. This habit shows that he had a meticulous and pedantic way of doing things. So, option (a) is the correct answer.
11. The paragraph talks about the discovery of Higgs Boson being one of the greatest intellectual works ever carried out. Option (d) is the most appropriate end to the paragraph as it talks about recognising this discovery as progress. All other options are out of context. So, option (d) is the correct answer.
12. The paragraph talks about the diversity of languages. The last line of the paragraph presents an idea about the hardwired linguistic aptitude of the human brain which is contradicted in the statement in option (a). Thus option)a) completes the paragraph and is the correct answer.
13. The paragraph talks about the Syrian people who are faced with a choice between Assad's dictatorship and US sponsored militants. Option (c) is the only option that talks about the Syrian people. It says that they have become pawns on a geopolitical chessboard. So, option (c) is the correct answer.
14. The passage talks about how in Rwanda though stress is laid on national rather than on ethnic identity,

there still exist some rules based on ethinicity. Thus option (a), which talks about political activity being tightly controlled, is the correct answer.

15. The paragraph talks about billboards of Greece whose condition reflects the decline of the country. Option (b) talks about these billboards serving as an eerie reminder of the country's economic plight. None of the other options talk about the billboard. So, option (b) is the correct answer.
16. The paragraph talks about a site started by Thrun that would offer "massive online open courses" (MOOCs) free of charge to the global 99 per cent, to the tech-savvy and web-illiterate alike. Option (a) carries forward the idea and talks about the barriers and privileges of the current education system and so option (a) is the correct answer. None of the other options are correct in the given context.
17. The paragraph talks highly of America as being a healthy and powerful nation. Option (d) takes this idea forward and is the correct answer.
18. The paragraph talks about India's bilateral relationship with China which is a subtle, unseen, but ongoing and deeply felt collision, the affects of which have left a convoluted lineage. Options (a), (b) and (c) all take this idea forward but option (c) talks about how the tension between the two countries have come to influence everything related to them and thus is the correct ending of the paragraph. So, option (c) is the correct answer.
19. The paragraph talks about Jewish people shifting to Florida when they get old after years of hard labour. Since option (a) continues this flow of ideas and talks about retirees, it is the correct answer.

Practice Exercise 2

1. Option (a) is the most suitable because it acts as an actual conclusion to the idea presented in the passage, offering a final thought on the resolution of this conflict. Option (d) is another close answer but does not finish the passage in what feels like a conclusive manner. Options (b) and (c) restate what is mentioned in the passage itself.
2. Option (b) continues and ends the thought expressed in the passage in the best way, while options (a), (c) and (d) take off on a different tangent altogether. Hence, (b) is the right answer.
3. Option (d) is an extension of the concept of the possibility of President's Rule mentioned in the paragraph and explains it in further detail, making it the best conclusion to the passage concerned.
4. From the given options, option (b) seems the most *conclusive* while the rest leave the thread loose, without providing a rounding off statement to the passage. Thus, (b) is the correct answer.
5. Option (d) best ends the passage, while (a), (c) and (d) continue the line of though expressed in the passage without providing the final link.
6. The crucial clue in the passage is provided by the direct mention of the border dispute. Option (d) is the only one that makes a direct reference to the same, providing the crucial link and conclusion to the passage.
7. Option (b) best sums up the idea presented in the passage.
8. Options (b), (c) and (d) are all sentences that could come before the paragraph, but not ideally conclude it. They leave the idea rather open-ended and incomplete, while A best puts forth a conclusion.
9. Options (a), (b) and (d) bear no direct relation with the content of the passage, nor do they extend the idea it presents. Option (b) is confusing because it does not directly allude to anything, but this also makes it a wrong option. Thus (c) is the best answer.
10. Option (a) is a *conclusion* while (b), (c) and (d) either build up or paraphrase what's been said in the passage.
11. The passage's contents are accurately summed up by option (b) while (a), (c) and (d) just reiterate parts of it.
12. The author's purpose and sentiment are expressed succinctly in option A's forceful concluding question.
13. The options (a). (b) and (d) can be eliminated on the basis that it does not add anything to the line of thought already being discussed in the passage. Option (c) is the only one that not only does that but goes a step further and provides an authoritative conclusion.
14. Option (d) talks of the future scenario with a thought for the reader to ponder over. Thus, option (d) is the best answer.
15. The conclusive tone of option (d) makes it the best option to the exclusion of the others.
16. The final option, (d), is the one that signs off the first-person address in the passage and is the best possible conclusion.
17. Option (a) speaks of a 'promise' and the 'future' providing us all the clues that it is indeed the concluding sentence of this passage. Options (b), (c) and (d) are either not conclusive or nature or too generic to wrap up the argument put forth.

18. Options (a), (b) and (c) are irrelevant and take a trajectory beyond the one drawn by the passage. Option (d) correctly connects the citizen to the government's legitimacy, making it the correct answer.

19. The writer in option (c) offers the 'author' he has discussed in the passage a suggestion in what is a strong judgment on his/her part. It is the best option as it is in keeping with the tone of the passage, which clearly expresses a view.

20. The logical end to the passage is option A that does not veer from the crux of the passage. It does not introduce unnecessary information or take a stand that cannot be conclusively taken as options (b), (c) and (d) do.

21. Option (a) is the best option here as it takes the most balanced stand and is reflective of the ending mood of the passage, that is more skeptical than laudatory. Thus options (b), (c) and (d) would be inappropriate choices.

22. Options (a), (b) and (c) reiterate what has been stated in the passage in a roundabout fashion. It is option (d) that adds a notable comment to tie up the arguments the writer has dealt with. Out of the given options it may not seem the only correct option, but it is the best one.

23. Only option (a) directly seems compatible with the intention of the passage, which is to decide whether even torture works, it is wrong. The other options describe factors or persons that are subsumed in the discussion presented in the discussion already and therefore cannot be treated as concluding remarks per se.

24. Option (a) and (b) merely restate what has already been said in the passage. Option (c) does bring in a new statement but more or less continues in the same strain. The concluding remark has to be thought packaged as advice or a strategy or something else to that effect. Option (d) fulfills this criteria.

25. Option (d) does not have much relevance to the content of the passage. Option (a) introduces a new angle and a new player, 'Washington', which cannot be seen as a final argument. Option (c) is an open-ended question, leaving the possibility of many interpretations. Thus option (b) is the correct choice, which summarizes and knits together the concerns and issues brought up by the passage.

26. Option (a) here best expresses the idea in the passage, which is a critique of a person called Adonis by the speaker, who contradicts himself at various points, an example of which is presented in Option (a). The other options don't use the material provided in the passage and hence cannot be sufficiently connected with it.

27. The passage analyses the relationship between Qatar and the Muslim Brotherhood. The passage clearly alludes to the fact that this relationship is a long-lasting one. Option (c) expresses this, while the others either leave the question open-ended or don't provide the closing statement that completes the passage satisfactorily.

28. After the passage analyses the entry of the internet as a major player in consumer preferences for obtaining their content, the passage is left at a more or less concluded point. Option (c) only expresses the best possible and most precise conclusion to the same. The other options seem ludicrous and don't fit the content of the passage well.

CHAPTER

23 Missing Sentence of the Paragraph

Exercise 1

Directions for Q 1-30. There is a sentence that is missing in the paragraph below. Look at the paragraph and decide in which blank (option 1, 2, 3 or 4) the following sentences would best fit.

Q1. Sentence: That the mayor, Sadiq Khan, has defied pressure to delay or weaken the scheme is to his credit.

Everyone who cares about public health and environmental regulation should welcome the expansion of London's ultra-low emission zone (Ulez), which launches on Tuesday. Air pollution is estimated to cause 4,000 premature deaths each year in the capital, with nitrogen dioxide from exhausts being the main danger, along with particulate matter whose effect is likened by scientists to inhaling tiny particles of tar. ___(1)___ Air pollution causes disproportionate harm to low-income families, who are most likely to live on main roads and least likely to own cars. It is particularly damaging to children's growing lungs. ___(2)___. In France, vehicles that do not meet new limits have been banned from urban areas. ___(3)___ In London, drivers of non-compliant vehicles - mostly petrol ones dating from before 2005, and diesel before 2015 - must pay a daily charge of £12.50, with higher charges for lorries and coaches. While no scheme is flawless, the improvements to air quality achieved by the existing scheme, covering inner London, mean that Londoners can be confident of the extension's health benefits. ___(4)___

(a) Option 1 (b) Option 2

(c) Option 3 (d) Option 4

Q2. Sentence: But the US alone had the same nominal GDP as the Brics countries in 2022.

Developing countries prize the bargaining power to gain better trade, technology and weapons deals. No doubt countries such as Argentina and Iran see Brics membership as a way to access Chinese investment. The club's original members had two things in common: they were large economies with high potential growth rates. ___(1)___ The addition of South Africa in 2010 did suggest that the club was interested in recasting the power structures of the international system. ___(2)___ Perhaps Brics' most tangible achievement has been the New Development Bank - an institution that has approved almost \$33bn of loans mainly for infrastructure projects since 2015. ___(3)___ Given that Brics operates on consensus, its 26-page Johannesburg declaration is a triumph of drafting rather than diplomacy. Where Brics members agree, for example on Syria and Libya, they make a collective pronouncement, and where they have diverging positions - such as on Ukraine - they do not. Getting agreement on a common currency across such a diverse grouping would dwarf the kind of problems encountered so far, rendering such an idea a pipe dream. ___(4)___ The next big international jamboree is the annual meeting of the G20, the group that contains most of the world's largest economies, and will be held in India in September. Just as with the Brics meeting, Russia's Vladimir Putin will not attend the G20 summit, although he did address Brics leaders by video link.

(a) Option 1 (b) Option 2

(c) Option 3 (d) Option 4

Q3. Sentence: The pitch is seductive.

Many sun-drenched countries, especially in the Maghreb, have been sold a future as export hubs for green hydrogen. __(1)__ As 1kg of hydrogen contains about three times as much energy as 1kg of petrol, it is no wonder that hydrogen is being touted as a fuel of the future. __(2)__ Europe's green deal, which aims to reduce greenhouse gas emissions by 55% by the end of the decade, relies on green hydrogen production in north Africa and Ukraine. Producing green hydrogen in Europe is not impossible. But it is expensive compared with fossil fuels, with even wind-based generation needing larger subsidies. Without big government support packages, it remains an open question whether European consumers would be prepared to foot the very significant price rises needed to go green in this way. Last year, the EU proposed doubling green hydrogen imports by 2030 to 10 m tonnes a year. __(3)__ The continent's heavy industries cannot use electricity, however environmentally friendly, for all their requirements; they need fuels for high-intensity heat. So to make sure that these energy sources are less carbon-intensive, Brussels is pushing industries - such as steel or petrochemical manufacturers - to adopt green hydrogen. __(4)__

(a) Option 1 (b) Option 2
(c) Option 3 (d) Option 4

Q4. Sentence: It is in setting and competitive solving that men dominate.

It is an old saw in the newspaper business that while you can get almost anything wrong - the scorers in the cup final, the winner of the 4.10 at Haydock - and few readers will bat an eyelid, if you make a mistake in the crossword puzzle then you will be dealing with complaints for weeks. Crossword lovers are obsessive, and their howls of displeasure if you put in the wrong answer for seven across will be anything but cryptic. By their followers, setters are regarded as something akin to folk heroes, even if they are only known to most by their aliases. __(1)__ When the great Guardian setter John Graham, universally known by his nom de plume Araucaria, announced in a series of clues in one of his puzzles that he had terminal cancer, it unleashed a flood of affection among readers. One said he had planted a monkey puzzle tree in honour of Mr Graham's moniker. As a Cambridge-educated pillar of the establishment, Graham - a Church of England priest - fitted the usual mental image of a crossword devotee, or cruciverbalist. Colin Dexter, the creator of Inspector Morse, was another enthusiast and named his detective after a fellow competitive solver, the Lloyds Bank chairman Sir Jeremy Morse. __(2)__ But this picture is deceptive: women are reckoned to be in the majority when it comes to getting a daily crossword fix. __(3)__ The erroneous but pervasive typecasting may explain the excitement among cruciverbalists at a recent tweet by the Canadian singer-songwriter Carly Rae Jepsen. "Once upon a time I was the answer in the New York Times crossword puzzle," she enthused. "A true career highlight. My father and I thought I had peaked." She appended her own puzzle, plugging her latest album to her 9.3 million Twitter followers. __(4)__

(a) Option 1 (b) Option 2
(c) Option 3 (d) Option 4

Q5. Sentence: Blurbs have always been controversial–too clichéd, too subject to cronyism–but lately, as review space shrinks and the noise level of the marketplace increases, the pursuit of ever more fawning praise from luminaries has become absurd.

If there's one thing authors love more than procrastinating, it's praising one another. During the Renaissance, Thomas More's Utopia got a proto-blurb from Erasmus ("divine wit"), while Shakespeare's First Folio got one from Ben Jonson ("The wonder of our stage!"). __(1)__ By the 18th century, the practice of selling a book based on some other author's endorsement was so well established that Henry Fielding's spoof novel Shamela even came with fake blurbs, including one from "John Puff Esq." __(2)__ Even the most minor title now comes garlanded with quotes hailing it as the most important book since the Bible, while authors report getting so many requests that some are opting out of the practice altogether. Publishers have begun to despair of blurbs, too. __(3)__ "You only need to look at the jackets from the 1990s or 2000s to see that even most debut novelists didn't have them, or had only one or two genuinely high-quality ones," Mark Richards, the publisher of the independent Swift Press, told me. "But what happened was an arms race. People figured out that they helped, so more effort was put into getting them, until a point was reached where they didn't necessarily make any positive difference; it's just that not having them would likely ruin a book's chances." __(4)__

(a) Option 1 (b) Option 2
(c) Option 3 (d) Option 4

Q6. Sentence: How could I not?

2018: I'm at a house party, and I'm characteristically nervous, despite knowing most everyone there. __(1)__ It's time to shake some ass, I'm informed–somebody's commandeered the aux cord and begun queuing up tracks, the first of which captures the room with a bouncing beat. Amid the chorus of drunk-girl "woos," I'm now wearing a shit-eating grin. __(2)__ Within the party anthem canon, "Ignition (Remix)" strikes a singular balance: both exceedingly danceable and mellow as a warm bath; at once a turn-up and a kickback, capturing in that cross section the irrepressible delight of each genre. __(3)__ Against the song's assuring swagger, the force of my self-doubt doesn't stand a chance: I'm bopping my head to the beat, feet planted, swaying from the shoulders. __(4)__.

It takes a moment, I think, for that second wave of recognition to dawn–for a few smiles to falter, and the flailing of limbs to grow stiff and muted.

(a) Option 1 (b) Option 2
(c) Option 3 (d) Option 4

Q7. Sentence: It's fair to say that the morbid fixation on mental health among a certain class of visible and voluble teenage girls has grown to be its own mental health crisis.

A common experience these days is being told that people don't talk about things that people are constantly talking about. "Let's Face It" – declared a recent headline on the website of McLean Hospital, the famous psychiatric facility in Boston where David Foster Wallace, Sylvia Plath, and Robert Lowell were patients – "No One Wants to Talk About Mental Health". This is an odd claim. If Sylvia Plath, for example, were revived after her six decades in the grave and made to listen to the streams of babble that course through our popular culture, one thing she would surely find remarkable is all the talk about mental health. She'd be amazed and maybe depressed at how avidly people diagnose (and how eagerly they invent) their own mental troubles, at how much jargon from psychotherapy circulates in everyday conversation, and with how much numbing regularity educators and other functionaries intone the phrase "mental health". __(1)__ Yet, the PR teams at psychiatric hospitals can say without laughing that people who would speak of mental health must first overcome a culture of silence, and that the people who do manage to pierce the layer of stigma, who defy the heavy shame to voice the forbidden theme, they are heroes. __(2)__ This includes those who celebrate the brave heroes mentioning mental health, since they also are mentioning mental health. __(3)__. I'm generally torn when I hear these solemn, delusional pronouncements. On the one hand, I find them irksome. However sincere or sympathetic the intention, they express the interests and ways of thinking of powerful institutions that are, I think, increasingly destructive. __(4)__.

(a) Option 1 (b) Option 2
(c) Option 3 (d) Option 4

Q8. Sentence: And then in the United States, liberalism generally means "New Deal liberalism."

Liberalism in Europe, today, is something like "libertarianism"–it is a right-wing ideology. There used to be a left libertarianism, which is probably better called anarchism, and that persists in various sectarian versions, but it isn't much in the public eye. __(1)__ It's our very modest version of social democracy, and it isn't a very strong doctrine, since many of its practitioners became neoliberals much too easily. So, the -ism is not a strong or coherent doctrine. That doesn't mean that there aren't liberals. But liberals are people who are best defined morally or psychologically; they're what Lauren Bacall, my favorite actress, called "people who don't have small minds." __(2)__ A liberal is someone who's tolerant of ambiguity, who can join arguments that he doesn't have to win, who can live with people who disagree, who have different religions or different ideologies. That's a liberal. __(3)__ But those liberal qualities don't imply any social or economic doctrine. So, there are liberals in the world, and I can recognize them, but liberalism does not describe their actual political commitment. __(4)__ The word is better used to qualify the kinds of commitments that I write about: democracy, socialism, nationalism, et cetera.

(a) Option 1 (b) Option 2
(c) Option 3 (d) Option 4

Q9. Sentence: Sontag and Malcolm wrote extensively about photography. Didion, very little.

"My mind veers inflexibly toward the particular," Joan Didion writes in her 1965 essay "On Morality." When it comes to the concrete and specific, you might say there's a continuum among her cohort (now mostly gone) of great American essayists. __(1)__ At one end, Susan Sontag's epigrammatic judgments, with their relative lack of empirical texture. In the middle, Janet Malcolm's fine attention to peculiarities of person or place. Then there is Didion, out along her own axis, where the essay is almost all detail. __(2)__ But such is her mix of vision, exactitude, and atmospheric effect that her work seems more suited than that of others to sit alongside paintings, drawings, and photographs, with an eye toward making connections. In their introduction to the catalog of Joan Didion: What She Means–a recent exhibition at the Hammer Museum, University of California, Los Angeles–the show's curators, Hilton Als and Connie Butler, speak of Didion's "acutely visual language." What does that mean? __(3)__ Als, a friend and literary peer of Didion's, has previously put together exhibitions about James Baldwin and Toni Morrison, authors whose power and presence we may imagine we glimpse in photographs of them. But Didion is something else: a writer whose talismanic image–in life, and even more so since her death, in December 2021–is the object of feverish projection and surmise. __(4)__ No wonder, when we survey celebrated portraits of her. In 1996, she sat for Irving Penn, who seems to have noticed that in many photographs of Didion it's her thin, bare arms that do the work of conveying brittle thought processes.

(a) Option 1 (b) Option 2
(c) Option 3 (d) Option 4

Q10. Sentence: Leonardo's caricatures, as they got called in the 18th century, are some of his most mind-bending and shockingly modern drawings.

It's a telling remark, but at first sight some of his most disturbing drawings suggest he shared those prejudices against people who look different. __(1)__

We think of him painting the beautiful: Ginevra de' Benci, Cecilia Gallerani and Salai glow with glossy hair and good bone structure. Yet alongside his fascination with youth and loveliness Leonardo was obsessed with irregular, diseased and aged faces whose "monstrous" distortions he drew with daunting precision. __(2)__

Their hypnotic power can be glimpsed in a new exhibition at the National Gallery in London, The Ugly Duchess: Beauty and Satire in the Renaissance. An Old Woman by Quinten Massys is nicknamed The Ugly Duchess because it inspired a John Tenniel illustration in Alice's Adventures in Wonderland. Massys, working in Antwerp in 1513, depicts a face that's a chaos of skeletal deformities under the skin, massive structural distortions that stretch the woman's upper lip, hollow her cheeks and inflate her forehead. Yet she is dressed to impress, including bulbous headgear that heightens her unusual features. Is she proud of them? In fact she appears to be selling herself on her looks, for she holds a flower, often an advert for sex work in Renaissance art. __(3)__ The painting is being shown with its pendant - an accompanying painting - which depicts an old man whose attentions she solicits. __(4)__

(a) Option 1 (b) Option 2
(c) Option 3 (d) Option 4

Q11. Sentence: But Sedatus lived a double life.

Gaius Verius Sedatus was a respectable citizen of the community of Chartres in the early 2nd century CE. __(1)__ He was a member of his local town council (a sort of mini-senate), where he and his colleagues presided over its laws and management, under the aegis of Roman law. Gaul had been conquered by Julius Caesar a century earlier and was now administered by trusted locals such as Sedatus, overseen by distant Roman officials. __(2)__ In the evening, he donned the mantle of a magician-priest and descended to his underground temple in the small cellar of his house. There he kept a group of four large incense-burners, placed symmetrically at the points of a square. He filled these vessels with aromatic, perhaps hallucinogenic herbs, and lit fires beneath them. When the drug-laden smoke was sufficiently dense for his needs, he and his followers began to summon the spirits by chanting their names and demanding that they provide him with guidance in the dark arts. __(3)__ Who were these spirits, who had to be contacted so secretly in a small space, dimly lit with oil lamps and flickering candles? Fortunately, one of the incense-burners is complete enough to study closely. __(4)__ The vessel is inscribed, telling us who Sedatus was: a Roman citizen (because of his triple name) and the presiding ritualist who summoned the spirits. Beneath this statement is a long list of spirit names, almost all of which are unknown to archaeologists. But one stands out: 'Dru'. If we are right in assuming this is an abbreviation of 'Druid' (and what else could it be?) then it is the only direct archaeological evidence for the existence of the Druids.

(a) Option 1 (b) Option 2
(c) Option 3 (d) Option 4

Q12. Sentence: The narrator lectures that the nucleus of an atom is tens of thousands of times smaller than the atom itself, and poetically concludes that we are made from emptiness.

The camera zooms in on the person's arm to reveal the cells, then a cell nucleus. __(1)__ A DNA strand grows on the screen. The camera focuses on a single atom within the strand, dives into a frenetic cloud of rocketing particles, crosses it, and leaves us in oppressive darkness. An initially imperceptible tiny dot grows smoothly, revealing the atomic nucleus. __(2)__ How often have you seen such a scene or read something equivalent to it in popular science? I am sure plenty, if you are fans of this genre like me. However, the narrative is wrong. Atomic nuclei in a molecule are not tiny dots, and there are no empty spaces within the atom. __(3)__ The empty atom picture is likely the most repeated mistake in popular science. It is unclear who created this myth, but it is sure that

Carl Sagan, in his classic TV series Cosmos (1980), was crucial in popularising it. After wondering how small the nuclei are compared with the atom, Sagan concluded that __(4)__ [M]ost of the mass of an atom is in its nucleus; the electrons are by comparison just clouds of moving fluff. Atoms are mainly empty space. Matter is composed chiefly of nothing.

(a) Option 1 (b) Option 2
(c) Option 3 (d) Option 4

Q13. Sentence: This may have sounded strange to Eliot's audience, who would have known his single most influential critical statement, made two decades before.

Addressing the Friends of the Irish Academy on the subject of W. B. Yeats in 1939, the year after the Irish poet's death, T. S. Eliot proclaimed that Yeats "was one of those few whose history is the history of their own time, who are a part of the consciousness of an age which cannot be understood without them." In making this point, he celebrated Yeats's work for its expression of the man's "unique personality."

__(1)__. In "Tradition and the Individual Talent" (1919), Eliot had announced the "impersonal theory of poetry," which held that poetry "is not the expression of personality, but an escape from personality."

__(2)__. Yeats was indeed an "impersonal" poet, Eliot explained, but by this he meant that, "out of intense and personal experience," Yeats was "able to express a general truth; retaining all the particularity of his experience, to make of it a general symbol." This was not an obvious claim. __(3)__. Yeats's dreamy and melancholy early work had seemed already antiquated to the poets of Eliot's generation. His concerns with Irish culture and politics were provincial. His mature poetic vision was in turn eccentric and gnostic, the doctrine of a church to which only he could belong. What Eliot intended by this remark, however, was Yeats's continuous growth over his long career. The poet indulged and then shook off the misty tastes of the nineteenth century, before striving to find a mode of expression suitably "hard" for an age of disillusion and violence, of the machine and total war. __(4)__

(a) Option 1 (b) Option 2
(c) Option 3 (d) Option 4

Q14. Sentence: We wonder where we can settle down that won't go to hell in a handbasket during our lifetime.

Each of us experiences the climate crisis. We try to adapt to it: buying face masks to brave smoke-filled air outdoors or air purifiers to clean it indoors, turning up the air conditioning to insulate ourselves from excessive heat, preparing to evacuate our homes, if need be, when another hurricane hits the coast. __(1)__ Some of us wonder whether we should bring children into this world. The climate crisis prompts questions that challenge our very being. We ask ourselves: 'Who am I in this increasingly unstable world? What is to become of me?' __(2)__ Such questions can lead to despair, or lead us to look away, but, as we will see, they can also positively challenge the way we think about ourselves. Our current political and economic circumstances lead us to think of ourselves as useful cogs in a machine, and of our identity in terms of certain hoops we need to jump through: go to college to get well-paying jobs, climb the property ladder, and make sure we have adequate savings for retirement. However, the climate crisis can prompt us to rethink these suppositions. What good are retirement savings if the world is burning? __(3)__ We need a much richer concept of self - a fully realised self that is worth preserving. __(4)__

(a) Option 1 (b) Option 2
(c) Option 3 (d) Option 4

Q15. Sentence: I, too, see a crisis brewing, among not only people my age but among the peers of my teenage children and the college students I teach.

It was time to consider calling it a night. Sheila Liming and I had talked all day–at a taco joint for lunch, and walking around Burlington, Vermont, running errands, and at dinner at a restaurant in a former warehouse. __(1)__ I had no shortage of good quotes for the story I planned to write about Liming and her interesting new book. Now, at 9 p.m., as I hopped my way around frigid puddles in the parking lot, laughing with Liming and her husband, I considered my 5:45 a.m. flight. __(2)__ For sure, the healthiest thing for me to do would be to get dropped off at my airport La Quinta. But it was not because I thought her book was interesting that I had reached out to Liming. It was because I passionately believed that her book was right. "I've become an accidental witness to a growing crisis," __(3)__ she writes in Hanging Out: The Radical Power of Killing Time. "People struggling to hang out, or else voicing concern and anxiety about how to hang out." __(4)__ Pushed further into isolation by the pandemic, we're all losing the ability to engage in what I view as the pinnacle of human interaction: sitting around with friends and talking shit.

(a) Option 1 (b) Option 2
(c) Option 3 (d) Option 4

Q16. Sentence: The photograph pictures Jerusalem Court in Clerkenwell, London.

__(1)__. A photograph taken in 1880 by Bedford Lemere, a renowned architectural photography firm of the late 19th and early 20th centuries, shows a dimly lit courtyard, narrow and surrounded on three sides by worn brick buildings. __(2)__ Uneven paving stones lead to a passageway, through which, barely visible, a man and a child watch the photographer from a distance, while a spectral presence in the foreground reveals itself to be another person, their form blurred, suggesting they moved during the long exposure time a camera of the era required. __(3)__ Most likely, it was commissioned by the Clerkenwell vestry to earmark Jerusalem Court as an area 'unfit for human habitation' - a phrase used by housing inspectors to describe dwellings deemed unhealthy for residents to live in. __(4)__ In the annual report for 1899, a special committee, commissioned by the Clerkenwell vestry to examine the condition of courts and blind alleys in the area, states that, according to 'medical men', the block of dwellings on the north side of Jerusalem court is 'very unhealthy, without through ventilation, and such as should never have been built'.

(a) Option 1 (b) Option 2
(c) Option 3 (d) Option 4

Q17. Sentence: While guilt, self-blame and anger rank high, one of the most prominent symptoms of pathological grief is the loss of meaning in life.

__(1)__ It's no surprise I had it wrong. Back in the day, even professional psychologists lacked an official diagnosis for persisting grief. That changed in March 2022, when the condition my mom most likely suffered from was added as 'prolonged grief disorder' to the latest revision of the psychologists' diagnostic manual, the DSM-5-TR. The diagnosis hinges on two factors. The first is denial: mourners cannot accept the death of the person they lost. This, in turn, causes symptoms like sadness, anger or guilt that last for more than 12 months. __(2)__ That persistence separates normal from prolonged grief. While the former is like a wave that occasionally flares up and then ebbs away, the latter runs like a horizontal line. Prolonged grief traps its sufferers in continuous rumination. __(3)__ This causes the second diagnostic factor: impairment. Some sufferers quit their jobs; others avoid people and places that remind them of their loss. Avoidance is just one of many hallmarks of this disorder. __(4)__

(a) Option 1 (b) Option 2
(c) Option 3 (d) Option 4

Q18. Sentence: As nationalism rises across the globe, many see 'cultural exchange' as the antidote to nationalist xenophobia.

Cultural exchange is often assumed to be progressive, but it has neither an inherent politics nor an inevitable outcome. __(1)__ Such exchange was, in fact, an integral part of the emergence of national literatures, cultures and identities in Iran and South Asia. Rather than resulting in greater cosmopolitanism, Indo-Iranian exchange fostered modern nationalism. __(2)__ Today, Persian is the national language of Iran. Although it has a long history there, its national status and close association with the country depend on events in the 19th century. __(3)__.As the Russian Empire swallowed up swathes of Iranian territory in the 1810s and '20s, and the sclerotic Qajar dynasty ruling Iran proved incapable of resistance, Iranian nationalism emerged to challenge both foreign imperialism and local despotism. __(4)__.

(a) Option 1 (b) Option 2
(c) Option 3 (d) Option 4

Q19. Sentence: We can't help but draw our own history to this specific moment, the dawn of the Age of Mammals, when fuzzy beasts could finally flourish.

__(1)__ The worst day in the entire history of life on Earth happened in the northern springtime. On that day, the last of the Age of Dinosaurs, a roughly seven-mile-wide chunk of rock that had been hurtling towards our orbit for millions of years slammed into Earth's midsection and immediately brought the Cretaceous to a close. The consequences were so dire that survival in the hours immediately following impact was merely a matter of luck. Of course, life wasn't totally extinguished on that day 66 million years ago. Some species survived, emerging into a transformed world. __(2)__ Dominant dinosaurs suffered a stroke of cosmic bad fortune, and our mammalian kin inherited a planet where they would no longer have to fear death in reptilian jaws. __(3)__ The image is of a great ecological cast change, different players continuing the evolutionary story. __(4)__ It's a very appealing distortion. The entire reason we so often fixate on the supposed dominance of the dinosaurs is because we now see ourselves in that position. For more than a century, the decimation of the 'ruling reptiles' has been taken as a cautionary tale of what could happen to us - not all that different from pundits who cry that the United States is set to topple like the Roman Empire.

(a) Option 1 (b) Option 2
(c) Option 3 (d) Option 4

Q20. Sentence: The report explores the interrelation of geopolitical, environmental and sociopolitical risks.

Sometimes words explode. It is a safe bet that, before 2022, you had never even heard the term 'polycrisis'. __(1)__ Now, there is a very good chance you have run into it; and, if you are engaged in environmental, economic or security issues, you most likely have - you might even have become frustrated with it. First virtually nobody was using polycrisis talk, and suddenly everyone seems to be.

But, as often happens, people seem to mean quite different things with the word. So, what does 'polycrisis' mean? __(2)__The term reverberated at the United Nations Climate Change Conference (COP27) in Sharm El-Sheikh in November 2022, and in Davos the following January, as The New York Times noted. In the Financial Times, Jonathan Derbyshire chose it for his 2022 'Year in a Word' piece, defining 'polycrisis' as a collective term for interlocking and simultaneous crises. Then 2023 opened with the World Economic Forum adopting this buzzword for its Global Risks Report, highlighting how '[c]oncurrent shocks, deeply interconnected risks and eroding resilience are giving rise to the risk of polycrises'. __(3)__ The World Economic Forum used the term to advertise the report, with headlines like 'We're on the Brink of a "Polycrisis" - How Worried Should We Be?' or 'Welcome to the Age of the Polycrisis'. __(4)__

(a) Option 1 (b) Option 2
(c) Option 3 (d) Option 4

Q21. Sentence: He emphasised that the 'Hashemites', his family, are the custodians of both Christian and Muslim sites in the holy city.

In December 2022, Abdullah II, the king of Jordan, gave an interview to the CNN anchor Becky Anderson. Sitting close to the Jordan River, not far from where Jesus is believed to have been baptised, this Muslim ruler expressed his concerns about the status of Jerusalem and the Christians under pressure from the new, extremist Israeli government. __(1)__. Abdullah II cited his great-great-grandfather Sharif Hussein. It was from Hussein's time, sometime at the end of the First World War, according to Abdullah II, that the Hashemite custodianship of Jerusalem's holy sites originates. __(2)__ His ancestor even gave sanctuary to Christian Armenian refugees in Jordan, said the king proudly on CNN.

Abdullah II's remarks presented him as a confident and reassuring monarch but they also refer to a history of modern Arab kingship and the modern Middle East that has mostly been forgotten. __(3)__ Wikipedia in English, for instance, tells us that the custodianship of the Muslim sites in Jerusalem by the Hashemites follows from a 'verbal agreement' of Hussein with the Supreme Muslim Council of Palestine in 1924. __(4)__

(a) Option 1 (b) Option 2
(c) Option 3 (d) Option 4

Q22. Sentence: Its advocates such as Dewey greatly affected nations such as China through his teaching and lecturing, leading us to see that pragmatism has a global narrative connected with it.

When one thinks of American pragmatism, one often puts too much emphasis on the American part. It might even stunt our enquiry, irrevocably fixating on thinkers such as John Dewey, William James, and Jane Addams. But there is more to the story of pragmatism than what happened in the United States around the turn of the 20th century. __(1)__ Pragmatism itself was a flexible, loosely allied approach to thinking that held few maxims in common other than the idea that our theorising and arguing ought to come from lived experience and ought to return back to experience as the ultimate test of its value. __(2)__ Is there a similar tale to be told about pragmatism and its interactions with India? Any narrative of pragmatism's influence and evolution in India will centre on Bhimrao Ambedkar, a student of Dewey's at Columbia University in New York. __(3)__ Some might recognise Ambedkar (1891-1956) as a chief architect of the Indian constitution in the 1940s. Others might recognise him as the indefatigable leader of India's 'untouchables' (now denoted by the self-chosen label 'Dalit'), given his constant advocacy for the rights of those oppressed by the complex and long-rooted caste system. __(4)__

(a) Option 1 (b) Option 2
(c) Option 3 (d) Option 4

Q23. Sentence: Secrets usually hurt their holders most

For the past decade, I've studied the psychology of secrecy. __(1)__. I know the story of Don and Judy's secret well because I'm their first child, and I learned about this secret the same day I gave an invited talk about my research on secrecy for a job interview. __(2)__. I was 26, and if you're wondering what it's like to learn such a major secret, I'll tell you this: it was surprising. It was shocking to learn that I was not biologically related to my father nor his parents with whom I was very close. And it was even more shocking to learn that my brother was, in fact, my half-brother, conceived from a different donor. But I had not been the keeper of the secret for all those years. And, while the revelation for me was jolting, the greater impact and harm came to my parents themselves. __(3)__. Keeping a secret is associated with lower life satisfaction, lower-quality relationships, and symptoms of poor psychological and physical health. Our secrets often hurt us, but not for the reasons you might think. While hiding a secret in conversation can feel uncomfortable, the hiding turns out to be the easy part. Simply thinking about a secret outside of a social interaction is associated with feelings of shame, isolation and inauthenticity. __(4)__. These experiences can leave us feeling helpless, at the mercy of our secrets, and unable to cope. And these harms can begin the very moment you decide to keep a secret.

(a) Option 1 (b) Option 2
(c) Option 3 (d) Option 4

Q24. Sentence: Delayed support is harming children's education and leaving many in distress.

For parents whose children have special educational needs or disabilities (Send), getting help can resemble an adversarial battle. __(1)__ Over the last decade, parents have increasingly resorted to taking councils to court for failing to carry out assessments for education, health and care plans (EHCPs), or for issuing a plan that fails to recognise their child's needs. __(2)__ Cases heard at tribunal have soared by 580% since 2011. __(3)__ Parents who don't have the time, money or confidence to fight their council, or who don't speak English as a first language, are especially likely to see their children go without the help they need. __(4)__.

(a) Option 1 (b) Option 2
(c) Option 3 (d) Option 4

Q25. Sentence: It is a point never reached.

An elusive point sits on the horizon. A deep yearning stirs within to move closer to this point, perhaps in search of the unknown, perhaps in search of questions without answers. It is a yearning that will never be fulfilled. __(1)__ This yearning is the all-too-human inclination for our lives to somehow be different than they are, and for the universe not to be indifferent to our cares and concerns. __(2)__ In her essay 'The Blue of Distance' (2005), the US author Rebecca Solnit associates this point never-reached with the colour blue. She writes: For many years, I have been moved by the blue at the far edge of what can be seen, that color of horizons, of remote mountain ranges, of anything far away. The color of that distance is the color of an emotion, the color of solitude and of desire, the color of there seen from here, the color of where you are not. And the color of where you can never go. __(3)__ When combined with the longing for something absent, for something that simply can't be, this is saudade, a Portuguese expression for a state akin to melancholic longing. A complex emotion where a melancholic grey seeps into the distant blue. __(4)__

(a) Option 1 (b) Option 2
(c) Option 3 (d) Option 4

Q26. Sentence: Like any U.S. city, Chicago has been beset by the constipated whimsy of as-seen-on-TV home renos: gray floors, gray counters, and the pallid ingenuity of an open floor plan.

__(1)__ A half-formed thought feels worse than an empty head–the tip-of-the-tongue sensation, the inkling of a there there without the foggiest notion of how to get, well, there. Especially dire is when the "what" that we wish to articulate feels half-formed itself, something observable yet emergent, for which the masses have yet to find language. But all we have is language, of course, and so we must muddle through, reaching for a word to serve as a placeholder for our idea until something better comes along. Some would say that finding new language is the work of scholars, but in the age of the Internet we may have lost track of who is leading whom. However provisional, the placeholders sometimes stick.

For example: I spent last month hunting for a new apartment in Chicago. __(2)__ All I wanted was a unicorn: an old building in a historic neighborhood, with humane updates and classic fixtures. Instead, I was confronted with a drab and seemingly ubiquitous new aesthetic. __(3)__ The look is "inoffensive, inexpensive, innocuous," as Amanda Mull described it recently in The Atlantic. Call it, as the headline of that piece does, the "HGTV-ification of America." __(4)__ .Have you noticed it, too? Not the gray laminate but that suffix: "-ification."

(a) Option 1 (b) Option 2
(c) Option 3 (d) Option 4

Q27. Sentence: Some of their most devoted contemporary readers were women and working men–readers with no access to higher education, who found in these books the intellectual and spiritual sustenance they craved

GEORGE ELIOT and Søren Kierkegaard were born in the same decade, six years apart: Kierkegaard in a smart townhouse in the center of Copenhagen in 1813, Mary Ann Evans–George Eliot's given name–in humbler circumstances in rural Warwickshire, England's "Midlands," in 1819. They both became philosophers. And they both wrote remarkable works animated by the marriage question–a question that continues to transgress the dubious boundary between philosophy and life. At a time when this boundary was being fixed and entrenched by an increasingly professionalized, specialized academic culture, Eliot and Kierkegaard leapt over it, bringing profound ideas to wide readerships. __(1)__ Academia boomed during the 19th century. New universities opened in cities across Europe and the United States, starting with Berlin in 1810. New academic disciplines were established: biology, sociology, geography, history, biblical studies, anthropology. Yet Kierkegaard and Eliot philosophized outside the university, for different reasons; they both voraciously pursued the life of the mind, while feeling deeply ambivalent towards it. __(2)__ After 10 years as a student, Kierkegaard was thoroughly disaffected by the systematic, scientific (or quasi-scientific) treatises and lectures that had become the gold standard of serious thought. His defiant, experimental works ridiculed salaried professors while tearing philosophy out of their hands. Marriages, engagements, seductions, and unrequited loves were Kierkegaard's subject matter. __(3)__ "A love affair is always an instructive theme regarding what it means to exist," he wrote at the age of 33, still struggling to come to terms with the failure of his own love affair five years earlier. __(4)__

(a) Option 1 (b) Option 2
(c) Option 3 (d) Option 4

Q28. Sentence: Some of this seems valuable for forming societies that are more inclusive and less abusive; some of it is reductive and beside the point.

The feminist writer Moira Donegan recently mocked contemporary social media reflexes in a tweet about Oedipus: "Wow, unfollowing now. I was a fan of his work solving the riddle of the Sphinx. Did not know he killed his father and married his mother." We are in an age of moralists; the standard question has become whether someone was virtuous, rather than whether they were interesting or useful or exhilarating. __(1)__ Being a moralist is a particularly fun and easy pursuit when it comes to the past, because pretty much everyone from the past comes up short when measured by present-day standards. __(2)__ Virtually no one in 1973, let alone 1923, had 2023 values about race, gender, sexuality and the rest, any more than they had search engines or Twitter accounts. __(3)__ It's not our individual virtue but our collective receipt of humane and egalitarian ideas worked out in recent decades that gives us our presumably splendid present-day beliefs. __(4)__

(a) Option 1 (b) Option 2
(c) Option 3 (d) Option 4

Q29. Sentence: In no other primate has the mathematics gone this wrong but, then again, no other primate has been as successful as we are in dominating the planet.

The average human spends at least one quarter of their life growing up. In the careful calculus of the animal kingdom, this is patently ridiculous. __(1)__ Even most whales, the longest of the long-lived mammals, spend a mere 10 per cent or so of their time growing into leviathans. __(2)__ Could the secret to our species' success be our slowness in growing up? And if so, what possible evolutionary benefit could there be to delaying adulthood - and what does it mean for where our species is going? __(3)__

The search for the secret to our success is at the heart of anthropology - the study of humans and their place in the world. __(4)__ This most narcissistic of disciplines piggybacked on the fascination for cataloguing and collecting the entirety of the world that rose up during the colonial expansions of 18th-century Europe and the growing popularity of 'natural laws' that explained the workings of the world in terms of immutable truths, discoverable to any man (and it was open largely only to men) with the wit and patience to observe them in nature.

(a) Option 1 (b) Option 2
(c) Option 3 (d) Option 4

Q30. Sentence: Plants experience pleasure and pain.

In 1870 the American Independent ran an article from Charles Dickens' magazine All the Year Round titled "Have Plants Intelligence?" The provocative question in the title was designed to spark intuitive negative responses, but the paragraphs that follow rehearse a clear argument in the affirmative. __(1)__ Life itself "presupposes in its possessor, whether animal or vegetable, a faculty of sensation that administers to its happiness, and that may consequently administer to its suffering," the author argues. __(2)__. Although the author suggests that the scientific community had dismissed the notion of feeling plants, in fact naturalists had been asking and debating this issue for decades, studying plants like the carnivorous flytrap that caught prey and the "sensitive" mimosa that shrank upon touch. __(3)__ By the mid-nineteenth century a number of scientists believed that plants could at least feel, if not think, and their findings were received by audiences whose own experiences cultivating plants had allowed them to observe a stunning array of plant behaviors. __(4)__ In the garden, the parlor, and the greenhouse, plants' living qualities became an object of fascination and raised questions like the one the article poses rhetorically. How to make sense of the behaviors of plants? Did they have an inner life? It could certainly appear so, though so much remained a mystery.

(a) Option 1 (b) Option 2
(c) Option 3 (d) Option 4

EXERCISE 2

Directions for Q 1-30. There is a sentence that is missing in the paragraph below. Look at the paragraph and decide in which blank (option 1, 2, 3 or 4) the following sentences would best fit.

Q1. Sentence: Details remain murky.

Nick Gibb, the long-serving Conservative schools minister, is right that safety is the most important consideration when deciding whether to close school buildings deemed to be dangerous. The public is all too familiar, post-Grenfell, with the horrific consequences that can follow from ignoring warnings that buildings are structurally unsound. __(1)__ But the announcement that more than 100 schools in England will not reopen next week, due to the possibility of concrete ceilings falling in, is enormously troubling. Not only will this last-minute decision disrupt thousands of children's education, with knock-on effects on parents and careers, it also points to the extent of the harm caused by the Conservatives' refusal to invest in the nation's schooling. __(2)__ The government has so far refused to reveal a full list of affected schools, although Essex is known to be the worst-hit county. Mr Gibb's explanation for the timing is that surveyors have been working over the summer, with findings delivered as recently as last week. __(3)__ The material under scrutiny is reinforced autoclaved aerated concrete (RAAC), which was widely used in schools, and some other public buildings, between the 1950s and mid-1990s. Previously, only RAAC judged by experts to be in "critical condition" was regarded as a threat - with 52 schools affected. __(4)__ But ministers have been forced to adopt a more conservative position after the recent collapse of a beam in a building previously thought to be safe.

(a) Option 1 (b) Option 2
(c) Option 3 (h) Option 4

Q2. Sentence: Though the majority of copies are in the US, more than a dozen have found their way to Japan.

Three years ago, a copy of William Shakespeare's First Folio exchanged hands for nearly $10m at Christie's, New York, becoming the most expensive work of literature ever sold at auction. What made the price all the more extraordinary was that this was not a unique artefact, like a medieval manuscript, but one of 233 known to have survived, from about 750 copies. __(1)__ The British Library alone owns five of them. Nevertheless, the First Folio holds a hallowed space, both within the English-speaking world and beyond. __(2)__ From today's perspective, this is not surprising. Shakespeare is the world's most performed playwright, whose name is as familiar in the classroom as on the stage. __(3)__ Published in the autumn of 1623, seven years after the playwright's death, the First Folio was not only responsible for preserving 16 of his plays, of which there was no previous record, for posterity - including Twelfth Night, Macbeth and The Tempest - but played a key role in doing the same for their author. "Without this book," wrote the Oxford professor Emma Smith, "half of Shakespeare's plays would have been lost, and without them, Shakespeare would not be a global cultural figure." __(4)__

(a) Option 1 (b) Option 2
(c) Option 3 (d) Option 4

Q3. Sentence: They are too real and too small, too specific and too discrete to be for all.

THE DREAM OF AN ARTWORK that encompasses the whole world; of a novel that tells everybody's story; of characters who feel and act and speak for us all; of the image that nobody doesn't recognize. __(1)__ Yet it is the world and characters and images and stories themselves that stand in the way of that dream. __(2)__ A person personifying history is still a person, history warped by and warping a personality. __(3)__ A dramatic narrative consists of speeches, acts, events. A consciousness is marred by the having of particular thoughts. An era is stained by its favorite clichés: the rise and fall, rags to riches, the trauma plot. Is there any escape from the contortions and inherited feelings of melodrama? What if it were the conventions of the novel themselves that obstructed the mission of telling the "inner life of the culture"?

Don DeLillo tells two stories about how and when he started writing novels (he wrote and published short fiction beforehand, but that's another story __(4)__): in 1966 while he was on vacation with friends sailing off the coast of Maine, they put in at Mount Desert Island and he sat on a railroad tie waiting to take a shower and "had a glimpse of a street maybe fifty yards away and a sense of beautiful old houses and rows of elms and maples and a stillness and a wistfulness–the street seemed to carry its own built-in longing."

(a) Option 1 (b) Option 2
(c) Option 3 (d) Option 4

Q4. Sentence: For the anthropologists who unearthed them thousands of years later, they were proof that our ability to count had manifested itself no later than 40,000 years ago.

Figuring out when humans began to count systematically, with purpose, is not easy. Our first real clues are a handful of curious, carved bones dating from the final few millennia of the three-million-year expanse of the Old Stone Age, or Paleolithic era. Those bones are humanity's first pocket calculators: For the prehistoric humans who carved them, they were mathematical notebooks and counting aids rolled into one. __(1)__ In 1973, while excavating a cave in the Lebombo Mountains, near South Africa's border with Swaziland, Peter Beaumont found a small, broken bone with twenty-nine notches carved across it. The so-called Border Cave had been known to archaeologists since 1934, but the discovery during World War II of skeletal remains dating to the Middle Stone Age heralded a site of rare importance. __(2)__ It was not until Beaumont's dig in the 1970s, however, that the cave gave up its most significant treasure: the earliest known tally stick, in the form of a notched, three-inch long baboon fibula. On the face of it, the numerical instrument known as the tally stick is exceedingly mundane. __(3)__ Used since before recorded history–still used, in fact, by some cultures–to mark the passing days, or to account for goods or monies given or received, most tally sticks are no more than wooden rods incised with notches along their length. They help their users to count, to remember, and to transfer ownership. All of which is reminiscent of writing, except that writing did not arrive until a scant 5,000 years ago–and so, when the Lebombo bone was determined to be some 42,000 years old, it instantly became one of the most intriguing archaeological artifacts ever found. Not only does it put a date on when Homo sapiens started counting, it also marks the point at which we began to delegate our memories to external devices, thereby unburdening our minds so that they might be used for something else instead. __(4)__

(a) Option 1 (b) Option 2
(c) Option 3 (d) Option 4

Q5. Sentence: 1989 thus ushered in the global triumph of freedom, but on Cold War liberalism's distorted terms.

Cold War liberalism was a catastrophe–for liberalism. This distinct body of liberal thought says that freedom comes first, that the enemies of liberty are the first priority to confront and contain in a dangerous world, and that demanding anything more from liberalism is likely to lead to tyranny. This set of ideas became intellectually trendsetting in the 1940s and 1950s at the outset of the Cold War, when liberals conceived of them as essential truths the free world had to preserve in a struggle against totalitarian empire. __(1)__ By the 1960s it had its enemies, who invented the phrase "Cold War liberalism" itself to indict its domestic compromises and foreign policy mistakes. __(2)__ That did not stop it from being rehabilitated in the 1990s, when it was repurposed for a post-political age. A generation of public intellectuals–among them Anne Applebaum, Timothy Garton Ash, Michael Ignatieff, Leon Wieseltier, and many others–styled themselves as successors to Cold War liberals, trumpeting the superiority of Cold War liberalism over illiberal right and left while obscuring just how distinctive it was within the broader liberal tradition. __(3)__ Then came the election of Donald Trump in 2016, which unleashed a great war over liberalism–a polemical one, at least–and prompted yet another resurgence of Cold War liberalism's core ideas. Patrick Deneen's much-discussed assault, Why Liberalism Failed (2018), was met by a crop of liberal self-defenses, almost all of them explicitly or implicitly attempted in Cold War terms. Francis Fukuyama, Adam Gopnik, and Mark Lilla all wrote book-length versions of why Cold War liberalism still had legs, but literally thousands of essays and websites, and even whole magazines such as The Atlantic, offered the same message in frantic response to Trump's breakthrough. Organized as much against the left as the right, these defenses not only rang hollow; they have failed to forestall the political crisis they promised to transcend. The result has been the reversal of Cold War liberal triumph into today's mood of desperation and despair that has left liberalism on the ropes, hated by a left and a right that now both propose to move beyond it. In the last several years, of course, a few right intellectuals of Deneen's ilk have continued to call for a vague "post-liberalism," the main actual function of which sometimes seems to be to bait Cold War liberals into reasserting their creed. __(4)__

(a) Option 1 (b) Option 2
(c) Option 3 (d) Option 4

Q6. Sentence: He oscillated back and forth between skepticism that anything certain could be known and his budding interest in the Christian faith, the latter nurtured by hearing the preaching of Ambrose, bishop of Milan.

In his Confessions, Saint Augustine describes a fascinating moment in his conversion to the

Christian faith. At the time, he was a successful teacher of rhetoric in Milan, living with his longtime concubine and their son. He had a group of close friends and was breaking away from the Manichaeans, the gnostic cult he had spent many years with, studying and teaching. Overwhelmed by the limits of human knowledge, he was increasingly skeptical that anyone could come to know the truth about how to live. __(1)__ He describes his internal dialogue at the time:

But where can truth be sought? When can it be sought? Ambrose has no time. __(2)__ There is no time for reading. Where should we look for the books that we need? Where and when can we obtain them? From whom can we borrow them? Fixed times must be kept free, hours appointed, for the health of the soul. Great hope has been aroused.... Why do we hesitate to knock at the door which opens the way to all the rest? Our pupils occupy the mornings; what should we do with the remaining hours? Why do we not investigate our problem? But then when should we go to pay respects to our more influential friends, whose patronage we need? When are we to prepare what our students are paying for? When are we to refresh ourselves by allowing the mind to relax from the tension of anxieties?

Augustine's language can be lofty and remote. But here is one of his great human moments. He wants to know how to live. __(3)__ He is not worried about discovering a truth that might spoil his career or require him to leave his concubine. Really! He doesn't have time, that's all - he's too busy, between his students and his patrons, oh, and Ambrose is too busy too. Everyone's too busy. He doesn't have time to read. Besides, he doesn't have time to get the books. Too bad for Augustine - he can't figure out the best way to live. He's too busy. __(4)__

(a) Option 1 (b) Option 2
(c) Option 3 (d) Option 4

Q7. Sentence: Reality, now more than ever, is contingent upon our own personal, collective, and sometimes even unconscious desires.

Reality is different these days. __(1)__ It isn't just that we have the tools to experience reality differently, or augment reality, by affixing a Meta Quest headset or an Apple Vision Pro to our skulls. It isn't just that we have the ability to quantify reality, through smartwatches and heart rate monitors and step counters and sleep trackers, or that we have the ability to manipulate people's perceptions of reality, through social media filters so ubiquitous that there is now a whole cottage industry of plastic surgery devoted to making people's fleshly faces match the selfies they post on Instagram. Nor is it just the fact that our social world includes the conversations we have with virtual personal assistants like Siri and Alexa, whose soothing voices greet us when we come home, or remind us of the weather. All of these, of course, play some role in the seismic reimaging of our selves, and our world, that the Internet – in particular, smartphone-enabled online culture – has engendered. But the shift we're experiencing is bigger, and more totalizing, than any single phenomenon. __(2)__ It's a spiritual shift, maybe even a metaphysical one. __(3)__ In *A Web of Our Own Making*, Antón Barba-Kay, a humanities professor at Deep Springs College in California and occasional contributor to this journal, offers a robust and comprehensive account of *what*, exactly, is going on. In a dense and penetrating book that feels, both in ambitious scope and granular detail, far more magisterial than its three hundred pages might suggest, Barba-Kay has produced both a convincing, citation-rich compendium of our digital experience, and a compelling piece of constructive philosophy. It is a philosophy that takes seriously the Internet's reshaping of human life – of the new ways we've come to understand our bodies, our relationships, our material nature, and our increasingly "data-driven" perspective. __(4)__ And it is a philosophy that offers, if not a cultural-level rejection of the morass, then at least the possibility of a personal way out: an escape Barba-Kay represents not as the breaking of an addiction nor an individualistic move toward wellness, but rather an existential – perhaps even *the* existential - choice.

(a) Option 1 (b) Option 2
(c) Option 3 (d) Option 4

Q8. Sentence: And then in the United States, liberalism generally means "New Deal liberalism."

Liberalism in Europe, today, is something like "libertarianism"–it is a right-wing ideology. There used to be a left libertarianism, which is probably better called anarchism, and that persists in various sectarian versions, but it isn't much in the public eye. __(1)__ It's our very modest version of social democracy, and it isn't a very strong doctrine, since many of its practitioners became neoliberals much too easily. So, the -ism is not a strong or coherent doctrine. That doesn't mean that there aren't liberals. But liberals are people who are best defined morally or psychologically; they're what Lauren Bacall, my favorite actress, called "people who don't have small minds." __(2)__ A liberal is someone who's tolerant of ambiguity, who can join arguments that he doesn't have to win, who can live with people who disagree, who have different religions or different ideologies. That's a liberal. __(3)__ But those liberal qualities don't imply any social or economic doctrine. So, there are liberals in the world, and I can recognize them, but liberalism does not describe their actual political commitment. __(4)__ The word is better used to qualify the kinds of commitments that I write about: democracy, socialism, nationalism, et cetera.

(a) Option 1 (b) Option 2
(c) Option 3 (d) Option 4

Q9. Sentence: Using metaphors derived from contemporary orders of hierarchy and subordination, medieval lyric not only sketches the feudal world but also documents its mood.

The enigma of courtly love poetry, according to the great mid-century medievalist Hugo Kuhn, is that its restraint transmits across centuries a sense of the existential terror and compensatory joie de vivre that must have characterized life in the Middle Ages. In their utterances of love, these formulaic, strangely contentless verses register what Kuhn called the 'objective social reality' of a poem. __(1)__ We have no idea what it was like to be alive at that time, and yet, in this poetry, the atmosphere of the age appears to vibrate through. __(2)__ The attempt to recover a felt sense of historical experience led Raymond Williams to invent the concept of a structure of feeling, which licenses a reading-backwards from 'the arts of a period' to its emotional ambience. 'We can learn a great deal of the life of other places and times', he wrote, 'but certain elements . . . will always be irrecoverable'. Moreover, Even those that can be recovered are recovered in abstraction, and this is of crucial importance. We learn each element as a precipitate, but in the living experience of the time every element was in a solution, an inseparable part of a complex whole. The most difficult thing to get hold of, in studying every past period, is this felt sense of the quality of life at a particular place and time: a sense of the ways in which the particular activities combined into a way of thinking and living. __(3)__.

Williams called this sense, inter alia, a 'colour', a 'style', a 'pattern', a 'characteristic', a 'culture', a 'particular living result of all the elements in the general organization'. Another term for it might be tone, a word with a heightened significance for poetry due to its association with song. In music, tone signifies pitch or key. In this century, Hans Ulrich Gumbrecht has proposed that we understand tone as the German Stimmung: mood, humour, temper, spirit, attitude, or tuning, as in the tuning of an instrument, a word closely related to Stimme or voice. Sianne Ngai, meanwhile, has articulated tone as 'a global and hyper-relational concept of feeling that encompasses attitude: a literary text's affective bearing, orientation, or "set toward" its audience and world.' __(4)__

(a) Option 1 (b) Option 2
(c) Option 3 (d) Option 4

Q10. Sentence: It is a topic of the salons, an amusement at the court, the subject of philosophical dissertations; and doctors talk incessantly about it in all their consultations.

Beginning in the spring of 1667, public opinion in Paris was rocked by a remarkable affair involving domesticated animals: the first practical experiments to transfuse animal blood into humans for therapeutic purposes. The experiments that came to be known as the "Transfusion Affair" were shrouded in the competing claims of a highly public controversy in which consensus and truth, alongside the animal subjects themselves, were the first victims. __(1)__. "There was never anything that divided opinion as much as we presently witness with the transfusions", wrote the Parisian lawyer at Parlement, Louis de Basril, late in the affair, in February 1668. __(2)__ At the center of the controversy was the young Montpellier physician and "most able Cartesian philosopher" Jean Denis, recently established in Paris, who experimented with animal blood to cure sickness, especially madness, and to prolong life. __(3)__ With the talented surgeon Paul Emmerez, Denis transfused small amounts of blood from the carotid arteries of calves, lambs, and kid goats into the veins of five ailing human patients between June 1667 and January 1668. __(4)__

(a) Option 1 (b) Option 2
(c) Option 3 (d) Option 4

Q11. Sentence: Something in me believed it was the way through the crucible, and stopping felt like relinquishing all control.

I can't remember a time when I didn't know that I was vulnerable. __(1)__ From childhood on, I felt stress as acutely as a needle puncture – the familiar tightness in my ribcage, the trembling in my upper arms. In an attempt to dull the pain, I'd obsess endlessly about the current subject of my worries, whether it was a guy who'd rejected me or the strange bruises that had appeared on my legs overnight. As an adult, I learned that ruminating – lingering over problems like a cow chewing cud – was linked to the depression and anxiety that I suffered in repeated bouts. But knowing this wasn't enough to halt my obsessing. __(2)__

Still, I've long known that not everyone responds to stress the way I do. __(3)__ I see the evidence every day in my own home. My husband, the descendant of laid-back Scandinavians, seems largely impervious to stresses and misfortunes. I think of him as a sturdy wagon, one that keeps rolling along, no matter the condition of the road. Then there's the author Kelly Hayes-Raitt, who has faced various slings and arrows through the years. Post-9/11, her consulting business went bottom-up, leaving her $90,000 in debt. After that, she ran for political office in Santa Monica in California, and lost after enduring multiple rounds of character assassination. But through it all, she says, she's never felt particularly anxious, depressed or otherwise unmoored – and she's never received any kind of psychiatric diagnosis. __(4)__

(a) Option 1 (b) Option 2
(c) Option 3 (d) Option 4

Q12. Sentence: It is an unmistakeable arrangement of attention and affect, a way of understanding and engaging with the world.

This portrait is beautiful. __(1)__ Sometimes, I find its beauty in the perfectly angled crook of the arm that rests easily across the sitter's lap. At other times, it is in the unstudied grace of the hand that props up the head, the long fingers curled in repose. Often, it's the dress that I find beautiful: expansive, heavy and brilliantly white, its generous skirt magnificently amassed around the seated figure. Occasionally, even the backdrop, an impassive flat wash of a blank summer blue that engages my attention. There are many ways to describe Amy Sherald's 2018 portrait of the former First Lady, Michelle Obama. It is regal, powerful, accomplished and imposing. But I absolutely know that it is also beautiful. __(2)__ I hold this judgment as a deep and sure conviction. I don't mean it as a casual pleasantry, a blandishment offered about the attractiveness of the sitter – although when we speak of beauty, we often mean only a narrowed notion of female physical appearance. __(3)__ I take beauty to refer instead to a peculiar and particular experience, both sensory and cerebral, often characterised by an inward responsiveness to an outward stimulation. __(4)__ In contemporary culture, we talk carelessly about beauty, dismissing it as a superficial concern or regarding it only as the special interest of art. But in philosophy, too, next to truth and morality, beauty can feel insubstantial, undeserving of our serious reflection.

(a) Option 1 (b) Option 2
(c) Option 3 (d) Option 4

Q13. Sentence: That's a particularly common view of the kind of Buddhist meditation known as mindfulness meditation – which is sometimes packaged in the frankly therapeutic form of 'mindfulness-based stress reduction'.

The concept of nirvana occupies a unique place in Buddhist thought – not just because it represents the culmination of the Buddhist path, and not just because it represents the nicest imaginable place to be, but also because of the way it straddles the two sides of Buddhism. There is, on the one hand, the naturalistic side of Buddhism, featuring ideas that would fit easily into a college psychology or philosophy course: ideas about the nature of the mind, about the causes of human suffering, and about how we should live our lives in light of these realities. These are the ideas that form the core of the 'secular Buddhism' that is practised by many in the West. __(1)__ Indeed, so naturalistic, so 'secular', is this set of ideas that some people see Buddhist meditation as more of a therapeutic than a spiritual undertaking, as basically palliative and not too profound. __(2)__ And then there is the more exotic side of Buddhism, which features supernatural, or at least mindbendingly metaphysical, ideas. These ideas include various cosmic realms and deities, but the most famous such idea is reincarnation – or, as Buddhists more commonly call it, rebirth. Nirvana certainly has its exotic aspects. Attaining it, according to traditional Buddhist belief, means being liberated from an otherwise endless cycle of rebirth. But this story about nirvana – the story about how exactly you find the escape hatch from recurring life cycles – leads seamlessly to a more naturalistic story about nirvana, a claim about the mechanics of suffering and of contentment. __(3)__ And in the process of following one story to the other, you can see mindfulness meditation in a new light, a light that emphasises how much more than casually therapeutic it can be; a light that shows it to be one of the most radical undertakings imaginable, a rebellion against the very laws that govern human existence. __(4)__

(a) Option 1 (b) Option 2
(c) Option 3 (d) Option 4

Q14. Sentence: What is the meaning of 'meaning' in 'the meaning of life'?

__(1)__ Philosophers ponder the meaning of life. At least, that is the stereotype. When I risk admitting to a stranger that I teach philosophy for a living and face the question 'What is the meaning of life?', I have a ready response: we figured that out in the 1980s, but we have to keep it secret or we'd be out of a job; I could tell you, but then I'd have to kill you. In fact, professional philosophers rarely ask the question and, when they do, they often dismiss it as nonsense. __(2)__ The phrase itself is of relatively recent origin. Its first use in English is in Thomas Carlyle's parodic novel Sartor Resartus (1836), where it appears in the mouth of a comic German philosopher, Diogenes Teufelsdröckh ('God-born devil-dung'), noted for his treatise on clothes. The question of life's meaning remains both easy to mock and paradigmatically obscure. __(3)__ We talk about the meaning of words, or linguistic meaning, the meaning of an utterance or of writing in a book. When we ask if human life has meaning, are we asking whether it has meaning in this semantic sense? Could human history be a sentence in some cosmic language? The answer is that it could, in principle, but that this isn't what we want when we search for the meaning of life. __(4)__ If we are unwitting ink in some alien script, it would be interesting to know what we spell out, but the answer would not have authority over us, as befits the meaning of life.

(a) Option 1 (b) Option 2
(c) Option 3 (d) Option 4

Q15. Sentence: Outside academia, for those who give it any thought, psychoanalysis is generally regarded as having followed phrenology and mesmerism into the dustbin of psychological enquiry.

An old therapist of mine had a signed photograph of Sigmund Freud hanging on her wall. A gift from a former patient who had employed forgery skills in a side business of dubious legality, it was the iconic Freud photo: full suit, blank scowl, half-smoked cigar. Once, mid-session, I asked my therapist what she thought of Freud's theories. 'I don't think much of them,' she replied. Her dismissiveness wasn't a surprise. By any measure, Freud was one of the most influential thinkers of the 20th century. Following his death in 1939, the British author W H Auden was able to declare in his poem 'In Memory of Sigmund Freud' (1939) that Freud had represented 'a whole climate of opinion', and the subsequent two decades represented the heyday of psychoanalysis. __(1)__ No longer. __(2)__ Boys lusting after their mothers; girls desiring a penis – such are the luridly risible impressions that persist in the popular imagination. What went wrong? In 1996, Tom Wolfe wrote that 'the demise of Freudianism can be summed up in a single word: lithium'. The American author described how in the early 1950s, after years of psychoanalytic ineffectiveness, rapid physical relief for sufferers of bipolar disorder arrived in the form of a pill. Wolfe's example is microcosmic of a wider state of affairs. The waning of psychoanalysis corresponds precisely to the rise of modern neuroscience, whose physicalist approach now drives psychiatry. __(3)__ Today, almost anyone could have a go at describing serotonin, or dopamine, or Prozac. Few of those same people could define the primal scene, or the super-ego. As the American author Siri Hustvedt puts it in The Shaking Woman, or a History of My Nerves (2010), Freud is now seen by many if not most as 'a mystic, a man whose ideas bear no relation to physical realities, a kind of monster of mirage who derailed modernity by feeding all kinds of nonsense to a gullible public until his thought was finally shattered by a new scientific psychiatry founded on the wonders of pharmacology'. __(4)__

(a) Option 1 (b) Option 2
(c) Option 3 (d) Option 4

Q16. Sentence: The same playbook may now be followed in Helsinki, after a cliffhanger vote delivered a similar electoral outcome.

For observers of a progressive persuasion, Sunday's Finnish election turned out to be an unwelcome repeat episode of Nordic noir. __(1)__. Last autumn, Sweden ejected a Social Democrat prime minister and installed a moderate Conservative successor, while at the same time empowering the radical right Sweden Democrats party. __(2)__. The high-profile casualty of this rightwards shift was Finland's millennial prime minister, Sanna Marin, who has been ousted four years after becoming the world's youngest political leader. __(3)__.Though Ms Marin's Social Democratic party actually improved its vote share, it narrowly came in third behind moderate conservatives and the radical right in what was a photo-finish. Her coalition government's fate was sealed by a collapse in support for allied leftwing parties, as the centre-right successfully mobilised fears over state borrowing levels. __(4)__.

(a) Option 1 (b) Option 2
(c) Option 3 (d) Option 4

Q17. Sentence: Paranoia doesn't dissipate, run down, run out of steam

Hatred is different from paranoia. Hatred can engulf a nation in a millions-strong frenzy of self-righteousness. Hatred can be held by one person all the way to the grave. It can be suddenly relinquished (sometimes beautifully); or it can just wear itself down like an overused axe blade. Paranoia, on the other hand, is a matter of self-defence: it assumes malice on the part of the other. __(1)__ My department chair, Torrone, wants to fire me. He's planted a graduate student in my Latin class. I'm thinking primarily of schizophrenic paranoia, such as my own. It is a red-hot drive that inhabits an individual and feels like it wants to take over his mind. When I'm paranoid, I travel on the horizon's edge, the line between all and nothing, between 'them' and me. __(2)__ That student is to observe me, to report back to Torrone. I travel that edge alone. Aloneness is of the essence. Paranoia has nothing to do with loneliness which, after all, seeks union. And it's seemingly forever. __(3)__ Logic is almost always pointless against it: I can no more will my paranoia away than I can will my thinking straight. Just yesterday I saw Torrone, out walking, all these years after the incident. I ducked down a side street. __(4)__

(a) Option 1 (b) Option 2
(c) Option 3 (d) Option 4

Q18. Sentence: The killer in El Paso, who law enforcement believes authored the memo, is apparently no exception.

"This attack is a response to the Hispanic invasion of Texas." Those were the words that appeared in a manifesto published shortly before the deadly shooting in El Paso on Saturday. More than half of so-called "alt-right killers" are motivated by the "white replacement" theory, which refers to the belief that white people will be systematically replaced by black and brown migrants. __(1)__ The white replacement theory is actually made up of two sub-conspiracies: "the great replacement" theory, which originated in France, and "the white genocide theory", which comes from the US. Together, the theories are among the most widespread ideologies in far-right spaces, and the primary catalysts of far-right mass violence. __(2)__ The great replacement can generally be understood as two core beliefs. The first is that "western" identity is under siege by massive waves of immigration from non-European/ non-white countries, resulting in a replacement of white European individuals via demographics. The second is that replacement has been orchestrated by a shadowy group as part of their grand plan to rule the world - which they will do by creating a completely racially homogenous society. This group is often overtly identified as being Jews, but sometimes the antisemitism is more implicit. These beliefs have proliferated in mass killer texts for the past eight years. __(3)__ They are generally understood as having begun with Anders Breivik, the Norwegian mass shooter whose 1,500-page manifesto expressed a fear of white ethnic replacement by migrants from the Middle East and North Africa. __(4)__ This same fear cropped up in the manifestos of several more mass killers in Europe, before making its way to the rambling screed published by the Christchurch shooter, which was titled The Great Replacement.

(a) Option 1 (b) Option 2
(c) Option 3 (d) Option 4

Q19. Sentence: The containers were still sealed, indicating that the evidence had never been sent to a lab.

Robert Spada walked into the decrepit warehouse in Detroit and surveyed the chaos: Thousands of cardboard boxes and large plastic bags were piled haphazardly throughout the cavernous space. The air inside was hot and musty. __(1)__ Spada, an assistant prosecutor, saw that some of the windows were open, others broken, exposing the room to the summer heat. Above the boxes, birds glided in slow, swooping circles. It was August 17, 2009, and this brick fortress of a building housed evidence that had been collected by the Detroit Police Department. Spada's visit had been prompted by a question: Why were police sometimes unable to locate crucial evidence? The answer lay in the disarray before him. As Spada wandered through the warehouse, he made another discovery, one that would help uncover a decades-long scandal, not just in Detroit but across the country. He noticed rows of steel shelving lined with white cardboard boxes, 10 inches tall and a foot wide, stacked six feet high. What are those? he asked a Detroit police officer who was accompanying him. Rape kits, the officer said. __(2)__

"I'm assuming they've been tested?" Spada said. "Oh, they've all been tested." Spada pulled out a box and peered inside. __(3)__ He opened four more boxes: the same. "I tried to do a quick calculation," he later told me. "I came up with approximately 10,000." Spada's estimate was conservative. Eventually 11,341 untested rape kits were found, some dating back more than 30 years–each one a hermetically sealed testament to the most terrifying minutes of a woman's life, each one holding evidence that had been swabbed or plucked from the most private parts of her body. And in all likelihood, some microscopic part of her assailant–his DNA, his identity–sat in that kit as well. __(4)__

(a) Option 1 (b) Option 2
(c) Option 3 (d) Option 4

Q20. Sentence: But his martyrdom represents more than the spread of a single oppressed religion: Polycarp's sacrifice in the 2nd century CE shows what it can mean to wield death as a form of resistance.

An octogenarian Christian bishop is condemned to death for his beliefs. Even while bound to a wooden stake, as Roman authorities order his immolation, the monk still refuses to blaspheme against his god. __(1)__ A crowd gathers to watch, including the monk's companions, who look on with horror and reverence as the pyre is lit. But the flames fail to extinguish his life, and a dagger finishes the job. The bishop Polycarp is dead. __(2)__ His companions rush to gather the body, creating a commotion so chaotic that Roman authorities must physically restrain them. They seek his remains, hoping to preserve Polycarp's bones as relics of suffering and dedication. Through death, the monk becomes a martyr, and Saint Polycarp's story begins to spread Christianity further across the Roman Empire. __(3)__ A form that will shape the ambit of political action in the millennia that follow. __(4)__

(a) Option 1 (b) Option 2
(c) Option 3 (d) Option 4

Q21. Sentence: That longstanding tradition of moral philosophy is an invaluable legacy of ancient Mediterranean civilisation.

In the Western world, only since the mid-18th century has it been possible to discuss ethical questions publicly without referring to Christianity. Modern thinking about morality, which assumes that gods do not exist, or at least do not intervene, is in its infancy. But the ancient Greeks and Romans elaborated robust philosophical schools of ethical thought for more than a millennium, from the first professed agnostics such as Protagoras (fifth century BCE) to the last pagan thinkers. __(1)__ The Platonists' Academy at Athens was not finally closed down until 529 CE, by the Emperor Justinian. __(2)__ It has prompted several contemporary secular thinkers, faced with the moral vacuum left by the decline of Christianity since the late 1960s, to revive ancient schools of thought. __(3)__ Stoicism, founded in Athens by the Cypriot Zeno in about 300 BCE, has advocates. Self-styled Stoic organisations on both sides of the Atlantic offer courses, publish books and blogposts, and even run an annual Stoic Week. Some Stoic principles underlay Dale Carnegie's self-help classic *How to Stop Worrying and Start Living* (1948). He recommended Marcus Aurelius' *Meditations* to its readers. But authentic ancient Stoicism was pessimistic and grim. It denounced pleasure. It required the suppression of emotions and physical appetites. __(4)__ It recommended the resigned acceptance of misfortune, rather than active engagement with the fine-grained business of everyday problem-solving. It left little room for hope, human agency or constructive repudiation of suffering.

(a) Option 1 (b) Option 2
(c) Option 3 (d) Option 4

Q22. Sentence: One of the big philosophical questions about holes is whether they are actually things themselves or, as the German-Jewish writer Kurt Tucholsky suggested in 'The Social Psychology of Holes' (1931), whether they are just 'where something isn't'.

__(1)__ It seems indisputable that there are holes. For example, there are keyholes, black holes and sinkholes; and there are holes *in* things such as sieves, golf courses and doughnuts. We come into the world through holes, and when we die many of us will be put into specially dug holes. But what *are* these holes and what are they made of? __(2)__ To help us investigate this issue, let us first dissect the anatomy of the hole. So, imagine a doughnut - the classic kind that is round with a hole in the middle, rather than the jam-filled kind. The dough of the doughnut is an example of what is called the 'host' of the hole - the stuff that surrounds the hole. Now imagine you put your finger through the hole in the doughnut, and wear the doughnut like a ring. Your finger is then an example of what is called a 'guest' in the hole - the stuff that is inside the hole. But now consider the doughnut in an early stage of its creation in a factory, about to get the hole cut out of the dough. What do we call the part of the dough that gets removed to create the hole? Should it be called a guest-in-residence, about to be evicted? These parts of the dough have been branded by food merchandisers as 'Timbits' and 'Munchkins', and are marketed as the actual hole of the doughnut. __(3)__ Yet surely they are not, as the hole is created by the Timbits' or Munchkins' removal, rather than being identified with what gets removed. __(4)__

(a) Option 1 (b) Option 2
(c) Option 3 (d) Option 4

Q23. Sentence: It is a panacea for the individual.

Among the promised psychological and physical benefits of meditation are the elimination or reduction of stress, anxiety and depression, as well as bipolar disorder, eating disorders, diabetes, substance abuse, chronic pain, blood pressure, cancer, autism and schizophrenia. __(1)__ There are also apparent interpersonal and collective effects. Mindfulness and other Buddhist-derived meditation techniques, such as compassion and loving-kindness meditation, can perhaps increase prosocial emotions and behaviours, yielding greater social connection and altruism, tampering aggression and prejudice. __(2)__ 'If every eight-year-old in the world is taught meditation,' the Dalai Lama purportedly said, 'the world will be without violence within one generation.' The quote is widely shared online. Such a useful activity naturally finds a variety of applications. __(3)__ Meditation techniques have been deployed in the military with the aim of increasing the wellbeing and work effectiveness of soldiers. Snipers are known to meditate in order to disengage emotionally from the act of killing, to steady the hand that takes a life (the element of peacefulness associated with meditation having been rather set aside). Corporations counteract stress and burnout with meditation which, on the surface, is an amiable aim, but it can also help create compliant workers. And in schools, meditation interventions aim to calm children's minds, offering students the ability to better deal with the pressure of attaining high grades. Here, too, the goal is to reduce misbehaviour and aggression in a bid to increase prosociality and compliance. __(4)__

(a) Option 1 (b) Option 2
(c) Option 3 (d) Option 4

Q24. Sentence: For two weeks, he worked as a guard in the cellblocks, monitoring men who had been captured on the battlefields of Afghanistan.

In 2004, Steve Wood was deployed to Guantánamo Bay, as a member of the Oregon National Guard. He and his comrades were told that many of the detainees were responsible for 9/11 and, given the opportunity, would strike again. "I just remember being super excited, because I thought, I'm going to be doing something important," Wood told me. __(1)__. Then a sergeant major pulled him aside for a brief interview, and assigned him to work the night shift in Echo Special, a secret, single-occupancy unit that had been built to house the United States military's highest-value detainee. __(2)__ The International Committee of the Red Cross–which has access to many of the world's most notorious detention sites, some of them in countries where there is no rule of law–had recently sent representatives to Guantánamo, but the base commander, citing "military necessity," had refused to allow them into Echo Special. The man confined there was referred to by his detainee number, 760. When Wood tried to search for 760 in Guantánamo's detainee database, he found nothing. __(3)__ Wood was the second of three boys. His father died in a plane crash when he was three years old, and his mother brought him and his brothers up in Molalla, Oregon, a lumber town about an hour south of Portland. In 1999, shortly after graduating from high school, Wood started a job at the local sawmill. Several of his co-workers were missing fingers, and the manager took every opportunity to denigrate the staff. After a few months, he signed up for the Oregon National Guard, on the military-police track. He sought structure and discipline–a life of pride, purpose, and clarity of mission. __(4)__

(a) Option 1 (b) Option 2
(c) Option 3 (d) Option 4

Q25. Sentence: Since then, scrutiny has only increased, with more questions being asked of the western businesses behind projects such as Kariba, a huge offset-promoted forest in Zimbabwe.

The emerging carbon offsets market is chaotic and dysfunctional. Problems need to be addressed openly, and resolved as quickly as possible. __(1)__. A joint investigation by the Guardian, the German weekly Die Zeit and SourceMaterial revealed in January that the vast majority of rainforest offset credits from the leading certifier - which are sold to companies that then use them to make claims about their overall emissions - do not offer the environmental benefits that they claim. __(2)__ Recognising the urgent need to rebuild flagging confidence, if the carbon-trading system is not to collapse as it did once before, the Integrity Council for the Voluntary Carbon Market last week announced that new rules for offset issuers will be announced in May. A separate process overseen by a different body is reviewing the claims that businesses make, based on their offset purchases. __(3)__. While all this might sound remote from the concerns of most people, the stakes could hardly be higher. Many environmentalists would prefer governments to oversee a transfer of resources from rich countries to the forested nations that need incentives to conserve precious carbon sinks. __(4)__ The reality is that due to the way our global economic system is organised, we all depend on market mechanisms.

(a) Option 1 (b) Option 2
(c) Option 3 (d) Option 4

Q26. Sentence: Google and Facebook were restructuring the world, not just solving its problems.

IN A SERIES of remarkably prescient articles, the first of which was published in the German newspaper Frankfurter Allgemeine Zeitung in the summer of 2013, Shoshana Zuboff pointed to an alarming phenomenon: the digitization of everything was giving technology firms immense social power. __(1)__ From the modest beachheads inside our browsers, they conquered, Blitzkrieg-style, our homes, cars, toasters, and even mattresses. Toothbrushes, sneakers, vacuum cleaners: our formerly dumb household subordinates were becoming our "smart" bosses. Their business models turned data into gold, favoring further expansion. __(2)__ The general public, seduced by the tech world's youthful, hoodie-wearing ambassadors and lobotomized by TED Talks, was clueless. __(3)__. Zuboff saw a logic to this digital mess; tech firms were following rational–and terrifying–imperatives. To attack them for privacy violations was to miss the scale of the transformation–a tragic miscalculation that has plagued much of the current activism against Big Tech. The imperatives of surveillance capitalism are almost of the evolutionary kind: no clever policy, not even in Congress, has ever succeeded in shortening the giraffe's neck (it has, however, done wonders for Mitch McConnell's). __(4)__

(a) Option 1 (b) Option 2
(c) Option 3 (d) Option 4

Q27. Sentence: What people don't know–or didn't until a recent biography of the then Prime Minister set the record right–is that Singh's first draft of the Budget was a socialist document.

JULY 2016 IS being celebrated, at least by the media, as the 25th aniversary of India's liberation from the dirigiste policies of the previous 40 years. The Budget of July 1991 has been made to go down in history as a 'pathbreaking' one, the Budget that set free, in then Finance Minister Manmohan Singh's words, the 'animal spirits' of Indian businessmen. At the end of his speech, he quoted Victor Hugo to say that no one can stop an idea whose time has come. __(1)__ The Prime Minister, says his biographer, asked Singh, "Is this for what I chose you?" Singh came back a couple of days later with the Budget that is now being feted. And for the last 25 years, he has taken all the credit for it. __(2)__ But the spirit of free enterprise about which Singh waxed so eloquent–and to which he did not fully subscribe– has never constituted what Germans would call India's *zeitgeist*, the driver of its inner spirit. That honour was long ago claimed by socialism, which believes that 'animal spirits' are best kept under check so that the state can work its magic in lifting the poor out of poverty. And, in varying degrees, this belief has permeated every Budget since the one of 1946, which was presented by Liaquat Ali Khan who went on to become the prime minister of Pakistan a year later. __(3)__ Narendra Modi's first Budget was not very different. And, for the very limited departure it showed from the past, his Government was excoriated for being a '*suit-boot ki sarkar*'. Modi and his Finance Minister have withdrawn hastily since then and gone back to the old, more politically acceptable style. His third Budget, in fact, truly revived the socialistic spirit and it became clear that the much hailed Budget of 1991 hadn't expelled the gorilla from the room. The state would continue to dominate the economy, thank you very much. __(4)__

(a) Option 1 (b) Option 2
(c) Option 3 (d) Option 4

Q28. Sentence: At its most basic level, mental hygiene refers to the branch of medicine that aspires to prevent psychiatric disorders.

In English, the term 'mental hygiene' likely sounds a bit stale. __(1)__ Having gained a brief but widespread ascendancy in the first half of the 20th century, the phrase gradually faded from popular memory and was replaced by the expression 'mental health' in the 1950s. In Chinese, however, mental hygiene is still alive and well. Translated as *xinli weisheng* or *jingshen weisheng*, the phrase has been a mainstay in Chinese psychiatric policy for close to a full century. __(2)__ The term was first coined in the late-19th century and became commonplace by the turn of the 20th. In contrast to mental health (the expression used by the World Health Organization today), early mental hygiene consisted of a prophylactic approach to insanity through education and eugenics, rather than a holistic emphasis on self-actualisation and self-care. Mental hygienists, promising an easy fix to mental illness, gained almost universal support by the 1920s and '30s. __(3)__ Yet the Second World War changed the course of their trajectory. Following the development of antipsychotic drugs and the discovery of Nazi war crimes, the discipline became both medically irrelevant and politically unpalatable. __(4)__

(a) Option 1 (b) Option 2
(c) Option 3 (d) Option 4

Q29. Sentence: It's startling that Broder's unabashed expression of sadness - and all the shitty emotions - has struck such a nerve in a world where people's social media profiles are immaculately curated to show their happiest selves.

In a Twitter account called So Sad Today, the American writer Melissa Broder has been sending out snippets of her daily inner life since 2012. Broder writes about mundane sadness - 'waking up today was a disappointment' or 'what you call a nervous breakdown I call oops, accidentally saw things as they are'- and she is brutally honest about her own shortcomings ('whoops, hurt myself conforming to socially accepted standards of beauty that I know are false but still feel compelled to fit into' or 'just felt a flicker of self-esteem and was like what the fuck is this'). __(1)__ The account has become a sensation, winning her more than 675,000 followers, and Broder's book of personal essays about her mental-health battles, also named *So Sad Today*, appeared in 2016. __(2)__ But clearly the growing rates of depression worldwide mean that we are struggling to be happy. Are we doing something wrong? Broder's popularity should compel us to cast a new look at sadness and its cousins. __(3)__. Perhaps we should consider realigning ourselves with the Romantics, who as a group found solace in freely expressing emotions in poetry. In his 'Ode on Melancholy' (1820), for example, John Keats wrote: 'Ay, in the very temple of Delight,/Veil'd Melancholy has her sovran shrine'. Pain and joy are two sides of the same coin - both are necessary for a fully lived life. __(4)__

(a) Option 1 (b) Option 2
(c) Option 3 (d) Option 4

Q30. Sentence: He is a garrulous, flirty raconteur.

Heavy-set, with a soft-jowled face, King has a distinctly ursine air about him. We first meet at a Wendy's in downtown Brooklyn, his teddy-bearishness rounded out by a plushy layer of cocoa-coloured velour tracksuit with a matching hoodie, T-shirt, and beanie hat. __(1)__ He leans in close over the small white plastic table in the corner and shares, in a gravelly voice, his penchant for Dominican women ('I'll take one as my next wife'), his distaste for Indian shop-owners ('They look at you like you in a zoo. Or the bottom of they shoe'), and his love for his two-year-old grandbaby Vanny. __(2)__ But when he talks about his three-decade long 'bid' in various upstate correctional facilities, punctuated by periods of isolation in 'the Box' - a solitary confinement cell - he gets quieter, and stares away, distracted and angry.

'I was in the Box a number of times,' he says, 'for dirty urine - when they find weed in your urine - and for arguing with the police over dumb shit. I was never there for stabbin' or nothin'.' __(3)__ He produces a long, thin Chick-O-Stick from his pocket and begins to chew on the bright orange flesh. 'I seen some people, they go into the Box with 30 days, and they in that box for three years because they went off on a police officer; took some shit or piss and slung it on 'em because they had nothin' better to do. Once they been there a minute, that's when they start to see shit, harm themselves, harm others. I wasn't in there banging my head on the wall, screaming and carrying on. I was chillin', readin', I ain't bother no people.' __(4)__

(a) Option 1 (b) Option 2
(c) Option 3 (d) Option 4

EXERCISE 3

Directions for Q 1-15. There is a sentence that is missing in the paragraph below. Look at the paragraph and decide in which blank (option 1, 2, 3 or 4) the following sentences would best fit.

Q1. Sentence: Between 1933 and 1938, more than 80,000 politicians, philosophers, communists and liberals flee from Germany to France.

Paris, France, 1933. __(1)__ The French newspaper Le Figaro reads: 'It's a wick to a barrel of powder' beneath the headline 'Hitler Is the New Master of Germany'. Terror sets in. __(2)__ The far-Right is growing. The economy is suffering. There is mass unemployment. There are workers' strikes. Fascism begins appealing to the middle classes. __(3)__ In Berlin, Stormtroopers are patrolling the streets. The Gestapo is detaining people and murdering them in cellars. Refugees from Germany arrive by train daily looking for asylum. __(4)__ There is anti-German sentiment. There are anti-immigrant protests.

(a) Option 1 (b) Option 2
(c) Option 3 (d) Option 4

Q2. Sentence: Vacancies in England have almost doubled since the pandemic, according to a recent report.

Do more with less. This has been the government's expectation of every public sector employee since 2010. In education, this has led to stagnant wages and unsustainable workloads, compounded by a punitive Ofsted inspection process that heaps stress upon teachers and can condemn a school to failure in a single sentence. Many are leaving the profession. __(1)__ As a result, teachers are being forced to teach more classes outside their specialism. __(2)__ The risk is a creeping deprofessionalisation of the sector that will have a negative impact on learning. This crisis has been building for years. Austerity has led to fewer support staff, leaving teachers to cope with a rising tide of mental health and social issues. Meanwhile, a succession of below-inflation pay rises over the last decade means teacher earnings have fallen by 13% in real terms since 2010. __(3)__. It is not just absolute pay that is forcing teachers to leave or dissuading people from applying, but the growing gap between teacher pay and salaries in other graduate professions. This is particularly acute in secondary schools, which have struggled to recruit maths and science graduates who can get better-paid jobs elsewhere. __(4)__

(a) Option 1 (b) Option 2
(c) Option 3 (d) Option 4

Q3. Sentence: Eyes might roll at yet another TV serialisation of Great Expectations, but experience has taught target-driven commissioners that it's hard to go wrong with Dickens.

Literary adaptations often turn out to be bankers on both stage and screen: they have the benefit of name recognition and established fanbases. __(1)__. Some - like another extended West End hit, To Kill a Mockingbird - have the advantage of featuring on school syllabuses. __(2)__ As a Shakespearean story that is being delivered by the RSC at the playwright's birthplace, Hamnet has hit a particular mark: it is an intelligent and timely reckoning with theatre's own history, accreted through generations of scholarship. __(3)__ As well as exploring the impact of his son's death, at the age of 11, on the tragedy he would premiere a few years later - Hamlet - it reclaims Anne Hathaway from the apparent ignominy of being bequeathed only her husband's second-best bed, by looking behind the recurring motifs of herbs and birds in his plays. __(4)__.

(a) Option 1 (b) Option 2
(c) Option 3 (d) Option 4

Q4. Sentence: But as a coalition partner in Olaf Scholz's Social Democrat-led government, it is taking environmental obstructionism to a new level.

Germany's pro-business Free Democratic party (FDP) has long been an uncompromising defender of the biggest domestic car industry in Europe. A couple of years ago, it campaigned against proposals for a national speed limit on autobahns - a move that would have helped reduce Germany's CO_2 emissions. __(1)__ The FDP is the driving force behind German opposition to Brussels' plans to ban sales of new cars with internal combustion engines from 2035. __(2)__ Until this month, the date was considered a done deal, and constitutes a vital pillar of the EU's strategy to reach net zero emissions by 2050. __(3)__ But Germany is now insisting that the European Commission offers a get-out clause, allowing car manufacturers to carry on producing the engines if they can find a way to deliver carbon-neutral "e-fuels" to run them. __(4)__

(a) Option 1 (b) Option 2
(c) Option 3 (d) Option 4

Q5. Sentence: One MP from the centre-right party Les Républicains - which Mr Macron's minority government needs onside to achieve majorities - accused the president of acting in an "isolated, narcissistic way, impervious to French people's lives".

A few months before sweeping to power in the 2017 presidential election, Emmanuel Macron published a memoir-cum-personal manifesto, Revolution. In it, he made the case for rebellion against allegedly outmoded institutions and ideas that were holding back France. Six years on, it is the popular revolts against Mr Macron's own policies which have taken centre-stage. __(1)__ Recent months have seen some of the largest protests in the history of the Fifth Republic, as Mr Macron has sought to push through a deeply unpopular plan to raise the retirement age from 62 to 64. On Monday, his government survived a related parliamentary motion of no confidence by the skin of its teeth. __(2)__ This followed the president's controversial - though constitutional - decision to use executive powers to get his way, bypassing a vote in the national assembly that he thought he might lose. Among his own MPs, the manoeuvre provoked public misgivings. __(3)__ Elsewhere, even allowing for the usual political game-playing, the response was authentically furious. __(4)__

(a) Option 1 (b) Option 2
(c) Option 3 (d) Option 4

Q6. Sentence: His genius poured forth in three dimensions, building on breakthroughs in painting and collage.

In 2015, New York's Museum of Modern Art mounted the first major retrospective of Pablo Picasso's sculpture in a half-century, with over 100 pieces, from stylized ceramic heads to "found" metal weldings to wood deconstructions. __(1)__ One period stood out for its darkened, austere galleries: the World War II years, when he remained in Paris during the Nazi occupation. __(2)__ The objects here were stripped-down, elemental, toying with minimalist representation during an epoch of maximalist anguish, as in "Bull's Head," which fuses a bicycle seat and handlebars, evoking his perennial theme of the bullfight, and opening a portal onto fear and vulnerability, a striking counterpoint to the self-assured, protean figure Picasso presented to the world. __(3)__ We're used to seeing the great man play offense, not defense. __(4)__

(a) Option 1 (b) Option 2
(c) Option 3 (d) Option 4

Q7. Sentence: I guessed not

In the summer of 2021, I experienced a cluster of coincidences, some of which had a distinctly supernatural feel. Here's how it started. I keep a journal and record dreams if they are especially vivid or strange. __(1)__ It doesn't happen often, but I logged one in which my mother's oldest friend, a woman called Rose, made an appearance to tell me that she (Rose) had just died. __(2)__ She'd had another stroke, she said, and that was it. Come the morning, it occurred to me that I didn't know whether Rose was still alive. __(3)__ She'd had a major stroke about 10 years ago and had gone on to suffer a series of minor strokes, descending into a sorry state of physical incapacity and dementia. __(4)__ I mentioned the dream to my partner over breakfast, but she wasn't much interested.

(a) Option 1 (b) Option 2
(c) Option 3 (d) Option 4

Q8. Sentence: Chinese Foreign Minister Qin Gang, who signed the communiqué with his Honduran counterpart Eduardo Reina, said it showed Honduras made "a choice to stand on the right side of history..."

By formally establishing diplomatic relations with China on March 26, 2023, Honduras has joined a growing list of countries that have recently switched recognition from Taipei to Beijing. __(1)__ Taiwan now has only 12 countries, besides the Vatican, with which it has diplomatic ties, including four small Pacific island nations, Eswatini in southern Africa, Paraguay, and six central American and Caribbean nations. __(2)__. Taiwan has accused Honduras of seeking financial assistance as a precondition to continue relations, and President Tsai Ing-wen said, after the switch, that Taiwan "will not engage in a meaningless contest of dollar diplomacy with China". __(3)__ She also accused China of "persistently [using] any and all means to suppress Taiwan's international participation, intensify its military intimidations... and disrupt regional peace". __(4)__

(a) Option 1 (b) Option 2
(c) Option 3 (d) Option 4

Q9. Sentence: He was a bloodhound in the library, hunting down fragments of Livy's Roman history, and discovering Cicero's "Pro Archia," in which the Roman statesman argued that the Greek poet Archias merited citizenship for his "human and literary studies."

For the Romans, Ms. Bakewell writes, the word humanitas meant being human, "but with added overtones of being refined, knowledgeable, articulate, generous, and well mannered." Her first humanists are the umanisti of 14th-century Italy, literary scholars specializing in studia humanitatis, or human studies, rather than Christian theology, for instance. __(1)__ Not that religious concerns were ignored: Dante may have been a "cosmic visionary," but his cosmos was Christian, so much so that he invented a Hell for his enemies and had to leave the pagan Virgil in Limbo. __(2)__ After Dante came Francesco Petrarca (Petrarch) and Giovanni Boccaccio. Petrarch (1304-1374), a poet and scholar, relished the peripatetic "literary life __(3)__ His biggest find was three of Cicero's letters in the cathedral library of Verona. These showed the private Cicero, the "informal writer and friend who reflected on human dilemmas and emotions," and mixed observations on current affairs with anecdotes from philosophy and literature. When Petrarch emulated Cicero in his letters, he revived the voice of humanitas. __(4)__

(a) Option 1 (b) Option 2
(c) Option 3 (d) Option 4

Q10. Sentence: It is a primal work of culture, a narrative cornucopia encompassing stories about the origins of heroes and kings; stories about nations, whose gnarly, almost metaphysical genealogical connections are bound up in the Latin root natus and its cognates; stories about ancestors told around campfires, in books and now in hyperspace.

Genealogy - the records of descent, the pedigrees of mortals and gods, of genos, race, kind and offspring - is one of the great feats of the human imagination: a vast collection of stories, both intimate and cosmic, __(1)__ that bind the living to the dead and to one another, the past to the present and the present to what is to come. __(2)__. The work of the imagination in metaphorical genealogies is obvious. In Hesiod and Homer, for instance, the gods of earth and sky produce the Titans, Cronus and his sister, Rhea, who gives birth to Zeus and other Olympian gods. __(3)__ Achilles is a great-grandson of Zeus through his grandfather Aeacus; through his mother, Thetis, he is a grandson of one of the gods of the sea. __(4)__

(a) Option 1 (b) Option 2
(c) Option 3 (d) Option 4

Q11. Sentence: Demolition squads of scholars have stencil-brushed the casing and every wire of the corpus; warning tape encircles the mother lode of fifty books, which are still capable of sending readers sky-high

Ernst Jünger is the intractable land mine of German literature. __(1)__. Millions of soldiers came home from the First World War missing a body part or a piece of their mind. __(2)__ Jünger, who learned not to flinch at the abyss–who positively courted shrapnel, was wounded seven times, and ended up one of the most decorated soldiers on the German side–came out with a style. Terse, clean, cool: he ran against the grain of the language and pressed the decadent accents of l'art pour l'art into the service of total war, treating incoming bombshells as if they were Madame Bovary's parasols. "The odd thing was that the little birds in the forest seemed quite untroubled by the myriad noise," he wrote of his first artillery onslaught on the Western Front. " (3) In the short intervals of firing, we could hear them singing happily or ardently to one another, if anything even inspired or encouraged by the dreadful noise on all sides." (4) .

(a) Option 1 (b) Option 2
(c) Option 3 (d) Option 4

Q12. Sentence: The updates follow edits made to books by Roald Dahl and Ian Fleming to remove offensive references to gender and race in a bid to preserve their relevance to modern readers.

(1) Several Agatha Christie novels have been edited to remove potentially offensive language, including insults and references to ethnicity. (2) Poirot and Miss Marple mysteries written between 1920 and 1976 have had passages reworked or removed in new editions published by HarperCollins to strip them of language and descriptions that modern audiences find offensive, especially those involving the characters Christie's protagonists encounter outside the UK. (3) Sensitivity readers had made the edits, which were evident in digital versions of the new editions, including the entire Miss Marple run and selected Poirot novels set to be released or that have been released since 2020, the Telegraph reported. (4)

(a) Option 1 (b) Option 2
(c) Option 3 (d) Option 4

Q13. Sentence: For instance, she insisted, contrary to some philosophers and theologians of her day, that mothers were not corrupting forces but foundational to the pursuit of knowledge.

In 1696, Damaris Cudworth Masham, an Englishwoman and a reluctant philosopher, stepped from obscurity to publish a book whose title - A Discourse Concerning the Love of God - concealed the feminist gems within. (1) . In 1705 she entered the public sphere again with another work, more radical than the first, titled Occasional Thoughts in Reference to a Vertuous or Christian Life, in which she argued that women should contribute to all intellectual subjects (2) 'I see no Reason why it should not be thought that all Science lyes as open to a Lady as to a Man.' (3) . Masham was also close to the Enlightenment philosopher John Locke. Their friendship endured for almost 20 years. (4) .

(a) Option 1 (b) Option 2
(c) Option 3 (d) Option 4

Q14. Sentence: highlighting the fragility of Puerto Rico's infrastructure and the paucity of United States federal aid to its citizens.

When Hurricane Fiona flooded regions of Puerto Rico with up to 30 inches of rain in September last year, the island was still recovering from hurricanes Irma and Maria, two catastrophic storms in 2017 during which nearly 3,000 people died. (1) . Fiona left close to 200,000 residents without drinkable water and 1.3 million without power, (2) . Puerto Rico has experienced intense tropical storms for centuries, but anthropogenic climate change is altering their frequency, strength and character. (3) . For the past few decades, for example, the island has suffered both monstrous hurricanes and deep droughts: an unusual combination. (4) .

(a) Option 1 (b) Option 2
(c) Option 3 (d) Option 4

Q15. Sentence: . While fertility issues cause many couples difficulty in becoming pregnant, it is still common that multiple viable embryos are available.

Since in vitro fertilisation was introduced in the late 1970s, more than 8 million children have been born using the process. During IVF, multiple eggs from the intended mother (or a donor) are fertilised by the sperm of the intended father. (1) . To decide which embryo should be transferred into the uterus of the mother, embryologists typically pick one based on morphology - the physical appearance of the embryo under the microscope, which can be suggestive of healthy development. (2) . In some IVF cases, the parents carry a genetic mutation that, if transmitted to the child, will lead to a severe early childhood disease (for example, cystic fibrosis). (3) . In these cases, an embryo is selected based on its DNA. A tiny biopsy of just a few cells is taken from the developing embryo, DNA is extracted from the cells, and only mutation-free embryos are considered for transfer. This form of preimplantation genetic testing (PGT) has been available for more than three decades, but it is irrelevant to most potential IVF parents, since only a minority of parents carry these rare mutations. (4) .

(a) Option 1 (b) Option 2
(c) Option 3 (d) Option 4

Answer Key

Exercise 1

1. (b)	2. (b)	3. (a)	4. (c)	5. (b)
6. (b)	7. (a)	8. (a)	9. (b)	10. (b)
11. (b)	12. (b)	13. (a)	14. (a)	15. (d)
16. (c)	17. (d)	18. (a)	19. (b)	20. (c)
21. (b)	22. (b)	23. (c)	24. (c)	25. (a)
26. (c)	27. (a)	28. (a)	29. (b)	30. (b)

Exercise 2

1. (b)	2. (b)	3. (b)	4. (a)	5. (c)
6. (a)	7. (c)	8. (a)	9. (a)	10. (b)
11. (b)	12. (d)	13. (b)	14. (c)	15. (b)
16. (b)	17. (c)	18. (a)	19. (c)	20. (c)
21. (b)	22. (b)	23. (a)	24. (a)	25. (b)
26. (b)	27. (a)	28. (b)	29. (b)	30. (a)

Exercise 3

1. (d)	2. (a)	3. (a)	4. (a)	5. (d)
6. (a)	7. (c)	8. (b)	9. (c)	10. (b)
11. (a)	12. (d)	13. (a)	14. (b)	15. (a)

Explanations

Exercise 1

1. Option (b) is correct as the statements before mention the negative impacts of air pollution and thus prove how "defying pressure to delay the scheme" is a good thing.

   Putting in (1) would disrupt the continuity of 1st and 2nd line that define the negative impacts.

   Similarly, (3) can be negated as it breaks the flaw between what is happening in London and what is happening in France.

   (4) may also seem like the correct place but putting in (2) forms a transition from "impacts of air pollution" to what the policies are as further sentences then define different policies; making (2) the better choice.

2. Option (b) is correct as the sentence provides contradiction to the statement "The addition of South Africa in 2010 did suggest that the club was interested in recasting the power structures of the international system." Therefore, the current power USA still holds better claim given its economic position.

   Putting in (1) breaks the flow as to who current members are and what they are planning to do by adding more countries.

   Putting in (3) is incorrect as the focus has now shifted on the achievements of BRICS and what they plan to do going forward.

   Putting in (4) is incorrect as the author is again discussing shortcomings of plans of BRICS nations and who current members are.

3. Option (a) is correct as "the pitch" is defined in the sentence "the Maghreb, have been sold a future as export hubs for green hydrogen". The pitch is seductive because of the future it proposes for that nation. Putting in (2), (3) and (4) does not clarify for whom the pitch is seductive, making them wrong.

4. Option (c) is correct as the sentence further elaborates on the statement "women are reckoned to be in the majority when it comes to getting a daily crossword fix."

   Putting in (4) is irrelevant as then we are talking about Carly Ray.

   Putting in (2) may seem correct but it disrupts the flow between "mental image" of Graham as a cruciverbalist as against women being better at solving crosswords.

   Similarly, putting in (1) is incorrect as the men dominate in solving crosswords and not making them, given the circumstances of being in a competitive environment.

5. Option (b) is correct as the statement "Even the most minor title now comes garlanded with quotes..." further elaborates on the fact as to how blurbs are controversial.

   Putting in (1) disrupts the flow of historical description as to how blurbs came into origination.

   Putting in (3) might seem suitable but it disrupts the flow of the view of publishers.

   The statement could be a conclusion in (4), but (2) seems to be a better place given the further elaboration.

6. Option (b) is correct as the question here refers to the grin the author had because of the famous song on which she starts to dance.

7. Option A is correct as the next statement then defines how psychiatric hospitals are still using PR on mental health for their benefits.

   Putting in (2) would break the flow about PR activities.

8. Option (a) is correct as the liberalism in Europe is compared with liberalism in United States.

   Putting in (2) would shift the discussion from "who a liberal is", making it the wrong place.

   Similarly, the question sentence doesn't have "qualities" mentioned in "but those liberal qualities....", making it the wrong place.

In the context of (4) "the word" refers to commitments which are not mentioned in the question statement.

9. The sentence fits best in (2) as it continues the comparison of Sontag, Malcolm and Didion. Putting in (1) is incorrect as the following sentence then has full names. (Rule of full name to surname should be followed).

   (3) and (4) do not mention Sontag and Malcolm at all, and hence should be avoided.

10. Option (b) is correct as "their" in "Their hypnotic power...." refers to the caricatures and elaborates on their exhibition.

    Putting in (1) would not be correct as further discussion is about paintings and not about the caricatures as mentioned in the question sentence.

    Similarly, putting in (3) would break the flow about an old woman by Quinten Massys.

    (4) is not the right place as the sentence is not a concluding one and the subject of caricatures has been discussed in the passage.

11. Option (b) is correct as the sentences "In the evening, he donned the mantle of a magician-priest and descended to his underground temple in the small cellar of his house..." define the double life.

    Putting in (1) would disrupt the reason as to why he was respectable. Putting in (3) is incorrect as the description is now about the spirits and not Sedatus.

    (4) may also seem appropriate but (2) is the better choice.

12. Option (b) is correct as the sentence previous to the blank mentions "atomic nucleus". (1) is negated as the question sentence does not talk about cell nucleus but talks about atomic nucleus.

    Putting in (3) and (4) is incorrect as the narrator's experiment/lecture is no longer being discussed.

13. Option (a) is correct as "In "Tradition and the Individual Talent" (1919), Eliot had announced the "impersonal theory of poetry," which held that poetry "is not the expression of personality, but an escape from personality."" This provides the "critical statement" referred to in question sentence.

    Putting in (2) would be incorrect as the next line then talks about Yeats and him being "impersonal"- without any reference to the question sentence.

    Putting in (3) and (4) would similarly be incorrect as there is no 'critical statement' to follow up then.

14. Option (a) is correct as the initial statements mention the doubts created in our minds because of climate crisis and the question statement is one such example. (2) may also seem lucrative but putting in (1) follows the same structure as "Some of us wonder whether we should bring children into this world." Making it the better choice.

    Given the above reasoning putting in (3) and (4) is irrelevant where the discussion has shifted to the life stages we go through.

15. Option (d) is correct as the "crisis" referred to in the question sentence is explained in the previous statement "The Radical Power of Killing Time." "People struggling to hang out, or else voicing concern and anxiety about how to hang out."

    Putting in (1) would obstruct the flow of activities that the author has been explaining. Same goes for (2). (3) is actually mid-sentence and should be avoided.

16. Option (c) is correct as the previous sentences give description of the photo.

    Putting in (1) is incorrect as "the photograph" cannot be followed by "a photograph". Putting in (2) is incorrect as it disrupts the flow of the "description" of the photo.

    Putting in (4) is incorrect as the discussion has now shifted to who commissioned the photo rather than what the photo is about.

17. Option (d) is correct as the sentence gives a conclusion of what "pathological" grief actually is.

    Putting in (1) may also seem correct given the generic statement but the passage defines "pathological or prolonged" grief later, making it unlikely to be the opening sentence.

    Putting in (2) would disrupt the flow about difference between normal and prolonged grief. Same goes for (3) - it disrupts the description of diagnosis.

18. Option (a) is correct as the question sentence is a general statement continuing the discussion on "cultural exchange".

    2 may seem lucrative as well but that would disrupt the shift to discussion about Iran/Persia. Same goes for (3).

    (4) is not correct as the question sentence is not a conclusion.

19. Option (b) is correct as the next statement defines how the dawn of age of Mammals happened.

    (3) may also seem lucrative but the question sentence is more titular in tone making it evident that it should come before the sentence "Dominant dinosaurs suffered a stroke of cosmic bad fortune, and our mammalian kin inherited a planet where they would no longer have to fear death in reptilian jaws." which defines how the dawn came.

Putting in (1) is incorrect as the flow is then shifted to fall of dinosaurs and not to the rise of mammals.

Similarly, putting in (4) is incorrect as the discussion has now shifted from the rise of mammals.

20. Option (c) is correct as "it" here refers to the "Global Risk Report" mentioned in the statement "Forum adopting this buzzword for its Global Risks Report, highlighting how '[c]oncurrent shocks, deeply interconnected risks and eroding resilience are giving rise to the risk of polycrises'."

Putting in (1) is incorrect as one is frustrated because of the term "polycrisis" and not by what it defines.

Putting in (2) would break the flow of "what polycrisis means" and the term reverberated. Also, the term cannot "explore" but can only refer to "interrelation of geopolitical, environmental and sociopolitical risks".

(3) is more appropriate than (4) as it connects to "Global Risk Report" in (3).

21. Option (b) is correct as the next statement then defines how they were the custodians.

Putting in (3) and (4) is irrelevant as the discussion is now focused on what kind of a monarch Abdullah is rather than on what he said.

(1) Might also seem correct but (2) is better-suited given the further explanation in coming sentences.

22. Option (b) is correct as "its" in the question sentence refers to "pragmatism" as defined in "Pragmatism itself was a flexible, loosely allied...."

Putting in (3) and (4) is incorrect as the passage then discusses Ambedkar and not pragmatism. (1) may seem correct but putting in (2) facilitates the transition of Global narrative from America to India.

23. Option (c) is correct as the statement "Keeping a secret is associated with lower life satisfaction..." continues the discussion on how the secret holders are hurt.

Putting in (1) and (2) would be incorrect as the author is discussing a specific incident here and does not require generic sentences like the question sentence.

4 seems lucrative as well but the question sentence is more of a beginning statement and fits (3) better.

24. Option (c) is correct as the statement "Parents who don't have the time, money or confidence to fight their council, or who don't speak English as a first language, are especially likely to see their children go without the help they need." explains the distress mentioned in the question statement.

Putting in (1) would disrupt the flow as to how the parents are trying to get help.

Putting in (2) would disrupt the flow of legal action.

(4) is negated as the question statement is neither a conclusion nor does it begin a new topic.

25. Option (a) is correct as it follows the parallelism: It is a yearning that will never be fulfilled. It is a point never reached. (2) may also seem appropriate but the previous sentence talks about the yearning and not the point. Putting in (3) and (4) would be incorrect as the point is now being referred to as "blue" and not "point".

26. Option (c) is correct as the question statement defines the ubiquitous drab aesthetic of Chicago as mentioned in the sentence "Instead, I was confronted with a drab and seemingly ubiquitous new aesthetic".

Putting in (2) may seem appropriate but (3) fits better given the adjectives in previous sentence.

Similarly, (4) may seem correct as well but "the look" should be defined before for the usage of "the".

(1) Is incorrect as the discussion there is about thoughts and not about Chicago apartments.

27. Option (a) is correct as "their" refers to Kierkegaard and Eliot as mentioned in previous sentence.

Similarly, (3) and (4) should be negated as both are mentioned singularly in previous sentence.

Option (b) may seem correct but the discussion has now moved to universities rather than the work by Kierkegaard and Eliot.

28. Option (a) is correct as "this" refers to "whether someone was virtuous, rather than whether they were interesting or useful or exhilarating. "

Putting in (2) would disrupt the flow of past to present day standards.

Putting in (3) and (4) is incorrect as the discussion has now shifted to present day virtue and beliefs and the question sentence does not fit there.

29. Option (b) is correct as the question sentence defines the success mentioned in "Could the secret to our species' success be our slowness in growing up?" (1) may seem appropriate but due to the above mentioned reason, (2) is better.

Similarly, (3) and (4) can be negated.

30. Option (b) is correct. As a continuation to "Life itself "presupposes in its possessor, whether animal or vegetable, a faculty of sensation that administers to its happiness, and that may consequently administer to its suffering," the author argues."- the question statement elaborates the fact that plants also have feelings.

Putting in (1) would be incorrect as the initial sentences talk about life/intelligence plants whereas question statement talks specifically about feelings.

Sentences around 3 then discuss the debate whereas the question statement states that plants do actually have feelings- this leads to contradictions.

(4) may seem lucrative but putting the question sentence there would then obstruct the flow of scientific experiments and findings.

EXERCISE 2

1. Option (b) is correct. Further sentences detail then why the details are murky. "The government has so far refused to reveal a full list of affected schools, although Essex is known to be the worst-hit county. Mr Gibb's explanation for the timing is that surveyors have been working over the summer, with findings delivered as recently as last week."

   Putting in (1) will disrupt the flow of "the announcement" related to structurally unsound buildings.

   Putting in (4) is irrelevant as no such details are mentioned in further sentences.

   (3) might also seem possible but "murky" means dark and the fact that the government is not providing any details makes it dark. So, (2) is more suitable.

2. Option (b) is correct as the sentences then follow "From today's perspective, this is not surprising. **Shakespeare is the world's most performed playwright**, whose name is as familiar in the classroom as on the stage."

   (1) also seems lucrative but putting in (2) would connect properly with Shakespeare being a world-famous playwright. Hence, the copies are not only in USA and Britain but also in Japan.

   Putting in (3) is incorrect as the discussion has now shifted to the fame of author due to First Folio.

   Putting in (4) is irrelevant as there are no related sentences around.

3. Option (b) is correct as "they" in the question sentence refers to "characters" mentioned in the statement "Yet it is the world and characters and images and stories themselves that stand in the way of that dream." Also, the question sentence explains how these characters stand in the way of that dream and the discussion is then continued in the sentence "A person personifying history is still a person, history warped by and warping a personality." Putting in (3) would be grammatically incorrect as "they" cannot refer to "a person" as mentioned in the previous sentence.

   Putting in (4) may also seem lucrative "they referring to short stories" but (2) is a better place given further sentences on the discussion.

   Putting in (1) would break the flow of contradiction brought in by the sentence "yet.."

4. Option (a) is correct and follows parallelism with the **sentence:** "For the prehistoric humans who carved them, they were mathematical notebooks and counting aids rolled into one."

   Putting In (2) is incorrect as a single bone is being discussed in previous sentences.

   On a similar line of grammatical errors, (3) is negated.

   Similarly, in (4) a single bone is described.

5. Option (c) is correct. The question sentence concludes the statements on how cold war liberalism was rehabilitated in 1990s.

   Putting in (1) would be incorrect time series representation.

   Putting in (2) would break the flow of the 3 sentences referring to the periods: 1940s and 1950s, 1960s and 1990s.

   Putting in (4) is irrelevant as the discussion has now shifted to the present.

6. Option (a) is correct. As the question sentence describes who Ambrose was, i.e., the bishop of Milan, it should come before "Ambrose has no time." This makes (1) the only viable choice.

7. Option (c) is correct as the sentence relates to "It's a spiritual shift, maybe even a metaphysical one."

   Putting in (1) may seem lucrative but further sentences define what reality is "not" whereas the question sentence defines "what reality is".

   Putting in (4) would be incorrect as it talks about Barba - Kay .

   (2) Was close but putting in (3) is better as it is more on a concluding note.

8. Option (a) is correct as the liberalism in Europe is compared with liberalism in United States.

   Putting in (2) would shift the discussion from "who a liberal is" making it the wrong place.

   Similarly, the question sentence doesn't have "qualities" mentioned in "but those liberal qualities...." making it the wrong place.

   In the context of (4) "the word" refers to commitments which are not mentioned in the question statement.

9. Option (a) is correct as the initial sentences talk about the importance of poetry historically and the question sentence talks about the same. It also explains the "objective social reality'

Other options may also seem lucrative but further sentences talk about the attempts to reinvent historical experience. Also these sentences do not comment on how poetry brought out the social reality.

So, (2), (3) and (4) can be negated.

10. Option (b) is correct as the statement "There was never anything that divided opinion as much as we presently witness with the transfusions", wrote the Parisian lawyer at Parlement, Louis de Basril, late in the affair, in February 1668 ...then the lines which tell what was discussed are in the present tense. The given statement which says "It is a topic of the salons, an amusement a" is apt here as this is also in the same tense and an extension of the statement. This is the correct position of the statement.

(1) is a little early to put in the statement as we have just begun talking about the topic.

(3) is negated as the context is about Deniz then and not about people talking about animal transfusion. (4) is negated as the given question sentence is not a conclusion sentence.

11. Option (b) is correct as the question statement complements the sentence "But knowing this wasn't enough to halt my obsessing." And explains why the author could not stop the obsessing, making it the best choice.

(1) May also seem appropriate but putting it there would break the flow of time periods when the author felt vulnerable.

Putting in (3) would break the flow of comparison of how others cope with stress.

(4) is irrelevant as the discussion is no more about the author's coping mechanism.

12. Option (d) is correct as the question sentence complements the statement "I take beauty to refer instead to a peculiar and particular experience, **both sensory and cerebral, often characterised by an inward responsiveness to an outward stimulation."**

Putting in (1) would break the flow as to how the portrait is beautiful. Putting in (2) would break the flow of the "judgement".

Putting in (3) would break the flow of what the author actually thinks of beauty.

13. Option (b) is correct as the question sentence elaborates on "...that some people see Buddhist meditation as more of a therapeutic than a spiritual undertaking, as basically palliative and not too profound"

Putting in (4) would be tempting but incorrect as now meditation is being shown as a rebellion against the very laws that govern human existence than being therapeutic.

Putting in (3) is negated on similar lines.

Putting in (1) would break the flow of "secular" ideas.

14. Option (c) is correct as the question is further elaborated in the sentences "We talk about the meaning of words, or linguistic meaning, the meaning of an utterance or of writing in a book. When we ask if human life has meaning, are we asking whether it has meaning in this semantic sense? Could human history be a sentence in some cosmic language?"

Putting in (1) would have been appropriate if the question was "What is meaning of life" as the further sentences then focus on that.

On similar lines (2) is negated.

Putting in (4) is negated as the answer has already been provided to the question asked in the sentence.

15. Option (b) is correct as "the dustbin of psychological enquiry" is then described in the sentence "Boys lusting after their mothers; girls desiring a penis - such are the luridly risible impressions that persist in the popular imagination."

Putting in (1) actually leaves the sentence "No longer" hanging.

Putting in (3) and (4) is incorrect as the discussion has now shifted to neuroscience.

16. Option (b) is correct as the "playbook" is defined in the sentence "Sweden ejected a Social Democrat prime minister and installed a moderate Conservative successor, while at the same time empowering the radical right Sweden Democrats party".

Putting in (1) would be incorrect as there is no description of what the playbook is, previously.

Putting in (3) would disrupt the discussion about Sanna Marin.

(4) is negated as the electoral outcome has been described in the passage already.

17. Option (c) is correct as the question statement defines how Paranoia is forever- as mentioned in the previous sentence.

Putting in (1) would break the flow of example as to how paranoia is a matter of self-defence.

Putting in (2) breaks the flow of the example.

Putting in (4) is tempting but (3) is more appropriate.

18. Option (a) is correct. Focus on the latter part of the question **sentence:** "The killer in El Paso, who law enforcement believes authored the memo, **is apparently no exception."** So, he is no exception to the belief, as mentioned in the previous sentence.

For (2) the white replacement theory is being explained and not a belief- so it can be negated. Similarly, (4) can be negated.

Putting in (3) would be tempting but then it would break the flow of "killer texts" and examples.

19. Option (c) is correct as "the containers" here refer to the rape kits. Putting in (1) would be tempting but (3) is more suitable as the later sentences then discuss the same that the evidence had not reached labs.

Putting in (2) is negated on the same grounds.

Putting in (4) is negated as this is not a concluding statement.

20. Option (c) is correct as the sentence continues the discussion on how the monk became a martyr and the aftereffects.

Putting in (1) would disrupt the flow about how his death took place. Same goes for (2). (4) is negated as the statement is not a conclusion.

21. Option (b) is correct as the sentence "It has prompted several contemporary secular thinkers..." explains how the legacy was formed. Putting in (3) and (4) is irrelevant as the discussion has now shifted to stoicism. (1) may be tempting as well but (2) is more appropriate given further elaboration.

22. Option (b) is correct as the question statement answers the question "But what *are* these holes and what are they made of?"

Putting in (1) may be tempting but the question statement is a specific one, making it less likely to be an opening statement.

Putting in (3) and (4) is irrelevant as doughnut holes are being described then.

23. Option (a) is correct. Panacea means "something that will cure all diseases or solve all problems and difficulties"- this relates to the previous sentence mentioning diseases.

On similar lines, (2), (3) and (4) should be negated.

24. Option (a) is correct as the sentence facilitates the transition to "Then a sergeant major pulled him aside for a brief interview, and assigned him to work the night shift in Echo Special......"

Putting in (2) may be tempting but the previous sentence mentions "single unit"- so Woods could not have guarded the "cellblocks".

Blanks (3) and (4) are irrelevant to the question sentence.

25. Option (b) is correct as "A joint investigation by the Guardian, the German weekly Die Zeit and SourceMaterial revealed in January that the vast majority of rainforest.." defines why the scrutiny has increased.

Putting in (1) would be incorrect as the question sentence is not a generic one (as is in the beginning of a passage) and provides more specific information.

Putting in (3) would be incorrect as in "all this might sound remote"- all this refers to the claims offset by business.

Putting in (4) is incorrect as the topic has now shifted to what environmentalists want and not the scrutiny.

26. Option (b) is correct as the question sentence relates to the statement "From the modest beachheads inside our browsers, they conquered, Blitzkrieg-style, our homes, cars, toasters, and even mattresses. Toothbrushes, sneakers, vacuum cleaners: our formerly dumb household subordinates were becoming our "smart" bosses. Their business models turned data into gold, favoring further expansion." Putting in (1) is tempting but should be negated as the flow should be "general to specific".

Putting in (3) is negated as "this mess" is defined in the previous sentence and not in the question sentence.

Putting in (4) is incorrect as the discussion is specifically on Google and not on Facebook.

27. Option (a) is correct as the further sentence then makes sense as to why the question was raised.

Putting in (2) would break the flow about the fate of the budget.

Putting in (3) and (4) is irrelevant as the discussion has now shifted to Modi's budget.

28. Option (b) is correct as the question sentence continues the discussion on how the term came into being and what it means.

Putting in (1) would be incorrect as there the author is trying to explain how the term has become "stale".

Putting in (3) and (4) would be incorrect as the question sentence gives a basic description about "mental hygiene" whereas the sentences around (3) and (4) give more specific details.

29. Option (b) is correct as the discussion then continues on the growing rate of depression.

Putting in (1) is tempting but the sentence talks about popularity of Broader's account which is mentioned in the sentence "The account has become a sensation, winning her more than 675,000 followers, and Broder's book of personal essays about her mental-health battles, also named *So Sad Today*, appeared in 2016." So, the question sentence should follow the given sentence.

Putting in (3) or (4) is irrelevant as in further sentences it has been established that Broader's popularity is a symbol of growing depression and putting the question sentence here would be redundant.

30. Option (a) is correct as the sentence "He leans in close over the small white plastic table in the corner and shares, in a gravelly voice, his penchant for Dominican women ('I'll take one as my next wife'), his distaste for Indian shop-owners ('They look at you like you in a zoo. Or the bottom of they shoe'), and his love for his two-year-old grandbaby Vanny." then elaborates on the question sentence. Putting in (2) would be tempting but then the discussion shifts to his days in the "box". On similar lines (3) and (4) are negated.

Exercise 3

1. Option (d) is correct as the line before talks about the movement of refugees and the question statement then further describes the types of refugees that are arriving.

   The statement we have is specific information whereas the passage begins with a generic statement such as "The French newspaper...". So, (1) is not correct.

   (2) and (3) may seem lucrative but (4) provides the best position given the subject is then continued.

2. Option (a) is correct as the statement then reads "Many are leaving the profession. Vacancies in England have almost doubled since the pandemic, according to a recent report."

   Therefore, the sentence becomes a natural successor of the statement "Many are leaving".

   As the sentence is not a conclusion- it cannot be the last sentence.

   Putting the sentence in (2) would obstruct the flow that teaching profession is losing its essence as teachers are being forced to teach outside their specialism.

   Similary, putting in (3) would obstruct the flow around discussions on salary of teachers.

3. Option (a) is correct. The sentence provides contradiction to the statement "Literary adaptations often turn out to be bankers on both stage and screen: they have the benefit of name recognition and established fanbases" giving the clue that adaptations are preferred and then brings us back to Literature with Dickens. The passage then continues the discussion around supremacy of literature. Hence, putting in (2), (3) and (4) would be incorrect given a would be incorrect because a generic sentence should be compared with a general statement itself and not with specific examples.

4. Option (a) is correct. The sentence provides contradiction to environmentally suitable actions as stated in "A couple of years ago, it campaigned against proposals for a national speed limit on autobahns - a move that would have helped reduce Germany's CO_2 emissions." making (1) the perfect gap for the sentence. "The FDP is the driving force behind German opposition to Brussels' plans to ban sales of new cars with internal combustion engines from 2035" and the question sentence have the same idea so they cannot be contradictory to each other, negating (2).

   (3) might seem correct as well. However, it would lead to 2 continuous sentences starting with "but", which is grammatically incorrect.

   It cannot be a concluding sentence as it has been further elaborated on in the passage. So, (4) should be negated.

5. Option (d) is correct as the sentence elaborates on the "furious response" mentioned in the line "Elsewhere, even allowing for the usual political game-playing, the response was authentically furious."

   As the statement is a specific example, it cannot be (1) as the passage is still stating a general idea in the initial sentences.

   Putting the sentence in (2) would obstruct the discussion on happenings in parliament.

   (3) seems lucrative but the MP being referred in the question here does not belong to Macron's MPs but to Les Republicans as per the question statement.

6. Option (a) is correct as further statements then define the "genius" mentioned in question sentence.

   Putting in (2) would obstruct the flow about "the objects in the galleries".

   If we put it in (3) there is no further explanation about how the genius poured and the same goes for (4).

7. Option (c) is correct. The statement should relate to something that the author is not sure about which leads him to "guess" something. Such is the situation in (3) blank. (1) would not make sense as he writes dreams that are vivid. So, he would not be guessing. Same goes for (2) and (4)

8. Option (b) is correct as the following statement then continues the discussion on Honduras. (1) also seems correct but if we put the question sentence in (1), it creates 2 continuous sentences starting with "Taiwan" at (2) which would be grammatically incorrect. Hence, there must be a sentence at (2). Using the same logic, (3) and (4) can be negated.

9. Option (c) is correct as the next line "His biggest find was three...." then continues the discussion on Cicero.

   Putting in (1) breaks the flow as we are still talking about Ms Bakewell there.

   Putting in (2) is misplaced as the sentence about Cicero comes back later.

   He should be followed by his and not vice versa. So, (4) can be negated.

10. Option (b) is correct as "it" in the question sentence refers to "Genealogy" and elaborates on it. Putting it in (1) would obstruct the flow of the starting sentence.

    Similarly, putting in (3) would obstruct the flow about Zeus and Achilles. Same goes for (4).

11. Option (a) is correct as the sentence elaborates about the present scenario of the land mine mentioned in the previous statement.

    Putting in (2) would be incorrect as the passage has then shifted to past tense whereas the question statement is in present tense.

    Same goes for (3) and (4).

12. Option (d) is correct as the question sentence changes the subject from stories of Agatha Christie to that of Roald Dahl and Ian Fleming. Therefore, it introduces a new topic making it the last sentence in the passage.

    Putting in (1) is not correct as further lines then discuss about characters from Agatha Christie's novels.

    Putting in (2) would break continuity about Agatha Christie.

    Putting in (3) might seem lucrative but the discussion again talks about Miss Marple- hence, it would disturb the flow of topics.

13. Option (a) is correct as the passage then continues how Damaris was a reluctant philosopher. Putting in (2) would disrupt the discussion around women getting access to science. Similar is the case with (3).

    Putting in (4) would be incorrect as the discussion is then about Damaris and her relations with Locke.

14. Option (b) is correct as "highlighting" in question statement refers to the problems created by Fiona mentioned in previous sentence.

    Putting in (1) would be incorrect as the flow of the paragraph would change.

    Putting in (3) would be incorrect as "highlighting refers to the problem", it does not refer to Puerto Rico. Same is the case with (4).

15. Option (a) is correct as the statement "To decide which embryo should be transferred..." the continues the discussion that an embryo needs to be chosen as there are viable options as mentioned in question sentence.

    Putting in (2) would be incorrect as the embryo has already been chosen here.

    Same goes for (3).

    Putting in (4) is incorrect as the question sentence is neither a conclusion nor does it start a new topic.

CHAPTER

24 Irrelevant Statement Questions

Find the Sentence that does not fit the Sequence in the Paragraph

This Question type made its appearance in the CAT 2011 and has been coming regularly ever since.

This question type is stated as follows: 'In each of the questions given below, four sentences are given labelled (a), (b), (c) and (d). Of these, three statements need to be arranged in a logical order to form a coherent paragraph/passage. From the given options, choose the option that does not fit the sequence'. The candidate has to choose one statement from a paragraph which is irrelevant.

The best way to solve this sentence is to use a strategy similar to Paragraph Jumbles with a combination of the Odd Man Out question type.

The most important step is to find the main idea in the paragraph that has been broken down into individual sentences and then find the sentence which is not aligned to either the main idea or the points of references.

Once the main idea has been identified and the supporting details are in place, it becomes easy to identify the sentence which is either not contributing to the paragraph or whose presence is making the paragraph lose its coherence.

That sentence which fits the above description will be the correct answer choice in this case.

LEVEL OF DIFFICULTY–I

Odd Man Out/Irrelevant Statement Questions

Directions for the questions (1-15): Five statements are given below, labelled as 1, 2, 3, 4 and 5. Of these, four statements are in logical order and form a coherent paragraph/passage. From the given options, choose the option that does not fit the sequence.

Q1.

1. When cheap imported honey began cutting into Arp's profits in the 1980s, he decided to send some of his hives with a beekeeper friend to pollinate in California.
2. In the early 1980s, when Mike Arp was just selling honey, he would lose about 5 per cent of his hives per year to disease or weather conditions. Around 2000, Arp's bees started dying in greater numbers.
3. And finally, what he still considers the bane of his business, a parasitic mite called Varroa destructor literally sucked the life out of his bees. The mite feeds on the bee's plump body, destroying the insect's immune system and other vital functions.
4. He experienced a nearly 100 per cent loss of his hives from an infestation of tracheal mites. Then he had to cope with the intrusion of Africanised 'killer' bees.
5. If Arp does not apply regular chemical treatments for the mites his colonies will die.

Q2.

1. What is not keeping CEOs up at night? Gender pay disparity.
2. Though CEOs seem to not, you know, care, regulators do: Many countries increasingly require companies to report gender pay data.
3. Female executives worldwide ranked it 6th.

4. A survey of the concerns of 740 CEOs and 780 C-suite executives worldwide found that US executives, who are overwhelmingly male, ranked 'implement equal pay for equal work' *last* on their list of 19 hot-button issues, rating it a half-dozen places below 'other'.
5. 'This disparity in rankings is cause for concern', write the authors of the report, which was commissioned by The Conference Board.

Q3.

1. I remember being depressed.
2. I felt like my mind suddenly became sick and twisted. I did not recognise my new self and wondered what had happened to the cheerful person I used to be.
3. It was a frightening state of mind that seemed to go on indefinitely. The very idea of waking up was riddled with dread.
4. A state of internal turbulence, apprehension and negativity about the future propelled the total collapse of a positive and optimistic attitude.
5. The past became meaningless, and the future ceased to exist. The world itself was not credible any more.

Q4.

1. Some people hear voices and believe others are plotting against them. Scientists do not know exactly what causes schizophrenia because the brain is so complex.
2. It is a severe mental illness affecting how a person thinks, feels and acts.
3. For those who already have schizophrenia, cannabis can trigger psychotic episodes.
4. Fewer than 1 per cent of Americans have schizophrenia, though the rate is difficult to measure because the illness can be hard to diagnose and many population studies omit people who are institutionalised, incarcerated, do not speak English or homeless, according to the National Alliance on Mental Illness.
5. In addition to delusions and hallucinations, symptoms can be as varied as a flat affect and lack of focus and motivation, disorganised thinking and speech, difficulty making decisions and expressing and managing emotions, and memory loss and other cognitive impairments.

Q5.

1. A study estimated that under current climate conditions and due to land clearing and fragmentation by dams, platypus numbers almost halved.
2. However, the platypus remains unlisted in most jurisdictions in Australia – except South Australia – where it is endangered.
3. The platypus is the sole living representative of its family, and genus, though a number of related species appear in the fossil record.
4. It is one of the five extant species of monotremes, the only mammals that lay eggs instead of giving birth to live young.
5. This led to the extinction of local populations across about 40 per cent of the species' range, reflecting ongoing declines since European colonisation, the researchers said.

Q6.

1. Chances are that if you are really following food trends, you will be discarding the piles of 'clean eating' recipe books in your kitchen in favour of a whole new swath of literature on dieting for mental health.
2. Which fad diet have you chosen to follow this year?
3. There is the 'Mad Diet', which promises 'easy steps to lose weight and cure depression', the 'Anti-Anxiety Diet', which is a 'Whole-Body Programme to Stop Racing Thoughts, Banish Worry and Live Panic-Free', or 'Food and Mood: Eating Your Way Out of Depression'.
4. One that helps you lose weight, or one that cures your mental health problems?
5. Of course, the food quacks are not the only ones cashing in on the current interest in mental health.

Q7.

1. It might well be that all moral agents would also accept a code of prudence or rationality, but this would not by itself show that prudence was part of morality.
2. So 'morality' cannot be taken to refer to every code of conduct put forward by a society.
3. Even in small homogeneous societies that have no written language, distinctions are sometimes made between morality, etiquette, law and religion.
4. Any definition of 'morality' in the descriptive sense will need to specify which of the codes put forward by a society or group count as moral.
5. And in larger and more complex societies, these distinctions are often sharply marked.

Q8.

1. A business is a productive organisation – an organisation whose purpose is to create goods and services for sale, usually at a profit.

2. Business ethics can thus be understood as the study of the ethical dimensions of productive organisations and commercial activities.
3. Business is also an activity.
4. Questions in business ethics are important and relevant to everyone.
5. One entity (for example, a person, an organisation) 'does business' with another when it exchanges a good or service for valuable consideration.

Q9.

1. The concept of eudaimonia, a key term in ancient Greek moral philosophy, is standardly translated as 'happiness' or 'flourishing' and occasionally as 'well-being'.
2. Each translation has its disadvantages.
3. The trouble with 'flourishing' is that animals and even plants can flourish but eudaimonia is possible only for rational beings.
4. The trouble with 'happiness' is that in ordinary conversation it connotes something subjectively determined.
5. A virtue is a trait that contributes to or is a constituent of eudaimonia and we ought to develop virtues, the eudaemonist claims, precisely because they contribute to eudaimonia.

Q10.

1. They then are in a position to assert that whatever choices increase the Good, that is, bring about more of it, are the choices that it is morally right to make and to execute.
2. The word deontology derives from the Greek words for duty (deon) and science (or study) of (logos).
3. In other words, deontology falls within the domain of moral theories that guide and assess our choices of what we ought to do (deontic theories), in contrast to those that guide and assess what kind of person we are and should be (aretaic [virtue] theories).
4. And within the domain of moral theories that assess our choices, deontologists - those who subscribe to deontological theories of morality - stand in opposition to consequentialists.
5. In contemporary moral philosophy, deontology is one of those kinds of normative theories regarding which choices are morally required, forbidden or permitted.

Q11.

1. It was less a polemic than a closely reasoned argument, fortified with lofty philosophic learning and grounded classroom experience.
2. Bloom took aim at my own generation (I was born in 1948), and its political complexion was anathema.
3. In 1987, it was a national sensation, a trigger-point for debate over the legacy of the sixties and its 'counter-culture'.
4. Looking for another book not long ago, I stumbled upon Allan Bloom's *The Closing of the American Mind.*
5. Subtitled 'How Higher Education Has Failed Democracy and Impoverished the Souls of Today's Students', Bloom's salvo attacked from the right.

Q12.

1. What's more, a 2017 Japanese government-commissioned study found that just over a third of new fathers wanted to take paternity leave, but didn't.
2. And in Japan in particular, where low birth rates have led to a scarcity of workers, if more fathers took parental leave and picked up more child-care responsibilities, mothers might have an easier time entering or staying in the workforce (and, in the longer run, Japanese families might be encouraged to have more children).
3. What's stopping Japanese dads from taking time off?
4. A country's work culture can limit the success of even generous policies.
5. Research indicates that dads who take leave are more involved as their kids grow up, which improves both the kids' and the dads' physical and mental health (and moms' too, no doubt).

Q13.

1. It is 1924.
2. Günter has come to Vienna from Coblenz specifically to meet the Professor, and a friend told him that Freud passes the corner of Hörlgasse and Liechtensteinstrasse everyday after lunch.
3. Günter Zeitz is thirty-three years old.
4. And, in the manner of certain very tall men, he habitually hunches his shoulders and lets his head hang forward.
5. His hair is black, unruly.

Q14.

1. The coronavirus (CoV) that is spreading panic across China and the world causes illnesses ranging from the common cold to more severe diseases such as Middle East Respiratory Syndrome (MERS-CoV) and Severe Acute Respiratory Syndrome (SARS-CoV).

2. The reason for panic in China is that the new strain of virus has been designated as a 'novel coronavirus' as it has not been previously identified in humans.
3. Chinese authorities have said that the strain of coronavirus is transmitted from person to person.
4. What makes it dangerous is that currently there is no specific treatment for the disease caused by this strain of coronavirus. But the symptoms can be treated based on the patient's clinical condition.
5. More than 200 cases have been reported across China and 4 people have died so far.

Q15.

1. I hated shaking hands with people because it was embarrassing.
2. And a happy examiner is always better than an indifferent one.
3. I was born with a condition called hyperhidrosis – a fancy word for sweaty palms.
4. I tried placing handkerchiefs between my hand and the paper, and I even tried those plastic gloves doctors wear – nothing helped. Eventually, I just had to grin and bear it, and my teachers had to accept puddles instead of papers.
5. Writing was even worse. Within minutes, my notebook would turn into a swimming pool.

IRRELEVANT STATEMENT QUESTIONS

CAT Level Exercises

Odd Man Out/Irrelevant Statement Questions

***Directions for the questions (16-45)*:** Five sentences are given below. Four of them can be re-arranged to form meaningful paragraph. Key in the number of the sentence which is out of context.

Q16.

1. I had grown up in a mountain town of the Dominican Republic and emigrated to New York City just before my 12th birthday.
2. As a high-school student with still-shaky English proficiency, I found a collection of Plato's dialogues in a garbage pile near my house in Corona, Queens.
3. My mother had left the Dominican Republic a few years earlier, secured the only job she could get, earning the minimum wage in a garment factory.
4. Like many immigrants, we were poor, exposed, and disoriented by our uprooting.
5. In 1985, we entered New York City's overcrowded public school system where the free lunches supplied a good portion of our sustenance.

Q17.

1. Her drive had been easily identified by her supervisors, and she was continually rewarded with broader responsibilities.
2. Melanie, a 47-year-old partner at a top civil engineering firm in Boston could not accept the fact that she was staring at tacky art in a physician's waiting room.
3. But she was a fighter and would not be deterred.
4. She could deal with the unexplained weight loss and the yellow tint that had altered the colour of her eyes.
5. Sitting there, her thoughts drifted back to her advisor in college, who cautioned her that it would not be easy to succeed in a male-dominated field.

Q18.

1. It was bell hooks who planted the seed of a book in my brain.
2. In a 2013 in-conversation event with Melissa Harris-Perry, she said she didn't trust the Internet, that a plug could be pulled at any time and that everything we put there could one day be lost.
3. But her writing wasn't only on feminist fractures. She was prolific, writing dozens of books across subjects – race, feminism, class, capitalism, masculinity, academia, children's rights, spirituality, and love.
4. I was writing for the Internet at the time – ephemeral articles that often got swept away on busy timelines.
5. Hearing her musings persuaded me to slow down on putting my work online, and instead seek to put my political energy towards writing something physical that could be held and referred to, handed to someone, used as a tool.

Q19.

1. Randy Blythe, frontman of the US metal band remembers the first time he performed live sober.
2. The music industry is full of high-risk situations when it comes to substance abuse and addiction. For many, touring is the most challenging aspect of what they do.

3. It was 18 October 2010 and the bands were opening for Metallica in Brisbane, Australia.
4. "I was thrown into the lion's den," he says.
5. "On stage in front of 14,000 people, weeping uncontrollably - thank God I had long hair so it covered my face."

Q20.

1. On Radio 4's Desert Island Discs last year, as in a speech given on Monday, he appeared most animated when speaking of his feelings towards his parents, wife, and children.
2. In 2021, our society is more honest than it used to be about the degree to which such relationships can and do go wrong.
3. Sir Keir Starmer's sincerity when he talks about family is palpable.
4. The bonds between generations, and couples, clearly mean a great deal to him, as they do to most people.
5. A progressive politics with a strong commitment to family relationships is certainly possible, but needs more details.

Q21.

1. Having gained a brief but widespread ascendancy in the first half of the 20th century, the phrase gradually faded from popular memory and was replaced by the expression "mental health" in the 1950s.
2. In English, the term "mental hygiene" likely sounds a bit stale.
3. Mental hygienists, promising an easy fix to mental illness, gained almost universal support by the 1920s and 1930s.
4. Translated as *xinli weisheng* or *jingshen weisheng,* the phrase has been a mainstay in Chinese psychiatric policy for close to a full century.
5. Yet the Second World War changed the course of their trajectory.

Q22.

1. "Yesterday was a really bad day for him," a Georgia sheriff's captain remarked of the suspect.
2. The fear, anger, and heartbreak felt when news broke that eight people had been killed in shootings in Atlanta on Wednesday, six of them women of Asian descent, was multiplied by the extraordinary response of authorities.
3. Police said that the suspect "gave no indicators" that his actions were racially motivated, talking of a sex addiction and saying he was trying "to take out that temptation."
4. Denouncing assaults and avoiding overtly racist terms such as "kung flu" is not enough.
5. For many Asian Americans, it was a further evidence that crimes against their community are not being taken seriously, even as they surge.

Q23.

1. A year ago, as the reality of Covid lockdown hits home, evangelists for the work of Marcel Proust spotted a window of opportunity.
2. A significant uplift in online sales was duly reported.
3. In the last years of his life, toiling incessantly on the vast text, Proust rarely left the cork-lined cocoon of his bedroom.
4. Domestic confinement had eliminated the usual distractions, and pandemic reading lists invariably carried a namecheck for Proust's monumental seven-volume classic, *In Search of Lost Time.*
5. Cynics might point out that most purchases were limited to Swann's Way, the first book in the series; only a post-pandemic audit will be able to establish how many readers journeyed through all 4,215 pages.

Q24.

1. A Hong Kong company named Hapilabs offers an electronic fork that tracks how many bites you take per minute in order to prevent hasty eating: shovel food in too fast and it vibrates to alert you.
2. Hand-in-glove with the authorities that promote self-scrutiny are the businesses that sell it, in the form of weight-loss foods, medicines, services, surgeries, and new technologies.
3. It is also true that the masters of the universe in business and government seem attracted to it, perhaps because stern self-discipline is how many of them attained their status.
4. A report by the consulting firm McKinsey & Co predicted in May 2012 that "health and wellness" would soon become a trillion-dollar global industry.
5. "Obesity is expensive in terms of health-care costs," it said before adding, with a consultantly chuckle, "dealing with it is also a big, fat market."

Q25.

1. We had school (which was not the big deal it is today), and we also had what I call a hunter-gatherer education.
2. When I was a child in the 1950s, my friends and I had two educations.

3. We played all weekend and all summer long.
4. We played in mixed-age neighbourhood groups almost every day after school, often until dark.
5. Over the same decades that children's play has been declining, childhood mental disorders have been increasing.

Q26.

1. In my book, *Free to Learn* (2013), I document these changes, and argue that the rise in mental disorders among children is largely the result of the decline in children's freedom.
2. School fosters competition, not co-operation and children there are not free to quit when others fail to respect their needs and wishes.
3. If we love our children and want them to thrive, we must allow them more time and opportunity to play, not less.
4. Yet policymakers and powerful philanthropists are continuing to push us in the opposite direction.
5. Toward more schooling, more testing, more adult direction of children, and less opportunity for free play.

Q27.

1. He vowed that he would do "whatever it takes" to protect the euro from aggressive speculation by bond markets.
2. Mr. Draghi eased the pressure and defused a crisis that, left unchecked, posed an existential threat to the European Union.
3. During the eurozone debt crisis, the then president of the European Central Bank, Mario Draghi, deployed a phrase that demonstrated the transformative power of strong leadership in dangerous circumstances.
4. Fall in indices of Wallstreet of the USA caused a global worry as well.
5. The spirit of "whatever it takes" is required this summer from richer nations, if a durable and morally just exit from the Covid-19 pandemic is to take place.

Q28.

1. Conveniently for a government that made cutting the deficit its raison d'etre, this manoeuvre took public spending on higher education off the books, and an accounting assumption was made that the government-backed loans would be repaid.
2. Around a decade has passed since David Cameron's coalition government tripled the cap on university tuition fees to £9,000, while drastically reducing direct grants to higher education institutions in England.
3. Ten years on, there are clear signs that this funding model and the marketised campus culture it created is becoming dysfunctional.
4. In Whitehall, alarm bells are ringing over the distinctly sub-prime state of the student loan book, which the Office for National Statistics now insists is included in national accounts.
5. The current estimate is well over 50 per cent, costing the public purse about £1 trillion by 2040.

Q29.

1. Some 2,700 years ago in the ancient city of Sam'al, in what is now modern Turkey, an elderly servant of the king sits in a corner of his house and contemplates the nature of his soul. His name is Katumuwa.
2. As I watched the irregular wavy lines march across the screen, with spikes provoked by his perceptions of events such as the banging of a door, I wondered at the nature of the consciousness that generated those signals.
3. It instructs his family, when he dies, to celebrate "a feast at this chamber: a bull for Hadad harpatalli and a ram for Nik-arawas of the hunters and a ram for Shamash, and a ram for Hadad of the vineyards, and a ram for Kubaba, and a ram for my soul that is in this stele."
4. Katumuwa believed that he had built a durable stone receptacle for his soul after death.
5. He stares at a basalt stele made for him, featuring his own graven portrait together with an inscription in ancient Aramaic.

Q30.

1. From Belfast's Botanic Gardens to the Royal Botanic Garden in Benmore, to the National Botanic Garden of Wales in Llanarthne and the Royal Botanic Gardens at Kew, they have given visitors precious space, greenery and fresh air.
2. For those fortunate enough to live within reach of one of them, the UK's botanical gardens have provided a remarkable escape from the travails of the pandemic.
3. Indeed, in the past they have most frequently been framed as mainly scientific institutions, important hubs of botanical research.
4. As spring arrives in its fickle fits and starts, they provide breathtaking displays of seasonal flora:
5. Kew, carpets of sky-blue scilla and groves of flowering magnolia; at Benmore, tides of rhododendrons.

Q31.

1. They have been more eagerly awaited than usual this year because the implosion of the England men's team in the Ashes.
2. This suggested there was something rotten in the state of the domestic game.
3. It may be a little early to be thinking about spring, but the publication of the first-class cricket fixtures hints that it is not too far away.
4. The ECB is trying to shoehorn four men's competitions into a packed summer: the championship; a 50-over cup; the 20-over blast.
5. Publication was delayed while different interest groups argued over what structure the sport should have.

Q32.

1. As grim as the crisis in Kazakhstan already appears, it could soon look much worse.
2. Modest concessions did not address the deeper grievances: corruption in a nation rich in oil, where many still struggle to get by while the elite cream off the cash.
3. Authorities reported on Thursday that dozens of protesters and at least 12 members of the police and security forces were dead.
4. At least 2,000 protesters have been arrested.
5. With the Internet largely blocked and other communications severely hampered and with reports of gunfire in Almaty, the country's largest city, the true toll may be much higher.

Q33.

1. The threat to American democracy may be greater today than when the insurrectionist mob swept into the US Capitol one year ago.
2. Attempting to prevent the peaceful transfer of power following a free and fair election.
3. It is hard to know where one might begin to tackle the sprawling right-wing disinformation ecosystem.
4. But if the danger appears less immediate, addressing it is no less urgent.
5. Joe Biden is ensconced in the White House and with the passage of time, the shock of their lethal assault has faded.

Q34.

1. And so here we are: among the dark, blustery, not so cold days of between-Christmas-and-new-year.
2. Though the one certainty of early 2022 is the Omicron variant.
3. A time to say goodbye to 2021, the year everyone hoped would be better than 2020, and that wasn't, really.
4. The temptation is to switch on the TV and to revel in the teeming joys of all that the bafflingly myriad streaming services have to offer.
5. The year many hoped would mean the end of the pandemic.

Q35.

1. For Christians, the Christmas narrative offers an annual reminder of the ethical duty to offer hospitality to the stranger.
2. Both identify Christ with the predicament of all who are vulnerable, exiled and in need.
3. The strained circumstances of the birth of Jesus in a Bethlehem stable and the holy family's subsequent flight from Herod into Egypt
4. But 70 years on, proliferating barriers and fences along European borders testify to a harsher mood.
5. For non-believers - most of us these days - there is always the reference point of international law.

Q36.

1. Russia's president has steadily broadened the scope of his demands to encompass defence and security arrangements in Europe as a whole.
2. What Putin wants, in effect, is to turn the clock back to the 1990s, before former Warsaw Pact countries such as Poland and ex-Soviet republics such as Estonia joined NATO.
3. Despite assurances at last summer's G7 summit in Cornwall that "America is back," Biden is focused primarily on his domestic agenda and on containing China.
4. The recent barrage of threats from Vladimir Putin is no longer solely to do with Ukraine.
5. Even if current tensions on Ukraine's borders do not ultimately result in open conflict, this deliberate escalation bodes ill for 2022.

Q37.

1. "And when human relations change there is at the same time a change in religion, conduct, politics and literature."
2. Virginia Woolf pinned it to "on or about" December 1910: the date at which human nature changed.
3. "All human relations have shifted," she wrote.
4. With less hyperbole, we might suggest that it was in the late 1950s that Black America transformed - not just with the civil rights movement, but across the whole spectrum of creativity and conduct.
5. But some of the most quotidian parts have gone under-examined, such as clothes.

Q38.

1. This gene encodes a transcription factor (p53) that normally regulates the cell cycle and prevents genomic mutations.
2. It was named after two American physicians, Frederick Pei Li and Joseph E Fraumenl, Jr.
3. These physicians recognised that the syndrome is linked to germline mutations of the p53 tumour suppressor gene.
4. Li-Fraumeni syndrome is a rare cancer predisposition hereditary disorder characterised as autosomal dominant.
5. Another variant of Li-Fraumeni that remains somewhat controversial is a mutation of the CHEK2 gene.

Q39.

1. The government's notice to Twitter after it reinstated several handles that mentioned a controversial hashtag, which the former wanted blocked, marks a critical point in an already uneasy relationship between a powerful government and an influential technology platform.
2. The issue pertains to tweets put out by some handles on the ongoing farmer protests as also a hashtag that suggested that a farmer genocide was being planned.
3. A showdown seems inevitable now, what with the government threatening Twitter with penal action for not complying with its orders.
4. The Ministry of Electronics and IT ordered these handles (257 URLs and one hashtag) to be blocked on the grounds that they were spreading dangerous misinformation about the protests.
5. In a very sensitive setting, one that at least at one point was simmering with the potential for large-scale violence, provocation of any kind is unacceptable.

Q40.

1. Scientists weren't sure what species the fossils belonged to.
2. Prior work suggested that the sediments in which the hobbit fossils were found were about 12,000 to 95,000 years old.
3. The first hobbit fossils were found in 2003 in Liang Bua cave on the Indonesian island of Flores.
4. Examination of the fossils suggested that Homo floresiensis belonged to a unique branch of the human lineage.
5. But they found that the individuals were equipped with grapefruit-size brains and would have stood just 3 feet (1 metre) tall.

Q41.

1. This time it is the Union Territory of Puducherry, and that too at a time when elections are expected soon.
2. After all, it does not have a single elected MLA here.
3. After Karnataka and Madhya Pradesh, yet another Congress government has fallen.
4. Now there is chatter that President's Rule will be used to delay elections, to help BJP build a base.
5. As the pygmification of India's biggest opposition party continues apace, it is non-party actors, such as Punjab farmers today, who will step into the vacuum to voice social and political grievances.

Q42.

1. Prayuth accused the demonstrators of bringing Thailand to the brink of collapse.
2. In the United States, the president Donald Trump recently levelled thinly veiled threats to would-be violent agitators as demonstrations over racial injustice unfolded.
3. Thailand's Prime Minister Prayuth Chan-ocha aired a dire warning to the thousands of protesters who thronged the streets of Bangkok for days in the summer of 2020 demanding his resignation.
4. "If that happens, just wait, everybody will be on fiery land, engulfed in flames," he said.
5. Prayuth and other political leaders eyeing masses of protesters often see forces of destruction lurking in even peaceful demonstrations.

Q43.

1. It is one of archaeology's great tasks to understand how this happened.
2. In the time before the invention of writing, communication was almost always person-to-person: people met with one another to transfer ideas, designs and technologies.
3. By excavating artefacts, archaeologists can examine the spread of a new pottery design, say, or the flourishing of a particular type of stone tool.
4. Here, archaeologists might refer to "diffusion" among the groups, a vague 19th-century term suggesting that the movement of cultural practices between peoples was an uncomplicated process, like ink moving across blotter paper.

5. My 'aha' moment about these questions came 20 years ago. I was visiting a small museum in southern Arizona and saw on the wall a 19th-century photo of a white woman with a tattooed face.

Q44.

1. Bitcoin, the first cryptocurrency, was introduced by Satoshi Nakamoto, a pseudonym used by the mysterious originator. It turned our understanding of currency on its head.
2. What we have are digital currencies designed for decentralised operations, cutting out a regulated intermediary like a bank.
3. Conventional money or fiat currency, is issued by the state.
4. In the flux after the 2008 financial crisis, an extraordinary instrument dubbed cryptocurrency was created.
5. Inspired by the philosophy of "self-sovereign identity" cryptocurrencies are an asset which are not anyone's liability, neither is there a single authority or institution to maintain records.

Q45.

1. With its richness of languages, nowhere is this simultaneously cognitive and romantic project more valid than in India.
2. Parents today are making widely varying language choices for their children, depending upon their different circumstances and desires.
3. International Mother Language Day is celebrated on 21 February to mark the centrality of multilingualism for building an inclusive world, where no child is left behind.
4. And while we absolutely must help diversity thrive, that cannot be by any narrow orthodoxy.
5. The medium of instruction often comes under flint-eyed scrutiny.

PRACTICE EXERCISES ON IRRELEVANT STATEMENT QUESTIONS

Exercise 1

Odd Man Out/Irrelevant Statement Questions

Directions for the questions (1-12): Four statements are given below, labelled (a), (b), (c) and (d). Of these, three statements are in logical order and form a coherent paragraph/passage. From the given options, choose the option that does not fit the sequence.

Q1.

(a) Ontology has frequently been understood as the theory of the ultimate classes of existents or entities and of characteristics of and structures that belong to all entities merely as such.

(b) Understood in these way acts of human cognition, for example, like all other events, obviously fall within the domain of ontology.

(c) There are, thus, also certain special or 'regional' ontology, which attempt to exhibit the essential characteristics and structures peculiar to the members of each of the ultimate classes of entities - of minds (and mental acts), physical bodies and so on.

(d) But even given this it is still not strictly true, as Gustav Bergmann has often said, that '...epistemology is but the ontology of the knowing situation'.

Q2.

(a) The discovery of the giant planet has puzzled the astronomers, effectively throwing a wrench in planet formation theories.

(b) Planets close to their stars, like Earth, coalesce from small asteroid-like bodies born in the primordial disk of dust and gas that surrounds a forming star.

(c) An international team of astronomers, led by a University of Arizona graduate student, discovered the planet HD 106906 b around a Sun-like star.

(d) 'This system is especially fascinating because no model of either planet or star formation fully explains what we see', said Vanessa Bailey, who led the research.

Q3.

(a) Governments, city-planners and conservationists can work together to predict and plan in advance for urbanisation's threats to nature.

(b) According to the report, humans are building the equivalent of a city the size of Vancouver every week.

(c) Having information on cities' impacts to these endangered species and protected areas enables planners to shape the growth of cities before it is too late and to implement more sustainable urban planning.

(d) However, a lack of funding, especially in developing countries, may prevent the implementation of smart-growth plans.

Q4.

(a) Philosophers and seers since long have mull over fundamental questions regarding our existence.
(b) Is our existence a random event in evolution or is there a greater principle in life with meaning and purpose?
(c) The Upanishads say, 'neti, neti' - not this, not this - that the true meaning of life is that something which is beyond our intellectual grasp, as it perhaps lies in the stillness beyond the workings of the mind.
(d) This enquiry has served as catalyst for evolution of ideas, philosophical and scientific quests, and a trigger for some of the greatest spiritual odysseys.

Q5.

(a) This can be or may not be the only way.
(b) By holding onto resentment, all you are doing is continuing and intensifying your own sadness.
(c) Learn to let things go, especially those which are unchangeable and that are in the past.
(d) This feeling will eat at you from the inside and cause stress.

Q6.

(a) Corporate Social Responsibility has entered India's legal corridors.
(b) In India, traditionally, pro bono legal work was carried out by lawyers who had dedicated themselves to helping society.
(c) Top law firms and lawyers are doing pro bono so that they can give back to society.
(d) There are a number of socially aware and generous souls who are increasingly lending their expertise for pro bono work.

Q7.

(a) Commuters today are more likely to be plugged into their phones, scrolling content compressed for our lowered attention spans.
(b) Penguin India has introduced Esingles, digital downloads described as 'byte-sized stories easily completed in the course of a daily commute or lunch hour'.
(c) The internet has created new demands on our time, and a stream of alerts, updates and tweets leave us impatient with the long-winded.
(d) As information is pared down, it seemed unlikely books would be left behind, so it is no surprise that 'byte-size' and 'quick' are adjectives now associated with a once-leisurely activity.

Q8.

(a) Dinets first observed the behaviour in 2007 when he spotted crocodiles lying in shallow water along the edge of a pond in India with small sticks or twigs positioned across their snouts.
(b) The behaviour potentially fooled nest-building birds wading in the water for sticks into thinking the sticks were floating on the water.
(c) The crocodiles remained still for hours and if a bird neared the stick, they would lunge.
(d) Crocodiles are way clever than thought about generally.

Q9.

(a) The competitive pressures in the environment have radically altered the context in which Human Resource services are delivered in Indian organisations.
(b) The HR Competencies, in other words, differentiate outstanding performers from average performers in the HR function.
(c) The traditional role of HR, based on the image of a transaction and administrative oriented HR practitioner providing services to a set of customers, is undergoing change.
(d) With the focus moving towards integrating HR into strategic planning of the organisation, another dimension is added to the picture of HR service delivery.

Q10.

(a) Every campaign leader knows how to pick up and kiss a child in the crowds, how to hug an old widow, how to chant with the pundits, and show abeyance to the Mullahs.
(b) Did anyone hit at 'quality' for infrastructure, amenities, education, health and finally governance.
(c) Politics is still a game of money, mind and manipulations.
(d) False promises are not entirely a sin, but let these be redeemed by true, professional and quality governance that shows at the end of the tenure.

Q11.

(a) The emerging web services paradigm offers the promise of new efficiencies and improve integration designed to enhance collaboration between internal and external applications.
(b) For example, web services can serve as a bridge between an e-procurement application and an internal inventory system.
(c) Although, web services are relatively nascent and adoption rates currently low, it is critical for ERP vendors to begin taking steps to prepare for their rapidly maturing initiative.
(d) As items are purchased through e-procurement application, a web service specific to inventory

reduction can be invoked to adjust inventory levels.

Q12.

(a) Much of the modern use of metals happens behind closed doors of corporations, under the veil of trade secrets.
(b) He chooses to restrict his analysis to metals and metalloids, which could face more critical constraints because many of them are relatively rare.
(c) Even if we can find out how certain metals are used, it may not always be possible to determine the proportions they are used in.
(d) The authors compromise was to account for the use of 80 per cent of the material that is made available each year through extraction and recycling.

EXERCISE 2

Odd Man Out/Irrelevant Statement Questions

Directions for the questions (1-9): Four sentences are given below. Four of them can be re-arranged to form meaningful paragraph. Key in the number of the sentence which is out of context.

Q1.

(1) The MOEF project itself is a professional ministry where executive decision-making with regard to environmental clearances is exercised.
(2) The Ministry of Environment and Forests has brought back the quota licencing regime.
(3) Projects have to be cleared or refused on the basis of an objective criteria and not ministerial discretions.
(4) It is time that heads of government took it upon themselves to establish an effective grievances redressal system.

(a) 1
(b) 2
(c) 3
(d) 4

Q2.

(1) Even London's latest pet project - proving that Russia cannot host an Olympics as successfully as Beijing or London - could easily backfire.
(2) For more than two decades, August has been the most cruel month for Russian leaders.
(3) The August 1991 coup led to the departure of President Mikhail Gorbachev and the end of the Soviet Union.
(4) The August 1998 debt default and ruble collapse laid waste to President Boris Yeltsin's free-market reforms and resulted in the sacking of his prime minister, Sergei Kiriyenko.

(a) 1
(b) 2
(c) 3
(d) 4

Q3.

(1) Commercial use of drones is banned by the Federal Aviation Administration (FAA), although it makes some exceptions such as for hobbyists' flights in unpopulated areas where the aircraft stays in sight of a human operator.
(2) These sites will help the FAA understand how to integrate UAS into American airspace, which Congress has told it to do by September 2015.
(3) It is believed that Amazon's new project will pose a new challenge to the FAA operations.
(4) But the skies are opening up: by the end of December, the FAA will select six UAS testing sites from a list of 25 applicants in 24 states.

(a) 1
(b) 2
(c) 3
(d) 4

Q4.

(1) The Assad regime depends on its patrons in Iran and the Iranian-backed Hezbollah militia in neighbouring Lebanon.
(2) The Sunni-led opposition is similarly turning to its regional patrons.
(3) These regional players, with their own agendas, will keep pulling Syria apart until a functioning national government can be re-established.
(4) Syrian society is considered fractured and dissonant.

(a) 1
(b) 2
(c) 3
(d) 4

Q5.

(1) It has become something of a cliché to predict that Asia will dominate the twenty-first century.
(2) It is a safe prediction, given that Asia is already home to nearly 60 per cent of the world's population and accounts for roughly 25 per cent of global economic output.

(3) Asia is also the region where many of this century's most influential countries - including China, India, Japan, Russia, South Korea, Indonesia and the United States - interact.

(4) These developments both reflect and reinforce heightened nationalism throughout the region.

(a) 1

(b) 2

(c) 3

(d) 4

Q6.

1. This indicates a deep lack of concern for citizens on the part of the administrators.
2. Before this year will have ended, the French parliament will have enacted a comprehensive pension overhaul, which is essential not only to putting France's public finances on a sound and sustainable footing, but also to shoring up confidence in the eurozone in 2014 and beyond.
3. This effort has gained broad public acceptance because it was fair; both retirees and working people will contribute, as will companies and households.
4. For the first time, pension reform has been carried out in France in continuous consultation with employers' associations and trade unions.

(a) 1

(b) 2

(c) 3

(d) 4

Q7.

(1) The concept of 'sustainable harmony' can be promoted by publishing indices of personal well-being and environmental preservation, alongside standard GDP data.

(2) The desire to help others without consideration for ourselves is not just a noble ideal.

(3) Selflessness raises the quality and elevates the meaning of our lives, and that of our descendants; in fact, our very survival may even depend on it.

(4) Studie's have shown that individuals and societies can learn to be more altruistic.

(a) 1

(b) 2

(c) 3

(d) 4

Q8.

(1) The problem with charities is that they have little incentive to become more efficient.

(2) Yet the real value is in training people to deliver for themselves, at a local scale - empowered rather than controlled, creative rather than rehearsed and working by choice rather than in desperation.

(3) There is no simple way to monitor the quality and efficiency of a charity - especially one devoted to long-term changes (that is, investments) rather than daily delivery of services.

(4) Since starting my own non-profit organisation, I look at other nonprofits with new eyes.

(a) 1

(b) 2

(c) 3

(d) 4

Q9.

(1) Nowadays, many people seem to be more relaxed than ever about nationality, with the Internet enabling them to forge close connections with distant cultures and people.

(2) But states remain extremely sensitive about their borders' inviolability.

(3) A great game is beginning among Asia's great powers, and there are scant rules in place to manage how it will be played.

(4) After all, territory - including land, oceans, air space, rivers and seabeds - is central to a country's identity, and shapes its security and foreign policy.

(a) 1

(b) 2

(c) 3

(d) 4

Exercise 3

Odd Man Out/Irrelevant Statement Questions

Directions for the questions (1-12): Four statements are given below, labelled (a), (b), (c) and (d). Of these, three statements are in logical order and form a coherent paragraph/passage. From the given options, choose the option that does not fit the sequence.

Q1.

(a) Heavy rain brought by cyclone Phailin, which hit the state coast led to floods in the city.

(b) Mohapatra said the government had provided relief to the flood-hit by road services and stooped air dropping operations.

(c) The Cyclone has claimed 21 lives.

(d) As thousands of marooned people cried for food, the State Government in tandem with Central agencies stepped up relief and rescue operations.

Q2.

(a) Basic problems of an economy are solved by a controlled and regulated price mechanism.
(b) In mixed economy, private and public sectors coexist.
(c) In mixed economy, basic economy problem are solved by both, price mechanism and economic planning.
(d) It is an economy characterised by existence of certain features of both capitalistic and socialistic economy.

Q3.

(a) Fifteen or twenty years ago, there were few summer camps for children.
(b) Some camps are also operated by welfare societies, boy scouts and girl guides.
(c) Because even those were expensive, only the wealthy could afford to send their son and daughter to them.
(d) Within the past ten years, however, the numbers of camps have greatly increased.

Q4.

(a) The rain forest contains more than half of Earth's plant and animal species, even though rain forests cover only about 6 per cent of the earth's surface.
(b) Many of the plants and foods in your home originated in the rain forests.
(c) Common house plants, such as bromeliads, African violets, periwinkle and the Christmas cactus, began in the rain forest.
(d) More than 1,400 varieties of tropical plants are thought to be potential cures for cancer.

Q5.

(a) Drivers chew some intoxicant, smoke, use pills and consume special drinks mainly to drive more, sleepless and deliver fast.
(b) A recent survey has found that truck and other vehicle drivers working overtime use intoxicants and suffer from health problems including sleeplessness and stress.
(c) Around 27 per cent of the drivers surveyed admitted that they consumed alcohol while driving, another 10 per cent said they chewed tobacco and 26 per cent smoked beedi, the survey in the states revealed.
(d) The survey was conducted as part of a project by the Institute of Road Traffic Education (IRTE) and Centre for Disease Control and Prevention of the US across states including Rajasthan, Maharashtra, and the NCR.

Q6.

(a) The book 'Knowing Christ Today' by Dallas Willard deals with the disastrous effects of divorcing the teachings of Jesus Christ and his people from the domain of human knowledge.
(b) Its aim is to reposition the substantial teachings of Christianity ('Mere' Christianity) as a body of knowledge in the contemporary world.
(c) It is Dr. Willard's hope that this book will put those who practice Christian discipleship in a different and much stronger position, and that it will be helpful for all areas of education, but especially for Christian schools, colleges and universities.
(d) In the process, it explains what knowledge is, as compared to belief, commitment and profession, and clarifies the difference it makes whether or not an area of thought and practice is regarded as an area of knowledge.

Q7.

(a) The 'Dare To Lead' conference was attended by more than 150 women executives spanning across various industries and touched upon issues pertaining to the challenges faced by women in the corporate world.
(b) An Executive Debani Ghosh said that women have to stop putting themselves down; no one else can banish their insecurities for them.
(c) Be confident in your competence that you do not need to play the gender card anymore, equality can only be demanded if women themselves stop expecting any special treatment.
(d) From the shop-flower to board room, women have proven that they are skilled.

Q8.

(a) Writers do not always express in direct words what they want to say; they depend on the common sense of the reader to be able to form total impression of whole writing.
(b) In a comprehension exercise, you may be asked all types of questions designed to test your knowledge of the passage.
(c) You may be asked to give the facts and interpretation of these facts.
(d) You may be asked to express the meaning of word or phrase as it is used in the passage.

Q9.

(a) It is tough to find another sportsperson who holds so many records, Given that cricket is a sport driven by numbers.
(b) He has made his fans fall in love with numbers because he kept clocking them one after

the other, with each figure seeming more incredible.

(c) I remember the time when he suffered the tennis elbow; it was a big concern for us as he had missed many matches.

(d) 100 hundreds in international cricket, 15,847 test runs, first to score a double hundred in ODIs, most runs in World Cup the list goes on and on for him.

Q10.

(a) A prototype of a thermoelectric refrigerant based on Peltier effect has been developed in an Indian company which does not require a compressor, expansion valves, absorbers or solution pumps necessary while using refrigerant liquid.

(b) The team worked on the idea for one-and-a-half years at the college's Innovation and Entrepreneurship Development Centre.

(c) They are now ready with a prototype labelled 'Photovoltaic-driven refrigerator-cum-warmer'.

(d) The device can achieve 200°C in a few seconds and cool down to 8°C in 40 minutes.

Q11.

(a) The NSA says its online surveillance programs have played an instrumental role in thwarting terrorism.

(b) Even when it is encrypted, online data can still be heisted, but the information looks like gibberish without the decoding keys.

(c) Facebook also has said it is cloaking its social networking network with greater encryption, but has not publicly set a timetable for getting all the added protection in place.

(d) The increased use of encryption technology is aimed at stymieing government surveillance that may be occurring without the companies' knowledge.

Q12.

(a) Bitcoin is a decentralised digital currency which is an open source peer-to-peer electronic mode of payment.

(b) The Reserve Bank of India (RBI) is, and rightly so, keeping an eye on the growing popularity of Bitcoin and is adopting a wait-and-watch approach.

(c) With many establishments in the United States, China and not to mention online sites accepting Bitcoin, pressure will increase for its transaction in India.

(d) But it is doubtful as to how long it can stay on the sidelines and observe the developments without intervening.

Exercise 4

Odd Man Out/Irrelevant Statement Questions

Directions for the questions (1-15): Five sentences related to a topic are given below. Four of them can be put together to form a meaningful and coherent short paragraph. Identify the odd one out.

Q1.

1. In general, the EB-5 visa is an entrepreneurial visa with an early investment of USD 5,00,000 and an assurance of at least ten full-time jobs in the US.
2. Additionally, there was a time when a prospective EB-5 visa holder was requested to pay the minimum investment in physical gold instead of cash – it encouraged or discouraged Black money laundering is a debate.
3. While Indian IT professionals fighting with the tightened norms of the US's most popular visa category, H-1B visa, the EB-5 visa is gaining popularity as an alternative.
4. Nowadays, children of high net worth people, officials and working class people believe that this visa is a gateway to a US Green Card.
5. Andrew Graves, Director of Business Development, US Immigration Fund said, 'Most people want to invest in EB-5 mainly for their children so they are able to go to the US and stay there and not be dependent on any other visa category'.

Q2.

1. Kerala has already been given a specific role in the Project Mausam (PM) launched by the Union Government in 2014 where a major goal was to revive the historical 'spice route' in a larger geopolitical and geo-economic context (India, Ministry of Culture 2014: 8).
2. This historical reference to the city has a particular context too, which not many would have noticed then, even in the spices-rich state.
3. However, the PM somehow remains a non-starter, and the interests of the state of Kerala – identified as a potential hub of spices trade – have been completely derailed with the central government's own import policy with regard to such vital commodities.

4. While inaugurating the Kochi Metro in June 2017, Indian Prime Minister, Mr. Narendra Modi had called Kochi 'the queen of the Arabian Sea, an important spice trading centre', (India, Press Information Bureau 2017).
5. Historically, Kerala has sustained a unique position in the global exchange relations between the two countries, both economically and culturally, and the 'spice route' connectivity goes back to two millennia between them.

Q3.

1. His signature style of minimal, geometric, modernist buildings, invariably all-white, has kept him at the top of his profession since the 1980s.
2. Four women who worked with Meier and a fifth who met him on a project have detailed encounters in which they say he sexually harassed them.
3. Richard Meier, one of the world's most renowned architects, has stepped down as head of his firm following sexual harassment accusations from several women going back decades.
4. 'While our recollections may differ, I sincerely apologise to anyone who was offended by my behaviour. Effective today, I am taking a six-month leave of absence as founder and managing partner', He added.
5. 'I am deeply troubled and embarrassed by the accounts of several women who were offended by my words and actions', said Meier in a statement on his website.

Q4.

1. These revised charges will be effective from 01 April 2018 and will benefit over 25 crore customers.
2. Also, the lender added that the decision of slashing AMB was taken keeping in view the feedback from various stakeholders.
3. State Bank of India has closed as many as 41.16 lakh savings accounts between April and January in the current fiscal year for not maintaining the average monthly balance, reveals an RTI query.
4. India's largest lender, State Bank of India (SBI), has slashed charges for non-maintenance of Average Monthly Balance (AMB) in savings accounts by nearly 75 per cent.
5. 'Our stakeholders were unhappy with the recently imposed heavy maintenance charges', the spokesperson for SBI said. Now charges for non-maintenance of AMB for customers in Metro and Urban centres have been reduced from a maximum of ₹50 per month to ₹15 per month. Similarly for Semi-Urban and Rural centres, the charges have been reduced from ₹40 every month to ₹12, and ₹10 GST charges will be applicable over and above the rates specified above.

Q5.

1. Less fond than her late husband of its uncompromising aesthetics, she had kept the vase in a cupboard after his death.
2. 'It was unprecedented: two very big buyers, who, from about the £50-60k mark, were just slugging it out. Quite often you'll get two people who are very keen for the same item, but that keen? It went for 20 times the estimate'.
3. Auctioneer Nic Saintey told the Guardian that he knew immediately that it was a Hans Coper, but thought the seller, who had brought it in a shoebox, might not.
4. This sale caught not just the seller - a pensioner whose husband had paid £250 for the item in the 1970s - but the entire market unawares, and the owner took the vase to an open valuation day at her local auction house, Bearnes Hampton and Littlewood in Exeter.
5. A Hans Coper vase has sold at auction in Devon for a record £3,81,000, the highest price ever paid for a piece of modern and contemporary studio pottery.

Q6.

1. Executive producers for the series made this disclosure when asked during a panel event in Jerusalem on Tuesday if Smith, who played a young Prince Philip in the first and second seasons, was paid more than Foy.
2. In response, the series' producers, Suzanne Mackie and Andy Harries, acknowledged the 35-year-old male English actor was paid more owing to his Doctor Who fame, but said the practice would be rectified in the future, according to the US entertainment magazine *Variety*.
3. Claire Foy, who plays the Queen in The Crown, was paid less than her co-star Matt Smith during the first two seasons of the hit show, producers of the Netflix series have revealed.
4. The first season of The Crown, which received widespread critical acclaim, is understood to be have been the most expensive series commissioned by Netflix at the time, reportedly costing the streaming company £100m.
5. 'Going forward, no one gets paid more than the Queen', Mackie told the audience.

Q7.

1. The rural economy was adversely affected in terms of employment, daily financial practices and social network use for over three months.
2. With cashless policies gaining currency in various parts of the world, we believe the era of digitisation is near.
3. Serious concerns arise with regard to the achievement of its stated goals.
4. People came to rely more strongly on their networks to sustain their economic and social activities.
5. Drawing on survey data from rural Tamil Nadu, the effects of demonetisation are documented.

Q8.

1. All governments support micro-irrigation because of its water use efficiency.
2. In this context, a study was undertaken in nine states, mainly to examine the actual area covered compared to the potential area and to understand the adoption level of mi as well as to analyse the cost and returns under different farm categories.
3. The results indicated that only about 9 per cent of the mi potential is covered in the country.
4. The adoption of micro-irrigation projects has resulted in water saving, yield and income enhancement at the farm level.
5. However, the overall impression is that they are capital-intensive and suited to large farms.

Q9.

1. US President Donald Trump's agenda for H-1B visa has affected people at large as there is a steep decline in a number of student visas approved in the Trump regime.
2. The United States Citizenship and Immigration Services (USCIS) handed out 4.21 lakh student visas last year.
3. Statistics for this financial year clearly suggest an aggregate decline of 16 per cent as compared to the previous year.
4. A year before that, the US Department of State had handed out 5.02 lakh visas.
5. Asian students contribute to 40 per cent of the total student visas.

Q10.

1. This change has come mainly due to two reasons. First - increasing population - and second - highly wasteful flood method of irrigation (FMI) thus depletion of groundwater.
2. Given that around 65 per cent of irrigation and 85 per cent of the drinking water comes from the groundwater resources, majority of the groundwater sources in the country are registering a fall in water levels.
3. Today, India is considered to be a water stressed country, though we were highly water-surplus in 1950s.
4. The government of India had launched a subsidy scheme for micro-irrigation called National Mission on Micro Irrigation (NMMI) in 2006.
5. To arrest the decline in per capita water availability and per capita foodgrain availability, we need to increase production with judicious water use in farming.

Q11.

1. There is no easy answer to this question.
2. 'How much money should I have when I retire?'
3. So what's the solution? According to Govila, if you have age on your side, that is if you start planning for your retirement early, you should invest more in equities and as you grow older, you should shift part of your corpus into Debt.
4. The retirement corpus - the amount of money one would require to have a peaceful retired life - varies from person to person, depending on a host of factors, primarily the lifestyle one wants to maintain post-retirement and hence the related expenses, said Sanjeev Govila, founder of Delhi-based Hum Fauji Initiatives that provides financial services solutions to people from the armed forces.
5. This is one of the most common questions that financial advisors and planner face when someone new approaches them for help with their future financial Goals.

Q12.

1. Owing to its scope, the Jawaharlal Nehru National Urban Renewal Mission is an excellent window for understanding the evolution of urban governance in India, despite its closing in 2014.
2. The JNNURM's aspirations were belied by its realities of progressive centralisation, degraded local capacities, commercially oriented infrastructure development, and intercity and intra-city inequalities.
3. These signatures appear to endure, to varying degrees, in new urban programmes, with potentially far-reaching ramifications for urban governance.

4. We identify and discuss three signatures that shaped its conceptualisation, operationalisation and outcomes: flexible networks of policy actors and advisors; mobile policy ideas, best practices, and norms; and the pervasive role of consultancies.
5. Jawaharlal Nehru National Urban Renewal Mission (JNNURM) was a massive city-modernisation scheme launched by the Government of India under Ministry of Urban Development that envisaged a total investment of over $20 billion over seven years.

Q13.

1. Success of BPO in India is the operational cost reduction by outsourcing the business process services to India that makes the country a suitable destination.
2. The paper also focuses on the role call centres play in unmooring local identities to construct transnational labour identities for a neo-colonialist workplace.
3. Through empirical research, this paper addresses the transformation of Indian urban labour into a global proletariat.
4. The phenomenal success of BPOs, particularly call centres, continues in 2005, offering high-school and college English-speaking graduates quick employment with comparatively high wages.
5. Following the short-lived dotcom boom in India (2000–02), Information Technology Enabled Services Business Process Outsourcing was first considered by many infotech industry watchers as a capricious venture, liable to crash due to poor infrastructure.

Q14.

1. This paper argues that the events in the Indian soft drinks market can only be explained with reference to the global fight between Coke and Pepsi and their respective global strategies.
2. After the second coming of the international varieties of Cola drinks, the market has witnessed a high profile tussle between the global giants - Coca-Cola and PepsiCo.
3. Moreover, these two firms are so dissimilar that their relative successes and failures can throw light on some of the important issues in industrial organisation.
4. This tussle and the respective problems faced by the two firms in the Indian market are extremely instructive.
5. For generations, the Cola war has been raging with soda enthusiasts taking sides of either Pepsi or Coke; customers are still non-conclusive on which is better.

Q15.

1. According to the taste expert - Malcolm Gladwell, there is a significant difference in flavour.
2. This gives Fanta a stronger blast of flavour while Coke is a lot smoother.
3. For generations, the Cola war has been raging with soda enthusiasts taking sides of either Pepsi or Coke.
4. In his 2005 book *Blink*, he confirms that Pepsi has more of a citrus flavour, while coke is characterised by a raisiny-vanilla tang.
5. But aside from the multi-million dollar advertising campaigns and packaging - can you really tell the difference?

Answer Key

Level Of Difficulty–I

1. (1)	**2.** (2)	**3.** (5)	**4.** (3)	**5.** (2)
6. (5)	**7.** (1)	**8.** (4)	**9.** (5)	**10.** (1)
11. (2)	**12.** (4)	**13.** (2)	**14.** (5)	**15.** (2)

Irrelevant Statement Questions

Cat Level Exercises

16. (2)	**17.** (4)	**18.** (3)	**19.** (2)	**20.** (5)
21. (4)	**22.** (4)	**23.** (3)	**24.** (3)	**25.** (5)
26. (2)	**27.** (4)	**28.** (5)	**29.** (2)	**30.** (3)
31. (4)	**32.** (2)	**33.** (3)	**34.** (4)	**35.** (4)
36. (3)	**37.** (5)	**38.** (5)	**39.** (5)	**40.** (2)
41. (5)	**42.** (2)	**43.** (5)	**44.** (3)	**45.** (5)

Practice Exercises On Irrelevant Statement Questions

Exercise 1

1. (d)	**2.** (b)	**3.** (b)	**4.** (c)	**5.** (a)
6. (d)	**7.** (b)	**8.** (d)	**9.** (b)	**10.** (b)
11. (c)	**12.** (b)			

Exercise 2

1. (d)	**2.** (a)	**3.** (c)	**4.** (d)	**5.** (d)
6. (a)	**7.** (a)	**8.** (b)	**9.** (c)	

Exercise 3

1. (b)	**2.** (a)	**3.** (b)	**4.** (d)	**5.** (a)
6. (c)	**7.** (a)	**8.** (a)	**9.** (c)	**10.** (d)
11. (c)	**12.** (a)			

Exercise 4

1. Odd **man** out **is** 2. **Correct** sequence **is** 3145.
2. Odd **man** out **is** 5. **Correct** sequence **is** 4213.
3. Odd **man** out **is** 1. **Correct** sequence **is** 3254.
4. Odd **man** out **is** 3. **Correct** sequence **is** 4125.
5. Odd **man** out **is** 2. **Correct** sequence **is** 5413
6. Odd **man** out **is** 4. **Correct** sequence **is** 3125.
7. Odd **man** out **is** 2. **Correct** sequence **is** 5314.
8. Odd **man** out **is** 1. **Correct** sequence **is** 4523.
9. Odd **man** out **is** 5. **Correct** sequence **is** 1324.
10. Odd **man** out **is** 4. **Correct** sequence **is** 3125.
11. Odd **man** out **is** 3. **Correct** sequence **is** 2514.
12. Odd **man** out **is** 5. **Correct** sequence **is** 1243.
13. Odd **man** out **is** 1. **Correct** sequence **is** 5432.
14. Odd **man** out **is** 5. **Correct** sequence **is** 2413.
15. Odd **man** out **is** 2. **Correct** sequence **is** 3514.

Explanations

Level Of Difficulty–I

1. The passage is talking about a bee cultivator named Mike Arp. The passage begins with the sentence 2 which talks about the loss of his bees due to weather conditions and the drastic fall in the number of bees around 2000. This is followed by sentence 4 which furthers the point that his bees died due to infestation of killer bees. This is then followed by sentence 3 which carries forward the threat to the bees. The paragraph ends with sentence 5 which depicts Arp's compulsion to use chemical treatments. 1 does not fit in this passage as it is talking about profits from honey which is nowhere mentioned in the passage.
2. The order of the passage is 1, 4, 3, 5 and 2 is the odd man out. The passage begins with a question and 4 carries the idea forward that CEO's are the least concerned about equal pay while females ranked it 6th which is stated in sentence 3. The disparity sentence 5 talks about is the disparity in rankings by males and females. Hence 2 does not fit into the passage.
3. The odd one out here is 5 and the order is 1, 3, 2, 4. 5 does not fit into the passage as it talks about the author's state of mind during depression and 5 does not fit into the tone of the passage. The author talks about depression here and recalls his experience as a never-ending loop which seemed to go on forever. It made the author think of his old self and how he had morphed himself into this new self. 5 may have been taken from another paragraph in which the author may have been describing his state of mind where nothing else mattered.
4. 3 is the odd one out here and the order of the passage is 4, 2, 5, 1. It begins with the current scenario of patients having schizophrenia, followed by 2 which describes what it is. 5 furthers the passage by taking forward the symptoms and ends with 1.

   3 here does not go with the flow of the passage as it abruptly describes the effect of drugs on the patient.
5. The order of the passage is 3, 4, 1, 5 and 2 is the odd one out as the passage talks generally about platypus and the causes for extinction of a few of its local populations while 2 talks specifically about platypus populations in South Australia. Sentence 3 introduces platypus as a species and 4 further carries its description ahead. 1 introduces the threat to the platypus which led to a fall in its population. 5 ends with the idea that talks about the extinction of 40 per cent of the species.
6. The order of the passage is 2, 4, 1, 3 and 5 is odd one out. The passage talks about the diet plans which is stated in sentence 2 which is then followed by sentence 4. Sentence 1 introduces a new diet and 3 carries forward its implications. 5 does not fit in the flow of the passage and may have been taken from a following paragraph.
7. The passage in general talks about how morality as a concept can be used in societies and how different codes of morality are specified in different societies. The correct order of the paragraph is 2, 4, 3, 5 and the odd sentence out is 1.
8. The passage describes what a business is and then further goes on to bifurcate business into 2 of its major activities and finally relates it to ethics. The order of the passage is 1, 3, 5, 2. 4 is the odd one out as it brings into picture the concept of questions in business ethics which may have been described in another paragraph.
9. The passage introduces the concept of Eudaimonia and its translation, as suggested in sentence 1. 2 then follows 1 which states the problems with

the translation of eudaimonia as a definition. 3 and 4 follow 2, respectively, and the order of the passage thus becomes 1, 2, 3, 4 and 5 is the odd one out as it talks of virtues which is nowhere mentioned in the aforesaid sentences.

10. 1 is the odd sentence out as it directly begins with a 'they' while none of the other sentences talks about what they are. The flow of the passage talks about what deontological ethics is and that stands in contrast to the consequentialists, which is another branch of philosophy. The correct order of the passage is 2, 5, 3, 4.

11. The passage is a book review and talks about Allan Bloom's 'The closing of the American Mind'. 4, 3, 5, 1 is the correct order of the passage as it begins with introducing the author and the book, followed by sentence 3 which gives an insight into the book's debatable nature and its familiarity in the age. Sentence 5 furthers the theme of the passage followed by 1. 2 is irrelevant in the paragraph.

12. The passage talks about work culture in Japan and about paternal leaves as an organisational policy. The correct order of the passage is 5, 2, 1, 3. Sentence 4 is a wrongly placed sentence and might have been taken from succeeding paragraphs. 1 and 3 form a mandatory pair and 5 is a general introductory sentence and hence should be placed at the beginning. 2 follows 5 which states the benefits of paternal leaves.

13. The passage flows like a story. The correct sequence of the passage is 1, 3, 5, 4. 2 is the odd one out as the passage is describing the man, Günter, while the sentence talks about his visit to Vienna, which has not been mentioned as of now anywhere in the paragraph.

14. 5 is the odd one out here as the passage is talking about the newly found illness, Coronavirus and how it is dangerous to the human race. 5 talks about the casualties and deaths due to the virus specifically in China. The passage otherwise is a generalisation of the disease, its spreading and its treatment.

15. The passage is about the author trying to describe his childhood problem of sweaty palms and how tried to deal with them. 3 is the introductory sentence followed by 1 and 5, respectively, which describe the problems he had to face because of it. 4 shows the remedies he tried. So the flow of the passage is 3, 1, 5, 4 and 2 is the odd sentence out as it talks randomly about a happy examiner and does not fit into the passage.

Irrelevant Statement Questions

Cat Level Exercises

16. Statements 1, 3, 5, and 4 form a meaningful paragraph by talking about the migration of the author from Dominican Republic to New York. Statement 2 talks about her later life. So, Statement 2 is odd one out.

17. Statements 2, 5, 3, 1 make a meaningful paragraph by talking about Melanie's career. Statement 4 is out of context. Also, if she can deal with her physical issues, why would she be waiting for a physician. Hence, Statement 4 is irrelevant.

18. Statements 1, 2, 4, 5 make a complete sequence about how the author was motivated by Melissa and changed her attitude about the Internet. Statement 3 talks about the writings of Melissa which is out of context here. Hence, Statement 3 is irrelevant.

19. Statements 1, 3, 4, 5 is the correct sequence talking about Randy and his performance, and how nervous he was. Statement 2 is not matching the sequence as it is talking about the music industry in general, whereas this paragraph is specifically about Randy. Hence, Statement 2 is irrelevant.

20. Statements 3, 1, 4, 2 form a meaningful paragraph as they talk about Sir Keir and his speech on family relations. Statement 5 brings politics in picture making it out of context.

21. Statements 2, 1, 3, 5 form a meaningful paragraph commenting on decline of "mental hygiene" whereas Statement 4 talks about it as mainstay in China making it out of context.

22. Statements 2, 3, 1, 5 form a meaningful paragraph by talking about crime that took place and how the police underplayed it. Statement 4 brings in new term of "kung flu" in picture making it out of context.

23. Statements 1, 4, 2, 5 make a meaningful paragraph talking about rise in Proust's book sales and comments of cynics on the same. Statement 3 talks about his personal life making it out of context.

24. Statements 2, 1, 4, 5 form a proper paragraph and focus on fitness industry whereas Statement 3 brings a different idea of self-discipline.

25. Statements 2, 1, 4, 3 form a meaningful paragraph describing the author's childhood whereas Statement 5 brings in a different concept of mental disorders.

26. Statements 1, 3, 4, 5 form a meaningful paragraph in that sequence. Statement 2 brings a description of activities at school which does not relate with other sentences.

27. Statements 3, 1, 2, 5 make a meaningful paragraph. Statements 3, 1, 2 follow a sequence going by the rule of full name to surname to pronoun. Statement 5 then connects the phrase "whatever it takes" in Statements 3, 1, 2 to current scenario. Statement 4 may seem to be related to Eurozone crisis but it focuses on the USA and then the world rather than Eurozone and Mr. Draghi's actions alone. Hence, Statement 4 is out of context.

28. Statements 2, 1, 3, 4 form a meaningful paragraph by talking about the actions of Cameron's actions and its impact on present. Statement 2 introduces the topic, i.e., actions of Cameron's government. Statement 1 carries the comment further. Statements 3, 4 then bring us to the present. Statement 5 looks like a disconnected sentence as it mentions "current estimate", but it is not clear what the estimate is for.

29. Statements 1, 5, 3, 4 make a meaningful paragraph by showing the contemplation of soul from past to the grave and the message written on it. Statement 1 begins the paragraph by introducing Katumuwa. Statement 5 should follow Statement 1 as "he" refers to Katumuwa and carries the idea stated in Statement 1 forward. Statement 3 follows 5 as "it" refers to the basalt stele mentioned in Statement 5. Statement 4 finishes the idea in Statements 1, 5, 3. Statement 2 is irrelevant as it talks about the author. Statement 4 brings in the belief of Katumuwa which is out of context.

30. Statements 2, 1, 4, 5 form a meaningful paragraph by talking about the beauties of botanical gardens. Statement 2 introduces the topic of the paragraph, i.e., UK's botanic gardens. Statement 1 follows 2 as "they" in Statement 1 refers to the gardens. Statements 4, 5 form a mandatory pair and should follow Statements 2, 1 taking the idea stated in that forward. Statement 3 brings in its scientific purposes which makes it out of context.

31. Statements 3, 1, 2, 5 make a meaningful paragraph talking about publication of spring and why they were delayed. Statement 4 talks about summer sports making it out of context.

32. Statements 1, 3, 5, 4 form a meaningful paragraph by describing the protests taking place in Kazakhstan. Statement 2 talks about deeper issues of the country making it out of context.

33. Statements 1, 2, 5, 4 form a meaningful paragraph by talking about riots that may take place in the USA. Statement 3 brings in the "rightwing information system" making it out of context.

34. Statements 1, 3, 5, 2 make a meaningful paragraph as these sentences talk about the specific period of Christmas to New Year and how these last two years have been different due to the corona virus and continues to 2022 with the Omicron. Statement 4 brings in the temptation about TV which changes the context.

35. Statements 1, 3, 2, 5 make a meaningful paragraph by talking about faith of Christians and how non-believers look at them. Statement 4 brings in issues between countries making it out of context.

36. Statements 4, 1, 5, 2 make a meaningful paragraph by talking about Putin's actions and how it can impact the world. Statement 3 however talks about the USA making it out of context.

37. Statements 2, 3, 1, 4 make a meaningful paragraph by talking about the time when Black America changed. Statement 5 talks about specific aspects such as clothes making it out of context. Also, there is no other sentence which could be contradicted by Statement 5.

38. Statements 4, 2, 3, 1 form a meaningful paragraph. Statement 5 is out of context as it introduces a new topic with mention of another variant.

39. Statements 1, 3, 2, 4 forms a meaningful paragraph by explaining the fight between the Indian government and Twitter. Statement 5 talks about the "provocation" which is not mentioned in the passage earlier.

40. Statement 2 is the odd sentence. Statement 3 begins the passage by telling us when and where hobbit fossils were first found. Statement 1 follows by saying that at the time hobbit fossils were found, scientists weren't sure about the species the fossils belonged to. Statement 5 follows sentence 1."But" is the key word here. It suggests that although the scientists were not sure of the species the fossils belonged to, they found that the individuals had grape-size brains and were 3 feet tall. Statement 4 will be followed by 5 because Statement 4 tells us that after examination the scientists have found out what species the hobbits belonged to. Statement 2, on the other hand, talks about some research that was conducted earlier. The sequence is Statements 3, 1, 5, 4.

41. Statements 3, 1, 4, 2 form a meaningful paragraph and explain the formation of government by various parties. Statement 5 brings in action of non-party actors making it out of context.

42. Statements 3, 1, 4, 5 form a meaningful paragraph bringing out what is happening in Thailand.

Statement 2 brings out what happened in the United States making it out of context.

43. Statements 2, 1, 4, 3 form a meaningful paragraph by explaining what archaeology needs to do and how they are approaching it. Statement 5 brings in an "aha" moment of the writer, which does not relate well with the remaining paragraph. So, Statement 5 is out of context.

44. Statements 4, 1, 5, 2 form a meaningful paragraph and talk about cryptocurrencies whereas Statement 3 introduces fiat money.

45. Statements 3, 1, 4, 2 form a meaningful paragraph by bringing out the state of mother tongues in India. Statement 5 specifically focuses on medium of instruction making it out of context.

Practice Exercises On Irrelevant Statement Questions

Exercise 1

1. Statement (d) explains the view of Gustav Bergmann regarding ontology as he assumes ontology is a part of epistemology. Epistemology is the branch of philosophy concerned with the nature and scope of knowledge and is also referred to as 'theory of knowledge', and ontology is the branch of philosophy which deals with nature of existence. While statements (a), (b), (c) explain about ontology.

2. Statement (a) mentions about discovery of a new planet. Statement (b) provides a general concept about planets that how planets are formed. Statement (c) mentions about who all were involved in discovering this planet while Statement (d) mentions about Bailey views who led this research. Statements (a), (c), (d) seem to be interconnected, so the logical order is (a), (c), (d).

3. Statements (a), (c) are related to how the planners and government can work together on gathered information regarding urbanisation and create a smart plan for development without affecting environment and biodiversity. Statement (d) tells that lack of funds affect implementation of such plans. Whereas statement (b) tells about a report on urbanisation and is illogical in context to the passage as statements (a), (c), (d) seem to be interconnected as they mention about plans and implementation of plans.

4. The passage is about Search for Meaning of Existence. Statements (a), (b), (d) are statements related to the main idea of passage. Statement (b) mentions about question relating to meaning and purpose of existence. Statement (a) also mentions about such questions over which philosophers have been pondering on since ages. Statement (d) also seems to be related as it mentions about enquiry and researches of the philosophers, etc. Statement (c) seems to be illogical as mentions about Upanishads and explains about meaning of life and not about questions or researches.

5. Statement (b), (d), (c) are interrelated as all three have a common idea about how to hold on resentment. If somebody is stressed, he becomes sad and at times misses the best opportunity in his/her way. While statement (a) talks about uncertainty and is thus the odd one out.

6. Statement (a) mentions about the term corporate social responsibility which is slowly creeping and becoming a part of India's business era. The term pro bono means, 'for the public good'; pro bono means a case is taken up for free or the rates are deeply discounted. Statements (c) and (b) mention about the legal system and pro bono work. Statement d is not about the legal system.

7. Statements (a), (c), (d) are interrelated as they mention about the increment in number of people who surf internet even for small matters, people are switching from thick books to e-books because they have become handy. Statement (b) specifically mentions about Penguin India, innovation while rest are a general statement.

8. Statement (d) is a general statement about crocodiles and their characteristic and tactics of attracting their prey. Statement (a) mentions about a researcher Dinet who carried out a research on crocodiles. Statement (b) and (c) support this statement.

9. Statements (a), (c), (d) are focussing upon the integration of HR techniques into strategic planning of the organisation, whereas Statement (b) focuses upon competencies in HR professionals that differentiates between outstanding and average performers.

10. Statements a, c, are in logical order as they explain the tactics applied by politicians to attract the voters towards them. Statement (b) stands out.

11. The logical order is (a), (b), (d).

The three options logically in order explain us about the advantages of applying web services in an enterprise while statement (c) stands out as it explains about the disadvantage of web service and what alternate step could be taken.

12. Statements (a), (c), (d) tell us about the analysis conducted by the author, while statement (b) tells us about the areas of limitation in the research.

Exercise 2

1. The fourth sentence talks of grievance redressal mechanisms, whereas the rest of the sentences refer to the decision-making process of the government, with special reference to quota licencing. Thus option (d) is the irrelevant sentence.
2. Sentence (a) addresses London's attempt at proving that Russia cannot host the Olympics. This is unlike the other three sentences that make direct references to the bad luck that the month of August brings to Russia in particular. Thus sentence (a) is irrelevant to the rest of the passage.
3. Option (c) is the answer as it speaks of Amazon, which is unaddressed in the other three sentences that deal with the operations of the FAA in the American airspace. Thus (c) is the irrelevant sentence.
4. While options (a), (b) and (c) describe the political regime in Syria, option (d) makes a remark about Syrian society, which is not in line with the theme followed by the rest of the sentences. Thus, it is the irrelevant sentence.
5. First, option (d) is unspecific in the region it speaks of. Second, it brings up nationalism which has no continuity with the rest of the sentences' ideas. Thus, it is the irrelevant sentence.
6. Option (a) directly contrasts what has been said in the other options, which is appreciative and laudatory of the French parliament's efforts at implementing a comprehensive pension overhaul. Thus, it is irrelevant in the given context.
7. While option (a) does seem connected to the rest of the sentences, it is still the most irrelevant from among the options present. It is an extension of the concept of altruism in discussion in the question, in that it discusses 'sustainable harmony'. Options (b), (c) and (d) hover around the same premise and thus constitute a consistent thought.
8. Option (b) is the answer because it diverges into a different direction from the one author takes in the other three sentences in his/her assessment of charities. It does not express an idea similar to these other sentences. It is thus the irrelevant sentence.
9. Options (a), (b) and (d) talk of interconnectedness and territorial concerns of countries across the world, in a broad way. There is no specific mention of any particular region or country. The mention of Asia's power games and focus on it is what makes option C the irrelevant sentence.

Exercise 3

1. Statements (a), (c), (d) talk about the cyclone and the current relief provided by the State Government and central agencies. Statement (b) is not fit as the paragraph does not talk about one's opinion (i.e., Mohapatra's).
2. Statements (d), (c), (b) are relevant as these sentences are descriptive and describes the characteristics of mixed economy while (a) does not follow the order as it focuses on price mechanism.
3. Statements (a), (c), (d) form mandatory pairs by focussing on the past and present conditions and increment in numbers of summer camps each year while statement (b) tells about various organisations and people who carry out these camps.
4. Out of the given statements, statement (a, b, c) are in logical order. Statement (d) does not fits the sequence as the para mentions the existence of various plants in rainforest and not their medicinal value.
5. The para is about the survey conducted on heavy vehicle drivers who work overtime and consume intoxicants. Statement (a) talks about drivers who drink and drive fast. While rest statement talk about survey conducted on heavy vehicle drivers, hence statement (a) is odd one out.
6. The para is based on the content of the book called 'Knowing Christ Today' by Dallas Willard. Statement (a), (b), (d) mentions about content of the book but Statement (c) mentions Dr.Willards percept for the book.
7. Statement (a) describes about conference held on women empowerment. While statements (b), (c), (d) mentions opinion of a women executive Debani Ghosh, the correct order is (b, c, d). All three are interrelated and focus on thoughts of Ghosh on women empowerment.
8. The logical order is b, c, d as it mentions what skills or knowledge is demanded on the part of the reader while he is solving a comprehension exercise. All the three sentences are interrelated and talk in the same sense while option (a) mentions a writer's tactics applied in a comprehension to make it trickier.

9. Statement (a) describes how the sportsperson made incredible record and made his fans fall in love with numbers. Statement (b) is also interconnected as it also talks about numbers 'sportsperson who holds so many records'. Statement (c) talks about the writer's memory about the sportsperson's injury. Statement (d) tells about the sportsperson's records in various groups of cricket scores.

10. Statements (a), (b), (c) mention about development of thermoelectric refrigerant invented to cope up with global warming, while Statement (d) does not fit the sequence because it mentions about particular characteristic of the device.

11. The statements focus on the enhancement of encryption techniques. Statement (c) stands out as it talks about the way Facebook is protecting the data of its users. Statements (a), (b) and (d) talk in particular about the techniques that NSA has used for encrypting data for security reasons.

12. The above statements explain about RBI's focus on the growth of a digital currency, Bitcoin. To this statement, (b), (c), (d) stand connected as they explain about the activities of RBI in connection with bitcoin whereas statement (a) defines bitcoin and stands out.

Exercise 4

1. Paragraph starts with statement 3, where the gist of the paragraph is introduced, gist of H-1B and its new alternative EB-5. Statement 1 goes on to elaborate about EB-5 visa, what type it is, its requirement. Statement 4 further explains who opts for this visa EB-5 - High net worth people who believe that this could get them Green Card. Statement 5 further supports the previous statement by stating the official statement of the Director of Immigration Fund.

   Statement 2 is irrelevant as it talks about how EB-5 investment would be taken in gold and not in cash - measure or counter measure to Black money laundering is debatable. The paragraph above does not talk about Black money laundering, thus this does not fit in.

2. Statement 4 introduces the subject and the key stakeholders - Kochi and Indian PM. Statement 2 states 'this historical reference' which refers to 'Queen of Arabian Sea', thus this follows 4. Statement 1 talks about Kerala as a state now, till now paragraph was talking about Kochi and its status. Also the goal of Project Mausam is stated here and Kerala's role in it. Statement 3 takes this further by stating 'However...'; this remains as a non-starter due to some political issues probably.

   Statement 5 mentions 'two countries' which are not mentioned which all in the paragraph, there is no correct references here, thus it does not follow any logic to be mentioned in the paragraph.

3. It is a press cover, introducing the accused Richard Meier in Statement 3 and what he is charged for. Statement 2 continues the news article elaborating the accusation, that is five women have accused him of harassment. Statement 5 covers the official statement by Richard and statement 4 adds another official statement by him. So the whole context of the article was 'Sexual harassment and actions' by Richard.

   Statement 1 mentions about the profession and style of Richard as an architect which may be relevant but out of context for this paragraph.

4. Statement 4 starts off with introducing India's largest lender - SBI, along with the main idea of passage that is 'slashing of imposition of charges for non-maintenance by SBI'. Statement 1 continue the idea of 'new revised charges' by mentioning the significance of these revised charges and how it will benefit its customers. Statement 2 adds why this step was taken. Statement 5 further continues the idea of consideration of SBI stakeholders.

   Statement 3 simply mentions the action taken by SBI for non-maintenance of accounts by account holders. It does not relate to the idea of 'slashed charges' but simply of non-activity/non-maintenance, thus it does not fit in the sequence above.

5. Statement 5 begins the paragraph with opening statement that a Hans Coper was sold for some record price. Now, this sale caught not just the seller but everyone else off guard because the vase was apparently bought at a much cheaper price back in 70's; this is mentioned in Statement 4. Also mention of woman's husband who bought this vase is done. Statement 1 continues by mentioning what the woman thought how ordinary the vase was to her. However, the auctioneer knew the value of the vase would be much unordinary on contrary to what the woman, also the seller, thought. This is stated in Statement 3. This forms a coherent paragraph.

   Statement 2 is irrelevant here, that is mentioning about 2 buyers who made unprecedented offers; however, offer in detail is not yet discussed anywhere in paragraph. 'It was unprecedented' implies that something of that sort would be mentioned before this statement, which is not.

6. Statement 3 starts off with the claim that the actress who plays the Queen in a TV show was paid less than her co-star. Statement 1 states 'this disclosure' which is what is mentioned in earlier statement. Statement 2 states 'In response' which is quite understandably here - In response to the claim made by the actress. The producers give their opinion on this claim now. Finally, paragraph is concluded with the statement of promise on the pay out by Mackie - One of the producers of the show, she was also earlier introduced in the paragraph. This is stated in Statement 5.

   Statement 4 talks about the series 'The Crown' in general and how widely acclaimed it is and that it is expensive. This is irrelevant to the paragraph in discussion.

7. Statement 5 starts off with the passage, that the effects of demonetisation are documented. Statement 3 starts drawing the effects which are serious. Statement 1 elaborates first such effect. Statement 4 concludes the paragraph with the conclusion that people relied more strongly on their network to sustain their economic and social activities during this time.

   Statement 2 talks about digitisation era, in general, globally. The paragraph thus formed is not relevant to this idea.

8. Paragraph starts off with Statement 4, with a major headline that Micro-irrigation has had positive effects. Statement 5 states the usual contrary opinion of micro-irrigation that it is expensive and suited only to large farms which is not true; thus in this context (to prove the point), a study was conducted in 9 states in India, this is mentioned in Statement 2. Finally, results of this study are discussed in Statement 3.

   Statement 1 is irrelevant here as it talks about government support and only one positive aspect of micro-irrigation.

9. Statement 1 opens the dialogue that the new agenda of H1B visas has affected at large the total number of student applications to US. Statement 3 mentions this decline in percentage terms that is 16 per cent drop. Statement 2 tells the number of applications last year and Statement 4 states the number of applications the year prior, thus the chronological order of events.

   Statement 5 talks about Asian students' percentage of students who come over to US; this is irrelevant in the context of the paragraph.

10. Statement 3 starts the paragraph talking about India and how it is a water stressed country today, on contrary to what it used to be in 1950's. Reasons for 'This change' from water surplus to water scarce are mentioned in Statement 1, also depletion of ground water. Why there is a depletion in ground water is mentioned in Statement 2. Finally, to control this, a few methods are suggested in Statement 5.

    Statement 4 talks about a new scheme by government of India, how significant it may sound; it does not fit into the context of the paragraph above.

11. Paragraph begins with a question as in Statement 2. Statement 5 mentions 'this is one....', refers to the question asked just before. Statement 1 states the conundrum that there is no easy or simple answer to this question. Statement 4 finally talks about the opinion of experts.

    Statement 3 talks about a 'problem' whereas there is not any. Paragraph simply talks about the retirement investment queries.

12. Paragraph starts off with introduction of the scheme for Urban Renewal, the full form of the scheme is mentioned, in Statement 1. Statement 2 next talks about aspirations of this scheme and few details are mentioned. Statement 4 further talks about the three signatures and Statement 3 elaborates these three signatures in detail.

    Statement 5 is simply a definition of this scheme and does not fit into the context in discussion here in this paragraph.

13. This is clearly a preface to a white paper. Statement 5 starts off the paragraph by stating the emergence of BPO in India post 2002. Statement 4 talks further about persistent success of BPOs through 2005. Statement 3 tells us what the central idea of the paper is. Statement 4 takes it further with the keyword 'also focusses on...'.

    Statement 1 merely talks about the key reason to success of BPO Industry in India. The paragraph does not talk about that.

14. This paragraph is clearly a preface to a white paper. Statement 2 introduces the theme of the paragraph - Tussle between Coca-Cola and Pepsi as global Cola giants. 'This tussle' in Statement 4 makes it immediately follow statement 1 which states what this paper will talk about in detail. 'Moreover' in Statement 3 further continues the paragraph on dissimilarities between the two companies that will be also discussed in the paper.

Statement 5. Merely talks about Cola war between the two companies and how customers are still non-conclusive on which one is better. It is irrelevant to this paragraph's context.

15. Statement 3 starts off the discussion by stating that for generations there has been this cola war between Coca-Cola and Pepsi over which is better in terms of taste, brand, etc. Statement 5 keeps aside the brand value which is almost the same, and states if one can really spot the difference now, in terms of taste. Statement 1 records the claim of this expert who claims there is a significant difference. Statement 4 states that difference.

    Statement 2 talks about difference in flavours of Fanta and Coke which is out of context here.

CHAPTER 25 Summary of the Passage Questions

QUESTIONS THAT ASK YOU TO SUMMARISE AN ARGUMENT

This is another important question type which has been regularly seen in the CAT and other top Management Entrance Exams. A summary is defined as the reduction of a large amount of information to its most important points. You need to remember the following points about summarising in order to be able to spot summaries effectively:

(1) While achieving a reduction of the passage into its summary, care is taken to ensure that the main idea of the passage is properly communicated - i.e. there is no compromise or dilution of the sense of the main idea communicated by the passage while framing the summary. The summary might have the main idea stated in the original words of the author or in fresh words which will essentially convey the same meaning. This factor should always be kept in mind while solving summary based questions. Hence, recognising the main idea of the passage while reading the original text for the first time is extremely crucial for identifying the correct summary.

A good process to follow in trying to recognise the summary is to go back to the questions:

- Who or what is the original text talking about? (Answer: Topic of the text)
- What is the main idea about the topic that is being conveyed by the original text? (Answer: Main idea of the text)

Then, you go on to the alternative summaries available and ask the same questions again with respect to the proposed summary.

- Who or what is the summary talking about? (Answer: Topic of the summary)
- What is the main idea about the topic that is being conveyed by the summary? (Answer: Main idea of the summary.)

For the correct option, the two answers that emerge out of these questions should be exactly the same as the two answers that emerged out of the original text.

(2) Significant reduction from the original text to the summary is generally achieved by either condensing or removing altogether the supporting details in the passage. In many cases, it is not even necessary to mention some of the details presented in the original paragraph in order to write a good summary.

(3) Very often, authors of texts repeat the main idea several times while writing. This is done to ensure that their main idea is hammered into the minds of the reader several times and in several ways so that the gaps (if any) in understanding the main idea may be removed.

Needless to say, in the summary, the main idea will be written only once - and that too in one sentence only. Any repetitions of ideas present in the original text are removed from the summary.

Consider the following example:

Jaya and Devika are both successful women who are also members of a socially disadvantaged section of the society. Jaya has a firm belief in positive discrimination. By positive discrimination she believes that the negative discrimination that society has subjected her section of the society to can only be offset through reverse discrimination. She believes that if positions of economic, social and political eminence, power and honour are offered principally to historically disadvantaged sections of society, then these groups will begin to play a more significant role in society today.

Devika, on the other hand, feels that she has succeeded in her chosen field of work on her hard work and on her own merits. She thinks that the principle of positive discrimination is flawed since it will result in the lowering of standards and decreases competition between similarly qualified personnel who will expect to achieve positions because of their factors rather than their suitability for the particular position.

Which of the following best sums up Jaya's argument?

(a) Positive discrimination will encourage more people to apply for jobs, previously unavailable to them.

(b) Positive discrimination will give extra opportunities to socially disadvantaged sections of the society.

(c) Quality and professionalism will improve because of the greater number of positions held by members of minority groups.

(d) Positive discrimination will remove deep-rooted prejudices against the weaker sections of society from the work arena.

The correct answer is (b).

EXERCISE 1

Read the paragraphs given in each question and choose a suitable summary from the given options:

Q1. It appears that there are basically two types of scientific innovators. The first ones are innovators in totality who conceive the idea that may have never existed before. They derive inspiration from events, incidents and traditions occurring in their surroundings or even from folk stories floating around. The other ones are the incremental innovators who work on existing objects and ideas to bring some newness therein. Development of several modern drugs from Ayurvedic texts and folklores falls in this category.

(a) Innovators in totality conceive new ideas from events and traditions such as the tradition of Ayurvedic medicine in ancient India. Incremental innovators improve existing ideas.

(b) Scientific innovation takes the form of inception and development of new ideas, and study for refining existing ideas. Application of Ayurveda in modern medicine is an example of the latter.

(c) Innovators are either incremental or total innovators. Incremental innovators conceptualise new ideas while total innovators utilise events, incidents and traditions to conceive improvements.

(d) Conception on new ideas and improvements of ideas are some of the several forms of scientific innovation. The former draws on events or incidents while the latter draws on existing objects.

Q2. Obama initially promised to close Guantanamo Bay within a year of entering the White House in 2009. Opposition to its closure involves two central issues which Obama has been unable to resolve. One is finding host countries to take in all the detainees. The other issue concerns whether some of the detainees can be moved to 'supermax' facilities within the US. Seventeen detainees who have received their final transfer approval are scheduled for release in the coming weeks. As many as an additional 30 more could be released by the summer. This would reduce the prison's population to 60, but still the question remains: Would the remaining prisoners be moved to prisons in the US, and would their legal status finally be addressed?

(a) The Obama administration has faced opposition to its decision to close the Guantanamo Bay facility as the legal status of the inmates has not been addressed.

(b) The Obama administration has not delivered on its promise to close Guantanamo Bay. Reasons cited for the same, inter alia, are lack of citizenship details of the inmates and convincing host countries to take them.

(c) President Obama has faced stiff criticism for closing down Guantanamo Bay as the question of legal status of the inmates has not been addressed. Further, the government cannot house the released inmates within the US.

(d) Questions pertaining to housing the detainees of Guantanamo Bay have created roadblocks for the Obama administration. Whether the remaining prisoners will be moved to other facilities or to their host countries remains to be seen.

Q3. While it is essential to follow through on the opportunity the Paris agreement has created to prevent a cataclysmic planetary collapse over the decades ahead, building climate change resilience can start now. Importantly, the agreement paid relatively scant attention to the need for more investment in resilience building to help communities, cities and countries manage the consequences of climate change that is already under way. Our experience of working in a diverse range of cities across Asia through the Asian Cities Climate Change Resilience

Network and the 100 Resilience Cities initiative - both pioneered by The Rockefeller Foundation - demonstrates that cities can take innovative, integrated and practical solutions, without always requiring a great deal of money. Indeed, the main investment has often been that of political will and active engagement by local citizens, businesses and experts.

(a) Climate change is one of the most important issues of our time and the experience of Foundations can be very useful in combating its immediate effects.

(b) Climate resilience refers to the ill effects of climate change that are already under way. Innovative and pragmatic solutions are imperative to tackle this problem while simultaneously addressing the problem of climate change.

(c) The recent climate convention in Paris has not taken into consideration combating the negative effects of climate change that have already started manifesting. Strategies to mitigate the same can be implemented through joint participation of various segments of society.

(d) Lack of political will and public participation has resulted in poor implementation of various solutions to combat climate change and build resistance.

Q4. Perrault was born in 1628, and worked as an adviser in the French court of Louis XIV. He only began to write his fairy stories, borrowing the plots and the well-known opening, 'once upon a time' or *il était une fois*, from folk tales, later in life. 'Perrault's stories set the standard for the modern fairy tale', said Google. The backbone of these fairy tales persists within contemporary novels and movies, making our reading or cinema-going a fundamentally optimistic venture: when we hear 'once upon a time', we've come to expect - and anxiously await - a 'happily ever after'.

(a) Perrault was an eminent novelist who compiled fairy tales which created the basic framework for several contemporary novels and movies as we know them today.

(b) Perrault's version of fairy tales has had a far greater influence on the human psyche than we realise. We find them to be a recurring theme in all our contemporary stories which leads us to seek a happily ever after ending in every book or movie we come across.

(c) The very fact that when we hear 'once upon a time' we are filled with optimism for a happy ending signifies how much the stories of our childhood influence us.

(d) Perrault's collection of fairy tales is largely responsible for the optimism of the cinema-going audience. This shows the significant impact of reading these stories at a young age.

Q5. You doubtless know the story by now: how Britons followed Americans into borrowing money they couldn't afford to buy stuff they didn't need. How shoppers went crazy and entire economies got off-kilter - until catastrophe hit. How the feckless Anglo-Americans now need to tighten their belts, stop maxing out their credit cards and start saving like Germans. This is that rare example of an account agreed by both the anti-consumerist left and the anti-welfarist right. And it is mostly tosh. It lacks history, and assumes that debt is a uniquely Anglo-American vice. It sits unnervingly close to hypocrisy: my necessary loan is your stupid debt.

(a) The assumption that the British and Americans should stop living beyond their means and adopt austerity measures exposes the hypocrisy of the capitalist and socialist segments.

(b) The assumption that the British followed the Americans into a debt crisis is unfair and rankles of hypocrisy.

(c) Both the capitalist right and the socialist left seem to agree that austerity measures are the need of the hour for the Americans and British. This is, however, an unresearched opinion bordering on hypocrisy.

(d) Living beyond their means is not a uniquely Anglo-American problem and attempts to cast it as such reveal a lack of understanding of the issue. An expenditure which is a necessity for one cannot be an extravagance of another.

Q6. For 45 years, Iran's most famous modern monument, the Azadi (Freedom) Tower in Tehran, has been the backdrop to every major news story coming out of the country. A plaza for celebrations, anniversaries, military parades and a gathering point for mass demonstrations, the 50 m (165 ft) tall tower has overlooked some of Iran's most important political events. Most recently, the mass demonstrations that followed the disputed presidential election of 2009 drew hundreds of thousands to Azadi Tower, where they demanded a recount of their votes.

(a) When their basic rights are threatened, people often find a national symbol as the rallying point to raise their protests.

(b) The Azadi Tower has become the symbol of the modern man's struggle against the conservative institutions of power to reclaim his rights.

(c) The Azadi Tower of Iran has become symbolic of the citizens' trials and tribulations as well as their triumphs over the years.

(d) All newsworthy incidents in Iran have taken place in the backdrop of the Azadi Tower.

Q7. A project aiming to revolutionise medicine by unlocking the secrets of DNA is under way in centres across England. Prime Minister David Cameron has said it 'will see the UK lead the world in genetic research within years'. The first genetic codes of people with cancer or rare diseases, out of a target of 1,00,000, have been sequenced. Experts believe it will lead to targeted therapies and could make chemotherapy 'a thing of the past'. Just one human genome contains more than 3 billion base pairs - the building blocks of DNA.

(a) Prime Minister Cameron has unveiled an ambitious genome project which has the potential to cure cancer.

(b) Sequencing genetic codes may hold the key to combating rare and fatal diseases. This idea is at the heart of a project launched in England, which, experts feel, will revolutionise medicine.

(c) Targeted therapy for rare diseases has been made possible by studying the genetic codes of people with cancer and rare diseases. A similar project is also under way in England.

(d) The 1,00,000 genome project could make chemotherapy a thing of the past as genetic code sequencing can provide targeted therapies for cancer and rare diseases.

Q8. Lego's decision to stop asking bulk customers what they want to do with the bricks is a 'victory for freedom of speech', Chinese artist Ai Weiwei has told the BBC. Last October, Ai accused Lego of censorship when it refused to sell its bricks directly to him. On Tuesday Lego said customers should instead make clear that the company does not endorse works shown in public. Ai, a leading artist, is also known for criticism of the Chinese government. He said Lego's U-turn would encourage people to use the product to express themselves.

(a) We live in truly strange times where even a child's plaything can turn into a medium of expression. The Chinese government discovered this when artist Ai Weiwei used it to criticise their policies.

(b) Business firms seldom side against the government to protect the interests of the consumers whose satisfaction is their ultimate aim. Lego, however, begs to differ.

(c) Lego bricks have recently been used by the Chinese to make political statements forcing Lego to impose restrictions on bulk buying. The toy major was forced to take this step.

(d) Lego has rolled back the controversial decision to seek information from customers purchasing in bulk. This was seen as a move encouraging the use of the product as a medium of expression.

Q9. 'Kooks', from the 1971 album *Hunky Dory*, looks ahead to parenthood, alongside his then wife Angie, with optimism. It offers advice to a child growing up in unconventional circumstances. 'Kooks' isn't among Bowie's most famous songs. 'The better known Changes', 'Life on Mars' and 'Oh, You Pretty Things' all appeared on the same album. But many of his fans have taken to Twitter to praise it in the wake of his death, noting its anthemic quality, its openness and acceptance of difference.

(a) Bowie's song 'Kooks' has always been a favourite with his fans, who have now taken to Twitter to praise the song in the wake of his death.

(b) Bowie's 'Kooks' has captured imaginations as a piece of advice to a child and for its quality of innocence and acceptance.

(c) The song, 'Kooks' was written by Bowie as a celebration of parenthood at the birth of his son. It offers advice and guidance and has become very popular after his death.

(d) 'Kooks' may not be Bowie's most famous song but its theme of optimism and open acceptance serve as a means of guidance to a growing child. This has made it one of his most memorable songs.

Q10. 'Jerusalem' is the musical setting of William Blake's poem Prelude to Milton. He was specifically thinking about a legend that as a boy, Jesus of Nazareth visited England with his great uncle, Joseph of Arimathea, who was a sailor and trader. So why did Blake spin a poem about a medieval myth? Probably because England at the time was a place of change and he wasn't entirely happy about the direction it was taking. It was the time of the Industrial Revolution, when factories - the dark Satanic Mills he wrote of - seemed to swallow people up and spit them out broken and mangled. As a nonconformist Christian, Blake looked back on a time when a religious figure could walk in barefoot simplicity on 'England's green and pleasant land'.

(a) Usually in times of political turmoil, poets and artists attempt to construct an alternate history through their works.

(b) Jerusalem is an expression of Blake's dissatisfaction with the Industrial Revolution taking place in England.

(c) Blake's Jerusalem explores a Christian myth to express his dissatisfaction about the dreary Industrial Revolution in England. Blake looked back at a time when there was more simplicity.

(d) Jerusalem was written to further popularise the legend of Jesus visiting England in a time when English society was suffering from the Industrial Revolution.

Q11. The Rainforest Alliance, an ethical certification organisation, has now stripped a group of Assam Company's plantations of its green frog seal. The Assam Company said the loss of its certification was because of a 'minor error' on one estate 'Hajua' while spraying a plant extract, which it understood did not require personal protective equipment. It said that because the Assam Company estates operate in a 'single cluster', the other estates were automatically decertified.

(a) The green frog seal is imperative for tea plantations to ensure demand from companies as it testifies to their ethical conduct.

(b) Minor errors may sometimes have far reaching consequences as the Assam Company has realised.

(c) Ethical conduct of business also includes their treatment of their staff. The Assam Company's green frog seal was revoked recently due to negligence in observing safety of employees.

(d) A minor error in wearing protective gear has resulted in revocation of the Assam Company's green frog seal. An incident on one estate has resulted in decertification of all the other estates held by the company.

Q12. We have songs for different moods and different times of day, and to achieve different objectives. I write to Bach, I run to Martin Solveig, maybe you sort the recycling to Senagalese pop music, or polish antique silverware to Nicky Minaj's Anaconda. The limitations of one song could never define even a single life, so the idea of trying to define a country with reference to just one song is laughably simplistic. Those calling for an English national anthem should give up now: it's a pointless, fruitless, unnecessary task.

(a) Different moods of a person can be defined by the promiscuous selection of songs they listen to.

(b) Songs are used as National Anthems for their ability to reflect our moods and ideas. Yet it may not be possible to adopt a single song to reflect the patriotism of an entire nation.

(c) No song can capture the entire range of emotions of an individual. How is it possible then for a song to represent the idea of their nation to the millions of individuals in England?

(d) While songs usually reflect most emotions in an individual, they usually cannot give a true picture of the patriotic spirit of a nation.

Q13. Stripping terrorists of their citizenship is tempting for governments and satisfying for voters. It allays concerns that jihadists may recruit and radicalise susceptible inmates while in prison, or that they might one day again roam France and wreak havoc. The symbolism - that a person waging war against France is no longer French - is politically popular: three-quarters of French people support Mr. Hollande's proposal, according to a recent poll. Yet many on France's left see it differently. They say that the planned law could foment radicalisation by sending the message to dual-citizen Muslims that they are less French than the rest of society and, by creating unequal categories of citizenship, betray the cherished 'egalité' enshrined in France's constitution.

(a) Revoking the citizenship of terrorists is a very popular idea in France. However, this could also have repercussions such as alienating citizens with dual citizenship and a violation of the 'egalite' principle.

(b) French President Hollande has proposed stripping jihadists of citizenship as this may be used to radicalise prison inmates. However, the decision could also create unequal categories of citizenship.

(c) In a symbolic gesture the French are demanding revoking the citizenship of known terrorists. This will prevent the recruit of prison inmates for antinational agendas.

(d) Francoise Hollande has proposed a new bill to strip terrorists of their citizenship. This is an intensely debated argument.

Q14. But there are solid reasons why the world has now convinced itself that oil is worth much less than before. On one side of the ledger there is supply, not only of oil itself, but also of the other fossil fuels which can often substitute for it, notably gas, which is more abundant than anyone would have imagined a few years ago, courtesy of the fracking boom. On the demand side, things have been developing even more rapidly, with a serious slowdown in the resource-intensive emerging economies, above all debt-laden China. The fracking revolution will not be reversed, and it increasingly looks like the Chinese Flu will be hard to shake. All of which suggests that low oil prices could be here for a while.

(a) Both demand and supply forces have resulted in the substantial reduction in global oil prices.
(b) The demand for oil has been slowing due to slowdown of resource-intensive economies and the supply has been hampered due to the availability of alternative resources, thus pushing prices down further.
(c) The fracking boom has restricted the supply of oil to debt-laden China resulting in lower oil prices.
(d) The fracking boom on the demand side and the Chinese Flu on the supply side have caused sharp decline in global oil prices.

Q15. Today we know much more about how and why HIV the virus that leads to AIDS has become a global pandemic. Unsurprisingly, sex workers unwillingly played a part. But no less important were the roles of trade, the collapse of colonialism and twentieth-century sociopolitical reform.

(a) Diseases do not assume epidemic proportions without the aid of sociopolitical and economic factors.
(b) Trade and commerce, among other factors, played an important role in the spread of the HIV which causes AIDS.
(c) The AIDS epidemic was also fanned by the decline of colonialism and trade and commerce along with social and political changes effected in the twentieth century.
(d) The chief reason for the spread of the AIDS causing HIV was sex workers and post-colonial reform measures of the twentieth century.

Q16. Surprisingly, it works. Repeating myself afterwards minus the cups I sound even more convincing about the specifics of my fish-and-chip dinner than I did the first time round. The cups device is just one of the many exercises taught in City Academy's 'How to Get Heard in Meetings' course, which, while open to anyone, is being marketed as an especially female-friendly way to apply performance techniques to everyday scenarios. Women have long struggled to make themselves heard in the workplace. In 2014, *Harvard Business Review* reported that 'we have consistently heard women say that they feel less effective in meetings than they do in other business situations. Some say that their voices are ignored or drowned out. Others tell us that they can't find a way into the conversation... In fact, several men reported seeing a female colleague get rattled or remain silent even when she was the expert at the table'.

(a) Executives with poor communication skills often struggle to get themselves heard at meetings. Female executives have been noted to get rattled and drowned out at such meetings.
(b) Male executives in modern business organisations do not allow their female counterparts the space to voice their thoughts in discussions. This causes women executives to feel less effective in meetings.
(c) Women often struggle to make their points in official meetings perhaps because they are outnumbered by their male colleagues or ignored. Communication exercises have become a popular method to set right this state of affairs.
(d) Female executives usually opt for performance techniques to improve their communication skills at meetings.

Q17. In a commentary, the Vatican daily *Osservatore Romano* said treatment of this kind towards religion 'is not new' and stressed that religious figures have repeatedly condemned violence in the name of God. 'Behind the deceptive flag of uncompromising secularism, the weekly is forgetting once more what religious leaders of every faith unceasingly repeat to reject violence in the name of religion using God to justify hatred is a genuine blasphemy, as pope Francis has said several times', it said. The commentary added: 'In Charlie Hebdo's choice, there is the sad paradox of a world which is more and more sensitive about being politically correct, almost to the point of ridicule, yet does not wish to acknowledge or to respect believers' faith in God, regardless of the religion'.

(a) Religion has recently been deemed the promoter of bloodshed because of the element of fanaticism without considering the ample examples of situations wherein religion has been the messiah of peace. Believers respect this power of God and religion, and this notion should be acknowledged.
(b) Religious leaders cite religion as the chief means of ensuring peace by evoking the name of God to stop violence. Yet the secular movement deceives people.
(c) We live in times where the greatest virtue among people is to be politically correct. Yet the media refuses to respect peoples' faith in God.

(d) The Charlie Hebdo incident has revealed the potential of religion to turn into a divisive force which permits violence to curb dissent. However, religious leaders continue to reject violence in the name of God and label it blasphemy.

Q18. University of Oregon's Lundquist College of Business and his co-authors compared the effective tax rates paid by a sample of American firms between 2002 and 2011 with a measure of those companies' CSR programmes compiled by MSCI, an index provider. It found that the companies which do the most CSR also make the most strenuous efforts to avoid paying tax - and that those with a high CSR score also spend more lobbying on tax. The most obvious explanation for this inverse relationship is hypocrisy. Surely CSR depends on the idea that firms have an obligation to society, not just to shareholders. And surely the most basic obligation to society is to pay the taxes that support the poor and vulnerable. Another explanation is that firms are not monoliths but collections of rival fiefs with different priorities. The department that oversees the CSR programmes, and thus has an interest in boosting their budgets, may never talk to those in the finance department who are paid to minimise the tax bill.

(a) A recent study by researchers at the University of Oregon has revealed that companies that do the most CSR also indulge in tax avoidance strategies, thereby exposing the hypocrisy of these corporate giants.

(b) A recent survey supports the public opinion that companies that do the most CSR also indulge heavily in aggressive tax planning to please shareholders. This state of affairs could be a result of double standards or lack of coordination in departmental goals.

(c) A recent study by researchers at the University of Oregon reveals an inverse relationship between expenditure on CSR and lobbying on tax. These findings are highly suggestive of conflicting interdepartmental goals in business firms and hypocrisy of the corporate class.

(d) The findings of a recent research suggest that companies with high expenditure on CSR also engage in greater tax lobbying. This could result from double standards or conflicting interdepartmental goals.

Q19. The concept of the modern, open democracy that embraces freedom, diversity and human rights is under threat. We live in a time of conflict unlike any other. A war is under way that is not just being fought out on conventional battlefields among state powers, but on the Internet and the streets of our towns and cities, as the citizens of Paris found to a shocking cost in November.

(a) The concept of modern society and freedom of speech are under threat due to the rise of modern forms of warfare.

(b) The ideals of democracy are at war with an emerging threat. Unlike previous wars, this war is not confined to secluded battlefields and has spread over the Internet and our homes.

(c) Cybercrimes have now taken precedence over conventional methods of warfare. This has restricted freedom and liberty.

(d) Terrorism, armed with modern technology and modern forms of warfare, has emerged as the greatest threat to the ideals of liberty.

EXERCISE 2

The following text is followed by four alternate summaries. Choose the option that best captures the essence of the text:

Q1. A newly opened glass elevator in a Dubai tourism spot has been closed by tourism officials after cracks appeared in the structure at the height of the week-long Ramadan holidays. The glass elevator in Burj Arab's scenic area had been supporting dozens of tourists on Monday when the cracks on its floor appeared with a loud bang. A single pane of the 3-m-long section shattered into coin-sized segments and fell from a great height on the ground, according to footage on state broadcaster CCTV. The area's management bureau said on its microblog on Thursday that there was no threat to safety because only one of the three layers of glass that make up the elevator floor was damaged.

(a) The newly opened glass elevator in Dubai has suffered cracks but the cracks are not a threat to safety.

(b) The newly opened glass elevator in Dubai has suffered cracks and even though it is not a threat to safety, the elevator has been shut down by the tourism officials.

(c) The tourism officials of Dubai have closed the newly opened glass elevator due to certain cracks appearing in the structure. These cracks were not considered a threat to safety by the area's management bureau.

(d) Despite the management bureau's assurance that the cracks in the newly opened glass elevator are superficial, the tourism officials of Dubai have closed it, until further notice.

Q2. In talks with Tsipras about struggling economy, Lagarde sets out fresh conditions for further financial aid. The European Union will need to provide significant debt relief for Greece if it is to persuade the International Monetary Fund to put its financial clout behind the country's third bailout package, the Washington-based organisation has said. After what was described as a cordial meeting between the IMF's managing director, Christine Lagarde, and the Greek prime minister, Alexis Tsipras, on the sidelines of the World Economic Forum in Davos, the fund said it was only prepared to support the recession-ravaged Eurozone country on a strings-attached basis. It said Greece had to be prepared to implement a tough package of economic reform and the country's Eurozone partners had to be willing to write down Greece's debts.

(a) In a discussion with Greece on the sidelines of World Economic Forum in Davos, IMF sets norms to provide financial aid to Greece on a conditional basis which includes Eurozone writing down its debts and Greece implementing stringent economic reforms.

(b) In a discussion between IMF and Greece on the sidelines of World Economic Forum in Davos, IMF declared publicly that it'll provide Greece financial aid only if Eurozone approves of this loan and takes guarantee of Greece's debt.

(c) In a discussion with Greece on the sidelines of World Economic Forum, IMF agrees to provide financial aid to Greece.

(d) Despite stringent Economic reforms and Eurozone writing down its debts, Greece needs financial aid from IMF which IMF promises it will provide. This has been decided on the sidelines of World Economic Forum in Davos.

Q3. Once upon a time, there was a Frenchwoman named Mathilda who made it her life's mission to save two of everything. Not just a spare for every possible eventuality - filling every cupboard to bursting, littering her cellar - but a twin for every object she owned, right down to table lamps. This hoarding made no sense at all, until it emerged that her grandfather once saved his family's lives during the war by producing a spare reel of thread for a German soldier who needed to repair his uniform. Without that favour, they could have died. And so even as an adult, she could only feel safe so long as she had one of everything in reserve.

(a) Learning from her grandfather's experience where he saved his family's lives during war, Frenchwoman Mathilda made it her mission to save two of everything she owned. She'd feel safe this way to have reserve of everything.

(b) Since her grandfather saved his family's lives during war, Frenchwoman named Mathilda has been saving two of everything. She feels safe this way that she has a reserve of everything she owns.

(c) Inspired by her grandfather's actions where he saved his family's lives during war by offering a spare reel to a German soldier, Mathilda made it her life's mission to save two of everything, keep a twin of every object she owned; this way she'd feel safe especially during war.

(d) Frenchwoman Mathilda saves two of everything and keeps a twin of everything she owns. This feeling of having reserve of everything makes her feel safe. She has learnt this from her grandfather who had a spare reel of thread to offer to a German soldier to repair his uniform during war. This action saved his family's lives from the German soldier.

Q4. Recent experiment shows that a group of people, say X who prepared their meals at home and regularly consumed breakfast and an evening meal, had overall better diet. They avoided fast food and high sugar content drinks and ate more fresh vegetables and fruits compared to a group of people, say Group Y who did not keep an eating routine. Y who ate on the run or used media while they ate or purchased food often ate less healthily.

(a) People who eat regular meals are healthier than the ones who eat less healthy food.

(b) People who keep an eating routine eat healthier food than the ones who do not eat healthy.

(c) People who eat home-cooked food and follow an eating routine eat healthier as compared to people who do not keep an eating routine.

(d) Fast food and sugary drinks are unhealthy as compared to vegetables and fruit. People should avoid them.

Q5. Questioning 5000 girls across Delhi about the various taxes they pay at their favourite restaurants, the respondents put the VAT at 12.5 per cent when it actually costs 14.5 per cent. They believed the service charge is another tax imposed by the State or Central Government when it is actually purely imposed by the restaurant for rendering its service to you; respondents estimated service charge to be at 2.5 per cent when it may vary from 4-10 per cent. The Service tax was estimated to be another 2.5 per cent when it is actually 12.36 per cent and payable on 40 per cent of your total bill (excluding taxes), which equals 4.96 per cent.

(a) According to a recent survey, girls in Delhi are not used to paying for their own restaurant bills.

(b) According to a recent survey, Delhi restaurants charge more taxes than in other states in India.

(c) According to a recent survey, Girls in Delhi are clearly ignorant about the taxes charged by the restaurants for the food and services.

(d) According to a recent survey, girls in Delhi hold a sense of disgust on knowing petty issues like restaurant taxes and ignore them deliberately.

Q6. Many regime loyalists of Xi Jinping are just going through the motions. It is hard to miss the theatre of false pretence that has permeated the Chinese body politic for the past few years. Last summer, I was one of a handful of foreigners (and the only American) who attended a conference about the 'China Dream', Mr. Xi's signature concept, at a party-affiliated think tank in Beijing. We sat through 2 days of mind-numbing, nonstop presentations by two dozen party scholars – but their faces were frozen, their body language was wooden and their boredom was palpable. They feigned compliance with the party and their leader's latest mantra. But it was evident that the propaganda had lost its power, and the emperor had no clothes.

(a) Mr. Xi is surrounded by supporters and well-wishers who pretend that they believe in his philosophy.

(b) The endgame of communist rule in China has begun, and Xi Jinping's ruthless measures are only bringing the country closer to a breaking point.

(c) Mr. Xi's reality is now known to close associates and regime loyalists.

(d) Mr. Xi's attempts to cover up the atrocities of his regime have now been exposed.

Q7. The common view of language is that any language is a set of arbitrary but conventionally agreed upon words or signs, linked to each other by a purely formal system of syntactic and grammatical rules. Language, thus, is like a code; it is a way of representing actual things and events around in the perceived world, but has no internal, no ulterior, no arbitrary connections to that world, and hence is readily separable from it.

(a) Language represents the world but is separable from it.

(b) Language is a set of rules is an assumption.

(c) Language is a set of rules and codes which represents the world.

(d) Language is universal and common to all in form of signs and signals, hence is understood by all.

Q8. The Andaman holiday island of Viber islands has been plunged into a poisonous grey haze caused by illegal forest fires in neighbouring Neil islands. Reduced visibility caused passenger planes from Thailand destined for Port Blair airport to turn around on Tuesday. The noxious fumes which have been spreading for weeks have shut down many other islands of south-east Asia. Tourist spots have been closed in, and the local swimming championship cup scheduled to be held on Rutland island was cancelled on Wednesday. A beach volleyball championship in Barren Island scheduled on Thursday was also abandoned.

(a) Illegal fires have resulted in poisonous smoke spreading through the neighbouring islands of Viber.

(b) A poisonous haze has spread over various islands of south-east Asia due to the fires in Viber islands – one of the biggest islands of Andaman – and it has interrupted certain activities in those islands.

(c) Forest fires of Viber islands have resulted in spread of poisonous gases across various parts of south-east Asia and have put a stop to all the normal activities across islands over the last few weeks.

(d) Illegal forest fires in Neil islands have spread poisonous gases across Viber islands and many south-east Asian islands over the last few weeks, and have caused shutdown of certain normal activities in these islands.

Q9. It was a good idea for Avery Fisher Hall that most often conducts shows of New York Philharmonic orchestra, one of the Big Five orchestras in the world, to invite East West players, a theatre group based in Los Angeles, to stage an abridged version of Shakespeare's play, *A Midsummer Night's Dream*, with Mendelssohn's entire score attached. Conducted by Muah Ling and directed by Jennifer Chang, the result is a perfect combination of words and music in a setting – with the local woods skirting one side of the theatre – that is close to ideal.

(a) The production of Shakespeare's play, complemented with a live backing of Mendelssohn's score, is as good as it is rare.

(b) East West Players joined hands with Avery Fisher Hall to stage, *A Midsummer Night's Dream*.

(c) East West Player's rendition of *A Midsummer Night's Dream*, complete with a live backing of Mendelssohn's score at Avery Fisher Hall, resulted in something close to ideal.

(d) East West Players in collaboration with Avery Fisher Hall has created a new version of *A Midsummer Night's Dream*.

Q10. Ramsey is a smart and brilliant scholar, always curious and public spirited. He is also the perfect spokesman for an approach that has come to be known as behavioural economics. He does not come across as someone preaching others about their shortcomings because they feel like his shortcomings too. Ramsey recounts a dispute at an academic conference with the orthodox economist John Thatcher: 'I said that the difference between our models was that he assumed that the subjects in his model were as smart as he was, and I assumed they were as dumb as I am. Thatcher agreed'.

(a) Ramsey has turned his weaknesses of being dumb into a new subject, a new branch of economic science - behavioural economics.
(b) Ramsey is a scholar of behavioural economics; also a great spokesman of it wherein he shows his weaknesses and makes his audience identify with the same.
(c) Ramsey is a brilliant scholar because he can connect with people, in this case subjects of his study.
(d) Ramsey is an excellent scholar whose ability to make jokes about himself has gained him popularity in one of the fields of economics - behavioural economics.

Exercise 3

The following text is followed by four alternate summaries. Choose the option that best captures the essence of the text:

Q1. State Government's plan to ban the sale of sugary drinks in cups more than 250 ml volume capacity was an overreach that was struck down by High Court in December 2015 just before it was to take effect. Now the State Government is talking to health advocates and beverage management about reviving the cup ban. If the aim is to persuade people to change their high sugar content soda drink consumption habits, prohibiting certain serving sizes is ineffective; a young soda lover or even a thirsty shopping patron in this scorching heat will still find his way to have his favourite drink till satisfaction, via refill of two or more such 250 ml cups. The State Government would do better to educate and encourage people, especially schoolchildren, to make smarter food choices.

(a) The State Government is on the right side of an urgent public health battle of high on sugar drinks by banning the cups of capacity more than 250 ml but he needs to use better weapons to counter this battle.
(b) People should be able to make wiser food choices themselves and not depend on governments to regulate their activities like the imposition of ban of soda cups of more than 250 ml capacity on public which was annulled by High Court.
(c) Bans are not an effective way to educate people to eat right but education is.
(d) Instead of reviving the big cup (of capacity more than 250 ml) ban which was first proposed and then struck down by High Court, the State Government should encourage people to make healthier choices.

Q2. Today we live in a progressive world where we have Internet that has made it smaller, telephones that are not mere communication channels but instruments to make the dear ones staying thousands of miles away appear live in front of you on screens and everything at push of button. But we're still battling a generation-old disease: Tuberculosis (TB). When I talk to patients, a million questions come to my mind. Why do we have a disease that is curable but has gone totally berserk? It doesn't matter who you are or from where you are, TB can still attack you. Obviously, people from the lower socio-economic ranks are more vulnerable because of various factors like poor sanitation, less space and overcrowding.

(a) The world is still plagued by certain diseases because of lack of cure.
(b) The people from lower socio-economic strata suffer more from fatal diseases like Tuberculosis.
(c) Irrespective of the progress made by mankind, certain social evils still exist.
(d) There is more to the treatment for a disease, like TB, than finding its cure; something not fully known yet in this progressive world.

Q3. Book sales depend crucially on buzz and word of mouth; you buy a book because you've heard about it, because other people are reading it or because it's made to the best-sellers list. And what Flipkart possesses is the power to kill the buzz. It's definitely possible, with some extra effort, to buy a book you've heard about even if Flipkart doesn't carry it; but if Flipkart doesn't carry that book, you're much less likely to hear about it in the first place. So can we trust Flipkart not to abuse that power? No, we can't. By putting the squeeze on publishers, Flipkart is ultimately hurting authors and readers.

(a) Book sales depend on word of mouth. Flipkart.com, the giant online book retailer in India, has too much power to control this book market.

(b) Flipkart.com, the giant online book retailer in India, is hurting authors by regulating the sale of books by publishing self-interest reviews.

(c) When it comes to publicity, Flipkart has market power.

(d) World of book sales depends on word of mouth. Flipkart, the giant online book retailer in India, has too much power, in case of books, and is hurting publishers through it.

Q4. All human rights are indivisible, such as the right to life and freedom of expression; economic, social and cultural rights, such as the rights to work, social security and education, or collective rights, such as the rights to development and self-determination, are indivisible, interrelated and interdependent. The improvement of one right facilitates advancement of the others. Likewise, the deprivation of one right adversely affects the others.

(a) Combination of economic, social and cultural rights are human rights, depriving a person of his rights facilitates improvement of other persons.

(b) Human rights are interdependent and interrelated. Deprivation or improvement of one right adversely affects or facilitates advancement of others, respectively.

(c) Rights of people are interdependent as deprivation and improvement of rights of one person adversely affects and facilitates advancement of rights of others.

(d) Depriving a person of his rights adversely affects rights of another person.

Q5. That South Korea, that country shrouded in incense and shadows, is but a distant memory. Now neon lights up the night. Sixty years after the Korean War, separation from North Korea, and its reunification and political rapprochement with the West, South Korea's population has more than doubled. Golf courses are replacing rice paddies. New cities have sprouted where only thatched-roof hamlets squatted. Even long-time residents fail to recognise their own city when they venture downtown.

(a) The increase in population has brought about various social, economic and political changes in South Korea.

(b) South Korea has changed in so many ways that it is difficult even for the long-time residents to recognise their own country now.

(c) There is a sea of change in South Korea 60 years after the Korean War ended and South Korea achieved cordial political relations with the Western World. So much so that even its own long-time citizens sometimes fail to recognise it.

(d) An increase in population has resulted in urbanisation in South Korea since it achieved cordial political relations with the West due to it.

Q6. New mobile phone devices come along once every 6-8 years or so. Starting around 1990, the first generation of cellular phones relied on small book-sized mobile phones. In 1997, smaller sizes with bigger antennas were introduced for better connectivity. By 2005, those black military equipment looking mobile phones were replaced by swanky colourful and inbuilt camera phones. Around 2011, fight in mobile market was not of size any more but of camera resolution and music quality. Today in 2015 it's more about design, brand, sound, camera, applications and features. What to expect by 2020? Well, we just can't predict any more, clearly what we have today must have never been expected 20 years back. We are moving fast in this technology driven industry.

(a) Mobile devices are constantly upgraded with introduction of new technology, better features, designs, applications, etc. It's hard now in this fast moving technology-driven industry to predict what new features in mobile phone devices will be introduced in future.

(b) Mobile devices see a change after every 6-8 years and this change is in line with the expectation of society. We can predict what features we'll have on our mobile phone devices by 2020.

(c) Mobile devices are invariably getting upgraded with variant features we thought of, what the industry introduces tomorrow is absolutely a matter of the discretion of industry; we as users can just be surprised now like we're are today by what these devices are now over 20 years back.

(d) Mobile networks are constantly upgraded with the introduction of new technology. It's difficult in this fast moving technology-driven world to predict what new features in mobile phone networks will be introduced in future.

Q7. Pakistani electoral college reasserted its commitment to democracy in Sunday's parliamentary elections. More than 91 per cent of them cast ballots, a level of participation far above the 86 per cent turnout posted by Indians in 2005. President Pervez Musharaf, an increasingly military-driven and authoritarian leader, was denied a parliamentary majority.

(a) Voters of electoral college in the parliamentary elections came out in huge numbers to deny President Pervez Musharaf majority and to reassert their support to democracy.

(b) Voters of electoral college in the parliamentary elections do not want President Pervez Musharaf to come into power.

(c) Voters of electoral college in Pakistan do not want an authoritarian President.

(d) A great turnout of voters of electoral college in the recent parliamentary elections is a reassertion of Pakistan's democratic status.

Q8. I was struck by not just the Wall Street's income disparity, but also by the lack of compassion that wealthy finance workers sometimes displayed towards the poor. P. K. Piff, a professor of psychology and social behaviour at the University of California, Irvine, believes all the money sloshing around Wall Street could make some consultants unaware of their surroundings. He has conducted several social experiments that consistently show that when people gain access to money, their empathy towards the less fortunate falls and, at the same time, their sense of entitlement and self-interest rises.

(a) Wall Street creates wealth at a staggering clip, but many of its companies' and executives' philanthropy has not kept pace.

(b) Wall Street exemplifies the assertion that access to money lowers the level of empathy with the poor.

(c) Wall Street is an apt example to prove that people who are rich do not empathise as much with those that are poor as much as author does.

(d) Wall Street has seen a steady increase in wealth and a steady decline in philanthropy.

Q9. The Egyptians cared about the mortal body; its very mortality mattered profoundly to them. Today we try to deny the body's movement towards death, its inevitable decay. The Egyptians, instead of fearing the process of dying and the corpse, felt reverence. These were stages in the life of a beloved body and should be treasured. What was beautiful - and tragic, but more lovely for all that - was the body's ephemerality, its being always on the way to disappearing. The Egyptians recognised that death's presence was woven into the texture of life, giving that life one of its essential meanings.

(a) The Egyptians believed that death was inevitable and hence, it should not be mourned.

(b) The Egyptians were not afraid of death but were amazed by it because they believed in afterlife.

(c) The Egyptians celebrated death as they believed it to be final destination of their beloved ones.

(d) The Egyptians understood that a corpse was just another stage of the body and the mortality of the body mattered to them. They accepted death as a truth of life.

Q10. The dramatic turn came hours after Greece missed a debt payment to the IMF, leaving Greece effectively in default and raising the pressure on the country to find a solution to its rapidly escalating financial squeeze. With its banking system shut down and access to further aid cut-off, Greece faced the prospect of further debt defaults and the possibility of being forced to abandon the euro as its currency.

(a) Greece may not have enough money to meet its international financial obligations, as the recent debt default with IMF showed. It is also facing the risk of being forced to leave the euro as its currency.

(b) Greece is in a financial crisis and is losing its financial status.

(c) Greece is not in a condition to repay any of the loans that it has taken to maintain its currency.

(d) Considering the financial difficulties faced by Greece, it is not unusual for the country to not be able to repay its debts rather it's not even the country's fault. International financial bodies should help Greece.

EXERCISE 4

According to the Latest CAT Pattern

Q1. The following text is followed by four alternate summaries. Choose the option that best captures the essence of the text.

NATO has strongly condemned Russia for violating Turkey's airspace after Ankara reported two incursions in two days - incidents that risk further inflaming tensions days after Russia's military intervention in Syria began. Ambassadors from the 28 NATO member states held an emergency meeting in Brussels to respond to what the NATO secretary general, Jens Stoltenberg, called 'unacceptable violations of Turkish airspace' by a Russian jet. A Russian warplane again violated Turkish airspace on Sunday, a Turkish foreign ministry official said late on Monday, prompting Ankara to summon Moscow's ambassador. It had done the same following a violation on Saturday, and said Russia would be held 'responsible for any undesired incident that may occur' if it were repeated.

(a) Twice has it happened that Russia has violated Turkey's airspace over which NATO has issued a warning to Russia about possible undesirable repercussions.

(b) Ankara is complaining to NATO about Russia that is violating its airspace in recent past. It has asked to take strict action against Russia with undesirable consequences.

(c) NATO has issued warning against Russia if it ever violates Turkey's airspace.

(d) Russia's military intervention in Syria has compelled NATO to issue warnings against Russia on undesirable consequences.

Q2. The following text is followed by four alternate summaries. Choose the option that best captures the essence of the text.

An important question is, for example, whether Christianity is true. This is not a question one can relate to theoretically or academically. For a person who 'understands himself in life', it is a question of life and death. It is not something you sit and discuss for discussion's sake. It is something to be approached with the greatest passion and sincerity. If you fall into the water, you have no theoretical interest in whether or not you will drown. It is neither 'interesting' nor 'uninteresting' whether there are alligators in the water. It is a question of life or death. So we must therefore distinguish between the philosophical question of whether God exists and the individual's relationship to the same question, a situation in which each and every man is utterly alone. Fundamental questions such as these can only be approached through faith.

(a) Faith is the only way one can understand religion.

(b) Fundamental questions of life like the value of religion can be approached via faith, in isolation from philosophical enquiries.

(c) We humans when we encounter imminent calamity naturally become religious.

(d) Desperate times bring desperate measures, thus a man in trouble always turns to religion and faith.

Q3. The following text is followed by four alternate summaries. Choose the option that best captures the essence of the text.

Questioning 4000 people across the UK about the costs of common procedures and treatments, the respondents put the cost of a liver transplant at £12,279 whereas it actually costs £70,000. They believed the number of annual NHS bariatric related surgeries to be about 25,000 when it is actually double that; last year it cost the NHS in excess of £25m. The average cost of a natural birth was estimated to be £1288, when it is instead £1824 - and that's without any complications.

(a) People in the UK are ignorant about the costs of treatment provided by the NHS.

(b) People in the UK don't pay for their own medical treatments.

(c) Healthcare in the UK is much more expensive than in other countries.

(d) NHS provides medical treatment to the UK public at a reasonable cost.

Q4. The following text is followed by four alternate summaries. Choose the option that best captures the essence of the text.

Roosevelt's presidential vision impressively combined philosophic principles with pragmatic effectiveness as a politician. Roosevelt's most fundamental political belief was an 'absolute acquiescence in the decisions of the majority'. Stemming from his deep optimism in human reason, Roosevelt believed that the will of the people, expressed through elections, provided the most appropriate guidance for directing the republic's course. Roosevelt also felt that the Central Government should be 'rigorously frugal and simple'. As president he reduced the size and scope of the Federal Government by ending internal taxes, reducing the size of the army and navy and paying off the government's debt. Limiting the Federal Government flowed from his strict interpretation of the Constitution.

(a) Roosevelt urges decadent and enfeebled modern government to forego obsession with power and give more importance to rigorously frugal and simple style of governance, he practiced what he preached.

(b) Roosevelt urges decadent and enfeebled modern government to respect the will of the absolute majority and ignite a zest of good governance. He exemplified his commitment during his tenure as president of the US.

(c) Roosevelt criticises the power hungry governance by not respecting the will of absolute majority. He practiced what he preached.

(d) Roosevelt believes in respecting the will of the majority and the benefits of a system of governance which is both frugal and simple. His tenure exemplifies his commitment to his ideology.

Q5. The following text is followed by four alternate summaries. Choose the option that best captures the essence of the text.

Current global efforts to cut greenhouse gas emissions leave about half of the reductions needed still to be found, according to a new analysis by the UN. The report suggests that governments will have to go much further in their pledges to limit future carbon dioxide emissions, which have been submitted to the UN ahead of the crunch conference on climate change taking place this December in Paris. Ways for governments to ramp up their commitments in future are one of the key components of the Paris talks. The UN Environment Programme (Unep) published a report showing that global emission levels should not exceed 48 gigatonnes (GT) of carbon dioxide equivalent by 2025, and 42 GT in 2030, if the world is to have a good chance of holding global warming to no more than 2°C on average above pre-industrial temperatures.

(a) The UN is forcing countries to see climate change as a threat to global environment ahead by raising voice in Paris summit.
(b) Paris summit will focus on how to control climate change, as is the need of the hour.
(c) Governments need to increase efforts to limit global carbon emissions so as to control climate change, says UN report ahead of Paris summit.
(d) If governments accede to UN's demands, world has a chance in fighting global warming.

Q6. The following text is followed by four alternate summaries. Choose the option that best captures the essence of the text.

Researchers in the US followed 90,000 nurses over 20 years who reported their diet in early adulthood. Half of the nurses involved also reported their typical diet throughout their adolescence. Researchers drew a link between high fruit consumption - 2.9 vs. 0.5 daily servings - and about 25 per cent reduced risk of breast cancer diagnosis in midlife. Drinking fruit juice didn't appear to affect disease risk, but eating apples, bananas, grapes, oranges and kale was associated with the greatest reduction in risk, according to a news release.

(a) Eating fruits between the ages of 20 through midlife may decrease the risk of breast cancer.
(b) Research conducted on nurses can help reduce cancer risk.
(c) Consuming fruit juice does not help reduce risk of cancer.
(d) People in early age should start eating fruits and vegetables, is the only definite way to avoid cancer later in life.

Q7. The following text is followed by four alternate summaries. Choose the option that best captures the essence of the text.

Scientists who study emotional reactions like crying have found that women have much smaller tear ducts than men. Both sexes may have a strong reaction to something - but men's tear ducts are so big that the liquid stays put and eventually drains away. In women the tears quickly overwhelm the duct and spill out down their cheeks. But, as females grow old, the size of their tear ducts becomes almost equal to that of their male counterparts. So, there is not much difference in crying pattern based on gender in older people.

(a) Biologically, women are designed to shed more tears than men; however, as they age it gets the same for both.
(b) Women cry more than men.
(c) Women have tendency to cry more than men. Scientists attribute this quality to women being more emotional than men.
(d) Women have smaller tear ducts than men so they cry more.

Q8. The following text is followed by four alternate summaries. Choose the option that best captures the essence of the text.

In some communities, elections for local office are held separately from all federal and state elections, so that the electorate pays attention to the local issues. However, in those cases, while citizens face shorter ballots, they are asked to go to the polls much more often, with a consequent drop-off in turnout. Citizens in Baton Rouge, Louisiana, where state elections are held separately from federal elections and local elections are held separately from state elections, were asked to go to the polls 11 times in the 2003-04 biennium. Citizens have the right to express their views, but because they are asked to so often, many choose not to exercise the franchise.

(a) Elections get more attention when Federal system is followed and more offices are kept up for contest.
(b) Public does not caste vote if asked to do so often.
(c) Frequent elections don't necessarily translate into public effectively expressing its consent and concern.
(d) Local, State and Federal are three separate offices to be contested for. More the offices, better it is for public to express its consent or disagreement towards the government.

Q9. The following text is followed by four alternate summaries. Choose the option that best captures the essence of the text.

Nestlé has failed in an attempt to convince European judges to let it trademark the shape of the four-fingered version of a KitKat in the UK. The European court of justice ruled that the KitKat's shape was not distinctive enough for consumers to associate it with the chocolate covered wafer. Nestlé is not seeking to trademark its two-fingered version of KitKat.

(a) Nestle could not succeed in its recent attempt to trademark a particular version of its chocolate due to lack of uniqueness as a chocolate covered wafer.

(b) Nestle recently lost the case of KitKat and its features.

(c) KitKat's four-fingered chocolate version is not unique.

(d) Nestle's KitKat case was unique in the sense that four-fingered chocolate wafer is different from two-fingered chocolate wafer; it's a trademark design.

Q10. The following text is followed by four alternate summaries. Choose the option that best captures the essence of the text.

Dementia is in the public and political spotlight like never before, as society wakes up to the fact that it poses one of the greatest threats to the health and wealth of our country. The numbers are stark: 8,50,000 people in the UK are currently living with dementia, at an estimated cost of more than £26bn a year. By 2021, 1 million people will have the condition. In response, there have been many commitments from the UK government and charities, which include making significantly more funding available for research.

(a) The UK is set to fund the research on Dementia in the country.

(b) The UK government has finally realised the extent of damage caused by Dementia in the country and is ready to wipe it off completely.

(c) The UK is gathering more funds in order to deal with Dementia - biggest threat to the country.

(d) The UK government and charities are keen on arranging more funds to conduct research on Dementia - one of the biggest diseases, in terms of cost and number, faced by the country.

Q11. The following text is followed by four alternate summaries. Choose the option that best captures the essence of the text.

Tourism officials have closed a newly opened glass walkway in a central China tourism spot after cracks appeared in the structure at the height of the week-long National Day holiday.

The glass walkway in Henan province's Yuntaishan scenic area had been supporting dozens of tourists on Monday when the cracks appeared with a loud bang. A single pane of the 68-m-long (223 ft.) section shattered into coin-sized segments, according to footage on state broadcaster CCTV. The area's management bureau said on its microblog on Thursday that there was no threat to safety because only one of the three layers of glass that make up the walkway was damaged.

(a) The tourism officials of China have closed the newly opened glass walkway due to certain cracks appearing in the structure. These cracks were not considered a threat to safety by the area's management bureau.

(b) The newly opened glass walkway in China has suffered cracks but fortunately these cracks are not safety threat.

(c) The newly opened glass walkway in China has been shut down by the tourism officials as it suffered cracks; however, it is not a threat to safety.

(d) The newly opened glass walkway in China has suffered cracks.

Q12. The following text is followed by four alternate summaries. Choose the option that best captures the essence of the text.

Thai holiday island of Phuket has been plunged into a poisonous grey haze caused by illegal forest fires in neighbouring Indonesia. Reduced visibility caused passenger planes from Singapore and Kuala Lumpur, and destined for Phuket airport to turn around on Thursday. The noxious fumes which have been spreading for weeks have shut down many other parts of south-east Asia. Schools have been closed in Malaysia and races in Singapore for the swimming world cup - the FINA world championship - were cancelled on Saturday. A marathon in Malaysia on Sunday was also abandoned.

(a) A poisonous haze has spread over various countries of south-east Asia due to the fires in Indonesia.

(b) Certain normal activities are affected in SE Asian countries due to illegal smoke in Indonesia.

(c) Illegal fires have caused poisonous smoke spreading through the neighbouring countries of Indonesia.

(d) Illegal forest fires in Indonesia have spread poisonous gases across many SE Asian countries over last few weeks that have caused a shut-down of a few normal activities in those countries.

Q13. The following text is followed by four alternate summaries. Choose the option that best captures the essence of the text.

Many meanings attach to the word democracy. If there is one true meaning then it is, indeed, as Plato might have said, stored up in heaven; but unhappily has not yet been communicated to us. The word is what some philosophers have called 'an essentially contested concept', one of those terms we can never all agree to define in the same way because the very definition carries a different social, moral or political agenda. But somehow, nowadays at least, we cannot live without it.

(a) Democracy, however necessary in the modern world, is a sham.
(b) Democracy is misunderstood by the world today.
(c) Democracy, however necessary in the modern world, is not a very clearly defined concept.
(d) Concept of Democracy confuses philosophers and the world.

EXERCISE 5

Directions for the questions: Four alternative summaries are given below the text. Choose the option that best captures the author's position.

Q1. The 2015 target to establish a universal moratorium on executions - proposed by the Spanish Prime Minister at the Fourth World Congress against the Death Penalty held recently in Geneva - is likely to revive momentum on the 2007 non-binding resolution adopted by the UN General Assembly to evolve a realistic strategy to discourage states from enforcing the ultimate sentence. Many promising developments in the principal retentionist countries, evidence of high cost of specialised expertise needed to handle death penalty cases, and the expensive business of maintaining the death row population as compared to imprisoning convicts for life not to mention the grave risk of miscarriage of justice add moral weight and urgency to the case for halting executions forthwith.

(a) The UN General Assembly adopted a non-binding resolution to evolve a strategy to discourage states from imposing the death penalty, in the year 2007. Many retentionist countries are now in favour of this resolution owing to the high cost involved in maintaining the death row, etc.
(b) The 2015 target to establish a worldwide ban on executions, proposed by the Spanish Prime Minister, is likely to revive momentum on the United Nations' 2007 resolution to evolve a strategy to discourage states from enforcing the death penalty. Further, many promising developments in retentionist countries, the high costs and procedural wrangles add weight to stop executions at the earliest.
(c) In the year 2007, the UN General Assembly adopted a non-binding resolution to evolve a strategy to prevent states from enforcing death sentence. This resolution was revived at the Fourth World Conference held in Geneva where it was made mandatory for all states to halt executions.
(d) The 2015 target, proposed by the Spanish Prime Minister at the Fourth World Conference in Geneva, to enforce a moratorium on death penalty has been acknowledged by the principal retentionist countries in the world due to the high costs involved in the procedure.

Q2. In the sixteenth, seventeenth, eighteenth and nineteenth centuries, music inspired writers, philosophers, aristocrats and other thinkers of the time. Music of a classical variation was not available to the public. One had to attend a performance to experience the work of composers such as Bach, Beethoven and Mozart. Such music was considered that of the upper class and the sounds coming from the peasant's homes and markets were lesser versions of these grand orchestras. As time progressed there was a shift. With the birth of radio, television, record players and electric instruments, the entire idea of music changed. Music in the twentieth century is built on popularity among the masses. One hit wonders rule the radio waves. Everyone, from the poorest of poor to the richest of rich has the ability and right to listen to music. Age matters not in music appreciation, the twentieth century marks the time when young children begin to learn the classics on the piano.

(a) Music in the twentieth century has all the aspects of something underground and music after the twentieth century is that underground becoming mainstream.
(b) Music before the twentieth century was a privilege of a chosen few but music in the twentieth century is accessible to and appreciated by a large section of the population.
(c) Music in the twentieth century has a much greater variety than that of previous centuries.
(d) Music wouldn't truly have a purpose without its audiences. Before the twentieth century, music was the indulgence of the upper class but in the twentieth century, everybody enjoys one hit wonders.

Q3. Economists face two competing criticisms. Either they are lambasted for their arrogance or accused of being unwilling to draw firm conclusions (in exasperation at the hedging of his economic adviser, President Harry Truman requested a one-handed economist). Dani Rodrik of Harvard University, drawing on an idea from Isaiah Berlin, splits economists into two camps: hedgehogs and foxes. Hedgehogs take a single idea and apply it to every problem they come across. Foxes have no grand vision but lots of seemingly contradictory views, as they tailor their conclusions to the situation. More foxlike behaviour will not by itself prevent the next crisis; politicians anyway will still be making the decisions. But it could help policymakers be better prepared.

(a) The world has seen two types of economists: hedgehogs and foxes. Their hedgehog or foxlike behaviour is what they face criticism for. Because of the hedging of his economic adviser, President Harry Truman requested a one-handed economist.

(b) There are two types of economists: hedgehogs and foxes. Hedgehogs are stubborn in nature. Foxes are able to draw a firm conclusion after a lot of dillydallying.

(c) On the one hand, economists can be single-minded like hedgehogs. On the other hand, they can also be likened to foxes. While seemingly having no objective and being unable to make up their minds, this foxlike behaviour might help them to be better prepared for a crisis.

(d) Economists are of two competing types. Some of them apply a single concept to all problems because they resemble hedgehogs. Others have no vision and are not able to take a fast decision because they resemble foxes.

Q4. Rapid urbanisation has converted fertile agriculture, forests and wetlands into concreted areas that are unable to retain rainwater or channel them into tributary streams that feed the Cauvery. Urbanisation demands concrete; concrete requires sand. In the districts surrounding the Cauvery, rampant sand mining has altered the natural topography of the river, eroding its banks, widening the river and altering water flow patterns. Despite warnings from environmentalist groups and farmer coalitions, and interventions by the court, this practice continues unchecked. It is no surprise that the wells that replenish farms across the basin are running dry – or that desperate farmers are reduced to abandoning agriculture and renting their farms to sand contractors for sand storage, thus becoming complicit in their own destruction.

(a) In order to meet the huge demand on sand, caused by rapid urbanisation, sand mining is taking place unrestrained in the districts surrounding the Cauvery, despite resistance from environmentalist groups and farmer coalitions, with the result, the wells that replenish farms across the Cauvery basin are running dry.

(b) Rapid urbanisation has placed huge demand on construction material like sand and in order to meet this demand rampant sand mining is taking place in fertile regions surrounding the Cauvery basin and farmers in this region are renting out their farms to sand contractors as they find it more lucrative than agriculture.

(c) To meet the huge demand on sand due to rapid urbanisation, rampant sand mining is done in the districts surrounding the Cauvery, despite resistance from environmentalists and farmer coalitions, and hence the wells that replenish farms are running dry, forcing farmers to abandon agriculture and rent their farms to sand contractors, thus conniving in their own destruction.

(d) Rapid urbanisation in the areas surrounding the Cauvery basin has led to a huge demand for sand; hence farmers in the region, in connivance with sand contractors, are involved in rampant sand mining, thus being a cause for their our destruction.

Q5. Our most elite universities are today running away from their elitism, denying it and doing their best to conceal or suppress it. In running away from it, they not only disown values and traditions that are an important part of their identity, but they also disserve the great democratic country in which they sit. These elite schools are national treasures. Their elitism is what makes them such. It's not a problem, it's an asset, a value, something to be cherished and cared for.

(a) Our elite universities should preserve their elitist ethos because it is this elitism which makes them centres of distinguished learning.

(b) In order to fit into the democratic milieu of the country, it is necessary for universities to jettison their elitist character.

(c) By concealing their elitism, universities are abandoning their traditional values and thereby doing a great disservice to the nation.

(d) Elite universities, which are cherished for championing traditional value systems, play a significant role in upholding the democratic spirit of a country.

Q6. When a court issues a decision, the judge writes an opinion, typically running into many pages, in which he explains his reasoning. He grounds the decision in law, precedent, common sense and principles that he feels obliged to articulate and defend. This is what transforms the decision from mere fiat into something that is politically legitimate, capable of securing the assent of free people. It constitutes the difference between simple power and authority. One distinguishing feature of a modern, liberal society is that authority is supposed to have this rational quality to it - rather than appealing to, say, a special talent for priestly divination. This is our Enlightenment inheritance.

(a) A judgement which is not based on sound reasoning fails to gain acceptance from the general public.

(b) When compared to the conservative societies of yore, which relied on priestly divination, authority in the modern liberal society is rooted in the principles of rationalism.

(c) Authority, entrenched in the principles of rationalism, is the hallmark of modern liberal society.

(d) A verdict passed by an authority ceases to be politically legitimate if it is not based on sound reasoning.

Q7. Attempting to explain the genesis of crime in the cultural context, rather than exploring it within the framework of culture, hardly seems to be level-headed. The recent data, which included inputs form psychology, criminology, sociology and cultural anthropology, suggest that the violence is, in part, a means of achieving identity, as well as a way of gaining social capital, which can be understood within the context of culture. Thus, taking a culturally situated approach to understanding criminal violence can facilitate a richer understanding of violence and its motivations by extending existing theory, which has implications for clinical practice, for criminal justice process and for the community as a whole.

(a) Understanding of criminal violence is better served by cultural context which is not contaminated by consideration of personal traits.

(b) Criminal violence can be prevented and criminal justice can prevail if the genesis of the criminal justice is identified in a cultural context.

(c) Culturally situated approach is the best way not only to identify the genesis of criminal violence but also serve criminal justice process as well as the community.

(d) Understanding of the roots of criminal violence should look for the psychological bases of the crime from an integrated approach.

Q8. The concept of democratic quality consists of two necessary, but independently insufficient, components. The first is an opportunity-structure component, which includes the institutional and structural opportunities that allow for democratic rule. The second is a citizen component, which refers to the ways in which citizens can and do breathe life into existing institutional opportunities for democratic rule. Different models of democracy place different demands on citizens as much as they do on institutions. Thus, the research of quality of democracy needs to engage with work in political behaviour and political psychology, from which it has traditionally been disconnected.

(a) Institutional opportunities should ideally be independent of the citizen component in a democracy.

(b) The quality of democracy depends on the models it chooses to depend on.

(c) The quality of democracy depends on the quality of both citizens and structure.

(d) Political behaviour and political psychology of citizens bear insignificant influence on quality of democracy.

Q9. While ancient philosophers might disagree about ethics and the best way to live, there were few moral relativists in Ancient Greece. Epicurus, Aristotle and Zeno, the founder of the Stoics, not to mention Plato, all believed that their moral values were objective truths, not simply opinions. For Plato, a transcendent exemplar of that is good lies externally. The Stoics believed that virtue was written into the very fabric of reality, waiting to be discovered by the wise sage. It followed that once you discovered how to be good, you had also discovered quite a lot about how the universe worked. Ethical precepts came first, and natural philosophy had to cohere with these moral commitments.

(a) Moral relativism is the hallmark of ancient philosophy and is decided by the discovery of truth about the universe.

(b) Moral values that were enshrined by ancient philosophers depended primarily on individual perspective, about which there was a lot of disagreement.

(c) For ancient philosophers, ethics and moral values were far more important than the fabric of reality that is transcendental and temporal.

(d) For ancient philosophers, the concepts of right and wrong needed to be grounded in something external to the human mind.

Q10. Legitimate research problems should be empirically answerable, and at present the question of whether there is a crisis in the classics in India today is only partly so. Not only is the question of the vitality of classical knowledge complex, but data on higher education in India are woefully inadequate to answer it. There is no systematic database or accurate metric to enable us to move beyond the subjective and actually measure the severity of this problem, or indeed, almost any problem of knowledge production in the social sciences and the humanities. Accordingly, our account will be largely personal and anecdotal, and limited in its truth value by the limits of a few persons' experience - though these experiences are real and have a certain heuristic value.

(a) Research problems from humanities are solved in a less acceptable way than those from the fields of sciences, the subjectivity being the main culprit for the deficiency.

(b) Higher education in India does not give adequate importance to classics in India, making them vulnerable to the subjectivity in their interpretation.

(c) Knowledge production in the social sciences is not amenable to empirical data, a case easily understood by studying the crisis in the classics in India today.

(d) For want of adequate empirical data, we need to depend on subjective perception about the crisis being faced by classics in India, but this serves the purpose of insight into the problem.

Q11. Marine mammals use echolocation, in which animals produce short pulses of sound that are reflected when they strike an object, giving information about a potential prey. Blainville's beaked whales actually produce two distinct click types: search clicks and buzz clicks. Each of the click types occurs during a different phase of the foraging dive. Search clicks are emitted during the approach phase, at intervals of 0.2-0.4 second and a frequency of 26-51 kHz. Since strong echoes are received from these clicks, they function to enhance prey detection and classification. When the target is about 5 m away, the whale switches to buzz clicks, short bursts of sound at a frequency of 45-90 kHz or higher. Buzz clicks are highly repetitive, and researchers estimate that the whales may click 300 or more times in the last 3 m of their approach to the target, whose echoes help the animal where to attack.

(a) Blainville's beaked whales are most successful in predation because of the varying frequencies of sound they produce for echolocation.

(b) Blainville's beaked whales enhance their success of predation by varying the frequencies of sound produced for echolocation.

(c) Echolocation enhances the possibility of escaping from predation, especially when the sounds produced are of varying frequencies.

(d) Blainville's beaked whales, using a unique mechanism, change the frequencies of sounds they produce for echolocation and enhance their predation success.

Q12. It is a truism that in any country including India, the coastal population inevitably focuses attention on maritime security, while those far from the sea remain fixated on the land borders. India's security challenges across its land borders with Pakistan and China have only accentuated this trend.

(a) India's security concerns are mostly concentrated on its land borders.

(b) India has strengthened the security of its sea-lanes.

(c) Countries all over the world attempt to safeguard their shores while India concentrates its forces on the land borders.

(d) Maritime and land border security are of paramount importance to any country.

Q13. Democracy thrives when there are major opportunities for the mass of ordinary people to participate, through discussion and autonomous organisations, in shaping the agenda of public life, and when these opportunities are being actively used by them. This is ambitious in expecting very large numbers of people to participate actively in serious political discussion and in framing the agenda, rather than be the passive respondents to opinion polls, and to be knowledgeably engaged in following political events and issues. This is an ideal model which can almost never be fully achieved, but like all impossible ideals, it sets a marker. It is always intensely practical to consider where our conduct stands in relation to an ideal, since in that way we can try to improve.

(a) The ideal of democracy can be a beacon light for us to guide us in our attempts to improve.

(b) Ideals, which are impossible to achieve, are just theoretical aspects serving little purpose.

(c) Democracy is a myth without participation of very large numbers of people.

(d) Democracy requires active participation in opportunities to maximise one's potential.

Q14. Even in the highest level of animal development, speech, although human-like in its phonetical aspect, is not yet connected with intellect. Probably in the first stages in the development of the child, there also exists a pre-intellectual period in speech and a pre-speech period in thinking. Thought and word are not connected with each other by a primary bond. A connection originates, changes and grows in the course of development of thinking and speech. Yet, it would be wrong to regard thinking and speech as two unrelated processes which either run parallel to each other or cross each other at certain points of their course, thus entering into a purely mechanical interrelation. The absence of a primary bond between thought and word does not mean at all that this connection can come into existence only in an external way.

(a) Thought and speech, thought distinct, are not mutually exclusive.
(b) In early development of humans, speech develops thought and vice versa.
(c) The lack of primary bond between thought and speech necessitates an external way.
(d) We can never exaggerate the significance of external connection between thought and speech.

Q15. Since prehistory, literature and arts have been drawn to portrayals of physical environments and human-environment interactions. The modern environmentalist movement as it emerged first in the late-nineteenth century and, in its more recent incarnation, in the 1960s, gave rise to a rich array of fictional and nonfictional writings, concerned with humans' changing relationship to the natural world. Only since the early 1990s, however, has the long-standing interest of literature studies in these matters generated the initiative most commonly known as 'ecocriticism', an eclectic and loosely coordinated movement whose contributions thus far have been most visible within its home discipline of literature, but whose interests and alliances extend across various art forms and media.

(a) Arts and literature have leaned solely on nature for inspiration and portrayal of that inspiration.
(b) Ecocriticism has been the brain child of literature and arts, which are designed to our appreciation of natural world.
(c) The scope of ecocriticism has widened due to the evolution of human perspective towards environment.
(d) Ecocriticism has been counter-productive because it has not been able to generate interest in the natural world.

Exercise 6

Read the paragraphs given in each question and choose a suitable summary from the given options:

Q1. Wild hippos are noisy creatures, their calls travelling long distances across lakes and rivers. But until now the precise function of the loud "wheeze honks" the animals make has been a mystery. Scientists studying hippos at a nature reserve in Africa say the distinctive honks enable the large mammals to tell friend from foe. And the team says the animals can probably recognise individuals from their "voices." Study leader, Prof Nicolas Mathevon, from the University of Saint-Etienne in France has studied the sounds animals make across the world, from leopard seals to hyenas. He said hippos have a wide vocal repertoire, including grunts, bellows, squeals and "wheeze honks," but very little is known about their social communication. "In their call, there is information about the identity of the individual - so they have 'voices' - and they are able to recognise each other by their voices," he said. "This recognition ability supports the social relationships between individuals."

(a) Wild hippos are noisy creatures, and they establish a social relationship with each other through the loud "wheeze honks."
(b) Hippos can recognise their friends voice through the wheeze honks-in their calls to make voices they make for their communication.
(c) Wild hippos are noisy creatures having a wide vocal repertoire, make wheeze honks - in their call have information about their identity - voices through which they recognise friends and support social relationships between individuals.
(d) Scientists studying hippos at a nature reserve in Africa say the distinctive honks enable the large mammals to tell if it's a friend.

Q2. On the backdrop of UNCTAD, recent publication on "Global Investment Trends", Global foreign direct investment (FDI) flows showed a strong rebound in 2021, up 77 per cent to an estimated $1.65 trillion, from $929 billion in 2020, surpassing their pre-COVID-19 level. The outlook for global FDI in 2022 is positive. Measures taken by the government on the fronts of FDI policy reforms, investment facilitation and ease of doing business have resulted in increased FDI inflows into the country. The following trends in India's FDI are an endorsement of its status as a preferred investment destination amongst global investors. India has attracted highest ever total FDI inflow of US$ 81.72 billion during the financial year FY 2020-21. Supported by a strong pace of vaccination, India's GDP growth at 9.2 per cent in 2021-22 is projected to be the highest among all large economies. With India moving up strongly and steadily in the ease of doing business, it gets an edge to attract private and foreign investors.

(a) India has attracted highest FDI inflow supported by a strong pace of vaccination, getting an edge to attract private investors.

(b) India has attracted greater FDI inflow supported by a strong pace of vaccination, getting an edge to attract private and foreign investors.

(c) The Global Foreign Direct Investments showed a strong rebound, in hands with an ease of doing business, political reforms, investment facilitation making India the fastest growing economy.

(d) Global foreign direct investment (FDI) flows showed a strong rebound in 2021, up 77 per cent to an estimated $1.65 trillion, from $929 billion in 2020, surpassing the pre-COVID-19 level.

Q3. Zero carbon flights are the ultimate goal for an airline industry that relies heavily on fossil fuels. Aviation pumps out at least 2.5 per cent of global carbon dioxide (CO_2) emissions today. Sustainable aviation fuels will shrink the industry's climate risk by 2030, but zero-emissions fuels like hydrogen are beginning to emerge. The US government says lowering aviation emissions 20 per cent by 2030 is realistic and the industry should achieve net zero emissions by 2050. To hit net zero - where carbon from jet fuel and other sources is balanced by removing an equal amount from the atmosphere - the airlines must cut fuel emissions and offset the rest.

(a) There should be an introduction to sustainable aviation fuels (Zero carbon flights) in order to lower the aviation emissions for combating the climate risks.

(b) The aviation pumps around 2.5 per cent of global carbon dioxide and probably there is a need for zero emissions fuels like hydrogen.

(c) In order to achieve zero emissions, the carbon emitted from jet fuels is balanced by removing equal amount from atmosphere.

(d) There should be a cut in the fuel emissions by the aviation industry since they are probably causing the climate risk.

Q4. One of the world's rarest sea lion species was driven into near extinction after being targeted by hunters. Now, New Zealand sea lions are repopulating the coasts - surprising locals in unexpected places. Surrounded by the South Pacific Ocean, sea lions were once found on every coast of the island nation of New Zealand. The once-flourishing species was hunted to the brink of extinction over a century ago. But since 1993, these rare animals have been making a comeback. The former breeding grounds of the once-flourishing species are now populated by humans. New Zealand's Department of Conservation is helping to fund research that can better predict the settling and habitation patterns of sea lions. By collaborating with sea lion experts and local wildlife rangers, the New Zealand government hopes to minimize threats to the endangered sea lions as their populations make a comeback.

(a) The rare sea lion species are now repopulating the coasts and taking back the main-lands which are now populated by humans.

(b) The New Zealand's Department of Conservation is helping to fund research on the settling and habitation patterns of the sea lions.

(c) The New Zealand's Department of Conservation is helping fund. research on settling and habitation patterns of the rare sea lions that were on the verge of extinctions a century ago, now which are taking back the mainland by spotting on various unexpected places.

(d) The New Zealanders will have to learn to cohabitate with the sea lions since they have been spotted at various unexpected places.

Q5. Talking about doomsday - the end of human civilisation - many scenarios don't measure up. People and machines might converge in ways that you and I would find ghastly, but in future, they would probably represent an adaptation. Environmental collapse might make parts of the globe unpleasant, but considering that the biosphere has survived ice ages, it wouldn't be the final curtain. Depression, which has become 10 times more prevalent in Western nations in the post war era, might grow so widespread that vast numbers of people would refuse to get out of bed, a possibility. But Marcel Proust, as miserable as he was, wrote *Remembrance of Things Past* while lying in bed. At a time of global unease, worst-case scenarios have a certain appeal, not unlike reality TV. And it's only natural to focus on danger; if nature hadn't programmed human beings to be wary, the species might not have gotten this far.

(a) Talking about doomsday - end of human civilisation - but human species is programmed by nature to be wary. Life would go on even when there are awful scenarios, the humans adapt or evolve and sustain.

(b) People and machines might converge in ghastly ways, but from the standpoint of the future, they would probably represent an adaptation.

(c) Talking about doomsday - end of human civilisation - but human species is programmed by nature to be wary. A single nuclear bomb ignited by terrorists, would be awful beyond words, but life would go on.

(d) At a time of global unease, worst-case scenarios have a certain appeal, And it's only natural to focus on danger; if nature hadn't programmed human beings to be wary, the species might not have gotten this far.

Q6. From mules to ligers, the list of human-made hybrid animals is long. And, it turns out, ancient. Meet the kunga, the earliest known hybrid animal bred by people. The ancient equine from Syro-Mesopotamia existed around 4,500 years ago and was a cross between a donkey and a hemippe, a type of Asiatic wild ass, researchers report January 14 in *Science Advances*. Horses didn't appear in this region of Asia until 4,000 years ago, centuries after their domestication in Russia. But dozens of equine skeletons were excavated in the early 2000s from a royal burial complex dating back to 2600 B.C. at Umm el-Marra in northern Syria. The animals, whose physical features didn't match any known equine species, appear to be "kungas" – horse-like animals seen in artwork and referenced in clay tablets predating horses by centuries. "They were highly valued, very expensive," says paleogeneticist Eva-Maria Geigl of Institut Jacques Monod in Paris.

(a) Kunga, A manmade hybrid animal is a horse-like animal seen in artwork and referenced in clay tablets predating horses by centuries.

(b) The ancient equine from Syro-Mesopotamia existed around 500 years ago and was cross between a donkey and a hemippe.

(c) The Kungas, man-made hybrid horse-like animal, a type of an Asiatic wild ass, were highly valued and expensive.

(d) The Kungas were manmade hybrid horse-like equine from Syro-Mesopotamia existed around 500 years ago and was cross between a donkey and a hemippe type of an Asiatic wild ass and were highly valued and expensive.

Q7. For years, scientists have argued over how organic chemicals in ALH 84001 formed. Possible explanations have included abiotic factors, such as volcanic activity or cosmic impacts, as well as ancient life on Mars or contamination from our planet after the meteorite fell to Earth.

To help solve this mystery, the researchers analysed tiny minerals within the meteorite. They discovered that organic compounds in the meteorite were associated with serpentine-like minerals. Serpentine is a dark green mineral, sometimes mottled or spotted like a snake's skin, which is associated with once-wet environments. These findings suggest the organic chemicals in ALH 84001 may have formed due to water-rock interactions similar to ones known to happen on Earth. One process, called serpentinization, happens when iron- or magnesium-rich volcanic rocks chemically interact with circulating water, changing their mineral nature and producing hydrogen. The other interaction, called carbonation, involves rocks reacting with slightly acidic water containing dissolved carbon dioxide to form carbonate minerals.

(a) The organic chemical in ALH 84001 are formed due to abiotic factors, such as volcanic activity or cosmic impacts, as well as ancient life on Mars or contamination from our planet after the meteorite fell to Earth.

(b) To solve the mystery of the formation of organic chemicals in ALH 84001, the researchers analysed and discovered from a meteorite that they were associated with serpentine-like minerals, and may have formed due to serpentinisation and carbonation.

(c) The organic compounds in the meteorite were associated with serpentine-like, dark green mineral, sometimes mottled or spotted like a snake's skin, that is associated with once-wet environments.

(d) The organic chemicals in ALH 84001 may have formed due to water-rock interactions similar to ones known to happen on Earth.

Q8. An anti-lock braking system (ABS) is a safety anti-skid braking method used on aircraft, now used in cars, Motorcycles, and buses. ABS functions by preventing the wheels from locking up while braking, through keeping a tractive connection with the road surface. ABS is an automatic system that uses principles of threshold braking and cadence braking, methods which are practiced by skilled riders. ABS generally offers advanced vehicle control and drops halting distances on dry and some smooth surfaces on loose gravel or snow-covered surfaces. ABS significantly increases braking distance, improving steering control. Since ABS was introduced in production vehicles, it has become increasingly advanced and powerful. Depending on its unique capabilities and combinations, it is also known as electronic brake force distribution, traction control system, emergency brake assist, or electronic stability control (ESC). In the future, it may not simply prevent wheel lock but may also change the front-to-rear brake bias.

(a) An anti-lock braking system (ABS) which has become increasingly advanced and powerful, uses principles of threshold and cadence braking, now is a widely used system that prevents the wheels from locking up while braking by keeping tractive connection with road surface - generally offers advanced vehicle control and drops halting distances on dry and some smooth surfaces.

(b) An anti-lock braking system (ABS), has now become advanced and powerful, uses principles of threshold and cadence braking, now is widely used system that prevents the wheels from locking up while braking through keeping a tractive connection with the road surface.

(c) An anti-lock braking system (ABS) is a safety anti-skid braking method used on aircraft, now it is used in Cars, Motorcycles, and buses, functions by preventing the wheels from locking up while braking, through keeping a tractive connection with the road surface.

(d) ABS significantly increases braking distance, improving steering control. Since ABS was introduced in production vehicles, it has become increasingly advanced and powerful. Depending on its unique capabilities and combinations, it is also known as electronic brake force distribution.

Q9. The real pirates of the Caribbean operated during the Golden Age of Piracy (1690-1730) terrorising merchant ships and colonial ports to grab gold, liquor and any cargo they fancied during their adventurous but almost always had short careers in crime. In this collection, we look at all the key aspects of being a pirate from wearing the flashiest clothes and handling the best weapons to saying the right maritime expressions. We look, too, at the havens they used, the treasure they captured, and the punishments they suffered. Finally, we showcase four of the most notorious pirates. There is the master of showmanship Blackbeard, Captain Kidd and his fabled buried treasure that still tantalises treasure-seekers today, Anne Bonny who fought with more courage than her male crewmates, and the most successful of them all, mad, bad Bartholomew Roberts.

(a) The real pirates of the Caribbean operated during the Golden Age of Piracy terrorising merchant ships and colonial ports to grab gold, liquor and any cargo they fancied during their adventurous but almost always had short careers in crime.

(b) All the key aspects of being a pirate were looked for, from wearing the flashiest clothes and handling the best weapons to saying the right maritime expressions.

(c) Four of the most notorious pirates are the master of showmanship Blackbeard, Captain Kidd and his fabled buried treasure that still tantalises treasure-seekers today, Anne Bonny who fought with more courage than her male crewmates, and the most successful of them all, mad, bad Bartholomew Roberts.

(d) The real pirates of the Caribbean operated during the Golden Age of Piracy befriending merchant ships and colonial ports to grab gold, liquor and any cargo they fancied during their adventurous but almost always short careers in crime.

Q10. Nearly a third of the world's oceans and land should be protected by 2030 to stem extinctions and ensure humanity lives in harmony with nature. That is the suggestion from 195 countries in a proposed United Nations plan to tackle the global destruction of nature. The measure is one of 21 targets in the first draft of the Global Biodiversity Framework (GBF). Others include reforming planning systems to protect species, ending farming subsidies that are driving wildlife losses, and boosting conservation funding by at least $200 billion a year. Overall funding today is about $100 billion a year. "Despite on-going efforts, biodiversity is deteriorating worldwide and this decline is projected to continue or worsen under business-as-usual scenarios," says the draft, which negotiators will need to finalise in time for a major UN biodiversity summit in October.

(a) The UN plan laid by 195 countries suggests that nearly a third of the world's ocean and land needs to be conserved in order to save stem extinctions and ensure harmony with nature.

(b) The UN plan suggests that the world's ocean and land should be protected in order to tackle the global destruction of nature and despite planning for the protection of the species, and boosting conservation funding, the biodiversity is deteriorating worldwide.

(c) The UN plan implements various measures and arranges conservation funding in order to tackle the global destruction and despite of the efforts, the biodiversity is deteriorating worldwide.

(d) The UN plan states that a third of the world's ocean and land needs to be conserved and despite of planning systems to protect the species, the biodiversity is endangered.

Q11. The age of the electric car is upon us. Earlier this year, General Motors announced that it aims to stop selling petrol-powered and diesel models by 2035. Audi, based in Germany, plans to stop producing such vehicles by 2033. Many other automotive multinationals have issued similar road maps. Suddenly, major carmakers' foot-dragging on electrifying their fleets is turning into a rush for the exit. The electrification of personal mobility is picking up speed in a way that even its most ardent proponents might not have dreamt of just a few years ago. In many countries, government mandates will accelerate change. But even without new policies or regulations, half of global passenger-vehicle sales in 2035 will be electric. This massive industrial conversion marks a shift from a fuel-intensive to a material-intensive energy system. In the coming decades, hundreds of millions of vehicles will hit the roads, carrying massive batteries inside them.

(a) The US automobile giant General Motors announced that it aims to stop selling petrol-powered and diesel models by 2035. Audi, based in Germany, plans to stop producing such vehicles by 2033.
(b) There will be a massive shift from a fuel- intensive to a material intensive energy system since major carmakers are foot-dragging on electrifying their fleets in hands with the government mandates that will accelerate the change.
(c) The electrification of personal mobility is picking up speed in a way that even its most ardent proponents might not have dreamt of just a few years ago.
(d) Even without the new policies or regulations given by many countries government, half of global passenger-vehicle sales in 2035 will be electric.

Q12. According to Duke University ecologist James Clark, many researchers think that, given the right conditions, trees can generally continue to grow for a very long time, producing more seeds all the while. But the common agricultural practice of replacing fruit and nut trees every few decades to avoid declining yields belies this dogma, he points out. "Nobody who's trying to produce seeds or nuts for a profession would rip out their trees and plant new ones if they didn't have to." The researchers found that although seed output, or fecundity, initially increased dramatically with tree size across all species, there was a point where fecundity started to decline in 63 per cent of the species they studied, while in another 17 per cent, the rate of fecundity instead plateaued at a certain size. In the remaining 20 per cent, there appeared to be no negative effect of tree size on fecundity, although the authors note this could have been due to the difficulty in finding larger members of those species.

(a) Researchers think that, given the right conditions, trees can generally continue to grow for a very long time, producing more seeds all the while, But the common agricultural practice of replacing fruit and nut trees every few decades to avoid declining yields belies this dogma.
(b) The fecundity increases with increase in the size of the tree across all species whereas at certain size of the tree it plateaus, contradicting the theory that given the right conditions, trees can generally continue to grow for a very long time, producing more seeds all the while.
(c) Researchers found that fecundity, initially increased dramatically with tree size across all species, there was a point where fecundity started to decline in 63 per cent of the species they studied, while in another 17 per cent, the rate of fecundity instead plateaued at a certain size.
(d) The fecundity increases with increase in the size of the tree across all species whereas at certain size of the tree it rises more, in agreement with the theory that given the right conditions, trees can generally continue to grow for a very long time, producing more seeds all the while.

Q13. How does political polarisation occur under repressive conditions? Drawing on psychological theories of social identity, the author posits that the nature of repression drives polarisation. Repression alters group identities, changing the perceived distance between groups and ultimately shaping the level of affective and preference polarisation between them through differentiation processes. The author tests the proposed causal relationship using mixed-method data and analysis. The results of a laboratory experiment reveal that exposure to a targeted repression prime results in greater in-group identification and polarisation between groups, whereas exposure to a widespread prime results in decreased levels of these same measurements. The effect of the primes appears to be mediated through group identification.

(a) Repression alters group identities, increasing the perceived distance between groups and ultimately shaping the level of affective and preference polarisation between them through differentiation processes.
(b) Repression alters group identities, changing the perceived distance between groups and ultimately shaping the level of affective and preference polarisation between them through differentiation processes.
(c) Exposure to a targeted repression prime results in greater in-group identification and polarisation between groups, whereas exposure to a widespread prime results in decreased levels of these same measurements.
(d) Exposure to a widespread prime results in greater in-group identification and polarisation between groups, whereas exposure to a targeted

repression prime results in decreased levels of these same measurements.

Q14. A new system helps labs determine the most efficient way to produce target molecules by utilising the strengths of humans and robots. Chemists have devised a new system to help robots and humans collaborate more efficiently in labs by recognising the strengths and weaknesses of each. Automation is a growing feature of chemistry labs, taking over many of the repetitive, complex and time-consuming tasks required to run experiments and measure results. In "self-driving laboratories," robots pour, mix, distil and titrate chemicals, while an artificial intelligence pores through data and highlights interesting experimental avenues.

(a) A new system is devised with collaboration of humans and robots using automation which takes over many repetitive, complex and time-consuming tasks while an artificial intelligence pores data highlighting interesting avenues.

(b) A new system helps labs determine the most efficient way to produce target molecules by utilising the strengths of humans and robots while Chemists have devised a new system to help robots and humans collaborate more efficiently in labs by recognising the strengths and weaknesses of each.

(c) Automation is a growing feature of chemistry labs, taking over many of the repetitive, complex and time-consuming tasks required to run experiments and measure results.

(d) A new system is devised with collaboration of humans and robots using automation which takes over many repetitive, complex and time consuming tasks while an artificial intelligence pores data highlighting interesting avenues.

Q15. Evolutionary perspectives suggest that participation in collective rituals may serve important communicative functions by signalling practitioners' commitment to the community and its values. While previous research has examined the effects of ritual signals at the individual and collective level, there has been limited attention directed to the impact of socio-environmental factors on the quality of ritual signalling. We show that participants' relative position in the social hierarchy systematically affects the form of ritual signalling. Moreover, signalling in each particular modality is stronger among individuals who participate in more public rituals, corresponding to their long-term commitment to the community. In sum, our results demonstrate that social hierarchies exact unequal requirements on ritual participants, who in turn modify their signalling strategies accordingly.

(a) Previously, there has been limited attention directed to the impact of socio-environmental factors on the quality of ritual signalling - whereas, Evolutionary perspectives suggest that participation in collective rituals may serve important communicative functions by signalling practitioners' commitment to the community and its values.

(b) There has been limited attention directed to the impact of socio-environmental factors on the quality of ritual signalling - whereas, Evolutionary perspectives implement the participation in collective rituals that serve communicative functions by signalling practitioners' commitment to the community and its values.

(c) Previously, there has hardly any attention directed to the impact of socio-environmental factors on the quality of ritual signalling - whereas Evolutionary perspectives suggest that participation in collective rituals may serve important communicative functions for the community and its values.

(d) There has been some attention directed to the impact of socio-environmental factors on the quality of ritual signalling And Evolutionary perspectives suggest that participation in collective rituals may serve important communicative functions by signalling practitioners' commitment to the community and its values.

Q16. The kangaroo's pouch is as a hoodie sweatshirt put on backwards. The hood of the sweatshirt is the pouch, and the drawstrings are the mother's muscles to open and close it. The inside of the pouch is the texture of the soft kangaroo's skin, but hairless. The pouch is very warm inside, the same as the mom's body temperature: about 105 degrees Fahrenheit (40.5 degrees Celsius). Because of this, it can get sweaty inside. When a mama kangaroo gives birth to a joey through the vaginal canal after 32 or 33 days of gestation, her baby is extremely undeveloped. About the size of a jellybean and weighing less than a gram, the new-born joey uses its forelimbs to crawl up into its mom's pouch. There, it latches onto an elongated teat, which swells and pokes down the throat of the baby, holding it in place for about three-and-a-half to four months.

(a) The kangaroo gives birth to an undeveloped joey, and the joey uses its forelimbs to crawl up to the soft and warm pouch - it latches onto an elongated teat which swells and pokes down the throat of the baby, holding it in place inside for about four months.

(b) The kangaroo's pouch is like a hoodie sweatshirt put on backwards – hood of the sweatshirt is the pouch, and the drawstrings are the mother's muscles she uses to open and close it.

(c) Inside of the kangaroo's very warm pouch is the texture of the skin, but hairless. It's soft and comparable with the skin on the inside of a person's wrist.

(d) Kangaroo gives birth to a joey through the vaginal canal after 32 or 33 days of gestation, her baby is undeveloped about the size of a jellybean and weighing less than a gram, the new born joey uses its forelimbs to crawl up into its mom's pouch.

Q17. The public distribution system in India is a major instrument for achieving the goal of "Zero Hunger". Despite the vast amounts of resources spent, the PDS suffers from several inefficiencies largely attributable to the monopoly of agents involved in the last-mile delivery of grains. To address this issue, several state governments in India have started implementing a novel intervention called portability. This intervention offers beneficiaries the choice of when and where they can avail of their food entitlements while the government controls what and how much.

(a) The public distribution system in India was designed to achieve the target of "Zero Hunger" - since there are hardly any amounts spent, PDS suffers from several inefficiencies due to the monopoly of the agents involved in the last-mile delivery of grains - to address this, novel intervention portability was implemented.

(b) The public distribution system in India was designed to achieve the target of "Zero Hunger" - although there are large amounts spent, PDS profits from several advantages due to the monopoly of the agents involved in the last-mile delivery of grains - to address this, novel intervention portability was implemented.

(c) The public distribution system in India was designed to achieve the target of "Zero Hunger" - although there are large amounts spent, PDS suffers from several inefficiencies due to the monopoly of the agents involved in the last-mile delivery of grains - to address this, novel intervention portability was implemented.

(d) The public distribution system in India was designed to achieve the target of "Zero Hunger" - although there are large amounts spent, PDS suffers from several inefficiencies due to the lack of the agents involved in the last-mile delivery of grains - to address this, novel intervention portability was implemented.

Q18. An innovative method of controlling a range of damaging crop diseases using native, beneficial soil bacteria has emerged from research-industry collaboration. The agri-tech innovation hopes to give farmers a way to reduce the cost and environmental damage caused by the chemical treatments currently in use to control crop diseases. The John Innes Centre team tested hundreds of strains of Pseudomonas bacteria from the soil of a commercial potato field, then sequenced the genomes of 69 of these strains. By comparing the genomes of strains shown to suppress pathogen activity with those that did not, the team were able to identify a key mechanism in some of strains that protected the potato crop from harmful disease-causing bacteria. Using a combination of chemistry, genetics and plant infection experiments they showed that the production of small molecules called cyclic lipopeptides is important to the control of potato scab, a bacterial disease that causes major losses to potato harvests.

(a) A combination of chemistry, genetics and plant infection experiments shows that the production of small molecules called cyclic lipopeptides is important to the control of potato scab, a bacterial disease that causes major losses to potato harvests.

(b) The agri-tech innovation hopes to give farmers a way to reduce the cost and environmental damage caused by the chemical treatments currently in use to control crop diseases.

(c) By comparing the genomes of strains shown to suppress pathogen activity with those that did not, it was able to identify a key mechanism in some of the strains that protected the potato crop from harmful disease-causing bacteria.

(d) Beneficial soil bacteria that aids in controlling the crop diseases in turn reducing the cost and environmental damage caused by the chemical treatments done to treat the harmful disease causing bacteria is an innovative method of controlling a range of damaging crop diseases done by the agri tech.

Q19. In 1993, South Africa announced that it had built nuclear weapons in the 1980s, before dismantling its arsenal, keeping matters secret from world. Till today, it remains the only country to have pulled off that exact trick. Other countries have gone nuclear in other ways. Countries with more economic and political clout have built weapons on their own timetables. Three other countries Israel, Pakistan, and North Korea have developed nuclear weapons while being supported by larger allies.

Many wealthy countries, including Australia, Brazil, Germany, Japan, and South Korea, have chosen not to pursue weapons programs. Recognising different paths to proliferation is an essential part of arms control: Grasping how one country is pursuing nuclear weapons can help other countries constrain that pursuit. There's meaningful variation in how states have thought about pursuing nuclear weapons and it changes how we think about stopping them. It changes how we think about managing them.

(a) Countries outside elite world powers kept nuclear weapons matters a secret - while many countries build weapons on their own timetables and some being supported by larger allies whereas many have chosen not to pursue weapons programs, Recognising these different paths to proliferation is an essential part of arms control: grasping how one country is pursuing nuclear weapons can help other countries constrain that pursuit.

(b) South Africa announced to world that it had built nuclear weapons in the 1980s, before dismantling its arsenal, for the first time, a country outside of the elite world powers had obtained nuclear capabilities while keeping matters a secret from almost everyone else.

(c) Some countries have developed nuclear weapons while being supported by larger allies, while many wealthy countries, including Australia, Brazil, Germany, Japan, and South Korea, have chosen not to pursue weapons programs.

(d) Recognising these different paths to proliferation is an essential part of arms control: Grasping how one country is pursuing nuclear weapons can help other countries constrain that pursuit. There's meaningful variation in how states have thought about pursuing nuclear weapons.

Q20. Little more than two months after it was first spotted in South Africa, the Omicron variant of the coronavirus SARS-CoV-2 has spread around the world faster than any previous versions. Scientists have tracked it in more than 120 countries, but remain puzzled by a key question: where did Omicron come from? There's no transparent path of transmission linking Omicron to its predecessors. Instead, the variant has an unusual array of mutations, which it evolved entirely outside the view of researchers. Omicron is so different from earlier variants, such as Alpha and Delta, that evolutionary virologists estimate its closest-known genetic ancestor probably dates back to more than a year ago, sometime after mid-2020 "It just came out of nowhere," says Darren Martin, a computational biologist at the University of Cape Town, South Africa.

(a) Little more than two months after it was first spotted in South Africa, the Omicron variant of the coronavirus SARS-CoV-2 has spread around the world faster than any previous versions.

(b) The Omicron variant of SARS-CoV-2 is the fastest growing mutant, found in South Africa, has no clue of its emergence and has an usual array of mutations that is very different from its predecessors Alpha and Delta.

(c) Omicron is so different from earlier variants, such as Alpha and Delta, that evolutionary virologists estimate its closest-known genetic ancestor probably dates back to more than a year ago, sometime after mid-2020.

(d) Scientists have tracked it in more than 120 countries, but remain puzzled by a key question: where did Omicron come from? There's no transparent path of transmission linking Omicron to its predecessors.

Q21. Twilight time between wakefulness and sleep is packed with creative potential. People drifting into light sleep were better problem solvers. The results help demystify the fleeting early moments of sleep and find ways to boost creativity. Rumour speaks that Thomas Edison used to chase the twilight moments between wakefulness and sleep. Supposedly, he used to fall asleep in a chair holding two steel balls. As he drifted off, the balls fell into metal pans, waking him up and he could write down his inventive ideas before falling asleep and forget them. Researchers tested Edison's method of cultivating creativity and volunteers came to solve tricky number problem. They were asked to convert a string of numbers into a shorter sequence. They weren't told that there was an easy trick to do this task. The second number in the sequence would always be the correct final number, too. Once discovered, this trick dramatically cut the solving time.

(a) It is believed that the twilight time is packed with creative potential and people who drifted into a light sleep were better problem solvers later and Thomas Edison used to chase these moments of creativity for his inventive ideas.

(b) Thomas Edison used to chase the twilight moments between wakefulness and sleep, he used to fall asleep in a chair holding two steel balls and as he drifted off, the balls fell into metal pans. The resulting clatter woke him. Then, he could write down his inventive ideas before he fell into a deep sleep and forgot them.

(c) Thomas Edison believed that the twilight time is packed with creative potential and people who drifted into a deep sleep were better problem solvers later.

(d) Thomas Edison believed that the twilight time is packed with creative potential and people who drifted into a light sleep were not better problem solvers later.

Q22. Archaeological excavations have discovered artefacts used by early humans, including stone tools, which suggest an extremely early date for human habitation and technology in the area. While the civilisations of Mesopotamia and Egypt have long been recognised for their celebrated contributions to civilisation, India has often been overlooked, especially in the West, though its history and culture is just as rich. The Indus Valley Civilisation (c. 7000–c. 600 BCE) was among the greatest of the ancient world, covering more territory than either Egypt or Mesopotamia, and producing an equally vibrant and progressive culture.

(a) Archaeological excavations have discovered artefacts used by early humans, including stone tools, which suggest an extremely early date for human habitation and technology in the area.

(b) The civilisations of Mesopotamia and Egypt have long been recognised for their celebrated contributions to civilisation, India has often been overlooked, especially in the West, though its history and culture is just as rich.

(c) Archaeological excavations have discovered human artefacts suggesting a date for human habitation and technology - Mesopotamia and Egypt recognised for their celebrated contributions to civilisation, India has its rich history and culture, the Indus Valley Civilisation among the greatest of the ancient world.

(d) Archaeological excavations have discovered human artefacts suggesting an extremely early date for human habitation and technology - Mesopotamia and Egypt recognised for their celebrated contributions to civilisation, India has its rich history and culture although overlooked by the West, the Indus Valley Civilisation among the greatest of the ancient world.

Q23. Drifting may seem somewhat random, but science can make useful predictions possible. In 1970s, people who managed ponds had problems with algae, plants and snails in water. To control the pests, managers brought four species of carp from Asia. But some of the fish escaped into rivers creating lots of troublesome fish. These non-native fish can bully ecosystems, growing fast and big, they scarf down lots of food on which the native fish would normally depend. Today, descendants of those carp remain a big problem. And as the fish spawn, their eggs have been drifting far and wide. Anticipating where something will drift can be a thorny challenge. But finding answers may head off crises. If science can solve problem, there's hope people may figure out how to stop it. Else, legions of carp eggs will grow into adults that out compete their neighbours. Stopping their spread would help reduce the overall damage they cause.

(a) Drifting may seem somewhat random, but science can make useful predictions possible - a species of carp, troublesome invasive species, growing fast and quickly taking over, drifting their eggs far away after spawning, has become a big problem.

(b) A species of carp, troublesome invasive species, growing fast and quickly taking over, drift their eggs far away after spawning, and that has become a big problem - If science can get ahead of the problem, there's hope people may figure out how to stop it, else, legions of carp eggs will grow into adults that out compete their neighbours.

(c) If science can get ahead of the problem, there's hope people may figure out how to stop it. But if science is too slow to answer this question, legions of carp eggs will grow into adults that out compete their neighbours.

(d) A species of carp, troublesome invasive species, a kind of non-native fish can bully ecosystems, quickly taking over. Growing fast and big, they scarf down lots of the food on which the native fish would normally depend. Today, the descendants of those carp remain a big problem.

Q24. The Portuguese built an empire largely composing of trade centres dotted around the coasts of three continents. The curiosity and expertise of Portuguese mariners like Vasco da Gama resulted in exploration of new sea routes down the coast of West Africa, around the Cape of Good Hope and across the Indian Ocean to India and beyond. The process by which the empire was built and maintained and its impact on local peoples, environments and trade networks were studied. Age of Exploration led to a new, more violent and disruptive world where colonial powers carved up the globe as they jostled to extract precious resources and to enslave and transport millions of people for use as free labour. This Age of Empires still has consequences today wherever colonial powers once imposed their language, culture and religion upon indigenous peoples worldwide.

(a) The Portuguese built an empire from 1420 onwards that was largely composed of trade centres dotted around the coasts of three continents and this colonial enterprise was driven by a search for African gold, Asian spices and Christian kingdoms in the east.

(b) The curiosity and expertise of Portuguese mariners like Vasco da Gama resulted in the exploration of new sea routes down the coast of West Africa, around the Cape of Good Hope and across the Indian Ocean to India and beyond.

(c) The Portuguese mariners had curiosity and explored various sea routes to continents in search of gold, spices and kingdoms - This Age of Empires, led to a new, more violent and disruptive world where colonial powers carved up the globe as they jostled to extract precious resources and enslaved various people for use of free labour.

(d) The Age of Empires, still has consequences today wherever colonial powers once imposed their language, culture and religion upon indigenous peoples worldwide.

Q25. Beginning with a survey of 80,000 managers, it is found that there is one quality that sets truly great managers apart from the rest: They discover what is unique about each person and then capitalise on it. Average managers play checkers, while great managers play chess. The difference? In checkers, all the pieces are uniform and move in the same way; they are interchangeable. You need to plan and coordinate their movements, certainly, but they all move at the same pace, on parallel paths. In chess, each type of piece moves in a different way, and you can't play if you don't know how each piece moves. More important, you won't win if you don't think carefully about how you move the pieces. Great managers know and value the unique abilities and even the eccentricities of their employees, and they learn how best to integrate them into a coordinated plan of attack.

(a) There is one quality that sets great managers apart from the rest: They discover what is common about each person and then capitalise on it - Great managers know and value the unique abilities and even the eccentricities of their employees, and they learn how best to integrate them into a coordinated plan of attack.

(b) While there are as many styles of management as there is one quality that sets truly great managers apart from the rest: They discover what is unique about each person and then stabilise on it - great managers know and value the unique abilities and even the eccentricities of their employees, and they learn how best to integrate them into a coordinated plan of attack.

(c) While there are as many styles of management as there is one quality that sets truly great managers apart from the rest: They discover what is unique about each person and then capitalise on it - great managers know and value the abilities and the eccentricities of their employees.

(d) While there are as many styles of management as there is one quality that sets truly great managers apart from the rest: They discover what is unique about each person and then capitalise on it - great managers know and value the unique abilities and even the eccentricities of their employees, and they learn how best to integrate them into a coordinated plan of attack.

Q26. Voltage, measured in Volts, is what pushes electrons to flow through a circuit called an electric current. The higher the voltage in a circuit, the more potential energy exists. Imagine a river running downhill. The height of the hill is voltage. The water is an electric current. A higher hill leads to a stronger river current. Likewise, a bigger voltage leads to a stronger electric current. Resistance in a circuit can slow the electric current generated by a voltage. But that current can still be harnessed to do useful work. A typical battery today might store a few volts of electricity. Long-distance power lines have high voltages that efficiently send electricity long distances. Devices called transformers step that voltage down to lower, safer levels before it travels through smaller lines to your home.

(a) Voltage, measured in Volts, pushes electrons to flow through a circuit, that flow of electrons is called an electric current - Higher the voltage in a circuit, the more potential energy exists to push electrons from one point to another - Long-distance power lines have high voltages that efficiently send electricity long distances. Devices called transformers step that voltage down to lower, safer levels before it travels through smaller lines to your home.

(b) Voltage, measured in Volts, pushes electrons to flow through a circuit, that flow of electrons is called an electric current - Higher the voltage in a circuit, the lesser potential energy exists to push electrons from one point to another - Long-distance power lines have high voltages that efficiently send electricity long distances. Devices called transformers step that voltage down to lower, safer levels before it travels through smaller lines to your home.

(c) Voltage, measured in Volts, pushes electrons to flow through a circuit, that flow of electrons is called an electric current - Higher the voltage in a circuit, the more potential energy exists to push electrons from one point to another - Short-distance power lines have high voltages that efficiently send electricity long distances. Devices called transformers step that voltage down to lower, safer levels before it travels through smaller lines to your home.

(d) Voltage, measured in Volts, pushes electrons to flow through a circuit, that flow of electrons is called an electric current - Higher the voltage in a circuit, the more potential energy exists to push electrons from one point to another - Long-distance power lines have high voltages that efficiently send electricity long distances. Devices called transformers step that voltage up to higher, safer levels before it travels through lines to your home.

Q27. At one extreme are people with prosopagnosia, or "face blindness". Present a prosopagnosic person with a photograph, and you'll find that she can answer a diverse range of questions about a person in the picture, from hair colour to expressed emotion. But ask her to identify that person, and she will struggle - whether the photo depicts a celebrity, a close friend, or even herself. At the other extreme are "super recognisers," whose ability to detect faces is so extraordinary that it comes with its own flavour of social problem: seeing people you recognise everywhere, even if you passed them only briefly on the subway several years ago. Most of us fall somewhere in between, able to recognise hundreds to thousands of individuals, but not every single one.

(a) People with prosopagnosia struggle to identify the peoples face though they can answer diverse questions about a person in the picture, similarly, many people are able to recognise hundreds, but not every single one.

(b) People vary in their ability to recognise particular kinds of faces or particular people, people who look different from those who surround us harder to distinguish.

(c) People with prosopagnosia easily identify the peoples face though they fail to answer diverse questions about a person in the picture, similarly, many people are able to recognise hundreds, but not every single one.

(d) People are similar in their ability to recognise particular kinds of faces or particular people, people who look different from those who surround us harder to distinguish.

Q28. Developers are required by the state to safely remove western burrowing owls - a federally protected subspecies - from their land. But there's often little guidance on how to do that, and even less information on what happens to the birds in their new homes. Despite their name, western burrowing owls - found across arid grasslands from Canada to South America - do not burrow, they borrow. The 10-inch-tall birds hole up in abandoned burrows made by prairie dogs and ground squirrels, hunting insects and small mammals during the day and nesting with up to a dozen of their chicks at night. Because they don't dig their own homes, their owl's adopted burrows are crucial to their survival; lose the host species who digs the hole, lose the owls, as has been the case with prairie dog declines throughout the Great Plains.

(a) The western burrowing owls hole up in the abandoned burrows made by dogs and ground squirrels, hunt insects during the day and nest the chicks at night - the owls adopted burrows are crucial to their survival. Developers are required by the state to safely remove western burrowing owls but often they do it with inadequate information.

(b) Developers are required by the state to safely remove western burrowing owls - a federally protected subspecies - from their land, but there's often little guidance on how to do that, and even less information on what happens to the birds in their new homes.

(c) The 10-inch-tall birds hole up in abandoned burrows made by prairie dogs and ground squirrels, hunting insects and small mammals during the day and nesting with up to a dozen of their chicks at night.

(d) The owls don't dig their own homes, their owl's adopted burrows are crucial to their survival; lose the host species who digs the hole, lose the owls, as has been the case with prairie dog declines throughout the Great Plains.

Q29. Many scholars have identified fundamental differences between the causes and consequences of issues experienced in the rural and urban sectors. The rural sector has five identifying characteristics. Firstly, people are either directly or indirectly dependent upon agriculture. Next, the upper caste citizens are the largest landholders. Thirdly, the roles and values of rural people are traditional. Also, the farmers receive inadequate compensation for their hard work. Finally, people are scattered in rural areas as compared to urban cities. This isolation means that their access to services like banks, hospitals and schools is also minimal.

(a) Several differences between the causes and consequences of issues experienced the in rural and urban sectors are identified such as agriculture dependency, upper caste being the largest landlords and traditional viewpoints of people.

(b) People are scattered in rural areas as compared to urban cities and this isolation means that their access to services like banks, hospitals and schools is also minimal.

(c) People are grouped in rural areas as compared to urban cities and this union means that their access to services like banks, hospitals and schools is also in abundance.

(d) Several differences between the causes and consequences of issues experienced the in rural and urban sectors are identified such as agriculture independency, lower caste being the largest landlords and modern viewpoints of people.

Q30. The undeniable environmental ramifications of continued dependence on oil-derived jet fuel have spurred international efforts in the aviation sector toward alternative solutions. Due to the limited options for decarbonisation, the successful implementation of bio-aviation fuel is crucial in contributing to the roster of greenhouse gas emissions mitigation strategies for the aviation sector. Since fleet replacement with low-carbon technologies may not be a feasible option, due to the long lifetime and significant capital cost of aircraft, "drop-in" alternatives, which can be used in the engines of existing aircraft in a seamless transition, may be required. The economic and environmental performance of different potential bio-feed stocks and technologies are investigated and compared in order to make recommendations on short- and long-term strategies that could be employed internationally.

(a) The undeniable environmental ramifications of continued dependence on oil-derived jet fuel have spurred international efforts in the aviation sector toward alternative solutions.

(b) The economic and environmental performance of different potential bio-feed stocks and technologies are investigated and compared in order to make recommendations on short- and long-term strategies that could be employed internationally.

(c) The aviation sector is facing challenges in replacing the oil derived jet fuel whereas the implementation of biofuels to mitigate the greenhouse gas emissions is practiced – technologies are investigated in order to make recommendations on short and long term strategies that could be employed.

(d) Due to the limited options for decarbonisation, the successful implementation of bio-aviation fuel is crucial in contributing to the roster of greenhouse gas emissions mitigation strategies for the aviation sector.

Answer Key

Exercise 1

1. (b)	**2.** (d)	**3.** (c)	**4.** (b)	**5.** (d)
6. (c)	**7.** (b)	**8.** (d)	**9.** (d)	**10.** (c)
11. (c)	**12.** (c)	**13.** (a)	**14.** (b)	**15.** (c)
16. (c)	**17.** (a)	**18.** (d)	**19.** (b)	

Exercise 2

1. (c)	**2.** (a)	**3.** (a)	**4.** (c)	**5.** (c)
6. (a)	**7.** (a)	**8.** (d)	**9.** (c)	**10.** (b)

Exercise 3

1. (d)	**2.** (d)	**3.** (d)	**4.** (b)	**5.** (c)
6. (a)	**7.** (a)	**8.** (b)	**9.** (d)	**10.** (a)

Exercise 4

1. (a)	**2.** (b)	**3.** (a)	**4.** (d)	**5.** (c)
6. (a)	**7.** (a)	**8.** (c)	**9.** (a)	**10.** (d)
11. (a)	**12.** (d)	**13.** (c)		

Exercise 5

1. (b)	**2.** (b)	**3.** (c)	**4.** (c)	**5.** (a)
6. (c)	**7.** (d)	**8.** (c)	**9.** (d)	**10.** (d)
11. (b)	**12.** (a)	**13.** (a)	**14.** (a)	**15.** (c)

Exercise 6

1. (c)	**2.** (c)	**3.** (a)	**4.** (c)	**5.** (a)
6. (d)	**7.** (b)	**8.** (a)	**9.** (a)	**10.** (b)
11. (b)	**12.** (b)	**13.** (b)	**14.** (b)	**15.** (a)
16. (a)	**17.** (c)	**18.** (d)	**19.** (a)	**20.** (b)
21. (a)	**22.** (d)	**23.** (b)	**24.** (c)	**25.** (d)
26. (a)	**27.** (a)	**28.** (a)	**29.** (a)	**30.** (c)

Explanations

Exercise 1

1. (a) is incorrect as application of Ayurveda to modern medicine is an example of incremental innovation. (c) is incorrect as the last sentence states that total innovators conceive improvements whereas they conceive ideas from scratch hence there is no scope

for improvements in those ideas. According to (d) there are several forms of innovation whereas the passage states that there are basically two types. Hence this is a distortion of the facts presented in the passage. (b) provides the summary of the points correctly.

2. (a) is incorrect because it does not mention the main idea of the passage, which is the decision to deal with the current inmates from the Guantanamo facility. There are two options to resolve the issue before the government - send the inmates to their host countries or shift them to other US prisons. (b) does not take into account the option of moving detainees to supermax facilities. (c) is a distortion of the passage - President Obama has not closed down the facility yet. (d) captures the essence of the paragraph in the best manner.
3. The main idea of the passage is that the prevention of climate change will involve solutions which will be implemented over the decades to come. It will be a long-term exercise. However, climate change already has had negative consequences. Resilience measures are required to mitigate the impact of these consequences. Innovative and practical solutions are available that can be implemented through the participation of politicians, citizens, business firms and experts (various segments of society). These points are best summarised in (c).
4. Main Idea: Perrault is the first known individual to have written some form of fairy stories which then evolved into the modern fairy tales that we read as children. These stories have lent a certain degree of optimism to the human mind. We look for a happy ending in every contemporary novel or movie we see. Thus in a way these fairy tales provide the basic framework for all our contemporary stories. (b) best captures the essence of the passage.
5. According to the passage a lot of people, including political factions, believe that Anglo-Americans living beyond their means through debt was the root cause that pushed the world economy into recession. Instead of spending on credit, these countries should focus on savings. However, this opinion is flawed and reveals a lack of knowledge about the history of such a crisis. There is also an element of hypocrisy in judging these consumers - something which constitutes a necessary expenditure for some cannot become a wasteful expenditure for others, those who lack the means. Option (d) captures the theme correctly.
6. The passage refers to the fact that the Azadi Tower is the rallying point for all major national celebrations and anniversaries as well as for staging mass demonstrations. Hence it symbolises both the struggles and the victories of the Iranian people. (a) is too broad in focus. The passage specifically mentions Iran. (d) and (b) do not capture the main idea.
7. (a) does not cover the main idea. (c) is a distortion of the passage - the results it speaks of have not been achieved yet but are likely to be achieved in the future. (d) mentions the 1,00,000 genome project whereas the same has not been mentioned in the passage.
8. The passage talks specifically of the Lego decision and its consequences. It does not explore the idea mentioned in (a) in detail. The idea in (b) is incomplete. (c) does not talk about the roll back and related consequences.
9. (a) is incorrect because 'Kooks' was not one of his most popular songs until after his death. (b) mentions the quality of innocence which has not been mentioned in the passage. (c) is an incomplete summary of the passage. The chief purpose of the song was not to celebrate parenthood, it was to offer advice.
10. (a) is too general. (b) is incomplete as it does not mention the importance of the myth about Jesus. (d) is a distortion. Blake did not intend to popularise the myth; he merely returned to it because he longed for simpler times.
11. (a) is not the main idea of the passage but an introduction. (b) is an incomplete summary. (d) does not touch upon the point of ethical conduct.
12. (a) is too general. (b) also gives the reason of why songs are used as national anthems the world over which is unnecessary. (d) is too general and does not consider the ongoing debate over the English National Anthem.
13. (a) best captures all the main points of the passage. The others are incomplete in some way or the other.
14. (a) does not give enough information. (b) best captures the essence of the passage. (c) is a distortion - the fracking boom has not restricted supply. (d) is a distortion - the fracking boom was on the supply side and China's reduction in demand on the demand side.
15. (a) is too general. (b) is too narrow and does not include the other factors. (c) does not include the sex workers but covers all important reasons apart from sex workers. This is the main idea of the passage. (d) does not contain enough information.
16. (a) is incorrect because it talks of executives with poor communication skills which is not the issue here. (b) is incorrect because it only considers the problem of females being 'drowned out' and

not of their opinions being ignored. It also does not mention the communication techniques being taught to remedy that. (d) is wrong because it partially captures the essence of the text.

17. (b) is incorrect because it takes too extreme a stance against secularism. (c) is incorrect because it deviates from the main idea and focuses primarily on political correctness. (d) is incorrect because Charlie Hebdo has not been mentioned in that context in the passage.
18. (a) only mentions the hypocrisy of companies but not the other reason, i.e. interdepartmental conflict. (b) talks about public opinion; however, the passage does not mention public opinion anywhere. (c) states that there is an inverse relationship between spending on CSR and tax lobbying whereas the passage points to a direct relationship, i.e. higher the CSR spending, higher the tax lobbying. (d) captures the relationship between CSR expenditure and tax avoidance correctly and also the two reasons for the same provided in the passage.
19. According to the passage, freedom, diversity and human rights form the essence or concept of modern democracy. Certain forces, by threatening these ideals, also threaten democracy. The passage also speaks of troubled times and that we are currently in a state of war against such forces; however, this war is being fought in a new battleground, namely the Internet and the streets of cities such as Paris.

    (a) is incorrect because it cites forms of modern warfare as the chief problem. (b) best captures the essence of the passage. (c) is too specific and off the main idea. (d) talks about terrorism which can be inferred from the passage but has not been specifically mentioned. It also only mentions a threat to liberty whereas the ideals of democracy are much broader in scope.

Exercise 2

1. (a) and (b) are incorrect because the options suggest that the management bureau's statement is true but the paragraph does not comment on its veracity. (c) is correct because it best captures the essence of the paragraph. It states that a newly opened glass elevator in Dubai has been closed now due to certain cracks that appeared on it. It also covers the part that the area's management bureau had assured later that the cracks do not pose any danger. (d) is incorrect as it states that the cracks are superficial, which might not be correct. Also, it suggests that the statement of the area management bureau came before the closing of the glass elevator but that cannot be inferred from the paragraph.
2. (a) best captures the essence of the paragraph. It states that in discussion between Greece and IMF, IMF has set out conditions for Greece if it needs financial aid from it to help it pull out of the struggling zone. Conditions are that Greece's partners in Eurozone should be convinced to write down Greece's debts and also that Greece should now be more stringent and tough with its economic reforms. These conditions, as can inferred, if put in place may help Greece to come out of the struggling economic zone. (b) is incorrect because nowhere it is mentioned that these conditions were declared publicly. Also it is mentioned in the paragraph that Eurozone must write down Greece's debts which means wavering off Greece's loan, it cannot be inferred that Eurozone must approve of this loan by IMF to Greece. (c) is incorrect as it missed out on the conditions set out by IMF to Greece. Option (d) changes the meaning of the paragraph. 'Despite...' means that these conditions are already up and running in Greece and despite that it needs a financial aid which is not what the paragraph means here.
3. Option (a) best captures the essence of the paragraph. Mathilda has this habit of saving two of everything, keeping a twin of everything. She has learnt this from her grandfather's experience where he offered a spare reel of thread to a German soldier who spared his and his family's life. Because of this she feels safe doing so. Option (b) is incorrect because it states that 'since' her grandfather saved his family's life, Mathilda is also saving a spare of everything, when nowhere is it mentioned in the passage that she is doing so since that incident. Option (c) is incorrect towards the end where it states that Mathilda feels safe saving a spare of everything especially during war. It cannot be inferred from the paragraph that Mathilda feels safe with this action of hers during war. War is mentioned in the context of her grandfather and her feelings of war times cannot be inferred. Option (d) is incorrect as the structure of this summary is redundant. It captures all the important points and essence of the paragraph fine but with a poor summary structure.
4. The passage clearly states that people who make their meals at home and follow an eating routine have better diets as compared to people who eat on the run or hastily. (c) best captures this essence. (a) is wrong because the passage does not suggest that the people who eat regular meals are healthier but that they eat healthier food than the other types in discussion. (b) is wrong because comparison is not just with the ones that eat unhealthy food but with

those who eat on the run or use media while eating. (d) is not even close to the discussion; in fact, it gives a different meaning; here it is comparing healthy and unhealthy food instead of people who eat it.

5. The passage shows that the girls in Delhi are not aware of the different taxes charged by restaurants. They believe them to be lower than they actually are. This idea is covered in (c). (a) is incorrect because paying for themselves or not, point is if they know these taxes or not. (b) is incorrect because there is no comparison in the passage between taxes charged in Delhi and other states. (d) is incorrect because the passage does not talk of a sense of disgust by Delhi girls, neither does it suggest that they 'deliberately' ignore the taxes' figures.
6. The paragraph states that party scholars in China pretended to be in agreement with the regime and their leader's latest thoughts but it was clear that they did not believe in it. 'The emperor had no clothes' hence indicates that Mr. Xi is surrounded by people who pretend to be supporters but are not really. Hence, he stands exposed to outsiders and, in reality, does not have the cover of his well-wishers. So (a) is the answer. (b) is incorrect because it refers to the breaking point for the country but does not indicate how Mr. Xi stands exposed. (c) is wrong because passage does not talk about Xi's reality getting exposed to all, his party members knowing his reality does not necessarily leave him exposed to everyone else. (d) is incorrect because one cannot infer that Xi has tried to cover up the atrocities of his regime.
7. (a) best summarises the passage. (b) is incorrect as it is too narrow. (c) is incorrect because it is incomplete. (d) is incorrect as the passage doesn't say this at all about language.
8. Illegal forest fires in the area have spread across poisonous gases in other neighbouring regions, due to which few normal societal activities have shut down. We can also infer that this fire has spread across various other islands in that area. (d) best captures the essence. (a) is narrow; it just talks about spreading of poisonous gases and not its consequence on human activities. (b) is narrow because it just talks about interrupted activities in Viber islands when the passage also mentions of other neighbouring islands. (c) is incorrect because it talks about interruption in all normal activities in the area whereas passage talks about only certain such activities; we cannot infer that all normal activities were interrupted.
9. The passage states that the mentioned play was good. (a) calls the idea rare which is out of scope. (b) merely mentions that the group conducted a play at Avery Fisher Hall, which is incomplete as the results are not mentioned. (c) is the correct answer as it states the play reaped great results with all the music and setting. (d) states that the group created a new version, which is not mentioned in passage.
10. Passage talks about Ramsey who is a perfect spokesman for behavioural economics. His audience never feels that he is pointing out their shortcomings, rather his own. (b) best mentions this essence. (a) is incorrect because the passage does not suggest that behavioural economics comprises Ramsey's weaknesses, he is just using his model to excel in this branch. (c) is incomplete as it does not mention behavioural economics, also the passage does not state why Ramsey is brilliant but just that he has is the perfect fit for the job here. (d) is incorrect because the passage does not mention Ramsey as popular, neither does it mention that he laughs at himself.

Exercise 3

1. (a) is negated because the paragraph does not talk about high on sugar drinks as an urgent public health battle. (b) is incorrect because it mentions that people should be able to make wiser health choices and not depend on government but the paragraph states on contrary that people should be educated by the government to be able to make wiser health choices. (c) is more of a conclusion than a summary and is too general. (d) is correct because it best summarises the issue of revival of big cups (of more than 250 ml capacity) ban and how it is better to encourage people to eat better than impose such bans.
2. (a) is incorrect as the passage suggests on the contrary that despite no lack of cure we have certain diseases like TB prevailing.

   (b) is incorrect because this option suggests only half the idea.

   (c) is incorrect because the passage does not talk of social evils.

   (d) is correct because the passage suggests that despite the availability of cure, a certain disease prevailing among the people means that in order to counter a disease one must look at other aspects too.
3. (a) is incomplete; it merely states that Flipkart has too much power but not that it is abusing that power.

   (b) is incorrect as the passage does not suggest that Flipkart is doing anything of that sort.

   (c) is also incomplete as like (a); it also refers to publicity in general and not that of books.

(d) is correct as it captures the essence of passage; it states that Flipkart has the power to kill the buzz made by books and is definitely abusing that power.

4. (a) is incorrect; passage does not suggest that.

   (b) is correct and best captures the essence of the passage.

   (c) is incorrect because deprivation/improvement of one person's rights does not affect other person's rights in any way. The passage does not suggest that.

   (d) is too narrow in scope.

5. The passage talks of South Korea which has seen drastic changes for 60 years after the Korean War ended and it made cordial political relations with the West.

   (a) is incorrect because increase in population has not brought any such change in South Korea according to passage.

   (b) is narrow in scope.

   (c) is correct as it best captures the essence of the passage and that it has seen changes 60 years after the Korean War and is making peaceful relations with the West.

   (d) is incorrect because an increase in population has not brought any such change in South Korea according to passage.

6. (a) best captures the essence of the passage. It talks about how we have progressed in mobile phone devices industry, and future technology is highly unpredictable in this fast moving technology-driven industry.

   (b) is incorrect because it states that the changes and innovations in this mobile phone devices industry are in line with the expectations of the people. Passage doesn't suggest that.

   (c) is incorrect because the passage does not suggest that the new features introduced tomorrow will be at the discretion of mobile phone industry but that we cannot predict that.

   (d) is incorrect as it talks about mobile networks, whereas passage talks about mobile phone devices.

7. The passage focuses on two points: firstly, that a large number of voters of electoral college of Pakistan cast ballots to reassert the support to democracy and as a result the authoritarian President was denied majority.

   (a) covers both these points and is the correct answer.

   (b) is incorrect as it is incomplete. They came out and denied him majority is not mentioned here.

   (c) is narrow in scope.

   (d) is narrow in scope.

8. The passage talks of the situation at the Wall Street and the professor quotes that this situation is in line with the results of the various social experiments that he has conducted. So, we can conclude that Wall Street is just an example of the general trend in which too much access to money lowers the level of empathy with the poor.

   (a) is too narrow in scope as it only talks about the example and not the assertion made by the professor.

   (b) best captures the assertion of the author and its example.

   (c) is incorrect because it does not compare the empathy level of the rich with that of the author.

   (d) is too narrow in scope as it only talks about the example and not the assertion made by the professor.

9. (a) is incorrect as the passage does not suggest that death should/should not be mourned but it talks of ephemerality of life as beautiful and tragic.

   (b) is incorrect as the passage does not suggest that Egyptians did/did not believe in afterlife.

   (c) is incorrect as the passage does not suggest that Egyptians did/did not believe in afterlife.

   (d) best captures the essence of the passage because it talks of the view of Egyptians in the context of the ephemerality of life and death being a stage of life, which even though tragic is beautiful.

10. (a) best captures the essence of the passage. It talks about Greece defaulting on IMF's debt repayment date, its probable inability to repay further debts and the possibility of Greece losing euro as its currency because of all this.

    (b) is incorrect because it is incomplete.

    (c) is incorrect because the passage does not suggest that Greece took loans to maintain its currency.

    (d) is incorrect as it is an opinion; passage is stating facts and is objective. Moreover nowhere is it mentioned that international financial bodies should help Greece.

Exercise 4

1. Option (a) is correct because it captures well what the paragraph states that Russia has violated Turkey's airspace twice which has resulted in NATO calling an urgent meeting of the ambassadors of the member nations. The ambassadors then summoned Moscow's ambassador to issue a warning about 'undesirable incidents' in case of any such repetitions.

   Option (b) is incorrect as paragraph doesn't suggest that Ankara has requested NATO to threaten Russia.

Option (c) is incomplete as it doesn't capture the past actions of Russia in terms of airspace violation.

Option (d) is incorrect because NATO issuing warnings to Russia has nothing to do with Russia's militia actions in Syria.

2. Option (a): Religion can be approached via faith and not understood.

   Option (b) talks about approaching fundamental questions and is the correct answer.

   Option (c) is narrow in scope.

   Option (d) is incorrect in delivering the gist of the passage.

3. Passage shows that the UK public is not aware of the costs of treatment provided by NHS to them; thus they are ignorant of these costs. This is covered in option (a).

   Option (b) is not mentioned in passage.

   Option (c) is incorrect as comparison of healthcare costs of the UK and other countries is not done in passage.

   Option (d) is incorrect as the costs being reasonable or not is not stated in passage.

4. Roosevelt is not urging or criticising the government or its ideology; he is just stating his beliefs of good governance.

   Option (a) and (b) are incorrect as it seems Roosevelt is appealing/urging to public/government to take action which is not the case.

   Option (c) is incorrect as Roosevelt is not criticising any form of governance in passage but he is only suggesting his way of governance.

   Option (d) captures the gist of the passage well as simply his beliefs are states here, also that his tenure exemplifies his thinking and beliefs.

5. Option (a) is incorrect as the UN is forcing countries to take any action; it is just presenting its findings and report.

   Option (b) is incorrect as it is narrow in scope; it doesn't state the details of the UN's report.

   Option (c) is correct as it captures the whole gist of the passage that the UN report, which states that more has to be done for arresting climate change, has come right before the Paris summit.

   Option (d) is incorrect as the UN is not demanding anything, nor does it state that the countries 'must' follow its directives.

6. Option (a) is correct as the passage talks about a research that was conducted and led to the conclusion that eating certain types of fruits and vegetables during early adulthood (20-40 years) 'may' result in a reduced risk of breast cancer.

   Option (b) is incorrect as it is narrow in scope.

   Option (c) is incorrect as it doesn't include benefits of including fruits in early age in decreasing the risk of cancer.

   Option (d) is incorrect as passage doesn't state the 'definite' way to reduce the risk of cancer but a probable suggestion.

7. Option (a) is correct as it captures the true essence of the passage that the tear ducts of women are smaller; hence the tears roll down the cheeks, also that as they age this becomes of same size as of men.

   Option (b) is incorrect as passage is talking about tears as a fact and not them crying. Crying may be one of the causes if tears but is not the only cause.

   Option (c) is incorrect as passage doesn't talk about emotions of men and women here.

   Option (d) is incorrect as it is too narrow in scope. The consequences of smaller tear ducts are not stated here.

8. Option (a) is incorrect as passage doesn't talk about significance and benefits of Federal system.

   Option (b) is incomplete, as passage doesn't necessarily state that public won't caste vote if asked to do so often, but that so many offices lead to so many elections, thus less turnout.

   Option (c) is correct as the passage state that how the frequency of elections affects the choice of voters to cast their votes. It says that in some communities, where local offices and federal and state elections are held together, voters do not pay sufficient attention to local issues. Also, sometimes voters choose not to cast their votes if they are frequently asked to do so. So if the voters do not exercise their right to vote, the election results will not necessarily reflect their choice.

   Option (d) is incorrect in complete sense to the passage.

9. Option (a) is the answer as passage states that Nestle has filed for trademark for the four-fingered version of KitKat in the UK but the European court has declined it stating that it does not have the features distinctive enough to be trademarked. This is captured in (a).

   Option (b) is incorrect as it's incomplete, yes Nestle may have lost the case but that's not what the whole passage was about.

   Option (c) is incorrect as it's too marrow to be stated as passage summary.

Option (d) is absolutely incorrect in the sense of the passage.

10. Option (a) is incorrect as passage doesn't state that the UK government is set to fund the research, but it is still arranging for them.

    Option (b) is incorrect as the extent of damage realisation is not the gist of the passage but working on gathering funds and doing more research is.

    Option (c) is incomplete as it doesn't mention other charities and that Dementia is one of the big diseases and not the 'only single biggest threat'.

    Option (d) is the answer as passage states that Dementia is one of the greatest threats to the health and wealth of the UK and in light of this fact, the government and charities are making more funds available for research.

11. Option (a) captures the gist of the passage in complete as the passage states that a newly opened glass walkway in China has been closed now due to certain cracks that appeared on it, also that area's management bureau had assured later that the cracks do not pose any danger or threat to safety.

    Options (b), (c) and (d) are just incomplete in their sense to summarise the passage.

12. Options (a), (b) and (c) are too narrow in scope. They mention correct facts but don't summarise the passage well.

    Option (d) is correct as passage mentions how the illegal forest fires have affected the normal activities across parts of south-east Asia, including Thailand, Malaysia and Singapore and how this has resulted in a spread of poisonous gases across the neighbouring countries of Indonesia, over the last few weeks causing a halt in certain normal activities.

13. Option (a) is clearly incorrect as passage doesn't state that Democracy is a sham.

    Option (b) is incorrect as Democracy is simply a not so clearly defined concept, nowhere does the passage states that it is misunderstood as concept can only be misunderstood if it has a definite meaning at first; Democracy doesn't.

    Option (c) is correct as it captures the gist perfectly.

    Option (d) is incomplete as it's not just philosophers but the world that has not understood the meaning of Democracy perfectly.

EXERCISE 5

1. The following are the main points of the passage: (1) The 2015 target to impose a ban on executions. (2) The adoption of the non-binding resolution imposed by the UN General Assembly. (3) The developments which contribute to the prevention of executions by retentionist states. Choice (a) cannot be called the best summary because it omits point 1 which is one of the main points of the passage. Choice (c) is a distortion of the original as it states that it has been made mandatory for all states to halt executions. Even choice (d) is a distortion of the original idea. Only choice (b) captures all the essential points of the passage.

2. In choice (a), the word 'underground' means exclusive privilege. So the inference from the paragraph would be that before the twentieth century, music was underground but in the twentieth century, music has become mainstream. Choice (a) has the wrong time periods mentioned. The correct time references should be 'before the twentieth century' and 'in the twentieth century' and not 'in the twentieth century' and 'after the twentieth century'. Choice (a) is incorrect as a summary. Choice (b) aptly and concisely summarises the content of the paragraph. Choice (c) is incorrect as a summary. The paragraph does not talk about the quality or variety of twentieth century music. It only highlights the fact that the reach and popularity of music has increased in the twentieth century. In choice (d), the first sentence is out of scope. Hence it cannot be a summary.

3. There are no two types of economists. It has only been mentioned that Dani Rodrik has split economists into two camps. So choices (a) and (b) are distorted. Choice (a) does not highlight the hedgehog and foxlike behaviour of the economists. The third sentence in choice (a) unnecessarily mentions an example or specific detail from the para (President Harry Truman requested a one-handed economist). There is no need of this example in the summary. 'after a lot of dillydallying' in choice (b) is not a correct way of mentioning the point. Choice (d) mentions a wrong cause and effect (because they resemble hedgehogs; because they resemble foxes). Only choice (c) covers the main points correctly. The last idea of the plus point, of foxlike behaviour, has found place only in choice (c).

4. The following are the main points of the paragraph: (1) Rampant sand mining is taking place in the districts surrounding the Cauvery despite resistance from environmentalists, etc. (2) With the wells running dry due to sand mining farmers are forced to rent their farms to sand contractors, thereby bringing their own destruction. Choice (a): This cannot be the best summary because it fails to mention the second point. Choice (b): This option, which states that farmers find sand mining more

lucrative, is a distortion of the original as this point is not mentioned in the paragraph. Choice (c): Correct. This option summarises the paragraph most appropriately. Choice (d): This option, which states that farmers connive with the sand contractors, is also a distortion.

5. The passage states that universities must not try to suppress their elitism because by doing so they disserve their democratic country. Therefore, they should preserve their elitist character because this is what gives them their unique identity. Choice (a): Correct. By stating that it is their elitism which makes elite universities centres of distinguished learning, this option captures the author's position correctly. Choice (b): This runs contrary to what the author is trying to convey through the passage. Choice (c): This option, which is rather categorical in stating that universities are doing a great disservice to the nation, is inappropriate as the answer. Choice (d): This option which focuses more on universities upholding the democratic spirit of the country does not capture the author's position correctly.
6. Choice (a): This is not the crux of what the author is trying to convey through the passage. Choice (b): The passage is not essentially about comparing the modern liberal society with the conservative societies of the past. Choice (c): CORRECT. This is what the author of the passage is likely to agree with. Choice (d): The example of the judge is given to emphasise that authority based on rationalism is the distinguishing feature of modern liberal societies.
7. The passage indirectly mentions that criminal behaviour should not be attributed to cultural context. Instead, we should consider the psychological factors related to 'identity'. This sense is given by Option (d), which is the best option. Option (a): incorrect because the last part says that personal traits should not be considered, an idea going against the general idea implied in the given paragraph. Option (b): incorrect because this is what the paragraph is arguing against. Option (c): incorrect because the use of superlative is not justified anywhere in the paragraph. Option (d): correct as per the reasons given above. Thus, the best option is option (d).
8. Overall, the passage says that citizen component and structural component are both required for the quality of democracy. Option (c), which states this, is the best option. Option (a): incorrect because the paragraph explicitly says that 'citizens breathe life into the existing institutional opportunities'. Option (b): incorrect because the dependence of democracy on models is not mentioned in the paragraph. Option (c): correct as per the reasons given above. Option (d): incorrect because the author actually suggests that these factors should be considered for good research on the quality of democracy. Thus, option (c) is the best option.
9. Overall, the paragraph posits that ethics depend on objective truths, not simply opinions. This implies that the values of right and wrong are decided by external factors from nature, which are to be discovered by us. This sense is given by option (d), which is the best option. Option (a): incorrect because the passage says that moral relativism was rare (this fact is implied by the use of 'few' moral relativists). Option (b): incorrect because this option states that moral values depended on individual perspective, a fact that is not endorsed by the given paragraph; in fact, it clearly states that ethics depend on the external universe. Option (c): incorrect because the importance of moral values to ancient philosophers is not hinted at anywhere in the passage. Option (d): correct as per the reasons given above. Thus, the best option is option (d).
10. The author asserts that the existence of the crisis cannot be answered by using empirical data, but the subjective experience helps us learn about the problem (...heuristic value is mentioned to imply this). Thus option (d), which states this view, is the best option. Option (a): incorrect because the comparison given in the option cannot be logically arrived at. Option (b): incorrect because the degree of importance given to classics by the universities is not the central point and moreover, this idea cannot be inferred from the passage. Option (c): incorrect because the passage does not support the view that knowledge production in humanities cannot be studied using empirical data. Option (d): correct as per the reasons given above. Thus, the best option is option (d).
11. The passage posits that echolocation is used by Blainville's beaked whales and they change the frequency of sound so that they can locate the prey correctly and attack it at the right place. This implies that their predation success improves by varying the frequencies. This sense is given by option (b), which is the best option. Option (a): incorrect because, basing on the given information, we cannot say that these whales are most successful. Option (b): correct as per the reasons given above. Option (c): incorrect because the information about escaping from predator is not there. Option (d): incorrect because the expression 'unique mechanism' cannot be justified. Thus, option (b) is the best option.

12. The paragraph argues that India's security challenges across its land borders with Pakistan and China have highlighted the general trend that people far from the sea focus attention on land border security. This idea is best summarised in option (a). Option (a): CORRECT based on the explanation given above. Option (b): This goes against the contents of the passage. Option (c): The comparison in option (c) is not attempted in the paragraph. Option (d): This is a general statement which doesn't reflect the central idea of the argument.
13. The paragraph posits that, ideally, most citizens should participate in democratic process, but this expectation is too ambitious. Alternately, the ideal, though not realistic, sets a marker, helping us to improve. This sense is given by option (a), which is the best option. Option (a) is correct as per the reasons given above. Option (b) is incorrect because the notion that ideals serve 'little' purpose goes against the positive tone of the paragraph towards ideals. Option (c) is incorrect because the author explicitly mentions that this kind of participation is 'ambitious' and so, he is not likely to endorse this view. Option (d) is incorrect because of the use of the expression 'one's potential'. Thus, the best option is option (a).
14. The first four sentences indicate that thought and word are different, but the later part says that a connection originates between them over period of development. Overall, the paragraph posits that thought and speech are different, but they depend on each other (not just by external way, but by the internal way - the last sentence implies this). This is the position the author presents. Option (a), which gives this sense, is the best option. Option (a) is correct as per the reasons given above. Option (b) is incorrect because the author mentions 'pre-intellectual period in speech' and 'pre-speech period in thinking'. This implies that either thought or speech does not give rise to the other. Option (c) is incorrect because the passage does not suggest that the lack of primary bond makes external connection essential. Option (d) is incorrect because this option gives the sense that external connection is 'extremely important', but the author does not give that much emphasis to the external way of connecting speech and thought. Thus, the best option is option (a).
15. The passage talks about arts and literature that portray physical environment and human-environment interactions. Then it talks about environmentalist movement and development of ecocriticism as the result of our interest in environment. Thus, the author overall argues that increasing human interest in environment has resulted in the development of ecocriticism. This sense is given by option (c), which best reflects the author's position as well as the central idea of the paragraph. Option (a) is incorrect because the use of 'solely' in this option makes this option incorrect because while it is true that arts and literature do depend on nature for inspiration, the passage does not support the use of 'solely' in this regard. Option (b) is incorrect because it is human perspective to environment, not arts and literature, that resulted in ecocriticism. Option (c) is correct as per the reasons given above. Option (d) is incorrect because the author's tone towards ecocriticism is not negative. Thus, the best option is option (c).

Exercise 6

1. In Option (a), only that the hippos communicate through loud wheeze honks is stated which does not derive a complete meaning of the paragraph

   In Option (b), the statement summarises the given para, whereas in Option (c), the summary looks more relevant since it talks about the social relationships between the individuals.

   Option (d) does not state how the hippos communicate to establish a social relationship and recognise the voice of hippos.
2. Option (a) and (b) are only considering the strong pace of vaccination for the growth of India whereas in option (c) all the factors are considered. Hence option (c) is a right answer that summarizes the para correctly. In option (d), the values for the growth is given while the reasons pertaining to that are not mentioned.
3. Option (a) clearly summarizes the paragraph best. There is a need for sustainable aviation fuels since the climate is at risk and it is necessary to hit net zero by removing equal amount of carbon dioxide from the atmosphere to achieve balance.

   In option (b), only the need of zero emission fuels like hydrogen is given. It doesn't summarize the paragraph.

   Option (c) talks about achieving the balance between the carbon emission and removal of the same from atmosphere, which doesn't really talk about the reason causing the pollution.

   Option (d) doesn't talk about the ideas to combat the climate risk.
4. Option (c) covers all the necessary points that are given in the above paragraph. It summarizes the para best.

In Option (a), the efforts by the government to minimize the threats to the endangered species is not mentioned.

In option (b), the rare endangered sea lion species who are now taking back the land of their habitat is not mentioned.

Option (d) summarizes an incomplete story of the given para.

5. In options (b) and (c), the human adaptation is mentioned but not how they evolved or sustained is. Hence, option (b) or (c) is not correct. Option (d) talks about how nature has made humans to be wary, they wouldn't have sustained during such type of uncertainty. This only talks about one aspect. Thus, option (d) is also not correct as it does not cover the essence of the paragraph. On the contrary, option (a) correctly summarizes the para and hence, it is correct.

6. Option (d) correctly summarizes the paragraph.

   In option (a), the human bred animal is a cross breed between a donkey and a hemippe is not mentioned.

   In Options (b) and (c), the options do not clearly summarize the given para.

7. In Option (a), the formation of organic chemicals in ALH 84001, which is a mystery, only certain possible explanations are given.

   In option (b), the research regarding the formation of organic chemicals is given and thus it correctly summarizes the paragraph.

   In Option (c), the other factors such as carbonisation aren't mentioned.

   Option (d) is incomplete as the summary should be inclusive of all the factors of research done to find out the presence of organic chemical ALH 84001.

8. Option (a) correctly summarizes the entire factual paragraph.

   Option (b) does not state that the ABS offers advanced vehicle control and drops halting distances on dry and some smooth surfaces. Similarly nor do options (c) and (d).

9. Options (b) and (c) do not talk about the terror that the pirates caused by looting merchant ships for gold and other treasures. Option (d) talks about befriending the merchant ships while the pirates used to terrorise the merchant ships. Hence, option (a) is correct.

10. In option (a), the summary doesn't state about the failed efforts to conserve the biodiversity. Option (b), correctly summarizes the given para. Option (c) also summarizes the para but it states that the UN plan implements, whereas in para it states about the UN plan suggests. Option (d) doesn't state the planning measures taken by the UN for instance the arrangement of the funding, to conserve the biodiversity.

11. Option (a) does not talk about the shift from a fuel- intensive to a material intensive energy system and the government regulations that will accelerate the change. Similarly, Option (c) only tells us about the electrification of the personal mobility vehicles. Option (d) somewhat summarizes the paragraph but option (b) correctly does it. Hence, option (b) is the correct answer.

12. Option (a) only states the thoughts of researchers, instead of stating the factual conclusions based on experiments. Hence, option (a) is not correct. Option (b) correctly summarizes the given para. Option (c) only states the findings of the researchers. Whereas, option (d) gives away incorrect data of fecundity rising more with increase in the size of the tree.

13. Option (a) talks about increasing the perceived distance between groups whereas in para it is mentioned that changing the perceived distance between groups. Hence, option (a) is not correct. Options (c) and (d) talk about the kind of exposure to the prime and its results, which does not correctly summarize the para. Hence, option (b) is the correct answer.

14. Option (b) covers all the important points like the target molecules, recognising the strength and weaknesses etc. of robot and humans. All other options are incomplete in that sense hence incorrect.

15. In option (a), the crux of the para, that is how the previous research as well as the evolutionary research impacts the socio environmental factors on the quality of ritual signalling. Hence, it summarizes the paragraph correctly.

    In option (b), the evolutionary perspectives only suggests, wherein the option says it implements the participation in collective rituals that serve communicative functions by signalling practitioners' commitment to the community and its values. Hence, it doesn't summarize the para correctly.

    In option (c), it is mentioned that has hardly any attention directed to the impact of socio-environmental factors on the quality of ritual signalling, whereas in paragraph it is stated collective ritual involvement may provide crucial communicative functions by signalling practitioners' commitment to the community and its values. Hence option (c) is not correct.

    In option (d), it is given that there has been some attention directed to the impact of socio-environmental factors whereas in paragraph it is stated that limited attention directed to the impact of socio-environmental factors. Hence option (d) too is not correct.

16. In option (a), the correct summary of the para is given.

    In option (b), the information about the baby joey is not mentioned, hence it will not be correct.

    Similarly in option (c), hence option (c) is also not correct.

    Option (d) could be correct but option (a) looks more relatable with the paragraph given.

17. In option (c), it is stated that there were large amounts spent on the PDS and this is correct. In option (a), it has been stated that there are hardly any amounts spent on PDS, whereas, in para it is mentioned that there were large amounts spent.

    In option (b), it is stated that PDS profits from several advantages due to the monopoly of the agents whereas in the given paragraph, it is stated that PDS suffers from several inefficiencies due to the monopoly of the agents.

    In Option (d), it is stated that PDS suffers from several inefficiencies due to the lack of the agents involved in the last-mile delivery of grains, whereas there has been a monopoly of agents as stated in the para. Hence, Option (c) is correct since it correctly summarises the para.

18. Option (a) does not state the real crux of the para which is the benefits of soil bacteria and the effect of harmful chemical treatments done to treat the diseases of crops. Similarly is the case with option (c). Option (b) only talks about the innovation to reduce the cost and environmental damage cause to treat the crop disease. Hence, option (b) is also not correct.

19. Option (a) talks about the choices that different countries have made in building weapons and how these different paths to proliferation is an essential part of arms control. Hence, option (a) is correct

    Option (b) only talks about South Africa who has secretly obtained nuclear capabilities. Hence, option (b) is not correct.

    Similarly, option (c) talks about only the countries who have chosen not to pursue weapons. Option (c) is also incorrect. Option (d) does not talk about the choices that different countries have made in building weapons. Hence, option (d) is also not correct.

20. Option (a) talks only about the fast spread of the Omicron Virus from South Africa. Option (c) talks about the different variants of SARS-CoV-2 and that Omicron is different. Option (d) talks about the origin of the Omicron virus. Whereas, option (b) talks about the fast growing variant omicron, where it was found first, how different it is from other mutants and a clue for its emergence. Hence, option (b) is the correct option that summarizes the paragraph.

21. Option (b) mentions the experiment carried out by Edison but does not tell about the outcomes of it. Hence, it does not summarize the para correctly. Option (c) states that people who drifted into a deep sleep were better problem solvers later, which is incorrect. In paragraph it is mentioned that people who drifted into a light sleep were better problem solvers later. Similarly is the case with option (d).

    Hence, option (a) is correct since it states all correct facts given in the para and summarizes the para correctly.

22. Option (a) does not talk about various civilisations and culture, hence it is not correct. Option (b) does not mention the Indus Valley Civilisation which is one of the greatest in the world. Option (c) rightly summarizes the para but it does not mention that the human artefacts suggest a very early date for human civilisation. Hence, option (c) is also not correct. Option (d) mentions all the facts mentioned in the para and thus, correctly summarizes the given paragraph.

23. Option (a) does not mention the possibility of the science going ahead of problem. Hence, it is incorrect.

    Options (c) and (d) do not mention about the spread of the carp eggs.

    Option (b) correctly summarizes the para.

24. In option (a) and (b), it is not mentioned that the colonial powers exploited the various global colonies. Hence, option (a) is not correct. Similarly is with Option (d). Option (c) correctly summarizes the given paragraph.

25. In option (a), it is stated that the managers discover what is common about each person and then capitalise on it whereas in para it is given that the managers discover what is unique about each person. In option (b), the managers discover what is unique about each person and then stabilise on it, whereas in paragraph it is given that the managers capitalise on it. In option (c), it fails to mention that the managers learn how best to integrate people into a coordinated plan of attack. Option (d) correctly summarises the paragraph since all the facts are correctly mentioned.

26. In option (b), it is given that Higher the voltage in a circuit, the lesser potential energy exists to push electrons from one point to another, whereas in

paragraph it is mentioned that Higher the voltage in a circuit, the higher potential energy exist. Thus, option (b) is incorrect.

In option (c), short-distance power lines have high voltages that efficiently send electricity long distances whereas in paragraph it is stated that long distance power lines have high voltages. Hence, option (c) is incorrect.

In option (d), it is given that devices called transformers step that voltage up to higher, safer levels before it travels through lines to your home, but in para it is mentioned that devices called transformers step that voltage up to lower, safer levels before it travels through lines to your home. Hence, option (d) is also incorrect.

Option (a) correctly summarizes the para as all the given facts are correctly stated in the option summary.

27. In options (c) and (d), incorrect facts are presented. The facts mentioned in option (b) are not found in the given para. Hence, option (a) is correct as it correctly possess the facts mentioned in the para.

28. Options (b), (c) and (d) do not summarize the para since they do not state all correct facts as mentioned in the para. Option (a) summarizes the para correctly.

29. Options (c) and (d) are factually incorrect. Option (b) does not speak about the differences in the urban and rural sectors and thus, Option (b) does not summarize the para. Hence, option (a) is the only factually correct option.

30. Option (a) does not include the alternative solution of using bio feed stocks. Hence, it is incorrect. Option (b) as well as option (d) does not talk about the environmental challenges the aviation industry is facing, hence, options (b) and (d) are also not correct. Option (c) correctly summarizes the paragraph including the environmental challenges faced by the aviation industry as well as the implementation strategies that can be developed to cope with it.

PART 3

Verbal Reasoning

Verbal Reasoning is an important component of the CAT examination and hence has been classified as a separate part of this book. This part contains Critical Reasoning, Syllogisms, Binary Logic, and Logical Deductions. In each section of this part you will get to:

- Learn what question types you can expect to see in various aptitude exams.
- Get an opportunity to practise and hone your skills in each question type.
- Experience and review the typical types of traps that are used by question-setters to induce mistakes in each question type.

Key Components of this part:

- **Critical Reasoning with its 10 question types, including the popular CAT question types of summary and concluding sentence in a paragraph.**
- **Syllogisms and extensive practise exercises on the same covering all varieties of questions.**
- **Binary Logic Problems and solving tricks for this tricky question type.**
- **Logical Deductions**

Go through the theory question types and exercises for Critical Reasoning

↓

Go through the theory question types and exercises for Syllogisms

↓

Go through the theory question types and exercises for Binary Logic

↓

Go through the theory question types and exercises for Logical Deduction

In This Part

Section 1: **Critical Reasoning**

SECTION 1: Critical Reasoning

Critical Reasoning is one of the most important areas of questioning in CAT. In this section we have given you the opportunity to learn about the various critical reasoning question types like Strengthening Arguments, Weakening Arguments, Identifying Assumptions; Identifying Inferences, Select the Best Concluding Sentence for a Paragraph, Summarising a Paragraph, Segregating Relevant and Irrelevant Information, Evaluating Method of the Argument, Identifying Flaws/Fallacies in the Argument, and Identifying Cause and Effect Relationships.

This section will help you in the following ways:

In the chapter on **Critical Reasoning/Paragraph Comprehension** the different question types on critical reasoning as well as the various techniques and methods to solve such questions are discussed.

Besides, you would also have ample opportunity to practise the same in the chapter on **Previous Years' Questions from CAT**.

CHAPTER 1 Critical Reasoning/ Paragraph Comprehension

INTRODUCTION

Over the past fifteen years, Critical Reasoning (CR) questions have been a consistent presence in the CAT and other exams like XAT, GMAT, IIFT, etc. The ability of the student to solve this question type depends on his/her ability to recognise and evaluate argumentative logic. The better you are at understanding arguments, the better you will be at questions related to critical reasoning. As a reader, you are likely to agree with the point that argumentation is essentially a social skill that depends on exposure and the logical ability to reason out, rather than on the knowledge of one particular language. Hence, doing well at CR questions depends more on your ability to reason out logically, than on your's specific knowledge of English.

This being so, CAT/MBA aspirants who consider themselves weak at the English section, should target these questions as possible scoring areas. Thus, strategically CR is one of the most important areas of the CAT exam.

A nice added benefit to preparing yourself for the critical reasoning questions on the CAT is that this preparation will also help you in your Management studies. Many of the techniques used to answer these test questions will come in handy when you are asked to do projects, case analyses and discussions in general.

WHAT IS CRITICAL REASONING?

The typical structure of CR questions is that of a short passage (mostly consisting of a single paragraph) followed by a question on the basis of the paragraph.

However, classifying them as short Reading Comprehension questions is not correct. They differ from Reading Comprehension in both the structuring of the passage and the types and variety of questions. The typical CR passage is anything between 50 words to 200 words long and necessarily contains an **argument**. As already mentioned in the chapter on Reading Skills Development, under Part I of this book, an argument will always have a **claim,** supported by **reasons/evidences**.

CHARACTERISTICS OF A CRITICAL REASONING PASSAGE

While writing argumentatively, the author's principal objective is to persuade the reader about his/her point of view. A successfully presented argument convinces the reader about the author's point of view. In order to do so, not only does the author have to present his point of view, but he also needs to support it with reasons–after all, the reader needs to know why he should agree with the author's points of view. Hence, the author has to provide enough support for his point of view in order to convince the reader. These supports may be in the form of reasons or evidences. The **supports** of an argument are also called as the **premises** of the argument.

The structure of the argument is:

Because of **these** (reasons or facts), we should conclude **this** (claim/conclusion)

Consider the following examples:

(A) Abortion should not be allowed **because** we have no right to end a human life.

The opposite argument for statement (A) would be:

(B) Abortion should be allowed **because** a woman has the right to decide what she wants to do with her body.

(C) Smoking and chewing of pan masala should be banned **because** they are harmful to the health of the consumer.

All the above arguments are in the form: "This because of that."

SUPPORTS OF AN ARGUMENT

The supports of an argument can be visualised as the foundations on the basis of which arguments are made. They are similar to the foundations of a building–the stronger the foundation, the stronger the building. Similarly, the stronger the support for an argument, the stronger the argument.

Consider the following passage that appeared in a newspaper editorial. The passage below has a claim supported by reasons.

Flexitime, or flexibility of working hours, has become popular amongst corporates in recent times. (This is the claim). Many corporates have found that flextime has several advantages. The most obvious advantage is less absenteeism. When employees can choose working hours that meet their needs, they are less likely to take time off. Another advantage of flextime is more efficient use of the business office. The additional hours that a company is "open for business" often converts into higher productivity and greater profits.

Besides giving employees a choice of their working hours, it allows them to exert more control over their working environment. This leads to increased job satisfaction and less employee turnover.

Similarly, there could be a passage having a claim supported by facts. (Please recollect that 'Facts' are statements/information that can be physically verified. They might prove to be true or false on verification.) Consider the following passage:

Country X's relations with Country Y have varied from being stormy and incordial at times to being icy cold and impersonal at other times. There have been periods in the histories of the two countries when their relationships have been dictated by the military maneuvers around their borders–for instance the times preceding the 1945, the 1957 and the Kampaundril wars–while at other times, the relationship has been cold and impersonal at best – due to Country X's constant refrain that Country Y has been instigating terrorism within its borders.

Let us now look at some additional points that you need to keep in mind while reading for the conclusion and the supports in a paragraph:

1. Try to identify the conclusion sentence/s within a paragraph. Many a time the conclusion sentence will be indicated by the use of signal words. While reading a CR paragraph, look for such words. Some of them are: *therefore, thus, hence, so, in conclusion, as a result of, in short, in sum, the point is.*

The consumption of tobacco is harmful to the health of the individual. Hence, smoking should be banned.

The signal word hence at the beginning of the second sentence, indicates the oncoming conclusion.

2. If no conclusion or main claim is stated, you can construct it by finding the main question which the essay directly addresses.

Let us now work out a few examples in spotting Conclusion and Reasons.

Directions: For each of the arguments given below, write down the conclusion and the reasons.

1. If any government becomes tyrannical, then the people governed under that government have a right to revolt. The government of France has become tyrannical. Therefore, the people governed by the government of France have a right to revolt against it.

   Conclusion:

   Reasons:

2. I don't care how many acting awards Salim Khan has won. He simply has no sense of acting. He looks like a dud in whatever roles he plays. Be it a romantic, action or a dramatic role, he simply is not able to act.

   Conclusion:

   Reasons:

3. If you haven't tried our Pack and Chew's Pastry, you simply must. It's the best pastry in town. We make it the home made way. Besides, it's good because we use vitamin enriched materials.

   Conclusion:

   Reasons:

Having recognized that every Conclusion-Reason passage is composed of an argument supported by its set of reasons/ facts, we need to look at two additional components which underlie every argument (Hence which are a part and parcel of every CR passage)–viz. **Assumptions and Inferences**.

WHAT ARE ASSUMPTIONS?

An *assumption* is the passage's "must have." In other words, if the assumption is not true, it follows that the conclusion is not true.

Assumptions can be defined as additional unstated evidence/information, which bridges the gap between the argument, its evidence presented and the conclusion.

In other words, you can also look at assumptions as additional information that the author has assumed the reader already knows while reading the argument. It is best explained through an example.

Argument: Since, India's time zone is five and a half hours ahead of GMT, we can conclude that India is to the East of the United Kingdom.

The unstated assumption here is that if the time of a country is ahead of the GMT, it lies to the east of the United Kingdom. Another, unstated assumption here is that the United Kingdom follows the GMT.

The assumption is a support to the argument, which must be true. Else the argument will fall apart. In the best case, the argument is seriously weakened if the assumption that the author assumes is false.

How do we spot assumptions? In order to deduce assumptions in an argument, you need to look for holes in the argument. Try to identify a missing support that would have the effect of providing a missing support to the argument. The author's belief about an unstated assumption is that it need not be explicitly stated. He believes that his reader will automatically assume the missing assumption. Hence, he does not feel the need to write it explicitly in the passage.

In order to find the hole, ask yourself the following question:

Is the evidence/supporting logic explicitly presented in the argument sufficient so as to support the argument? Is any additional evidence/supporting logic necessary to justify the argument? If yes, an assumption has been made.

Once you have identified a hole, your next objective is to try to word the additional evidence/supporting logic that you need to assume for the argument to make sense. For this purpose, ask yourself the following question:

What additional evidence/supporting logic do I as a reader, need to assume for the argument to make sense?

The answer to the above question gives you a possible assumption. Before you accept that assumption, however, you might need to test whether your assumed assumption is valid or not. In order to do so, try to **deny or negate** the assumption.

What happens when you negate the assumption? Does it weaken your argument?

If yes, then your assumption is correct, i.e., in case the assumption is not true, then the argument makes no sense. Hence, you have a valid assumption.

If no, then the assumption you have identified is not correct, i.e., the argument continues to make sense even if the assumption is not true. In such a case, you should realise that your assumption is wrong.

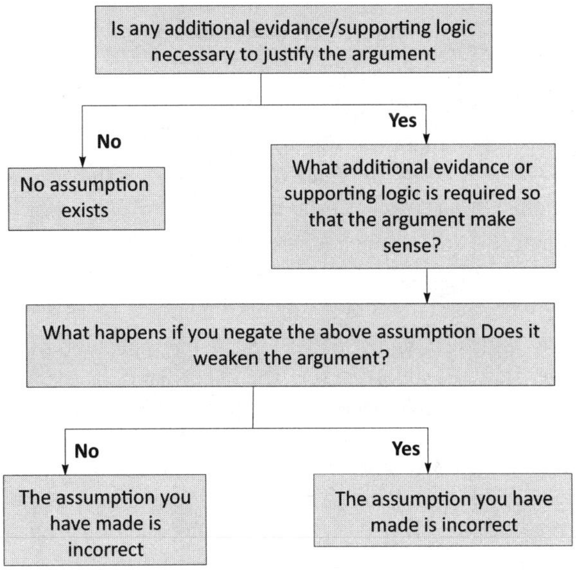

Fig. 1.1 Identifying an Assumption in an Argument

Let us now move on to the next issue–inferences.

What are Inferences?

An inference can be defined as an unstated extension of the argument. In other words, it can also be seen as an implied conclusion.The inference may be about the main point in the paragraph or it could be about a less central issue. This factor does not affect the fact that an inference is an implied conclusion.

The Cream of the Piece

Unlike assumptions which are the basis of the argument and hence, come before the argument, inferences come after the argument.

Figuratively speaking, imagine a three-storey building as an argument. The assumptions can be seen as the foundation of the building. At the same time, an inference would be akin to the fourth storey of the building. While the building would not exist without a foundation, the shape and size of the fourth storey can be logically deduced from that of the third storey.

Further, unlike assumptions, which you have to find, an inference will show itself to you when you read the entire argument. Inferences emerge out of a combination of the statements in the paragraph. If all the statements in the passage are true, the inferences which emerge out of the combination of some or all of the statements must also be true.

The Cream of the Piece

The logic of an inference (or an implied conclusion) can be captured as follows:

If **A** (statement in a paragraph) and **B** (statement in the paragraph) **are true,** then **C** (inference or the implied conclusion) is automatically true.

Hence, in order to check whether the inference you have drawn is correct, try to deny the inference.

i.e. given that **A** and **B** are true, **C** need not be true.

If this logic can be justified, then the inference you might have drawn is incorrect. On the other hand, if this logic cannot be justified, then the inference is correct.

As a recap of this section, we would like to remind you that in order to be able to solve a CR question, you should be reading the CR paragraph with four basic objectives.

These are:

(1) What is the claim/argument made by the author of the paragraph?

(2) What are the supports the author is providing to the claim/argument?

(3) What are the assumptions the author is making while making the claim/argument?

(4) What unstated inferences/conclusions should you draw from the statements contained in the paragraph?

The principles elucidated above are principles associated with good reading of arguments. Initially, you will need to practice applying these principles consciously. Like any other activity, the more you apply these principles, the better you will become at them. You need to continue practicing these principles consciously till you feel that they have become a part of your reflexes. After that, all these principles will apply intuitively, i.e., you will be able to spot the claim, its supports, the assumptions as well as the inferences, as a reflex to the reading of the question. When you reach that stage, you will realise that you have become good at solving CR questions.

We now move on to the typical question types asked under CR.

QUESTION TYPES IN CRITICAL REASONING

Critical reasoning questions will ask you to do any of the following:

(1) Test for the strengthening of an argument with (a) additional evidence (b) additional reasons/ arguments.

(2) Test for the weakening of an argument with (a) additional evidence (b) additional reasons/arguments.

(3) Identify an assumption.

(4) Identify an inference.

(5) Select the best concluding statement for a paragraph.

(6) Summarise the argument.

(7) Segregate relevant and irrelevant information.

(8) Evaluate the method of the argument.

(9) Identify the flaws/fallacies in an argument.

(10) Identify Cause and Effect relationships.

QUESTION TYPE 1: THE STRENGTHENING OF AN ARGUMENT

The claim of an argument is supported by reasons or evidences. In questions on strengthening of the argument, the question will ask you to select from amongst the four/five options, the one that strengthens the argument. Arguments can be strengthened in two ways: either through the introduction of some supporting evidence or the introduction of some supporting reasons. Hence, these questions might ask you to select an option that provides either supporting evidence or supporting reasons.

Besides, if we have an option that strengthens an assumption that is the key to the argument's claim, then that option will also strengthen the argument.

In a figurative sense, if you look at the argument as a building with supports, then supporting evidences/reasons provide us with additional supports to the claim of the question. In such questions, while evaluating the options, you should try to assess which option best supports the claim of the argument. The strengthening evidence/reason might be stronger/equal to/or weaker than the explicitly stated evidences/reasons in the argument. However, in order to find out the correct answer to such questions, you do not need to compare the quality of the support an option provides with respect to the explicitly stated supports. All you need to do is compare the respective options and try to see which option best supports the claim of the argument. By evaluating the relative strengths of the support provided to the claim of the argument, you can easily identify the correct option. The following question will make this question type clear to you:

One of the most important and constructive reforms in National Politics has been the abolition of the post of State Ministers in the various departments.

Each of the following, if true, would strengthen the above argument, except

(A) There are few, if any, specific duties or responsibilities assigned to the State Minister in any department.

(B) A historian claimed that the post was "superfluous."

(C) People of Cabinet minister caliber normally refuse the post if offered a ministership in the guise of a State Minister.

(D) The office is used as a means of appeasing regional parties, by giving their MPs ministerial status and perks without giving them, any significant responsibilities.

The correct answer is B.

Question Type 2: The Weakening of an Argument

These questions are very similar to strengthening argument questions–the only difference being that they are on the other side of the fence. Similar to the strengthening of arguments, weakening of arguments can also be done by the introduction of additional evidence and/or reasons that attack the basis of the claim of the argument.

After identifying the claim in an argument and the supports provided for the claim, you will need to evaluate each option for the degree to which it goes towards weakening the argument. The evidence/reason that most/least seriously weakens, the supports of the argument's claim would be the answer (depending upon what you have been asked to identify).

In a figurative sense, the weakening evidence/reasons are like attacks on the pillars of the building–(i.e., they attack the supports of the argument's claim). Your judgment needs to tell you how serious the attack is.

Besides, if we have an option that weakens an assumption that is key to the argument's claim, then that option will also have the effect of weakening the argument. Let us look at a few examples that will make this question type clear to you:

Before the arrival of a new trainer, the sales output in Mindworkzz Learning Systems Ltd had been rising by 20 percent per year on the average over the past ten years. However, after new training innovations by the trainer (which included computerisation of training processes and reductions in the need for additional work force) annual sales output has only risen by 10 percent this year. It appears that Joe's innovations have caused the reduction in the annual growth rate.

Which of the following, if true, would most seriously weaken the conclusion above?

(A) The investment in computerisation has a provision for depreciation of the cost of the computers.

(B) Increases in selling price did not follow increases in the cost of the inputs.

(C) The innovations brought in by the new trainer were intended as long-term investments and not made for short-term profit growth.

(D) General demand for the training provided by the company has declined.

The correct answer is D.

In the past, to run for one's country in the Asiad was the ultimate achievement of any athlete. Nowadays, an athlete's motives are more and more influenced by financial gain, and consequently, we do not see our best athletes in the Asiad, which is still only for amateurs.

Which of the following will most weaken the above conclusion?

(A) The publicity and fame that can be achieved by competing in the Asiad makes the athletes who do so, more "marketable" by agents and potential sponsors. Thus, they can earn a lot of money even while retaining their amateur status.

(B) The spirit of the Asiad places emphasis on participation rather than on the winning of the race.

(C) A leading columnist recently argued on the basis of concrete evidence that our best Asiad athletes already receive enough in terms of promotions and sponsorships.

(D) It has been suggested that professional athletes should be allowed to compete in the games.

The correct answer is A.

In these times of growing economic turbulence, unless new reserves are found soon, the world's supply of natural gases is being depleted in such a way that with demand continuing to grow at the present rates, reserves will be exhausted by the year 2200 AD.

Which of the following, if true, will most weaken the above argument?

(A) There has been a slowdown in the rate of increase in world demand for natural gases over the last decade, from 20 per cent to 10 per cent.

(B) It has been known for many years that there are vast stocks of natural gases under Antarctica, which have yet to be economically exploited.

(C) Electricity is being used increasingly in place of natural gases for many industrial and domestic uses.

(D) None of the above.

The correct answer is D.

In accordance with their powers, many zilla panchayats are introducing chlorination of the drinking water provided to families through the water supply system. This follows the conclusion of 10 years of research that the process ensures that children and adults receive the required intake of fluoride that will strengthen teeth. The maximum level has been set at one part per million. However, there are many who object, claiming that chlorination removes freedom of choice.

Which of the following will weaken the claim of the proponents of chlorination?

(A) Chlorination over a certain prescribed level has been shown to lead to a general weakening of teeth.
(B) There is no record of the long-term effects of drinking chlorinated water on dental and general health.
(C) In a study done at the grassroots level, it was found that some people to be affected by chlorination claim that they have not had sufficient opportunity to voice their views about the issue.
(D) Water already contains natural chlorine.

The correct answer is B.

Question Type 3: Identify an Assumption

We have already looked at assumptions in details. This question type asks you to identify the assumption in the paragraph. The following examples will make it clear to you:

In response to the criticism about the methods used by his poll predicting agency, a leading psephologist Mannoy Toy, replied: "I realise there are some shortcomings to the questionnaire method that we have applied to do the survey. However, since we have ensured that we send a copy of the questionnaire to every home in each of the constituency where we have carried out our survey, we believe the results to be quite representative... We think the numbers received are so large that it overcomes the lack of a scientific approach that might have crept into our survey.

The writer of the above statement makes which of the following assumptions?

(A) A high proportion of the respondents who have received the questionnaire have replied to the same.
(B) A majority of the voters in the constituency live in homes.
(C) The method of data collection used by the agency is unscientific.
(D) A large, absolute number of replies automatically guarantees the accuracy of the results.

The correct answer is D.

A recent survey by a leading NGO came to the following conclusion about donor psychology:

If you are interested in getting a good donation, you need to realise that Donors are almost never disturbed by being asked for too much. In fact, the result is the opposite–they are flattered. Besides, if you ask for too much, the donor can always suggest a smaller amount. On the other hand, if you ask for too little, the donor is usually offended. A common reaction to being asked too little is "so that's all he thinks I'm worth."

The above statement assumes that

(A) Donors are usually never asked for enough.
(B) A good fund raiser will value the worth of the donor.
(C) It is worth the gamble to ask for large donations.
(D) None of these.

The correct answer is C.

New age problems require new age solutions. Further new age problems arise with new age populations and new age technologies. In order to find solutions to these problems we need to build new age institutions as well as new age political, economic and social mechanisms. Yet, institutions and political and economic mechanisms grow slowly and die slowly. Hence, new age institutions should be given every chance of trying to achieve success in their objectives.

The argument above rests on which of the following assumptions:

(A) New age institutions are needed because old institutions are inefficient.
(B) New age institutions are created in order to solve existing problems.
(C) Over a course of time, as an institution grows, it has chances of succeeding in its objectives.
(D) None of these.

The correct answer is C.

In its quest to go global, once an Indian company has established an extensive sales network in a foreign market and therefore, has achieved substantial sales, it seems that these markets should be treated in a very similar fashion to those in India. It is therefore only in those countries where only initial sales networks have been developed, where marketing methods will have to differ from the methods applied in India.

The above statement assumes that:

(A) Sales networks can be the same in both foreign countries and in India.
(B) Extensive sales networks are preferable to less developed ones.
(C) The markets of some countries will develop faster than others.
(D) None of these.

The correct answer is D.

The main monetary policy objective is to reduce substantially, the import surplus of the coming years while resuming economic growth. Realisation of this goal entails a marked structural change of the economy, which can be brought about by freezing the standard of living (per capita private consumption plus public services) and restricting investments that do not further exports.

The writer of the above policy assumes that:

(A) Economic growth will lead to structural changes in the economy.
(B) If people consume less, the economy grows.
(C) In order to reduce import surplus investment needs to be restricted.
(D) People should be persuaded to give up consumption in order to achieve the national good.

The correct answer is B.

The reason that is most commonly quoted for nationalisation of foreign companies is a change in governance. Nationalisation tends to cover a wide range of industries and is not selective to the country of ownership of the foreign company.

The above statement assumes that:

(A) Some critical industries are more likely to be nationalised than others which might not be so critical.
(B) The process of nationalisation is not limited to any particular industry or country.
(C) Nationalisation of businesses is so widespread as to cause concern at the international level.
(D) Sharing ownership with local nationals will forestall takeovers by foreign governments.

The correct answer is B.

QUESTION TYPE 4: IDENTIFY AN INFERENCE/ CONCLUSION

We have already discussed inferences and conclusions in details. Questions related to these will ask you to spot the option that is/is not an inference or a conclusion that can be drawn from the details mentioned in the paragraph. Consider the following examples, which will clarify to you how questions about inferences are structured:

A pill that can induce abortions in pregnant women has become available in Australia. The drug Antiperphrine, has proved more than 98.9 per cent effective in tests conducted by a scientific team in Sydney. The drug is an anti hormone and disrupts pregnancy by blocking the implantation of a fertilized egg in the wall of the uterus. In Australia, the pill will be available to women who are upto 42 days late in their menstrual cycle. The company that manufactures the pill, states however, that the pill is not a "morning after" pill for use as a contraceptive.

Which of the following statements can be correctly deduced from the text above?

(A) The drug Antiperphrine uses a new type of contraceptive method.
(B) The drug Antiperphrine blocks egg production.
(C) The drug Antiperphrine has the effect of termination of pregnancy.
(D) The drug is only available in Australia.

The correct answer is C.

One of the most important measures of a country's trading strength is the measurement of its net exports. Net exports are defined as exports less imports. It is important since the figure measures the net effect of a nation's trade in goods and services vis-a-vis the world. In 1998, the country's net exports were 7 percent of its GDP (Gross Domestic Product) and in 2005, they were 14 percent.

If the information above is accurate, which of the following must be true?

(A) If GDP was constant from 1998 to 2005, net exports were greater in 2005 than in 1998.
(B) Exports were greater than imports in 2005, but not in 1998.
(C) Exports doubled from 1998 to 2005.
(D) In 1998, net exports were lower than in 2005.

The correct answer is A.

About 40 percent of urban Indian husbands think it is a good idea for wives with school age children to work outside the home. Only about ten percent of rural Indian husbands approve of the same. Every second urban Indian wife, and one in four rural Indian wives with school age children has a job outside her home.

If the information above is correct, which of the following can be inferred?

(A) Rural Indian families have more children than urban Indian families.
(B) Employment opportunities for urban Indian wives are greater than for rural Indian wives.
(C) Urban Indian husbands have a less conservative attitude than rural Indian husbands.
(D) Rural Indian husbands would seem to be less satisfied about working wives who have school age children than urban Indian husbands.

The correct answer is D.

Paro overslept. Therefore, she was late for school by the time she got ready. Hence, she did not eat her breakfast. As she realised that she was late for her school bus, she ran as fast as she could from her home to the bus stop and did not see a banana skin that was lying on the ground in her path. She slipped on the banana skin and fractured her leg. Some passersby took her to the hospital and while lying in bed she was visited by her friend Dhanno, who wanted to know why she had got up so late.

Which of the following conclusions can be made from the above passage?

(A) Because Paro did not eat her breakfast, she broke her ankle.

(B) Paro's friend visited her in the hospital because she wanted to know why she was in the hospital.

(C) Paro did not notice the banana skin because she overslept.

(D) Paro's fractured leg meant that she did not go to school that day.

The correct answer is D.

A recent study on medicine addiction found out that there are principally three main factors that determine the risk of becoming dependant on or addicted to medicines. The first factor is the type of medicine, the second is the personality of the individual, and the third factor is controlled by the circumstances in which the medicine is taken. As a parallel example, we only need to look as far as alcohol. While it could be safely said that the majority of the adult population have taken alcohol, yet only a small proportion of these go on to get addicted to alcohol. Besides, it is well documented that many strong medicines that have been used for medical purposes have not caused the patient to become addicted.

However, the study found that people who took medicines for the heck of it were more likely to become dependent on the same. The dependence need not be restricted to the physiological side but may become psychological, although the effects are still essentially the same. People with psychopathic, immature or otherwise unstable personalities were shown to be at the greatest risk of becoming addicted.

Which of the following conclusions can be drawn from the text?

(A) One becomes addicted to certain medicines only if one has a weak personality.

(B) Taking medicines for the fun of it increases the possibility of becoming dependent on medicines.

(C) Alcohol is a safe medicine since very few people become dependent on it.

(D) Long-term use of certain drugs for medical purposes does not cause addiction.

The correct answer is B.

An advertisement for a leading racquet manufacturer made the following claim:

The last five Wimbledon men's single champions have all changed to Head's new tennis rackets–the only racket that uses genuine nano technology in its frame. In that case, isn't now the time to add power to your tennis strokes and to trade in your old racket for a Head?

Which of the following claims is not made and cannot be inferred from the above ad?

(A) Frames strengthened by nano-technology are used only in Head's new rackets.

(B) Nano technology strengthened frames make tennis rackets stronger and allow the player to make more powerful strokes.

(C) Former Wimbledon champions know a great deal about tennis and their equipment.

(D) Head tennis rackets helped the last five Wimbledon men's singles champions achieve their status.

The correct answer is D.

Question Type 5: Select the Best Concluding Statement of a Paragraph

In this type of question, a paragraph is given and four alternative concluding statements are given for the same. You are required to choose the option that best concludes the paragraph. These questions first made their appearance in the CAT 2005 examination and sparked huge debates amongst the student community about their answers.

The reason for the confusion was that when read normally, each of the four options for the concluding sentence, logically followed the material of the text in the paragraph. However, in these questions the key to deducing the one correct option is the ability to understand the author's opinion (Advanced Reading Skill 5 from Part I of this book). Once you have identified the author's opinion, you can evaluate the options for the concluding sentence by trying to fit in the one option that made the most 'concluding sense' in the context of the author's opinion about the topic.

By trying to fit the concluding sense of each option, we mean to say that you need to compare how each sentence concludes the argument, i.e., winds up the points made by the author and best conveys the author's opinion about the topic.

Further, the concluding sentence also needs to be a conclusion of the paragraph. It should not leave the scope of further carrying the paragraph's discussion forward. The following examples will help you understand this type of question:

Complete the following paragraph with the most suitable sentence.

In order to boost sales of toys at times other than the peak sale time, toy-manufacturers take recourse to the use of several techniques. Some of these include promoting character toys from Bollywood and Hollywood movies or TV series. All these sets are marketed as "collectibles" for the young consumers. The collections within a family of Collectibles, however, never appear to be complete (especially to the parents). As soon as all the characters are acquired, the child then requires the associated gadgets and gizmos that are bundled into the collectible set. Thus parents go shopping for the "car," the "home," the "mobile home," and even the "airplane" to ensure a happy homely environment for the toys. Ultimately, just as the elusive final piece of the series is attained, the manufacturer and promoter release the next series of "collectibles".

The prime aim of the manufacturer and promoter is to ensure that

(A) all children should be happy and no child can be happy without a complete series of toys.

(B) as soon as one set is complete or almost complete, then the next one arrives on the scene.

(C) children should be encouraged to complete their collections of toys.

(D) sales need to be artificially bolstered throughout the year.

The correct answer is D.

Let us now look at the following examples from the CAT 2005:

Federer's fifth grand slam win prompted a reporter to ask whether he was the best ever. Federer is certainly not lacking in confidence, but he wasn't about to proclaim himself the best ever. "The best player of this generation, yes" he said, "But nowhere close to ever. Just look at the records that some guys have. I'm a minnow." ________

1. His win against Agassi, a genius of the previous generation, contradicts that.
2. Sampras, the king of an earlier generation, was as humble.
3. He is more than a minnow to his contemporaries.
4. The difference between 'the best of this generation' and 'the best ever' is a matter of perception.

The correct answer is 3. You need an answer that concludes the passage. While option 1 and 2 take the paragraph into a new direction, 4 is irrelevant in the context provided–it is too general in nature.

Thus the end of knowledge and the closing of the frontier that it symbolizes is not a looming crisis at all, but merely one of many embarrassing fits of hubris in civilization's long industry. In the end, it will pass away and be forgotten. Ours is not the first generation to struggle to understand the organizational laws of the frontier, deceive itself that it has succeeded, and go to its grave having failed. ________

1. One would be wise to be humble.
2. But we might be the first generation to actually reach the frontier.
3. But we might be the first generation to deal with the crisis.
4. However, this time the success is not illusory.

Options 2 and 4 seem to indicate that we might have reached the frontier. But by it's very definition, the frontier of knowledge can never be reached. Hence, you can eliminate these answers. Further, if you consider option 3, it talks about dealing with the crisis–which does not exist at all according to the first sentence of the paragraph. Thus, the correct answer is option 1.

Most firms consider expert individuals to be too elitist, temperamental, egocentric, and difficult to work with. Force such people to collaborate on a high stakes project and they just might come to fisticuffs. Even the very notion of managing such a group seems unimaginable. So most organizations will fall into default mode, setting up project teams of people who get along nicely. ________

1. The result however is disastrous.
2. The result is mediocrity.
3. The result is the creation of experts who then become elitists.
4. Naturally, they drive innovations.

The paragraph clearly states that teams are formed on the basis of people's ability to get along with each other (rather than on their merit with respect to the task at hand). Obviously, this leads to a compromise in the quality of the work being performed. Hence, Option 4 is eliminated. Option 1 simply does not follow from the previous sentence since the word however indicates that the author should be contradicting his previous idea with this sentence. However, if you analyse the ideas in the last sentence of the paragraph and the Option 1, you will clearly see that there is no contrast between the two ideas.

Option 3 talks about an effect that is highly improbable in the context. Option 2 is perfect since you will expect mediocrity when you create a team on the basis of parameters other than ability.

The audiences for crosswords and sudoku, understandably, overlap greatly, but there are differences, too. A crossword attracts a more literary person, while sudoku appeals to a keenly logical mind. Some crossword enthusiasts turn up their noses at sudoku because they feel it lacks depth. A good crossword requires vocabulary, knowledge, mental flexibility and sometimes even a sense of humor to complete it. It touches numerous areas of life and provides an 'Aha!' or two along the way.________

1. Sudoku, on the other hand, is just a logical exercise, each one similar to the last.
2. Sudoku, incidentally, is growing faster in popularity than crosswords even among the literate.
3. Sudoku, on the other hand, can be attempted and enjoyed even by children.
4. Sudoku, however, is not exciting in any sense of the term.

In order to solve the above question, you need to understand that you are looking for the option that best 'completes' the paragraph. The structural construct under which we reach the last sentence of the paragraph is that of a comparison between crosswords and sudokus. The author has shown a clear bias towards crosswords–and in fact is in the process of explaining his sentence 'Some crossword enthusiasts turn up their noses at sudoku because they feel it lacks depth.' So obviously, after praising crosswords, he has to talk in a dark light about sudoku. Option 1 has the perfect fit under this structure. Although Option 4 is also negative in its construction, it is unlikely to be the answer because of the fact that it is too crude and direct–something that you cannot associate with the author's style of writing. Options 2 and 3 get eliminated because they are talking positively about sudokus–something that goes against our expectations of what the author is likely to convey.

QUESTION TYPE 6: QUESTIONS THAT ASK YOU TO SUMMARISE AN ARGUMENT

This is another important question type which has been regularly seen in the CAT and other top Management Entrance Exams. A **summary** is defined as the reduction of a large amount of information to its most important points. You need to remember the following points about summarising in order to be able to spot summaries effectively:

(1) While achieving a reduction of the passage into its summary, care is taken to ensure that the main idea of the passage is properly communicated–i.e., there is no compromise or dilution of the sense of the main idea communicated by the passage while framing the summary. The summary might have the main idea stated in the original words of the author or in fresh words which will essentially convey the same meaning. This factor should always be kept in mind while solving summary based questions. Hence, recognising the main idea of the passage while reading the original text for the first time is extremely crucial for identifying the correct summary.

A good process to follow in trying to recognise the summary is to go back to the questions:

- Who or what is the original text talking about? (Answer: TOPIC of the text); and
- What is the main idea about the topic that is being conveyed by the original text? (Answer: MAIN IDEA of the text)

Then, you go on to the alternative summaries available and ask the same questions again with respect to the proposed summary.

- Who or what is the summary talking about? (Answer: TOPIC of the summary) and;
- What is the main idea about the topic that is being conveyed by the summary? (Answer: MAIN IDEA of the summary.)

For the correct option, the two answers that emerge out of these questions should be exactly the same as the two answers that emerged out of the original text.

(2) Significant reduction from the original text to the summary is generally achieved by either condensing or removing altogether the supporting details in the passage. In many cases, it is not even necessary to mention some of the details presented in the original paragraph in order to write a good summary.

(3) Very often, authors of texts repeat the main idea several times while writing. This is done to ensure that their main idea is hammered into the minds of the reader several times and in several ways so that the gaps (if any) in understanding the main idea may be removed.

Needless to say, in the summary, the main idea will be written only once–and **that too in one sentence only.** Any repetitions of ideas present in the original text are removed from the summary.

Consider the following example:

Jaya and Devika are both successful women who are also members of a socially disadvantaged section of the society. Jaya has a firm belief in positive discrimination. By positive discrimination she believes that the negative discrimination that society has subjected her section of the society to can only be offset through reverse discrimination. She believes that if positions of economic, social and political eminence, power and honor are offered principally to historically disadvantaged sections of society, then these groups will begin to play a more significant role in society today.

Devika, on the other hand, feels that she has succeeded in her chosen field of work on her hard work and on her own merits. She thinks that the principle of positive discrimination is flawed since it will result in the lowering of standards and decreases competition between similarly qualified personnel who will expect to achieve positions because of their factors other than rather than their suitability for the particular position.

Which of the following best sums up Jaya's argument?

(A) Positive discrimination will encourage more people to apply for jobs, previously unavailable to them.

(B) Positive discrimination will give extra opportunities to socially disadvantaged sections of the society.

(C) Quality and professionalism will improve because of the greater number of positions held by members of minority groups.

(D) Positive discrimination will remove deep rooted prejudices against the weaker sections of society from the work arena.

The correct answer is B.

The Question Type 7: Questions that Ask You to Identify the Relevance of the Argument

Relevant information questions are framed with the objective of testing the student's abilities to understand the main idea of the passage. The student is expected to test various options for their relevance to the arguments presented.

A relevant piece of information can be defined as something that affects the argument–either positively by strengthening it or negatively by weakening it. The degree to which the argument is affected in either direction is not a factor while testing the relevance of the information.

In some cases, information is relevant to the argument simply because it has the effect of either elaborating or explaining or expanding the main point.

Obviously, when the argument is not affected by the information provided in any way, it becomes irrelevant in the context of the text provided.

Another way in which you will have to test the reasonableness of an argument is by linking the information to how it helps you judge an assumption in the argument. Does the information whose relevance you have to judge have any effect on how reasonable an assumption underlying the argument is? Does it make the assumption more valid and reasonable? Does it reduce the reasonableness of the assumption of the argument? If the answer to either of these is yes, then it automatically makes the information reasonable.

Consider the following example:

A service oriented company, Bharadwaj Inc., included in its annual balance sheet and P&L accounts presented to its shareholders at it's AGM, the following note on its policy of accounting:

Fixed assets are stated in the consolidated balance sheet at cost minus accumulated depreciation and amortization. Depreciation is provided on all fixed assets, except land. This is done to reflect the true value of the asset. The writing off of their cost is done by using the Straight Line Method of depreciation over the estimated economically useful lives of the respective assets.

The cost of leasehold improvements, if any, is amortized over the term of the remaining number of years of the lease in equal annual installments.

Which of the following statements is relevant to, but not consistent with, the above accounting policy?

(A) The economic useful life of land and buildings is assumed to be 40 years, and Bharadwaj Inc., therefore, employs a depreciation rate of 2.5 per cent per annum.

(B) Bharadwaj Inc. include in their plant, equipment whose historical cost is ₹1.5 crore. This is mentioned at it's historical cost itself, even though this equipment is more than 10 years old and the depreciation rate on plant and machinery has been 1.5 per cent for many years.

(C) The company spent ₹30 lakh on improving a building, which is leased. The period of the lease was seven years, but the lease must be renewed in two years time. The company provided for amortization at 50 per cent of the amount for this year.

(D) None of these.

The correct answer is B.

Question Type 8: Questions that Ask You to Evaluate the Method of the Argument

Questions based on the method of the argument, ask the student to identify the technique applied by the author of the argument in order to make his argument, i.e., the logic for the support of the claim that the author is making.

Method questions are normally general about the entire argument, but can be sometimes specific about a part of the argument.

Some examples of the kinds of options the method-based questions might give are as follows:

(1) The author argues from a small sample to a large population.

(2) The author compares two parallel events and argues on the basis of parallels and contrasts.

(3) The author uses an analogy to present his case.

(4) The author transfers a cause and effect relationship from one field to another.

(5) The author uses an appeal to popular opinion in order to make his point.

(6) The author is making a prediction based on the evidence from events of the past.

(7) The author attacks the opponent rather than attacking his argument.

(8) The author discusses two diverse issues by comparing commonalities between them.

(9) The author makes an extrapolation of a personal experience into a general case.
(10) The author argues from the specific to the generic.
(11) The author argues from the generic to the specific.

In order to solve questions based on Method, ask yourself how the author has reached the conclusion and in what context each part of the evidence is presented.

A famous judge stated that if murder is a worse crime than blackmail and blackmail is a worse crime than theft, then murder is a much worser crime than theft.

Which is a correct analysis of the above argument?

(A) A case operating in one situation will also be operative in another situation, if both situations are characterised in identical terms.
(B) A case that operates under certain conditions will surely be operative in other situations in which the same conditions are present in a more acute form.
(C) A case that clearly expresses the purpose it was meant to serve will also apply in other situations in which the identical purpose may be served.
(D) None of the above.

The correct answer is D.

Question Type 9: Questions that Ask You to Identify the Flaws/Fallacies in an Argument

Flaw based questions are similar to method based questions. The only difference is that unlike in the case of method questions where the validity of the argument does not matter, in flaw based questions, the validity of the argument matters. You need to identify whether there is an error in the entire argument or whether it is in a specific part of the argument.

Consider the following questions based on flaws/fallacies in an argument.

Roma: The number of accidents on state and national highways this year in the state of Karnataka, where the speed limit was lowered to fifty kmph an hour two years ago, is clear evidence that speed restrictions rigorously enforced, make drivers more aware of the dangers of going too fast.

Aamir: Wrong. If you take a close look at the records it will show you that the number of accidents has been falling ever since the introduction of newer and stricter penalties for traffic rules violations, which happened two years before the lowering of the speed limit.

Which of the following best describes the weak point in Roma's statement upon which Aamir focuses?

(A) The decrease in highway accidents may be a temporary phenomenon.
(B) The evidence Roma cites comes only from one area.
(C) No exact statistics for freeway accidents are given by Roma.
(D) Roma fails to provide concrete evidence to prove a direct causative relationship between the cause and the effect.

The correct answer is D.

Question Type 10: Questions that Ask you to Identify Cause-Effect Relationships

Cause-effect relationships are commonly used in all types of argumentations. We have studied this in detail under Reading Comprehension as well as under the chapter on Paragraph Jumbles. Questions of this type will ask you to spot/reason out causal relationships between diverse events/phenomena. Look at the following question in order to get a clearer picture of such questions:

In India in 1990, there were, on an average 14 deaths at birth (infant mortality) per 1,00,000 population. By 2000 there were 11, and by 2001, 8. Today, there are 5 deaths at birth per 1,00,000 population, and it is anticipated that the downward trend will continue.

Each of the following, if true, would help account for this trend except:

(A) Medical care is more widespread and available.
(B) More effective birth control methods have been implemented.
(C) The number of pediatricians per 10,000 population has increased.
(D) Midwifery has declined in favor of doctors.

The correct answer is D.

General Approach for Solving Critical Reasoning Questions

The Cream of the Piece

Step 1: Read the question stem first. This will help you to decide what you are going to be looking for in the paragraph when you read it for the first time.

Step 2: Next read the passage, identifying the claim, the supporting reasons/evidence, the assumptions inherent in the argument and the inferences that can be made from the argument.

Step 3: Pre-phrase your answer–Knowing what you are going to be looking for while reading the options is helpful in order to get the correct answer. Then, check the options to see which one best fits your opinion.

ELEMENTARY PRACTICE EXERCISE

1. The best movie showing in the country right now is *Black and Red*–it has been in the #1 position for three weeks.
   - How can we weaken this argument?
   - How can we strengthen this argument?
2. All mammals have red blood. Therefore, deers have red blood.
   - If so, what is the "missing step," or "hidden assumption"?
3. The Education Minister has recently suggested that all people should go to school for at least 15 years. However, this argument is clearly wrong since the minister himself is educated only upto the sixth class.
   - How can we weaken this argument?
   - How can we strengthen this argument?
4. It is a well accepted fact that in order to raise your scores in the CAT, you should study and practice the question types in the test a lot. However, Motilal used this strategy and he did not get the score that he wanted. Therefore, this strategy is not helpful.
   - How can we weaken this argument?
   - How can we strengthen this argument?
5. It is a commonly known fact that most people do not obey traffic signals when they drive on the roads. Isn't it very often that you have noticed people disobey signals and get away scot-free? We can therefore conclude that the system of traffic signals is entirely useless.
   - How can we weaken this argument?
   - How can we strengthen this argument?
6. Frozen water is less dense than liquid water. Therefore, frozen water will float in liquid water.
   - If so, what is the "missing step," or "hidden assumption"?
7. The President has recently suggested adding fluoride to all public water sources. This is obviously a bad idea since many of the former communist and fascist countries also added fluoride to all their public water sources.
   - How can we weaken this argument?
   - How can we strengthen this argument?
8. Four hours ago I had a bad cold and headache, so I took six Dercold tablets. I still have the cold and the headache. Therefore, Dercold is a useless medicine.
   - How can we weaken this argument?
   - How can we strengthen this argument?
9. In an attempt to increase sales, HTR Ltd. implemented a new customer service policy that required all sales representatives to address all prospective clients by name. Within three months of this step, sales had risen by over 25 per cent, something that had never happened in the company's history. The new policy was therefore a success.
   - How can we weaken this argument?
   - How can we strengthen this argument?
10. It is obvious to everyone who can reason that Einstein could not have formulated the theory of relativity. It is a common fact that Einstein did not receive a passing grade in math class as a child.
    - What is the "missing step" or "hidden assumption" in this argument?
    - How can we weaken this argument?
    - How can we strengthen this argument?

Practice Exercises

Q1. Oligopoly is the state where there are many competitors within a single market. The Pepsi Company realizes that its operations are in competitive industries.

Which of the following conclusions may be inferred from the above?

(a) Pepsi's market is not oligopolistic.

(b) Monopoly is defined as one seller in a market.

(c) The Pepsi Company has a lot of domestic competition.

(d) The Pepsi Company is operating in an oligopolistic market.

(e) Monopoly and oligopoly are similar markets.

Q2. People in a South African tribe have observed that heavy rains are usually preceded by claps of thunder. They are convinced that the heavy rains are somehow caused by the claps of thunder.

Which of the following, if true, would weaken the tribals, conviction?

(a) The temperature must fall below 20 degrees Celsius for both heavy rains and claps of thunder to occur.

(b) The presence of rain bearing clouds is the reason for the heavy rains as well as the claps of thunder.

(c) The tribals of the particular tribe are unscientific people prone to superstitions.

(d) It is as yet to be proved that claps of thunder precede and hence, cause heavy rains.

(e) Claps of thunder actually cause heavy rains.

Q3. Professor Krithileshwar Jhamb argued that that the method of evaluation for teachers, used at IIM Bangalore where students evaluated the teachers, was not a valid measure of teaching quality. Students should fill out questionnaires at the end of the term when the courses have been completed.

Which of the following, if true, provides support for Professor Jhamb's proposal?

(a) Professor Jhamb received low ratings from a majority of his students.

(b) Under the present system, students were made to evaluate their teachers mid-term.

(c) Students at IIM Bangalore are not interested in evaluating their teachers.

(d) The institution should have more methods to evaluate teachers.

(e) A new proposal for methods of evaluation is being decided.

Q4. PM Manmohan Singh lobbied for the inclusion of India amongst the set of ASEAN countries. This would help develop and liberalize trade with countries such as Japan, China and other prominent members of the ASEAN group.

Each of the following, if true, could account for the above, except:

(a) The PM is up for re-election and needs to show results.

(b) The PM's United Party Alliance had promised the creation of new jobs in the economy.

(c) The inclusion of India in the ASEAN would be a major achievement on the economic and political front for Manmohan Singh.

(d) Being a shrewd economist, Manmohan Singh realised that trade agreements with prominent nations of the ASEAN would definitely lead to an increase in the trade deficit of the country.

(e) None of these.

Q5. "If the islanders are doomed to have local self governance–and it is the islanders who have determined this–then they should be ready to bear the negative consequences of local self governance." said a British colonist as he left the shores of the island he was governing.

Which of the following, if true, would weaken his argument?

(a) Local rulers are always more interested in the development of their country than foreign colonists.

(b) Local self governance is not child's play.

(c) The islanders are equally qualified and competent, if not more than the colonists, to run their own government.

(d) A group of islanders were against the transfer of power.

(e) The islanders were not working to form their own government.

Q6. Amrinder Singh is no big catch for the Tongress Party in Uttam Pradesh. Even though he is the brother of the Chief Minister of the opposing Bhrasthwadi Party, he himself has no political clout and was not even important organizationally for his own party.

Which of the following statements is inconsistent with the above?

(a) Amrinder Singh is the brother of the present Chief Minister of Uttam Pradesh.

(b) The Bhrastwadi Party and the Tongress Party are political rivals.

(c) Amrinder Singh is being touted as the next leader of the Bhrasthwadi Party.

(d) Amrinder Singh has not been interested in politics.

(e) Amrinder Singh is not treated as very important by his own party men.

Q7. Stock market analyst Dhirubhai Mehta: "We believe that company's stock will appreciate at 35 per cent a year for the next 10–12 years. The company just became the leader in its industry and we expect its sales to continue to grow at 8 per cent a year over this period."

Investor: "But how can the stock's price be expected to grow more quickly than the company's underlying sales?"

Which of the following facts would best support the stock analyst?

(a) The company's expenses will be declining over the next 5 to 10 years.

(b) The company just won a patent on a new product.

(c) Company A's stock is currently overvalued by a significant amount.

(d) The company's industry peer group is expected to experience stock appreciation rates of 30 per cent over the same time horizon.

(e) The company is expecting some losses in the coming season.

Q8. A car magazine report: 'The average mileage in the small car market was found to be 18 kilometres per litre.

The average mileage was calculated by taking cars of all manufacturers in the segment, filling them with 10 litres of fuel and driving them along the Mumbai-Pune expressway. However, for the Karuti, the mileage was 22 kilometres per litre. Clearly, if you want to buy a new car, you should buy the Karuti.'

Which of the following assumptions does the magazine make?

(a) The reader is interested in buying a car.

(b) Mileage is the sole consideration for the readers of the magazine who intend to buy a car.

(c) No other car in the segment had a mileage better than the Karuti's mileage.

(d) None of these.

(e) The readers might also look for other factors as comfort, etc.

Q9. For the above question, which of the following additional information makes the argument stronger?

I. Petrol prices have touched the sky, and hence the reader should be primarily interested in saving on fuel costs while purchasing a new car.

II. Besides mileage, Karuti scored the best on 9 out of 10 performance indicators used by the survey.

III. The article is titled–"Your first Car"

(a) I and II (b) II and III

(c) II only (d) All of these

(e) None of these

Q10. Per-capita income in India last year was ₹17,600. Real median income for female headed families was ₹38,000. Therefore, women wage-earners are paid more than the national average.

Which of the following would, if true, weaken the above conclusion?

(a) Only a small proportion of the total wage earners are women family heads.

(b) In 99 percent of the cases, families headed by a female included other wage-earners.

(c) Average income is significantly different from median income.

(d) All of these.

(e) None of these.

Q11. The head of the NCAER was quoted as saying that the Consumer Price Index (CL) will go down next month because of a recent drop in the price of petrol and steel.

Which of the following cannot be inferred from the statement?

(a) The cost of petrol and steel has gone down sharply.

(b) Consumption of petrol and steel has gone up.

(c) Petrol and steel are major items in the CPI.

(d) The changes in the cost of petrol is reflected quickly in the CPI.

Q12. "There has been a high incidence of traffic accident related deaths last year." Hence, the chairman of the CBDT suggested that excise taxes on cars and automobiles should not be reduced as planned by the government.

Which of the above statements weakens the argument above?

(a) Although there was a high incidence of traffic accident related deaths last year, it was not significantly higher than the previous years.

(b) Compulsory insurance covered most physical damage to automobiles and property.

(c) A Government of India report has shown that the demand for automobiles was highly inelastic.

(d) It was found in a study that an inadequate road network accounted for 30 per cent of the accidents last year.

(e) Higher prices would definitely deter lawyers.

Q13. The Incandescent brand fruit juice claims to be the most original fruit juice available on the market today. To prove this claim, the company marketing Incandescent called 10 people and asked them about their thoughts on fruit juices available on the market today. Nine of them stated that they unequivocally drink Incandescent brand fruit juices on a regular basis because it is closest to the taste of real fruits.

Which of the following would most weaken this argument?

(a) The Incandescent brand fruit juice is highly addictive.

(b) The 10 people called were related closely to top executives of the company.

(c) Most people prefer cola drinks to fruit juices. Here, Incandescent is a poor third to Coke and Pepsi.

(d) The 10 people were selected at random.

(e) All of these.

Q14. For the above question, which of the options actually strengthen the argument?

(a) A and B (b) C and D
(c) D only (d) A and D
(e) A, B and D

Q15. Chewing tobacco has many benefits. However, the primary benefits occur in the area of mental health. The habit originates in a search for contentment. The life expectancy of our people has increased greatly in recent years; it is possible that the relaxation and contentment and enjoyment produced by tobacco chewing has lengthened many lives. Hence, chewing tobacco is beneficial.

Which of the following, if true, would weaken the above conclusion?

(a) The government earns millions of dollars from the sales of chewing tobaccos.
(b) The evidence cited in the statement covers only one example of the effects of tobacco chewing.
(c) There is as yet no statistical evidence to prove a link between chewing and longevity.
(d) None of these.
(e) Chewing tobacco satiates the longing in a person.

Q16. Which of the following if true would best support the above argument?

(a) Chewing tobacco has proved to be less harmful than smoking.
(b) In a survey of 100 people, it was found that people who chewed tobacco had longer lives than people who drank Pepsi.
(c) A study conducted by the National Institute of Health Research found a link between chewing tobacco and longevity.
(d) Chewing tobacco leads to happier individuals. Happiness is proven to be a cause for longevity.
(e) None of these.

Q17. Many of the junk foods on the market today, doughnuts, burgers and pizza, have less nutrients than natural foods, which were dominant a decade or two ago. Many nutritionists claim that pizza and doughnuts give less nourishment than natural foods. A spokesman of a leading junk food Company–Pizza House–stated recently that an examination of grade-school students shows less nutritional deficiency than in their parents' time. Hence, junk foods are not as bad as made out to be.

Which of the following, if true, would tend to strengthen the view of the spokesman?

(a) Grade school children reported eating no breakfast at all.
(b) Fewer junk foods were available to the parents.
(c) Adults claim to eat junk foods as well as natural foods.
(d) Both (b) and (c).
(e) Only (a) and (c).

Q18. My neighbour, Mr. Kohli's dogs bark and howl every time he lets them outside. My class teacher told me that dogs tend to bark and howl when they see other dogs eating biscuits sitting in their owner's laps. I personally believe they bark and howl because they enjoy disrupting my meditations.

Which of the following can be inferred from the preceding passage?

(a) Mr. Kohli lets out his dogs very often.
(b) The dogs are always howling and barking to disturb neighbours.
(c) The dogs enjoy being outside.
(d) Mr. Kohli's dogs bark and howl whenever they are outside.
(e) None of these.

Q19. The argument for liberalization which answers the worries of the left parties about the possible trade deficits created by the opening up of the Indian economy goes thus: 'In today's economic scenario, where there are many trading countries, the trade between two specific countries need not be balanced. The differing demands of goods and services and the differing productive capabilities of the same among different countries will cause a country like India to have trade deficits with some countries and surpluses with other countries. On the whole, the trade deficits and surpluses will balance out in order to give a trade balance'.

Which of the following conclusions best summarises the argument presented in the passage above?

(a) Left parties need not worry about trade deficits in India since its trade will always be in balance even though it runs a deficit with a single country.
(b) India's trade deficits and surpluses with other countries always balance out.
(c) The left parties in India should not be concerned about India's trade deficits with specific countries because they will balance out in the long run.
(d) None of these.
(e) Only (a) and (b).

Q20. Most citizens are very conscientious about observing a law when they can see the reason behind it. For instance, there has been very little need to actively enforce the recently implemented law that increased the penalty for godmen duping people of their money by playing with their emotions. This is because citizens are very conscientious about duping someone in the name of religion, as it leaves their religious gurus with a bad name.

Which of the following statements would the author of this passage be most likely to believe?

(a) The increased penalty alone is a significant motivation for most citizens to obey the law.

(b) There are still too many inconsiderate citizens in the society.

(c) Godmen should not be allowed to play with the emotions of the people.

(d) Society should make an effort to teach citizens the reasons for its laws.

(e) People would be more likely to listen to genuine religious gurus than self proclaimed godmen.

Q21. Throughout the first decade of the 21st century, net increases in Indian direct investments in the Far East (funds outflows) exceeded net new Far East direct investment in India.

Each of the following, if true, could help to account for this trend except:

(a) Land values in the Far East were increasing at a faster rate than in India.

(b) Labor mobility was higher in India than in the Far East.

(c) The cost of labor (wages) was consistently lower in the Far East than in India.

(d) Corporate liquidity was lower in India than in the Far East.

(e) Labour and land values were increasing at a faster rate in the Far East.

Q22. Inflation can only be fundamentally caused by two factors–Supply side factors and demand side factors. These factors are either reductions in the supply of goods and services or increases in demand due to either the increased availability of money or the reallocation of demand. Unless other compensating changes also occur, inflation is bound to result if either of this occurs. In economies prior to the introduction of banks (a pre banking economy) the quantity of money available, and hence, the level of demand, was equivalent to the quantity of gold available. If the statements above are true, then it is also true that in a pre banking economy.

(a) any inflation would be the result of reductions in the supply of goods and services.

(b) if other factors in the economy are unchanged, increasing the quantity of gold available would lead to inflation.

(c) if there is a reduction in the quantity of gold available, then, other things being equal, inflation would result.

(d) Whatever changes in demand occur, there would be compensating changes in the supply of goods and services.

(e) All of the above.

Q23. Which of the following best completes the argument below?

One effect of the FM radio was a collapse in the market for audio cassettes. Formerly, people had to buy audio cassettes in order to listen to their favorite music, but the advent of FM radio changed all that by 'giving people music on tap'. Similarly, the introduction of crops genetically engineered to be resistant to pests will

(a) increase the size of crop harvests.

(b) increase the cost of seeds.

(c) reduce demand for chemical pesticides.

(d) reduce the value of farmland.

(e) None of the above.

Q24. Most large retail stores of all goods and brands hold discount sales in the month of November. The original idea of price reduction campaigns in November became popular when it was realized that the sales of products would generally slow down following the Diwali rush, were it not for some incentive. The lack of demand could be solved by the simple solution of reducing prices.

There is now an increasing tendency among major chains of stores across the country to have their "November sales" begin before Diwali. The idea behind this trend is to endeavor to sell the maximum amount of stock at a profit, even if that may not be at the maximum profit.

Which of the following conclusions cannot be drawn from the above?

(a) The incidence of "early" November sales results in lower holdings of stocks with the corollary of lower stock holding costs.

(b) Demand is a function of price; as you lower price, demand increases.

(c) Major stores seem to think it makes sense to have the November sales campaigns pre-Diwali.

(d) The major department stores do not worry as much about profit maximisation as they do about sales maximisation.

(e) A price cut offers an incentive to buy for the customs.

Q25. Of the world's largest AIDS cases countries in 2010, three had the same share of world AIDS patients as they had in 2000. These three countries may serve as examples of countries that succeeded in holding steady their share of the AIDS disease.

Which of the following, if true, would most seriously undermine the idea that these countries serve as examples as described above?

(a) Of the three countries, two had a much larger share of world AIDS incidence in 2000 than in 2010.

(b) Countries should strive to reduce their share of the total AIDS patients in the world, rather than try to hold it constant.

(c) The three countries have different rates of population growth.

(d) None of these.

Q26. In a famous experiment at the IISC campus, when a cat smelled milk, it salivated. In the experiment, a bell was rung whenever food was placed near the cat. After a number of trials, only the bell was rung, whereupon the cat would salivate even though no food was present. Such behaviour has been observed in other animals such as dogs, monkeys, etc. and is a vital input for training domesticated animals.

Which of the following conclusions may be drawn from the above experiment?

(a) Cats and other animals can be easily tricked.

(b) The ringing of a bell was associated with food in the mind of the Cat.

(c) A conclusion cannot be reached on the basis of one experiment.

(d) Two stimuli are stronger than one.

Q27. At a rally in the Moinul Haque Stadium, candidate Laloo exclaimed: "Nearly everyone at the rally is behind me. It looks like I am going to be elected."

Which of the following statements, if true, best supports the above conclusion?

(a) Laloo's opponent also appeared at the rally.

(b) The rally was attended by almost all the residents of Laloo's constituency.

(c) Laloo was never defeated in an election.

(d) Laloo was supported by the MLA.

(e) Laloo was an undesirable candidate.

Q28. Ram is a terrible driver. He has had at least five traffic violations in the past year.

Which of the following can be said about the above claim?

(a) This is an example of an argument that is directed against the person making an argument rather than the argument itself.

(b) The argument is fallacious because it contains an illegitimate parallelism.

(c) The above argument obtains its strength from a similarity of two compared situations.

(d) The argument is built upon an assumption that is not stated but is concealed.

Q29. Since the late 1970s, there has been a dramatic decline in the incidence of traditional childhood diseases such as chicken pox, in India. This decline has been accompanied by an increased incidence of scleroid malaria, a hitherto rare viral infection among children. Few adults, however, have been affected by the disease. Which of the following, if true, would best help to explain the increased incidence of scleroid malaria among children?

(a) Hereditary factors determine in part, the degree to which a person is susceptible to the virus that causes scleroid malaria.

(b) The decrease in traditional childhood diseases and the accompanying increase in scleroid malaria have not been found in any other country.

(c) Children who contract chicken pox develop an immunity to the virus that causes scleroid malaria.

(d) None of these.

(e) Children who get a ruebella infection don't get chicken pox.

Questions 30 and 31 are based on the following:

An annually conducted nationwide survey by a leading health research organization, shows a continuing marked decline in the use of illegal drugs like hashish and charas by high school seniors over the last five years.

Q30. In using the results of the survey described above, in order to make conclusions about illegal drug use in the teenage population as a whole, which of the following, if true, casts most doubt on the relevance of the survey results?

(a) Because of cuts in funding, no survey of illegal drug use by high school seniors will be conducted next year.

(b) Another survey found an increase in the rate of smoking amongst the high school seniors.

(c) Illegal drug use by teenagers is highest in those areas of the country where teenagers are least likely to stay in high school for their senior year.

(d) The proportion of high school seniors who say that they strongly disapprove of illegal drug use has declined over the last three years.

(e) Both (a) and (c).

Q31. Which of the following, if true, would provide most support for concluding from the survey results described above that the use of illegal drugs by people below the age of 20 is declining?

(a) Another survey found an increase in the rate of smoking amongst the high school seniors.

(b) In the past, high school seniors were consistently the population group most likely to use illegal drugs and most likely to use them heavily.

(c) The percentage of high school seniors who use illegal drugs is consistently very similar to the percentage of all people below the age of 20 who use illegal drugs.

(d) Both (b) and (c).

(e) All of (a), (b) and (c).

Q32. The local education authorities in India have recently issued a "prescribed" list of books that are approved for reading in schools by children aged between 5 and 11.

A furor has arisen among many parents because an authoress by the name of Pooja Mehta, very popular with children, has been omitted from the said list. When asked to comment on the omission, the head of the committee that was responsible for preparing the list of books said that the books of Mrs Pooja Mehta have been omitted because "we thought they are of an inferior quality and do not sufficiently stimulate the children's intellectual ability and not because they contain characters which are stereotypes or may show racial prejudice."

Which one of the following statements can be inferred from the above paragraph?

(a) There was an opinion that Mrs Mehta's books were omitted because they contained characters that were stereotypes or showed racial prejudice.

(b) The parents' view is that Mrs Pooja Mehta's books might have been left off the list because some of her characters were racist.

(c) Mrs Pooja Mehta was popular with children and parents because she included stereotype characters in her books.

(d) None of these.

(e) Mrs. Pooja Mehta's speciality was the ability to write about racial prejudice.

Q33. All televisions emit sounds. And all radios emit sounds. Therefore, I conclude that all televisions are radios.

The argument above is invalid because

(a) the writer bases his argument on another argument that contains circular reasoning.

(b) the writer has illogically classified two disparate groups together when there is no relationship between them, except that they both have the same attribute.

(c) the writer has made a mistaken analogy between two dissimilar objects.

(d) the writer has failed to express his reasoning fully.

(e) The writer has failed to express a relation between the two objects.

Q34. In elections in a democratic set up, the proper role of the press is to cover only those factors in the campaign which bear on the eventual outcome. Since the outcome is invariably a victory for the candidate of one of two major parties, the press should not cover the campaigns of candidates of minor parties. The argument above relies on which of the following assumption?

(a) It is unlikely that there will be more than three candidates in any given race.

(b) Candidates of minor parties will never win elections.

(c) The number of votes cast for a candidate of a minor party is not likely to affect the outcome of the contest between the candidates of the two major parties.

(d) Both (b) and (c).

(e) None of the above.

Q35. The daily journey from his home to his office takes Shyam on an average fifty five minutes by car. Shyam learns about a different route from a neighbour. This route is longer in distance, but will only take thirty five minutes on the average, because it contains stretches of roads where it is possible to drive at higher speeds. Shyam's only consideration apart from the time factor, is the cost. He calculates that his car will consume 10 per cent less gasoline if he takes the suggested new route. Shyam decides to take the new route for the next two weeks as an experiment.

If the above were the only considerations, which one of the following may have an effect on the decision Shyam has made?

(a) Major road work is begun on the shorter distance route, which holds up traffic for an extra ten minutes. The project will take six months, but after it, the improvements will allow the journey to be made in half an hour less than at present.
(b) Re-routing of heavy vehicular traffic from the shorter route to a new route, is expected to reduce the amount of traffic to one third of the current levels
(c) Shyam finds a third route which is slightly longer than his old route, but shorter than the suggested route.
(d) Both (a) and (b).
(e) Shyam suffers from an eye problem which makes it difficult for him to drive longer distances.

Q36. The cost of housing in many urban parts of India has become so excessive that many young couples, with above-average salaries, can only afford small apartments. EMI and rent commitments are so huge that they cannot consider the possibility of starting a family since a new baby would probably mean either the mother or father giving up a well-paid position–something they can ill afford. The lack of or great cost of child-care facilities further precludes the return of both parents to work.

Which of the following adjustments could practically be made to the situation described above which would allow young couples to improve their housing prospects?

(a) Encourage couples to remain childless.
(b) Encourage couples to have one child only.
(c) Encourage young couples to move to cheaper areas for living.
(d) None of these is likely to have an impact on the current situation.
(e) Both (a) and (c).

Q37. By the early 1990s, the services sector contributed approximately 20 percent of India's GDP. Still, no coherent system of rules, principles, and procedures exist to govern the service sector.

Which of the following best summarises the argument?

(a) Regulatory systems lag behind reality.
(b) A regulatory system ought to reflect the importance of the service sector.
(c) India's GDP was five times its service sector.
(d) None of these.
(e) The service sector contributes insignificantly to the GDP.

Q38. In 1980, Uttam Pradesh earned ₹17 million in tourist revenue. By 1990, tourist revenue doubled and in 2000, it reached the sum of ₹132 million.

Each of the following, if true, may explain the trend in tourist revenue except:

(a) The number of tourists has increased from 1940 to 1980.
(b) Average expenditure per tourist has increased.
(c) Average stay per tourist has increased.
(d) The number of total hotel rooms has increased.
(e) Only (a) and (b).

Q39. Following the massive earthquake in Gujarat, building rules in Gujarat required all apartment buildings constructed after 2002 to have earthquake resistant designs.

From which of the following can the statement above be inferred?

(a) Apartment buildings built after 2002 had to be earthquake resistant.
(b) All apartment buildings built in Gujarat after 2002 have to have earthquake resistant designs.
(c) Some apartment buildings constructed before 2002 had earthquake resistant designs.
(d) Both A and B.
(e) Building rules require the buildings to have fixed number of floors.

Q40. In 1980, the average per capita telephone consumption in India was one telephone per hundred people. By 2005, the figure became one telephone per 8 people.

Each of the following, if true, could explain this trend except:

(a) The cost of owning telephones has gone down to one fifth of its earlier values.
(b) There has been a privatisation of the telecom sector in the 1990s.
(c) Getting a telephone connection has been simplified, and waiting lines have been eliminated.
(d) There has been an increase in affluence and disposable income amongst the country's vast middle class.
(e) Only (a) and (b).

Answer Key

1. (d)	**2.** (b)	**3.** (b)	**4.** (d)	**5.** (c)
6. (c)	**7.** (a)	**8.** (b)	**9.** (c)	**10.** (d)
11. (b)	**12.** (c)	**13.** (b)	**14.** (c)	**15.** (c)
16. (c)	**17.** (b)	**18.** (d)	**19.** (b)	**20.** (d)
21. (d)	**22.** (b)	**23.** (c)	**24.** (a)	**25.** (b)
26. (b)	**27.** (b)	**28.** (d)	**29.** (c)	**30.** (c)
31. (c)	**32.** (a)	**33.** (b)	**34.** (d)	**35.** (a)
36. (c)	**37.** (b)	**38.** (d)	**39.** (b)	**40.** (b)

CHAPTER

2 Previous Years' Questions from CAT

CAT 2003

Directions for the questions (1-2): Four alternative summaries are given below each text. Choose the option that best captures the essence of the text.

Q1. You seemed at first to take no notice of your school-fellows, or rather to set yourself against them because they were strangers to you. They knew as little of you as you did of them; this would have been the reason for their keeping aloof from you as well, which you would have felt as a hardship. Learn never to conceive a prejudice against others because you know nothing of them. It is bad reasoning, and makes enemies of half the world. Do not think ill of them till they behave ill to you; and then strive to avoid the faults which you see in them. This will disarm their hostility sooner than pique or resentment or complaint.

(a) The discomfort you felt with your school fellows was because both sides knew little of each other. You should not complain unless you find others prejudiced against you and have attempted to carefully analyse the faults you have observed in them.

(b) The discomfort you felt with your school fellows was because both sides knew little of each other. Avoid prejudice and negative thoughts till you encounter bad behaviour from others, and then win them over by shunning the faults you have observed.

(c) You encountered hardship amongst your school fellows because you did not know them well. You should learn to not make enemies because of your prejudices irrespective of their behaviour towards you.

(d) You encountered hardship amongst your school fellows because you did not know them well. You should learn to not make enemies because of your prejudices unless they behave badly with you.

Q2. The human race is spread all over the world, from the polar regions to the tropics. The people of whom it is made up eat different kinds of food, partly according to the climate in which they live, and partly according to the kind of food which their country produces. In hot climates, meat and fat are not much needed; but in the Arctic regions they seem to be very necessary for keeping up the heat of the body. Thus, in India, people live chiefly on different kinds of grains, eggs, milk, or sometimes fish and meat. In Europe, people eat more meat and less grain. In the Arctic regions, where no grains and fruits are produced, the Eskimo and other races live almost entirely on meat and fish.

(a) Food eaten by people in different regions of the world depends on the climate and produce of the region, and varies from meat and fish in the Arctic to predominantly grains in the tropics.

(b) Hot climates require people to eat grains while cold regions require people to eat meat and fish.

(c) In hot countries, people eat mainly grains while in the Arctic, they eat meat and fish because they cannot grow grains.

(d) While people in Arctic regions like meat and fish and those in hot regions like India prefer mainly grains, they have to change what they eat depending on the local climate and the local produce.

CAT 2004

Directions for the questions (3-5): Four alternative summaries are given below each text. Choose the option that best captures the essence of the text.

Q3. Although almost all climate scientists agree that the Earth is gradually warming, they have long been of two minds about the process of rapid climate shifts within larger periods of change. Some have speculated that the process works like a giant oven or freezer, warming or cooling the whole planet at the same time. Others think that shifts occur on opposing schedules in the Northern and Southern Hemispheres, like exaggerated seasons. Recent research in Germany examining climate patterns in the Southern Hemisphere at the end of the last Ice Age strengthens the idea that warming and cooling occurs at alternate times in the two hemispheres. A more definitive answer to this debate will allow scientists to better predict when and how quickly the next climate shift will happen.

(a) Scientists have been unsure whether rapid shifts in the Earth's climate happen all at once or on opposing schedules in different hemispheres; research will help find a definitive answer and better predict climate shifts in future.

(b) Scientists have been unsure whether rapid shifts in the Earth's climate happen all at once or on opposing schedules in different hemispheres; finding a definitive answer will help them better predict climate shifts in future.

(c) Research in Germany will help scientists find a definitive answer about warming and cooling of the Earth and predict climate shifts in the future in a better manner.

(d) More research rather than debates on warming or cooling of the Earth and exaggerated seasons in its hemispheres, will help scientists in Germany predict climate changes better in future.

Q4. Local communities have often come in conflict with agents trying to exploit resources, at a faster pace, for an expanding commercial-industrial economy. More often than not, such agents of resource-intensification are given preferential treatment by the state, through the grant of generous long leases over mineral or fish stocks, for example, or the provision of raw material at an enormously subsidized price. With the injustice so compounded, local communities at the receiving end of this process, have no recourse except direct action, resisting both the state and outside exploiters through a variety of protest techniques. These struggles might perhaps be seen as a manifestation of a new kind of class conflict.

(a) A new kind of class conflict arises from preferential treatment given to agents of resource-intensification by the state, which the local community sees as unfair.

(b) The grant of long leases to agents of resource-intensification for an expanding commercial-industrial economy leads to direct protests from the local community, which sees it as unfair."

(c) Preferential treatment given by the state to agents of resource-intensification for an expanding commercial-industrial economy exacerbates injustice to local communities and leads to direct protests from them, resulting in a new type of class conflict.

(d) Local communities have no option but to protest against agents of resource-intensification and create a new type of class conflict when they are given raw material at subsidised prices for an expanding commercial-industrial economy.

Q5. Modern bourgeois society, said Nietzsche, was decadent and enfeebled–a victim of the excessive "development of the rational faculties at the expense of will and instinct." Against the liberal-rationalist stress on the intellect, Nietzsche urged recognition of the dark mysterious world of instinctual desires–the true forces of life. Smother the will with excessive intellectualizing and you destroy the spontaneity that sparks cultural creativity and ignites a zest for living. The critical and theoretical outlook destroyed the creative instincts. For man's manifold potential to be realized, he must forego relying on the intellect and nurture again the instinctual roots of human existence.

(a) Nietzsche urges the decadent and enfeebled modern society to forego intellect and give importance to creative instincts.

(b) Nietzsche urges the decadent and enfeebled modern society to smother the will with excessive intellectualising and ignite a zest for living.

(c) Nietzsche criticizes the intellectuals for enfeebling the modern bourgeois society by not nurturing man's creative instincts.

(d) Nietzsche blames excessive intellectualisation for the decline of modern society and suggests nurturing creative instincts instead.

CAT 2003

Directions for the questions (6-9): Four alternative summaries are given below each text. Choose the option that best captures the essence of the text.

Q6. Some decisions will be fairly obvious–"no-brainers." Your bank account is low, but you have a two-week vacation coming up and you want to get away to some place warm to relax with your family. Will you accept your in-laws' offer of free use of their Florida beachfront condo? Sure. You like your employer and feel ready to move forward in your career. Will you step in for your boss for three weeks while she attends a professional development course? Of course.

I. Some decisions are obvious under certain circumstances. You may, for example, readily accept a relative's offer of free holiday accommodation. Or step in for your boss when she is away.

II. Some decisions are no-brainers. You need not think when making them. Examples are condo offers from in-laws and job offers from bosses when your bank account is low or boss is away.

III. Easy decisions are called "no-brainers" because they do not require any cerebral activity. Examples such as accepting free holiday accommodation abound in our lives.

IV. Accepting an offer from in-laws when you are short on funds and want a holiday is a no-brainer. Another no-brainer is taking the boss's job when she is away.

(a) I (b) II
(c) III (d) IV

Q7. Physically, inertia is a feeling that you just can't move; mentally, it is a sluggish mind. Even if you try to be sensitive, if your mind is sluggish, you just don't feel anything intensely. You may even see a tragedy enacted in front of your eyes and not be able to respond meaningfully. You may see one person exploiting another, one group persecuting another, and not be able to get angry. Your energy is frozen. You are not deliberately refusing to act; you just don't have the capacity.

I. Inertia makes your body and mind sluggish. They become insensitive to tragedies, exploitation, and persecution because it freezes your energy and decapacitates it.

II. When you have inertia, you don't act although you see one person exploiting another or one group persecuting another. You don't get angry because you are incapable.

III. Inertia is of two types–physical and mental. Physical inertia restricts bodily movements. Mental inertia prevents mental response to events enacted in front of your eyes.

IV. Physical inertia stops your body from moving; mental inertia freezes your energy and stops your mind from responding meaningfully to events, even tragedies, in front of you.

(a) I (b) II
(c) III (d) IV

Q8. Try before you buy. We use this memorable saying to urge you to experience the consequences of an alternative before you choose it, whenever this is feasible. If you are considering buying a van after having always owned sedans, rent one for a week or borrow a friend's. By experiencing the consequences first hand, they become more meaningful. In addition, you are likely to identify consequences you had not even thought of before. May be you will discover that it is difficult to park the van in your small parking space at work, but that, on the other hand, your elderly father has a much easier time getting in and out of it.

I. If you are planning to buy a van after being used to sedans, borrow a van or rent it and try it before deciding to buy it. Then you may realise that parking a van is difficult while it is easier for your elderly father to get in and out of it.

II. Before choosing an alternative, experience its consequences if feasible. If, for example, you want to change from sedans to a van, try one before buying it. You will discover aspects you may never have thought of.

III. Always try before you buy anything. You are bound to discover many consequences. One of the consequences of going in for a van is that it is more difficult to park than sedans at the office car park.

IV. We urge you to try products such as vans before buying them. Then you can experience consequences you have not thought of such as parking problems. But your father may find vans more comfortable than cars.

(a) I (b) II
(c) III (d) IV

Q9. It is important for shipping companies to be clear about the objectives for maintenance and materials management–as to whether the primary focus is on service level improvement or cost minimization. Often, when certain systems are set in place, the cost minimization objective and associated procedures become more important than the flexibility required for service level improvement. The problem really arises since cost minimization tends to focus on out of pocket costs which are visible, while the opportunity costs, often greater in value, are lost sight of.

I. Shipping companies have to either minimize costs or maximize service quality. If they focus on cost minimization, they will reduce quality. They should focus on service level improvement, or else opportunity costs will be lost sight of.

II. Shipping companies should determine the primary focus of their maintenance and materials management. Focus on cost minimization may reduce visible costs, but ignore greater invisible costs and impair service quality.

III. Any cost minimization program in shipping is bound to lower the quality of service. Therefore, shipping companies must be clear about the primary focus of their maintenance and materials management before embarking on cost minimization.

IV. Shipping companies should focus on quality level improvement rather than cost cutting. Cost cutting will lead to untold opportunity costs. Companies should have systems in place to make the service level flexible.

(a) I (b) II
(c) III (d) IV

CAT 1999

Directions for the questions (10-17): Read each of the eight short passages given below and answer the questions that follows it.

Q10. Three airlines–IA, JA and SA–operate on the Delhi-Mumbai route. To increase the number of seats sold, SA reduced its fares and this was emulated by IA and JA immediately. The general belief was that the volume of air travel between Delhi and Mumbai would increase as a result.

Which of the following, if true, would add credence to the general belief?

(a) Increase in profitability of the three airlines.
(b) Extension of the discount scheme to the other routes.
(c) A study that shows that air travelers in India are price-conscious.
(d) A study that shows that as much as 80 per cent of air travels in India are company-sponsored.

Q11. According to Mc Neil, a Brahmin priest was expected to be able to recite at least one of the Vedas. The practice was essential for several centuries when the Vedas had not yet been written down. It must have had a selective effect since priests would have been recruited from those able or willing to memorize long passages. It must have helped in the dissemination of the work, since a memorized passage can be duplicated many times.

Which one of the following can be inferred from the above passage?

(a) Reciting the Vedas was a 'Brahmin's obligation.'
(b) The Vedic priest was like a recorded audio cassette.
(c) Mc Neill studied the behavior of the Brahmin priests.
(d) Vedic hymns had not been scripted.

Q12. Developed countries have made adequate provisions for social security of senior citizens. State insurers (as well as private ones) offer Medicare and pension benefits to people who can no longer earn. In India, with the collapse of the joint family system, the traditional shelter of the elderly has disappeared. And a state faced with a financial crunch is not in a position to provide social security. So it is advisable that the working population give serious thought to building a financial base for itself.

Which one of the following, if it were to happen, weakens the conclusion drawn in the above passage the most?

(a) The investable income of the working population as a proportion of its total income will grow in the future.
(b) The insurance sector is underdeveloped and trends indicate that it will be extensively privatised in the future.
(c) India is on a path of development that will take it to a developed country's status with all its positive and negative implications.
(d) If the working population builds a stronger financial base, there will be revival of the joint family system.

Q13. Various studies have shown that our forested and hilly regions and, in general, areas where biodiversity–as reflected in the variety of flora–is high, are the places where poverty appears to be high. And these same areas are also the ones where educational performances seem to be poor. Therefore, it may be surmised that, even disregarding poverty status, richness in biodiversity goes hand in hand with educational backwardness.

Which of the following statements, if true, can be said to best provide supporting evidence for the surmise mentioned in the passage?

(a) In regions where there is little variety in flora, educational performance is seen to be as good as in regions with high variety in flora, when poverty levels are high.

(b) Regions which show high biodiversity, also exhibit poor educational performance, at low level of poverty.

(c) Regions which show high biodiversity reveal high levels of poverty and poor educational performance.

(d) In regions where there is low biodiversity, at all levels of poverty, educational performance is seen to be good.

Q14. Cigarettes constitute a mere 20 per cent of tobacco consumption in India, and fewer than 15 per cent of the 200 million tobacco users consume cigarettes. Yet these 15 per cent contribute nearly 90 per cent of the tax revenues to the exchequer from the tobacco sector. The punitive cigarette taxation regime has kept the tax base narrow, and reducing taxes will expand this base.

Which one of the following best bolsters the conclusion that reducing duties will expand the tax base?

(a) The cigarette manufactures' association has decided to indulge in aggressive promotion.

(b) There is a likelihood that tobacco consumers will shift to cigarette smoking if cigarette prices were to reduce.

(c) The cigarette manufacturers are lobbying for a reduction on duties.

(d) An increase in duties on non-cigarette tobacco may lead to a shift in favour of cigarette smoking.

Q15. Thomas Malthus, the British clergyman turned economist, predicted that the planet would not be able to support the human population for long. His explanation was that human population grows at a geometric rate, while the food supply grows only at an arithmetic rate.

Which one of the following, if true, would not undermine the thesis offered by Malthus?

(a) Population growth can be slowed down by the voluntary choices of individuals and not just by natural disasters.

(b) The capacity of the planet to feed a growing human population can be enhanced through biotechnological means.

(c) Human systems, and natural systems like food supply, follow natural laws of growth, which have remained constant, and will remain unchanged.

(d) Human beings can colonise other planetary systems on a regular and ongoing basis to accommodate a growing population.

Q16. The company's coffee crop for 1998-99 totalled 8079 tonnes, an all-time record. The increase over the previous year's production of 5830 tonnes was 38.58 per cent. The previous highest crop was 6089 tonnes in 1970-71. The company had fixed a target of 8000 tonnes to be realized by the year 2000-01, and this has been achieved two years earlier; thanks to the emphasis laid on the key areas of irrigation, replacement of unproductive coffee bushes, intensive refilling and improved agricultural practices. It is now our endeavour to reach the target of 10,000 tonnes in 2001-02.

Which one of the following would contribute most to making the target of 10,000 tonnes in 2001-02 unrealistic?

(a) The potential of the productivity enhancing measures implemented up to now has been exhausted.

(b) The total company land under coffee has remained constant since 1969 when an estate in the Nilgiri Hills was acquired.

(c) The sensitivity of the crop to climatic factors makes predictions about production uncertain.

(d) The target-setting procedures in the company have been proved to be sound by the achievement of the 8000 tonne target.

Q17. Animals, in general, are shrewd in proportion as they cultivate society. Elephants and beavers show the greatest signs of this sagacity when they are together in large numbers, but when man invades their communities, they lose all their spirit of industry. Among insects, the labours of the bee and the ant have attracted the attention and admiration of naturalists, but all their sagacity seems to be lost upon separation, and a single bee or ant seems destitute of every degree of industry. It becomes the most stupid insect imaginable and it languishes and soon dies.

Which of the following can be inferred from the above passage?

(a) Humankind is responsible for the destruction of the natural habitat of animals and insects.

(b) Animals, in general, are unable to function effectively outside their normal social environment.

(c) Naturalists have great admiration for bees and ants, despite their lack of industry upon separation.

(d) Elephants and beavers are smarter than bees and ants in the presence of human beings.

CAT ARCHIVES

Directions for the questions (18-19): For each of the two questions, indicate which of the statements given with that particular question is consistent with the description of the unreasonable man in the passage below.

Unreasonableness is a tendency to do socially permissible things at the wrong time. The unreasonable man is the sort of person who comes to confide in you when you are busy. He serenades his beloved when she is ill. He asks a man who has just lost money by paying a bill for a friend to pay a bill for him. He invites a friend to go for a ride just after the friend has finished a long car trip. He is eager to offer services which are not wanted but which cannot be politely refused. If he is present at an arbitration, he stirs up dissension between the two parties, who are really anxious to agree. Such is the unreasonable man.

Q18. He tends to:

(a) entertain women.

(b) be a successful arbitrator when dissenting parties are anxious to agree.

(c) be helpful when solicited.

(d) tell a long story to people who have heard it many times before.

Q19. The unreasonable man tends to:

(a) bring a higher bidder to a salesman who has just closed a deal.

(b) disclose confidential information to others.

(c) sing the praises of the bride when he goes to a wedding.

(d) sleep late and rise early

Directions for the questions (20-24): Read each of the short passages given below and answer the questions that follow.

Q20. The Kolahal party had to fight the Golmal party bitterly to win the mayoral electrons. One of the main features of its campaign was that it would make public all the papers related to a scandal during the regime of the Golmal party. After the victory, however, the new mayor got busy introducing many schemes, both liked and not liked by the public. The Golmal party made only mild protests but refrained from tabling a serious no-confidence motion in the council which it could have won by obtaining the support of the independent members.

Which of the following statements, if true, implies that the Kolahal party is blackmailing the Golmal party?

(a) The papers mentioned in the election campaign are prepared and ready.

(b) Some members of the public disliked the reforms made by the new mayor.

(c) People complained about collusion between the two parties.

(d) Independent members were not keen on supporting the Golmal party.

Q21. Cellular phone services are being provided by two companies in each telecom circle. These companies were awarded the contracts based on the licence fees they agreed to pay the government and were selected on a competitive basis. Cellular phone service providers have found that their profits are much less than they expected–in fact, in most cases they are losing money.

Which of the following can be inferred from the above passage?

(a) All the cellular phone service providers have been operating inefficiently.

(b) The government was wrong in allowing private provision of cellular services.

(c) Cellular service providers have been unable to match performance to plan.

(d) Paging services have eaten into the revenue of the cellular service.

Q22. Organizations are often defined as groups of people who come together to pursue a common goal. But more often than not, goals diverge as much as they converge, making the rationality of the overall organization no more than an elusive ideal. Beneath the collective irrationality, however, organizations are often operating in a way that is eminently rational from the standpoint of the individuals, groups and coalitions directly involved.

Which of the following can be inferred from the above passage?

(a) If all employees of an organization pursue their individual goals, one can never have an organization that behaves rationally.

(b) Although conceptually, an organization may appear to be irrational–behaviors of individuals, groups and coalitions in the organization may be rational.

(c) As individuals, groups or coalitions in an organization pursue their own interests, the conceptual issues of rational behavior get blurred.

(d) Since people are essentially irrational, the ideal of building a rational organization is elusive.

Q23. BSE officials point out that ever since on-line trading took off, surveillance isn't difficult any more. Sophisticated software has been installed for continuous monitoring of stock prices. If that is so, how could the unnatural spurt in prices of operator-driven stock go unnoticed? There does not seem to be regular checks or supervision.

Which of the following can be inferred from the above passage?

(a) The software used at BSE is not as sophisticated as it is claimed to be.

(b) The operators can drive stock prices crazy irrespective of the kind of software installed.

(c) Nobody can ever predict how stock prices move in the market.

(d) Having the infrastructure in place is one thing, but proper utilization is another.

Q24. At a movie theatre in Bangalore, last year, the proprietor decided to sell about one-third of his total balcony capacity on the internet. The response was tremendous. On every new release, the entire on-line capacity was sold out. Today, there are at least 2 million educated and well-heeled consumers in India who are ordering everything from cinema tickets to paan and tennis racquets to shirts from the comfort of their offices or homes.

Which of the following can be inferred from the above passage?

(a) There is a growing breed of computer-savvy consumers in Bangalore.

(b) It is more comfortable to purchase movie tickets through the internet.

(c) A retailing revolution is underway in India, with the advent of the internet.

(d) The proprietor of the theatre can profitably decide to sell all the balcony tickets through the internet.

Directions for the questions (25-26): Each passage below is followed by a question and four alternative answers. Select the best alternative.

Q25. In the Panchatantra, a woodpecker offered the following words of consolation to a hen sparrow whose eggs had been crashed by an elephant with spring fever:

For the lost and dead and past
The wise have no laments:
Between the wise and fools
Is just this difference.

This stanza highlights an important lesson that:

(a) Wisdom is a direct function of retaining the lessons contained in the past.

(b) There is no end to the reward of discriminating judgement.

(c) One must be sensitive to the past only in so far as it offers wisdom, not as an object of brooding or regret.

(d) Joy results from resolute yet circumspect use of the active powers; only the foolish would do otherwise.

Q26. The Sanskrit text of the Laws of Manu were first translated into English in 1794 and translations into other European languages swiftly followed. For Nietzsche, the humane wisdom of Manu far surpassed that of the New Testament; for the British Raj, it seemed to be the perfect tool with which to rule the Hindu. No understanding of modern India is possible without it and in the richness of its ideas, its aphoristic profundity and its relevance to universal human dilemmas, Manu stands beside the great epics, the Ramayana and the Mahabarata. The author of this passage

(a) believes that the Laws of Manu are greater than the epics.

(b) exaggerates the importance of Manu in Hinduism by declaring it to be the last word on the subject.

(c) states that Manu's work is comparable to the great epics.

(d) believes that the British could not have ruled India without reading the Laws of Manu; so great was its importance.

Answer Key

CAT 2003

1. (b)	**2.** (a)			

CAT 2004

3. (b)	**4.** (c)	**5.** (a)		

CAT 2003

6. (a)	**7.** (d)	**8.** (b)	**9.** (b)	**10.** (c)

CAT 1999

11. (b)	**12.** (c)	**13.** (d)	**14.** (b)	**15.** (c)
16. (a)	**17.** (b)			

CAT ARCHIVES

18. (d)	**19.** (a)	**20.** (a)	**21.** (c)	**22.** (b)
23. (d)	**24.** (c)	**25.** (c)	**26.** (c)	

PART 4

The CAT Experience

This chapter has been added to the book to create a clarity in the mind of the students about the kind of level of questions they can expect in the actual exam itself.

We have named it the CAT experience and designed it in the form of a mock test so that after completing the chapters the students cam test themselves in this chapter which will provide a simulated CAT experience. The number of questions from each topic and the difficulty level of these questions are very similar to the actual latest CAT exam. Detailed solutions are provided so that the students can understand the questions better, and analyse their errors which is an important factor in the preparation process.

The students should try to attempt these questions like a mock test and learn from their mistakes about areas of improvement.

We hope this will help them to gain more confidence about the exam and their preparation.

CHAPTER

1 The CAT Experience

Test 1

Directions for Q 1-4. Read the following passage and answer the questions that follow.

'As long as it's healthy!' Up until now, this cliché was merely a generic - if somewhat ominous - way for expecting parents and their loved ones to talk about their future children. But what if that outcome was not merely an expression of wishful thinking, but something that parents could control? Imagine a fertility doctor examining the embryos that could develop into your children, providing you with a menu. One has a heightened risk for schizophrenia but a very low risk for cancer; another has relatively low risks for these diseases but a three-fold increased risk for Alzheimer's disease; and a third has roughly average risks for all of these diseases. Oh, and the first two are boys, while the third is a girl.

While this may sound like a science-fiction movie, several private companies have begun selling services that resemble this scenario. Such companies cater to couples undergoing in vitro fertilisation (IVF), offering to generate a genetic risk profile for each of their frozen, days-old embryos. It's estimated that more than 100 families have already taken these tests, and some resulting babies have been announced. But is it really possible to offer such a 'menu' in a way that provides meaningful, scientifically valid information? This question has been the focus of our work as geneticists in the past few years. To the extent that the answer is yes, it raises an even more challenging question: should this be allowed?

To better consider these questions, we'll review some key arguments for and against this kind of risk profiling - called 'polygenic embryo screening', or PES. (Terminology in this new field is not fixed, and the procedure is also sometimes called 'preimplantation genetic testing for polygenic diseases', or PGT-P.) We will attempt to clarify which arguments are relevant and convincing, and which require further study. We will also consider this technology in the context of the historical evils of eugenics. Since the word eugenics is too often used in a manner that sheds more heat than light in discussions of genetic technologies, we will first lay out what is known (and not yet known), before engaging with the most inflammatory aspects of the debate.

Despite ample initial scepticism, recent science has demonstrated the potential utility of profiling human embryos for disease risk. Importantly, if these profiles are used to select the 'healthiest' embryo from a given IVF cycle, the child to be born is expected to have better health than a randomly selected sibling embryo. However, unbridled enthusiasm would be misguided: these bright predictions might only be fulfilled under certain conditions, and there is a risk that consumers using these services will be misled about their benefits. Further, widespread implementation of embryo screening will not only complicate IVF clinical procedures, it could also have social and psychological effects that reverberate far beyond the clinic.

Q1. What is "polygenic embryo screening" as per the passage?

(a) It is a technique used by IVF clinics to ensure successful implantation of the embryo.

(b) It is a technique used to understand the various features of an embryo.

(c) It is a technique used to decide which embryo would lead to the healthiest child

(d) It is a technique used to understand the science of fertilization in humans.

Q2. "We will also consider this technology in the context of the historical evils of eugenics." What could be eugenics?

(a) The system of planned breeding for improvement of a particular race.

(b) The system of knowing the sex of the child before birth.

(c) The system of knowing whether the baby would probably be a transgender.

(d) The word "eugenics" does not relate to any of the above mentioned systems.

Q3. "However, unbridled enthusiasm would be misguided". Which of the following statements, if proved to be false, would support the author's claim.

(a) The success of predictions made about an embryo's health depends on fulfillment of certain conditions.

(b) An embryo, once having formed its features, can be altered by the prevailing conditions in which it survives.

(c) An embryo is largely not affected by the environment/circumstances in which it is grows.

(d) An embryo's risk profiling cannot give us an idea about its success.

Q4. Which of the following can be definitely understood about the author from the passage?

(a) He is a critic of new scientific methods.

(b) He is involved in the field of genetics.

(c) He is against the system of embryo profiling.

(d) He is against the usage of science when it comes to breeding.

Directions for Q 5-8. Read the following passage and answer the questions that follow.

Suppose a person is very concerned about the ethical issues around food and farming, especially animal welfare, but for whatever reason finds that a wholly plant-based diet does not work for them. What is the most defensible step away from veganism - the best compromise to make, if it is a compromise at all?

About a year ago, this question became vivid to me soon after I set out on an experiment: a near-vegan diet for a month. For some time, I have tried to eat in a way mindful of ethical issues, avoiding, albeit imperfectly, the products of inhumane factory farming. But I have eaten animal products, including meat and fish, regularly. After spending a lot of time in recent years working on questions about animal minds (initially trying to understand octopuses and other cephalopods, and then moving on from there), the ethical questions around food began to feel quite pressing. So I wanted to find out how I felt on a diet with almost no animal products.

My plan was near vegan, as I allowed myself two eggs each day, and some minor deviations (didn't worry if I was given butter for my toast, didn't query the details of Thai sauces, and stayed with my usual fish oil tablets). The eggs were included because, ever since another series of dietary experiments a few decades earlier, I have found that a high-protein and fairly high-fat diet is best for my general wellbeing. So, I thought, two eggs would help smooth the transition, along with protein supplements. Free-range eggs I see as the most ethical of all widely available animal products. Some vegans hold that eating eggs of any kind is unethical, while others at least see this choice as more defensible than other animal foods. (Peter Singer, in his book Animal Liberation, regards free-range egg production as acceptable.)

The aim of the experiment was to look at the possibility of heading towards veganism, and to do this primarily for animal welfare reasons. I accept some of the arguments against meat made on environmental grounds, but the issues around animal suffering are primary for me.

To my surprise, the experiment quickly became an illuminating failure. The regime was, after just a few days or so, much harder than I had expected. I felt unsettled, tired, and much of the time quite cold, surprisingly (in February in Australia). Heartburn, headaches, inattention... it did not go well. On day 10, I decided to change plans, and add some dairy products to the diet for the middle third of the month. This transition was just as surprising as the previous one. Immediately I felt fine, with all those problems out of the picture. I felt better than fine, in fact - very sharp. Ten days after that, I resumed the near-vegan regime. The results were as discouraging as before, and I switched back. By the end of the month, I'd spent half of it mostly vegan and half as a vegetarian.

Perhaps I should have stuck with the first, mostly vegan diet, and waited to get used to it. (My understanding is that one's microbiome, one's gut ecology, has to make a shift.) But I was reluctant to do this, especially during the COVID-19 pandemic. With that unsettled feeling, day after day, I suspected I was more vulnerable to pathogens than usual. I expected to catch COVID-19 at some stage (as I did, a month or so later), and wanted to be physically well-equipped to fight it off.

I realise that this was a very short experiment. But the moments of transition between the various diets posed some choices in a clear way. Suppose one decides that a wholly plant-based or near-vegan diet is not going to work, and something must be added. If one is looking for one step away, thinking primarily about animal welfare questions, then three options appear that have completely different kinds of justification:

- humanely farmed meat (especially beef)
- wild-caught fish
- dairy products (conventionally farmed)

These aren't really the only three options (I will look at others below), but they are some obvious and available ones, within a developed-world urban or suburban setting. Let's say, initially, that the goal is to choose one of these as the step away. Which should it be?

Q5. What is the purpose of the author in the passage?

(a) The author is trying to justify the non-vegan diet as a vegan diet may not be sustainable for many.
(b) The author is just penning down his experiments with the vegan diet.
(c) The author is trying to find ways to encourage people to adopt "near-vegan" diet if not going completely vegan.
(d) The author is trying to bring out the pain of animals.

Q6. "For some time, I have tried to eat in a way mindful of ethical issues, avoiding, albeit imperfectly, the products of inhumane factory farming." What could be the products of inhumane factory farming according to the passage/author?

(a) Vegan options that are made in factories to replace the non-vegan options such as beef.
(b) Meat and other animal products factory farmed that lead to suffering for animals.
(c) Non-vegan dairy products that are not made in factory but traditionally farmed.
(d) Both B and C are products of inhumane factory farming.

Q7. Which of the following can be definitely concluded on the basis of the passage?

A. Being vegan is not sustainable as human body cannot adapt to it.
B. Being vegetarian would be an easier choice than being a vegan for a non-vegetarian.
C. One's body demands a certain diet which cannot be altered later once the habits have been formed.

(a) Only A (b) Only B
(c) B and C (d) Only C

Q8. Which of the following if proved wrong would go against the idea of the passage?

A. Being vegan is not easy for people who are conditioned to a non-vegetarian lifestyle.
B. A lifestyle change is never difficult for everyone if you make up your mind irrespective of the difficulties you face.
C. Being vegan is a choice and the author was trying it because he was against the animal suffering in the meat products that are produced.

(a) Only A
(b) Only B
(c) Only A and C
(d) All of the above

Directions for Q 9-12. Read the following passage and answer the questions that follow.

In 1932, Matsushita Kōnosuke, the founder of Panasonic, had an epiphany. On visiting the headquarters of the religion Tenrikyō, he was inspired by the sense of collective commitment he witnessed there. In a subsequent speech to Panasonic employees, Matsushita laid out a new guiding philosophy for his fledgling corporation: 'Human beings need both material and spiritual prosperity. Religion guides people out of suffering toward happiness and peace of mind. And business, too, can contribute by providing physical necessities required for happiness. This should be its primary mission.' For Matsushita, work was none other than a 'holy pursuit' (sei naru jigyō).

Matsushita later attributed the stunning financial success of his corporation to this 1932 epiphany. He equated corporate flourishing with improvements in national standards of living, and he conflated Panasonic's ascendancy with global salvation. For him, everyone benefited when people had been trained to work indefatigably for a collective mission.

In a speech on 21 April 1961, Matsushita pushed the idea further, impressing upon his employees that their job was to 'make people before products'. Panasonic certainly made goods, the corporate magnate acknowledged, but the company also made the assiduous individuals who manufactured its cutting-edge electronics and marketed them to the world. By extension, Panasonic sales teams 'made people' (hitozukuri) in another sense, using skilful marketing to form the very consumers who dutifully purchased Panasonic's wares.

As a corporate ethos, Matsushita's hitozukuri concept was groundbreaking, and over the years many other corporations borrowed his philosophy and leadership style. But the concept of 'making persons' achieved even broader reach as national policy. Just a year after Matsushita's epochal declaration, Japan's prime minister Ikeda Hayato adopted hitozukuri in 1962 as a guiding principle for his administration, describing the concept as 'gaining trust from the world by valuing morality, cultivating virtue, loving the nation and its people, and developing skills and techniques.' As this rather ambiguous definition reveals, the hitozukuri slogan was both vague and inspiring. As politics, it made for a good soundbite, but as policy it was difficult to explain. Its outcomes were impossible to measure, and the phrase also did not translate well: members of Ikeda's cabinet struggled to find a suitable English rendition as they prepared for a diplomatic trip to the United States in 1962.

The notion of 'making persons' had a certain logic that did translate across borders in that early 1960s Cold War context. It reflected the shared presupposition among the capitalist nations that 'religious capitalism' was the antithesis of 'godless communism'. According to this vision, First World prosperity emerged directly from piety, and religiosity favourably distinguished capitalists from their allegedly amoral communist counterparts.

To be sure, politicians asserted this causal relationship more than they actually explained it. With the benefit of historical hindsight and critical distance, it is clear that there was always a preposterous quality to the ideological claim. It was preposterous because it literally put ends before beginnings: post/pre. We are rich because we are religious. We must become religious if we want to get rich.

Q9. Which of the following can be definitely inferred from the line "'religious capitalism' was the antithesis of 'godless communism'."

(a) Communists did not believe in the existence of god which led to their decline.
(b) Capitalism combined wealth with religion to become popular, whereas communism negated religion as well as wealth.
(c) Communism and capitalism are different because one does not believe in god whereas the latter does.
(d) Capitalism believes in personal well being whereas communism believes in the society's well being.

Q10. How did Panasonic "make people before products"?

A. Panasonic's created hardworking employees who created cutting edge technology for the world.
B. Panasonic's employees inspired/encouraged their buyers and influenced them.
C. Panasonic's policies created several nations.

(a) A and B (b) B and C
(c) A and C (d) A, B and C

Q11. Why does the author state "the hitozukuri slogan was both vague and inspiring"?

(a) Because the outcome of the concept could not be quantified but the concept sounded nice.
(b) Because it was used by politicians as per their convenience.
(c) Because the concept was used by other corporates and countries simultaneously.
(d) The author calls the concept inspiring but not vague.

Q12. Why does the author state "We are rich because we are religious. We must become religious if we want to get rich."

(a) To highlight the importance of religion.
(b) It is an outrageous statement aimed at bringing out the shrewd usage of the 'causal relationship' by the politicians.
(c) It is a sarcastic statement aimed at ridiculing Panasonic's concepts.
(d) It brings out the uselessness of "hitozukuri".

Directions for Q 13-16. Read the following passage and answer the questions that follow.

In late-1940s Jamaica, when my mother, Ethlyn Adams, was a teenager and began to think about courtships, she was summoned to the dining room by her father. He'd recently been promoted to inspector of police in the Jamaican constabulary, allegedly (in family lore) the island's first black man to be appointed to such a senior position. Inspector Vivian Wellington Adams tapped his finger on the sandalwood dining table and warned his daughter: 'I don't want you bringing anyone into the house darker than this.' My grandfather would brook no questioning of his version of the brown paper-bag test. He was a black man but he would not have answered to that description; he'd have considered it an insult.

Jamaica was a pigmentocracy – it still is – and a premium was placed on fair skin, a societal code that Frantz Fanon in Black Skin, White Masks (1952) calls an 'epidermal schema'. Inspector Adams was a cinnamon-coloured brown man. His daughter Ethlyn, by her own estimation, as well as her family's, 'had good colour', and no right-thinking person would allow their family-line to be contaminated by those of a darker hue. This, after all, was colonial Jamaica, at a time when the journalist and historian Vivian Durham observed cogently: 'It was the ambition of every black Jamaican to be white.'

It is commonly agreed that race is a social construct. If, as sociologists such as Alondra Nelson tell us, there is more difference within groups than between groups – so that, as the child of dark-skinned Jamaican parents, I have more in common genetically with a red-haired Scot than a sub-Saharan African – then why do I still feel obliged to accept the primacy of race, and the notion that any distancing from those of my own phenotype is a betrayal? If my ornery old grandfather was still alive, I suspect he'd be enraged. Inspector Adams would have been more impressed by the attitude of Britain's first prime minister of colour. Unlike the 1987 breakthrough, when four black and brown MPs – Diane Abbott, Keith Vaz, Bernie Grant and Paul Boateng: the first elected in modern times – emphasised the importance of their race and ethnicity, Rishi Sunak has dialled down his. Further, Sunak has signalled his allegiance to British Conservatives' anti-immigrant, nativist tribe, such that his Hindu wristband and alignment with people of his complexion and diminished social capital among them are all but invisible.

Unexpectedly, I seem to have gone the other way and become even more black as I've aged – especially through others' perception of me – and that process appears to have accelerated since the murder of George Floyd and the rise of the Black Lives Matter movement. But, and it's a big but, it's complicated.

While I enjoy the freedoms and vibrancy of black culture, I resist the tyrannies of the promotion and exclusive embrace of 'Black' – a descriptor, now capitalised by a growing number of papers (both Right- and Left-wing), journals and individuals, even though I never got the memo. What are we supposed to do about the perverse domain assumptions that underpin the adoption of an old racial taxonomy long past its sell-by date, as well as its triumphant inversion: the ambition to be Black fuelled by the old sentiment: 'Fuck you, white people. You reject us? Nah, we reject you!' But this notion of blackness is defined and limited by its opposition to whiteness, encouraging silos of separation. This surely highlights one of the central questions of blackness: what do you let go of, what and who do you allow to define you?

Q13. What is pigmentocracy as per the passage?

(a) Favouring a specific skin colour over others.
(b) Favouring fairer skin than dark complexion.
(c) Rule of a certain colour on a diverse region.
(d) The passage is ambiguous about pigmentocracy.

Q14. Which of the following would aptly define the author.

(a) She accepts her colour but is embarrassed by certain notions related to the same.
(b) She embraces her colour and culture and is proud of it.
(c) She has similar views regarding colour as was her grandfather's.
(d) She feels embarrassed by her colour and the ideology of "her people".

Q15. Why would Inspector Adams be inspired by Rishi Sunak's methods?

A. Because the British PM rose to power despite being of a darker colour.
B. Because the British PM downplayed his ethnicity to relate more to those in power.
C. Because the British PM tries to bring all ethnic groups on the central stage.

(a) Only B (b) A and B
(c) A and C (d) B and C

Q16. Which of the following, if proven to be true, would falsify the author's claim that "Black people" tend to be more separatists/aloof at times?

(a) As per recent surveys, it has been found that black people prefer to stay within their communities.
(b) As per recent surveys, it has been found that more and more coloured communities are being formed in metropolitan areas of USA.
(c) As per recent polls, blacks tend to elect people of brown colour.
(d) All of the above would support the author's claims.

Directions for Q 17-18. There is a sentence that is missing in the paragraph below. Look at the paragraph and decide in which blank (option 1, 2, 3 or 4) the following sentences would best fit.

Q17. Sentence: The fact of such a meeting taking place is naturally surprising.

In September 1943, as the tide of the Second World War was turning in the Soviet Union's favour, the Soviet leader Joseph Stalin called a meeting at the Kremlin. __(1)__ Alongside the foreign minister Vyacheslav Molotov and the head of the secret police Vsevolod Merkulov were three men in Stalin's office for the first time: Metropolitan Sergius, Metropolitan Aleksey, and Metropolitan Nikolay, three of the few Orthodox Church hierarchs left in the Soviet Union. __(2)__ Even those who know little about the Soviet Union are familiar with its anti-religious policies, especially thanks to Cold War rhetoric about 'godless communists'. __(3)__ Indeed, this meeting was being held after decades of persecution of the Russian Orthodox Church by the officially atheist Soviet state. The three Metropolitans came to this meeting after decades of watching their Church decimated all around them. __(4)__.

(a) Option 1 (b) Option 2
(c) Option 3 (d) Option 4

Q18. Sentence: They're wandering across a steppe covered in short, dry grasses and pine trees.

The sun rises on the Palaeolithic, 14,000 years ago, and the glacial ice that once blanketed Europe continues its slow retreat. In the daylight, a family begins making its way toward a cave at the foot of a mountain near the Ligurian Sea, in northern Italy. __(1)__ Ahead, the cave's entrance is surrounded by a kaleidoscope of wildflowers: prickly pink thistles, red-brown mugworts, and purple cornflowers. __(2)__. But before entering, this hunter-gatherer family stops to collect the small, thin branches of a pine tree. __(3)__. Bundled together, covered with resin and set alight, these branches will become simple torches to illuminate the cave's darkened galleries. The group is barefoot and the path into the cave is marked by footprints in the soft earth and mud. There are traces of two adults, a male and female, with three children: a three-year-old toddler, a six-year-old child, and an adolescent no older than 11. __(4)__. Canine paw prints nearby suggest they may be accompanied by pets.

(a) Option 1 (b) Option 2
(c) Option 3 (d) Option 4

Q19. The passage given below is followed by four alternate summaries. Choose the option that best captures the essence of the passage.

The ways that animals move are just about as myriad as the animal kingdom itself. They walk, run, swim, crawl, fly and slither – and within each of those categories lies a tremendous number of subtly different movement types. A seagull and a hummingbird both have wings, but otherwise their flight techniques and abilities are poles apart. Orcas and piranhas both have tails, but they accomplish very different types of swimming. Even a human walking or running is moving their body in fundamentally different ways.

(a) There are myriad movement types in an animal's life.
(b) Different species use the same organs to move differently.
(c) The degree of each movement in an animal's life cannot be compared to another.
(d) The type of movement of animals are many and each movement type moves the body is different ways.

Q20. The passage given below is followed by four alternate summaries. Choose the option that best captures the essence of the passage.

It appears to be going about its usual business, transcribing genes and making proteins. The powerhouse organelles called mitochondria are dutifully churning out energy. But then a mitochondrion receives a signal, and its typically placid proteins join forces to form a death machine. They slice through the cell with breathtaking thoroughness. In a matter of hours, all that the cell had built lies in ruins. A few bubbles of membrane are all that remains. Apoptosis, as this process is known, seems as unlikely as it is violent. And yet some cells undergo this devastating but predictable series of steps to kill themselves on purpose. When biologists first observed it, they were shocked to find self-induced death among living, striving organisms. And although it turned out that apoptosis is a vital creative force for many multicellular creatures, to a given cell it is utterly ruinous. How could a behaviour that results in a cell's sudden death evolve, let alone persist?

(a) Apoptosis is a life ruining process for cells and still it might be evolving.
(b) Apoptosis is a self-induced death process as well as a vital creative force for some cells.
(c) Apoptosis and its evolution has puzzled scientists as it has evolved from the mitochondria which is the power house of cells.
(d) Apoptosis is an enigmatic process and scientists at large are trying to figure out what it is and what it will evolve into.

Q21. Five sentences are given below out of which four are part of a paragraph. From the given options, choose the statement that does not fit in the paragraph

(a) One of the first things I try to do in the book is to break that dichotomy down.
(b) Because we do have this tendency to think about the universe writ large, this big place that we live in.
(c) That we don't just create things in it, but we grow from it in a very meaningful sense.
(d) And then there's kind of this tiny stuff going on inside of us or inside of the materials around us, and we don't really connect them.
(e) But of course, they are profoundly connected.

Q22. Five sentences are given below out of which four are part of a paragraph. From the given options, choose the statement that does not fit in the paragraph.

(a) Some years ago, Christina Dhanuja saw a video on a WhatsApp group that she was a part of, which left her troubled.
(b) In the video, Dhanuja explained, an elderly woman spoke of the caste system and declared that "work is worship".
(c) The woman in the video claimed that depending on the kind of work she was performing at any given time, she belonged to a different caste group.
(d) For instance, Dhanuja recounted, the woman said that when she did intellectual work, she became a Brahmin and that when she did manual labour she became a Shudra.
(e) Dhanuja found it disturbingly ironic that a member of the group would share a video that so fundamentally misrepresented the caste system.

Q23. Rearrange the following sentences in a logical order to form a coherent paragraph.

(a) "We are keeping this," she is supposed to have said.

(b) Literary wives are a unique breed, writes Carmela Ciuraru in the introduction to her strange new book - at which point the reader pictures Véra Nabokov either licking Vladimir's stamps, or pulling the pages of an early draft of Lolita from the fire in which he was attempting to burn it.

(c) It's not true, is it, this statement of hers? And what's more, she must know it.

(d) But no sooner has the smoke faded than alarm bells start to ring.

(e) The women in Lives of the Wives, all of them the long-suffering partners of writers, could not be more different from one another if they tried; each one, in fact, is what my late father-in-law would have described wryly as a breed apart.

Q24. Rearrange the following sentences in a logical order to form a coherent paragraph.

(a) Few people know whether they will have the same job in five years. Many aren't sure whether they will be living in the same place.

(b) This sense of uncertainty and stasis, of a present that stretches on without end, is particularly disorientating because elsewhere time is speeding up.

(c) Recently, it has been difficult to plan for the future.

(d) The delicate clocks that determine when a flower blooms or a bird migrates are accelerating and unwinding at an erratic pace.

(e) Few politicians speak about it, preferring to invoke nostalgia in place of new ideas.

TEST 2

Directions for Q 1-4. Read the following passage and answer the questions that follow.

A great artist said artworks are not to be experienced but to be understood: From all directions, across the visual art world's many arenas, the relationship between art and the viewer has come to be framed in this way. An artwork communicates a message, and comprehending that message is the work of its audience. Paintings are their images; physically encountering an original is nice, yes, but it's not as if any essence resides there. Even a verbal description of a painting provides enough information for its message to be clear.

This vulgar and impoverishing approach to art denigrates the human mind, spirit, and senses. From where did the approach originate, and how did it come to such prominence? Historians a century from now will know better than we do. What can be stated with some certainty is the debasement is nearly complete: The institutions tasked with the promotion and preservation of art have determined that the artwork is a message-delivery system. More important than tracing the origins of this soul-denying formula is to refuse it–to insist on experiences that elevate aesthetics and thereby affirm both life and art.

In the popular imagination, the great corrupter of the visual arts is the art market, with its headline-making, eight-figure auction house sales of works by living artists. The secondary art market is indeed obscene, but to blame the market for all that's wrong with contemporary art is to disregard the no less pernicious motives of the apparatus of messaging that is foisted upon artworks by nonmarket institutions and their attendant bureaucracies. Private and public museums and galleries; colleges and universities; the art media; nonprofit, for-profit, and state-run agencies and foundations: These institutions adjudicate which living artists are backed financially, awarded commissions, profiled, taught in classrooms, decorated with prizes, publicized, and exhibited.

Institutional bureaucrats, not billionaires, have the power to constrain the possibilities for aesthetic development in the present. The figure of the contemporary artist we know today is an invention of the bureaucrats. He, like them, is a managerial type: polished, efficient, a very moderate, top-shelf drinker. His CV is always up to date. He worries about climate change. The likelihood he graduated from an Ivy League university is especially high; he may himself be a tenured professor (a near given for literary artists).

The nonmarket institutions of the art world, all vanguards of the progressive movement, have telegraphed that such a profile is compulsory for artists. They should be camera-ready and, if nonwhite, eager to discuss matters of identity. Like shrapnel, the words "justice," "legacies," "confront," and "decenter" ideally will litter any personal statements on their work. To conform to these expectations is to be savvy, a prerequisite for success. Such is the figure of the institutionally backed artist.

We derive meaning from artworks privately. The experience is interior and unfolding, often difficult to describe to others. Meanings can strike us, entering our psyches in a moment, involuntarily, driven by some hidden force. More commonly, meaning opens up within us slowly: on the third, closer read of the poem; after evaluating a painting for some time, once the eye has roamed and settled and roamed again, noticed detail, related parts to their whole. After an initial sensual impression, our faculties that make meaning are gradually enlivened–emotional, psychological, spiritual, intellectual.

Q1. Why does the artist state "Paintings are their images; physically encountering an original is nice, yes, but it's not as if any essence resides there."

(a) To highlight how paintings have become redundant art forms.

(b) To show that the relevance of an art piece lies in its interpretation by its audience.

(c) To highlight that the essence of an art work lies in its message.

(d) To highlight that beauty of an artwork is irrelevant.

Q2. The author of the passage is most likely to agree with which of the following statement(s)?

A. Personal interpretation of art is irrelevant to the message of the artwork.

B. Institutional bureaucrats are to blame for the present state of art world.

C. True artists do not exist as they cannot come into limelight.

(a) Only A (b) Only B

(c) Only C (d) A and B

Q3. What is the purpose of the author in the passage?

(a) To show how certain institutions rule the world of art.

(b) To show how certain norms have become "rules" in the world of at despite not serving any useful purpose.

(c) To highlight how the institutions tasked with the preservation of art are reducing great works to moralizing message-delivery systems

(d) To raise voice for the artists who are deemed irrelevant by institutions controlling the world of art.

Q4. Which of the following, if falsified, would jeopardize the author's claim that bureaucrat institutes do not preserve art?

(a) It has been observed that art institutes have contributed heavily to the growth of new artists.

(b) It has been found in a recent survey that more and more audience have started visiting museums showing contemporary art.

(c) It has been noticed that the more the people can relate to art's message rather than personal interpretation, the more they are inclined to preserve it.

(d) None of these.

Directions for Q 5-8. Read the following passage and answer the questions that follow.

The period of human history when European people could confidently characterise themselves as 'modern' lasted barely a hundred years, from the upheavals of the 1870s to those of the 1970s. This was the era in which the bureaucratic nation-state appeared to have been secured as the building block of geopolitical power, and the welfare state became essential to the pursuit of social justice. Liberal democracy was to be realised via the steady expansion of suffrage and legally protected human rights. Experts in both the natural and social sciences (newly divided into separate disciplines) would bend their knowledge to the development of richer, healthier, happier societies. Industry would drive a steady expansion in productive possibilities. Artists, having lost their function of depicting the world, or of celebrating political or religious authority, were free to invent alternative forms of expression.

As Mike Savage emphasises in The Return of Inequality, the 'modern' also manifested itself as a distinctive relationship to time and space, felt most acutely when wandering the streets of the great European and American cities. Modern society existed in a condition of constant flux, between a past that was now defunct, and a future fraught with uncertainty yet full of possibility. The 'premodern' or 'traditional' was over, and therefore of little concern. Fatefully, as Gurminder Bhambra and John Holmwood show, this was also the way many non-European peoples were seen: as relics to be overhauled or replaced.

The hundred-year period that began around 1870 also witnessed the birth and growth of sociology, the discipline most preoccupied with 'modernity'. Karl Marx produced his mature scientific writings between the late 1860s and his death in 1883, while the other two giants of the sociological canon, Max Weber and Émile Durkheim, wrote their most important works between 1890 and 1920. As Bhambra and Holmwood show, this canon wasn't established until after 1945, and then only thanks to the American sociologist Talcott Parsons, who led the effort to establish sociology as a credible scientific discipline. It was during the postwar period that the original vows of modernity were most energetically renewed, in the form of expanded welfare states, the progressive planning of economic and urban life, and the deliberate 'modernisation' of developing economies by newly independent governments. Sociology had much to offer governments that were committed to alleviating poverty and maintaining social cohesion, and that didn't want to rely only on traditional (patrimonial, religious or otherwise irrational) solutions to social ills.

What happened to this project? The multiple crises that occurred in the wake of 1968 - economic, political and cultural - have been examined time and again. They include, inter alia, the inability of governments to deliver prosperity for all in the face of slowing productivity growth; the fear that welfare states were generating as many problems as they solved; the emergence of a political generation that prioritised cultural differences over collective needs; the perceived decline of urban community, rooted in the hubris of planners and modern architecture; the steady offshoring of manufacturing industries; and the feeling that experts - especially in such fields as psychiatry - had become flushed with power. The neoliberalism of Thatcher and Reagan may not have had answers to these problems, but it was at least willing to name them in ways that facilitated its political hegemony.

Sociologists responded in various ways. For those with the deepest professional investment in the discipline as it existed, Anthony Giddens, for example, the task was to work even harder at establishing sociology as the primary explainer and navigational aid of modern societies. What role did statisticians play in the creation of this thing called 'society' that they claimed to know so much about? What power were doctors accruing to themselves when they promised to make people 'healthy'? What were scientists doing to make 'nature' speak with such clarity in their laboratories and papers?

Q5. The author is most likely to AGREE with which of the following statements?

A. Present day society draws more inspiration from the history rather than the modern era.

B. Margaret Thatcher was an unsuccessful leader as the world grappled with many problems while under her leadership.

C. Sociology has had a prevalent role to play from the "modern" era to the present day world.

(a) A and B (b) A and C

(c) B and C (d) A, B and C

Q6. Which of the following is NOT a reason for the decline of "modern" era as per the passage?

A. Rise of a political state that thrived on cultural differences of people.

B. Neoliberal policies of political leaders that had no answers for the political hegemony.

C. Reliance on other nations for manufacturing activities.

(a) Only A (b) Only B

(c) Only C (d) A and C

Q7. Why does the author state "Modern society existed in a condition of constant flux, between a past that was now defunct, and a future fraught with uncertainty yet full of possibility."?

(a) To bring out that modern society was not concerned with its history or the possibilities of future.

(b) To bring out that modern society was not concerned with its history and planned for an uncertain future.

(c) To bring out that modern society was concerned with its history and planned for an uncertain future.

(d) To bring out that modern society had moved past its history while bracing for an uncertain future.

Q8. Which of the following can be definitely concluded from the passage?

(a) The "modern era" led to great developments in the field of sociology.

(b) Sociology got its history, value and importance in the "modern" era.

(c) Sociology was not established as a separate branch of study in the "modern era".

(d) Sociology evolved and evoked radicalization in the modern era.

Directions for Q 9-12. Read the following passage and answer the questions that follow.

Intelligent decision-making doesn't require a brain. You were capable of it before you even had one. Beginning life as a single fertilised egg, you divided and became a mass of genetically identical cells. They chattered among themselves to fashion a complex anatomical structure - your body. Even more remarkably, if you had split in two as an embryo, each half would have been able to replace what was missing, leaving you as one of two identical (monozygotic) twins. Likewise, if two mouse embryos are mushed together like a snowball, a single, normal mouse results. Just how do these embryos know what to do?

This is intelligence in action: the ability to reach a particular goal or solve a problem by undertaking new steps in the face of changing circumstances. It's evident not just in intelligent people and mammals and birds and cephalopods, but also cells and tissues, individual neurons and networks of neurons, viruses, ribosomes and RNA fragments, down to motor proteins and molecular networks.

But how did intelligence emerge in biology? The question has preoccupied scientists since Charles Darwin, but it remains unanswered. The processes of intelligence are so intricate, so multilayered and baroque, no wonder some people might be tempted by stories about a top-down Creator.

Darwin's best shot at an explanation was that random mutations changed and rearranged genes, altered the structure and function of bodies, and so produced adaptations that allowed certain organisms to thrive and reproduce in their environment. In the end, somehow, intelligence was the result. But there's plenty of natural and experimental evidence to suggest that evolution doesn't just select hardwired solutions that are engineered for a specific setting. For example, lab studies have shown that perfectly normal frog skin cells, when liberated from the instructive influence of the rest of the embryo, can reboot their cooperative activity to produce a novel proto-organism, called a 'xenobot'.

The urgency of understanding intelligence in biological terms has become more acute with the 'omics' revolution, where new techniques are amassing enormous amounts of fresh data on the genes, proteins and connections within each cell. Yet the deluge of information about cellular hardware isn't yielding a better explanation of the intelligent flexibility we observe in living systems. Nor is it yielding sufficient practical insights, for example, in the realm of regenerative medicine. We think the real problem is not one of data, but of perspective.

From the earliest metabolic cycles that kept microbes' chemical parameters within the right ranges, biology has been capable of achieving aims. Yet generation after generation of biologists have been trained to avoid questions about the ultimate purpose of things. Biologists are told to focus on the 'how', not the 'why', or risk falling prey to theology. Students must reduce events to their simplest components and causes, and study these mechanisms in piecemeal fashion. Talk of 'goals', we are told, skirts perilously close to abandoning naturalism; the result is a kind of 'teleophobia', a fear of purpose, based on the idea that attributing too much intelligence to a system is the worst mistake you can make.

But the converse is just as bad: failing to recognise intelligence when it's right under our noses, and could be useful. Not only is 'why' always present in biological systems – it is exactly what drives the 'how'. Once we open ourselves up to that idea, we can identify two powerful tricks, inspired by computer science and cybernetics, that allowed evolution to 'hack' its way to intelligence from the bottom up.

Q9. Why has the author used the example of the normal frog skin cells in the 3rd paragraph?

(a) The author has used the example to establish that evolution is flexible.

(b) The author has used the example to establish that it is always the environment which determines evolution.

(c) The author has used the example to corroborate the statement that decision making does not need brain.

(d) The author has used the example to show that all cells are intelligent.

Q10. What does the author imply by "Darwin's best shot at an explanation was that random mutations changed and rearranged genes, altered the structure and function of bodies, and so produced adaptations that allowed certain organisms to thrive and reproduce in their environment."?

(a) Evolution is a completely random process.

(b) Environment plays a pivotal role in determining the type of species that could adapt to survive.

(c) No on exactly knows what evolution is.

(d) Adaptations happen as genes always change.

Q11. Which of the following is definitely TRUE regarding the author as per the passage?

A. He/She may be skeptical about the existence of a "creator" of life.

B. He/She is urging scientists to focus on "why" along with "how" of biology.

C. He/She is a student of biology.

(a) Only A (b) A and B

(c) Only B (d) A, B and C

Q12. What is "teleophobia" according to the passage?

(a) Fear of abandoning naturalism

(b) Fear of attributing too much intelligence to a system.

(c) Fear of not recognizing intelligence.

(d) Fear of purpose

Directions for Q 13-16. Read the following passage and answer the questions that follow.

Technology exists to expand and sustain our capabilities. Therefore, doing technology well contributes to our hopes for leading an ethically good life: developing the right capabilities in the right ways – and using them for good ends. Videoconferencing could make a significant contribution to this. However, the essential capability I'm concerned about is not videoconferencing in itself, but rather the humanisation of technologies for everyone's benefit. This is, I argue, one of the most pressing issues we have to deal with, as technology becomes ever more entangled into our lives. But to do so successfully, we need to think more deeply and creatively, using techniques from the interdisciplinary field we call design research – applying a blend of psychology, philosophy, anthropology, engineering and aesthetics.

In this essay, I will explore how the experience of videoconferencing points, in one way, towards the limits of human adaptability and, in the other, to a liberating human capability that we must collectively cultivate and sustain – as an innovative extension to the ethical framework described by the philosopher Martha Nussbaum in Creating Capabilities (2011). As the designer Jon Kolko says in Well-Designed (2014), we should adopt an 'optimistic stance' and 'seek to explore the situation space, to see multiple potentials for improvement, and to always consider what might be' through systematic empathy and 'integrative thinking'.

How important is this? The impact of bad design is massive – multiplied across the billions of people striving to flourish online, not only when we need the technology as a stop-gap measure to alleviate disruptions to everyday life, but also when we want to use it for more socially progressive purposes. Videoconferencing, and the telepresence experience it can enable, promises to facilitate the formation of communities and partnerships that escape the boundaries of time and distance. It can even help us overcome social and economic barriers. School teachers, for example, can struggle to achieve meaningful dialogue with busy working parents. Governments are breezily assuming this is made easy with technology. Teachers are discovering the truth. But it could be better.

In many ways, the impact of the technology could be revolutionary. It could help us create and sustain capabilities of the kind identified by Nussbaum: a case can easily be made for its positive contribution to any of her list of 10. The more seemingly foundational capabilities, including 'life' and 'bodily health' are clear, for example, in enabling remote access to medical services. But videoconferencing could also expand the development of 'senses, imagination and thought', 'practical reason' and 'play' through widening access to cultural and educational opportunities. In countries where the internet isn't tightly policed by the state, it's having a huge impact on the capability for 'affiliation' between people who wouldn't be able to collaborate otherwise.

But what of the expression and development of 'emotions', Nussbaum's fifth capability? In education (my field), there is a need to include an emotional dimension to what we do, to communicate to students (and academics) that emotions are essential ingredients, not to be ashamed about but to be developed. My colleagues at the Institute for Advanced Teaching and Learning at the University of Warwick have worked hard to create pedagogical practices aligned with this in traditional teaching spaces. But we find it harder to make this work online at a distance. Videoconferencing could be great. If only we could get the thing to work properly. But for now, it's quite often just painful.

Q13. What is the main idea of the passage related to video conferencing?

(a) To comment on the importance of video conferencing in the development of technology.

(b) To comment on how videoconferencing can be "improved" with ethics and innovation.

(c) To comment on the limitations of videoconferencing and how to overcome them.

(d) To comment on the role of videoconferencing in modern-day teaching.

Q14. "But for now, it's quite often just painful." Why does the author call 'it' painful?

(a) The author calls modern day teaching practices painful as they do not accommodate emotions.

(b) The author calls ban on internet in certain countries to be painful.

(c) The author calls videoconferencing painful as it does not accommodate emotions.

(d) The author calls the practice of online teaching though videoconferencing painful as it does not accommodate emotions.

Q15. Which of the following can be definitely inferred from the passage?

(a) The author is focusing on the humanization of technology.

(b) Technology is being effectively used to alleviate poverty worldwide.

(c) Governments are participating actively in improvement of modern technology.

(d) None of the above can be definitely inferred from the passage.

Q16. The author is most likely to AGREE with which of the following:

A. Effective capability is needed to provide effective education.

B. Emotion needs to be specifically focused on while providing education.

C. Technology and certain aspects of human life need to be separate.

(a) Only A (b) A and B
(c) Only B (d) A, B and C

Q17. Five sentences are given below out of which four are part of a paragraph. From the given options, choose the statement that does not fit in the paragraph.

(a) Because you're dealing with variable factors like humidity and the arbitrary whims of the baking gods, sourdough is not a process that will bend to your will.

(b) Even control freaks will be humbled by sourdough's unpredictability, and that's a good thing.

(c) I am, finally, leaving the dough alone during the fermentation process instead of fretting endlessly about its rise, and my bread is much better for it. Patience, it turns out, *is* a virtue.

(d) You can do everything "right," and your loaf might still collapse into a dense, misshapen mess in the oven. But even if your bread is ugly and a little burned on the bottom, it will probably still taste pretty damn good.

(e) Realizing that even if you "fail," you have still succeeded, is a beautiful thing.

Q18. Five sentences are given below out of which four are part of a paragraph. From the given options, choose the statement that does not fit in the paragraph.

(a) It sounds like a cheap true-crime conspiracy: An international network of predators steeped in Satanism lure children from seemingly harmless online platforms like Discord, Minecraft, and Roblox and extort them to sexually exploit and grievously harm themselves.

(b) Some victims are even pushed to suicide. Except it's true.

(c) Victims have flushed their heads in toilets, attacked their siblings, killed their pets, and in some extreme instances, attempted or died by suicide.

(d) A reporting consortium including *Der Spiegel*, Recorder, *The Washington Post*, and WIRED has unearthed a sprawling ecosystem that has targeted thousands of people and victimized dozens, if not hundreds, of children using some of the internet's biggest platforms.

(e) Law enforcement believes the "com" network encompasses a swath of interlocking groups with thousands of users, including hundreds of hardcore members who victimize children through coordinated online campaigns of extortion, doxing, swatting, and harassment.

Q19. The passage given below is followed by four alternate summaries. Choose the option that best captures the essence of the passage.

Stop. Think. Fraud. You may well have seen or heard the Home Office advert in recent weeks that's trying to educate us in all the ways online crooks are out to cheat us. They seem so plausible, these cyber crooks, as they try to trick us into handing over our passwords, bank details, PIN numbers, identities and cash. The website tells us that one in 17 adults in England and Wales were victims of fraud in one year–nearly three million of us. That's a lot of people, but a drop in the ocean compared with the number of us being fooled and deceived in other ways. One respected survey showed that nearly two thirds of us can no longer tell the difference between good journalism and falsehood. Around the same are finding it harder to tell if a piece of news was produced by a respected news organisation. So that's about 24m adults–never mind kids or teenagers–in the dark about who to believe. And if that doesn't make you "stop, think, fraud", then nothing will. This week I found myself with a bunch of smart 19-year-olds, all starting life at uni. Where, I asked them, did they get their news? For most of them the answer was a social media channel–Instagram, Reddit, TikTok.

(a) The increasing difficulty of online security due to cybercrime.

(b) The importance of campaigns to educate the public about online safety.

(c) The need for stronger passwords and PINs to protect personal information.

(d) The growing popularity of social media as a source of news.

Q20. The passage given below is followed by four alternate summaries. Choose the option that best captures the essence of the passage.

In the end, it only took two months of heel-dragging for Polish president Andrzej Duda, a staunch supporter of the populist Law and Justice Party (PiS), to finally accept that–despite all attempts to rig the election in their favour–the authoritarian incumbents had lost. Eventually, he swore in Donald Tusk (Civic Platform, PO) as the new prime minister on 13th December. Shortly afterwards, the newly minted premier thanked the country's head of state, saying he hoped their working relationship would be constructive, cooperative and in the service of the Polish people. Tusk appeared to be struggling to control his facial expressions during this speech: he seemed unconvinced that either the president or the PiS was interested in constructive cooperation

(a) With a focus on fostering a spirit of unity, Donald Tusk, leader of the opposition Civic Platform party, takes over as Prime Minister of Poland, expressing hope for a new era of cooperation despite some past tensions

(b) Following a period of political uncertainty that stretched for two months, Polish President Andrzej Duda, a member of the Law and Justice Party (PiS), finally concedes defeat and inaugurates Donald Tusk, leader of the rival Civic Platform (PO), as the new Prime Minister.

(c) The Law and Justice Party (PiS), known for its populist stances, faces accusations of attempting to influence the recent Polish election in their favor. Despite these allegations, the party ultimately concedes defeat, leading to the appointment of Donald Tusk from the opposition Civic Platform (PO) as the new Prime Minister.

(d) Following a contentious election and a two-month delay, Poland has a new Prime Minister, Donald Tusk, who expresses cautious optimism for cooperation, despite being doubtful about the President's willingness.

Q21. Rearrange the following sentences in a logical order to form a coherent paragraph

(a) Under rightwing Coalition governments - an enduring alliance between the Liberal and National parties - Australia was seen as a climate pariah on the world stage. The new prime minister will have to do very little to raise his country's standing.

(b) This was good news.

(c) In his victory speech on election night last Saturday, Labor's Anthony Albanese promised to turn Australia into a "renewable energy superpower" and end a decade of "climate wars".

(d) From a global perspective, Mr Albanese's most important policy is to cut greenhouse gas emissions by 43% by 2030 compared with 2005 levels.

(e) It is a marked improvement on the last government and will be well received in neighbouring Pacific nations tired of seeing existential threats from rising sea levels dismissed in Canberra.

Q22. Rearrange the following sentences in a logical order to form a coherent paragraph

(a) Amid all this wizardry, some aspects of the Elizabeth line remain reassuringly true to the finest traditions of British infrastructure.

(b) Even if you live hundreds of miles from Paddington or Stratford, you may know that London has just opened a vast and shiny new rail line.

(c) Naturally enough, it is years over deadline and billions above budget.

(d) Once the 100 km track is all joined up, a banker flying into Heathrow will be able to take one train directly into Canary Wharf, while a resident of Southall will be able to visit relatives in Seven Kings without ever having to change carriages, let alone lines.

(e) But one innovation especially worth highlighting lies not in its engineering but its economics. A big chunk of the cash for building came from businesses along the route.

Q23. There is a sentence that is missing in the paragraph below. Look at the paragraph and decide in which blank (option 1, 2, 3 or 4) the following sentences would best fit.

Sentence: This study demonstrates that bumblebees possess a level of social learning previously thought to be exclusive to humans

Led by Dr Alice Bridges and Professor Lars Chittka, the research team designed a two-step puzzle box requiring bumblebees to perform two distinct actions in sequence to access a sweet reward at the end. ___(1)___. Training bees to do this was no easy task, and bees had to be helped along by the addition of an extra reward along the way. ___(2)___. This temporary reward was eventually taken away, and bees subsequently had to open the whole box before getting their treat. ___(3)___. Surprisingly, while individual bees struggled to solve the puzzle when starting from scratch, those allowed to observe a trained "demonstrator" bee readily learned the entire sequence - even the first step - while only getting a reward at the end. ___(4)___. They can share and acquire behaviours that are beyond their individual cognitive capabilities: an ability thought to underpin the expansive, complex nature of human culture, and one previously thought to be exclusive to us.

(a) Option 1 (b) Option 2
(c) Option 3 (d) Option 4

Q24. There is a sentence that is missing in the paragraph below. Look at the paragraph and decide in which blank (option 1, 2, 3 or 4) the following sentences would best fit.

Sentence: Many envisioned an equal-opportunity society of small producers and consumers, where no one would have undue market power, and where prices would be determined by the "invisible hand."

Does free-market capitalism buttress democracy, or does it unleash anti-democratic forces? ___(1)___. This question first emerged in the Age of Enlightenment, when capitalism was viewed optimistically and welcomed as a vehicle of liberation from the rigid feudal order. ___(2)___. Under such conditions, democracy and capitalism are two sides of the same coin. Domestic propaganda in the United States has pushed the same optimistic vision over the past century, aiming to convince voters that free-market capitalism is essential to the "American Way," and that their liberty depends on supporting unfettered free enterprise and distrusting government. ___(3)___. But economic developments in recent decades suggest that we should re-examine such beliefs. To see why, allow me first to clarify some background ideas about what I call technological competition among innovating companies seeking to amass market power. ___(4)___. Such competition differs from conventional price competition by producing only one or a few winners, rather than permitting all firms to survive with lower profits.

(a) Option 1 (b) Option 2
(c) Option 3 (d) Option 4

TEST 3

Directions for Q 1-4. Read the following passage and answer the questions that follow.

I have only the highest respect for the documentarian Ken Burns. He's America's storyteller: an unrivalled filmmaker whose creativity, passion and style shine through every history he portrays. My intent is not to dunk on anyone, but rather to start a conversation about how Americans as a society grapple with our own contentious history. Our identities are shaped by the collective experiences of our past, and how we see ourselves in relation to them. Together, we constantly reframe and revise the past to make it make sense to us in the present.

It just so happens that the best place to start that conversation is with Burns and Lynn Novick's five-and-a-half-hour TV miniseries Prohibition (2011), which covers that most misunderstood chapter in US history, from the 1919 ratification of the 18th Amendment - prohibiting 'the manufacture, sale, or transportation of intoxicating liquors' - until its repeal by the 21st Amendment in 1933. Prohibition deserves our attention because it reflects what we think we know about history, rather than the actual history itself. It is what the comedian Stephen Colbert called 'truthiness' in truth's stead. The problems start within the first five seconds of the film. The filmmakers set the narrative tone for the entire series with an epigraph - stark white letters centered against a black background:

Nothing so needs reforming as other people's habits.

Fanatics will never learn that, though it be written in letters of gold across the sky.

It is the prohibition that makes anything precious.

- Mark Twain

Direct. Eloquent. Authoritative. Damning. The framing is clear: temperance activists are the bad guys, 'fanatics' hellbent on changing other people's habits who are dumb enough to 'never learn' the most obvious lessons staring them right in the face. The problem is that Twain never really said that. Instead, it is a mosaic of unconnected quotes, spanning different works of fiction and nonfiction over the years.

'Nothing so needs reforming as other people's habits' comes from Pudd'nhead Wilson (1894): Twain's serialised novel about race, slavery and small-town religion. 'Fanatics will never learn that ...' was scrawled in Twain's travel notebook while in London in November 1896 as he extolled the virtues of 'temperate temperance'. And 'it is the prohibition that makes anything precious' came 11 months earlier while in India, as Twain ruminated about Adam, Eve and forbidden fruit during his visit to Allahabad.

When stitched together, they make for a compelling framework for what we feel to be true about temperance and prohibitionism. In the 11 years since the release of the TV series, nobody seems to have noticed this. Still, the epigraph sets the stage for what's to come. Burns and Novick are gifted storytellers, and every story needs conflict - heroes versus villains, good guys versus bad guys. They've cast prohibitionists as the bad guys, as they so often are when prohibition is remembered: hard-headed fanatics intent on dictating 'other people's habits' in a manner most undemocratic and un-American.

Q1. How do Americans deal with their own history?

(a) They accept their history with a tinge of nostalgia.

(b) They struggle with their own history, trying to make sense of it.

(c) They are very proud of their glorious past.

(d) None of the above.

Q2. "It is what the comedian Stephen Colbert called 'truthiness' in truth's stead." What is truthiness?

(a) The actual history

(b) The real interpretation of history

(c) The interpretation of truth in history that is shown to general public.

(d) The truth that one should understand.

Q3. Which of the following can be definitely inferred from the passage?

A. Film- makers tend to twist words of artists to suit their messages.

B. Mark Twain was a great supporter of prohibition of alcohol.

C. People tend to be affected by words easily, even when they are twisted.

(a) A and B (b) B and C

(c) A and C (d) None of these

Q4. What is the attitude of the author towards Burns and Novick?

(a) He despises them for their twisting of words.

(b) He admires them for their smart usage of content.

(c) He appreciates them for their story telling abilities.

(d) Both (a) and (c)

Directions for Q 5-8. Read the following passage and answer the questions that follow.

Learning styles theory contends that people learn in different ways, mainly through visual, auditory or kinaesthetic modes, and so material should be presented to students to accommodate these differences, consistent with the 'meshing hypothesis' where instruction is tailored to preferences. Teachers should provide visual learners with visual representations of content, such as diagrams; auditory learners with lectures or audio recordings; and, for the kinaesthetic learner, the opportunity to have a hands-on approach where they can move around.

The Institute for Learning Styles Research, where you can become a certified 'Multi-Modal Paired Associates Learning Test' practitioner for just $1,895, claims that there are in fact seven different 'perceptual styles', including the olfactory learner who 'learns best through the sense of smell and taste'. This may well have been the inspiration for a satirical article in The Onion from 2000 on 'odour-based' learning, which claims that 'Reyna Panos, director of the Nasal/Olfactory Secondary Education (NOSE) certification program at Brown University' said that 'nasal learners do best when they are encouraged to use odour-based recall techniques in testing situations, and are allowed to organise and prioritise items by scent'. The biggest challenge now, the article quotes her apparently saying, 'is to educate the educators'. It's a farcical and humorous piece but one that sadly contains a disturbing reality when we look at just how prevalent learning styles theory is within education.

Learning styles theory has enjoyed extraordinary success over the past 50 years, and not just in the classroom. Not only did the theory become uncritically accepted on teacher training courses for many years and subsequently in the classroom, but it was also widely adopted in the mainstream media. As recently as 2014, it was featured on the BBC as a 'key skill'. Depressingly, the theory was also a central part of classroom practice. Even august institutions such as the British Council have information about learning styles on their 'Teaching English' website. Despite the fact that 'educating the educators' on key findings from cognitive science has been a core aim of various strands of education reform over the past 20 years, a study in 2012 showed that more than 90 per cent of teachers believed that students learn best when material is presented in their preferred learning style: visual, auditory or kinaesthetic.

Learning styles theory represents a form of retrospective absolution

There's little sign of the situation changing. A systematic review in 2020 found that 95.4 per cent of trainee teachers agreed that matching instruction to learning styles is effective.

The broad, intuitive appeal of the theory stems from the fact that it seems self-evidently true. Many people will say that they cannot learn by listening to a lecture and that they 'learn by doing', or that they need to move around or listen to music while studying. Others will contend that they are 'verbal learners' who learn best through reading or listening to an audiobook. For many adults, school was a frustrating experience where they did not learn as much as they could, and their sense of individual agency was negated. Learning styles theory represents a form of retrospective absolution where, if only their teachers had tailored instruction to match their learning style, then they could have achieved their potential.

Yet, despite its appeal, there is simply no credible evidence to support the idea that attending to learning styles actually supports learning, regardless of how well-intentioned the teacher might be. To paraphrase the physicist Wolfgang Pauli, not only is it not right, it's not even wrong.

The fact that so many teachers continue to practise and endorse methods that have no discernible beneficial impact on their students is as scandalous as it sounds. How have we reached this point? To answer this question, it is necessary to look beyond the superficial appeal of learning styles, to consider the historical developments that provided the fertile soil into which such a misguided approach has taken root.

Q5. What is correct regarding "meshing hypothesis" as per the passage?

(a) It states how various learning methods compare to each other.

(b) It summarizes the various learning methods.

(c) It acts as a guide for teachers to understand the various learning methods.

(d) The meshing hypothesis is related to learning instructions are attuned to preferences.

Q6. Why does the author call learning theory a "form of retrospective absolution"?

(a) Because it is not highly effective in the real context.

(b) Because it tries to shift the blame of learning on the methods rather than the learner.

(c) Because it brings out the fallacies of learning methods that were used earlier.

(d) Because it leads to an illusion of absolution on the part of the learner.

Q7. The author is MOST LIKELY to agree with which of the following statements?

A. The self-evident theory creates a mass appeal.

B. Being self-evident does not mean that a theory is actually effective.

C. A self-explanatory theory may be effective in the long run.

(a) A and B (b) B and C

(c) A and C (d) A, B and C

Q8. The lines: "not only is it not right, it's not even wrong.", imply that....

(a) Something is totally wrong which is not right.

(b) Something is wrong but it could be right.

(c) Something could be both not wrong and not right.

(d) None of the above.

Directions for Q 9-12. Read the following passage and answer the questions that follow.

We'll start with a natural thought. Many of our alternative energy technologies are already highly developed. Solar panels, for example, represent a good option today, and are appearing more and more on the roofs of houses and businesses. It's tempting to think that a rebooted society could simply pick up where we leave off. Why couldn't our civilisation 2.0 just start with renewables?

Well, it could, in a very limited way. If you find yourself among the survivors in a post-apocalyptic world, you could scavenge enough working solar panels to keep your lifestyle electrified for a good long while. Without moving parts, photovoltaic cells require little maintenance and are remarkably resilient. They do deteriorate over time, though, from moisture penetrating the casing and from sunlight itself degrading the high-purity silicon layers. The electricity generated by a solar panel declines by about 1 per cent every year so, after a few generations, all our hand-me-down solar panels will have degraded to the point of uselessness. Then what?

New ones would be fiendishly difficult to create from scratch. Solar panels are made from thin slices of extremely pure silicon, and although the raw material is common sand, it must be processed and refined using complex and precise techniques - the same technological capabilities, more or less, that we need for modern semiconductor electronics components. These techniques took a long time to develop, and would presumably take a long time to recover. So photovoltaic solar power would not be within the capability of a society early in the industrialisation process.

Perhaps, though, we were on the right track by starting with electrical power. Most of our renewable-energy technologies produce electricity. In our own historical development, it so happens that the core phenomena of electricity were discovered in the first half of the 1800s, well after the early development of steam engines. Heavy industry was already committed to combustion-based machinery, and electricity has largely assumed a subsidiary role in the organisation of our economies ever since. But could that sequence have run the other way? Is there some developmental requirement that thermal energy must come first?

On the face of it, it's not beyond the bounds of possibility that a progressing society could construct electrical generators and couple them to simple windmills and waterwheels, later progressing to wind turbines and hydroelectric dams. In a world without fossil fuels, one might envisage an electrified civilisation that largely bypasses combustion engines, building its transport infrastructure around electric trains and trams for long-distance and urban transport. I say 'largely'. We couldn't get round it all together.

While the electric motor could perhaps replace the coal-burning steam engine for mechanical applications, society, as we've already seen, also relies upon thermal energy to drive the essential chemical and physical transformations it needs. How could an industrialising society produce crucial building materials such as iron and steel, brick, mortar, cement and glass without resorting to deposits of coal?

You can of course create heat from electricity. We already use electric ovens and kilns. Modern arc furnaces are used for producing cast iron or recycling steel. The problem isn't so much that electricity can't be used to heat things.

An alternative is to generate high temperatures using solar power directly. Rather than relying on photovoltaic panels, concentrated solar thermal farms use giant mirrors to focus the sun's rays onto a small spot. The heat concentrated in this way can be exploited to drive certain chemical or industrial processes, or else to raise steam and drive a generator.

Q9. Which time period is being talked about mostly by the author in the passage?

(a) The author is talking about the present era where we have many alternatives of green energy.

(b) The author is talking about a future world where the world might have experienced destruction.

(c) The author is talking about the historical era when invention of electricity took place.

(d) Nothing can be said definitely as there is no clear mention of an era.

Q10. "The problem isn't so much that electricity can't be used to heat things." What could be the problem then?

(a) The problem would be that the heat needs to be generated in huge amounts which may be difficult with electricity.

(b) The problem would be that electricity produces by- products which are not desired.

(c) The problem would be that electricity is not a viable source of energy.

(d) The problem would be that enough electricity cannot be generated.

Q11. The author is most likely to AGREE with which of the following statement(s)?

A. Electricity generation would ultimately prove to be pivotal for a society starting from scratch.

B. Human race cannot survive without fossil fuels in a post-apocalyptic world.

C. Solar power would prove to be the ultimate source of energy in a post-apocalyptic world.

(a) Only A (b) Only B
(c) Only C (d) B and C

Q12. What can be inferred by the "rebooted society" as mentioned in the passage?

A. A new society free from the constraints of the older one.

B. An experimental society in the beta 2.0 phase.

C. A future society which might emerge after the current one is destroyed.

(a) Only B and C (b) Only B
(c) Only C (d) Only A

Directions for Q 13-16. Read the following passage and answer the questions that follow.

In ancient Greek mythology, Diana was a patroness of virgins and goddess of the hunt, and any man who trespassed upon her privacy was likely to be punished by death. In our less supernal era, Princess Diana had been a virgin cynically used by the so-called "royal family" of Britain, of whom her husband Prince Charles was the most manipulative. And she was the one to be hunted, both symbolically and with a terrifying literalness, to her death. If Diana had possessed any flickering consciousness in these last minutes of her life, it would have been of those human jackals known as paparazzi gloating over their prey: the bitterly ironic end of the hunt.

But wasn't the princess complicit in her fate? Didn't she, by courting the tabloid media, not only bring her fate upon herself, but deserve it? So commentators have begun to speculate, with that instinct for blaming the victim that characterizes the most puritanical sense of justice. By refusing to live a lie for the sake of patriarchal order, Princess Diana exposed the hypocrisy of the Establishment to the glare of commoners. She did not, or could not, play the role of Prince Charles' wife, but chose rather to live by the truth. And the bad luck, the repeated "poor judgment" of the princess in choosing lovers–isn't this too a symptom of a complicit fate? Isn't such chronic behavior the result of self-loathing?

In fact, the hunt that resulted in Princess Diana's death began almost 20 years ago. When Diana was in her late teens, and Prince Charles was turning 30, royal courtiers were casting about for a worthy (i.e., unsullied, virginal) bride for the heir to the throne. It would not matter, evidently, that these courtiers, like the members of the royal family, knew of Charles' semisecret relationship with the married woman Camilla Parker Bowles. The princess-to-be was required to be virginal in every sense–to be ignorant of the very conditions of her marriage. With the cruel logic of those fairy tales that don't end happily, the princess-to-be was intended as a sacrifice to the Establishment. Of Diana at the time of the wedding, it was said by a former classmate that she was "one of the few virgins of her age around. She was a complete romantic, and she was saving herself for the love of her life, which she knew would come one day." There is no evidence that Diana would have behaved other than devotedly to her husband and family if she hadn't been forced to acknowledge that her husband wasn't only having a clandestine affair with another man's wife, but had been having this affair for years.

The drama in the princess's life had exclusively to do, it seems, with her often desperate search for love. This hope to be loved is in fact a wish to be loved for "what I am." Yet for one of Diana's status, to be loved would be as difficult as manning a canoe through treacherous whitewater rapids; for most people, paddling in calmer waters, with no distractions, no temptations, no ravenous paparazzi, no billionaire playboys pressing $205,000 diamond rings into our hands, this quest for love is not nearly so difficult. The paradox of the celebrity's quest is that she must realize that her "admirers" are drawn to her for the very reasons that the crowd is drawn to her; yet she wants to believe that, no, in fact she is loved for herself. (Most of us know we are only loved for ourselves–for what else is there?)

Q13. What does the author imply by "The princess-to-be was required to be virginal in every sense."

(a) Princess Diana was supposed to be unaware of the situation of her husband for her marriage to be successful.

(b) Princess Diana was supposed to be only a virgin and unsullied.

(c) Princess Diana was supposed to be "not a royal".

(d) Princess Diana was supposed to be a novice in royal methods.

Q14. "But wasn't the princess complicit in her fate?" Why does the author think that the princess was complicit in her fate?

(a) Because she married Prince Charles despite the latter having an affair.

(b) Because the Princess was too naïve to be a part of the royal family.

(c) Because the Princess shared her personal life with the media.

(d) Both B and C

Q15. What is the "paradox of the celebrity's quest according to the passage?

(a) The celebrity are loved for their power and position.

(b) The celebrity want to be loved for themselves like a normal person, but they are loved because they are famous.

(c) The celebrity want to be loved by everyone but the people love them for what they are.
(d) The people love the celebrity because they idolize them but the celebrity want something else.

Q16. The author would AGREE that:

(a) Princess Diana lived a lie in her marriage for her family's sake.
(b) Prince Charles became a scapegoat for the media because of Princess Diana.
(c) Princess Diana may have suffered from low self-esteem.
(d) The author would not agree with any of the above.

Q17. Five sentences are given below out of which four are part of a paragraph. From the given options, choose the statement that does not fit in the paragraph.

(a) Over two decades, social media has become a powerful and much discussed force. Networks like Facebook and LinkedIn keep us connected to school friends and former colleagues, and to their sometimes problematic political and scientific beliefs.
(b) Instagram and X give us glimpses into the lives of people that we admire, as well as the lives of those that we loathe.
(c) Studies link a rise in teen anxiety and depression to content that promotes an unhealthy body image
(d) A common ground between these disparate platforms is their need to serve audiences in the hundreds of millions or billions, in order to support a revenue model in which services are free and supported by advertising.
(e) They are, necessarily, big rooms that welcome everyone and offer few indicators of what the room should be used for.

Q18. Five sentences are given below out of which four are part of a paragraph. From the given options, choose the statement that does not fit in the paragraph.

(a) Think back to the last time you fell over in a public place. What did you do next?
(b) Perhaps you immediately righted yourself and carried on exactly as before. I bet you didn't, though.
(c) I bet you first stole a furtive glance at your surroundings to see if there were witnesses. If there were, then you may well have bent over and inspected the ground as if to figure out why you tripped, even if you already knew why.
(d) We do this by conforming to all manner of invisible rules, governing, for example, the distance we maintain from one another, where we direct our eyes and how we carry ourselves
(e) Or maybe you smiled or laughed to yourself or uttered a word like 'Oops!' or 'Damn'. At the very least, I bet your heart rate increased.

Q19. The passage given below is followed by four alternate summaries. Choose the option that best captures the essence of the passage.

The Hungarian folktale Pretty Maid Ibronka terrified and tantalised me as a child. In the story, the young Ibronka must tie herself to the devil with string in order to discover important truths. These days, as a PhD student in philosophy, I sometimes worry I've done the same. I still believe in philosophy's capacity to seek truth, but I'm conscious that I've tethered myself to an academic heritage plagued by formidable demons. The demons of academic philosophy come in familiar guises: exclusivity, hegemony and investment in the myth of individual genius. As the ethicist Jill Hernandez notes, philosophy has been slower to change than many of its sister disciplines in the humanities: 'It may be a surprise to many ... given that theology and, certainly, religious studies tend to be inclusive, but philosophy is mostly resistant toward including diverse voices.'

(a) Philosophy although has been resistant towards diverse voices has been an object of interest to the author because of its demons.
(b) Philosophy has not been able to change fast as a discipline but the author seeks answers to her questions through the study of its many demons plaguing it.
(c) The demons of philosophy are always making it difficult for people to study it but the author is still mystified by it.
(d) Philosophy as a subject has excited the author to pursue it inspite of its inherent demons and she is confident to overcome them and find what she needs to know.

Q20. The passage given below is followed by four alternate summaries. Choose the option that best captures the essence of the passage.

The homunculus - meaning *little man* - is the brainchild of the Canadian neurosurgeon Wilder Penfield (1891-1976), who co-founded the Montreal Neurological Institute at McGill University in 1934 and became its first director. There, he developed a pioneering technique for identifying, and then surgically removing, abnormal brain tissue causing epileptic seizures. Using this method over the course of his career, he and his colleagues produced early detailed maps of the functions of various regions of the cerebral cortex.

(a) Penfield created the homunculus and developed a technique for removing the part of the brain tissue causing epileptic seizures.

(b) Penfield was instrumental in creating the homunculus which was a breakthrough in the field of brain surgery.

(c) Penfield was the director of the Montreal Neurological Institute and he was successful in creating the detailed maps of cerebral cortex useful in neurosurgery.

(d) Penfield is a renowned neurosurgeon and has contributed mostly to his field in many ways, the primary being the creation of the homunculus.

Q21. Rearrange the following sentences in a logical order to form a coherent paragraph

(a) For reasons including timing, the existence of upsetting video footage showing both children being assaulted, and the fact that in each case a woman who was not a relative was convicted of murder, these tragedies received far more attention than is typical.

(b) The purpose of a just-published report on these cases, by the safeguarding practice review panel, is to bring together lessons and suggest how to make similarly awful events less likely in future.

(c) Star Hobson and Arthur Labinjo-Hughes, whose murderers were convicted last December, were among the 223 children who were killed.

(d) There were 536 incidents involving serious harm to a child, where abuse was a factor, in the year to March 2021 in England.

(e) How urgently this needs to happen was further illustrated this week when Laura Castle was convicted of murdering Leiland-James Corkill, a baby she was in the process of adopting.

Q22. Rearrange the following sentences in a logical order to form a coherent paragraph

(a) A low ceiling fan blows germfree air down onto the stainless-steel countertop and over three mice in an open cage, and their sister wriggling between my thumb and index finger.

(b) Then, with a hole punch that I could use for office paper, I divot the lower edge of her right ear.

(c) She pumps her hind legs as if swimming. I hesitate.

(d) As I pinch back the loose skin over her shoulders, her forearms splay outward.

(e) Of the thousands of bodies in this room, only five of us reflect the fluorescent lights.

Q23. There is a sentence that is missing in the paragraph below. Look at the paragraph and decide in which blank (option 1, 2, 3 or 4) the following sentences would best fit.

Sentence: The air was full of fragments of her life; one knew this, and the other that.

Details of Benedictsson's death detonated through the Nordic cultural bourgeoisie. ___(1)___. Famous friends published obituaries in the Scandinavian newspapers, and her portrait was on display in bookstore windows. ___(2)___. Speculations as to the cause of her death crossed each other like arrows of gossip. Bad finances was one theory, unhappy love another. ___(3)___. In the scandalous newspaper *Aftenbladet*, the owner of the Leopold Hotel declared that Mrs Benedictsson was undeniably tense and hysterical. ___(4)___. There were two beings in her, he claimed, that fought each other: her father had cultivated a wildness in her nature, while her mother taught her only to pray.

(a) Option 1 (b) Option 2
(c) Option 3 (d) Option 4

Q24. There is a sentence that is missing in the paragraph below. Look at the paragraph and decide in which blank (option 1, 2, 3 or 4) the following sentences would best fit.

Statement: But in ancient times, the spectacle of the sun disappearing in the middle of the day would have been a thing of wonder, even something to be feared.

This April 8, millions of people will watch in awe as the sun disappears behind the moon in a total solar eclipse. ___(1)___ These days, of course, we understand what's going on–the moon's orbit is carrying it in between the sun and the Earth, with the moon's shadow striking our planet's surface. ___(2)___ "Imagine you're a farmer–you're out there, and all of a sudden sky goes dark," says Bradley Schaefer, an astronomer at Louisiana State University who has studied the history of solar and lunar eclipses. "It can only be a message from the gods." ___(3)___ To our ancestors, an eclipse would almost certainly have been seen as an omen, Schaefer says. "The sun and the moon are typically the chief gods in your pantheon–and there's the sun, dying in front of your eyes. That's not good." ___(4)___

(a) Option 1 (b) Option 2
(c) Option 3 (d) Option 4

Answer Key

Test 1

1. (c)	2. (a)	3. (c)	4. (b)	5. (c)
6. (b)	7. (b)	8. (c)	9. (b)	10. (a)
11. (a)	12. (b)	13. (b)	14. (a)	15. (a)
16. (a)	17. (b)	18. (a)	19. (d)	20. (b)
21. (c)	22. (e)	23. (b, a, d, c, e)		
24. (c, e, a, b, d)				

Test 2

1. (c)	2. (b)	3. (c)	4. (d)	5. (b)
6. (b)	7. (d)	8. (a)	9. (a)	10. (b)
11. (b)	12. (d)	13. (b)	14. (d)	15. (a)
16. (c)	17. (c)	18. (c)	19. (b)	20. (d)
21. (c, b, a, d, e)		22. (b, d, a, c, e)		23. (d)
24. (b)				

Test 3

1. (b)	2. (c)	3. (d)	4. (c)	5. (d)
6. (b)	7. (a)	8. (c)	9. (b)	10. (a)
11. (a)	12. (c)	13. (a)	14. (c)	15. (b)
16. (c)	17. (c)	18. (d)	19. (d)	20. (a)
21. (d, c, a, b, e)		22. (e, a, d, c, b)		23. (a)
24. (b).				

Explanations

Test 1

1. Option (c) is correct. Read the lines "But what if that outcome was not merely an expression of wishful thinking, but something that parents could control? Imagine a fertility doctor examining the embryos that could develop into your children, providing you with a menu. One has a heightened risk for schizophrenia but a very low risk for cancer; another has relatively low risks for these diseases but a three-fold increased risk for Alzheimer's disease; and a third has roughly average risks for all of these diseases. Oh, and the first two are boys, while the third is a girl. To better consider these questions, we'll review some key arguments for and against this kind of risk profiling – called 'polygenic embryo screening', or PES. (Terminology in this new field is not fixed, and the procedure is also sometimes called 'preimplantation genetic testing for polygenic diseases'"

   Option (b) is a close one, but the usage of "various features" makes it a vague option.

   Option (a) is not mentioned in the passage, and option (d) is not related to the question.

2. Option (a) is correct. Read the lines "We will attempt to clarify which arguments are relevant and convincing, and which require further study. We will also consider this technology in the context of the historical evils of eugenics. Since the word eugenics is too often used in a manner that sheds more heat than light in discussions of genetic technologies, we will first lay out what is known (and not yet known), before engaging with the most inflammatory aspects of the debate."

   As the word refers to history – option (a) is the apt choice here.

3. Option (c) is correct. Read the lines "However, unbridled enthusiasm would be misguided: these bright predictions might only be fulfilled under certain conditions, and there is a risk that consumers using these services will be misled about their benefits. Further, widespread implementation of embryo screening will not only complicate IVF clinical procedures, it could also have social and psychological effects that reverberate far beyond the clinic."

   Falsifying (a) and (b) would mean that the embryo is not affected by the "conditions" as mentioned in the lines above, whereas falsifying (c) would imply that an embryo is affected by its environment, supporting the author's claim.

   Option (d) is not related to the author's claim.

4. Option (b) is correct. Read the lines "This question has been the focus of our work as geneticists in the past few years. To the extent that the answer is yes, it raises an even more challenging question: should this be allowed?"

   Option (c) and (d) are extreme and cannot be inferred definitely on the basis of the passage.

   Option (a) is not mentioned in the passage at all.

5. Option (c) is correct. In the last paragraph, the author is trying to give options to people trying to shift to a vegan diet so that the transition can be smooth.

   Option (a) is not correct as the author is still trying for a "near-vegan" diet.

   Option (c) is a better choice than (b) and (d).

6. Option (b) is correct. Read the lines "About a year ago, this question became vivid to me soon after I set out on an experiment: a near-vegan diet for a month. For some time, I have tried to eat in a way mindful of ethical issues, avoiding, albeit imperfectly, the products of inhumane factory farming. But I have eaten animal products, including meat and fish, regularly. After spending a lot of time in recent years working on questions about animal minds

(initially trying to understand octopuses and other cephalopods, and then moving on from there), the ethical questions around food began to feel quite pressing. So I wanted to find out how I felt on a diet with almost no animal products."

As the author was trying to avoid animal products of "inhumane factory farming," it would definitely include option (b). Traditional farming is not so inhumane, according to the passage; hence, options (c) and (d) are negated.

7. Option (b) is correct. Read the lines "The regime was, after just a few days or so, much harder than I had expected. I felt unsettled, tired, and much of the time quite cold, surprisingly (in February in Australia). Heartburn, headaches, inattention... it did not go well. On day 10, I decided to change plans, and add some dairy products to the diet for the middle third of the month. This transition was just as surprising as the previous one. Immediately I felt fine, with all those problems out of the picture. I felt better than fine, in fact - very sharp. Ten days after that, I resumed the near-vegan regime. The results were as discouraging as before, and I switched back. By the end of the month, I'd spent half of it mostly vegan and half as a vegetarian.

Perhaps I should have stuck with the first, mostly vegan diet, and waited to get used to it. (My understanding is that one's microbiome, one's gut ecology, has to make a shift.) But I was reluctant to do this, especially during the COVID-19 pandemic."

8. Option (c) is the correct answer.

(a) and (c) are correct because this is what the author believes. If we negate it, it would go against the message of the passage.

Option (b) is talking about everyone in a general way, which is incorrect, even if we prove it wrong, it will be irrelevant.

9. Option (b) is correct. Read the lines "The notion of 'making persons' had a certain logic that did translate across borders in that early 1960s Cold War context. It reflected the shared presupposition among the capitalist nations that 'religious capitalism' was the antithesis of 'godless communism'. According to this vision, First World prosperity emerged directly from piety, and religiosity favourably distinguished capitalists from their allegedly amoral communist counterparts."

(a), (c) and (d) cannot be definitely inferred on the basis of the passage.

10. Option (a) is correct. Read the lines "Matsushita pushed the idea further, impressing upon his employees that their job was to 'make people before products'. Panasonic certainly made goods, the corporate magnate acknowledged, but the company also made the assiduous individuals who manufactured its cutting-edge electronics and marketed them to the world. By extension, Panasonic sales teams 'made people' (hitozukuri) in another sense, using skilful marketing to form the very consumers who dutifully purchased Panasonic's wares."

Option (c) was not directly related to Panasonic.

11. Option (a) is correct. Read the lines "Just a year after Matsushita's epochal declaration, Japan's prime minister Ikeda Hayato adopted hitozukuri in 1962 as a guiding principle for his administration, describing the concept as 'gaining trust from the world by valuing morality, cultivating virtue, loving the nation and its people, and developing skills and techniques.' As this rather ambiguous definition reveals, the hitozukuri slogan was both vague and inspiring. As politics, it made for a good soundbite, but as policy it was difficult to explain. Its outcomes were impossible to measure, and the phrase also did not translate well: members of Ikeda's cabinet struggled to find a suitable English rendition as they prepared for a diplomatic trip to the United States in 1962.

The notion of 'making persons' had a certain logic that did translate across borders in that early 1960s Cold War context. It reflected the shared presupposition among the capitalist nations that 'religious capitalism' was the antithesis of 'godless communism'. According to this vision, First World prosperity emerged directly from piety, and religiosity favourably distinguished capitalists from their allegedly amoral communist counterparts."

12. Option (b) is correct. Read the lines "The notion of 'making persons' had a certain logic that did translate across borders in that early 1960s Cold War context. It reflected the shared presupposition among the capitalist nations that 'religious capitalism' was the antithesis of 'godless communism'. According to this vision, First World prosperity emerged directly from piety, and religiosity favourably distinguished capitalists from their allegedly amoral communist counterparts.

To be sure, politicians asserted this causal relationship more than they actually explained it. With the benefit of historical hindsight and critical distance, it is clear that there was always a preposterous quality to the ideological claim. It was preposterous because it literally put ends before beginnings: post/pre. We are rich because we are religious. We must become religious if we want to get rich."

13. Option (b) is correct. Read the lines "Jamaica was a pigmentocracy - it still is - and a premium was placed on fair skin, a societal code that Frantz Fanon in Black Skin, White Masks (1952) calls an 'epidermal schema'. Inspector Adams was a cinnamon-coloured brown man. His daughter Ethlyn, by her own estimation, as well as her family's, 'had good colour', and no right-thinking person would allow their family-line to be contaminated by those of a darker hue. This, after all, was colonial Jamaica, at a time when the journalist and historian Vivian Durham observed cogently: 'It was the ambition of every black Jamaican to be white.'"

Options (a) and (c) are more indirect while (b) directly answers the question.

14. Option (a) is correct. Read the lines "Unexpectedly, I seem to have gone the other way and become even more black as I've aged - especially through others' perception of me - and that process appears to have accelerated since the murder of George Floyd and the rise of the Black Lives Matter movement. But, and it's a big but, it's complicated.

While I enjoy the freedoms and vibrancy of black culture, I resist the tyrannies of the promotion and exclusive embrace of 'Black' - a descriptor, now capitalised by a growing number of papers (both Right- and Left-wing), journals and individuals, even though I never got the memo. What are we supposed to do about the perverse domain assumptions that underpin the adoption of an old racial taxonomy long past its sell-by date, as well as its triumphant inversion: the ambition to be Black fuelled by the old sentiment: 'Fuck you, white people. You reject us? Nah, we reject you!' But this notion of blackness is defined and limited by its opposition to whiteness, encouraging silos of separation. This surely highlights one of the central questions of blackness: what do you let go of, what and who do you allow to define you?"

15. Option (a) is correct. Read the lines "Inspector Adams was a cinnamon-coloured brown man. His daughter Ethlyn, by her own estimation, as well as her family's, 'had good colour', and no right-thinking person would allow their family-line to be contaminated by those of a darker hue. This, after all, was colonial Jamaica, at a time when the journalist and historian Vivian Durham observed cogently: 'It was the ambition of every black Jamaican to be white.'

Unlike the 1987 breakthrough, when four black and brown MPs - Diane Abbott, Keith Vaz, Bernie Grant and Paul Boateng: the first elected in modern times - emphasised the importance of their race and ethnicity, Rishi Sunak has dialled down his. Further, Sunak has signalled his allegiance to British Conservatives' anti-immigrant, nativist tribe, such that his Hindu wristband and alignment with people of his complexion and diminished social capital among them are all but invisible."

16. Option (a) is correct, as this shows that the blacks do not want to mingle with people of other races generally, which supports the author's claim.

(b) and (c) do not imply the above.

17. Option (b) is correct, as ": Metropolitan Sergius, Metropolitan Aleksey, and Metropolitan Nikolay, three of the few Orthodox Church hierarchs left in the Soviet Union," describes the nature of the meeting, which makes it surprising. Putting in (2) is incorrect as it disrupts the flow about Orthodox Church in Russia.

The same goes for (3).

Putting in (4) is incorrect, as the question sentence is neither a conclusion nor does it start a new topic.

18. Option (a) is correct as "they" in the question sentence refers to the 'family" mentioned in "In the daylight, a family begins making its way toward a cave at the foot of a mountain near the Ligurian Sea, in northern Italy."

Using the same logic, (2) and (3) can be negated.

4 may seem lucrative, but (1) is better placed as (1) provides a complete picture while (4) talks about specifics.

19. Option (d) is the answer.

Although option (a) is a very close option, option (d) has more points together with the main idea.

20. Option (b) is the correct answer. Options (a), (c) and (d) are not incorrect, but they are more generic in nature.

21. Option (c) is the irrelevant statement. Here the creation of things are irrelevant in the context of what the author has written.

See the original paragraph: "One of the first things I try to do in the book is to break that dichotomy down. Because we do have this tendency to think about the universe writ large, this big place that we live in. And then there's kind of this tiny stuff going on inside of us or inside of the materials around us, and we don't really connect them. But of course, they are profoundly connected. And, you know, the universe–we used to call it outer space, and we think of it as mostly a vacuum. It's emptiness."

22. Option (e) is the irrelevant statement as in the other statements the author is still talking about what the video was. Her own reaction to it will come later, hence this statement is the irrelevant one. The correct sequence is (a) (b) (c) (d).

23. (TITA: (b) (a) (d) (c) (e))

(b) introduces the topic of the passage i.e. "literary wives." (a) follows (b) as "this" refers to the early draft of Lolita, which was being burnt in fire. (d) then further elaborates on the burning, making bad the right sequence. (c) comes after (d), which shows the thought after the smoke has faded, and then a series of thoughts start coming to the mind. (e) gives a concluding sentence as it introduces a new subject, "Lives of the Wives," making badce the right sequence.

24. (TITA: (c) (e) (a) (b) (d))

(c) starts the paragraph with a generic statement. (e) and (a), then follow (c) as they elaborate on the "difficulty to plan future". (e) comes before (a) as it has "speak about it," wherein it refers to the plan for the future.

(b) then follows (a), as "the sense of uncertainty" has been described in (a). So, ceab is the right sequence. (d) follows (b) and talks about the "speeding up" of time. So, ceabd is the right sequence.

Test 2

1. Option (c) is correct. Read the lines "Artworks are not to be experienced but to be understood: From all directions, across the visual art world's many arenas, the relationship between art and the viewer has come to be framed in this way. An artwork communicates a message, and comprehending that message is the work of its audience. Paintings are their images; physically encountering an original is nice, yes, but it's not as if any essence resides there. Even a verbal description of a painting provides enough information for its message to be clear."

The author clearly states that the message of the artwork is more important.

(b) might be tempting but the interpretation of the audience may not be the correct message being communicated by the artwork.

(a) and (d) are exaggerated choices and should be negated.

2. Option (b) is correct.

(c) cannot be inferred from the passage as it is too extreme.

(a) is mentioned in an opposite sense directly in the passage.

Read the lines "How any one individual chooses to pursue his career is not of particular interest to me. There will always be artists who are, and those who are not, corruptible, whether their patrons are the Medici, the CIA, or the Mellon Foundation. Bad art, wonderfully, is in the end forgotten. As tiresome, didactic, and predictable as much contemporary art may be, I venture that a different corruption by the institutional bureaucrats should trouble art lovers more. While the market has turned artworks into mere commodities, the vast machinery of the art world has turned artworks into artifacts, by zealously, and almost exclusively, upholding the artwork as an entity with a message to convey.

We derive meaning from artworks privately. The experience is interior and unfolding, often difficult to describe to others. Meanings can strike us, entering our psyches in a moment, involuntarily, driven by some hidden force. More commonly, meaning opens up within us slowly: on the third, closer read of the poem; after evaluating a painting for some time, once the eye has roamed and settled and roamed again, noticed detail, related parts to their whole. After an initial sensual impression, our faculties that make meaning are gradually enlivened–emotional, psychological, spiritual, intellectual."

3. Option (c) is correct.

Throughout the passage the author has talked about how art works have been reduced to just "message-providing" systems and not considered anything more than that.

All other factors contribute to this theme.

4. Option (d) is correct.

All of the above, if falsified, would actually support the author's claim and here we have to jeopardize, which means go against the author.

Falsifying (a) would mean that art institutes have not contributed to the growth of new artists, which goes in line with author's claim.

Falsifying (b) would mean that more and more audience have not started visiting the museums, which goes in line with the author's claim.

Falsifying (c) would mean that people are inclined to preserve art when they do not relate to message but with own interpretation which is again in line with author's claim.

5. Option (b) is correct.

Statement A is correct on the basis of the line "At the very least, these events render unsustainable any terminological equivalence between 'society' and 'nation-state'. In subtle ways, they have also contributed to a new type of sociological thinking, which doesn't rely on concepts of the premodern, the modern or the postmodern. Instead, it draws insight and inspiration from a discipline that isn't so invested in the conceptualisation of modern society: history."

Statement B is negated as the author does not call Thatcher unsuccessful.

Statement C is correct as throughout the passage the author has mentioned various instances as to how sociology has contributed to the society.

6. Option (b) is correct. Read the lines "What happened to this project? The multiple crises that occurred in the wake of 1968 - economic, political and cultural - have been examined time and again. They include, inter alia, the inability of governments to deliver prosperity for all in the face of slowing productivity growth; the fear that welfare states were generating as many problems as they solved; the emergence of a political generation that prioritised cultural differences over collective needs; the perceived decline of urban community, rooted in the hubris of planners and modern architecture; the steady offshoring of manufacturing industries; and the feeling that experts - especially in such fields as psychiatry - had become flushed with power. The neoliberalism of Thatcher and Reagan may not have had answers to these problems, but it was at least willing to name them in ways that facilitated its political hegemony."

(a) and (c) are clearly stated as the reasons.

(b) is not a reason per se as it just states that Thatcher and Reagan brought neoliberalism in politics.

7. Option (d) is correct. Read the lines ". Modern society existed in a condition of constant flux, between a past that was now defunct, and a future fraught with uncertainty yet full of possibility. The 'premodern' or 'traditional' was over, and therefore of little concern. Fatefully, as Gurminder Bhambra and John Holmwood show, this was also the way many non-European peoples were seen: as relics to be overhauled or replaced."

It is clear that the modern society was not tied with the past but it does not state that they were not concerned with or planned for the future. They were just bracing/preparing for an uncertain future.

8. Option (a) is correct.

Read the lines "The hundred-year period that began around 1870 also witnessed the birth and growth of sociology, the discipline most preoccupied with 'modernity'. Karl Marx produced his mature scientific writings between the late 1860s and his death in 1883, while the other two giants of the sociological canon, Max Weber and Émile Durkheim, wrote their most important works between 1890 and 1920. As Bhambra and Holmwood show, this canon wasn't established until after 1945, and then only thanks to the American sociologist Talcott Parsons, who led the effort to establish sociology as a credible scientific discipline. It was during the postwar period that the original vows of modernity were most energetically renewed, in the form of expanded welfare states, the progressive planning of economic and urban life, and the deliberate 'modernisation' of developing economies by newly independent governments. Sociology had much to offer governments that were committed to alleviating poverty and maintaining social cohesion, and that didn't want to rely only on traditional (patrimonial, religious or otherwise irrational) solutions to social ills."

(b), (d) and (c) are not stated in the passage at all.

9. Option (a) is correct. Read the lines "But there's plenty of natural and experimental evidence to suggest that evolution doesn't just select hardwired solutions that are engineered for a specific setting. For example, lab studies have shown that perfectly normal frog skin cells, when liberated from the instructive influence of the rest of the embryo, can reboot their cooperative activity to produce a novel proto-organism, called a 'xenobot'."

Option (b) is close but not directly related to the example.

Options (c) and (d) are not related to the example at all.

10. Option (b) is correct. The line here implies that adaptations happen to survive in the given environment and thus environment decides what kind of organisms can survive to reproduce and form a species.

Statement (a) is stated in the line and is not an "implication".

(c) is wrong as we know "what" evolution is, we need to understand how it takes place. (d) is wrong as genes re-arrange and not always "change".

11. Option (b) is correct.

Statement A is true as per the lines "But how did intelligence emerge in biology? The question has preoccupied scientists since Charles Darwin, but it remains unanswered. The processes of intelligence are so intricate, so multilayered and baroque, no wonder some people might be tempted by stories about a top-down Creator. "

It becomes evident that the author does not believe[may not believe] in the existence of a "creator" as he states that some might be "tempted".

B is true as per the last 2 paragraphs of the passage.

C is not directly stated in the passage and cannot be said to be definitely true.

12. Option (d) is correct. Read the lines "Biologists are told to focus on the 'how', not the 'why', or risk falling prey to theology. Students must reduce events to their simplest components and causes, and study these mechanisms in piecemeal fashion. Talk of 'goals', we are told, skirts perilously close to abandoning naturalism; the result is a kind of 'teleophobia', a fear of purpose, based on the idea that attributing too much intelligence to a system is the worst mistake you can make."

(b) is close but is the idea on which teleophobia is based and not the exact meaning of the concept.

All other options can be negated on the basis of above-mentioned lines.

13. Option (b) is correct. Read the lines "In this essay, I will explore how the experience of videoconferencing points, in one way, towards the limits of human adaptability and, in the other, to a liberating human capability **that we must collectively cultivate and sustain - as an innovative extension to the ethical framework** described by the philosopher Martha Nussbaum in Creating Capabilities (2011). As the designer Jon Kolko says in Well-Designed (2014), we should adopt an 'optimistic stance' **and 'seek to explore the situation space, to see multiple potentials for improvement, and to always consider what might be' through systematic empathy and 'integrative thinking'."**

[The above lines in bold give a hint towards the main idea.]

Option (a) does talk about videoconferencing in the development of technology, which is incorrect and should be negated.

Option (c) mentions only "limitations" which is not what the author wants.

Option (d) is a sub-theme of the passage.

14. Option (d) is correct.

Read the lines "But what of the expression and development of 'emotions', Nussbaum's fifth capability? In education (my field), there is a need to include an emotional dimension to what we do, to communicate to students (and academics) that emotions are essential ingredients, not to be ashamed about but to be developed. My colleagues at the Institute for Advanced Teaching and Learning at the University of Warwick have worked hard to create pedagogical practices aligned with this in traditional teaching spaces. But we find it harder to make this work online at a distance. Videoconferencing could be great. If only we could get the thing to work properly. But for now, it's quite often just painful."

The main concern here is online teaching and not just videoconferencing. So, (c) can be negated.

(b) is not related to the question. (d) is more specific than (a) making it the right choice.

15. Option (a) is correct. Read the lines "However, the essential capability I'm concerned about is not videoconferencing in itself, but rather the humanisation of technologies for everyone's benefit. This is, I argue, one of the most pressing issues we have to deal with, as technology becomes ever more entangled into our lives. But to do so successfully, we need to think more deeply and creatively, using techniques from the interdisciplinary field we call design research - applying a blend of psychology, philosophy, anthropology, engineering and aesthetics."

(a) can be inferred as philosophy's framework, and educational needs are being used to improve technology.

(b) can be negated as the author mentions "it needs" to do so.

(c) can also be negated on the basis of above mentioned lines.

16. Option (c) is correct. Read the lines "In education (my field), there is a need to include an emotional dimension to what we do, to communicate to students (and academics) that emotions are essential ingredients, not to be ashamed about but to be developed. My colleagues at the Institute for Advanced Teaching and Learning at the University of Warwick have worked hard to create pedagogical practices aligned with this in traditional teaching spaces. But we find it harder to make this work online at a distance."

Statements A and C are not mentioned in the passage at all.

Only Statement B is correct.

17. Option (c) is the irrelevant statement because in this statement the author is mentioning how she is cooking whereas in the other statements she is generally talking to the reader about the baking process.

Hence option (c) is the answer and the sequence is abde.

18. Option (c) is the irrelevant statement. (c) is very specific about the harm done, which might come later in the paragraph but not at this stage where the crime is being introduced.

The correct sequence is abde, and c is the irrelevant statement.

19. The passage discusses the prevalence of online scams and fake news, highlighting the difficulty people have in distinguishing real information from deception. Option (a) focuses solely on cybercrime, while the passage talks about a broader issue of online safety.

Option (c) is a specific detail mentioned within online safety, but not the main takeaway. Option (d) describes a source of the problem (social media), but the passage emphasizes the need for education, not just the source. Therefore, option (b) best captures the overall message about the importance of public education regarding online safety in a world filled with scams and misinformation.

20. (a) Focuses on Tusk's hope for cooperation, ignoring the contested election and the delay. (b) Captures some aspects with the delay and inauguration, but misses the accusations of manipulation and Tusk's scepticism. (c) While mentioning the PiS's loss and Tusk's appointment, it misses the delay, Tusk's scepticism, and focuses heavily on the allegations. Option (d) best summarises the paragraph because it is concise (mentions election issues, delay, new leader, Tusk's hope and doubt). Others miss key details or focus too much on side points.

21. (TITA: (c) (b) (a) (d) (e))

(c) should be the opening sentence due to the usage of full name "Anthony Albanese". (b) follows (c) as the "news" has been defined in (c). (a) then describes why it is good news. So, (c) (b) (a) is the right sequence. (e) is the concluding sentence. Now, (d) describes Mr. Albanese's policy and should come somewhere after (c). As (c) (b) (a) is the right sequence, (d) follows (c) (b) (a). So, (c) (b) (a) (d) (e) is the correct sequence.

22. (TITA: (b) (d) (a) (c) (e))

(b) starts the passage by stating a recent event. (d) then defines the "new rail line" mentioned in (b). (a) should follow (d) as the "wizardry" mentioned in (a) is defined in (d). So, (b) (d) (a) is the right sequence. (c) and (e) form a mandatory pair as (e) provides a contradiction to (c) and should follow (b) (d) (a). So, (b) (d) (a) (c) (e) is the right sequence.

23. Placing the sentence "This study demonstrates that bumblebees possess a level of social learning previously thought to be exclusive to humans" at the end (option (d)) is the most effective way to structure the paragraph as it emphasizes the paradigm shift - bumblebees exhibiting a level of social learning once thought to be unique to humans. This placement strengthens the impact of the research findings. The paragraph progressively reveals the key finding. It starts with the puzzle box experiment, then details the challenges faced by individual bees, and introduces the concept of social learning through observation. Explaining the difficulty faced by individual bees (option (c)) logically precedes introducing social learning as a solution (option (d)). While option (b) (after explaining the difficulty for individual bees) creates a logical flow, it weakens the paragraph's concluding impact. Option (d) positions the key finding from the research at the forefront, leaving a lasting impression on the reader.

24. The paragraph starts with a question about the relationship between free-market capitalism and democracy. Option (b) positions the sentence as a direct answer, providing a historical context for the optimistic view of free-market capitalism. Also, the paragraph seems to be setting up a discussion that explores contrasting viewpoints on the relationship. Option (b) creates a clear division between the idealized view presented in the missing sentence and the subsequent discussion of historical perspectives (option (c)) and modern realities (option (d)). Option (a) is incorrect because both the missing sentence and the opening question address the idealistic view of free-market capitalism. Placing them together creates a slight repetition. Option (b) positions the missing sentence as an elaboration on the question, avoiding redundancy. The paragraph's core theme seems to be the current debate about free-market capitalism and democracy. Option (a) starts with the idealized view, which might slightly delay the reader's focus on the present-day complexities. Option (b) introduces the question about the present right away, creating a more immediate focus. Option (a) also introduces the idea, which is then being built upon by the second sentence, and then placing the missing sentence in option (b) completes the flow.

TEST 3

1. Option (b) is correct.

See the following lines from the passage: "My intent is not to dunk on anyone, but rather to start a conversation about how Americans as a society grapple with our own contentious history. Our identities are shaped by the collective experiences of our past, and how we see ourselves in relation to them. Together, we constantly reframe and revise the past to make it make sense to us in the present." Option (b) is the most suitable answer. Options (a) and (c) are not hinted or mentioned in the passage.

2. Option (c) is correct. Read the lines "It just so happens that the best place to start that conversation is with Burns and Lynn Novick's five-and-a-half-hour TV miniseries Prohibition (2011), which covers that most misunderstood chapter in US history, from the 1919 ratification of the 18th Amendment - prohibiting 'the manufacture, sale, or transportation of intoxicating liquors' – until its repeal by the 21st Amendment in 1933. Prohibition deserves our attention because it reflects what we think we know about history, rather than the actual history itself. It is what the comedian Stephen Colbert called 'truthiness' in truth's stead."

3. Option (d) is correct.

   Statement A is true for Novick and Burns but cannot be generalized to all " film-makers".

   B and C are not explicitly stated in the passage.

4. Option (c) is correct. Read the lines "Burns and Novick are gifted storytellers, and every story needs conflict – heroes versus villains, good guys versus bad guys. They've cast prohibitionists as the bad guys, as they so often are when prohibition is remembered: hard-headed fanatics intent on dictating 'other people's habits' in a manner most undemocratic and un-American."

   (a) and (b) cannot be definitely concluded on the basis of the passage.

5. Option (d) is correct. Read the lines "Learning styles theory contends that people learn in different ways, mainly through visual, auditory or kinaesthetic modes, and so material should be presented to students to accommodate these differences, consistent with the 'meshing hypothesis' where instruction is tailored to preferences. Teachers should provide visual learners with visual representations of content, such as diagrams; auditory learners with lectures or audio recordings; and, for the kinaesthetic learner, the opportunity to have a hands-on approach where they can move around."

6. Option (b) is correct. Read the lines "For many adults, school was a frustrating experience where they did not learn as much as they could, and their sense of individual agency was negated. Learning styles theory represents a form of retrospective absolution where, if only their teachers had tailored instruction to match their learning style, then they could have achieved their potential."

   Option (a) does not relate to the absolution part.

   Option (c) is not related to the question.

   Option (b) is a better choice than (d), since it specifically explains the absolution.

7. Option (a) is correct. Read the lines "The broad, intuitive appeal of the theory stems from the fact that it seems self-evidently true. Many people will say that they cannot learn by listening to a lecture and that they 'learn by doing', or that they need to move around or listen to music while studying. Others will contend that they are 'verbal learners' who learn best through reading or listening to an audiobook. For many adults, school was a frustrating experience where they did not learn as much as they could, and their sense of individual agency was negated. Learning styles theory represents a form of retrospective absolution where, if only their teachers had tailored instruction to match their learning style, then they could have achieved their potential.

   Yet, despite its appeal, there is simply no credible evidence to support the idea that attending to learning styles actually supports learning, regardless of how well-intentioned the teacher might be. To paraphrase the physicist Wolfgang Pauli, not only is it not right, it's not even wrong."

   Statements A and B are mentioned in the passage.

   Statement C is not stated in the passage at all.

8. Option (c) is correct as the following lines show: "Yet, despite its appeal, there is simply no credible evidence to support the idea that attending to learning styles actually supports learning, regardless of how well-intentioned the teacher might be. To paraphrase the physicist Wolfgang Pauli, not only is it not right, it's not even wrong."

   Thus, it can be inferred that something could be neither wrong nor right.

   Options (a) and (b) are changing the idea and are incorrect.

9. Option (b) is correct. Read the lines "It's tempting to think that a rebooted society could simply pick up where we leave off. Why couldn't our civilisation 2.0 just start with renewables?

   Well, it could, in a very limited way. If you find yourself among the survivors in a post-apocalyptic world, you could scavenge enough working solar panels to keep your lifestyle electrified for a good long while. Without moving parts, photovoltaic cells require little maintenance and are remarkably resilient. They do deteriorate over time, though, from moisture penetrating the casing and from sunlight itself degrading the high-purity silicon layers. The electricity generated by a solar panel declines by about 1 per cent every year so, after a few generations, all our hand-me-down solar panels will have degraded to the point of uselessness. Then what?"

10. Option (a) is correct. Read the lines "How could an industrialising society produce crucial building materials such as iron and steel, brick, mortar, cement and glass without resorting to deposits of coal?

    You can of course create heat from electricity. We already use electric ovens and kilns. Modern arc furnaces are used for producing cast iron or recycling steel. The problem isn't so much that electricity can't be used to heat things.

An alternative is to generate high temperatures using solar power directly. Rather than relying on photovoltaic panels, concentrated solar thermal farms use giant mirrors to focus the sun's rays onto a small spot. The heat concentrated in this way can be exploited to drive certain chemical or industrial processes, or else to raise steam and drive a generator." As the author gives solution to generate more heat, that has to be the problem with electricity.

(b) is not mentioned in the passage at all.

(c) and (d) can be negated on the basis of the passage.

11. Option (a) is correct. Read the lines "Perhaps, though, we were on the right track by starting with electrical power. Most of our renewable-energy technologies produce electricity. In our own historical development, it so happens that the core phenomena of electricity were discovered in the first half of the 1800s, well after the early development of steam engines. Heavy industry was already committed to combustion-based machinery, and electricity has largely assumed a subsidiary role in the organisation of our economies ever since. But could that sequence have run the other way? Is there some developmental requirement that thermal energy must come first?"

(b) can be negated as it is an exaggerated statement and, the author provides alternate sources to produce electricity.

(c) can be negated on similar grounds as the author also mentions wind energy and hydroelectricity.

12. Option (c) is correct as the author talks about a society which might emerge after an apocalypse of today's world. See the lines: "It's tempting to think that a rebooted society could simply pick up where we leave off. Why couldn't our civilisation 2.0 just start with renewables?

Well, it could, in a very limited way. If you find yourself among the survivors in a post-apocalyptic world, you could scavenge enough working solar panels to keep your lifestyle electrified for a good long while."

Option (b) talking about the experimental society is incorrect as no experimentation has been mentioned here, since the passage talks about the issues an actual society would face.

Statement A [option (d)] is talking about constraints which are not mentioned or hinted in the passage.

13. Option (a) is correct. Read the lines "When Diana was in her late teens, and Prince Charles was turning 30, royal courtiers were casting about for a worthy (i.e., unsullied, virginal) bride for the heir to the throne. It would not matter, evidently, that these courtiers, like the members of the royal family, knew of Charles' semisecret relationship with the married woman Camilla Parker Bowles. The princess-to-be was required to be virginal in every sense–to be ignorant of the very conditions of her marriage."

14. Option (c) is correct. Read the lines "But wasn't the princess complicit in her fate? Didn't she, by courting the tabloid media, not only bring her fate upon herself, but deserve it? So commentators have begun to speculate, with that instinct for blaming the victim that characterizes the most puritanical sense of justice."

15. Option (b) is the correct answer according to the following lines: "The paradox of the celebrity's quest is that she must realize that her "admirers" are drawn to her for the very reasons that the crowd is drawn to her; yet she wants to believe that, no, in fact she is loved for herself. (Most of us know we are only loved for ourselves–for what else is there?)"

Option (c) is the complete opposite of the answer that is needed.

Option (d) is ambiguous; hence incorrect.

16. Option (c) is correct. Read the lines "She did not, or could not, play the role of Prince Charles' wife, but chose rather to live by the truth. And the bad luck, the repeated "poor judgment" of the princess in choosing lovers–isn't this too a symptom of a complicit fate? Isn't such chronic behavior the result of self-loathing?"

Option (a) is negated by the following lines: "By refusing to live a lie for the sake of patriarchal order, Princess Diana exposed the hypocrisy of the Establishment to the glare of commoners. She did not, or could not, play the role of Prince Charles'"

Option (b) is incorrect and not mentioned.

17. Option (c) is the irrelevant statement. Statement (c) is talking about the studies related to teen anxiety, whereas the other statements talk about social media in general. Hence, the irrelevant statement is (c), whereas the correct sequence is (a) (b) (d) (e).

18. Option (d) is the irrelevant statement. The other statements of the paragraph are directed towards 'you', whereas the statement (d) is directed towards 'we'. This means that it is not part of this particular paragraph and may come later. The correct sequence is (a) (b) (c) (e), and d is the irrelevant statement.

19. Option (d) is correct.

Option (a) mentions the interest because of the demons, which is incorrect.

Option (b) is tempting but the answers will not be possible by the study of the demons.

Option (c) is a general statement and does not cover the actual idea.

20. Option (a) is the correct summary as it covers the main idea about the surgery of and the removal of the abnormal brain tissue causing epileptic seizures.

The other options are incomplete and do not have the main idea.

Thus, option (a) is the correct answer.

21. (TITA: (d) (c) (a) (b) (e))

(d) starts the passage by introducing the topic - "incidents with harm to children". (c) then provides more specific information on that making (d) (c) the right sequence. (a) should follow (c) as "the murder" mentioned in (a) has been defined in (c). So, (d) (c) (a) is the right sequence. (b) then gives the action that has taken place. (e) should be the last sentence as it is introducing a new case and therefore a new topic. So, (d) (c) (a) (b) (e) is the correct sequence.

22. (TITA: (e) (a) (d) (c) (b))

(d) (c) (b) form a sequence in that order as they define a process. (b) defines what the author did after hesitation as mentioned in (c). (c) (b) should follow (d) as (c) defines the reaction to (d). (a) should come before (d) (c) (b) as the "sister" is then referred to as "she" in (d) (c) (b). So, (a) (d) (c) (b) is the right sequence.

(e) should be followed by (a) (d) (c) (b) as the (e) bodies mentioned in (e) are then defined in (a) (d) (c) (b). So, (e) (a) (d) (c) (b) is the right sequence.

23. Option (a). The sentence "The air was full of fragments of her life; one knew this, and the other that." would best fit in blank number (1)

Let's look at the context of the paragraph:

The first sentence sets the stage for the aftermath of Benedictsson's death. There is a sense of mystery and fragmented information surrounding her life. The second sentence talks about how news of her death spread and how she was honored. The third sentence talks about the rumors surrounding her death. Placing the sentence "The air was full of fragments of her life; one knew this, and the other that." at the beginning establishes the atmosphere of uncertainty and speculation that surrounded Benedictsson's life and death. It introduces the idea that there is no single, definitive narrative about her, but rather many different pieces that people are trying to put together.

24. Option (b) Is the answer

See the original paragraph: "This April 8, millions of people will watch in awe as the sun disappears behind the moon in a total solar eclipse. These days, of course, we understand what's going on–the moon's orbit is carrying it in between the sun and the Earth, with the moon's shadow striking our planet's surface. But in ancient times, the spectacle of the sun disappearing in the middle of the day would have been a thing of wonder, even something to be feared. "Imagine you're a farmer–you're out there, and all of a sudden sky goes dark," says Bradley Schaefer, an astronomer at Louisiana State University who has studied the history of solar and lunar eclipses. "It can only be a message from the gods." To our ancestors, an eclipse would almost certainly have been seen as an omen, Schaefer says. "The sun and the moon are typically the chief gods in your pantheon–and there's the sun, dying in front of your eyes. That's not good."

The first sentence talks about how we understand eclipses today, and logically the second sentence provides a contrast about our ancestors, which is logically followed by an example about a farmer understanding it to be a message from the gods. Then the next statement continues the theme of our ancestors.

PART 5 CAT Papers with Solutions

- This section contains the original CAT English papers from 2021-2023 and also their detailed solutions. It helps you check your level of score you are at in the CAT and also get a feel of the paper.

SOLVE the original CAT 2021, 2022, and 2023 paper in 40 minutes.

IN THIS PART

Section 1: **CAT Papers**

SECTION 1: CAT Papers

This section contains the original CAT English papers from 2021 to 2023, reproduced as a full section. All the chapters in this part will help you to test your level of preparation by

- Giving you an opportunity to check what level of score you are at in the CAT.
- Helping you to assess your score as each of the questions carries +4 marks for a correct answer and -1 mark for a wrong answer.

Key Components of this Section:

The size of the comprehension passages in the latest papers have reduced to a maximum of one-page passage as opposed to longer passages in the earlier CAT exam.

- The number of questions in the comprehension section is now limited to 16-18 questions with a break up of 3-6 questions per passage.
- The verbal section fluctuates between 8 to 10 questions.
- The VARC Section had a total of 34 questions in CAT 2015, 2016, 2017, 2018 and 2019.
- CAT 2019, like CAT 2018 had 24 questions on Reading Comprehension and 10 questions on Verbal Ability.
- CAT 2021, 2022 and 2023 had 24 questions in total. Comprising of 16 questions in Reading Comprehension and 8 questions in Verbal Ability.

All the slots from CAT 2021 to 2023 have been added in this section with detailed solutions.

CHAPTER 1

CAT Paper 2021 (Slot 1) VARC Section Questions and Solutions

Comprehension:

The passage below is accompanied by a set of questions. Choose the best answer to each question.

For the Maya of the Classic period, who lived in Southern Mexico and Central America between 250 and 900 CE, the category of 'persons' was not coincident with human beings, as it is for us. That is, human beings were persons - but other, nonhuman entities could be persons, too. . . . In order to explore the slippage of categories between 'humans' and 'persons', I examined a very specific category of ancient Maya images, found painted in scenes on ceramic vessels. I sought out instances in which faces (some combination of eyes, nose, and mouth) are shown on inanimate objects. . . . Consider my iPhone, which needs to be fed with electricity every night, swaddled in a protective bumper, and enjoys communicating with other fellow- phone-beings. Does it have personhood (if at all) because it is connected to me, drawing this resource from me as an owner or source? For the Maya (who did have plenty of other communicating objects, if not smartphones), the answer was no. Nonhuman persons were not tethered to specific humans, and they did not derive their personhood from a connection with a human. . . . It's a profoundly democratising way of understanding the world. Humans are not more important persons - we are just one of many kinds of persons who inhabit this world. . . .

The Maya saw personhood as 'activated' by experiencing certain bodily needs and through participation in certain social activities. For example, among the faced objects that I examined, persons are marked by personal requirements (such as hunger, tiredness, physical closeness), and by community obligations (communication, interaction, ritual observance). In the images I examined, we see, for instance, faced objects being cradled in humans' arms; we also see them speaking to humans. These core elements of personhood are both turned inward, what the body or self of a person requires, and outward, what a community expects of the persons who are a part of it, underlining the reciprocal nature of community membership. . . .

Personhood was a nonbinary proposition for the Maya. Entities were able to be persons while also being something else. The faced objects I looked at indicate that they continue to be functional, doing what objects do (a stone implement continues to chop, an incense burner continues to do its smoky work). Furthermore, the Maya visually depicted many objects in ways that indicated the material category to which they belonged - drawings of the stone implement show that a person-tool is still made of stone. One additional complexity: the incense burner (which would have been made of clay, and decorated with spiky appliques representing the sacred ceiba tree found in this region) is categorised as a person - but also as a tree. With these Maya examples, we are challenged to discard the person/nonperson binary that constitutes our basic ontological outlook. The porousness of boundaries that we have seen in the Maya world points towards the possibility of living with a certain uncategorisability of the world.

Q1. Which one of the following best explains the "additional complexity" that the example of the incense burner illustrates regarding personhood for the Classic Maya?

(a) The example provides an exception to the nonbinary understanding of personhood that the passage had hitherto established.

(b) The example adds a new layer to the nonbinary understanding of personhood by bringing in a third category that shares a dissimilar relation with the previous two.

(c) The example adds a new layer to the nonbinary understanding of personhood by bringing in a third category that shares a similar relation with the previous two.

(d) The example complicates the nonbinary understanding of personhood by bringing in the sacred, establishing the porosity of the divine and the profane.

Q2. Which one of the following, if true, would not undermine the democratising potential of the Classic Maya worldview?

(a) They believed that animals like cats and dogs that live in proximity to humans have a more clearly articulated personhood.

(b) They understood the stone implement and the incense burner in a purely human form.

(c) They depicted their human healers with physical attributes of local medicinal plants.

(d) While they believed in the personhood of objects and plants, they did not believe in the personhood of rivers and animals.

Q3. On the basis of the passage, which one of the following worldviews can be inferred to be closest to that of the Classic Maya?

(a) A tribe that perceives plants as person-plants because they form an ecosystem and are marked by needs of nutrition.

(b) A tribe that perceives its hunting weapons as sacred person- artefacts because of their significance to its survival.

(c) A futuristic society that perceives robots to be persons as well as robots because of their similarity to humans.

(d) A tribe that perceives its utensils as person-utensils in light of their functionality and bodily needs.

Q4. Which one of the following, if true about the Classic Maya, would invalidate the purpose of the iPhone example in the passage?

(a) Classic Maya songs represent both humans and non-living objects as characters, talking and interacting with each other.

(b) Unlike modern societies equipped with mobile phones, the Classic Maya did not have any communicating objects.

(c) The clay incense burner with spiky appliques was categorised only as a person and not as a tree by the Classic Maya.

(d) The personhood of the incense burner and the stone chopper was a function of their usefulness to humans.

Comprehension:

The passage below is accompanied by a set of questions. Choose the best answer to each question.

Cuttlefish are full of personality, as behavioral ecologist Alexandra Schnell found out while researching the cephalopod's potential to display self-control. "Self-control is thought to be the cornerstone of intelligence, as it is an important prerequisite for complex decision- making and planning for the future," says Schnell . . .

[Schnell's] study used a modified version of the "marshmallow test" . . . During the original marshmallow test, psychologist Walter Mischel presented children between age four and six with one marshmallow. He told them that if they waited 15 minutes and didn't eat it, he would give them a second marshmallow. A long-term follow-up study showed that the children who waited for the second marshmallow had more success later in life. The cuttlefish version of the experiment looked a lot different. The researchers worked with six cuttlefish under nine months old and presented them with seafood instead of sweets. (Preliminary experiments showed that cuttlefishes' favorite food is live grass shrimp, while raw prawns are so-so and Asian shore crab is nearly unacceptable.) Since the researchers couldn't explain to the cuttlefish that they would need to wait for their shrimp, they trained them to recognize certain shapes that indicated when a food item would become available. The symbols were pasted on transparent drawers so that the cuttlefish could see the food that was stored inside. One drawer, labeled with a circle to mean "immediate," held raw king prawn. Another drawer, labeled with a triangle to mean "delayed," held live grass shrimp. During a control experiment, square labels meant "never".

"If their self-control is flexible and I hadn't just trained them to wait in any context, you would expect the cuttlefish to take the immediate reward [in the control], even if it's their second preference," says Schnell and that's what they did. That showed the researchers that cuttlefish wouldn't reject the prawns if it was the only food available. In the experimental trials, the cuttlefish didn't jump on the prawns if the live grass shrimp were labeled with a triangle–many waited for the shrimp drawer to open up. Each time the cuttlefish showed it could wait, the researchers tacked another ten seconds on to the next round of waiting before releasing the shrimp. The longest that a cuttlefish waited was 130 seconds.

Schnell [says] that the cuttlefish usually sat at the bottom of the tank and looked at the two food items while they waited, but sometimes, they would turn away from the king prawn "as if to distract themselves from the temptation of the immediate reward." In past studies, humans, chimpanzees, parrots and dogs also tried to distract themselves while waiting for a reward.

Not every species can use self-control, but most of the animals that can share another trait in common: long, social lives. Cuttlefish, on the other hand, are solitary creatures that don't form relationships even with mates or young. "We don't know if living in a social group is important for complex cognition unless we also show those abilities are lacking in less social species," says comparative psychologist Jennifer Vonk.

Q5. In which one of the following scenarios would the cuttlefish's behaviour demonstrate self-control?

(a) raw prawns are released while an Asian shore crab drawer labelled with a triangle is placed in front of the cuttlefish, to be opened after one minute.

(b) raw prawns are released while a live grass shrimp drawer labelled with a square is placed in front of the cuttlefish.

(c) live grass shrimp are released while two raw prawn drawers labelled with a circle and a triangle respectively are placed in front of the cuttlefish; the triangle-labelled drawer is opened after 50 seconds.

(d) Asian shore crabs and raw prawns are simultaneously released while a live grass shrimp drawer labelled with a triangle is placed in front of the cuttlefish, to be opened after one minute.

Q6. Which one of the following, if true, would best complement the passage's findings?

(a) Cuttlefish live in big groups that exhibit sociability.

(b) Cuttlefish cannot distinguish between geometrical shapes.

(c) Cuttlefish are equally fond of live grass shrimp and raw prawn.

(d) Cuttlefish wait longer than 100 seconds for the shrimp drawer to open up.

Q7. All of the following constitute a point of difference between the "original" and "modified" versions of the marshmallow test EXCEPT that:

(a) the former was performed over a longer time span than the latter.

(b) the former used verbal communication with its subjects, while the latter had to develop a symbolic means of communication.

(c) the former had human subjects, while the latter had cuttlefish.

(d) the former correlated self-control and future success, while the latter correlated self-control and survival advantages.

Q8. Which one of the following cannot be inferred from Alexandra Schnell's experiment?

(a) Like human children, cuttlefish are capable of self-control.

(b) Intelligence in a species is impossible without sociability.

(c) Cuttlefish exercise choice when it comes to food.

(d) Cuttlefish exert self-control with the help of diversions.

Comprehension:

The passage below is accompanied by a set of questions. Choose the best answer to each question.

We cannot travel outside our neighbourhood without passports. We must wear the same plain clothes. We must exchange our houses every ten years. We cannot avoid labour. We all go to bed at the same time . . . We have religious freedom, but we cannot deny that the soul dies with the body, since 'but for the fear of punishment, they would have nothing but contempt for the laws and customs of society'. In more's time, for much of the population, given the plenty and security on offer, such restraints would not have seemed overly unreasonable. For modern readers, however, Utopia appears to rely upon relentless transparency, the repression of variety, and the curtailment of privacy. Utopia provides security: but at what price? In both its external and internal relations, indeed, it seems perilously dystopian.

Such a conclusion might be fortified by examining selectively the tradition which follows More on these points. This often portrays societies where . . . 'it would be almost impossible for man to be depraved, or wicked'. . . . This is achieved both through institutions and mores, which underpin the common life. . . . The passions are regulated and inequalities of wealth and distinction are minimized. Needs, vanity, and emulation are restrained, often by prizing equality and holding riches in contempt. The desire for public power is curbed. Marriage and sexual intercourse are often controlled: in Tommaso Campanella's *The City of the Sun* (1623), the first great literary utopia after More's, relations are forbidden to men before the age of twenty- one and women before nineteen. Communal child-rearing is normal; for Campanella this commences at age two. Greater simplicity of life, 'living according to nature', is often a result: the desire for simplicity and purity are closely related. People become more alike in appearance, opinion, and outlook than they often have been. Unity, order, and homogeneity thus prevail at the cost of individuality and diversity. This model, as J. C. Davis demonstrates, dominated early modern utopianism. And utopian homogeneity remains a familiar theme well into the twentieth century.

Given these considerations, it is not unreasonable to take as our starting point here the hypothesis that utopia and dystopia evidently share more in common than is often supposed. Indeed, they might be twins, the progeny of the same parents. Insofar as this proves to be the case, my linkage of both here will be uncomfortably close for some readers. Yet we should not mistake this argument for the assertion that all utopias are, or tend to produce, dystopias. Those who defend this proposition will find that their association here is not nearly close enough. For we have only to acknowledge the existence of thousands of successful intentional communities in which a cooperative ethos predominates and where harmony without coercion is the rule to set aside such an assertion. Here the individual's submersion in the group is consensual (though this concept is not unproblematic). It results not in enslavement but voluntary submission to group norms. Harmony is achieved without harming others.

Q9. Following from the passage, which one of the following may be seen as a characteristic of a utopian society?

(a) Institutional surveillance of every individual to ensure his/her security and welfare.
(b) The regulation of homogeneity through promoting competitive heterogeneity.
(c) A society where public power is earned through merit rather than through privilege.
(d) A society without any laws to restrain one's individuality.

Q10. All of the following statements can be inferred from the passage EXCEPT that:

(a) utopian and dystopian societies are twins, the progeny of the same parents.
(b) many conceptions of utopian societies emphasise the importance of social uniformity and cultural homogeneity.
(c) it is possible to see utopias as dystopias, with a change in perspective, because one person's utopia could be seen as another's dystopia.
(d) utopian societies exist in a long tradition of literature dealing with imaginary people practicing imaginary customs, in imaginary worlds.

Q11. Which sequence of words below best captures the narrative of the passage?

(a) Curtailment of privacy - Dystopia - Utopia - Intentional community.
(b) Relentless transparency - Homogeneity - Utopia - Dystopia.
(c) Utopia - Security - Dystopia - Coercion.
(d) Utopia - Security - Homogeneity - Intentional community.

Q12. All of the following arguments are made in the passage EXCEPT that:

(a) there have been thousands of communities where homogeneity and stability have been achieved through choice, rather than by force.
(b) the tradition of utopian literature has often shown societies in which it would be nearly impossible for anyone to be sinful or criminal.
(c) in More's time, there was plenty and security, so people did not need restraints that could appear unreasonable.
(d) in early modern utopianism, the stability of utopian societies was seen to be achieved only with individuals surrendering their sense of self.

Comprehension:

The passage below is accompanied by a set of questions. Choose the best answer to each question.

The sleights of hand that conflate consumption with virtue are a central theme in A Thirst for Empire, a sweeping and richly detailed history of tea by the historian Erika Rappaport. How did tea evolve from an obscure "China drink" to a universal beverage imbued with civilising properties? The answer, in brief, revolves around this conflation, not only by profit-motivated marketers but by a wide variety of interest groups. While abundant historical records have allowed the study of how tea itself moved from east to west, Rappaport is focused on the movement of the idea of tea to suit particular purposes.

Beginning in the 1700s, the temperance movement advocated for tea as a pleasure that cheered but did not inebriate, and industrialists soon borrowed this moral argument in advancing their case for free trade in tea (and hence more open markets for their textiles). Factory owners joined in, compelled by the cause of a sober workforce, while Christian missionaries discovered that tea "would soothe any colonial encounter". During the Second World War, tea service was presented as a social and patriotic activity that uplifted soldiers and calmed refugees.

But it was tea's consumer-directed marketing by importers and retailers - and later by brands - that most closely portends current trade debates. An early version of the "farm to table" movement was sparked by anti-Chinese sentiment and concerns over trade deficits, as well as by the reality and threat of adulterated tea containing dirt and hedge clippings. Lipton was soon advertising "from the Garden to Tea Cup" supply chains originating in British India and supervised by "educated Englishmen". While tea marketing always presented direct consumer benefits (health, energy, relaxation), tea drinkers were also assured that they were participating in a larger noble project that advanced the causes of family, nation and civilization. . . .

Rappaport's treatment of her subject is refreshingly apolitical. Indeed, it is a virtue that readers will be unable to guess her political orientation: both the miracle of markets and capitalism's dark underbelly are evident in tea's complex story, as are the complicated effects of British colonialism. Commodity histories are now themselves commodities: recent works investigate cotton, salt, cod, sugar, chocolate, paper and milk. And morality marketing is now a commodity as well, applied to food, "fair trade" apparel and eco- tourism. Yet tea is, Rappaport makes clear, a world apart - an astonishing success story in which tea marketers not only succeeded in conveying a sense of moral elevation to the consumer but also arguably did advance the cause of civilisation and community.

I have been offered tea at a British garden party, a Bedouin campfire, a Turkish carpet shop and a Japanese chashitsu, to name a few settings. In each case the offering was more an idea - friendship, community, respect - than a drink, and in each case the idea then created a reality. It is not a stretch to say that tea marketers have advanced the particularly noble cause of human dialogue and friendship.

Q13. This book review argues that, according to Rappaport, tea is unlike other "morality" products because it:

(a) was actively encouraged by interest groups in the government.

(b) appealed to a universal group and not just to a niche section of people.

(c) was marketed by a wide range of interest groups.

(d) had an actual beneficial effect on social interaction and society in general.

Q14. According to this book review, A Thirst for Empire says that, in addition to "profit-motivated marketers", tea drinking was promoted in Britain by all of the following EXCEPT:

(a) manufacturers who were pressing for duty-free imports.

(b) factories to instill sobriety in their labour.

(c) the anti-alcohol lobby as a substitute for the consumption of liquor.

(d) tea drinkers lobbying for product diversity.

Q15. The author of this book review is LEAST likely to support the view that:

(a) tea became the leading drink in Britain in the nineteenth century.

(b) tea drinking was sometimes promoted as a patriotic duty.

(c) the ritual of drinking tea promotes congeniality and camaraderie.

(d) tea drinking has become a social ritual worldwide.

Q16. Today, "conflat[ing] consumption with virtue" can be seen in the marketing of:

(a) travel to pristine destinations.

(b) sustainably farmed foods.

(c) ergonomically designed products.

(d) natural health supplements.

Q17. The passage given below is followed by four alternate summaries. Choose the option that best captures the essence of the passage.

Foreign peacekeepers often exist in a bubble in the poor countries in which they are deployed; they live in posh compounds, drive fancy vehicles, and distance themselves from locals. This may be partially justified as they are outsiders, living in constant fear, performing a job that is emotionally draining. But they are often despised by the locals, and many would like them to leave. A better solution would be bottom-up peacebuilding, which would involve their spending more time working with communities, understanding their grievances and earning their trust, rather than only meeting government officials.

(a) Peacekeeping forces in foreign countries have tended to be aloof for valid reasons but would be more effective if they worked more closely with local communities.

(b) Extravagant lifestyles and an aloof attitude among the foreigners working as peacekeepers in poor countries have justifiably make them the target of local anger.

(c) Peacekeeping duties would be more effectively performed by local residents given their better understanding, knowledge and rapport with their own communities.

(d) The environment in poor countries has tended to make foreign peacekeeping forces live in enclaves, but it is time to change this scenario.

Q18. Five jumbled up sentences, related to a topic, are given below. Four of them can be put together to form a coherent paragraph. Identify the odd one out and key in the number of the sentence as your answer:

(a) There is a dark side to academic research, especially in India, and at its centre is the phenomenon of predatory journals.
(b) But in truth, as long as you pay, you can get anything published.
(c) In look and feel thus, they are exactly like any reputed journal.
(d) They claim to be indexed in the most influential databases, say they possess editorial boards that comprise top scientists and researchers, and claim to have a rigorous peer-review structure.
(e) But a large section of researchers and scientists across the world are at the receiving end of nothing short of an academic publishing scam.

Q19. Five jumbled up sentences, related to a topic, are given below. Four of them can be put together to form a coherent paragraph. Identify the odd one out and key in the number of the sentence as your answer:

(a) The legal status of resources mined in space remains ambiguous; and while the market for asteroid minerals is currently nonexistent, this is likely to change as technical hurdles diminish.
(b) Outer space is a commons, and all of it is open for exploration, however, space law developed in the 1950s and 60s is state-centric and arguably ill-suited to a commercial future.
(c) Laws adopted by the US and Luxembourg are first steps, but they only protect firms from competing claims by their compatriots; a Chinese company will not be bound by US law.
(d) Critics say the US is conferring rights that it has no authority to confer; Russia in particular has condemned this, citing the US' disrespect for international law.
(e) At issue now is commercial activity, as private firms–rather than nation states–look to space for profit.

Q20. The four sentences [labelled (a), (b), (c), (d)] below, when properly sequenced would yield a coherent paragraph. Decide on the proper sequencing of the order of the sentences and key in the sequence of the four numbers as your answer:

(a) The work is more than the text, for the text only takes on life, when it is realized and furthermore the realization is by no means independent of the individual disposition of the reader.
(b) The convergence of text and reader brings the literary work into existence and this convergence is not to be identified either with the reality of the text or with the individual disposition of the reader.
(c) From this polarity it follows that the literary work cannot be completely identical with the text, or with the realization of the text, but in fact must lie halfway between the two.
(d) The literary work has two poles, which we might call the artistic and the aesthetic; the artistic refers to the text created by the author, and the aesthetic to the realization accomplished by the reader.

Q21. The passage given below is followed by four alternate summaries. Choose the option that best captures the essence of the passage.

McGurk and MacDonald (1976) reported a powerful multisensory illusion occurring with audio-visual speech. They recorded a voice articulating a consonant 'ba-ba-ba' and dubbed it with a face articulating another consonant 'ga-ga-ga'. Even though the acoustic speech signal was well recognized alone, it was heard as another consonant after dubbing with incongruent visual speech i.e., 'da-da-da'. The illusion, termed as the McGurk effect, has been replicated many times, and it has sparked an abundance of research. The reason for the great impact is that this is a striking demonstration of multisensory integration, where that auditory and visual information is merged into a unified, integrated percept.

(a) Visual speech mismatched with auditory speech can result in the perception of an entirely different message: this illusion is known as the McGurk effect.
(b) The McGurk effect which is a demonstration of multisensory integration has been replicated many times.
(c) When the quality of auditory information is poor, the visual information wins over the auditory information.
(d) When the auditory speech signal does not match the visual speech movements, the acoustic speech signal is confusing and integration of the two is imperfect.

Q22. The four sentences [labelled (a), (b), (c), (d)] below, when properly sequenced would yield a coherent paragraph. Decide on the proper sequencing of the order of the sentences and key in the sequence of the four numbers as your answer:

(a) A popular response is the exhortation to plant more trees.

(b) It seems all but certain that global warming will go well above two degrees–quite how high no one knows yet.
(c) Burning them releases it, which is why the scale of forest fires in the Amazon basin last year garnered headlines.
(d) This is because trees sequester carbon by absorbing carbon dioxide.

Q23. The four sentences (labelled (a), (b), (c), (d)) below, when properly sequenced would yield a coherent paragraph. Decide on the proper sequencing of the order of the sentences and key in the sequence of the four numbers as your answer:

(a) In the central nervous systems of other animal species, such a comprehensive regeneration of neurons has not yet been proven beyond doubt.
(b) Biologists from the University of Bayreuth have discovered a uniquely rapid form of regeneration in injured neurons and their function in the central nervous system of zebrafish.
(c) They studied the Mauthner cells, which are solely responsible for the escape behaviour of the fish, and previously regarded as incapable of regeneration.
(d) However, their ability to regenerate crucially depends on the location of the injury.

Q24. The passage given below is followed by four alternate summaries. Choose the option that best captures the essence of the passage.

Developing countries are becoming hotbeds of business innovation in much the same way as Japan did from the 1950s onwards. They are reinventing systems of production and distribution, and experimenting with entirely new business models. Why are countries that were until recently associated with cheap hands now becoming leaders in innovation? Driven by a mixture of ambition and fear they are relentlessly climbing up the value chain. Emerging-market champions have not only proved highly competitive in their own backyards, they are also going global themselves.

(a) Competition has driven emerging economies, once suppliers of cheap labour, to become innovators of business models that have enabled them to move up the value chain and go global.
(b) Innovations in production and distribution are helping emerging economies compete with countries to which they once supplied cheap labour.
(c) Production and distribution models are going through rapid innovations worldwide as developed countries are being challenged by their earlier suppliers from the developing world.
(d) Developing countries are being forced to invent new business models which challenge the old business models, so they can remain competitive domestically.

Answer Key

1. (c)	**2.** (c)	**3.** (a)	**4.** (d)	**5.** (d)
6. (a)	**7.** (d)	**8.** (b)	**9.** (a)	**10.** (a)
11. (d)	**12.** (c)	**13.** (d)	**14.** (d)	**15.** (a)
16. (b)	**17.** (a)	**18.** (e)	**19.** (d)	
20. (d, c, a, b)		**21.** (a)	**22.** (b, a, d, c)	
23. (b, c, d, a)		**24.** (a)		

Explanations

1. In the example which talks about the incense burner, the 'additional complexity' is that, in addition to being categorised as a person, it is also categorised as a tree with spiky appliques representing the sacred ceiba tree. The third categorisation is the classification as a tree is similar to the other two classifications; the same object being referred to a tree and a person-tool. So, option (c) is the correct answer. All the other options do not fall in the same explanation and hence are incorrect.

2. This is an example of a trick question. The question asks for the option that *does not undermine* the democratising potential of the Maya worldview. In other words, *it should be in line with* the Maya view. Going through the options one by one.
Option (a) suggests that cats and dogs would be considered superior to other nonpersons. An unequal world is suggested by this option and hence option (a) would undermine the 'democratising' potential of the Maya worldview and is incorrect.
Option (b) suggests that the stone implement and incense burner were regarded as humans and not objects, which implies that humans are in a way superior to nonpersons. So, option (b), too, would undermine the 'democratising' potential of the Maya worldview and hence is incorrect.
Option (d) suggests that some objects 'deserve' to be persons, while others did not. This too would undermine the 'democratising' potential of the Maya worldview.
Only option (c), if true, is in line with the essence of the Maya worldview. Human healers being given the physical attributes of local medicinal plants

suggests that these plants are equal in status to humans.

3. Read the lines from the passage, "The Maya saw personhood as 'activated' by experiencing certain bodily needs and through participation in certain social activities."
Personhood was not based on the usefulness of nonpersons to humans or their similarity to humans. So, options (b) and (c) are easily ruled out.
While both options (a) and (d) talk about the 'bodily needs' of nonpersons, only (a) relates to the idea of social participation. Plants form an ecosystem, participating in a community. Option (d), on the other hand, talks about the functionality of utensils being a reason why they are regarded as persons. So, the correct answer is option (a).

4. Read the lines from the passage, "Consider my iPhone, which needs to be fed with electricity every night, swaddled in a protective bumper, and enjoys communicating with other fellow phone-beings. Does it have personhood (if at all) because it is connected to me, drawing this resource from me as an owner or source? For the Maya (who did have plenty of other communicating objects, if not smartphones), the answer was no. Nonhuman persons were not tethered to specific humans, and they did not derive their personhood from a connection with a human."

The Maya would not have treated the iphone as a nonhuman person; personhood would be 'activated' only when the nonhuman person experiences certain bodily needs or participates in certain social activities.
If option (d) were true "if the incense burner and stone chopper were regarded as persons just because of their usefulness to humans" then the iPhone example would be invalidated.
All other options given do not relate to the reason why Maya categorised objects as persons and hence are incorrect.

5. Only option (d) lies in line with the idea that the passage gives out. Check the order of preferences of sea food by the cuttlefish; live grass shrimp, king prawns and then Asian shore crab, which is the most hated.
Option (a) talks about raw prawns and Asian crab wherein obviously raw prawns, which are being released first, would be taken up by the cuttlefish. Hence, it is negated since the idea of self control does not arise here.
Similarly, option (b) places a square on the drawer of live grass shrimp indicating it will never be released. The cuttlefish would then prefer the raw prawns. Hence, is negated.
Only option (d) talks implies and idea of self control wherein the least 2 preferences are released first while the shrimp is to be opened 50 seconds later and hence would require the cuttlefish to wait. This hence is the correct answer.

6. Read the lines, "We don't know if living in a social group is important for complex cognition unless we also show those abilities are lacking in less social species".

If option (a) is true, it will prove the above uncertainty and hence would complement the idea in the passage.
All other options do not add value and hence are incorrect.

7. All other options except option (d) are part of the modified marshmallow test conducted on the cuttlefish. Hence, (d) is the correct answer.

8. Read the lines, "We don't know if living in a social group is important for complex cognition unless we also show those abilities are lacking in less social species".

It can be seen that option (b) cannot be inferred from the passage with surety.

9. Read the lines, 'Utopia appears to rely upon relentless transparency, the repression of variety, and the curtailment of privacy. Utopia provides security: but at what price?' So, institutional surveillance in the name of security can be seen as a characteristic of a Utopian society. Options (b) and (d) are ruled out from these lines. In the second paragraph, the passage mentions that Utopia curbs the desire for public power and promotes equality. So, option (c) is also incorrect. The correct answer is option (a).

10. Although the author states that utopia and dystopia share a lot of things in common but it does not lead to the conclusion that these two are twins. Although it has been mentioned that the two are uncomfortably close, but the author also says, "we should *not mistake this argument for the assertion that all utopias are, or tend to produce, dystopias*".

It will hence be unreasonable to call them twins. Hence option (a) can be safely rejected.

11. Options (b) and (c) do not mention the key word 'intentional communities' which is an essential idea in the passage and hence can be eliminated. Option (a) does not mention 'homogeneity' and hence can be rejected. Only option (d) contains all the essential ideas and hence is the correct answer.

12. Read the lines, "in More's time, for much of the population, given the plenty and security on offer, *such restraints would not have seemed overly unreasonable.*" Option (c) changes a few words in the sentence that alters the meaning of this idea. People do not 'need' constraints and hence this is the incorrect answer.

13. The author talks about morality marketing and states that 'tea is. . . . . .*a world apart* "an *astonishing* success story in which tea marketers not only succeeded in conveying a sense of moral elevation to the consumer but also arguably did advance the cause of civilisation and community'. So, the correct choice is option (d).

14. The second paragraph talks about 'the temperance movement' (anti-alcohol lobby) advocating tea as it 'cheered but did not inebriate', industrialists supporting free trade in tea in order to gain 'open markets' (duty-free markets) for textiles and factory owners joining the group advocating tea, as it meant 'a sober workforce'. So, options (a), (b) and (c) are correct. The passage does not talk about tea drinkers lobbying for product diversity. So, the correct choice is (d).

15. Except option (a), all other options have been talked about in the passage.
'I have been offered tea at a British garden party, a Bedouin campfire, a Turkish carpet shop and a Japanese chashitsu, to name a few settings. In each case the offering was more an idea "friendship, community, respect" than a drink, and in each case the idea then created a reality.' From these lines, (b) and (c) both can be inferred.
The author, however, does not say anywhere that tea became the leading drink in Britain in the nineteenth century. So, the author is least likely to support option (a).

16. The word conflating means to combine or confuse between 2 different things. 'Conflating consumption with virtue' means combining consumption of something with virtuous. The consumption of sustainably farmed foods is marketed as the right thing to do, so option (b) is the correct answer.

17. The only justified summary is option (a) which captures the entire idea that foreign peacekeepers remain aloof and in a bubble, live in posh areas and are distant from locals. But a major reason for this aloofness is the despise they receive from locals which could be debilitated if they are allowed to work more closely with the local communities.

18. Sentence (a) states the main idea of the paragraph. Sentences (d) and (c) form a unit: (d) explains how the journals are indexed and structured and (c) follows this up stating that they have the look and feel of any reputed journal. This begs the question, ˜What is then wrong with these journals?™ Sentence (b) answers this. (a), (d), (c), (b) forms a cogent paragraph. Sentence (e) talks of an ˜academic publishing scam™ but none of the other sentences shed any light on this. So, (e) is the sentence to be eliminated.

19. All given sentences apart form sentence (d) relate to private commercial activity in space and the limitations of outdated space laws. Sentence (d) opens up with critics which has not been talked about in other sentences and hence is a new idea. Sentences (e), (b) and (c) relate to commercial activity by private firms as opposed to nation states in space and the ill-suitability of existing state-centric laws. Sentence (a), on the legal status of space mining, follows (b). The order becomes (e), (b), (a), (c); (d) is the odd one out.

20. Sentences (d) and (c) form a mandatory pair: the 'polarity' talked about in sentence (d) is carried forward in (c).
Sentence (d) opens up with the main idea of the paragraph "the two poles of every literary work, the text by the author and the realisation accomplished by the reader". Sentences (a) and (b) form a mandatory: sentence (a) talks about the fact life only when it is realised and that the realisation itself depends on the reader's disposition. Sentence (b) follows (a) and talks about the convergence of the text and the reader.
(d), (c), (a), (b) is the correct order.

21. The passage talks about how a dubbed voice, paired with a different visual message generates a unified but a completely different sound. This multisensory illusion is called the McGurk Effect. Only option (a) captures this idea perfectly and hence is the correct summary.

22. The paragraph talks about how high the global temperatures could rise and the possible measures that can be taken to atleast lower it. Hence, (b) becomes the opening sentence. (d), (c) forms a mandatory pair since 'it' in Sentence (c) refers to carbon dioxide sequestered by trees. (d) is an explanation to statement (a) and hence the order becomes (b), (a), (d), (c).

23. The paragraph opens up with the introduction of a new study by biologists in zebrafish which is then followed by Sentence (c) which refers to 'they' as biologists. (a) is the ending sentence which talks about the uncertainty of existence of such a process in other animals. (d) effectively follows (c) since it talks about how regeneration is dependent on the place of injury. Hence, (b), (c), (d), (a) becomes the order.

24. The entire idea of the paragraph is that the developing nations, which were unti recently, only responsible for supplying cheap labour to developed nations, are now improving their production and distribution and are now gradually climbing up the value chain. One other aspect which is enabling them to do so is ambition and fear and are slowly going global. Only option (a) captures this idea entirely and hence is the correct summary.

CHAPTER 2

CAT Paper 2021 (Slot 2) VARC Section Questions and Solutions

Comprehension:

The passage below is accompanied by a set of questions. Choose the best answer to each question.

It has been said that knowledge, or the problem of knowledge, is the scandal of philosophy. The scandal is philosophy's apparent inability to show how, when and why we can be sure that we know something or, indeed, that we know anything. Philosopher Michael Williams writes: 'Is it possible to obtain knowledge at all? This problem is pressing because there are powerful arguments, some very ancient, for the conclusion that it is not ... Scepticism is the skeleton in Western rationalism's closet'. While it is not clear that the scandal matters to anyone but philosophers, philosophers point out that it should matter to everyone, at least given a certain conception of knowledge. For, they explain, unless we can ground our claims to knowledge as such, which is to say, distinguish it from mere opinion, superstition, fantasy, wishful thinking, ideology, illusion or delusion, then the actions we take on the basis of presumed knowledge - boarding an airplane, swallowing a pill, finding someone guilty of a crime - will be irrational and unjustifiable.

That is all quite serious-sounding but so also are the rattlings of the skeleton: that is, the sceptic's contention that we cannot be sure that we know anything - at least not if we think of knowledge as something like having a correct mental representation of reality, and not if we think of reality as something like things-as-they-are-in-themselves, independent of our perceptions, ideas or descriptions. For, the sceptic will note, since reality, under that conception of it, is outside our ken (we cannot catch a glimpse of things-in-themselves around the corner of our own eyes; we cannot form an idea of reality that floats above the processes of our conceiving it), we have no way to compare our mental representations with things-as they-are-in-themselves and therefore no way to determine whether they are correct or incorrect. Thus the sceptic may repeat (rattling loudly), you cannot be sure you 'know' something or anything at all - at least not, he may add (rattling softly before disappearing), if that is the way you conceive 'knowledge'.

There are a number of ways to handle this situation. The most common is to ignore it. Most people outside the academy - and, indeed, most of us inside it- are unaware of or unperturbed by the philosophical scandal of knowledge and go about our lives without too many epistemic anxieties. We hold our beliefs and presumptive knowledges more or less confidently, usually depending on how we acquired them (I saw it with my own eyes; I heard it on Fox News; a guy at the office told me) and how broadly and strenuously they seem to be shared or endorsed by various relevant people: experts and authorities, friends and family members, colleagues and associates. And we examine our convictions more or less closely, explain them more or less extensively, and defend them more or less vigorously, usually depending on what seems to be at stake for ourselves and/or other people and what resources are available for reassuring ourselves or making our beliefs credible to others (look, it's right here on the page; add up the figures yourself; I happen to be a heart specialist).

Q1. The author discusses all of the following arguments in the passage, EXCEPT:

(a) sceptics believe that we can never fully know anything, if by "knowing" we mean knowledge of a reality that is independent of the knower.

(b) the best way to deal with scepticism about the veracity of knowledge is to ignore it.

(c) philosophers maintain that the scandal of philosophy should be of concern to everyone.

(d) if we cannot distinguish knowledge from opinion or delusion, we will not be able to justify our actions.

Q2. According to the last paragraph of the passage, "We hold our beliefs and presumptive knowledges more or less confidently, usually depending on" something. Which one of the following most broadly captures what we depend on?

(a) Remaining outside the academy; ignoring epistemic anxieties.

(b) How we come to hold them; how widely they are held in our social circles.

(c) How much of a stake we have in them; what resources there are to support them.

(d) All of the options listed here.

Q3. The author of the passage is most likely to support which one of the following statements?

(a) The confidence with which we maintain something to be true is usually independent of the source of the alleged truth.

(b) For the sceptic, if we think of reality as independent of our perceptions, ideas or descriptions, we should aim to know that reality independently too.

(c) The scandal of philosophy is that we might not know anything at all about reality if we think of reality as independent of our perceptions, ideas or descriptions.

(d) The actions taken on the basis of presumed knowledge are rational and justifiable if we are confident that that knowledge is widely held.

Q4. ". . . we cannot catch a glimpse of things-in-themselves around the corner of our own eyes; we cannot form an idea of reality that floats above the processes of our conceiving it . . ." Which one of the following statements best reflects the argument being made in this sentence?

(a) Our knowledge of reality floats above our subjective perception of it.

(b) If the reality of things is independent of our perception, logically we cannot perceive that reality.

(c) If the reality of things is independent of our eyesight, logically we cannot perceive our perception.

(d) Our knowledge of reality cannot be merged with our process of conceiving it.

Comprehension:

The passage below is accompanied by a set of questions. Choose the best answer to each question.

It's easy to forget that most of the world's languages are still transmitted orally with no widely established written form. While speech communities are increasingly involved in projects to protect their languages - in print, on air and online - orality is fragile and contributes to linguistic vulnerability. But indigenous languages are about much more than unusual words and intriguing grammar: They function as vehicles for the transmission of cultural traditions, environmental understandings and knowledge about medicinal plants, all at risk when elders die and livelihoods are disrupted.

Both push and pull factors lead to the decline of languages. Through war, famine and natural disasters, whole communities can be destroyed, taking their language with them to the grave, such as the indigenous populations of Tasmania who were wiped out by colonists. More commonly, speakers live on but abandon their language in favor of another vernacular, a widespread process that linguists refer to as "language shift" from which few languages are immune. Such trading up and out of a speech form occurs for complex political, cultural and economic reasons - sometimes voluntary for economic and educational reasons, although often amplified by state coercion or neglect. Welsh, long stigmatized and disparaged by the British state, has rebounded with vigor.

Many speakers of endangered, poorly documented languages have embraced new digital media with excitement. Speakers of previously exclusively oral tongues are turning to the web as a virtual space for languages to live on. Internet technology offers powerful ways for oral traditions and cultural practices to survive, even thrive, among increasingly mobile communities. I have watched as videos of traditional wedding ceremonies and songs are recorded on smartphones in London by Nepali migrants, then uploaded to YouTube and watched an hour later by relatives in remote Himalayan villages ...

Globalization is regularly, and often uncritically, pilloried as a major threat to linguistic diversity. But in fact, globalization is as much process as it is ideology, certainly when it comes to language. The real forces behind cultural homogenization are unbending beliefs, exchanged through a globalized delivery system, reinforced by the historical monolingualism prevalent in much of the West.

Monolingualism - the condition of being able to speak only one language - is regularly accompanied by a deep-seated conviction in the value of that language over all others. Across the largest economies that make up the GS, being monolingual is still often the norm, with multilingualism appearing unusual and even somewhat exotic.

The monolingual mindset stands in sharp contrast to the lived reality of most the world, which throughout its history has been more multilingual than unilingual. Monolingualism, then, not globalization, should be our primary concern.

Multilingualism can help us live in a more connected and more interdependent world. By widening access to technology, globalization can support indigenous and scholarly communities engaged in documenting and protecting our shared linguistic heritage. For the last 5,000 years, the rise and fall of languages was intimately tied to the plow, sword and book. In our digital age, the keyboard, screen and web will play a decisive role in shaping the future linguistic diversity of our species.

Q5. The author mentions the Welsh language to show that:

(a) efforts to integrate Welsh speakers in the English-speaking fold have been fruitless.
(b) while often pilloried, globalisation can, in fact, support linguistic revival.
(c) vulnerable languages can rebound with state effort.
(d) languages can revive even after their speakers have gone through a "language shift".

Q6. The author lists all of the following as reasons for the decline or disappearance of a language EXCEPT:

(a) governments promoting certain languages over others.
(b) the focus on only a few languages as a result of widespread internet use.
(c) a catastrophic event that entirely eliminates a people and their culture.
(d) people shifting away from their own language to study or work in another language.

Q7. From the passage, we can infer that the author is in favour of:

(a) an expanded state role in the preservation of languages.
(b) "language shifts" across languages.
(c) cultural homogenisation.
(d) greater multilingualism.

Q8. We can infer all of the following about indigenous languages from the passage EXCEPT that:

(a) they are in danger of being wiped out as most can only be transmitted orally.
(b) people are increasingly working on documenting these languages.
(c) they are repositories of traditional knowledge about the environment and culture.
(d) their vocabulary and grammatical constructs have been challenging to document.

Comprehension:

The passage below is accompanied by a set of questions. Choose the best answer to each question.

Many people believe that truth conveys power. Hence sticking with the truth is the best strategy for gaining power. Unfortunately, this is just a comforting myth. In fact, truth and power have a far more complicated relationship, because in human society, power means two very different things.

On the one hand, power means having the ability to manipulate objective realities: to hunt animals, to construct bridges, to cure diseases, to build atom bombs. This kind of power is closely tied to truth. If you believe a false physical theory, you won't be able to build an atom bomb. On the other hand, power also means having the ability to manipulate human beliefs, thereby getting lots of people to cooperate effectively. Building atom bombs requires not just a good understanding of physics, but also the coordinated labor of millions of humans. Planet Earth was conquered by Homo sapiens rather than by chimpanzees or elephants, because we are the only mammals that can cooperate in very large numbers. And large-scale cooperation depends on believing common stories. But these stories need not be true. You can unite millions of people by making them believe in completely fictional stories about God, about race or about economics. The dual nature of power and truth results in the curious fact that we humans know many more truths than any other animal, but we also believe in much more nonsense. . . .

When it comes to uniting people around a common story, fiction actually enjoys three inherent advantages over the truth. First, whereas the truth is universal, fictions tend to be local. Consequently if we want to distinguish our tribe from foreigners, a fictional story will serve as a far better identity marker than a true story The second huge advantage of fiction over truth has to do with the handicap principle, which says that reliable signals must be costly to the signaler. Otherwise, they can easily be faked by cheaters If political loyalty is signaled by believing a true story, anyone can fake it. But believing ridiculous and outlandish stories exacts greater cost, and is therefore a better signal of loyalty Third, and most important, the truth is often painful and disturbing. Hence if you stick to unalloyed reality, few people will follow you. An American presidential candidate who tells the American public the truth, the whole truth and nothing but the truth about American history has a 100 percent guarantee of losing the elections An uncompromising adherence to the truth is an admirable spiritual practice, but it is not a winning political strategy. . . .

Even if we need to pay some price for deactivating our rational faculties, the advantages of increased social cohesion are often so big that fictional stories routinely triumph over the truth in human history. Scholars have known this for thousands of years, which is why scholars often had to decide whether they served the truth or social harmony. Should they aim to unite people by making sure everyone believes in the same fiction, or should they let people know the truth even at the price of disunity?

Q9. The central theme of the passage is about the choice between:

(a) leaders who unknowingly spread fictions and those who intentionally do so.
(b) attaining social cohesion and propagating objective truth.
(c) truth and power.
(d) stories that unite people and those that distinguish groups from each other.

Q10. The author would support none of the following statements about political power EXCEPT that:

(a) people cannot handle the unvarnished truth, so leaders retain power by deviating from it.
(b) while unalloyed truth is not recommended, leaders should stay as close as possible to it.
(c) manipulating people's beliefs is politically advantageous, but a leader who propagates only myths is likely to lose power.
(d) there are definite advantages to promoting fiction, but there needs to be some limit to a pervasive belief in myths.

Q11. The author implies that like scholars, successful leaders:

(a) need to leverage both types of power to remain in office.
(b) use myths to attain the first type of power.
(c) know how to balance truth and social unity.
(d) today know how to create social cohesion better than in the past.

Q12. Regarding which one of the following quotes could we argue that the author overemphasises the importance of fiction?

(a) "scholars often had to decide whether they served the truth or social harmony. Should they aim to unite people by making sure everyone believes in the same fiction, or should they let people know the truth?"
(b) "In fact, truth and power have a far more complicated relationship, because in human society, power means two very different things."
(c) "Hence sticking with the truth is the best strategy for gaining power. Unfortunately, this is just a comforting myth."
(d) "On the one hand, power means having the ability to manipulate objective realities: to hunt animals, to construct bridges, to cure diseases, to build atom bombs."

Comprehension:

The passage below is accompanied by a set of questions. Choose the best answer to each question.

I have elaborated . . . a framework for analyzing the contradictory pulls on [Indian] nationalist ideology in its struggle against the dominance of colonialism and the resolution it offered to those contradictions. Briefly, this resolution was built around a separation of the domain of culture into two spheres-the material and the spiritual. It was in the material sphere that the claims of Western civilization were the most powerful. Science, technology, rational forms of economic organization, modern methods of statecraft-these had given the European countries the strength to subjugate the non-European people. . . To overcome this domination, the colonized people had to learn those superior techniques of organizing material life and incorporate them within their own cultures But this could not mean the imitation of the West in every aspect of life, for then the very distinction between the West and the East would vanish-the self-identity of national culture would itself be threatened. . . .

The discourse of nationalism shows that the material/spiritual distinction was condensed into an analogous, but ideologically far more powerful, dichotomy: that between the outer and the inner Applying the inner/outer distinction to the matter of concrete day-to-day living separates the social space into ghar and bahir, the home and the world. The world is the external, the domain of the material; the home represents one's inner spiritual self, one's true identity. The world is a treacherous terrain of the pursuit of material interests, where practical considerations reign supreme. It is also typically the domain of the male. The home in its essence must remain unaffected by the profane activities of the material world-and woman is its representation. And so one gets an identification of social roles by gender to correspond with the separation of the social space into ghar and bahir. . . .

The colonial situation, and the ideological response of nationalism to the critique of Indian tradition, introduced an entirely new substance to [these dichotomies] and effected their transformation. The material/spiritual dichotomy, to which the terms world and home corresponded, had acquired a very special significance in the nationalist mind. The world was where the European power had challenged the non-European peoples and, by virtue of its superior material culture, had subjugated them. But, the nationalists asserted, it had failed to colonize the inner, essential, identity of the East which lay in its distinctive, and superior, spiritual culture [I]n the entire phase of the national struggle, the crucial need was to protect, preserve and strengthen the inner core of the national culture, its spiritual essence. . . .

Once we match this new meaning of the home/world dichotomy with the identification of social roles by gender, we get the ideological framework within which nationalism answered the women's question. It would be a grave error to see in this, as liberals are apt to in their despair at the many marks of social conservatism in nationalist practice, a total rejection of the West. Quite the contrary: the nationalist paradigm in fact supplied an ideological principle of selection.

Q13. Which one of the following best describes the liberal perception of Indian nationalism?

(a) Indian nationalism embraced the changes brought about by colonialism in Indian women's traditional gender roles.

(b) Indian nationalist discourses provided an ideological principle of selection.

(c) Indian nationalism's sophistication resided in its distinction of the material from the spiritual spheres.

(d) Indian nationalist discourses reaffirmed traditional gender roles for Indian women.

Q14. On the basis of the information in the passage, all of the following are true about the spiritual/material dichotomy of Indian nationalism EXCEPT that it:

(a) helped in safeguarding the identity of Indian nationalism.

(b) represented a continuation of age-old oppositions in Indian culture.

(c) was not as ideologically powerful as the inner/outer dichotomy.

(d) constituted the premise of the ghar/bahir dichotomy.

Q15. Which one of the following, if true, would weaken the author's claims in the passage?

(a) The Industrial Revolution played a crucial role in shaping the economic prowess of Britain in the eighteenth century.

(b) The colonial period saw the hybridisation of Indian culture in all realms as it came in contact with British/European culture.

(c) Indian nationalists rejected the cause of English education for women during the colonial period.

(d) Forces of colonial modernity played an important role in shaping anti-colonial Indian nationalism.

Q16. Which one of the following explains the "contradictory pulls" on Indian nationalism?

(a) Despite its fight against colonial domination, Indian nationalism had to borrow from the coloniser in the material sphere.

(b) Despite its spiritual superiority, Indian nationalism had to fight against colonial domination.

(c) Despite its fight against colonial domination, Indian nationalism had to borrow from the coloniser in the spiritual sphere.

(d) Despite its scientific and technological inferiority, Indian nationalism had to fight against colonial domination.

Q17. The four sentences [labelled (a), (b), (c) and (d)] below, when properly sequenced would yield a coherent paragraph. Decide on the proper sequencing of the order of the sentences and key in the sequence of the four numbers as your answer:

(a) Look forward a few decades to an invention which can end the energy crisis, change the global economy and curb climate change at a stroke: commercial fusion power.

(b) To gain meaningful insights, logic has to be accompanied by asking probing questions of nature through controlled tests, precise observations and clever analysis.

(c) The greatest of all inventions is the iiber-invention that has provided the insights on which others depend: the modern scientific method.

(d) This invention is inconceivable without the scientific method; it will rest on the application of a diverse range of scientific insights, such as the process transforming hydrogen into helium to release huge amounts of energy.

Q18. The passage given below is followed by four alternate summaries. Choose the option that best captures the essence of the passage.

Creativity is now viewed as the engine of economic progress. Various organizations are devoted to its study and promotion; there are encyclopedias and handbooks surveying creativity research. But this proliferating success has tended to erode creativity's stable identity: it has become so invested with value that it has become impossible to police its meaning and the practices that supposedly identify and encourage it. Many people and organizations committed to producing original thoughts now feel that undue obsession with the idea of creativity gets in the way of real creativity.

(a) The obsession with original thought, how it can be promoted and researched, has made it impossible for people and organizations to define the concept anymore.

(b) The value assigned to creativity today has assumed such proportions that the concept itself has lost its real meaning and this is hampering the engendering of real creativity.

(c) The industry that has built up around researching what comprises and encourages creativity has destroyed the creative process itself.

(d) Creativity has proliferated to the extent that is no longer a stable process, and its mutating identity has stifled the creative process.

Q19. Five jumbled up sentences, related to a topic, are given below. Four of them can be put together to form a coherent paragraph. Identify the odd one out and key in the number of the sentence as your answer:

(a) It has taken on a warm, fuzzy glow in the advertising world, where its potential is being widely discussed, and it is being claimed as the undeniable wave of the future.

(b) There is little enthusiasm for this in the scientific arena; for them marketing is not a science, and only a handful of studies have been published in scientific journals.

(c) The new, growing field of neuromarketing attempts to reveal the inner workings of consumer behaviour and is an extension of the study of how choices and decisions are made.

(d) Some see neuromarketing as an attempt to make the "art" of advertising into a science, being used by marketing experts to back up their proposals with some form of real data.

(e) The marketing gurus have already started drawing on psychology in developing tests and theories, and advertising people have borrowed the idea of the focus group from social scientists.

Q20. The passage given below is followed by four alternate summaries. Choose the option that best captures the essence of the passage.

The unlikely alliance of the incumbent industrialist and the distressed unemployed worker is especially powerful amid the debris of corporate bankruptcies and layoffs. In an economic downturn, the capitalist is more likely to focus on costs of the competition emanating from free markets than on the opportunities they create. And the unemployed worker will find many others in a similar condition and with anxieties similar to his, which will make it easier for them to organize together. Using the cover and the political organization provided by the distressed, the capitalist captures the political agenda.

(a) An economic downturn creates competition because of which the capitalists capture the political agenda created by the political organisation provided by the unemployed.

(b) An unlikely alliance of the industrialist and the unemployed happens during an economic downturn in which they come together to unite politically and capture the political agenda.

(c) The purpose of an unlikely alliance between the industrialist and the unemployed during an economic downturn is to stifle competition in free markets.

(d) In an economic downturn, the capitalists use the anxieties of the unemployed and their political organisation to set the political agenda to suit their economic interests.

Q21. The four sentences [labelled (a), (b), (c) and (d)] below, when properly sequenced would yield a coherent paragraph. Decide on the proper sequencing of the order of the sentences and key in the sequence of the four numbers as your answer:

(a) The US has long maintained that the Northwest Passage is an international strait through which its commercial and military vessels have the right to pass without seeking Canada's permission.

(b) Canada, which officially acquired the group of islands forming the Northwest Passage in 1880, claims sovereignty over all the shipping routes through the Passage.

(c) The dispute could be transitory, however, as scientists speculate that the entire

(d) Arctic Ocean will soon be ice-free in summer, so ship owners will not have to ask for permission to sail through any of the Northwest Passage routes.

(e) The US and Canada have never legally settled the question of access through the Passage, but have an agreement whereby the US needs to seek Canada's consent for any transit.

Q22. The passage given below is followed by four alternate summaries. Choose the option that best captures the essence of the passage.

Biologists who publish their research directly to the Web have been labelled as "rogue", but physicists have been routinely publishing research digitally ("preprints"), prior to submitting in a peer-reviewed journal. Advocates of preprints argue that quick and open dissemination of research speeds up scientific progress and allows for wider access to knowledge. But some journals still don't accept research previously published as a preprint. Even if the idea of preprints is gaining ground, one of the biggest barriers for biologists is how they would be viewed by members of their conservative research community.

(a) Compared to biologists, physicists are less conservative in their acceptance of digital pre-publication of research papers, which allows for faster dissemination of knowledge.

(b) One of the advantages of digital preprints of research is they hasten the dissemination process, but these are not accepted by most scientific communities.

(c) While digital publication of research is gaining popularity in many scientific disciplines, almost all peer-reviewed journals are reluctant to accept papers that have been published before.

(d) Preprints of research are frowned on by some scientific fields as they do not undergo a rigourous reviewing process but are accepted among biologists as a quick way to disseminate information.

Q23. Five jumbled up sentences, related to a topic, are given below. Four of them can be put together to form a coherent paragraph. Identify the odd one out and key in the number of the sentence as your answer:

(a) The care with which philosophers examine arguments for and against forms of biotechnology makes this an excellent primer on formulating and assessing moral arguments.

(b) Although most people find at least some forms of genetic engineering disquieting, it is not easy to articulate why: what is wrong with re-engineering our nature?

(c) Breakthroughs in genetics present us with the promise that we will soon be able to prevent a host of debilitating diseases, and the predicament that our newfound genetic knowledge may enable us to enhance our genetic traits.

(d) To grapple with the ethics of enhancement, we need to confront questions that verge on theology, which is why modern philosophers and political theorists tend to shrink from them.

(e) One argument is that the drive for human perfection through genetics is objectionable as it represents a bid for mastery that fails to appreciate the gifts of human powers and achievements.

Q24. The four sentences (labelled (a), (b), (c) and (d)) below, when properly sequenced would yield a coherent paragraph. Decide on the proper sequencing of the order of the sentences and key in the sequence of the four numbers as your answer:

(a) But today there is an epochal challenge to rethink and reconstitute the vision and practice of development as a shared responsibility - a sharing which binds both the agent and the audience, the developed world and the developing, in a bond of shared destiny.

(b) We are at a crossroads now in our vision and practice of development.

(c) This calls for the cultivation of an appropriate ethical mode of being in our lives which enables us to realize this global and planetary situation of shared living and responsibility.

(d) Half a century ago, development began as a hope for a better human possibility, but in the last fifty years, this hope has lost itself in the dreary desert of various kinds of hegemonic applications.

Answer Key

1. (b)	**2.** (b)	**3.** (c)	**4.** (b)	**5.** (d)
6. (b)	**7.** (d)	**8.** (d)	**9.** (b)	**10.** (a)
11. (c)	**12.** (a)	**13.** (d)	**14.** (b)	**15.** (b)
16. (a)	**17.** (c, b, a, d)		**18.** **(b)**	**19.** (e)
20. (d)	**21.** (b, a, d, c)		**22.** **(a)**	**23.** (a)
24. (b, d, a, c)				

Explanations

1. Note that the question has the word "except". The correct answer is the option which is not a statement made by the author. The author says that the "most common" way of dealing with scepticism about the veracity of knowledge is to ignore it. Option (b) states that it is "the best way". Clearly, option (b) hence cannot be an argument made by the author and is the correct answer. All the other options have some ideas that have been mentioned in the passage.

2. Read the lines, "We hold our beliefs and presumptive knowledges more or less confidently, usually *depending on how we acquired them* (I saw it with my own eyes; I heard it on Fox News; a guy at the office told me) and *how broadly and strenuously they seem to be shared or endorsed by various relevant people:*

experts and authorities, friends and family members, colleagues and associates." Option (b) talks about examining or defending our convictions and hence is the correct answer.

3. Read the lines, "And we examine our convictions more or less closely, explain them more or less extensively, and defend them more or less vigorously, usually depending on . . . . *what resources are available for reassuring ourselves or making our beliefs credible to others* (look, it's right here on the page; add up the figures yourself; I happen to be a heart specialist)." This is exactly opposite to what option (a) states and hence is incorrect. Option (c) would be something which the author would support. Read the lines, "For, the sceptic will note, *since reality, under that conception of it, is outside our ken,* we have no way to compare our mental representations with things-as-they-are-in-themselves and therefore *no way to determine whether they are correct or incorrect.*" Options (b) and (d) are incorrect since the ideas mentioned do not lie in line with the passage.

4. The idea in the passage is that if anything is outside our perceptions, descriptions or ideas, it is something which lies outside the realm of our understanding, we will then be unable to perceive it. Option (b) is the correct idea and hence is the correct answer.

5. The idea mentioned in the passage states that there are a few languages which do not get impacted by the forced language shift and can revive themselves. Welsh is an example of such a language which revived even after a language shift and hence is the correct answer.

6. Read the lines, "through war, famine and natural disasters," and language shift "for complex political, cultural and economic reasons - sometimes voluntary for economic and educational reasons, although often amplified by state coercion or neglect." Only option (b) has not been mentioned in these factors and hence option (b) is the correct answer.

7. The last and the second last paragraphs talk about multilingualism as an idea and how it can benefit us instead of sticking to one language. The idea propagated has been mentioned in option (d) and hence is the correct answer.

8. Read the lines, indigenous languages have "unusual words and intriguing grammar." It cannot be inferred from these lines that these languages are difficult to document. It just states that these languages have unusual words and grammar. Option (d) hence cannot be inferred.

9. Read the lines, "Even if we need to pay some price for deactivating our rational faculties, the advantages of increased social cohesion are often so big that fictional stories routinely triumph over the truth in human history." It is a constant debate that when it comes to uniting people over a common stand, fiction plays a more convincing role over actual facts. Option (b) is hence the right answer here.

10. Read the lines, "An uncompromising adherence to the truth is an admirable spiritual practice, but it is not a winning political strategy." This line indirectly states that since it is not a winning political strategy, the political powers retain their supremacy by not sticking to truth but by moulding it and hence concealing the unvarnished truth. Option (a) is hence correct.

11. According to the passage, "Even if we need to pay some price for deactivating our rational faculties, the advantages of increased social cohesion are often so big that fictional stories routinely triumph over the truth in human history. Scholars have known this for thousands of years, which is why scholars often had to decide whether they served the truth or social harmony." The author implies that scholars have been aware of the fact that fictional stories hold supremacy over the truth but they had to decide whether to put forward the social harmony inducing fiction or the hard bound truth. Hence, the gist of the idea has been mentioned in option (c).

12. In this option, the author equates fiction with social harmony and unity while he associates truth with disharmony among the people. Hence, we can say that out of all the options, option (a) gives the most importance to fiction and hence is the correct answer.

13. Read the lines, "Once we match this new meaning of the home/world dichotomy with the identification of social roles by gender, we get the ideological framework within which nationalism answered the women's question. It would be a grave error to see in this, as liberals are apt to in their despair at the many marks of social conservatism in nationalist practice, a total rejection of the West." We can infer from these lines that liberals stick to the social gender roles and hence is the correct answer.

14. Read the lines, "The discourse of nationalism shows that the material/spiritual distinction was condensed into an analogous, but ideologically far more powerful, dichotomy: that between the outer and the inner. . . . Applying the inner/outer distinction to the matter of concrete day-to-day

living separates the social space into ghar and bahir, the home and the world. The world is the external, the domain of the material; the home represents one's inner spiritual self, one's true identity." These lines have been discussed in options (c) and (d). Option (a) can be inferred from the lines.

"But, the nationalists asserted, it had failed to colonise the inner, essential, identity of the East which lay in its distinctive, and superior, spiritual culture. . . ." Only option (b) has not been discussed in the passage and hence is the correct answer.

15. According to the passage, "European power failed to colonise the inner, essential, identity of the East which lay in its distinctive, and superior, spiritual culture." If option (b) is true, it would undermine the idea of inner/outer dichotomy and hence would weaken the author's claim. Option (b) is hence the correct answer.

16. The author begins the passage by describing the "contradictory pulls" on Indian nationalist ideology. In science, technology, economic organisation and modern methods of statecraft, the West dominated. In fact, to overcome this domination, instead of fighting the colonialists on this front, colonised people "had to learn those superior techniques of organising material life and incorporate them within their own cultures." In other words, despite its fight against colonial domination, Indian nationalism had adopt Western ideas in the material sphere.

17. Correct sequence is (c), (b), (a), (d).

Sentence (c) is the opening sentence of the paragraph and talks about the modern scientific method. This idea is further carried forward in sentence (b). (a), (d) form a mandatory pair where the invention of fusion has been further explained in (d). Hence, (c), (b), (a), (d) is the correct order.

18. The gist of the paragraph is that the importance that is being attributed to creativity has led to an over investing study of the idea itself. This is leading to the erosion of creativity as an idea and is seemingly hampering with the original creativity. This has been mentioned in option (b) and hence is the correct answer. Option (a) is very generic and can be ruled out. Option (c) focuses solely on the research of creativity and not the idea of it hampering real creativity.

19. All the sentences talk about neuromarketing and (e) is the odd one out which talks about the drawing on results from scientific methods from focus groups. This hence can be ruled out.

20. During an economic downturn, the capitalists realise it is beneficial for them to pair with the distressed in order to benefit from the pollical and economic situation. Option (d) sums this up and hence is the correct answer.

21. The correct sequence is (b), (a), (d), (c).

Sentence (b) is an opening sentence which talks about Canada taking over the Northwest passage islands and now claiming sovereignty over the shipping routes. This is carried forward in sentence (a) which talks about the US previously having the claim that the passage is an international strait through which any vessel can pass without any permission. (d), (c) forms a mandatory pair where (d) talks about the unsettled dispute between the US and Canada and (c) talks about the melting of the strait which will make it free of ice and would not require any permission.

22. Only option (a) summarises the idea of physicists being more acceptable towards the preprints than biologists and which helps in the better dissemination of knowledge and speeds up the research process.

Option (b) focuses only on preprints and also generalises the idea that preprints are not accepted by most journals and hence is incorrect. Similarly, option (c) talks about all journals not accepting the preprints. Option (d) talks about an idea completely opposite to what the passage talks about. Option (a) is hence the correct answer.

23. Sentence (a) talks about a broader and a newer idea while other sentences talk about genetics and genetic engineering. Sentences (b) and (e) form a mandatory pair where (d) answers the question posed in sentence (b). Similarly (c), (d) form a mandatory pair. Sentence (a) is hence the odd one out.

24. The correct sequence is (b), (d), (a), (c).

Sentence (b) starts with the main idea of the passage hence is best opening sentence. (d), (a) forms a mandatory pair: sentence (d) talks about the idea of development began half a century ago and how it lost its way. Sentence (a) talks about the view on the vision and practice of development today. Sentence (c) carries forward the idea in (b) and states what the rethinking and reconstitution of development has. Hence, (b), (d), (a), (c) is the correct order.

CHAPTER 3

CAT Paper 2021 (Slot 3) VARC Section Questions and Solutions

Comprehension:

The passage below is accompanied by a set of questions. Choose the best answer to each question.

Today we can hardly conceive of ourselves without an unconscious. Yet between 1700 and 1900, this notion developed as a genuinely original thought. The "unconscious" burst the shell of conventional language, coined as it had been to embody the fleeting ideas and the shifting conceptions of several generations until, finally, it became fixed and defined in specialized terms within the realm of medical psychology and Freudian psychoanalysis.

The vocabulary concerning the soul and the mind increased enormously in the course of the nineteenth century. The enrichments of literary and intellectual language led to an altered understanding of the meanings that underlie time-honored expressions and traditional catchwords. At the same time, once coined, powerful new ideas attracted to themselves a whole host of seemingly unrelated issues, practices, and experiences, creating a peculiar network of preoccupations that as a group had not existed before. The drawn-out attempt to approach and define the unconscious brought together the spiritualist and the psychical researcher of borderline phenomena (such as apparitions, spectral illusions, haunted houses, mediums, trance, automatic writing); the psychiatrist or alienist probing the nature of mental disease, of abnormal ideation, hallucination, delirium, melancholia, mania; the surgeon performing operations with the aid of hypnotism; the magnetizer claiming to correct the disequilibrium in the universal flow of magnetic fluids but who soon came to be regarded as a clever manipulator of the imagination; the physiologist and the physician who puzzled over sleep, dreams, sleepwalking, anesthesia, the influence of the mind on the body in health and disease; the neurologist concerned with the functions of the brain and the physiological basis of mental life; the philosopher interested in the will, the emotions, consciousness, knowledge, imagination and the creative genius; and, last but not least, the psychologist.

Significantly, most if not all of these practices (for example, hypnotism in surgery or psychological magnetism) originated in the waning years of the eighteenth century and during the early decades of the nineteenth century, as did some of the disciplines (such as psychology and psychical research). The majority of topics too were either new or assumed hitherto unknown colors. Thus, before 1790, few if any spoke, in medical terms, of the affinity between creative genius and the hallucinations of the insane . . .

Striving vaguely and independently to give expression to a latent conception, various lines of thought can be brought together by some novel term. The new concept then serves as a kind of resting place or stocktaking in the development of ideas, giving satisfaction and a stimulus for further discussion or speculation. Thus, the massive introduction of the term unconscious by Hartmann in 1869 appeared to focalize many stray thoughts, affording a temporary feeling that a crucial step had been taken forward, a comprehensive knowledge gained, a knowledge that required only further elaboration, explication, and unfolding in order to bring in a bounty of higher understanding. Ultimately, Hartmann's attempt at defining the unconscious proved fruitless because he extended its reach into every realm of organic and inorganic, spiritual, intellectual, and instinctive existence, severely diluting the precision and compromising the impact of the concept.

Q1. "The enrichments of literary and intellectual language led to an altered understanding of the meanings that underlie time-honored expressions and traditional catchwords." Which one of the following interpretations of this sentence would be closest in meaning to the original?

(a) All of the options listed here.

(b) The meanings of time-honored expressions were changed by innovations in literary and intellectual language.

(c) Time-honored expressions and traditional catchwords were enriched by literary and intellectual language.

(d) Literary and intellectual language was altered by time-honored expressions and traditional catchwords.

Q2. Which one of the following statements best describes what the passage is about?

(a) The identification of the unconscious as an object of psychical research.

(b) The collating of diverse ideas under the single term: unconscious.

(c) The growing vocabulary of the soul and the mind, as diverse processes.

(d) The discovery of the unconscious as a part of the human mind.

Q3. Which one of the following sets of words is closest to mapping the main arguments of the passage?

(a) Unconscious; Latent conception; Dreams.

(b) Imagination; Magnetism; Psychiatry.

(c) Literary language; Unconscious; Insanity.

(d) Language; Unconscious; Psychoanalysis.

Q4. All of the following statements may be considered valid inferences from the passage EXCEPT:

(a) Without the linguistic developments of the nineteenth century, the growth of understanding of the soul and the mind may not have happened.

(b) New conceptions in the nineteenth century could provide new knowledge because of the establishment of fields such as anaesthesiology.

(c) Eighteenth century thinkers were the first to perceive a connection between creative genius and insanity.

(d) Unrelated practices began to be treated as related to each other, as knowledge of the mind grew in the nineteenth century.

Comprehension:

The passage below is accompanied by a set of questions. Choose the best answer to each question.

Starting in 1957, [Noam Chomsky] proclaimed a new doctrine: Language, that most human of all attributes, was innate. The grammatical faculty was built into the infant brain, and your average 3-year-old was not a mere apprentice in the great enterprise of absorbing English from his or her parents, but a "linguistic genius." Since this message was couched in terms of Chomskyan theoretical linguistics, in discourse so opaque that it was nearly incomprehensible even to some scholars, many people did not hear it. Now, in a brilliant, witty and altogether satisfying book, Mr. Chomsky's colleague Steven Pinker . . . has brought Mr. Chomsky's findings to everyman. In "The Language Instinct" he has gathered persuasive data from such diverse fields as cognitive neuroscience, developmental psychology and speech therapy to make his points, and when he disagrees with Mr. Chomsky he tells you so. . . .

For Mr. Chomsky and Mr. Pinker, somewhere in the human brain there is a complex set of neural circuits that have been programmed with "super-rules" (making up what Mr. Chomsky calls "universal grammar"), and that these rules are unconscious and instinctive. A half-century ago, this would have been pooh-poohed as a "black box" theory, since one could not actually pinpoint this grammatical faculty in a specific part of the brain, or describe its functioning. But now things are different. Neurosurgeons [have now found that this] "black box" is situated in and around Broca's area, on the left side of the forebrain. . . .

Unlike Mr. Chomsky, Mr. Pinker firmly places the wiring of the brain for language within the framework of Darwinian natural selection and evolution. He effectively disposes of all claims that intelligent nonhuman primates like chimps have any abilities to learn and use language. It is not that chimps lack the vocal apparatus to speak; it is just that their brains are unable to produce or use grammar. On the other hand, the "language instinct," when it first appeared among our most distant hominid ancestors, must have given them a selective reproductive advantage over their competitors (including the ancestral chimps). . . .

So according to Mr. Pinker, the roots of language must be in the genes, but there cannot be a "grammar gene" any more than there can be a gene for the heart or any other complex body structure. This proposition will undoubtedly raise the hackles of some behavioral psychologists and anthropologists, for it apparently contradicts the liberal idea that human behavior may be changed for the better by improvements in culture and environment, and it might seem to invite the twin bugaboos of biological determinism and racism. Yet Mr. Pinker stresses one point that should allay such fears. Even though there are 4,000 to 6,000 languages today, they are all sufficiently alike to be considered one language by an extraterrestrial observer. In other words, most of the diversity of the world's cultures, so beloved to anthropologists, is superficial and minor compared to the similarities. Racial differences are literally only "skin deep." The fundamental unity of humanity is the theme of Mr. Chomsky's universal grammar, and of this exciting book.

Q5. According to the passage, all of the following are true about the language instinct EXCEPT that:

(a) not all intelligent primates are gifted with it.
(b) it confers an evolutionary reproductive advantage.
(c) developments in neuroscience have increased its acceptance.
(d) all intelligent primates are gifted with it.

Q6. On the basis of the information in the passage, Pinker and Chomsky may disagree with each other on which one of the following points?

(a) The language instinct.
(b) The Darwinian explanatory paradigm for language.
(c) The possibility of a universal grammar.
(d) The inborn language acquisition skills of humans.

Q7. Which one of the following statements best summarises the author's position about Pinker's book?

(a) Culture and environment play a key role in shaping our acquisition of language.
(b) The universality of the "language instinct" counters claims that Pinker's book is racist.
(c) Anatomical developments like the voice box play a key role in determining language acquisition skills.
(d) The evolutionary and deterministic framework of Pinker's book makes it racist.

Q8. From the passage, it can be inferred that all of the following are true about Pinker's book, "The Language Instinct", EXCEPT that Pinker:

(a) writes in a different style from Chomsky.
(b) draws from behavioural psychology theories.
(c) draws extensively from Chomsky's propositions.
(d) disagrees with Chomsky on certain grounds.

Comprehension:

The passage below is accompanied by a set of questions. Choose the best answer to each question.

Keeping time accurately comes with a price. The maximum accuracy of a clock is directly related to how much disorder, or entropy, it creates every time it ticks. Natalia Ares at the University of Oxford and her colleagues made this discovery using a tiny clock with an accuracy that can be controlled. The clock consists of a 50-nanometre-thick membrane of silicon nitride, vibrated by an electric current. Each time the membrane moved up and down once and then returned to its original position, the researchers counted a tick, and the regularity of the spacing between the ticks represented the accuracy of the clock. The researchers found that as they increased the clock's accuracy, the heat produced in the system grew, increasing the entropy of its surroundings by jostling nearby particles . . . "If a clock is more accurate, you are paying for it somehow," says Ares. In this case, you pay for it by pouring more ordered energy into the clock, which is then converted into entropy. "By measuring time, we are increasing the entropy of the universe," says Ares. The more entropy there is in the universe, the closer it may be to its eventual demise. "Maybe we should stop measuring time," says Ares. The scale of the additional entropy is so small, though, that there is no need to worry about its effects, she says.

The increase in entropy in timekeeping may be related to the "arrow of time", says Marcus Huber at the Austrian Academy of Sciences in Vienna, who was part of the research team. It has been suggested that the reason that time only flows forward, not in reverse, is that the total amount of entropy in the universe is constantly increasing, creating disorder that cannot be put in order again.

The relationship that the researchers found is a limit on the accuracy of a clock, so it doesn't mean that a clock that creates the most possible entropy would be maximally accurate - hence a large, inefficient grandfather clock isn't more precise than an atomic clock. "It's a bit like fuel use in a car. Just because I'm using more fuel doesn't mean that I'm going faster or further," says Huber.

When the researchers compared their results with theoretical models developed for clocks that rely on quantum effects, they were surprised to find that the relationship between accuracy and entropy seemed to be the same for both. We can't be sure yet that these results are actually universal, though, because there are many types of clocks for which the relationship between accuracy and entropy haven't been tested. "It's still unclear how this principle plays out in real devices such as atomic clocks, which push the ultimate quantum limits of accuracy," says Mark Mitchison at Trinity College Dublin in Ireland. Understanding this relationship could be helpful for designing clocks in the future, particularly those used in quantum computers and other devices where both accuracy and temperature are crucial, says Ares. This finding could also help us understand more generally how the quantum world and the classical world are similar and different in terms of thermodynamics and the passage of time.

Q9. The author makes all of the following arguments in the passage, EXCEPT that:

(a) The relationship between accuracy and entropy may not apply to all clocks.

(b) Researchers found that the heat produced in a system is the price paid for increased accuracy of measurement.

(c) There is no difference in accuracy between an inefficient grandfather clock and an atomic clock.

(d) In designing clocks for quantum computers, both precision and heat have to be taken into account.

Q10. Which one of the following sets of words and phrases serves best as keywords of the passage?

(a) Electric current; Heat; Quantum effects.

(b) Silicon Nitride; Energy; Grandfather Clock.

(c) Measuring Time; Accuracy; Entropy.

(d) Membrane; Arrow of time; Entropy.

Q11. "It's a bit like fuel use in a car. Just because I'm using more fuel doesn't mean that I'm going faster or further" What is the purpose of this example?

(a) If you go faster in a car, you will tend to consume more fuel, but the converse is not necessarily true. In the same way, increased entropy does not necessarily mean greater accuracy of a clock.

(b) The further you go in a car, the more fuel you use. In the same way, the faster you go in a car, the less time you use.

(c) If you measure the speed of a car with a grandfather clock, the result will be different than if you measured it with an atomic clock.

(d) The further and faster you go in a car, the greater the amount of fuel you will use, the greater the amount of heat produced and, hence, the greater the entropy.

Q12. None of the following statements can be inferred from the passage EXCEPT that:

(a) the arrow of time has not yet been tested for atomic clocks.

(b) quantum computers are likely to produce more heat and, hence, more entropy, because of the emphasis on their clocks' accuracy.

(c) grandfather clocks are likely to produce less heat and, hence, less entropy, because they are not as accurate.

(d) a clock with a 50-nanometre-thick membrane of silicon nitride has been made to vibrate, producing electric currents.

Comprehension:

The passage below is accompanied by a set of questions. Choose the best answer to each question.

Back in the early 2000s, an awesome thing happened in the *New X-Men* comics. Our mutant heroes had been battling giant robots called Sentinels for years, but suddenly these mechanical overlords spawned a new threat: Nano-Sentinels! Not content to rule Earth with their metal fists, these tiny robots invaded our bodies at the microscopic level. Infected humans were slowly converted into machines, cell by cell.

Now, a new wave of extremely odd robots is making at least part of the Nano-Sentinels story come true. Using exotic fabrication materials like squishy hydrogels and elastic polymers, researchers are making autonomous devices that are often tiny and that could turn out to be more powerful than an army of Terminators. Some are 1-centimetre blobs that can skate over water. Others are flat sheets that can roll themselves into tubes, or matchstick-sized plastic coils that act as powerful muscles. No, they won't be invading our bodies and turning us into Sentinels - which I personally find a little disappointing - but some of them could one day swim through our bloodstream to heal us. They could also clean up pollutants in water or fold themselves into different kinds of vehicles for us to drive. . . .

Unlike a traditional robot, which is made of mechanical parts, these new kinds of robots are made from molecular parts. The principle is the same: both are devices that can move around and do things independently. But a robot made from smart materials might be nothing more than a pink drop of hydrogel. Instead of gears and wires, it's assembled from two kinds of molecules - some that love water and some that avoid it - which interact to allow the bot to skate on top of a pond.

Sometimes these materials are used to enhance more conventional robots. One team of researchers, for example, has developed a different kind of hydrogel that becomes sticky when exposed to a low-voltage zap of electricity and then stops being sticky when the electricity is switched off. This putty-like gel can be pasted right onto the feet or wheels of a robot. When the robot wants to climb a sheer wall or scoot across the ceiling, it can activate its sticky feet with a few volts. Once it is back on a flat surface again, the robot turns off the adhesive like a light switch.

Robots that are wholly or partly made of gloop aren't the future that I was promised in science fiction. But it's definitely the future I want. I'm especially keen on the nanometre-scale "soft robots" that could one day swim through our bodies. Metin Sitti, a director at the Max Planck Institute for Intelligent Systems in Germany, worked with colleagues to prototype these tiny, synthetic beasts using various stretchy materials, such as simple rubber, and seeding them with magnetic microparticles.

They are assembled into a finished shape by applying magnetic fields. The results look like flowers or geometric shapes made from Tinkertoy ball and stick modelling kits. They're guided through tubes of fluid using magnets, and can even stop and cling to the sides of a tube.

Q13. Which one of the following statements best captures the sense of the first paragraph?

(a) The X-Men were mutant heroes who now had to battle tiny robots called Nano-Sentinels.

(b) Tiny sentinels called X-Men infected people, turning them into mutant robot overlords.

(c) None of the options listed here.

(d) People who were infected by Nano-Sentinel robots became mutants who were called X-Men.

Q14. Which one of the following statements best summarises the central point of the passage?

(a) Once the stuff of science fiction, nano-robots now feature in cutting-edge scientific research.

(b) The field of robotics is likely to be feature more and more in comics like the *New X-Men.*

(c) Robots will use nano-robots on their feet and wheels to climb walls or move on ceilings.

(d) Nano-robots made from molecules that react to water have become increasingly useful.

Q15. Which one of the following scenarios, if false, could be seen as supporting the passage?

(a) Nano-Sentinel-like robots are likely to be used to inject people to convert them into robots, cell by cell.

(b) Some hydrogels turn sticky when an electric current is passed through them; this potentially has very useful applications.

(c) Robots made from smart materials are likely to become part of our everyday lives in the future.

(d) There are two kinds of molecules used to make some nano-robots: one that reacts positively to water and the other negatively.

Q16. Which one of the following statements, if true, would be the most direct extension of the arguments in the passage?

(a) Sentinel robots will be used in warfare to cause large-scale destructive mutations amongst civilians.

(b) 1-centimetre blobs of gel that have nano-robots in them will be used to send messages.

(c) X-Men may be created by injecting people with mutant nano-gels that will respond to the brain's magnetic field.

(d) In the future, robots will be used to search and destroy diseases even in the deepest recesses of the human body.

Q17. The four sentences [labelled (a), (b), (c) and (d)] below, when properly sequenced would yield a coherent paragraph. Decide on the proper sequencing of the order of the sentences and key in the sequence of the four numbers as your answer:

(a) Restitution of artefacts to original cultures could faces legal obstacles, as many Western museums are legally prohibited from disposing off their collections.

(b) This is in response to countries like Nigeria, which are pressurising European museums to return their precious artefacts looted by colonisers in the past.

(c) Museums in Europe today are struggling to come to terms with their colonial legacy, some taking steps to return artefacts but not wanting to lose their prized collections.

(d) Legal hurdles notwithstanding, politicians and institutions in France and Germany would now like to defuse the colonial time bombs, and are now backing the return of part of their holdings.

Q18. The passage given below is followed by four alternate summaries. Choose the option that best captures the essence of the passage.

People view idleness as a sin and industriousness as a virtue, and in the process have developed an unsatisfactory relationship with their jobs. Work has become a way for them to keep busy, even though many find their work meaningless. In their need for activity people undertake what was once considered work (fishing, gardening) as hobbies. The opposing view is that hard work has made us prosperous and improved our levels of health and education. It has also brought innovation and labour and time- saving devices, which have lessened life's drudgery.

(a) While the idealisation of hard work has propelled people into meaningless jobs and endless activity, it has also led to tremendous social benefits from prosperity and innovation.

(b) Some believe that hard work has been glorified to the extent that it has become meaningless, and led to greater idleness, but it has also had enormous positive impacts on everyday life.

(c) Hard work has overtaken all aspects of our lives and has enabled economic prosperity, but it is important that people reserve their leisure time for some idleness.

(d) Despite some detractors, hard work is essential in today's world to enable economic progress, for education and health and to propel innovations that make life easier.

Q19. The passage given below is followed by four alternate summaries. Choose the option that best captures the essence of the passage.

The human mind is wired to see patterns. Not only does the brain process information as it comes in, it also stores insights from all our past experiences. Every interaction, happy or sad, is catalogued in our memory. Intuition draws from that deep memory well to inform our decisions going forward. In other words, intuitive decisions are based on data, and not contrary to data as many would like to assume. When we subconsciously spot patterns, the body starts firing neurochemicals in both the brain and gut. These "somatic markers" are what give us that instant sense that something is right ... or that it's off. Not only are these automatic processes faster than rational thought, but our intuition draws from decades of diverse qualitative experience (sights, sounds, interactions, etc.) - a wholly human feature that big data alone could never accomplish.

(a) Intuition draws from deep memory, and may not be related to data, but to decades of diverse qualitative experience.

(b) Intuitions are neuro-chemical firings based on pattern recognition and draw upon a rich and vast database of experiences.

(c) Intuition is infinitely richer than big data which is based on rational thought and accomplishes more than what big data can.

(d) Intuitions are automatic processes and are therefore faster than rational thought, and so decisions based on them are better.

Q20. The four sentences [labelled (a), (b), (c) and (d)] below, when properly sequenced would yield a coherent paragraph. Decide on the proper sequencing of the order of the sentences and key in the sequence of the four numbers as your answer:

(a) Businesses find automation, such as robotic employees, a big asset in terms of productivity and efficiency.

(b) But in recent years, robotics has had increasing impacts on unemployment, not just of manual labour, as computers are rapidly handling some white-collar and service-sector work.

(c) For years politicians have promised workers that they would bring back their jobs by clamping down on trade, offshoring and immigration.

(d) Economists, based on their research, say that the bigger threat to jobs now is not globalisation but automation.

Q21. The four sentences [labelled (a), (b), (c) and (d)] below, when properly sequenced would yield a coherent paragraph. Decide on the proper sequencing of the order of the sentences and key in the sequence of the four numbers as your answer:

(a) It is regimes of truth that make certain relationships speakable - relationships, like subjectivities, are constituted through discursive formations, which sustain regimes of truth.

(b) Relationships are nothing without the communication that brings them into being; interpersonal communication is connected to knowledge shared by interlocutors, and scholars should attend to relational histories in their analyses.

(c) A Foucauldian approach to relationships goes beyond these conceptions of discourse and history to macrolevel regimes of truth as constituting relationships.

(d) Reconsidering micropractices within relationships that are constituted within and simultaneously contributors to regimes of truth acknowledges the central position of power/knowledge in the constitution of what has come to be considered true and real.

Q22. Five jumbled up sentences, related to a topic, are given below. Four of them can be put together to form a coherent paragraph. Identify the odd one out and key in the number of the sentence as your answer:

(a) They often include a foundation course on navigating capitalism with Chinese characteristics and have replaced typical cases from US corporates with a focus on how Western theories apply to China's buzzing local firms.

(b) The best Chinese business schools look like their Western rivals but are now growing distinct in terms of what they teach and the career boost they offer.

(c) Western schools have enhanced their offerings with double degrees, popular with domestic and overseas students alike–and boosted the prestige of their Chinese partners.

(d) For students, a big draw is the chance to rub shoulders with captains of China's private sector.

(e) Their business courses now largely cater to the growing demand from China Inc which has become more global, richer and ready to recruit from this sinocentric student body.

Q23. The passage given below is followed by four alternate summaries. Choose the option that best captures the essence of the passage.

Brazil's growth rate has been low, yet most Brazilians say their financial situation has improved, and they expect it to get even better. This is because most incomes are rising fast, with higher minimum wages and very low unemployment. The result is falling inequality and a growing middle class – the result of economic stabilization, improved social security and universal primary education. But despite recent improvements the Brazilian economy is still painfully unequal, with poor Brazilians paying the biggest share of their income in taxes and getting the least back in government services.

(a) Economic reforms have benefitted many Brazilians, but they are unaware of the impending problems from rising inequalities in their society.

(b) Most Brazilians feel they have benefitted from recent economic events, but the poor continue to be dealt unfairly by the state.

(c) Good economic indicators have masked the unfair taxation of the poor that is likely to destabilise the Brazilian economy in the next few years.

(d) With rising incomes and falling unemployment, most Brazilians are being misled into thinking that their economy is doing well.

Q24. Five jumbled up sentences, related to a topic, are given below. Four of them can be put together to form a coherent paragraph. Identify the odd one out and key in the number of the sentence as your answer:

(a) A typical example is Wikipedia, where the overwhelming majority of contributors are male and so the available content is skewed to reflect their interests.

(b) Without diversity of thought and representation, society is left with a distorted picture of future options, which are likely to result in augmenting existing inequalities.

(c) Gross gender inequality in the technology sector is problematic, not only for the industry-wide marginalisation of women, but because technology designs embody the values of their makers.

(d) While redressing unequal representation in the workplace is a step in the right direction, broader social change is needed to address the structural inequalities embedded within the current organisation of work and employment.

(e) If technology merely reflects the perspectives of the male stereotype, then new technologies are unlikely to accommodate the diverse social contexts within which they operate.

Answer Key

1. (b)	**2.** (b)	**3.** (d)	**4.** (b)	**5.** (d)
6. (b)	**7.** (b)	**8.** (b)	**9.** (b)	**10.** (c)
11. (a)	**12.** (b)	**13.** (a)	**14.** (a)	**15.** (a)
16. (d)	**17.** (a)	**18.** (a)	**19.** (b)	**20.** (a)
21. (a)	**22.** (c)	**23.** (b)	**24.** (d)	

Explanations

1. The given sentence states that the enrichment/improvement/refinement of literary and intellectual language changed the understanding of the meaning of time-honoured expressions and traditional catchwords. Hence, option (b) is the correct answer.

2. The passage very clearly mentions that unconscious 'burst the shell of conventional language, coined as it had been to embody the fleeting ideas and the shifting conceptions of several generations until, finally, it became fixed and defined in specialized terms within the realm of medical psychology and Freudian psychoanalysis.' It further talks about how various ideas developed through 1700 to 1900, and how the 'massive introduction of the term unconscious by Hartmann in 1869 appeared to focalize many stray thoughts'. Option (b) summarizes the ideas best and hence is the correct answer.

3. The passage very clearly mentions that unconscious 'burst the shell of conventional language, coined as it had been to embody the fleeting ideas and the shifting conceptions of several generations until, finally, it became fixed and defined in specialized terms within the realm of medical psychology and Freudian psychoanalysis.' It further talks about how various ideas developed through 1700 to 1900. The words imagination, magnetism, dreams, literary language and insanity are nowhere close to this idea and hence options (a), (b) and (c) can be eliminated.

4. Option (b) cannot be inferred from the passage since it does not talk about the term anaesthesiology.

It only says that with the introduction of the term 'unconscious', it seemed that this new knowledge could, with further elaboration and exploring, provide a bounty of higher understanding. Option (d) can be easily inferred based on the examples in the second paragraph. Similarly, options (a) and (c) can also be inferred.

5. The question is trickily worded asks to pick an option which is incorrect.

   According to the passage, Pinker 'effectively disposes of all claims that intelligent nonhuman primates like chimps have any abilities to learn and use language.' Reading this idea,it can be seen that option (d) is not true and hence is the correct answer.

6. Read the following line, 'Unlike Mr. Chomsky, Mr. Pinker firmly places the wiring of the brain for language within the framework of Darwinian natural selection and evolution.' It can hence be stated that option (b) is the correct answer.

7. From the passage, it can be seen that the author calls Pinker's book 'brilliant, witty and altogether satisfying'. Even though the common notion is that the book is racist, the author states that Pinkers talks about the 'fundamental unity of humanity' and 'the universal grammar' of language- the universality of 'the language instinct', in other words, to oppose such claims. So, option (b) is the correct answer.

8. Read the lines from the passage, where the author talks about how roots of language must be in the genes will '*undoubtedly raise the hackles* of some behavioral psychologists and anthropologists, for it apparently contradicts the liberal idea that human behavior may be changed for the better by improvements in culture and environment'. So, Pinker's position is at variance with that of behavioural psychologists. Hence option (b) is not true about Pinker's book.

9. Read the lines in the first paragraph: '...the researchers found that as they increased the clock's accuracy, the heat produced in the system grew, increasing the entropy of its surroundings by jostling nearby particles . . . "If a clock is more accurate, you are paying for it somehow," says Ares.' It can hence be stated that option (b) is the correct answer.

10. 'Measuring time', 'accuracy' and 'entropy' are key ideas in the passage. None of the given options apart from option (c) includes 'measuring time' and hence can be ruled out.

11. Read the lines, 'The relationship that the researchers found is a limit on the accuracy of a clock, so it doesn't mean that a clock that creates the most possible entropy would be maximally accurate'. The author tries to draw a parallel that just as increased fuel does not mean an increase in speed, an increase in entropy does not imply an increase in accuracy. Hence, option (a) is the correct answer.

12. Upon reading the lines, "Keeping time accurately comes with a price. The maximum accuracy of a clock is directly related to how much disorder, or entropy, it creates every time it ticks," it can be said that sincw quantum computers are, 'devices where both accuracy and temperature are crucial', it can be inferred that quantum computers are likely to produce more heat and, hence, more entropy, because of the importance accuracy would play in this case. Hence option (b) can be said to be the right choice.

13. The lines in the first paragraph state 'Our *mutant heroes* had been battling giant robots called Sentinels for years, but suddenly these mechanical overlords *spawned a new threat: Nano-Sentinels!*' From these lines, option (a) can be said to be the correct answer.

14. The central idea of the passage is that nano robots, which were at one point of time, only included in science fiction and comics, are now a reality. They are an idea come true with the researchers making these using molecular parts. Option (a) captures this idea well and hence is the correct answer.

15. Keep in mind what the question is asking out of you. It is asking for an option which if true, is against the ideas in the passage. Talking about the idea of Nano sentinels, the passage states that 'No, they won't be invading our bodies and turning us into Sentinels'. That is, these Nano-Sentinel robots do not turn the body they are injected into to robots. So, option (a), if true, goes against the passage. Hence, this is the correct answer choice.

16. Read the lines 'some of them could one day swim through our bloodstream to heal us. They could also clean up pollutants in water or fold themselves into different kinds of vehicles for us to drive.' Now read option (d). It can be easily agreed to that option (d) is the correct answer.

17. The correct sequence is (c), (b), (a), (d).

    Sentence (c) is the best opening sentence and talks about some European museums taking steps to return artefacts. Sentence (b) takes the idea forward and talks about these steps. So, (c), (b) forms a mandatory pair. (a), (d) is a mandatory pair, with (a) talking about the legal hurdles in the restitution of artefacts and (d) talking about what some countries would like to do, legal hurdles notwithstanding. So, (c), (b), (a), (d) is the correct order.

18. The paragraph talks about how the notion of idleness is seen as something to avoid and in contrast how the idea of keeping oneself busy is seen as the right thing to do. The activities which were once seen as work have now transformed into hobbies for people. Even after these opposing views, it can also be said that it is hard work which has brought prosperity and improved the conditions. Option (a) catches this idea well and hence is the correct summary.

19. The paragraph talks about the idea of intuition and how it is not something which occurs to us out of the blue but is based on patterns and in built memories and incidents which gets stored in our brains. Whenever something relatable or based on a pattern is observed, there are neurochemicals released in the brain which tells us if something is right or off. This is what we misunderstand as our intuition. Option (b) is the correct answer.

20. The correct sequence is (c), (d), (a), (b).

Sentence (c) is the best opening sentence. (c), (d) is a mandatory pair where sentence (c) identifies trade, offshoring and immigration as threats to jobs, while (d) talks about an even bigger threat which is automation. Sentence (a) carries forward the idea being talked about in sentence (d) and states the value that businesses find in automation. Sentence (b) follows sentence (a) and ends the paragraph, elaborating on the impact of robotics on unemployment. (c), (d), (a), (b) is hence the correct order.

21. Correct sequence is (b), (c), (a), (d).

Sentence (b) is the best opening sentence and talks about the importance of relational histories and how it is significant in the analysis of interpersonal communication. Sentences (a), (c) and (d) bring forward the idea of 'regimes of truth', which is first talked about in sentence (c), and sentence (b) follows sentence (c). Sentence (a) furthers the idea of 'regimes of truth' and how they make relationships sustainable. Sentence (d) follows sentence (a) and concludes the paragraph.

22. Statement (c) is irrelevant.

This is easily decipherable. While all other sentences talk about Chinese business schools and the courses they offer, sentence (c) brings the idea of Western schools and their offerings. The correct sequence is (b), (e), (a), (d).
So, (c) is the odd one out.

23. Option (a) talks about economic reforms benefitting the citizens of Brazil which is a false statement and hence can be ruled out. Similarly, option (c) talks about good economic indicators which becomes vague. The paragraph talks about how the Brazilians feel their financial situation has improved. The reason for this believable scenario is that there are low employment levels and high minimum wages. The poor however remains poor with them letting go of a huge part of their incomes in taxes.

Hence, option (b) is the correct summary here.

24. Statement (d) is irrelevant.

While all other sentences talk about the idea of gender inequality in the technology sector and its impact on society, sentence (d) is more vague and generalized. It talks about structural inequalities in the current organisation of work and employment. (c), (e), (a), (b) is the correct sequence.
(d) is hence the odd one out.

CHAPTER 4

CAT Paper 2022 (Slot 1) VARC Section Questions and Solutions

Comprehension:

The passage below is accompanied by a set of questions. Choose the best answer to each question.

Critical theory of technology is a political theory of modernity with a normative dimension. It belongs to a tradition extending from Marx to Foucault and Habermas according to which advances in the formal claims of human rights take center stage while in the background centralization of ever more powerful public institutions and private organizations imposes an authoritarian social order.

Marx attributed this trajectory to the capitalist rationalization of production. Today it marks many institutions besides the factory and every modern political system, including so-called socialist systems. This trajectory arose from the problems of command over a disempowered and deskilled labor force; but everywhere [that] masses are organized - whether it be Foucault's prisons or Habermas's public sphere - the same pattern prevails. Technological design and development is shaped by this pattern as the material base of a distinctive social order. Marcuse would later point to a "project" as the basis of what he called rather confusingly "technological rationality." Releasing technology from this project is a democratic political task.

In accordance with this general line of thought, critical theory of technology regards technologies as an environment rather than as a collection of tools. We live today with and even within technologies that determine our way of life. Along with the constant pressures to build centers of power, many other social values and meanings are inscribed in technological design. A hermeneutics of technology must make explicit the meanings implicit in the devices we use and the rituals they script. Social histories of technologies such as the bicycle, artificial lighting or firearms have made important contributions to this type of analysis. Critical theory of technology attempts to build a methodological approach on the lessons of these histories.

As an environment, technologies shape their inhabitants. In this respect, they are comparable to laws and customs. Each of these institutions can be said to represent those who live under their sway through privileging certain dimensions of their human nature. Laws of property represent the interest in ownership and control. Customs such as parental authority represent the interest of childhood in safety and growth. Similarly, the automobile represents its users in so far as they are interested in mobility. Interests such as these constitute the version of human nature sanctioned by society.

This notion of representation does not imply an eternal human nature. The concept of nature as non-identity in the Frankfurt School suggests an alternative. On these terms, nature is what lies at the limit of history, at the point at which society loses the capacity to imprint its meanings on things and control them effectively. The reference here is, of course, not to the nature of natural science, but to the lived nature in which we find ourselves and which we are. This nature reveals itself as that which cannot be totally encompassed by the machinery of society. For the Frankfurt School, human nature, in all its transcending force, emerges out of a historical context as that context is [depicted] in illicit joys, struggles and pathologies. We can perhaps admit a less romantic . . . conception in which those dimensions of human nature recognized by society are also granted theoretical legitimacy.

Q1. All of the following claims can be inferred from the passage, EXCEPT:

(a) analyses of technologies must engage with their social histories to be able to reveal their implicit and explicit meanings for us.

(b) technologies seek to privilege certain dimensions of human nature at a high cost to lived nature.

(c) the significance of parental authority to children's safety does not therefore imply that parental authority is a permanent aspect of human nature.

(d) the critical theory of technology argues that, as issues of human rights become more prominent, we lose sight of the ways in which the social order becomes more authoritarian.

Q2. Which one of the following statements contradicts the arguments of the passage?

(a) Paradoxically, the capitalist rationalisation of production is a mark of so-called socialist systems as well.

(b) Marx's understanding of the capitalist rationalisation of production and Marcuse's understanding of a "project" of "technological rationality" share theoretical inclinations.

(c) The problems of command over a disempowered and deskilled labour force gave rise to similar patterns of the capitalist rationalisation of production wherever masses were organised.

(d) Masses are organised in patterns set by Foucault's prisons and Habermas' public sphere.

Q3. Which one of the following statements best reflects the main argument of the fourth paragraph of the passage?

(a) Automobiles represent the interest in mobility present in human nature.

(b) Technology, laws, and customs are comparable, but dissimilar phenomena.

(c) Technological environments privilege certain dimensions of human nature as effectively as laws and customs.

(d) Technology, laws, and customs are not unlike each other if considered as institutions.

Q4. Which one of the following statements could be inferred as supporting the arguments of the passage?

(a) The romantic conception of nature referred to by the passage is the one that requires theoretical legitimacy.

(b) Technologies form the environmental context and shape the contours of human society.

(c) Nature decides the point at which society loses its capacity to control history.

(d) It is not human nature, but human culture that is represented by institutions such as law and custom.

Comprehension:

The passage below is accompanied by a set of questions. Choose the best answer to each question.

Stories concerning the Undead have always been with us. From out of the primal darkness of Mankind's earliest years, come whispers of eerie creatures, not quite alive (or alive in a way which we can understand), yet not quite dead either. These may have been ancient and primitive deities who dwelt deep in the surrounding forests and in remote places, or simply those deceased who refused to remain in their tombs and who wandered about the countryside, physically tormenting and frightening those who were still alive. Mostly they were ill-defined–strange sounds in the night beyond the comforting glow of the fire, or a shape, half-glimpsed in the twilight along the edge of an encampment. They were vague and indistinct, but they were always there with the power to terrify and disturb. They had the power to touch the minds of our early ancestors and to fill them with dread. Such fear formed the basis of the earliest tales although the source and exact nature of such terrors still remained very vague.

And as Mankind became more sophisticated, leaving the gloom of their caves and forming themselves into recognizable communities–towns, cities, whole cultures–so the Undead travelled with them, inhabiting their folklore just as they had in former times. Now they began to take on more definite shapes. They became walking cadavers; the physical embodiment of former deities and things which had existed alongside Man since the Creation. Some still remained vague and ill-defined but, as Mankind strove to explain the horror which it felt towards them, such creatures emerged more readily into the light.

In order to confirm their abnormal status, many of the Undead were often accorded attributes, which defied the natural order of things–the power to transform themselves into other shapes, the ability to sustain themselves by drinking human blood, and the ability to influence human minds across a distance. Such powers–described as supernatural–only [lent] an added dimension to the terror that humans felt regarding them.

And it was only natural, too, that the Undead should become connected with the practice of magic. From very early times, Shamans and witchdoctors had claimed at least some power and control over the spirits of departed ancestors, and this has continued down into more "civilized" times. Formerly, the invisible spirits and forces that thronged around men's earliest encampments, had spoken "through" the tribal Shamans but now, as entities in their own right, they were subject to magical control and could be physically summoned by a competent sorcerer. However, the relationship between the magician and an Undead creature was often a very tenuous and uncertain one. Some sorcerers might have even become Undead entities once they died, but they might also have been susceptible to the powers of other magicians when they did.

From the Middle Ages and into the Age of Enlightenment, theories of the Undead continued to grow and develop. Their names became more familiar–werewolf, vampire, ghoul–each one certain to strike fear into the hearts of ordinary humans.

Q5. Which one of the following statements best describes what the passage is about?

(a) The passage discusses the evolution of theories of the Undead from primitive thinking to the Age of Enlightenment.
(b) The passage describes the failure of human beings to fully comprehend their environment.
(c) The writer describes the ways in which the Undead come to be associated with Shamans and the practice of magic.
(d) The writer discusses the transition from primitive thinking to the Age of Enlightenment.

Q6. Which one of the following observations is a valid conclusion to draw from the statement, "From out of the primal darkness of Mankind's earliest years, come whispers of eerie creatures, not quite alive (or alive in a way which we can understand), yet not quite dead either."?

(a) Long ago, eerie creatures used to whisper in the primal darkness that they were not quite dead.
(b) Mankind's early years were marked by a belief in the existence of eerie creatures that were neither quite alive nor dead.
(c) Mankind's primal years were marked by creatures alive with eerie whispers, but seen only in the darkness.
(d) We can understand the lives of the eerie creatures in Mankind's early years through their whispers in the darkness.

Q7. "In order to confirm their abnormal status, many of the Undead were often accorded attributes, which defied the natural order of things . . ." Which one of the following best expresses the claim made in this statement?

(a) Human beings conceptualise the Undead as possessing abnormal features.
(b) The Undead are deified in nature's order by giving them divine attributes.
(c) According the Undead an abnormal status is to reject the natural order of things.
(d) The natural attributes of the Undead are rendered abnormal by changing their status.

Q8. All of the following statements, if false, could be seen as being in accordance with the passage, EXCEPT:

(a) the relationship between Shamans and the Undead was believed to be a strong and stable one.
(b) the growing sophistication of Mankind meant that humans stopped believing in the Undead.
(c) the transition from the Middle Ages to the Age of Enlightenment saw new theories of the Undead.
(d) the Undead remained vague and ill-defined, even as Mankind strove to understand the horror they inspired.

Comprehension:

The passage below is accompanied by a set of questions. Choose the best answer to each question.

Stoicism was founded in 300 BC by the Greek philosopher Zeno and survived into the Roman era until about AD 300. According to the Stoics, emotions consist of two movements. The first movement is the immediate feeling and other reactions (e.g., physiological response) that occur when a stimulus or event occurs. For instance, consider what could have happened if an army general accused Marcus Aurelius of treason in front of other officers. The first movement for Marcus may have been (internal) surprise and anger in response to this insult, accompanied perhaps by some involuntary physiological and expressive responses such as face flushing and a movement of the eyebrows. The second movement is what one does next about the emotion. Second movement behaviors occur after thinking and are under one's control. Examples of second movements for Marcus might have included a plot to seek revenge, actions signifying deference and appeasement, or perhaps proceeding as he would have proceeded whether or not this event occurred: continuing to lead the Romans in a way that Marcus Aurelius believed best benefited them. In the Stoic view, choosing a reasoned, unemotional response as the second movement is the only appropriate response.

The Stoics believed that to live the good life and be a good person, we need to free ourselves of nearly all desires such as too much desire for money, power, or sexual gratification. Prior to second movements, we can consider what is important in life. Money, power, and excessive sexual gratification are not important. Character, rationality, and kindness are important. The Epicureans, first associated with the Greek philosopher Epicurus . . . held a similar view, believing that people should enjoy simple pleasures, such as good conversation, friendship, food, and wine, but not be indulgent in these pursuits and not follow passion for those things that hold no real value like power and money. As Oatley (2004) states, "the Epicureans articulated a view–enjoyment of relationship with friends, of things that are real rather than illusory, simple rather than artificially inflated, possible rather than vanishingly unlikely–that is certainly relevant today" . . . In sum, these ancient Greek and Roman philosophers saw emotions, especially strong ones, as potentially dangerous. They viewed emotions as experiences that needed to be [reined] in and controlled.

As Oatley (2004) points out, the Stoic idea bears some similarity to Buddhism. Buddha, living in India in the 6th century BC, argued for cultivating a certain attitude that decreases the probability of (in Stoic terms) destructive second movements. Through meditation and the right attitude, one allows emotions to happen to oneself (it is impossible to prevent this), but one is advised to observe the emotions without necessarily acting on them; one achieves some distance and decides what has value and what does not have value. Additionally, the Stoic idea of developing virtue in oneself, of becoming a good person, which the Stoics believed we could do because we have a touch of the divine, laid the foundation for the three monotheistic religions: Judaism, Christianity, and Islam . . . As with Stoicism, tenets of these religions include controlling our emotions lest we engage in sinful behavior.

Q9. "Through meditation and the right attitude, one allows emotions to happen to oneself (it is impossible to prevent this), but one is advised to observe the emotions without necessarily acting on them; one achieves some distance and decides what has value and what does not have value." In the context of the passage, which one of the following is not a possible implication of the quoted statement?

(a) Emotional responses can make it difficult to distinguish valuable experiences from valueless experiences.

(b) "Meditation and the right attitude", in this instance, implies an initially passive reception of all experiences.

(c) The observation of emotions in a distant manner corresponds to the second movement referred to earlier in the passage.

(d) Meditation allows certain out-of-body experiences that permit us to gain the distance necessary to control our emotions.

Q10. Which one of the following statements, if false, could be seen as contradicting the facts/arguments in the passage?

(a) In the Epicurean view, indulging in simple pleasures is not desirable.

(b) The Greek philosopher Zeno survived into the Roman era until about AD 300.

(c) In the Stoic view, choosing a reasoned, unemotional response as the first movement is an appropriate response to emotional situations.

(d) Despite practising meditation and cultivating the right attitude, emotions cannot ever be controlled.

Q11. Which one of the following statements would be an accurate inference from the example of Marcus Aurelius?

(a) Marcus Aurelius was humiliated by the accusation of treason in front of the other officers.

(b) Marcus Aurelius was one of the leaders of the Roman army.

(c) Marcus Aurelius was a Stoic whose philosophy survived into the Roman era.

(d) Marcus Aurelius plotted revenge in his quest for justice.

Q12. On the basis of the passage, which one of the following statements can be regarded as true?

(a) There were no Stoics in India at the time of the Roman civilisation.

(b) The Epicureans believed in controlling all emotions.

(c) The Stoics valorised the pursuit of money, power, and sexual gratification.

(d) The Stoic influences can be seen in multiple religions.

Comprehension:

The passage below is accompanied by a set of questions. Choose the best answer to each question.

The Chinese have two different concepts of a copy. Fangzhipin . . . are imitations where the difference from the original is obvious. These are small models or copies that can be purchased in a museum shop, for example. The second concept for a copy is fuzhipin . . . They are exact reproductions of the original, which, for the Chinese, are of equal value to the original. It has absolutely no negative connotations. The discrepancy with regard to the understanding of what a copy is has often led to misunderstandings and arguments between China and Western museums. The Chinese often send copies abroad instead of originals, in the firm belief that they are not essentially different from the originals.

The rejection that then comes from the Western museums is perceived by the Chinese as an insult. . . .

The Far Eastern notion of identity is also very confusing to the Western observer. The Ise Grand Shrine [in Japan] is 1,300 years old for the millions of Japanese people who go there on pilgrimage every year. But in reality this temple complex is completely rebuilt from scratch every 20 years. . . .

The cathedral of Freiburg Minster in southwest Germany is covered in scaffolding almost all year round. The sandstone from which it is built is a very soft, porous material that does not withstand natural erosion by rain and wind. After a while, it crumbles. As a result, the cathedral is continually being examined for damage, and eroded stones are replaced. And in the cathedral's dedicated workshop, copies of the damaged sandstone figures are constantly being produced. Of course, attempts are made to preserve the stones from the Middle Ages for as long as possible. But at some point they, too, are removed and replaced with new stones.

Fundamentally, this is the same operation as with the Japanese shrine, except in this case the production of a replica takes place very slowly and over long periods of time In the field of art as well, the idea of an unassailable original developed historically in the Western world. Back in the 17th century [in the West], excavated artworks from antiquity were treated quite differently from today. They were not restored in a way that was faithful to the original. Instead, there was massive intervention in these works, changing their appearance. . . .

It is probably this intellectual position that explains why Asians have far fewer scruples about cloning than Europeans. The South Korean cloning researcher Hwang Woo-suk, who attracted worldwide attention with his cloning experiments in 2004, is a Buddhist. He found a great deal of support and followers among Buddhists, while Christians called for a ban on human cloning. Hwang legitimised his cloning experiments with his religious affiliation: 'I am Buddhist, and I have no philosophical problem with cloning. And as you know, the basis of Buddhism is that life is recycled through reincarnation. In some ways, I think, therapeutic cloning restarts the circle of life.'

Q13. Based on the passage, which one of the following copies would a Chinese museum be unlikely to consider as having less value than the original?

(a) Pablo Picasso's photograph of Vincent van Gogh's original painting, printed to exactly the same scale.

(b) Pablo Picasso's miniaturised, but otherwise faithful and accurate painting of Vincent van Gogh's original painting.

(c) Pablo Picasso's painting of Vincent van Gogh's original painting, bearing Picasso's signature.

(d) Pablo Picasso's painting of Vincent van Gogh's original painting, identical in every respect.

Q14. Which one of the following scenarios is unlikely to follow from the arguments in the passage?

(a) A 17th century French artist who adhered to a Christian worldview would need to be completely true to the original intent of a painting when restoring it.

(b) A 21st century Christian scientist is likely to oppose cloning because of his philosophical orientation.

(c) A 20th century Japanese Buddhist monk would value a reconstructed shrine as the original.

(d) A 17th century British painter would have no problem adding personal touches when restoring an ancient Roman painting.

Q15. Which one of the following statements does not correctly express the similarity between the Ise Grand Shrine and the cathedral of Freiburg Minster?

(a) Both were built as places of worship.

(b) Both can be regarded as very old structures.

(c) Both will one day be completely rebuilt.

(d) Both are continually undergoing restoration.

Q16. The value that the modern West assigns to "an unassailable original" has resulted in all of the following EXCEPT:

(a) it discourages them from carrying out human cloning.

(b) it discourages them from making interventions in ancient art.

(c) it discourages them from simultaneous displays of multiple copies of a painting.

(d) it allows regular employment for certain craftsmen.

Q17. The four sentences [labelled (a), (b), (c) and (d)] below, when properly sequenced, would yield a coherent paragraph. Decide on the proper sequencing of the order of the sentences and key in the sequence of the four numbers as your answer:

(a) Fish skin collagen has excellent thermo-stability and tensile strength making it ideal for use as bandage that adheres to the skin and adjusts to body movements.

(b) Collagen, one of the main structural proteins in connective tissues in the human body, is well known for promoting skin regeneration.

(c) Fish skin swims in here as diseases and bacteria that affect fish are different from most human pathogens.

(d) The risk of introducing disease agents into other species through the use of pig and cow collagen proteins for wound healing has inhibited its broader applications in the medical field.

Q18. The passage given below is followed by four alternate summaries. Choose the option that best captures the essence of the passage.

It's not that modern historians of medieval Africa have been ignorant about contacts between Ethiopia and Europe; they just had the power dynamic reversed. The traditional narrative stressed Ethiopia as weak and in trouble in the face of aggression from external forces, so Ethiopia sought military assistance from their fellow Christians to the north. But the real story, buried in plain sight in medieval diplomatic texts, simply had not yet been put together by modern scholars. Recent research pushes scholars of medieval Europe to imagine a much more richly connected medieval world: at the beginning of the so-called Age of Exploration, there is evidence that the kings of Ethiopia were sponsoring their own missions of diplomacy, faith and commerce.

(a) Medieval texts have been 'cherry-picked' to promote a view of Ethiopia as weak and in need of Europe's military help with aggressive neighbours, but recent studies reveal it was a well-connected and outward-looking culture.

(b) Medieval texts have documented how strong connections between the Christian communities of Ethiopia and Europe were invaluable in establishing military and trade links between the two civilisations.

(c) Medieval historical sources selectively promoted the narrative that powerful European forces were called on to protect weak African civilisations such as Ethiopia, but this is far from reality.

(d) Historians were under the illusion that Ethiopia needed military protection from their neighbours, but in fact the country had close commercial and religious connections with them.

Q19. There is a sentence that is missing in the paragraph below. Look at the paragraph and decide in which blank (option 1, 2, 3, or 4) the following sentence would best fit.

Sentence: Having made citizens more and less knowledgeable than their predecessors, the Internet has proved to be both a blessing and a curse.

Paragraph: Never before has a population, nearly all of whom has enjoyed at least a secondary school education, been exposed to so much information, whether in newspapers and magazines or through YouTube, Google, and Facebook. __(1)__. Yet it is not clear that people today are more knowledgeable than their barely literate predecessors. Contemporary advances in technology offered more serious and inquisitive students access to realms of knowledge previously unimaginable and unavailable. __(2)__. But such readily available knowledge leads many more students away from serious study, the reading of actual texts, and toward an inability to write effectively and grammatically. __(3)__. It has let people choose sources that reinforce their opinions rather than encouraging them to question inherited beliefs. __(4)__.

(a) Option 1 (b) Option 2

(c) Option 3 (d) Option 4

Q20. The passage given below is followed by four alternate summaries. Choose the option that best captures the essence of the passage.

Petitioning is an expeditious democratic tradition, used frequently in prior centuries, by which citizens can bring issues directly to governments. As expressions of collective voice, they support procedural democracy by shaping agendas. They can also recruit citizens to causes, give voice to the voteless, and apply the discipline of rhetorical argument that clarifies a point of view. By contrast, elections are limited in several respects: they involve only a few candidates, and thus fall far short of a representative democracy. Further, voters' choices are not specific to particular policies or laws, and elections are episodic, whereas the voice of the people needs to be heard and integrated constantly into democratic government.

(a) Citizens become less inclined to petitioning as it enables vocal citizens to shape political agendas, but this needs to change to strengthen democracies today.

(b) By giving citizens greater control over shaping political and democratic agendas, political petitions are invaluable as they represent an ideal form of a representative democracy.

(c) Petitioning is definitely more representative of the collective voice, and the functioning of democratic government could improve if we relied more on petitioning rather than holding periodic elections.

(d) Petitioning has been important to democratic functioning, as it supplements the electoral process by enabling ongoing engagement with the government.

Q21. The four sentences [labelled (a), (b), (c) and (d)] below, when properly sequenced, would yield a coherent paragraph. Decide on the proper sequencing of the order of the sentences and key in the sequence of the four numbers as your answer:

(a) The creative element in product design has become of paramount importance as it is one of the few ways a firm or industry can sustain a competitive advantage over its rivals.

(b) In fact, the creative element in the value of world industry would be larger still, if we added the contribution of the creative element in other industries, such as the design of tech accessories.

(c) The creative industry is receiving a lot of attention today as its growth rate is faster than that of the world economy as a whole.

(d) It is for this reason that today's trade issues are increasingly involving intellectual property, as Western countries have an interest in protecting their revenues along with freeing trade in non-tangibles.

Q22. There is a sentence that is missing in the paragraph below. Look at the paragraph and decide in which blank (option 1, 2, 3, or 4) the following sentence would best fit.

Sentence: Easing the anxiety and pressure of having a "big day" is part of the appeal for many couples who marry in secret.

Paragraph: Wedding season is upon us and - after two years of Covid chaos that saw nuptials scaled back- you may think the temptation would be to go all out. __(1)__. But instead of expanding the guest list, many couples are opting to have entirely secret ceremonies. With Covid case numbers remaining high and the cost of living crisis meaning that many couples are feeling the pinch, it's no wonder that some are less than eager to send out invites. __(2)__. Plus, it can't hurt that in celebrity circles getting married in secret is all the rage. __(3)__. "I would definitely say that secret weddings are becoming more common," says Landis Bejar, the founder of a therapy practice, which specialises in helping brides and grooms manage wedding stress. "People are looking for ways to get out of the spotlight and avoid the pomp and circumstance of weddings. __(4)__. They just want to get to the part where they are married."

(a) Option 1 (b) Option 2
(c) Option 3 (d) Option 4

Q23. The four sentences [labelled (a), (b), (c) and (d)] below, when properly sequenced, would yield a coherent paragraph. Decide on the proper sequencing of the order of the sentences and key in the sequence of the four numbers as your answer:

(a) Some company leaders are basing their decisions on locating offices to foster innovation and growth, as their best-performing inventors suffered the greatest productivity losses when their commutes grew longer.

(b) Shorter commutes support innovation by giving employees more time in the office and greater opportunities for in-person collaboration, while removing the physical strain of a long commute.

(c) This is not always the case: remote work does not automatically lead to greater creativity and productivity as office water-cooler conversations are also very important for innovation.

(d) Some see the link between long commutes and productivity as support for work-from-home scenarios, as many workers have grown accustomed to their commute- free arrangements during the pandemic.

Q24. The passage given below is followed by four alternate summaries. Choose the option that best captures the essence of the passage.

All that we think we know about how life hangs together is really some kind of illusion that we have perpetrated on ourselves because of our limited vision. What appear to be inanimate objects such as stones turn out not only to be alive in the same way that we are, but also in many infinitesimal ways to be affected by stimuli just as humans are. The distinction between animate and inanimate simply cannot be made when you enter the world of quantum mechanics and try to determine how those apparent subatomic particles, of which you and everything else in our universe is composed, are all tied together. The point is that physics and metaphysics show there is a pattern to the universe that goes beyond our capacity to grasp it with our brains.

(a) The inanimate world is both sentient and cognizant like its animate counterpart.

(b) Arbitrary distinctions between inanimate and animate objects disappear at the scale at which quantum mechanics works.

(c) The effect of stimuli is similar in inanimate objects when compared to animate objects or living beings.

(d) Quantum physics indicates that an astigmatic view of reality results in erroneous assumptions about the universe.

Answer Key

1. (b)	**2.** (d)	**3.** (d)	**4.** (b)	**5.** (a)
6. (b)	**7.** (a)	**8.** (c)	**9.** (d)	**10.** (a)
11. (b)	**12.** (d)	**13.** (d)	**14.** (a)	**15.** (d)
16. (a)	**17.** (b, d, c, a)		**18.** (a)	**19.** (d)
20. (d)	**21.** (c, b, a, d)		**22.** (b)	
23. (b, a, d, c)		**24.** (b)		

Explanations

1. Option (b) is correct.

If we see the following lines: "The reference here is, of course, not to the nature of natural science, but to the lived nature in which we find ourselves and which we are.".... These lines do not talk about the high cost to nature here or anywhere else in the passage; thus, option (b) cannot be inferred and is the right answer.

"advances in the formal claims of human rights take center stage while in the background centralization of ever more powerful public institutions and private organizations imposes an authoritarian social order"... - option (d) is inferred.

"A hermeneutics of technology must make explicit the meanings implicit in the devices we use and the rituals they script. Social histories of technologies such as the bicycle, artificial lighting or firearms have made important contributions to this type of analysis. Critical theory of technology attempts to build a methodological approach on the lessons of these histories." - option (a) is inferred.

'interest of childhood in safety and growth', and goes on to say that 'this notion of representation does not imply an eternal human nature'. - option (c) is inferred.

Thus, option (b) is the correct answer, since it cannot be inferred.

2. Option (d) is correct.

Option (d) says that masses are organized in patterns set by Foucault's prisons and Habermas' public sphere. This is incorrect because the passage says a different thing in this context, which we can see in the following lines taken from the passage: "everywhere [that] masses are organized - whether it be Foucault's prisons or Habermas' public sphere - the same pattern prevails."

This is distorted in the option; thus, option (d) is the answer.

3. Option (d) is correct.

Read the following lines from the passage: "As an environment, technologies shape their inhabitants. In this respect, they are comparable to laws and customs."....Option (d) clearly states this idea, which is the main argument there; hence it is correct.

4. Option (b) is correct.

The main argument of the passage is of course related to technology as we are analysing the Critical theory of Technology. So the supporting idea must be related to the main argument in the passage which is: "In accordance with this general line of thought, Critical theory of Technology regards technologies as an environment rather than as a collection of tools. We live today with and even within technologies that determine our way of life."

Thus, option (b) is correct and will support the main argument.

Option (c) is wrong as it says nature 'decides' what lies at the limit of history. The passage mentions that, nature is what lies at the limit of history.

The last line of the passage makes option (a) incorrect. According to the 4th paragraph, laws and customs represent the dimensions of human nature; this proves option 4 wrong.

5. Option (a) is correct.

The whole passage is about the undead who have been a mysterious presence right from the early ages of civilisation till today's modern world.

Thus, option (a) is correct.

6. Option (b) is correct.

It is very clear that in those times there was belief in the presence of eerie creatures who were neither alive nor dead. Hence, option (b) is correct.

7. Option (a) is correct.

The lines in the question can be understood in the sense that since the undead were not normal living beings, they were thought to have features which were not normal either.

Hence, option (a) is correct.

8. Option (c) is correct.

Options (a), (b) and (d) if made false would be in agreement with what is mentioned in the passage. Option (c) already is in accordance with the passage, and if we make it false it will go against the passage. Thus, the correct answer is option (c).

9. Option (d) is correct.

Meditation in the passage is not mentioned in the sense of out of the body experiences, rather it is mentioned in the context of a practice for controlling one's emotions. Option (d) talks about the out of body experiences in the context of meditation and is incorrect.

Since we have to find the incorrect answer, option (d) is the answer.

10. Option (a) is correct.

Option (a) says that according to the epicureans, indulging in simple pleasures is not desirable; now this is not true as the epicureans said the exact opposite that indulging in simple pleasures is desirable. So if we made option (a) false, it would actually become correct, and here we are looking for an option that, made false, would disagree with the passage; hence, option (a) is the opposite of that and the correct answer.

11. Option (b) is correct.

If we see the following lines from the passage: "For instance, consider what could have happened if an army general accused Marcus Aurelius of treason in front of other officers. ... Examples of second movements for Marcus might have included a plot to seek revenge, actions signifying deference and appeasement, or perhaps proceeding as he would have proceeded whether or not this event occurred: continuing to lead the Romans in a way that Marcus Aurelius believed best benefited them."

From the above lines, option (b) seems to be the correct answer.

12. Option (d) is correct.

From the following lines of the passage: "Additionally, the Stoic idea of developing virtue in oneself, of becoming a good person, which the Stoics believed we could do because we have a touch of the divine, laid the foundation for the three monotheistic religions: Judaism, Christianity, and Islam . . . As with Stoicism, tenets of these religions include controlling our emotions lest we engage in sinful behavior." - option (d) is absolutely right.

13. Option (d) is correct.

The following lines from the passage make the answer clear.: "The Chinese have two different concepts of a copy. Fangzhipin . . . are imitations where the difference from the original is obvious. These are small models or copies that can be purchased in a museum shop, for example. The second concept for a copy is fuzhipin . . .

They are exact reproductions of the original, which, for the Chinese, are of equal value to the original. It has absolutely no negative connotations."

For the Chinese, an exact copy is as good as an original; thus, option (d) is correct.

14. Option (a) is correct.

"In the field of art as well, the idea of an unassailable original developed historically in the Western world. Back in the 17th century [in the West], excavated artworks from antiquity were treated quite differently from today. They were not restored in a way that was faithful to the original. Instead, there was massive intervention in these works, changing their appearance."

These lines from the passage show that in the 17th century, European restorers were not averse to making alterations while restoring things. Thus option (a) is contrary to the passage and is the right answer. The other options are clearly mentioned in the correct manner; hence, they cannot be the answer.

15. Option (d) is correct.

The cathedral in Germany is always under restoration whereas the Japanese shrine is completely rebuilt every 20 years right from scratch and this is the difference between the two. Thus, option (d) is correct.

16. Option (a) is correct.

The unassailable original is the western concept which says that the value of the original is very important, whereas in Asia, copies are also not looked down upon. These ideas have been explicitly mentioned in the passage, hence options (b), (c) and (d) are true.

Human cloning is a new concept and there is not enough data or material to justify the 1st option; hence, the option (a) is the answer.

17. (b), (d), (c), (a) is the correct sequence.

Sentence (b), which is an introduction to collagen, is the starting idea and it is followed by how cow and pig collagen are avoided in use for humans due to the spread of the chances of infection which is sentence (d). Sentence (c) introduces the idea that fish collagen is different as the diseases affecting the fish are not affecting the humans and this is clearly followed by sentence (a) which closes the argument by explaining how good fish collagen is.

Thus, (b), (d), (c), (a) is the right sequence.

18. Option (a) is correct.

The main theme of the paragraph is that Ethiopia had been portrayed as a weak country which needed military help from the Christian countries and in reality it was quite different as Ethiopia is supposed to have been rich and outward looking. Option (d) has some points but option (a) portrays the idea in a better manner. Hence, option (a) is correct.

19. Option (d) is correct.

The given sentence is clearly a concluding sentence because the sentences before it are discussing the issue about internet which has been concluded in the given statement, hence it has to come at the end in blank 4.

20. Option (d) is correct.

Petitioning is an important part of democratic functioning as it gets the issues of the people directly to the government. It is a positive add-on to the electoral process. This is the theme of the paragraph and this is best communicated in option (d).

21. (c), (b), (a), (d) is the correct sequence.

(c), (b), (a) is a total sequence. Sentence (c) is clearly the starting sentence about creative design and is followed by (b) which carries the idea forward. Sentence (a) talks about its importance and introduces the new element of competitive advantage and this is carried in sentence (d) as the reason, and (d) also completes the idea.
Hence, (c), (b), (a), (d) is the right sequence.

22. Option (b), blank 2 is correct.

If we see the sentence before the 2nd blank, it says that people are less eager. The given statement fits exactly after that describing why they are less eager and they want to avoid the stress of the big weddings.
Option (b), blank 2 is the correct answer.

23. (b), (a), (d), (c) is the correct sequence.

There is a clear link between sentences (b) and (a) as both are talking about the positive effect of shorter commutes on employee performance. Sentence (c) provides the contrasting idea to (d) and hence will come after sentence (d). The correct sequence will be (b), (a), (d), (c).

24. Option (b) is correct.

Option (b) captures the important points of the paragraph like how limited our capacity to understand the universe is when we enter the world of quantum mechanics and find that arbitrary distinctions between animate and inanimate simply cannot be made.
Thus, option (b) is correct.
Other options talking about the inanimate being cognizant and the distinction between animate and inanimate are not correct.

CHAPTER 5

CAT Paper 2022 (Slot 2) VARC Section Questions and Solutions

Comprehension:

The passage below is accompanied by a set of questions. Choose the best answer to each question.

When we teach engineering problems now, we ask students to come to a single "best" solution defined by technical ideals like low cost, speed to build, and ability to scale. This way of teaching primes students to believe that their decision-making is purely objective, as it is grounded in math and science. This is known as technical-social dualism, the idea that the technical and social dimensions of engineering problems are readily separable and remain distinct throughout the problem-definition and solution process.

Nontechnical parameters such as access to a technology, cultural relevancy or potential harms are deemed political and invalid in this way of learning. But those technical ideals are at their core social and political choices determined by a dominant culture focused on economic growth for the most privileged segments of society. By choosing to downplay public welfare as a critical parameter for engineering design, we risk creating a culture of disengagement from societal concerns amongst engineers that is antithetical to the ethical code of engineering.

In my field of medical devices, ignoring social dimensions has real consequences. . . . Most FDA-approved drugs are incorrectly dosed for people assigned female at birth, leading to unexpected adverse reactions. This is because they have been inadequately represented in clinical trials.

Beyond physical failings, subjective beliefs treated as facts by those in decision-making roles can encode social inequities. For example, spirometers, routinely used devices that measure lung capacity, still have correction factors that automatically assume smaller lung capacity in Black and Asian individuals. These racially based adjustments are derived from research done by eugenicists who thought these racial differences were biologically determined and who considered nonwhite people as inferior. These machines ignore the influence of social and environmental factors on lung capacity.

Many technologies for systemically marginalized people have not been built because they were not deemed important such as better early diagnostics and treatment for diseases like endometriosis, a disease that afflicts 10 percent of people with uteruses. And we hardly question whether devices are built sustainably, which has led to a crisis of medical waste and health care accounting for 10 percent of U.S. greenhouse gas emissions.

Social justice must be made core to the way engineers are trained. Some universities are working on this. . . . Engineers taught this way will be prepared to think critically about what problems we choose to solve, how we do so responsibly and how we build teams that challenge our ways of thinking.

Individual engineering professors are also working to embed societal needs in their pedagogy. Darshan Karwat at the University of Arizona developed activist engineering to challenge engineers to acknowledge their full moral and social responsibility through practical self-reflection. Khalid Kadir at the University of California, Berkeley, created the popular course Engineering, Environment, and Society that teaches engineers how to engage in place-based knowledge, an understanding of the people, context and history, to design better technical approaches in collaboration with communities. When we design and build with equity and justice in mind, we craft better solutions that respond to the complexities of entrenched systemic problems.

Q1. In this passage, the author is making the claim that:

(a) technical-social dualism has emerged as a technique for engineering students to incorporate social considerations into their technical problem-solving processes.

(b) engineering students today are taught to focus on objective technical outcomes, independent of the social dimensions of their work.

(c) engineering students today are trained to be non-subjective in their reasoning as this best enables them to develop much-needed universal solutions.

(d) the objective of best solutions in engineering has shifted the focus of pedagogy from humanism and social obligations to technological perfection.

Q2. All of the following are examples of the negative outcomes of focusing on technical ideals in the medical sphere EXCEPT the:

(a) neglect of research and development of medical technologies for the diagnosis and treatment of diseases that typically afflict marginalised communities.

(b) exclusion of non-privileged groups in clinical trials which leads to incorrect drug dosages.

(c) incorrect assignment of people as female at birth which has resulted in faulty drug interventions.

(d) continuing calibration of medical devices based on past racial biases that have remained unadjusted for changes.

Q3. We can infer that the author would approve of a more evolved engineering pedagogy that includes all of the following EXCEPT:

(a) moving towards technical-social dualism where social community needs are incorporated in problem-definition and solutions.

(b) making considerations of environmental sustainability intrinsic to the development of technological solutions.

(c) a more responsible approach to technical design and problem-solving than a focus on speed in developing and bringing to scale.

(d) design that is based on the needs of communities using local knowledge and responding to local priorities.

Q4. The author gives all of the following reasons for why marginalised people are systematically discriminated against in technology-related interventions EXCEPT:

(a) "Beyond physical failings, subjective beliefs treated as facts by those in decision-making roles can encode social inequities."

(b) "And we hardly question whether devices are built sustainably, which has led to a crisis of medical waste and health care accounting for 10 percent of U.S. greenhouse gas emissions."

(c) "These racially based adjustments are derived from research done by eugenicists who thought these racial differences were biologically determined and who considered nonwhite people as inferior."

(d) "But those technical ideals are at their core social and political choices determined by a dominant culture focused on economic growth for the most privileged segments of society."

Comprehension:

The passage below is accompanied by a set of questions. Choose the best answer to each question.

[Octopuses are] misfits in their own extended families . . . They belong to the Mollusca class Cephalopoda. But they don't look like their cousins at all. Other molluscs include sea snails, sea slugs, bivalves - most are shelled invertebrates with a dorsal foot. Cephalopods are all arms, and can be as tiny as 1 centimetre and as large at 30 feet. Some of them have brains the size of a walnut, which is large for an invertebrate. . . .

It makes sense for these molluscs to have added protection in the form of a higher cognition; they don't have a shell covering them, and pretty much everything feeds on cephalopods, including humans. But how did cephalopods manage to secure their own invisibility cloak? Cephalopods fire from multiple cylinders to achieve this in varying degrees from species to species. There are four main catalysts - chromatophores, iridophores, papillae and leucophores. . . .

[Chromatophores] are organs on their bodies that contain pigment sacs, which have red, yellow and brown pigment granules. These sacs have a network of radial muscles, meaning muscles arranged in a circle radiating outwards. These are connected to the brain by a nerve. When the cephalopod wants to change colour, the brain carries an electrical impulse through the nerve to the muscles that expand outwards, pulling open the sacs to display the colours on the skin. Why these three colours? Because these are the colours the light reflects at the depths they live in (the rest is absorbed before it reaches those depths). . . .

Well, what about other colours? Cue the iridophores. Think of a second level of skin that has thin stacks of cells. These can reflect light back at different wavelengths. . . . It's using the same properties that we've seen in hologram stickers, or rainbows on puddles of oil. You move your head and you see a different colour. The sticker isn't doing anything but reflecting light - it's your movement that's changing the appearance of the colour. This property of holograms, oil and other such surfaces is called "iridescence". . . .

Papillae are sections of the skin that can be deformed to make a texture bumpy. Even humans possess them (goosebumps) but cannot use them in the manner that cephalopods can. For instance, the use of these cells is how an octopus can wrap itself over a rock and appear jagged or how a squid or cuttlefish can imitate the look of a coral reef by growing miniature towers on its skin. It actually matches the texture of the substrate it chooses.

Finally, the leucophores: According to a paper, published in Nature, cuttlefish and octopuses possess an additional type of reflector cell called a leucophore. They are cells that scatter full spectrum light so that they appear white in a similar way that a polar bear's fur appears white. Leucophores will also reflect any filtered light shown on them If the water appears blue at a certain depth, the octopuses and cuttlefish can appear blue; if the water appears green, they appear green, and so on and so forth.

Q5. All of the following are reasons for octopuses being "misfits" EXCEPT that they:

(a) do not possess an outer protective shell.
(b) have several arms.
(c) are consumed by humans and other animals.
(d) exhibit higher intelligence than other molluscs.

Q6. Which one of the following statements is not true about the camouflaging ability of Cephalopods?

(a) Cephalopods can change their colour.
(b) Cephalopods can take on the colour of their predator.
(c) Cephalopods can blend into the colour of their surroundings.
(d) Cephalopods can change their texture.

Q7. Based on the passage, it can be inferred that camouflaging techniques in an octopus are most dissimilar to those in:

(a) squids
(b) cuttlefish
(c) polar bears
(d) sea snails

Q8. Based on the passage, we can infer that all of the following statements, if true, would weaken the camouflaging adeptness of Cephalopods EXCEPT:

(a) the temperature of water at the depths at which Cephalopods reside renders the transmission of neural signals difficult.
(b) the number of chromatophores in Cephalopods is half the number of iridophores and leucophores.
(c) the hydrostatic pressure at the depths at which Cephalopods reside renders radial muscle movements difficult.
(d) light reflects the colours red, green, and yellow at the depths at which Cephalopods reside.

Comprehension:

The passage below is accompanied by a set of questions. Choose the best answer to each question.

We begin with the emergence of the philosophy of the social sciences as an arena of thought and as a set of social institutions. The two characterisations overlap but are not congruent. Academic disciplines are social institutions. . . . My view is that institutions are all those social entities that organise action: they link acting individuals into social structures. There are various kinds of institutions. Hegelians and Marxists emphasise universal institutions such as the family, rituals, governance, economy and the military. These are mostly institutions that just grew. Perhaps in some imaginary beginning of time they spontaneously appeared. In their present incarnations, however, they are very much the product of conscious attempts to mould and plan them. We have family law, established and disestablished churches, constitutions and laws, including those governing the economy and the military. Institutions deriving from statute, like joint-stock companies are formal by contrast with informal ones such as friendships. There are some institutions that come in both informal and formal variants, as well as in mixed ones. Consider the fact that the stock exchange and the black market are both market institutions, one formal one not. Consider further that there are many features of the work of the stock exchange that rely on informal, noncodifiable agreements, not least the language used for communication. To be precise, mixtures are the norm . . . . From constitutions at the top to by-laws near the bottom we are always adding to, or tinkering with, earlier institutions, the grown and the designed are intertwined.

It is usual in social thought to treat culture and tradition as different from, although alongside, institutions. The view taken here is different. Culture and tradition are sub-sets of institutions analytically isolated for explanatory or expository purposes. Some social scientists have taken all institutions, even purely local ones, to be entities that satisfy basic human needs – under local conditions. . . . Others differed and declared any structure of reciprocal roles and norms an institution. Most of these differences are differences of emphasis rather than disagreements. Let us straddle all these versions and present institutions very generally . . . as structures that serve to coordinate the actions of individuals. . . . Institutions themselves then have no aims or purpose other than those given to them by actors or used by actors to explain them . . .

Language is the formative institution for social life and for science . . . . Both formal and informal language is involved, naturally grown or designed. (Language is all of these to varying degrees.) Languages are paradigms of institutions or, from another perspective, nested sets of institutions. Syntax, semantics, lexicon and alphabet/character-set are all institutions within the larger institutional framework of a written language. Natural languages are typical examples of what Ferguson called 'the result of human action, but not the execution of any human design'[;] reformed natural languages and artificial languages introduce design into their modifications or refinements of natural language. Above all, languages are paradigms of institutional tools that function to coordinate.

Q9. Which of the following statements best represents the essence of the passage?

(a) It is usual in social thought to treat culture and tradition as different from institutions.

(b) Language is the fundamental formal institution for social life and for science.

(c) Institutions are structures that serve to coordinate the actions of individuals.

(d) The stock exchange and the black market are both market institutions.

Q10. "Consider the fact that the stock exchange and the black market are both market institutions, one formal one not." Which one of the following statements best explains this quote, in the context of the passage?

(a) Market instruments can be formally traded in the stock exchange and informally traded in the black market.

(b) The stock exchange and the black market are both organised to function by rules.

(c) The stock exchange and the black market are both dependent on the market to survive.

(d) The stock exchange and the black market are examples of how, even within the same domain, different kinds of institutions can co-exist.

Q11. In the first paragraph of the passage, what are the two "characterisations" that are seen as overlapping but not congruent?

(a) "individuals" and "social structures".

(b) "academic disciplines" and "institutions".

(c) "an arena of thought" and "academic disciplines".

(d) "the philosophy of the social sciences" and "a set of social institutions".

Q12. All of the following inferences from the passage are false, EXCEPT:

(a) the institution of friendship cannot be found in the institution of joint-stock companies because the first is an informal institution, while the second is a formal one.

(b) institutions like the family, rituals, governance, economy, and the military are natural and cannot be consciously modified.

(c) "natural language" refers to that stage of language development where no conscious human intent is evident in the formation of language.

(d) as concepts, "culture" and "tradition" have no analytical, explanatory or expository power, especially when they are treated in isolation.

Comprehension:

The passage below is accompanied by a set of questions. Choose the best answer to each question.

Humans today make music. Think beyond all the qualifications that might trail after this bald statement: that only certain humans make music, that extensive training is involved, that many societies distinguish musical specialists from nonmusicians, that in today's societies most listen to music rather than making it, and so forth. These qualifications, whatever their local merit, are moot in the face of the overarching truth that making music, considered from a cognitive and psychological vantage, is the province of all those who perceive and experience what is made. We are, almost all of us, musicians – everyone who can entrain (not necessarily dance) to a beat, who can recognize a repeated tune (not necessarily sing it), who can distinguish one instrument or one singing voice from another. I will often use an antique word, recently revived, to name this broader musical experience. Humans are musicking creatures. . . .

The set of capacities that enables musicking is a principal marker of modern humanity. There is nothing polemical in this assertion except a certain insistence, which will figure often in what follows, that musicking be included in our thinking about fundamental human commonalities. Capacities involved in musicking are many and take shape in complicated ways, arising from innate dispositions . . . Most of these capacities overlap with nonmusical ones, though a few may be distinct and dedicated to musical perception and production. In the area of overlap, linguistic capacities seem to be particularly important, and humans are (in principle) language-makers in addition to music-makers – speaking creatures as well as musicking ones.

Humans are symbol-makers too, a feature tightly bound up with language, not so tightly with music. The species Cassirer dubbed Homo symbolicus cannot help but tangle musicking in webs of symbolic thought and expression, habitually making it a component of behavioral complexes that form such expression. But in fundamental features musicking is neither language-like nor symbol-like, and from these differences come many clues to its ancient emergence.

If musicking is a primary, shared trait of modern humans, then to describe its emergence must be to detail the coalescing of that modernity. This took place, archaeologists are clear, over a very long durée: at least 50,000 years or so, more likely something closer to 200,000, depending in part on what that coalescence is taken to comprise. If we look back 20,000 years, a small portion of this long period, we reach the lives of humans whose musical capacities were probably little different from our own. As we look farther back we reach horizons where this similarity can no longer hold – perhaps 40,000 years ago, perhaps 70,000, perhaps 100,000. But we never cross a line before which all the cognitive capacities recruited in modern musicking abruptly disappear. Unless we embrace the incredible notion that music sprang forth in full-blown glory, its emergence will have to be tracked in gradualist terms across a long period.

This is one general feature of a history of music's emergence . . . The history was at once sociocultural and biological . . . The capacities recruited in musicking are many, so describing its emergence involves following several or many separate strands.

Q13. Which one of the following statements, if true, would weaken the author's claim that humans are musicking creatures?

(a) As musicking is neither language-like nor symbol-like, it is a much older form of expression.

(b) Nonmusical capacities are of far greater consequence to human survival than the capacity for music.

(c) From a cognitive and psychological vantage, musicking arises from unconscious dispositions, not conscious ones.

(d) Musical capacities are primarily socio-cultural, which explains the wide diversity of musical forms.

Q14. Based on the passage, which one of the following statements is a valid argument about the emergence of music/musicking?

(a) Anyone who can perceive and experience music must be considered capable of musicking.

(b) 20,000 years ago, human musical capacities were not very different from what they are today.

(c) All musical work is located in the overlap between linguistic capacity and music production.

(d) Although musicking is not language-like, it shares the quality of being a form of expression.

Q15. Which one of the following sets of terms best serves as keywords to the passage?

(a) Musicking; Cognitive psychology; Antique; Symbol-makers; Modernity.

(b) Humans; Capacities; Language; Symbols; Modernity.

(c) Humans; Musicking; Linguistic capacities; Symbol-making; Modern humanity.

(d) Humans; Psychological vantage; Musicking; Cassirer; Emergence of music.

Q16. "Think beyond all the qualifications that might trail after this bald statement . . ." In the context of the passage, what is the author trying to communicate in this quoted extract?

(a) Although there may be many caveats and other considerations, the statement is essentially true.

(b) A bald statement is one that is trailed by a series of qualifying clarifications and caveats.

(c) A bald statement is one that requires no qualifications to infer its meaning.

(d) Thinking beyond qualifications allows us to give free reign to musical expressions.

Q17. There is a sentence that is missing in the paragraph below. Look at the paragraph and decide in which blank (option 1, 2, 3, or 4) the following sentence would best fit.

Sentence: This was years in the making but fast-tracked during the pandemic, when "people started being more mindful about their food", he explained.
Paragraph: For millennia, ghee has been a venerated staple of the subcontinental diet, but it fell out of favour a few decades ago when saturated fats were largely considered to be unhealthy. __(1)__ But more recently, as the thinking around saturated fats is shifting globally, Indians are finding their own way back to this ingredient that is so integral to their cuisine. __(2)__ For Karmakar, a renewed interest in ghee is emblematic of a return-to- basics movement in India. __(3)__ This movement is also part of an overall trend towards "slow food". In keeping with the movement's philosophy, ghee can be produced locally (even at home) and has inextricable cultural ties. __(4)__ At a basic level, ghee is a type of clarified butter believed to have originated in India as a way to preserve butter from going rancid in the hot climate.

(a) Option 1

(b) Option 2

(c) Option 3

(d) Option 4

Q18. The passage given below is followed by four alternate summaries. Choose the option that best captures the essence of the passage.

Several of the world's earliest cities were organised along egalitarian lines. In some regions, urban populations governed themselves for centuries without any indication of the temples and palaces that would later emerge; in others, temples and palaces never emerged at all, and there is simply no evidence of a class of administrators or any other sort of ruling stratum. It would seem that the mere fact of urban life does not, necessarily, imply any particular form of political organization, and never did. Far from resigning us to inequality, the picture that is now emerging of humanity's past may open our eyes to egalitarian possibilities we otherwise would have never considered.

(a) The lack of hierarchical administration in ancient cities can be deduced by the absence of religious and regal structures such as temples and palaces.

(b) The emergence of a class of administrators and ruling stratum transformed the egalitarian urban life of ancient cities to the hierarchical civic organisations of today.

(c) We now have the evidence in support of the existence of an egalitarian urban life in some ancient cities, where political and civic organisation was far less hierarchical.

(d) Contrary to our assumption that urban settlements have always involved hierarchical political and administrative structures, ancient cities were not organised in this way.

Q19. The four sentences [labelled (a), (b), (c) and (d)] below, when properly sequenced, would yield a coherent paragraph. Decide on the proper sequencing of the order of the sentences and key in the sequence of the four numbers as your answer:

(a) From chemical pollutants in the environment to the damming of rivers to invasive species transported through global trade and travel, every environmental issue is different and there is no single tech solution that can solve this crisis.

(b) Discourse on the threat of environmental collapse revolves around cutting down emissions, but biodiversity loss and ecosystem collapse are caused by myriad and diverse reasons.

(c) This would require legislation that recognises the rights of future generations and other species that allows the judiciary to uphold a much higher standard of environmental protection than currently possible.

(d) Clearly, our environmental crisis requires large political solutions, not minor technological ones, so, instead of focusing on infinite growth, we could consider a path of stable-state economies, while preserving markets and healthy competition.

Q20. The four sentences [labelled (a), (b), (c) and (d)] below, when properly sequenced, would yield a coherent paragraph. Decide on the proper sequencing of the order of the sentences and key in the sequence of the four numbers as your answer:

(a) Women may prioritize cooking because they feel they alone are responsible for mediating a toxic and unhealthy food system.

(b) Food is commonly framed through the lens of individual choice: you can choose to eat healthily.

(c) This is particularly so in a neoliberal context where the state has transferred the responsibility for food onto individual consumers.

(d) The individualized framing of choice appeals to a popular desire to experience agency, but draws away from the structural obstacles that stratify individual food choices.

Q21. The four sentences [labelled (a), (b), (c) and (d)] below, when properly sequenced, would yield a coherent paragraph. Decide on the proper sequencing of the order of the sentences and key in the sequence of the four numbers as your answer:

(a) The trajectory of cheerfulness through the self is linked to the history of the word 'cheer' which comes from an Old French meaning 'face'.

(b) Translations of the Bible into vernacular languages, expanded the noun 'cheer' into the more abstract 'cheerful-ness', something that circulates as an emotional and social quality defining the self and a moral community.

(c) When you take on a cheerful expression, no matter what the state of your soul, your cheerfulness moves into the self: the interior of the self is changed by the power of cheer.

(d) People in the medieval 'Canterbury Tales' have a 'piteous' or a 'sober' cheer; 'cheer' is an expression and a body part, lying at the intersection of emotions and physiognomy.

Q22. The passage given below is followed by four alternate summaries. Choose the option that best captures the essence of the passage.

Today, many of the debates about behavioural control in the age of big data echo Cold War- era anxieties about brainwashing, insidious manipulation and repression in the 'technological society'. In his book Psychopolitics, Han warns of the sophisticated use of targeted online content, enabling 'influence to take place on a pre-reflexive level'. On our current trajectory, "freedom will prove to have been merely an interlude." The fear is that the digital age has not liberated us but exposed us, by offering up our private lives to machine- learning algorithms that can process masses of personal and behavioural data. In a world of influencers and digital entrepreneurs, it's not easy to imagine the resurgence of a culture engendered through disconnect and disaffiliation, but concerns over the threat of online targeting, polarisation and big data have inspired recent polemics about the need to rediscover solitude and disconnect.

(a) The notion of freedom and privacy is at stake in a world where artificial intelligence is capable of influencing behaviour through data gathered online.
(b) With big data making personal information freely available, the debate on the nature of freedom and the need for privacy has resurfaced.
(c) The role of technology in influencing public behaviour is reminiscent of the manner in which behaviour was manipulated during the Cold War.
(d) Rather than freeing us, digital technology is enslaving us by collecting personal information and influencing our online behaviour.

Q23. The passage given below is followed by four alternate summaries. Choose the option that best captures the essence of the passage.

There's a common idea that museum artworks are somehow timeless objects available to admire for generations to come. But many are objects of decay. Even the most venerable Old Master paintings don't escape: pigments discolour, varnishes crack, canvases warp. This challenging fact of art-world life is down to something that sounds more like a thread from a morality tale: inherent vice. Damien Hirst's iconic shark floating in a tank - entitled The Physical Impossibility of Death in the Mind of Someone Living - is a work that put a spotlight on inherent vice. When he made it in 1991, Hirst got himself in a pickle by not using the right kind of pickle to preserve the giant fish. The result was that the shark began to decompose quite quickly - its preserving liquid clouding, the skin wrinkling, and an unpleasant smell wafting from the tank.

(a) Museums have to guard timeless art treasures from intrinsic defects such as the deterioration of paint, polish and canvas.
(b) The role of museums has evolved to ensure that the artworks are preserved forever in addition to guarding and displaying them.
(c) Museums are left with the moral responsibility of restoring and preserving the artworks since artists cannot preserve their works beyond their life.
(d) Artworks may not last forever; they may deteriorate with time, and the challenge is to slow down their degeneration.

Q24. There is a sentence that is missing in the paragraph below. Look at the paragraph and decide in which blank (option 1, 2, 3, or 4) the following sentence would best fit.

Sentence: Most were first-time users of a tablet and a digital app.

Paragraph: Aage Badhein's USP lies in the ethnographic research that constituted the foundation of its development process. Customizations based on learning directly from potential users were critical to making this self-paced app suitable for both a literate and non-literate audience. __(1)__ The user interface caters to a Hindi-speaking audience who have minimal to no experience with digital services and devices. __(2)__ The content and functionality of the app are suitable for a wide audience. This includes youth preparing for an independent role in life or a student ready to create a strong foundation of financial management early in her life. __(3)__ Household members desirous of improving their family's financial strength to reach their aspirations can also benefit. We piloted Aage Badhein in early 2021 with over 400 women from rural areas. __(4)__ The digital solution generated a large amount of interest in the communities.

(a) Option 1
(b) Option 2
(c) Option 3
(d) Option 4

Answer Key

1. (b)	**2.** (c)	**3.** (a)	**4.** (b)	**5.** (c)
6. (b)	**7.** (d)	**8.** (b)	**9.** (c)	**10.** (d)
11. (b)	**12.** (c)	**13.** (d)	**14.** (b)	**15.** (c)
16. (a)	**17.** (c)	**18.** (c)	**19.** (b, a, d, c)	
20. (b, d, c, a)		**21.** (c, a, d, b)		**22.** (b)
23. (d)	**24.** (d)			

Explanations

1. Option (b) is correct.
The main idea here is that engineers are taught to be only focusing on the objective part of the sciences and not look at the socio-political or cultural aspects.
This is clearly mentioned in option (b). The other options are incorrect as they are inconsistent with the ideas mentioned in the passage.

2. Option (c) is correct.
The options (a), (b) and (d) are clearly mentioned in the passage as negative outcomes of focusing on technical ideals in medicine.
Option (c) is mentioned in the context of not using female parameters but in this option it is mentioned in an incorrect manner. Hence, option (c) is the answer.

3. Option (a) is correct.
The author has advised moving away from technical-social dualism. Option (a) mentions the opposite.
Other options (b), (c) and (d) mention points such as environmental sustainability, local community needs and priorities together with a responsible approach to technical design, all of which the author mentions or hints that should be included engineering pedagogy.
So option (a) is the answer.

4. Option (b) is correct.
Look at the following lines from the passage: "Many technologies for systemically marginalized people have not been built because they were not deemed important such as better early diagnostics and treatment for diseases like endometriosis, a disease that afflicts 10 percent of people with uteruses. And we hardly question whether devices are built sustainably, which has led to a crisis of medical waste and health care accounting for 10 percent of U.S. greenhouse gas emissions."
Here in the above lines, devices being made sustainably are related to greenhouse emissions and not to marginalised people. Hence, option (b) is the answer.

5. Option (c) is correct.
Option (c) mentions that they are eaten by humans and other animals but this is true for most molluscs and cephalopods, so that is not an exception. Hence, option (c) is correct.

6. Option (b) is correct.
Cephalopods can camouflage and take the colour of their surroundings etc. but they cannot take the colour of what is preying on them, that is, they cannot take the colour of their predator. Hence, option (b) is correct.

7. Option (d) is correct.
Squids, cuttlefish and polar bears are mentioned in the passage in direct comparison with octopus' in terms of their camouflaging techniques. Sea snails are not mentioned in comparison with octopus' in terms of their camouflaging techniques. Hence, option (d) is correct.

8. Option (b) is correct.
The number of chromatophores, iridophores and leucophores etc. are not integral to the camouflaging capacity of the cephalopods and they have not been mentioned in the passage also as being important in that sense. Hence, option (b) is the answer.
The other options are clearly mentioned or hinted in the passage as important for their ability to camouflage.

9. Option (c) is correct.
If we see the following lines from the passage where the main idea is discussed, it is clear that option (c) is the essence or the central idea.
: "Let us straddle all these versions and present institutions very generally . . . as structures that serve to coordinate the actions of individuals. . . . Institutions themselves then have no aims or purpose other than those given to them by actors or used by actors to explain them . . ."

10. Option (d) is correct.
Let us consider the following lines from the passage : "There are some institutions that come in both informal and formal variants, as well as in mixed ones. Consider the fact that the stock exchange and the black market are both market institutions, one formal one not."
It is absolutely clear from the above lines that option (d) is correct.

11. Option (b) is correct.
According to the passage: "We begin with the emergence of the philosophy of the social sciences as an arena of thought and as a set of social institutions. The two characterisations overlap but are not congruent."
The two characterisations are social sciences as an arena of thought (or academic discipline) and social sciences as a set of social institutions. Option (b) has both these points and is correct.

12. Option (c) is correct.
Options (a) and (b) are portrayed in a wrong manner and option (d) is ambiguous and not mentioned

in the context of the option. The passage says: "Natural languages are typical examples of what Ferguson called "the result of human action, but not the execution of any human design". Option (c) is correct according to the lines mentioned above.

13. Option (d) is correct.

If musicking capacities become socio-cultural then music is not natural/biological to humans, rather it is learnt behaviour, hence, in that sense we are not naturally musical or musicking creatures. Thus, option (d) is the answer.

14. Option (b) is correct.

See the following lines from the passage: "If musicking is a primary, shared trait of modern humans, then to describe its emergence must be to detail the coalescing of that modernity. This took place, archaeologists are clear, over a very long durée: at least 50,000 years or so, more likely something closer to 200,000, depending in part on what that coalescence is taken to comprise. If we look back 20,000 years, a small portion of this long period, we reach the lives of humans whose musical capacities were probably little different from our own."
Option (b) clearly follows from the argument given in the above lines about the emergence of musicking.

15. Option (c) is correct.

If we look at the passage and do paragraph mapping we find the lines from each paragraph as significant ideas of the passage:

a. Humans are musicking creatures. . . .
b. linguistic capacities seem to be particularly important, and humans are (in principle) language-makers in addition to music-makers – speaking creatures as well as musicking ones.
c. Humans are symbol-makers too, a feature tightly bound up with language, not so tightly with music
d. If musicking is a primary, shared trait of modern humans, then to describe its emergence must be to detail the coalescing of that modernity.

Now let's pick the key words from these key ideas of the passage:
Humans - musicking - linguistic capacity - symbol makers - modernity.
If we check the options, option (c) has all these key points. Hence, option (c) is the correct answer.

16. Option (a) is correct.

A bald statement is one which does not have any extra information or arguments but can lead to many arguments and caveats like what if etc... the author wants us to look beyond those considerations and caveats to look at the truth in the statement. Hence, option (a) is correct.

17. Option (c), blank 3 is correct.

The sentence after blank 2 says: "For Karmakar, a renewed interest in ghee is emblematic of a return-to basics movement in India". . . the given statement mentions "he", which is definitely referring to Karmakar, hence the deleted statement has to come after this statement and that is at the option (c), 3rd blank.

18. Option (c) is correct.

Options (a) and (b) are not giving the correct summary. [the paragraph does not mention how hierarchical civic organisations emerged]
Options (c) and (d) are close but (c) is a better option than (d).
Option (d) is more generic in nature.

19. (b), (a), (d), (c) is the correct sequence.

Sentences (b), (a) (d) and (c) are clearly linked and are mandatory pairs.
While (b) talks about ecosystem collapse caused by diverse reasons, (a) takes it forward by saying that there is no single solution to the problems.
Sentence (d) hints at large political solutions and (c) clearly supports and follows it by mentioning about the required legislation for it.
Clearly, (b), (a), (d), (c) is the correct sequence.

20. (b), (d), (c), (a) is the correct sequence.

Sentence (b) is the most plausible starting sentence talking about food as an individual choice. This is carried forward in sentence (d). Sentence (d) mentions about focus on individual choice drawing away from the 'structural obstacles' that stratify food choices. Sentence (c) adds to Sentence (d) saying that this is mostly in neoliberal societies where the state has transferred responsibility for food to individuals. So the sequence (b), (d), (c) makes a coherent link here. Sentence (c) leads to sentence (a) which mentions about the responsibility being passed on from the state to women.
(b), (d), (c), (a) is the correct sequence of the paragraph.

21. (c), (a), (d), (b) is the correct sequence

Statements (a), (d), (b) are linked to one another very clearly. Statement (a) talks about the history of the word 'cheer'; statement (d) adds to the statement 1 with different interpretations of 'cheer' in the medieval times and then statement (b) talks about how 'cheer' as a noun expanded into 'cheerfulness'. Statement (c) is better as a starting statement than a concluding statement. Thus, the correct sequence is (c), (a), (d), (b).

22. Option (b) is correct.

The key ideas of the paragraph are nature of freedom and privacy, and the big data exposing all our personal information.

If we consider the following lines from the passage: "warns of the sophisticated use of targeted online content, enabling 'influence to take place on a pre-reflexive level". On our current trajectory, "freedom will prove to have been merely an interlude..... but concerns over the threat of online targeting, polarisation and big data have inspired recent polemics about the need to rediscover solitude and disconnect."

Option (b) best covers the key points of the paragraph and is the best summary.

23. Option (d) is correct.

The options (a), (b) and (c) only mention the importance of museums preserving art forms but the passage was in general mentioning art forms and their preservation; hence, option (d) captures the idea of the paragraph in the best manner.

24. Option (d), blank 4 is correct.

The missing statement talks about "most were first-time users"; this refers to a group of people. The 1st or the 4th blank were the best places to put the deleted statement. But (d) looks better since the line before it is talking about a group of women who could be the first-time users. The 1st blank is not a good choice because we are not looking at a targeted group like in (d). Lines before options (b) and (c) are in present tense; hence, the given statement would not fit there too.

Thus option (d), blank 4 is correct.

CHAPTER 6

CAT Paper 2022 (Slot 3) VARC Section Questions and Solutions

Comprehension:

The passage below is accompanied by a set of questions. Choose the best answer to each question.

Interpretations of the Indian past . . . were inevitably influenced by colonial concerns and interests, and also by prevalent European ideas about history, civilization and the Orient. Orientalist scholars studied the languages and the texts with selected Indian scholars, but made little attempt to understand the world-view of those who were teaching them. The readings therefore are something of a disjuncture from the traditional ways of looking at the Indian past. . . .

Orientalism [which we can understand broadly as Western perceptions of the Orient] fuelled the fantasy and the freedom sought by European Romanticism, particularly in its opposition to the more disciplined Neo-Classicism. The cultures of Asia were seen as bringing a new Romantic paradigm. Another Renaissance was anticipated through an acquaintance with the Orient, and this, it was thought, would be different from the earlier Greek Renaissance. It was believed that this Oriental Renaissance would liberate European thought and literature from the increasing focus on discipline and rationality that had followed from the earlier Enlightenment . . . [The Romantic English poets, Wordsworth and Coleridge,] were apprehensive of the changes introduced by industrialization and turned to nature and to fantasies of the Orient.

However, this enthusiasm gradually changed, to conform with the emphasis later in the nineteenth century on the innate superiority of European civilization. Oriental civilizations were now seen as having once been great but currently in decline. The various phases of Orientalism tended to mould European understanding of the Indian past into a particular pattern . . . There was an attempt to formulate Indian culture as uniform, such formulations being derived from texts that were given priority. The so-called 'discovery' of India was largely through selected literature in Sanskrit. This interpretation tended to emphasize non-historical aspects of Indian culture, for example the idea of an unchanging continuity of society and religion over 3,000 years; and it was believed that the Indian pattern of life was so concerned with metaphysics and the subtleties of religious belief that little attention was given to the more tangible aspects.

German Romanticism endorsed this image of India, and it became the mystic land for many Europeans, where even the most ordinary actions were imbued with a complex symbolism. This was the genesis of the idea of the spiritual east, and also, incidentally, the refuge of European intellectuals seeking to distance themselves from the changing patterns of their own societies. A dichotomy in values was maintained, Indian values being described as 'spiritual' and European values as 'materialistic', with little attempt to juxtapose these values with the reality of Indian society. This theme has been even more firmly endorsed by a section of Indian opinion during the last hundred years.

It was a consolation to the Indian intelligentsia for its perceived inability to counter the technical superiority of the west, a superiority viewed as having enabled Europe to colonize Asia and other parts of the world. At the height of anti-colonial nationalism it acted as a salve for having been made a colony of Britain.

Q1. It can be inferred from the passage that the author is not likely to support the view that:

(a) India's culture has evolved over the centuries.

(b) India became a colony although it matched the technical knowledge of the West.

(c) Indian culture acknowledges the material aspects of life.

(d) The Orientalist view of Asia fired the imagination of some Western poets.

Q2. In the context of the passage, all of the following statements are true EXCEPT:

(a) Orientalist scholarship influenced Indians.

(b) Orientalists' understanding of Indian history was linked to colonial concerns.

(c) Indian texts influenced Orientalist scholars.

(d) India's spiritualism served as a salve for European colonisers.

Q3. It can be inferred from the passage that to gain a more accurate view of a nation's history and culture, scholars should do all of the following EXCEPT:

(a) examine the complex reality of that nation's society.

(b) develop an oppositional framework to grasp cultural differences.

(c) read widely in the country's literature.

(d) examine their own beliefs and biases.

Q4. Which one of the following styles of research is most similar to the Orientalist scholars' method of understanding Indian history and culture?

(a) Analysing Hollywood action movies that depict violence and sex to understand contemporary America.

(b) Studying artefacts excavated at a palace to understand the lifestyle of those who lived there.

(c) Reading 18th century accounts by travellers to India to see how they viewed Indian life and culture of the time.

(d) Reading about the life of early American settlers and later waves of migration to understand the evolution of American culture.

Comprehension:

The passage below is accompanied by a set of questions. Choose the best answer to each question.

Nature has all along yielded her flesh to humans. First, we took nature's materials as food, fibers, and shelter. Then we learned to extract raw materials from her biosphere to create our own new synthetic materials. Now Bios is yielding us her mind–we are taking her logic.

Clockwork logic–the logic of the machines–will only build simple contraptions. Truly complex systems such as a cell, a meadow, an economy, or a brain (natural or artificial) require a rigorous nontechnological logic. We now see that no logic except bio-logic can assemble a thinking device, or even a workable system of any magnitude.

It is an astounding discovery that one can extract the logic of Bios out of biology and have something useful. Although many philosophers in the past have suspected one could abstract the laws of life and apply them elsewhere, it wasn't until the complexity of computers and human-made systems became as complicated as living things, that it was possible to prove this. It's eerie how much of life can be transferred. So far, some of the traits of the living that have successfully been transported to mechanical systems are: self-replication, self-governance, limited self-repair, mild evolution, and partial learning.

We have reason to believe yet more can be synthesized and made into something new. Yet at the same time that the logic of Bios is being imported into machines, the logic of Technos is being imported into life. The root of bioengineering is the desire to control the organic long enough to improve it. Domesticated plants and animals are examples of technos-logic applied to life. The wild aromatic root of the Queen Anne's lace weed has been fine-tuned over generations by selective herb gatherers until it has evolved into a sweet carrot of the garden; the udders of wild bovines have been selectively enlarged in a "unnatural" way to satisfy humans rather than calves. Milk cows and carrots, therefore, are human inventions as much as steam engines and gunpowder are. But milk cows and carrots are more indicative of the kind of inventions humans will make in the future: products that are grown rather than manufactured.

Genetic engineering is precisely what cattle breeders do when they select better strains of Holsteins, only bioengineers employ more precise and powerful control. While carrot and milk cow breeders had to rely on diffuse organic evolution, modern genetic engineers can use directed artificial evolution–purposeful design–which greatly accelerates improvements.

The overlap of the mechanical and the lifelike increases year by year. Part of this bionic convergence is a matter of words. The meanings of "mechanical" and "life" are both stretching until all complicated things can be perceived as machines, and all self-sustaining machines can be perceived as alive. Yet beyond semantics, two concrete trends are happening: (1) Human-made things are behaving more lifelike, and (2) Life is becoming more engineered. The apparent veil between the organic and the manufactured has crumpled to reveal that the two really are, and have always been, of one being.

Q5. Which one of the following sets of words/phrases best serves as keywords to the passage?

(a) Complex systems; Carrots; Milk cows; Convergence; Technos-logic

(b) Complex systems; Bio-logic; Bioengineering; Technos-logic; Convergence

(c) Nature; Bios; Technos; Self-repair; Holsteins
(d) Nature; Computers; Carrots; Milk cows; Genetic engineering

Q6. None of the following statements is implied by the arguments of the passage, EXCEPT:

(a) historically, philosophers have known that the laws of life can be abstracted and applied elsewhere.
(b) the biological realm is as complex as the mechanical one; which is why the logic of Bios is being imported into machines.
(c) purposeful design represents the pinnacle of scientific expertise in the service of human betterment and civilisational progress.
(d) genetic engineers and bioengineers are the same insofar as they both seek to force evolution in an artificial way.

Q7. The author claims that, "Part of this bionic convergence is a matter of words". Which one of the following statements best expresses the point being made by the author?

(a) A bionic convergence indicates the meeting ground of genetic engineering and artificial intelligence.
(b) "Mechanical" and "life" were earlier seen as opposite in meaning, but the difference between the two is increasingly blurred.
(c) "Mechanical" and "life" are words from different logical systems and are, therefore, fundamentally incompatible in meaning.
(d) "Bios" and "Technos" are both convergent forms of logic, but they generate meanings about the world that are mutually exclusive.

Q8. The author claims that, "The apparent veil between the organic and the manufactured has crumpled to reveal that the two really are, and have always been, of one being." Which one of the following statements best expresses the point being made by the author here?

(a) The crumpling of the organic veil between apparent and manufactured reality reveals them to have the same being.
(b) Organic reality has crumpled under the veil of manufacturing, rendering the apparent and the real as the same being.
(c) Apparent reality and organic reality are distinguished by the fact that the former is manufactured.
(d) Scientific advances are making it increasingly diffcult to distinguish between organic reality and manufactured reality.

Comprehension:

The passage below is accompanied by a set of questions. Choose the best answer to each question.

As software improves, the people using it become less likely to sharpen their own know-how. Applications that offer lots of prompts and tips are often to blame; simpler, less solicitous programs push people harder to think, act and learn.

Ten years ago, information scientists at Utrecht University in the Netherlands had a group of people carry out complicated analytical and planning tasks using either rudimentary software that provided no assistance or sophisticated software that offered a great deal of aid. The researchers found that the people using the simple software developed better strategies, made fewer mistakes and developed a deeper aptitude for the work. The people using the more advanced software, meanwhile, would often "aimlessly click around" when confronted with a tricky problem. The supposedly helpful software actually short-circuited their thinking and learning.

[According to] philosopher Hubert Dreyfus . . . our skills get sharper only through practice, when we use them regularly to overcome different sorts of diffcult challenges. The goal of modern software, by contrast, is to ease our way through such challenges. Arduous, painstaking work is exactly what programmers are most eager to automate–after all, that is where the immediate effciency gains tend to lie. In other words, a fundamental tension ripples between the interests of the people doing the automation and the interests of the people doing the work.

Nevertheless, automation's scope continues to widen. With the rise of electronic health records, physicians increasingly rely on software templates to guide them through patient exams. The programs incorporate valuable checklists and alerts, but they also make medicine more routinized and formulaic–and distance doctors from their patients. . . . Harvard Medical School professor Beth Lown, in a 2012 journal article . . . warned that when doctors become "screen-driven," following a computer's prompts rather than "the patient's narrative thread," their thinking can become constricted. In the worst cases, they may miss important diagnostic signals. . . .

In a recent paper published in the journal Diagnosis, three medical researchers . . . examined the misdiagnosis of Thomas Eric Duncan, the first person to die of Ebola in the U.S., at Texas Health Presbyterian Hospital Dallas. They argue that the digital templates used by the hospital's clinicians to record patient information probably helped to induce a kind of tunnel vision. "These highly constrained tools," the researchers write, "are optimized for data capture but at the expense of sacrificing their utility for appropriate triage and diagnosis, leading users to miss the forest for the trees." Medical software, they write, is no "replacement for basic history-taking, examination skills, and critical thinking." . . .

There is an alternative. In "human-centered automation," the talents of people take precedence . . . In this model, software plays an essential but secondary role. It takes over routine functions that a human operator has already mastered, issues alerts when unexpected situations arise, provides fresh information that expands the operator's perspective and counters the biases that often distort human thinking. The technology becomes the expert's partner, not the expert's replacement.

Q9. It can be inferred that in the Utrecht University experiment, one group of people was "aimlessly clicking around" because:

(a) they wanted to avoid making mistakes.
(b) they did not have the skill-set to address complicated tasks.
(c) the other group was carrying out the tasks more effciently.
(d) they were hoping that the software would help carry out the tasks.

Q10. From the passage, we can infer that the author is apprehensive about the use of sophisticated automation for all of the following reasons EXCEPT that:

(a) it stunts the development of its users.
(b) it could mislead people.
(c) computers could replace humans.
(d) it stops users from exercising their minds.

Q11. In the Ebola misdiagnosis case, we can infer that doctors probably missed the forest for the trees because:

(a) they were led by the data processed by digital templates.
(b) they used the wrong type of digital templates for the case.
(c) the data collected were not suffcient for appropriate triage.
(d) the digital templates forced them to acquire tunnel vision.

Q12. In the context of the passage, all of the following can be considered examples of human-centered automation EXCEPT:

(a) software that auto-completes text when the user writes an email.
(b) medical software that provides optional feedback on the doctor's analysis of the medical situation.
(c) a smart-home system that changes the temperature as instructed by the resident.
(d) software that offers interpretations when requested by the human operator.

Comprehension:

The passage below is accompanied by a set of questions. Choose the best answer to each question.

Sociologists working in the Chicago School tradition have focused on how rapid or dramatic social change causes increases in crime. Just as Durkheim, Marx, Toennies, and other European sociologists thought that the rapid changes produced by industrialization and urbanization produced crime and disorder, so too did the Chicago School theorists. The location of the University of Chicago provided an excellent opportunity for Park, Burgess, and McKenzie to study the social ecology of the city. Shaw and McKay found . . . that areas of the city characterized by high levels of social disorganization had higher rates of crime and delinquency.

In the 1920s and 1930s Chicago, like many American cities, experienced considerable immigration. Rapid population growth is a disorganizing influence, but growth resulting from in-migration of very different people is particularly disruptive. Chicago's in-migrants were both native-born whites and blacks from rural areas and small towns, and foreign immigrants. The heavy industry of cities like Chicago, Detroit, and Pittsburgh drew those seeking opportunities and new lives. Farmers and villagers from America's hinterland, like their European cousins of whom Durkheim wrote, moved in large numbers into cities. At the start of the twentieth century, Americans were predominately a rural population, but by the century's mid-point most lived in urban areas. The social lives of these migrants, as well as those already living in the cities they moved to, were disrupted by the differences between urban and rural life. According to social disorganization theory, until the social ecology of the "new place" can adapt, this rapid change is a criminogenic influence. But most rural migrants, and even many of the foreign immigrants to the city, looked like and eventually spoke the same language as the natives of the cities into which they moved. These similarities allowed for more rapid social integration for these migrants than was the case for African Americans and most foreign immigrants.

In these same decades America experienced what has been called "the great migration": the massive movement of African Americans out of the rural South and into northern (and some southern) cities. The scale of this migration is one of the most dramatic in human history. These migrants, unlike their white counterparts, were not integrated into the cities they now called home. In fact, most American cities at the end of the twentieth century were characterized by high levels of racial residential segregation . . . Failure to integrate these migrants, coupled with other forces of social disorganization such as crowding, poverty, and illness, caused crime rates to climb in the cities, particularly in the segregated wards and neighborhoods where the migrants were forced to live.

Foreign immigrants during this period did not look as dramatically different from the rest of the population as blacks did, but the migrants from eastern and southern Europe who came to American cities did not speak English, and were frequently Catholic, while the native born were mostly Protestant. The combination of rapid population growth with the diversity of those moving into the cities created what the Chicago School sociologists called social disorganization.

Q13. Which one of the following is not a valid inference from the passage?

(a) The differences between urban and rural lifestyles were crucial factors in the disruption experienced by migrants to American cities.
(b) According to social disorganisation theory, fast-paced social change provides fertile ground for the rapid growth of crime.
(c) According to social disorganisation theory, the social integration of African American migrants into Chicago was slower because they were less organised.
(d) The failure to integrate in-migrants, along with social problems like poverty, was a significant reason for the rise in crime in American cities.

Q14. A fundamental conclusion by the author is that:

(a) the best circumstances for crime to flourish are when there are severe racial disparities.
(b) to prevent crime, it is important to maintain social order through maintaining social segregation.
(c) rapid population growth and demographic diversity give rise to social disorganisation that can feed the growth of crime.
(d) according to European sociologists, crime in America is mainly in Chicago.

Q15. Which one of the following sets of words/phrases best encapsulates the issues discussed in the passage?

(a) Rapid population growth; Heavy industry; Segregation; Crime
(b) Durkheim; Marx; Toennies; Shaw
(c) Chicago School; Native-born Whites; European immigrants; Poverty
(d) Chicago School; Social organisation; Migration; Crime

Q16. The author notes that, "At the start of the twentieth century, Americans were predominately a rural population, but by the century's mid-point most lived in urban areas." Which one of the following statements, if true, does not contradict this statement?

(a) A population census conducted in 1952 showed that more Americans lived in rural areas than in urban ones.
(b) The estimation of per capita income in America in the mid-twentieth century primarily required data from rural areas.
(c) Economists have found that throughout the twentieth century, the size of the labour force in America has always been largest in rural areas.
(d) Demographic transition in America in the twentieth century is strongly marked by an out-migration from rural areas.

Q17. The four sentences [labelled (a), (b), (c) and (d)] below, when properly sequenced, would yield a coherent paragraph. Decide on the proper sequencing of the order of the sentences and key in the sequence of the four numbers as your answer:

(a) If I wanted to sit indoors and read, or play Sonic the Hedgehog on a red-hot Sega Mega Drive, I would often be made to feel guilty about not going outside to "enjoy it while it lasts".
(b) My mum, quite reasonably, wanted me and my sister out of the house, in the sun.
(c) Tales of my mum's idyllic-sounding childhood in the Sussex countryside, where trees were climbed by 8 am and streams navigated by lunchtime, were passed down to us like folklore.
(d) To an introverted kid, that felt like a threat – and the feeling has stayed with me.

Q18. The passage given below is followed by four alternate summaries. Choose the option that best captures the essence of the passage.

Tamsin Blanchard, curator of Fashion Open Studio, an initiative by a campaign group showcasing the work of ethical designers says, "We're all drawn to an exquisite piece of embroidery, a colourful textile or even a style of dressing that might have originated from another heritage. [But] this magpie mentality, where all of culture and history is up for grabs as 'inspiration', has accelerated since the proliferation of social media... Where once a fashion student might research the history and traditions of a particular item of clothing with care and respect, we now have a world where images are lifted from image libraries without a care for their cultural significance. It's easier than ever to steal a motif or a craft technique and transfer it on to a piece of clothing that is either mass produced or appears on a runway without credit or compensation to their original communities."

(a) Media has encouraged mass production; images are copied effortlessly without care or concern for the interests of ethnic communities.
(b) Copying an embroidery design or pattern of textile from native communities who own them

is tantamount to stealing and they need to be compensated.

(c) Taking fashion ideas from any cultural group without their consent is a form of appropriation without giving due credit, compensation, and respect.

(d) Cultural collaboration is the need of the hour. Beautiful design ideas of indigenous people need to be showcased and shared worldwide.

Q19. The passage given below is followed by four alternate summaries. Choose the option that best captures the essence of the passage.

To defend the sequence of alphabetisation may seem bizarre, so obvious is its application that it is hard to imagine a reference, catalogue or listing without it. But alphabetical order was not an immediate consequence of the alphabet itself. In the Middle Ages, deference for ecclesiastical tradition left scholars reluctant to categorise things according to the alphabet - to do so would be a rejection of the divine order. The rediscovery of the ancient Greek and Roman classics necessitated more effcient ways of ordering, searching and referencing texts. Government bureaucracy in the 16th and 17th centuries quickened the advance of alphabetical order, bringing with it pigeonholes, notebooks and card indexes.

(a) The alphabetic order took several centuries to gain common currency because of religious beliefs and a lack of appreciation of its efficacy in the ordering of things.

(b) While adoption of the written alphabet was easily accomplished, it took scholars several centuries to accept the alphabetic sequence as a useful tool in their work.

(c) Unlike the alphabet, once the efficacy of the alphabetic sequence became apparent to scholars and administrators, its use became widespread.

(d) The ban on the use by scholars of any form of categorisation - but the divinely ordained one - delayed the adoption of the alphabetic sequence by several centuries.

Q20. The four sentences [labelled (a), (b), (c) and (d)] below, when properly sequenced, would yield a coherent paragraph. Decide on the proper sequencing of the order of the sentences and key in the sequence of the four numbers as your answer:

(a) Various industrial sectors including retail, transit systems, enterprises, educational institutions, event organizing, finance, travel etc. have now started leveraging these beacons solutions to track and communicate with their customers.

(b) A beacon fixed on to a shop wall enables the retailer to assess the proximity of the customer, and come up with a much targeted or personalized communication like offers, discounts and combos on products in each shelf.

(c) Smart phones or other mobile devices can capture the beacon signals, and distance can be estimated by measuring received signal strength.

(d) Beacons are tiny and inexpensive, micro-location-based technology devices that can send radio frequency signals and notify nearby Bluetooth devices of their presence and transmit information.

Q21. The passage given below is followed by four alternate summaries. Choose the option that best captures the essence of the passage.

"It does seem to me that the job of comedy is to offend, or have the potential to offend, and it cannot be drained of that potential," Rowan Atkinson said of cancel culture. "Every joke has a victim. That's the definition of a joke. Someone or something or an idea is made to look ridiculous." The Netflix star continued, "I think you've got to be very, very careful about saying what you're allowed to make jokes about. You've always got to kick up? Really?" He added, "There are lots of extremely smug and self-satisfied people in what would be deemed lower down in society, who also deserve to be pulled up. In a proper free society, you should be allowed to make jokes about absolutely anything."

(a) Victims of jokes must not only be politicians and royalty, but also arrogant people from lower classes should be mentioned by comedians.

(b) All jokes target someone and one should be able to joke about anyone in the society, which is inconsistent with cancel culture.

(c) Every joke needs a victim and one needs to include people from lower down the society and not just the upper class.

(d) Cancel culture does not understand the role and duty of comedians, which is to deride and mock everyone.

Q22. There is a sentence that is missing in the paragraph below. Look at the paragraph and decide in which blank (option 1, 2, 3, or 4) the following sentence would best fit.

Sentence: When people socially learn from each other, they often learn without understanding why what they're copying–the beliefs and behaviours and technologies and know-how–works.

Paragraph: __(1)__. The dual-inheritance theory . . . says . . . that inheritance is itself an evolutionary system. It has variation. What makes us a new kind of animal, and so different and successful as a species, is we rely heavily on social learning, to the point where socially acquired information is effectively a second line of inheritance, the first being our genes . . . __(2)__. People tend to home in on who seems to be the smartest or most successful person around, as well as what everybody seems to be doing–the majority of people have something worth learning. __(3)__. When you repeat this process over time, you can get, around the world, cultural packages–beliefs or behaviours or technology or other solutions – that are adapted to the local conditions. People have different psychologies, effectively. __(4)__.

(a) Option 1
(b) Option 2
(c) Option 3
(d) Option 4

Q23. The four sentences [labelled (a), (b), (c) and (d)] below, when properly sequenced, would yield a coherent paragraph. Decide on the proper sequencing of the order of the sentences and key in the sequence of the four numbers as your answer:

(a) The more we are able to accept that our achievements are largely out of our control, the easier it becomes to understand that our failures, and those of others, are too.
(b) But the raft of recent books about the limits of merit is an important correction to the arrogance of contemporary entitlement and an opportunity to reassert the importance of luck, or grace, in our thinking.
(c) Meritocracy as an organising principle is an inevitable function of a free society, as we are designed to see our achievements as worthy of reward.
(d) And that in turn should increase our humility and the respect with which we treat our fellow citizens, helping ultimately to build a more compassionate society.

Q24. There is a sentence that is missing in the paragraph below. Look at the paragraph and decide in which blank (option 1, 2, 3, or 4) the following sentence would best fit.

Sentence: This has meant a lot of uncertainty around what a wide-scale return to office might look like in practice.

Paragraph: Bringing workers back to their desks has been a rocky road for employers and employees alike. The evolution of the pandemic has meant that best laid plans have often not materialised. __(1)__ The flow of workers back into offices has been more of a trickle than a steady stream. __(2)__ Yet while plenty of companies are still working through their new policies, some employees across the globe are now back at their desks, whether on a full-time or hybrid basis. __(3)__ That means we're beginning to get some clarity on what return-to-office means – what's working, as well as what has yet to be settled. __(4)__

(a) Option 1
(b) Option 2
(c) Option 3
(d) Option 4

Answer Key

1. (b)	**2.** (d)	**3.** (b)	**4.** (a)	**5.** (b)
6. (d)	**7.** (b)	**8.** (d)	**9.** (d)	**10.** (c)
11. (a)	**12.** (a)	**13.** (c)	**14.** (c)	**15.** (d)
16. (d)	**17.** (b, c, a, d)		**18.** (c)	**19.** (a)
20. (d, c, a, b)		**21.** (b)	**22.** (b)	
23. (c, b, a, d)		**24.** (b)		

Explanations

1. Option (b) is correct.

From the following lines of the passage, it is clear that the west was technically superior to India: "It was a consolation to the Indian intelligentsia for its perceived inability to counter the technical superiority of the west, a superiority viewed as having enabled Europe to colonize Asia and other parts of the world"

Thus, option (b) goes against the passage and is the answer.

2. Option (d) is correct.

"This was the genesis of the idea of the spiritual east, and also, incidentally, the refuge of European intellectuals seeking to distance themselves from the changing patterns of their own societies"... these lines show that the European intellectuals used the spiritual east to distance themselves from the changing patterns of their society but it did not serve as a "salve[balm]" for them. So option (d) is not in accordance with what is mentioned.

The other options are clearly mentioned. Hence, (a), (b) and (c) cannot be the answer.

3. Option (b) is correct.

If we look at the following lines from the passage we come to certain conclusions:

"Interpretations of the Indian past . . . were inevitably influenced by colonial concerns and interests, and also by prevalent European ideas about history, civilization and the Orient.

Orientalist scholars studied the languages and the texts with selected Indian scholars, but made little attempt to understand the world-view of those who were teaching them. The readings therefore are something of a disjuncture from the traditional ways of looking at the Indian past"

Thus, it can be concluded from the above lines that to gain a better and more precise view of a nation's history and culture, scholars should not try to develop an oppositional framework to grasp cultural differences.

Thus, option (b) is the correct answer.

4. Option (a) is correct.

The orientalist scholars were selectively analysing material that conformed to a particular view of India, without looking at the reality of Indian life. Analysing Hollywood action movies that depict violence and sex to understand contemporary America is also just looking at a partial aspect of America and could be called as similar to the style of the orientalist scholars. Thus option 1 is correct.

5. Option (b) is correct.

Words used the options (a), (c) and (d) like cows, carrots, Holsteins are part of examples and not the key words or ideas. Hence, those options are irrelevant.

Complex systems, bioengineering, bio-logic, technos-logic etc. are key words used in the passage to convey important ideas.

Hence, option (b) is correct.

6. Option (d) is correct.

Option (a) is wrong because philosophers had "suspected" not known that laws of life can be applied elsewhere.

Option (b) is incorrect because the passage clearly mentions that the bios and its logic is more intricate than the logic of machines.

Option (c) is incorrect because the passage mentions that directed artificial evolution or purposeful design is used by genetic engineers but it does not mention or hint that this is "the pinnacle of scientific expertise".

Option (d) is the correct answer as can be inferred from the following lines of the passage:

"Genetic engineering is precisely what cattle breeders do when they select better strains of Holsteins, only bioengineers employ more precise and powerful control. While carrot and milk cow breeders had to rely on diffuse organic evolution, modern genetic engineers can use directed artificial evolution–purposeful design–which greatly accelerates improvements."

7. Option (b) is correct.

Read the following lines from the passage: "The overlap of the mechanical and the lifelike increases year by year. Part of this bionic convergence is a matter of words. The meanings of "mechanical" and "life" are both stretching until all complicated things can be perceived as machines, and all self-sustaining machines can be perceived as alive. Yet beyond semantics, two concrete trends are happening: (a) Human-made things are behaving more lifelike, and (b) Life is becoming more engineered. The apparent veil between the organic and the manufactured has crumpled to reveal that the two really are, and have always been, of one being."

The above lines from the passage convey that mechanical and lifelike were concepts which were supposed to be almost opposite of one another but in today's world the distinction is becoming less and less. Option (b) encapsulates the message in the best manner.

8. Option (d) is correct.

The lines in the question taken from the passage imply that the supposed [apparent] veil which was distinguishing the organic [meaning natural] and manufactured [meaning man made] has been crumpled [broken] and it is now seen that they both are similar and have always been, so it is now difficult to know the difference between the two, that is between the organic and the manufactured.

Option (d) best expresses the point made in the passage.

9. Option (d) is correct.

The lines in the passage state that the person was hopelessly "clicking around" because he was hoping that he would get some helpful prompts from the software as he was so dependent and used to getting help from more sophisticated software and he was not used to using his own mind to find the solutions for the problems he was facing. Thus, option (d) is correct.

10. Option (c) is correct.

Computers replacing humans is neither mentioned nor hinted at in the passage as the author's concern. Hence, option (c) is the answer.

11. Option (a) is correct.

The digital software was excessively relied upon too much and the clinicians did not use their own discerning powers hence they missed the 'forest for the trees'.

If we see the following lines from the passage it is clear that option (a) is correct.

"They argue that the digital templates used by the hospital's clinicians to record patient information probably helped to induce a kind of tunnel vision". "These highly constrained tools," the researchers write, "are optimized for data capture but at the expense of sacrificing their utility for appropriate triage and diagnosis, leading users to miss the forest for the trees." Medical software, they write, is no "replacement for basic history-taking, examination skills, and critical thinking".

12. Option (a) is correct.

Human-centred here means that human beings are directing the machine or software to help them. An automatic procedure which is installed to help everyone using that program which is not tailor made will not be human-centred. In this case, an auto correct program is not human-centred. Thus, option (a) is correct.

13. Option (c) is correct.

The social integration of African American migrants into Chicago was slower because they were less organised is not mentioned or hinted in the passage at all. Hence, option (c) is correct.

14. Option (c) is correct.

The passage mentions that rapid or dramatic social change causes increase in crime. So, it can be concluded by the author that rapid population growth and demographic diversity leads to social disorganisation that can be the reason for growth in crime.

Thus, option (c) is correct.

15. Option (d) is correct.

The key ideas of the passage are: Chicago school tradition, the great migration, social disorganisation theory, social organisation, crime.

Option (d) has the maximum points and is the best answer.

The other options talk about Durkheim, heavy industry, European immigrants which are part of supporting examples but not part of the key ideas. Hence, they are incorrect.

16. Option (d) is correct.

Options (a), (b) and (c) are saying that the rural population was high in the mid-20th century which is against the lines in the question, so they are not correct.

Option (d) says that there was an out migration from rural areas, and this supports the lines from the passage.

17. (b), (c), (a), (d) is the right sequence.

Sentences (b) and (c) mentioning the author's mother wanting them to go out and her tales of her childhood summers being spent outdoors are linked. Hence, sentences (b) and (c) have to be together. Sentences (a) and (b) talking about the author's feeling about going out and it feeling like a threat are linked so sentences (a) and (d) are together. The idea and story of the paragraph moves from the mother to the child; hence, the sequence starts with the mother. Thus, (b), (c), (a), (d) is the right sequence.

18. Option (c) is correct.

The idea of the paragraph is that social media has facilitated and encouraged people picking up and copying any art work or original idea without giving due credit to the culture of ethnic community to which it belongs.

Options (a) says media, whereas the paragraph says social media, hence it is incorrect.

Option (b) is very specific and not covering the whole idea, so it not the right answer.

Option (d) is totally unrelated to the theme of the paragraph.

Option (c) covers most of the points correctly, hence it is correct .

19. Option (a) is correct.

The main idea of the paragraph is that though alphabets were there the alphabetical order was not accepted and put into practice because of religious and other constraints. Later on it was accepted when the need was felt for ordering things for efficiency.

Option (a) has most of the important points, hence is the best answer.

Option (b) is not complete. Option (c) is giving a wrong idea which contradicts the paragraph.

Option (d) talks about a ban but that was never mentioned or hinted in the paragraph.

20. (d), (c), (a), (b) is the correct sequence.

Sentence (d) is clearly the starting idea which introduces a beacon, sentence (c) takes it forward by mentioning how its signal can be received on common devices. Sentence (a) mentions its usage in the industrial sector and finally sentence (a) talks about how it can be used in normal retail stores too. So clearly, the correct sequence is (d), (c), (a), (b).

21. Option (b) is correct.

The theme of the paragraph is that we should be allowed to joke about anyone and anything and each joke needs a target. This may not be the case of 'cancel culture' about whom the said person is talking.

Option (b) covers all the points and is the correct answer.

22. Option (b), blank (b) is correct.

The paragraph starts with the dual inheritance theory and mentions the two types of inheritance namely our genes and social learning. This is the correct point where the given missing statement fits because it talks about how we unconsciously imbibe through the social learning. Then the paragraph talks about how we notice people who are strong and can be emulated etc. The given missing statement is neither the starting, nor the concluding idea, so options (a) and (d) are eliminated. Option (c) follows best after the missing statement in the second blank. Thus, option (b), blank (b) is the correct point to put the given deleted statement.

23. (c), (b), (a), (d) is the correct sequence.

Sentence (c) is the best starting sentence as it talks about meritocracy and why it is an important indication of success. The 2nd sentence gives the contrary view about luck playing an important role in success not just merit. Sentence (a) clearly follows the 2nd sentence as it explains (b). So, (c), (b), (a) are clearly connected to each other. Sentence (d) is an extension of (a) talking about humility, respect and a more compassionate society. clearly, sentence (d) is the closing sentence. Thus the correct sequence is (c), (b), (a), (d).

24. Option (b), blank (b) is correct.

The statement after the 1st blank: "The flow of workers back into offices has been more of a trickle than a steady stream."...this statement has a direct correlation with the given statement which says that: "This has meant a lot of uncertainty around what a wide-scale return to office might look like in practice.". These two statements are clearly linked. The sentence after the second blank also has a link with the given statement, that their employees are either working from office, home or in the hybrid mode. Thus, the option (b), blank (b) is the right placement for the missing statement.

CHAPTER 7

CAT Paper 2023 (Slot 1) VARC Section Questions and Solutions

Comprehension:

The passage below is accompanied by four questions. Based on the passage, choose the best answer for each question.

RESIDENTS of Lozère, a hilly department in southern France, recite complaints familiar to many rural corners of Europe. In remote hamlets and villages, with names such as Le Bacon and Le Bacon Vieux, mayors grumble about a lack of local schools, jobs, or phone and internet connections. Farmers of grazing animals add another concern: the return of wolves. Eradicated from France last century, the predators are gradually creeping back to more forests and hillsides. "The wolf must be taken in hand," said an aspiring parliamentarian, Francis Palombi, when pressed by voters in an election campaign early this summer. Tourists enjoy visiting a wolf park in Lozère, but farmers fret over their livestock and their livelihoods. . . .

As early as the ninth century, the royal office of the Luparii–wolf-catchers–was created in France to tackle the predators. Those official hunters (and others) completed their job in the 1930s, when the last wolf disappeared from the mainland. Active hunting and improved technology such as rifles in the 19th century, plus the use of poison such as strychnine later on, caused the population collapse. But in the early 1990s the animals reappeared. They crossed the Alps from Italy, upsetting sheep farmers on the French side of the border. Wolves have since spread to areas such as Lozère, delighting environmentalists, who see the predators' presence as a sign of wider ecological health. Farmers, who say the wolves cause the deaths of thousands of sheep and other grazing animals, are less cheerful. They grumble that green activists and politically correct urban types have allowed the return of an old enemy.

Various factors explain the changes of the past few decades. Rural depopulation is part of the story. In Lozère, for example, farming and a once-flourishing mining industry supported a population of over 140,000 residents in the mid-19th century. Today the department has fewer than 80,000 people, many in its towns. As humans withdraw, forests are expanding. In France, between 1990 and 2015, forest cover increased by an average of 102,000 hectares each year, as more fields were given over to trees. Now, nearly one-third of mainland France is covered by woodland of some sort. The decline of hunting as a sport also means more forests fall quiet. In the mid-to-late 20th century over 2m hunters regularly spent winter weekends tramping in woodland, seeking boars, birds and other prey. Today the Fédération Nationale des Chasseurs, the national body, claims 1.1m people hold hunting licences, though the number of active hunters is probably lower. The mostly protected status of the wolf in Europe–hunting them is now forbidden, other than when occasional culls are sanctioned by the state–plus the efforts of NGOs to track and count the animals, also contribute to the recovery of wolf populations.

As the lupine population of Europe spreads westwards, with occasional reports of wolves seen closer to urban areas, expect to hear of more clashes between farmers and those who celebrate the predators' return. Farmers' losses are real, but are not the only economic story. Tourist venues, such as parks where wolves are kept and the animals' spread is discussed, also generate income and jobs in rural areas.

Q1. Which one of the following has NOT contributed to the growing wolf population in Lozère?

(a) The shutting down of the royal office of the Luparii.

(b) A decline in the rural population of Lozère.

(c) An increase in woodlands and forest cover in Lozère.

(d) The granting of a protected status to wolves in Europe.

Q2. The author presents a possible economic solution to an existing issue facing Lozère that takes into account the divergent and competing interests of:

(a) tourists and environmentalists.

(b) environmentalists and politicians.

(c) politicians and farmers.

(d) farmers and environmentalists.

Q3. Which one of the following statements, if true, would weaken the author's claims?

(a) The old mining sites of Lozère are now being used as grazing pastures for sheep.

(b) Wolf attacks on tourists in Lozère are on the rise.

(c) Unemployment concerns the residents of Lozère.

(d) Having migrated out in the last century, wolves are now returning to Lozère.

Q4. The inhabitants of Lozère have to grapple with all of the following problems, EXCEPT:

(a) poor rural communication infrastructure.

(b) lack of educational facilities.

(c) decline in the number of hunting licences.

(d) livestock losses.

Comprehension:

The passage below is accompanied by four questions. Based on the passage, choose the best answer for each question.

For early postcolonial literature, the world of the novel was often the nation. Postcolonial novels were usually [concerned with] national questions. Sometimes the whole story of the novel was taken as an allegory of the nation, whether India or Tanzania. This was important for supporting anti-colonial nationalism, but could also be limiting - land-focused and inward - looking.

My new book "Writing Ocean Worlds" explores another kind of world of the novel: not the village or nation, but the Indian Ocean world. The book describes a set of novels in which the Indian Ocean is at the centre of the story. It focuses on the novelists Amitav Ghosh, Abdulrazak Gurnah, Lindsey Collen and Joseph Conrad [who have] centred the Indian Ocean world in the majority of their novels. ...... Their work reveals a world that is outward-looking - full of movement, border-crossing and south-south interconnection. They are all very different - from colonially inclined (Conrad) to radically anti-capitalist (Collen), but together draw on and shape a wider sense of Indian Ocean space through themes, images, metaphors and language. This has the effect of remapping the world in the reader's mind, as centred in the interconnected global south. . . .

The Indian Ocean world is a term used to describe the very long-lasting connections among the coasts of East Africa, the Arab coasts, and South and East Asia. These connections were made possible by the geography of the Indian Ocean. For much of history, travel by sea was much easier than by land, which meant that port cities very far apart were often more easily connected to each other than to much closer inland cities. Historical and archaeological evidence suggests that what we now call globalisation first appeared in the Indian Ocean. This is the interconnected oceanic world referenced and produced by the novels in my book.

For their part Ghosh, Gurnah, Collen and even Conrad reference a different set of histories and geographies than the ones most commonly found in fiction in English. Those [commonly found ones] are mostly centred in Europe or the US, assume a background of Christianity and whiteness, and mention places like Paris and New York. The novels in [my] book highlight instead a largely Islamic space, feature characters of colour and centralise the ports of Malindi, Mombasa, Aden, Java and Bombay. . . . It is a densely imagined, richly sensory image of a southern cosmopolitan culture which provides for an enlarged sense of place in the world.

This remapping is particularly powerful for the representation of Africa. In the fiction, sailors and travellers are not all European. . . . African, as well as Indian and Arab characters, are traders, nakhodas (dhow ship captains), runaways, villains, missionaries and activists. This does not mean that Indian Ocean Africa is romanticised. Migration is often a matter of force; travel is portrayed as abandonment rather than adventure, freedoms are kept from women and slavery is rife. What it does mean is that the African part of the Indian Ocean world plays an active role in its long, rich history and therefore in that of the wider world.

Q5. All of the following claims contribute to the "remapping" discussed by the passage, EXCEPT:

(a) the global south, as opposed to the global north, was the first centre of globalisation.

(b) the world of early international trade and commerce was not the sole domain of white Europeans.

(c) Indian Ocean novels have gone beyond the specifics of national concerns to explore rich regional pasts.

(d) cosmopolitanism originated in the West and travelled to the East through globalisation.

Q6. All of the following statements, if true, would weaken the passage's claim about the relationship between mainstream English-language fiction and Indian Ocean novels EXCEPT:

(a) most mainstream English-language novels have historically privileged the Christian, white, male experience of travel and adventure.
(b) the depiction of Africa in most Indian Ocean novels is driven by an Orientalist imagination of its cultural crudeness.
(c) the depiction of Africa in most Indian Ocean novels is driven by a postcolonial nostalgia for an idyllic past.
(d) very few mainstream English-language novels have historically been set in American and European metropolitan centres.

Q7. Which one of the following statements is not true about migration in the Indian Ocean world?

(a) The Indian Ocean world's migration networks connected the global north with the global south.
(b) The Indian Ocean world's migration networks were shaped by religious and commercial histories of the region.
(c) Geographical location rather than geographical proximity determined the choice of destination for migrants.
(d) Migration in the Indian Ocean world was an ambivalent experience.

Q8. On the basis of the nature of the relationship between the items in each pair below, choose the odd pair out:

(a) Postcolonial novels : Anti-colonial nationalism
(b) Indian Ocean novels : Outward-looking
(c) Postcolonial novels : Border-crossing
(d) Indian Ocean world : Slavery

Comprehension:

The passage below is accompanied by four questions. Based on the passage, choose the best answer for each question.

[Fifty] years after its publication in English [in 1972], and just a year since [Marshall] Sahlins himself died– we may ask: why did [his essay] "Original Affluent Society" have such an impact, and how has it fared since? . . . Sahlins's principal argument was simple but counterintuitive: before being driven into marginal environments by colonial powers, hunter- gatherers, or foragers, were not engaged in a desperate struggle for meager survival. Quite the contrary, they satisfied their needs with far less work than people in agricultural and industrial societies, leaving them more time to use as they wished. Hunters, he quipped, keep bankers' hours. Refusing to maximize, many were "more concerned with games of chance than with chances of game." . . . The so-called Neolithic Revolution, rather than improving life, imposed a harsher work regime and set in motion the long history of growing inequality . . .

Moreover, foragers had other options. The contemporary Hadza of Tanzania, who had long been surrounded by farmers, knew they had alternatives and rejected them. To Sahlins, this showed that foragers are not simply examples of human diversity or victimhood but something more profound: they demonstrated that societies make real choices. Culture, a way of living oriented around a distinctive set of values, manifests a fundamental principle of collective self-determination. . . .

But the point [of the essay] is not so much the empirical validity of the data–the real interest for most readers, after all, is not in foragers either today or in the Paleolithic–but rather its conceptual challenge to contemporary economic life and bourgeois individualism. The empirical served a philosophical and political project, a thought experiment and stimulus to the imagination of possibilities.

With its title's nod toward *The Affluent Society* (1958), economist John Kenneth Galbraith's famously skeptical portrait of America's postwar prosperity and inequality, and dripping with New Left contempt for consumerism, "The Original Affluent Society" brought this critical perspective to bear on the contemporary world. It did so through the classic anthropological move of showing that radical alternatives to the readers' lives really exist. If the capitalist world seeks wealth through ever greater material production to meet infinitely expansive desires, foraging societies follow "the Zen road to affluence": not by getting more, but by wanting less. If it seems that foragers have been left behind by "progress," this is due only to the ethnocentric self-congratulation of the West. Rather than accumulate material goods, these societies are guided by other values: leisure, mobility, and above all, freedom.

Viewed in today's context, of course, not every aspect of the essay has aged well. While acknowledging the violence of colonialism, racism, and dispossession, it does not thematize them as heavily as we might today. Rebuking evolutionary anthropologists for treating present-day foragers as "left behind" by progress, it too can succumb to the temptation to use them as proxies for the Paleolithic. Yet these characteristics should not distract us from appreciating Sahlins's effort to show that if we want to conjure new possibilities, we need to learn about actually inhabitable worlds.

Q9. The author mentions Tanzania's Hadza community to illustrate:

(a) that forager communities' lifestyles derived not from ignorance about alternatives, but from their own choice.
(b) that hunter-gatherer communities' subsistence-level techniques equipped them to survive well into contemporary times.
(c) how pre-agrarian societies did not hamper the emergence of more advanced agrarian practices in contiguous communities.
(d) how two vastly different ways of living and working were able to coexist in proximity for centuries.

Q10. The author of the passage criticises Sahlins's essay for its:

(a) cursory treatment of the effects of racism and colonialism on societies.
(b) critique of anthropologists who disparage the choices of foragers in today's society.
(c) outdated values regarding present-day foragers versus ancient foraging communities.
(d) failure to supplement its thesis with robust empirical data.

Q11. We can infer that Sahlins's main goal in writing his essay was to:

(a) counter Galbraith's pessimistic view of the inevitability of a capitalist trajectory for economic growth.
(b) highlight the fact that while we started off as a fairly contented egalitarian people, we have progressively degenerated into materialism.
(c) hold a mirror to an acquisitive society, with examples of other communities that have chosen successfully to be non-materialistic.
(d) put forth the view that, despite egalitarian origins, economic progress brings greater inequality and social hierarchies.

Q12. The author of the passage mentions Galbraith's "The Affluent Society" to:

(a) contrast the materialist nature of contemporary growth paths with the pacifist content ways of living among the foragers.
(b) show how Sahlins's views complemented Galbraith's criticism of the consumerism and inequality of contemporary society.
(c) document the influence of Galbraith's cynical views on modern consumerism on Sahlins's analysis of pre-historic societies.
(d) show how Galbraith's theories refute Sahlins's thesis on the contentment of pre-hunter-gatherer communities.

Comprehension:

The passage below is accompanied by four questions. Based on the passage, choose the best answer for each question.

Many human phenomena and characteristics – such as behaviors, beliefs, economies, genes, incomes, life expectancies, and other things – are influenced both by geographic factors and by non-geographic factors. Geographic factors mean physical and biological factors tied to geographic location, including climate, the distributions of wild plant and animal species, soils, and topography. Non-geographic factors include those factors subsumed under the term culture, other factors subsumed under the term history, and decisions by individual people. . . .

[T]he differences between the current economies of North and South Korea . . . cannot be attributed to the modest environmental differences between [them] . . . They are instead due entirely to the different [government] policies . . . At the opposite extreme, the Inuit and other traditional peoples living north of the Arctic Circle developed warm fur clothes but no agriculture, while equatorial lowland peoples around the world never developed warm fur clothes but often did develop agriculture. The explanation is straightforwardly geographic, rather than a cultural or historical quirk unrelated to geography......Aboriginal Australia remained the sole continent occupied only by hunter/gatherers and with no indigenous farming or herding ...... [Here the] explanation is biogeographic: the Australian continent has no domesticable native animal species and few domesticable native plant species. Instead, the crops and domestic animals that now make Australia a food and wool exporter are all non-native (mainly Eurasian) species such as sheep, wheat, and grapes, brought to Australia by overseas colonists.

Today, no scholar would be silly enough to deny that culture, history, and individual choices play a big role in many human phenomena. Scholars don't react to cultural, historical, and individual-agent explanations by denouncing "cultural determinism," "historical determinism," or "individual determinism," and then thinking no further. But many scholars do react to any explanation invoking some geographic role, by denouncing "geographic determinism" . . .

Several reasons may underlie this widespread but nonsensical view. One reason is that some geographic explanations advanced a century ago were racist, thereby causing all geographic explanations to become tainted by racist associations in the minds of many scholars other than geographers. But many genetic, historical, psychological, and anthropological explanations advanced a century ago were also racist, yet the validity of newer non-racist genetic etc. explanations is widely accepted today.

Another reason for reflex rejection of geographic explanations is that historians have a tradition, in their discipline, of stressing the role of contingency (a favorite word among historians) based on individual decisions and chance. Often that view is warranted. . . . But often, too, that view is unwarranted. The development of warm fur clothes among the Inuit living north of the Arctic Circle was not because one influential Inuit leader persuaded other Inuit in 1783 to adopt warm fur clothes, for no good environmental reason.

A third reason is that geographic explanations usually depend on detailed technical facts of geography and other fields of scholarship. . . . Most historians and economists don't acquire that detailed knowledge as part of the professional training.

Q13. All of the following can be inferred from the passage EXCEPT:

(a) agricultural practices changed drastically in the Australian continent after it was colonised.

(b) while most human phenomena result from culture and individual choice, some have bio-geographic origins.

(c) several academic studies of human phenomena in the past involved racist interpretations.

(d) individual dictat and contingency were not the causal factors for the use of fur clothing in some very cold climates.

Q14. The examples of the Inuit and Aboriginal Australians are offered in the passage to show:

(a) how environmental factors lead to comparatively divergent paths in livelihoods and development.

(b) human resourcefulness across cultures in adapting to their surroundings.

(c) how physical circumstances can dictate human behaviour and cultures.

(d) that despite geographical isolation, traditional societies were self-sufficient and adaptive.

Q15. All of the following are advanced by the author as reasons why non-geographers disregard geographic influences on human phenomena EXCEPT their:

(a) disciplinary training which typically does not include technical knowledge of geography.

(b) belief in the central role of humans, unrelated to physical surroundings, in influencing phenomena.

(c) dismissal of explanations that involve geographical causes for human behaviour.

(d) lingering impressions of past geographic analyses that were politically offensive.

Q16. The author criticises scholars who are not geographers for all of the following reasons EXCEPT:

(a) their labelling of geographic explanations as deterministic.

(b) their rejection of the role of biogeographic factors in social and cultural phenomena.

(c) the importance they place on the role of individual decisions when studying human phenomena.

(d) their outdated interpretations of past cultural and historical phenomena.

Q17. There is a sentence that is missing in the paragraph below. Look at the paragraph and decide where (option 1, 2, 3, or 4) the following sentence would best fit.

Sentence: This philosophical cut at one's core beliefs, values, and way of life is difficult enough.
Paragraph: The experience of reading philosophy is often disquieting. When reading philosophy, the values around which one has heretofore organised one's life may come to look provincial, flatly wrong, or even evil. __(1)__. When beliefs previously held as truths are rendered implausible, new beliefs, values, and ways of living may be required. __(2)__. What's worse, philosophers admonish each other to remain unsutured until such time as a defensible new answer is revealed or constructed. Sometimes philosophical writing is even strictly critical in that it does not even attempt to provide an alternative after tearing down a cultural or conceptual citadel. __(3)__. The reader of philosophy must be prepared for the possibility of this experience. While reading philosophy can help one clarify one's values, and even make one self-conscious for the first time of the fact that there are good reasons for believing what one believes, it can also generate unremediated doubt that is difficult to live with. __(4)__.

(a) Option 4
(b) Option 3
(c) Option 1
(d) Option 2

Q18. There is a sentence that is missing in the paragraph below. Look at the paragraph and decide where (option 1, 2, 3, or 4) the following sentence would best fit.

Sentence: The discovery helps to explain archeological similarities between the Paleolithic peoples of China, Japan, and the Americas.
Paragraph: The researchers also uncovered an unexpected genetic link between Native Americans

and Japanese people. __(1)__. During the deglaciation period, another group branched out from northern coastal China and travelled to Japan. __(2)__. "We were surprised to find that this ancestral source also contributed to the Japanese gene pool, especially the indigenous Ainus," says Li. __(3)__. They shared similarities in how they crafted stemmed projectile points for arrowheads and spears. __(4)__. "This suggests that the Pleistocene connection among the Americas, China, and Japan was not confined to culture but also to genetics," says senior author Qing-Peng Kong, an evolutionary geneticist at the Chinese Academy of Sciences.

(a) Option 3 (b) Option 4
(c) Option 1 (d) Option 2

Q19. Five jumbled up sentences [labelled (a), (b), (c), (d) and (e)], related to a topic, are given below. Four of them can be put together to form a coherent paragraph. Identify the odd sentence and key in the number of that sentence as your answer.

(a) In English, there is no systematic rule for the naming of numbers; after ten, we have "eleven" and "twelve" and then the teens: "thirteen", "fourteen", "fifteen" and so on.

(b) Even more confusingly, some English words invert the numbers they refer to: the word "fourteen" puts the four first, even though it appears last.

(c) It can take children a while to learn all these words, and understand that "fourteen" is different from "forty".

(d) For multiples of 10, English speakers switch to a different pattern: "twenty", "thirty", "forty" and so on.

(e) If you didn't know the word for "eleven", you would be unable to just guess it - you might come up with something like "one-teen".

Q20. Five jumbled up sentences [labelled (a), (b), (c), (d) and (e)], related to a topic, are given below. Four of them can be put together to form a coherent paragraph. Identify the odd sentence and key in the number of that sentence as your answer.

(a) Having an appreciation for the workings of another person's mind is considered a prerequisite for natural language acquisition, strategic social interaction, reflexive thought, and moral judgment.

(b) It is a 'theory of mind' though some scholars prefer to call it 'mentalizing' or 'mindreading', which is important for the development of one's cognitive abilities.

(c) Though we must speculate about its evolutionary origin, we do have indications that the capacity evolved sometime in the last few million years.

(d) This capacity develops from early beginnings in the first year of life to the adult's fast and often effortless understanding of others' thoughts, feelings, and intentions.

(e) One of the most fascinating human capacities is the ability to perceive and interpret other people's behaviour in terms of their mental states.

Q21. The four sentences [labelled (a), (b), (c) and (d)] given below, when properly sequenced, would yield a coherent paragraph. Decide on the proper sequencing of the order of the sentences and key in the sequence of the four numbers as your answer.

(a) What precisely are the "unusual elements" that make a particular case so attractive to a certain kind of audience?

(b) It might be a particularly savage or unfathomable level of depravity, very often it has something to do with the precise amount of mystery involved.

(c) Unsolved, and perhaps unsolvable cases offer something that "ordinary" murder doesn't.

(d) Why are some crimes destined for perpetual re-examination and others locked into permanent obscurity?

Q22. The four sentences [labelled (a), (b), (c) and (d)] given below, when properly sequenced, would yield a coherent paragraph. Decide on the proper sequencing of the order of the sentences and key in the sequence of the four numbers as your answer.

(a) Algorithms hosted on the internet are accessed by many, so biases in AI models have resulted in much larger impact, adversely affecting far larger groups of people.

(b) Though "algorithmic bias" is the popular term, the foundation of such bias is not in algorithms, but in the data; algorithms are not biased, data is, as algorithms merely reflect persistent patterns that are present in the training data.

(c) Despite their widespread impact, it is relatively easier to fix AI biases than human-generated biases, as it is simpler to identify the former than to try to make people unlearn behaviors learnt over generations.

(d) The impact of biased decisions made by humans is localised and geographically confined, but with the advent of AI, the impact of such decisions is spread over a much wider scale.

Q23. The passage given below is followed by four alternate summaries. Choose the option that best captures the essence of the passage.

Manipulating information was a feature of history long before modern journalism established rules of integrity. A record dates back to ancient Rome, when Antony met Cleopatra and his political enemy Octavian launched a smear campaign against him with "short, sharp slogans written upon coins." The perpetrator became the first Roman Emperor and "fake news had allowed Octavian to hack the republican system once and for all". But the 21st century has seen the weaponization of information on an unprecedented scale. Powerful new technology makes the fabrication of content simple, and social networks amplify falsehoods peddled by States, populist politicians, and dishonest corporate entities. The platforms have become fertile ground for computational propaganda, 'trolling' and 'troll armies'.

(a) Disinformation, which is mediated by technology today, is not new and has existed since ancient times.

(b) People need to become critical of what they read, since historically, weaponization of information has led to corruption.

(a) Use of misinformation for attaining power, a practice that is as old as the Octavian era, is currently fueled by technology.

(a) Octavian used fake news to manipulate people and attain power and influence, just as people do today.

Q24. The passage given below is followed by four alternate summaries. Choose the option that best captures the essence of the passage.

Colonialism is not a modern phenomenon. World history is full of examples of one society gradually expanding by incorporating adjacent territory and settling its people on newly conquered territory. In the sixteenth century, colonialism changed decisively because of technological developments in navigation that began to connect more remote parts of the world. The modern European colonial project emerged when it became possible to move large numbers of people across the ocean and to maintain political control in spite of geographical dispersion. The term colonialism is used to describe the process of European settlement, violent dispossession and political domination over the rest of the world, including the Americas, Australia, and parts of Africa and Asia.

(a) Technological advancements in navigation in the 16th century, transformed colonialism, enabling Europeans to establish settlements and exert political dominance over distant regions.

(b) Colonialism, conceptualized in the 16th century, allowed colonizers to expand their territories, establish settlements, and exercise political power.

(c) Colonialism surged in the 16th century due to advancements in navigation, enabling British settlements abroad and global dominance.

(d) As a result of developments in navigation technology, European colonialism, led to the displacement of indigenous populations and global political changes in the 16th century.

Answer Key

1. (a)	**2.** (d)	**3.** (b)	**4.** (c)	**5.** (d)
6. (a)	**7.** (a)	**8.** (c)	**9.** (a)	**10.** (a)
11. (c)	**12.** (b)	**13.** (b)	**14.** (c)	**15.** (c)
16. (d)	**17.** (d)	**18.** (a)	**19.** (c)	**20.** (b)
21. (d, a, b, c)		**22.** (d, a, b, c)		**23.** (c)
24. (a)				

Explanations

1. Option (a) is the correct answer.
The closing of the royal office cannot be said to contribute to the growth of the growing population of wolves because the office was never directly related to the growth of the wolves; rather, they had finished their job of hunting them down.
Options (b), (c) and (d) are directly mentioned as related to the reasons for the growth.

2. Option (d) is the correct answer.

If you see the last paragraph it mentions the competing interests of the "clashes between farmers and those who celebrate the predators' return", which means farmers and environmentalists.

3. Option (b) is correct.

The passage clearly mentions options (a), (c) and (d); but if option (b) was correct then it would go against the claims of the author about the positives related to the wolves' return. Hence, option (b) is correct.

4. Option (c) is correct.

The problems about communication and educational facilities are mentioned in the first paragraph.

Livestock and cattle losses are clearly mentioned as the problem. The option (c) talking about the decline in the licenses for killing is just mentioned as a factual data and not as a problem that the people have to deal with.

5. Option (d) is correct.

Here we have to find an option which is not contributing to the remapping as suggested in the last paragraph.
Options (a), (b) and (c) are talking about the remapping in terms of the trade, the globalization and exploration of the rich regional past.
The 4th option says that cosmopolitanism [which is an aspect of globalization] originated in the west, and this is totally opposite to the thought of the passage.

6. Option (a) is correct.

The passage's claim about the relationship between mainstream English-language fiction and Indian Ocean novels has always been that it has been written from a western perspective. If we use any of the options (b), (c) and (d), it would weaken the claim of the passage as it is against what he has said.
Here as the right answer we have to find the exception, which is option (a) and is totally in sync with what the author claims and so it will strengthen rather than weaken the claim.
Hence, option (a) is correct.

7. Option (a) is correct.

The passage never states or hints that the Indian Ocean travel or migration connected the north and south; hence, option (a) is the answer which states that.
Option (b) is stated in the passage in the following lines "For their part Ghosh, Gurnah, Collen and even Conrad reference a different set of histories and geographies than the ones most commonly found in fiction in English. Those [commonly found ones] are mostly centred in Europe or the US, assume a background of Christianity and whiteness, and mention places like Paris and New York. The novels in [my] book highlight instead a largely Islamic space, feature characters of colour".
Option (c) is stated in the following lines: "For much of history, travel by sea was much easier than by land, which meant that port cities very far apart were often more easily connected to each other than to much closer inland cities"
Option (d) is stated in the line: "Migration is often a matter of force"

8. Option (c).

If we check in the passage post-colonial novels were not connected with border crossing, rather they were connected with "the world of the nation". See the lines: "For early postcolonial literature, the world of the novel was often the nation. Postcolonial novels were usually [concerned with] national questions."

9. Option (a).

The answer is clear from these lines from the passage: "Moreover, foragers had other options. The contemporary Hadza of Tanzania, who had long been surrounded by farmers, knew they had alternatives and rejected them. To Sahlins, this showed that foragers are not simply examples of human diversity or victimhood but something more profound: they demonstrated that societies make real choices.".

10. Option (a) is correct.

The answer is evident from the last paragraph from the following lines: "Viewed in today's context, of course, not every aspect of the essay has aged well. While acknowledging the violence of colonialism, racism, and dispossession, it does not thematize them as heavily as we might today."

11. Option (c) is correct.

The following lines show that option (c) is correct: ""The Original Affluent Society" brought this critical perspective to bear on the contemporary world. It did so through the classic anthropological move of showing that radical alternatives to the readers' lives really exist. If the capitalist world seeks wealth through ever greater material production to meet infinitely expansive desires, foraging societies follow "the Zen road to affluence": not by getting more, but by wanting less."
Option (b) is incorrect. The passage never mentions that foragers had an 'egalitarian' society. Nor does the essay, according to the passage, state that we have 'progressively degenerated' into materialism.
Option (d) implies that, according to Sahlins' essay, economic progress had egalitarian origins. This is incorrect.
The passage states that the title of Sahlins' essay is a 'nod toward' Galbraith's work. That is, Sahlin concurs with Galbraith. So, option (a) is also incorrect.

12. Option (b) is correct.

The following lines show that option (b) is correct. "With its title's nod toward *The Affluent Society* (1958), economist John Kenneth Galbraith's famously skeptical portrait of America's postwar prosperity and inequality, and dripping with New Left contempt for consumerism, "The Original Affluent Society" brought this critical perspective to bear on the contemporary world. Its "title's nod" means he was in agreement with Galbraith.
He was not influenced with Galbraith hence, option (c) is incorrect.

13. Option (b) is correct.

The passage does not mention or hint that 'most' human phenomena are a result of culture and individual choice and only some by biogeographic factors. The theme of the passage is that human phenomena are influenced both by geographic factors and by non-geographic factors and that underestimating geographic determinism is not right.

The use of the word 'most' here exaggerates the option and thus it cannot be inferred,

hence it is the right answer.

The other options (a), (c) and (d) are clearly understood from the passage.

14. Option (c) is correct.

The following lines clearly make option (c) as the correct choice: "At the opposite extreme, the Inuit and other traditional peoples living north of the Arctic Circle developed warm fur clothes but no agriculture, while equatorial lowland peoples around the world never developed warm fur clothes but often did develop agriculture. The explanation is straightforwardly geographic, rather than a cultural or historical quirk unrelated to geography"

15. Option (c) is correct.

Since options (a), (b) and (d) are clearly mentioned in the passage in the following lines : 'One reason is that some geographic explanations advanced a century ago were racist, thereby causing all geographic explanations to become tainted by racist associations in the minds of many scholars other than geographers. But many genetic, historical, psychological, and anthropological explanations advanced a century ago were also racist, yet the validity of newer non-racist genetic etc. explanations is widely accepted today. Another reason for reflex rejection of geographic explanations is that historians have a tradition, in their discipline, of stressing the role of contingency (a favorite word among historians) based on individual decisions and chance. Often that view is warranted . . . But often, too, that view is unwarranted.'....it is clear that these options cannot be the answer.

Option (c) is not mentioned or hinted in the passage; hence it is correct.

16. Option (d) is correct.

The non-geographer scholars are not criticised in the passage by the author for using outdated interpretations; hence, option (d) is correct.

All the other options are in agreement with the passage.

17. Option (d), which is the 2nd blank is correct.

The original paragraph states "The experience of reading philosophy is often disquieting. When reading philosophy, the values around which one has heretofore organised one's life may come to look provincial, flatly wrong, or even evil. When beliefs previously held as truths are rendered implausible, new beliefs, values, and ways of living may be required. This philosophical cut at one's core beliefs, values, and way of life is difficult enough. What's worse, philosophers admonish each other to remain unsutured until such time as a defensible new answer is revealed or constructed. Sometimes philosophical writing is even strictly critical in that it does not even attempt to provide an alternative after tearing down a cultural or conceptual citadel. The reader of philosophy must be prepared for the possibility of this experience. While reading philosophy can help one clarify one's values, and even make one self-conscious for the first time of the fact that there are good reasons for believing what one believes, it can also generate unremediated doubt that is difficult to live with."

If we see the deleted statement which says:

"This philosophical cut at one's core beliefs, values, and way of life is difficult enough". . .

This sentence is clearly linked with the lines after blank 2 . . . which states . . .

"What's worse, philosophers admonish each other to remain unsutured until such time as a defensible new answer is revealed or constructed"

The "what's worse" phrase is clearly a link with the deleted statement.

18. The third blank is correct, hence option (a) which denotes the third blank is the answer.

If you see the original paragraph: "The researchers also uncovered an unexpected genetic link between Native Americans and Japanese people. During the deglaciation period, another group branched out from northern coastal China and traveled to Japan. "We were surprised to find that this ancestral source also contributed to the Japanese gene pool, especially the indigenous Ainus," says Li. This discovery helps to explain archeological similarities between the Paleolithic peoples of China, Japan, and the Americas. Specifically, the three regions share similarities in how they crafted stemmed projectile points for arrowheads and spears. "This suggests that the Pleistocene connection among the Americas, China, and Japan was not confined to culture but also to genetics," says senior author Qing-Peng Kong, an evolutionary geneticist at the Chinese Academy of Sciences."

The given statement talks about the discovery and the sentence before it talks about how the groups went from China to Japan; hence, blank 3 is the right place to put the missing statement.

19. Option (c) is the answer.

In the other sentences the mentioned numbers are 10, 11, 12, 13, 14 and so on. In statement (c), suddenly a comparison is made with 40 which seems a little odd; hence, the irrelevant statement is statement (c).

20. Option (b) is the answer.

Sentence (e) mentions 'the ability to perceive and interpret other people's behaviour in terms of their mental states' and this looks clearly as the starting sentence of the paragraph. Sentence (d) follows (e) as it relates to how 'this capacity' develops. Sentence (a) follows (d), explaining how this capacity is useful and sentence (c) ends the paragraph saying when this capacity evolved. So, the correct sequence is (e), (d), (a), (c).

Sentence (b) is irrelevant as the point mentioned about the theory of the mind which is more generic in nature than the other sentences talking about the ability or capacity.

21. (d), (a), (b), (c) is the correct sequence.

(d) is clearly the starting sentence which is introducing the theme as a question, sentence (a) takes the question forward. Sentence (c) is the concluding sentence and since sentence (b) gives the answer, it has to come before (c) and after (a). Hence, the correct sequence is (d), (a), (b), (c).

22. (d), (a), (b), (c) is the correct sequence.

(d) is the starting idea and (a) clearly follows it explaining the impact.

(c) has to come at the end as it is comparing the biases between humans and AI. (b) will come before (c) and after (a) as it continues the idea of (a). Thus, (d), (a), (b), (c) is the correct sequence.

23. Option (c) is correct.

The theme of the paragraph is that technology is used to carry manipulated information in today's world in an unprecedented scale and that manipulation of information for gains is as old as the Octavian times.

Option (c) has both the points which make it the most suitable summary.

24. Option (a) is correct.

The paragraph mentions that colonialism is not a modern phenomenon but it has surely changed in the sixteenth century due to technological developments in navigation, which enabled Europeans to make their settlements and create political control over the other parts of the world.

Option (a) is the best as it has most of the points.

Option (c) mentions about 'British' settlements, but the paragraph talks more generally about European settlements.

Option (d) refers only to 'European colonialism' and does not mention that colonialism as such is not a modern phenomenon or one restricted to Europe.

Option (b) is incorrect as it states that colonialism was conceptualized in the 16th century, which is not mentioned or implied in the passage.

CHAPTER 8

CAT Paper 2023 (Slot 2) VARC Section Questions and Solutions

Comprehension:

The passage below is accompanied by four questions. Based on the passage, choose the best answer for each question.

The Second Hand September campaign, led by Oxfam . . . seeks to encourage shopping at local organisations and charities as alternatives to fast fashion brands such as Primark and Boohoo in the name of saving our planet. As innocent as mindless scrolling through online shops may seem, such consumers are unintentionally – or perhaps even knowingly – contributing to an industry that uses more energy than aviation. . . .

Brits buy more garments than any other country in Europe, so it comes as no shock that many of those clothes end up in UK landfills each year: 300,000 tonnes of them, to be exact. This waste of clothing is destructive to our planet, releasing greenhouse gasses as clothes are burnt as well as bleeding toxins and dyes into the surrounding soil and water. As ecologist Chelsea Rochman bluntly put it, "The mismanagement of our waste has even come back to haunt us on our dinner plate."

It's not surprising, then, that people are scrambling for a solution, the most common of which is second-hand shopping. Retailers selling consigned clothing are currently expanding at a rapid rate . . . If everyone bought just one used item in a year, it would save 449 million lbs of waste, equivalent to the weight of 1 million Polar bears. "Thrifting" has increasingly become a trendy practice. London is home to many second-hand, or more commonly coined 'vintage', shops across the city from Bayswater to Brixton.

So you're cool and you care about the planet; you've killed two birds with one stone. But do people simply purchase a second-hand item, flash it on Instagram with vintage and call it a day without considering whether what they are doing is actually effective?

According to a study commissioned by Patagonia, for instance, older clothes shed more microfibres. These can end up in our rivers and seas after just one wash due to the worn material, thus contributing to microfibre pollution. To break it down, the amount of microfibres released by laundering 100,000 fleece jackets is equivalent to as many as 11,900 plastic grocery bags, and up to 40 per cent of that ends up in our oceans. So where does this leave second-hand consumers? [They would be well advised to buy] high-quality items that shed less and last longer [as this] combats both microfibre pollution and excess garments ending up in landfills. . . .

Luxury brands would rather not circulate their latest season stock around the globe to be sold at a cheaper price, which is why companies like ThredUP, a US fashion resale marketplace, have not yet caught on in the UK. There will always be a market for consignment but there is also a whole generation of people who have been taught that only buying new products is the norm; second-hand luxury goods are not in their psyche. Ben Whitaker, director at Liquidation Firm B-Stock, told Prospect that unless recycling becomes cost-effective and filters into mass production, with the right technology to partner it, "high-end retailers would rather put brand before sustainability."

Q1. According to the author, companies like ThredUP have not caught on in the UK for all of the following reasons EXCEPT that:

(a) luxury brands do not like their product to be devalued.
(b) recycling is currently not financially attractive for luxury brands.
(c) the British don't buy second-hand clothing.
(d) luxury brands want to maintain their brand image.

Q2. he act of "thrifting", as described in the passage, can be considered ironic because it:

(a) is an anti-consumerist attitude.
(b) is not cost-effective for retailers.
(c) has created environmental problems.
(c) offers luxury clothing at cut-rate prices.

Q3. The central idea of the passage would be undermined if:

(a) second-hand stores sold only high-quality clothes.
(b) clothes were not thrown and burnt in landfills.
(c) Primark and Boohoo recycled their clothes for vintage stores.
(d) customers bought all their clothes online.

Q4. Based on the passage, we can infer that the opposite of fast fashion, 'slow fashion', would most likely refer to clothes that:

(a) do not shed microfibres.
(b) do not bleed toxins and dyes.
(c) are sold by genuine vintage stores.
(d) are of high quality and long lasting.

Comprehension:

The passage below is accompanied by four questions. Based on the passage, choose the best answer for each question.

Over the past four centuries liberalism has been so successful that it has driven all its opponents off the battlefield. Now it is disintegrating, destroyed by a mix of hubris and internal contradictions, according to Patrick Deneen, a professor of politics at the University of Notre Dame. Equality of opportunity has produced a new meritocratic aristocracy that has all the aloofness of the old aristocracy with none of its sense of noblesse oblige. Democracy has degenerated into a theatre of the absurd. And technological advances are reducing ever more areas of work into meaningless drudgery. "The gap between liberalism's claims about itself and the lived reality of the citizenry" is now so wide that "the lie can no longer be accepted," Mr Deneen writes. What better proof of this than the vision of 1,000 private planes whisking their occupants to Davos to discuss the question of "creating a shared future in a fragmented world"? . . .

Deneen does an impressive job of capturing the current mood of disillusionment, echoing left- wing complaints about rampant commercialism, right-wing complaints about narcissistic and bullying students, and general worries about atomisation and selfishness. But when he concludes that all this adds up to a failure of liberalism, is his argument convincing? . . . He argues that the essence of liberalism lies in freeing individuals from constraints. In fact, liberalism contains a wide range of intellectual traditions which provide different answers to the question of how to trade off the relative claims of rights and responsibilities, individual expression and social ties. . . . liberals experimented with a range of ideas from devolving power from the centre to creating national education systems.

Mr Deneen's fixation on the essence of liberalism leads to the second big problem of his book: his failure to recognise liberalism's ability to reform itself and address its internal problems. The late 19th century saw America suffering from many of the problems that are reappearing today, including the creation of a business aristocracy, the rise of vast companies, the corruption of politics and the sense that society was dividing into winners and losers. But a wide variety of reformers, working within the liberal tradition, tackled these problems head on. Theodore Roosevelt took on the trusts. Progressives cleaned up government corruption. University reformers modernised academic syllabuses and built ladders of opportunity. Rather than dying, liberalism reformed itself.

Mr Deneen is right to point out that the record of liberalism in recent years has been dismal. He is also right to assert that the world has much to learn from the premodern notions of liberty as self-mastery and self-denial. The biggest enemy of liberalism is not so much atomisation but old-fashioned greed, as members of the Davos elite pile their plates ever higher with perks and share options. But he is wrong to argue that the only way for people to liberate themselves from the contradictions of liberalism is "liberation from liberalism itself". The best way to read "Why Liberalism Failed" is not as a funeral oration but as a call to action: up your game, or else.

Q5. All of the following statements are evidence of the decline of liberalism today, EXCEPT:

(a) ". . . the creation of a business aristocracy, the rise of vast companies"
(b) "And technological advances are reducing ever more areas of work into meaningless drudgery."

(c) "'The gap between liberalism's claims about itself and the lived reality of the citizenry' is now so wide that 'the lie can no longer be accepted,'. . . . "

(d) "Democracy has degenerated into a theatre of the absurd."

Q6. The author of the passage refers to "the Davos elite" to illustrate his views on:

(a) the unlikelihood of a return to the liberalism of the past as long as the rich continue to benefit from the decline in liberal values.

(b) the hypocrisy of the liberal rich, who profess to subscribe to liberal values while cornering most of the wealth.

(c) the way the debate around liberalism has been captured by the rich who have managed to insulate themselves from economic hardships.

(d) the fact that the rise in liberalism had led to a greater interest in shared futures from unlikely social classes.

Q7. The author of the passage faults Deneen's conclusions for all of the following reasons, EXCEPT:

(a) its extreme pessimism about the future of liberalism today and predictions of an ultimate decline.

(b) its repeated harking back to premodern notions of liberty.

(c) its failure to note historical instances in which the process of declining liberalism has managed to reverse itself.

(d) its very narrow definition of liberalism limited to individual freedoms.

Q8. The author of the passage is likely to disagree with all of the following statements, EXCEPT:

(a) liberalism was the dominant ideal in the past century, but it had to reform itself to remain so.

(b) the essence of liberalism lies in greater individual self-expression and freedoms.

(c) claims about liberalism's disintegration are exaggerated and misunderstand its core features.

(d) if we accept that liberalism is a dying ideal, we must work to find a viable substitute.

Comprehension:

The passage below is accompanied by four questions. Based on the passage, choose the best answer for each question.

Umberto Eco, an Italian writer, was right when he said the language of Europe is translation. Netflix and other deep-pocketed global firms speak it well. Just as the EU employs a small army of translators and interpreters to turn intricate laws or impassioned speeches of Romanian MEPs into the EU's 24 official languages, so do the likes of Netflix. It now offers dubbing in 34 languages and subtitling in a few more. . . .

The economics of European productions are more appealing, too. American audiences are more willing than before to give dubbed or subtitled viewing a chance. This means shows such as "Lupin", a French crime caper on Netflix, can become global hits. . . . In 2015, about 75% of Netflix's original content was American; now the figure is half, according to Ampere, a media-analysis company. Netflix has about 100 productions under way in Europe, which is more than big public broadcasters in France or Germany. . . .

Not everything works across borders. Comedy sometimes struggles. Whodunits and bloodthirsty maelstroms between arch Romans and uppity tribesmen have a more universal appeal. Some do it better than others. Barbarians aside, German television is not always built for export, says one executive, being polite. A bigger problem is that national broadcasters still dominate. Streaming services, such as Netflix or Disney+, account for about a third of all viewing hours, even in markets where they are well-established. Europe is an ageing continent. The generation of teens staring at phones is outnumbered by their elders who prefer to gawp at the box.

In Brussels and national capitals, the prospect of Netflix as a cultural hegemon is seen as a threat. "Cultural sovereignty" is the watchword of European executives worried that the Americans will eat their lunch. To be fair, Netflix content sometimes seems stuck in an uncanny valley somewhere in the mid-Atlantic, with local quirks stripped out. Netflix originals tend to have fewer specific cultural references than shows produced by domestic rivals, according to Enders, a market analyst. The company used to have an imperial model of commissioning, with executives in Los Angeles cooking up ideas French people might like. Now Netflix has offices across Europe. But ultimately the big decisions rest with American executives. This makes European politicians nervous.

They should not be. An irony of European integration is that it is often American companies that facilitate it. Google Translate makes European newspapers comprehensible, even if a little clunky, for the continent's non-polyglots. American social-media companies make it easier for Europeans to talk politics across borders. (That they do not always like to hear what they say about each other is another matter.) Now Netflix and friends pump the same content into homes across a continent, making culture a cross-border endeavour, too. If Europeans are to share a currency, bail each other out in times of financial need and share vaccines in a pandemic, then they need to have something in common–even if it is just bingeing on the same series. Watching fictitious northern and southern Europeans tear each other apart 2,000 years ago beats doing so in reality.

Q9. Based only on information provided in the passage, which one of the following hypothetical Netflix shows would be most successful with audiences across the EU?

(a) A trans-Atlantic romantic drama set in Europe and America.

(b) A murder mystery drama set in North Africa and France.

(c) An Italian comedy show hosted by an international star.

(d) An original German TV science fiction production.

Q10. The author sees the rise of Netflix in Europe as:

(a)a looming cultural threat.

(b) a unifying force.

(c) filling an entertainment gap.

(d) an economic threat.

Q11. Which one of the following research findings would weaken the author's conclusion in the final paragraph?

(a) Research shows that Netflix hits produced in France are very popular with North American audiences.

(b) Research shows that Netflix has been gradually losing market share to other streaming television service providers.

(c) Research shows that older women across the EU enjoy watching romantic comedies on Netflix, whereas younger women prefer historical fiction dramas.

(d) Research shows there is a wide variance in the popularity and viewing of Netflix shows across different EU countries.

Q12. Based on information provided in the passage, all of the following are true, EXCEPT:

(a) national broadcasters dominate in the EU in terms of total television viewing hours.

(b) European television productions have the potential to become global hits.

(c) only half of Netflix's original programming in the EU is now produced in America.

(d) Netflix has been able to transform itself into a truly European entity.

Comprehension:

The passage below is accompanied by four questions. Based on the passage, choose the best answer for each question.

The Positivists, anxious to stake out their claim for history as a science, contributed the weight of their influence to the cult of facts. First ascertain the facts, said the positivists, then draw your conclusions from them. . . . This is what may [be] called the common-sense view of history. History consists of a corpus of ascertained facts. The facts are available to the historian in documents, inscriptions, and so on . . . [Sir George Clark] contrasted the "hard core of facts" in history with the surrounding pulp of disputable interpretation forgetting perhaps that the pulpy part of the fruit is more rewarding than the hard core. . . . It recalls the favourite dictum of the great liberal journalist C. P. Scott: "Facts are sacred, opinion is free.". .

What is a historical fact? . . . According to the common-sense view, there are certain basic facts which are the same for all historians and which form, so to speak, the backbone of history–the fact, for example, that the Battle of Hastings was fought in 1066. But this view calls for two observations. In the first place, it is not with facts like these that the historian is primarily concerned. It is no doubt important to know that the great battle was fought in 1066 and not in 1065 or 1067, and that it was fought at Hastings and not at Eastbourne or Brighton. The historian must not get these things wrong. But [to] praise a historian for his accuracy is like praising an architect for using well-seasoned timber or properly mixed concrete in his building. It is a necessary condition of his work, but not his essential function. It is precisely for matters of this kind that the historian is entitled to rely on what have been called the "auxiliary sciences" of history–archaeology, epigraphy, numismatics, chronology, and so forth. . . .

The second observation is that the necessity to establish these basic facts rests not on any quality in the facts themselves, but on an apriori decision of the historian. In spite of C. P. Scott's motto, every journalist knows today that the most effective way to influence opinion is by the selection and arrangement of the appropriate facts. It used to be said that facts speak for themselves. This is, of course, untrue. The facts speak only when the historian calls on them: it is he who decides to which facts to give the floor, and in what order or context. . . . The only reason why we are interested to know that the battle was fought at Hastings in 1066 is that historians regard it as a major historical event. . . . Professor Talcott Parsons once called [science] "a selective system of cognitive orientations to reality." It might perhaps have been put more simply. But history is, among other things, that. The historian is necessarily selective. The belief in a hard core of historical facts existing objectively and independently of the interpretation of the historian is a preposterous fallacy, but one which it is very hard to eradicate.

Q13. According to this passage, which one of the following statements best describes the significance of archaeology for historians?

(a) Archaeology helps historians to interpret historical facts.

(b) Archaeology helps historians to carry out their primary duty.

(c) Archaeology helps historians to ascertain factual accuracy.

(d) Archaeology helps historians to locate the oldest civilisations in history.

Q14. If the author of the passage were to write a book on the Battle of Hastings along the lines of his/her own reasoning, the focus of the historical account would be on:

(a) deriving historical facts from the relevant documents and inscriptions.

(b) producing a detailed timeline of the various events that led to the Battle.

(c) exploring the socio-political and economic factors that led to the Battle.

(d) providing a nuanced interpretation by relying on the auxiliary sciences.

Q15. All of the following describe the "common-sense view" of history, EXCEPT:

(a) history can be objective like the sciences if it is derived from historical facts.

(b) only the positivist methods can lead to credible historical knowledge.

(c) history is like science: a selective system of cognitive orientations to reality.

(d) real history can be found in ancient engravings and archival documents.

Q16. All of the following, if true, can weaken the passage's claim that facts do not speak for themselves, EXCEPT:

(a) a fact, by its very nature, is objective and universal, irrespective of the context in which it is placed.

(b) the order in which a series of facts is presented does not have any bearing on the production of meaning.

(c) facts, like truth, can be relative: what is fact for person X may not be so for person Y.

(d) the truth value of a fact is independent of the historian who expresses it.

Q17. There is a sentence that is missing in the paragraph below. Look at the paragraph and decide where (option 1, 2, 3, or 4) the following sentence would best fit.

Sentence: Dualism was long held as the defining feature of developing countries in contrast to developed countries, where frontier technologies and high productivity were assumed to prevail.

Paragraph: __(1)__. At the core of development economics lies the idea of 'productive dualism': that poor countries' economies are split between a narrow 'modern' sector that uses advanced technologies and a larger 'traditional' sector characterized by very low productivity.__(2)__. While this distinction between developing and advanced economies may have made some sense in the 1950s and 1960s, it no longer appears to be very relevant. A combination of forces have produced a widening gap between the winners and those left behind. __(3)__. Convergence between poor and rich parts of the economy was arrested and regional disparities widened. __(4)__. As a result, policymakers in advanced economies are now grappling with the same questions that have long preoccupied developing economies: mainly how to close the gap with the more advanced parts of the economy.

(a) Option 1

(b) Option 2

(c) Option 3

(d) Option 4

Q18. There is a sentence that is missing in the paragraph below. Look at the paragraph and decide where (option 1, 2, 3, or 4) the following sentence would best fit.

Sentence: And probably much earlier, moving the documentation for kissing back 1,000 years compared to what was acknowledged in the scientific community.

Paragraph: Research has hypothesised that the earliest evidence of human lip kissing originated in a very specific geographical location in South Asia 3,500 years ago.__(1)__. From there it may have spread to other regions, simultaneously accelerating the spread of the herpes simplex virus 1. According to Dr Troels Pank Arbøll and Dr Sophie Lund Rasmussen, who in a new article in the journal Science draw on a range of written sources from the earliest Mesopotamian societies, kissing was already a well-established practice 4,500 years ago in the Middle East. __(2)__. In ancient Mesopotamia, people wrote in cuneiform script on clay tablets. __(3)__. Many thousands of these clay tablets have survived to this day, and they contain clear examples that kissing was considered a part of romantic intimacy in ancient times. __(4)__. "Kissing could also have been part of friendships and family members' relations," says Dr Troels Pank Arbøll, an expert on the history of medicine in Mesopotamia.

(a) Option 2
(b) Option 1
(c) Option 4
(d) Option 3

Q19. Five jumbled up sentences [labelled (a), (b), (c), (d) and (e)], related to a topic, are given below. Four of them can be put together to form a coherent paragraph. Identify the odd sentence and key in the number of that sentence as your answer.

(a) The banning of Northern Lights could be considered a precursor to censoring books for "moral", world view or religious reasons.
(b) Attempts to ban books are attempts to silence authors who have summoned immense courage in telling their stories.
(c) Now the banning and challenging of books in the US has escalated to an unprecedented level.
(d) The widely acclaimed fantasy novel Northern Lights was banned in some parts of the US, and was the second most challenged book in the US.
(e) The American Library Association documented an unparalleled number of reported book challenges in 2022, about 2,500 unique titles.

Q20. Five jumbled up sentences [labelled (a), (b), (c), (d) and (e)], related to a topic, are given below. Four of them can be put together to form a coherent paragraph. Identify the odd sentence and key in the number of that sentence as your answer.

(a) Self-care particularly links to loneliness, behavioural problems, and negative academic outcomes.
(b) "Latchkey children" refers to children who routinely return home from school to empty homes and take care of themselves for extended periods of time.
(c) Although self-care generally points to negative outcomes, it is important to consider that the bulk of research has yet to track long-term consequences.
(d) In research and practice, the phrase "children in self-care" has come to replace latchkey in an effort to more accurately reflect the nature of their circumstances.
(e) Although parents might believe that self-care would be beneficial for development, recent research has found quite the opposite.

Q21. The four sentences [labelled (a), (b), (c) and (d)] given below, when properly sequenced, would yield a coherent paragraph. Decide on the proper sequencing of the order of the sentences and key in the sequence of the four numbers as your answer.

(a) Contemporary African writing like 'The Bottled Leopard' voices this theme using two children and two backgrounds to juxtapose two varying cultures.
(b) Chukwuemeka Ike explores the conflict, and casts the Western tradition as condescending, enveloping and unaccommodating towards local African practice.
(c) However, their views contradict the reality, for a rich and sustaining local African cultural ethos exists for all who care, to see and experience.
(d) Western Christian concepts tend to deny or feign ignorance about the existence of a genuine and enduring indigenous African tradition.

Q22. The four sentences [labelled (a), (b), (c) and (d)] given below, when properly sequenced, would yield a coherent paragraph. Decide on the proper sequencing of the order of the sentences and key in the sequence of the four numbers as your answer.

(a) Like the ants that make up a colony, no single neuron holds complex information like self-awareness, hope or pride.
(b) Although the human brain is not yet understood enough to identify the mechanism by which emergence functions, most neurobiologists agree that complex interconnections among the parts give rise to qualities that belong only to the whole.
(c) Nonetheless, the sum of all neurons in the nervous system generate complex human emotions like fear and joy, none of which can be attributed to a single neuron.
(d) Human consciousness is often called an emergent property of the human brain.

Q23. The passage given below is followed by four alternate summaries. Choose the option that best captures the essence of the passage.

Heatwaves are becoming longer, frequent and intense due to climate change. The impacts of extreme heat are unevenly experienced; with older people and young children, those with pre-existing medical conditions and on low incomes significantly more vulnerable. Adaptation to heatwaves is a significant public policy concern. Research conducted among at-risk people in the UK reveals that even vulnerable people do not perceive themselves as at risk of extreme heat; therefore, early warnings of extreme heat events do not perform as intended. This suggests that understanding how extreme heat is narrated is very important. The news media play a central role in this process and can help warn people about the potential danger, as well as about impacts on infrastructure and society.

(a) News stories help in warning about heatwaves, but they have to become more effective.

(b) Protection from heat waves is important but current reports and public policies seem ineffective.

(c) People are vulnerable to heatwaves caused due to climate change, measures taken are ineffective.

(d) Heatwaves pose an enormous risk; the media plays a pivotal role in alerting people to this danger.

Q24. The passage given below is followed by four alternate summaries. Choose the option that best captures the essence of the passage.

People spontaneously create counterfactual alternatives to reality when they think "if only" or "what if" and imagine how the past could have been different. The mind computes counterfactuals for many reasons. Counterfactuals explain the past and prepare for the future, they implicate various relations including causal ones, and they affect intentions and decisions. They modulate emotions such as regret and relief, and they support moral judgments such as blame. The ability to create counterfactuals develops throughout childhood and contributes to reasoning about other people's beliefs, including their false beliefs.

(a) Counterfactual alternatives to reality are created for a variety of reasons and is part of one's developmental process.

(b) People create counterfactual alternatives to reality for various reasons, including reasoning about other people's beliefs.

(c) Counterfactual thinking helps to reverse past and future actions and reason out false beliefs.

(d) Counterfactuals help people to prepare for the future by understanding intentions and making decisions.

Answer Key

1. (c)	**2.** (c)	**3.** (a)	**4.** (d)	**5.** (b)
6. (b)	**7.** (b)	**8.** (a)	**9.** (b)	**10.** (b)
11. (d)	**12.** (d)	**13.** (c)	**14.** (c)	**15.** (c)
16. (c)	**17.** (b)	**18.** (a)	**19.** (b)	**20.** (c)
21. (d, c, a, b)		**22.** (d, a, c, b)		**23.** (d)
24. (a)				

Explanations

1. Option (c) is correct.

We have to find the option which is not the reason why companies like ThredUP have not caught on in the UK. Option (c) which says people in Britain do not buy second-hand clothes is the right option here as this is a false option according to the passage. Some people in Britain definitely buy second-hand clothes. Option (c) contradicts what the passage says. Thus, it will be the right answer. All other options are mentioned in the last paragraph.

2. Option (c) is correct.

"Thrifting" as a concept was used in the passage to show how buying used clothes could help the environment but in reality it may not be so, rather it may be contributing to environmental damage in some ways. Hence, it may not be serving the actual purpose for which it is being employed. Thus, it is ironic in that sense.

3. Option (a) is correct.

If second-hand clothes only sold high-quality clothes, then the central idea of the passage, that not all second-hand clothing purchases are effective is saving the planet, would be undermined. Hence, option (a) is correct.

4. Option (d) is correct.

'fast fashion' brands are those that sell inexpensive, low-quality trendy clothing, in opposition to that 'slow brands' should be those that sell high quality and long lasting clothes. Thus, option (d) is correct. The other options are irrelevant.

5. Option (b) is correct.

All options except (b) are very well related to liberalism and the negatives caused by its decline. Technological advances cannot be considered evidence of the decline of liberalism.
We have to find which option is not an evidence of decline of liberalism; hence, option (b) is correct.

6. Option (b) is correct.

The following lines from the passage clearly show that the greed of the Davos elite is a problem: "The biggest enemy of liberalism is not so much atomisation but old-fashioned greed, as members of the Davos elite pile their plates ever higher with perks and share options"
Thus, option (b) is correct.

7. Option (b) is correct.

Options (a), (c) and (d) are clearly mentioned in the passage by the author as aspects of Deneen's theory which are faulty but he does not talk about option (b); hence, option (b) is correct.

8. Option (a) is correct.

The author argues at the start of the passage by saying, 'Over the past four centuries liberalism has been so successful that it has driven all its opponents off the battlefield'. He also says in the second last paragraph that liberalism has the ability to reform itself to remain dominant. So, the author is likely to agree with the 1st option; hence, option (a) is correct.
The author disagrees with the options (b), (c) and (d), hence they are incorrect.

9. Option (b) is correct.

If we see the following lines from the passage: "Not everything works across borders. Comedy sometimes struggles. Whodunits and bloodthirsty maelstroms between arch Romans and uppity tribesmen have a more universal appeal. Some do it better than others. Barbarians aside, German television is not always built for export,"....options (c) and (d) are clearly eliminated. Option 1 is not hinted at in the passage. But we surely get hints about option (b) in the passage.
Hence, option (b) is the best option here.

10. Option (b) is correct.

See the following lines from the passage: "If Europeans are to share a currency, bail each other out in times of financial need and share vaccines in a pandemic, then they need to have something in common–even if it is just bingeing on the same series" The above lines from the passage clearly make option (b) correct.

11. Option (d) is correct.

In the concluding paragraph of the passage, the author says that Netflix is a unifying force in Europe, making culture "a cross-border endeavour". If there were a wide variance and gap in the popularity and viewing of Netflix shows across the many countries of the EU, then the author's supposition that Netflix is popular across Europe, giving Europeans something to share across borders, is negated or at least weakened. Option (d) is thus the correct answer.

12. Option (d) is correct.

Options (a), (b) and (c) are clearly mentioned in the paragraph, but option (d) is something which Netflix may be aspiring for, but is not true in the present scenario.
Thus, option (d) is the answer.

13. Option (c) is correct.

If we see the following lines from the passage: "According to the common-sense view, there are certain basic facts which are the same for all historians and which form, so to speak, the backbone of history. . . But [to] praise a historian for his accuracy is like praising an architect for using well-seasoned timber or properly mixed concrete in his building. It is a necessary condition of his work, but not his essential function. It is precisely for matters of this kind that the historian is entitled to rely on what have been called the "auxiliary sciences" of history–archaeology, epigraphy, numismatics, chronology, and so forth"
This clearly shows that archaeology helps historians to check the facts or factual accuracy.
Thus, option (c) is correct.

14. Option (c) is correct.

"The facts speak only when the historian calls on them: it is he who decides to which facts to give the floor, and in what order or context. . . . The only reason why we are interested to know that the battle was fought at Hastings in 1066is that historians regard it as a major historical event" . . . these lines from the passage clearly show that not just facts but the interpretation of them would be of interest and in this case the other aspects of the war or the history like the socio-economic aspects would be worth considering.
Hence, option (c) is correct.

15. Option (c) is correct.

The passage says that the common sense view is very much an aspect of the positivist view focussing on facts, methods and archaeology. The author's view is quite opposite here and he mentions a selective system of orientation of facts and thus option (c) is correct.

16. Option (c) is correct.

If a fact is different for different people and is thus relative then the passage's claim will be totally weakened that facts speak for themselves. Thus, option (c) is correct.

17. Option (b), blank 2 is correct.

The paragraph starts with what is dualism and the missing statement tells how dualism was used in developing countries whereas it was not used in developed countries. Now this statement is rightly placed before the sentence which talks about the distinction between the developing and advanced economies. Hence, option (b) is correct.

18. Option (a), blank 2 is correct.

The correct placement of the missing sentence is the second blank right before ancient Mesopotamia because if we look at the sentence, "from the earliest Mesopotamian societies, kissing was already a well-established practice 4,500 years ago in the Middle East."

Now this statement is moving back the timeline from 3500 to 4500 hence the missing statement talking about the 1000 years displacement is best fitting here.

Hence, option (a), blank 2 is correct.

19. Option (b) is correct.

Sentence (c) is the best starting sentence as it is the more generic in nature. (e) adds to (c), and supports (c) with data. Sentences (d) and (a) discuss a very specific case-the banning of the book Northern Lights. (c), (e), (d), (a).

Sentence (b) although related to the paragraph is talking in general about authors having courage to tell their stories is not fully part of this specific paragraph. Thus, sentence (b) is the irrelevant statement.

20. Option (c) is correct.

(b), (d), (e), (a) is the correct sequence. (b), (d) is the starting link. (b) and (d) discuss the main focus of the paragraph, that is: children who routinely return home from school to empty homes and take care of themselves for extended periods of time.

(e), (a) is also a correct link, with (e) stating that self-care is not beneficial for development and (a) explaining why so. Thus, sentence (c) is the irrelevant statement.

21. The correct answer is (d), (c), (a), (b).

(d) is clearly the starting sentence. It is followed by the statement (c). (d), (c) together talk about the two opposing views.

(a), (b) are a close link as they are specifically exploring the conflict. (d), (c) are general and must come before (a), (b) which are specific. Thus, (d), (c), (a), (b) is the correct sequence.

22. The correct answer is (d), (a), (c), (b)

(a), (c) have to be together as they are talking about the neurons. (d) is the general starting idea and (b) clearly ends the paragraph. The correct sequence thus is (d), (a), (c), (b).

23. Option (d) is correct.

The two main themes here in the paragraph were that heat waves are creating a big risk and that the media have an important role to play in warning the people properly.

The 4th option conveys the above points in the best possible manner.

The other options are either half ideas or not so clear, hence option (d) is the answer.

24. Option (a) is correct.

The 1st option is correct because it covers the important ideas of the paragraph that there are many reasons why the mind creates counterfactuals and says that this develops throughout childhood and contributes to reasoning about other people's beliefs.

The 2nd and 3rd are partially correct as they do not talk about counterfactuals developing throughout childhood. The 4th option is also ambiguous.

CHAPTER 9 CAT Paper 2023 (Slot 3) VARC Section Questions and Solutions

Comprehension:

The passage below is accompanied by four questions. Based on the passage, choose the best answer for each question.

The biggest challenge [The Nutmeg's Curse by Ghosh] throws down is to the prevailing understanding of when the climate crisis started. Most of us have accepted . . . that it started with the widespread use of coal at the beginning of the Industrial Age in the 18th century and worsened with the mass adoption of oil and natural gas in the 20th.

Ghosh takes this history at least three centuries back, to the start of European colonialism in the 15th century. He [starts] the book with a 1621 massacre by Dutch invaders determined to impose a monopoly on nutmeg cultivation and trade in the Banda islands in today's Indonesia. Not only do the Dutch systematically depopulate the islands through genocide, they also try their best to bring nutmeg cultivation into plantation mode. These are the two points to which Ghosh returns through examples from around the world. One, how European colonialists decimated not only indigenous populations but also indigenous understanding of the relationship between humans and Earth. Two, how this was an invasion not only of humans but of the Earth itself, and how this continues to the present day by looking at nature as a 'resource' to exploit. . . .

We know we are facing more frequent and more severe heatwaves, storms, floods, droughts and wildfires due to climate change. We know our expansion through deforestation, dam building, canal cutting – in short, terraforming, the word Ghosh uses – has brought us repeated disasters. . . . Are these the responses of an angry Gaia who has finally had enough? By using the word 'curse' in the title, the author makes it clear that he thinks so. I use the pronoun 'who' knowingly, because Ghosh has quoted many non-European sources to enquire into the relationship between humans and the world around them so that he can question the prevalent way of looking at Earth as an inert object to be exploited to the maximum.

As Ghosh's text, notes and bibliography show once more, none of this is new. There have always been challenges to the way European colonialists looked at other civilisations and at Earth. It is just that the invaders and their myriad backers in the fields of economics, politics, anthropology, philosophy, literature, technology, physics, chemistry, biology have dominated global intellectual discourse. . . .

There are other points of view that we can hear today if we listen hard enough. Those observing global climate negotiations know about the Latin American way of looking at Earth as Pachamama (Earth Mother). They also know how such a framing is just provided lip service and is ignored in the substantive portions of the negotiations. In The Nutmeg's Curse, Ghosh explains why. He shows the extent of the vested interest in the oil economy – not only for oil-exporting countries, but also for a superpower like the US that controls oil drilling, oil prices and oil movement around the world. Many of us know power utilities are sabotaging decentralised solar power generation today because it hits their revenues and control. And how the other points of view are so often drowned out.

Q1. All of the following can be inferred from the reviewer's discussion of "The Nutmeg's Curse", EXCEPT:

(a) the contemporary dominant perception of nature and the environment was put in place by processes of colonialism.

(b) academic discourses have always served the function of raising awareness about environmental preservation.

(c) environmental preservation policy makers can learn a lot from non-European and/or pre-colonial societies.

(d) the history of climate change is deeply intertwined with the history of colonialism.

Q2. Which one of the following best explains the primary purpose of the discussion of the colonisation of the Banda islands in "The Nutmeg's Curse"?

(a) To illustrate the role played by the cultivation of certain crops in the plantation mode in contributing to climate change.

(b) To illustrate how colonialism represented and perpetuated the mindset that has led to climate change.

(c) To illustrate the first instance in history when the processes responsible for climate change were initiated.

(d) To illustrate how systemic violence against the colonised constituted the cornerstone of colonialism.

Q3. On the basis of information in the passage, which one of the following is NOT a reason for the failure of policies seeking to address climate change?

(a) The decentralised characteristic of renewable energy resources like solar power.

(b) The global dominance of oil economies and international politics built around it.

(c) The marginalised status of non-European ways of looking at nature and the environment.

(d) The greed of organisations benefiting from non-renewable energy resources.

Q4. Which one of the following, if true, would make the reviewer's choice of the pronoun "who" for Gaia inappropriate?

(a) Non-European societies have perceived the Earth as a non-living source of all resources.

(b) Ghosh's book has a different title: "The Nutmeg's Revenge".

(c) There is a direct cause-effect relationship between human activities and global climate change.

(d) Modern western science discovers new evidence for the Earth being an inanimate object.

Comprehension:

The passage below is accompanied by four questions. Based on the passage, choose the best answer for each question.

Steven Pinker's new book, "Rationality: What It Is, Why It Seems Scarce, Why It Matters," offers a pragmatic dose of measured optimism, presenting rationality as a fragile but achievable ideal in personal and civic life Pinker's ambition to illuminate such a crucial topic offers the welcome prospect of a return to sanity It's no small achievement to make formal logic, game theory, statistics and Bayesian reasoning delightful topics full of charm and relevance.

It's also plausible to believe that a wider application of the rational tools he analyzes would improve the world in important ways. His primer on statistics and scientific uncertainty is particularly timely and should be required reading before consuming any news about the [COVID] pandemic. More broadly, he argues that less media coverage of shocking but vanishingly rare events, from shark attacks to adverse vaccine reactions, would help prevent dangerous overreactions, fatalism and the diversion of finite resources away from solvable but less-dramatic issues, like malnutrition in the developing world.

It's a reasonable critique, and Pinker is not the first to make it. But analyzing the political economy of journalism – its funding structures, ownership concentration and increasing reliance on social media shares – would have given a fuller picture of why so much coverage is so misguided and what we might do about it.

Pinker's main focus is the sort of conscious, sequential reasoning that can track the steps in a geometric proof or an argument in formal logic. Skill in this domain maps directly onto the navigation of many real-world problems, and Pinker shows how greater mastery of the tools of rationality can improve decision-making in medical, legal, financial and many other contexts in which we must act on uncertain and shifting information. . . .

Despite the undeniable power of the sort of rationality he describes, many of the deepest insights in the history of science, math, music and art strike their originators in moments of epiphany. From the 19th-century chemist Friedrich August Kekulé's discovery of the structure of benzene to any of Mozart's symphonies, much extraordinary human achievement is not a product of conscious, sequential reasoning. Even Plato's Socrates – who anticipated many of Pinker's points by nearly 2,500 years, showing the virtue of knowing what you do not know and examining all premises in arguments, not simply trusting speakers' authority or charisma – attributed many of his most profound insights to dreams and visions. Conscious reasoning is helpful in sorting the wheat from the chaff, but it would be interesting to consider the hidden aquifers that make much of the grain grow in the first place.

The role of moral and ethical education in promoting rational behavior is also underexplored. Pinker recognizes that rationality "is not just a cognitive virtue but a moral one." But this profoundly important point, one subtly explored by ancient Greek philosophers like Plato and

Aristotle, doesn't really get developed. This is a shame, since possessing the right sort of moral character is arguably a precondition for using rationality in beneficial ways.

Q5. The author endorses Pinker's views on the importance of logical reasoning as it:

(a) focuses public attention on real issues like development rather than sensational events.

(b) helps people to gain expertise in statistics and other scientific disciplines.

(c) provides a moral compass for resolving important ethical dilemmas.

(d) equips people with the ability to tackle challenging practical problems.

Q6. According to the author, for Pinker as well as the ancient Greek philosophers, rational thinking involves all of the following EXCEPT:

(a) the belief that the ability to reason logically encompasses an ethical and moral dimension.

(b) an awareness of underlying assumptions in an argument and gaps in one's own knowledge.

(c) the primacy of conscious sequential reasoning as the basis for seminal human achievements.

(d) arriving at independent conclusions irrespective of who is presenting the argument.

Q7. The author refers to the ancient Greek philosophers to:

(a) indicate the various similarities between their thinking and Pinker's conclusions.

(b) reveal gaps in Pinker's discussion of the importance of ethical considerations in rational behaviour.

(c) highlight the influence of their thinking on the development of Pinker's arguments.

(d) show how dreams and visions have for centuries influenced subconscious behaviour and pathbreaking inventions.

Q8. The author mentions Kekulé's discovery of the structure of benzene and Mozart's symphonies to illustrate the point that:

(a) it is not just the creative arts, but also scientific fields that have benefitted from flashes of creativity.

(b) Pinker's conclusions on sequential reasoning are belied by European achievements which, in the past, were more rooted in unconscious bursts of genius.

(c) unlike the sciences, human achievements in other fields are a mix of logical reasoning and spontaneous epiphanies.

(d) great innovations across various fields can stem from flashes of intuition and are not always propelled by logical thinking.

Comprehension:

The passage below is accompanied by four questions. Based on the passage, choose the best answer for each question.

Understanding romantic aesthetics is not a simple undertaking for reasons that are internal to the nature of the subject. Distinguished scholars, such as Arthur Lovejoy, Northrop Frye and Isaiah Berlin, have remarked on the notorious challenges facing any attempt to define romanticism. Lovejoy, for example, claimed that romanticism is "the scandal of literary history and criticism" . . . The main difficulty in studying the romantics, according to him, is the lack of any "single real entity, or type of entity" that the concept "romanticism" designates. Lovejoy concluded, "the word 'romantic' has come to mean so many things that, by itself, it means nothing" . . .

The more specific task of characterizing romantic aesthetics adds to these difficulties an air of paradox. Conventionally, "aesthetics" refers to a theory concerning beauty and art or the branch of philosophy that studies these topics. However, many of the romantics rejected the identification of aesthetics with a circumscribed domain of human life that is separated from the practical and theoretical domains of life. The most characteristic romantic commitment is to the idea that the character of art and beauty and of our engagement with them should shape all aspects of human life. Being fundamental to human existence, beauty and art should be a central ingredient not only in a philosophical or artistic life, but also in the lives of ordinary men and women. Another challenge for any attempt to characterize romantic aesthetics lies in the fact that most of the romantics were poets and artists whose views of art and beauty are, for the most part, to be found not in developed theoretical accounts, but in fragments, aphorisms and poems, which are often more elusive and suggestive than conclusive.

Nevertheless, in spite of these challenges the task of characterizing romantic aesthetics is neither impossible nor undesirable, as numerous thinkers responding to Lovejoy's radical skepticism have noted. While warning against a reductive definition of romanticism, Berlin, for example, still heralded the need for a general characterization: "[Although] one does have a certain sympathy with Lovejoy's despair . . . [he is] in this instance mistaken. There was a romantic movement . . . and it is important to discover what it is" . . .

Recent attempts to characterize romanticism and to stress its contemporary relevance follow this path. Instead of overlooking the undeniable differences between the variety of romanticisms of different nations that Lovejoy had stressed, such studies attempt to characterize romanticism, not in terms of a single definition, a specific time, or a specific place, but in terms of "particular philosophical questions and concerns" . . .

While the German, British and French romantics are all considered, the central protagonists in the following are the German romantics. Two reasons explain this focus: first, because it has paved the way for the other romanticisms, German romanticism has a pride of place among the different national romanticisms . . . Second, the aesthetic outlook that was developed in Germany roughly between 1796 and 1801-02 – the period that corresponds to the heyday of what is known as "Early Romanticism" . . . – offers the most philosophical expression of romanticism since it is grounded primarily in the epistemological, metaphysical, ethical, and political concerns that the German romantics discerned in the aftermath of Kant's philosophy.

Q9. Which one of the following statements is NOT supported by the passage?

(a) Many romantics rejected the idea of aesthetics as a domain separate from other aspects of life.

(b) Characterising romantic aesthetics is both possible and desirable, despite the challenges involved.

(c) Romantic aesthetics are primarily expressed through fragments, aphorisms, and poems.

(d) Recent studies on romanticism seek to refute the differences between national romanticisms.

Q10. The main difficulty in studying romanticism is the:

(a) controversial and scandalous history of romantic literature.

(b) absence of written accounts by romantic poets and artists.

(c) lack of clear conceptual contours of the domain.

(d) elusive and suggestive nature of romantic aesthetics.

Q11. According to the passage, recent studies on romanticism avoid "a single definition, a specific time, or a specific place" because they:

(a) understand that the variety of romanticisms renders a general analysis impossible.

(b) prefer to highlight the paradox of romantic aesthetics as a concept.

(c) seek to discredit Lovejoy's scepticism regarding romanticism.

(d) prefer to focus on the fundamental concerns of the romantics.

Q12. According to the romantics, aesthetics:

(a) is primarily the concern of philosophers and artists, rather than of ordinary people.

(b) permeates all aspects of human life, philosophical and mundane.

(c) is widely considered to be irrelevant to human existence.

(d) should be confined to a specific domain separate from the practical and theoretical aspects of life.

Comprehension:

The passage below is accompanied by four questions. Based on the passage, choose the best answer for each question.

In 2006, the Met [art museum in the US] agreed to return the Euphronios krater, a masterpiece Greek urn that had been a museum draw since 1972. In 2007, the Getty [art museum in the US] agreed to return 40 objects to Italy, including a marble Aphrodite, in the midst of looting scandals. And in December, Sotheby's and a private owner agreed to return an ancient Khmer statue of a warrior, pulled from auction two years before, to Cambodia.

Cultural property, or patrimony, laws limit the transfer of cultural property outside the source country's territory, including outright export prohibitions and national ownership laws. Most art historians, archaeologists, museum officials and policymakers portray cultural property laws in general as invaluable tools for counteracting the ugly legacy of Western cultural imperialism.

During the late 19th and early 20th century – an era former Met director Thomas Hoving called "the age of piracy" – American and European art museums acquired antiquities by hook or by crook, from grave robbers or souvenir collectors, bounty from digs and ancient sites in impoverished but art-rich source countries. Patrimony laws were intended to protect future archaeological discoveries against Western imperialist designs. . . .

I surveyed 90 countries with one or more archaeological sites on UNESCO's World Heritage Site list, and my study shows that in most cases the number of discovered sites diminishes sharply after a country passes a cultural property law. There are 222 archaeological sites listed for those 90 countries. When you look into the history of the sites, you see that all but 21 were discovered before the passage of cultural property laws. . . .

Strict cultural patrimony laws are popular in most countries. But the downside may be that they reduce incentives for foreign governments, nongovernmental organizations and educational institutions to invest in overseas exploration because their efforts will not necessarily be rewarded by opportunities to hold, display and study what is uncovered. To the extent that source countries can fund their own archaeological projects, artifacts and sites may still be discovered The survey has far-reaching implications. It suggests that source countries, particularly in the developing world, should narrow their cultural property laws so that they can reap the benefits of new archaeological discoveries, which typically increase tourism and enhance cultural pride. This does not mean these nations should abolish restrictions on foreign excavation and foreign claims to artifacts.

China provides an interesting alternative approach for source nations eager for foreign archaeological investment. From 1935 to 2003, China had a restrictive cultural property law that prohibited foreign ownership of Chinese cultural artifacts. In those years, China's most significant archaeological discovery occurred by chance, in 1974, when peasant farmers accidentally uncovered ranks of buried terra cotta warriors, which are part of Emperor Qin's spectacular tomb system.

In 2003, the Chinese government switched course, dropping its cultural property law and embracing collaborative international archaeological research. Since then, China has nominated 11 archaeological sites for inclusion in the World Heritage Site list, including eight in 2013, the most ever for China.

Q13. It can be inferred from the passage that archaeological sites are considered important by some source countries because they:

(a) give a boost to the tourism sector.
(b) are subject to strict patrimony laws.
(c) generate funds for future discoveries.
(d) are a symbol of Western imperialism.

Q14. Which one of the following statements best expresses the paradox of patrimony laws?

(a) They were intended to protect cultural property, but instead resulted in the withholding of national treasure from museums.
(b) They were intended to protect cultural property, but instead resulted in the neglect of historical sites.
(c) They were aimed at protecting cultural property, but instead reduced business for auctioneers like Sotheby's.
(d) They were aimed at protecting cultural property, but instead reduced new archaeological discoveries.

Q15. Which one of the following statements, if true, would undermine the central idea of the passage?

(a) UNESCO finances archaeological research in poor, but archaeologically-rich source countries.
(b) Western countries will have to apologise to countries for looting their cultural property in the past century.
(c) Museums established in economically deprived archaeologically-rich source countries can display the antiques discovered there.
(d) Affluent archaeologically-rich source countries can afford to carry out their own excavations.

Q16. From the passage we can infer that the author is likely to advise poor, but archaeologically-rich source countries to do all of the following, EXCEPT:

(a) to find ways to motivate other countries to finance archaeological explorations in their country.
(b) allow foreign countries to analyse and exhibit the archaeological finds made in the source country.
(c) fund institutes in other countries to undertake archaeological exploration in the source country reaping the benefits of cutting-edge techniques.
(d) adopt China's strategy of dropping its cultural property laws and carrying out archaeological research through international collaboration.

Q17. There is a sentence that is missing in the paragraph below. Look at the paragraph and decide where (option 1, 2, 3, or 4) the following sentence would best fit.

Sentence: For theoretical purposes, arguments may be considered as freestanding entities, abstracted from their contexts of use in actual human activities.

Paragraph: __(1)__. An argument can be defined as a complex symbolic structure where some parts, known as the premises, offer support to another part, the conclusion. Alternatively, an argument can be viewed as a complex speech act consisting of one or more acts of premising (which assert propositions in favor of the conclusion), an act of concluding, and a stated or implicit marker ("hence", "therefore") that indicates that the conclusion follows from the premises. __(2)__. The relation of support between premises and conclusion can be cashed out in different ways: the premises may guarantee the truth of the conclusion, or make its truth more probable; the premises may imply the conclusion; the premises may make the conclusion more acceptable (or assertible). __(3)__. But depending on one's explanatory goals, there is also much to be gained from considering arguments as they in fact occur in human communicative practices. __(4)__.

(a) Option 3
(b) Option 1
(c) Option 4
(d) Option 2

Q18. There is a sentence that is missing in the paragraph below. Look at the paragraph and decide where (option 1, 2, 3, or 4) the following sentence would best fit.

Sentence: Beyond undermining the monopoly of the State on the use of force, armed conflict also creates an environment that can enable organized crime to prosper.

Paragraph: __(1)__. Linkages between illicit arms, organized crime, and armed conflict can reinforce one another while also escalating and prolonging violence and eroding governance. __(2)__. Financial gains from crime can lengthen or intensify armed conflicts by creating revenue streams for non-State armed groups (NSAGs). __(3)__. In this context, when hostilities cease and parties to a conflict move towards a peaceful resolution, the widespread availability of surplus arms and ammunition can contribute to a situation of 'criminalized peace' that obstructs sustainable peacebuilding efforts.__(4)__.

(a) Option 1
(b) Option 3
(c) Option 4
(d) Option 2

Q19. Five jumbled up sentences [labelled (a), (b), (c), (d) and (e)], related to a topic, are given below. Four of them can be put together to form a coherent paragraph. Identify the odd sentence and key in the number of that sentence as your answer.

(a) Although hard skills have traditionally ruled the roost, some companies are moving away from choosing prospective hires based on technical abilities alone.
(b) Companies are shaking off the old definition of an ideal candidate and ditching the idea of looking for the singularly perfect candidate altogether.
(c) Now, some job descriptions are frequently asking for candidates to demonstrate soft skills, such as leadership or teamwork.
(d) That's not to say that practical know-how is no longer required - some jobs still call for highly specific expertise
(e) The move towards prioritising soft skills "is a natural response to three years of the pandemic" says a senior recruiter at Cenlar FSB.

Q20. Five jumbled up sentences [labelled (a), (b), (c), (d) and (e)], related to a topic, are given below. Four of them can be put together to form a coherent paragraph. Identify the odd sentence and key in the number of that sentence as your answer.

(a) Boa Senior, who lived through the 2004 tsunami, the Japanese occupation and diseases brought by British settlers, was the last native of the island chain who was fluent in Bo.
(b) The indigenous population has been steadily collapsing since the island chain was colonised by British settlers in 1858 and used for most of the following 100 years as a colonial penal colony.
(c) Taking its name from a now-extinct tribe, Bo is one of the 10 Great Andamanese languages, which are thought to date back to pre-Neolithic human settlement of south-east Asia.
(d) The last speaker of an ancient tribal language has died in the Andaman Islands, breaking a 65,000-year link to one of the world's oldest cultures.
(d) Though the language has been closely studied by researchers of linguistic history, Boa Senior spent the last few years of her life unable to converse with anyone in her mother tongue.

Q21. The four sentences [labelled (a), (b), (c) and (d)] given below, when properly sequenced, would yield a coherent paragraph. Decide on the proper sequencing of the order of the sentences and key in the sequence of the four numbers as your answer.

(a) Veena Sahajwalla, a materials scientist at the University of New South Wales, believes there is a new way of solving this problem.
(b) Her vision is for automated drones and robots to pick out components, put them into a small furnace and smelt them at specific temperatures to extract the metals one by one before they are sent off to manufacturers for reuse.
(c) E-waste contains huge quantities of valuable metals, ceramics and plastics that could be salvaged and recycled, although currently not enough of it is.
(d) She plans to build microfactories that can tease apart the tangle of materials in mobile phones, computers and other e-waste.

Q22. The four sentences [labelled (a), (b), (c) and (d)] given below, when properly sequenced, would yield a coherent paragraph. Decide on the proper sequencing of the order of the sentences and key in the sequence of the four numbers as your answer.

(a) Centuries later formal learning is still mostly based on reading, even with the widespread use of other possible education-affecting technologies such as film, radio, and television.
(b) One of the immediate and recognisable impacts of the printing press was on how people learned; in the scribal culture it primarily involved listening, so memorization was paramount.

(c) The transformation of learners from listeners to readers was a complex social and cultural phenomenon, and it was not until the industrial era that the concept of universal literacy took root.

(d) The printing press shifted the learning process, as listening and memorisation gradually gave way to reading and learning no longer required the presence of a mentor; it could be done privately.

Q23. The passage given below is followed by four alternate summaries. Choose the option that best captures the essence of the passage.

The weight of society's expectations is hardly a new phenomenon but it has become particularly draining over recent decades, perhaps because expectations themselves are so multifarious and contradictory. The perfectionism of the 1950s was rooted in the norms of mass culture and captured in famous advertising images of the ideal white American family that now seem self-satirising. In that era, perfectionism meant seamlessly conforming to values, behaviour and appearance: chiselled confidence for men, demure graciousness for women. The perfectionist was under pressure to look like everyone else, only more so. The perfectionists of today, by contrast, feel an obligation to stand out through their idiosyncratic style and wit if they are to gain a foothold in the attention economy.

(a) The image of perfectionism is reflected in and perpetuated by the media; and people do their best to adhere to these ideals.

(b) Though long-standing, the pressure to appear perfect and thereby attract attention, has evolved over time from one of conformism to one of non-conformism.

(c) The pressure to appear perfect has been the cause of tension and conflict because the idea itself has been in a state of flux and hard to define.

(d) The desire to attract attention is so deep-rooted in individual consciousness that people are willing to go to any lengths to achieve it.

Q24. The passage given below is followed by four alternate summaries. Choose the option that best captures the essence of the passage.

Gradually, life for the island's birds is improving. Antarctic prions and white-headed petrels, which also nest in burrows, had managed to cling on in some sites while pests were on the island. Their numbers are now increasing. "It's fantastic and so exciting," Shaw says. As birds return to breed, they also poo. This adds nutrients to the soil, which in turn helps the plants to grow back stronger. Tall plants then help burrowing birds hide from predatory skuas. "It's this wonderful feedback loop," Shaw says.

Today, the "pretty paddock" that Houghton first experienced has been transformed. "The tussock is over your head, and you're dodging all these penguin tunnels," she says. The orchids and tiny herb that had been protected by fencing have started turning up all over the place.

(a) There is a huge positive transformation of the ecosystem of the island when brought under environmental protection.

(b) There is an increasing number of predatory birds and plants on the island despite the presence of pests which is a positive development.

(c) In the absence of pests, life on the island is now protected, and there has been a revival of a variety of birds and plants.

(d) Flowering plants, herbs and birds are now being protected on this wonderful Antarctic island.

Answer Key

1. (b)	**2.** (b)	**3.** (a)	**4.** (a)	**5.** (d)
6. (c)	**7.** (b)	**8.** (d)	**9.** (d)	**10.** (c)
11. (d)	**12.** (b)	**13.** (a)	**14.** (d)	**15.** (a)
16. (c)	**17.** (a)	**18.** (a)	**19.** (b)	**20.** (b)
21. (c, a, d, b)		**22.** (b, d, c, a)		**23.** (b)
24. (c)				

Explanations

1. Option (b) is correct.

Option (b) is completely opposite of what the passage mentions. The passage shows how European colonialists have been instrumental in our way of looking at Earth as a 'resource' to exploit. Though there have been opposition to this way of thinking, the passage says, "the invaders and their myriad backers in the fields of economics, politics, anthropology, philosophy, literature, technology, physics, chemistry, biology have dominated global intellectual discourse."

Option (b) cannot be inferred from the passage and is the correct answer choice.

2. Option (b) is correct.

Look at the following lines from the passage: "These are the two points to which Ghosh returns through examples from around the world. One, how European colonialists decimated not only indigenous populations but also indigenous understanding of the relationship between humans and Earth. Two, how this was an invasion not only of humans but of the Earth itself, and how this continues to the present day by looking at nature as a 'resource' to exploit. . ."

The above lines clearly show that option (b) is correct.

Option (b), although tempting, talks about the first instance, which is not clear from the passage.

3. Option (a) is correct.

Read the following lines from the passage: "Those observing global climate negotiations know about the Latin American way of looking at Earth as Pachamama (Earth Mother). They also know how such a framing is just provided lip service and is ignored in the substantive portions of the negotiations. In The Nutmeg's Curse, Ghosh explains why. He shows the extent of the vested interest in the oil economy - not only for oil-exporting countries, but also for a superpower like the US that controls oil drilling, oil prices and oil movement around the world. Many of us know power utilities are sabotaging decentralised solar power generation today because it hits their revenues and control"

Options (b), (c) and (d) are clearly inferred from the above lines but the solar power decentralisation is mentioned in the context of how it is made inaccessible as it is a threat to the giant power suppliers, not in the context of its characteristics as mentioned in option (a).

Hence, option (a) is correct.

4. Option (a) is correct.

The reason mentioned by the reviewer for the choice of the pronoun, "who" in the passage is in the following lines: 'I use the pronoun 'who' knowingly, because Ghosh has quoted many non-European sources to enquire into the relationship between humans and the world around them..' ......

The reviewer concludes his choice is based on the understanding of Earth as a living entity by non-European societies. Thus, if option (a) was true, it would make the reviewer's choice of the pronoun "who" for Gaia incorrect. Thus option (a) is the correct answer.

5. Option (d) is correct.

If we read the following lines from the passage: "Pinker's main focus is the sort of conscious, sequential reasoning that can track the steps in a geometric proof or an argument in formal logic. Skill in this domain maps directly onto the navigation of many real-world problems, and Pinker shows how greater mastery of the tools of rationality can improve decision-making in medical, legal, financial and many other contexts in which we must act on uncertain and shifting information." . . . these lines clearly show that the option (d) is correct.

6. Option (c) is correct.

Options (a), (b) and (d) can be inferred from the passage if you read the following extracts from the passage: 'Pinker recognizes that rationality "is not just a cognitive virtue but a moral one." But this profoundly important point, one subtly explored by ancient Greek philosophers . . .'. . . . "Even Plato's Socrates – who anticipated many of Pinker's points by nearly 2,500 years, showing the virtue of knowing what you do not know and examining all premises in arguments, not simply trusting speakers' authority or charisma".

Now when we see the following line: "Plato's Socrates – who anticipated many of Pinker's points by nearly 2,500 years, showing the virtue of knowing what you do not know and examining all premises in arguments, not simply trusting speakers' authority or charisma – attributed many of his most profound insights to dreams and visions.".... this differentiates Pinker from the Greek philosophers. This is mentioned in option (c), thus option (c) is correct.

7. Option (b) is correct.

When we see the lines: "The role of moral and ethical education in promoting rational behavior is also underexplored. Pinker recognizes that rationality "is not just a cognitive virtue but a moral one." But this profoundly important point, one subtly explored by ancient Greek philosophers like Plato and Aristotle, doesn't really get developed".

This clearly shows that option (b) is correct.

8. Option (d) is correct.

See the following lines from the passage: "Despite the undeniable power of the sort of rationality he describes, many of the deepest insights in the history of science, math, music and art strike their originators in moments of epiphany. From the 19th-century chemist Friedrich August Kekulé's discovery of the structure of benzene to any of Mozart's symphonies, much extraordinary human achievement is not a product of conscious, sequential reasoning.". . . These lines clearly show that option (d) is correct. The other options have errors or ambiguities.

9. Option (d) is correct.

(a), (b) and (c) are mentioned or hinted in the passage, but option (d) is clearly not a part of the passage. Thus, the correct answer is option (d).

10. Option (c) is correct.

If we see the following lines from the passage: "The main difficulty in studying the romantics, according to him, is the lack of any "single real entity, or type of entity" that the concept "romanticism" designates.'."
These lines clearly show that option (c) is correct.

11. Option (d) is correct.

According to the following lines from the passage: 'While warning against a reductive definition of romanticism, Berlin, for example, still heralded the need for a general characterization: "[Although] one does have a certain sympathy with Lovejoy's despair . . . [he is] in this instance mistaken. There was a romantic movement . . . and it is important to discover what it is". . .'
These lines clearly point towards option 4 as the correct option.

12. Option (b) is correct.

Read the following lines from the passage : "The more specific task of characterizing romantic aesthetics adds to these difficulties an air of paradox. Conventionally, "aesthetics" refers to a theory concerning beauty and art or the branch of philosophy that studies these topics. However, many of the romantics rejected the identification of aesthetics with a circumscribed domain of human life that is separated from the practical and theoretical domains of life. The most characteristic romantic commitment is to the idea that the character of art and beauty and of our engagement with them should shape all aspects of human life. Being fundamental to human existence, beauty and art should be a central ingredient not only in a philosophical or artistic life, but also in the lives of ordinary men and women."
The above lines clearly show that option (b) is correct.

13. Option (a) is correct.

If we see the following lines from the passage: "suggests that source
countries, particularly in the developing world, should narrow their cultural property laws so that they can reap the benefits of new archaeological discoveries, which typically increase tourism and enhance cultural pride." These lines clearly show that archaeological sites are important because they give a boost to tourism. Thus, option (a) is correct.

14. Option (d) is correct.

A paradox is something which is intended for a particular reason but it undermines that in some way. Here in the passage it is said that the culture patrimony laws were made to protect poor countries from being exploited by the richer countries for their archaeological artifacts. But the laws had a counter effect because they diminished the resources coming to these countries for archaeological research. Thus, option (d) is correct.

15. Option (a) is correct.

The theme of the passage is that stringent culture patrimony laws lessen the incentives for foreign investment in archaeological research, thus depriving poor, but archaeologically-rich source countries of the benefits of new archaeological research. Thus if UNESCO finances archaeological research in poor, but archaeologically-rich source countries then there would be no reason for these countries to stop or loosen the strict cultural property laws. So, option (a), if true, would weaken the main idea of the passage.

16. Option (c) is correct.

Options (a), (b) and (d) could be a likely advice to poor, but archaeologically-rich source countries. Since we have to find which option would not be an advice, option (c) is the correct option because they already have a financial problem; hence, that would not be correct.
Thus option (c) is the right option.

17. Option (a) is correct [blank 3].

The sentences before the 3rd blank are considering arguments in the context of premises and conclusions. So the blanks 1 and 2 are not the right place for the missing statement.
After the 3rd blank, there is an idea change talking about the purpose/goals of the argument and the missing statement should be just before it as it is talking about the theoretical purpose and is more generic in nature. The sentence before blank 4 already is in a conclusive style, so putting the statement in the 4th blank would be incorrect.
Thus the 3rd blank mentioned in option 1 is correct.

18. Option (a) [blank 1]

Clearly, the given statement is the starting idea and has to be placed at the start in the 1st blank as the

sentences after it are related and extend the idea of the given statement.
Option (a) stating the 1st blank is correct.

19. Option (b) is the irrelevant statement.

(a), (d), (c), (e) is the sequence which starts with hard skills being important but soft skills are also being seen as important. Option (b) which talks about the singularly perfect candidate is a related idea but is not seen as part of the sequence and is too specific. Hence, statement (b) is the odd one out.

20. Option (b) is the irrelevant statement.

(d), (c), (a), (e) is the correct sequence.
(d) is the best opening statement as it mentions 'an ancient tribal language'. (c) names this language and so it is placed after (d). (d), (c) are followed by (a), and (e), both are mentioning and explaining about Boa Senior, the last speaker of the language.
Statement (b) is the odd one out.

21. (c), (a), (d), (b) is the correct sequence

Sentence (c) talks about the problem of e-waste and how it contains materials that should be salvaged. Sentence (a) introduces the solution to the problem with the introduction of Veena. Sentence (d) mentions how she plans to build factories to untangle and this is followed by (b) which further elaborates how the process will be executed.
Hence, (c), (a), (d), (b) is the correct sequence.

22. (b), (d), (c), (a) is the correct sequence

Sentence (b) has to be the starting idea as it talks about how the printing press transformed the learning process from listening and memorisation to reading, and sentence (a) ends the paragraph as it talks about the situation today, centuries later. (d), (c) are a mandatory pair and have to be together. (b), (d) are also linked together and as (c) follows it with (a) as the ending idea, (b), (d), (c), (a) is the correct sequence.

23. Option (b) is correct

The idea of the paragraph is that the expectation to be perfect earlier was to conform to values and now in contrast it is non-conformation. Option (b) best captures the main idea and message of the paragraph. Hence, option (b) is the answer.

24. Option (c) is correct

The paragraph describes how the plants are again growing, birds etc. are coming back to breed and this has happened due to the absence of the pests who had most probably put a stop to all these things. Option (c) best captures the idea of the paragraph.